How
COLLEGE
AFFECTS
STUDENTS

Ernest T. Pascarella
Patrick T. Terenzini

Foreword by Kenneth A. Feldman

How COLLEGE AFFECTS STUDENTS

*Findings and Insights
from Twenty Years of Research*

 Jossey-Bass Publishers

San Francisco • Oxford • 1991

HOW COLLEGE AFFECTS STUDENTS
Findings and Insights from Twenty Years of Research

by Ernest T. Pascarella and Patrick T. Terenzini

Copyright © 1991 by: Jossey-Bass Inc., Publishers
350 Sansome Street
San Francisco, California 94104
&
Jossey-Bass Limited
Headington Hill Hall
Oxford OX3 0BW

Library of Congress Cataloging-in-Publication Data

Pascarella, Ernest T.
How college affects students : findings and insights from twenty
years of research / Ernest T. Pascarella, Patrick T. Terenzini;
foreword by Kenneth A. Feldman.
p.   cm.—(The Jossey-Bass higher and adult education series)
Includes bibliographical references and index.
ISBN 1-55542-304-3
ISBN 1-55542-338-8 (paperback)
1. College students—United States.   I. Terenzini, Patrick T.
II. Title.   III. Series.
LA229.P34   1991
378.1'98'0973—dc20   90-46068
                                                                CIP

Manufactured in the United States of America

The paper in this book meets the guidelines for
permanence and durability of the Committee on
Production Guidelines for Book Longevity of the
Council on Library Resources.

JACKET DESIGN BY WILLI BAUM

FIRST EDITION
First paperback printing: April 1991

Code 9105
Code 9141 (paperback)

The Jossey-Bass
Higher and Adult Education Series

Consulting Editor

Kenneth A. Feldman
State University of New York, Stony Brook

Contents

Foreword

Some fifty-five years ago, Stephen M. Corey (1936) published a ten-page article entitled "Attitude Differences Between College Classes: A Summary and Criticism" in the *Journal of Educational Psychology*. Reviewing seventeen studies published between 1925 and 1935, Corey found that many of them showed students in upper-level college classes to be somewhat more socially, politically, or religiously liberal than students in lower-level classes. He had only one methodological comment to make, but it was an important one. Because each of the studies collected cross-sectional data rather than longitudinal data, Corey warned that the results of the various bodies of research did not necessarily show that the colleges under study had actually produced changes in their students. Rather, differences between upper- and lowerclassmen might have resulted merely from selective attrition of students: "To conclude, from a comparison of scores made by freshmen, sophomores, juniors, and seniors, that education either has or has not been effective in engendering or qualifying certain attitudes is to overlook the very obvious fact that the differences between these scores, or for that matter, the absence of differences, might quite possibly be due to selection brought about by academic mortality" (p. 327). There may have been earlier studies of college impacts on students' attitudes and earlier reviews of these studies; Corey did not mention any, however.

To go from this early review (with its exclusive focus on student attitudes, its summary of a mere handful of studies, and its one methodological comment) to the present book (with its consideration of roughly 2,600 pieces of research, its ten chapters on different student characteristics potentially influenceable by college, its chapter reviewing relevant theoretical models, its appendix on methodological concerns, and its chapter on policy implications) is to make a vast jump, perhaps even a quantum leap. Of course, there have been other reviews and syntheses along the way. One thinks of Philip Jacob's *Changing Values in College* (1957), my own work with Theodore Newcomb (*The Impact of College on Students*, 1969), and Howard Bowen's *Investment in Learning* (1977), to name only three of the more comprehensive efforts. None of these, however, is on quite the same scale as the present volume.

In synthesizing the research of the late sixties through the seventies and eighties, Pascarella and Terenzini have cast an especially wide net in selecting for review the student characteristics potentially affected by the college experience. They consider the following sets of student outcomes: verbal skills, quantitative skills, and knowledge of specific subject matter; general cognitive competence and cognitive skills; self-conceptions and self-evaluations; psychosocial characteristics and personality traits; attitudes and values; moral reasoning, moral judgment, and moral behavior; educational attainment; career choice and career attainment; economic returns and benefits; and nonmonetary benefits, life satisfaction, and quality of life. Whenever possible, for each of these sets of characteristics, the research summarized is subdivided into the separate considerations of overall change and stability during college, net effects of college, between-college effects, within-college effects, conditional effects of college, and long-term effects of college. This particular arrangement, besides helping to systematize and clarify an otherwise confusing array of studies, enhances one of the main benefits of reviews or syntheses: The amount of research that has or has not been done in an area is clearly highlighted, thereby making evident which topics of interest have been the object of little or no research and which bear a surfeit.

How College Affects Students may be monumental, but it is also accessible. The authors have made sure it will appeal to readers of differing involvement. Even the most casual of readers can learn much by reading no more than the book's summary chapter (Chapter Thirteen), although such readers may also want to look at the introductory chapter and the chapter on implications for policy and practice (Chapters One and Fourteen). The somewhat more invested reader may want to add the thorough summaries at the end of each substantive chapter (Chapters Three through Twelve). The most avid readers, of course, will enjoy delving into the details of these substantive chapters.

The serious reader will also want to examine Chapter Two, which offers an elegant distillation and comparison of various psychological and sociological models of student development and collegiate impact. In this chapter, the authors note that most of the prominent contributors to theory development and to research into the impact of college on students have been psychologists. The authors note further that "as a consequence, the study of college students and the training of many higher educational researchers and administrators for the last quarter-century have been based largely on one theoretical genre." This genre has been challenged and modified by alternative approaches (primarily sociological) for studying student change and for planning educational programs and services. A psychological orientation—in particular, a developmental perspective—is an important aspect of Pascarella and Terenzini's own view of the interplay between student and college and subtly underlies their analysis of college student change and stability. Yet they are anything but doctrinaire or one-sided in their analysis. Indeed, their psychological approach is heavily tempered by considerations of the nature of interpersonal settings of colleges, the structural and organizational features of colleges' social environments, and the institutional characteristics of college. Incidentally, I might note that Newcomb and I essentially took the reverse tack in synthesizing the research on college impacts: We heavily tempered our more sociological approach with psychological considerations. To put the matter in its briefest formulation, whereas Pascarella and Terenzini lean toward *psychological* social psychology, we leaned toward *sociological* social psychology (compare House, 1977).

The authors have been most shrewd in handling methodological considerations; they are careful not to overwhelm those readers less than expert in their knowledge of research design and data analysis. As the authors themselves state in Chapter One, "Throughout our synthesis of the evidence, we attempt to deal with issues and problems of research design, measurement, and data analysis as they arise and then as simply and benignly as possible." They have also written a technical appendix that addresses in considerable detail the major methodological and analytical issues in assessing the influence of college on students. Even this section makes only minimal assumptions about the reader's statistical or mathematical knowledge and is both readable and lucid.

Pascarella and Terenzini are to be applauded for skillfully drawing out the implications of their synthesis for public policy and institutional practice. They are stalwart in raising policy issues concerning equality and inequality in postsecondary educational outcomes, institutional tolerance of individual student differences, and tensions between educational effectiveness and economic efficiency. Moreover, they use their findings to spell out how the faculty and administrators on individual campuses might best shape the educational and interpersonal settings of their campuses to promote learning and achievement of each institution's goals as well as to induce more students to become involved in the activities of these settings and thus benefit from the proffered opportunities.

How College Affects Students will be of enormous value to researchers, educators, administrators, and others interested in higher education. Its publication is indisputably a milestone in the analysis of college effects on students. More than ever before, we now know how students change at college and understand why they change as they do. At the same time, we are also more aware of *exactly* what we do *not* know about college impacts on students and of *precisely* what gaps in knowledge need filling in. With respect, then, to the influence on students that colleges do have and could have, the present book helps set the research and policy agenda for this, the last decade of the twentieth century.

February 1991   Kenneth A. Feldman
                                                 State University of New York, Stony Brook

We dedicate this book to the memory of
Lance Corporal Michael Doane
United States Marine Corps
Killed in action, Republic of Vietnam, spring 1968
In gratitude for the life of Ernest T. Pascarella

Preface

"If one believes in the cumulative nature of science, then periodic stock-taking becomes essential for any particular arena of scientific endeavor. The cumulation of knowledge in an area may, of course, occur more or less haphazardly—but this does not and should not preclude more systematic attempts by laborers in the field to determine where they have arrived and where they might go." With these words, Kenneth Feldman and Theodore Newcomb (1969) opened the preface to their landmark work, *The Impact of College on Students,* in which they reviewed and synthesized the findings of more than 1,500 studies conducted over four decades on the influence of college on students. They succeeded not only in providing the first comprehensive conceptual map of generally uncharted terrain but also in generating a number of interesting hypotheses about the ways in which college influences students. Moreover, along with the earlier pioneering empirical work of such scholars as Astin (1961, 1962, 1963a, 1963c); Dressel and Mayhew (1954); Eddy (1959); Jacob (1957); Newcomb, Koenig, Flacks, and Warwick (1967); Pace and Stern (1958); Sanford (1956), and Thistlethwaite (1959a, 1959b, 1960, 1962), Feldman and Newcomb were instrumental in precipitating a virtual torrent of studies on the characteristics of collegiate institutions and their students and how students change and benefit during and after their college years from college attendance.

The Impact of College on Students is now a classic, a standard text in graduate courses dealing with college students, as well as a standard and frequently cited reference for scholars, students, and administrators of higher education. Much of what those in the field of higher education currently understand about the developmental influence of college is based on the work of Feldman and Newcomb.

More than twenty years have now passed since the publication of the *Impact of College on Students*. In the intervening decades, the number of empirical studies added to the literature has surpassed the number produced in the preceding four decades reviewed by Feldman and Newcomb. Moreover, major areas of inquiry, such as the effects of college on learning, cognitive development, moral reasoning, and various indexes of status attainment, have reached maturity largely since the late 1960s. These facts in themselves suggest the need for a current synthesis of what we have learned about the influence of college on student development in the last twenty years.

The warrant for this book, however, lies in more than the publication of the many hundreds of studies on the influence of college on students conducted since Feldman and Newcomb's review. The impact of college on students as an area of inquiry has grown qualitatively as well as quantitatively since 1969, in both theory and method. Theories of student development and change have emerged in sometimes daunting number and variety. Multivariate statistical procedures, necessary for testing and extending these emergent theories, have become increasingly accessible to scholars (a development that has yielded mixed blessings). History-altering progress in both mainframe and microcomputing hardware and software has been the handmaiden of these advances, facilitating both the complex statistical analyses needed for testing complex theories and the analysis of large, nationally representative data bases. This happy, phenomenally productive conjunction of theory development, increased design and statistical sophistication, and data management capabilities has produced a research environment and resources that twenty years ago would have been well beyond the reach of all but a handful of well-funded scholars. Today, they are within reach of virtually anyone with interest, talent, and modest support.

Over the last decade, the increasing costs of college attendance and operation, plus mounting criticism of the quality of undergraduate education in the United States, have also spurred research on college outcomes. As computing equipment and management information systems have given college and university administrators and state and federal policymakers greater understanding of and control over college operating budgets and expenditures, the character of the questions asked of higher education has also changed. Questions about cost have increasingly been followed by questions about worth and value, education's "return on investment" in both economic and noneconomic terms. "Assessment" of undergraduate student learning has gained in popularity as a vehicle for a public accounting of an institution's stewardship of its resources and as a mechanism for improving the quality of the education offered.

Increases in all of these areas—in theory, methodological sophistication, computing, cost, criticism, and external oversight—have contributed to the burgeoning literature on the effects of college on students. What have we learned from this enormous volume of research? *Does* college make a difference? In all its simplicity and all its complexity, that is the question we have tried to answer.

The appeal of its straightforwardness notwithstanding, the question is really a naive one. In fact, we have tried to answer six questions. These are discussed more fully in the introductory chapter, but they are reducible to three: Do students change in various ways during the college years? To what extent are changes attributable to the collegiate experience and not to other influences (like growing up)? And finally, what college characteristics and experiences tend to produce changes? Our interest in this last question focuses particularly on institutionally manipulable influences on student change: those sources of change that are amenable to systematic institutional intervention through programmatic and policy decision making.

Audience

We believe our findings will be useful to a wide spectrum of people involved in or responsible for higher education. The full range of academic and student affairs administrators and staff—from middle-level administrators to vice-presidents and presidents—will find the current empirical foundations (or lack thereof) for many of their institutions' student-related activities, programs, and policies. Graduate students preparing for administrative or research positions in higher education, as well as researchers in such fields as psychology, sociology, anthropology, economics, public administration, and business administration who have an interest in the effects of college on students, will find a comprehensive analysis of the literature for a wide variety of student outcome areas, identification of areas in this literature where research is most needed, a conceptual framework (provided by the six questions we pose) for thinking about college effects, and a comprehensive bibliography. State and federal policymakers and their staffs—perhaps better able than we to extract the policy significance of this literature—will gain insight into the sources of influence on student change and what we consider to be the major implications of this body of evidence for administrative practice and public and institutional policy. Anyone interested in higher education in America and its effects on students will, we hope, find here a useful reference book and guide to understanding one of America's most important social institutions.

Overview of the Contents

The introductory chapter (Chapter One) provides a detailed discussion of the evolution of research on college outcomes as an area of study and outlines the conceptual framework that guided our review. Each of the six questions we pose in each college impact area is explained. These questions, we believe, provide a useful way to think about college effects, whether retrospectively (as we have done) or in planning future research. This first chapter also describes our search and review methods and defines key terms used throughout the book.

Chapter Two summarizes the major theoretical models of college effects on student change. These include the "developmental" models of Chickering, Kohlberg, and Perry and the college "impact" models of Astin,

Pascarella, Tinto, and Weidman. A number of less prominent theories and models of student change are also identified.

Chapters Three and Four address the influence of college on learning and cognitive development. Chapter Three focuses on the academic subject matter and skills learned during college, while Chapter Four is concerned with the development of more generalizable intellectual skills and analytical competencies.

Chapters Five through Eight deal with the influence of college on various dimensions of personal growth and change. Chapters Five and Six focus primarily on psychosocial changes, with Chapter Five examining changes in students' self systems (for example, their sense of identity and their self-evaluation), while Chapter Six reviews the research on changes in students' relational systems (for example, the ways they relate to people and institutions outside themselves). Included in the latter chapter are such topics as autonomy, locus of control, authoritarianism, interpersonal relations, personal adjustment, and maturity. Chapter Seven examines changes in students' cultural, aesthetic, and intellectual values; educational and occupational values; political and social attitudes and values; religious values and activities; and gender role orientations. Chapter Eight assesses the impact of college on moral development.

Chapters Nine through Eleven deal with the influence of college on the socioeconomic attainment process, primarily for educational, occupational, and economic attainments. Chapter Nine examines the impact of college on educational attainment. The focus here is on factors that influence educational aspirations, persistence, completion of college, and attainment of graduate and professional degrees. Chapter Ten reviews the contributions of college to career choice and the noneconomic aspects of career achievement and career progression. Here the focus is on factors that influence choice of a career and the various noneconomic dimensions of career success (for example, occupational status, rate and level of promotion, job productivity, and job satisfaction). Chapter Eleven summarizes the various economic returns of college attendance and different collegiate experiences.

Chapter Twelve synthesizes what is known about the long-term impact of college on the quality of life. Included are such factors as subjective well-being, health, marriage, family planning and child nurturance, consumer behavior, savings and investment behavior, and leisure.

Chapter Thirteen summarizes the total body of evidence pertaining to what we know about the impact of college. In the process, the chapter emphasizes the extent to which the evidence corroborates or amplifies the earlier syntheses of Feldman and Newcomb (1969) and Bowen (1977). The chapter also delineates a few of the ways in which certain evidence supports theoretical models of student development and the impact of college.

Chapter Fourteen discusses implications of the evidence for institutional practice and public policy. With regard to institutional practice, we review the findings of our synthesis that have implications for academic and student affairs policy formulation, program and service development, and program evaluation at the level of the individual campus. The key focus is on how the impact of college can be enhanced by administrative action at the campus level. With regard to public policy, we discuss and analyze the implications of the major findings for state and federal policy. Emphasis is on directions the evidence indicates should be taken in state and federal legislation and governmental program development and evaluation.

Following Chapter Fourteen is a technical appendix that addresses in considerable detail some of the major methodological and analytical issues in assessing the influence of college on students. Included is a discussion of such factors as research design, problems in attributing causality, statistical control, residual analysis, regression procedures, commonality analysis, causal modeling and path analysis, unit of analysis, change scores, and conditional versus general effects. This section is intended to be didactic and makes only minimal assumptions about the reader's statistical or mathematical knowledge. It is something of a primer for the nonquantitatively inclined.

Levels of Detail Within Each Chapter

Chapters devoted to a synthesis of the evidence (that is, Chapters Three through Twelve) are written on two levels as far as detail is concerned. On one level, we review the literature within the framework of our six guiding questions, giving attention to theoretical and methodological considerations that often determine the reliability and validity of findings. This detailed presentation of the evidence constitutes the major portion of each chapter. On a second level, we provide a comprehensive summary of our conclusions about the evidence, generally purged of methodological discussion. Such a summary appears at the end of each chapter.

Although many readers will approach each chapter by reading first the detailed synthesis of studies and then the summary, that is by no means the only effective way to digest the large amount of information in the book. Some may find that they gain more from reading the detailed discussion of studies *after* they read the comprehensive summary. We also recognize that a considerable number of readers may be most interested in the comprehensive summary and will use the detailed discussion of evidence in each chapter primarily as an elaborative selective reference. For this group of readers, we have taken pains to ensure that the summary section is in fact a comprehensive rather than a cursory review of our conclusions.

Acknowledgments

Publication of this volume is the culmination of some eight person-years of work, but its completion would have been impossible altogether without the assistance of a large number of people. We cannot possibly acknowledge our indebtedness to everyone who helped us in one way or another, such as the millions of students who agreed to participate in the more than 2,600 studies we reviewed, our graduate students who understood what we were about and respected our need for time and privacy, and the many scholars in the field who supplied us with fugitive conference papers, technical reports, unpublished papers, and original data for our review.

There are some, however, whose contributions to our work require special recognition. We are most deeply indebted to the College of Education at the University of Illinois, Chicago, and to the Institute of Higher Education at the University of Georgia, particularly to Cameron Fincher, for their sustained financial support of our efforts over the last four years. We highly value and appreciate the exceptional quality of the staff they made available to us at various times and in various capacities. Mary Sue Love of the University of Georgia's Institute of Higher Education patiently typed the original text and numerous changes for half of the chapters and made extensive revisions on five more. Yolanda Doyle and Aurelia Jones of the University of Illinois, Chicago, typed and maintained our bibliography, perhaps the most ponderous and cumbersome of its kind anywhere in captivity, as if it were their own. Joyce Placek, Susan Sheffield, and Mary Snyder, all from the University of Georgia, provided various kinds of technical support, from dealing with balky word processors to overseeing institute budgets and ensuring that we had what we needed when we needed it.

We are also deeply grateful to our graduate research assistants: Leslie Herzog of the University of Illinois, Chicago, and Ronald Core, Frances Rauschenberg, and Betty Watts-Warren of the University of Georgia. Collectively, they spent thousands of hours locating, copying, and abstracting journal articles, setting up computerized bibliographic systems, verifying references, and doing countless other tasks that attract little attention but without which competent library research is impossible. We appreciate their enthusiasm for our project and their good humor as much as their competence and attention to detail.

As these young scholars supported our efforts, so were they themselves (and through them were we) supported by the outstanding reference and interlibrary loan librarians and higher education bibliographers of the University of Illinois, Chicago, and University of Georgia libraries. The higher education collections of these two fine research libraries are exceeded only by the competence and patience of their librarians, and on behalf of our graduate assistants and for ourselves, we thank and applaud them.

A literature review of this magnitude requires about equal measures of dedication, hubris, and foolhardiness, and we are indebted to numerous colleagues who encouraged and supported our efforts over the period of the study. From the start, Gale Erlandson, higher education editor for Jossey-Bass, was as enthusiastic about the idea for this volume as we were.

She gave us valuable advice and encouragement throughout the project. We are particularly appreciative of the conscientious and constructive reviews of various chapters that we received from John P. Bean, John M. Braxton, Sven Groennings, Patricia M. King, George D. Kuh, Marcia Baxter Magolda, Theodore K. Miller, James L. Ratcliff, James R. Rest, John C. Smart, Daryl G. Smith, Herbert J. Walberg, and Roger B. Winston, Jr. Their knowledge of their scholarly areas, their thoughtfulness, and their insights contributed substantially to our thinking and writing. Any major oversights or analytical failures we will (good-naturedly, of course) attribute to them.

Special thanks are due to Leonard Baird and Oscar Lenning, who reviewed all chapters and made numerous important suggestions for revisions and improvements in the manuscript. We expected no less from these two meticulous scholars, and we certainly were not disappointed.

We are particularly grateful to Kenneth Feldman. His and Theodore Newcomb's prescience, their dedication to the study of college impacts on students, and their courage in taking on the tasks that produced *The Impact of College on Students* were inspirational in many ways. Our volume, of course, owes its intellectual genesis to theirs. Although there are some fundamental differences between the two books, together they contain a comprehensive analysis and history of the research on college students from its inception to the present. Ken Feldman read all our chapters and made numerous substantive and editorial suggestions that improved both the quality of our thinking and the tightness of our prose. On many occasions we benefited from the insights he had gained from producing his own review, from his encyclopedic knowledge of the research on college students, from his good humor and encouragement when our intellectual reach seemed to exceed our grasp, and from the example of the almost unattainably high standards his work has set for reviews of the literature.

Finally, we are most deeply indebted to our families for the sacrifices they have made. Our wives, Diana Pascarella and Caroline Terenzini, know better than all others what has gone into the preparation of this manuscript. Through it all, they were unfailingly supportive, understanding, and patient. Our children—Andy, Allison, and Emily Pascarella and Eden, John, and Drew Terenzini—made their own special contributions. Although they may not have fully understood what their absentee fathers were up to, their patience and enthusiasm for seeing what came to be called simply "the Book" provided a kind of encouragement that can come only from one's children.

To all these people we extend heartfelt thanks.

February 1991

Ernest T. Pascarella
Chicago, Illinois

Patrick T. Terenzini
State College, Pennsylvania

The Authors

Ernest T. Pascarella is professor of educational psychology at the University of Illinois, Chicago. Previously, he was associate director for research at the Center for Instructional Development at Syracuse University, where he received his Ph.D. degree (1973) in higher education. He received his A.B. degree (1965) in religion from Princeton University and his M.S. degree (1970) in psychological measurement from the University of Pennsylvania.

For the past seventeen years, Pascarella has focused his research and writing on student persistence in higher education and the impact of college on students. He has received awards for outstanding research from the International Reading Association (1981), the Association for Institutional Research (1987), the National Association of Student Personnel Administrators (1988), and the American Educational Research Association, Division J (1989). In 1986 he received the Distinguished Scholar-Teacher Award from the College of Education at Illinois and in 1989–90 served as president of the Association for the Study of Higher Education.

Patrick T. Terenzini is professor of higher education and senior scientist at the Center for the Study of Higher Education at The Pennsylvania State University. During most of the writing of this volume (1986–1989), he was professor of higher education at the Institute of Higher Education of the University of Georgia. Previously, he was assistant to the president for planning (1984–1986) and director of institutional research (1978–1984) at the State University of New York, Albany. Terenzini received his A.B. degree (1964) in English from Dartmouth College, his M.A.T. degree (1965) in English education from Harvard University, and his Ph.D. degree (1972) in higher education from Syracuse University.

Terenzini has received both the Sidney Suslow Award and two Forum Best Paper Awards from the Association for Institutional Research. He is editor-in-chief of *New Directions for Institutional Research,* associate editor of *Higher Education: Handbook of Theory and Research,* and a consulting editor for *Research in Higher Education.*

How
COLLEGE
AFFECTS
STUDENTS

1

Studying
College Outcomes:
Overview and
Organization
of the Research

Americans have traditionally had a special relationship with their colleges and universities. Public and private financial support for the nation's more than 3,000 postsecondary institutions has been massive. In some cases institutions have become quite wealthy, with endowments in excess of 500 million or even a billion dollars. But the relationship goes beyond simple financial support and often enters the realm of the emotional. Alma maters frequently use the words *loyal, faithful, love,* and *giving* in musically describing one's presumed lifetime bond to an undergraduate college or university. Songs written to spur on athletic teams call upon individuals to "fight for" and, in some extreme cases, make the ultimate sacrifice for their school. Perhaps nothing captures this so simply and directly as Daniel Webster's words about Dartmouth College before John Marshall and the Supreme Court in 1818: "It is, sir, as I have said, a small college, and yet there are those who love it" (Rudolph, 1962).

That a social institution can engender such fervent and magnanimous support attests to the generally high regard in which Americans hold postsecondary institutions in this country. And, indeed, we do often expect our colleges and universities to accomplish great things. In terms of educating undergraduate students, these include (but are certainly not limited to) such lofty goals as transmitting the intellectual heritage of Western civilization; fostering a high level of verbal and mathematical skills; developing an in-depth understanding of social, cultural, and political institutions; facilitating one's ability to think reflectively, analytically, critically, synthetically, and evaluatively; developing one's value structures and moral sensibilities; facilitating personal growth and self-identity; and fostering one's sense of career identity and vocational competence. In addition, there are

1

the less lofty but fully appreciated goals of socializing the individual for effective functioning in the middle class and acting as an important entrée to positions of status, influence, and wealth in American society.

The fact that until recently American postsecondary education has enjoyed such a long tradition of public and private support is perhaps one strong indicator of the general belief that undergraduate education does, in fact, accomplish these goals. But to what extent can we actually substantiate our beliefs? What systematic evidence do we have that undergraduate education influences individuals in the lofty ways so often claimed in college catalogues? This book is the outcome of a five-year effort to review and synthesize the recent evidence addressing these questions. As such, it is the most recent of a series of works (of varying degrees of comprehensiveness) that have similarly been concerned with an inventory of what we know and do not know about the influence of college on student development.

Twenty years have passed since the publication of *The Impact of College on Students* (Feldman & Newcomb, 1969). In that time, a number of important theoretical, methodological, and substantive contributions to research on the impact of college have appeared. These advances have combined to produce a body of studies that differs in significant ways from the vast preponderance of studies reviewed by Feldman and Newcomb (1969). Perhaps the single most important of these recent contributions has been the development of theoretical frameworks to guide and focus inquiry. Since the late 1960s an impressive number of formal theories (and some less well developed but still useful "models") of student development have been advanced. When informed and guided by these theoretical structures, inquiry has moved sharply away from descriptive, bivariate analyses, becoming more conceptually complex yet simultaneously more parsimonious. The trend has been decidedly away from random, opportunistic analyses and toward more focused, systematic, planned, and controlled studies. In short, the past twenty years have seen theories and models increasingly used to guide the designs of studies. Instead of simply describing what changes occur, the focus of these studies has been on understanding or explaining the complex longitudinal process of college impact. It should be pointed out, however, that only a minority of the total body of studies we review are theory driven. Nevertheless, we believe that the development of a theory base to guide inquiry on the impact of college has been an important contribution to knowledge in its own right. One chapter of this book (Chapter Two) is devoted to a discussion of several of the major or representative theoretical statements, and at least a small part of the evidence we review speaks to the validity of these models.

A second major advance has been in the sophistication and complexity of the analytical tools brought to bear on empirical questions in the social and behavioral sciences. This increased complexity is directly related to dramatic advances in computing hardware and software. Prior to the end of the 1960s only a few "canned" statistical packages existed, and of those that did, many (perhaps most) were incapable of performing multivariate analyses such as multiple group discriminant function analysis or the more complex forms of covariance and regression analysis. Such analyses often required specially written or borrowed programs.

With the development of more sophisticated, user-oriented statistical packages such as SPSS (Nie, 1983) and SAS (SAS Institute, 1985), the power of multivariate analysis has become available to novitiate and experienced researchers alike. Arguably, the consequences of this have not been uniformly positive. The uninformed use of sophisticated analytical routines is often more likely to obfuscate and mislead than to clarify. Nevertheless, the impressive advances in computing power during the last twenty years have permitted scholars to analyze large and complex national data sets with relative (though perhaps not absolute) ease and efficiency. Such analyses have made major contributions to our understanding of such issues as the impact of college on status attainment and the influence of institutional characteristics on learning. Moreover, they represent a new emphasis or direction in the research literature, which is not nearly so apparent in the studies reviewed by Feldman and Newcomb.

Third, and perhaps stemming from the confluence of theoretical and computing advances, the complexity of analytical or research designs has increased. The late 1960s and early 1970s saw the increased use of various regression analysis procedures to study the "unique," "net," or "unconfounded" effects of such factors as college characteristics or individual collegiate experiences on student development. With the development of theoretically guided causal models, regression procedures were used to estimate the "causal paths" among variables, which in turn permitted the researcher to portray the potential direct and indirect effects of different influences on student development. Often such "path analyses" took a multilevel approach that allowed one to assess aggregate (for example, institution, academic major, classroom) as well as individual level influences. More recently, path analysis has been refined to yet more powerful and complex causal modeling such as that available through linear structural relations (LISREL) and other structural equation models.

The adaptation of multiple regression procedures to the estimation of theoretical, causal models of college impact has been an important evolutionary change in the research literature during the past two decades. It is the hallmark of what could be described as a change from analytical designs that permit one to describe to designs that permit one to attempt to explain or understand.

Aside from dramatic growth in the body of existing evidence and significant developments in the nature of inquiry, external factors have contributed additional pressure for a reassessment of the impact of college. For example, the funding climate for higher education has been substantially transformed. Over the last two decades, inflation has driven up the cost of most things—including a college education. The postwar "baby boom" has largely passed through the postsecondary system, and the number of high school graduates has headed steadily downward. The combined effect of these two forces has been an erosion in the strength of higher education's claim for public and private support. This was brought into sharp relief in the mid 1980s by the publication of several national reports generally critical of American postsecondary education (for example, *Involvement in Learning* [National Institute of Education Study Group, 1984], *To Reclaim a Legacy* [Bennett, 1984], and *Integrity in the College Curriculum* [Association of American Colleges, 1985]). As a consequence, higher education coordinating boards, legislators, taxpayers, parents, and students have become increasingly concerned with evidence supporting college and university claims about the benefits of college attendance. From their perspective it is clearly legitimate to ask the question, What value (in the broadest sense of the term) does college add to an individual's life?

The impetus for this book stems largely from the confluence of the trends discussed above: (1) the growth of a large and significant body of additional evidence on the impact of college since Feldman and Newcomb's (1969) synthesis; (2) theoretical, analytical, and methodological contributions that have moved inquiry on the impact of college in new and productive directions; and (3) recent external pressures for accountability in terms of the various benefits attributable to college attendance. The book attempts to review and synthesize the evidence on the impact of college that has accumulated from 1967 to the present (because the Feldman and Newcomb synthesis was published in 1969, the literature it reviews generally stops at 1967).

To be sure, this is not the first work since Feldman and Newcomb (1969) to summarize the evidence on the impact of college. Other useful summaries include (but are by no means limited to) Chickering's *Education and Identity* (1969); Spaeth and Greeley's *Recent Alumni and Higher Education* (1970); Withey's *A Degree and What Else* (1971); Solmon and Taubman's *Does College Matter?* (1973); Lenning, Munday, Johnson, Vander Well, and Brue's *The Many Faces of College Success and Their Nonintellectual Correlates* (1974b); Bowen's *Investment in Learning* (1977); and Pace's *Measuring the Outcomes of College: Fifty Years of Findings and Recommendations for the Future* (1979). Of such summaries, Bowen (1977), in reviewing approximately 600 studies, makes the strongest attempt at comprehensiveness in terms of the body of evidence synthesized and the breadth of outcomes considered. His synthesis, however, focuses largely on the global outcomes of college attendance, that is, the various intellectual, personal, and economic benefits that accrue to those who attend college versus those who do not. The present volume is, of course, also concerned with this question. It moves beyond it, however, in also attempting to identify the specific institutional determinants of student change—those specific aspects of the collegiate experience that make a difference and over which institutions may have some control. Indeed, the identification (if not the unequivocal establishment) of links between institutional policies and programs and student change may constitute one of the major contributions of this book, the feature that perhaps sets it apart from its estimable predecessors.

Conceptual Framework

The second most difficult decision to make in attempting a synthesis of an extremely large body of research is the adoption of a guiding conceptual or organizational framework. (The most difficult decision, of course, is deciding whether or not to attempt it in the first place.) We considered two major issues in developing the conceptual framework for the present synthesis. The first was the organizing principle for presenting findings. After a fairly lengthy consideration, we decided to organize the evidence in terms of different types of outcomes rather than the potential sources of institutional influence on college outcomes (for example, major field, place of residence during college, student-faculty interactions).

In determining what types of outcomes to consider in our synthesis, we were guided by the thinking of various scholars concerned with taxonomies of the outcomes of college (for example, Astin, 1973a; Brown & DeCoster, 1982; Ewell, 1984, 1985a, 1985b, 1988; Hanson, 1982; Jacobi, Astin, & Ayala, 1987; Lenning, Lee, Micek, & Service, 1977; Parker & Schmidt, 1982). Of these, Astin's (1973a) taxonomy of outcomes was particularly influential in defining the content and scope of our synthesis. Astin suggests that college outcomes can be conceptualized along three dimensions: type of outcome, type of data, and time span. The first two dimensions can be visualized as a 2 × 2 matrix where type of outcome tends to be either cognitive or affective and type of data tends to be either psychological or behavioral. The temporal dimension makes less sense as a dichotomy and instead can be considered a continuous variable tapping the time span over which outcomes are assessed. Cognitive outcomes have to do with the utilization of higher-order intellectual processes such as knowledge acquisition, decision making, synthesis, and reasoning. Affective outcomes are attitudes, values, self-concepts, aspirations, and personality dispositions. The second dimension of Astin's taxonomy refers to the operations required to assess the cognitive or affective outputs under consideration. Psychological data reflect the internal states or traits of the individual and are typically assessed indirectly by means of a test or examination. Thus, an individual's level of skill in critical thinking is inferred from responses to a set of questions. Behavioral measures, on the other hand, are based on direct observation of the individual. Consequently, there is little to infer.

Astin's (1973a) 2 × 2 taxonomy of college outcomes, then, permits one to look at four different types of outcomes based on the intersection of the two dimensions: *cognitive-psychological* (for example, subject matter knowledge, critical thinking), *cognitive-behavioral* (level of educational attainment, occupational attainment, income, and the like), *affective-psychological* (for example, values, attitudes, personality orientations), and *affective-behavioral* (leadership, choice of major, choice of career, use of leisure time, and so on). Using Astin's model as a guide for defining the parameters of the evidence to be considered, the chapters of this book address different broad categories of college outcomes designed to provide coverage of the four taxonomic cells. Some chapters fit rather neatly into a single cell. For example, chapters on the acquisition of subject matter knowledge and academic skills and on the development of general cognitive competencies and skills (Chapters Three and Four) fall into the cognitive-psychological cell; chapters on psychosocial development and values and attitudes (Chapters Five through Seven) fit generally into the affective-psychological cell; and chapters on educational attainment and economic returns (Chapters Nine and Eleven) fall into the cognitive-behavioral cell. Other chapters, however, include elements from more than one cell. The chapter on moral development (Chapter Eight) probably taps both the cognitive-psychological and affective-psychological cells. Similarly, the chapters on career and quality of life (Chapters Ten and Twelve) tap both the cognitive-behavioral and affective-behavioral cells.

Obviously, some artificiality is inherent in any separation of the outcomes of college into discrete categories. A student does not develop in separate unrelated pieces but rather grows as an integrated whole. Development in one area is often highly related to, perhaps even dependent upon, development in other areas. Nevertheless, some reasonable taxonomy or categorization of outcomes is necessary if one is to make any sense of the vast amount of evidence available.

It is important to state explicitly that the focus of the present synthesis is on the outcomes of college for individual students. Certainly, evidence concerning the effects of postsecondary education on society is a scholarly topic worthy of considerable attention (for example, Bowen, 1977). However, we judged a synthesis of the societal benefits of college to be beyond the scope of this book.

The second major dimension of the conceptual framework of our synthesis concerned critical questions to be asked of the evidence within each of the various broad categories of outcomes. Here we were directly aided by the questions that guided some of our own previous research reviews (for example, Pascarella, 1985a; Nucci & Pascarella, 1987), and we decided to adapt that framework to the present synthesis.[1] Therefore, to the extent applicable within each category of outcomes, six basic questions guided the synthesis of evidence:

1. *What evidence is there that individuals change during the time in which they are attending college?* This, of course, is a fundamental question and one on which hinges the relevance of many subsequent questions that might be asked concerning college impact. For some outcomes, unless there is reason to believe that individuals change during college, questions regarding the effects of college versus noncollege or the effects of different institutional environments are essentially moot. A shorthand expression for the question will be "Change During College."

2. *What evidence is there that change or development during college is the result of college attendance?* This question is more specific (and therefore more difficult to answer) than our first one. It is not merely concerned with whether change or development occurs during college but instead focuses on the extent to which whatever change does occur can be attributed to college attendance rather than other influences (for example, normal maturation, differences in background traits between those who attend and do not attend college). In different contexts and in different disciplines this has been referred to as the "unique," "net," or "value-added" effects of college (Pascarella, 1986b). Our shorthand label for this question will be "Net Effects of College."

3. *What evidence is there that different kinds of postsecondary institutions have a differential influence on student change or development during college?* This question is essentially asking whether or not discernible differences in student development or the outcomes of college are attributable to the characteristics of the particular institution attended (institutional type, student body selectivity, size, financial resources, and the like). Since this question is primarily concerned with differential impacts between and among institutions, the shorthand phrase for this question will be "Between-College Effects."

4. *What evidence exists on effects of different experiences within the same institution?* This question is concerned with identifying different subenvironments or experiences within the institution (for example, residence arrangement, academic major, peer group involvement, extracurricular activities, interaction with faculty) that may have influences on student change or development. The shorthand expression will be "Within-College Effects."

5. *What evidence is there that the collegiate experience produces conditional, as opposed to general, effects on student change or development?* This question essentially asks whether various influential collegiate experiences have the same aggregate or general effect for all students or whether these experiences vary in their influence for different kinds of students (for example, men versus women, minority versus nonminority, low- versus high-aptitude students). While a general effect suggests that a particular experience is the same for all students experiencing it, a conditional

effect suggests that the magnitude of the effect is conditioned by or varies according to the specific characteristics of the individuals being considered. Thus, for example, a particular experience may have stronger developmental effects for male than for female students. Conditional effects are sometimes referred to as interaction effects in that individual subject differences are said to interact with the particular experience or exposure thought to influence a particular outcome. Our shorthand label will be "Conditional Effects of College."

6. *What are the long-term effects of college?* This question addresses the durability or permanence of the collegiate experience, or differences in that experience, on students' postcollege activities, attitudes, beliefs, and behaviors. Our shorthand phrase will be "Long-Term Effects of College."

Obviously, not all questions will be meaningful in terms of each category of college outcome considered. The influence of college is manifest much earlier on such outcomes as cognitive or moral development than it is on occupational or economic attainments. Indeed, for the latter two outcomes it makes little to sense to talk about development or changes during college.

Scope of the Evidence Reviewed

As previously indicated, the temporal, chronological focus of the synthesis is the evidence produced from 1967 to the present. In several instances, however, we review studies conducted prior to 1967 if that particular area of research has been untouched by existing syntheses or in order to place more recent evidence in context. To identify applicable investigations we initially conducted searches of various abstracting documents and data bases (for example, *Sociological Abstracts, Psychological Abstracts, Sociology of Education Abstracts, Dissertation Abstracts, College Student Personnel Abstracts, Higher Education Abstracts*). We also reviewed recent conference proceedings from such scholarly and professional associations as the American Educational Research Association, the Association for the Study of Higher Education, and the Association for Institutional Research. This allowed us to obtain studies that had yet to be published or that had never been published. Finally, we also used an extensive network of colleagues to obtain unpublished papers and technical reports that deal with college impact.

We believe these efforts yielded nearly every *major* research report concerned with the impact of college on students in books, monographs, journals, and nonpublished sources since 1967. It would be foolhardy to claim that the results of our literature search were completely exhaustive (although we have tried to approach this goal). With such a mass of literature to screen, it is likely that some studies were missed. Nevertheless, we do feel that our search has been thorough and that the studies we review here are at least a comprehensive representation of the existing literature.

Analysis of the Evidence

The two most comprehensive syntheses of the evidence on the impact of college on students, those of Feldman and Newcomb (1969) and Bowen (1977), are what has been termed narrative or explanatory literature reviews. That is, the syntheses and conclusions are based on a logical, explanatory analysis of the literature and are presented in narrative form. That this type of literature review or research synthesis has a strong and lengthy tradition in education and the social and behavioral sciences is evidenced by scanning such journals as *Review of Educational Research* and *Psychological Bulletin* and annual reviews such as *Review of Research in Education, Annual Review of Sociology,* and *Higher Education: Handbook of Theory and Research.*

About a decade ago, however, Glass and his colleagues introduced the concept of meta-analysis as an alternative methodology to the narrative synthesis of research findings (Glass, 1977; Glass, Cahen, Smith, & Filby, 1982; Glass, McGaw, & Smith, 1981). The primary purpose of meta-analysis is to apply systematic and scientific techniques and standards to the evaluation and summary of research (Walberg, 1985). Not surprisingly, it depends heavily on the quantification of the results of each study into a metric that permits aggregation and comparison across studies. The basic metric used is the effect size. This can be thought of as a standardized or z score expressed as the difference between the mean of an experimental group (for example, college attenders) and the mean of a control group (for example, nonattenders) divided by the standard deviation of the control group or in some situations the pooled standard deviation of both groups. By consulting the area under the normal curve, one can use this z score to determine the percentile point improvement or advantage accruing to the experimental group. Effect sizes can also be computed from correlation coefficients, thus permitting one to conduct quantitative research syntheses with correlational data.

Clearly, there are advantages to the use of meta-analysis in synthesizing a large body of literature. Among these are greater standardization in the reporting of results and conclusions, ease of comparability of conclusions across different bodies of research, an objective method for resolving conflicting findings in a body of evidence, and less dependence on the subjective biases of the person(s) conducting the synthesis (Glass, 1977; Jackson, 1980; Pillemer & Light, 1980; Light & Pillemer, 1982; Cooper, 1982).

In view of these potential advantages, we gave lengthy and serious consideration to the use of meta-analysis as the dominant approach to our synthesis. A number of factors, however, led us to decide against it. First, applications of meta-analysis have come under close and often critical scrutiny in terms of their producing a truly objective and meaningful synthesis of evidence (for example, Cook & Leviton, 1980; Eysenck, 1978; Gallo, 1978; Presby, 1978; Slavin, 1984; Wortman, 1983). These criticisms revolve largely around the following issues: (1) the forced combination of studies so different that the conclusions may make little conceptual sense (that is, the apples and oranges issue), (2) the failure to detect or take into account systematic bias in the underlying studies reviewed, and (3) the failure to discuss adequately the quality of studies being reviewed and to place greater weight on the studies that use stronger designs. These and related criticisms of meta-analysis are cogently reviewed by Slavin (1984), who concludes that meta-analysis can be a useful supplement to traditional narrative, explanatory reviews but should not be seen as a replacement for them.

The second, and perhaps more important, reason for our deciding against meta-analysis as the primary method of synthesizing the evidence was simply the remarkable diversity of ways in which research on the impact of college on students is reported. To some extent, of course, this may reflect the interdisciplinary nature of research on college students. The simple fact is that in many areas of inquiry the broad range of statistical evidence employed to report results makes the use of quantitative synthesis impractical if not impossible. For example, in some of the status-attainment research, results are variously reported in terms of partial correlations, increases in variance explained, unstandardized regression weights, standardized regression weights, or direct, indirect, and total effects in path analysis. Moreover, researchers who study the same status attainment outcomes with correlational data often differ in the variables that they control to estimate the net effects of college. This further complicates any quantitative aggregation of results. Such variety in statistical procedures used and statistics reported is not unique to this content area. Confronted with such overwhelming complexity and diversity, we judged it virtually impossible to compute comparable study effect sizes or to aggregate them in a manner that would yield meaningful conclusions. Related to this issue was our concern that the requirements of quantifying study results in a comparable metric would exclude studies based on naturalistic inquiry or other relevant investigations whose results were simply not amenable to the computation of effect sizes.

Having considered and decided against meta-analysis as our major methodology, we turned to a narrative explanatory synthesis as our primary approach to the analysis of evidence. In this approach we were guided by the criterion of "weight of evidence." That is, given a logical analysis of the studies conducted, what does the weight of evidence suggest about the influence of college or the influence of different aspects of the collegiate experience? It is interesting that when operationalized as "box scores" or "vote counts" (that is, the percentage or proportion of studies that show positive results versus those that do not), the simple criterion of weight of evidence has been found to yield conclusions quite similar to those based on effect sizes computed in meta-analysis. Indeed, the correlations between the two approaches are in the .77 to .87 range (Walberg, 1985).

Our own operationalization of the weight of evidence criterion, while not always in the form of box scores or vote counts, nevertheless has two important dimensions. First, it is not exclusionary in that we attempt to synthesize all the available studies pertaining to an outcome, not just certain ones. Second, we attempt to take into account variations in the methodological characteristics of studies and to give greater inferential weight to those investigations that are the most methodologically sound. This is particularly important in those instances where findings conflict. However, as we will see, it is sometimes the case that the weight of evidence is clear irrespective of the methodological attributes of the studies considered.

Although we have chosen a narrative, explanatory approach to our synthesis, we have still made supplementary use of meta-analytical techniques and results. In several of our chapters we review the results of meta-analytical work, and in at least one case we conduct our own meta-analysis to corroborate findings. We have also used a subset of studies in another synthesis to conduct our own meta-analysis of studies in that area that pertain directly to postsecondary education.

A Brief Note on Methodology

To those who conduct research on the effects of college on students and to those who are about to read the remainder of this book, there is simply no escaping the fact that what we can confidently conclude about the influence of college or the influence of different collegiate experiences on student development is in large measure determined by methodological issues. Throughout our synthesis of the evidence, we attempt to deal with issues and problems of research design, measurement, and data analysis as they arise and then as simply and benignly as possible. (This is, after all, a synthesis of research evidence, not a research design or statistics text.) Nevertheless, since we employ several terms frequently throughout the book, it is important to define them here.

The first of these terms is *net effect*. The easiest way to explain net effect is through an example. Suppose one wishes to estimate the effect of attending versus not attending college on cognitive development while at the same time controlling for the confounding influence of differences in initial intelligence between college and noncollege groups. If one were to compute the association between college attendance and a measure of cognitive development while statistically controlling for intelligence, the result would be an estimate of the effect of college on cognitive development *net* of (or independent of) the confounding influence of initial intelligence. Thus, the term *net effect* has a relative meaning, depending upon what confounding variables are controlled.

The second term is *direct effect*. A direct effect can be thought of as the unmediated influence of one variable on another (that is, the impact is direct and does not pass through an intervening variable). Although the descriptor *direct* is seldom used in the research literature, direct effects are by far the most frequently estimated effects in educational and social science research. Using our previous example, if going to college has a significant association with cognitive development when intelligence is controlled, then it can be said to have a direct effect on cognitive development net of intelligence. Conversely, if the association between college attendance is nonsignificant when intelligence is taken into account, then college can be said to have no direct effect on cognitive development net of intelligence. Throughout the text we frequently employ the complete descriptor *direct effect*. For purposes of brevity and variety, however, we also use the shorthand (and more common) term *effect* to stand for a "direct effect." Thus, whenever the term *effect* is used without an antecedent modifier, it signifies the direct or unmediated effect of a variable.

Although it is seldom estimated in the existing research, a variable may also have an "indirect" or mediated effect on an outcome. This occurs when the effect is transmitted through an intervening variable or variables. For example, it is possible that college attendance may have an important indirect effect on adult cognitive development by influencing a person's reading habits. Thus, the path of indirect influence would be college attendance directly affecting reading habits, and reading habits in turn directly affecting cognitive development. In this and similar ways college could have a significant impact on a range of outcomes without having a direct effect on them. In our synthesis of the research evidence, we have been impressed by how many of the effects of college are, or could be, indirect. Consequently, the term *indirect effect* is employed frequently throughout the book.

A final term is *total effect*. This is nothing more than the sum of the direct and indirect effects of one variable on another. In some instances the total effect of a variable will consist largely of its direct effect on an outcome. In other instances most of the total effect may be indirect. In still other cases a variable may have substantial direct and indirect impacts.

Our brief introduction of the above terms should afford the reader a basic understanding of them when they are used in the remainder of the book. Nevertheless a more detailed discussion of each is presented in the Appendix. Moreover, while we provide a brief working definition of each new statistical or methodological term as it is introduced in the text, we will often refer the reader to the Appendix for a more detailed presentation.

A Brief Note on the Evidence

As one might imagine, evidence on such a broad topic as the impact of college varies not only in methodological rigor but also in the focus of research, the nature of the samples, and the operational definitions of variables. Consequently, it may be useful for the reader to be aware of several general limitations or problems in the overall body of evidence.

First, the evidence has a bias. It focuses largely (although not exclusively) on nonminority students of traditional college age (eighteen to twenty-two), attending four-year institutions full-time and living on campus. This is not to say that the research literature has ignored the increasing numbers of students in American postsecondary education who fall outside these "traditional student" categories (for example, minority and older students, students attending college part-time while holding a job, commuter students, community college students). That would overstate the case. It is clear, nonetheless, that the impacts of college on such "nontraditional" students are underrepresented in the existing evidence.

A second problem with the evidence is that the characteristics of samples in the research vary dramatically, from single-institution samples with only a few students to multi-institution, nationally representative samples with hundreds and often thousands of students. In some areas of research, such as the impact of college on moral development, synthesizing the evidence is largely a task of finding common threads among many small-sample, single-institution studies. Here, the key problem, a problem that is not always resolved, is the generalizability of findings. In other areas of research, such as attitudes and values, psychosocial characteristics, educational attainment, and career, we tend to give greater credence to the findings from secondary analyses of large, nationally representative samples. Although such samples increase generalizability, this can come with a price. Secondary analysis often requires the construction of scales from items that may not have been intended for the purpose to which they will be put in a particular study. Consequently, the items may end up having only a marginal or surface relationship with the construct they are purported to measure. In short, the price one often pays for the generalizability inherent in national samples is problematic measurement of salient variables.

Third, researchers and lay readers alike must be wary of the potential in large national studies for identifying statistically significant differences or changes that may or may not have comparable educational, administrative, or policy significance. This potential is an artifact of the sensitivity of tests of statistical significance to large sample sizes: The larger the sample size, the more likely one is to detect statistically significant relations between and among variables. To minimize the risk of finding a mountain in a molehill, wherever possible we have estimated average effect sizes and based our conclusions on those estimates of the magnitudes of college impact.[2]

Fourth, with a few exceptions, such as the research on moral reasoning and reflective judgment, studies often differ substantially in their operational measurement of the same construct. For example, variables such as critical thinking, college "quality," liberalism, formal education, and subjective well-being are measured in a number of different ways in different studies. Such multiple assessment versions of the same construct present a challenge for the reviewer not unlike that of the problematic measurement of constructs in secondary analysis. The challenge is essentially one of determining replicability of results. Can one uncover consistent findings across studies that differ in the instruments used or the validity of operational definitions employed to assess the same construct?

Finally, in some areas of study, particularly those assessing change in cognitive skills, psychosocial development, or attitudes and values, the evidence is sometimes derived from instruments that place a premium on stability of measurement. Thus, some of these instruments may have a built-in bias *against* reflecting educational change. Consequently, evidence that suggests virtually no shifts in certain student traits may not necessarily mean that no change in fact occurred. There is at least the possibility that the full magnitude of the change is only partially reflected by the measure in use (Winter, 1979; Winter, McClelland, & Stewart, 1981).

Notes

1. It should be noted that Gurin (1971) developed somewhat similar questions at an earlier time.
2. Effect sizes were estimated as the average (across studies) change in freshman-to-senior scores calculated in terms of standard deviation units. More specifically, an effect size was estimated by subtracting a freshman-year mean score from the senior-year mean and then dividing that difference by the freshman-year standard deviation. The effect sizes from each study for a given outcome variable were then averaged across studies. When expressed in standard deviation units, effect sizes can be converted (using the area under the normal curve) to an estimate of the percentile point change. For example, given an estimated effect size equal to one standard deviation, the area under the normal curve extends from the 50th to the 84th percentile, indicating a change of 34 percentile points. Where possible and appropriate in subsequent chapters, we report estimated average college effect sizes in terms of both standard deviation and percentile point units.

2

Theories and Models
of Student Change
in College

Two decades ago, Chickering (1969) reflected on the flood of research on college students precipitated by Jacob (1957) and wrote, "These burgeoning efforts, almost without exception, have been exploratory. Few theories have been framed, few hypotheses tested. Thus, though much useful knowledge has been generated, it has remained in unintegrated form" (pp. 4–5). At about the same time, Keniston (1971a) lamented the absence of any "psychology, apart from the work of Erik Erikson, to adequately understand the feelings and behavior of today's American youth" (p. 3). Singer (1968) reviewed all the chapters on developmental psychology in the *Annual Review of Psychology* from 1950 to 1968 and found "almost no discussion of development after adolescence" (p. 608).

Since the late 1960s and early 1970s, however, an impressive number of formal theories (and some less well developed but still useful "models") of student change have been advanced. Indeed, the growth in theory development is one of the most striking and significant trends in the study of collegiate impact over the last two decades. In fact, depending upon how strictly one defines *theory,* twenty or more candidates are identifiable to guide an inquiry into how students change in the collegiate setting or to suggest what sorts of policy or programmatic interventions might be the most effective in promoting an institution's educational goals.

In addition to their number, these theories are distinguished by their almost exclusively psychological character. Most of the prominent contributors to theory development and research on the impact of college on students are psychologists. As a consequence, the study of college students and the training of many higher educational researchers and administrators for the last quarter-century have been based largely on one theoretical genre. Theories from other fields have only more recently begun to receive attention.

Despite the overall dominance of the psychological paradigm for explaining student change, a variety of theories have emerged, even within the developmental psychology tradition. All attempt to explain essentially similar processes, but they do so in ways that involve apparently different approaches and dimensions and manifestly different nomenclatures. Unless one wishes to assume that one theory or conception is as good as another, however, researchers and practitioners alike now confront questions about the similarities and differences among these models and the appropriateness of each for any given piece of research, program, or policy being considered.

The overall objective of this chapter is to review the theoretical ground upon which the study and practice of undergraduate education stands and to give some coherent shape to the conceptual diversity that tends to cloud our understanding and discussions of how college students change and why. Subsequent chapters in this book summarize the research of the last twenty years and shed some light on the conceptual validity of many of the theories reviewed in this chapter. No attempt is made, however, to develop a comprehensive, integrated theory, something that would probably be an impossible task anyway.

Change Versus Development

Before proceeding, it is important to differentiate between change and development. *Change* refers to alterations that occur over time in students' internal cognitive or affective characteristics. Change may be quantitative or qualitative, and it implies no directionality, encompassing both regression and progression. It is a descriptive, value-free term. *Development,* on the other hand, has generated considerable philosophical and theoretical debate among psychologists, sociologists, and others for some time. No attempt is made here to settle the matter. According to Learner (1986), however, some general agreement exists on the basic characteristics of development regardless of the disciplinary lens through which it is viewed. Those basic agreements, when aggregated, suggest that development involves changes in an organism that are "systematic, [organized, and] successive . . . and are thought to serve an adaptive function, i.e., to enhance survival" (p. 41). Intrapersonal changes may be a consequence of physical maturation (or deterioration), environmental influences, or the interaction of the individual and the environment (Kitchener, 1982). Embedded in this concept is a presumption of "growth," or the potential for growth, toward maturity, toward greater complexity through differentiation and integration. Development also implies that growth is to be valued and pursued as a desirable psychological and educational end, perhaps even as a moral end (Perry, 1970; Feldman, 1972).

Categories of Theories of College Student Change

Because the vast majority of studies of college students have focused on traditional-aged undergraduates (that is, those eighteen to twenty-two years old), the theories and models selected for review in this chapter deal principally with change or growth among that group of undergraduates. We do not intend to suggest by this that older students are unimportant in higher education or that theories of change over the full, human life span are without merit for understanding the effects of postsecondary education on individuals (including traditional-aged undergraduates). Indeed, these life-span theories are becoming increasingly important as larger numbers of older students enter (or return to) college. Similarly, we have chosen not to discuss theories of more generalized human change or development that apply to all individuals, whether in college or not (for example, Erikson, 1959, 1963, 1968). For practical reasons and with one or two exceptions, we have limited our discussion to those theories that are specific to traditional-aged college students, that have received widespread attention in the research literature on college students to date, or that have been widely adopted in the development of academic and nonacademic programs and services intended to facilitate educationally desirable changes in students. As will be seen below and in subsequent chapters, however, readers should understand that the evolving character of higher education's clientele, specifically the growing numbers of minority group and older students, raises serious questions about the universal applicability of these theories and models.

While a number of taxonomies of theories and models of student change might be developed, at least two general families are discernible in the literature on college students. One addresses the nature, structure, and processes of individual human growth. These "developmental" theories typically describe the dimensions of student development and the phases of individual growth along each dimension. This class of theories has been dominated by but is not restricted to psychological "stage" theories, which posit one or another level of development through which individuals pass in a presumably invariant and hierarchical sequence.

A second general class of models for the study of college student change focuses less on intra-individual development than on the environmental or sociological origins of student change (which need not be seen in all instances as developmental). These "college impact" models tend to be more eclectic and to identify sets of variables that are presumed to exert an influence on one or more aspects of student change, with particular emphasis on between- and within-institutional effects on change or development. These variable sets may be student related (sex, academic aptitude and achievement, socioeconomic status, race or ethnicity, and so on), structural and organizational (size, type of control, selectivity, and the like), or environmental (for example, the academic, cultural, social, and/or political climate created by faculty and students on a campus). Typically, these models also specify and provide for the interaction of student and environmental characteristics within the organizational context. Whereas "developmental" models concentrate attention on outcomes or the nature of student change (including identity formation, moral or cognitive development), "college impact" models focus more on the sources of change (for example, institutional characteristics, program and services, students' experiences, faculty members).

Developmental Theories of Student Change

As noted earlier, developmental theories and models seek to identify the dimensions and structure of growth in college students and to explain the dynamics by which that growth occurs.[1] While theorists vary in the degree to which they subscribe to certain characteristics or features of the developmental process, most theories view development as a general movement toward greater differentiation, integration, and complexity in the ways that individuals think, value, and behave. This movement is typically seen as orderly, sequential, and hierarchical, passing through ever-higher levels or stages of development, and to some extent as age related. Developmental theorists disagree over whether these progressions are irreversible, as well as over whether the progression is continuous and gradual or disjunctive and abrupt. Developmental change may be due to biological and psychological maturation, to individual experiences and the environment, or to the interaction of individual and environment.

Several taxonomies have been offered for the developmental theories or models of college student change, each with its own merits (see, for example, Drum, 1980; Knefelkamp, Widick, & Parker, 1978; Learner, 1986; Moore & Upcraft, 1990; Rodgers, 1980, 1989, 1990a, 1990b; Strange & King, 1990; Widick, Knefelkamp, & Parker, 1980). In this chapter, we adopt the four-family structure originated by Knefelkamp, Widick, and Parker (1978), as modified by Rodgers (1989).[2] The four clusters of theories and models we consider are (1) psychosocial theories, (2) cognitive-structural theories, (3) typological models, and (4) person-environment interaction models. Within certain of these families, as appropriate, relatively greater attention is given to the theories of Arthur Chickering, Lawrence Kohlberg, and William Perry, who have probably had more influence than any others on the study of college's impact on students and on institutional policies and programs specifically designed to shape student development. Indeed, wags have variously dubbed these individuals as the "Triumvirate" and the "Gang of Three."

Psychosocial Theories

The family of psychosocial theories includes theories that view individual development essentially as a process that involves the accomplishment of a series of "developmental tasks." Partly as a consequence of age progression and partly as a consequence of sociocultural or environmental influences, individuals over the life span are confronted by a series of developmental challenges to their current identity or developmental status that require some form of response. The nature of the tasks or challenges varies with an individual's age and developmental status. While developmental tasks tend to be presented in a sequence heavily influenced by biological and psychological maturational processes or by sociocultural influences (for example, rites of passage to adulthood and associated societal expectations), they may not be resolved in the order of their presentation, and the pattern may vary by sex and culture. In addition, most psychosocial theories assert that the individual's success in resolving each task can significantly affect the resolution of succeeding tasks and, consequently, the rate and extent of psychosocial development (Rodgers, 1989).

Three elements in the work of Erikson (1959, 1963, 1968) have exerted considerable influence on most psychosocial theories of college student development. The first is Erikson's articulation of the "epigenetic principle," which states that "anything that grows has a ground plan, and that out of this ground plan the parts arise, each part having its time of special ascendancy, until all parts have arisen to form a functioning whole" (1968, p. 92). This principle implies not only the notion of sequential, age-related, biological and psychological development but also the view that the particular character and extent of development are shaped in important ways by the individual's personal environment.

The second influential element of Erikson's work is his conception of developmental tasks or "crises." He theorizes eight stages[3] or periods in psychosocial development when biological and psychological changes interact with sociocultural demands to present a "crisis" that is characteristic of a given stage. For Erikson, a crisis does not mean a physical or psychological emergency but rather a time for decision requiring serious consideration of and a significant choice among alternative courses of action. The individual's choice at each crisis stage determines developmental progression, regression, or stasis. Embedded in this conception, of course, is the view that developmental change involves stimulus (or challenge) and response, with development (or the lack thereof) being determined by the nature of the response (see, also, Sanford, 1962, 1967; Cottle, 1974).

Erikson's third important influence on psychosocial theory development relating to college students is his identification of the "identity versus identity confusion" crisis (Stage 5) as the dominant developmental task for people of traditional college age (although not necessarily students). As will be seen below, identity development occupies a central place in most psychosocial theories of change among college students.

Probably no other psychosocial theorist has had a greater influence than Arthur Chickering (1969) on the study of college student development or on administrative programming intended to promote it. Ellison and Simon (1973, p. 50) refer to Chickering's theory as "the 'modal' model." For that reason, we review Chickering's theory in some detail. (Research evidence relating to Chickering's theory is reviewed in Chapter Six.)

Chickering's Seven Vectors of Student Development

Recognizing the absence of any systematic framework for integrating or synthesizing the abundant empirical evidence on college students and based on his review of that literature, Chickering (1969) identified seven "vectors of development" (each with its own subcomponents). These vectors were so labeled "because each seems to have direction and magnitude— even though the direction may be expressed more appropriately by a spiral or by steps than by a straight line" (p. 8). "Identity" development occupies a central place in Chickering's theory, and his seven vectors can be viewed as giving greater specificity to this central construct. For Chickering, "development along each vector involves cycles of differentiation and integration. . . . [T]he student continually apprehends more complexity. . . . These more differentiated perceptions and behaviors are subsequently integrated and organized so that a coherent picture of himself is established. Growth along the vectors is not simple maturational unfolding but requires stimulation" (Widick, Parker, & Knefelkamp, 1978a, p. 21).

Vector 1: Achieving Competence. According to Chickering, the progression in the college years is toward increased competence in intellectual areas, in physical and manual skills, and in social and interpersonal relations. Central to all three is the growth in a student's "*sense* of competence, the confidence one has in one's ability to cope with what comes and to achieve successfully what [one] sets out to do" (Chickering, 1969, p. 9). The sense of intellectual competence is particularly important. Because development depends on the ability to symbolize events and objects, growth in intellectual competence influences development along other vectors of development. Reflecting on *Education and Identity* (Chickering, 1969) some fifteen years after its publication, Chickering indicated that both intellectual and interpersonal competence probably should be given more attention than he gave them in 1969 and that the concept of competence may be particularly salient in the development of minority group members and women (Thomas & Chickering, 1984).

Vector 2: Managing Emotions. In the precollege and college years, according to Chickering, students must wrestle with a variety of intense emotions that have both biological and social origins. Emotions that involve aggression and sex are particularly salient in this period. During college, the rigid, reflexive controls inculcated by parents and society during childhood are examined, understood, and eventually replaced by internally adopted behavioral standards and controls. According to Chickering (1969, p. 53), "the task is to develop increasing capacity for passion and commitment accompanied by increasing capacity to implement passion and commitment through intelligent behavior." This capacity may be particularly important, says Chickering, given the cultural changes that have occurred since the initial formulation of his model and that have complicated the way our culture deals with lust and hate (Thomas & Chickering, 1984).

Vector 3: Developing Autonomy. Autonomy is "the independence of maturity, . . . it requires both emotional and instrumental independence, and recognition of one's interdependence" (Chickering, 1969, p. 12). As competence develops, the individual disengages from parents and the need for approval and reassurance and simultaneously recognizes the importance of others. Relationships based on mutual respect and helpfulness are established as the individual confronts the paradox of personal independence and interdependence. Recognition of interdependence is so critical, says Chickering, that the label for this vector could be changed from "autonomy" to "interdependence" to emphasize its importance (Thomas & Chickering, 1984).

Vector 4: Establishing Identity. Vector 4 is a pivotal one. Establishment of identity depends in part on growth along the competence, emotions, and autonomy vectors, and development on this vector fosters and facilitates changes along the remaining three vectors (described below). For young men or women, clarifications of their conceptions of their physical characteristics and personal appearance and of appropriate sexual roles and behaviors are important psychosocial events. The concept of identity remains general, however, a "solid sense of self" (Chickering, 1969, p. 80), and one that may undergo change over a lifetime. The issues confronted at this stage of development during the college years are not limited to college students or to this phase of one's life cycle. They are encountered in later life phases as well (Thomas & Chickering, 1984).

Vector 5: Freeing Interpersonal Relationships. As a personal identity is shaped, an increased ability to interact with others emerges; this interaction reveals "increased tolerance and respect for those of different backgrounds, habits, values, and appearance, and a shift in the quality of relationships with intimates and close friends" (Chickering, 1969, p. 94).

Tolerance is understood to be not merely the ability to withstand the unpleasant but rather greater openness and acceptance of diversity. Chickering believes the growing cultural diversity in recent years makes the development of tolerance particularly important and development of the capacity for intimacy even more complex than when he first formulated his theory (Thomas & Chickering, 1984).

Vector 6: Developing Purpose. Expanding competencies, identity, and interpersonal relationships require some sense of future direction and purpose. Development along the sixth vector occurs as the individual develops answers not only to the question "Who am I?" but also to "Who am I going to be?" Not just "Where am I?" but "Where am I going?" (Chickering, 1969, p. 16). Growth requires the development of plans that integrate priorities in recreational and vocational interests, vocational plans and aspirations, and life-style choices.

Vector 7: Developing Integrity. Growth along the seventh vector involves "the clarification of a personally valid set of beliefs that have some internal consistency and that provide at least a tentative guide for behavior" (1969, p. 17). An absolutistic reliance on rules yields to more relativistic consideration of rules and the purposes they are intended to serve. Values taken on authority in an earlier time are reviewed. Some are rejected, and those found suitable to the emerging identity are retained, personalized, and internalized. Although Chickering believes his general framework has stood up well, he also thinks any revisions on this vector would have to take into account the work of Perry and Kohlberg (Thomas & Chickering, 1984).

Chickering has also expressed the belief that *Education and Identity,* were he to rewrite it, would probably include two additional chapters. In one, he would shift the entire emphasis of the book toward a broader conception of "college students" to reflect the greatly increased variety of individuals attending college, including a large number of older students. His second additional chapter would deal "with ego development as a systematic set of theories that describe how [his] different vectors of development interact with one another—the ways they seem to be part of a larger structure" (Thomas & Chickering, 1984, p. 396).

Conditions for Impact. Chickering (1969) sought to bring knowledge and practice closer together. To do so, he identified six major areas in which colleges and universities exert an influence (positive or negative) on student growth along each of his seven vectors. These areas of influence (and their presumed effects) include (1) clarity of institutional objectives and the internal consistency of policies, practices, and activities (clarity, consistency, and seriousness about objectives, policies, programs, and practices are positively related to institutional impact); (2) institutional size (when size restricts opportunities for participation, impact is diminished); (3) curriculum, teaching, and evaluation (curricular flexibility, variety in instructional styles and modes, student participation in learning, and learning-oriented evaluation promote impact); (4) residence hall arrangements (the close friendships and reference groups that develop can promote or inhibit personal development, depending upon the diversity, attitudes, and values of the occupants); (5) faculty and administration (frequent, friendly contact in diverse settings with psychologically accessible adults will promote development); and (6) friends, groups, and student culture (student cultures amplify or attenuate other institutional influences on development, depending upon the degree of congruence between student and institutional values).

While a detailed critique of this theory, as well as others to follow, is beyond the scope of this chapter, critics have tended to focus on the theory's failure to treat cognitive or intellectual development in greater detail than as simply one subtask of the "developing competence" vector. Critics have also noted the absence of any detailed consideration of the underlying processes relating to change on each vector. Indeed, some individuals believe Chickering's vectors constitute not so much a theory (with the attendant specification of the systemic relations between and among variables and outcomes) as a description of what ideally happens to students during the college years. (Chickering, it should be noted, readily acknowledges the origins of his framework in the then-extant research literature.) Critics have also noted the lack of sufficient specificity in Chickering's model for easy application in research and administrative programming. These and other limitations (and strengths) of the theory are discussed in greater detail elsewhere (Ellison & Simon, 1973, pp. 50–53; Rodgers, 1980, pp. 51–52; Thomas & Chickering, 1984; Knefelkamp, Widick, & Parker, 1978, pp. 27–28).

Other Psychosocial Theories and Models

While Chickering's work has attracted greater attention and inspired more research and administrative programming than other psychosocial theories or models, several others merit attention. Space precludes detailed discussion of them, however.

Marcia's Model of Ego Identity Status. Building on Erikson's (1956, 1963, 1968) proposition that the definition of one's identity constitutes the central "crisis" of adolescence, James Marcia (1965, 1966) reasoned that "ego identity status" formation is a dynamic process that involves the resolution of two psychosocial tasks. The first is the experience of "crisis," understood in its Eriksonian sense as the engagement of and choice among meaningful but competing alternatives. The second task involves the making of occupational and ideological (that is, religious and political) commitments. *Commitment* refers to the level of the individual's personal investment in each of the three areas. Shortly after the model's initial explication and early testing, a fourth area—sexual values—was added so that its theoretical and operational forms would be as applicable to women as to men (Marcia, 1980; Marcia & Friedman, 1970; Schenkel & Marcia, 1972). Crisis is presumed to lead to differentiation and individualization, while commitment is assumed to result in stability, continuity, and comfort (Prager, 1986).

In his juxtaposition of these two psychosocial tasks, Marcia identifies four different responses to the need for identity and the process of identity formation. "Identity-diffused" individuals have neither experienced the crisis of the search for an identity nor made commitments to an identity in any of the occupational or value areas. Such people tend either to be uninterested in occupational or ideological matters or to accept all positions as more or less equal. "Foreclosed" individuals have not undergone any crisis, but they have made commitments. The commitments upon which their identities rest, however, tend to be those of their parents and have been accepted without question or examination. People in "moratorium" status are actively involved in a crisis period, searching for a defining identity, evaluating possible alternatives. These individuals are distinguished from identity-diffused people by the presence of their conscious search, but their commitments remain unformed or, at best, emergent. "Identity-achieved" individuals have both successfully weathered a crisis and made personal occupational, religious, political, and sex role commitments. These commitments have been independently arrived at, may be at variance with those of parents or others, and form a basis for independent action. Marcia (1976) notes, however, that identity achievement probably is not a permanent state. Rather, he suggests that individuals may shift through various statuses as they accommodate changes associated with the life cycle. Bourne (1978b) gives a conceptual and methodological critique of Marcia's model. The research on it relating to college effects is reviewed in Chapter Five of this volume (see also Bourne, 1978a; Marcia, 1980; Matteson, 1975; Waterman, 1982). Josselson (1987) offers a research-based discussion of Marcia's theory as it applies specifically to women.

Cross's Model of Black Identity Formation. Current research and theory on college student change and development appear quite clearly to assume that the nature and processes of identity development among black and other nonwhite students are essentially the same as those for whites. Others have reached a similar conclusion (Carter & Helms, 1987; Semmes, 1985; Stikes, 1984; Taylor, 1976; Wright, 1987). In the last two decades, however, a literature specifically addressing the characteristics of black identity and proposing models of its development has begun to emerge. Helms (1990b, p. 5) identifies three components of racial identity: (1) a personal identity (consisting of "one's attitudes and feelings about oneself"), (2) a reference group orientation (the extent to which one uses a particular racial group to define one's personal identity; it is reflected in one's values, attitudes, and behaviors), and (3) an ascribed identity ("the individual's deliberate affiliation or commitment to a particular racial group"). Racial identity is presumed to derive from the particular weightings the individual assigns to these three components. The possible variations in weightings give rise to different models, or racial identity "resolutions" (Helms, 1990b).

Helms (1990c) identifies two theoretical racial identity strands running through the variety of potential "resolutions." The first is a "type" perspective that consists of essentially taxonomic models that seek to classify individuals according to their characteristic racial beliefs, attitudes, feelings, and behaviors. Models in this category tend to focus on the implications of identity status for counseling and psychotherapeutic purposes. Because of this tendency and because these models have attracted virtually no attention in the study of the fact or process of identity development among black college students, we do not consider such models further. Helms labels the second theoretical strand the "Nigrescence or racial identity development (NRID) perspective," which seeks to describe "the developmental process by which a person 'becomes Black' where Black is defined in terms of one's manner of thinking about and evaluating oneself and one's reference groups rather than in terms of skin color per se" (p. 17). Most models fall into this second, stage category of black identity formation (Baldwin, 1980, 1981, 1984; Banks, 1981; Cross, 1971a, 1971b, 1978, 1980, 1985; Gay, 1984; Hauser & Kassendorf, 1983; Jackson, 1975; Sherif & Sherif, 1970; Taylor, 1976, 1977; Thomas, 1971; Toldson & Pasteur, 1975; White & Burke, 1987; see also Wyne, White, & Coop, 1974, for a discussion of black self-concept formation in the childhood and early adolescent years).

Of these, Cross's model has attracted more research attention than any other. According to Cross (1971a, pp. 100–107), individuals pass through five stages as their personal black identity takes shape. In Stage 1, "Preencounter" (or prediscovery), the individual's worldview is dominated by Euro-American determinants, with the emphasis in life on being assimilated or integrated into the dominant, white world. Stage 2, "Encounter," involves some experience (for example, the assassination of Martin Luther King, Jr.) that confronts the individual's understanding of blacks' place in the world and triggers a reinterpretation of initial views and beliefs. In Stage 3, "Immersion-Emersion," the individual searches for a new understanding of self as black. The immersion in "the world of Blackness" (p. 102) involves a turning inward and the view that everything of value must be black. In the emersion phase, the individual emerges from "the dead-end, either/or, racist, oversimplified aspects of the immersion experience . . . [and] begins to 'level off' and control his experiences" (p. 104). In Stage 4, "Internalization," four outcomes are possible: (1) continuation and rejection; (2) continuation and fixation at Stage 3; (3) internalization that brings an inner security and satisfaction with self but involves only a receptivity to discussions and plans for action, but no commitment to action; and (4) movement to what is actually Stage 5, "Internalization-Commitment." This is the most desirable outcome of the process and differs from Stage 4 in that the individual has a plan for participation in the reformation of the black community. While the individual's values may yet be Western, the individual now "represents a 'relevant' as opposed to a 'token' reformer" (p. 106). Because of measurement difficulties in differentiating Stage 5 from earlier states, however, doubts have been raised about whether Stage 5 constitutes a discrete identity level (Helms, 1990c). The research based on Cross's model is summarized in Chapter Five.

Descriptions and models relating to the psychosocial development of other minority groups have been offered, including ones specific to Asian Americans (for example, Sue & Sue, 1971), Hispanics (for example, Martinez, 1988), and Native Americans (for example, Johnson & Lashley, 1988), as well as several dealing with development in racial or ethnic groups more broadly defined (for example, Atkinson, Morten, & Sue, 1983; Ho, 1987). Moore (1990) provides a review of recent theories of student development that relate specifically to groups based on gender, age, sexual orientation, and ethnicity. Much of this thinking and writing focuses heavily on counseling and psychotherapeutic applications, although some attention is also given to the programmatic implications of group-specific student development models. Their utility for research on the psychosocial development of students over time remains unexamined.

Heath's Maturity Model. Douglas Heath (1968, 1978) offers a "dimensional" (as opposed to "stage") model of student development similar in many ways to Chickering's (1969) theory. Heath (1965) reviewed "clinical, theoretical, and empirical literature" in biology, psychoanalysis, psychology, anthropology, education, and mental health "for the traits describing mentally healthy, psychologically sound, optimally functioning, self-actualizing, fulfilled, emotionally mature, 'ideal' persons" (Heath, 1978, pp. 193–194). His review of this literature, his synthesis of what twenty-five educational philosophers throughout history have suggested are the goals of a liberal education, and his research led him to construct a model of the person as "a maturing system who can be described in terms of five interdependent dimensions in the four principal sectors of his life" (1977b, p. 7).

The five dimensions of maturing include becoming (1) more able to symbolize one's experiences (for example, through writing, speech, art, music, mathematics), (2) more allocentric (or "other centered"), (3) more integrated, (4) more stable, and (5) more autonomous. Maturing along each of these dimensions occurs in four "self system" (Widick, Knefelkamp, & Parker, 1980, pp. 99–100) sectors or structures: cognitive skills, values, self-concept, and interpersonal relations. Heath's emphasis is clearly on "becoming," or, as he prefers, "maturing." Maturing, as Heath sees it, is an organismic, systemic, reciprocal, and unending process. His theory "assumes that the development of one structure is not independent of the development of others" (1968, p. 5). Indeed, extreme development or lag along one dimension or in one structure will eventually inhibit development along other dimensions or in other sectors.

A distinctive feature of Heath's (1965, 1968, 1978) work is his persistent efforts to relate his model's constructs to the tenets of a liberal education as he discerns them in the writings of major educational philosophers and thinkers since Plato. Heath believes a liberal education is a powerful force toward maturity, and he offers a detailed analysis of his model with specific reference to various philosophers over the centuries (see Heath, 1968, appendix A). He also sets forth three conditions that define "a particularly powerful liberally educating environment: the educability of its students, its communal educative conditions, and the coherence of its purposes and means" (1968, p. 264). (The research evidence on Heath's model is reviewed in Chapter Six.)

The last two decades have seen both an explosive growth in the number of older people returning to (or beginning) college and the emergence of life-span theories of psychosocial development. The focus of this book and space limitations preclude discussion of these theories. Interested readers should consult Chickering and Havighurst (1981), Gould (1972), Levinson (1978), Neugarten (1964, 1968, 1975), Sheehy (1974), and Vaillant (1977).

Cognitive-Structural Theories

Whereas Erik Erikson is a significant progenitor of psychosocial theories and models, virtually all cognitive-structural theories of student development owe their origins to Jean Piaget (1964). Whereas psychosocial theorists focus on the content of development (for example, vectors, identity statuses, dimensions), cognitive-structural theorists seek to describe the process of change, concentrating on the cognitive structures individuals construct in order to give meaning to their worlds. Indeed, the psychosocial and cognitive-structural families appear to be complementary. "One describes what students will be concerned about and what decisions will be primary; the other suggests how students will think about those issues and what shifts in reasoning will occur" (Knefelkamp, Widick, & Parker, 1978, p. xii).

Cognitive-structural theories have several things in common. They all posit a series of stages through which an individual passes in the developmental process. In most theories, these stages are hierarchical, the successful attainment of one being a prerequisite to movement on to the next, and in most the progression is irreversible. Because of their foundations in cognition, one simply cannot "go home again" because one now perceives, structures, and gives meaning to one's world in a way that is fundamentally different from what it was at earlier stages. Because of this fundamental character of "making meaning," the stages of development are believed to be universal and transcultural, and some evidence exists to support that belief. All focus on *how* meaning is structured, not on what is known or believed.

Finally, as with psychosocial theories, cognitive-structural theories assume that developmental change involves a chain of stimulus (challenge) and response. As individuals develop, they encounter new information or experiences that conflict with or challenge the validity of their current cognitive structure. Adaptive responses to conflict or challenge may involve either of two processes: assimilation or accommodation. In assimilation, the individual perceptually reorders or reinterprets the source of conflict to make it consistent with current knowledge, belief, or value structures. In accommodation, the individual changes presently held cognitive or belief structures to admit or be consistent with the new experience presenting the conflict. The developmental process is seen as a series of constructions and reconstructions. "Healthy" responses to cognitive or affective conflict are presumed to lead to a reformation of existing structures that incorporates new and old knowledge, attitudes, values, and self-concepts in revised, coherent, integrated perceptual structures at the next, more advanced stage or developmental condition.

William Perry and Lawrence Kohlberg, the other two members of the "Triumvirate" or "Gang of Three," are both cognitive-structural developmentalists. Because of their prominence in the research literature, their theories are examined at some length.

Perry's Scheme of Intellectual and Ethical Development

On the basis of an extensive series of interviews with Harvard College students, William Perry (1970, 1981) sought to map conceptually the development he observed clinically in the "structures which the students explicitly or implicitly impute to the world, especially those structures in which they construe the nature and origins of knowledge, of value, and of responsibility" (1970, p. 1). Perry maintains that such structures transcend content and thus are less likely to be socially, culturally, or otherwise temporally dependent. His theory is clearly a stage model, although he prefers the term *position* because it implies no assumptions about duration and is "happily appropriate to the image of 'point of outlook' or 'position from which a person views his world' " (1970, p. 48).

Perry's model, or "scheme," asserts that the developmental sequence of forms "manifests a logical order—an order in which one form leads to another through differentiations and reorganizations required for the meaningful interpretation of increasingly complex experience" (1970, p. 3). Perry (1970) identified nine positions. At the broadest conceptual level, he has suggested that development can be conceived as comprising two major parts, with the pivotal stage (his Position 5) being the perception of all knowledge and values (including authority's) as relative.

Prior to the attainment of Position 5, cognitive structures or ways of perceiving one's world are dominated by a dualistic perception: Things are either right or wrong, good or bad, and knowledge of which is which is derived from "Authority." The dichotomous categories include knowledge, values, and people, and they are absolute. At Position 5, the individual begins to perceive not only the presence of multiple points of view but the indeterminacies of "Truth." The relative character of knowledge and values is recognized. Following this recognition, the individual follows a progression through the last four positions, moving toward higher developmental levels according to the extent to which the individual can cope with a relativistic world and begin to develop personal commitments (1970, p. 57). Perry (1981, p. 79) grouped his original nine positions into the following three clusters (King, 1978, offers four clusters).

Dualism Modified (Positions 1–3). In the early positions, students order their worlds in dualistic, dichotomous, and absolute categories. Knowledge is presumed to be absolute and known to authorities. Alternative views or different perspectives on the same phenomenon create discomfort and confusion. To students at these levels, learning means catching whatever the instructor pitches. By Position 3, however, "Multiplicity," the existence of multiple perspectives on any given issue, is recognized, and others holding an opinion contrary to one's own are no longer seen as simply wrong, but as entitled to their views. Indeed, all opinions are seen as having comparable claims on correctness.

Relativism Discovered (Positions 4–6). Recognition of multiplicity in the world leads to understanding that "knowledge is contextual and relative" (King, 1978, p. 38). Analytical thinking skills emerge, and students are able to critique their own ideas and those of others. They recognize that not all positions are equally valid. This stage can be problematic, however, since the discovery of relativism in ideas and values can lead to a resistance to choose among presumably equal alternatives. Subsequent development may be delayed at this stage.

Commitments in Relativism Developed (Positions 7–9). Students moving through Positions 7 through 9 "have made an active affirmation of themselves and their responsibilities in a pluralistic world, establishing their identities in the process" (King, 1978, p. 39). Commitments are made to ideas, to values, to behaviors, to other people (for example, in marriage and careers). According to Perry (1970), perhaps 75 percent of the students in his studies had reached the level of commitment denoted by Positions 7 and 8 by their senior year. Subsequent research, however, has found virtually no students scoring at these levels (P. M. King, letter to one of the authors, October 10, 1988).

Like students' cognitive structures, their commitments must be seen as dynamic and changeable, not in any capricious, fast-paced fashion but as a series of constructions and reconstructions, "differentiations and reorganizations" (Perry, 1970, p. 3). Commitments are modifiable, subject to new evidence and understanding about who one is and how the world is. Commitments may be made, but they are not immutable; they are alterable in the face of new evidence about the world. This process of construction and reconstruction does not end with college. Indeed, it may be a lifelong process (Perry, 1981).

More recently, Perry (1981) appears to attach greater significance to the transitions between positions: "Positions are by definition static, and development is by definition movement" (p. 78). He stresses that each position "both includes and transcends earlier positions, as the earlier ones cannot do with the later [ones]. This fact defines the movement as *development* rather than mere changes or 'phases' " (p. 78). Perry also suggests that development is recurrent: The discovery and reconstruction of "forms" that characterize the development of college students can also be experienced at later points in the life span. He concludes: "Perhaps the best model for growth is neither the straight line nor the circle, but a helix, perhaps with an expanding radius to show that when we face the 'same' old issues we do so from a different and broader perspective" (p. 97).

A persistent criticism of Perry's scheme has been the difficulty of operationalizing and measuring position change, particularly with large samples, although a number of different approaches have been attempted (King, 1978). The shift in the scheme's focus between Positions 5 and 6, from cognitive and intellectual growth to identity formation, has also been noted (see the discussion of Kitchener and King's reflective judgment model below). Studies of change during college based on Perry's scheme are reviewed in Chapter Four.

Kohlberg's Theory of Moral Development

Whereas Perry's theory seeks to explain cognitive and ethical growth, Lawrence Kohlberg's theory focuses somewhat more narrowly on moral development (Kohlberg, 1969, 1972, 1975, 1981a, 1981b, 1984; Kohlberg, Levine, & Hewer, 1983). Kohlberg sought to delineate the nature and sequence of progressive changes in individuals' cognitive structures and rules for processing information on the basis of which moral judgments are made. His principal concern, however, was not with the content of moral choice (which may be socially or culturally determined) but with modes of reasoning, with the cognitive *processes* (thought to be universal) by which moral choices are made.

Kohlberg's is a cognitive "stage" theory that identifies three general levels of moral reasoning, with two stages at each level, for a total of six stages, although in his later writings the sixth stage has been dropped from the formal model because of the absence of empirical evidence to support its existence as a distinct stage (Kohlberg, Levine, & Hewer, 1983). At each stage, the primary concern is with the principle of justice. Kohlberg (1972, p. 14) distinguishes between a "rule," which prescribes action, and a "principle," which affords "a guide for choosing among behaviors." Passage through the presumably invariant sequence of stages involves an increasingly refined, differentiated set of principles and sense of justice. At the earlier stages, this sense is based on considerations of self-interest and material advantage. At the opposite end of the moral development continuum, an internalized, conscience-based set of moral principles guides an individual's actions. A more detailed summary of the levels and component stages follows.

Level I: Preconventional. At Stage 1 ("Obedience and Punishment Orientation"), the physical consequences determine whether behavior is "good" or "bad." The individual recognizes and defers to superior physical strength out of self-interest. Any concern for laws or rules is based on the consequences of violations of those rules. At Stage 2 ("Naively Egoistic Orientation"), "right" actions are those that satisfy one's needs, but signs of an emerging relativism are apparent. The needs of others might be acknowledged, but any reciprocity is based not on a sense of the rights of others but on a "You-scratch-my-back-and-I'll-scratch-yours" bargain.

Level II: Conventional. At Stage 3 ("The 'Good Boy' Orientation"), the expectations of others are recognized as valuable in their own right, not merely for what obedience to them will return to the individual. Behavior is guided by a need for approval and to please others, particularly those closest to the individual (for example, parents and peer groups). The "intention" behind an action is considered important. At Stage 4 (which Kohlberg [1975] terms the "Authority and Social-Order Maintaining Orientation"), respect for authority as a social obligation emerges. "Moral judgments are based on concerns to maintain the social order and to meet the expectations of others. Law is seen . . . as necessary to protect and maintain the group as a whole" (Nucci & Pascarella, 1987, p. 273). Kohlberg (1975, p. 571) has characterized this stage as the " 'Law and Order' Orientation."

Level III: Postconventional. At Stage 5 ("Contractual Legalistic Orientation"), duty is seen as a social contract, which is acknowledged to have an arbitrary starting point, with an emphasis on democratically agreed upon, mutual obligations. Violations of the rights of others or the will of the majority are avoided. Because of the emphasis given at this third level of development to "equality and mutual obligation within a democratically established order," Kohlberg (1972, p. 15) has referred to the morality of this stage as "the morality of the American Constitution." Behavior at Stage 6 ("Conscience or Principle Orientation"), the highest level, is guided not by social rules but by principles thought to be logical and universal. "Highest value [is] placed on human life, equality, and dignity" (Kohlberg, 1972, p. 15). Right action is guided by personally chosen ethical principles and the dictates of conscience. As noted earlier, however, this stage has been dropped from more recent formal statements of the theory because of the lack of empirical evidence of its existence. (Studies of change in moral development during college, most of which are based on Kohlberg's theory, are reviewed in Chapter Eight.)

Other Cognitive-Structural Theories

As one might expect, both Perry's and Kohlberg's work have their critics. In some instances, critiques have spawned new theoretical statements that merit attention, although space constraints prohibit detailed discussion.

Kitchener and King's Reflective Judgment Model. Kitchener and King (1981, 1990; see also King, 1977; King, Kitchener, Davison, Parker, & Wood, 1983; Kitchener, 1978, 1986; Kitchener, King, Wood, & Davison, 1989) have argued that the Perry (1970) scheme shifts its focus between Positions 5 and 6 from cognitive or intellectual growth to identity development, leaving unspecified the nature and processes of any cognitive growth beyond that point. Rodgers (1989) has noted that this confounding of cognitive-structural and psychosocial development leaves two questions unanswered: "What does the psychosocial development of college students look like prior to Perry's Stage 6? What does their intellectual cognitive-structural development look like after Perry's Stage 5?" (p. 142). Rodgers suggests that Chickering's (1969) vectors answer the first question, and Kitchener and King's theory deals with the second.

Kitchener and King (1981) offer a model of "reflective judgment," defining a hierarchical, seven-stage sequence of increasingly complex stages relating to what people "know" or believe and how they justify their knowledge claims and beliefs. "Each stage represents a logically coherent network of assumptions and corresponding concepts that are used to justify beliefs" (p. 91). Each stage consists of a set of assumptions about reality and knowledge that the individual "uses to perceive and organize available information and to make judgments about an issue. The process of forming judgments becomes increasingly complex, sophisticated, and comprehensive from lower to higher stages" (p. 92).

The lowest three stages of Kitchener and King's model appear to coincide rather closely with Perry's first three positions (Rodgers, 1989). For example, in both models truth is seen as coming from authorities and is accepted without inspection by the individual. For Kitchener and King, individual beliefs are justified in terms of their conformity to an authority's truths. At Perry's Position 4, however, differences between the two frameworks begin to appear, with Kitchener and King continuing to focus on cognitive-structural changes (Rodgers, 1989). At the highest stage of Kitchener and King's model, "reality is understood as existing objectively" (Kitchener & King, 1981, p. 92). Knowledge statements are understood to have varying degrees of accuracy, and those with the highest claims on acceptance are those that are based on "a rational process of conjecture that demonstrates the use of evidence and rules of inquiry appropriate for the issue at hand" (Kitchener & King, 1981, p. 92). Knowledge claims must be evaluated and open to scrutiny by others. Rodgers (1989, pp. 142–146) compares and contrasts these two theories in greater detail, but he is unable to conclude whether they represent two distinct theories or one theory (Perry's) clarified by the other (Kitchener and King's).

Gilligan's "Different Voice" Model. Kohlberg's (1969) theory has also attracted critical attention that has led to a refined, if not an alternative, theoretical formulation. For some time, when interviews have been analyzed by means of instruments operationalizing Kohlberg's theory of moral development, women have consistently been scored at lower stages of development than men. This finding has typically been interpreted as evidence of a problem in women's development. Carol Gilligan in her research, however (1977, 1982a, 1982b, 1986a, 1986b), observed persistent discrepancies between women's concepts of self and morality and the major theories of human and moral development, including those of Piaget, Erikson, Kohlberg, and others, but particularly that of Kohlberg. Gilligan suggests the problem lies not with women but with conceptually biased theories, all of which emerged from studies of the moral development of male subjects. While these accepted theories purport to explain a universal developmental sequence, Gilligan argues that they do not accurately describe the experience of women, their sense of self, or the bases of their moral reasoning.

Gilligan's (1977) critique of Kohlberg's theory focuses on its "subordination of the interpersonal to the societal definition of the good" (p. 489). The problem, says Gilligan, is that for women the perception of the self is "tenaciously embedded in relationships with others" and women's judgments of what is moral are "insistently contextual" (1977, p. 482). The values of justice and autonomy that are given center stage in Kohlberg's theory "imply a view of the individual as separate and of relationships as either hierarchical or contractual, bound by the alternatives of constraint and co-operation. In contrast, the values of care and connection that emerge saliently in women's thinking imply a view of self and other as interdependent and of relationships as networks sustained by activities of care-giving and response" (1986a, p. 40). For Gilligan, women's concern with the well-being of others constitutes a "different voice" from that used by males: Women's moral reasoning is in the "care voice," while men tend to reason in the "justice voice." Similar observations of the central importance of interpersonal relations in women's sense of themselves are reported by Douvan and Adelson (1966) and Josselson (1987).

Gilligan's own model resembles other social development theories, with developmental movement "from an egocentric through a societal to a universal perspective" (1977, p. 483). Her first level ("Orientation to Individual Survival") focuses squarely and clearly on the self. As development occurs, there is a transition period ("From Selfishness to Responsibility"), characterized by the discovery of responsibility as a new basis for defining relations between self and others. The second level ("Goodness as Self-Sacrifice") focuses on the incorporation of a maternal concept of morality that involves the perception of the importance of protecting "the dependent and unequal." At this stage, "the feminine voice" emerges clearly, and "the good is equated with caring for others" (p. 492). The inequality inherent in this stage leads to a second transition ("From Goodness to Truth"), which seeks to resolve the conflict between selfishness and responsibility. Resolution is achieved at the third level ("The Morality of Nonviolence"), when an equilibrium is found between the expectations of conformity and caring in conventional notions of womanhood and individual needs. That equilibrium is found in nonviolence as a moral principle and a basis for decision making. "Judgment remains psychological in its concern with the intention and consequences of action, but it now becomes universal in its condemnation of exploitation and hurt" (Gilligan, 1977, p. 492).

The differences between Kohlberg and Gilligan are the differences between the morality of rights and the morality of responsibility, between concepts of autonomy and separation and concepts of connectedness and relationships. Gilligan, however, does not see these differences as reflecting any conflict; it is not a case of one theory being more or less adequate than the other. Rather, she believes they represent two different ways of viewing the world. Moreover, despite her focus on women, she asserts that both voices are inherent in the life cycle, constituting alternative grounds on which to evaluate the moral. She believes all individuals reason in both voices, although one is preferred and tends to dominate. Some men will tend to use the feminine "care" voice, while some women will prefer the "justice" voice. The care voice, however, is more frequently found among women and the justice voice among men. Gilligan's point is that by emphasizing one dimension, the other is neglected, leading "to the casting of all problems as problems of dominance and subordination" (Gilligan, 1986a, p. 54).

Kohlberg (1984) has responded by asserting that there is no need for two structures, that differences in the two voices merely constitute different styles of moral reasoning. Brabeck (1983b) and Walker (1984) present evidence in support of Kohlberg's position, whereas Baumrind (1986) supports Gilligan's position. While the issue remains unresolved (see Kerber et al., 1986), the possibility that the differences are substantive has implications for academic and student affairs programs (see Rodgers, 1989, p. 141; 1990b).[4]

Jane Loevinger's Theory of Ego Development. Loevinger (1976), focusing on ego development, offers a theory that is more comprehensive than Perry's or Kohlberg's. Loevinger does not offer any detailed definition of ego development, something she believes may not be possible, but her theory subsumes moral growth and interpersonal relations, as well as cognitive development. She sees the ego as a general organizing framework by means of which individuals view themselves and their worlds, and "ego development" connotes "the course of character development within individuals" (1976, p. 3).

Loevinger (1976) postulates nine stages, the first three of which ("Symbiotic," "Impulsive," and "Self-Protective") are generally found in individuals of precollege age. The three middle stages are the most frequently observed ones among traditional-age college students (see Chapter Five). Most new freshmen are at the "Conformist" stage, wherein individual behavior is largely determined by group behaviors, values, and attitudes. The need for acceptance and approval is high, and individual differences are not recognized. The developing individual then passes through the "Self-Aware" level in a transition from the the "Conformist" to the "Conscientious" stage. The transition's salient characteristics are "an increase in self-awareness and the appreciation of multiple possibilities in situations" (Loevinger, 1976, p. 19). It is a precursor of movement from the unexamined assumptions of the "Conformist" level toward the more complex reasoning required by the "Conscientious" level. At the "Conscientious" stage, rules and values have been internalized, and the individual has attained the capacity for detachment and empathy. Reasoning is more complex, and responsibility for one's actions is recognized. Our review identified no research that found college students at any of the final three stages of Loevinger's model (the "Individualistic" level [another transition] and the "Autonomous" and "Integrated" stages).

Loevinger (1976) sees the individual throughout as a unified but dynamic whole. Each of the nine stages has distinctive manifestations in terms of impulse control and character development, interpersonal style, conscious preoccupations, and cognitive style, although she sees these four components as really "four facets of a single coherent process" (p. 26). Chapter Five reviews the research using Loevinger's theory in the study of change among college students, and Hauser (1976) provides a critique of both Loevinger's theory and its measurement with the Sentence Completion Test (SCT). Loevinger (1979) also reviews the literature on the SCT's construct validity.

Other Models. Still other cognitive-structural theories or models have been developed. Harvey, Hunt, and Schroder (1961), with subsequent refinements by Hunt (1966, 1970), view cognitive development in terms of "conceptual levels" or stages based on cognitive complexity. The stages relate to the complexity of the information the individual can process and to the flexibility and sophistication of the processing itself. Hunt emphasizes ways in which instructional environments can be tailored to the level of the individual's conceptual functioning (see Hunt, 1976). Kegan (1979, 1980, 1982) offers a "constructive-developmental" framework for ego development that focuses on the processes by means of which individuals simultaneously "make meaning" of their world and define themselves in subject-object relationships. For Kegan, developmental stages are less interesting than the often painful and disorienting transitions that separate them, marking the terminus of one stage and the origin of the next. Stages mark developments in "the process of the restless, creative *activity* of personality, which is first of all about the making of meaning" (Kegan, 1980, p. 374). Kegan's model was developed more with counseling and psychotherapeutic applications than with research applications in mind.

Typological Models

Whereas psychosocial and cognitive-structural theories focus on the nature and processes of change (respectively), a third family of theories or models emphasizes distinctive but relatively *stable* differences among individuals. These models categorize individuals into groups based on these distinctive characteristics and thus are considered typological models. Typically, they focus on characteristic differences in the ways individuals perceive their world or respond to conditions in it. They may focus on cognitive style (Witkin, 1962, 1976), learning style (Kolb, 1976, 1984; see Claxton & Murrell, 1987, for a review of these models), maturity level and personal style (Heath, 1964, 1973), personality (Myers, 1980a, 1980b; Myers & McCaulley, 1985), or sociodemographic characteristics (Cross, 1971, 1981).

Type models have several characteristics in common (Rodgers, 1989). First, the styles or preferences that characterize people of a given type and differentiate them from people of another type are believed to develop relatively early and to be comparatively stable (although not unchanging) over time. Second, an individual may have or demonstrate characteristics indicative of other types within the taxonomy, but that individual tends to think, choose, or behave in ways consistent with the distinctive characteristics or preferences of the dominant type. Third, type categories describe areas of tendencies or preferences that people have in common. They do not explain idiosyncratic differences among individuals. They constitute "various tracks to wholeness, 'zip code' areas within which we grow and develop" (Rodgers, 1989, p. 153). Finally, these models generally do not attempt to explain either the content or processes of change (developmental or otherwise) in students. If change is treated at all, it is not central to the typology.

Nonetheless, typological models can be useful in understanding differences among college students and in illuminating why students respond differently to their college experiences. Indeed, as will be seen in subsequent chapters in this book, we still know comparatively little about the conditional effects of college, that is, how similar interpersonal and organizational experiences have varying effects related to differences in students' personal characteristics (for example, sex, race, aptitude, or psychological type). Because individual differences shape both cognitive and affective learning, typological models serve as a reminder of the need to take these differences into account in academic and nonacademic policies and practices. Because typological models do not seek to explain changes in students, however, we do not discuss them in any detail. Here, we briefly describe one such typology that has been particularly prominent in the college student research literature, that of Isabel Briggs Myers.

The Myers-Briggs typology follows the work of Carl Jung, as interpreted and given operational expression by Isabel Briggs Myers and her mother, Katharine Cooke Briggs (Myers, 1980a, 1980b; Myers & McCaulley, 1985; see also Lawrence, 1982, 1984). Jung believed that apparently random behaviors are, in fact, attributable to orderly and observable differences in mental functioning. Differences originate in the ways individuals prefer to receive information (the perception functions) and to reach conclusions or make decisions (the judgment functions). Within each of these functional areas are two preferences. In using the perception functions, one may prefer "sensing," or using the five senses, or alternatively, one may prefer "intuition," involving insight and unconscious associations. In exercising the judgment functions, an individual may prefer either "thinking" (that is, logic) or "feeling" (that is, affective values) as a basis for choosing or making decisions.

Type is presumed to be dynamic, not static. An individual may use all four functions at different times. Each individual, however, has a preference for using one or the other perception function and one or the other judgment function. Writers in this area sometimes use the analogy of handedness to illustrate the point: While an individual is capable of using both hands, one or the other tends to be preferred for certain functions, such as writing. "The favorite function is called *dominant* and will be either a perception process, Sensing (S) or Intuition (N), or a judgment process, Thinking (T) or Feeling (F). The dominant function is the unifying process in one's life" (Lynch, 1987, p. 7). The auxiliary function is not forgotten, however; it supplements the dominant.

The Myers-Briggs typology also includes two additional dimensions, called attitudes or orientations (Lynch, 1987). These attitudes reflect which function is dominant and which auxiliary, as well as where they are used. The first attitude, Extraversion (E) or Introversion (I), describes the individual's focus of attention and source of energy in the world, whether outward toward people, objects, and actions or inward toward ideas and concepts. The second attitude, Judgment (J) or Perception (P), reflects the individual's preferences for interacting with the external world. A Judgment orientation is toward organization, planning, and control of one's world, while a Perception orientation is toward openness, flexibility, and spontaneous reactions to events.

Knowledge of an individual's preferences within each of the two functions (perception and judgment), as well as his or her preferences on the two attitudinal dimensions, permits classification of that individual into one of sixteen types. These types can be used for research purposes or in the design of academic and nonacademic programs and activities. Provost and Anchors (1987) discuss some of the higher educational applications of the Myers-Briggs Type Indicator (MBTI), an instrument for operationalizing the theory. Lynch (1987) discusses type development and student development. Lawrence (1982) discusses use of the MBTI in instructional settings, and Lawrence (1984) and Claxton and Murrell (1987) review the MBTI-based research in this area.

Person-Environment Interaction Theories

Strictly speaking, person-environment theories[5] are not developmental in the sense that they do not attempt to explain in detail either the nature or specific processes of student "development" or growth. They are included here, however, because they do attempt to explain human behavior and provide frameworks for thinking about student change and college effects.

To varying degrees, all the theories and models discussed to this point acknowledge the role of the individual's environment in shaping human behavior and development. Certain theories and models, however, focus specifically and in detail on the environment and how it, through its interactions with characteristics of the individual, influences behavior. The extent to which person and environment receive equal attention in these theories varies, sometimes substantially. Within this general family of models, several subcategories are identifiable (Baird, 1988; Huebner, 1980, 1989;

Strange & King, 1990). Some of their differences derive from writers' decisions about whether the environment should be defined objectively, as a reality external to the individual, or perceptually, reality being whatever the individual perceives and believes it to be. Baird (1988) provides an extensive discussion and critique of a number of models that fall into this general category, as well as of some of the important theoretical and technical issues involved in measuring person-environment interactions and their effects.

Physical Models

Physical theories and models focus on the external, physical environment, whether natural or man-made, and how it shapes behavior by permitting certain kinds of activities while limiting or making impossible other kinds. The physical environment may be conceived rather specifically, as in the architectural features of residence halls (for example, Heilweil, 1973; Schroeder, 1980a), or quite broadly, as in urban settings (Michelson, 1970; Sommer, 1969).

Perhaps the most fully developed theory in this category is Barker's (1968; Barker & Associates, 1978) theory of "behavior settings." According to Barker, environments select and shape the behavior of the people occupying any given setting, tending to influence them in similar ways despite their individual differences. Behavior settings are bounded, "standing patterns of behavior . . . [such as] a basketball game, a worship service, a piano lesson . . . that persist when the participants change" (1968, p. 18). Such settings also have a "milieu [that is] an intricate complex of times, places, and things" (1968, p. 19) that surrounds or encloses the behavior and that exists independently of the standing pattern of behavior and of anyone's perception of the setting. Wicker (1973) and Wicker and Kirmeyer (1976) report evidence indicating that a setting's influence is to some extent dependent upon the balance between the number of people in the setting, the activities to be performed, and the physical size of the setting. In this refinement of Barker's ideas, a setting can be "undermanned" or "overmanned," depending on the number of people the setting's activities and physical space can accommodate. Behavior is shaped accordingly.

Human Aggregate Models

Authors of human aggregate models describe an environment and its influences in terms of the aggregate characteristics (for example, sociodemographic characteristics, goals, values, attitudes) of the people who inhabit it. Astin (1968b) and Holland (1966, 1985) are examples, but Holland's work on vocational choice has attracted the most attention and underpins a substantial body of research on college students.

Holland (1966, 1985) argues that choosing a vocation is also a manifestation of personality: "The choice of an occupation is an expressive act which reflects the person's motivation, knowledge, personality, and ability" (1966, p. 4). His theory rests on four "working assumptions" (1985, pp. 2–4). First, most people can be categorized into one of six theoretical "types": realistic, investigative, artistic, social, enterprising, or conventional.[6] Each type reflects a distinctive constellation of preferences, activities, interests, and dispositions, and each corresponds to a given category of vocations. The types are derived from observation of the characteristics of individuals in those occupations, and "each type has a characteristic repertoire of attitudes and skills for coping with environmental problems and tasks. Different types select and process information in different ways, but all types seek fulfillment by exercising characteristic activities, skills, and talents and by striving to achieve special goals" (1985, p. 3). An individual may have certain of the characteristics of more than one type, and while one type is likely to be more prominent than the others, an individual's personality pattern is one of similarity and dissimilarity with each of the six types.

Second, six "model environments" correspond to the six individual types. Environments are determined by the personality types of the individuals who dominate them (for example, "Realistic" environments are dominated by Realistic type people, "Investigative" environments are dominated by Investigative types, and so on). According to Holland, "where people congregate, they create an environment that reflects the types they are, and it becomes possible to assess the environment in the same terms as we assess people individually" (1985, p. 4).

Third, people seek out those environments that permit them to use their skills, exercise their attitudes and values, and play desirable roles. Through their particular constellation of characteristics and friendship networks, environments also recruit and select individuals for membership.

Finally, the interaction of personality and environment determines behavior. Where the individual's personality pattern is similar to the pattern of others who define the environment, stability is likely. Where there are inconsistencies, some sort of change can be forecast, either in the individual or, more likely, in the setting as the individual withdraws from an incompatible setting in search of one more congruent with his or her type pattern. Theoretically, then, given knowledge of an individual's pattern and environment, certain occupational, social, personal, and educational outcomes are predictable.

Perceptual Models

In perceptual models, definitions of the environment are related in some fashion to the individual student's perception and interpretation of the external world, whether behavioral or psychosocial. While each student's perceptions are subjective and particular to that individual, in the aggregate they theoretically become and define the culture or environment in which the individual lives and that is presumed to influence in various ways that individual's psychosocial development in a range of areas. Most of the originators of theories in this subcategory owe some debt to the work of Kurt Lewin (1936, 1951) and Henry Murray (1938, 1951). The most prominent writers in this subcategory include Moos, Pervin, and Stern.

Moos (1976, 1979; Insel & Moos, 1974) focuses on the social climate's influences on the people who inhabit it. Social climate is considered to have three broad dimensions: a relationship dimension (which involves the interpersonal relations among the people in the environment), a personal development dimension (the growth opportunities afforded by the environment), and a system maintenance and change dimension (which relates to behavioral expectations within the environment, the control it exercises over its occupants, and the manner in which it responds to change).

Stern (1970; Pace & Stern, 1958) developed a "needs-press" model of college students and their environments. According to Stern (1970, p. 6), psychological needs are "organizational tendencies which appear to give unity and direction to a person's behavior." Needs are inferred from students' self-reported preferences for different kinds of activities. An environmental "press" is a situational pressure to behave in certain ways, manifested by the collective activities and interpersonal interactions of the individuals who occupy the environment. The press of any given environment may facilitate or impede the satisfaction of an individual's needs. While the concepts of need and press and Stern's operationalization of them were intended to make possible investigations of the interaction of people and their environments, few studies have actually done so (Walsh, 1973).

Pervin's (1967, 1968a, 1968b) "transactional" theory is based on his belief that behavior is best understood in terms of both the interactions (cause-effect relations) and transactions (reciprocal relations) between the individual and the environment. Pervin's approach is a phenomenological one that focuses on imbalances in or discrepancies between the individual's perceptions of an actual and ideal self, as well as perceived discrepancies between self and other students, self and faculty, and self and administration. Discrepancies, when great enough, lead to psychological conflict, strain, and dissatisfaction. Interpersonal and other environments with promise for bringing an individual's actual and ideal selves closer together (or to reduce perceived discrepancies between self and other dimensions or occupants of the college environment) tend to attract the individual and to produce satisfaction and improved functioning. Environments seen as having the potential of moving the actual and ideal selves (or self and other environmental occupants) farther apart, however, tend to reduce performance and satisfaction and to be avoided.

Pace (1969, 1984; Pace & Stern, 1958) has devoted considerable time and attention to the description and study of collegiate environments, and his work relies heavily on student perceptions of their environments. He has not, however, articulated any comprehensive or systemic theory of person-environment interactions and their presumably predictable consequences for students.

Structural Organizational Models

The fourth subcategory in Strange and King's (1990) typology of person-environment interaction models denotes theories or models that look to organizational structures and characteristics to explain the behavior of the people in those organizations. Because these frameworks typically focus on the organization's employees and managers, however, and because they are rarely used in the study of change among college students, they are referred to here only to alert the reader to their existence and to complete the Strange and King taxonomy. James and Jones (1974) provide a somewhat dated review of this literature. Readers interested in this approach should also see Kuh (1987).

Commonalities in Developmental Theories

As even the foregoing brief summaries make clear, the most prominent and influential theories of college student growth vary in a number of important ways, including the structure of the developmental process, its end points, the number of developmental stages or dimensions, the origins of developmental growth or stage change, and the characterization and labeling of each dimension or stage. At the same time, however, it is also apparent that certain commonalities in substance and process exist among most of these theories and models. This section identifies both substantive and process themes that appear with some consistency in many developmental theories. Rodgers (1980) gives a similar but more extensive analysis than is possible here.

Similarities in Substance

Within the cognitive-structural family of developmental theories, several authors have constructed what are essentially tables of conceptual concordance that equate stages across theoretical models.[7] In addition to the stage similarities, however, several substantive themes are discernible in many developmental theories and models. Common to several theories of college student development is the emergence during the college years of self-understanding and awareness that one's feelings and behaviors may not always conform to some set of ideal standards. Externally originated controls on behavior slowly give way to internal controls. This theme is identifiable in Marcia's notions of experiencing crisis and making of commitments in identity formation, in Chickering's (1969) "Managing Emotions" vector, in Loevinger's "Self-Aware" transitional phase (Stage 5), and in Heath's (1968) growing allocentricism, particularly with respect to the student's self-concept.

A second substantive theme common to several theories is not only the increase in consciousness of self during the college years but also the emergence of an understanding and appreciation of the roles of and obligations to other people in one's life. The growth of individuality is accompanied by expanded interpersonal horizons and a growing understanding and appreciation of the paradoxical merger of dependence and independence in the concept of interdependence. This theme is identifiable in Chickering's "Autonomy" and "Identity" vectors; Heath's "Becoming Integrated" and "Becoming Autonomous" dimensions; Loevinger's "Self-Aware," "Conscientious," and "Individualistic" stages (5–7); Kohlberg's "Authority and Social-Order Maintaining Orientation" and "Contractual Legalistic Orientation" stages (4 and 5); and Perry's "Relativism" and "Commitment Foreseen" positions (5 and 6).

Third, a high degree of similarity exists across developmental theories at the highest stages of development. For most, the higher levels of growth mark a progression toward self-definition and integration. Indeed, while the precise specification of the developmental end points varies across these theories, the progression is invariably toward greater differentiation and complexity accompanied by greater integration. A number of progressive developmental sequences are apparent: from cognitive and affective simplicity to complexity, from personal irresponsibility to responsibility, from dependence to autonomy and interdependence, from impulsiveness to self-control, from immaturity to maturity, from external controls to internal controls and self-determination, from self-interestedness to a sense of justice and responsibility for others, from instinctual behavior to principled action.

Similarities in Process

Similarities across theories and models also exist in their conceptions of the processes of student development (Blocher, 1978; Rodgers, 1980). Miller and Winston (1990, p. 101) identify five "fundamental developmental principles that reappear throughout the literature on human development." (In the following, Miller and Winston use a somewhat broader definition of *psychosocial* than we have in this chapter.)

1. *Psychosocial development is continuous in nature,* and normal maturation leads to developmental changes regardless of the environment, but not independent of it. [Individual experiences and responses determine the extent to which growth is promoted or impeded.] . . .
2. *Psychosocial development is cumulative in nature,* and life experiences tend to

represent "building blocks" [Certain tasks must be accomplished before higher level ones can be taken on.] . . .

3. *Psychosocial development progresses along a continuum from simpler to more complex behavior. . . .*
4. *Psychosocial development tends to be orderly and stage related. . . .*
5. *Psychosocial development is reflected in developmental tasks.*

[Miller & Winston, 1990, p. 102]

Four additional process commonalities are also apparent in developmental theories of student growth:

6. Cognitive readiness is a necessary, but not sufficient, condition for development.

Sanford (1962) has stated that two conditions are necessary for the kind of developmental progress described by most of the theories reviewed here that deal with student change. The first "is the idea of *readiness,* the notion that certain kinds of response cannot be made unless certain states or conditions have been built up in the person" (p. 258). While the notion of readiness may be both biological and psychological, Sanford appears to be concerned primarily with psychosocial readiness and to consider such readiness to change to be critical to both cognitive and affective development. Most of the change-oriented theories reviewed here implicitly assume or explicitly assert some notion of psychological, *cognitive* readiness to be primary and necessary (although not sufficient) for developmental progress. Each theory presumes possession of cognitive and analytical capabilities sufficient to recognize and understand (if not articulate) emerging internal or external challenges to the balance or stability of an individual's current intellectual and emotional structures—the way one interprets and organizes knowledge and experience in order to make them understandable. It is these challenges or imbalances in cognitive structures, of course, that are presumed to initiate a potentially developmental response. For such a response to occur, however, the individual must be cognitively capable of recognizing the conflict(s) inherent in retaining the structures of the current developmental stage or condition in the face of evidence suggesting that to do so is to take an intellectually untenable position. Thus, the state of cognitive development may set a ceiling on further growth, at least until the individual is cognitively ready for stage or condition change. The individual may be ready and yet choose *not* to change, but the intellectual ability to recognize the possible need for change and actually to revise present cognitive structures must exist if growth is to occur.

7. Recognition of complexity precedes higher-level developmental change.

Cognitive capacity and readiness for change are intimately related to development because of their necessity for the perception of the complexity of one's world, as well as of one's place in it. For Perry, recognition of alternative, differentiated ideas or beliefs is one of the major steps in his conception of students' growth—the perception of the relativity of knowledge and values that is required before choices can be discerned and initial commitments made. For Kohlberg (1975) the capacity for reasoning and differentiation puts a ceiling on the moral stage an individual can attain. Chickering (1969, p. 92), while less explicit than the others, clearly recognizes that "conflicting values, diverse behaviors and mutually exclusive models combine to offer multiple alternatives from which a particular identity must be constructed." If one can truly choose among alternatives, it seems reasonable to assume also the ability to differentiate among alternatives. Heath (1968, p. 253) asks: "Is not the process of maturing one of reaching successively more complex and stable equilibrium levels at which a person's growth may 'pause' temporarily—or forever?"

Thus, developmental theories presume a recognition of complexity in knowledge and values. The individual's growing awareness of this complexity and also the cognitive readiness for change constitute the developmental trigger. Both are necessary but not sufficient conditions for growth.

8. Developmental movement originates in a challenge to the current state of development.

If cognitive readiness and the perception of complexity make up the developmental trigger, then cognitive or affective conflict is the finger that pulls it. Fundamental to virtually all of the change-oriented theories is the proposition that developmental movement requires the experience of conflict, the awareness of a challenge to the integrity and stability of the developmental stage or condition at which the individual currently functions. This concept, of course, is not new. In fact, it is the second of Sanford's (1962) two conditions alluded to earlier for explaining developmental changes among students: "Whatever the stage of readiness in the personality, further development will not occur until stimuli arrive to upset the existing equilibrium and require fresh adaptation" (p. 258). Sanford (1967, p. 49) asserts the functionalist view that "a person strives to reduce the tension caused by a challenge and thus to restore equilibrium," and the theorists who dominate the conceptual scene in college student research clearly subscribe to this view (see Rodgers, 1980; Caple, 1987a).

Thus, most change-oriented theories hold an almost Newtonian view of developmental change: A structure at rest will remain at rest unless confronted by experiences or perceptions that challenge its ability to explain them and thus remain internally consistent. The individual may simply assimilate the new knowledge or experience into current structures and beliefs, perhaps even altering its content somewhat in order to do so. Such a response is unlikely to lead to developmental change. However, the individual may recognize the magnitude of the conflict and accommodate to it through the reformation of existing beliefs or knowledge structures. Such reconstructions are considered the essence of developmental growth. Whether growth occurs depends upon the nature of the individual's response to the conflict. Not all changes are "growth" experiences.

9. The capacity for detachment from self and for empathy controls access to higher developmental levels.

Recognition of the pluralism of knowledge and values, the ability to differentiate among alternatives, and the capacity to deal with the conflicts that may exist among alternatives are preconditions for another important process common to developmental models: the ability to separate from self and empathize with others, to put oneself in the place of another, to adopt another's point of view. For most developmental writers, the capacity for empathy with others represents a major determinant of higher-level individual development. Most importantly, the capacity for empathy is presumed to lead not only to a better understanding of self and a wider appreciation of the ideas and rights of others but also to the development of more mature interpersonal relationships and ultimately to the development of commitments.

The Role of the Environment in Developmental Change

Depending upon which theoretical tradition is consulted, development may be seen to have physiological, psychological, or sociocultural origins. Virtually no theorist puts all of the conceptual eggs in only one of these baskets, of course, but the focus of attention in explaining human behavior can vary considerably. Among the developmentalists discussed here, the major concern is with describing the dimensions (content) of student development or the cognitive and epistemological functioning (process) that produces it. In the examination of these important components of student change, attention is necessarily concentrated on changes that occur within the individual student.

Consequently, perhaps unavoidably, virtually none of these theories examines in any detailed fashion the environmental conditions and processes that might lead to development of any particular kind or at any particular stage. This is not to say that these writers ignore the influence of the individual's environment on behavior. Indeed, in nearly every case, the environment is acknowledged to have an important influence on development. The point is that intra-individual growth dimensions and changes in epistemological structures receive closer attention than do the sources of any changes. While the individual's environment is recognized to be an important determinant of development, it tends nonetheless to be treated theoretically as an amorphous set of conditions. As will become apparent below, sociological writers focus less on the specific nature of changes than on their origins.

Other Perspectives

Despite the substantive and process commonalities discussed in the preceding sections and despite the fact that psychologically based, developmental theories of student growth have to date dominated study and practice in this area of higher education, there is far from complete agreement, even within the developmentalist community, on a number of issues. The disputed ground includes whether the developmental course and process are the same for men and women and for whites and nonwhites, whether movement across stages is irreversible, and whether the character of cognitive structures is transcultural and universal. Questions also remain about whether structures are domain or content specific and how growth actually occurs. Not everyone sees the world as Piaget did (see, for example, Gelman & Baillargeon, 1983).

Indeed, more recently a "theory of self-organization," offering a view of student growth dramatically different from the ones summarized here, has attracted some attention (see Caple, 1987a, 1987b; Kuh, Whitt, & Shedd, 1988). According to this view, the growth tendency is not toward equilibrium but toward disequilibrium, and the sorts of structural changes considered to be developmental by the theorists reviewed here do *not* occur in some systematic, patterned, cumulative process. For self-organization theorists, development-producing changes are, in fact, random and unpredictable.

A review (much less a resolution) of these disputed points is beyond the scope and intent of this chapter, but researchers and practitioners alike need at the least to be aware of their presence. In addition, the developmentalists and others who seek psychological explanations for college student change face theoretical challenges from outside the fold as well as from within. Critiques of the dominance of the developmentalist perspective in the research on college students come from sociologists and others who seek the origins of change in students' external rather than internal worlds.

Feldman (1972) identifies several troublesome problems in the adoption of developmental models for understanding the change process in college students. One problem, says Feldman, is that much of the research based on a developmental theory of change is not neutral. Evidence tends to be interpreted in developmental terms, as reflecting movement toward a more advanced stage of growth, even when the changes are not in theoretically expected directions. It is quite possible, of course, that regressive changes in fact occur; yet the positive, developmental bias, says Feldman, militates against such interpretations of the evidence. For example, Heath (1968) found that entering freshmen scored higher on various measures of autonomy and emotional independence than they did seven months later. Despite this evidence, however, he concludes that "the apparent 'regression' in autonomy was necessary to become more autonomous. Similarly, the apparent 'integration' of the entering freshmen's talents, values, and interests may have been a less mature form of integration than the 'disintegration' the same men experienced later in the year" (p. 253).

Feldman (1972) believes that in addition to the tendency to "psychologize" student change, such models also ignore a variety of other changes that college students experience. He suggests that "some (many?) of the imputed or actual changes in students, prompted by their moving into new [social and preoccupational] positions in college or by their anticipation of future roles, imply little or nothing about development; these changes simply may lie outside the developmental (growth) framework" (p. 17).

Dannefer (1984a), while writing specifically about adult development, offers a similar but even sharper critique. Dannefer considers the entire developmental approach to be flawed. The conception's propositions of "sequentiality, unidirectionality, an end state, irreversibility, qualitative-structural transformation, and universality" (p. 103) do not take into account the powerful influence exerted by the environment. Dannefer charges that while developmentalists acknowledge environmental influences, that role typically is a supporting, instrumental one, a necessary but not sufficient condition providing opportunities that trigger internal, growth-determining mechanisms.

What *are* the origins of the impetus for change and growth? Dannefer (1984a) suggests that environmental structures influence the social organization of developmental opportunities at each of three levels: (1) at the societal level (for example, via stratification patterns based on social class, sex, race, or age), (2) at the organizational level (for example, in bureaucracies, schools, and social service agencies), or (3) at the micro level, where peer and other small group dynamics operate through a variety of mechanisms. In the traditional micro-level view, educational institutions socialize students through a series of experiences in a wide variety of environmental settings that instill in students knowledge, attitudes, values, and skills through the influences of faculty, other students, and other socializing agents. In these ways, schools shape the content and direction of student change and growth.

A common organizational-level perspective (for example, Feldman, 1972; Clark, 1960) conceives of colleges and universities as "gatekeepers," a sort of social and occupational sieve controlling who is certified for access to various socioeconomic status and occupational positions and benefits.

Through such controls, institutions are also presumed to exert considerable influence on students' present and future behaviors, attitudes, values, beliefs, interests, and even cognitive preferences. Through their social "charters" to produce certain kinds of students (Kamens, 1971, 1974), colleges not only "allocate" students to various and select adult roles but also thereby induce adoption of behaviors, attitudes, goals, and values appropriate to the roles and expectations of the station and status assigned them by their education (Meyer, 1977).

Traditional approaches to individual development, the critics say, do not take adequate account of "(1) the malleability of the human organism in relation to environments; (2) the structural complexity and diversity of the social environment; [or] (3) the role of the symbolic—of social knowledge and human intentionality—as factors mediating development" (Dannefer, 1984a, pp. 106–107). According to Dannefer (1984b, p. 847), developmental theories fall into the trap of "ontogenetic reductionism—the practice of treating socially produced and patterned phenomena as rooted in the characteristics of the individual organism. . . . To state that the environment is important, to mention it often, and to include it in definitional statements do not together mean that research will be designed, nor findings interpreted, in a way that apprehends social structure as a constitutive force in development, and that views the social environment as more than a setting that facilitates maturational unfolding."

Feldman (1972, p. 18) proposes that attention be focused on social organizations and the variations among them, with differential student change and stability "inferred *directly* in terms of the differences among colleges, rather than in terms of the 'preconceived' notions [of development]." For example, differences among students at different institutions with respect to most variables of interest in student change research would be interpreted as consequences of the variations in institutional characteristics (for example, size, the status system, normative values of faculty, and student cultures) rather than necessarily as signs of "growth" or development. While certain of the differential impacts observed may be developmental in nature, "In general the social organizational orientation is neutral about or orthogonal to a developmental approach. . . . [N]othing is implied by the investigators about which shifts do or do not represent development in personality" (Feldman, 1972, p. 19).

Feldman's (1972) overriding point is that the developmental conception of student change is only one of several possible conceptual paradigms. The various theories and models reviewed here, as well as those proposed by critics, differ in their assumptions, tenets, structures, dynamics, and inferences. As Feldman notes, however, this is not to say that they are completely distinct or incompatible. The important lesson is to understand what the constraints are on any approach and to bear in mind that reliance on developmental models may lead to misspecification of the origins of student change and growth. "Each [approach] may be necessary to the study of student change and stability during college, but none of them is sufficient" (Feldman, 1972, p. 21).

College Impact Models of Student Change

Theories of the environmental or sociological origins of change in college students constitute a second general family of models of student change. These "impact models" concentrate not so much on any particular internal process or dimension of student change as on the processes and origins of change. These models are much less specific than theories of individual development in their explication of the particular changes students undergo, are less detailed in their overall exposition, and have a less explicit base in other theories (for example, sociology, organizational impact, or industrial psychology).

Astin's Theory of "Involvement"

Astin (1970c) proposed one of the earliest college impact models, the now-familiar "input-process-output" model. More recently, Astin (1984, 1985a; Jacobi, Astin, & Ayala, 1987) has come to view the purpose of higher education as one of talent development. On the basis of his own research and consistent with Pace's (1984) work on the quality of student effort, Astin has proposed a "theory of involvement" to explain the dynamics of how students develop. According to Astin (1985a, p. 133), his theory "can be stated simply: *Students learn by becoming involved.*" He sees in his theory elements of the Freudian notion of cathexis (the investment of psychological energy), as well the learning theory concept of time-on-task. He suggests five "basic postulates": (1) involvement requires the investment of psychological and physical energy in "objects" (for example, tasks, people, activities) of one sort or another, whether specific or highly general; (2) involvement is a continuous concept—different students will invest varying amounts of energy in different objects; (3) involvement has both quantitative and qualitative features; (4) the amount of learning or development is directly proportional to the quality and quantity of involvement; and (5) educational effectiveness of any policy or practice is related to its capacity to induce student involvement (Astin, 1985a, pp. 135–136).

Astin's (1985a) conception occupies something of a middle ground between psychological and sociological explanations of student change. His earlier formulations suggested an almost passive role for students in their own development, a role analogous to that of raw materials (the "inputs") in a production process (Astin, 1970c) or as the hospital patient whose improvement depends primarily upon the skill and prescriptions of the physician (Astin, 1977a). In his more recent thinking, however, Astin (1985a) assigns the institutional environment a critical role in that it affords students a great number and variety of opportunities for encounters with other ideas and people. Now, however, the student clearly plays a central role inasmuch as change is likely to occur to the extent that the student becomes involved in those encounters. The student must actively exploit the opportunities presented by the environment. Thus, development or change is not seen merely as the consequence of collegiate "impact" on a student. Rather, the individual plays a central role in determining the extent and nature of growth according to the quality of effort or involvement with the resources provided by the institution.

Whether Astin's propositions constitute a "theory," however, is open to question. While they are included here because of the attention they have attracted from higher educational researchers and administrators, they probably do not meet generally accepted definitions of theory. Kerlinger (1986, p. 9), for example, defines a theory as "a set of interrelated constructs (concepts), definitions, and propositions that present a systematic view of phenomena by specifying relations among variables, with the purpose of explaining and predicting the phenomena." (See also Walsh, 1973.) Astin offers a general dynamic, a principle, rather than any detailed, systemic description of the behaviors or phenomena being predicted, the variables presumed to influence involvement, the mechanisms by which those variables relate to and influence one another, or the precise nature of the process by which growth or change occurs. It remains to be seen whether Astin's involvement propositions are useful in guiding research beyond providing a general, conceptual orientation.

Tinto's Theory of Student Departure

A more explicit model of institutional impact, yet one quite similar to Astin's in its dynamics, is a longitudinal model given by Tinto (1975, 1987) that seeks specifically to explain the college student attrition process (see Figure 2.1). Building upon the work of Spady (1970), Tinto theorizes that students enter a college or university with varying patterns of personal, family, and academic characteristics and skills, including initial dispositions and intentions with respect to college attendance and personal goals. These intentions and commitments are subsequently modified and reformulated on a continuing basis through a longitudinal series of interactions between the individual and the structures and members of the academic and social systems of the institution. Satisfying and rewarding encounters with the formal and informal academic and social systems of the institution are presumed to lead to greater integration in those systems and thus to student retention. The term *integration* can be understood to refer to the extent to which the individual shares the normative attitudes and values of peers and faculty in the institution and abides by the formal and informal structural

Figure 2.1. A Model of Institutional Departure.

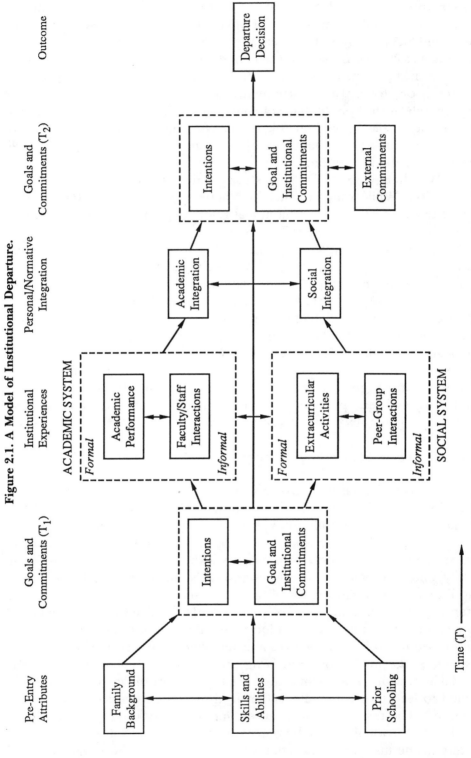

| Pre-Entry Attributes | Goals and Commitments (T₁) | Institutional Experiences | Personal/Normative Integration | Goals and Commitments (T₂) | Outcome |

requirements for membership in that community or in the subgroups of which the individual is a part. Academic and social integration may describe a condition (that is, the individual's place in the academic and social systems) or an individual perception (that is, the individual's personal sense of place in those systems). Negative interactions and experiences tend to reduce integration, to distance the individual from the academic and social communities of the institution, promoting the individual's marginality and, ultimately, withdrawal.

Although Tinto focuses on the college attrition process, his model has been successfully employed to study other student outcomes, such as students' reports of academic skill acquisition (for example, Terenzini & Wright, 1987a; Volkwein, King, & Terenzini, 1986), personal change (for example, Terenzini & Wright, 1987b), and major field changes (Theophilides, Terenzini, & Lorang, 1984b). Indeed, the underlying dynamic of Tinto's theory of departure—student integration into the academic and social systems of an institution—is quite similar to Astin's (1984, 1985a) "involvement" and Pace's (1984) "quality of effort," although the importance of the investment of physical and psychological energy postulated by Astin and Pace is only implied in Tinto's concept of integration. Tinto's more explicit theoretical structure, compared to that given by Astin (1985a), however, offers significant opportunities both to researchers who wish to study the college student change process and to administrators who seek to design academic and social programs and experiences intended to promote students' educational growth.

Pascarella's General Model for Assessing Change

Tinto's (1975, 1987) model is largely (although not exclusively) concerned with intra-institutional influences on students and with the influences exerted on students by other individuals (primarily students and faculty members but also family and noncollege peers). Less attention is devoted to specification of the nature or strength of the influences of an institution's structural/organizational characteristics or to the role of individual student effort.

Pascarella (1985a) has suggested a general causal model that includes more explicit consideration of both an institution's structural characteristics and its general environment but that is also amenable to multi-institution studies of collegiate impact. Drawing on his own work (Pascarella, 1980), as well as that of Lacy (1978), Pace (1979), Weidman (1984), and others, Pascarella suggests that growth is a function of the direct and indirect effects of five major sets of variables (see Figure 2.2). Two of those sets, students' background and precollege characteristics and the structural and organizational features of the institution (for example, size, selectivity, residential

Figure 2.2. A General Causal Model for Assessing the Effects of Differential College Environments on Student Learning and Cognitive Development.

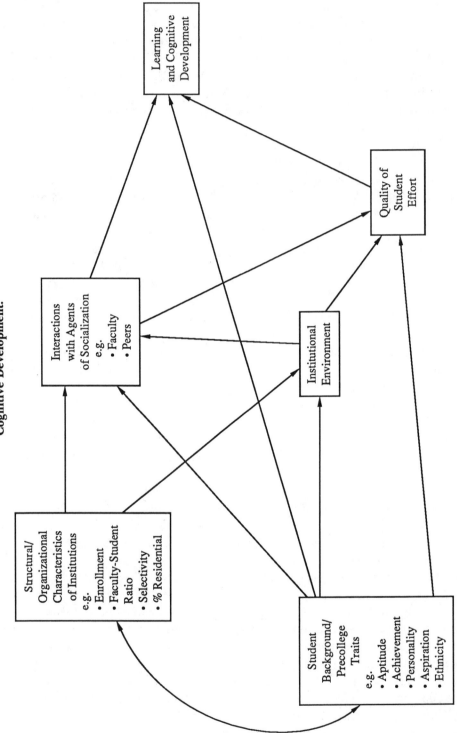

Source: Pascarella, 1985a, p. 50.

character), together shape the third variable set: a college's or university's environment.

These three clusters of variables, in turn, influence a fourth cluster that involves both the frequency and content of students' interactions with the major socializing agents on campus (the faculty and other students). Quality of effort, the fifth constellation of variables, is shaped by students' background traits, by the general institutional environment, and by the normative influences of peers and faculty members. Student change is seen as a function of students' background characteristics, interactions with major socializing agents, and the quality of students' efforts in learning and developing. The structural features of an institution are believed to have an indirect rather than a direct influence on student development, their effect being mediated through the institution's general environment, the quality of student effort, and students' interactions with peers and faculty members. While initially designed to explain changes in students' learning and cognitive development, Pascarella's model is equally appropriate for the study of other college outcomes (see Pascarella, 1985c, 1985d; Pascarella, Smart, Ethington, & Nettles, 1987; Pascarella, Ethington, & Smart, 1988).

Weidman's Model of Undergraduate Socialization

Most recently, Weidman (1989a) has proposed a model of undergraduate socialization that seeks to incorporate both psychological and social structural influences on student change. The model gives particular attention to noncognitive changes, such as those involving career choices, life-style preferences, values, and aspirations (see Figure 2.3). Weidman's model, however, is somewhat more explicit than those summarized above in its explication of the process of undergraduate socialization—the acquisition of the knowledge, attitudes, and skills that are valued by the society (or important subgroups) in which the individual lives.

Weidman's model is based primarily on his own research (Weidman, 1984, 1989b; Weidman & Friedman, 1984; Weidman & White, 1985), as well as the models of Chickering (1969) and Astin (1977a, 1984) and the sociological literature on adult socialization (Brim & Wheeler, 1966; Mortimer & Simmons, 1978). Like Tinto and Pascarella, Weidman hypothesizes that students bring with them to college a set of important orienting background characteristics (socioeconomic status, aptitudes, career preferences, aspirations, values, and the like) but also normative pressures deriving from both parents and other noncollege reference groups (for example, peers, employers, community). These characteristics and shaping forces constitute predisposing and, to a certain extent, constraining forces on students' choices within the college's structural and organizational settings. These contexts may be both formal and informal, and they are the occasions for exposure to normative pressures through students' social and academic encounters

Figure 2.3. A Conceptual Model of Undergraduate Socialization.

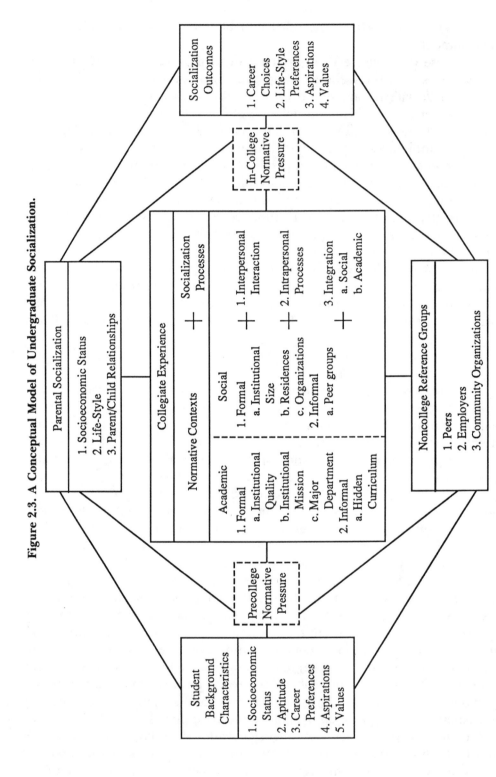

Source: Weidman, 1989a. Used by permission.

with faculty members and student peers. The mechanisms by means of which these normative pressures are exerted may involve interpersonal interactions, intrapersonal processes and changes, or the normative order and expectations implied within an institution with a given mission, faculty, and both organizational and faculty expectations of students.

In addition to within-institutional socializing forces and to a greater extent than either Tinto or Pascarella, Weidman also hypothesizes important noncollege influences on students. The model explicitly posits a continuing socializing role for parents (even when students live away from home) and for other noncollege reference groups, such as peers, current and potential future employers, and community organizations.

According to Weidman, the socialization process fosters students' evaluations and balancing of these various normative influences for attaining personal goals. Decisions are then made to maintain or change values, attitudes, or aspirations held at the time of matriculation. This process is seen as both longitudinal and reciprocal, with the salience of segments of the model varying over time and both influencing and being influenced by other components of the socialization structure. Because of its recent introduction into the literature, however, the validity of this model and its utility for research and/or practical purposes remain unexamined.

Commonalities in College Impact Models

Like the developmental models reviewed earlier, the primarily sociological, "impact" models discussed in the preceding section have several characteristics or propositions in common. For example, compared with the developmental frameworks, each of these alternative conceptions assigns a much more prominent and specific role to the context in which the student acts and thinks. Institutional structures, policies, programs, and services (whether academic or nonacademic), as well as the attitudes, values, and behaviors of the people who occupy (and to some extent define) institutional environments, are all seen as potential sources of influence in students' cognitive and affective changes. These sociological models resemble the developmental theories in that students are seen as active participants in their own growth, but the environment is also seen as an active force that not only affords opportunities for change-inducing encounters but can also on occasion require a student to respond. Thus, change is influenced not only by whether and how the student responds but also by the nature and intensity of the environmental stimulus. Specification of potential areas of variation in institutional environments (both within and across institutions) is a much more salient characteristic of sociological models than of developmental models.

At the same time, the specification of those facets of the student that are considered to be important tends to be general and somewhat simplistic. To be sure,. variations in student change attributable to sex, race or ethnicity, socioeconomic status, academic aptitude and achievement, and so on have been empirically well established, but developmental theories and the research based on them suggest that other important student traits may be overlooked if the perspective is strictly sociological. For example, sociological models probably give less attention than is warranted to consideration of such student traits as cognitive and emotional readiness for intellectual, academic, or psychosocial change; to current levels of intellectual curiosity; or to students' capacities for empathy or role playing. At the least, it would appear that the student traits to which attention might profitably be given in the study of change probably should be expanded beyond the current reliance on demographic and background characteristics.

Conclusions

This chapter has summarized the most prominent theories of the origins and nature of student change and sought to reduce the apparent conceptual diversity among them by identifying substantive and process features they have in common. Knowledge of these theories and their commonalities will serve as a useful backdrop against which our review of the last twenty years of research on the influences of college on student change can be examined. An understanding of the general nature of change in college students is also fundamental to the design and development of academic and nonacademic policies, programs, and practices, as well as to fruitful research on student change during the college years.

Some writers suggest that the college years function as something of a developmental testing ground between adolescence and adulthood, a time to examine and test new roles, attitudes, beliefs, and behaviors, a time when an individual can give full attention to change and development. White (1980, p. 29), for example, has characterized higher education as "an institutionalized form of psychosocial moratorium (a breathing period, a growing space). It embodies experiences which should promote development in . . . cognition, identity, and moral judgment." The phrase *psychosocial moratorium* is borrowed from Erikson (1968), of course, and means "a delay of adult commitments," but it also describes "a period that is characterized by a selective permissiveness on the part of society and of provocative playfulness on the part of youth" (Erikson, 1968, p. 157). According to Erikson (p. 157), "Each society and each culture institutionalizes a certain moratorium for the majority of its young people. For the most part, these moratoria coincide with apprenticeships and adventures that are in line with the society's values."

For other writers, the transition from high school to college is viewed as a form of culture shock involving significant social and psychological relearning in the face of encounters with new ideas, new teachers and friends with quite varied values and beliefs, new freedoms and opportunities, and new academic, personal, and social demands. Indeed, Heath (1968) believes one of the central functions of a liberal education is specifically to provide such "shocks." Feldman and Newcomb (1969) characterize the freshman year as a combination of "desocialization" (pressures to unlearn certain current attitudes, values, beliefs, and behaviors) and "socialization" (pressures to learn and participate in a new culture and social order). From the perspective of the theories and models of institutional impact summarized here, the potency of colleges and universities for influencing student change and growth appears to lie in the exposure they afford their students to diversity, presenting opportunities to explore, peer and adult models to emulate, and experiences that challenge currently held values, attitudes, and beliefs.

It seems entirely reasonable to expect colleges and universities to promote and facilitate cognitive readiness for development through student encounters with various bodies of knowledge and modes of inquiry, as well as training in logic, critical thinking, and the evaluation of alternative ideas and courses of action. Higher educational institutions can also be expected to contribute to the recognition of complexity and the ability to deal with it through the opportunities they give students for testing ideas and beliefs, for practicing new roles, for developing interpersonal relations at levels of maturity quite above those that were possible in high school, and by providing services and advisers to help students through the periods of personal and intellectual conflict and disorientation that are thought to be necessary for change and development. In short, the college environment presumably offers a setting in which the impetus and opportunities for change are substantial, perhaps unsurpassed by those of any other social institution.

The substantive and procedural elements common to the developmental theories reviewed in this chapter, as well as the socializing structures and forces that underlie the potential of colleges and universities to shape student change in a variety of ways and settings, suggest that the diversity of theoretical propositions, dimensions, and nomenclatures may not be so great as first thought. Indeed, Korn (1986, p. 13) has identified in recent theories of student change what he considers to be manifestations of a " 'cognitive revolution' in psychology," a key element of which "is understanding an individual's active transaction/interaction with significant aspects of his or her environment." Significant theoretical work remains to be done, however. As noted earlier in this chapter, considerable uncertainty exists about whether the developmental paths of men and women are the same. In addition, the nature of identity development among black and other nonwhite students remains virtually unknown territory and constitutes a glaring and embarrassing gap in our theoretical knowledge.

But while there is yet much work to be done to develop new theories, as well as to consolidate psychological and sociological paradigms, each of the two generic approaches to the study of change among college students has much to offer the other. Focusing on one to the exclusion of the other is not only likely to result in misspecification of the college student change process but also to be dysfunctional, leading to poor theory, poor research, and poor practice.

As subsequent chapters will demonstrate, there is ample evidence that students do indeed change in a number of ways during the college years. Many of those changes are independent of what students are like when they enter college. The evidence also strongly suggests that the nature and origins of these changes are frequently both psychological and sociological. As will become apparent, college and university campuses constitute powerful and highly varied settings for student change—developmental and otherwise.

Notes

1. Discussion of how these theories might be applied in practice is beyond the scope of this chapter. Readers interested in such linkages should consult Brown & Barr (1990); Drum (1980); Huebner (1979, 1989); Knefelkamp, Widick, & Parker (1978); Kuh, Whitt, & Shedd (1988); Rodgers (1980, 1983, 1989, 1990a, 1990b, 1990c); Strange (1987); and Strange & King (1990). Readers are forewarned, however, by Parker's (1937,$p. 420) ijsightful$paradox: "Phe natura of theory is sqch that$ip does not lead directly to practice and the nature of practice is such that it does not proceed without theory."

2. Knefelkamp, Widick, and Parker (1978) originally included a fifth category for "maturity" models. That category contained only Heath's (1968) theory, however, and in the present treatment, Heath's framework is included in the section on psychosocial theories.

3. Erikson's eight stage-crises, in their theorized developmental order and with approximate, associated age ranges, are (1) basic trust versus mistrust (birth to two years), (2) autonomy versus shame and doubt (ages three to six), (3) initiative versus guilt (ages six to ten), (4) industry versus inferiority (ages ten to fourteen), (5) identity versus identity confusion (ages fourteen to twenty), (6) intimacy versus isolation (ages twenty to forty), (7) generativity versus stagnation (ages forty to sixty-five), (8) integrity versus despair (ages sixty-five and older) (Rodgers, 1989, p. 123).

4. Rodgers (1990b) provides a more extensive discussion of the theoretical literature relating to differences in the psychosocial and cognitive-structural development of women and men. See also Belenky, Clinchy, Goldberger, & Tarule (1986) for a discussion of women's five "ways of knowing," derived from their research.

5. Walsh (1973, 1975) provides a useful summary and review of the origins

and relevant research relating to selected theories in this family, including those of Astin (1968b), Barker (1968), Clark and Trow (1966), Holland (1966), Newcomb (Newcomb, Koenig, Flacks, & Warwick, 1967), Pervin (1968a, 1968b), and Stern (1970). Feldman (1969) and Baird (1988) both provide excellent critiques of environmental models and theories. Walsh (1973, 1975) and Huebner (1980, 1989) both give useful critiques of selected person-environment interaction theories.

6. "Realistic" types tend to be physically strong, mechanically inclined, conventionally "masculine," aggressive, and unsociable, with good motor skills but poor verbal and interpersonal skills, and a preference for concrete problems over abstract ones. "Intellectual" types are task oriented and asocial, prefer thinking and understanding over action in problem solving, enjoy ambiguous tasks, and have unconventional values. "Social" model types are sociable, humanistic, religious, and "feminine"; need attention; have good verbal and interpersonal skills; avoid the intellectual and physical; and prefer feeling and interpersonal approaches to problem solving. "Conventional" types prefer structured verbal and numeric activities, are conforming, identify with power, and value material possessions and status. They prefer well-structured tasks and avoid problems that require interpersonal or physical skills. "Enterprising" model types have good verbal skills for selling, dominating, and leading. They prefer organizing and directing, are persuasive, seek power and status, and avoid well-defined work situations and problems that require prolonged intellectual effort. "Artistic" types have a high need for originality and self-expression. They are asocial, impulsive, and unconventional and avoid highly structured problems or those requiring gross physical skills (Holland, 1966, pp. 16–17).

7. Knefelkamp, Parker, and Widick (1978, p. 76), for example, compare Erikson, Perry, Kohlberg, and Loevinger's stages. See also Loevinger (1976, p. 109) and Chickering (1976, pp. 72–73). While Chickering's (1969) vectors of development are usually excluded from such tables because they are not offered as stages, Chickering (1969, p. 8) himself has suggested that growth along his vectors "may be expressed more appropriately by a spiral or by steps than by a straight line." Elsewhere, Chickering has agreed that while his vectors "are not hierarchical in the sense that Perry's or Loevinger's . . . stages are . . . [his vectors] are developmentally sequential in a general way. They stimulate thinking in a logical progression" (Thomas & Chickering, 1984, pp. 396–397).

3

Development of Verbal,
Quantitative,
and Subject Matter
Competence

There is little doubt that the enhancement of student learning is central to
the mission of colleges and universities. This chapter reviews the evidence
pertaining to the influence of college on the acquisition of subject matter
knowledge and academic skills. (Chapter Four focuses on more general
cognitive development and skills less directly tied to the academic program.) The phrase "subject matter knowledge and academic skills" casts a
wide conceptual net. This seems appropriate, however, as the knowledge
and skill outcomes of college have been assessed in diverse ways. Examples
include but are not limited to the general and specific academic knowledge
and skills assessed by standardized tests (such as the Graduate Record Examination), measures of specific course learning, level of verbal and mathematical competence, and individual self-reports of gains in general and
specific dimensions of academic knowledge and skills.

Our review in this chapter covers studies that employ these and related measures of knowledge and academic skill acquisition. While it might
seem appropriate to consider cumulative grade point average within this
rubric as well, we have chosen not to do so. Despite an earlier stance on
this issue (Pascarella, 1985a), we have concluded from our current review
of the literature that there may be too many problems in the reliability and
validity of grade point average to consider it solely, or perhaps even primarily, as a measure of how much was learned during college. To some
extent, grades clearly do reflect learning and may well be our most readily
available measure. At the same time, however, it is equally clear that grades

Note: Sections of this chapter appeared in Pascarella, E. (1985). College en-
vironmental influences on learning and cognitive development. In J. Smart
(Ed.), *Higher Education: Handbook of theory and research*, Vol. 1. New York:
Agathon.

are influenced by many other factors. These include the type, racial composition, and academic selectivity of the institution attended (Astin, 1971b, 1972b; Aulston, 1974; Bassis, 1977; Cohen & Brawer, 1982; Kintzer & Wattenbarger, 1985; Lara, 1981; Pascarella, Smart, Ethington, & Nettles, 1987; Perrucci, 1969; Webb, 1971); the student's major field of study (Astin, 1982; Cunningham & Lawson, 1979; Goldman & Hewitt, 1975; Goldman & Widawski, 1976; Prather, Smith, & Kodras, 1979; Prather, Williams, & Wadley, 1979); predominant mode of course instruction (Cunningham & Lawson, 1979); course grading policies (Sgan, 1970; Von Wittich, 1972); instructor rank (Prather & Smith, 1976); and professorial style and personality (Theodory & Day, 1985).

Because of these potential confounding influences, it is extremely difficult to make standardized comparisons of learning based on student grade point average either between or within institutions. Consequently, we have not considered grades primarily as a measure of knowledge acquisition. Rather, we have chosen to treat grade point average primarily as a measure of the extent to which the student successfully complies with the academic norms or requirements of the institution. Thus, grades are viewed as one among a number of dimensions of the collegiate experience (both academic and extracurricular) where the student may demonstrate different levels of involvement or achievement (for example, Willingham, Young, & Morris, 1985). In subsequent chapters we review the evidence pertaining both to the range of institutional effects on grades and to the influence of college grades on various dimensions of postcollege achievement.

Change During College

Overall Change

As with few areas of research on the impact of college on students, findings from studies that investigate gains in subject matter knowledge and academic skill acquisition during college, as measured by standardized tests, are close to being unequivocal. Students appear to make statistically significant (that is, nonchance) gains during college in many areas of subject matter knowledge and academic skills. Moreover, this finding is consistent across nearly five decades of research (McConnell, 1934; Hartson, 1936; Learned & Wood, 1938; Flory, 1940; Hunter, 1942; Barnes, 1943; Heston, 1950; Silvey, 1951; Lannholm, 1952; Lannholm & Pitcher, 1959; Harvey & Lannholm, 1960; Campbell, 1965; Lenning, Munday, & Maxey, 1969; Harris, 1970; Harris & Hurst, 1972; Powers, 1976; Dumont & Troelstrup, 1981).

These studies have employed a wide range of standardized instruments to measure learning gains during college. Included are the Ohio State University Psychological Examination, the Psychological Examination of the American Council on Education, the Graduate Record Examination, the Otis Intelligence Test, the American College Testing Program Achievement Test, and the Nelson-Denny Reading Test. Despite the fact that all these instruments have a strong loading on verbal and/or quantitative competencies, they nevertheless have somewhat different emphases. Moreover, a number of the studies cited above do not provide complete information on sample variation (that is, sample standard deviations). These two characteristics of the body of research make it extremely difficult to estimate the typical magnitude of learning gains during college. In a synthesis of some (though not all) of the studies conducted through the 1960s, Bowen (1977) concludes that average freshman-to-senior gains are .50 of a standard deviation (SD) for verbal skills, .20 of a standard deviation for mathematical skills, and one standard deviation for measures of specific knowledge (for example, history, humanities, social sciences). These represent improvements over the freshman-year score of 19, 8, and 34 percentile points, respectively. (Percentile point improvement is estimated by converting gains from standard deviation units to the area under the normal curve. For example, the area under the normal curve for one standard deviation extends from the 50th to the 84th percentile, or 34 percentile points.)

Based on those studies conducted prior to 1970 that provide sufficient information and more recent studies that were not reviewed by Bowen (1977) (for example, Harris & Hurst, 1972; Dumont & Troelstrup, 1981), our own estimates of the average magnitude of gains in verbal and mathematical skills during college generally concur with those of Bowen. Our estimates are somewhat higher, .56 of a standard deviation for verbal gains and .24 of a standard deviation for mathematics gains, but the differences are so small as to be of little or no practical consequence. Compared to Bowen's estimate of the magnitude of gains in measures of specific knowledge (one standard deviation), our own are somewhat lower, .87 of a standard deviation. Again, however, the difference between our estimate and that of Bowen may not have much substantive meaning.

It is interesting to consider why average gains on measures of specific knowledge appear to be larger in magnitude than gains in more general verbal and mathematical skills. One possible explanation is that the measures that essentially tap more general verbal and quantitative skills are designed to emphasize reliability or stability over time. Consequently, they may be less sensitive to the effects of college than measures of subject matter knowledge.

Patterns of Change

Does any particular time during the student's college experience appear to be linked with greater gains in learning than other periods? Here the evidence is somewhat inconsistent. Earlier studies that examined this issue (Learned & Wood, 1938; Lannholm & Pitcher, 1959) suggest that somewhat greater gains may occur during the first two years of college than during the last two. However, more recent evidence from two studies that used the same instrument but covered different time periods during college suggests a somewhat different conclusion. Lenning, Munday, & Maxey (1969) investigated gains during the first two years with the tests of the American College Testing Program, while Dumont & Troelstrup (1981) employed the same test to study gains from freshman to senior year. Although the two studies used different samples, one can indirectly estimate relative gains from freshman to sophomore and from sophomore to senior year by comparing the magnitude of gains between studies. When this is done, it would appear that on the English, mathematics, and composite sections, gains from the sophomore to senior year are approximately equal to or slightly larger than those from freshman to sophomore year. On the social studies and natural sciences sections, it would appear that freshman-to-sophomore gains are somewhat larger than sophomore-to-senior gains.

The inconsistent findings make it difficult to form a firm conclusion as to differential patterns of gains in knowledge acquisition during college. However, it is clearly the case that even if somewhat greater gains occur during the first two years of college, students continue to make significant gains in their junior and senior years. This conclusion is further supported by a substantial number of cross-sectional studies that compare samples of freshmen or underclassmen with concurrent samples of upperclassmen or seniors on various standardized measures of subject matter knowledge commonly included in college curricula (Barrows et al., 1981; Barrows, Clark, & Klein, 1980; Barrows, Klein, Clark, & Hartshorne, 1981; Cogan, Torney-Purta, & Anderson, 1988; College Entrance Examination Board, 1968; Educational Testing Service, 1954, 1976, 1978; Sharon, 1971). The findings of these studies, many based on large, national samples, clearly suggest that the longer a student attends college, the more he or she knows. Sophomores tend to score significantly higher than freshmen, and juniors and seniors tend to score significantly higher than sophomores.[1]

Relationship of Change to Major

It would further appear that the more a student studies in a particular area of knowledge (for example, majoring in humanities, social sciences, mathematics, physical sciences; or the number of courses taken in a particular field of study), the more the student knows in terms of knowledge and skills specific to that area (Cohen, 1986; Educational Testing Service, 1954; Haven, 1964; Learned & Wood, 1938). This is hardly surprising in that the more one is exposed to an environment that emphasizes comprehension of a specific body of knowledge and methods, the more likely one is to internalize the normative values of that environment and to learn from it (Coleman, 1960). The only evidence inconsistent with this generalization is reported by Palmer (1984) in a study of students from three metropolitan community college districts. The number of reading and writing courses taken in college was not significantly related to the English usage score on a standardized measure of knowledge in general education (the General Academic Assessment). The Palmer study, however, deals with much more general courses and outcomes than do the investigations of Cohen (1986), Educational Testing Service (1954), Haven (1964), and Learned and Wood (1938).

The inescapable conclusions that students make statistically significant gains in academic knowledge and skill acquisition during college, that seniors tend to know more than freshmen, and that one tends to be most knowledgeable in those academic areas where one has studied most are not exactly earthshaking. Indeed, it would be quite surprising, perhaps even shocking, if the evidence were to suggest otherwise.

Design Issues Affecting Interpretation of Results

Concluding that increases in knowledge occur *during college* is quite a different matter from concluding that they occur *because of college*. A number of fundamental research design problems plague the studies reviewed above and prevent the unequivocal attribution of the increases, or freshman versus senior differences, to the college experience. In cross-sectional designs (for example, those comparing scores of separate samples of freshmen and seniors at the same time), differential institutional recruiting standards for successive comparison classes and/or the natural attrition of less capable students from freshman to senior year may yield a substantially more selective population of seniors than the population of freshmen with whom they are compared. Consequently, the differences observed between freshmen and seniors could simply be the result of comparing samples from populations differing in ability or motivation instead of reflecting the influence of college.

Although longitudinal designs (for example, those following the same panel of subjects from freshman to senior year) generally control for this threat to the internal validity of the study, the attrition of students other than those for whom one has both freshman and senior scores may yield a sample that is no longer representative of the appropriate population. (By "internal validity" we mean the extent to which gains in learning can be attributed to the impact of college and not other influences.) Moreover, in the absence of a control group of similar individuals who do not attend college (a characteristic of all the studies cited above), longitudinal investigations are vulnerable to a number of other threats to internal validity. Perhaps the most important of these is the potential confounding influence of maturation. As students grow older, from freshman to senior year, the natural process of maturation could lead to a certain amount of increased knowledge and skill acquisition independent of exposure to college. This might occur through such mechanisms as work, travel, or personal reading, quite apart from one's formal course of study. To the extent that freshman-to-senior gains in knowledge acquisition capture normal maturation as well as the influence of college itself, they may spuriously overestimate the latter.

A second but perhaps less obvious confounding influence is that due to regression artifacts. Regression artifacts are based on the compounded unreliability in standardized measures when used to estimate change or gain. They are often manifest in a negative correlation between initial (for example, freshman) score and amount of change or gain (for example, freshman to senior year). That is, samples that start lower as freshmen will tend to show greater freshman-to-senior gains than samples that start higher. Thus, for example, we find strong negative correlations between initial American College Test (ACT) composite scores and amount of freshman-to-senior gain in the Dumont and Troelstrup (1981) investigation. Under certain conditions, regression artifacts can lead to some bizarre and misleading estimations of the influence of college on subject matter learning. For example, from differences in amount of change that are due largely to differences in regression artifacts, one might erroneously conclude that colleges with a less selective admissions policy are more effective in facilitating learning and knowledge acquisition than are very selective colleges (Banta, Lambert, Pike, Schmidhammer, & Schneider, 1987). When one is considering simple freshman-to-senior (or freshman-to-sophomore) gains in learning on the same instrument, it is often difficult, if not impossible, to separate regression effects from the unique or net effect of college. As with maturation, this too may lead to a spuriously inflated estimate of the influence of college on learning. However, in other circumstances (for example, a sample from a very selective institution), it may lead one to underestimate the true influence of college.

Net Effects of College

Studies that attempt to determine whether differential gains in academic knowledge and skill acquisition are attributable to differences in exposure to postsecondary education (that is, the net effect of college) are, by necessity, more complex in scope and design than investigations that show only that students change during college. Typically, such studies are longitudinal and attempt to include control groups of subjects who do not attend college or who have less than four years' exposure to postsecondary education. Because it is nearly impossible to control individual differences among subjects by random assignment to different levels of exposure to college, these studies often rely on various forms of statistical control (for example, multiple regression, analysis of covariance) to estimate the unique or net effects of college attendance. (See the Appendix for a fuller discussion of these procedures.)

Much of the most important research on the impact of college on learning has been conducted by Wolfle (1980b, 1983, 1987). In an example combining meticulous scholarship with careful empirical analysis, Wolfle (1980b) constructed a correlation matrix based on published evidence from eight different sources. Using this matrix, he tested the validity of a causal model (shown in Figure 3.1) that posited that verbal skills (vocabulary) were a function of adult intelligence, formal education, age, gender, and father's education. Adult intelligence, in turn, was a function of formal education, age, and childhood intelligence, and formal education (through the bachelor's degree level, mean = 12.29, standard deviation = 2.66) was a function of childhood intelligence, age, gender, father's education, and father's socioeconomic status. Wolfle solved each equation with multiple regression analysis and found that amount of formal education had only a small (.03) direct effect on verbal skills when childhood intelligence, age, gender, father's education and socioeconomic status, and adult intelligence were controlled statistically. (The direct effect in this particular study was the standardized regression, or beta, weight for a variable. It indicates the part of a standard deviation change in the dependent variable for every increase of one standard deviation in the predictor variable, holding constant the

Figure 3.1. Wolfle's Causal Model.

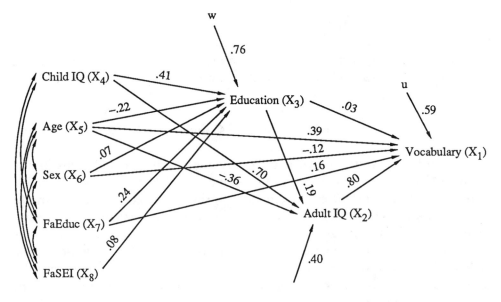

Source: L. Wolfle, "The Enduring Effects of Education on Verbal Skills," *Sociology of Education, 53,* p. 107. Copyright 1980, American Sociological Association. Reprinted by permission of the publisher.

influence of all other variables in the equation. See the Appendix for a fuller discussion of how this and similar analyses are done.)

Although the direct effect of formal education on verbal achievement was relatively small, education nevertheless had a moderate direct effect on adult intelligence (.19), and adult intelligence, in turn, had a strong direct effect on achievement (.80). This means that amount of formal education also *indirectly* influenced verbal achievement through its direct influence on adult intelligence. The indirect effect of education on achievement, through intelligence, was .15 (the product of .19 × .80). This gave a total effect of formal education on verbal achievement of .18 (that is, the sum of the direct effect, .03, plus the indirect effect, .15). (Indirect and total effects are discussed in greater detail in the Appendix.) Unfortunately, Wolfle (1980b) used a continuous variable (years of formal education) as his measure of exposure to education. Thus, it is difficult to separate the impact due to college attendance from that due to secondary education.

Evidence more directly pertaining to the net effect of college on knowledge and skill acquisition is presented by Wolfle (1983, 1987) and Robertshaw and Wolfle (1982), who used the 1979 follow-up of the National Longitudinal Study of the High School Class of 1972 (NLS-72). The dependent measures in all three studies were a fifteen-item vocabulary test and a twenty-five-item mathematics test administered in 1979. (The vocabulary test was specially designed *not* to have a "collegiate bias," and the math test required basic computational skills.) In his 1983 analyses, Wolfle controlled for race, parents' education, father's occupation, and 1972 scores on each 1979 outcome measure. Net of these influences, amount of formal postsecondary education beyond secondary school had a significant positive association with both 1979 vocabulary and 1979 mathematics scores. No significant differences in the effect of college were noted between black and white students. Wolfle (1983) concludes that individuals who completed a four- or five-year college degree program scored on the average 2.48 points higher on the vocabulary test and 3.41 points higher on the mathematics test than individuals who were similar in age to college graduates but who only completed high school. Since it is unclear how Wolfle coded amount of formal education, it is not entirely clear what the magnitude of this advantage amounts to, although Wolfle suggests that it may be as much as half a standard deviation for each measure.

A less ambiguous estimate of the magnitude of the verbal and mathematics achievement advantage attributable to a bachelor's degree is available in Wolfle (1987). In reanalyses of the same NLS data, Wolfle controlled for the same variables as in his 1983 analyses plus gender, handicapped status, region of the country, semesters of exposure to secondary school mathematics, and whether or not the individual attended a public or private secondary school. Educational level was coded as follows: 0 = no college, 1 = less than two years of college, 2 = two years of college or more, 3 = B.A. degree, 4 = M.A. degree, 5 = Ph.D. or professional degree. Net of other variables, amount of postsecondary education had statistically significant positive associations with both the 1979 verbal and mathematics scores. Using the statistics reported by Wolfle, we estimated the advantage associated with obtaining a B.A. degree (versus not attending college) to be between .26 and .32 of a standard deviation for the 1979 verbal scores and between .29 and .32 of a standard deviation for the 1979 mathematics score. These convert to percentile advantages of between 10.3 percentile points and 12.6 percentile points on the verbal test and between 11.4 percentile points and 12.6 percentile points on the mathematics test. In other words, if the person whose formal education stops with secondary school is functioning at the 50th percentile seven years after high school, those with a B.A. degree are between the 60th and 63rd percentiles on verbal skills and between the 61st and 63rd percentiles on mathematics skills.

Wolfle (1983, 1987) also reports an additional finding of interest. While verbal scores for the entire sample appeared to increase over the seven years from 1972 to 1979, overall mathematics scores tended to decline. Using the statistics reported by Wolfle (for example, means, standard deviations, and regression weights), we estimated that the advantage in 1979 mathematics achievement attributable to four years of college was more a matter of maintaining approximate 1972 levels than of substantially increasing mathematics competencies. The statistically significant net difference found between those individuals who completed a B.A. degree and those whose formal education ended with secondary school was largely a function of the college degree recipients maintaining 1972 levels, while the high school graduates retrogressed. Of course, as Pace (1979) and Ethington and Wolfle (1986) have pointed out, for certain subgroups, such as those majoring in mathematics, science, or engineering in college, the net effect of postsecondary education is likely to produce substantial gains in mathematics skills.

This evidence suggests that the net advantage in mathematics knowledge attributable to attending college (versus not going to college) may in fact be greater than that estimated from simple freshman-to-senior gains. Indeed, the simple freshman-to-senior mathematics gains estimated by Bowen (1977) and by ourselves are somewhat smaller than the net college effect estimated by Wolfle (1983, 1987) on the basis of the NLS data. (Recall that Bowen estimated this effect size at .20 of a standard deviation, we estimated it at .24 of a standard deviation, and the estimate from Wolfle's analysis is between .29 and .32 of a standard deviation.) It may well be that simple gains in mathematics scores during college tend to *underestimate* the actual effect of college on knowledge acquisition in this area.

A different picture emerges, however, when one compares the net effect of college on verbal scores estimated from the Wolfle (1987) analyses with that from typical freshman-to-senior gains estimated by Bowen (1977) and ourselves. Recall that Bowen estimated the simple gain effect size to be .50 of a standard deviation and we estimated it to be .56 of a standard deviation. In contrast, based on Wolfle's (1987) analyses, which took important confounding variables into account, the estimated advantage attributable to a B.A. degree was substantially smaller, less than .33 of a standard deviation. Although such a comparison is somewhat tenuous, it nevertheless suggests that the net effect of college on verbal skills may be considerably less than what is indicated by simple freshman-to-senior gains.

A somewhat different approach to estimating the net effects of college was taken by Owings and Fetters (1983). They employed the same data set (NLS-72) and asked essentially the same questions as Wolfle did, but they disaggregated the data by race (black and white) and gender. Controlling for 1972 vocabulary and mathematics scores, family socioeconomic status, employment experience, occupational level, marital status, and number of children, the researchers found that amount of postsecondary education beyond high school had a statistically significant positive association with 1979 vocabulary and mathematics scores for all groups except black men. While such results suggest that the impact of college on verbal and mathematics skills is less pronounced for black men than for other race or gender groups, it is unclear from Owings and Fetters' analyses whether such a difference is statistically significant or merely the result of chance. Recall that with the same basic data Wolfle (1983) found no significant difference in the influence of college on verbal and mathematics skills for blacks or whites.

A final analysis of the NLS-72 data was conducted by Robertshaw and Wolfle (1982) in an attempt to estimate the effect of two-year colleges as well as four-year colleges on knowledge acquisition for black and white students. Amount of schooling was coded as follows: 1 = high school only, 2 = noncollege vocational school, 3 = two-year college vocational, 4 = two-year college academic, 5 = four-year college. Analysis of covariance was used to control statistically for parents' education, father's occupational level, and 1972 verbal and mathematics scores. Comparison of covariate-adjusted 1979 achievement scores for whites indicated significantly higher verbal and mathematics achievement for all groups with some education beyond secondary school (as compared to the group with none). The greatest differences on both tests, however, were between the group with no postsecondary schooling and the group with four years of college. Based on adjusted means, four years of college was worth 2.15 points (out of 15) on the vocabulary score and 2.66 points (out of 25) on the mathematics test. These translate into estimated advantages of 12 and 18 percentile points, respectively.

For blacks, the only statistically significant mean achievement differences on either test were between the group with four years of college and the group with no postsecondary schooling. Four years of college was associated with an advantage of 2.08 points (20 percentile points) on the verbal test and an advantage of 2.97 points (26 percentile points) on the mathematics test. Blacks who had exposure to two years of college did have somewhat higher mathematics scores than those whose formal education ended with secondary school; the differences, however, were not statistically significant and were smaller in absolute magnitude than the corresponding differences for whites. Thus, while both blacks and whites generally benefited about the same in verbal and mathematics achievement from four years of college, the corresponding achievement benefits from two-year colleges were somewhat more pronounced for whites. In both the black and white samples students benefited more from four years of college than from two years of college.

It is interesting to consider why white students appear to benefit more in terms of verbal and mathematics gains from two-year colleges than do black students. One possible explanation is that this finding may reflect differences in the course work pursued by black and white students in two-year colleges. Unfortunately, Robertshaw and Wolfle (1982) did not consider differential course work in their analyses; and, indeed, it is not clear to what extent such considerations were possible with their data.

Because they permit comparison among those with differing levels of exposure to postsecondary education, these secondary analyses of the National Longitudinal Study of the High School Class of 1972 constitute major contributions to our knowledge concerning the net effect of college on the acquisition (or maintenance) of verbal and mathematical skills. The results of these analyses tend to confirm the theoretical contention that the intellectual environment to which one is exposed makes a measurable contribution to the development of verbal comprehension and numerical abilities through young adulthood (Bloom, 1964; Horn, 1970; Horn & Donaldson, 1976; McGinn, Viernstein, & Hogan, 1980; Willis, Blieszner, & Baltes, 1981). At the same time, however, there is an obvious limitation to the results. While the measures in the NLS-72 data have the advantage of being standardized across a large national sample, they are nevertheless limited as measures of verbal and mathematical skills. The verbal test contained only fifteen items and was limited to vocabulary, while the mathematics test had only twenty-five items and was limited largely to computational skills. As Robertshaw and Wolfle (1982) point out, more comprehensive tests designed to assess greater breadth and depth of verbal and quantitative knowledge might have shown greater sensitivity to the full range of knowledge and skill acquisition fostered by college attendance.

A second limitation of the findings from the NLS-72 analyses is that the time period covered is approximately seven years, from 1972 until 1979. This means that to some extent at least, the effects attributed to college attendance may be confounded by differential postcollege experiences (for example, type of employment, military service, graduate school). For instance, college graduates on the average may have entered occupations that require a greater use of verbal and quantitative skills than those who ended their formal education with high school. This may have contributed to the net achievement advantage associated with four years of college. Such a confounding influence, however, may not be as serious as it first appears. If college tends to enhance the likelihood that individuals will enter postcollegiate environments that accentuate, or at least maintain, verbal and quantitative skills learned in college, one might reasonably consider that in itself an important added benefit of college attendance. We will have more to say about this in the section on long-term effects in this chapter and, indeed, throughout the remainder of the book.

Between-College Effects

Since the early 1960s, a modest but important body of research has developed that specifically addresses the influence of different postsecondary institutions on student learning. As with the investigations focusing on the net effects of college attendance in general on student learning, this research is also hindered by the inability to randomly assign individuals to different comparative conditions. In the previous section on the net effect of college attendance, the problem involved the self-selection of people with different characteristics, motivations, and academic aptitudes to college and noncollege conditions. In this section the problem is manifest in the fact that students who do attend college are not randomly distributed across different postsecondary institutions (for example, Astin, 1965c). Consequently, the achievement outcomes associated with different types of postsecondary institutions are likely to be confounded by differences in the motivations, academic aptitudes, and aspirations of the students they enroll (Astin, 1970a, 1970b; Chickering, 1971b).

Attempting to separate these confounding influences from the effects attributable to exposure to different institutional environments entails the use of rather complex statistical controls (for example, regression analysis, analysis of covariance, clustering of residual scores) as opposed to those more internally valid controls achieved by true experimental designs. Although there are a number of variations on the basic theme, the typical study we reviewed used some form of multiple regression analysis (or analysis of regression residuals) to control statistically for differences in student precollege characteristics. With student precollege characteristics controlled statistically, different measures of college characteristics or environmental dimensions can then be checked for their net association with various achievement outcomes. The studies vary in their use of the institution or the student as the unit of analysis. When the student is the unit of analysis, one is essentially asking whether different college environments have different influences on individual student behavior. When the institution is used as the unit of analysis, the question is whether different college environments have different influences on aggregate or collective student behavior (Burstein, 1980a). In the first type of analysis, the outcome is *individual* student achievement; in the second, the outcome is typically the *average* student achievement for a particular institution. A fuller discussion of these procedures is presented in the Appendix.

Perhaps the first methodologically sound study to address the issue of differences in achievement outcomes across various postsecondary institutions was conducted by Nichols (1964). Nichols used a sample of 356 National Merit Scholarship finalists from ninety-one institutions to assess the effects of different colleges on the verbal and quantitative scores of the Graduate Record Examination (GRE). A large battery of student precollege characteristics (for example, Scholastic Aptitude Test scores, high school rank in class, National Merit Scholarship Qualifying Test scores, family characteristics) was statistically controlled by multiple regression and partialing techniques. Partial correlations (controlling for precollege traits) were then computed between GRE scores and an extensive list of institutional structural/organizational characteristics and environmental measures. The structural/organizational characteristics included such factors as private versus public control, faculty-student ratio, enrollment, and library books per student. Environmental factors were measured by means of the Environmental Assessment Technique (EAT) (Astin & Holland, 1961; Astin, 1963b). The EAT is based on Holland's (1959, 1973, 1984, 1985) theory of personality types and consists of six orientations derived from the distribution of major fields at the institution: realistic, investigative, artistic, social, enterprising, and conventional. Students were the unit of analysis.

Two general trends can be gleaned from Nichols's (1964) findings, and these trends are generally replicated by the research that followed Nichols. First, the amount of variance in GRE scores associated with differences among colleges was quite small relative to the amount associated with differences in the precollege characteristics of students entering different institutions. In short, nearly all of the output achievement differences among students at different institutions was explainable by differences in the precollege characteristics of the students they enrolled four years earlier.

The second major finding was that none of the college structural/organizational characteristics had statistically significant partial correlations with verbal or mathematics achievement when the confounding influence of student precollege characteristics was held constant. The only significant (at $p < .05$) partial correlations were between the GRE verbal score and three dimensions of the EAT: social orientation (proportion of students majoring in education, nursing, social sciences, and so on, $r = .14$); enterprising orientation (proportion of students majoring in advertising, prelaw, and the like, $r = .13$); and realistic orientation (proportion of students majoring in engineering, agriculture, and so forth, $r = -.13$). Such findings are not very dramatic, particularly when one considers the fact that of some 116 partial correlations computed, at least 6 should be statistically significant by chance at $p < .05$. At the very best, then, Nichols's (1964) study presents only marginally suggestive evidence that environmental factors measuring the dominant intellectual orientation of the student culture on a campus have unique influence on learning.

Rather meager evidence with respect to differential institutional influence on knowledge acquisition is also reported by Astin (1968c, 1969b, 1971a) and Astin and Panos (1969). Using a design quite similar to Nichols's and a sample of 669 students from thirty-eight institutions who had taken the National Merit Scholarship Qualifying Test in secondary school, Astin and Panos sought to determine whether traditional indexes of institutional quality (for example, academic aptitude of the student body, financial resources, library size, student-faculty ratio) were associated with the knowledge acquisition of individual students. The dependent measures were scores on the humanities, social sciences, and natural sciences area tests of the Graduate Record Examination. Nearly all of the indexes of institutional excellence had statistically significant simple (or zero-order) correlations with the three GRE scores. However, when a battery of 103 student precollege variables (for example, academic aptitude, secondary school achievement, aspirations, family background) was controlled statistically, nearly all of the correlations became trivial in magnitude (average partial $r = .05$), with no single quality index consistently related to more than one of the three GRE scores. Further, Astin found no evidence to suggest that the magnitude of the influence of quality indexes such as student body selectivity varied significantly for students with different levels of academic aptitude.

Additional analyses by Astin and Panos (1969) suggested that GRE achievement may be influenced by institutional characteristics other than commonly accepted "quality" indexes. Considering only those factors having statistically significant partial correlations with at least two of the three GRE area scores (controlling for student precollege characteristics), Astin and Panos found that learning was enhanced at institutions where students made frequent use of automobiles and were undecided about their careers. It was also enhanced at institutions having a generally flexible curriculum with a realistic (technical) emphasis and a relatively large total enrollment. Achievement was negatively associated with student independence and verbal aggressiveness in the classroom, the severity of administrative controls over heterosexual and cheating behavior, and sectarian (Catholic) control. These partial correlations, however, were quite modest in magnitude (average partial $r = .10$). Indeed, when Astin (1968c) held precollege characteristics constant in a hierarchical regression analysis, sixty-nine separate indexes of institutional characteristics and environment increased the explained variance in achievement only 3.3 percent for the social science score, 5.6 percent for the humanities score, and 3.4 percent for the natural science score. These are quite modest percentages compared to the corresponding percentages of 48.2 percent, 43.0 percent, and 49.6 percent attributable to student precollege characteristics alone. Thus, consistent with Nichols's (1964) findings, Astin and Panos's analyses suggest that the net influence of differences in institutional characteristics on student knowledge acquisition is quite small relative to the influence of differences in the precollege traits of students enrolled in different institutions.

Centra, Linn, and Parry (1970) were interested in the influence of college racial composition on knowledge acquisition. To estimate this influence, seven predominantly white colleges were matched (according to purposes, type of control, and ability level of students) with seven predominantly black colleges. The sample consisted of 406 students from the white colleges and 327 from the black colleges. Students were the unit of analysis. At the time this study was conducted the Office of Civil Rights indicated that 97 percent of the students enrolled at the seven black institutions were black, while 99 percent of the students at five of the white institutions were white. The dependent measures were the three area tests of the Graduate Record Examination administered when the students were seniors. When academic ability (SAT scores) was controlled statistically, no significant differences were found between students from the two groups of colleges on either the GRE social science or natural science test. Further, a correction for unreliability indicated only trivial differences between the college groups on the humanities test. Generally, there was little evidence to suggest that either group of colleges was more or less effective in fostering student learning as measured by the GRE area tests. Similar results are also reported by Astin (1968c).

While Nichols (1964), Astin and Panos (1969), and Centra, Linn, and Parry (1970) were concerned with the influence of institutional characteristics on individual student learning and consequently used the student as the unit of analysis, other investigations by Rock, Centra, and Linn (1970), Centra and Rock (1971), and Rock, Baird, and Linn (1972) examined the relationship between college characteristics and student learning with the institution as the unit of analysis. All three studies report analyses that appear to be based on the same data set: 6,855 students from ninety-five small, essentially private liberal arts colleges, 50 percent of which were church related and only ten of which had enrollments in excess of 2,000 students. In the Rock, Centra, and Linn and the Centra and Rock studies the dependent measures were a form of residual scores on the three area tests of the GRE. These residual scores were developed by first regressing the average GRE area score for each institution on the average Scholastic Aptitude Test verbal and mathematics scores for each institution and the proportion of students at each institution majoring in the three areas (humanities, social sciences, or natural sciences). The regression yielded predicted GRE scores for each institution that, when subtracted from the actual score, produced the residual score. Such residual scores have two properties. First, they are statistically independent of the predictor variables. Thus, the investigators had a measure of institutional achievement that was statistically purged of the influence of the aptitude and academic major of the students enrolled. Second, despite problems in the reliability of residual scores, they can nevertheless be used as an estimate of institutional productivity or value added. Positive residual scores indicate higher institutional achievement than would be expected on the basis of student aptitude and major, while negative residuals would indicate lower than expected achievement. (A fuller discussion of residual scores is found in the Appendix.)

Rock, Centra, and Linn (1970) used a sophisticated grouping procedure to relate the three residual GRE scores to a battery of college characteristics traditionally associated with institutional "quality" (for example, number of books in the library, faculty-student ratio, proportion of faculty with doctoral degrees). Only two institutional factors, however, college income per student and proportion of faculty with a doctorate, tended consistently to identify colleges with high residual achievement scores. This tendency was somewhat stronger for achievement in the natural sciences and humanities than it was for achievement in the social sciences.

Centra and Rock (1971) used the same three dependent variables and much the same analytical procedures as Rock, Centra, and Linn (1970) but focused on measures of the institutional environment rather than on traditional indexes of institutional "quality." The investigators used a subsample of the larger sample described above, which consisted of 1,064 students from twenty-seven small liberal arts colleges with enrollments of less than 1,500. Measures of the college environment were five factors from the Questionnaire on Student and College Characteristics completed by students in the sample: faculty-student interaction, curriculum flexibility, cultural facilities, student activism, and degree of academic challenge. The residual GRE scores for each institution were related to the five environmental factors. Faculty-student interaction tended to be linearly related to residual achievement in that colleges with high scores on this dimension tended to overachieve (that is, to have positive achievement residuals) on the humanities and natural science tests, while institutions with low levels of faculty-student interaction tended to underachieve (that is, to have negative residuals) on all three GRE area tests. This finding is consistent with an ancillary finding reported by Astin (1968c). Using multiple regression to control salient student precollege characteristics, Astin found that a variable termed "familiarity with the instructor" had a statistically significant (and positive) partial regression coefficient with the humanities score of the GRE. (The "familiarity with the instructor" scale was a measure of the degree of student-faculty informal interaction at the institution.)

Centra and Rock (1971), too, found that curriculum flexibility was further related to higher than predicted institutional achievement on the natural science and social science tests. (This finding was also consistent with the positive partial correlations reported between flexibility of the curriculum and the GRE area tests by Astin [1968c].) Colleges with relatively high scores on the cultural facilities scale tended to overachieve on the humanities test but had lower than predicted scores on the natural science test. Finally, institutions with relatively high levels of challenge in their academic course work tended to overachieve on the humanities test. Thus, based on Centra and Rock's findings, a college environment particularly effective in fostering learning is one with the following characteristics: frequent student-faculty interaction, with faculty perceived as being interested in teaching and treating students as individuals; a relatively flexible curriculum in which students have freedom in choosing courses and can experiment before selecting a major; an intellectually challenging academic program with a stress on intellectual rather than social matters; and strong cultural facilities (for example, lectures, concerts, plays).

The final analysis of the sample of the ninety-five liberal arts colleges was conducted by Rock (1972) and Rock, Baird, and Linn (1972). With initial academic ability of students controlled, colleges were clustered by means of a taxonomic technique. Discriminant analysis was then used to determine the institutional characteristics that best distinguished the groups on GRE achievement. It was found that in all three achievement areas one group or cluster of colleges could be identified as being more effective than the remaining groups of colleges. Perhaps the most important finding of the study, however, was the fact that there was no one group of colleges that was highest in all three GRE area tests. Moreover, the institutional characteristics associated with high net achievement in one area test were not necessarily the same ones associated with high net achievement in another area. For example, on the humanities area test the most effective group of colleges was characterized by a higher proportion of faculty with doctorates, greater selectivity (average SAT scores in the student body), and a larger total budget. On the social science test, however, the most effective group (of four groups of colleges) had the second lowest student body selectivity and proportion of faculty with a doctorate. Budget did not discriminate among the groups. On both the social science and natural science tests the proportion of social science and natural science majors, respectively, was the characteristic that best discriminated the most effective from the least effective institutions. These particular effects were small, however, as indeed were all effects in the study.

To date, the most recent research focusing on institutional characteristics and student learning was conducted by Ayres and Bennett (1983), who used a sample of 2,229 students from fifteen public institutions in North Carolina, ten predominantly white and five predominantly black. Institutions were the unit of analysis, which meant that the analyses had relatively little chance of finding statistically significant trends because of the extremely small sample size. Unlike previous studies, which employed various forms of the Graduate Record Examination, the dependent variable Ayres and Bennett used was the National Teacher Examination (NTE). The NTE is designed to measure college achievement in professional education, English expression, science, mathematics, social studies, literature, and fine arts. Thus, the investigators judged it to be a reasonable outcome estimate of a general undergraduate education program.

A regression equation that included the average SAT score of each institution, average number of credit hours taken in general education, average educational attainment of the faculty, average faculty salary, institutional age, library size, and institutional size explained 88 percent of the variance in NTE achievement. Net of the influence of all other variables, the average educational attainment of faculty accounted for the largest percentage of unique variance in NTE achievement of all institutional variables. Using the statistics reported by Ayres and Bennett, we calculated the unique variance explained by the faculty degree index at 4.8 percent, which was marginally significant at $p < .14$. No other institutional variable in the equation approached statistical significance. Although the institutional sample size of the Ayres and Bennett study was quite small ($n = 15$), their study does have the advantage of a relatively large sample of individual students from each institution (233 students per campus). More important, perhaps, is the fact that the major finding of the study is consistent with the earlier results reported by Rock, Centra, and Linn (1970), that a greater proportion of faculty with a doctorate tended to identify institutions that overachieved on the three area scores of the Graduate Record Examination.

The weight of evidence from investigations designed to estimate the effects of different institutional characteristics on student learning clearly suggests that for four-year institutions at least, such effects are both small and inconsistent. Regardless of whether individual students or institutions were the unit of analysis, when student precollege traits were controlled statistically, measures of institutional "quality" or environmental characteristics accounted for a relatively minor percentage of the variance in standardized measures of learning. Furthermore, if one considers only those findings consistent across studies based on independent samples, only measures of student-faculty interaction, degree of curricular flexibility, and faculty formal education (that is, percentage with a doctorate) had significant associations with learning when salient student precollege traits were taken into account. The magnitude of these associations was small, however, perhaps even trivial in terms of a meaningful impact on learning.

One obvious interpretation of such evidence is that when statistical controls are made for the capabilities of the students enrolled, different kinds of four-year postsecondary institutions appear to have essentially the same general influence on student knowledge acquisition. That is, two students of equal academic aptitude, one attending a high "quality" institution (for example, selective admission, large library, abundant financial resources) and the other attending a college of lesser "quality," might not generally differ in how much they learned during college. One implication of this interpretation is that indexes of an institution's "quality"—or perhaps more accurately, its stock of human, educational, and financial resources—tend to have a diminishing return rather than a linear relationship with student learning. A library of one million volumes, for example, may be adequate to support effectively nearly any undergraduate curriculum. While the addition of another two million volumes is unlikely to be detrimental, the incremental benefits it provides for student learning beyond the first one million volumes may be relatively small. Thus, substantial differences in "quality" indexes or resources among colleges may not be matched by similar differences in measures of student learning.

In a related sense, the absence of important net differences in student learning among different colleges tends to confirm Pace's (1974) findings of increasing homogeneity and conformity among American four-year postsecondary institutions. If one assumes diminishing diversity and distinctiveness in the nation's four-year colleges and universities, it follows that institutional effects on student learning (or other areas of development, for that matter) will also become increasingly indistinguishable (Birnbaum, 1983; Bowen, 1980, 1981; Chickering, McDowell, & Campagna, 1969; Newman, 1971; Stadtman, 1980).

Alternative Explanations for the Absence of Between-College Effects

There is a certain appeal to the conclusion that differences in institutional characteristics or environments have few independent effects on student learning during college, most notably in that it agrees with existing evidence. On the other hand, given the fact that such a conclusion is based on studies from only five different samples carried out over a period of nearly two decades, it is worth at least positing several alternative explanations or hypotheses for the results. Most of these alternative hypotheses are bound up in the methodological problems of existing investigations. One of the most obvious is the restricted range of the samples used. In the Nichols (1964) and the Astin (1968c) and Astin and Panos (1969) investigations (which used students as the unit of analysis), the sample was either National Merit Scholarship finalists or students who took the Merit Scholarship Qualifying Test in secondary school. Selectivity of this sort in a sample will typically attenuate the correlations in any analysis (Cohen & Cohen, 1975). Thus, even if these students attend very different kinds of institutions, environmental effects on individual outcomes are likely to be suppressed by the relatively restricted range of aptitude represented. In short, analyses of samples consisting largely of the most academically able students may mask important institutional effects that might be discernible in a sample representing a broader range of talent.

An analogous problem exists in those studies that use the institution as the unit of analysis. The ninety-five institutions in the Rock, Centra, and Linn (1970) and the Rock, Baird, and Linn (1972) studies were really all small, private liberal arts colleges, as were the twenty-seven institutions employed by Centra and Rock (1971). Restricting the range of institutions sampled may have the same masking tendency on environmental effects as does restricting the range of students sampled.

A second potential methodological problem in existing research concerns the analytical approaches used. When student precollege characteristics are not independent of the type of institution attended, a considerable part of the explained variance in achievement or learning is likely to be the result of the *joint* influence of student precollege traits and the institutional environment. This joint influence cannot be uniquely attributed either to the college environment or to student precollege traits. However, the analytical approaches used in nearly all existing studies tend either to disregard joint effects or to attribute them to student precollege traits. This is understandable because the studies reviewed were primarily interested in estimating the unique or net effects of college environments on learning. Unfortunately, and perhaps unavoidably, this approach produces a somewhat conservative estimate of institutional effects. Because of this methodological problem, for which there is no easy or simple remedy, the existing body of evidence may be underestimating the extent and magnitude of institutional effects on learning. In short, the existing evidence may be reporting a lower-bounds estimate of between-college effects. (For a fuller discussion of this issue, see the Appendix.)

A third methodological problem concerns the level of organizational specificity on which existing studies focus in attempting to estimate the effects of institutional or environmental factors on student learning. Given evidence to suggest that a substantial number of distinguishable subenvironments exist in many institutions (for example, Feldman & Newcomb, 1969; Lacy, 1978; Pascarella, 1976; Phelan, 1979; Weidman, 1979), one might legitimately question the sensitivity of existing studies that assess the effects of environmental dimensions or other characteristics at the institutional level. This level of aggregation may simply be too gross to capture the influence of differential subenvironments or subcultures in the institution. It seems reasonable that if students have more intensive exposure to these subenvironments or subcultures, they are more likely to be influenced by them than they are by the total campus environment (Baird, 1974, 1988; Newcomb, 1968; Newcomb & Wilson, 1966). Indeed, at many institutions the "average" or "typical" environmental stimuli may have little to do with the reality impinging on students in different campus subenvironments (different academic majors, residential arrangements, and so forth).

Thus, another alternative explanation for the general absence of consistent institutional effects on student learning is that the institution is simply too general a level of aggregation. Evidence for this is offered by Hartnett (1976) and Hartnett and Centra (1977). Their study estimated the effects of academic departments (rather than entire colleges) and employed as a criterion standardized measures of achievement tests appropriate for individual departments. The dependent variables were field test scores of the Educational Testing Service Undergraduate Assessment Program. The achievement tests for each department were residualized on SAT scores, and departments were the unit of analysis. The findings revealed substantial between-department variation in net achievement within the same institution. For example, many institutions that had departments with achievement in the top 20 percent of positive residuals (that is, better than predicted departmental achievement based on students' SAT scores) also had departments in the lower 20 percent of negative residuals. It is likely that such marked differences within institutions would have been masked in studies where mean institutional score on characteristics such as student body selectivity and educational resources per student was employed as the unit of analysis. Even within institutions that are most advantaged in terms of overall human, educational, and financial resources, there are likely to be distinguishable differences in the effectiveness with which individual departments foster learning.

Similarly, it is unclear that many colleges, particularly large research institutions, provide much of a common learning experience for their students. With hundreds of courses available, few students may really have a common curricular experience that lasts throughout college. Evidence for this is provided by Ratcliff and Associates (1988) in their analysis of the course transcripts of a sample of graduating seniors at a large, urban, doctorate-granting university. These investigators examined the transcripts of 151 graduating seniors and found that they had collectively enrolled in 1,358 unduplicated courses during college. Of these 1,358 courses, there were only 282 (20.8 percent) in which five or more of the students had enrolled. If students have such different formal academic experiences within the same institution, it seems reasonable that this would produce differential effects on knowledge acquisition. A similar case might be made for the influence of different student subcultures within the same institution. Thus, another plausible explanation for why between-college effects on learning are so small is that important influences on learning within any particular college may be quite heterogeneous (J. Ratcliff, personal communication, July 24, 1988).

A final problem with existing research may stem from the instruments used to assess the learning outcomes of college. Typically, these have been standardized measures of rather broad academic achievement (for example, Graduate Record Examination verbal and quantitative tests, National Teacher Examination) or level of knowledge in somewhat more focused subject matter or curricular areas (for example, Graduate Record Examination area tests in the natural sciences, social sciences, and humanities). While such instruments tend to be strong in terms of psychometric reliability and content validity, one might question whether they are sensitive or focused enough to capture those aspects of environmentally induced impacts on learning that may be unique to some institutions. It may well be that the GRE and related standardized achievement tests used in the studies reviewed above are measuring a relatively common body of knowledge and academic skills; and there may not be a great deal of variation among preparation programs at the four-year institutions sampled in terms of the effectiveness with which they impart this body of knowledge and skills. This may, in part at least, account for the relative absence of substantial and consistent institutional differences in GRE (or NTE) performance when student precollege aptitude is controlled. Existing studies may have simply focused on a "common core" of subject matter knowledge and skill outcomes in which we should expect only minimal differences among institutions.

Related to this notion is the argument that some institutions, most notably those with highly selective student bodies, are capable of inducing levels of intellectual development that are qualitatively different from those fostered by less selective institutions. Warren (1984) has argued that the learning achievements of poorly prepared students in unselective institutions cannot be compared with the accomplishments of well-prepared students in selective institutions as though they were distances each group of students has moved along the same dimension. The content, objectives, and activities of upper-division courses in selective institutions, he argues, are often *qualitatively* different from any encountered in unselective institutions. (Braxton and Nordvall [1985] provide evidence from liberal arts colleges to support this argument.) These qualitative differences in the types of knowledge or learning fostered by highly selective institutions may not be adequately captured by standardized indicators such as the GRE area scores or subscores. Some recent evidence in this regard suggests that item-type scores within the GRE (for example, quantitative comparisons, analytical reasoning, data interpretation) may capture discrete forms of learning that the GRE subscores do not effectively differentiate (Ratcliff & Associates, 1988; Wilson, 1985).

Within-College Effects

In commenting on the body of research on the college environment conducted in the early and mid-1960s, Berdie (1967) made a particularly cogent point in a paper entitled "A University Is a Many Faceted Thing." He argued that most institutions are not monolithic organizations with a single uniform set of environmental stimuli impinging equally on all members. Rather, individuals are members of different subenvironments within the same institution that may have substantially different influences on growth and development. In terms of the acquisition of subject matter knowledge and skills, the academic program is perhaps the most salient of these subenvironments. Obviously, not all learning occurs as a result of the academic program or in classroom settings. Students clearly learn a range of valuable skills from peers, work, and extracurricular and athletic involvements, to name only a few. Yet it is undeniably the college's academic program, with its courses, classroom, laboratory, library, and related experiences, that is the major vehicle through which subject matter knowledge and skills are transmitted (for example, Bisconti, 1987; Bisconti & Kessler, 1980). This section will focus primarily on ways in which differences in the individual student's academic experience influence learning in college. Emphasis will be placed on the influence of differences in patterns of course work, the teaching/learning context, instructional approaches, teaching behavior, and the extent of student involvement or engagement in academic and related experiences. Although there are other conceptual schemes for organizing the effects of college experiences on learning (for example, Bergquist, Gould, & Greenberg, 1981), we think these categories most accurately reflect both where the preponderance of evidence exists and how it is clustered.

Patterns of Course Work

It seems reasonable to expect that what a student learns during college will depend largely on the nature of the courses he or she takes. Different patterns of courses taken should lead to the development of different kinds of knowledge and skills. The hypothesis that differential course work accounts for much of the differences in learned abilities has had considerable attention in research on the impact of secondary education (for example, Fennema & Sherman, 1977; Pallas & Alexander, 1983; Steel & Wise, 1979). While there has been a growing interest in course work patterns in postsecondary education, the bulk of inquiry has been descriptive (for example, Beeken, 1982; Blackburn, Armstrong, Conrad, Didham, & McKune, 1976; Dressel & DeLisle, 1969; Prather, Williams, & Wadley, 1976; Warren, 1975). Comparatively little attention has been devoted to determining whether differential course work leads to differential learning.

One notable exception to this is the work of Ratcliff and Associates (1988) on a single-institution sample. These researchers first residualized the nine item types of the Graduate Record Examination on student Scholastic Aptitude Test scores to produce measures of senior-year learning statistically independent of precollege academic ability. They then cluster analyzed courses on student transcripts by the residual scores on the nine item types of the GRE: quantitative comparison, antonyms, regular mathematics, analytical reasoning, sentence completion, analogies, data interpretation, reading comprehension, and logical reasoning.

The results yielded two major findings. First, high residual GRE achievement generally did not appear to be associated with course work taken in any one year. Rather, a spread of course work taken from the freshman to the senior year was most consistently associated with high GRE residuals on seven of the nine item types. This further supports the notion that significant academic learning is not concentrated in any one period during college but instead occurs over the entire span of the college years.

The second major finding of the Ratcliff and Associates (1988) study was that high residual scores on specific GRE item types were associated with specific sets of course work differing by discipline, level (that is, freshman, sophomore, junior, senior), and sequence. One course work cluster consisted primarily of lower-division courses in the arts and sciences and was associated with high residual achievement on antonyms and low achievement in analytical reasoning. A second cluster consisted primarily of business courses evenly distributed between lower and upper divisions. This group was associated with high performance in analytical reasoning and quantitative comparisons and low performance on antonym items. A third cluster consisted primarily of upper-division business and social science courses and was associated with high achievement on analytical reasoning and regular mathematics items. The fourth cluster was defined primarily by lower-division course work in mathematics and the natural sciences and was linked to high residual performance in regular mathematics. A final cluster was largely made up of lower- and upper-division courses in journalism, English, and mathematics and was associated with strong performance in regular mathematics and weak performance in analytical reasoning.

Ratcliff and Associates' (1988) findings are preliminary, and although there is some evidence of their generalizability across institutions (Ratcliff, 1988), they await more definitive replication before any but the most tentative conclusion can be made. They nevertheless provide support for a differential course work hypothesis at the postsecondary level. While a consistent pattern may not necessarily emerge, the results clearly suggest that the pattern of course work taken during college may have important implications for the types of learning that occur, independent of student academic ability.

The Teaching/Learning Context

Perhaps the most obvious contextual difference in the academic experience of students within the same institution is one's major field of study. The vast majority of colleges and universities require students to select a primary field of study, and this represents a significant portion of the student's total formal course work. Although the extent of requirements for majors varies, it is generally quite substantial: 30 to 40 percent of the total undergraduate course load for the typical B.A. degree and from 40 to 50 percent of the total load for the B.S. degree (Levine, 1978; Jacobs, 1986). As such, the academic major represents an important social and intellectual subenvironment for the student. For example, the major facilitates frequent contact between peers with similar academic and career interests, thus shaping acquaintance networks and reinforcing initial interests (Jacobs, 1986; Feldman & Newcomb, 1969). Moreover, it would appear that majors form somewhat distinctive instructional environments in terms of classroom environments (Astin, 1965a), the nature of the interaction between students and faculty (Gamson, 1966; Hearn & Olzak, 1981; Vreeland & Bidwell, 1966), the effort devoted to instruction (Stark & Morstain, 1978; Trow, 1977), and students' cognitive preferences and strategies for meeting course demands (Barrall & Hill, 1977; Goldman & Hudson, 1973; Goldman & Warren, 1973; Tamir & Kempa, 1977).

Given this evidence, it would seem reasonable to anticipate that one's major would provide distinctive learning outcomes during college. However, beyond the rather obvious and unsurprising finding (cited earlier) that students demonstrate the highest levels of proficiency on subject matter tests most congruent with their academic major, there is little to suggest that students become *generally* more knowledgeable during college *because* of what they major in. Again, the problem is one of separating the socialization effect of different major fields of study from the recruitment effect of students with different characteristics entering different majors to begin with. Unfortunately, in terms of estimating effects on knowledge acquisition, the few existing studies have generally not addressed this issue. In a single-institution study, for example, Dumont and Troelstrup (1981) found no statistically significant differences in average freshman-to-senior gains on the ACT achievement test composite score across five broad academic fields of study. Since amount of change is a function of a group's initial score, however, it is somewhat difficult to interpret these findings, particularly in the absence of some control for initial score.

Perhaps the most extensive evidence concerning major field of study and academic learning is provided by Adelman (1984). Adelman conducted a secondary analysis of student performance between 1964 and 1982 on the Graduate Record Examination, the Graduate Management Admission Test, the Medical College Admission Test, the Law School Admission Test, and fifteen tests of advanced achievement in specific subject areas. With the exception of engineering, students majoring in professional or occupational fields consistently had lower scores on these tests than did those majoring in traditional arts and science fields. Students majoring in engineering, science, and mathematics consistently scored the highest of all major fields. Since Adelman was unable to adjust for initial academic aptitude, however, it is difficult to causally attribute these differences to the effect of one's academic major. If not totally, then at least to a great extent, they probably reflect initial differences in academic aptitude or proficiency among students entering different major fields of study.

If there is little solid evidence one way or the other to suggest that one's academic major has a significant impact on what is generally learned in college outside of one's major field, this should not be construed as indicating that major is unimportant. As we shall see throughout the remainder of this book, one's academic major has a set of influences that extends beyond the college experience to such salient outcomes as one's career choice and income.

Class Size

A somewhat narrower context for teaching and learning than academic major is class size. Here there has been a substantial amount of research over the last sixty years concerning the influence of class size on learning in college (for example, Edmonson & Mulder, 1924; Mueller, 1924; Hudelson, 1928; Cheydleur, 1945; Nachman & Opochinsky, 1958; Simmons, 1959; Siegel, Adams, & Macomber, 1960; Hoover, Baumann, & Schafer, 1970; Attiyeh & Lumsden, 1972; Karp & Yoels, 1976; Williams, Cook, Quinn, & Jensen, 1985). In addition to the body of empirical evidence, there have been a number of reviews of the research on class size and learning (Dubin & Taveggia, 1968; Laughlin, 1976; McKeachie, 1978, 1980; Milton, 1972; Witmer & Wallhaus, 1975). The consensus of these reviews—and of our own synthesis of the existing evidence—is that class size is not a particularly important factor when the goal of instruction is the acquisition of subject matter knowledge and academic skills. Moreover, this finding appears to hold across class type (for example, lecture, discussion) and when measures of learning were standardized across content areas (Williams, Cook, & Jensen, 1984). It is probably the case, however, that smaller classes are somewhat more effective than larger ones when the goals of instruction are motivational, attitudinal, or higher-level cognitive processes (McKeachie, 1980).

Instructional Approaches

Not surprisingly, the question of the effects of different instructional approaches on academic learning and skill acquisition has been the focus of much research. This large body of research is as diverse as it is extensive. Indeed, it may well merit a book-length synthesis in and of itself. Fortunately, however, a number of scholars have undertaken syntheses of different segments of this evidence, upon which our own analysis substantially relies.

Lecture Versus Discussion. One of the initial areas of inquiry into the effects of different instructional approaches on learning is that of lecturing versus discussion. It is reasonably clear that lecturing is the overwhelming method of choice for undergraduate teaching in most institutions. Pollio (1984), for example, estimates that teachers in the typical classroom spend about 80 percent of their time lecturing to students, who in turn are attentive to what is being said about 50 percent of the time. Even so, there is little consistent evidence to suggest that lecturing is any less efficient in imparting subject matter knowledge to students than is instruction that emphasizes class discussion (Dunkin & Barnes, 1985; Kulik & Kulik, 1979; McKeachie, 1962; Ryan, 1969). The weight of evidence, as well as the findings of most literature reviews, tends to converge on this conclusion. The evidence also appears to be consistent in indicating that lecturing is a somewhat less effective instructional approach than classroom discussion when the goal of instruction is higher-order cognitive skills (critical thinking, problem solving, and the like) rather than the transmission of factual information.

Here we see a conclusion quite similar to that of the cognitive benefits of large versus small classes. Since instructional approach is not independent of class size (that is, small classes are more conducive to discussion than large classes), it is likely that these two conclusions are mutually confounding. Nevertheless, the weight of evidence makes it reasonably clear that in postsecondary education neither large or small classes nor lecture or discussion formats are more effective than the other in fostering the mastery of factual subject matter material.

Team Teaching. Another instructional approach that has received some attention in postsecondary education has been that of team teaching. By team teaching we mean the use of two or more people assigned to the same class *at the same time* for instructional purposes. Schustereit (1980) conducted a synthesis of studies pertaining to the influence of team teaching on subject matter achievement. He divided the studies reviewed into two types, those comparing classes taught by a team and those taught by one teacher and studies comparing different teaching techniques, including team teaching. Using the box score method of synthesizing research, he found inconsistent results from the studies reviewed. There were generally as many studies favoring team teaching as favoring solitary teaching. Thus, any generalization about team teaching being a consistently superior or inferior instructional technique for enhancing subject matter learning appears unwarranted.

Individualized Instruction. One characteristic of most traditional lecture or discussion instructional approaches (whether individually or team taught) has been that the pace at which instruction is provided tends to be a constant for all students, while level of achievement or subject matter proficiency tends to vary among students (Cross, 1976, 1981). In the early 1960s, however, Carroll (1963) developed a learning model that essentially reversed the relationship between what is constant and what varies in instruction. In brief, he argued that learners will succeed in learning a given task to the extent that they receive proper instruction and that they spend the amount of time they individually need to learn it. Therefore, according to Carroll, virtually all students can achieve mastery of any learning task if each is given enough time and receives competent instruction.

Although Carroll's (1963) model was developed primarily to address elementary and secondary school learning, it and the closely related mastery concepts of Bloom (1968) have significantly influenced collegiate instruction during the last two decades. Indeed, it is probably safe to say that one important strand of the intellectual heritage of Carroll and Bloom has been the development of various approaches to individualized instruction in postsecondary education. These approaches have taken various forms and are exemplified, though not necessarily exhausted, by the following:

1. *Audio-tutorial instruction (AT):* This instructional method, as developed by Postlethwaite (Postlethwaite, Novak, & Murray, 1972), involves three main components. The independent study session is the primary activity in audio-tutorial instruction. Students work independently on learning tasks in a learning center equipped with laboratory materials, audio tapes, and visual aids. The small assembly session is a weekly meeting of six to ten students and an instructor for the purpose of discussion and quizzing. A weekly meeting, the general assembly session, is used for motivational lectures, films, and major examinations.

2. *Computer-based instruction (CBI):* This approach involves the interactive use of a computer. Programmed instruction, drill and practice, and/or tutorial exercises are frequently implemented in CBI.

3. *Personalized system of instruction (PSI):* This approach was first described by Keller (1968) and has frequently been termed the Keller Plan. PSI involves the following components: (1) small modularized units of instruction, (2) study guides, (3) mastery orientation and immediate feedback on unit tests, (4) self-pacing through the material, (5) student proctors to help with individual problems, and (6) occasional lectures for motivation.

4. *Programmed instruction (PI):* This approach involves the presentation of material in a step-by-step sequential manner. It is a procedure employed in many types of individualized instructional methods.

5. *Visual-based instruction (VI):* This approach relies heavily on visually based materials (for example, slide tapes, films, and other visual instructional technology) as the main instructional vehicle for a course.

While these instructional methods or approaches differ from each other in some specific respects, they have many similarities. Perhaps the primary one is the acknowledgment of individual differences among students coupled with a concern for adapting instruction to the individual learner (Goldschmid & Goldschmid, 1974). Second, the different methods tend to modularize the course content into reasonably small, self-contained units (Dunkin & Barnes, 1985). Third, most of the methods tend to require mastery of material presented in the small units and typically provide immediate (or at least timely) feedback to students concerning their performance on mastery tests (Aiello & Wolfe, 1980; Rowe & Deture, 1975). Finally, the different methods all appear to emphasize active individual student involvement in the learning process, a feature consistent with what is known about effective learning environments (for example, McKeachie, Pintrich, Lin, & Smith, 1986; Rosenshine, 1982). Consequently, there is often less emphasis on employing the teacher in formal or traditional teaching situations such as lectures (Dunkin & Barnes, 1985).

It is our view that these and related attempts to individualize instruction constitute the single most dramatic shift in college teaching over the last two decades. Moreover, the weight of evidence from experimental studies would suggest that such approaches are reasonably effective in improving the acquisition of subject matter content (at least as measured by course-specific tests) over more traditional instructional approaches such as lecture, discussion, and combinations of lecture and discussion. The magnitude of the improvement, however, is not uniform across the different implementations of individualized instruction.

Kulik, Kulik, and Cohen (1979b) and Kulik (1983) summarized the results of forty-two studies employing the audio-tutorial (AT) method in college courses. The major criterion for a study's inclusion in this synthesis was that it had a control group taught by more traditional methods (for example, lecture, discussion) and reported the results of a common course examination. Although there was considerable variation across studies in the magnitude of the effect size (that is, the average of the AT group minus the average of the conventional group divided by the pooled standard deviation of both groups), the average effect size was .20 of a standard deviation favoring the AT group. This effect size was statistically significant (that is, non-zero) and represented an achievement advantage attributable to the AT approach of 8 percentile points. In other words, if the conventionally taught group was achieving at the 50th percentile, the AT group was, on the average, at the 58th percentile. Quite similar results have been reported by Mintzes (1975) in a narrative review of research on the audio-tutorial method and by Aiello and Wolfe (1980) in another meta-analysis based on twenty-seven studies. Aiello and Wolfe report an effect size favoring the AT group of .21, almost exactly the same as that found by Kulik and colleagues. It is also important to note that Kulik, Kulik, and Cohen (1979b) found no statistically significant differences between AT and conventional methods in the attitudes of students toward instruction or their rates of withdrawal from the course. Thus, the modest learning advantages associated with the audio-tutorial approach do not appear to come at the cost of increased course withdrawal rates or negative student attitudes toward the instruction received.

Aiello and Wolfle (1980) and Kulik, Kulik, and Cohen (1980) conducted independent meta-analyses of the effects of computer-based instruction (CBI). The former synthesis was based on eleven studies, while the latter was based on fifty-nine studies. This may account for the substantial difference in effect sizes reported: .42 for Aiello and Wolfle and .25 for Kulik, Kulik, and Cohen. Because the Kulik, Kulik, and Cohen synthesis is based on nearly five times as many studies as the Aiello and Wolfle synthesis, we are inclined to have greater faith in the representativeness of its findings. The statistically significant effect size of .25, favoring CBI over conventional instruction, represents an advantage of 10 percentile points in course achievement. Furthermore, across those studies that address the questions, computer-based instruction showed a positive and significant effect on student attitudes toward instruction and a significant reduction in the hours per week needed for instruction.

Meta-analyses of research on programmed instruction (PI) have been conducted by Aiello and Wolfle (1980) on the basis of twenty-eight studies and by Kulik, Cohen, and Ebeling (1980) on the basis of fifty-seven studies. The results of these two independent syntheses are remarkably similar. The effect size favoring PI over conventional instruction reported by Aiello and Wolfle is .27 of a standard deviation, while that reported by Kulik, Cohen, and Ebeling is .26. Again, this represents an achievement advantage attributable to the PI approach of 10 percentile points. Kulik, Cohen, and Ebeling also report the same achievement advantage for both immediate and delayed measures of achievement and no statistically significant differences between PI and conventional approaches in attitudes toward instruction, course withdrawal rates, and hours per week required for instruction.

Evidence from sixty-five studies that focused on the effects of visual-based instruction (VI) on subject matter learning has been synthesized by Cohen, Ebeling, and Kulik (1981). They report a statistically significant effect size of .15, favoring VI over conventional instructional approaches. While the typical student in the conventional approach functioned at the 50th percentile in learning, the typical student exposed to visual-based instruction was functioning at the 56th percentile (an advantage of 6 percentile points in learning). Cohen, Ebeling, and Kulik also report no significant differences between VI and conventional methods across studies in course withdrawal rate or attitudes toward the instruction received.

Finally, a substantial amount of interest has focused on synthesizing evidence that addresses the effectiveness of the Keller Plan, or personalized system of instruction (PSI), on subject matter learning (for example, Aiello & Wolfle, 1980; Block & Burns, 1976; Johnson & Ruskin, 1977; Kulik, 1982; Kulik, Kulik, & Carmichael, 1974; Kulik, Kulik, & Cohen, 1979a; Robin, 1976). This is probably due to the fact that with the possible exception of the audio-tutorial approach, PSI tends to be the most fully developed and elaborated system of instruction. Thus, it is perhaps the easiest to implement and has the added advantage of not being overly dependent on instructional hardware. Whatever the reason, there is striking consensus in each individual synthesis we reviewed to suggest that PSI is effective in fostering improved subject matter mastery over more conventional instructional approaches. This is true regardless of whether the synthesis is quantitative or narrative.

The meta-analytical syntheses of PSI and learning have been conducted by Aiello and Wolfle (1980) on the basis of nineteen studies and by Kulik, Kulik, and Cohen (1979a) on the basis of sixty-one studies. The former report an effect size of .42, favoring PSI over conventional instruction, while the latter report an effect size of .49. Because of Kulik, Kulik, and Cohen's more extensive sampling of the evidence, we are inclined to have somewhat more faith in the effect that they report (although the difference in effect sizes between the two syntheses is probably trivial). Kulik, Kulik, and Cohen's statistically significant effect size translates into an achievement advantage of 19 percentile points attributable to the personalized system of instruction. They also found that across relevant studies, PSI was associated with a statistically significant advantage of 18 percentile points over conventional methods in students' attitudes toward the instruction received. No statistically significant differences were found between PSI and conventional methods in terms of course withdrawal rates or time required for instruction. (It is noted a recent synthesis by Kulik, Kulik, and Bangert-Drowns (1990) suggests a reconsideration of this conclusion.)

In addition to analyses of the overall effects of the personalized system of instruction on subject matter learning, there has been at least some interest in discovering which particular components of PSI contribute most to its effectiveness (Kulik, 1982; Kulik, Jaksa, & Kulik, 1978; Robin, 1976). The studies cited tend to agree that the most salient aspects of PSI in terms of enhancing learning are the mastery requirement and immediate feedback on tests and quizzes. Thus, students in PSI approaches may perform better on common final examinations than students in conventional instruction, in part, at least, because they are forced to study more and have more opportunities to practice the criterion behavior (for example, Cline & Michael, 1978). There is less support for the idea that PSI features such as self-pacing and optional lectures are essential for improving learning, although they may have indirect effects by fostering greater motivation or satisfaction with instruction.

One can conclude from the extensive syntheses of research on the various forms of individualized instruction that each appears to enhance subject matter learning over traditional approaches such as lectures and/or discussion sections. Moreover, this learning advantage appears to occur without giving rise to undesirable side effects in terms of negative student attitudes toward instruction, increased course withdrawal rates, or increased time required to meet course demands. It is also clear, however, that the relative magnitude of the learning advantages attributable to individualized instruction varies quite markedly across its different implementations. Four of the five approaches reviewed (audio-tutorial, computer-based, programmed instruction, and visual-based) provide learning advantages over conventional instruction that are consistent but modest, ranging from 6 to 10 percentile points. In comparison, the learning advantage attributable to the personalized system of instruction (19 percentile points) is twice as great as any of the other approaches.[2]

A second conclusion is that the magnitude of the estimated advantage for each of the different implementations of individualized instruction is essentially independent of study characteristics. Typically, this is determined by regressing effect size on certain design characteristics of the studies included (for example, subject self-selection, randomized assignment to conditions, pretreatment equivalence of experimental and control groups). When this was done, the study design characteristics contributed little to explaining differences in study outcomes (Aiello & Wolfle, 1980; Kulik, Kulik, & Cohen, 1979a, 1979b, 1980). Consequently, one can reasonably conclude that the effects of the different forms of individualized instruction on subject matter learning are not generally biased in their direction by the methodological rigor of the research.

There is one possibly important exception to this conclusion in the research on computer-based instruction, visual-based instruction, and the personalized system of instruction. In these areas student achievement results somewhat more favorable to individualized approaches were found if different instructors implemented individualized and conventional approaches than if the same instructor implemented both. Dunkin and Barnes (1985) argue that this suggests the possibility of an instructor self-selection effect, with individualized approaches tending to attract the most motivated or effective instructors.

A final conclusion about the effects of individualized instructional approaches on student learning is that they tend to be essentially independent of the teaching/learning context. There is little evidence from any of the syntheses that individualized approaches tend to be more effective in some content areas than in others. The one exception to this is that the personalized system of instruction appeared to have stronger positive effects on learning in mathematics, engineering, and psychology than in other social sciences or the natural sciences (Dunkin & Barnes, 1985; Kulik, Kulik, & Cohen, 1979a). Of course, there is a caveat to this conclusion: Individualized instructional approaches are, by their very nature, more likely to be implemented in some content areas and/or course levels than in others.

It is probably much more likely, for example, that PSI would be implemented in an introductory calculus course than in a literature course on modern European writers. Indeed, the evidence from most reviews suggests this. Consequently, although it is safe to conclude that individualized instructional approaches are equally effective across nearly all content areas *where they have been implemented,* it is also important to acknowledge that they have not been implemented equally across all possible content areas in the curriculum.

Teacher Behavior

Do differences in teaching behavior systematically influence the acquisition of subject matter knowledge by students? The answer to this question appears to be yes; and it is based on a substantial body of evidence. By and large, this evidence has focused on answering two related questions. First, what are the dimensions of more effective (versus less effective) teaching behavior? Second, how are these various dimensions of teaching behavior related to subject matter learning?

Given the concerns of this book, the first question is perhaps less important than the second. Suffice it to say that reviews of the factor-analytical studies of the dimensions of student evaluations of teaching yield about six general dimensions (Cohen, 1981; Doyle, 1975; Feldman, 1976; Kulik & McKeachie, 1975; Marsh, 1984, 1986a). While different studies employ different names for what may be the same construct, the taxonomy offered by Cohen (1981) is useful and parsimonious. His labels for the dimensions are as follows:

1. *Skill:* This dimension represents the instructor's overall pedagogical adroitness. Typical items are "the instructor has good command of subject matter"; "the instructor gives clear explanations."
2. *Rapport:* This dimension assesses the instructor's empathy, accessibility, and friendliness; for example, "the instructor is available to talk with students outside of class."
3. *Structure:* This dimension measures how well the instructor planned and organized the course; for example, "the instructor uses class time well."
4. *Difficulty:* This dimension assesses the amount and difficulty of work expected in the course; for example, "the instructor assigns difficult reading."
5. *Interaction:* This dimension measures the extent to which students are encouraged to become actively involved in class sessions; for example, "the instructor facilitates classroom discussion."
6. *Feedback:* This dimension measures the extent to which the instructor

provides feedback on the quality of a student's work; for example, "the instructor keeps students informed of their progress."

In terms of the second question, the evidence suggests that while these dimensions of students' perceptions of teaching behavior are largely independent of class size (Feldman, 1984), they have statistically significant positive correlations with course achievement (for example, Benton, 1982; Centra, 1977, 1979; Cohen, 1972; Costin, Greenough, & Menges, 1971; Follman, 1974; Frey, Leonard, & Beatty, 1975; Gage, 1974; Marsh, 1984; Marsh, Fleiner, & Thomas, 1975; McKeachie & Lin, 1978; Mintzes, 1982; Murray, 1985; Sullivan, 1985; Sullivan & Skanes, 1974). Cohen (1981) conducted a meta-analytical synthesis of much of the research on the relationship between student perceptions of teaching behavior and subject matter achievement. His overall synthesis was based on forty-one independent validity studies reporting data from sixty-eight separate multisectional courses. Of the six dimensions of teaching behavior named above, only instructor skill and course structure or organization had statistically significant mean correlations with course achievement, .50 and .47, respectively. More modest correlations were found for such dimensions of teacher behavior as rapport (average correlation = .31), feedback (r = .31), and interaction (r = .22). Cohen also reports statistically significant mean correlations between course achievement and overall student ratings of the course instructor (r = .43) and the course (r = .43).

Additional analysis by Cohen (1981) suggests that the magnitude of the association between student perceptions of instructor proficiency and course achievement is influenced by a number of study characteristics. (In this analysis only overall rating of instructor was employed as a measure of instructor proficiency.) Most notably, correlations between instructor rating and achievement were larger for full-time (versus part-time) faculty,[3] when an external evaluator (not an instructor) graded students' course achievement, and when students knew their final grades before rating the instructor. The last finding, in particular, suggests that knowledge of one's grade may bias perceptions of the quality of instruction received. Additional study characteristics such as statistical control for ability, course level, institutional setting, and a measure of the overall quality of the study had only trivial influences on the magnitude of the correlation between rating of instructor proficiency and subject matter achievement.[4]

Despite the suggestion in Cohen's (1981) synthesis that knowledge of one's grade may bias perceptions of the quality of instruction received, the body of evidence clearly suggests that subject matter learning has a nontrivial relationship with the quality of instruction received. Two dimensions of teacher behavior stand out as being particularly salient in terms of potential influence on learning. These are skill, the general classroom adroitness and pedagogical clarity of the teacher, and structure, the degree of clear organization in the course. Other factors such as instructor rapport, interpersonal accessibility, and feedback to students also appear to be positively associated with achievement but less strongly than instructor skill and course structure.

A recent synthesis of an expanded data base of studies by Feldman (1989, in press) provides an important refinement to the above conclusion regarding instructor skill and course structure. Feldman's analyses suggest that the positive association found between instructor skill and student learning depends more on instructor clarity and understandability than on other constituent factors such as instructor subject matter knowledge or sensitivity to class level and progress. Likewise, the positive association between course structure and learning is more dependent on instructor preparation and organization than on clarity of course objectives and requirements.

Teacher Clarity. Research on student evaluations of teaching is only one source of evidence on the relationship between variations in teaching behavior and variations in achievement. Other researchers have come at the issue from a somewhat different perspective. Interestingly, however, the findings from this research are in rather close agreement with the evidence just reviewed.

One perspective is to take a very micro view of teaching and focus on the effects of specific, observable behaviors on subject matter learning. One of the most developed lines of research in this area is that concerned with teacher clarity. Most of the original work on the influence of teacher clarity and achievement was conducted by Land and Smith and their colleagues (Denham & Land, 1981; Land, 1979, 1980, 1981a, 1981b; Land & Smith, 1979a, 1979b, 1981; L. Smith, 1977, 1982; Smith & Edmonds, 1978; Smith & Land, 1980). They have attempted to identify specific teacher behaviors that present clear and unambiguous learning stimuli to students versus behaviors that lead to ambiguity and confusion. Examples of the former are using examples to illustrate concepts, identifying key points, and clearly signaling topic transitions. Examples of the latter are using "vagueness terms" and "mazes." Vagueness terms are imprecise terms that confuse the learner, such as *basically, you know, so to speak, usually, kind of, I'm not sure,* and so on (Hiller, Fisher, & Kaess, 1969). Mazes are units of discourse that do not make sense, such as starts or halts in speech, redundantly spoken words, and complex tangles of words (L. Smith, 1977).

Land and Smith have attempted to estimate the effects of teacher clarity (versus vagueness or lack of clarity) on subject matter achievement through the series of experimental studies just cited. In the typical study the same instructional content was purposefully taught under different levels of teacher clarity. The basic results of this body of research suggest that independent of other influences, degree of teacher clarity has a statistically significant positive effect on subject matter achievement. Conversely, high frequencies of teacher vagueness terms and mazes, in particular, appear to inhibit learning by college students.

More recent research on teacher clarity by Hines, Cruickshank, and Kennedy (1982, 1985) has broadened the operational definition of the term to include twenty-nine different low-inference (observable) variables thought to comprise clarity in instruction. To determine the independent effect of these variables on subject matter learning, the researchers conducted a complex experiment in which thirty-two student teachers were randomly assigned to classes to teach a twenty-five-minute lesson in matrix multiplication to peers. The teachers were free to select any instructional strategy they believed effective, and all instructional sessions were videotaped so that the teacher clarity behaviors could be recorded by independent observers. Net of student perceptions of teacher clarity and student satisfaction with the instruction, observer ratings of teacher clarity accounted for a statistically significant 52 percent of the variance in mean class achievement on a common posttest. Individual teacher behaviors most strongly and positively related to achievement were using relevant examples during explanation, reviewing material, asking questions to find out if students understood, teaching in a step-by-step manner, explaining things and then stopping so that students could think about the explanation, presenting the lesson in a logical manner, and informing students of lesson objectives or what they were expected to be able to do on completion of instruction. Such behaviors, as well as those uncovered by Land and Smith, are quite consistent with student perceptions of faculty behaviors (for example, skill, structure) that are also positively associated with student learning.[5] Moreover, given the fact that many of the teaching behaviors found to be associated with enhanced subject matter learning are themselves learnable, the research on teacher clarity may have potentially important implications for the pedagogical training of college faculty. Dalgaard (1982), for example, has experimentally demonstrated that teaching-training interventions can significantly improve the classroom effectiveness of graduate teaching assistants.

Student-Faculty Informal Interaction and Effective Teaching. Another perspective on the relationship between teacher behavior and student learning takes a somewhat more macro view. Typical of this approach is the research on the relationship between student-faculty informal interaction and effective teaching conducted by Wilson, Wood, and Gaff (1974) and Wilson, Gaff, Dienst, Wood, and Bavry (1975). In a comprehensive multi-institutional study the researchers had faculty and students identify faculty members whom they (faculty and students) regarded as having a particularly significant impact on students. These "effective teachers" were then compared with other faculty not so identified on a number of teaching dimensions.[6] Aside from factors such as using examples and analogies in teaching and efforts to make courses interesting, effective teachers were also characterized by accessibility to students outside of class. Thus, not only were the effective teachers the most skillful and interesting in the classroom; they also tended to extend their contact with students to nonclassroom situations. Moreover, faculty who interacted frequently with students outside of class tended to give cues as to their "social-psychological accessibility" for such interaction through their in-class teaching behaviors.

Such teaching behaviors and personal traits are not restricted to effective teachers in four-year institutions. Guskey and Easton (1983) report markedly similar behaviors and traits as also characterizing effective teachers in urban community colleges.

Student Involvement

Several recent models of learning and student development have suggested the importance of student involvement or engagement as a key determinant of the outcomes of education (for example, Astin, 1984; Friedlander, 1980; Pace, 1976, 1984; Parker & Schmidt, 1982; Rosenshine, 1982). Not surprisingly, perhaps, a substantial body of evidence exists to suggest that the greater the student's involvement in academic work or in the academic experience of college, the greater his or her level of knowledge acquisition. This evidence is consistent whether extent of involvement is measured at the class level or in terms of broader-based types of involvement.

At the class level, for example, substantial experimental evidence suggests that students are more attentive and involved in what transpires in class when they are required to take notes, and in turn note taking has positive effects on course subject matter achievement (for example, Hult, Cohn, & Potter, 1984; Kiewra, 1983; King, Biggs, & Lipsky, 1984; Locke, 1977; Weiland & Kingsbury, 1979). Similarly, evidence reported by Johnson (1981) and Johnson and Butts (1983) suggests that the greater the proportion of time in which the student is actually engaged in learning activities (taking notes, engaging in discussion, answering questions, and the like), the greater the level of content acquisition.

Peer Teaching or Tutoring. One method by which faculty have sought to increase students' active involvement or engagement in learning is through peer teaching or tutoring (Goldschmid and Goldschmid, 1976). Most of the recent research has suggested that peer teaching and peer tutorial programs have a positive impact on learning. Bargh and Schul (1980) conducted an experiment in which one group of undergraduates studied verbal material to learn it themselves while another group studied the material for the purpose of teaching it to another person. When pretest scores were controlled statistically, students who were preparing to teach scored significantly higher on a subsequent test of content retention than their counterparts who studied only to learn it for themselves. Similar results have been reported by Annis (1983), who compared comprehension knowledge in history among randomly assigned groups of sophomore women who differed in whether they read a passage for the purpose of teaching it to another student or not. With initial reading comprehension scores controlled statistically, students who read the passage with the purpose of teaching it or who actually taught it to another student scored significantly higher on a test of comprehension than students who merely read the passage or who read it and were taught.

Perhaps the most comprehensive study in this area of research was conducted by Benware and Deci (1984). They hypothesized that learning in order to teach facilitates greater intrinsic motivational processes than simply learning to be tested and that intrinsically motivated learning is more active and results in greater conceptual learning. In order to create an intrinsic or active orientation, randomly assigned students in an introductory psychology course were asked to learn material with the purpose of teaching it to another student, while the passive orientation asked students merely to learn material in order to be tested. The results indicated significantly higher conceptual learning of the material read for the group learning to teach but no statistically significant differences in rote learning between the group learning to teach and the group learning to be tested. The group learning to teach also perceived themselves to be more actively engaged in the course than the group learning to be tested, even though they spent equal time with the material.

The experimental research on peer teaching provides reasonably strong evidence that learning material in order to teach it not only increases student involvement in the process of learning but also enhances mastery of the material itself, particularly at the conceptual level. A possible explanation suggested by Bargh and Schul (1980) is that the cognitive benefits of learning to teach result from the use of a different and more comprehensive method of study than that employed when one is merely learning material in order to be tested. This may, in part, account for the finding that tutors in PSI courses benefit even more in terms of content mastery from these courses than do students who take them (Johnson, Sulzer-Azaroff, & Mass, 1977; McKeachie, Pintrich, Lin, & Smith, 1986).

Extent and Quality of Student Effort. A somewhat more broadly based perspective on student involvement and learning has been taken by Pace (1980, 1984). A basic assumption of Pace's work is that what a student gets out of college is dependent not only upon what the college does or does not do but also on the extent and quality of effort that the student puts into college. Thus, extent of subject matter learning, as well as other outcomes of college, is a function of what the institution offers and what the student does with those offerings. To assess involvement Pace has developed fourteen "quality of effort" scales that estimate a student's use of an institution's facilities and opportunities. The scales consist of items that vary according to complexity or "quality of effort" involved in a specific activity; and the respondent indicates level of involvement on a "never" to "very often" continuum. For example, items on the classroom involvement scale range from relatively simple activities such as taking notes or underlining to more complex or higher-level cognitive activities such as efforts to explain, organize, and go beyond assignments. The fourteen scales cluster into three factors: (1) academic and intellectual experiences (for example, library, faculty, classrooms), (2) personal and interpersonal experiences (for example, student acquaintances, conversation topics), and (3) group facilities and opportunities (for example, student union, clubs).

Pace (1980) administered the quality of effort scales to a sample of more than 4,000 students at all class levels at thirteen institutions. He also attempted to assess student knowledge acquisition by means of self-reported gains on two scales: general education (gaining broad general knowledge and cultural awareness) and academic and intellectual outcomes (acquiring field-specific knowledge and intellectual skills). (While there are assessment problems with such self-reports, most evidence suggests that they have moderately positive correlations, $r = .25$ to $r = .65$, with objective measures of knowledge [for example, Baird, 1976a; Berdie, 1971; Dumont & Troelstrup, 1980; McMorris & Ambrosino, 1973; Pohlmann & Beggs, 1974].) Pace found that the quality of effort students put into the academic or intellectual aspects of the college experience had statistically significant correlations of .39 with both the general education and the academic (intellectual) outcome scales. It was also the case, however, that the student's quality of effort in personal and interpersonal experiences and group facilities and opportunities had statistically significant positive correlations with the same two outcomes (ranging from $r = .19$ to $r = .40$).

To Pace, such findings suggest a basic wholeness about the college experience. In addition to academic and intellectual effort, involvement in personal and social experiences in college may contribute to learning and the development of intellectual skills. An alternative hypothesis, of course, is that involvement in personal and social experiences is associated with learning and intellectual skill development only because students who are highly involved in the academic and intellectual experience of college tend also to be involved in the personal and social experience of college (for example, Pace, 1987; Pascarella, 1985c; Pascarella & Terenzini, 1980a; Stage, 1987). Thus, if academic and intellectual efforts directly influence learning, personal and social involvements are also likely to correlate with learning but not necessarily in a causal sense.

Despite this alternate hypothesis, Pace's findings on quality of effort and learning are important, particularly since they have been supported by other studies. For example, a series of single-institution, longitudinal analyses by Terenzini and colleagues (Terenzini, Pascarella, & Lorang, 1982; Terenzini, Theophilides, & Lorang, 1984a; Terenzini & Wright, 1987a; Volkwein, King, & Terenzini, 1986) sought to determine the kinds of college experiences that were related to student self-reports of progress in academic and intellectual skill development. Using regression analysis to control statistically for salient background characteristics (for example, race, gender, secondary school achievement) and personal goals, the investigators found that a measure of classroom involvement had generally consistent, positive associations with the academic and intellectual progress measure. The classroom involvement scale measures such factors as how frequently students express their ideas in class and are intellectually stimulated by material covered in class.

Student Interactions with Faculty. Related to the concept of classroom involvement and effort is that of students' interactions and relationships with faculty. If one is willing to assume that faculty generally attach substantial value to student behaviors and attitudes that increase effort and learning (for example, Wallace, 1963, 1967a, 1967b; Pascarella, 1980) and that faculty influence on student values, behaviors, and attitudes is enhanced through informal contact beyond the classroom, it would seem to follow that student interaction with faculty is a potentially important influence on learning. A number of studies tend to confirm this notion, although the evidence is not totally consistent. Endo and Harpel (1982, 1983) conducted two longitudinal studies that looked at the influence of different measures of student-faculty interaction on self-report measures of knowledge acquisition in the senior and freshman years, respectively. Controlling for student precollege characteristics and expectations of college, Endo and Harpel (1982) found that frequency of informal contact with faculty had statistically significant positive associations with seniors' self-reports of adequacy of general knowledge and adequacy of mathematics skills. With similar statistical controls, Endo and Harpel (1983) found that frequency of informal contact with faculty also had a statistically significant positive association with freshmen's reports of their knowledge of basic facts. The researchers also found that perceived quality of relationships with faculty was significantly associated with this outcome.

In terms of the influence of *frequency* of student-faculty informal contact on self-reports of progress in academic and intellectual skill development, similar results have been reported in the longitudinal investigations of Terenzini, Theophilides, and Lorang (1984a) and Terenzini and Wright (1987a). Less supportive evidence, however, has been reported by Terenzini, Pascarella, and Lorang (1982) and Volkwein, King, and Terenzini (1986). In terms of the *quality* of students' relationships with faculty, the findings of Terenzini and colleagues are quite consistent with those of Endo and Harpel (1982, 1983). Controlling for student precollege characteristics,

Terenzini and colleagues found that a measure of the extent to which a student had developed a friendly, informal, influential relationship with at least one faculty member was a statistically significant positive predictor of perceived gains in academic skill development.

In addition to the possible problems of reliability and validity of student self-reports (discussed previously), much of the research on student involvement or quality of effort and learning is plagued by potential ambiguity in causal direction. This is particularly evident in those studies that find statistically significant associations between frequency of student-faculty informal interaction and various measures of gains in academic knowledge and skills. Do frequency and quality of informal interaction with faculty enhance students' academic competence, or do initial perceptions of gains in academic knowledge and skills eventually lead students to seek informal contact with faculty beyond the classroom? Unfortunately, the designs of existing studies make it difficult, if not impossible, to answer this question.

Despite this and related methodological problems, the research that links broad-based student involvement or quality of effort during college and increases in academic knowledge and skills opens a potentially significant new area of inquiry. This is particularly true if we can gain a better understanding of those institutional policies, practices, and organizational structures that facilitate involvement or quality of effort. Some evidence does exist to suggest two important influences: living on campus (versus commuting to college) and both institutional and major department size. The former tends to facilitate involvement (for example, Astin, 1973b; Chickering, 1974a; Chickering & Kuper, 1971; Pace, 1980; Pascarella, 1984b), while the latter factors tend to inhibit it (for example, Hearn, 1987; Pascarella, 1985c; Stoecker, Pascarella, & Wolfle, 1988). Moreover, evidence from Pascarella (1985d) suggests that the effect of place of residence on student involvement during college persists irrespective of institutional size, while the inhibiting effect of attending a large institution holds even when place of residence is held constant. Chapman and Pascarella (1983) have suggested that the factors that influence different types of student involvement during college depend on a complex pattern of interactions (conditional effects) between student precollege characteristics and the type of institution attended (four-year residential, four-year commuter, two-year commuter). It is difficult, however, to draw any clear generalizations from their findings.

Conditional Effects of College

Student-by-Institution Effects

We found little consistent evidence to suggest the presence of conditional effects in the influence of college on student subject matter learning.

A study by Robertshaw and Wolfle (1982), reviewed earlier, found that with secondary school achievement controlled, white students derived greater verbal and mathematics knowledge from attendance at two-year colleges than did black students. This finding, however, has not been replicated.

Another investigation by Ayres (1982, 1983) suggests that black students may not benefit the same amount from attendance at different kinds of institutions. Using the same sample as Ayres and Bennett (1983) but with students ($n = 3,426$ from fifteen institutions) rather than the institutions as the unit of analysis, Ayres sought to determine whether the racial composition of a college influences achievement on the National Teacher Examination. Using analysis of covariance to control for differences in entering aptitude (SAT scores), black students at predominantly white institutions tended to score higher on the NTE than students of similar aptitude at predominantly black institutions. This finding is only partially supported by Davis (1977) with samples of black physical education majors at predominantly black and predominantly white colleges. Controlling for entrance examination scores, Davis found that blacks at predominantly white institutions had significantly higher NTE scores on competencies necessary for effective teaching. However, no statistically significant differences were found between blacks at predominantly black and predominantly white institutions with respect to NTE area (physical education) scores.

The study by Rock, Baird, and Linn (1972) reviewed earlier presents evidence to suggest that students initially highest in precollege academic aptitude may benefit slightly more in terms of GRE achievement from attending an academically selective rather than a nonselective liberal arts college. (Selectivity here is operationally defined as the average SAT score of the institution's student body.) Astin (1968c), however, found no evidence to suggest that the academically most capable student benefited more in terms of GRE achievement from attending a selective rather than a nonselective college. Since Astin's study used students rather than institutions as the unit of analysis, his test for conditional effects is probably more definitive than that of Rock, Baird, and Linn.

Student-by-Instructional Approach Effects

One area that has received considerable attention with respect to the possibility of conditional effects is that of instructional approach, particularly for various forms of individualized instruction. Since a major characteristic of much individualized instruction is to ensure subject matter mastery irrespective of student ability, one plausible hypothesis is that the academically least well prepared students will benefit relatively more from individualized instruction than the better prepared. There is some support for this hypothesis from individual studies. For example, Pascarella (1977a, 1978) compared calculus achievement between similar students in a personalized system of instruction versus a traditional lecture and recitation format. While PSI generally outperformed the traditional approach, the greatest advantage was for the mathematically least well prepared student. As level of precourse mathematics preparation increased, the relative advantage of PSI tended to decrease. Similar findings are reported by Born, Gledhill, and Davis (1972); Gay (1986); Ross and Rakow (1981); Stinard and Dolphin (1981).

Despite the findings of these selected individual studies, the weight of evidence nevertheless suggests that the generally positive effects of individualized instruction on subject matter learning do not vary significantly with student aptitude or prior subject matter preparation. In each of the five meta-analyses of various forms of individualized instruction previously reviewed, effect sizes for conditional effects based on prior aptitude on subject matter achievement were computed. In all cases the effect sizes were statistically nonsignificant and trivial. This indicates that the magnitude of the effect of each of the five forms of individualized instruction reviewed does not depend on student aptitude or prior subject matter preparation (Cohen, Ebeling, & Kulik, 1981; Kulik, Cohen, & Ebeling, 1980; Kulik, Kulik, & Cohen, 1979a, 1979b, 1980). Overall, the best- and least-prepared students apparently derive equal learning benefits from individualized instruction.

Some evidence does suggest that different instructional approaches may be differentially effective for students with different personality characteristics. Most of the consistent findings in this area have focused on the degree to which the student is characterized as independent, internally motivated, flexible, or having a high need for achievement. The weight of evidence would appear to indicate that students who come to a course high on any or all of these characteristics tend to derive greater achievement benefits when the instructional approach stresses learner self-direction and participation. Conversely, students who score low on such traits tend to have higher achievement under more structured or teacher-directed approaches. Experimental evidence reported by Domino (1968, 1971) and Peterson (1979), for example, shows that students high in need for achievement via independence demonstrate greater subject matter achievement in instructional conditions that stress student self-direction and participation than in more structured or teacher-directed formats. Conversely, students high in need for achievement via conformity have higher achievement in structured rather than more independent instructional approaches. With the exception of Goldberg (1972), strikingly consistent results have been reported by Daniels and Stevens (1976); Horak and Horak (1982); Parent, Forward, Canter, and Mohling (1975); and Van Damme and Masui (1980) using learner internal versus external locus of control, by Pascarella (1977b) using a motivation construct, and by Charkins, O'Toole, and Wetzel (1985) using students' preferences for dependent, collaborative, or independent learning style.

Though not extensive, the body of research on the interaction of student personality traits and instructional approaches underscores the importance of being sensitive to individual differences in college instruction. Not all students may benefit equally from the same instructional format. The research further suggests that it may be possible to enhance subject matter learning by adapting instruction to individual differences among learners.[7]

Long-Term Effects of College

A substantial part of the evidence pertaining to the long-term effects of college on knowledge acquisition is based on surveys of college graduates. Typically, graduates are asked to indicate the extent to which their undergraduate experience influenced a number of educational objectives, including knowledge acquisition. The use of retrospective self-reports of college impact on learning is a strategy employed in national surveys of college graduates by Bisconti and Solmon (1976), Pace (1974), and Spaeth and Greeley (1970). All three studies report evidence indicating that college alumni attribute their undergraduate experience with substantially increasing the acquisition of both general and specific knowledge. In 1968 Spaeth and Greeley (1970), for example, surveyed nearly 5,000 alumni who graduated from 135 colleges or universities in 1961. Of those surveyed, 41 percent said that college "greatly affected" and 46 percent said that it "somewhat affected" their ability to think and express themselves. Similarly, 35 percent reported that college "greatly affected" and 42 percent reported that it "somewhat affected" the development of a broad knowledge of the arts and sciences.

Consistent findings are reported by Pace (1974) in a nineteen-year follow-up study of alumni from seventy-nine institutions. In his study the percentage of alumni who reported deriving "very much" or "quite a bit" of benefit from college in different areas of development was as follows: 79 percent for vocabulary, terminology, and facts in various fields of knowledge; 64 percent for awareness of different philosophies, cultures, and ways of life; 62 percent for broadened literary acquaintance and appreciation; and 54 percent for understanding and appreciating science and technology.

The study by Bisconti and Solmon (1976) followed up more than 4,000 individuals approximately fourteen years after they had entered college in 1961. The authors report that 73 percent of those surveyed said that their college experiences were "very useful" in increasing their general knowledge.

Such consistent evidence from national surveys is, of course, encouraging. The possibility nevertheless exists that equally capable individuals who did not go to college would feel equally influenced by their various noncollegiate experiences. This issue was addressed, at least to some extent, in a massive secondary analysis by Hyman, Wright and Reed (1975). Using data on Caucasian individuals, aged thirty-seven to forty-eight, from fifty-four Gallup, National Opinion Research Center, and Institute for Social Research samples covering twenty-two years (1949–1971), Hyman, Wright, and Reed analyzed individuals' responses to a battery of factual questions in three general areas. These areas measured each individual's ability to (1) identify correctly prominent public figures and major public events; (2) answer correctly questions on vocabulary, humanities, history, civics and government, geography, science, and so on; and (3) respond correctly to questions on popular culture and sports. On nearly all questions in these areas, correct responses were closely related to formal education, with differences between college and high school graduates being substantial. For example, the advantage in percentage correct for college versus high school graduates was 20 percent in history, 32 percent in humanities, 24 percent in geography, and 34 percent in civics. More important, these differences remained even after statistical or design controls were made for race, gender, religion, native or foreign born, geographical origin, age, socioeconomic origin, and current socioeconomic status. Unfortunately, not all controls could be made on the same surveys.

The Hyman, Wright, and Reed (1975) analyses also report two additional findings. First, while the differences in knowledge between college and high school graduates continued into the oldest age brackets, they were somewhat more pronounced for the younger respondents than for the older ones. This perhaps suggests that the influence of college on knowledge acquisition is partially diluted over time in the general population by intervening life experiences. How much this occurs for individuals, or whether it occurs at all, however, may depend to a great extent on the nature of those intervening experiences. Second, although the differences in knowledge between college and high school graduates held for all levels of current socioeconomic status, they tended to be greatest for the highest levels. To Hyman, Wright, and Reed this suggests that the effects of education on knowledge are frequently enhanced among those whose social and economic circumstances are advantaged. Such individuals may be in the best position to engage in cultural, intellectual, and artistic activities that both further enhance interests and tastes developed in college and expand their knowledge base.

There is, of course, an important potential limitation to the findings of Hyman, Wright, and Reed (1975). It is not apparent that the most important confounding variables are controlled in their analyses. In the absence of controls for potentially confounding background factors such as intelligence, motivation, and aspiration, strict attribution of differences in knowledge to level of formal education is somewhat risky. The results might simply reflect systematic differences in these and similar traits among those who seek varying levels of formal education.

Despite this limitation, the analyses of Hyman, Wright, and Reed (1975) are a major contribution and probably represent our single most comprehensive source of evidence on the long-term impact of postsecondary education on knowledge acquisition. Moreover, they also present an additional set of findings that suggests that college attendance is associated with postcollege experiences that are likely to accentuate this impact even further. Compared with high school graduates, college graduates were more likely to (1) read newspapers, magazines, and books; (2) remain more informed about public affairs; and (3) participate in both formal and informal continuing education.[8] These differences tended to remain even after statistical controls were made for background variables. This suggests that an important part of the long-term influence of college on knowledge acquisition is that it creates an interest in and a receptivity to further learning. (As we shall see in subsequent chapters, a college degree is also more likely to provide the economic advantages that permit one to procure the goods and services necessary for additional learning.) Consequently, the wide-ranging knowledge differences that Hyman, Wright, and Reed found between college and high school graduates are probably not just the direct result of what is learned *during* college. Rather, it is likely that the differences also reflect important variations in posteducation attitudes, interests, activities, and life-styles attributable, at least in part, to whether or not one attends college (for example, Anderson & Darkenwald, 1979; Bowen, 1977; Guthrie, Seifert, & Kirsch, 1986; Withey, 1971). Such indirect effects of college attendance, transmitted through college's influence on postcollege experiences, are an important if often overlooked part of the total impact of postsecondary education.

Summary

Change During College

Evidence from a substantial number of studies conducted over a fifty-year period is quite consistent in suggesting that students make statistically significant gains in general and more specific subject matter knowledge during their undergraduate years. Our best estimate of freshman-to-senior gains is that they average approximately .56 of a standard deviation for general verbal skills, .24 of a standard deviation for general mathematical or quantitative skills, and .87 of a standard deviation for specific subject matter knowledge. These represent improvements over entering freshman competencies of approximately 21 percentile points, 9.5 percentile points, and 30.8 percentile points, respectively; and they are reasonably consistent with Bowen's (1977) estimates.

Net Effects of College

Given certain methodological problems, it is possible that the magnitude of the gains for verbal and quantitative skills indicated above may not accurately reflect the net effect of college. The most methodologically sound research suggests that the net effect of college on verbal skills may be somewhat smaller and the effect on mathematical skills may be somewhat larger than that indicated by typical freshman-to-senior gains. For verbal skills, the estimated net effect of graduating from college compared to not attending college was between .26 and .32 of a standard deviation. This converts to an advantage of between 10.3 and 12.6 percentile points. For mathematical skills, the estimated net effect of college was between .29 and .32 of a standard deviation, which converts to an advantage of between 11.4 and 12.6 percentile points. The instruments used to assess verbal and mathematical knowledge in this research are not particularly comprehensive. Consequently, they may not fully capture the impact of college.

Between-College Effects

Our synthesis found little consistent evidence to suggest that measures of institutional "quality" or environmental characteristics have more than a small, perhaps trivial, net influence on how much a student learns during four years of college. When student precollege traits were controlled statistically, only three variables had statistically significant positive associations with standardized measures of achievement across at least two independent samples. These were frequency of student-faculty interaction, degree of curricular flexibility, and faculty members' formal educational level. The magnitude of these associations, however, was quite small and perhaps of questionable practical importance.

In this chapter we have suggested and discussed a number of methodological problems in the existing research that may account for the general absence of differential effects between institutions. Despite these problems, however, it may be incorrect simply to dismiss the weight of evidence, even if it is counterintuitive. It may well be that with differences in the academic capabilities of student bodies taken into account, four-year institutions with substantial differences in their stock of human, financial, and educational resources have essentially the same impact on how much students learn as undergraduates. Consistent with this conclusion we have suggested the possibility of a diminishing return relationship between institutional resources (for example, number of books in the library) and learning that may at least partially explain why a high level of resources is not necessarily matched by a proportional increase in measured student learning.

Within-College Effects

Some recent evidence suggests that what is learned during college is differentially influenced by the pattern of courses taken, even when student ability is held constant. This research is in its nascent stages, however, and it may be some time before we can determine whether clearly replicable patterns of differential course work effects on learning exist across institutions.

Although it is likely that students learn the most during college in the subject matter specific to their academic major, we found little methodologically sound evidence to indicate that academic major had a differential influence on the acquisition of subject matter knowledge or academic skills outside the major. Similarly, we found little consistent evidence to suggest that mastery of factual subject matter content is accomplished any more efficiently in small, discussion-oriented classrooms than in large, lecture-oriented classrooms. At the same time, the evidence does suggest that the former may be preferable when the goal of instruction is affective or higher-order cognitive skills such as critical thinking.

Considerable evidence exists to suggest that certain individualized instructional approaches or systems that emphasize small, modularized units of content, mastery of one unit before moving to the next, immediate and frequent feedback to students on their progress, and active student involvement in the learning process are consistently effective in enhancing subject matter learning over more traditional instructional formats such as lecture and recitation. Some variation exists in the relative effectiveness of these approaches, however. Of the five individualized instructional approaches reviewed, four of them, audio-tutorial, computer-based, programmed, and visual-based instruction, showed statistically significant modest learning advantages over traditional approaches of from 6 to 10 percentile points. In contrast, the typical advantage attributable to the personalized system of instruction (Keller Plan) was 19 percentile points, approximately twice as large as any of the other forms of individualized instruction.

It also appears that despite the findings of a few studies to the contrary, the learning advantages attributable to the various forms of individualized instruction are the same for students at different levels of precourse aptitude or subject matter competence. Similarly, with a few exceptions, the advantages attributable to individualized instruction do not seem to depend on content area. It is likely, however, that the nature of many of the forms of individualized instruction make their use more probable in some subject areas or disciplines than in others. The natural sciences, engineering, mathematics, and some of the social sciences appear to be the areas where the greatest implementation of individualized approaches has taken place.

Although it may be overstated to say that we know what causes effective teaching, we do know much about what effective teachers do and how they behave in the classroom. Student subject matter learning seems to be enhanced when teachers (1) have a good command of the subject matter and are enthusiastic in its presentation, (2) are clear in their explanation of concepts, (3) structure and organize class time well, (4) present unambiguous learning stimuli to students (for example, use examples and analogies to identify key points, signal a topic transition clearly), (5) avoid vagueness terms and language mazes, and (6) have good rapport with students in class (are open to student opinions and encourage class discussion and the like) and are accessible to students in nonclassroom settings. Perhaps the most important finding in research on teacher behaviors that are associated with student learning is that some may themselves be learnable (for example, structuring and organizing class time efficiently, teacher clarity).

Not all subject matter learning in college, however, can be seen simply as a function of what the institution does to the student in instructional or noninstructional settings. Rather, much depends on the quality of the student's effort in making use of the range of learning opportunities provided by the institution. Instructional strategies such as tutoring and studying material for the purpose of teaching it to someone else appear to enhance student involvement or effort in learning, thereby enhancing subject matter mastery. Course work, however, may not be the only arena where student involvement or effort is associated with increased learning. Though not as methodologically sound as that from instructional experiments, there is nevertheless a considerable body of correlational evidence to suggest that how much a student perceives himself or herself as having learned in college is a function of his or her effort in the social as well as the academic system of the institution. Such effort seems to be independently and positively influenced by living on campus (versus commuting to college) and by attending a small institution.

Conditional Effects

There is little consistent evidence to suggest that either postsecondary education in general or the type of institution attended in particular has a differential effect on knowledge acquisition for different kinds of students. Some evidence exists to suggest that black students may make greater knowledge gains at predominantly white colleges than at predominantly black institutions, but the findings are not compelling. In the area of instructional research, on the other hand, there is a reasonably consistent body of evidence to suggest that certain kinds of students learn more from one instructional approach than from another. Students high in need for independent achievement or internal locus of control appear to learn more from instructional approaches that stress student independence, self-direction, and participation than from more structured or teacher-directed approaches. Conversely, students high in need for conforming or dependent achievement or external locus of control appear to benefit more from structured, teacher-directed instructional formats than from approaches that emphasize independent learning.

Long-Term Effects

Finally, while flawed to some degree by lack of controls for aptitude, motivation, and aspiration, a comprehensive body of evidence indicates that college graduates have a more substantial factual knowledge base than those whose formal education ends with secondary school. This difference remains statistically significant over a fairly wide age range. Moreover, there is additional consistent evidence to suggest that college graduates are much more inclined than high school graduates to engage in activities that are likely to add to their knowledge (for example, serious reading, continuing education) after graduation. The implication from these findings is that the total effect of college on knowledge acquisition is not simply limited to what occurs while the student is in attendance. Rather, by influencing postcollege interests and activities that enhance learning, college may also have an important indirect effect on one's knowledge that extends well into one's adult life. Astin (1977a) refers to this and similar long-term effects of college as channeling. That is, the college experience tends to channel individuals into postcollege experiences that further accentuate interests, capabilities, and values crystallized during one's college years. While our tendency is to refer to such impacts as indirect effects, we agree with Astin that they are an important consideration in estimating the influence of college. Indeed, this becomes a recurring theme in subsequent chapters.

Notes

1. See Pace (1979) for a detailed review of more than fifty years of standardized testing with college samples. See also Astin (1977a), Friedlander (1982), and Pace (1974) for evidence indicating gains during college in academic knowledge acquisition and skills based on student self-reports.

2. Research on the personalized system of instruction or its components not included in the syntheses reviewed would not appear to change this conclusion (for example, Canelos & Ozbeki, 1983; Cline & Michael, 1978; Eniaiyeju, 1983; Freeman, 1984; Guskey, 1987; Guskey, Benninga, & Clark, 1984; Guskey & Monsaas, 1979; Haemmerlie, 1985;

Najmaie & Dolphin, 1983; Rysberg, 1986; Smith, 1987; Yeany, Waugh, & Blalock, 1979).

3. It does not appear that students taught by part-time faculty learn any less than those taught by full-time faculty (Davis, Belcher, & Mc-Kitterick, 1986).

4. It also appears that the quality of instruction received (at least as measured by student ratings) is largely independent of other faculty characteristics, most notably scholarly productivity (for example, Aleamoni & Yimer, 1973; Centra, 1981; Crimmel, 1984; Dent & Lewis, 1976; Feldman, 1987; Finkelstein, 1984; Friedrich & Michalak, 1983; Hicks, 1974; Hoyt & Spangler, 1976; Linsky & Straus, 1975; Marsh, 1984; Rossmann, 1976; Rothman & Preshaw, 1975; Stallings & Singhal, 1970; Webster, 1985, 1986). These studies suggest that, at best, the association between ratings of undergraduate instruction and scholarly productivity is a small, positive one (correlations in the .10 to .16 range). Thus, if research activity does not appear to be a major asset in a faculty member's capacity for effectively teaching undergraduates, so too it certainly does not appear to be a detriment. It is also possible, of course, that in advanced seminars or graduate courses, scholarly or research activity is more important to effective teaching than it is in the vast majority of undergraduate courses. The research evidence is largely silent on this point, however.

5. To be sure, there are other specific teacher behaviors that have positive associations with student learning in college. Merlino (1977), for example, found that the use of higher-level questioning (analysis, synthesis, and so on) was positively related to students' understanding of biological concepts. Such evidence, however, tends to be based on isolated studies and does not constitute a body of evidence from which clear generalizations can be made.

6. It is important to note that these "effective teachers" were not necessarily those whose students learned the most on objective measures of achievement. Thus, this is a somewhat broader and more subjective measure of teaching effectiveness than that used by other studies of the relationship between teacher behavior and student learning.

7. This may be particularly important for nontraditional and/or adult students. See, for example, Mickler and Zippert (1987), whose research suggests that adult students' learning is enhanced when teaching strategies are matched with learning styles.

8. Hyman, Wright, and Reed (1975) are not the only researchers to report these findings. The fact that college educated people are significantly more likely than those with less formal education to participate in various types of formal and informal continuing education is well documented (for example, Boaz, 1978; Carp, Peterson, & Roelfs, 1974; Cross, 1981; National Center for Education Statistics, 1980; Knapp,

1977; Okes, 1976). Furthermore, evidence presented by Anderson and Darkenwald (1979) and Felmlee (1988) indicates that this tendency is essentially independent of one's income and occupation or, in the case of women, age, marital status, intelligence, and number of children. Similarly, evidence from national surveys clearly suggests that individuals with a college education are more likely than others to be knowledgeable about political candidates and civic and political issues (Campbell, Converse, Miller, & Stokes, 1960; Key, 1961). Finally, there is also additional evidence that both volume and type of reading are associated with college attendance. For example, controlling for gender, occupational level, and subject matter content, Guthrie, Seifert, and Kirsch (1986) found that those with at least some college spent a significantly greater part of their day reading than did those with no college. They also found that the college group read significantly more than the noncollege group in the areas of news, business, society, science, and fiction. The education groups did not differ in volume of recreational or reference reading. Interestingly, there is little evidence that college "quality" is related to amount of serious reading. Controlling for gender, career choice, religion, socioeconomic origin, and college grades, Spaeth and Greeley (1970) found only a trivial and statistically nonsignificant relationship between the student body selectivity of the college one attended and amount of serious reading (for example, nonfiction, poetry, and number of books read).

4

Cognitive Skills
and Intellectual Growth

In Chapter Three we focused on the learning outcomes typically thought
to be directly related to the curriculum or academic program of a college,
namely, the acquisition of subject matter knowledge and academic (usually
verbal and quantitative) skills. Obviously, imparting such academically oriented knowledge is a central concern of most postsecondary institutions.
On the basis of recent findings and conceptions of cognitive structure and
process in competent individuals, such a concern seems reasonably well
founded. A growing body of evidence suggests that sound content knowledge is a necessary foundation for highly competent and creative intellectual performance (Rabinowitz & Glaser, 1985). It has been argued that
without a sufficient background of facts, data, and information, one's intellectual structure may simply be too flimsy to sustain clear and serious thought
about complex problems and issues (for example, Bloom, 1987; Bok, 1978;
Hirsch, 1987).

Yet, abundant evidence suggests that much factual material is forgotten rather soon after it is presented in educational settings (Blunt & Blizard, 1975; Brethower, 1977; Gustav, 1969; McLeish, 1968). Thus, beyond
postsecondary education's undeniably significant role in the imparting of
specific subject matter knowledge, claims for the enduring influence of
postsecondary education on learning must be based, to some extent at least,
on the fostering of a repertoire of general intellectual or cognitive competencies and skills. These cognitive skills go by a number of different names
(reasoning skills, critical thinking, intellectual flexibility, reflective judgment, cognitive complexity, and so on), and they differ somewhat in the
types of problems or issues they address. Nevertheless, most, if not all, seem
to have as a common theme the notion of applicability and utility across a
range of different content areas. As suggested by Michael (1975a), these
cognitive competencies and skills represent the general intellectual outcomes of college that permit individuals to process and utilize new information; communicate effectively; reason objectively and draw objective
conclusions from various types of data; evaluate new ideas and techniques
efficiently; become more objective about beliefs, attitudes, and values; eval-

114

uate arguments and claims critically; and make reasonable decisions in the face of imperfect information. These and related general cognitive skills are a particularly important resource for the individual in a society and world where factual knowledge is becoming obsolete at an accelerated rate (Rosen, 1975). In this chapter we synthesize evidence on the extent to which such general cognitive competencies and skills are fostered by college attendance.

Change During College

The reliable and valid measurement of general cognitive competencies and skills is often a difficult and highly complex psychometric task. One must infer the presence of sophisticated constructs or underlying psychological traits from an individual's responses to questions on a paper and pencil instrument or in an interview. Thus, an issue in summarizing the evidence on how much students gain in general cognitive skills during college concerns exactly what is being measured by the various instruments used. Unfortunately, the names of the various measurement instruments do not always provide a clear description of the traits assessed. Consequently, in this section we give a brief description of the major instruments used and present a synthesis of the evidence pertaining to change during college. The research can be seen as falling into the following six categories: communication skills, Piagetian formal operational reasoning, critical thinking, learning new concepts, postformal reasoning, and conceptual complexity. These form the framework for our synthesis.

Communication Skills

The most extensive evidence available on the gains made during college in communication skills is presented by Steele (1986) in a cross-sectional investigation of 1,589 freshmen from thirteen institutions and 1,366 seniors from ten institutions. Steele measured communication skills with the speaking and writing assessments of the American College Testing Program (ACT) College Outcome Measures Program (COMP) (Forrest & Steele, 1978, 1982). The COMP assessments of speaking and writing are defined as the ability to communicate effectively about social institutions, science and technology, and the arts. Three samples of writing and three samples of speaking are taken from a number of standardized role-playing tasks in which the student is asked to endorse a particular point of view by making a persuasive argument. In both the speaking and writing tasks equal emphasis is given to rhetorical concerns (discourse or organization of ideas), psychological concerns (making contact with and attending to the perspective of the relevant audience), and practical concerns (such as using vivid language and illustrations to dramatize and create an effect). Little emphasis is given to errors such as mispronounced or misspelled words unless they noticeably detract from or obscure the message.

On both the speaking and writing tests seniors scored significantly higher than freshmen. The freshman-senior difference on the speaking skills test was approximately two-thirds of a freshman standard deviation, which translates to a senior advantage of 24.5 percentile points above the freshman average score. On the writing skills test, the freshman-senior difference was approximately one-half of a freshman standard deviation, which translates to a senior advantage of about 19 percentile points above the average freshman. Although there is not a great deal of additional evidence from use of the relatively new ACT COMP, similar results have been reported in a single-institution, cross-sectional comparison of freshmen and seniors by Jones (1982).

Whitla (1978) used a somewhat different instrument, the Test of Logic and Rhetoric, to assess cross-sectionally freshman-sophomore and freshman-senior differences in written communication at three institutions: a private college, a state college, and a two-year college. The Test of Logic and Rhetoric purports to assess one's ability to communicate in writing with clarity and style. It consists of five different essays on various standardized topics coded for spelling, grammar, organization, quality of arguments, and quality of counterarguments. Although the students at different class levels were matched on academic ability and secondary school rank in class, statistically significant differences were found in their ability to communicate effectively. With the exception of those majoring in the natural sciences, seniors (or sophomores) at all three institutions composed more forceful and logical essays and made fewer syntactical mistakes than did freshmen.

Piagetian Formal Operational Reasoning

In Piaget's highly influential theory, human intellectual development is posited as moving through four major periods (Inhelder & Piaget, 1958): sensorimotor (birth to two years of age), preoperational (two to seven years), concrete operational (seven to eleven years), and formal operational (eleven years and up). Some have called the final period the "crowning achievement" of intellectual development (Flavell, 1963). This is essentially the ability to reason abstractly and deductively and to move one's intellectual orientation from "what is" to "what could be" (King, 1986).

The basis of formal reasoning is the capacity for scientific reasoning in solving problems. It involves such elements as hypothetico-deductive reasoning, proportional thinking, combinational analysis, isolation and control of variables, and probability (Lawson, 1985). As suggested by King (1986), mature problem solving may exhibit any or all of these traits. For example, determining whether a burned-out bulb or a dead battery is causing a flashlight to malfunction requires isolation and control of variables.

Despite the fact that Piaget's model posits adolescence as the period of time when formal operational reasoning is most likely to develop, an impressive body of evidence suggests that perhaps half of entering college students (or upperclassmen, for that matter) are not yet functioning at this stage (for example, Chiappetta, 1976; Cohen, Hillman, & Agne, 1978; Dettloff, 1982; Kolodiy, 1975; Lawson, Nordland, & DeVito, 1974; Neimark, 1975; Piaget, 1972; Robbins, 1981). King (1986), in a synthesis of sixteen other studies that covered a period from 1962 to 1981, estimates that only about 55 percent of all college students are operating at the formal reasoning level, with the range being from 10 percent to 100 percent across samples. Consequently, it is not surprising that gains in formal reasoning during college have been the concern of a number of researchers. The results of this research are somewhat mixed.

Waite (1975) used a semiclinical method of assessing science students' performance on five Piagetian-type tasks designed to measure an individual's ability to perform at the formal operational level. No statistically significant relationship was found between class level and performance on the test. Similar cross-sectional results have been reported by Williams, Turner, Debreuil, Fast, and Berestiansky (1979). Here there was no clear pattern of performance on a test eliciting six logical operations described by Piaget's theory between first- and third-year science students. On some operations third-year students outperformed first-year students, while on other operations the reverse was true.

Somewhat less ambiguous cross-sectional evidence has been reported by Dunlop and Fazio (1976) with a sample of 466 students enrolled in general college chemistry or college physical science. Seniors tended to have higher scores than freshmen had on a measure of formal or abstract reasoning that consisted of eighteen problem-solving tasks.

Longitudinal investigations of gains in formal reasoning during college have been conducted by Eisert and Tomlinson-Keasey (1978) and Mentkowski and Strait (1983). Eisert and Tomlinson-Keasey gave a measure of formal reasoning to fifty-five freshmen at the beginning and end of their freshman year. The measure of formal reasoning was typical of those used in the other studies previously reviewed, and it assessed the student's ability to separate variables, test variables in an unconfounded way, generate hypotheses, draw conclusions, conduct tests of hypotheses, demonstrate an understanding of probability, and ascertain the relationship between two variables. The average formal reasoning score at the end of the freshman year was approximately .40 of a standard deviation greater than the score at the beginning of the year. This statistically significant gain translates into an improvement in formal reasoning of about 15.5 percentile points during the freshman year.

In the investigation by Mentkowski and Strait (1983), the same sample of students was assessed at entrance to college and at the end of their sophomore and senior years with a measure of formal reasoning. This measure included two problems in proportionality, two problems in conservation of volume, and one problem on the separation of variables. Repeated measures of analysis of variance indicated a statistically significant freshman-to-senior increase in formal reasoning of slightly more than .27 of a standard deviation (an improvement of 10.6 percentile points over the freshman year). Interestingly, however, about 85 percent of the total freshman-to-senior gain occurred during the freshman and sophomore years. The gain in formal reasoning that occurred during the junior and senior years was relatively smaller and nonsignificant.[1]

Critical Thinking

Related conceptually to the concept of abstract or formal reasoning as developed by Piaget is that of critical thinking. Critical thinking has been measured in a number of different ways (McMillan, 1987) but typically involves the individual's ability to do some or all of the following: identify central issues and assumptions in an argument, recognize important relationships, make correct inferences from data, deduce conclusions from information or data provided, interpret whether conclusions are warranted on the basis of the data given, and evaluate evidence or authority (Furedy & Furedy, 1985). (There are, of course, variations in the ways in which critical reasoning skills are measured, and we tend to take a fairly broad view in terms of their inclusion in this section.) While formal reasoning ability is typically assessed by having the individual solve operational tasks or problems, critical thinking appears to stress the individual's ability to interpret, evaluate, and make informed judgments about the adequacy of arguments, data, and conclusions. Typical in the measurement of both formal reasoning and critical thinking is the notion that some answers or solutions are more verifiably correct than others (Brabeck & Wood, 1990).

Research on student gains in critical thinking during college has a fairly long history; and some of the most convincing evidence comes from studies conducted prior to 1967. Perhaps the first and clearly the most comprehensive investigation in this area was conducted by Dressel and Mayhew (1954) on a total sample of more than 1,700 students from eleven institutions. Using a test of critical thinking in the social sciences, the investigators found statistically significant freshman-year gains of about half a standard deviation or better in all eleven institutions. This translates into an improvement of about 19 percentile points in critical thinking during the freshman year. There was a tendency for students who initially scored low to change the most, but this could have been the effect of regression artifacts. A test of critical thinking in reading and writing that involved the critical analysis of passages (for example, "The Sermon on the Mount," *The Rubáiyát*, Thoreau's *Walden*) also showed statistically significant freshman-year gains in nine of the institutions. Again, the gains were about half a standard deviation, with the initially lowest scoring students showing the greatest gains.

Dressel and Mayhew (1954) also administered a test of science reasoning and understanding, designed to measure critical thinking in science, to 470 students in seven colleges and universities. They found statistically significant freshman-year gains of about half a standard deviation in six of the institutions. Finally, Dressel and Mayhew administered a general test of critical thinking to 1,000 entering freshmen in seven colleges and readministered it at the end of the freshman year. The general measure of critical thinking was based on fifty-seven items and assessed one's ability to define a problem, select information pertinent to the problem, recognize assumptions, formulate relevant hypotheses, and draw valid conclusions. Statistically significant freshman-year gains were made at all seven institutions. Once again the gains were about half a standard deviation or larger, and those students initially lowest showed the largest gains.

Lehmann (1963, 1968) conducted a study quite similar to that of Dressel and Mayhew (1954) except that he traced gains in critical thinking from freshman to senior year at a single large public university. The American Council on Education's Test of Critical Thinking Ability was administered to a sample of 1,051 freshmen upon entrance to college and again at the end of the freshman and subsequent years in college. The ACE Test of Critical Thinking Ability consists of fifty-two verbal, situational-type items designed to test the same five areas of critical thinking as the general measure of critical thinking that Dressel and Mayhew (1954) used earlier. Both men and women made statistically significant gains in critical thinking from the freshman to the senior year of approximately one standard deviation (1.02 SD for men and .93 SD for women). This translates into an improvement of about 34 percentile points during the four years of college. The greatest gain for both men and women, however, appeared to occur sometime between the beginning and end of the freshman year. The freshman-year gain alone was .67 of a standard deviation (.69 SD for men and .64 SD for women), which constituted an improvement of about 25 percentile points. Thus, of the total gain in critical thinking from freshman to senior year, about two-thirds occurred while the students were freshmen.

More recent longitudinal research on critical thinking has yielded results generally, though not totally, consistent with those of earlier investigations. Studying a single-institution sample, Mentkowski and Strait (1983) found freshman-to-senior gains on the inference, recognition, and deduction scales of the Watson-Glaser Critical Thinking Appraisal (Watson & Glaser, 1980) of .32, .19, and .33 of a standard deviation, respectively. These are somewhat smaller than those of either Dressel and Mayhew (1954) or Lehmann (1963). Mentkowski and Strait also found that only about half of this gain or less occurred in the first two years of college, a finding different from the pattern of gains shown by Lehmann (1968). Pascarella (1989), on the other hand, found a freshman-year gain of about .70 of a standard deviation on the Watson-Glaser total score and gains on the inference, recognition, and deduction scales of .27, .60, and .58 of a standard deviation, respectively. These are much closer to the magnitude of the freshman-year gains in critical thinking reported by Dressel and Mayhew (1954) and Lehmann (1963, 1968).[2]

It is also interesting to note that gains in critical thinking are not simply limited to traditional-age college students attending college full-time. Klassen (1983–1984) conducted a longitudinal study of returning adult students who completed the "Weekend Social Science Option" at a large community college. This program included courses in social science, applied statistics, and speech and required individual research on a personally selected question. Pre- and posttesting with the Watson-Glaser Critical Thinking Appraisal showed a statistically significant average gain in overall critical thinking for the sixty-seven adults in the program.

A somewhat different approach to assessing the gains in critical thinking that occur during college is found in cross-sectional investigations by Keeley, Browne, and Kreutzer (1982) and Steele (1986). Keeley, Browne, and Kreutzer administered open-ended and essay measures of critical thinking to separate cohorts of 145 freshmen and 155 seniors at a large state university. The two samples were each randomly divided in half with one half receiving general instructions and the other half receiving multiple, specific instructions for writing critical evaluations of an essay. The resultant critical essays were scored for eight separate items and total score in the specific-question condition, and for various levels of criticism in the general-question condition. Because of the cross-sectional nature of the design, analysis of covariance was employed to control statistically for freshman-senior differences in academic aptitude (ACT composite score). After statistical adjustments for differences in initial aptitude, seniors scored significantly higher than freshmen on two questions (identifying the controversy and conclusions of the essay and identifying assumptions) and on total score in the specific-question condition. In the general-question condition seniors had significantly higher aptitude-adjusted scores on six of seven criticism categories: general criticism, specific criticisms, understanding of structure, logical consistency, explicit criticism strategy, and essay length. In the specific-criticism subcategory seniors pointed out more ambiguities, logical flaws, and misuses of data than did the freshman cohort. Since Keeley, Browne, and Kreutzer report no standard deviations in their data, it is not possible to estimate the magnitude of the freshman-senior differences.

In Steele's (1986) cross-sectional study of freshmen and seniors at thirteen institutions, he also administered an assessment of reasoning skills in social, scientific, and artistic areas designed to measure traits similar to those captured by the concept of critical thinking (for example, problem solving, identification of principles, discussion of reasonable and appropriate benefits and solutions, identification of relationships). The measure was embedded in the writing and speaking tasks that were also used to assess communication skills. Steele's data show that the freshman-senior difference on the reasoning skills measure was .90 of a standard deviation favoring the seniors. This represents an improvement during college of 31 percentile points.

The use of essays to measure the development of critical thinking during college has also been employed by Winter and McClelland (1978) and Winter, McClelland, and Stewart (1981). Their sample included students drawn from an academically selective liberal arts college, a state teachers' college, and a community college. The design was cross-sectional at the teachers' college and the community college and both cross sectional and longitudinal at the liberal arts college. The measure of critical thinking was the Test of Thematic Analysis (Winter & McClelland, 1978), an essay measure of critical thinking that assesses the "ability to form and articulate complex concepts in drawing contrasts among examples and instances in the real world" (p. 9). The test presents a person with two different groups of Thematic Apperception Test stories. Subjects are then asked to formulate and describe the differences between the groups of stories in a thirty-minute essay, which is subsequently judged against nine criteria: parallel comparison, exceptions or qualifications, examples, overarching issues, redefinition, subsuming alternatives, nonparallel comparisons (for example, apples and oranges), affective reactions, and subjective reactions. (The Test of Thematic Analysis is an obvious variation on the general theme of critical thinking, yet it has enough common conceptual elements with better-known and more typical measures of critical thinking to be included in this section.)

A panel of eighty students at the selective liberal arts college showed statistically significant increases on the total Test of Thematic Analysis score between the freshman year and senior year. In the cross-sectional comparisons of separate samples of freshmen and seniors at the three institutions, seniors had significantly higher Thematic Analysis scores than freshmen at the selective liberal arts college. The freshman-senior differences at the teachers' college and the freshman-sophomore differences at the community college were in the right direction but were smaller and not statistically significant. Although no statistical control procedure was used to adjust for possible differences between the freshman and senior samples, the various background and aptitude (SAT) differences noted between freshman and senior (or sophomore) samples at the same institution were not statistically significant. Thus, it is unlikely that differences between freshman and upperclassman samples on Thematic Analysis scores (particularly at the liberal arts college) were simply the result of systematic differences in recruitment or attrition that might have produced a more academically selective upper-classman population.

Whitla (1978) also reports that seniors scored higher on the Test of Thematic Analysis than did freshmen, even when the two groups were matched on SAT scores and secondary school rank. Mentkowski and Strait (1983), however, found only marginally significant freshman-to-senior gains and no significant differences between separate cohorts of freshmen and seniors in a cross-sectional analysis. In the latter analysis the differences were nevertheless in the expected direction.

Learning New Concepts

Whitla (1978) and Winter, McClelland, and Stewart (1981) have been concerned with the development of college students' abilities to attain concepts and learn new material. In Whitla's cross-sectional study of three institutions, freshmen and seniors were given the Heidbreder Concept Learning Test (Heidbreder, 1946), which measures the extent and speed with which one learns abstract concepts. Freshman-senior differences on this measure were statistically nonsignificant. Remarkably similar cross-sectional results are reported by Winter, McClelland, and Stewart with what appears, however, to be the same sample. In addition, Winter, McClelland, and Stewart also found only small, chance freshman-to-senior gains on the Concept Learning Test in their liberal arts college sample.

Postformal Reasoning

Piagetian formal reasoning, critical thinking (as it has typically been assessed), and related measures of abstract reasoning and concept learning focus to a great extent on what a number of cognitive developmental theorists characterize as the individual's ability to solve puzzles (for example, Churchman, 1971; Kitchener, 1986). Such puzzles may come in many forms and require the application of sophisticated reasoning and information processing; yet they typically have the common trait of a verifiably correct or at least more valid answer. Although the cognitive skills involved in puzzle solving are an invaluable addition to the individual's stock of intellectual resources, they are not always those best suited to addressing the real-world problems of adults (such as poverty, alcoholism, pollution, crime). For these and similar "ill-structured" or "wicked" problems, there is likely to be conflicting or incomplete information, unspecifiable parameters, and a number of possible solutions, none of which may be verifiably correct (Kitchener, 1986; Wood, 1983). Formal rules and logic may not suffice; and tentative answers typically need to be "constructed" rather than "discovered."

A number of cognitive development theorists (for example, Arlin, 1975; Basseches, 1980, 1984; Kitchener & King, 1981; Kitchener & Kitchener, 1981; Labouvie-Vief, 1980; Perry, 1970, 1981) have argued that such adult problem solving requires cognitive capacities beyond those described by formal reasoning, information processing, or critical thinking (hence the descriptive term *postformal reasoning*). These cognitive capacities have been operationally defined in a number of ways, but perhaps the best known and most extensively studied is the reflective judgment model (King, 1977; Kitchener, 1977; Kitchener & King, 1981). This model can be thought of as a scheme to understand the development of complex reasoning and judgment skill that draws on the thinking of a number of cognitive developmental psychologists (for example, Basseches, 1980; Loevinger, 1976; Perry, 1970). In this scheme, reasoning is seen as developing along a multilevel continuum. At the lowest levels, reality is what the individual observes, and truth is what authorities say it is. Personal beliefs either exist as a given or are based on the absolute knowledge of an authority. At the highest level, personal beliefs are seen as variable approximations of an objective truth. Beliefs are justifiable to the extent that they are based on a rational process that involves appropriate forms of inquiry and use of the rules of evidence. (See Chapter Two for a fuller description of this model; see also Kitchener, 1986; Schmidt & Davison, 1981, 1983.)

Reflective judgment is measured by the Reflective Judgment Interview (RJI) (Kitchener & King, 1981). The RJI consists of four dilemmas and a set of standardized probe questions designed to tap level of reasoning. Each dilemma is defined by two contradictory points of view and represents an ill-structured problem. Subjects are asked to state and justify their points of view about the issues in each dilemma. The four dilemmas represent different content domains: science, current events, religion, and history. Because the measurement of reflective judgment requires an interview approach, most research on the topic has been limited to small samples. At the same time, there is a considerable body of research that links postsecondary education with increases in reflective judgment. Much of this research is summarized in reviews by Brabeck (1983, 1984b) and Kitchener and King (1990).

A large number of cross-sectional studies have addressed the issue of whether increases in reflective judgment are associated with amount of formal postsecondary education (Brabeck, 1983a; Glatfelter, 1982; Griffith, 1984; Hayes, 1981; King & Parker, 1978; Kitchener & King, 1981; Kitchener & Wood, 1987; Lawson, 1980; Mines, 1980; Sakalys, 1982; Schmidt, 1985; Shoff, 1979; Strange & King, 1981; Welfel, 1982). These various studies compared high school students with college students, college freshmen with college seniors or upperclassmen, and undergraduate students with master's and doctoral students. With only occasional and inconsistent exceptions (for example, Brabeck, 1983a), students at higher levels of post-secondary education had significantly higher reflective judgment scores than did students at lower levels.

The longitudinal research on reflective judgment is consistent with the cross-sectional findings. Studies by Brabeck and Wood (1983); King, Kitchener, Davison, Parker, and Wood (1983); King, Kitchener, and Wood (1985); Kitchener, King, Wood, and Davison (1985, 1989); Schmidt (1985); Polkosnik and Winston (1989); and Welfel and Davison (1983, 1986) all show statistically significant gains in reflective judgment either from the beginning to the end of the freshman year, from the freshman year to the senior year, or from the freshman to upperclassman years in college. Since not all the longitudinal studies cover the same time period during college, it is difficult to estimate the magnitude of freshman-to-senior gains in reflective judgment. Our best though tentative estimate is that traditional-age freshmen gain about one standard deviation in reflective judgment during college and advance about half a stage on the reflective judgment schema. At first glance the latter gain seems quite small and perhaps trivial. As pointed out by Kitchener and King (1990), however, the magnitude of the gain may not be as important as the fact that in college students such a gain typically reflects a qualitative shift from a style of reasoning based largely on personal beliefs to one that explicitly uses evidence in making judgments. This shift therefore represents a major prerequisite for the development of a rational approach to problem solving.

Although the reflective judgment model has been the dominant focus of inquiry, there have been other attempts to estimate how college students develop in the area broadly conceived as postformal reasoning. Baxter Magolda and Porterfield (1985) employed the Measure of Epistemological Reflection (MER), and Baxter Magolda (1987a) used both the MER and a semistructured interview to specifically assess student status on the first five positions of the Perry (1970) scheme of intellectual and ethical development. The MER is a written instrument that assesses the respondent's views in six domains of thinking related to learning and elicits specific justification for the respondent's thinking. The semistructured interview also addressed the same six domains but was somewhat more open-ended in subjects' responses and justification for their responses. In a series of three cross-sectional studies, Baxter Magolda and Porterfield found that group means generally increased on both these instruments with increasing levels of postsecondary education. Seniors were more advanced on the Perry scheme than freshmen, and graduate students were more advanced than college seniors. The freshman-senior differences were about one standard deviation in magnitude. Similar cross-sectional results have been reported by Blake (1976), Meyer (1977), and Moore (1989). The first two studies used semistructured interviews, while the third used a paper and pencil instrument called the Learning Environment Preferences to measure student position on the Perry model.

Baxter Magolda (1988) also reports the results of a longitudinal study that found statistically significant freshman-to-sophomore gains on both the MER and the semistructured interview for both men and women. The overall freshman-year gain was about one standard deviation on the MER and .60 of a standard deviation on the structured interview.

Somewhat less positive results are reported by Mentkowski and Strait (1983). They used an essay measure of development on the Perry continuum termed the Measure of Intellectual Development (MID), initially developed by Knefelkamp (1974) and Widick (1975). The MID requires the writing of three short essays that are scored according to how one construes the nature and origin of knowledge and responsibility in decision making. A cross-sectional analysis found seniors to be significantly higher than freshmen on two of the three essays. The findings of the longitudinal analysis, however, were more ambiguous. Students increased about .40 of a standard deviation from freshman to senior year on one essay but actually decreased .20 of a standard deviation on another.

Perkins and his colleagues (Perkins, 1985, 1986; Perkins, Allen, & Hafner, 1983; and Perkins, Bushey, & Faraday, 1986) have developed and operationally defined the concept of informal reasoning. Informal reasoning is not unlike reflective judgment in that it deals with reasoning about ill-structured problems for which there may be no verifiably correct answers. The emphasis in informal reasoning is the degree of sophistication that the individual demonstrates in developing the pros and cons of both sides of an issue or argument and the adequacy with which he or she supports the final conclusion reached. In measuring informal reasoning an individual is asked to give oral or written arguments on controversial issues (for example, the military draft, a nuclear freeze, a ban on handguns). These arguments are then judged along a number of criteria (for example, overall quality of argument, lines of argument for or against own personal view, strength with which conclusions are supported).

In a cross-sectional investigation of sex-balanced groups of secondary school, undergraduate, and graduate students, Perkins (1985) found that level of informal reasoning tended to increase significantly with formal education. He also found that college seniors supported their conclusions significantly better than college freshmen did. In a related longitudinal investigation of a liberal arts college sample, Perkins, Bushey, and Farady (1986) found statistically significant freshman-year gains on three dimensions of informal reasoning: number of lines of argument supporting the subject's stance on the issue, number of lines of argument supporting both sides of the issue, and the quality with which the individual's own stance on the issue was elaborated and supported in his or her argument.

The capacity for seeing more than one side of a controversial issue has also been the focus of Winter, McClelland, and Stewart (1981) and Mentkowski and Strait (1983). To measure this capacity, both groups used the Analysis of Argument (AOA) (A. Stewart, 1977). This instrument measures relativism of judgment or commitment to one position on an issue while understanding diverse views. Respondents are asked to attack and defend a complex and controversial issue on which they may have a view, such as birth control. Separate scores are given for the quality of the individual's arguments both against the issue (attack) and for the issue (defense). In their three-institution study, Winter, McClelland, and Stewart found statistically significant cross-sectional differences favoring seniors over freshmen on both the attack and defense scores of the AOA at all institutions. Moreover, in their longitudinal study of a single liberal arts college, they found statistically significant freshman-to-senior gains on both scores of the AOA.

The findings of Mentkowski and Strait (1983) are not totally consistent with those of Winter, McClelland, and Stewart (1981). In their cross-sectional analysis, seniors were significantly higher then freshmen only on the defense score of the AOA. Scores on the attack score were in the right direction, but the difference was small and statistically nonsignificant. No overall statistically significant differences were found in freshman-to-senior gains in the longitudinal analysis. Scores on the defense scale changed in the right direction, but scores on the attack scale were counter to expectations, though the difference was not a statistically significant one.

Conceptual Complexity

A final dimension of cognitive development that does not fit neatly into any of the above categories (though it is perhaps assumed by each) is that of conceptual complexity. Conceptual complexity is the extent to which a person is capable of attending to a large variety of cognitive stimuli and organizing his or her dealings with the external environment in increasingly abstract, complex, and varied ways (Harvey, Hunt, & Schroder, 1961). Individuals with a high level of conceptual complexity can generate their own criteria for organizing and evaluating their dichotomous distinctions, they can view more subtle relationships between elements in their environment, and they can synthesize these elements more fully (Khalili & Hood, 1983, p. 389). In short, they can deal more proficiently and abstractly with increasing complexity.

Both cross-sectional evidence and longitudinal evidence suggest that students make statistically significant gains in conceptual complexity during college. In a cross-sectional study at two institutions, P. Meyer (1977) administered an early version of the Paragraph Completion Method (PCM) (Hunt, 1971; Hunt, Butler, Noy, & Rosse, 1978) to individual cohorts of freshmen and seniors at two colleges. The PCM is a semiprojective measure designed to test conceptual level by having subjects complete sentence stems. The responses are scored according to a protocol scheme by independent judges, whose average ratings yield a conceptual level. Meyer found that at both institutions seniors had significantly higher conceptual levels than did freshmen.

Similar findings are presented in a longitudinal investigation by Khalili and Hood (1983). They administered the PCM to separate panels of students at the beginning and end of the freshman year and again at the end of the senior year. A statistically significant freshman-to-senior gain in conceptual complexity of approximately 1.33 of a standard deviation was reported. However, about half of this gain (.72 SD) occurred during the freshman year.

Net Effects Of College

It is quite clear from the weight of evidence presented in the preceding section that students make statistically significant and, in some cases, substantial gains during college on a number of dimensions of general cognitive capabilities and skills. As indicated in Chapter Three, however, finding that such gains are coincident with college attendance is not the equivalent of being able to causally attribute them to college attendance. Cross-sectional designs that compare freshmen with seniors confound the effects of college with differential recruitment standards, the attrition of less academically competent students between the freshman year and senior year, the addition of new students via transfer, and maturation or chronological age (that is, the fact that seniors are typically older than freshmen). Longitudinal studies without a control group confound the effects of college with those of regression artifacts and maturation. The confounding effects of maturation are particularly troublesome in that growth in many dimensions of cognitive skills that appear to change during college is thought to be developmentally based. Consequently, one would expect certain gains to occur simply through the normal maturation that accompanies an individual's growing older. Attempts to estimate the net effect of college on general cognitive skills need to develop some reasonable controls for these various confounding influences and in particular, we believe, the effects of maturation.

Communication Skills

In Steele's (1986) multi-institution, cross-sectional study of freshman-senior differences in speaking and writing skills, he conducted a series of additional analyses to determine whether the differences found were simply the result of differential aptitude or age. With freshmen and seniors matched on aptitude (that is, ACT scores), there were still statistically significant differences in speaking and writing skills favoring the seniors of about two-thirds and one-half of a standard deviation, respectively. Thus, the freshman-senior differences in communication skills did not appear to be simply a function of differential aptitude. This is consistent with the findings of Whitla (1978), who reported statistically significant differences in writing skill for freshmen and seniors matched on academic aptitude and secondary school rank in class.

In order to estimate the confounding effects of age, Steele divided seniors into three age ranges (twenty through twenty-two, twenty-three through thirty, and over thirty). There were only trivial and inconsistent differences among the three groups in speaking and writing skills, and the magnitude of these differences was not nearly as large as the freshman-senior differences. Though one might wish that Steele had made the same kind of comparison among freshmen or between freshmen and seniors in the same age range, this evidence nevertheless suggests that effects due to maturation are substantially less than effects due to degree of exposure to college.

General Intellectual and Analytical Skills

We uncovered one study that sought to determine the net effects of community college attendance on general intellectual and analytical skills. Capoor and Gelfman (1988) conducted a cross-sectional investigation that compared the general intellectual development of entering freshmen and graduating sophomores at seven community colleges. General intellectual development was assessed with the ACT College Outcomes Measures Program (COMP) (Forrest, 1982). The COMP, as a total measure, is designed to assess general intellectual and analytical skills that are presumed to be necessary for the individual to function and adapt in a complex society. Included are such areas as communication, reasoning and solving problems, functioning within social institutions, and using science and technology. Capoor and Gelfman matched 250 pairs of freshmen and sophomores on such factors as sex, age, curriculum, and precollege verbal and mathematical abilities. Within each category of matching, graduating sophomores were found to have significantly higher total COMP scores than freshmen. Unfortunately, group standard deviations were not presented in the results, so it is difficult to estimate the magnitude of freshman-sophomore differences.

Piagetian Formal Operational Reasoning

Little research has directly addressed the net influence of college on Piagetian formal reasoning. Mentkowski and Strait (1983) found that when differences in secondary school academic achievement were controlled statistically, differences found between separate cohorts of freshmen and seniors on a measure of formal reasoning became statistically nonsignificant.

Critical Thinking

The weight of evidence clearly supports the notion that college has a net positive influence on the development of critical thinking. Of the five studies we located that directly address the issue, four suggest that freshman-senior differences on various measures of critical thinking are not simply the result of differential academic ability or maturation effects.

Whitla (1978) matched separate cohorts of freshmen and seniors on academic aptitude and secondary school rank in class and found that seniors still had significantly higher scores on the Test of Thematic Analysis than did freshmen. Net of aptitude and prior achievement, seniors were more adept than freshmen in mounting effective and logical arguments. Similarly, Keeley, Browne, and Kreutzer (1982) found that seniors scored significantly higher than freshmen on an essay measure of critical thinking, even when differences in academic aptitude were controlled statistically.

Although the Whitla (1978) and Keeley, Browne, and Kreutzer (1982) studies suggest that freshman-senior differences in critical thinking cannot be explained by differential academic ability, they did not address the confounding influence of age or maturation. More recent studies by Steele (1986) and Pascarella (1989), however, did attempt to control for age, or at least take it into account, in estimating the net effect of college on critical thinking. In a cross-sectional analysis, Steele found that when freshmen and seniors were matched on academic aptitude, seniors still had significantly higher COMP reasoning scores than did freshmen. He also divided seniors into three age-groups (twenty through twenty-two, twenty-three through thirty, and over thirty) and found that the largest difference among age-groups in reasoning skills was less than a tenth of the difference found between freshmen and seniors on reasoning skills.

Pascarella (1989) conducted a longitudinal quasi-experiment in which he matched samples of secondary school seniors who attended and did not attend college on senior-year Watson-Glaser Critical Thinking Appraisal total score, academic aptitude, and family socioeconomic status. He then followed the samples for the entire academic year subsequent to their secondary school graduation. At the end of this period he readministered the Critical Thinking Appraisal to those who attended college full-time and those who did not attend college at all. (The individuals who enrolled in college full-time after graduation from secondary school attended eighteen different institutions throughout the country.) Statistically controlling for secondary school critical thinking scores, secondary school grades, academic aptitude, socioeconomic status, and initial educational aspirations, Pascarella found that the students with one year of college had significantly higher Critical Thinking Appraisal total scores at the second testing than did those not attending college. The net difference due to the first year of college attendance was .44 of a standard deviation, which translates into an advantage of 17 percentile points. Interestingly, this is only slightly smaller in magnitude than the simple (unadjusted) freshman-year critical thinking gains of .50 of a standard deviation reported in the multi-institution study of Dressel and Mayhew (1954).

Pascarella (1989) also found that the net effect of the first year of college on critical thinking was selective. Statistically controlling for the same variables (and substituting subscale for total score), he ascertained that the college group had significantly higher scores on the interpretation and evaluation of arguments subscales of the Critical Thinking Appraisal. These subscales measure the individual's ability to weigh evidence, determine the validity of data-based generalizations or conclusions, and distinguish between strong and weak arguments. The estimated net effect of the first year of college on the inference, recognition, and deduction subscales of the Critical Thinking Appraisal, however, was statistically nonsignificant. These scales measure the ability to discriminate the truth or falsity of inferences, recognize assumptions, and determine whether stated conclusions follow from the information provided.

Mentkowski and Strait (1983) report the only study uncovered that failed to support the notion of a significant net effect of college on critical thinking. When they statistically controlled for differences in secondary school academic achievement, cross-sectional freshman-senior differences on the inference, recognition, and deduction scales of the Watson-Glaser Critical Thinking Appraisal became statistically nonsignificant. These findings correspond closely with those of Pascarella (1989). Unfortunately, Mentkowski and Strait did not examine the Critical Thinking Appraisal total score or the interpretation and evaluation of arguments subscales, measures on which Pascarella did find evidence of a net positive effect attributable to college attendance. Consequently, their investigation cannot provide additional confirmatory evidence for a selective effect of college on critical thinking.

Postformal Reasoning

A considerable amount of research on Kitchener and King's (1981) reflective judgment model has been concerned with separating the effects of formal education from those of other factors such as age or academic ability. Evidence presented by Shoff (1979), Strange (1978), and Strange and King (1981) tends to support the contention that growth in reflective judgment is more closely related to amount of postsecondary education than to increasing age. Shoff (1979), as reviewed by Kitchener and King (1990), compared senior college students with two groups of adult students entering college for the first time. The college seniors were found to have significantly higher reflective judgment scores than either adult freshmen who were the same age or those who were ten or more years older.

Strange (1978) and Strange and King (1981) used a sex-balanced cross-sectional design with sixty-four liberal arts college students in four groups: sixteen traditional-age freshmen (age eighteen), sixteen nontraditional-age freshmen (age twenty-two), sixteen traditional-age seniors (age twenty-two), and sixteen nontraditional-age seniors (age twenty-six). For both the traditional and nontraditional age-groups, seniors had significantly higher reflective judgment scores than did freshmen. Conversely, students who were four years apart in age but who were in the same college class (freshmen or seniors) did not differ significantly in reflective judgment scores.

More recent research by Glatfelter (1982) and Schmidt (1985) has been less clear in indicating that formal education level is more important than maturation in influencing the development of reflective judgment. Glatfelter, for example, found a statistically significant education effect for traditional-age students but not for older women students. Schmidt combined a cross-sectional and longitudinal design that had three groups: traditional-age freshmen (age eighteen), traditional-age juniors (age twenty-one), and nontraditional-age freshmen (age twenty-one). All three groups were matched on verbal aptitude. When pooled, both freshman groups made statistically significant gains in reflective judgment through their junior year. However, in the cross-sectional analysis, nontraditional-age freshmen did not differ significantly in reflective judgment from either the traditional-age freshmen or juniors. Schmidt concludes that the findings suggest that both age and education affect the development of reflective judgment.

In an attempt to draw firmer conclusions about the relative roles of age and education in the development of reflective judgment, Kitchener and King (1990) averaged the mean reflective judgment scores for older, nontraditional-age first-year college students across the studies reviewed above. They then compared this average with the means of traditional-age freshmen and traditional-age seniors taken from fourteen studies of reflective judgment. While the means of the traditional and nontraditional/older freshmen were almost the same (3.57 and 3.60, respectively), they were substantially lower than those of seniors (3.99). Thus, older adults returning to school had levels of reflective judgment quite consistent with traditional-age entering freshmen and substantially lower than those of seniors. Overall, this suggests that college may have a greater effect on the development of reflective judgment than does maturation.

Other research has attempted to determine whether freshman-senior differences in reflective judgment are the result of differential aptitude or ability between the two groups. Most of these studies have controlled for such differences through matching or statistical means. The weight of evidence from this body of research suggests that freshman-senior differences in reflective judgment are reduced, but cannot be totally explained away, by verbal ability or fluency (Kitchener, 1977; Kitchener & King, 1981; King, Kitchener, Davison, Parker, & Wood, 1983), by academic aptitude or socioeconomic status (King, Taylor, & Ottinger, 1989), by academic achievement (Welfel, 1982; King, Taylor, & Ottinger, 1989), or by level of Piagetian formal reasoning (King, 1977).

Perhaps the most convincing evidence of the effect of college on the development of reflective judgment comes from a longitudinal study conducted by Kitchener, King, Wood, and Davison (1985, 1989). In this study, two groups of subjects of the same age—one group who attended and one who did not attend college—were matched on academic aptitude. While those individuals who did not attend college showed some increase in reflective judgment, those who earned a bachelor's degree showed significantly greater gains.

The influence of college on measures of postformal reasoning other than reflective judgment has been the focus of research by Whitla (1978), Perkins (1985), and Parker and Thorndike (1989). Whitla matched separate cohorts of freshmen and seniors at three institutions on academic aptitude and secondary school achievement. With those two variables held constant, seniors at all three institutions had significantly higher scores than freshmen on the Analysis of Argument Test. These differences could still be confounded by age, however.

In an effort to control for maturation as well as ability, Perkins (1985) developed a series of regression equations in which the various dimensions of informal reasoning were regressed on individual intelligence, age, and number of years of formal education (from secondary school through graduate school). With age and intelligence controlled statistically, years of formal education had statistically significant positive associations with four dimensions of informal reasoning: overall quality of argument, number of sentences of argument, number of lines of argument, and number of objections raised by the individual to his or her own position. Thus, net of age and intelligence, amount of formal education was positively associated with the overall quality and complexity with which one developed and supported arguments about controversial issues.

Parker and Thorndike (1989) present some of the only evidence that fails to support the hypothesis that college has a net positive impact on postformal reasoning. While they found that upperclassmen (juniors and seniors) at a single institution had generally higher scores on the Measure of Epistemological Reasoning than lowerclassmen (freshmen and sophomores), the differences became small and statistically nonsignificant when age was held constant statistically.

Between-College Effects

In Chapter Three we saw that a focused series of studies has systematically addressed the question of differences among institutions (and institutional characteristics) in their influence on student learning. Most of these studies were similar and quite sophisticated in design and yielded notably consistent findings. In contrast, the evidence concerning differences among colleges in effects on general cognitive skills is limited and lacks this coherent focus and methodological rigor. Indeed, in order to draw conclusions one must be willing to rely on indirect as well as direct evidence. Much of the indirect evidence comes from research on instructional practices at different types of institutions. The underlying assumption here is that differences in the extent to which instructional practices elicit higher-level cognitive processes on the part of students will lead to differences in the development of general cognitive skills.

Instructional Practices

Coordinated studies by Barnes (1980, 1983) and Fischer and Grant (1983) sought to assess the cognitive level of instruction carried out in classes at four different institutions. The sample was 155 class sections of forty randomly selected professors at two public and two private undergraduate institutions. Attempts were made to obtain an even distribution of beginning and advanced courses in all disciplines across each institution. The classes were audiotaped and then scored according to the cognitive level of instruction (for example, questioning, verbal exchanges between professors and students) that occurred. Overall cognitive level was categorized according to Bloom's taxonomy of educational objectives (Bloom, Englehart, Furst, Hill, & Krathwohl, 1956). The cognitive processes required were, in ascending order of complexity, knowledge or recall, comprehension, application, analysis, synthesis, and evaluation. The only institutional factor found to be related to cognitive level of instruction was institutional size. Classrooms in the larger colleges (independent of private or public control) provided significantly greater opportunity for students to apply higher-order cognitive processes to subject matter than did corresponding classrooms in the smaller colleges. Unfortunately, no controls appear to have been made for differential student aptitude across institutions in the sample. Consequently, it is difficult to tell whether cognitive level differences in classrooms are really a function of institutional size or differential student body selectivity (Hegarty, 1978).

College Selectivity

The issue of college selectivity has been dealt with more directly in a creative study by Braxton and Nordvall (1985). They attempted to determine the cognitive level of instruction at liberal arts colleges of different levels of student body selectivity by analyzing the cognitive content of final examinations. Analyses were made of forty-three course final examinations from twenty-two selective liberal arts colleges and forty examinations from thirty less selective liberal arts colleges. (Selectivity was based on the Carnegie Classification of liberal arts colleges.) Examination questions were coded by independent judges according to the levels of the Bloom taxonomy. Controlling for the academic discipline of the course, class level (introductory or advanced), and intent of course (for majors or nonmajors), Braxton and Nordvall found that exams at selective (versus less selective) liberal arts colleges asked a significantly lower percentage of knowledge (recall) questions and a significantly higher percentage of critical thinking questions (that is, a combination of analysis and synthesis levels). The differences between both percentages were about half a standard deviation in magnitude.

Braxton and Nordvall (1985) conclude from their findings that examination questions given at more selective liberal arts colleges tend to demand higher-order levels of understanding and cognitive processing than do those given at less selective liberal arts colleges. The latter tend to stress content recall over those processes typically associated with critical thinking. One would assume that such differences in the cognitive level of examination would indicate similar differences in the cognitive level of instruction received at selective and less selective colleges. Given Braxton and Nordvall's research design, however, this can only be inferred indirectly. It is unclear from their findings whether the differences in examinations do in fact represent actual differences in the cognitive level of instruction received at colleges of different selectivity. An alternative explanation is that the cognitive level of instruction at selective and less selective colleges is essentially the same. Professors at selective colleges, however, ask a larger number of high-level cognitive processing questions on their exams because they perceive that the students in their institution are generally capable of handling such questions.

Regardless of whether Braxton and Nordvall's (1985) findings represent the effect of differential instructional environments that are associated with student body aptitude or simply professorial perceptions of student capabilities, the hypothesis that selective institutions enhance the development of general cognitive skills has been the focus of a small body of research. Recall from the first section of this chapter that Winter, McClelland, and Stewart (1981) found that seniors at a small, highly selective liberal arts college (average SAT score of 600 or higher) had significantly higher scores on the Test of Thematic Analysis (an essay measure of critical thinking) than did freshmen. The same cross-sectional comparison at a less selective state teachers' college (average SAT score of high 400s) showed much smaller differences, which were not statistically significant. Similarly, while seniors at both institutions had significantly higher scores than freshmen on the Analysis of Argument Test (an essay measure of intellectual flexibility in analysis), the magnitude of the freshman-senior difference was significantly greater at the selective liberal arts college than at the state teachers' college.

Since freshmen at the selective liberal arts college had somewhat higher scores on both measures, it would be hazardous to attribute these variations in cross-sectional freshman-senior differences to institutional effects. Uncontrolled recruitment and attrition influences may confound the results. At the same time, however, additional findings consistent with those of Winter, McClelland, and Stewart have been reported by Pace (1984). Recall from Chapter Three that Pace (1984) focused on the quality of student effort during college along different dimensions (for example, classroom, courses, libraries, cultural facilities, clubs) and its relationship to student-reported gains in a number of areas. In further analyses of student effort in this sample of nineteen diverse colleges, he found that small and highly selective liberal arts colleges, as compared to all other institutions, had significantly higher scores not only on many of the quality of effort scales but also on student self-reported gains on an intellectual skills scale (for example, ability to think analytically and logically). Quite similar results have recently been reported by Pace (1990) in an analysis of seventy-four diverse colleges and universities. Thus, if small, selective liberal arts colleges produce greater growth in general cognitive development, they may do so, in part at least, by fostering higher levels of involvement and effort in the academic and social life of the institution.

The finding that students from selective liberal arts colleges report greater gains in intellectual skills than those from other institutions is consistent with earlier findings of surveys of upperclassmen in a national sample of colleges and universities (Pace, 1974). A slightly higher percentage of upperclassmen at selective institutions than at less selective ones indicated that they had received "very much" or "quite a bit of" benefit from college in terms of critical thinking. The average was 75 percent at selective liberal arts colleges. This compared to a baseline of 72 percent at all institutions.

Somewhat less convincing evidence concerning the influence of institutional selectivity on general cognitive skills is reported by Pascarella (1989). In his quasi-experimental study estimating the net effects of the first year of college on critical thinking, he collected considerable information on the college attended and the student's freshman-year experience. The college subjects in this study attended eighteen different colleges throughout the country differing in average student body selectivity from an ACT of 17 to 29. Statistically controlling for secondary school level of critical thinking (Watson-Glaser Critical Thinking Appraisal), academic aptitude, secondary school grades, socioeconomic status, and educational aspirations, Pascarella found that the partial correlations between institutional selectivity and critical thinking at the end of the freshman year were statistically nonsignificant and trivial in magnitude—ranging from .10 to -.08 for CTA total and subscale scores. Thus, when important precollege characteristics were held constant, there was no statistically significant relationship between college selectivity and the development of critical thinking.

Curricular Emphasis

Another approach to investigating the effects of different colleges on general cognitive development has been to focus on curricular emphasis. In extensive, multi-institution analyses of critical thinking, Dressel and Mayhew (1954) found statistically significant freshman-year gains in a global measure of critical thinking at seven colleges. The greatest gains, however, were found at those colleges with courses specifically organized for general education purposes and with definite core requirements (for all students) involving the completion of all or a major portion of these courses in the freshman year. (General education curricula tend to involve the study of basic liberal arts and sciences in an integrative fashion. The purpose is to foster the integration and synthesis of knowledge rather than learning discrete bits of specialized information. Emphasis is therefore placed on the development of more general intellectual skills and orientations such as analytical and critical skills and tolerance for ambiguity [Gaff, 1983].)

Similar findings have been reported by Forrest (1982), who used the total score of the ACT COMP. Recall that the COMP, as a total measure, is designed to assess general intellectual and analytical skills that are presumed to be necessary for the individual to function and adapt in a complex society. The COMP was taken by samples of seniors (or sophomores at two-year institutions) at forty-four colleges and universities. Forrest then used the correlation between ACT score and COMP score to derive an estimated freshman COMP score. The difference between the estimated freshman COMP score and the actual senior COMP score was an estimated gain score. Structural and curricular differences among the forty-four institutions were then analyzed in relationship to the estimated COMP gain.

A major feature that distinguished institutions with large versus small estimated COMP gain scores was the degree of balanced curricular emphasis on general education. For example, a group of eight institutions devoting an average of 46 percent of the required curriculum to general education with even content distribution in four areas (written and oral communication, social science and history, science and mathematics, and fine arts and humanities) had gain scores twice as large as a group of nine institutions devoting only 31 percent of their curriculum to general education and with uneven distribution. There were no systematic differences between the two groups of institutions on student body ACT or SAT scores. Forrest also found that typical measures of institutional "quality" were largely unrelated to estimated COMP gains. Thirteen institutions highest in financial expenditures per student and student body selectivity (based on ACT or SAT scores) did not differ in estimated COMP gains from eighteen institutions lowest on these two traits.

There are nontrivial methodological problems with both Dressel and Mayhew's (1954) and Forrest's (1982) studies. In the former, it is possible that some of the institutional differences in critical thinking gains were confounded by regression effects (that is, initially lower scoring institutions exhibiting the largest changes). In the latter investigation, there is some disagreement about the reliability and meaning of estimated gain scores based on the COMP (Banta, Lambert, Pike, Schmidhammer, & Schneider, 1987; J. Steele, 1989). Despite such problems, these studies are potentially important in that they suggest the possibility that an institution's curricular emphasis influences the development of general cognitive skills.

College Social Structure

Other research had been concerned with the extent to which an institution's social structure might influence the development of cognitive skills. In addition to their three-institution study, Winter, McClelland, and Stewart (1981) also studied seven additional institutions to determine the correlates of cross-sectional freshman-senior differences on the Test of Thematic Analysis. The researchers found a statistically significant negative correlation between the magnitude of such differences and both the percentage of students on campus belonging to fraternities or sororities and the percentage of students living in dormitories or fraternity or sorority houses. Winter, McClelland, and Stewart interpret this as indicating that the "collegiate" aspects of college may function to retard some aspects of cognitive development. The cross-sectional nature of their data, however, and the apparent absence of controls for freshman-senior differences in confounding variables (for example, academic aptitude) make this conclusion tenuous.

College Racial Composition

Yet another investigation of the effects of different colleges on general cognitive skills is that conducted by Fleming (1982, 1984). The focus of her study was the influence of college racial composition on the intellectual development of black students. A cross-sectional design compared separate cohorts of black freshmen and seniors at a predominantly black and a predominantly white institution, both located in the Southwest. The groups were compared on three measures of general cognitive development: the Test of Concept Formation (a measure of the ability to formulate concepts), the Test of Thematic Analysis (a written measure of critical thinking), and the Analysis of Argument (a measure of intellectual flexibility). In an analytical design that statistically controlled for group differences on socioeconomic status and SAT scores, Fleming found generally greater freshman-senior differences on the cognitive development measures at the predominantly black institution than at the predominantly white one. At the black institution seniors had significantly higher scores than freshmen on the Test of Concept Formation and the Test of Thematic Analysis. There were no statistically significant overall freshman-senior differences at the white institution on any of the three measures.

Within-College Effects

Research on individual experiences during college that enhance the development of general cognitive skills is similar in emphasis to the body of evidence concerned with influences on knowledge acquisition. Consequently, in synthesizing the evidence we will use the same general organizational structure used in Chapter Three (that is, the categories of teaching/ learning context, instructional approaches, teacher behavior, and student involvement).

Teaching/Learning Context

Several of the general cognitive skills we have considered in this chapter emphasize scientific reasoning (for example, Piagetian formal operational reasoning and some dimensions of critical thinking). It thus seems reasonable that scholars would be interested in whether majoring in the sciences or related fields of concentration enhances cognitive development more than majoring in other areas. The findings of this research are mixed. Cross-sectional studies of Piagetian reasoning or problem solving by Enwieme (1976), Maier and Casselman (1971), and White and Ferstenberg (1978) suggest that science majors are more likely to be formal reasoners than those majoring in nonscience fields. However, no statistically significant differences between science and nonscience majors were found in similar cross-sectional studies by Dunlop and Fazio (1976) and Fuqua (1983).

One possible explanation for these equivocal findings is that a student's major may influence formal reasoning selectively, with the strongest impact being in content areas most consistent with the major. DeLisi and Staudt (1980) administered three formal reasoning tasks to students in three different majors: physics, political science, and English. The tasks consisted of a pendulum problem, a political socialization concepts task, and a literary analysis task and were designed to correspond in content to the physics, political science, and English majors, respectively. The analysis found no total score difference in formal reasoning by major, but students were significantly more likely to perform at the level of formal operations on the tasks related to their own academic area than on tasks outside their area. For example, on the pendulum problem, 90 percent of the physics majors performed at the formal operations level versus 60 percent of the political science majors and 40 percent of the English majors. In contrast, 90 percent of the English majors performed at the formal operations level on the literary analysis task versus 40 percent of the physics majors and 40 percent of the political science majors.

There are, of course, important methodological problems with the cross-sectional evidence reviewed above. Most important, perhaps, is the difficulty in separating the actual effects of majoring in a particular area from the effects of differences in the individual characteristics of students initially selecting various majors. Watson (1984) addressed this problem in a longitudinal study that traced the development of formal reasoning for small samples of science and humanities majors from the freshman to the senior year. The measure of formal operations used during the freshman year and senior year was a combination of the chemical combinations task and the inclined plane task. Scores of the science and humanities groups were quite similar in the freshman year, but the science group had significantly higher scores than the humanities group in the senior year. These findings indicate greater development in formal reasoning by science majors than by nonscience majors. However, the tasks used to measure formal operational reason were taken from the science domain. Consequently, these results do not necessarily conflict with those of DeLisi and Staudt (1980); indeed, they should be expected given the latters' finding that major has its strongest impact on formal reasoning in content areas consistent with the major.

A small body of research has also been concerned with the influence of academic major or concentration on critical thinking. Simon and Ward (1974), for example, tested the performance of a sample of senior students on the Watson-Glaser Critical Thinking Appraisal (CTA). They found no statistically significant difference between science and nonscience majors on CTA total score or on four of the five subscores. Only on the inference scale did one group, science majors, score significantly higher than the other. Similar results have been reported by Bietter (1970–1971) and more recently by Pascarella (1989) in a longitudinal study of the freshman year. Controlling for initial Watson-Glaser CTA score, as well as aptitude, Pascarella found only trivial and statistically nonsignificant associations between number of science and logic courses taken during the freshman year and either CTA total or subscale scores at the end of the freshman year.

Some studies, such as Burns (1974), Bennett (1975–1976), and, King, Wood, and Mines (1990), have uncovered differences among students in different academic majors on the Watson-Glaser CTA and other measures of critical thinking. However, when initial student academic aptitude is controlled statistically (a secondary analysis possible from the descriptive statistics provided by King, Wood, and Mines), the link between academic major and critical thinking tends to become small and statistically nonsignificant. Thus, we are disposed to conclude that differences in critical thinking found among seniors or other upperclassmen in different academic concentrations in these studies may be more attributable to recruitment than to socialization. Consistent with this conclusion, Donald and Bateman (1989) found no statistically significant differences among science, social science, and commerce majors in gains on the Watson-Glaser CTA during the first two years of college.

As suggested by McMillan (1987), the Watson-Glaser CTA is a very general, broad-based measure of critical thinking that may not be sufficiently domain specific to capture the influence of academic major or academic concentration. More domain-specific measures of critical thinking, however, have shown a sensitivity to a student's academic experience. Most of this evidence is reported by Dressel and Mayhew (1954) in their study of increases in critical thinking during the first year of college. When academic aptitude and pretest scores were controlled statistically, amount of exposure to science courses within specific institutions was found to be significantly and positively associated with freshman-year gains in a critical thinking measure based on science content (the Test of Science Reasoning and Understanding). Similarly, amount of exposure to humanities courses (music, literature, art) was significantly and positively associated with freshman-year gains in a critical thinking measure based on humanities content (the Test of Critical Judgement in the Humanities).

Similar results have been reported by Pike and Phillippi (1988) in an analysis of the influence of course work patterns on subscale scores of the COMP. Net of entering ability, motivation, and age, seniors whose course work was strongly oriented toward the humanities tended to have the highest scores on a scale measuring use of the arts, those with course work based strongly on mathematics and science courses had the highest scores on a scale measuring use of science and technology, and those with course work that emphasized either the humanities or social sciences had the highest scores on a scale measuring functioning within social institutions. Similar, if not totally consistent, results are also reported by Pike and Banta (1989) for an independent sample and by Pike (1989) for a comprehensive multi-year sample of college seniors from a single university.

Finally, a small amount of research has focused on the influence of academic major on level of development in postformal reasoning, specifically, reflective judgment. Here both cross-sectional evidence and longitudinal evidence suggest that differences in reflective judgment have little to do with one's undergraduate academic major or area of concentration (King & Parker, 1978; King, Wood, & Mines, 1990; Schmidt, 1983; Welfel, 1982; Welfel & Davison, 1986).

Instructional Approaches

Though not as extensive as the research on subject matter learning, a considerable body of evidence focuses on the effects of different instructional or curricular approaches on the development of general cognitive skills. Consistent with previous sections of this chapter, our synthesis of this evidence is organized according to category of cognitive skill.

Communication Skills. Trank and Steele (1983) sought to determine whether a one-semester course in rhetoric would influence the development of students' speaking and writing skills. Students were given pre- and posttests with alternate forms of the ACT COMP speech and writing tests. There was a statistically significant improvement in total score, but the effect was somewhat stronger in speaking than in writing. Trank and Steele also noted that the students who initially scored lowest showed the greatest gain. In the absence of a control group, however, it is difficult to determine whether this is a differential course effect or simply the result of regression artifacts.

Piagetian Formal Reasoning. A considerable body of inquiry has focused on the effectiveness of instructional interventions designed to increase students' formal reasoning. In our synthesis of this evidence we found one particular approach, termed *inquiry* or *learning cycle* (Karplus, 1974), to have the most consistently positive effects. The purpose of the learning cycle–inquiry approach is to move students from concrete to formal reasoning. It does this essentially by making the learning process highly inductive, or concrete, in nature. Concepts are taught in three stages: (1) exploration—students participate in an activity or laboratory with concrete materials (for example, collect data or conduct an experiment); (2) invention—students draw together ideas and/or concepts out of the concrete activities; and (3) discovery—students generalize or apply the concept (Lawson & Snitgen, 1982). For example, one might introduce the general concept of protective coloration in biology by first throwing equal numbers of red, yellow, blue, white, and green toothpicks on the grass and then seeing which color is least likely to be found.

A number of experimental and quasi-experimental studies (based largely on science content) have compared the effects of the learning cycle–inquiry approach on formal reasoning with that of the more traditional lecture/discussion approach. With the exception of Blake and Nordland (1978) and McMeen (1983), the weight of evidence indicates that the learning cycle–inquiry approach is the more effective in enhancing students' transition from concrete to formal reasoning (Baker, 1978; Campbell, 1978; Killian & Warrick, 1980; Lawson & Snitgen, 1982; McKinnon & Renner,

1971; Mele, 1978; Renner & Lawson, 1975; Renner & Paske, 1977). Although lack of complete data (for example, standard deviations) in some studies makes it difficult to determine the size of the advantage in formal reasoning due to the learning cycle–inquiry approach, our best estimate from available data is that it is about .25 of a standard deviation. This translates to an advantage of about 10 percentile points. We also found little to suggest differences in the quality of the research design between those studies that found the learning cycle–inquiry approach the more effective and those studies that did not.[3]

The learning cycle–inquiry approach was expanded into an entire freshman-year curriculum at a large state university. The purpose of this experimental curriculum (Accent on Developing Abstract Processes of Thought, or ADAPT) was to assist students in moving from concrete to formal (abstract) reasoning (Tomlinson-Keasey & Eisert, 1978a). The ADAPT program combined six disciplines (anthropology, economics, English, history, mathematics, and physics). In each discipline area, courses were taught in an inductive manner consistent with the learning cycle–inquiry approach. An additional aspect of the ADAPT program was that all freshmen enrolled in it formed a social cluster that took classes together and had close contact with peers and professors.

In order to estimate the net impact of the ADAPT curriculum on general cognitive skills, Tomlinson-Keasey and Eisert (1978a) and Tomlinson-Keasey, Williams, and Eisert (1978) conducted a quasi-experiment. The control group included freshman students who had applied to the ADAPT program but were not in the final group of participants. The two groups did not differ significantly in ACT scores or secondary school class percentile rank. Both the ADAPT and control students made statistically significant freshman-year gains on a measure of Piagetian formal reasoning, but the gains of the former were significantly greater. These results were generally replicated in a second-year evaluation of the program (Tomlinson-Keasey & Eisert, 1978b). However, in this instance the APAPT students were initially much lower in formal reasoning than the control students. Thus, the significantly greater gains for the ADAPT group may have been the result of regression to the mean.

Critical Thinking. A substantial amount of research has been concerned with the influence of specific instructional or curricular interventions on critical thinking.[4] Much of this research has been reviewed in a synthesis by McMillan (1987). Of the twenty-seven studies McMillan reviewed, thirteen focused on the influence of specific instructional variables, and seven focused on the effect of courses. Only two of the studies used true experimental designs (random assignment of subjects to treatments); the rest were either pretest-posttest nonequivalent control group quasi-experiments or simple pre-post designs without a control group. The primary (though not exclusive) criterion measure used was the Watson-Glaser Critical Thinking Appraisal, a very broad-based, general measure of critical thinking that is not tied to academic content. In terms of specific instructional variables, six studies found no statistically significant differences, three reported mixed findings, and four found statistically significant differences favoring a particular instructional variable. However, no single instructional variable was found consistently to enhance critical thinking. Similarly, in terms of course interventions, three studies found no significant effects, three found mixed effects, and only one found significant effects.

One conclusion that can be drawn from the McMillan (1987) review is that specific instructional and course interventions have little consistent impact on the development of critical thinking. The major reason for this may be that a one-quarter or one-semester instructional experience is simply too brief and isolated to have a discernible impact on a general cognitive skill such as critical thinking. This may be particularly true as the instrument of choice for assessing critical thinking in these studies is the Watson-Glaser CTA, a measure that is oriented toward critical thinking in everyday matters rather than in academic matters.

The McMillan (1987) synthesis takes a box score approach (that is, number of studies showing significant results, number showing mixed results, and number showing no significant differences). It therefore tends to be conservative in that studies with statistically nonsignificant findings are considered to indicate a zero effect for the experimental intervention. A meta-analysis, on the other hand, would take a more liberal (Bayesian) approach and consider the size of an intervention's effect even if it were not significantly different from zero. McKeachie, Pintrich, Lin, and Smith (1986) reconsidered an unpublished version of McMillian's review from this perspective and concluded that instruction that stresses student discussion and/or places explicit emphasis on problem-solving procedures and methods may enhance critical thinking. Additional studies not included in McMillian's synthesis would lend at least some support for this position (for example, Holloway, 1976; Moll & Allen, 1982).

There has been less research on the influence of purposeful curricular interventions on critical thinking. In their second-year evaluation of the ADAPT curriculum, Tomlinson-Keasey and Eisert (1978b) compared freshman-year change scores on the Watson-Glaser CTA between students in the ADAPT program and control groups of regular university freshmen. The ADAPT students showed a statistically significant gain of more than one standard deviation, while the gains for the control groups were essentially trivial and statistically nonsignificant, averaging only about .05 of a standard deviation. Unfortunately, the pretest of the ADAPT group was more than a full standard deviation lower than that of the control groups. Consequently, the greater improvement in critical thinking for the ADAPT students may have been, in large part, the result of regression artifacts.

Somewhat more impressive evidence concerning the effects of curricular interventions on critical thinking is presented by Winter, McClelland, and Stewart (1981). They hypothesized that a curriculum experience that requires the integration of ideas, courses, and disciplines would enhance critical thinking over the more typical curriculum, which merely provides a checklist of requirements without any integrative rationale. To test this hypothesis, they compared students in two different curricula within the same institution on gains on the Test of Thematic Analysis. (Recall that the TTA is an essay measure of critical thinking.) The experimental curriculum was a joint humanities program in which students took a group of two or more courses from different but complementary subject areas. The courses focused on an integrative theme relevant to the different disciplines. The control group was made up of students in the regular courses in the same general area, covering the same material, over the same period of time. While students in the integrative program started out on the TTA higher than the controls (1.66 versus 1.22), they also showed significantly greater gains (average increase of .50 versus .08 for the controls). This is the opposite of what one would expect from regression artifacts and represents reasonably impressive evidence of a real effect, despite the absence of an equivalent control group. Winter, McClelland, and Stewart conclude from this evidence that the experience of having to integrate two or more disciplines at the same time elicits greater cognitive growth than does simply studying the same material in separate courses without a consciously integrative structure. This is consistent with the evidence reported by Dressel and Mayhew (1954) and Forrest (1982) concerning the marked effects on critical thinking and reasoning skills of colleges that stress integrative general education in their curricula.

Postformal Reasoning. A small body of evidence suggests that college instruction can be designed to facilitate development along Perry's (1970) scheme of intellectual development. (Recall that this scheme views intellectual development as advancing through three basic stages: a dualistic right-versus-wrong stage, a relativistic stage in which facts are seen in terms of their context, and a stage in which the individual can make intellectual commitments within a context of relative knowledge.) Stephenson and Hunt (1977) report the results of a course-based intervention founded on a theory of cognitive developmental instruction. This type of instruction assumes that intellectual development occurs as a result of "cognitive conflict or dissonance which forces individuals to alter the constructs they have used to reason about certain situations" (Widick, Knefelkamp, and Parker, 1975, p. 291). The experimental intervention was a freshman social science course that focused on human identity within the context of literature and psychology (readings were from such authors as Edward Albee, James Baldwin, Arthur Miller, and Sylvia Plath). The method of instruction was specifically intended to advance dualistic students toward the relativistic stage of the Perry continuum. As such, the instruction emphasized challenges to the students' values and cognitive constructs within a supportive teaching paradigm. The control groups were made up of students in a humanities class and an English class that focused on similar course content but did not include cognitive developmental instruction.

Students in both instructional conditions were pre- and posttested with an instrument developed specifically to measure position on the Perry continuum. Even though the groups were generally equal to begin with, the experimental group exhibited substantially greater stage movement (mean change of +.85 stage) than the control groups (mean change of +.25 stage). Since students self-selected themselves into both the experimental and control conditions, however, there is still the possibility that the findings may be confounded by the interaction of selection and change (that is, the reason why an individual chooses a particular mode of instruction may be a determinant of the degree of change).

Findings generally consistent with those of Stephenson and Hunt (1977) have been reported in two additional course interventions described by Knefelkamp, (1974); Widick, Knefelkamp, and Parker (1975); and Widick and Simpson (1978). As with the Stephenson and Hunt study, the two course interventions sought to determine whether cognitive developmental instruction matched to the student's initial stage on the Perry scheme could facilitate progress along the continuum. Once again the instruction emphasized challenges to the students' cognitive and value structure within an overall supportive learning environment. In one intervention, without a control group, there was a pre- to postcourse gain of slightly more than .75 of a stage in the Perry continuum.[5] In the second intervention study, a greater percentage of those exposed to cognitive developmental instruction exhibited progress on the Perry continuum (63 percent) than those in the control sections (51.5 percent). The second study, however, was unclear as to how students were placed in the experimental and control sections. More recent findings similar to those of Knefelkamp (1974); Widick, Knefelkamp, and Parker (1975); and Widick and Simpson (1978) have been reported for an application of cognitive developmental instruction in an introductory course on educational foundations (Mortensen & Moreland, 1985, as reviewed in Kurfiss, 1988).

Conceptual Complexity. We uncovered only one study that dealt with the effects of instructional interventions on conceptual complexity, and that involved the ADAPT curriculum described earlier in the chapter. Tomlinson-Keasey and Eisert (1978a) compared changes in freshman-year scores on the Test of Conceptual Complexity for students in the ADAPT curriculum and regular freshmen. The Test of Conceptual Complexity appears to be a version of the Paragraph Completion Method. (Recall that conceptual complexity assessed in this manner measures the extent to which a person is capable of conceptualizing complex issues on increasingly abstract levels.) Although the ADAPT and control groups were not significantly different on the pretest, the ADAPT students increased approximately .50 of a standard deviation during the freshman year, while the control group actually decreased. The difference in the change in scores was statistically significant. Again, however, these results may be confounded by the fact that students selected the ADAPT or control curriculum. Although students in both groups were similar in conceptual complexity at the beginning of the freshman year, the reasons for their selection of one curriculum rather than the other could have been a determinant of differential change.

Teacher Behavior

As indicated in Chapter Three, there is a considerable body of research on teacher behavior and its relationship to students' learning of subject matter content. In contrast, there has been surprisingly little inquiry concerning the influence of teacher behavior on general cognitive skills. Perhaps the most useful research in this area has been conducted by D. Smith (1977, 1981), who employed a correlational design to assess the relationship between college classroom interactions and critical thinking. Critical thinking was measured by the Watson-Glaser CTA and Chickering's (1972) self-report index of critical thinking behavior. The Flanders (1970) Interaction Analysis System was used to assess four dimensions of classroom interactions. These interactions were related to changes between precourse and postcourse scores on the critical thinking appraisal and to postcourse scores on the six dimensions of the self-report index of critical thinking by means of canonical correlation (akin to multiple regression analysis with more than one dependent variable). The sample included twelve classes (138 students) distributed across disciplines, with analyses conducted at both individual and classroom levels of aggregation. The results suggest that at both levels three types of instructor-influenced classroom interactions were consistently and positively related to gains in critical thinking and to the analysis and synthesis dimensions of critical thinking behavior: the degree to which faculty encouraged, praised, or used student ideas; the degree to which students participated in class and the cognitive level of that participation; and the extent of peer-to-peer interaction in the class.

Clearly, the D. Smith (1977, 1981) research has an important methodological limitation, namely, the absence of controls for possible confounding differences in student precourse levels of critical thinking. (Indeed, research with samples of medical students suggests that student classroom participation is significantly and positively associated with precourse levels of critical thinking [Foster, 1981, 1983].) Nevertheless, the results do suggest that student critical thinking may be enhanced by teacher classroom behaviors that foster active student involvement in the learning process at a rather high level of interchange between student and teacher and between student and student. In this sense Smith's findings are quite consistent with earlier research suggesting that student-initiated discussions or verbal interactions in the classroom enhance the development of higher-order problem-solving skills over more traditional lecture approaches (for example, Beach, 1968; Romig, 1972; C. Smith, 1970). In fact, it may well be that increased student participation is an important causal mechanism underlying the positive association found between small classes and the development of higher-order cognitive processes (Dunkin & Barnes, 1985; McKeachie, 1978, 1980). Other factors being equal, student discussion is probably more likely in a class of 15 to 20 than in one of 250. The D. Smith findings, however, further suggest that amount of student-faculty and student-student interchange may not be particularly influential unless that interchange is at a reasonably high cognitive level.

Student Involvement

Consistent with the theoretical propositions of Astin (1984) and Pace (1980), as well as with the findings of studies synthesized in Chapter Three, a considerable body of evidence suggests that a student's quality of effort or level of involvement in college has a significant and positive influence on various dimensions of general cognitive development. Much of this research uses student self-reports of intellectual or cognitive development during college. As we suggested in Chapter Three, there are some psychometric problems with this approach; yet there also tend to be moderate positive correlations between self-reports and more objective measures of growth during college. Consequently, student self-reports provide a reasonable, if not totally adequate, indicator of cognitive growth.

Self-reports were used in an eight-institution study of college impact reported by Gaff, Wilson, and their colleagues (Gaff, 1973; Wilson, Wood, & Gaff, 1974; Wilson, Gaff, Dienst, Wood, & Bavry, 1975). Seniors at the eight institutions were asked to indicate both the extent of their campus involvement in nine different activities (intellectual, vocational, athletic, political, social, and so on) and the extent of their progress during college on a number of different dimensions of cognitive growth (for example, learning abstractions, applying principles, evaluating materials and methods). Degree of involvement was found to be significantly associated with cognitive growth but in a somewhat selective way. Specifically, perceived growth tended to be commensurate with involvement in activities that were consistent with it and supported it. For example, regardless of academic or vocational interests, students who were most involved in the pursuit of intellectual activities reported the most progress in learning abstractions, comprehending ideas, and applying principles. Conversely, students who had become the most deeply involved in social and athletic activities reported the least cognitive growth.

Similar results have been reported by Volkwein, King, and Terenzini (1986) in a single-institution study of students who transferred to a large state university and were followed over their first year of attendance. The study assessed student background characteristics (for example, age, socioeconomic status, secondary school achievement, intended major, and educational/vocational goals) and campus experiences (classroom involvement, relations with peers, extracurricular activities, social involvement, and so forth). The dependent measure was termed intellectual skill development and was a self-report scale of progress that focused on cognitive skills (for example, thinking analytically, critically evaluating ideas). Statistically controlling for background characteristics, the researchers found that a measure of classroom involvement had the strongest statistically significant association with the scale of intellectual skill development. The net association of other campus experiences such as social involvement or extracurricular activities was generally much smaller and statistically nonsignificant. Additional evidence from a related series of single-institution studies (Terenzini, Theophilides, & Lorang, 1984a; Volkwein, Wright, & Agrotes, 1987) and a study based on a national sample (Anaya, 1989) tend to support this finding. Each of these investigations relies on similar self-report measures of cognitive development.

Less supportive evidence concerning the role of student involvement in facilitating the development of cognitive skills has been reported by Hood (1984) in a study of freshman-to-senior gains in cognitive complexity (assessed with the paragraph completion method). Gain in cognitive complexity for each student was examined in relation to involvement in various undergraduate experiences such as major, type of residence, work experience, and participation in various campus activities. None of the specific college experiences, however, had a statistically significant correlation with the gain scores.

At first glance, results similar to those of Hood's (1984) investigation are apparently reported by Pascarella (1989) in a study of growth in critical thinking during the freshman year. (Critical thinking was measured by the Watson-Glaser CTA.) Nine individual measures of the undergraduate academic or social experience—residence arrangement, time spent studying, extracurricular activities, number of intellectually focused interactions with faculty and peers, and the like—had only trivial and statistically nonsignificant relationships with critical thinking at the end of the freshman year when the initial level of critical thinking was taken into account. However, when Pascarella combined the individual experience variables into a composite estimate of student social and intellectual involvement, it yielded a statistically significant positive association (partial $r = .34$) between involvement and critical thinking at the end of the freshman year. This association remained significant even when precollege critical thinking, academic aptitude, socioeconomic status, and college selectivity were controlled statistically. These findings, like those of Pace (1980, 1984) reported in Chapter Three, suggest a certain wholeness to student involvement or quality of effort in terms of its impact on cognitive development.

Pascarella's (1989) findings are also similar to those of Ory and Braskamp (1988) and Pace (1987, 1990). In these three studies level of student involvement or effort in both academic (intellectual) and interpersonal experiences had significant positive correlations with a measure of intellectual skill development (analysis, synthesis, and so on) that were markedly similar in magnitude. Thus, while it may well be, as indicated by the work of Wilson, Volkwein, Terenzini, and their colleagues, that a student's academic involvement holds the greatest potential for fostering growth in intellectual skills, it is also the case that the student is a member of a larger social system in which interpersonal interactions with the major agents of socialization (faculty and student peers) may provide an important influence on student intellectual growth in their own right. This influence may have both direct and indirect components. In the case of the latter, interpersonal interactions with faculty and peers may indirectly influence intellectual growth by influencing students' levels of involvement in academic or intellectual experiences.

Substantial evidence exists to suggest that interactions with major socializing agents (faculty and peers) are, in fact, significantly linked to the development of general cognitive skills during college. In an eight-institution study, for example, Wilson, Gaff, Dienst, Wood, and Bavry (1975) found that seniors who reported the greatest gains in such areas as ability to comprehend, interpret, or extrapolate; ability to evaluate materials and methods; and ability to apply abstractions or principles also had the highest amount of informal, nonclassroom interaction with faculty. This relationship appears to hold even when controls are made for differences among students in salient precollege characteristics. Pascarella and Terenzini (1978) controlled for fourteen such precollege characteristics (academic ability, secondary school achievement, race, socioeconomic status, personality characteristics, and the like) and found that frequency of student nonclass contact with faculty to discuss intellectual matters had a statistically significant positive association with reported gains in intellectual development during the freshman year. (The measure of intellectual development included such items as critical evaluation of ideas and applying abstractions or principles in problem solving.) This finding, replicated on an independent sample by Terenzini and Pascarella (1980a), and generally consistent findings with respect to the association between informal contact with faculty and perceived gains in cognitive development have also been reported in longitudinal studies by Endo and Harpel (1982, 1983); Elfner, McLaughlin, Williamsen, and Hardy (1985); and Spady (1971). Each of these studies attempted to control for important confounding variables (including academic ability, aspirations, major) in estimating the association in question.

A related line of longitudinal inquiry has focused primarily on the relationship between the *quality* of interactions between students and major agents of socialization on campus and perceived growth in cognitive skills (Endo & Harpel, 1983; Pascarella, Duby, Terenzini, & Iverson, 1983; Terenzini & Pascarella, 1980a; Volkwein, King, & Terenzini, 1986). The analytical designs of these studies typically regress measures of perceived student cognitive growth (thinking critically, thinking analytically, evaluating ideas, and so forth) on student precollege characteristics and measures of the quality of interaction with faculty and student peers. This permits statistical control of important confounding influences when estimating the association between the measures of interaction and measures of development. The general results of this body of evidence suggest that net of the effects of confounding variables, students who reported the greatest cognitive development were also most likely to (1) perceive faculty as being concerned with teaching and student development, (2) report developing a close, influential relationship with at least one faculty member, and (3) find their interactions with peers to have had an important influence on their development.

The potential impact of developing a close relationship with a faculty member is further suggested by Baxter Magolda (1987b) in an analysis of student intellectual development on the Perry scheme as assessed by the Measure of Epistemological Reflection. Students at the highest level of complexity in intellectual development preferred a relationship with faculty that emphasized working together as colleagues. In contrast, students at the lowest level preferred the relationship to be comfortable and relaxed but not too personal.

As suggested in Chapter Three, there are problems in drawing conclusions from this body of evidence because of ambiguities in the direction of causal influence. Do the extent and quality of student-faculty informal interactions influence cognitive growth, or do increases in cognitive skills lead to closer relationships and more frequent interactions with faculty? It is also possible that the causal linkages could be circular or reciprocal—interaction influencing growth, which in turn fosters even more interaction. Despite this ambiguity, the evidence does underscore the potential importance of the collegiate social environment and the extent and focus of interactions within that environment as an influence on student cognitive development.

One area in which colleges have at least some reasonable policy control over the student social environment is in residence halls. Indeed, a substantial amount of research has addressed ways in which residence halls might be structured to enhance the normative press for academic values and academic achievement.[6] Surprisingly little inquiry, however, has addressed the influence of residential living on the development of more general cognitive skills. As reported earlier in this chapter, Winter, McClelland, and Stewart (1981) found statistically significant freshman-to-senior changes on the Test of Thematic Analysis at a selective liberal arts college. To determine the institutional experiences that accounted for those changes, the researchers regressed student TTA gain scores on seven different scales derived from a factor analysis of a seventy-item measure of college experiences. Net of the other influences, a scale measuring the students' involvement in dormitory-sponsored activities (the dormitory-centered life scale) had a statistically significant negative association with gains on the TTA. Winter, McClelland, and Stewart suggest that one explanation for this finding is that a college's dormitories may often be a constraining influence that prolongs an overly protective, quasi-familial living atmosphere (for instance, residence staff *in loco parentis*). Thus, rather than providing an intellectually challenging environment, many dormitory activities may simply provide an insulated, comfortable, and unchallenging niche for students.

With respect to Winter, McClelland, and Stewart's (1981) findings, it is important to point out that residence arrangements within the same institution can differ substantially in the extent of their intellectual or traditional collegiate press (for example, Moos, 1976, 1979). Thus, some residential environments may be more conducive than others to the kinds of experiences and interactions that foster intellectual growth. Pascarella and Terenzini (1980b) addressed this issue in a quasi-experimental study that compared freshmen in traditional residence hall settings with those in a "living-learning" residence on self-reported gains in applying abstractions and principles in problem solving, critical evaluation of ideas, and other aspects of cognitive development. The living-learning residence was structured to integrate the students' academic and residential life and to enhance the intellectual impact of interactions between students and faculty and between students and their peers. Because of self-selection of freshmen into the traditional and living-learning residences, statistical controls were made for fifteen precollege variables (including academic aptitude, socioeconomic status, secondary school academic and social achievement, expectations of college). Net of these influences, students in the living-learning residence rated the institutional environment significantly stronger in intellectual press and sense of community and also reported significantly greater freshman-year gains on the measure of cognitive development.

A final piece of evidence on student involvement and cognitive development during college concerns the potential role of athletic participation. Winter, McClelland, and Stewart (1981), in their investigation of gains in critical thinking (as measured by the Test of Thematic Analysis) at a selective liberal arts college, also found that increases on the TTA were positively associated with varsity athletic participation, particularly for men. They explain this finding as follows (p. 134): "Success in athletics [requires] at least two qualities of mind: disciplined, thorough practice and adaptability to complex and rapidly changing circumstances. Applied to mental life, this practice and adaptability should enhance a person's ability to form and articulate abstract cognitive concepts to organize complex experience. (Thus coaches in many sports, for example, speak of a player's ability to diagnose or 'read' the other team's intentions or the course of the game.)"

This would seem to suggest that the student-athlete has a set of experiences during college that are particularly rich in terms of their potential for impact on adaptive and critical thinking processes. It is likely, however, that the institutional ethos, particularly with respect to the importance of athletics in the total scheme of things, may be a significant moderator of this impact. At the particular college in which these analyses were conducted, the varsity athletes did not receive athletic scholarships, live in special dormitories, or take special academic programs. Indeed, they were a representative cross section of the entire student body and, as such, were likely to be active participants in the academic as well as the athletic life of the institution. Whether varsity sports participation would have a similar impact on the cognitive development of student-athletes at institutions where varsity athletics are emphasized at the price of the individual's academic life is problematic.

Conditional Effects of College

We uncovered almost no evidence to suggest that the effects of college on the development of general cognitive skills differ for different kinds of students. The one study that made a concerted effort to investigate conditional effects found none. In a quasi-expermental study of the effect of the first year of college on critical thinking, Pascarella (1989) also attempted to determine whether different students benefited differentially from attending versus not attending college, from attending colleges of different selectivity, and from involvement in various social and academic activities in college. The magnitude of the influence of these factors on the development of critical thinking did not differ for students of different races or genders or for students with different levels of secondary school critical thinking, academic aptitude, academic achievement, family socioeconomic status, or educational aspirations. In short, the effects were the same for all students. It is important to point out, however, that this study had a very small, matched sample ($n = 47$) that did not afford it great statistical power to detect conditional effects. Because of this constraint, the Pascarella study may have failed to detect statistically significant conditional effects that were in fact present, if perhaps modest in magnitude.

Some scattered evidence concerning the impact of different instructional approaches suggests the possibility that certain kinds of students may benefit more than others from these approaches. For example, in a quasi-experimental investigation to estimate the comparative effects on Piagetian formal reasoning of a learning cycle–inquiry approach versus a traditional lecture/demonstration approach, Renner and Paske (1977) found that less advanced (concrete) reasoners benefited more from learning cycle instruction while students with some initial expertise in formal reasoning made greater progress in the traditional approach. In short, students advanced most in instruction matched to their initial level of reasoning. Similar if not totally parallel findings have been reported by Lawrenz (1985) in an experimental study of the use of student groupings in a learning cycle–inquiry type of science instruction. In each phase of instruction students worked and interacted in small groups. All students tended to make statistically significant gains in formal reasoning during the instruction. Greater gains were made, however, when students were homogeneously grouped by initial reasoning ability than when the reasoning ability in the small group was heterogeneous.

Long-Term Effects of College

In attempting to synthesize the evidence on the long-term effects of college on the development of general cognitive skills, we must rely almost totally on surveys that ask alumni about their retrospective perception of the influence or benefits of college. The sheer weight of evidence from this research suggests that college alumni perceive their undergraduate experience as having an important influence on their general cognitive development. Pace (1979), for example, reviewed the results of five surveys (three of which were based on national samples) of college alumni conducted from 1948 through 1976. The percentage of alumni in these surveys who reported that college affected them "greatly" or "somewhat" in critical thinking and analytical skills ranged from 72 to 96 percent. Similarly, the percentage reporting that college helped them "very much" or "quite a bit" in written and oral communication varied from 63 to 85 percent. Our own further analysis of this data suggests no statistically significant relationship between the perceived effect of college on these competencies and how long it had been since the various samples graduated from college, a time period ranging from about six to twenty years.

If alumni do not appear to differ significantly in their perceptions of the effectiveness of college on cognitive development on the basis of the time period since graduation (at least between six and twenty years since graduation), there are nevertheless some modest differences based on the student body selectivity of the college attended. Pace (1974), for example, found that 74 percent of alumni from selective universities and 77 percent from selective liberal arts colleges indicated that their institution provided "very much" or "quite a bit of" benefit in the development of critical thinking compared to a national baseline of 72 percent for all institutions in the sample. Similarly, in a ten-year follow-up of a national sample of college graduates, Bisconti and Solmon (1976) found that 51 percent of those graduating from highly selective institutions felt their undergraduate experience had been "very useful" in increasing their ability to think clearly. This compared to 42 percent of those graduating from less selective institutions. This relationship remained statistically significant even after controls were made for the individual's family background, gender, college grades, and academic major. Such statistical controls notwithstanding, it would be hazardous to attribute the differences in alumni perceptions to environmental differences between selective and less selective colleges. A plausible alternative explanation is that selective colleges simply recruit and enroll academically able students who are more open to the intellectual impacts of college to begin with. Thus, the findings could be the result of differential student recruitment rather than differential environmental or socialization effects.

Although the evidence from alumni surveys is impressive, at least in terms of how these individuals retrospectively perceive the impact of college on their cognitive development and thinking skills, it is not clear that it fully captures the total effect of college. As stressed in Chapter Three, a major if often ignored impact of college is transmitted through its influence on the graduate's postcollege experiences (further schooling, occupation, leisure activities, continuing intellectual interests). A large part of the long-term impact of college on cognitive development may take this indirect path of college influencing the nature of postcollege experiences, experiences that have a continuing influence on cognitive growth. For example, consider the evidence reported by Kohn and Schooler (1978, 1983) that intellectually and socially stimulating work makes an independent contribution to continued cognitive development in adult life. One important indirect effect of college on cognitive development, then, may be through the channeling of its graduates into occupations with relatively high ideational content, demanding social interaction and substantial self-direction (Beaton, 1975; Lindsay & Knox, 1984). Indeed, as we shall see in a subsequent chapter, a college degree may be the crucial entry criterion for many such jobs (for example, Bowen, 1977; Jencks et al., 1979; Sewell, Haller, & Portes, 1969; Sewell & Hauser, 1975).

This channeling effect perhaps helps to explain the findings of Heath (1976c). In his follow-up of male graduates of a liberal arts college who were in their early thirties, Heath discovered that the most important enduring effect of the institution (from a graduate's perspective) was its impact on intellectual maturation (relating ideas to each other at increasingly abstract levels, thinking logically, and the like). Even so, the undergraduate experience was ranked behind other factors (such as wife, graduate or professional school, occupation) in terms of its relative impact on intellectual maturation. It is likely, however, that graduation from college (or perhaps even that particular college) enhanced the likelihood of postgraduate educational and occupational experiences that in turn had an accentuating effect on trends in intellectual development initiated during the undergraduate years.

Summary

Change During College

Our synthesis suggests that students make statistically significant gains during the college years on a number of dimensions of general cognitive capabilities and skills. Compared to freshmen, seniors have better oral and written communication skills, are better abstract reasoners or critical thinkers, are more skilled at using reason and evidence to address ill-structured problems for which there are no verifiably correct answers, have greater intellectual flexibility in that they are better able to understand more than one side of a complex issue, and can develop more sophisticated abstract frameworks to deal with complexity. Since not all the studies we reviewed provided the necessary statistical data (for example, standard deviations), estimates of the magnitude of these freshman-to-senior gains are tenuous at best. Nevertheless, our best estimate is that the magnitude of the gains made are as follows: oral communication, .60 SD (an improvement of 22 percentile points); written communication, .50 SD (an improvement of 19 percentile points); Piagetian formal (abstract) reasoning, .33 SD (an improvement of 13 percentile points); critical thinking, 1 SD (an improvement of 34 percentile points); using reason and evidence to address ill-structured problems, 1 SD (an improvement of 34 percentile points); and ability to deal with conceptual complexity, 1.2 SD (an improvement of 38 percentile points). It is also our best estimate that about 50 percent or more of the gains made in abstract reasoning, critical thinking, and ability to conceptualize complexity occur during the freshman and sophomore years of college. One must keep in mind, however, that only a portion of these gains can be attributed to the influence of college.

Net Effects of College

The body of evidence concerning the net effects of college on the development of general cognitive skills is small and limited in scope. From this evidence, however, we offer the following conclusions.

1. When both age and academic ability are taken into account, seniors still have significantly better written and oral communication skills than freshmen. Similarly, graduates of community colleges score higher than incoming freshmen on a measure of general intellectual and analytical

skill development, even when age, verbal ability, and mathematical ability are held constant.

2. There is reasonably sound and consistent evidence to suggest that college has a net positive influence on diverse measures of critical thinking that cannot be explained away by differences among those who attend and do not attend college in initial critical thinking, academic aptitude, maturation, socioeconomic status, or aspirations. The effect of college on critical thinking, however, seems to be selective. It appears to enhance one's ability to weigh evidence, to determine the validity of data-based generalizations or conclusions, and to distinguish between strong and weak arguments. There is less support for the claims that college has a unique effect on one's ability to discriminate the truth or falsity of inferences, recognize assumptions, or determine whether stated conclusions follow from information provided.

3. The weight of evidence suggests that attending college has a stronger influence than normal maturation on reflective judgment, one's ability to use reason and evidence in making judgments about controversial issues. It would appear that those who attend college not only make greater gains in reflective judgment than those who do not but also that these gains cannot be explained away by differences in initial academic ability between those who attend college and those who do not.

4. Net of age, intelligence, and academic aptitude, attending college appears to influence one's intellectual flexibility (ability to comprehend and effectively argue both sides of a complex or controversial issue) positively and significantly.

The research on the net effects of college sheds little light on *why* college attendance fosters greater average growth in general cognitive skills than other post–high school experiences. One reasonable explanation, however, is that of all the experiences a student could have after secondary school, college is the one that most typically provides an overall environment where the potential for intellectual growth is maximized. To be sure, a diverse array of noncollege experiences might exert substantial impact on an individual's intellectual growth. The advantage of college, however, is that salient intellectual, cultural, and interpersonal influences (for example, courses, libraries, laboratories, faculty, and other similarly engaged peers) tend to be concentrated in one place. Given this concentration of influences, evidence supporting a net positive impact of college on a range of general cognitive competencies and skills may not be particularly surprising.

Between-College Effects

We found only a limited amount of consistent evidence to suggest that institutional characteristics have an important influence on the development of general cognitive skills. A number of studies indicate that general cognitive growth is maximally enhanced at institutions with selective undergraduate student bodies, particularly when cognitive growth is assessed by student or alumni self-reports of gains made during college. However, more methodologically sound studies, using objective measures and/or controlling for important precollege characteristics, have found little relationship between institutional selectivity and objective measures of cognitive development. It may be that selectivity only has a discernible impact on student cognitive development when it is combined with other factors such as small size and an institutional ethos that encourages a high level of student effort and involvement. Certain selective liberal arts colleges tend to combine these traits, though methodologically sound and replicated findings concerning their direct impact on cognitive development are sparse. It does appear that selective liberal arts colleges tend to give examinations that stress more higher-order cognitive skills than do less selective liberal arts colleges. Whether this reflects actual differences in the level at which courses are taught or simply professorial perceptions of students' capabilities, however, is still unclear.

There is some evidence that institutions with a strong emphasis on fraternity or sorority life tend to inhibit growth in critical thinking. Nevertheless, the apparent absence in this evidence of controls for freshman-cohort differences within and among institutions makes any firm conclusions difficult. Similarly, there is cross-sectional evidence, paired with appropriate cohort statistical controls, to suggest that black students demonstrate greater development in critical thinking and concept attainment at predominantly black institutions than at predominantly white ones. This finding awaits replication, however.

The only area where we found consistent evidence with respect to between-college effects (and it is based on only two studies) was in the influence of institutional curricular emphasis. Despite some methodological problems, it would appear that students at institutions with a strong and balanced curricular commitment to general education show particularly large gains in measures of critical thinking and adult reasoning skills. The two studies that provide this evidence were conducted nearly thirty years apart.

Within-College Effects

The weight of evidence would suggest that one's major course of study influences the development of general cognitive skills but that the influence is selective. A student's cognitive growth is greatest on measures where the content is most consistent with his or her academic major or course work emphasis. Thus, for example, science majors tend to outperform others on measures of formal reasoning and critical thinking when these skills are applied to sciencelike tasks or problems. In contrast, when the tasks or problems are presented in the form of social science content, social science majors tend to perform best. On general measures of critical thinking (for example, the Watson-Glaser Critical Thinking Appraisal) or postformal reasoning (for example, reflective judgment), one's academic major has little consistent relationship with gains.

A reasonably consistent body of experimental evidence suggests that the learning cycle–inquiry approach to science instruction is effective in moving students from concrete to formal (abstract) operational reasoning. This approach stresses an inductive learning process that is geared to concrete reasoning and in which actual experiments or other concrete activities are used to introduce concepts and abstractions. The learning cycle–inquiry approach has also been shown to enhance the development of formal reasoning and conceptual complexity when implemented in a general freshman-year curriculum not restricted to science courses.

Whether one concludes that there are instructional approaches that consistently enhance critical thinking depends on how one reads the evidence. From a conservative perspective, where statistically nonsignificant findings equal a zero treatment effect, no one instructional or curricular approach appears consistently to facilitate the growth of critical thinking, particularly when critical thinking is measured by general, nonacademic instruments such as the Watson-Glaser Critical Thinking Appraisal. A more liberal perspective, which considers experimental control differences as being non-zero even if the differences are not statistically significant, would suggest that instruction that stresses student discussion at a relatively high level of cognitive activity and/or instruction that places emphasis on problem-solving procedures and methods may enhance critical thinking.

There is evidence that a curriculum experience that requires the integration of ideas and themes across courses and disciplines enhances critical thinking over simply taking a distribution of courses without an integrative rationale or theme. Although this evidence is based on only one study, it is nevertheless of some importance because of its consistency with evidence suggesting that colleges stressing integrative general education in their overall curriculum are particularly effective in promoting growth in critical thinking.

A small body of research suggests that specially structured course interventions may enhance the development of postformal reasoning, specifically, stage movement on the Perry continuum. These interventions, which have been termed cognitive developmental instruction, focus on providing challenges to the individual's initial cognitive and value structures paired with instructional supports appropriate for the individual's initial level of cognitive development. The internal validity of experiments that assess the influence of these interventions, however, is not particularly strong. Thus, causal attribution is tenuous.

It is important to point out that the estimated magnitude of instructional or curricular effects on measures of general cognitive skills tends to be smaller than that of the effect of the overall college experience. This would suggest that growth in many areas of cognitive development may be a gradual process characterized by a period of rapid advancement followed by a period of consolidation (Kitchener, 1982). Fundamental shifts in thought processes may proceed slowly and irregularly. Thus, a single instructional or curricular experience over a limited period may not provide the developmental impact of a cumulative set of mutually reinforcing experiences over an extended period of time (Kitchener, 1983; White, 1980).

Consistent with theoretical expectations, extent of growth in general cognitive skills during college appears to be a direct result of a student's quality of effort or level of psychological and social involvement in college. Involvement in intellectual and cultural activities may be more important to general cognitive development than other types of involvement (social, athletic, and so on). Yet it also appears that the nature and quality of social interactions with faculty members and student peers play a role of some consequence in one's cognitive growth. These interactions are of particular salience if they focus on ideas or intellectual matters. The weight of evidence, we believe, suggests that the more one's social experience reflects and reinforces one's academic experience, the greater will be the possibilities for intellectual development. Put another way, the more complete the integration between a student's academic life and social life during college, the greater the likelihood of his or her general cognitive and intellectual growth.

One place where some institutions can influence this integration is student residence facilities. What evidence does exist suggests that when this academic and social integration is purposefully and successfully implemented in a residence hall environment, student cognitive growth can be facilitated. To the extent that residential life simply functions as a comfortable, protective, anti-intellectual niche for students, however, it may actually inhibit cognitive growth.

Conditional Effects

We found little consistent evidence to indicate that the effects of college on general cognitive skills differ for different kinds of students. Similarly, little evidence exists to suggest that the characteristics of the college attended have a differential influence on general cognitive skills for different kinds of students. There is, nonetheless, a small body of evidence suggesting that learning cycle–inquiry instruction has its most pronounced influence on the development of Piagetian formal reasoning either for students who are initially at the concrete reasoning stage or for students grouped with others at the same initial Piagetian reasoning level.

Long-term Effects

Although the evidence (from national samples) on long-term effects of college is based largely on alumni perceptions, its clear weight indicates that the undergraduate experience is seen as having an important influence on general cognitive development and thinking skills. These perceptions do not appear to be a function of time elapsed since graduation, but there is a slight trend for alumni from academically selective institutions to report greater impact than alumni from less selective institutions. The latter finding is consistent with differences in retrospective reports of seniors or other upperclassmen from selective and less selective institutions. It should be underscored that this modest association between self-reports of impact and college selectivity may not be due to environmental or socialization differences between selective and less selective colleges. The nature of the evidence makes differential student recruitment by selective and less selective colleges as plausible an explanation for these findings as any differential socialization that might take place in colleges of varying selectivity.

Finally, there is evidence to suggest that intellectually and socially stimulating work environments make an independent contribution to cognitive development in adult life. We have suggested that a major, though indirect, long-term effect of college on cognitive development comes through its power to position graduates in intellectually and socially demanding employment.

Notes

1. There is also evidence to suggest that students make statistically significant gains in purely verbal measures of abstract reasoning during college. Welfel and Davison (1986) found that engineering majors and humanities and social science majors made statistically significant freshman-to-senior gains on the Concept Mastery Test of about one standard deviation. The Concept Mastery Test is a measure of verbal abstract reasoning that consists of synonyms and antonyms and the completion of analogies.

2. There is also corroborating evidence from self-reports to suggest that students make nontrivial gains in the general ability to think critically. Heath (1968), in an extensive analysis of student maturation during college, suggests that increasing integration of intellectual skills (a broad notion of intellectual development that includes critical thinking) was one of the major and most significant maturing effects of college as perceived by students. Similarly, in a longitudinal study of 311 students, Endo and Harpel (1980) found that seniors were significantly more likely than freshmen to indicate capabilities typically associated with critical thinking (for example, recognizing assumptions, detecting

faulty reasoning, examining statements critically). (See also Bisconti & Solmon, 1976; Coles, 1983; Gaff, 1973; Hesse-Biber, 1985.)

3. We also found several studies that suggested that such approaches as remedial instruction in natural science and mathematics (Reif, 1984), practice in Piagetian tasks (Thomas & Grouws, 1984), modeling principles of formal thought (Wilson, 1987), and instruction in logic (Enyeart, 1981) enhanced progress from concrete to formal reasoning. However, these studies lacked the independent replication that characterized the evidence on the learning cycle–inquiry approach.

4. See Bailey (1979); Beckman (1956); Coscarelli and Schwen (1979); Gressler (1976); Hancock (1981); Hancock, Coscarelli, and White (1983); Hardin (1977); Hayden (1978); Jackson (1961); Jones (1974); Logan (1976); Lyle (1958); Moll and Allen (1982); Shuch (1975); Tomlinson-Keasey and Eisert (1978b). See also Kurfiss (1988) for an excellent discussion of different instructional strategies designed to improve problem solving and critical thinking in various disciplines.

5. Similar results are also reported by Stonewater and Daniels (1983) for a course based on psychosocial theory and designed to help students understand the process of career decision making and acquire skills useful in making appropriate career decisions. There were statistically significant advances on the Perry scheme, but there was no control group for comparative purposes.

6. See Ainsworth and Maynard (1976); Blai (1971); Blimling and Hample (1979); Brown (1968); Centra (1968); DeCoster (1968, 1979); Duncan and Stoner (1977); Gifford (1974); Gerst and Moos (1972); Golden and Smith (1983); McIntire (1973); Magnarella (1975); Moos, DeYoung, and Van Dort (1976); Pugh and Chamberlain (1976); Scott (1975); Schrager (1986); Schroeder (1980b); Snead and Caple (1971); Taylor and Hanson (1971); Williams and Reilly (1972); Winston, Hutson, and McCaffrey (1980).

5

Psychosocial Changes:
Identity, Self-Concept,
and Self-Esteem

Historically, America's colleges and universities have had an educational and social mission to "educate" in a sense that extends beyond the cognitive and intellectual development of students. That broader mission has defined education to include increased self-understanding; expansion of personal, intellectual, cultural, and social horizons and interests; liberation from dogma, prejudice, and narrow-mindedness; development of personal moral and ethical standards; preparation for useful and productive employment and membership in a democratic society; and the general enhancement of the quality of graduates' postcollege lives. In this and the next three chapters, we focus on the changes college students experience in the psychosocial, attitudinal, and moral areas sometimes referred to as the affective or non-cognitive domains.

Our understanding of these phases and processes of student change may be in transition. Keniston (1970, 1971a, 1971b), for example, believes that social and cultural transformations have produced a new phase that he calls *youth* to characterize "a growing minority of post-adolescents today . . . [who] have not settled the questions whose answers once defined adulthood: questions of relationship to the existing society, questions of vocation, questions of social role and life-style" (1970, p. 634). Others (Sanford, 1962; Chickering, 1969; Freedman, 1965; Goldscheider and Da Vanzo, 1986; Miller & Winston, 1990) share Keniston's view of a distinctive and evolving developmental period between adolescence and young adulthood. Holt (1980, p. 919) offers some supportive empirical evidence. Parsons and Platt (1970, chap. 4), witnessing the same phenomenon through the eyes of sociologists, believe that mass higher education has created a social situation in which colleges and universities are the primary vehicles of a newly emergent phase ("studentry") in the socialization process.

The literature on college students comes from diverse and evolving disciplinary and theoretical origins (Kitchener, 1982) that have produced varying conceptions of change or growth in human dimensions given varying names. Methodological problems also abound, including (among others) the confounding of sociocultural changes with ontogenetic patterns (that is, maturational sequences embedded in every living organism), the comparison of nonequivalent groups in cross-sectional studies, and the interaction of ontogenetic development with historical events that can vary across cohorts of students under study (Huston-Stein & Baltes, 1976; see also Moss & Sussman, 1980). As if that were not enough, developmental researchers are sometimes inclined to reinterpret results that deviate from theoretical expectations in a manner that *is* consistent with developmental theory (Feldman & Newcomb, 1969, pp. 346–351; Feldman, 1972).

As used in this and the next chapter, the term *psychosocial* is broadly understood to have two components. The first, referred to in the first two syllables of the term, consists of the personal, internal, psychologically oriented aspects of individual being that dispose an individual to act or respond in certain ways. This portion of the term includes such constructs as self, ego, and identity. *Psychosocial* also contains a second component, one that refers to the individual's personal orientations to the external world, to the relationships between the self and society. The term is close in meaning to what some call "personality," although we use *psychosocial* as being a more fully descriptive term (and one over which there are fewer definitional disputes).

This chapter examines the effects of college on those psychosocial aspects of students' lives that Inkeles (1966) referred to as the "self" system (the sense of identity, self, and self-esteem). Chapter Six examines the evidence on change in students' "relational" systems (how students relate to people and institutions outside themselves).[1] Changes in two components of students' self and relational systems are treated in separate chapters in this book: (1) students' values and attitudes (because of the extensive literature and because we consider attitudes and values to be less central to the character of the individual, more specific in their content, and more changeable over time; see Chapter Seven) and (2) students' moral development (also because of the extensive research on this topic in the last two decades; see Chapter Eight).

Within the category of self systems, the vast majority of research examines change in one or more of five major areas: (1) identity status, (2) ego development, (3) academic self-concept, (4) social self-concept, and (5) self-esteem. Each of these areas is examined within the six-question structure established for this book (see Chapter One).

Change During College

Identity Status

Before 1968, "personality development" theories were sparse, and the dominant presumption was that personality had pretty much assumed its final shape by late adolescence (Singer, 1968). Much has changed since then.

A substantial proportion of the identity development research has been based on the theoretical model of James Marcia (1965, 1966). As may be recalled from Chapter Two, Marcia considers identity formation to be a function of the resolution of two psychosocial tasks: the experience of "crisis," understood in its Eriksonian sense as the engagement of and choice among meaningful but competing alternatives, not as some psychological emergency,[2] and the making of personal commitments in occupational, religious, political, and sexual areas. Depending upon whether a crisis has been experienced (or is in progress) and whether commitments have been made, four identity development statuses can be discerned. "Diffusion" status is defined by the absence of any crisis period and the absence of commitments. "Foreclosure" status applies to individuals who have made commitments (usually to positions similar to those of their parents) without having seriously engaged the alternatives as possibilities. "Moratorium" status describes people who are actively considering and weighing identity alternatives (that is, are in "crisis") but who have not yet committed themselves to any particular identity. "Identity achievement" refers to the state of having made commitments that evolved out of a period of crisis (Marcia, 1966).[3] A substantial portion of the literature based on Marcia's (1965, 1966) model is correlational, describing characteristics of individuals in the various identity status categories.[4] Far fewer studies examine either the fact of change in identity status or the processes by which such change might occur.

With only one exception (Adams & Shea, 1979), the research using Marcia's model supports the presumption of identity status change during the college years, indicating shifts toward identity resolution and achievement during varying periods of college attendance. This evidence is consistent whether based on cross-sectional designs (for example, Adams, Shea, & Fitch, 1979; Prager, 1986; Henry & Renaud, 1972; Meilman, 1979), short-term (one or two years) longitudinal designs (Adams & Fitch, 1982, 1983; Donovan, 1970; Fitch & Adams, 1983; Kroger & Haslett, 1988; Waterman & Waterman, 1971), or longer-term (four or more years) longitudinal inquiries (Waterman, Geary, & Waterman, 1974; Waterman & Goldman, 1976; Marcia, 1976). Indeed, Waterman (1982) concluded from his review that the greatest gains in identity formation occur during the traditional college years (ages eighteen to twenty-three), perhaps because collegiate settings afford students diverse environments, successful role models, and opportunities to examine and test alternatives.

Estimating the magnitude of identity change, whether its intensity (degree to which the average individual changes) or its extensity (the proportion of students who change), however, is problematic. Studies based on Marcia's model typically involve interviews and, consequently, some very small samples. Thus, estimates of the magnitude of change vary considerably across studies. Some sense can be gotten from several studies, although we hasten to caution readers about the high instability of these estimates. Using a sample larger than most ($n = 148$), Adams and Fitch (1982) report that about half of their respondents in a large, midwestern university remained in the same identity status over a two-year period. Another 15 to 20 percent changed statuses toward greater identity differentiation and integration, while about 10 percent evidenced regression (change among the rest was either theoretically uninterpretable or attributed to measurement error). These percentage shifts were almost identical for men and women. Waterman, Geary, and Waterman (1974) found that while as freshmen only 2 percent of their fifty-three students had attained identity-achieved status in both occupational and ideological areas, by the senior year that percentage had increased to 19 percent. The percentage who had achieved identity status in neither area dropped from 60 percent during the freshman year to 38 percent among the seniors. Waterman and Goldman (1976) report consistent freshman-to-senior increases in the percentage of students ($n = 59$) in the identity achievement status in each of the three identity subareas: occupational choice, 60 to 80 percent; religious beliefs, 21 to 54 percent; and political beliefs, 35 to 62 percent. Across categories, the percentage of achievers increased from 40 percent as freshmen to 61 percent as seniors. In his review, Waterman (1982) concludes that the moratorium identity status was the least stable (less than 10 percent remained in this status at a four-year technological institute and at a four-year private liberal arts college). Four-year stability rates were roughly comparable (45 to 60 percent) in the other status categories.

The effects of college appear to be greatest in the vocational area. The only studies of four-year changes (Waterman, Geary, & Waterman, 1974; Waterman & Goldman, 1976) found significant increases in the proportion of students in the achiever status, with declines in the proportion in the moratorium status. The proportion of foreclosure-status students in the religious area declined significantly over four years, but there was no clear tendency for these declines to be accompanied by increases in identity achievement across the schools in these studies. In the political area over a four-year period, more than half of the students formed no clear commitments (Waterman, 1982).

A similar and generally consistent picture of identity development during the college years emerges from a number of studies of identity and self-actualization based on approaches and instruments other than Marcia's (many of them, however, also derived from Erikson's theory of identity formation). With some exceptions (for example, Erwin & Delworth, 1980; the cross-sectional results of Hood, 1986a; Wilson, Anderson, & Fleming, 1987; urban students in Fry, 1974), this body of research suggests that student identity tends to change in developmentally positive directions during the college years over both the short term (one or two years) (Erwin, 1982; Erwin & Delworth, 1982; Whitbourne, Jelsma, & Waterman, 1982) and the longer term (four or more years) (Constantinople, 1969, 1970; Erwin & Kelly, 1985; among rural students in Fry, 1974; Gaff, 1973; the longitudinal results of Hood, 1986a; Hood, Riahinejad, & White, 1986; King, 1973; Mulford, 1967; Offer & Offer, 1975; Pace, 1974, 1984; Schubert, 1975b; Stark & Traxler, 1974; Wilson, Gaff, Dienst, Wood, & Bavry, 1975; Winter, McClelland, & Stewart, 1981; see also Moffatt, 1989, pp. 40–45).

The most convincing evidence comes from Constantinople (1969). Using a measure of Erikson's fourth, fifth, and sixth stages of psychosocial development (industry versus inferiority, identity versus identity diffusion, and intimacy versus isolation) in a combination cross-sectional and longitudinal study of 952 students in all four class years at the University of Rochester, Constantinople found consistent increases in the successful resolution of identity issues from freshman through senior years across subjects and from one year to the next within subjects. She also reports similar results from a smaller sample (Constantinople, 1970). The findings of both studies were replicated some ten years later by Whitbourne, Jelsma, and Waterman (1982).

Black Identity Development. A substantial literature portrays the characteristics of black students (and to a significantly lesser extent, other minority group students) and contrasts black and white students on a wide variety of demographic, psychological, and social dimensions. One of the most noteworthy results of our review of the research literature on identity formation, however, is the *absence* of studies dealing with identity development among black (or other minority) students. As noted in Chapter Two, very few studies examine the nature of changes among black or other nonwhite minority students during college or try to identify the factors that might promote (or attenuate) those changes. Current theory and research on college student change and development appear quite clearly to assume that the identity development–related characteristics and backgrounds students bring with them to college, their experiences while there, and the process of such development are more or less uniformly the same for minority group students as for white, middle-class students. Yet a number of studies offer rather dramatic evidence that such is not the case: Black and other students of color differ from whites in a variety of personal and socioeconomic characteristics upon matriculation, and their experiences of college differ in important ways from those of their white peers.[5]

In the last two decades, however, a literature specifically addressing the characteristics of black identity and its development has begun to emerge (Baldwin, 1980, 1981, 1984; Baldwin, Duncan, & Bell, 1987; Banks, 1981; Branch-Simpson, 1985; Cheatham, Slaney, & Coleman, 1990; Cross, 1971a, 1971b, 1978, 1980, 1985; Gay, 1984; Hauser & Kassendorf, 1983; Jackson,

1975; Taylor, 1976, 1977; Thomas, 1971; Toldson & Pasteur, 1975; White & Burke, 1987; Wyne, White, & Coop, 1974). (A considerably smaller literature related to psychosocial development in other minority groups, such as Hispanics, Native Americans, and Asian Americans, is now developing; see Chapter Two.) Of the available models of black identity formation, Cross's has attracted the most research attention.

As may be recalled from Chapter Two, the Cross model consists of five stages through which individuals pass as their personal black identity takes shape: (1) "Preencounter" (when a black person's worldview is a Euro-American one, with an emphasis on assimilation and integration into the white world), (2) "Encounter" (when some experience, such as the assassination of Martin Luther King, Jr., forces a rethinking of blacks' place in the world), (3) "Immersion-Emersion" (involving first a search for self, or immersion, in the world of blackness, followed by an emersion as the individual takes control of his or her experiences), (4) "Internalization" (where rejection, a Stage 3 fixation, or superficial internalization of a black identity all are possible), and (5) "Internalization-Commitment" (involving a serious and personal commitment to active political and sociocultural reform in one's community). The final stage has received less attention, however, because of empirical difficulties in differentiating it from earlier stages (Helms, 1990c).

Several studies have been undertaken to develop instruments operationalizing Cross's stages (Cross, 1979; Davidson, 1974; Milliones, 1974, 1980) or to validate his conceptions (Carter & Helms, 1987; Cross, 1979; Hall, Cross, & Freedle, 1972; Hall, Freedle, & Cross, 1972; Krate, Leventhal, & Silverstein, 1974; Parham & Helms, 1981, 1985a, 1985b; Polite, Cochrane, & Silverman, 1974; Williams, 1975). The latter group is generally supportive of Cross's propositions, but most examine only the correlates of each stage. Only three studies (Cheatham, Slaney, & Coleman, 1990; Cross, 1979; Krate, Leventhal, & Silverstein, 1974) examine individual status change over time, and these studies produced conflicting findings. Cheatham and his colleagues, in a cross-sectional study, found no differences in Cross model identity status across class year (or between institutions) among 250 African-American students attending a traditionally black institution and a predominantly white institution. The studies by Cross and by Krate, Leventhal, and Silverstein, on the other hand, found changes reported retrospectively over varying periods of time that were consistent with Cross's stages. Supporting Cross's and Krate and colleagues' conclusions concerning the model's construct validity but in contrast to Cheatham and colleagues, studies of changes in students' degree of subscription to various black ideological positions have found significant increases in the salience of black ideology among black students at predominantly white institutions but not among blacks at predominantly black colleges or universities (Baldwin, Duncan, & Bell, 1987; Fleming, 1977, cited in Fleming, 1981; Ramseur, 1975; Cross, 1978, reviews early efforts to validate his model). Cheatham, Tomlinson, and Ward (1990) tried to replicate the findings of Baldwin and his associates. They succeeded in finding a significant main effect for academic class (higher African self-consciousness scales among upper-division [versus lower-division] students), but they failed to find a significant class × school interaction—an indication that students' black identities underwent no greater change at a traditionally black institution than at a predominantly white one.

In all these studies, however, changes in black identity status are confounded with a variety of other potentially influential variables (for example, entering identity status, age, enrollment in black studies courses). Thus, while the available evidence appears to support the construct validity of Cross's model, it is not clear whether changes in identity status are related to college attendance, to the racial/ethnic mix of students at the institution attended, or to sociocultural and economic conditions external to postsecondary educational institutions.

Taken together, these studies clearly indicate that black identity comprises idiosyncratic and personal elements, as well as components derived from membership in a historically disadvantaged, racially based collectivity (see, especially, Gurin & Epps, 1975). Nevertheless, the interactions among these components and the variables mediating their formation are as yet only dimly understood. There is also reason to believe, however, that the psychological tensions between individual and collective identities can, in some cases, be counterdevelopmental. Excessive allegiance to a group identity, when it leads to separatism, may also serve to isolate black students from social and academic contacts, experiences, and environments that while being aversive may also constitute socially and academically developmental opportunities (Fleming, 1981; Monroe, 1973; Kilson, 1973a, 1973b; S. Steele, 1989).

Ego Development

In contrast to the foregoing picture of fairly consistent, if modest, change in identity status over the college years, the evidence in another major area of inquiry, based almost exclusively on Loevinger's (1966, 1976) model of ego development, paints a portrait of relative stability rather than change. In brief, Loevinger offers a comprehensive model of ego development that includes moral, interpersonal, and cognitive growth, where "ego" constitutes a central organizing framework that provides structure and meaning for one's self and one's world. Ego development refers to the *totality* of intraindividual development (see Chapter Two for a somewhat fuller definition and description of Loevinger's model; see also Josselson, 1980). Although Loevinger's model consists of nine stages, the three middle stages are of greatest interest here. The "Conformist" stage (designated I-3) is essentially a period in which rules are obeyed without questioning and the individual's ego development is group centered. Individual differences have not emerged, and the need for acceptance and approval by peers is high. At the "Self-Aware" level (actually a transition phase, designated I-3/4), self-awareness increases and alternatives are recognized. At the "Conscientious" stage (I-4), the individual has internalized a set of rules and values, reasoning has become more complex, and a sense of responsibility for one's actions emerges.

Redmore (1983), in a four-and-one-half-year study of fifty-seven pharmacy college students, found a significant increase in ego development, as measured by the Sentence Completion Test (SCT) (Loevinger & Wessler, 1970; Loevinger, Wessler, & Redmore, 1970), but the changes were primarily among the men, whose ego development appeared to be catching up to that of the women, who did not change over the period of the study. In a second study in the same report, Redmore also found a statistically significant increase in ego development over four years among forty students in psychology classes at two community colleges. Adams and Fitch (1982), using a cross-sectional sample of freshmen, sophomores, and juniors, found that 22 percent of their students showed gains in ego development one year later, 17 percent regressed, and the majority (61.4 percent) showed no change over the year. While other studies (Mentkowski, 1988; Mentkowski & Doherty, 1984; Mentkowski & Strait, 1983) contain some evidence suggesting increases in ego development, that evidence derives from cross-sectional designs and analyses and is generally not sustained by subsequent longitudinal analyses from the same project, with or without a control for age. These results suggest the cross-sectional analyses may have been detecting cohort rather than maturational differences. Hood (1984) reports freshman-senior changes in ego development, but other longitudinal studies that found no change in ego development stage are reported by Whiteley (1982), Tomlinson-Keasey and Eisert (1978b), and Kitchener, King, Davison, Parker, and Wood (1984). Loxley and Whiteley (1986) and Whiteley and Yokota (1988), however, do report a statistically significant longitudinal increase from freshman to senior year in a relatively small sample ($n = 75$) of students who had followed an experimental curriculum as freshmen. Nonetheless, the magnitude of the changes (.39 of a stage on Loevinger's Sentence Completion Test) led to the conclusion that "the college years do not appear to be a time of fundamental progression in ego development" (Whiteley & Yokota, 1988, p. 15).

A combined cross-sectional and longitudinal study, conducted between 1971 and 1979 at two institutions—one an engineering school, the other a selective, private liberal arts university—produced mixed results (Loevinger, 1979; Loevinger et al., 1985). In a meta-analysis of combined freshman-senior change data from a succession of cohorts entering the two schools during the middle to late 1970s, Loevinger and her colleagues found that the men at the engineering college gained significantly in ego development, while their female peers also gained but not significantly. At the liberal arts university, men gained (but not significantly), while the women lost significantly.

In most of these analyses, the modal developmental status was in the "Self-Aware" transition level (I-3/4) between the "Conformist" (I-3) and "Conscientious" (I-4) stages (see also Redmore & Waldman, 1975; Weathersby, 1981), although there is evidence that the distribution of noncollege people may be skewed toward the lower stage, while that of college students is skewed toward the higher one (Holt, 1980, table 4). Changes that were identified were generally from the "Conformist" (I-3) stage to the "Self-Aware" level (I-3/4) and generally on the order of one-half a stage (or standard deviation) in magnitude or less (Redmore, 1983; Loxley & Whiteley, 1986; Whiteley & Yokota, 1988).

The pattern of differences in measured identity and ego development over the elementary, high school, and college years suggests the possibility that the rate of change in ego development may level off by the end of high school (see, for example, Archer, 1982; Goldberger, 1980; LaVoie, 1976; Martin & Redmore, 1978; Redmore & Loevinger, 1979; Redmore & Waldman, 1975). Newman and Newman (1978) reached a similar conclusion in their review of literature dealing with identity formation.[6] The high similarity in the proportions of students who remain stable and who change in ego development status over two years (see, for example, Kitchener, King, Davison, Parker, & Wood, 1984) and over four years (Redmore, 1983) offers tentative support for this proposition.

One must conclude from these rather disparate studies, however, that there is insufficient evidence to indicate reliable gains in ego development during the college years. Indeed, the work of Loevinger and her colleagues (1985) suggests that for some (particularly women), ego development during college *may* even be a regressive experience, although the research on this point awaits replication (perhaps even reinterpretation; see, for example, Gilligan, 1977, 1982a, 1982b, 1986a).

One might explain the differences in the findings between the "identity" and "ego development" research as a function of the latter's psychosocially more global character and, perhaps, its consequently greater resistance to change. It may also be, however, that the relative stability of ego status is a function of attenuated variance in the measures currently in use (see Holt, 1980). Thus, the question of whether the contrasts are substantive or artifactual remains open.

Self-Concept: Definitions and Structure

As Hansford and Hattie (1982, p. 123) aptly put it, the self-concept literature is "a somewhat ill-disciplined field," but "it is clear that the area cannot be ignored." The self-concept literature's sheer volume, its centrality to most notions of psychosocial development, and the value attached to it as an educational outcome in its own right command attention. The principal difficulty in any review such as this, however, is the slipperiness of the concepts and terms used. In the course of their meta-analyses of the relationship between self and achievement or performance measures, Hansford and Hattie counted fifteen different "self-" terms, *self-concept* and *self-esteem* being the two most frequent. The terms are often used interchangeably. Our uses of *self-concept* and *self-esteem* should not be taken to imply any assertion on our part of theoretically different foundations for these two terms. Quite the contrary. There may well be none! Precisely because of this theoretical confusion, this review distinguishes between the two terms on empirical grounds: how the terms are given operational expression in the literature.

In very broad terms, self-concept is a person's self-perceptions, formed through experiences with his or her environment, particularly with significant others (Shavelson, Hubner, & Stanton, 1976; Shavelson, Burnstein, & Keesling, 1977). Most writers agree that self-concept is also multifaceted (one's general self-concept can be theoretically and empirically differentiated from one's academic self-concept) and hierarchical (from general self-concept at the top of a pyramidal structure to individual experiences in particular situations at the base) (Byrne, 1984; Gergen, 1971; Fleming, 1986; Markus, 1977; Marsh, 1986b; Marsh & Parker, 1984; Shavelson, Hubner, & Stanton, 1976; Shavelson & Bolus, 1982). As will be seen, in a substantial body of research, *self-concept* is a relational term that is used to denote students' judgments of their competence or skills (whether academic or social) *relative to those of other students*. It refers to the determination of one's comparative standing in any given area of competence or skill. The research on college students typically examines their self-concepts in either or both academic and social areas.

If academic and social self-concepts refer to a student's "comparative" self vis-à-vis other students, then *self-esteem* operationally has a more internal referent based on the student's comparison of a "real" with an "ideal" self. Self-esteem is at once a more generalized and more personalized evaluation of self. The term *self-esteem*, as used here, is not specific to any particular dimension of self, and judgment is based less on one's standing relative to others (although that clearly will affect self-esteem) than on internal standards or the level of satisfaction with "self" as one is. Self-esteem is "the evaluation which the individual makes and customarily maintains with regard to himself: it expresses an attitude of approval or disapproval, and indicates the extent to which the individual believes himself to be capable, significant, successful, and worthy. In short, self-esteem is a *personal* judgment of worthiness that is expressed in the attitudes the individual holds toward himself" (Coopersmith, 1967, pp. 4–5). Wells and Marwell (1976), after listing a sample dozen synonyms for *self-esteem*, suggest that all of them denote some process of self-evaluation and self-affection. Our use of *self-esteem* certainly involves the former, but it is closer to the latter.

Thus, given the variety and often imprecise definitions of terms relating to individuals' self systems, our categorizations are empirically based. All three constructs involve self-evaluation. If the self-evaluative referent in a study is operationalized as external to the self and involves other individuals, then we label it self-concept (whether academic or social). If the referent is some internal standard (typically involving more generalized judgments of self-worth or value), then we treat it under the rubric of self-esteem.

Academic Self-Concept

As noted earlier, studies of changes in academic self-concept typically have a "social comparison" character, asking students to rate themselves "compared to other students you know" on various items reflective of academic skill or performance (for example, writing ability, mathematical ability, achievement motivation, intellectual self-confidence). In some studies, these items are treated separately; in others, they are aggregated into scales.

Overall, the general picture this body of evidence paints is one of growth over the four years of college, but the nature of the changes appears not to be entirely linear or monotonic. The conventional wisdom would suggest that the academic self-concepts of freshmen would probably not increase during the year and might even suffer some damage as students move from high school into the presumably more academically competitive environment of college (see, for example, Komarovsky, 1985). That may to some extent be true. For example, Baird (1969b), studying freshmen entering twenty-nine colleges, found a decline after one year in students' self-ratings of their "scholarship," even after controlling for precollege ratings. He found no change, however, on a measure of academic self-confidence. In a study of nearly 35,000 freshmen entering 307 institutions in 1966, Bayer, Drew, Astin, Boruch, and Creager (1970) found that after one year the percentage of students rating themselves above average in various areas either stayed the same or increased only slightly (somewhat larger increases were reported in artistic and writing abilities). Bassis (1977), using a large, nationally representative data base, reports findings indicating that students' academic self-concepts may change very little over the first year. Indeed, indirect evidence from one national study (Werts & Watley, 1969) and direct evidence from a number of smaller-scale or single-institution studies suggest that the conventional wisdom may be right: Students' academic self-concepts, for some at least, may even decline during the first year (Chickering, 1974a; Gadzella & Fournet, 1975; Komarovsky, 1985; Skager, Holland, & Braskamp, 1966). Ten institutions' averages reported in Skager, Holland, & Braskamp indicate early drops in academic self-confidence on the order of .21 and .34 of a standard deviation (or 8 and 13 percentile points) among freshman men and women, respectively.

While Komarovsky (1985) identifies at least three possible responses to experiences that threaten one's academic self-concept (a maladaptive withdrawal, the mobilization of resources to improve one's standing and self-concept, or readjustment of one's self-image), the reasons behind any declines in self-concept remain largely unexamined. It is quite possible that such "declines" reflect not so much "real" changes in students' self-concepts as temporary adjustments in their comparative standards. For example, the very bright freshman who in high school might have rated himself or herself among the top 1 percent of students academically, upon entering a highly selective institution (with many other equally bright students) might adjust that "top 1 percent" rating downward to "average," at least temporarily (L. Baird, personal communication, March 1990).

Whatever the reason for early declines in academic self-concept, the weight of evidence clearly and consistently indicates that in the ensuing years students' academic self-images become progressively more positive over time, recovering perhaps as quickly as by the end of the sophomore year (Pascarella, 1985c, 1985d, undated). After four or more years, academic self-concepts are consistently higher than they were during the freshman year. This conclusion is supported by large, nationally representative studies over a four-year period (Astin, 1977a, 1982; Chickering, 1974a) and in studies based on data from the Cooperative Institutional Research Program (CIRP) that covered a nine-year period (Astin & Kent, 1983; McLaughlin & Smart, 1987; Pascarella, Smart, Ethington, & Nettles, 1987; Smart, 1985; Smart & Pascarella, 1986a). Results from single-institution or smaller-scale cross-sectional and longitudinal studies also indicate positive change in students' assessments of academic competence and self-worth after four years of college (Bailey & Minor, 1976; Fleming, 1984; Gadzella & Fournet, 1975; Gurin & Epps, 1975; Hood & Jackson, 1986a; Komarovsky, 1985; Schmidt, 1970).

Information on the intensity and extensity of change in academic self-concept over four years is scarce, however. The best estimates of the degree of change over the four years of college come from Astin (1977a). On the basis of data from some 25,000 freshmen who entered more than 300 institutions in 1961 and were followed up five years later, Astin reports an increase of 14 percentage points from the freshman to the senior year in the proportion of students who rated themselves "above average" in intellectual self-confidence. The percentage who rated their academic ability above average increased 4 percentage points over the period, while self-evaluations of artistic and writing abilities climbed 6 to 7 points. Self-ratings of mathematical ability dropped by 2.2 percentage points. Such evidence must be interpreted cautiously, however. Not only is students' reference group becoming increasingly competent over time, but it is also changing in composition as some students drop out and others continue their education.

Interestingly, Astin (1977a) found that for a third of the self-concept items (covering academic, social, and other areas), the percentages of students rating themselves above *and* below average increased. As he suggests, these findings may indicate that students' self-concepts tend to become more differentiated during the college years. They may also reflect an increase in students' sense of reality, that one cannot be above average in all areas and that one may excel in some areas while doing poorly in others.

Social Self-Concept

While fewer studies have examined changes in students' social as compared with academic self-concepts, the patterns of change that emerge from the studies in both areas are highly similar. The transition from high school to college appears to be as hard on students' social self-concepts (popularity, popularity with the opposite sex, leadership ability, social self-confidence, understanding others, and the like) as it is on their academic self-images. With some exceptions that indicate relative stability or slight declines (for example, Bayer, Drew, Astin, Boruch, and Creager, 1970), the evidence indicates that students' social self-concepts are likely to become somewhat less positive initially. Baird (1969b), in a study of more than 5,000 freshmen (drawn randomly from a larger, nationally representative study) entering twenty-nine colleges around the country, identified a general trend toward lower self-concepts in popularity after one year on campus. Skager, Holland, and Braskamp (1966) found similar results (with institutions as the unit of analysis, self-ratings of popularity dropped .22 and .25 of a standard deviation, or 9 and 10 percentile points, among freshman men and women, respectively). Lokitz and Sprandel (1976) report similar directional results in a single-institution study. Their interview data indicate that students feel stripped of their social identities by the move to college, having lost the social identity moorings afforded by parents' place in the community and by their own place in their high schools and among their peers.

The dawn of an increasingly more positive social self-image, however, eventually relieves these darker hours for students' social self-concepts. Like that related to academic self-image, the change probably occurs by the end of the sophomore year (Pascarella, 1985d). The evidence from large, national studies is clear and consistent that as seniors, students' social identities are much more positive than they were as entering freshmen (Astin, 1977a; Chickering, 1974a). Results from single-institution studies are consistent with these findings (Heath, 1968; Schmidt, 1970; Fleming, 1984), as are several national studies covering a nine-year period (Astin & Kent, 1983; McLaughlin & Smart, 1987; Smart & Pascarella, 1986a; Pascarella, Smart, Ethington, & Nettles, 1987).

Over the four-year period of college, according to Astin's (1977a) data, the percentage of students reporting themselves "above average" in five areas of social self-concept increases from 4 to 11 percentage points, an average gain of about 7 points. At the same time, the percentage reporting themselves "below average" in the same five areas declines by less than a percentage point in three areas (social self-confidence, popularity, and leadership ability) to nearly 8 points in public speaking ability.

Self-Esteem

As noted earlier, *self-esteem,* as used here, is an empirically based term and category. In contrast to studies of change in students' academic and social self-concepts (studies that typically ask students to compare themselves with other students), studies of self-esteem examine students' generalized judgments of their own worth or merit, evaluated not in terms of their position relative to others but with reference to an internal, personal standard. While studies of changes in students' self-esteem adopt various measurement schemes,[7] an individual with high self-esteem is typically characterized as having feelings of worth, being able to do things as well as others, having a number of good qualities, having much to be proud of, having a positive attitude toward oneself, feeling useful to others, feeling self-confident, and being satisfied with oneself (Bachman & O'Malley, 1977; Smart, Ethington, & McLaughlin, undated).

A voluminous literature on self-esteem exists, most of it reporting on elementary and secondary school students (Wylie, 1979). However, several studies of college students, based on nationally representative samples and employing sophisticated analytical techniques, have been published. These studies consistently indicate increases in students' self-esteem during the college years (Bachman, 1972; Bachman & O'Malley, 1977; Bachman, O'Malley, & Johnston, 1978; Kanouse et al., 1980; Knox, Lindsay, & Kolb, 1988; O'Malley & Bachman, 1979; Smart, Ethington, & McLaughlin, undated; Wolfle, in press). The studies by Bachman and his colleagues are particularly informative about change during the college years. In 1966, these researchers studied a panel of more than 2,200 white, male tenth graders in eighty-seven nationally representative high schools who were followed up at various intervals until 1974 (five years after high school graduation). A generally linear increase in self-esteem was found over the eight-year period of the study. Gains were monotonic (always increasing or not changing at all) through the senior year of high school, with a more substantial jump over the next four years. Over the eight years, a gain of .92

of a standard deviation was recorded for the entire study group, which included high school graduates who did not go on to college. Our estimate, based on a bar graph (Bachman & O'Malley, 1977, p. 370), indicates that the magnitude of the gain between high school graduation and five years later was approximately .60 of a standard deviation (an increase of 23 percentile points). Kanouse et al. (1980) report four-year gains of .50 of a standard deviation (an increase of 19 percentile points) averaged across postsecondary "tracks" (for example, full-time employment, enrollment in two-year colleges, enrollment in four-year colleges, military service). Despite these upward shifts in absolute self-esteem scores, however, the evidence also indicates a good deal of relative stability (that is, the relative position, or rank order, of individuals within the group). After adjustments for measurement reliability, Bachman, O'Malley, and Johnston (1978) estimate that self-esteem had a stability coefficient of .90 for one-year intervals, with a stability of .40 over the entire eight-year period of their study. Change did occur, but it appeared to be gradual, in relatively equal intervals, and to be "developmental rather than revolutionary" (p. 115).

Other large-scale studies, all but one based on data from the National Longitudinal Study of the High School Class of 1972 (NLS-72), corroborate the findings of Bachman and his colleagues (Behuniak & Gable, 1981; Knox, Lindsay, & Kolb, 1988; Smart, Ethington, & McLaughlin, undated; Wolfle, in press; Weidman, Phelan, & Sullivan, 1972). None of these studies, however, reports information that could be used to cross-validate the estimate of the magnitude of the changes in self-esteem during the college years derived from Bachman and O'Malley's (1977) study.

With one exception (Whiteley, 1982), the results of a sizable number of smaller-scale or single-institution studies, using a considerable variety of measures of self-esteem, provide additional, consistent evidence of statistically significant increases during the college years in students' evaluations of themselves as worthy, competent, equal to others, and having reason to be proud of their accomplishments during the college years (Edwards & Tuckman, 1972; Finnie, 1970; Graffam, 1967; Heath, 1968; Hess & Bradshaw, 1970; Katz & Associates, 1968; King, 1970, 1973; Knox, 1971; Manis, 1985; Marron & Kayson, 1984; Moos, 1979; Moos & Lee, 1979; Mortimer & Lorence, 1981; Priest, Prince, & Vitters, 1978; Reid, 1974; Schmidt, 1970; Stikes, 1984; Valine, 1976; Winter, McClelland, & Stewart, 1981). King (1970, 1973), in his interviews with Harvard College students, found reason to speculate that the gains in self-esteem over time may be less an increase than a change in other components of a student's self-image. He noted that fewer fluctuations from doubt to self-regard were accompanied by students' more realistic appraisals of their aptitudes and personality strengths and weaknesses. By the senior year, students' self-esteem appeared to be better anchored in a realistic appraisal of themselves, a conclusion similar to that noted earlier by Astin (1977a).

Net Effects of College

Erikson (1968) asserts that individuals develop psychosocially according to an "epigenetic principle," some internal set of developmental, ontogenetic laws that shape psychosocial change, doing so to some extent (but not entirely) independently of environmental and sociohistorical influences. An alternative perspective (see Chapter Two) maintains that students (and people in general) adapt and change as a consequence of various socializing forces exerted by family, peers, schools, and other social groups and agencies. While no one appears to be willing to argue that change is produced exclusively by one or the other of these sources of influence, the assignment of degrees of influence is problematic in the extreme, particularly in "self system" areas, where the evidence is probably the least rigorous methodologically.

Differentiating ontogenetic and educational effects is particularly difficult with respect to identity and ego development inasmuch as most of the research literature in these two areas deals with structures rather than processes (Bourne, 1978b). Most studies have sought to identify sociodemographic, cognitive, psychological, or behavioral correlates of varying identity and ego development stages. Only a handful of studies have sought to illuminate the processes mediating identity formation or ego development, and fewer still have focused on the role of education in that process. With respect to black identity development, we found no studies that addressed the question of net college effects. In all studies of change in black identity status over time, precollege identity status and other background variables are left uncontrolled, and educational level remains confounded with age and with other potential sources of influence, such as enrollment in black studies courses.

Identity Development

Adams and Shea (1979), using cross-sectional data from 294 freshmen, sophomores, and juniors in eight departments and five colleges of Utah State University, found no main effect for class on measures of Marcia's ego identity status. In a subsequent study, using one-year-later longitudinal information from 148 of these same subjects in longitudinal and cross-sequential analyses, Adams and Fitch (1982) report a significant cohort effect in which juniors were most likely to be identity achievers and least likely to be foreclosed. The difference in the findings of these two studies, however, may well be due to attrition-related sample changes.

While number of years of education has been positively associated with identity status among elementary and secondary school students (Archer, 1982), as well as among undergraduate students (Prager, 1986), the evidence indicates that age is also positively related to identity status (Prager,

1986; Meilman, 1979). Meilman, for example, found that the largest increases in identity achievement status and the largest drops in diffused and foreclosed status appear to occur between the ages of eighteen and twenty-one, the period coterminous with the college years. In all these studies, regrettably, age and education remain confounded, no attempt being made to control either one while examining the effects of the other, in some cases even when information on both variables is available. Nor are other potentially confounding variables (such as socioeconomic status, intellectual ability, race/ethnicity) controlled.

Munro and Adams (1977) contrasted the identity status of an opportunity sample of college students and working people aged eighteen to twenty-one and found that the students were significantly more likely to be in the diffused or moratorium status (that is, had not made commitments). While one might infer from these results that education tends to slow identity development, it is also possible that the social, occupational, and possibly family demands on working youth are such that they require identity resolutions sooner than does the college environment, which has frequently been characterized as a "psychosocial moratorium" in which students are permitted by society and their own expectations to explore and experiment with various possible identities. In any event, the Munro and Adams study suggests that the process of identity development among college and working youth may be neither parallel nor isomorphic: Rates of development varied across areas.

Equally equivocal is the evidence of net college impacts from cross-sectional studies that used models and measures of identity different from those of Marcia (although still usually Eriksonian based). Constantinople (1969) used both cross-sectional and longitudinal evidence in her assessment of more than 950 University of Rochester undergraduates on a measure of successful and unsuccessful resolutions of Erikson's fourth, fifth, and sixth developmental stages. She found that seniors scored significantly higher than freshmen in the successful resolution of industry and identity "crises" and lower on the unsuccessful resolution of inferiority crises. Analyses of her longitudinal data over two- and three-year periods supported the interindividual comparisons. Constantinople (1969, p. 367) concluded that her analyses "raised some questions . . . specifically about the potency of the social environment as a factor affecting personality development." Evidence consistent with this is reported in other cross-sectional studies of four-year change (Mulford, 1967; Stark & Traxler, 1974). Stark and Traxler, who studied 507 midwestern college students in a cross-sectional design, found that both age and educational attainment were related to identity crystallization, although they concluded that the age effects may have been somewhat stronger than the college effects.

With some exceptions (for example, Hood, 1984), other cross-sectional, freshman-senior comparisons fail to show statistically significant changes in identity during college (Erwin & Delworth, 1980; Hood, 1986a; Wilson, Anderson, & Fleming, 1987). In none of these studies, however, were there controls for age, precollege scores, or other potentially confounding precollege variables.

Turner (1975) took a novel approach to the question of identity development and reports evidence that supports the view of the college years as a psychosocial moratorium, a period of exploration and testing. On the basis of a survey of adults in the Los Angeles metropolitan area and questionnaires completed by students at the University of California, Los Angeles, two Australian universities, and one British university, Turner explored the popular assumption that the "search for identity" is a widespread phenomenon. In the Los Angeles sample, he found the frequency of asking, "Who am I really?" was inversely related to age, but even among the youngest group, two-thirds denied asking the question. Educational attainment was positively related to "questing," but the effect was smaller (gamma = .22) than for age (gamma = .51). When age was controlled, Turner still found a positive educational effect on questing. The greatest jump in the percentage of those questing occurred between grade school and high school; the increase was smaller from high school to college. Within the several college samples studied, however, Turner found that most students acknowledged a personal search for identity but that class year was consistently unrelated to questing.

Ego Development

Evidence relating to the net effects of college on students' ego development is similarly meager and inconclusive. Redmore and Waldman (1975) found an association between educational level and stage of ego development, but educational level was confounded with age in this study. Mentkowski and Strait (1983) studied more than 750 Alverno College students (all women, ranging in age from seventeen to fifty-five) in three entering cohorts. When ego development scores of freshmen and seniors were contrasted after removing the effects of age and sample bias due to attrition, seniors scored significantly higher than freshmen. However, when Mentkowski and Strait studied these ego stage changes longitudinally, they found no statistically significant shifts over a period of three and a half years, suggesting that the changes observed in their cross-sectional analyses may have been due more to cohort differences than to educational effects.

Kitchener, King, Davison, Parker, and Wood (1984) found neither cross-sectional differences in ego development stage scores across groups of high school juniors, college juniors, and graduate students nor any significant group-by-time interaction when these groups were tested longitudinally two years later. Indeed, correlations of pre- and posttest SCT scores within each group produced coefficients of .56, .80, and .48 for the three groups, respectively. These results indicate greater stability over the two-year period among college juniors than among either high school juniors or graduate students. This finding is consistent with that reported earlier indicating the possibility of some leveling off in SCT scores after the first two years of college and with evidence reported by Adams and Shea (1979), who found no cross-sectional differences among freshmen, sophomores, and juniors in either identity or ego development. Neither age nor other potentially confounding variables were controlled in these studies, however, and some evidence exists to suggest at least a modest correlation between age and ego development as measured by the Sentence Completion Test total protocol scores (Sullivan, McCullough, & Stager, 1970; Weathersby, 1981).

Academic and Social Self-Concept

Compared to studies of college's effects on students' identity and ego development, even fewer examine the influence of college attendance on academic and social self-concepts net of students' precollege self-concepts and other background characteristics. These studies are methodologically stronger, however, and more consistent in their findings.

Two studies (Smart & Pascarella, 1986a; Pascarella, Smart, Ethington, & Nettles, 1987) drew on nationally representative samples of college students assembled by the University of California, Los Angeles, and the American Council on Education as part of the Cooperative Institutional Research Program (CIRP) directed by Alexander Astin (1977a). The CIRP data base used in these studies includes more than 10,000 freshmen who entered 487 U.S. colleges and universities in 1971 and were followed up nine years later. Both studies used highest degree earned as an index of educational attainment. Pascarella, Smart, Ethington, and Nettles (1987), who studied nearly 4,600 students enrolled in nearly 400 four-year institutions and followed up on them nine years later, found that the positive relation between degree attainment and increased academic and social self-concepts persisted even in the presence of controls for sex, race, secondary school academic achievement and social accomplishment, socioeconomic status, and precollege degree aspirations. Moreover, the educational effects also persisted after controls for any effects of postcollege occupational status. As will be seen in later sections of this chapter, however, the collegiate effects vary, depending upon students' experiences while in college, as well as their sex and race. Smart and Pascarella (1986a) report similar results with nearly 9,600 students in both academic and social self-concepts, even after taking into account students' precollege self-concepts in each area but leaving occupational activities and status uncontrolled. Multiple regression analyses identified a number of college experiences, and characteristics of the institution attended were also related to 1980 self-concepts, tending to support the conclusion of college effects.[8]

More importantly for present purposes, the Pascarella, Smart, Ethington, and Nettles (1987) study indicates that collegiate effects net of precollege self-concepts and other background characteristics are largely *indirect* (through students' college experiences) rather than direct and then only for white, not black, students. Educational attainment's only direct effect was on the social self-concepts of white males. Thus, it appears that the effects of college attendance net of other salient variables are discernible, but they are not global influences deriving from the simple fact of attendance. Rather, they appear to be related to the nature of the experiences students have while in college and to certain of the personal characteristics students bring with them to college. These differential impacts are discussed below in the sections on within-college and conditional effects.

Single-institution, cross-sectional studies (Bailey & Minor, 1976; Gadzella & Fournet, 1975) also report evidence that indicates significant and positive increases from freshman to senior to graduate status in students' academic self-concepts. These studies do not, however, control for precollege academic self-concept or for other variables that might confound the estimation of the net impact of college.

Self-Esteem

Research on the net effects of college on students' self-esteem comes from three national data bases and several single-institution studies. Overall, the evidence points to statistically significant and positive, but probably small and to some extent indirect, effects of college on self-esteem.

Bachman and his colleagues (Bachman, 1972; Bachman & O'Malley, 1977; Bachman, O'Malley, & Johnston, 1978; O'Malley & Bachman, 1979), following more than 2,200 tenth graders through high school graduation and five years beyond, found educational level significantly and positively related to self-esteem after controlling family socioeconomic status and also high school ability and achievement. When precollege self-esteem scores of the junior and senior years of high school are added to the regression model, however, the direct effect of educational attainment on self-esteem becomes trivial. But the evidence also suggests that the relationship is stronger in the earlier educational years than in later ones. While the groups' trend lines over time are almost perfectly linear and parallel across groups, there is a tendency for the lines to converge somewhat over time and for the correlations between education and self-esteem to decline (from .27 in 1966 to .14 in 1974). Bachman, O'Malley, and Johnston (1978, p. 211) conclude that "the pattern suggests that the rise in self-esteem may reflect a gradually increasing maturity and the corresponding increases in status, opportunities, and privileges." These results also suggest that educational attainment shifts in its centrality over time. That is, educational attainment declines in its impact on self-esteem as young men move through the final years of high school and beyond and is based on a shifting set of factors that less and less involve academic or educational achievements. In the presence of occupational status, educational attainment has no direct impact on self-esteem and only a trivial indirect impact (.04) via occupational status (Bachman & O'Malley, 1977). Other studies in this series tend to support these conclusions, extend them to women, and appear to rule out the possibility that the findings discussed above reflect cohort effects (O'Malley & Bachman, 1979).

Findings from studies based on data from the National Longitudinal Study of the High School Class of 1972 are generally consistent with those of Bachman and his associates (Kanouse et al., 1980; Knox, Lindsay, & Kolb, 1988; Smart, Ethington, & McLaughlin, undated; Wolfle, in press). Knox, Lindsay, and Kolb (1988)[9] and Wolfle (in press) controlled race, parental socioeconomic status, academic ability, and precollege self-esteem and found educational attainment to have small but statistically significant effects on self-esteem seven years after high school graduation (Wolfle) and fourteen years after (Knox, Lindsay, and Kolb). Wolfle, however, found that only about half of the net relation between attainment and self-esteem represented direct causal effects ("seems to be so modest as not to warrant serious consideration" [p. 8]). The other half was spurious and due to the mutual dependence of precollege and college self-esteem on antecedent causes in the model, including family background, a finding consistent with that of Bachman and his colleagues. Knox and his colleagues found that having two or more years of postsecondary schooling made the greatest difference in self-esteem (net of background factors). Kanouse et al., however, found that differences in self-esteem at the end of high school (college-going students being generally higher) grew smaller or disappeared over time, within the first year among men. They concluded, as did Wolfle, that global self-esteem is not appreciably affected by post–high school "track."

Other studies drawing on national data bases (Weidman, Phelan, & Sullivan, 1972; Yankelovich, 1974b) and, with one exception (Hess & Bradshaw, 1970), on single-institution studies (Knox, 1971; Marron & Kayson, 1984; Valine, 1976) report an association between educational attainment and gains in self-esteem. These studies, however, employed fewer controls than those just reviewed, and none controlled for precollege level of self-esteem.

While it appears that education probably is indirectly, if not directly, related to gains in students' self-esteem net of precollege characteristics, Wylie's (1979) comprehensive and rigorous review of the developmental literature on self-regard (a term she uses interchangeably with self-concept) clearly suggests that changes in self-esteem are not related to age. Such a conclusion tends to rule out simple maturational or ontogenetic explanations of observed changes in self-esteem during college.

Between-College Effects

Identity and Ego Development

Little can be said with any confidence about differential effects of varying college characteristics on changes in students' identity status or in their ego development. This is probably due to the fact that research in both of these areas is still in its nascent stages. As noted in the previous section, much of the identity research focuses on the structural characteristics and correlates of identity status and ego development. A comparatively small portion of these studies focused on education's effects on change in these areas of psychosocial development, and none systematically and rigorously examined differential educational effects related to varying institutional characteristics.

We identified only one possible exception: a study that examined between-college effects on black students' identity development. Cheatham, Slaney, and Coleman (1990), using an instrument derived from Cross's model, studied 250 African-American undergraduates attending a traditionally black and a predominantly white institution. Using a 2 (institution) × 2 (sex) × 4 (class) multivariate analysis of variance (MANOVA), these researchers found no statistically significant main or interaction effects on black identity status, indicating (among other things) no differences in black identity development based on the type of institution black students attended.

Some evidence does indicate that the "search for identity" is a far more common practice among college students than among similarly aged young people or in the general population. Moreover, it appears to be a process common across institutions: No differences were found in the rate of "questing" among students at the University of California, Los Angeles, and one British and two Australian universities (Turner, 1975). It is worth remembering, however, that if identity development is defined as the simultaneous achievement of an identity in the occupational, religious, political, and sexual realms, then it remains a relatively infrequent occurrence during the traditional college years.

Academic and Social Self-Concept

Substantially more and better evidence exists concerning between-institutional effects on changes in students' academic and social self-concepts. Most of this evidence is based on nationally representative data gathered by the University of California, Los Angeles, and the American Council on Education's Cooperative Institutional Research Program (Astin, 1977a). The studies drawing on this rich data base quite consistently indicate that, net of a wide variety of students' background characteristics and the kinds of experiences they have while in college (regardless of the kind of institution attended), institutional characteristics (with one or two possible exceptions) are *in*directly related to changes in students' academic and social self-concepts. Where direct institutional effects are discernible (Bassis, 1977; Smith, 1990), they tend to be small.

For example, in a series of studies of nearly 5,200 students who entered seventy-four four-year colleges and universities in 1975 and were followed up two years later, Pascarella (1985c, 1985d, undated) found that with a variety of students' precollege traits controlled, measures of institutional selectivity, size, and type of control accounted for less than 1 percent of the variance in students' academic self-concept after two years. These structural and organizational characteristics did, however, have indirect effects on self-concepts through their influence on the kinds of academic and social experiences students had, which were in turn related to students' self-concepts. For example, selective institutions appear to have a negative indirect influence on students' academic self-concept because of the inverse relationship between selectivity and level of academic achievement, which is positively related to academic self-concept. Similarly, public institutions with large enrollments and high student-faculty ratios had a negative indirect effect on social self-concept through their negative effects on students' social integration with both peers and faculty members (Pascarella, 1985d, p. 297, table 2). The latter variables tend to enhance social self-concept.

Similar findings emerge from a series of studies (varying in sample composition, sizes, and analytical designs and methods) based on CIRP data from some 9,500 students who entered 487 U.S. colleges and universities in 1971 and were followed up nine years later (Pascarella, Smart, Ethington, & Nettles, 1987; Smart, 1985; Smart & Pascarella, 1986a), as well as from a CIRP-based, four-year (1982–1986) longitudinal study of women attending women's colleges and coeducational institutions (Smith, 1990). These studies consistently indicate that, net of entering characteristics, what happens to students after they arrive on campus has a greater influence on academic and social self-concepts than does the kind of institution students attend. Net of background characteristics, college experiences, academic major, and postbaccalaureate occupational status, Pascarella and colleagues found that with some few exceptions, institutional selectivity or prestige, the predominant race of a school, and size and type of control had no direct effect on academic or social self-concept among men or women, whites or blacks. McLaughlin and Smart (1987), who used the same nine-year CIRP data base previously described, report findings that indicate less growth in both academic and social self-concepts among male graduates of major research universities than among their peers at four other types of institutions, but there is some reason to believe that this finding is artifactual (reflecting a selection and ceiling effect) rather than substantive.

There are several notable exceptions to the general conclusion that institutional characteristics exert little influence on changes in self-image. The first is the positive but indirect effect of attending a predominantly black institution on both the academic and social self-concepts of black women. For academic self-concept, the effect was transmitted through academic integration, and for social self-concept, through academic integration, social leadership and involvement, and postcollege occupational status (Pascarella, Smart, Ethington, & Nettles, 1987).

Second, with respect to social self-concept, only the college's size/type of control (a single factor) had any effect, and it was negative (and indirect, via lower social leadership or involvement) across all groups (Pascarella, Smart, Ethington, & Nettles, 1987). And finally, while Smart and Pascarella (1986a) found size positively related to social self-concept and selectivity positively related to academic self-concept nine years later, these effects were also only one-third to one-half the size of effects related to various college experiences. These findings are generally consistent with those of Astin (1977a) and Astin and Kent (1983), who found few institutional or structural characteristics related to changes in academic or social self-concept (although Astin and Kent's data indicate some variability by sex).

Astin (1977a), however, also reports that given their precollege characteristics, students attending a two-year college or a predominantly black institution showed smaller than expected changes in social self-concept. His finding concerning the predominant race of an institution conflicts with that of Pascarella, Smart, Ethington, and Nettles (1987), who found no significant negative effects (direct or indirect) of attending a predominantly black college. Indeed, attending a predominantly black college had a significant and positive *in*direct effect on the academic and social self-concepts of black female students and a significant and positive direct effect on the academic self-concept of white male students, findings generally consistent with those of Fleming (1984). Given the wide variety of methodological differences between these studies, it is difficult to know how much substantive meaning to attach to this discrepancy in what are otherwise generally consistent findings.

The common thread running through these studies is the apparently greater importance of what happens to students after they enroll rather than the characteristics of the institutions they attend. It seems clearly possible that the global institutional descriptors typically used to study between-college effects may simply be incapable of detecting real or meaningful differences in institutional effects on self-concept. It seems to us that the use of more specific descriptors and ones that focus on institutional subenvironments holds greater promise of detecting institutional effects.

The "Frog-Pond" Effect

Reference group theory asserts that individuals' self-evaluations are based not only on information about their absolute standing on some variable but also on their relative position when comparing themselves with important others, such as peers. Davis (1966), in his classic study applying this theoretical perspective to students' career aspirations and choices, employed the metaphor of a frog pond and sought to determine whether one is better off (by some standard) being a big frog in a small pond or a small frog in a big pond. Two different theoretical frameworks underlie the question. One school of thought, the "relative deprivation" model (see Davis), argues that college selectivity has a negative influence on academic self-concept because of its negative effect on grade performance (that is, the same student has a harder time getting good grades at a selective institution than at a less selective one). An alternative perspective, the "environmental-press" model (see Thistlethwaite & Wheeler, 1966), argues that selectivity has a positive influence on a student's academic self-concept through the context it creates, with students spurred to higher achievement levels by the presence of their able peers and confirmed in a positive self-image by their admission to the company of intellectually talented students and faculty.

Astin (1977a) found little support for the popular view that institutional selectivity negatively affects academic self-concept, particularly among able students. Nor did he find any evidence to support the environmental-press hypothesis. Indeed, selectivity in his nationally representative study had no effect—one way or the other—on the academic self-concept of able students, although there were some variations within certain institutional types and among middle-ability students. Astin does not, however, specifically examine the effects on academic self-concept of the interrelations among precollege self-concept, institutional selectivity, and college grade performance. He reports no tests of possible indirect effects of selectivity on self-concept.

Pascarella (undated) reports evidence consistent with Astin's results in that selectivity had no effect (positive or negative) on academic self-concept among men, but its effect on women was direct and negative. The possibility of indirect effects (untested in Astin, 1977a, and Pascarella, undated) is suggested in other studies by Pascarella (1985c, 1985d) of a similar data base. In a later, specific test for such effects, however, and after controlling a variety of relevant precollege characteristics, college experiences, and postcollege occupational status, Pascarella, Smart, Ethington, and Nettles (1987) found that institutional selectivity/prestige had neither a direct nor an indirect effect on the academic self-concepts of black or white men or women.

The above findings are at odds with those of other studies supporting the relative deprivation theory as it applies to occupational aspirations (Davis, 1966), motivation for graduate study (Werts & Watley, 1969; see also Astin, 1969d), and the academic self-concepts of tenth- and eleventh-grade students (Bachman & O'Malley, 1986). In these three studies, it appeared that it was better to be a big frog in a small pond than a small frog in a big pond, but in the Davis and Werts and Watley studies, the negative effects of performance on academic self-concept had to be assumed, and in the Bachman and O'Malley study the effects of institutional quality were weak.[10]

Only two studies specifically tested the competing "frog-pond" models with large samples of college students and direct measures of pre- and post-test academic self-concept. Drew and Astin (1972), using data from a random sample of 4,400 students who entered 246 institutions in 1966 and were followed up a year later, report generally strong support for the relative deprivation model and equivocal support for the environmental-press theory. They found the partial correlation of college selectivity and follow-up academic self-rating (net of initial rating and other relevant precollege characteristics) to be nonsignificant (.007), while the partial correlation between college grades and follow-up rating was .27. However, Drew and Astin did not report any test for an indirect relation between selectivity and self-evaluation. They also found evidence supporting an environmental-press function for selectivity. They may have underestimated the influence of selectivity, however, as a consequence of partialling it out of the follow-up measure of self-concept (Bassis, 1977).

In what appears to be the most rigorous test of the frog-pond effect on academic self-concept, a path-analytical study of some 5,600 freshmen entering ninety schools randomly selected from the CIRP data base tested in 1966 and again in 1967, Bassis (1977) reports evidence generally (but not totally) supportive of the relative deprivation theory. Institutional selectivity had a negative direct effect (-.25) on college grades, which in turn had a positive effect (.24) on academic self-evaluation after the freshman year. Thus, the indirect effect of selectivity on self-evaluation is negative (-.06), but its statistical significance is not reported. Additionally, however, Bassis found that selectivity directly and positively (.13) influenced academic self-evaluation net of high school and college achievement, at least modest support for the environmental-press model. This finding indicates that the reference group that students use in evaluating themselves does not consist solely of their classmates. Indeed, Bassis's findings suggest that students' academic self-concepts may be based not only on how well they perform relative to their proximate peers but also on adjustments of those comparisons, taking into account the academic quality and competitiveness of the college they attend. Thus, the weight of evidence on this issue is far from conclusive, although it tends to support the relative deprivation model. We conclude, as did Drew and Astin (1972) and Bassis (1977), that the frog pond's dynamics are more complicated than usually propounded and tested. Although the metaphor is popular, the dynamics underlying it remain relatively murky.

Self-Esteem

Only one study of a nationally representative sample has examined between-institution effects on student's self-esteem (Knox, Lindsay, & Kolb, 1988). This investigation was based on the National Longitudinal Study of the High School Class of 1972 and involves data collected at various points between 1972 and 1986 from 12,841 graduates from more than 1,300 high schools. Net of race, gender, parental socioeconomic status, academic ability, and precollege self-esteem, Knox and his colleagues found measures of institutional selectivity, cohesion (for example, proportion of freshmen living on campus, ratio of full-time to total students), vocational emphasis, enrollment size, proportion of freshmen working, and private versus public control to be unrelated to self-esteem in 1986. Attendance at three Carnegie-type institutions had small (and approximately equal) positive effects on self-esteem, but there was no apparent commonality among the three types: Research University II, Comprehensive University II, and Liberal Arts College II. Given these findings and the evidence indicating that the importance of educational attainment to self-esteem appears to decline after high school graduation (Bachman & O'Malley, 1977; Bachman, O'Malley, & Johnston, 1978), the length of time covered in this study, and the absence of controls for postcollege employment or other activities (which would be expected to reduce institutional effects even more), we are inclined to conclude that the evidence suggests that institutional differences have little or no effect on students' self-esteem.[11]

Within-College Effects

Studies of within-college effects on changes in students' identity and ego stage development, academic and social self-concepts, and self-esteem fall into three general groups. One set examines the effects of different curricula or academic majors. The second cluster focuses on the effects of different kinds of residence arrangements, and the third deals with levels of social and academic integration and students' interactions with peers and faculty members.[12]

Identity and Ego Development

Little has changed since Adams and Fitch (1982) concluded that "A serious test of environmental or social systems that affect identity or ego stage development is yet to be completed" (p. 582). Regrettably, because of

the tendency of researchers in this area to focus on the structural characteristics of identity and ego development, few studies have examined the
processes of such development, and even fewer analyze characteristics of
the higher educational setting that might be related to identity or ego development change.

Sargent (in Loevinger et al., 1985) found some freshman-senior declines in ego development stage among business majors, but no other
subgroup showed any consistent declines, and any consistent major-related
gains are unreported. Hood, Riahinejad, and White (1986) found significant freshman-year differences by major (humanities and social science majors being higher than natural science and business majors), but these differences had disappeared by the senior year (see also Hood, 1984). Two
projects (see Moshman, Johnston, Tomlinson-Keasey, Williams, & Eisert,
1984; Loxley & Whiteley, 1986; Tomlinson-Keasey & Eisert, 1978b; Whiteley & Yokota, 1988) examined the effects of participation in experimental
learning programs on ego development, but the results are inconsistent.
These studies present such different findings, vary so widely in their designs and samples, leave so many relevant variables uncontrolled, and make
up such a tiny body of literature that one can conclude only that nothing is
yet known about the effects (if any) of academic curriculum or major on
identity or ego stage development during the college years.

At the same time, as is suggested elsewhere in this volume, academic
discipline may be less influential than the environment of and the attitudes
and values of students and faculty within a department regardless of the
discipline. Adams and Fitch (1983) found that different departments attract students at varying identity and ego development stages. The researchers also found that once students are in a departmental program,
different interpersonal and contextual factors emerge to encourage or facilitate change in identity formation; the same relation did not hold for ego
stage development, however.

With respect to residence arrangement, Pace (1984) analyzed data
from 14,600 students at sixty-two colleges over the period from 1979 to
1982. He found that the largest differences in self-reported gains in personal and social development (primarily a "self-understanding" dimension)
were between campus (residence hall, Greek society) and off-campus groups.
A smaller study (n = 115 students in a large undergraduate course) that
used a residence × class year factorial analysis of variance found a main
effect for residence but not a significant residence × year interaction (Wilson, Anderson, & Fleming, 1987). These results suggest the residence effect could be as much a matter of student self-selection as anything else. It
may also be, as in other areas reviewed in this volume, that the residence
hall effects are indirect, mediated by the interpersonal relations they facilitate.

Indeed, evidence consistent with the findings of Adams and Fitch

(1983) reported earlier indicates that the people—faculty and peers—with whom students come into contact play an important role in changes in identity and ego development during college (Erwin & Delworth, 1982; Henry & Renaud, 1972; Komarovsky, 1985; Madison, 1969; Newman & Newman, 1978). The potency of these socializing agents in a variety of areas of change is documented in this volume and others, and it appears that these agents' influence is equally potent for identity formation and ego stage development. Several studies (Henry & Renaud, 1972; Komarovsky, 1985; Madison, 1969; Newman & Newman, 1978) suggest that the influences of students' peers may be stronger than those of faculty. These studies suggest that it is the *diversity* of individuals (particularly other students) that developmentally challenges students' conceptions of themselves and that requires adaptation and commitment to certain attitudes, values, beliefs, and actions. Studies of the effects of students' participation in campus and recreational activities and organizations, however, have produced conflicting results (Hood, Riahinejad, & White, 1986; Erwin & Kelly, 1985).

Academic and Social Self-Concept

While only a small number of studies examine the relation between academic major or curriculum and intellectual self-concept, they are methodologically sound and based on the large and nationally representative CIRP data bases. These studies are also generally consistent in finding that majoring in mathematics, the physical or natural sciences, engineering, or another technical field is positively related to increased academic self-concept (Astin, 1977a; Astin & Kent, 1983; Smart, 1985; Pascarella, Smart, Ethington, & Nettles, 1987), although there is evidence that the positive net effect of a scientific or technical major on academic self-concept may vary somewhat according to sex and race (Pascarella, Smart, Ethington, & Nettles, 1987).[13]

In all these studies, this relation is evident while controlling for precollege intellectual self-concept, as well as a wide variety of other salient student background characteristics. Astin (1977a) also found that, net of other factors, being in an honors curriculum was associated with larger than expected gains in academic self-image. Astin and Kent (1983) report similar results, although only for women. As might be expected, however, there is reason to believe that the effects of academic major on intellectual self-ratings are not unidimensional. Students' self-concepts are highest in those skill and content areas that are congruent with those stressed by the major field (Smart, 1985).

Only Pascarella and his colleagues (Pascarella, Smart, Ethington, & Nettles, 1987) specifically examined the effects of academic major on social self-concept. They found only one (net of initial social self-ratings and other background and institutional characteristics): Majoring in a scientific or technical field had a significant direct and negative effect on the social self-evaluations of white male college students. Major had no effect on white women or on black students of either sex.

The effects of student residence arrangement on changes in academic and social self-concepts have attracted somewhat more research attention than academic major. Chickering (1974a), in a major study of differences in the experiences and consequences of commuting versus living on campus, studied nearly 27,000 freshmen who entered 179 schools in nine types of two- and four-year institutions in 1965. Using a random sample of 6,700 of these students and after controlling for information on the student's high school, family background, and attitudes and activities, including precollege self-concept, Chickering found commuting to be inversely related to freshmen's year-end self-ratings of their artistic ability, academic self-confidence, and public speaking ability; but only the last difference was statistically significant. Baird (1969b) found similarly weak effects in another national study of the freshman year.

Over a four-year period and with the same controls as in the freshman-year analyses, however, Chickering (1974a) found campus residents rated themselves higher than apartment dwellers or commuters on six of eight skills, including academic, writing, artistic, public speaking, and leadership skills, all except artistic at statistically significant levels. In contrast, Astin (1977a), after elaborate controls for precollege characteristics, found no statistically significant relation between residence arrangement and academic self-concept.[14]

Other evidence from the CIRP data base indicates that residential effects on academic or intellectual self-concept may be more indirect than direct. Pascarella (1985d) analyzed data from nearly 4,200 freshmen who entered seventy-four universities and four-year colleges and were followed up two years later. After controlling for eight relevant background characteristics, institutional selectivity/prestige, and large enrollment/public control (both factorially derived measures), he found that living on campus had no significant direct effect on academic self-concept, although it had a significant *in*direct effect via its significant direct influence on students' social integration with peers, which *was* positively related to academic self-concept.

The evidence on the effects of place of residence during college on changes in students' social self-concepts is no clearer or more consistent than that on academic or intellectual self-evaluations. Baird (1969b) reports that declines in freshmen's ratings of their popularity were relatively independent of residence (except that students living in fraternities and sororities declined less than those in other groups). Moos (1979) found various types of residence hall environment uncorrelated with several measures of students' social self-concepts after controlling sex, socioeconomic status, and initial status on those measures. Moos and Lee (1979) found that the amount of variance in three measures of social self-concept uniquely due to residence was from only 2 to 6 percent.

Chickering (1974a), in contrast, after controlling for each student's high school, family background, attitudes, and values, found living at home during the freshman year negatively related to measures of social confidence and popularity, with initial differences growing during the year. His data through senior year reveal the same relationships: Gains in social self-confidence and popularity are greatest among residence students and lowest among commuter students, with off-campus apartment dwellers intermediate. Astin (1973b, 1977a) found similar results, even after extensive controls for students' precollege characteristics.

As with academic self-ratings, Pascarella's (1985d) path analysis of data from a nationally representative sample of students studied over a two-year period indicates that living on campus has no direct relation to social self-concept but may have a significant *in*direct effect. The effect of on-campus residence was exerted through its influence on students' interactions with the major agents of socialization—their peers and faculty members, with the influence of peers being nearly twice that of faculty members. Thus, it would appear that students' involvement with these socializing agents, not the mere fact of on-campus residence, is the mechanism that underlies institutional influence on students' social self-concepts.

All of these studies deal with residential arrangement globally conceived. Only the work of Moos and his colleagues (Moos, 1979; Moos & Lee, 1979; Moos, DeYoung, & Van Dort, 1976; Moos & Otto, 1975) has systematically sought to explore internal residential conditions that exert influence. These investigators report differential effects across residential environment types in a variety of areas (most not dealing with self-concepts). However, they also found, consistent with the evidence reviewed above indicating indirect residential effects, that significant portions of the variability across residential environments are explainable on the basis of the characteristics of the students occupying them. In addition, Moos and his colleagues have suggested that because of the tendency for like-inclined students to seek each other out, residence settings may not only facilitate certain kinds of change, but they can also insulate students from pressures to change in other areas. Lozoff (in Katz & Associates, 1968, chap. 7) observed the same effect among students who lived in residence halls for four years. As yet, however, we know very little about exactly how residence arrangement exerts its influence, the nature of the influence, the areas in which it is felt, or the conditions under which it is felt. Moffatt (1989), however, provides rich, anthropological insight into these issues.

A small (but growing) and consistent body of research indicates that the most powerful forces acting on academic and social self-images may flow from students' involvement in the formal and informal academic and social systems of their institutions. These formal "systems" consist of the institutional mechanisms and activities for shaping students' academic and nonacademic lives (classes, grades, cocurricular activities, academic and nonacademic rules and regulations, and so on). Informal systems involve the ongoing interaction patterns students have with other students and faculty members, as well as the normative pressures on students exerted by the dominant academic and social values and attitudes of these important socializing agents. Students' interactions with other students and faculty members appear to be particularly influential. Pascarella (1985c, 1985d, undated) analyzed data from some 5,200 students studied over two years as part of the CIRP studies. Even with eight precollege family and student characteristics and two factorially derived measures of institutional characteristics held constant, he found that a student's level of academic integration (a seven-item measure of academic interest, satisfaction, and success) was the best predictor of academic and intellectual self-concept (path coefficient of .27 to .31 across the three studies). This was at least twice as powerful as any precollege trait except academic aptitude. Academic achievement consistently had the strongest effect on academic self-concept, but knowing a professor or administrator personally also had a significant influence. Net of other factors, students' interactions with their peers (for example, studying with other students, participating in a subject matter or special-interest club) were also positively and significantly related to academic self-image (.06), although social involvement with faculty members was not. These findings are supported by evidence from studies of national samples of entering freshmen followed over a nine-year period (Pascarella, Smart, Ethington, & Nettles, 1987; Smart & Pascarella, 1986a), regardless of whether occupational status was controlled.

Astin and Kent (1983), on the other hand, followed a nationally representative sample of students over a four-year period and found that academic self-evaluations, net of other factors, were enhanced among women at institutions with faculty members who had a research orientation *and* who socialized with students. Among men, positive self-images were associated with knowing faculty or administrators personally. Komarovsky (1985) provides additional evidence relating to the positive effects of student-faculty interaction on women students' intellectual self-images, and Gurin and Epps (1975) report similar findings relating to black students' self-images.

The evidence of the effects of students' involvement in institutional social systems on their social self-evaluations is equally clear and consistent. National studies indicate that interpersonal and social self-concept appears to be most influenced by students' integration in the social systems of the institutions attended, whether studied over a two-year period (Pascarella, 1985d) or a nine-year period (Smart & Pascarella, 1986a). Students' social involvement with their peers and their interaction and familiarity with faculty and staff members were both uniquely and significantly associated with students' interpersonal and social self-concepts, net of various background and institutional characteristics, with the influence of peers being a third again as powerful as that of faculty. The conclusion that faculty play a secondary role in this area is reinforced by Endo and Harpel (1982).

Pascarella, Smart, Ethington, and Nettles (1987) and Astin and Kent (1983) report similar findings consistent with those just summarized and based on studies of students over longer periods of time. More importantly, perhaps, both studies, as well as Astin's (1977a), found that students' involvement in social leadership activities (for example, being president of a student organization, having a role in a play, winning a varsity letter, or editing a school publication) was an important predictor of their social self-images, particularly for women students.

Self-Esteem

Only a handful of studies have examined within-institution effects on changes in students' self-esteem as defined here (having a positive attitude toward oneself, general feelings of worth, feeling oneself the equal of others, and the like). While these studies tend to fall into the same general categories as those dealing with academic and social self-concepts (curriculum or major field, residence, and interpersonal interactions), they are so few in number as to constitute a severely limited pool of evidence in any area.

We identified no study that specifically tested for differences in self-esteem related to academic major. Behuniak and Gable (1981) examined data from nearly 2,500 students enrolled in four-year colleges randomly sampled from the NLS-72 data base, but their interest was in whether students who persisted in a major experienced greater change in self-esteem than students who changed majors after their sophomore year. Behuniak and Gable report statistically significant increases in self-esteem over a four-year period for all six major areas tested (precollege level was uncontrolled), but the statistical significance of differences in the amount of change across majors was never tested. Regardless of whether the differences were statistically significant or not, however, they were relatively small in size.

The only other relevant studies indicated that increases in self-esteem were associated with participation in an honors program, particularly the writing of the senior honors thesis (King, 1973), with intervention counseling for underachieving freshman students (Valine, 1976), and with freshman-year participation in an experimental, "character development" program (Whiteley, 1982).

Whiteley's (1982) finding that freshmen in a character development program showed greater gains in self-esteem than students in other housing settings is clouded by the fact that program membership and residence arrangement are confounded. The "Sierra" (experimental) group and two control groups lived in halls that differed both programmatically and compositionally: One control hall had only freshmen, as did the experimental hall, and the other had students from various class years. The fact that changes in self-esteem in the all-freshman control group more closely resembled those of the Sierra group suggests that living in an all-freshman hall may bolster self-esteem, while mixed-class halls may diminish it. As Whiteley suggests, it may be that living with other freshmen has generally positive effects on students' comparisons of themselves with other freshmen, while simultaneously insulating them from less flattering contrasts with upper-division students, a possibility consistent with Moos and Lee's (1979) suggestion that residence halls can promote both change and stability.

We found only one study that contrasted the effects on self-esteem of commuting and living away from home (either on or off campus) during college. Marron and Kayson (1984) report finding significant positive effects over time, but neither the residence nor the residence × time interaction was significant, indicating residence was unrelated to changes in self-esteem. Initial level of self-esteem, however, was uncontrolled, as were a number of other student background characteristics. The effects of interpersonal interactions on self-esteem remain largely unexamined.

Conditional Effects of College

Identity and Ego Development

Virtually without exception, studies of students' identity status and/or ego stage development that consider individuals' characteristics focus on sex-related differences. Despite this single-minded concentration on gender, however, the literature sheds little light on any differences in identity or ego development change rates. For example, a significant portion of the work done on Marcia's model is based only on males, while Loevinger's studies have tended to concentrate on varied groups of females who also differ substantially in age. Furthermore, these studies select males and females from different populations, use different data collection procedures and instruments, and contrast the sexes on different variables (Bourne, 1978b). Most problematic of all, a significant number of the studies that do investigate change in identity and/or ego development do *not* examine whether the *rate of change* (that is, the time × sex interaction) is significantly different between the sexes, or, in other words, whether women change significantly more or less than men change.[15]

We identified eleven studies that specifically tested for a time × sex interaction and used a measure of identity/ego development other than Marcia's. Four found significant interactions, while seven did not. Constantinople (1967, 1969, 1970) provides the strongest evidence that identity development proceeds at different rates among males and females during the college years. In a cross-sectional study of 952 full-time University of Rochester undergraduates in 1965, she found that at time of matriculation women evinced more mature levels of identity development than men but men showed significantly greater gains in identity formation over the four years of college. Because length of time in college was confounded with admissions- and retention-related variations in the composition of the classes, Constantinople undertook a series of longitudinal follow-ups, obtaining results generally supportive of her cross-sectional findings (Constantinople, 1969). She was inclined to speculate that the college environment's emphasis in many quarters on vocational preparation, a focal point of male identity, may promote greater identity change in males than in females. Loevinger et al. (1985) reached a similar conclusion but (unlike Constantinople) did not specifically test a time × sex interaction. Other studies that have tested for a significant interaction have produced results similar to Constantinople's, indicating greater identity or ego stage development among men than among women during four years of college (Constantinople, 1970; Loxley & Whiteley, 1986; Whiteley & Yokota, 1988; Redmore, 1983).

The apparent consistency of this research, however, is challenged by another set of studies that are generally as consistent in their failure to find statistically significant time × sex interactions on various measures of identity and ego stage development. Whitbourne, Jelsma, and Waterman (1982) call Constantinople's (1969) findings into question. They reanalyzed her cross-sectional data, identifying apparent variations by cohort in sex differences across the sophomore, junior, and senior years that suggest Constantinople's results may reflect more cohort differences than ontogenetic or education-based changes. Using their own data and attempting a partial replication of the longitudinal portion of Constantinople's study, Whitbourne, Jelsma, and Waterman found additional evidence that sex differences varied across cohorts. Each of these analyses suggests that differences between the sexes may be due not so much to gender as to the particular cohorts analyzed.

Other studies also challenge the proposition of sex-based differences in the rates of identity and ego stage development during the college years. Some of these studies are based on Marcia's model and instrumentation (Adams & Shea, 1979; Adams & Fitch, 1982), others on the Erwin Identity Scale (Erwin, 1982; Hood, 1986a; Hood, Riahinejad, & White, 1986), and still others on Loevinger's Sentence Completion Test of Ego Development (Adams & Fitch, 1982; Kitchener, King, Davison, Parker, & Wood, 1984). Some are cross-sectional; others are longitudinal.

Virtually without exception, however, these studies also adopted factorial analysis of variance designs, leaving a number of potentially confounding, precollege student characteristics uncontrolled. Thus, in all these studies, age and educational level remain confounded, regrettably leaving the issue of maturational versus educational effects very much unresolved.

Academic and Social Self-Concept

As with studies of the conditional effects of age and/or education on changes in students' identity status or ego development stage, inquiries concerning the differential effects of college on academic and social self-concept that depend on student characteristics also focus primarily on sex-based differences, although one study examined race-based differential effects as well (Pascarella, Smart, Ethington, & Nettles, 1987). All of these studies are derived from the large, nationally representative CIRP data base.

Only three studies (Bailey & Minor, 1976; Pascarella, Smart, Ethington, & Nettles, 1987; Smart & Pascarella, 1986a) specifically tested sex (or race) × educational attainment interactions to determine whether the rates of change in self-concept varied over time by sex (or race). Pascarella and his colleagues analyzed academic and social self-concept data from 4,600 freshmen who entered 379 four-year colleges and universities in 1971 and were followed up nine years later. These researchers controlled throughout for precollege academic and social self-concept, gender and race (as appropriate), socioeconomic status, high school achievement, high school social accomplishment, and degree aspiration, as well as institutional selectivity/prestige, enrollment and type of control (public versus private), predominant institutional race, and students' occupational status.

Net of these controlled variables, Pascarella, Smart, Ethington, and Nettles (1987) found no statistically significant gender or racial differences in the impact of educational attainment on academic self-concept. Other studies that found no statistically significant differences between the sexes in the impact of college on academic self-image are reported by Smart and Pascarella (1986a) and by Bailey and Minor (1976).[16]

Net of these same student background and institutional characteristics (and occupational status nine years later), the effects of educational attainment on students' social self-images also appear to be general across the sexes and races (Pascarella, Smart, Ethington, & Nettles, 1987; see also Cheatham, Slaney, & Coleman, 1990). Pascarella and his colleagues did, however, identify several conditional effects related to certain college experiences. For example, social leadership or involvement during college had a significantly stronger positive influence on the social self-concepts of black men than of white men and black women; attending a predominantly black institution had a more positive impact on social self-concept for white men than for white women or black men. Furthermore, majoring in a scientific or technical field had a significantly more negative effect on social self-image for white men than for white women. Conversely, academic integration had a significantly more positive impact on social self-concept for black women than for black men. Smart and Pascarella (1986a) also report finding no sex-based conditional college effects on social self-concept.[17]

McLaughlin and Smart (1987), using the same 1971–1980 CIRP data base as Pascarella and others described above, found statistically significant interactions between sex and type of institution in their effects nine years later on both academic and social interaction. Male graduates of major research universities exhibited less growth in both self-concepts than their counterparts at four other types of schools, and all of them appeared to gain about equally in academic and social self-image. No differences were apparent in the effects of type of institution on the academic or social self-concepts among women students. There is reason to believe, however, that the results for males may be artifactual, due to selection and ceiling effects (men attending major research universities had the highest scores on both self-concept measures). Nor has this interaction been replicated: No other study was identified that tested it.

Self-Esteem

No unambiguous evidence relating to sex-based, differential educational effects on self-esteem was identified. Two large-scale studies (O'Malley & Bachman, 1979; Smart, Ethington, & McLaughlin, undated) and two single-institution studies (Marron & Kayson, 1984; Whiteley, 1982) touch on the issue. All suggest that the effects of educational attainment on self-esteem are probably general rather than conditional on sex, but this conclusion is based on indirect evidence and therefore inferential. Literature reviews (for example, Maccoby & Jacklin, 1974; Wylie, 1979) conclude that few differences in self-esteem exist between men and women "across age levels through college age" (Maccoby & Jacklin, 1974, p. 153). But it should be noted that much of the literature covered in these reviews is based on elementary and secondary school students and does not examine sex-based, differential change over time. We identified no study that searched for racially based conditional effects of college.

Long-Term Effects of College

Identity and Ego Development

We uncovered few studies that specifically examined the durability of college effects on identity status and ego stage development during the post-college years. This is not to say that changes in these areas of psychosocial development have not been studied, only that such studies have not examined the role of education in identity and ego development. Bourne (1978a), in his review of the literature on ego identity, found only two longitudinal studies that used Marcia's (1965, 1966) identity status paradigm in following subjects over more than three years. One of these (Waterman, Geary, & Waterman, 1974) was a freshman-senior study, while the other (Marcia,

1976) was a six-year follow-up of a cross-sectional sample of thirty male undergraduates. While the evidence reviewed earlier indicated relative stability in identity status during the college years, Marcia found greater instability over the six-year period among subjects with higher identity status (moratorium and identity achievers) than among low-status individuals (diffused or foreclosed identities). Marcia concluded that achieving an identity during college may or may not yield continued identity achievement in later years, while *not* achieving an identity during college seems to mean not achieving one six or seven years later. Only two additional studies published since Bourne's review were identified. Josselson (1987), following up on thirty-four women interviewed as college seniors twelve years earlier (Josselson, 1973), found that "Women characterized as Foreclosures, Identity Achievements, or Diffusions at the end of college [are] likely to remain so, although the women who are Diffuse in identity may, through luck, find a benevolent organizing force" (1987, pp. 168–169). Some of those characterized as "moratoriums" at graduation subsequently reached identity achievement, but others returned to their precrisis status. A cross-sectional study by Meilman (1979) also produced no evidence of backsliding in overall status beyond the college years.

While the studies of Josselson (1987) and Meilman (1979) tend to call into question Marcia's (1976) conclusion of postcollege identity status stability, one must remember that all these studies are based on *very* small samples. Given the evidence available elsewhere (and much depends upon the definitions of terms), it seems reasonable to conclude that identity formation, ego development, and other forms of psychosocial development probably do not end with graduation (Chickering & Havighurst, 1981; Levinson, 1978; Levinson, Darrow, Klein, Levinson, & McGee, 1974; Neugarten, 1969, 1977; Neugarten & Datan, 1973; Vaillant, 1977; Whitbourne & Tesch, 1985; Whitbourne & Waterman, 1979). While these studies are consistent in their indications of continuing identity development after college, any effects related to educational attainment level were, regrettably, untested.

Academic and Social Self-Concept

Somewhat more information is available on the durability of collegiate effects on students' academic and social self-concepts. While only three studies (McLaughlin & Smart, 1987; Pascarella, Smart, Ethington, & Nettles, 1987; Smart & Pascarella, 1986a) provide reasonably definitive evidence on the topic, they are generally consistent in finding college effects in the postcollege years. All three studies were based on a nine-year follow-up of participants in the 1971 CIRP data collection.

Pascarella, Smart, Ethington, and Nettles (1987) analyzed data from

4,600 students who had enrolled in 1971 in 379 four-year colleges and universities and were followed up nine years later. They controlled for students' precollege academic and social self-concepts, high school academic achievement and social accomplishment, socioeconomic status, and initial degree aspirations, as well as for a measure of occupational status, thereby holding constant to some extent, at least, postbaccalaureate experiences. Net of these variables, Pascarella and his colleagues found that educational attainment nine years later was positively related to the academic self-concepts of white students but not black students. Education's effect was only indirect, however, mediated through its positive influence on occupational status. Educational attainment was also positively related to the social self-images of white men and women and of black women but not black men nine years after matriculation. While education's effects on white males were both direct and indirect, its effects on women of both races were indirect only, again through occupational status. Corroborative findings based on a different sample but with fewer controls are reported in Smart and Pascarella (1986a).

Thus, it would appear that college attendance has a positive net influence on students' social and academic self-images nearly a decade after matriculation. However, that effect seems to be relatively modest and to be mediated by postcollege employment, perhaps reflecting the sense of accomplishment that might be expected to come with ascendence to more socially prestigious and monetarily rewarding occupational positions. Education's positive effects on self-concept appear to come about by helping students obtain relatively higher status employment, which in turn has a direct and positive effect on the academic self-images of whites but not blacks. Occupational status also has a positive and direct effect on the social self-concepts of all groups except black male students.

Self-Esteem

Three large-scale studies (Knox, Lindsay, & Kolb, 1988; Smart, Ethington, & McLaughlin, undated; Wolfle, in press), all of which drew on NLS-72 data, and two studies of the same set of graduates of the same institution (Mortimer & Lorence, 1979a, 1981) indicate that postsecondary educational attainment has a small but statistically significant effect on self-esteem, whether measured seven or ten years after high school graduation. For example, Wolfle (in press) examined the self-esteem of 8,650 white males seven years after high school. After controlling for parents' education, father's occupational status, reading and math ability, and precollege self-esteem, Wolfle found that educational attainment had a statistically significant but small (path coefficient = .074) direct impact on postcollege self-esteem. Findings consistent with these are reported by Smart, Ethington, and McLaughlin (undated); by Bachman, O'Malley, and Johnston (1978);

and by Knox, Lindsay, and Kolb (1988), who also report regression coefficients comparable to those obtained by Wolfle. None of these studies, however, controls for the influence of postcollege experiences, particularly occupational ones, on self-esteem.

In a study of "personal efficacy" or "self-competence" dimensions of self-concept (labels operationally consistent with our definition of self-esteem), Mortimer and Lorence (1979a) studied the role of both educational attainment and occupational autonomy on the self-esteem levels of 435 members of the 1966–67 University of Michigan graduating class, who were followed up in 1976. After controlling family income, mother's education, college GPA, senior-year intrinsic and extrinsic work values, occupational autonomy and income, and postbaccalaureate educational attainment, Mortimer and Lorence found senior-year self-esteem still had a direct effect of .78 on self-esteem ten years later. In a related study of the same group of subjects, Mortimer and Lorence (1981), using a broad measure of "well-being," estimated the ten-year stability coefficient to be .79 on a competence dimension, with an estimated yearly stability of .977 (the highest among five self-concept constructs). Over one-third of the variability in 1976 self-esteem was predictable from 1966–67 scores. Indeed, there is some evidence to suggest that the dimensions of self-esteem become more stable as the individual moves into adulthood. Mortimer and Lorence concluded that self-esteem's persistence over time suggests that it is relatively independent of social and environmental influences.

Given the results reported earlier relating to the modest but statistically significant gains in self-esteem made during the college years, and given the findings above, the weight of evidence points to modest but statistically significant net effects of the college years on students' self-images as they move into and through the early adult years. Only the work of Mortimer and Lorence (1981), however, considers the extent to which the apparent persistence of the college influence also reflects a supportive family, social, and occupational environment. It seems likely, consistent with Newcomb, Koenig, Flacks, and Warwick (1967), that to some extent college's effects persist through the influence of spouses, friends, neighbors, and work colleagues who are similarly educated and share the positive self-esteem that tends to come with higher levels of educational and occupational attainment.

Summary

In this chapter, our attention has focused on student change in areas Inkeles (1966) referred to as the "self system"—the sense of self, personal identity, ego development, self-concept, and self-esteem. While a number of taxonomies might be constructed to categorize changes among students in this area, the research falls rather clearly into four general categories:

identity status and ego development, academic self-concept, social self-concept, and generalized self-esteem.

Change During College

Despite some nontrivial conceptual and methodological problems (for example, ambiguous concepts and terms, small samples, uncontrolled variables) and with the exception of the evidence relating to ego stage development (where the findings are mixed), the research on identity development, academic and social self-concept, and self-esteem consistently indicates that students, as a group, change during the college years. Students successfully resolve identity-related issues, become more positive about their academic and social competencies, and develop a greater sense of self-worth and value. The trend line in each area is not always consistently upward in all cases, however, and for some individuals college may even produce decreases in these areas (Bird, 1975; Timmons, 1978; Wagner, 1970; Wright, 1973).

The identity status literature, based largely on a model developed by Marcia (1965, 1966, 1967), virtually without exception reports students' resolution of identity issues and the forging of commitments to a personal identity in political, religious, sexual, and, particularly, occupational areas. Although there is considerable variation across studies and across identity areas within studies, the percentage of seniors who have successfully examined and resolved their identity within occupational, ideological, or sexual areas is probably some 20 to 25 percentage points higher than among freshmen, with the senior percentages highest in the occupational category and lowest in the religious one. Studies based on theoretical conceptions and measures of identity and self-actualization different from those of Marcia are also generally (but not entirely) consistent in indicating positive developmental change during the college years. There is some modest evidence, however, that from two-fifths to two-thirds of entering freshmen may enter college and leave four years later with their identity status relatively unexamined (Waterman, 1982, table 1; Goethals & Klos, 1970).

The evidence regarding change during the college years in students' ego stage development (where ego is understood to refer to a central organizing framework that provides structure and meaning for one's self and world) is less consistent than that dealing with changes in identity status. Some studies report increases in ego development, but more of them do not. Other studies detect some limited upward movement in the early college years, with no apparent change after that. The general weight of evidence indicates little if any change during the college years. Such movement as may occur is unlikely to be dramatic, perhaps half a stage or less. There is also some tentative evidence that college *may* be a regressive experience for some female students. It is unclear, however, whether these general findings are substantive, because of a plateauing during the late adolescent period that spans the high school and early college years, or artifactual, because of the use of small samples, weak statistical procedures, and the global character of measures used to assess a complex and subtle process.

One of the most striking findings of our review is how few of the extant studies examine identity formation among black and other minority students. A literature that focuses on the characteristics and formation of black identity has emerged in the last two decades and is closely tied to the development of individual identity as it evolves from an examination of collective or group identities. This nascent literature, however, has not yet examined in detail the interactions between and among individual and group components, the conditions and processes of change, or the timing of black identity formation. The paucity of studies in this area constitutes a major weakness in our knowledge of the effects of college on students and will become increasingly more pressing in future years as the number and proportion of black students and other students of color increase.

The research regarding changes in students' academic and social self-concepts (how students evaluate their competencies and skills relative to those of their peers) is methodologically stronger and generally consistent in indicating increasingly more positive self-evaluations in students' writing and mathematical abilities, their achievement motivation, and their intellectual self-confidence. Consistent gains are also recorded in students' beliefs about themselves in such areas as their popularity in general and with the opposite sex, their leadership abilities, their social self-confidence, and their understanding of others. In both academic and social areas, however, the increases in the percentage of students rating themselves "above average" are small and not very dramatic (4 to 8 percentage points from freshman to senior year).

Studies of change during the college years in students' self-esteem (generalized self-evaluations with a more internal standard for judgment) are consistent with those relating to self-concept and point to a generally linear increase over time. However, these studies also indicate a substantial jump in the five years following high school graduation, with gains over this period on the order of .60 of a standard deviation (or about 22 percentile points). Yet not all of these gains are attributable to educational attainment.

Net Effects of College

Little can be said with confidence about the unique effects of college on identity status and ego development. The reason is partly a function of the evolution of the research in these areas. During the last twenty years, the concern has been with issues of structure rather than process. Most studies investigate the existence of hypothesized statuses or stages, the actual occurrence of theorized progressions from one status stage to the next, or the sociodemographic, cognitive, affective, or behavioral correlates of each status or stage. Only a handful of studies illuminate the processes by means of which status or stage change occurs or the factors that mediate that process. Even fewer examine the role of college in that process, and most of those lack methodological rigor. In virtually all of these studies, college effects are left confounded with those of age and normal maturation. Taken together, these studies do not constitute a body of research upon which conclusions about college effects can be confidently made.

The evidence for collegiate effects on students' academic and social self-concepts net of potentially confounding variables is also limited, but it is based on methodologically rigorous analyses and large data bases representative of the national population of college students. Net of the influence of such variables as sex, race, secondary school academic achievement and social accomplishment, socioeconomic status, precollege degree aspirations, and postbaccalaureate occupational status, postsecondary educational attainment appears to be related positively to changes in students' ratings of themselves relative to their peers. This positive relation appears to hold true in terms of both academic self-concept (writing and mathematical abilities, general academic abilities, and intellectual self-confidence) and social self-concept (leadership ability, popularity in general and with the opposite sex, public speaking ability, and general social self-confidence). The collegiate influence appears to be indirect rather than direct, however, being mediated through certain characteristics students bring with them to college and certain within-college experiences to be summarized shortly.

While a number of studies report positive college effects on students' self-esteem, the more rigorously controlled studies (which also tend to draw on national data bases) indicate that college's effects, while statistically significant, are small and complexly interrelated with students' family background, ability, and previous achievement. Some evidence indicates that education's effects diminish shortly after high school graduation, although there is reason to believe that they may increase in potency again as a consequence of postgraduate study.

Between-College Effects

Little if anything can be said about between-college effects on students' identity status or ego development, however it is measured. Only a very small number of investigations have examined identity or ego status at more than one institution (in some cases no more than two or three), precluding reliable and meaningful generalization. Even if generalization were possible, it would be unwise given the absence of controls in these studies for initial differences among entering students.

With some exceptions, the research on the effects of between-college differences on students' academic and social self-concepts is reasonably consistent in indicating that when various prematriculation characteristics are held constant, what happens to students after they enroll has greater influence on them than where they enroll. Several studies of nationally representative samples found few direct effects of college size, type of control, predominant race, single-sex versus coed status, or academic selectivity on students' self-evaluations in either the academic or social sphere. Where such effects are found, they are small. Several institutional characteristics do appear to have an *in*direct effect on self-concept through their influence on the kinds of academic and social experiences students have, which are in turn related to students' self-concepts. For example, institutional selectivity appears to have a slight negative effect on academic self-concept because of its inverse relationship with grades and academic integration levels, which themselves are positively related to academic self-concept. Similarly, large public institutions appear to have a negative indirect effect on students' social self-concepts by inhibiting social interaction with faculty and peers. A noteworthy exception to the conclusion that there are few between-college effects involves black female students. Although it has not been replicated, there is some evidence that attendance at a predominantly black institution has a positive if indirect influence on both the academic and social self-concepts of black women.

Although the evidentiary base is extremely small, such institutional characteristics as selectivity, cohesion, vocational emphasis, size, proportion of freshmen employed, and type of control are all apparently unrelated to self-esteem after a variety of student precollege characteristics have been controlled. While attendance at certain Carnegie-type institutions may be associated with increased self-esteem, the differences across types present no clear pattern.

From this evidence, we conclude that there are few changes in students' self-images and self-esteem associated with attending various kinds of colleges or universities. Both in this area and in the other areas, however, it seems possible—indeed, perhaps likely—that the global characteristics typically used to characterize colleges and universities are insufficiently precise to differentiate among institutions in their effects on students' self-perceptions.

Within-College Effects

Little research explores the kinds of college experiences that might be associated with changes in students' identity status, ego development stage, or self-esteem. Extant studies are often methodologically suspect, limited in generalizability, or conflicting in results, whether the effects of major field, curriculum, or place of residence are under investigation. Some evidence does suggest that students' interpersonal experiences with faculty and other students are associated with changes in identity status and level of ego functioning. Interactions with other students (particularly the diversity of the students with whom the individual has contact) may be more influential than contacts with faculty members.

The research on within-college effects on students' academic and social self-concepts is somewhat more illuminating. Majoring in mathematics, the physical or natural sciences, engineering, or other technical fields is associated with larger than expected gains in academic self-concept (given students' precollege characteristics). With the exception of white males (for whom majoring in the sciences has a negative effect), however, major field appears to be unrelated to students' social self-concepts.

Studies of the effects of where one lives while in college are not entirely consistent. Earlier research found that on-campus residents enjoyed an advantage over their commuting peers in the likelihood that they would develop more positive academic and social self-concepts. More recent studies, however, controlling for students' background characteristics, have refined our understanding of the nature of the effects of place of residence. They indicate that the residential advantage is indirect rather than direct, more one of environment than of place. These more recent investigations find that residential effects are mediated by students' levels of academic and social involvement with faculty members and peers. To some extent, the research on residential effects based solely on place of residence (rather than the nature of the residence experience) suffers from the same constraints as that seeking relationships of self-concepts with academic majors and curricula: The independent measures may simply lack the necessary power to detect real differences, being too global, inclusive, and distal to be effective predictors.

What consistency exists in the within-college evidence of effects on academic and social self-concepts can be found in the growing body of evidence that the most powerful forces involve other people and students' levels of involvement or integration in the academic and social systems of the institutions they attend. With a variety of precollege characteristics held constant, including initial academic and social self-evaluations and net of selected institutional characteristics, the evidence quite consistently indicates that levels of academic and social integration, particularly the degree of involvement with peers and faculty members, are positively related to gains in students' academic and social self-concepts. Peers appear to be particularly influential. The effects of academic and social integration are direct and substantial on both types of self-concept. Such involvement in campus life may be especially important to the social self-image of female students, for whom social leadership activities may be particularly influential in enhancing positive self-concepts.

Conditional Effects of College

Although research on the conditional effects of college has focused almost exclusively on differences between the sexes, whether sex is differentially related to the degree of change in students' identity status or ego development stage nevertheless remains an open question. Some studies suggest that males experience greater gains than females (for whom college may even have a slightly regressive effect), while others indicate no differential effects.

The evidence is more consistent and persuasive (albeit limited) in suggesting that with salient student background and institutional characteristics held constant, the effects of educational attainment on academic and social self-concepts are general rather than conditional. Sex- and race-related differences in the rates of change in social (but not academic) self-concept do, however, appear to be associated with certain college experiences. For example, social leadership or involvement has a stronger positive effect for black men than for white men and for black men compared to black women. Academic integration has a stronger positive impact on black women than on black men, and majoring in a scientific or technical field appears to have a stronger negative effect on social self-concept for white men than for white women.

While the evidence is extremely limited, it suggests no sex-related differences in self-esteem associated with educational attainment. This conclusion is highly tentative, however.

Long-Term Effects of College

Virtually nothing is known about the long-term effects of educational attainment on changes in students' ego development stage or identity status. There is ample reason to believe that identity formation does not end with the college years, but college's effects on those changes remain largely unexplored and consequently unknown.

Although only a few studies have examined the long-term effects of college on academic and social self-concepts, they have been methodologically rigorous and based on large, representative, national samples. After holding constant students' precollege background characteristics, certain structural and organizational features of the schools attended, and postcollege occupational status, the net effects of postsecondary educational attainment on academic and social self-concepts are still discernible nearly a decade later. In the case of academic self-evaluations, however, college's influence appears to be indirect rather than direct and to affect white but not black students. The effects of postsecondary educational attainment on social self-image are only marginally more general or direct. College's positive effects on white males are both direct and indirect, but the effects on white and black women are only indirect. The amount of formal education appears to have no effects, positive or negative, direct or indirect, on black male students' self-concepts. For both academic and social self-images, education's indirect effects tend to be mediated through postcollege occupational status.

Statistically significant, if small, associations between educational attainment and self-esteem are found seven and ten years after college. These associations are detectable even after holding constant a variety of relevant precollege individual characteristics, including precollege self-esteem levels. The major benefits appear to accrue to individuals who persist into the upper-division years or who go on for postgraduate study. Some ambiguity remains, however, since the role played by postcollege experiences, particularly occupationally related ones, remains unclear.

Some Concluding Thoughts

Taken together, this body of research offers few opportunities for claims of significant benefits of college attendance in students' self systems: their sense of personal identity, their ego functioning, and their self-evaluations. There are several reasons for this conclusion.

First, and particularly in the areas of identity formation and ego development, these are relatively new fields of inquiry, and theoretical foundations are still being laid and explored as researchers focus on basic, often descriptive questions. For the most part, questions about whether any changes are attributable to college attendance itself, to the kind of institution attended, or to the experiences students have while in college have not even been asked, much less answered.

Methodological constraints in the literature as a whole constitute a second reason. Many of the studies (especially in the identity and ego research areas) rest on opportunity samples, frequently small and ungeneralizable to any population of significance. Moreover, many of the studies are based on research designs and analytical procedures that are ill-suited to addressing questions of net college effects. Most problematic of all in attempting to understand the unique effects of college and university attendance, age and educational attainment often remain confounded. This is sometimes true even when the data for partitioning out the effects of maturation and education are available. Controls for students' backgrounds and precollege levels on dependent measures are absent or weak. Noncollege comparison groups are extremely rare. Taken as a whole and evaluated against the generally accepted canons of social science research, this body of evidence is not impressive.

Nevertheless, there are some rigorous and generalizable studies, and their results constitute the third reason for our inability to claim much in the way of significant college effects on students' self systems. These studies generally indicate that after holding constant various relevant student background characteristics, the discernible direct effects of college attendance tend to be small. Much of the evidence simply will not sustain claims of substantial and direct collegiate effects. At the same time, however, reasonably consistent evidence indicates that college attendance does make a difference, albeit small. But its effects appear to be more indirect than direct, being mediated largely by the academic and social interactions students have with one another and with faculty members.

Finally, it is neither unreasonable nor novel to argue that it may be unrealistic to expect the college experience to have an effect much greater than that revealed by the available research. Self systems are complex, poorly understood, and generally believed to reach deeply into an individual's being. As such, they are not likely to be easily touched, changed, or measured, especially over comparatively short periods of time. If this is so, then we ought not to be too surprised by the apparently modest effects of college in these areas. It may also be, however, that as this general area of inquiry matures, as theories are tested, clarified, and refined, as more psychometrically sound instruments and more rigorous designs and analytical procedures are adopted, the effects of college attendance will be more clearly discernible than they are at present.

Notes

1. Other authors have suggested taxonomies consistent with Inkeles's (1966) model and the focus on self and relational systems in this chapter and the next. See Drum (1980); Heath (1968); Kuh, Krehbiel, and MacKay (1988, p. 94); and Trent and Medsker (1968, p. 9).
2. Indeed, the authors of several studies of psychosocial change specifically comment on the *absence* of crisis in the sense of a psychological emergency, noting the comparatively smooth transition from one condition or phase to another (Freedman, 1967; Katz & Associates, 1968; King, 1973; Offer & Offer, 1975).
3. Matteson (1975), Bourne (1978a, 1978b), Marcia (1980), and Waterman (1982) review the literature on Marcia's (1965, 1966) model. Bourne (1978b) also provides a conceptual and methodological critique.
4. The bulk of this research examines the relationships between identity status and self-esteem (Fannin, 1977; Marcia, 1967; Marcia & Friedman, 1970; Orlofsky, 1977; Prager, 1982; Schenkel & Marcia, 1972). However, a number of researchers have studied the relation between identity status and a considerable variety of other variables, including anxiety (Schenkel & Marcia, 1972), authoritarianism (Marcia, 1967; Marcia & Friedman, 1970; Schenkel & Marcia, 1972), autonomy and

conformity (Toder & Marcia, 1973; Waterman, Buebel, & Waterman, 1970), decision-making style (Waterman & Waterman, 1974), expressive writing (Waterman & Archer, 1979; Waterman, Kohutis, & Pulone, 1977), intimacy and isolation (Orlofsky, Marcia, & Lesser, 1973), locus of control (Adams & Shea, 1979; Waterman, Buebel, & Waterman, 1970), academic major (Marcia & Friedman, 1970; Fannin, 1977; Waterman & Waterman, 1972), moral development (Podd, 1972), sex role orientation (Orlofsky, 1977), and work role salience (Fannin, 1977).

5. A considerable literature examines the undergraduate experience of black students at both black and white institutions (for example, Allen, 1986, 1987; Astin, 1982; Beckham, 1987; Burbach & Thompson, 1971; Centra, 1970; Davis & Borders-Patterson, 1973; Edwards, 1970; Epps, 1972; Fleming, 1981, 1984; Gibbs, 1973, 1974, 1975; Gurin & Epps, 1975; Hedegard & Brown, 1969; Kiernan & Daniels, 1967; Loo & Rolison, 1986; McSwine, 1971; Monroe, 1973; Moore, 1972; Semmes, 1985; Sowell, 1972; Stikes, 1984; Thomas, 1981a; Willie & Levy, 1972; Willie & McCord, 1972). Several reviews of the research literature on black students in higher education are available (Fleming, 1981; Harper, 1975; Ramseur, 1975; Sedlacek, 1987; Stikes, 1975; Willie & Cunnigen, 1981). See Duncan (1976) for a discussion of psychosocial conditions for minority graduate students. Several sources discuss the particular needs of various minority group students, including black students (Pounds, 1987; Sedlacek, 1987), Hispanic students (Olivas, 1986; Quevedo-Garcia, 1987), Asian Americans (Chew & Ogi, 1987), and Native Americans (LaCounte, 1987). This list is not exhaustive.

6. Freedman (1965) reached this conclusion on the basis of the timing of change along various dimensions of "personality."

7. Wylie (1974) offers an extensive critique of the various research methodologies employed in the study of self-esteem, or what she frequently refers to as self-regard. Wylie (1979) has also given a comprehensive review of studies of the self-concept or self-esteem of people six through fifty years of age, with particular emphasis on self-concept/esteem as a function of age and developmental level. See also Wells and Marwell (1976) and Dickstein (1977).

8. Astin (1977a) reports similar findings and reaches similar conclusions. His evidence tends to be somewhat indirect, however, being based on positive relations between senior-year self-concepts (net of precollege levels and a host of other background variables) and such variables as involvement in college (greater change among students who were also more involved in college is presumed to indicate college effects) and persistence (higher self-concepts among persisters than dropouts, implying college effects). Because Astin does not report a relation between increases in academic and/or social self-concept and some specific measure of educational attainment (for example, number of years

enrolled, highest degree earned), however, we do not discuss his results in detail. Astin does report finding no relation between changes
in academic or social self-concept and age, which argues against a
"maturation" explanation (and strengthens the "college effects" explanation) of the observed changes. Thus, while Astin does not report
specific tests of a relation between educational attainment and positive
changes in self-concepts, his data tend to support a conclusion of college effects net of other variables.

9. While this study was competently conducted, Knox, Lindsay, and Kolb
    consider their findings preliminary and expect to report additional
    analyses in a forthcoming book entitled *The Way Up: The Long-Term
    Effects of Higher Education on Students.*

10. See Marsh (1986b), Marsh and Parker (1984), and other references in
    those papers for related studies based on elementary and high school
    students.

11. The only other study identified that deals with between-college effects
    on self-esteem as defined here (Edwards & Tuckman, 1972) con-
    trasted community college and university liberal arts students after
    two years. Initially, community college students had lower self-esteem
    than the university students, but after two years, these differences dis-
    appeared as community college students showed marked increases and
    the university students remained unchanged.

12. A considerable number of studies examine the effects of what Thrasher
    and Bloland (1989) call intentional interventions, specially developed
    courses or programs intended (or perhaps implicitly expected) to alter
    in some fashion students' psychosocial development. Because these in-
    terventions take such diverse, often idiosyncratic forms (see below),
    are often of very brief duration, frequently employ opportunity sam-
    ples of questionable representativeness for any larger population, and
    use widely varied designs and analytical procedures, no attempt is made
    here to summarize their findings. Overall, our review leads us to agree
    with Thrasher and Bloland, who reviewed the literature on such in-
    tervention programs published between 1973 and 1987 and con-
    cluded that while program effects were found, they tended to be small,
    perhaps because most studies examined change over a short period
    of time. Studies of the effects of interventions on various dimensions
    of students' identity or ego development, academic and/or social self-
    concept, and self-esteem fall into the following general categories (ref-
    erences are not exhaustive within categories): formal courses (Brush,
    Gold, & White, 1978; Kammer, 1984; King, Walder, & Pavey, 1970;
    Loeffler & Feidler, 1979; McClaran & Sarris, 1985; Parish, 1988b;
    Plummer & Koh, 1987; Stake & Gerner, 1985; Tracy, 1975; West &
    Kirkland, 1986), periods of study abroad (Barnhart & Groth, 1987;
    Carsello & Creaser, 1976; Hensley & Sell, 1979; Hull & Lemke, 1975;

Hull, Lemke, & Houang, 1977; Juhasz & Walker, 1988; Kuh & Kauffman, 1985; McEvoy, 1986; Morgan, 1972, 1975; Nash, 1976; Stauffer, 1973), various forms of personal counseling (Cooker & Caffey,
1984; Guller, 1969; Heppner & Krause, 1979; Locke & Zimmerman,
1987; McWilliams, 1979; Terranova, 1976), marathon and encounter
group sessions (Culbert, Clark, & Bobele, 1968; Foulds, 1971; Guinan
& Foulds, 1970; Kimball & Gelso, 1974; Lieberman, Yalom, & Miles,
1973; Meador, 1971; Treppa & Fricke, 1972; University of Massachusetts Counseling Center, 1972; Young & Jacobson, 1970), remediation
or compensatory programs (Fennimore, 1968; Leib & Snyder, 1967;
Olsen, 1972; Peterson, 1973), generalized psychosocial development
programs (Loeffler & Feidler, 1979; Ohlde & Vinitsky, 1976; Parrott
& Hewitt, 1978; Walsh, 1985), cooperative education or community
work experiences (Hursh & Borzak, 1979), student exchange programs within the United States (Hull, Lemke, & Houang, 1977; Worley, 1978), and wilderness training programs (Heaps & Thorstenson,
1972; Lambert, Segger, Staley, Spencer, & Nelson, 1978; Robbins, 1976;
Vander Wilt & Klocke, 1971). McHugo and Jernstedt (1979) review
the literature on field experiences (including study abroad and wilderness training).

13. It should be noted that Smart (1985) and Pascarella, Smart, Ethington, and Nettles (1987) examined academic self-concept nine years
after matriculation. They also controlled for postcollege educational
attainment (highest degree earned) and employment (job status). Thus,
while some of these results may be influenced to an unknown degree
by postcollege activities, two important sources of bias—postbaccalaureate education and employment—have been at least partially controlled.

14. This finding is inferred from the absence of any mention by Astin
(1977a) of finding a statistically significant relation between residence
and change in academic self-concept (Astin uses the term *intellectual
self-esteem,* but the operational form of this term is equivalent to what
we have labeled *academic self-concept*). The correctness of this inference
was confirmed in a telephone conversation with Astin on April 9, 1990.

15. A number of studies of college students have explored differences
between the sexes in various facets of identity formation and ego development but do not directly test differences between the sexes in
the amount of change over time. Because this volume is concerned
with the fact and determinants of college student changes in a number of areas, these studies are only tangentially related to the question
of differential change conditional on sex. However, readers interested
in questions relating to sex-based differences in identity status and
ego stage development might find one or more of the following studies of use: Alishio and Schilling (1984); Allen (1986); Belenky, Clin-

chy, Goldberger, and Tarule (1986); Douvan and Adelson (1966); Gilligan (1982a); Hodgson and Fischer (1979); Rodgers (1990b); Stark and Traxler (1974); W. Stewart (1977); and Waterman and Nevid (1977). This listing is neither an exhaustive nor a comprehensive collection of such studies. See also the sections on conditional effects in Chapters Three, Four, Six, Seven and Eight of this volume.

16. The findings of these studies may appear to conflict with those of large, national studies of self-concept change over four years by Astin (1977a) and over nine years by Astin and Kent (1983), both of which suggest that men increase their positive academic self-concepts more than women. The discrepancies, however, are due to different analytical strategies. Astin (1977a) appears to have tested the main effect of sex on senior-year self-concepts (both academic and social) after holding constant the effects of numerous other background variables on the follow-up measure. It is not clear whether he included in this particular analysis some measure of educational attainment (for example, number of years enrolled, whether a degree had been earned). Astin and Kent (1983) base their conclusions on a comparison of changes in the percentage of respondents rating themselves "above average" on a variety of items relating to academic and social self-concept. Thus, based on his report, it appears doubtful that Astin specifically tested the significance of any differences in the *rates* of change between the sexes (the years of education × sex interaction term). It is clear that Astin and Kent did not.

17. Bragg (1976) summarizes the literature on socializing processes related to identity development. While her review concentrates on the development of professional identities in graduate education programs, it has some generalizability to undergraduate settings and identity more broadly conceived.

6

Psychosocial Changes:
Relating to Others
and the External World

Whereas Chapter Five deals with changes in students' conscious and unconscious conceptions and evaluations of themselves, this chapter examines
changes in what Inkeles (1966) referred to as individuals' "relational systems." These include changes in students' relationships with other students
and in their orientations to authority figures, intimates, peers, and collectivities. In short, this chapter deals with changes in the ways students relate to
their external world.

The literature on these changes is both extensive and varied in the
particular aspects of psychosocial development that are the object(s) of study.
Moreover, the research is based on varying theoretical or conceptual perspectives that in turn beget different constructs, terminologies, and instrumentation. Much of this research is also based on pencil and paper tests,
the construct validity of which is frequently unestablished. In addition, the
connections between the psychosocial characteristics presumably measured
by these instruments and actual student behaviors have frequently not been
shown.

Our review indicates that the research concerning relational systems
falls into six categories, dealing with issues of (1) autonomy, independence,
and locus of control; (2) authoritarianism, dogmatism, and ethnocentricism; (3) intellectual orientation (considered part of the relational system
because of its generally external thrust); (4) interpersonal relations; (5) personal adjustment and psychological well-being; and (6) maturity and general personal development.

Change During College

Autonomy, Independence, and Locus of Control

Studies in autonomy, independence, and locus of control examine
the extent to which students change in their susceptibility to external influ-

ences, whether human or institutional. Most studies focus on changes in students' levels of autonomy and/or independence, that is, their degree of freedom from the influence of others in their choices of attitudes, values, and behaviors. (Note that the emphasis here is on students' general orientation, not on specific areas of belief, which are reviewed in Chapter Seven.) Agents of outside influence might be parents, peers, and institutions, with their formal rules, regulations, and laws. The terms *autonomy* and *independence* are subject to some ambiguity. For example, taken to their logical extreme, they could denote antisocial behavior. For Chickering (1969), however, autonomy, in its highest form, is synonymous with interdependence, which involves not simply one's freedom to choose or act free of outside influences but rather a freedom that also recognizes one's dependence on and obligations to others, both individuals and societal collectivities and conventions.

Other studies examine locus of control, a concept based on social learning theory and referring to the extent to which one is self-directed or believes oneself to be the determiner of one's own fate. Internally directed people tend to believe that they can control what happens to them, while externally directed individuals believe that their destiny is determined more by luck, chance, or fate (Rotter, 1966, 1975; Phares, 1973, 1976).

For centuries, independence of thought and action has been considered an important characteristic in most conceptions of adulthood and psychosocial health. As such, independence has long been an educational goal. Changes in the extent to which students think and behave in ways that reflect independence of the influence of others have been an object of study for more than thirty years. Few psychosocial traits have received more attention, and the evidence—from whichever decade—consistently indicates changes along this personal dimension during the college years.

Wolfle and Robertshaw (1982), Knox, Lindsay, and Kolb (1988),[1] and Nichols (1967), all drawing on large, national data bases, have provided the most persuasive evidence on changes in students' autonomy, independence, or locus of control. Wolfle and Robertshaw studied some 8,650 white males who participated in the National Longitudinal Study of the High School Class of 1972 (NLS-72) and who were tested again in 1976 with a short form of Rotter's (1966) locus of control scale. About 60 percent of the respondents had had some postsecondary schooling. Wolfle and Robertshaw found a statistically significant (but slight) shift from external to internal locus of control, indicating an increase in students' sense of control over what happens to them and a decline in their sense that their world is controlled by luck, fate, chance, or other external forces. Kanouse and colleagues (Kanouse et al., 1980), Knox, Lindsay, and Kolb (1988), Behuniak and Gable (1981), and Smart, Ethington, and McLaughlin (undated), who all used NLS-72 data, report findings consistent with those of Wolfle and Robertshaw, although they employ somewhat different samples, designs, and analytical approaches. Nichols (1967), who studied more than 600 National Merit Scholarship finalists in more than 100 colleges, also reports evidence consistent with these findings.

With some exceptions (for example, Adams & Shea, 1979; Watkins, 1987; Whiteley, 1982), single-institution or small-scale studies of students' locus of control status generally report increases in internality during the college years that are consistent both with the studies reported above and within this set of studies (Finnie, 1970; Goldman & Olczak, 1976, 1980; King, 1970; Knoop, 1981; Leon, 1974; Linder, 1986; Olczak & Goldman, 1975; Priest, Prince, & Vitters, 1978; Schroeder, 1973; Schroeder & Lemay, 1973; Scott, 1975).[2]

Our analysis of data reported by Wolfle and Robertshaw (1982) indicates an increase in internality of .26 of a standard deviation (10 percentile points). However, this estimate includes nonstudents as well as students. It was not possible to estimate the effect sizes for the two groups separately. Nichols's (1967) data, on the other hand, do indicate four-year declines on a measure of "dependence" of .28 and .29 of a standard deviation (-11 percentile points) among male and female National Merit finalists, respectively, accompanied by gains of .25 and .49 of a standard deviation (10 and 19 percentile points) for men and women, respectively, on a measure of "self-sufficiency." Thus, it appears that during the college years, students experience statistically significant but relatively small gains in internality.

With respect to changes in autonomy, the second edition of the Student Developmental Task Inventory, or SDTI-2 (Winston, Miller, & Prince, 1979), is designed to operationalize three of Chickering's (1969) seven vectors: achieving autonomy, freeing interpersonal relations, and developing purpose. Our synthesis of results from four studies (Greeley & Tinsley, 1988; Jordan-Cox, 1987; Straub & Rodgers, 1986; Winston, Miller, & Prince, 1979) that used the autonomy scale of the SDTI-2, as well as the autonomy scale norms of the Student Developmental Task and Lifestyle Inventory, a major revision of the SDTI-2 (Winston & Miller, 1987), indicates average freshman-to-senior differences of .59 of a standard deviation (22 percentile points). Other studies that used the SDTI-2 consistently indicate gains in autonomy during the college years, but the information needed to estimate effect sizes is not given (Itzkowitz & Petrie, 1986, 1988; Polkosnik & Winston, 1989). Still other single-institution studies that employed quite varied instruments and methodologies support the conclusion that students gain in their freedom from the influence of others during the college years (Chickering, 1967; Constantinople, 1967, 1970; Fry, 1976, 1977; Graffam, 1967; Heath, 1968; Hood & Jackson, 1986c; Lokitz & Sprandel, 1976; Matteson, 1977; Montgomery, McLaughlin, Fawcett, Pedigo, & Ward, 1975; Offer & Offer, 1975; Stikes, 1984; Straub, 1987; Pemberton, as cited in Williams & Reilly, 1972).

While the concept of autonomy implies a freedom from the influence of various individual and institutional sources (parents, peers, friends, teachers, schools, governments), most studies treat autonomy, independence, or locus of control as a global construct. Only a small group of studies, all of which used the College Student Questionnaire's (Peterson, 1968) peer independence and family independence scales, differentiate changes in students' degree of independence from parents as well as from peers. The psychological separation from parents is a common theme in the theoretical literature on adolescence. On the basis of various theories of identity development discussed in Chapter Two and the research on that topic reviewed in Chapter Five, one might predict that students would gain their independence from family before they would from peers. As the psychological (and sometimes physical) distance between the individual and parents increases, the individual turns increasingly to people outside the home (primarily but not exclusively peers) as psychosocial referents. Indeed, the departure from home experienced by many (but by no means all) students and the socialization processes of the college years provide ample opportunities for students to begin, if not consummate, the emotional and psychological separation from family. Whether that is, in fact, what happens, however, remains something of an open question.

Of the nine studies identified that spoke directly to the issue of change in level of independence from family and peers, six report statistically significant increases in family independence. Changes with respect to peers were smaller and either statistically nonsignificant or ignored in the presentation of results, thereby suggesting statistical nonsignificance (Hatch, 1970; Miller, 1973; Newcomb, Brown, Kulik, Reimer, & Revelle, 1970; Peterson, 1968; Wilder, Hoyt, Doren, Hauck, & Zettle, 1978; Wilder, Hoyt, Surbeck, Wilder, & Carney, 1986). Newcomb and his colleagues, as well as Heath (1968), report a decline in peer independence scores among freshmen. Hatch found this to be true only among women, while the men in her study increased in peer independence. Fry (1974) reports statistically significant increases in family independence among students from rural but not urban backgrounds. The remaining two studies (Nelsen & Johnson, 1971; Nelsen & Uhl, 1977) found statistically significant increases on both the family and peer independence scales, although in both studies the increases in independence from family exceeded those relating to peers. Across the few studies reporting data that can be used to estimate magnitudes, it appears that students gain in independence from family on the order of .60 of a standard deviation (29 percentile points) and from peers by about .20 of a standard deviation (8 percentile points). With one exception (Wilson, Anderson, & Fleming, 1987), studies based on other measures also report freshman-senior increases in autonomy in students' interpersonal relations with their parents (Heath, 1968; Lokitz & Sprandel, 1976).

Thus, the weight of evidence tends to support the proposition that students gain greater independence from parents than from peers during the college years. The research on this point is not yet conclusive, however.

Authoritarianism, Dogmatism, and Ethnocentricism

The studies reviewed in this section deal with one or another form of narrow-mindedness. Definitions of *authoritarianism* generally include such personal descriptors as an undemocratic orientation, obedience and submissiveness toward authority, rigid adherence to rules, intolerance of ambiguity and points of view contrary to one's own, and general anti-intellectualism.[3] *Dogmatism* (see Rokeach, 1960) is a somewhat broader term that reflects the closed character of an individual's belief systems, nonreceptivity to relevant information, and inability to evaluate and act on the inherent merits of information, unaffected by irrelevant considerations originating inside or outside the individual. The term *ethnocentricism* typically denotes an individual's tendency to view social interactions in terms of in-groups and out-groups, where in-groups are seen as dominant and perceptions of individuals' characteristics are determined on the basis of stereotypic positive or negative images of the groups to which they belong. The ethnocentric individual tends to be submissive to the in-group and hostile to the out-group.

As will become evident shortly, a significant amount of the research conducted in these areas has focused on changes in authoritarianism and employed the Omnibus Personality Inventory (OPI) (Heist & Yonge, 1968), particularly the autonomy and social maturity scales. "High scorers [on the autonomy scale] show a tendency to be independent of authority as traditionally imposed through social institutions" (Heist & Yonge, 1968, p. 4). They also tend to "feel that disobedience to government is sometimes justified, and do not favor strict enforcement of all laws no matter what the consequences" (Heist & Yonge, 1968, p. 6). "High scorers [on the social maturity scale] tend to be uncompulsive, nonpunitive, independent, and not subject to feelings of victimization. . . . Low scorers tend to be more judgmental, intolerant, and conventional in their thinking" (Trent & Medsker, 1968, p. 149). Because of the substantive similarity between the content of these scales and generally accepted definitions of authoritarianism described above and for other empirical reasons,[4] results obtained by means of the OPI autonomy and social maturity scales are reviewed here as reflecting students' authoritarian orientations despite the fact that the scales' labels imply that somewhat different traits are being measured.

The only multi-institutional (or otherwise large-scale) studies to investigate four-year changes in students' levels of authoritarianism are those of Chickering and his colleagues (Chickering, 1969, 1971b, 1974b; Chickering & Kuper, 1971; Chickering & McCormick, 1973; Chickering, McDowell, & Campagna, 1969); Clark, Heist, McConnell, Trow, and Yonge (1972); and Trent and Medsker (1968). (See also Trent & Craise, 1967; Walizer & Herriott, 1971.) Chickering's analyses are based primarily on longitudinal data from thirteen institutions (or subsets of them) that were part of his Project on Student Development, a five-year research project begun in 1965 (Chickering, 1969). Those of Clark and his colleagues draw on cross-sectional data from eight institutions (also studied in the late 1960s). Although these institutions were not chosen to be representative of higher educational institutions in America, they are quite diverse with respect to student and institutional characteristics. Trent and Medsker followed some 10,000 1959 high school graduates from sixteen communities throughout the United States over a five-year period. All three of these projects used the Omnibus Personality Inventory.

Virtually without exception, the analyses from these three projects found statistically significant changes away from authoritarian thinking from freshman to senior year. Our synthesis of data reported by Clark, Heist, McConnell, Trow, and Yonge (1972) and by Chickering (1974b) indicates that the average magnitudes of the four-year increases on the autonomy scale (indicating gains in nonauthoritarianism) were .72 of a standard deviation (26 percentile points) in the Chickering data and .80 of a standard deviation (29 percentile points) among the students studied by Clark and his colleagues. Evidence from several single-institution studies of four-year change, also based on the OPI's autonomy scale, suggests that increases in autonomy may even be somewhat higher (Bennett & Hunter, 1985; Kuh, 1976; Yonge & Regan, 1975). The average four-year increase in OPI autonomy scores across five studies, regardless of sample size or number of institutions, was .88 of a standard deviation (31 percentile points), with the range from .51 to 1.52 standard deviations (19 to 43 percentile points).

Similar results, both in direction and in magnitude, are reported in studies that used OPI social maturity scores (Korn, 1968; Ellis, 1968; Levin, 1967; Trent & Golds, 1967; Trent & Medsker, 1968).[5] Our synthesis of data reported in these studies indicates an average increase in nonauthoritarianism (across eight groups) of .90 of a standard deviation (about 32 percentile points). Except for Levin, these same studies gathered data on four-year change on the California F-scale measure of authoritarianism. Our synthesis of these changes (averaged across eleven groups) indicates a decrease in authoritarianism of .73 of a standard deviation (−27 percentile points). Caution is warranted, however, since the Trent and Golds and Trent and Medsker studies in some instances drew on the same data base. Nonetheless, the similarities of the magnitudes of the four-year changes on these scales and across multiple samples are striking.

Our synthesis of Korn's (1968, p. 167) and Ellis's (1968, pp. 327–330) data on four-year changes on the E (ethnocentricism) scale among men and women attending the University of California, Berkeley, and Stanford University indicates a drop (averaged across the four groups) of .45 SD (−17 percentile points). No studies were identified that would permit responsible estimation of the magnitudes of the changes in dogmatism. Although data to estimate effect sizes were not reported, a number of single-institution or small-scale studies that used the OPI's autonomy and/or social maturity scales, the California F scale or E scale, or other measures report evidence substantially consistent in their indications of declines (over varying periods of time) from freshman-year scores in authoritarianism, dogmatism, and/or ethnocentricism (Alfert & Suczek, 1971; Ayers & Turck, 1976; Baker, 1976a, 1976b; Brawer, 1973; Cade, 1979; Elton, 1969, 1971; Elton & Rose, 1969; Feldman & Weiler, 1976; Finnie, 1970; Freedman, 1967; Katz & Associates, 1968; Lacy, 1978; Newcomb, Brown, Kulik, Reimer, & Revelle, 1971; Ogle & Dodder, 1978; Rich & Jolicoeur, 1978; Schmidt, 1970, 1971; Suczek, 1972).

Regrettably, there is little evidence upon which to base a firm conclusion concerning the timing of changes in these general areas. Feldman and Newcomb (1969, pp. 96–104) concluded that there was more evidence for gradual change over the college years than for greater changes in some years than in others. The research completed in the last twenty years sheds little light on this question. Most studies in this and other areas of student change did not examine variations in the rate of change over the college years. Some evidence does *suggest* that changes may be greater in the first two years of college than in the later years. Data reported by Chickering, McDowell, and Campagna (1969) and by Newcomb, Brown, Kulik, Reimer, and Revelle (1971) on the degree of change in these areas over two years (gains of .73 and .68 SD in OPI autonomy scores and a decline of .66 SD on an "authoritarian cluster" of scales), when compared to the estimates of four-year change in authoritarianism reported earlier, suggest that most or all of the change away from authoritarianism occurs in the first two years of college. Clearly, however, two studies do not constitute conclusive evidence, and more extensive and current research will be needed before this proposition can be accepted with confidence.

Intellectual Orientation

In Chapter Four, we reviewed studies that examined changes in students' general cognitive skills (communication skills, Piagetian formal reasoning, critical thinking, postformal reasoning, and so on). In this section, we examine another dimension of intellectual change, that which deals more with students' general intellectual orientation to their world. The term *intellectual orientation* is used here to characterize students' intellectual approaches to their world, including their intellectual curiosity, inclination to be skeptical and critical of information, analytical orientation, and intellectual flexibility and complexity. The studies reviewed here examined students' general disposition to be inquisitive, reflective, rational, logical, analytical, critical, and skeptical.

As in the preceding section, much of the research in this area has relied on the use of several scales from the Omnibus Personality Inventory (Heist & Yonge, 1968). Such studies typically involve one or more of six OPI scales: thinking introversion (TI), theoretical orientation (TO), estheticism (Es), complexity (Co), autonomy (Au), and religious orientation (RO). Because of these scales' content, the evidence from the autonomy scale is discussed in this chapter with other measures of authoritarianism (see note 4), and evidence from the aestheticism and religious orientation scales is reviewed in Chapter Seven. In this section we focus on the evidence from the remaining three OPI scales and other sources.

Before doing so, however, it may be helpful to briefly describe the general content of these three OPI scales.

Thinking Introversion (TI): [High scorers] are characterized by a liking for reflective thought and academic activities. . . . Their thinking is less dominated by immediate conditions and situations, or by commonly accepted ideas, than that of thinking extroverts [low scorers]. Most thinking extroverts show a preference for overt action and tend to evaluate ideas on the basis of their practical, immediate applications, or to entirely reject or avoid dealing with ideas and abstractions.
Theoretical Orientation (TO): This scale measures an interest in, or orientation to, a more restricted range of ideas than is true of TI. High scorers indicate a preference for dealing with theoretical concerns and problems and for using the scientific method in thinking; . . . High scorers are generally logical, analytical, and critical in their approach to problems and situations.
Complexity (Co): This measure reflects an experimental and flexible orientation rather than a fixed way of viewing and organizing phenomena. High scorers are tolerant of ambiguities and uncertainties; they are fond of novel situations and ideas. Most persons high on this dimension prefer to deal with complexity, as opposed to simplicity, and very high scorers are disposed to seek out and to enjoy diversity and ambiguity [Heist & Yonge, 1968, p. 4].

As with the research on authoritarianism, dogmatism, and ethnocentricism, the best evidence on changes in students' general intellectual orientations comes from four major sources: Chickering and colleagues' thirteen-college study (Chickering, 1974b; Chickering & Kuper, 1971; Chickering & McCormick, 1973; Chickering, McDowell, & Campagna, 1969), the eight-college study done at the University of California, Berkeley's Center for Research and Development in Higher Education (Clark, Heist, McConnell, Trow, & Yonge, 1972; McConnell, 1972; Wilson, Gaff, Dienst, Wood, & Bavry, 1975), Trent and Medsker's (1968) classic five-year longitudinal study of high school seniors who graduated in 1959 (see also Trent & Craise, 1967), and samples of "West Coast" institutions and National Merit Scholars analyzed and reported by Trent and Golds (1967). Excepting Trent and Medsker (1968), we identified no nationally representative study of general intellectual disposition conducted in the last two decades.

Virtually without exception, the OPI-based evidence indicates consistent but modest increases in students' intellectual orientations during the college years. On the basis of change estimates averaged across ten groups in four national studies (Chickering, 1974b; Clark, Heist, McConnell, Trow, & Yonge, 1972; Trent & Golds, 1967; Trent & Medsker, 1968), our analyses indicate four-year average increases of .34 of a standard deviation (13 percentile points) in thinking introversion and .36 of a standard deviation (14 percentile points) in complexity. Interestingly, the gains in thinking orientation tended with reasonable consistency to be only one-half to one-third the size of the gains on the other two scales: an average increase of only .19 of a standard deviation (8 percentile points) across the groups in these studies. No particular reason for these differences in scale results is readily apparent.

Whatever the reason, it is clear that students as a group consistently increase modestly in their general intellectual orientations during the college years when tested by means of these three OPI scales. McConnell (1972) and Wilson, Gaff, Dienst, Wood, and Bavry (1975) report similar and consistent evidence based on these and other OPI scales aggregated to form "Intellectual Disposition Categories" (IDCs). Wilson and his colleagues found that of the 1,033 students in their sample, 47 percent increased one IDC or more over the four years, but 53 percent remained the same or declined. With some exceptions (Brawer, 1973; Snyder, 1968), results from a number of smaller-scale investigations, also based on these OPI scales, provide evidence substantially consistent with that of the large-scale studies (Bennett & Hunter, 1985; Elton, 1969, 1971; Feldman & Weiler, 1976; Kuh, 1976; Lacy, 1978; Newcomb, Brown, Kulik, Reimer, & Revelle, 1971; Welty, 1976; Yonge & Regan, 1975). Similarly consistent evidence (with the exception of Tomlinson-Keasey, Williams, & Eisert, 1978; and Schmidt, 1970, 1971) is provided by additional studies that examined change over varying periods of time using measures of intellectual disposition other than the OPI (Barton, Cattell, & Vaughan, 1973; Burton & Polmantier, 1973; Eisert & Tomlinson-Keasey, 1978; Friedlander & Pace, 1981; Hummel-Rossi, 1976; Magnarella, 1975; Regan, 1969; Schmidt, 1971; Smith, 1971).[6]

We identified only one study that shed any light on the timing of change in intellectual disposition over the traditional four-year period of college. Our analysis of data in Chickering, McDowell, and Campagna (1969) indicates one-year increases of .12 and .18 of a standard deviation (5 and 7 percentile points) in thinking introversion and complexity, respectively, with gains of .18 and .24 of a standard deviation (7 and 9 points) over a two-year period. Comparing these effect sizes with the four-year change estimates of .34 and .36 SD reported earlier, one might speculate that perhaps half to two-thirds of the gains occur in the first two years. While this finding is consistent with that of Lehmann (1963) in terms of changes in students' critical thinking abilities, the body of evidence on this point can hardly be characterized as convincing. Although there is little on the point, it is entirely possible that these rather modest group gains mask more substantial individual changes, both upward and downward.

Interpersonal Relations

Changes in individuals' self and relational systems such as those discussed in Chapter Five and here are complex and interconnected. The self is not defined in isolation but at least partially by one's interactions with others. Perceptions of self and beliefs about others' perceptions of oneself shape not only individuals' internal, psychological structures but also their responses to and interactions with their external social world. In this section, we review the research literature that deals with changes in students' social adjustment and interpersonal relations.

Only Chickering (1974b) reports evidence from a large-scale study of four-year changes in students' social and interpersonal interactions. His study of thirteen small colleges relied heavily on the Omnibus Personality Scale, and his evidence on interpersonal relations comes from that measure's social extroversion (SE) scale. High SE scores indicate a preference for being with people, seeking social activities, and deriving satisfaction from them, while the low-scoring introvert tends to withdraw from such social interaction. The students in the institutions studied by Chickering showed no freshman-senior change in their interest in being with people or in seeking out and deriving pleasure from social activities. Indeed, our analyses of data in two single-institution studies (Kuh, 1976; Yonge & Regan, 1975) indicate a *drop* in social extroversion of about .20 of a standard deviation (-8 percentile points) across the two studies. Brawer (1973) and Hatch (1970) also report declines in social extroversion during the early college years.

The meaning of such stability (possibly even declines) on this psychosocial dimension is difficult to interpret with confidence. Stability or small declines might suggest a certain developmental regression or withdrawal from other people and social activities in general, a withdrawal into oneself, and possibly greater self-centeredness rather than the social and interpersonal expansion often expected in the college years (for example, Chickering, 1969). At the same time, one might reasonably argue that the scores reflect not so much a shift toward introversion as an increase in students' interpersonal maturity, in their selectivity of friends, and in increased intimacy with that smaller circle of close friends. This latter interpretation, of course, is consistent with the successful resolution of Erikson's (1956, 1963)

"intimacy versus isolation" crisis, and with Chickering's (1969) "freeing interpersonal relationships" vector, particularly the component relating to
changes in the quality of intimate relations with others. It is also possible
that the college experience may be anchoring these dimensions, preventing
regression or decline.

Possible answers to the nature of the changes reflected by the OPI's
social extroversion scores are suggested in a series of small-scale studies
based on the SDTI-2 (Winston, Miller, & Prince, 1979), which constitutes
another body of research dealing with freshman-senior changes in students'
interpersonal relations. Of interest here is the SDTI-2's "developing mature
interpersonal relations" (MIR) scale, which characterizes students' relationships with the opposite sex, mature relationships with peers, and tolerance
(the capacity to respond to others as individuals rather than stereotypes).
Our analyses of MIR data in four studies of freshman-to-senior changes
(Greeley & Tinsley, 1988; Itzkowitz & Petrie, 1986; Jordan-Cox, 1987;
Winston, Miller, & Prince, 1979) indicate average increases in developing
mature interpersonal relations on the order of .16 of a standard deviation
(6 percentile points). It is worth noting that the Winston, Miller, and Prince
study was the only one reporting a four-year decline (−.04 SD) on this
scale, while the estimated gains in the other three studies (each of which
used a sample rather different from the others) ranged from .17 to .26 of
a standard deviation. Freshman-senior increases on the MIR scale in a revised version of the SDTI-2, the Student Developmental Task and Lifestyle
Inventory, or SDTLI, mentioned earlier, averaged .57 of a standard deviation (22 percentile points) among undergraduates at twenty different colleges in the United States and Canada (Winston & Miller, 1987). Still other
studies, based on a considerable variety of samples and instruments and
covering varying periods of time, give generally consistent evidence of increases in students' capacities for more mature interactions with their peers
and others (Fisher, 1981; George & Marshall, 1972; Hanson, 1988; Hood
& Mines, 1986; J. Katz, 1974; King, 1970, 1973; McArthur, 1970; Reid,
1974; Riahinejad & Hood, 1984; Rich & Jolicoeur, 1978; Schmidt, 1970,
1971; Spaeth & Greeley, 1970; Theophilides, Terenzini, & Lorang, 1984b;
Withey, 1971).

When the stability of or small declines in students' OPI social extroversion scale scores are considered with the increases reported by more
numerous (if smaller) studies that used other measures of students' interpersonal relations, the evidence (some of which is examined below) leads
us to conclude that changes in students' interpersonal relations probably
involve shifts toward more mature relations with peers and others. Fleming
(1984) is a notable exception to this pattern. In her study of black students
at predominantly black and predominantly white institutions, she found
that the nature and degree of change depended largely upon the social
context in which it occurred.

Personal Adjustment and Psychological Well-Being

As with other dimensions of students' "relational systems," a substantial portion of the literature relating to changes in students' personal adjustment and general psychological well-being during the college years is based on the Omnibus Personality Inventory, particularly the impulse expression (IE), anxiety level (AL), schizoid functioning (SF), and personal integration (PI) scales. The general conceptual relatedness of these scales has been suggested by Yonge and Regan (1975), and generally moderate correlations among the scales are given in the OPI's technical manual (Heist & Yonge, 1968, p. 50).

Only two large-scale research projects (neither of which can be considered nationally representative) dealt with changes in students' emotional adjustment: Clark and his colleagues' (1972) study of students at eight diverse institutions and Chickering and his associates' studies of thirteen small colleges (Chickering, 1969, 1971b, 1974b; Chickering & Kuper, 1971; Chickering & McCormick, 1973; Chickering, McDowell, & Campagna, 1969). Our analyses of data reported in Clark, Heist, McConnell, Trow, and Yonge, (1972) and in Chickering (1974b; Chickering & McCormick, 1973) indicate average increases on the impulse expression scale of .40 of a standard deviation (16 percentile points). High scores on this scale reflect a "readiness to express impulses and to seek gratification in thought and action . . . have an active imagination, [and] value sensual reactions and feelings"; very high scores indicate a tendency toward aggression (Heist & Yonge, 1968, p. 5). Although there is considerable variability among individual estimates, our synthesis of increases (no declines were found) in impulse expression across nine samples in five single-institution studies indicates average four-year gains of .37 of a standard deviation (14 percentile points). A comparison of these estimates of four-year change with estimated shifts of +.25 and +.41 of a standard deviation on the same scale over a one- and a two-year period, respectively (Chickering, McDowell, & Campagna, 1969), suggests the possibility that half or more of any shift in impulse expression may occur in the first two years of college, stabilizing in the latter two years. Evidence consistent with this possibility is reported by Newcomb, Brown, Kulik, Reimer, and Revelle (1971).

With some exceptions (such as Brawer, 1973), smaller-scale studies, covering varying periods of time, also report evidence of increases in students' willingness to express impulses (Bennett & Hunter, 1985; Cade, 1979; Freedman, 1967; Offer & Offer, 1975; Snyder, 1968; Suczek, 1972). Nichols (1967), in a study of National Merit Scholarship finalists, also reports declines on measures of superego strength (.26 and .38 of a standard deviation [−10 and −15 percentile points] among males and females, respectively) and deferred gratification (.36 and .33 of a standard deviation; −14 and −13 percentile points among males and females, respectively).

As with social extroversion, however, the interpretation of these changes is ambiguous. Gains might reflect a general increase in students' comfort with normal and natural feelings and concomitant gains in self-confidence, spontaneity, and self-esteem, as well as an emergent personal identity. Conversely, one might infer that observed gains reflect declines in self-control and a shift toward aggressiveness, disruptiveness, rebellion, hostility, or other form of social deviancy. Indeed, the IE scale correlates negatively with the self-control, socialization, responsibility, and good impression scales of the California Psychological Inventory (Heist & Yonge, 1968, p. 31). The antisocial tendencies tapped by this scale are apparent primarily in people who score two or more standard deviations above the mean. Thus, caution is advised in inferring developmentally or socially desirable changes from the results summarized above.[7]

Some insight into the nature of these psychological changes may also be gained by considering the shifts in scores on other, related scales. Freshman-senior changes in score on the OPI's schizoid functioning scale averaged across eight samples on ten campuses (Clark, Heist, McConnell, Trow, & Yonge, 1972; Korn, 1968; Ellis, 1968), according to our estimates, indicate declines of about .41 and .45 of a standard deviation (−16 and −17 percentile points) among men and women, respectively. Higher scores indicate social alienation, with feelings of isolation, loneliness, hostility, and aggression. Chickering's (1974b) data, however, indicate much more modest freshman-senior declines in students' sense of isolation, tension, and difficulty in adjusting to their social environment, as reflected on the OPI's anxiety level scale. (Higher scores on this scale reflect *less* anxiety, nervousness, or difficulty in adjusting to one's social environment.) Our synthesis indicates an increase of only .10 of a standard deviation. Three studies that used the anxiety level scale indicate somewhat larger reductions in anxiety levels over the four years of college (Bennett & Hunter, 1985; Kuh, 1976; Yonge & Regan, 1975), although only the Yonge and Regan study was based on a sample of more than 175 students.

Consistent with the above findings, Chickering's (1974b) data on the OPI's personal integration scale (on which high scorers admit to *few* behaviors or attitudes that characterize socially alienated or emotionally disturbed individuals) suggest an average increase of .41 of a standard deviation (16 percentile points). Studies by Kuh (1976) and Yonge and Regan (1975) also reflected freshman-senior gains, but these increases were about half the size of those indicated by Chickering's (1974b) data. Taken together, these estimates of average change in impulse expression (+.37 SD), schizoid functioning (−.43 SD), and personal integration (+.41 SD) are strikingly similar to the estimated overall change in psychological well-being (+.40 SD) reported by Bowen (1977, p. 134). With one exception (Cade, 1979), other smaller-scale studies that used the personal integration scale or other similar scale scores over varying periods of time also report increases in students' self-understanding and control of emotions and gains in personal integration over varying periods of time (Brawer, 1973; Bennett & Hunter, 1985; Heath, 1968; Hood & Jackson, 1986b; King, 1970, 1973; Newcomb, Brown, Kulik, Reimer, & Revelle, 1971).

Our analyses of one- and two-year changes in personal integration scale data from Chickering, McDowell, and Campagna (1969) suggest, as they did with the impulse expression scale, that perhaps half to two-thirds of these changes may occur in the first two years of college (+.24 and +.31 standard deviations after one and two years, respectively). This speculation, however, awaits more rigorous verification.

Glenn and Weaver (1981) and Witter, Okun, Stock, and Haring (1984) provide strong evidence of educational-related increases in generalized psychological well-being. However, because their data were collected primarily in the postcollege years, these studies are discussed in detail in Chapter Twelve. Several single-institution studies (Hearn, 1980; Martin & Light, 1984; Schubert, 1975b) also provide evidence of increases in students' general psychological well-being during the college years.

Given this evidence, let us now return to the question of whether the freshman-senior increases in impulsivity reported earlier reflect developmentally and socially desirable change. From the gains on the OPI's impulse expression scale, together with the evidence of declines in seniors' social alienation (for example, schizoid functioning) and increases in general psychological well-being, we conclude that the weight of evidence suggests general increases in areas most people would consider desirable psychosocial change during the college years. The inverse relation between impulse expression and schizoid functioning, together with the decline in anxiety levels and gains in personal integration and general psychological well-being, is, we believe, generally indicative of healthy impulsivity, spontaneity, and individual emotional expression. It is worth recalling, however, that changes in this area during college may vary considerably, depending upon the context and the characteristics of the individuals involved (see the discussion of black identity formation in Chapter Five and Lamont, 1979).

Maturity and General Personal Development

Several studies have examined students' psychosocial development not in specific areas but as more globally conceived. In the only "national" study of students' more generalized personal development, Pace (1990) analyzed data from a nonrandom (but probably reasonably representative) 25,427 undergraduates at seventy-four colleges and universities between 1983 and 1986. The data were accumulated from responses to his College Student Experience Questionnaire (CSEQ). Pace found that between 62 and 81 percent of his respondents (depending upon the kind of institution they attended) reported making "substantial progress" in "developing [their] own values and ethical standards," in "understanding [themselves]—[their] abilities, interests, and personality," and in "understanding other people and [in] the ability to get along with different kinds of people" (p. 58).

Pascarella, Terenzini, and their associates report a series of studies based on data from three large research universities (two residential and one commuter) conducted over nearly a decade with a half-dozen independent samples of students who were followed up over varying periods of time. The dependent measure in these studies, with minor variations, was a factorially derived measure of "personal development," consisting of items that ask respondents to report the amount of progress (on a 1–4 scale, from "none" to "a great deal") they believe they have made during the academic year just ending. Progress is reported in such areas as developing a clearer understanding of oneself, developing interpersonal skills, increased openness to new ideas, a growing sense of self-reliance and personal discipline, and a clearer idea of abilities and career goals. Without exception, students in these studies reported gains on this measure of personal change over varying periods of time (Pascarella & Terenzini, 1978, 1980b, 1981; Pascarella, Duby, Terenzini, & Iverson, 1983; Terenzini & Pascarella, 1980a; Terenzini, Pascarella, & Lorang, 1982; Terenzini, Theophilides, & Lorang, 1984b; Terenzini & Wright, 1987b, 1987c). The magnitudes of these changes, however, cannot be estimated in a way that would be meaningfully comparable to those reported elsewhere in this book. Similar evidence of increases in perceived maturity are reported in other single-institution studies, such as Benezet (1976), Shields (1972), and Zirkle and Hudson (1975).

Perhaps the best known and most sustained series of studies of changes in students' "maturity" are those of Douglas Heath. On the basis of an earlier study (Heath, 1965) and a synthesis of what twenty-five educational philosophers throughout history have said about the goals of a liberal education, Heath (1968, 1977b, 1978) developed a comprehensive, dimensional model of college student "maturity." For Heath, maturing is a process that takes place in four major "personality sectors" (cognitive skills, self-concept, values, and interpersonal relations) and, within each of these sectors, along five interdependent dimensions: symbolization, allocentricism, integration, stability, and autonomy. (See Chapter Two for a more detailed description of Heath's model.)

Heath's (1968) most important report of research on maturity during the college years was based on a cross-sectional study of 25 percent samples of two Haverford College graduating classes (n = 24 each) and a 20 percent sample (n = 25) of freshmen, who were followed up one year later. His data collections have all been multifaceted, based on standard psychological tests, projective and semiprojective measures, and measures and questionnaires specially designed to examine change in the twenty specific sectors of his model. Heath drew three general conclusions from his intensive analyses: (1) seniors were more mature than freshmen, and both groups were more mature than they were upon entry to Haverford; (2) seniors reported greater advances toward maturity after four years than did the freshmen after one year; and (3) the rate of maturing varies across the different sectors of the personality. Interestingly, students believed themselves to have matured even more than Heath's objective data indicated. Unfortunately, data that would permit estimation of the magnitude of the increases in maturity were not reported.

Heath's students matured most in their attitudes about themselves, their interpersonal relations, and their values and least in cognitive and intellective skills. This finding is consistent with the relative magnitudes of changes reviewed earlier in this chapter in intellectual orientation and, say, autonomy and independence or authoritarianism and dogmatism. However, the finding is contrary to findings reported by studies reviewed in Chapters Three and Four of this volume. The differences in these findings may be related to the specificity of the cognitive skills measured and reviewed in the earlier chapters. Seniors ranked gains in the integration of intellectual skills, awareness and understanding of themselves and the development of a more conscious self-concept, and integration and other-centered maturation of interpersonal skills as the three areas of greatest change during their college years. Heath (1968, p. 133) identified the progressive psychosocial integration of both seniors and freshmen as "the most important maturational change in college," a process that affected all other sectors of the personality in different but important ways. Maturation occurred "more in one sector of [the students'] personality than in another at different times, depending upon the demands of the environment and their readiness to respond to those demands" (p. 118).

Heath (1968) concluded that the freshman year was particularly important, a conclusion reached by Lehmann (1963) and consistent with the evidence reported in several areas above. The pattern of subsequent growth, Heath found, was set in the freshman year, possibly even the first few months of college. He considered much of the later growth a movement toward greater stabilization and integration of growth patterns established in the earlier college years.

Because Heath's (1968) research was based on a small sample of men from a single, highly selective liberal arts college and because his freshman-senior comparisons were cross-sectional rather than longitudinal, care must be taken not to overgeneralize his findings to college students at large. His results are, however, generally consistent with those of other researchers who have studied larger samples on different campuses around the country. Regrettably, we identified only two studies by other authors who used Heath's model in dealing with change in college students (Erwin, 1983; Jones, 1987). Jones concluded from his review of the published literature "that no one has independently tested the model empirically" (p. 206). The systemic complexity of Heath's model, some of its terminology, and the multiple measures needed to operationalize it may have deterred other researchers from adopting it.

Net Effects of College

Autonomy, Independence, and Locus of Control

Whether the observed gains in personal independence and autonomy are in fact due to the college experience, to normal maturation, or to other influences remains an open question. We identified no studies of net college effects based on anything resembling a nationally representative sample. In the largest study in this area, Barton, Cattell, and Vaughan (1973) focused on 573 subjects recruited from high schools in three major New Zealand cities. Of these subjects, 355 went on to college and 218 went directly to work. Both groups had a mean age of eighteen years at the time of the first testing in 1965. At this time there were no differences between the groups on a measure of independence. Five years later, however, respondents who went on to college showed no change, while those who went straight into a job showed a significant drop from their original scores. The authors speculate that these findings may reflect employed respondents' increased marital obligations or the nature of their low-status jobs. If this is the case, then the effect of college attendance on postsecondary school levels of autonomy and independence would appear to be an anchoring one, while high school graduates who do not go on to college decline in these areas. In any event, it is not possible to attribute these findings to educational attainment with great confidence inasmuch as various alternative explanations (socioeconomic status, cognitive development, or other personality traits) were untested or uncontrolled.

Several studies that used the SDTI-2 found generally consistent, significant, and positive relationships between academic class level and scores on overall and subtask scales of that measure's developing autonomy scale (Greeley & Tinsley, 1988; Itzkowitz & Petrie, 1986, 1988; Straub & Rodgers, 1986; Winston, Miller, & Prince, 1979). All of these studies, however, were cross-sectional, employed simple one-way analysis of variance, and controlled neither for precollege autonomy levels nor for other factors that might be associated with changes in autonomy scores. Winston, Miller, and Prince (1979) found autonomy scores unrelated to age, but Straub and Rodgers (1986) and Hood and Jackson (1986c) report contrary evidence. Hood and Jackson used the Iowa Developing Autonomy Inventory and found that autonomy scores correlated .50 and .43 with age and academic class, respectively. In none of these three studies, however, was class or age controlled while the relation between autonomy and the other variable was being tested.

The evidence on the effects of college on students' locus of control, net of other possible influences, is much more conclusive than that dealing with autonomy and independence. With one exception (Kanouse et al., 1980), studies of net college effects on locus of control indicate that college attendance has a statistically significant and positive effect on students' internality, but education's direct effect is probably quite small.

The most definitive evidence comes from Wolfle and Robertshaw (1982), who analyzed data from a subsample of 8,650 white males randomly drawn from the NLS-72 data base of seniors at 1,318 public and private high schools who were tested in 1972 and again in 1976. Wolfle and Robertshaw used a short form of Rotter's (1966) locus of control scale as a dependent measure and dichotomized postsecondary educational attainment into one category of respondents who had had no schooling beyond high school and another group who had had any postsecondary schooling from a four-year college or university or from a two-year college or vocational or technical school. Using LISREL (a sophisticated analytical procedure that controls for a variety of statistical artifacts commonly left uncontrolled), Wolfle and Robertshaw also held constant students' precollege vocabulary, reading, and math ability; socioeconomic status; and 1972 locus of control status. They found that postsecondary attendance and 1976 locus of control correlated .252, but only about one-fifth (.054) of this was the direct effect of college attendance on locus of control. The remainder was due to other sources—particularly 1972 level of locus of control—upon which educational attainment and 1976 locus of control were mutually dependent. Results consistent with these are reported by Smart, Ethington, and McLaughlin (undated) and by Knox, Lindsay, and Kolb (1988). These studies also used NLS-72 data but followed subjects over seven and fourteen years, respectively. Knox, Lindsay, and Kolb report regression coefficients (estimated effect sizes net of several background characteristics) for different levels of postsecondary educational attainment ranging from .028 for less than two years to .070 for holding an advanced degree. After fourteen years, having two or more years of postsecondary education had the largest impact (.083) on locus of control. While all of these studies left occupational variables uncontrolled, their inclusion could only have reduced the already small educational effect sizes. Thus, it would appear that while college may have a statistically significant positive impact on internal locus of control, the magnitude of that impact is small.

Smart, Ethington, and McLaughlin (undated) also found that the pattern of change was not the same across groups that varied by postsecondary educational attainment. For respondents with no postsecondary education, the rate of increase in locus of control[8] was greater than that of all others in the first (post–high school) interval. Yet four to seven years later, their rate of increase in internality was the lowest of all groups.

It is noteworthy that these changes toward internality, net of other salient variables, were consistent (if small) across the two-decade period covered by this review. Moreover, during the first of those decades, the intra-individual shifts appear to have occurred simultaneously with an inter-individual trend in scores on Rotter's (1966) I-E scale among successive cohorts in the general student population toward greater *external* control. This phenomenon is perhaps related to a sense of loss of control associated with the war in Vietnam and with Watergate (Phares, 1976; Schneider, 1971). Given the ambiguous evidence on whether age and locus of control are related (Lefcourt, 1982), these contrary intra- and inter-individual shifts, taken together, constitute strong evidence of the presence of college effects independent of changes in the population.

Authoritarianism, Dogmatism, and Ethnocentrism

In the late 1950s and early 1960s, Walter Plant and his colleagues conducted an extended series of what have become classic studies of the net effects of college on changes in students' levels of authoritarianism, dogmatism, and ethnocentrism (Plant, 1958a, 1965; Plant & Telford, 1966; Telford & Plant, 1968; for related studies, see McCullers & Plant, 1964; Plant, 1958b; Plant & Minium, 1967). The substantive significance of these studies is that except for Plant (1958a), they indicate that the declines consistently reported in other studies of students' levels of authoritarianism, dogmatism, and/or ethnocentrism were also observable among groups of age-mates who did *not* go to college. Plant concluded that the reported changes were probably due to general personality changes under way among college-age individuals and were independent of educational attainment level.

As Trent and Medsker (1968, p. 156) have pointed out, however, Plant's conclusion rests on tests of pre- and posttest differences *within* groups that differed in educational attainment. While all groups showed statistically significant declines (Plant, 1965; Plant & Telford, 1966; Telford & Plant, 1968), leading to the conclusion of general maturational changes, the differences in the *amounts* of change across groups were never tested, despite their sometimes substantial size and the general tendency for the amount of change to have been positively related to educational attainment.

Only the Trent and Medsker (1968) study addressed the net effects of college on changes in authoritarianism and dogmatism using a nationally representative sample. Analyzing the responses of 1959 high school graduates to the Omnibus Personality Inventory's nonauthoritarianism and social maturity scales, Trent and Medsker compared the changes among 1,301 respondents who persisted in college throughout the four-year period with those of 922 continuously employed individuals. College men and women were significantly more nonauthoritarian than their employed counterparts in 1959 (by 3.2 and 3.7 standard score points for men and women, respectively). Moreover, four years later the differences between the groups were even greater: more than 10 and 12 points, over a full standard deviation (34 and 38 percentile points), respectively. While the college groups had increased their scores by 6 and 8 points (for men and women, respectively) over the period, their employed peers' scores had decreased (−.99 and −.32 standard score points, both nonsignificant) (see also Trent & Craise, 1967). Similar differences were observed in the groups' social maturity scores: Although both groups increased at statistically significant levels, the rate of increase for the college group was significantly greater than that of the employed group. These differences were observed after controlling for academic ability and socioeconomic status, although initial OPI scores were not controlled. Given that the college students' scores were initially higher than the scores of their employed peers, these findings are at odds with any expectations of regression to the mean, providing further support for the hypothesis of net college effects. Evidence consistent with the net college effect hypothesis is also found in the twelve-institution study conducted by Rich and Jolicoeur (1978).

Intellectual Orientation

Trent and Medsker (1968), using the thinking introversion (TI) and complexity (Co) scales of the OPI, also provide the most definitive evidence of net college impact on students' intellectual orientation. The TI scale reflects an interest in reflective and abstract thinking and in thought that is less dominated by immediate conditions or practical considerations. High scores on the Co scale reflect an experimental and flexible orientation toward reality rather than a fixed way of viewing and organizing phenomena. Trent and Medsker contrasted the scores on these two scales of 1,300 individuals who had persisted in college for four years after high school graduation with those of age-mates who had been employed full-time since graduation. Persisting college men and women showed statistically significant, if modest, gains (.31 and .35 of a standard deviation, or 12 and 14 percentile points, for men and women, respectively) in reflective thinking (TI). The college women also gained significantly over four years in their interest in inquiry and tolerance for ambiguity (Co), although the college men showed no changes on this scale. By comparison and with one exception, those who were continuously employed full-time over the four years after high school showed statistically significant declines (a range of −.07 to −.29 across sexes) in their intellectual dispositions. The exception was employed men, who gained in their interest in reflective thinking over the period at a rate only slightly lower than that of their male college counterparts (.23 versus .31 of a standard deviation, or 9 versus 12 percentile points). The declines among employed individuals were particularly sharp on the complexity scale (−.29 and −.20 of a standard deviation, or −11 and −8 percentile points, for males and females, respectively). Declines on both scales among women who became homemakers and had had no outside work experience were greater than those of any other group of women (including groups who had any combination of college, work, and/or homemaking).

Thus, over a four-year period, those who went on to college, as a group, increased in their intellectual dispositions, while those who went to work tended to show less tolerance for ambiguity and less interest in intellectual inquiry. Statistical tests indicate that these differences in change rates (with the exception of the males on the TI scale) are all statistically significant. Other tests indicate that these difference tend to persist even when intellectual disposition scores at time of high school graduation, socioeconomic status, and ability are taken into account. Analyses of students who attended college for varying amounts of time produced results consistent with those described above, indicating positive net college effects on intellectual disposition. Generally similar results are reported by Barton, Cattell, and Vaughan (1973) and by Friedlander and Pace (1981).

Interpersonal Relations

The evidence on the net effects of college on student abilities to interact in mature ways with their peers and others is mixed, methodologically weak, and thus inconclusive. A dozen studies contain evidence germane to this point. Six of them suggest a positive relation between academic class level and increases in the maturity of students' interpersonal relationships (Friedlander & Pace, 1981; George & Marshall, 1972; Hood, 1984; Hood & Jackson, 1986a; Itzkowitz & Petrie, 1988; Jordan-Cox, 1987). Three reports found no relationship (Greeley & Tinsley, 1988; Straub & Rodgers, 1986; Winston, Miller, & Prince, 1979). The other three studies (one based on our own analyses of data reported) produced mixed results (Itzkowitz & Petrie, 1986; Kuh, 1976; Yonge & Regan, 1975). More important in determining the presence (or absence) of college effects net of other student characteristics, none of these studies controlled for any precollege student traits, leaving amount of postsecondary education confounded with age and normal maturation. Moreover, many of these studies were based on relatively small samples, and all were conducted at single institutions, from which generalizations to a national population would be tenuous at best. Thus, little is known with any degree of confidence about the net effects of college on students' development of mature interpersonal relations.

Personal Adjustment and Psychological Well-Being

A substantial body of evidence based on national samples indicates that educational attainment is positively related to psychological well-being, although the magnitude of education's effects appears to be slight, if statistically significant. Because these studies examined psychological well-being during the postcollege years, however, they are discussed in Chapter Twelve. Only a handful of single-institution studies have addressed the question of net college effects. With one exception (Hood & Jackson, 1986b), these studies also lend support to the conclusion that education is reliably, if modestly, related to general psychological well-being (Martin & Light, 1984; Schubert, 1975b), although the studies were not based on rigorous designs or analytical procedures.

Maturity and General Personal Development

No studies were identified with samples or designs strong enough to support even tentative conclusions about the effects of educational attainment on students' personal development or changes in levels of maturity net of normal maturation or other potentially confounding influences. Most studies dealing with change in this area employed longitudinal, freshman-senior designs in which all subjects received equal exposure to the influences of college.

Between-College Effects

Autonomy, Independence, and Locus of Control

We identified only one study that used a national data base and dealt with the effects of institutional characteristics on students' independence from parents or peers. Knox, Lindsay, and Kolb (1988) analyzed data from 7,500 participants in the NLS-72 study who had attended some type of postsecondary institution and were followed up periodically over the next fourteen years. Net of race, sex, parental socioeconomic status, academic abilities, and precollege locus of control, the 1986 internality level was found to be positively and significantly related to institutional cohesion (a factorially derived measure based on the proportion of freshmen on campus, the "full-timeness" of the student body, and the proportion of out-of-state freshmen), the proportion of freshmen working, and institutional selectivity (median SAT score). The magnitudes of these effects were quite modest, however, with beta weights ranging from .077 to .103.

In a separate analysis, Knox, Lindsay, and Kolb (1988) also examined differential institutional effects by means of the nine-category Carnegie Foundation typology of colleges and universities. Controlling for the same student characteristics as in their other analysis, these investigators found internal locus of control to be higher among individuals who attended most types of postsecondary institutions than among high school graduates, but no one type showed any distinctive amount of influence over the others. Only attendance at (Carnegie classification type) Comprehensive Colleges and Universities-II (those that enroll 1,500–2,500 full-time students, more than half of whom graduate in occupational or professional disciplines) or, interestingly, Liberal Arts I (highly selective) institutions was *un*related to higher internality when compared to those whose formal education ended with high school.

Authoritarianism, Dogmatism, and Ethnocentrism

The evidence on between-college effects in the areas of authoritarianism, dogmatism, and ethnocentrism comes from three major research projects: Trent and Medsker's (1968), Clark, Heist, McConnell, Trow, and Yonge's (1972), and Chickering's study of thirteen small colleges (Chickering, 1969, 1971b, 1974b; Chickering, McDowell, & Campagna, 1969; Chickering & McCormick, 1973). These studies are virtually unanimous in finding statistically significant declines in measures of authoritarianism (largely OPI based) at all kinds of institutions over varying periods of time. There is less agreement, however, on whether differences exist among institutions.

Trent and Medsker (1968), while controlling academic ability and socioeconomic status, found only minor variations in freshman-senior increases on the social maturity scale across the six different types of institutions (public, nonsectarian, and church-related colleges and universities). These researchers report somewhat larger variations across institutional types on the nonauthoritarianism scale. They also found some evidence of less positive effects being associated among women (but not men) with attendance at Catholic colleges. Trent and Golds (1967) even found some evidence of increases in authoritarianism among students at Catholic colleges. Trent and Medsker, however, concluded that changes in nonauthoritarian attitudes were more closely related to the type of institution chosen and to persistence in that institution than to changes associated with the experiences at a particular kind of institution.

Clark, Heist, McConnell, Trow, and Yonge (1972) report findings essentially consistent with Trent and Medsker's (1968). However, Clark and his colleagues also report evidence suggesting some variations across institutions, depending on the liberal or conservative climate of the school. This association between institutional environment and impact on students' levels of authoritarianism is also reported by Chickering (1974b). Despite the differences among his thirteen small liberal arts colleges in their educational missions, institutional characteristics, and kinds of students enrolled, Chickering found few substantial differences in the amount or nature of change for a majority of the students across institutions (Chickering, 1974b; Chickering, McDowell, & Campagna, 1969). When students' precollege autonomy levels were controlled, however, Chickering found evidence of institutional effects on the amount of student change over both two- and four-year periods. Larger increases in autonomy were discovered on campuses with a higher proportion of nonconformist students with already high autonomy scores and where teaching practices that give ample time for classroom discussions and course assignments that require complex mental activities were more likely to be found. Increases on the autonomy scale are less likely at institutions with a practical, instrumental orientation; with a mannerly, "proper" atmosphere; and with a heavy reliance on lectures, memorization, and extrinsic motivations (Chickering, 1974b). Rich and Jolicoeur (1978) found some suggestion that declines in dogmatism were more likely on small than on large campuses, but otherwise they uncovered little evidence of any effects related to selectivity or type of control.[9]

Intellectual Orientation

It is clear that different kinds of institutions attract and enroll students with widely varying intellectual orientations. It is equally clear that there are substantial differences among institutions in the intellectual dispositions of their graduates. The limited existing evidence on change indicates quite consistently, however, that net of students' precollege intellectual orientations, the *rates* of increase in this area are approximately the same across kinds of institutions. For example, Trent and Golds (1967) found few statistically significant differences in the amount of changes in three OPI measures of intellectualism (thinking introversion, theoretical orientation, and complexity) among students attending Catholic institutions, Catholics at secular institutions, and non-Catholics at public institutions. These findings persisted when Trent and Golds corrected for ability and were observable in three independent samples, one consisting of five West Coast Catholic colleges plus one public college and one public university. The second of these was the national data base developed by Trent and Medsker (1968). The third was a sample of National Merit Scholarship winners. In virtually all instances, students at Catholic colleges matriculated with lower levels of intellectual curiosity than their Catholic and non-Catholic peers at nondenominational institutions. Four years later they were still below their peers, with the size of the differences among them having changed little, if at all.

Clark and his colleagues (Clark, Heist, McConnell, Trow, & Yonge, 1972), in their study of eight disparate institutions, and Chickering and his colleagues (Chickering, 1974b; Chickering, McDowell, & Campagna, 1969), in their thirteen-college study, report essentially the same findings. Clark and his associates also found no evidence that relatively small group gains were masking more substantial, though counterbalancing, individual changes over the college years. Moreover, between-institution differences in the percentages decreasing in intellectual curiosity disappeared when freshman-year levels were controlled.

Interpersonal Relations

Several studies report evidence gathered from multiple institutions relating to changes in the nature or maturity of students' interpersonal relations with their peers and others. For various reasons, however, most provide little evidence that can be generalized to college students en masse (Brawer, 1973; Cheatham, Slaney, & Coleman, 1990; Fleming, 1984; Itzkowitz & Petrie, 1986, 1988; Jordan-Cox, 1987; McLeish, 1970). The only national evidence is provided by Nichols (1967), who analyzed data from 297 men entering 104 different colleges and 128 women entering 86 colleges. All were National Merit Scholarship finalists. After controlling for students' precollege personality characteristics, high school rank, academic aptitude (SAT scores), and parents' education, Nichols found few college characteristics significantly related to freshman-senior changes in students' scores on a measure of dominance or extraversion (the latter reflecting sociability and some degree of status seeking). Institutional affluence was positively related to larger than predicted gains in extroversion (given precollege characteristics) among both sexes and larger than predicted gains in dominance among the women. Attending a university (private for men, public for women), in contrast to other types of institutions, was positively associated with gains in extroversion. Among women, coed liberal arts college attendance was negatively related to extroversion. Other structural characteristics (size and ability level of the study body and so on), however, were largely unrelated to changes in either sex. Certain other variables characterizing the environment of a campus appeared to have an influence net of students' background characteristics, but no clear pattern was apparent. Chickering and his associates (Chickering, 1974b; Chickering, McDowell, & Campagna, 1969) found little change in students' scores on the OPI's social extraversion scale over one-, two-, or four-year periods and only minor variations across the thirteen small colleges studied. No clear pattern was discernible. Rich and Jolicoeur (1978), in a study of twelve California colleges and universities, found no relation between the degree of change in students' interpersonal skills and institutional size, type, or selectivity.

Thus, limited evidence indicates little if any between-institution effects on students' development of mature interpersonal relations. It may well be that the development of such relations is highly individualistic and responsive to an individual's specific circumstances rather than to more global conditions or influences.

Personal Adjustment and Psychological Well-Being

A relatively small but consistent body of evidence indicates that net of various precollege characteristics, where one goes to college probably does have a differential effect upon one's personal adjustment and general psychological well-being. The literature in this area relies more on environmental characterizations of institutions, however, than on the more global structural variables typically used to differentiate among institutions.

In the largest and best-controlled study in this area, Nichols (1967) residualized National Merit Scholarship finalists' senior-year OPI scores on thirty-eight personality scales, mothers' and fathers' education, high school rank, and SAT scores. With these influences controlled, he found that the scores of both men and women on a factorially derived measure of anxiety increased at colleges where many students majored in "realistic" or intellectually oriented subjects (for example, engineering and the sciences). Men's anxiety scores decreased at institutions where majors in artistic and social fields were more dominant. Women's scores decreased at institutions with an "enterprising orientation" (those with many majors in law, political science, or history). Nichols found *no* statistically significant correlations between residualized change scores and such conventional characteristics of institutions as student body ability, size, or type of control.

Similar evidence suggesting that institutional environment or ambience is related to changes in various measures of personal adjustment or psychological well-being is reported by Chickering (1974b; Chickering & McCormick, 1973), Clark, Heist, McConnell, Trow, and Yonge (1972), and Winter, McClelland, and Stewart (1981). Chickering found that (over both a two- and a four-year period) students' OPI impulse expression (IE) scale scores were likely to increase at colleges where a large proportion of students already score high on the IE scale, where students often participate in class discussions and decisions about course content and procedures, where the amount of time invested in more complex study activities is relatively high, and where intrinsic reasons for study predominate. Taken together, the results of all these studies indicate that there probably are between-college differences in personal adjustment and psychological well-being. However, contrary to what one might expect, the differences are more likely due to environmental differences than to structural or organizational ones. Nevertheless, little can be said with confidence about which sorts of environments promote adjustment and which impede it.

Maturity and General Personal Development

Only two studies (Ewell, 1989; Pace, 1990) were identified that examined differential institutional effects on students' general personal development or maturity. Without exception, all other studies identified in this area were conducted on a single campus.

Pace (1990) analyzed aggregated (1983–1986) College Student Experience Questionnaire (CSEQ) data from more than 25,000 students at seventy-four colleges and universities, grouped into five types of institutions: research universities, doctoral universities, comprehensive colleges and universities, general liberal arts colleges, and selective liberal arts colleges. Three of his outcome measures dealt with students' reported progress in their personal development. With the exception of the selective liberal arts colleges (which had the largest percentage of students reporting "substantial progress" on all three items), Pace found virtually no differences among the other four types of institutions. He did find considerable variability in the amount of progress students reported *within* category types, indicating that *which* institution a student attends may indeed make a difference, although the *type* of institution attended probably does not.

Ewell (1989) explored the influences of four sets of institutional variables on faculty and administrators' perceptions of their institution's effectiveness in enhancing students' personal development: (1) institutional characteristics (for example, size, type of control, selectivity, curricular emphasis); (2) mission (identity, distinctiveness, degree of consensus on mission, and so forth); (3) institutional culture or environment; and (4) "institutional functioning" (degree of trust, student-faculty contact, information flow, and the like). Ewell conducted a secondary analysis of 320 four-year institutions using data from the Assessment of Performance of Colleges and Universities (APCU) survey and from the U.S. Department of Education's 1983 Higher Education General Information Survey (HEGIS). He found that both public control and the percentage of part-time students were consistently important—and negative—sources of influence on each of three one-item indicators of institutional effectiveness in promoting students' general personal development (or providing opportunities for same). The presence of a "clan" (or extended familylike) culture was also associated with each outcome measure, but on only one item did the effect persist in the presence of various "institutional functioning" variables, such as high student-faculty contact and high levels of organizational information and feedback (the sense of being kept informed). The latter two variables were identified as important mediators of perceptions of institutional effectiveness. Each set of "nonmaterial" variables (mission direction and specificity, clanlike versus hierarchical culture, organizational feedback, and student-faculty interaction) made statistically significant and unique contributions to perceptions of institutional effectiveness above and beyond such structural characteristics as size, control, selectivity, and curricular emphasis. Although the validity of Ewell's findings is open to challenge as evidence of between-college effects on students' personal development, the findings are consistent with Pace's (1990) and with the evidence in other areas of psychosocial development that suggests the importance of interpersonal contacts and institutional environments in psychosocial change among students.

Within-College Effects

With a few exceptions, studies of the within-college sources of change in students' relational systems fall into two categories: one dealing with the effects of academic majors or curricular programs or experiences and the other focusing on the effects of place of residence. Several studies examined the effects of "living-learning" centers, thus combining curricular and residential effects. In a few areas, some attention was also focused on the effects of students' membership in fraternities or sororities and students' interpersonal experiences with faculty and peers.

Autonomy, Independence, and Locus of Control

Studies that examine academic program or curricular experiences are few in number and disparate in focus. Behuniak and Gable (1981) analyzed freshman-to-senior locus of control data from more than 5,600 NLS-72 participants, but they did so without controls of any kind. They found that across six major fields, most groups showed freshman-senior increases in internality (ranging from −.01 to +.18 of a standard deviation, or 0 to 7 percentile points). Business majors showed the largest gains, and students majoring in the natural and physical sciences, mathematics, and the social sciences recorded the smallest gains. Surprisingly, however, no tests were conducted on the significance of the differences in the amount of change across the major fields. King (1973) reports that increases in internal locus of control were greater among honors program participants than among regular curriculum students, but Graffam (1967) concluded that increases in independence, net of age, were due more to the general institutional environment than to degree program (A.B. versus B.S.). Neither study controlled initial levels of autonomy or independence, however, and given the heterogeneity of these studies, little can be concluded with any confidence.

Somewhat greater clarity exists among studies that examined the effects of experimental, living-learning programs on changes in student autonomy and independence, but the picture is somewhat ambiguous. Evidence from 197 freshmen who entered the University of Michigan's Residential College (RC) in 1967 and from 410 freshmen in three different control groups indicates that while the scores of all groups on the College Student Questionnaire's family independence scale increased, gains among the RC students were more substantial, although they fell narrowly short of statistical significance after adjustment for initial level of family independence. On the peer independence scale, scores for all groups decreased, but there were no appreciable differences in adjusted scores among the groups in the amount of change. In this area, as in others, there were indications that the experimental college had a slight accentuation effect—initial differences becoming greater over time (Newcomb, Brown, Kulik, Reimer, & Revelle, 1970, 1971). Pemberton (cited in Williams & Reilly, 1972) found small increases in peer independence among the residents of a living-learning center compared to those in a conventional residence hall.

In two studies (the second a replication of the first), Goldman and Olczak (1976, 1980) found that freshmen in a living-learning center showed smaller gains (or no gains at all) on Shostrom's (1966) inner-directedness scale. It is quite possible, however, that the differences between these studies and those just discussed are artifactual, due to sample and contextual differences among the studies.[10]

We identified only two studies that specifically examined differences in changes in independence among residential and commuting students. Sullivan and Sullivan (1980) and Scott (1975) found that increases in inner-directedness occurred more often among residence hall students than among commuters or students living off campus. Straub's (1987) study of critical incidents related to the development of autonomy produced evidence consistent with this finding: Moving away from home was a prominent factor for many. None of these studies, however, controlled for precollege independence levels of other potential confounding variables (Sullivan and Sullivan controlled only for SAT scores).[11]

A small body of research has examined the effects over time of Greek fraternity and/or sorority membership on autonomy (Hughes & Winston, 1987; Miller, 1973; Wilder, Hoyt, Doren, Hauch, & Zettle, 1978; Wilder, Hoyt, Surbeck, Wilder, & Carney, 1986). The most convincing evidence is presented in the two studies of Bucknell University students by Wilder and his associates (the second study a replication of the first). In each of the seven cohorts of entering freshmen studied over the period from 1965 to 1981, Greeks were significantly lower than non-Greeks upon entry to college in both family and peer independence, as measured by the Educational Testing Service's College Student Questionnaire (CSQ). Moreover, both investigations found significantly larger freshman-senior gains among non-Greeks than among Greeks on the family independence scale. Neither study, however, recorded statistically significant differences between the groups in the amount of change on the CSQ's peer independence scale.

In the more recent Bucknell study (Wilder, Hoyt, Surbeck, Wilder, & Carney, 1986), a third group, ex-Greeks (students who had joined but then withdrew from the organization or became inactive), did show significantly greater increases in peer independence than either Greeks or non-Greeks and significantly greater gains than Greeks on the family independence scale. Wilder and his colleagues concluded that the impact of Greek membership was modest and to a large extent dependent upon how one defined "Greek membership."[12]

Caution is warranted in interpreting these and similar findings (for example, Miller, 1973; Schmidt, 1971). Controls for students' self-selection into Greek membership or independent status or for other precollege characteristics were rarely employed. Moreover, none of these studies differentiated between being a Greek and living in Greek housing (versus living off campus or in a traditional residence hall), thereby leaving residential effects uncontrolled. We concur with Winston and Saunders (1987), who concluded that while there is little evidence to support the view that Greek society membership promotes the development of students' independence or autonomy, neither is there much evidence to suggest that Greek societies constitute major obstacles to such changes. Indeed, there is "little credible research . . . in the current literature, . . . [and] very little research on the impact of sororities and fraternities on students [has been done] in the past ten years" (p. 11).

Authoritarianism, Dogmatism, and Ethnocentrism

Only a handful of studies specifically examined the differential effects of college major on changes in authoritarianism during college. Yet with one exception (Elton, 1971), they are consistent in their findings that academic major field is probably not a net determinant of changes in authoritarianism (Elton & Rose, 1969; Feldman & Weiler, 1976; Levin, 1967; Yonge & Regan, 1975). In the most rigorous investigation, Feldman and Weiler (1976) studied 826 University of Michigan students who completed the OPI as freshmen in 1962 or 1963 and again as seniors in 1966 or 1967. Controlling for initial scores on the OPI's autonomy scale (considered a measure of nonauthoritarianism in this review), Feldman and Weiler focused on the changes among male and female "primary recruits" (those who had not changed majors during the period under study) in ten academic major fields. While statistically significant differences existed across majors among the women at the time of entry and among men both upon entry and four years later, there was no evidence of differential rates of change across majors within either sex when initial level of autonomy was held constant. Feldman and Newcomb (1969) found a number of studies reporting major-related differential effects, specifically, accentuation effects: Initial differences between major fields became greater over time. However, Feldman and Weiler believe that these effects may have been exaggerated by most earlier studies' inclusion of students who had changed into their major fields from other fields. When such "primary" and "secondary" recruits were combined in their study, Feldman and Weiler found evidence more consistent with that reviewed by Feldman and Newcomb. The disappearance of major-related accentuation effects when only primary recruits were studied indicates that influences other than major field may have been at work or that the differences across majors found in the earlier studies reflected changes in composition of the groups rather than major field effects.[13]

With one exception that may have been due to insufficient differences between experimental and control group treatments (Cade, 1979), evaluative studies of the effects of residence in a living-learning center (LLC) suggest that such facilities probably lead to larger drops in authoritarianism than do more traditional residential settings. These studies were based on LLCs at the University of California, Berkeley (Suczek, 1972) and the University of Michigan (Lacy, 1978; Newcomb, Brown, Kulik, Reimer, & Revelle, 1971). While all three studies report reductions in authoritarianism across LLC and control groups, the drops were greater among students living in LLC environments, even when initial differences in authoritarianism were controlled. However, Lacy found that when variables reflecting students' interpersonal relations with faculty members and peers were added to his path model, the direct effects of place of residence were reduced to small, nonsignificant components (range of .02 to .08, with three of four direct effects being less than .03). Such findings indicate that the impact of structural residential arrangements are indirect, being mediated by the peer and faculty interactions they facilitate (and that exert strong, direct influences). This conclusion is supported by research on other educational outcomes (Ogle & Dodder, 1978; Pascarella & Terenzini, 1980b, 1981).

Evidence pertaining to the effects of place of residence on students' levels of authoritarianism and dogmatism is inconsistent. Some studies indicate that levels of authoritarianism decline more among on-campus residents than among commuting students (Chickering & Kuper, 1971; Chickering, McDowell, & Campagna, 1969; Matteson, 1974; Rich & Jolicoeur, 1978). Other studies report no residence-related differences (Katz and Associates, 1968; Levin, 1967). While one might be inclined to invest greater confidence in Chickering's evidence since it is based on students in several (five and thirteen) institutions (all small liberal arts colleges) whereas Levin's data come from only two schools (Berkeley and Stanford), neither study controlled for initial levels of authoritarianism or for differences between residential groups on other potentially confounding precollege characteristics.

We identified only one study (Schmidt, 1971) that examined differential changes in dogmatism between Greek social society members and independents. In that study, both sorority members and independents declined in dogmatism between their freshman and senior years, but there was no statistically significant difference in the groups' rates of decline.

Intellectual Orientation

Although limited to a small number of single-institution studies, the available evidence is quite consistent in suggesting that major field of study has little or no impact on differential changes in students' intellectual orientations (Brown, 1968; Feldman & Weiler, 1976; Burton & Polmantier,

1973; Yonge & Regan, 1975). All these studies with the exception of Burton and Polmantier's were based on data from the Omnibus Personality Inventory's thinking introversion, theoretical orientation, and (except for Brown's study) complexity scales. Moreover, all these studies (except Burton and Polmantier's) controlled for students' precollege scores on these scales. Feldman and Weiler, in the most rigorous of the studies, were looking for evidence of major-related accentuation effects. While no such effects were found among men, some of Feldman and Weiler's findings suggested that among women academic major might have been related to somewhat higher gains in an experimental and flexible approach to viewing one's world (complexity). Women majoring in English language and literature and in the Romance languages and literature appeared to have experienced the largest gains, while those in elementary education experienced declines. The relation was a weak one, however. Yonge and Regan found statistically significant differences during both the freshman and senior years among majors classified according to the six Holland (1966, 1973, 1985) environments (realistic, investigative, conventional, enterprising, social, and artistic). While significant differences across groups in the amount of freshman-senior change were found on the complexity scale, however, similar differential changes were not found in thinking introversion or theoretical orientation.

Studies of the influences of participation in experimental curricula or living-learning programs are also few in number but consistent in finding that student participants in such programs show significantly larger gains in intellectual orientation than do students in traditional curricular programs (Bennett & Hunter, 1985; Lacy, 1978; Newcomb, Brown, Kulik, Reimer, & Revelle, 1971; Tomlinson-Keasey, Williams, & Eisert, 1978). In the studies by Lacy and by Newcomb and his colleagues, these effects persisted in the presence of controls for precollege levels of intellectual orientation. Lacy's evidence, as with other outcomes discussed earlier, however, indicates that the effects of such living-learning experiences may be *indirect* rather than direct. That is, the effects may be mediated by interpersonal contacts with peers and faculty and thus derive more from the socialization processes they tend to facilitate than from any of the structural characteristics (for example, size, rules and regulations governing activities, structured activities) of the program itself. While scores on the OPI's complexity, thinking introversion, and theoretical orientation scales after two years were all positively associated with living in a living-learning residence environment (net of initial scores), the direct effects were reduced to small, nonsignificant components when variables characterizing the interpersonal relations among students and faculty were introduced.[14]

Place of residence also appears to have a reliable, if modest, effect on changes in students' intellectual dispositions. As with other within-college effects in this area, the research is meager but consistent in indicating that students living on campus are more likely than their commuting peers to gain on measures of intellectual orientation, even when precollege dispositions are controlled (Chickering & Kuper, 1971; Welty, 1976). Welty's findings suggest that these effects are a function of the living situation and the interactions it fosters with other students and faculty. Moreover, the findings of both studies are clearly consistent with the evidence discussed above relating to the relative advantages of participating in living-learning programs.

The degree of change in intellectual orientation appears more clearly to be related to the socializing influences within various college settings that involve the interaction of people—students and faculty members. The role of interpersonal relationships within living-learning programs was just noted (Lacy, 1978; Newcomb, Brown, Kulik, Reimer, & Revelle, 1971). Other studies lead to the same conclusion (Brown, 1968; Clark, Heist, McConnell, Trow, & Yonge, 1972, chap. 9; Hummel-Rossi, 1976; Wilson, Gaff, Dienst, Wood, & Bavry, 1975). In the work of Lacy, Newcomb and his associates, and Hummel-Rossi, moreover, the influence of students' peers appears to exceed that of faculty members, although both Lacy's and Hummel-Rossi's data indicate that the degree of influence depends to some extent on the area of change and the nature of the student-faculty interaction, with content appearing to be somewhat more important than frequency.

Interpersonal Relations

Few studies exist on academic major–related changes in students' interpersonal development. The clearest evidence comes from Yonge and Regan (1975), who tested freshman-senior change scores on the OPI's social extroversion scale, a measure of interest in being with other people and in seeking social activities, and of the satisfaction students derive from such activities. Using data from 833 males in three entering classes at the University of California, Davis (1964–1966), Yonge and Regan found statistically significant differences in social extroversion in both the freshman and the senior years across majors categorized by the six Holland types, but there were no significant differences across types in the amount of freshman-senior change. Hood (1984) and Hood and Mines (1986) also found no differences by major field in seniors' tolerance of others or the quality of their relationships with friends, but it is not clear whether differences were tested across senior-year scores or across freshman-senior *change* scores. While both of these studies have limitations, neither provides any basis for believing that academic major has any systematic or unique effect on students' interpersonal development.

The evidence relating to residence effects is only slightly more rigorous but tends to indicate that where one lives during the college years is also probably not related to changes in the character of students' interpersonal relations. In the strongest studies on this matter, Newcomb and his colleagues (Newcomb, Brown, Kulik, Reimer, & Revelle, 1971), after adjusting for precollege scores on each outcome measure, found that students in a living-learning center declined somewhat on measures of sociability and social extroversion while students in a conventional residence hall increased slightly. The differences in the change scores, however, were nonsignificant. Rich and Jolicoeur (1978), in their study of a dozen California colleges and universities, found no differences between residential and commuting students in the size of their gains in interpersonal competence. Riahinejad and Hood (1984) report that freshman-senior increases in tolerance of others and in the quality of interpersonal relations were unrelated to various but unspecified types of college residence. Similarly, Chickering and Kuper (1971) did not include the social extroversion scale on a list of OPI scales on which residential and commuter students differed in their rates of change, implying that there were no differences.

Several studies suggest, however, that the character of the residence arrangement may be more important than its location. Evidence relating to the differential effects of single-sex versus coeducational housing suggests that coed arrangements may have more beneficial influences: In coed housing, opposite-sex relationships are more easily formed (Brown, Winkworth, & Braskamp, 1973), sex-stereotyping declines (J. Katz, 1974), and self-consciousness and anxiety in social settings diminish (Reid, 1974).[15]

Personal Adjustment and Psychological Well-Being

Evidence concerning the effects of academic major field on changes in students' personal adjustment and psychological well-being is limited and not entirely consistent. Studies that used the OPI's impulse expression (IE) scale have consistently found statistically nonsignificant differences across groups, whether grouping majors according to Holland's six personality types (Yonge & Regan, 1975) or by school within a university (Snyder, 1968) or when using majors as intact groups (Feldman & Weiler, 1976). Suczek (1972) found no differences on change in impulse expression scores relating to interest and participation in a nonresidential experimental college.

Yonge and Regan (1975) report similar nonsignificant differences across majors on the OPI's anxiety level and personal integration scales, two additional measures used to assess psychological "health." Moreover, the findings obtained by Yonge and Regan and by Feldman and Weiler remained even after precollege scores on these dependent variables were controlled.

It may be, however, as suggested elsewhere in this volume, that the characteristics of a particular major or discipline, however grouped, are less important than the environment *within* a department, whatever the discipline. Hearn (1980), who studied departmental influences on changes in the psychological well-being of 394 students in twenty-eight major departments in a large state university and a smaller church-related university, reports evidence in support of this speculation. Controlling for family socioeconomic status, job experience in the major field, grade performance in the major field, parental support for the student's major and career choice, and the student's perception of the department's orientation toward students, Hearn found that department contextual variables contributed significantly to the explanation of variance in students' senior-year scores on measures of negative and positive sense of well-being. The R^2 changes in negative and positive affect ranged from .040 to .067 across the sexes. Among the men, psychological well-being was promoted by departments with lenient grading practices, a vocational orientation, predominantly other-sex faculty members, and—surprisingly—a relatively weak emphasis on student support. For the women, general well-being was promoted by departments with more stringent grading practices, opposite-sex faculty members, and a concern for student support. Thus, it appears at least possible that students' general sense of psychological well-being may be more closely associated with the *qualitative character* of their major department than with its structural or organizational characteristics or its particular disciplinary emphasis.

The evidence relating to the effects of place of residence on changes in students' personal adjustment and general psychological well-being is limited and contradictory. Chickering and Kuper (1971) report that students living on campus, compared to commuters, showed greater increases on the OPI's impulse expression and personal integration scales, but these analyses involved no controls for differences in entering characteristics. Welty (1976), on the other hand, after controlling precollege status on the criterion measure, found no differences between commuters and on-campus residents on either the anxiety level or personal integration scale of the OPI. Cade (1979) (like Chickering) found differences on the impulse expression scale but (like Welty) found no differences on the anxiety level and personal integration scales in a study of student mix and program combinations within residence halls.

In a somewhat more controlled study but one without a comparison group of commuting students, Newcomb and his associates (Newcomb, Brown, Kulik, Reimer, & Revelle, 1971) examined differences in the amount of change between freshman residents of a living-learning center and their peers in traditional housing. After controlling precollege scores on the dependent variables, these investigators found that students in the living-learning center were significantly more likely to report symptoms of stress or anxiety on a factorially derived cluster of "anxiety" measures and a significantly greater tendency to experience feelings of hostility, aggression, isolation, loneliness, and rejection. Students in traditional housing arrangements moved in the opposite direction on these variables.

Maturity and General Personal Development

Pascarella and Terenzini (1980b, 1981), in studies of two independent samples of freshmen residing in a living-learning center at a large northeastern university, found consistent evidence that such specialized living arrangements had positive effects on generalized measures of students' personal development during the freshman year. With fifteen preenrollment characteristics held constant, they found residence in the living-learning center (versus a conventional residence hall) positively, if marginally ($p < .10$), associated with students' year-end self-reports of progress in such areas as gaining a better understanding of self, developing interpersonal skills, and developing increased self-reliance and personal discipline (Pascarella & Terenzini, 1981). More revealing, the evidence in both studies indicated that the structural and organizational influences of residence arrangement were mediated by the quality and impact of students' interpersonal relations with important agents of socialization—faculty members and peers, particularly the latter. These interpersonal variables not only had significant positive associations with reported personal development, but they also differentiated the climate of the living-learning center from that of traditional residences. These findings and those of Lacy (1978) suggest that environmental effects of differing organizational arrangements in undergraduate residences, and perhaps broader campus environments as well (Erwin, 1983; Zirkle & Hudson, 1975), may be largely accounted for by students' interactions with major socializing agents.

The possibility that increases on measures of generalized personal development are more a function of students' interpersonal relations than where they live receives support in the findings reported by Pascarella, Duby, Terenzini, and Iverson (1983). As in the studies by Pascarella and Terenzini (1980b, 1981), the evidence suggested that students' peer interactions, net of background and other college experience variables, exerted more influence on personal growth than did faculty contacts and that the quality of students' interactions with faculty was more influential than its frequency. Student-faculty discussions of intellectual or course-related matters and career-related issues consistently appeared to be particularly influential. Similar findings are reported in other studies of the freshman year (Pascarella & Terenzini, 1978), even when independent samples of students on another (but similar) campus were used (Terenzini & Pascarella, 1980a; Terenzini, Pascarella, & Lorang, 1982), and in studies that examined within-college effects over three and four years (Terenzini, Theophilides, & Lorang, 1984b; Terenzini & Wright, 1987b, 1987c). The latter studies suggest that the rate of students' reported personal growth is relatively constant across the college years, although each year appears to make its own unique contribution and the specific sources of influence within each year vary over time (Terenzini, Theophilides, & Lorang, 1984b; Terenzini & Wright, 1987b, 1987c).

Douglas Heath (1968, 1977c) reports similar findings from his comprehensive and detailed studies of Haverford College students. Among the interpersonal determinants of students' increases in various dimensions of maturity, Heath cited the following as most important: (1) students' roommates, (2) the type of student attracted to Haverford, (3) students' close male friends, and (4) students' close female friends. Among the academic and intellectual determinants of increased maturity, he listed the campus's intellectual atmosphere, certain courses, and contacts with faculty members. While faculty and peer relations each played significant roles in students' intellectual development, peers and close friends (male or female) clearly played the dominant role in students' interpersonal growth, with faculty influence appearing to be modest outside the intellectual sphere.

Heath (1977c) also identified important avenues of institutional influence. He concluded that the three most important routes were (in order) the college's religious-ethical tradition; the coherence between institutional values and the way those values are implemented in specific activities, including the classroom; and the sense of community among the students and faculty at the college. These institutional characteristics are similar to those identified as significant by Chickering (1969) in his study of thirteen small colleges and by Kuh and his colleagues (Kuh et al., in press) in their study of fourteen institutions identified as particularly successful in involving students in their own intellectual and psychosocial education. The thread running throughout all these studies is the potency of interpersonal context on psychosocial changes among students.

Conditional Effects of College

Autonomy, Independence, and Locus of Control

While a number of studies examine the varying effects of college on autonomy, independence, or locus of control that are related to individual characteristics, drawing conclusions is problematic because of the considerable variety in samples, analytical procedures, periods of time over which change is measured, institutional settings, and the particular variables involved. Only Smart, Ethington, & McLaughlin (undated) offer a rigorous test for conditional effects. Using data from some 10,800 students whom they followed over a seven-year period as part of the NLS-72 project, Smart and his colleagues found a statistically significant sex by educational attainment interaction. After adjusting for socioeconomic status and initial locus of control and self-confidence, the researchers concluded that postsecondary educational attainment had a significantly stronger positive effect on increased locus of control for women than for men. However, the study left postcollege experiences, such as employment, uncontrolled. Thus, whether these differential effects are in fact due to education remains uncertain.

Other, smaller-scale or single-institution studies of the joint effects of sex and educational attainment on autonomy or independence constitute a conflicting body of research. One can find evidence of (1) nonsignificant differences between the sexes in the effects of years of college on autonomy (Greeley & Tinsley, 1988); (2) significant differences between the sexes, with men making greater gains than women during the college years (Hatch, 1970; Montgomery, McLaughlin, Fawcett, Pedigo, & Ward, 1975); and (3) significant differences between the sexes, with men gaining in peer independence while women declined during the first year, but with women's scores increasing somewhat more than those of men in the succeeding three years (Nelsen & Uhl, 1977).

In short, the research on the conditional effects of college on students' levels of autonomy, independence, and internality is highly inconsistent. No statistically significant interaction has been replicated on a comparable sample or over a comparable period of time.

Maturity and General Personal Development

Only four studies were identified that specifically tested the statistical significance of the interaction of student characteristics and various dimensions of the college experience in influencing student maturity or personal development (Pascarella & Terenzini, 1978, 1980b; Terenzini & Pascarella, 1980a; Terenzini, Pascarella, & Lorang, 1982). Pascarella and Terenzini (1980b) found that net of salient background characteristics and various college experience variables, the greatest benefits in terms of student-reported personal growth accrued to students in a living-learning residence who had initially high educational aspirations. As educational aspirations declined, so did the beneficial effects of the living-learning center on personal development. This differential, conditional effect has not been replicated, however.

Terenzini and Pascarella (1980a), in a study of 763 freshmen entering a large, private, residential university, found that net of student background characteristics and other college experience variables, the *frequency* of student contact with faculty members to discuss personal problems was more likely to contribute to the personal development of women, nonwhites, and students with high entering SAT scores than other groups of students. The *quality* of faculty relations had the most positive influence on the personal development of men and students who, on entrance to the university, attached a relatively low level of importance to graduation. In two other studies, however, no statistically significant interaction effects on personal development were found between the frequency and nature of student-faculty interactions and sex (Pascarella & Terenzini, 1978; Terenzini, Pascarella, & Lorang, 1982), race or major field (Pascarella & Terenzini, 1978), or academic aptitude and high school achievement (Terenzini, Pascarella, & Lorang, 1982).

Other Facets of Students' Relational Systems

We found few studies of change in students' authoritarianism, dogmatism, ethnocentrism, intellectual orientations, interpersonal relations, or personal adjustment and psychological maturity that rigorously examined differential college effects that were conditional on individual characteristics. As one might expect, a number of studies compared the scores of men and women on various measures in each of these areas at time of entry and at various points subsequent to matriculation. Many, if not most, of these same studies also contrasted freshman-senior scores among men and among women. Most of the studies found statistically significant, if sometimes small, freshman-senior increases (declines in the cases of authoritarianism, dogmatism, and ethnocentrism) among both men and women in these several areas. Some found differences in the amount of change between the sexes, but with *very* few exceptions (for example, Cade, 1979; Greeley & Tinsley, 1988), the statistical significance of the differences between the sexes (or races) in the *amount* of change (the time by sex, or race, interaction) went untested. Where tested, these interactions remain unreplicated. Thus, nothing can be said with any confidence about the effects of college in these several areas that might be differentially related to students' individual characteristics.

Long-Term Effects of College

More than two decades ago, Freedman (1967, p. 60) wrote: "Unlike the situation of the undergraduate years, there is a dearth of research dealing with personality change after college." So far as the long-term effects of college on students' relational systems are concerned, little has changed.

Autonomy, Independence, and Locus of Control

We identified only three studies that dealt with the long-term effects of college on students' levels of autonomy, independence, or locus of control. Two of them examined changes in locus of control using the NLS-72 data base (Knox, Lindsay, & Kolb, 1988; Smart, Ethington, & McLaughlin, undated). Smart and his colleagues studied high school graduates over a seven-year period, and Knox and his associates followed respondents over a fourteen-year period. After controlling socioeconomic status, Smart and his colleagues found modest increases for all study participants after high school, with the relative position of groups based on education holding nearly constant at each time interval. The evidence indicates a reduction in group differences immediately after high school but a tendency among those with greater exposure to postsecondary education (compared to those with little or no exposure) to develop higher levels of internality over the longer term. The study also indicates that college's effects on long-term changes in self-esteem may be greater than its effects on changes in internal locus of control.

Knox, Lindsay, and Kolb (1988) found similar results over a fourteen-year period even with additional controls for race, gender, academic abilities, and precollege level of internality. Despite these controls, the effects of educational attainment were still discernible (if small) fourteen years after high school graduation, with the largest increases among those with two or more years of postsecondary education. Similar findings are reported in a study of twenty-two autobiographical accounts of enduring college effects (Powell, 1985).

While the large-scale studies of Smart, Ethington, and Kolb and Knox, Lindsay, and Kolb were well designed and executed and their results were consistent (despite differences in the composition of their samples, their methodologies, and the periods of time over which changes were monitored), neither study controlled for the potentially confounding effects of occupational status on internality. Thus, increases in internality may be due as much to occupational circumstances as to educational attainment. While one might predict at least an indirect relation between education and increased internality (via occupation), the relative importance of education and occupation awaits further clarification.

Authoritarianism, Dogmatism, and Ethnocentrism

More than two decades ago, Freedman (1967) followed up three cohorts of Vassar College alumnae. He found an upward trend in scores on the Omnibus Personality Inventory's social maturity scale (reflecting increased nonauthoritarianism) in all three cohorts, but the shift was statistically significant for only one class. In contrast to the widespread movement away from authoritarianism during the undergraduate years, the alumnae years appeared to produce neither a continuation in those changes nor their reversal.

More recent research has produced substantially (but not entirely) similar findings. Kuh (1976, 1981), in the only studies we identified that dealt with changes in authoritarianism during the postbaccalaureate years, analyzed OPI data for 170 male and female alumni of Luther College (Iowa) who had been tested as freshmen in 1966, as seniors in 1970, five years after graduation (Kuh, 1976), and ten years after graduation (Kuh, 1981). Five years after graduation and compared to themselves as seniors, males as a group showed a slight (but nonsignificant) increase in authoritarianism (OPI's autonomy scale; see note 4), while females showed a modest (but statistically significant) increase (.23 of a standard deviation, or 9 percentile points, according to our analyses of Kuh's 1976 data). Ten years after graduation, however, in contrast with the women, who showed no change on this variable over the intervening five years, the men had continued to increase in authoritarianism, to a point virtually identical to that of the women five years earlier and significantly above where they had been upon graduation. Thus, after ten years (and according to our analyses of Kuh's 1981 data), both men and women in this study were approximately one-third of a standard deviation (13 percentile points) higher in authoritarianism than they were at the end of their undergraduate years. The differences between the Kuh and Freedman findings could be due to differences in the samples used, the period of time over which change was examined, the historical periods in which the studies were conducted, or all of these factors.

In the only other relevant research identified, Fry (1976) reports three studies indicating that one year after graduation the attitudes toward authority among college graduates who went on to graduate or professional school remained relatively negative when compared to those of graduates who took employment (the latter group's attitudes became more positive). Fry (1977) explains his results in terms of graduates' socialization to their postbaccalaureate environments: Undergraduate and graduate students can be critical of authority with impunity while in school (indeed, such a trait is even seen as a sign of intellectual independence), but graduates entering employment may find it prudent (if not necessary) to moderate any negative feelings about authority.

Intellectual Orientation

Kuh (1976, 1977, 1981), using the single-institution data base described in the preceding section, provides the only evidence we found on the durability of college's effects on changes in students' intellectual dispositions as they enter their adult years. No controls were employed for pretest differences in any pre-post comparisons. Kuh (1976) found no statistically significant changes among men or women between the time of graduation and five years later with respect to their interest in ideas or scholarly orientation (OPI's thinking introversion scale) or preference for the use of logic in problem solving (theoretical orientation). While women's scores dropped slightly on both measures, the declines were statistically nonsignificant, although they appear to have declined still further after that point, reaching statistical significance ten years after graduation. Both sexes declined significantly and substantially in the first five years after graduation ($-.39$ and $-.46$ of a standard deviation, or -15 and -18 percentile points, for men and women, respectively) in the extent to which they viewed and organized their worlds experimentally and flexibly (complexity). These declines appear to have bottomed out by this point, however. Our analyses of data in Kuh (1981) indicate no statistically significant changes for either sex between the five- and ten-year measurement points. In another study of the same graduates, Kuh (1977) found the five-year changes to be generally unrelated to respondents' political affiliation, type of postbaccalaureate institution attended, or current occupation. It is doubtful that Kuh's findings can be generalized much beyond small, church-related, liberal arts colleges, however. This leaves us with little to say with confidence about the durability of college effects on their graduates' intellectual dispositions into the alumni years, where much may also depend upon type of job, family life, leisure activities, and so on.

Interpersonal Relations

Kuh (1976, 1981) found no statistically significant changes in alumni scores on the OPI's social extroversion scale, whether five or ten years after graduation. Freedman (1967), however, in the only other study of long-term effects in this area, reports a trend across the classes suggesting gains on a measure of "social integration." In a finding that may partially explain the nonsignificant difference in Kuh's results, Freedman reports that the changes were not all in the same direction: The scores of 62 percent of the Vassar alumnae increased, but those of a third declined. Less than 5 percent remained unchanged. Thus, a number of individual shifts in opposite directions may have counterbalanced one another, producing little or no apparent group change in Kuh's study.

Personal Adjustment and Psychological Well-Being

Kuh (1976, 1981) and Freedman (1967) also dealt with changes during the postbaccalaureate years in areas related to personal adjustment and general psychological well-being. Both report results that suggest a postcollege decline in expressiveness. Kuh's respondents declined in their readiness to express impulses and to seek gratification either in conscious thought or overt action (OPI impulse expression scale), but the changes appear to have occurred within the first five years after graduation. According to our analyses, Kuh found no additional statistically significant changes in the second five years after receipt of the baccalaureate degree. Freedman's Vassar College alumnae showed a significant increase on a measure of personal "repression and suppression." Kuh also found statistically significant increases among both male and female alumni in their social and emotional integration and significant reductions among the men in symptoms of anxiety, nervousness, tension, and worry. As with impulse expression, these changes appear to have occurred within five years of graduation and to have stabilized over the next five years. Although neither the Kuh nor the Freedman study controlled for graduates' postcollege occupational experiences, which might have had a major influence on individuals' sense of adjustment and well-being, there is reason to believe that net of occupational status and income, educational attainment still exerts a positive influence on adults' sense of well-being (Witter, Okun, Stock, & Haring, 1984). This evidence is discussed more fully in Chapter Twelve.

Maturity and General Personal Development

Only the sustained research of Heath (1968, 1976c, 1977a, 1977c) sheds any light on the durability into the adult years of the overall maturing processes begun during the college years. In a series of studies that used quantitative and interview techniques with sixty-eight Haverford College students who were followed into their adult years, Heath found evidence of persistent college effects on the continuing maturation of his students. Studied in their early thirties, Heath's subjects were found to be significantly more mature on every measure as adults than they were when they graduated (Heath, 1976a). Moreover, the effects of college appeared to be the same over three decades of graduates, but the pattern of effects varied between undergraduates and alumni. As undergraduates, these individuals appeared to be primarily concerned with the maturation of self-concepts and the development of interpersonal relations. In retrospect, however, alumni reported that college's primary effects had been in the stabilization and integration of values, about which self-concepts subsequently coalesced. As Heath suggests, these variations are probably attributable to the dominant preoccupation of the time: Undergraduates are concerned with themselves and their relations with others, while as alumni, their focus is on careers, family, and community. The evidence indicated that the main effects of college for alumni lay in their increased abilities to relate ideas to one another at increasingly higher levels of abstraction, the clarification of and ability to articulate personal values, the stabilization and internalization of these values, and the integration of these values into a coherent system. However, when the subjects were asked to identify the major determinants of their maturation since graduation, spouses and type of occupation ranked first and second, respectively. While alumni reported that Haverford's impact (ranked ninth) was distinctive and enduring, it was nonetheless judged to be rather more modest than that of spouses and occupations on postbaccalaureate maturation. It is impossible to say how much these rankings may be due to the temporal proximity of spouses and jobs. It seems likely that the durability of any college effect may depend to a large degree upon the extent to which it is supported or reinforced by postcollege experiences and friends, as well as by one's spouse.

Summary

This chapter has reviewed the research on the relationship between college attendance and changes in what Inkeles (1966) referred to as people's "relational systems," the ways in which students interpret and respond to people, conditions, and institutions in their external world. Studies in this area focus on six general areas: (1) autonomy, independence, and locus of control; (2) authoritarianism, dogmatism, and ethnocentrism; (3) intellectual orientation; (4) interpersonal relations; (5) personal adjustment and psychological well-being; and (6) maturity and general personal development.

Change During College

There can be little doubt that students' relational systems change during the college years. Indeed, the research in this general area is remarkably consistent. With very few exceptions, large-scale, nationally representative studies and smaller-scale, single-institution studies alike find general increases in students' freedom from the influences of others (although changes in peer independence appear to be either statistically nonsignificant or small), in nonauthoritarian thinking and tolerance for other people and their views, in intellectual orientation to problem solving and their own world in general, in the maturity of their interpersonal relations, in their personal adjustment skills and general sense of psychological well-being, and in their more globally measured levels of maturity and personal development. Changes in students' social extroversion is an exception. Here there is some evidence of decline during the college years. Nevertheless, there is reason to believe that these declines may reflect less any tendency toward social introversion than decreased dependence upon groups, increased selectivity in students' choices of friends, and increased intimacy within those friendships, whether with individuals of the same or opposite sex.

The largest freshman-senior changes appear to be away from authoritarian, dogmatic, and ethnocentric thinking and behavior. Declines in authoritarianism and dogmatism (with some variations across different scales) appear to be on the order of .70 to .90 of a standard deviation (or 26 to 32 percentile points). Declines in ethnocentrism may be somewhat smaller (around $-.40$ of a standard deviation, or -15 percentile points). Intermediate increases appear to occur in intellectual orientation (approximately .33 of a standard deviation, or 13 percentile points), personal adjustment and psychological well-being (about .40 of a standard deviation, or 15 percentile points), and autonomy and family independence (.60 of a standard deviation, or 22 percentile points). The smallest shifts seem to occur in locus of control (increases in internality of .25 to .30 of a standard deviation, or 10 to 12 percentile points), peer independence (.20 of a standard deviation, or 1 percentile point), and interpersonal relations (.16 of a standard deviation, or 6 percentile points). While one might wonder about the range and variability of these estimates (some of which is no doubt due to the roughness of our estimates), it is important to keep in mind, as Feldman and Newcomb (1969) point out, that there is really little reason to expect the rates of change to be the same in all change areas. Indeed, one might reasonably *expect* them to vary, even substantially, across areas. Similarly, there is ample evidence to indicate that students coming to college vary considerably on any given individual characteristic, including the readiness and willingness to change. Under the circumstances, some students will change sooner (or later) than others, and individuals themselves will vary across characteristics in their readiness to change.

Feldman and Newcomb (1969, pp. 100–102) found more evidence of gradual rather than discontinuous change over the college years. The only exception was in students' nonauthoritarianism scores, which increased more dramatically during the freshman year than during later years. Our review suggests a similar conclusion. It is true that there is some basis for believing that the early college years may be somewhat more influential than the later ones on intellectual orientation and personal adjustment and general psychological well-being, as well as on authoritarianism and dogmatism. This evidence, however, is largely indirect and based on a comparison of the findings of independent studies that explored change over varying periods of time. What *is* striking is how few studies conducted in the last two decades examine the *timing* of student change in virtually all areas or the extent to which change is conditional on students' individual characteristics. We still know relatively little about *when* and *who* changes psychosocially.

Net Change

Despite the large and consistent volume of evidence indicating statistically significant changes in a wide variety of facets of students' relational systems during the college years, only the increases in internality (locus of control), intellectual disposition, and personal adjustment and general psychological well-being and the declines in authoritarianism and dogmatism can be attributed with any confidence to college attendance. Moreover, even here, college's net effects on locus of control and personal adjustment and psychological well-being appear to be small.

The relation between college attendance and declines in authoritarianism and dogmatism is strong, however, even after controlling initial level, academic ability, and socioeconomic status. While the body of research upon which this conclusion is based is small, it is generally rigorous and derived from a nationally representative study that included respondents who did not attend college. College's effects on intellectual disposition is similarly clear, although the magnitude of the effect is more modest. Net of ability and socioeconomic status, people who complete college show significant gains in their tolerance for ambiguity, flexibility of thought, and preference for reflective and abstract thought, as well as for logical, rational, and critical approaches to problem solving. High school graduates who go directly into employment tend to show either no gains or sometimes even modest declines in these areas. Women who become homemakers and have no work experience outside the home appear to decline most of all.

Little can be said with any confidence about net college effects on changes in autonomy and independence, interpersonal relations, or overall maturity and personal development. The major constraints on our knowledge in these areas are methodological. There are few studies with sufficiently rigorous designs and analytical procedures and generalizable samples upon which to base reasonably confident conclusions. With very few exceptions, studies in these areas are cross-sectional, utilizing few controls (often none) for initial levels on the dependent variables or other salient background characteristics. Consequently, college and age or maturational effects remain confounded. Results could be due to college, to maturation, or to differences in the composition of the comparison groups. While more studies of college's net effects deal with students' interpersonal relations than with their autonomy or overall personal development, the results are inconsistent. Moreover, most studies of change in levels of maturity and general personal development are longitudinal and based on a single institution, thus shedding no light on the question of net effects.

The weight of evidence therefore fairly clearly supports popular beliefs about the effects of college in helping to reduce students' authoritarianism, dogmatism, and (perhaps) ethnocentrism and in increasing their intellectual orientation, personal psychosocial adjustment, and sense of psychological well-being. Empirical support for beliefs and claims about college's net influence on students' autonomy and independence, the maturity of their interpersonal relations, and their general maturity and personal development, however, is either inconsistent or nonexistent.

Between-College Effects

Evidence on whether the kind of institution a student attends makes a difference in his or her relational system presents a mixed picture, depending upon the outcome under study. The literature is nearly silent on between-college effects on changes in maturity or general personal development: With two exceptions, the studies in these areas are all single-institution studies or, for one reason or another, are of questionable generalizability. Several studies examine change in students' development of mature interpersonal relations, but for various reasons their results are also of questionable generalizability. The soundest inquiries report either few differences across kinds of institution or inconsistent and ambiguous patterns of small differences.

The literature on changes in students' intellectual dispositions and orientations is not silent, but the most definitive evidence indicates that college's effects are general. Once students' prematriculation characteristics are taken into account, the observed increases in reflective and abstract thinking, in preference for logical and rational approaches to problem solving, and in general intellectual flexibility are about the same regardless of the kind of institution attended. Limited evidence indicates that where one goes to school may make a statistically significant difference in autonomy, independence, or internal locus of control. Selective and "cohesive" institutions (those with relatively high proportions of full-time students and freshmen living on campus and low percentages of students working) appear to promote an internal locus of control somewhat more effectively than other kinds of institutions, but the difference is small.

It is possible, of course, that such findings are less a function of reality than of the inadequacy of the measures typically used to differentiate institutions (for example, size, type of control, selectivity). The research in four areas of relational change provides modest support for such speculation, finding differences across institutions to be based on institutional environments or contexts. For example, as just noted, increases in internality are associated with institutional "cohesion," and the largest declines in authoritarianism and dogmatism have been found on campuses with a large number of nonconforming students, teaching practices that encourage student participation in classroom discussions and course decision making, and class assignments that require complex mental activities. Increases appear to be less likely on campuses with a "collegiate," practical, vocational, or instrumental orientation and with an emphasis on extrinsic motivations.

Similar findings that suggest the importance of contextual rather than structural or organizational differences among institutions are reported in the area of students' personal adjustment and general psychological well-being and in studies of general personal development. In the former area, differences in size, type of control, and selectivity appear to have little or no influence on student change once aptitude, achievement, socioeconomic status, and other personality traits are held constant. By contrast, male students' anxiety levels appear to be higher at schools with a realistic or intellectual orientation (Holland types) but lower on campuses where artistic and social majors are more prevalent. Among women, increased anxiety levels are more common on campuses with proportionally more students majoring in "enterprising" fields (law, political science, and history). The two large-scale studies on general personal development indicate that with the exception of the combination of selectivity and curricular mission in the selective liberal arts colleges, conventional descriptors of institutional characteristics appear not to be useful predictors. Between-institution differences in effects on general personal development appear more likely to be a function of institutional environment than of structural characteristics.

It would appear, then, that where a student goes to college *may* make a difference in the kinds of change that are likely to occur in the relational facets of that student's psychosocial makeup. That difference, however, is likely to be slight. Moreover, any such effects are not likely to be a consequence of differences on those characteristics typically used to distinguish among institutions (size, selectivity, type of control, and the like). Rather, institutional effects appear more likely to follow from differences in institutional context—the organizational policies, practices, and interpersonal climate—that students find on campus. These may vary substantially for institutions of similar type, size, or selectivity.

Within-College Effects

The cumulative weight of evidence on within-college effects indicates few, if any, significant differences in the rates of change related to academic major fields in any of the six general areas of psychosocial growth reviewed. The evidence is more abundant in some areas than in others, but the consistency of the findings across areas is striking, coming as it does from both poorly and moderately well controlled studies, the vast majority of which are single-institution investigations. One study, however, examined the effects of departmental environments on students' psychological well-being and found statistically significant, contextually related variations. This finding is consistent with the findings of studies in other areas of psychosocial change that suggest that departmental environment may be more influential than a particular discipline in shaping students' psychosocial lives. It is also consistent with the between-college evidence that indicates that psychosocial changes may be influenced more by contextual differences than by structural or organizational differences.

While academic major may not be related to changes in the several areas reviewed in this chapter, a small but reasonably consistent body of research indicates that residence in a living-learning center (LLC) has positive and significant effects on students' gains in autonomy and personal independence, intellectual dispositions and orientations, and generalized personal development, as well as on declines in authoritarianism and dogmatism. Moreover, these effects are discernible even when precollege scores on these variables are controlled. There is no evidence, however, that LLCs have any influence on changes in students' development of more mature interpersonal relations or their personal adjustment or general psychological well-being.

More important, perhaps, a growing body of evidence indicates that when students' interpersonal contacts and relations with other students and faculty members are also taken into account, the beneficial effects of LLC residence tend to diminish, sometimes to disappear. These findings are significant because of their suggestion that the effects of LLC residences may be more indirect than direct. The structural, organizational, and programmatic features of living-learning centers, it would appear, exert their influence on student change through the interpersonal relations they foster or facilitate among the major socializing agents—other students, faculty members, and administrators (although the influences of administrators have not been specifically studied). These findings are, of course, clearly supportive of our earlier speculation on the greater importance of environmental and contextual conditions as opposed to organizational or programmatic considerations.

When one considers the cumulative evidence relating to the effects of living in traditional residence halls versus living in off-campus quarters and commuting, it appears that living on campus tends to promote somewhat greater increases in personal autonomy and independence, intellectual disposition, and the development of more mature interpersonal relationships. The evidence is mixed, however, with respect to on-campus advantages relating to gains in personal adjustment and psychological well-being, gains in generalized personal development, and declines in authoritarianism and dogmatism.

More striking, again, is the importance of students' interpersonal relations with peers and faculty, a theme previously alluded to in the context of living-learning centers but frequently found as well in studies of the effects of residence arrangement on students' psychosocial development. That motif is particularly apparent in the general body of research reporting gains in intellectual orientation and in maturity and general personal development. It is somewhat more muted in the evidence on increases in autonomy and independence and is barely audible in studies finding declines in authoritarianism and dogmatism, partly because it is not specifically considered in many studies. As one might expect, the relative influence of peers and faculty members varies across the areas, with a general tendency for faculty influence to be greater in intellectual areas and peer influence more dominant in noncognitive areas (although there is some evidence to the contrary). In addition, there is reason to believe that the nature or character of students' contacts with peers may exert a greater influence than their frequency, although the evidence on this point is equivocal.

Conditional Effects of College

Nothing can be said with confidence about college effects in any of the six areas reviewed that might be dependent on students' individual characteristics. Numerous studies in each area contrast males and females as freshmen and as seniors or test for significant differences between freshman and senior years for each sex separately. But the questions answered by such tests (Do men and women differ as freshmen or as seniors on some attribute? Do men (or women) change significantly over the college years?) are really "main effect" questions and do not deal with the issue of conditional (or interaction) effects. Only a small handful test such effects: the statistical significance of the *difference* between the sexes (or occasionally the races) in the *amount* of change due to college attendance. Most of the studies in that handful relate to changes in students' levels of autonomy, independence, or locus of control. While the only study based on a nationally representative sample indicates that women make significantly larger gains in these areas than men, a number of single-institution studies produce conflicting findings of no differences, larger gains among males, or larger gains among females. Thus, we can conclude only that the investigation of conditional college effects in these several areas constitutes uncharted research territory.

Long-Term Effects of College

A dozen studies, drawing on six separate data bases, have dealt with the long-term effects of college in the six areas of psychosocial change. Within any of these areas, however, no more than two studies contain relevant information, and those (with two exceptions) are single-institution studies with sometimes idiosyncratic samples of questionable generalizability. The two exceptions drew on a national data base, and both found statistically significant but small positive effects of college attendance on internal locus of control seven and fourteen years after graduation. Neither study, however, controlled for the potentially confounding effects of occupational status and other noncollege or postcollege experiences. Thus, the long-term durability of college effects on locus of control remains unclear.

Across the smaller, single-institution studies of other areas of relational system change, there is some evidence of stability three, five, and ten years after graduation in graduates' levels of authoritarianism, with very limited evidence hinting at a possible (but small) drop in intellectual disposition. A very small body of evidence also provides some basis for the belief that alumni become somewhat more conservative in their willingness to express impulses than they were in their senior year and to enjoy slightly higher levels of personal integration and lower levels of stress and anxiety than they did in their senior year. Controls for occupation reduce but do not entirely eliminate these educational effects on psychological well-being.

Thus, it would appear that college has some long-term effects in several areas of graduates' relational systems. This is a highly tentative conclusion, however, based on a small number of studies with limited samples. Most of the findings of these studies may be only marginally generalizable. These findings are, however, consistent with those of Schaie and Parham

(1976), who examined personality characteristics in a seven-year longitudinal study of a sample of 2,500 individuals who ranged in age from twenty-one to eighty-four years. These authors concluded that "stability of personality traits is the rule rather than the exception" (p. 157). They did not, unfortunately, examine any differences that might have been related to educational attainment.

In sum, the evidence is clear and consistent in indicating that statistically significant changes occur in a variety of externally oriented psychosocial areas during the college years, all of them in directions that most people would agree are educationally and socially relevant and desirable. Although the evidence regarding education's effect on these changes is considerably smaller and somewhat less persuasive, we conclude there are sound grounds for claiming that education, above and beyond other relevant variables, has a discernible, if generally small, effect in each area of change. With a few exceptions, what happens to students after they arrive on campus clearly has a more potent influence in each area of change than where students go to school. Moreover, the dominant source of within-college effects consistently appears to be the frequency and nature of the contacts undergraduates have with the major agents of socialization: their peers and faculty members. Indeed, taken together, the evidence reviewed here indicates that the structural, organizational, and programmatic effects of college are largely indirect ones, being mediated through the influence they exert on the nature and frequency of students' interpersonal interactions, as well as institutional and subgroup environments.

To a certain extent, however, this overall body of evidence is a dated one. A substantial portion of it, particularly that dealing with the changes in autonomy, independence, intellectual orientation, and authoritarianism, is drawn from studies that were conducted in the 1970s. More worrisome is the fact that much of the early research, for obvious reasons, was based on narrowly generalizable samples and employed what today would be considered low-powered analytical procedures. With some exceptions, one is left with the feeling that in the last decade the knowledge development curve in these dimensions of psychological change has leveled off. One might reasonably argue that what we now know about these dimensions is only modestly greater than what we knew fifteen years ago.

Notes

1. Although this study was competently conducted, the authors consider these findings and conclusions to be tentative. They expect to publish additional analyses in a forthcoming book entitled *The Way Up: The Long-Term Effects of Higher Education on Students* (W. E. Knox, telephone communication, June 1990).
2. Priest, Prince, and Vitters (1978) used Rotter's (1966) Internal-External

Scale. The others' findings are based on the Personal Orientation Inventory (POI), developed by Shostrom (1966). The POI contains 150 paired, opposing statements that comprise multiple scales, including two major scales: inner-directedness and time competence. The conclusions reached in this review are based on changes in scores on the inner-directedness scale.

3. Although typically treated as a unitary construct, authoritarianism can be conceptualized and shown to have multiple dimensions (see, for example, Adorno, Frenkel-Brunswick, Levinson, & Sanford, 1950; Baker, 1976a).

4. Baker (1976a) provides a succinct history of the evolution of the OPI. According to her and others (for example, Trent & Medsker, 1968), the social maturity (SM) scale had its origins in earlier, more ideological measures of authoritarianism. The SM scale, however, is scored on the basis of nonauthoritarian rather than authoritarian responses. Subsequent revisions of the SM scale led to the development of the OPI autonomy scale, the validational correlations of which indicated that it measures a general nonauthoritarianism (Baker, 1976a, p. 627). Levin (1967) reports correlations between the SM and F scales ranging from .67 to .75 over a variety of independent samples. Trent and Medsker (1968, p. 285) also report moderate to high correlations between the social maturity and nonauthoritarianism scales (.61), the autonomy and social maturity scales (.82), and the autonomy and nonauthoritarianism scales (.70). Moreover, studies by Clark, Heist, McConnell, Trow, and Yonge (1972), which included two of the creators of the OPI on the project staff, and by Trent and Medsker (1968) discuss autonomy scale results in the context of a general examination of authoritarian or nonauthoritarian changes in students.

5. Mean scores in Trent and Medsker (1968), Trent and Golds (1967), and Yonge and Regan (1975) are not reported in raw score form but rather in OPI standard score form based on original OPI normative data having a mean of 50 and a standard deviation of 10 (Trent & Medsker, 1968, p. 132). Given Trent's senior authorship in the 1967 and 1968 publications, we presume the transformation of raw to standard scores in the two publications is based on the same normative data set, although nothing specific is said on this point. Similarly, the data in Yonge and Regan (1975), given Yonge's contributions to the development of the OPI, are also presumed to be based on OPI normative data. On that assumption, we divided the freshman-senior scale score differences in these three studies by 10 (the presumed freshman-year standard deviation) in order to estimate the magnitudes of changes. Evidence from other large- and small-scale studies suggests, however, that a standard deviation of 10 may be somewhat high. Thus, our estimates of change derived from these three studies may be slightly

underestimated, although the magnitude of the underestimation is not likely to be much more than .10 of a standard deviation.

6. Several studies employed the "theoretical" scale of the Allport, Vernon, and Lindzey (1960) Study of Values (SOV) (Arsenian, 1970; Cox, 1988; Huntley, 1967; May & Ilardi, 1970, 1973). People who score high on this scale are concerned with discovering truth; they are critical, analytical, rational, and concerned with ordering and systematizing their knowledge. The evidence from the SOV is inconsistent, however, perhaps because of its ipsative scoring (see Heist, 1968, pp. 214–218). Feldman and Newcomb (1969, p. 8) concluded that "Freshman-senior differences on the theoretical . . . values [scale] are not only inconsistent across samples but are almost never statistically significant." We found no evidence to challenge that conclusion.

7. Feldman and Newcomb (1969, appendix C) offer a more extended discussion of the problems of inferring changes in "maturity" from changes in personality scale scores.

8. Smart, Ethington, and McLaughlin (undated) label their dependent variable "self-confidence." Their description of the scale, however, includes references to being "internally motivated" and believing "hard work to be more important to future success than luck" (table 1). Because of this content, their findings based on the use of this scale are included in the sections dealing with locus of control.

9. In a study of the relative contributions of individual and institutional variables to the development of social competence, Walizer and Herriott (1971) found that a set of college structural variables made statistically significant and unique contributions (11.3 percent versus 11.7 percent explained by students' background characteristics) to the explained variations in OPI social maturity scale scores four years after high school graduation. The joint contribution was 2.8 percent, indicating that the two variables sets made relatively independent contributions. Regrettably, Walizer and Heriott's report sheds no light on which specific structural characteristics were the most influential or on the nature or direction of that influence.

10. Several studies present information on the effects of various other course and programmatic academic experiences on changes in students' autonomy, independence, or locus of control, but because of their considerable heterogeneity in both substance and methodology, generalization would be little more than speculation. These academic experiences include (but are not limited to) developmental and remedial programs (Leon, 1974; Yarbrough, Ragan, & Wilson, 1984), "field" and study-abroad programs (Billigmeier & Forman, 1975; Hursh & Borzak, 1979; Nash, 1976; Pyle, 1981), instructional approach (Guskey, Benninga, & Clark, 1984; Duby, 1981; Mullins & Perkins, 1973), specific course content (Dignan & Adams, 1979; Franks, Falk,

& Hinton, 1973; Harris, 1983; Parish, 1988a; Stonewater & Daniels, 1983), psychosocial development courses and programs (Försterling, 1985; Kleeman, 1974; Lynch, Ogg, & Christensen, 1975; Trueblood & McHolland, cited in Kleeman, 1974; Mitchell, Reid, & Sanders, cited in Kleeman, 1974; Perry & Penner, 1989; West & Kirkland, 1986), and group encounters (Aronson, 1971; Blume, 1981; Diamond & Shapiro, 1973; Foulds, 1971; Foulds, Guinan, & Warehime, 1974; Smith, 1970). While these studies are generally consistent in suggesting that these various activities have positive effects on students' independence levels, little is known about the longevity of the effects or about the mediating processes that make up the various activities.

11. Other residence-related studies have examined the effects on autonomy of varying parental visitation policies (Montgomery, McLaughlin, Fawcett, Pedigo, & Ward, 1975), single-sex versus coeducational halls (Schroeder & LeMay, 1973), participation in residence assistant programs (Scott, 1975), and living in a fraternity or sorority versus living in a traditional residence hall (Rago, 1973). Because of the small number of studies dealing with any specific topic, however, it is impossible to draw definitive conclusions.

12. Jakobsen (1986), Strange (1986), and Wilder and Hoyt (1986) provide a dialogue on the meaning and implications of the findings of Wilder, Hoyt, Surbeck, Wilder, and Carney (1986).

13. Several studies have investigated the effects of special, short-term interventions on students' levels of authoritarianism or dogmatism. These interventions include experimental courses (Berdie, 1974), women's studies courses (Lenihan & Rawlins, 1987), personal growth groups (Blume, 1981), a career decision-making course (Stonewater & Daniels, 1983), simulation gaming (Bredemeier, Bernstein, & Oxman, 1982), study abroad (Marion, 1980), and student teacher training programs (Borgers, 1979; Campbell & Williamson, 1973; Johnson, 1969). In all these studies, the changes were generally toward nonauthoritarianism or a reduction in dogmatism, but nothing is known about the generalizability of these interventions, their effects, or the durability of any effects.

14. Changes in intellectual orientation have also been associated with shorter-term, academically related interventions, including personal growth or encounter groups (Blume, 1981; Foulds, Guinan, & Hannigan, 1974), a physical fitness class (Gondola & Tuckman, 1985), joint faculty/student-designed academic programs (Magnarella, 1975), a program of residence hall–based, informal series of discussions with faculty members (Brown, 1968), a "creative studies" project (Parnes & Noeller, 1973), and study-abroad experiences (James, 1976; Kuh & Kauffman, 1985).

15. The effects of various interventions on students' interpersonal rela-

tions have also been studied, although summary conclusions are not attempted here because of their substantive and methodological heterogeneity. These interventions include (but are not limited to) formal course work (Whitla, 1981; Yarbrough, Ragan, & Wilson, 1984), study abroad (Hull & Lemke, 1975; Hull, Lemke, & Houang, 1977; Kuh & Kauffman, 1985; Pelowski, 1979; Pyle, 1981), and counseling or structured program interventions (Alberti, 1972; Allred & Graff, 1980; Grant & Eigenbrod, 1970; Hipple, 1973; Martinson & Zerface, 1970).

7

Attitudes and Values

There can be little doubt that American colleges and universities are and have been deeply concerned with shaping the attitudes, values, and beliefs of their students (Rudolph, 1962; McBee, 1980; Morrill, 1980; Sloan, 1980). While there may be little agreement inside or outside the academy on precisely which attitudes and values colleges and universities should teach (or how energetically), there probably is substantial agreement among faculty and administrators, as well as parents, legislators, alumni, and students themselves, that higher educational institutions should be involved in the shaping of values.

The extent to which these purposes are being achieved, however, has been the subject of considerable debate. Jacob (1957, pp. xiii, 4), noting that values "are a *subject* of instruction . . . a specific *motivation* of instruction [and] also a *consequence* of instruction," reviewed the research literature dealing with value change during college and concluded that college's main effect appears to be "to bring about general acceptance of a body of standards and attitudes characteristic of college-bred men and women in the American community." Indeed, Jacob reported finding greater value homogeneity and consistency among students at the end of their four years of college than when they entered college. What changes he did find, he believed could as reasonably be attributed to the selection and retention of students as to college effects.

These conclusions precipitated a torrent of additional studies of attitude and value change among college students, and Feldman and Newcomb (1969) identified a substantial body of evidence at variance with Jacob's conclusions. This chapter reviews the research reported since the publication of Feldman and Newcomb's book that deals with changes in students' attitudes and values. Before turning to that review, however, we need to keep in mind that meaningful measurement of the extent to which value or attitude change occurs during college confronts at least three difficult issues.

The first issue is the specification and definition of precisely what is being measured (see Grandy, 1988). Terms like *values* and *attitudes* have multiple meanings. Values have been specified to be "preferences, criteria, or choices of personal or group conduct" (Jacob, 1957, p. xiii); "a cluster of attitudes organized around a conception of the desirable" (Feldman & Newcomb, 1969, p. 7); and a "strong preference based on a conception of what is desirable, important, and worthy of esteem" (Lenning, Lee, Micek, and Service, 1977, pp. 58–59). Rokeach (1971, p. 453) believes that "an attitude represents an organization of interrelated beliefs that are all focused on a specific object or situation, while . . . values are generalized standards of the means and ends of human existence that transcend attitudes toward specific objects and situations." Because many studies use these terms interchangeably, we have made no attempt to differentiate them. Instead, we include in our review studies of college student change in areas that might reasonably be said to be covered by one or more of these definitions.

The second difficult issue besetting research on attitude and value change concerns the degree of correspondence between the attitudes and values held and their consequent influence on individual action. Do students (or anyone else, for that matter) really practice what they preach? If value or attitude change is apparent on some measure, is that shift also reflected in altered behavior? Compared to the volume of research on changes in values and attitudes, very little study has been given to their effects on behavior (see also Chapter Eight). As will be seen later in this chapter, the correspondence is probably far from perfect. At the same time, perhaps one ought not to expect a high degree of correspondence between professed values and behavior since a wide variety of general and situationally specific factors converge to shape discrete individual actions. Thus, what one sees in manifest behavior may reflect only attitudinal or value tendencies that are dominant at the time (Feather, 1980).

Finally, the study of college effects on attitude and value change is complicated by the need to control for historical and/or generational influences. Briefly, the issue is whether changes observed in college students are, in fact, a consequence of the collegiate experience or simply a reflection of changes occurring in the larger society. Given the social and political turmoil in the United States over the last two decades, this issue is particularly acute in the study of change in students' attitudes and values. The measurement problem here and what the research has to say about the origins of effects of observed changes are discussed in greater detail later in this chapter. Nonetheless, readers should be sensitive to this interpretive problem throughout the chapter.

Change During College

Our review indicates that the bulk of the empirical literature of the last twenty years relating to changes in attitudes and values falls generally into five categories: (1) cultural, aesthetic, and intellectual; (2) educational and occupational; (3) social and political; (4) religious; and (5) gender roles.[1]

Cultural, Aesthetic, and Intellectual Attitudes and Values

Feldman and Newcomb (1969) found almost universal increases in students' aesthetic interests and values during college, and the evidence reported since that time consistently indicates the same effects. Indeed, in only a handful of studies (Baumgartel & Goldstein, 1967; Bradshaw, 1975; Jones & Finnell, 1972; Moos & Otto, 1975) were declines or no changes in cultural, aesthetic,[2] or intellectual[3] attitudes and values observed during some portion of the college years. Otherwise, the literature is remarkably consistent in indicating increases in students' interests and activities in creative writing, reading, classical music, art, and other cultural and aesthetic experiences and activities. In some instances, the changes involve a growth in students' cultural and aesthetic appreciation; in others, the changes are behavioral (for example, attending concerts or art shows, writing poetry). In all cases, the changes are toward a greater valuing of cultural and aesthetic experiences and activities.

The evidence comes from a number of multi-institution or national population studies (Astin, 1977a; Bayer, Royer, & Webb, 1973; Chickering, 1971a, 1974b; Chickering, McDowell, & Campagna, 1969; Clark, Heist, McConnell, Trow, & Yonge, 1972; Cobern, Salem, & Mushkin, 1973; Hyman, Wright, & Reed, 1975; Pace, 1972, 1974, 1984; Nelsen & Johnson, 1971; Peterson, 1968; Rich & Jolicoeur, 1978; Solmon & Ochsner, 1978a, 1978b; Trent & Golds, 1967; Weidman, 1979; Wilson, Gaff, Dienst, Wood, & Bavry, 1975; Winston & Miller, 1987). Other evidence of significant increases in aesthetic and cultural values and interests during the college years is reported in a number of single-institution studies (Cox, 1988; Endo & Harpel, 1980, 1982; Feather, 1975; Fry, 1974; Heath, 1968; Huntley, 1967; Korn, 1968; Mentkowski & Doherty, 1984; Miller, 1973; Newcomb, Brown, Kulik, Reimer, & Revelle, 1970, 1971; May & Ilardi, 1973; Lacy, 1978; Marion & Cheek, 1985; Moos, 1978, 1979; Ory & Braskamp, 1988; Regan, 1969; Stakenas, 1972; Wilder, Hoyt, Doren, Hauck, & Zettle, 1978; Wilson, 1974).

Astin (1977a), for example, used data from the Cooperative Institutional Research Program (CIRP), an unequaled series of studies of more than 200,000 students who entered more than 300 institutions between 1961 and 1969 and were followed up at intervals varying from one to five years. Although Astin found declines of 1 to 5 percentage points in students' interests in becoming accomplished in the performing arts, he also found consistent, if modest, increases in students' artistic interests over the four years of college (up to 6 percentage points). Similarly, Peterson (1968) reports statistically significant freshman-to-senior increases on the CSQ's cultural sophistication scale in a random subset of 700 undergraduates at eleven colleges who were generally representative of American college students. Again, however, the freshman-senior differences were not large. Other multi-institution studies, using different measures, have produced results consistent with these (Chickering, McDowell, & Campagna, 1969; Chickering, 1971a; Clark, Heist, McConnell, Trow, & Yonge, 1972, especially chap. 7).

The evidence from these multi-institution studies is supported by that of Hyman, Wright, and Reed (1975). Drawing on the information in fifty-four national surveys conducted between 1949 and 1971 by various national polling organizations, these authors found significant and substantial differences across educational strata in people's knowledge and receptivity to knowledge in such areas as current affairs, domestic and foreign policy, and popular culture and in their reported use of the print media (especially magazines and books). Sizable advantages over an elementary school education were associated with graduation from high school, but the gains associated with college graduation were even greater. Although the advantages of a college education varied across topical areas, in a number of instances they were half-again or twice the size of the advantage of high school graduation over only an elementary school education.

Several single-institution studies contain information that can be used to estimate the magnitudes of observed freshman-to-senior increases, and our reanalyses of reported data reveal some consistency: .33 of a standard deviation (13 percentile points) on the CSQ's (see note 2) cultural sophistication scale (Nelsen & Uhl, 1977) and .39 of a standard deviation (15 percentile points) on the Study of Value's aesthetic scale (Arsenian, 1970), both with men and women combined. Gains of .49 of a standard deviation (19 percentile points) are reported by Winston and Miller (1987) on a measure of cultural participation completed by freshmen and seniors on twenty campuses in the United States and Canada.

Freshman-senior changes on the estheticism scale of the Omnibus Personality Inventory (OPI) (Heist & Yonge, 1968), averaged across seventeen samples in eight studies, indicate gains of .30 of a standard deviation (12 percentile points). These estimated effect sizes are from half to two-thirds the size of that reported by Bowen (1977, p. 98) for "esthetic sensibility." Bowen's estimate appears to be partly based on judgment and on fewer studies than our own (see Bowen, 1977, p. 82). Either or both of these facts might explain the differences between his estimate and ours.

Modest group changes may, of course, mask a considerable number of individual changes that offset one another in the calculation of group means. Chickering (1971a) controlled for this possibility, as well as for "floor" and "ceiling" effects, and still found gains in cultural sophistication similar to those obtained when only sex and college were controlled: small but significant gains, although they varied in degree across the seven colleges in his research. These findings are consistent with those published in an earlier study (Chickering, McDowell, and Campagna, 1969).

Although the evidence of change over the college years is consistent across studies, few shed light on whether the rate of change in cultural, aesthetic, and intellectual attitudes and values is constant over the college years. Nelsen and Uhl (1977), May and Ilardi (1973), and Chickering, McDowell, and Campagna (1969) all found year-to-year variations in the increases in cultural and aesthetic interests, but there was no consistency across studies to suggest whether more change is likely in the early or later college years.

Educational and Occupational Values

Educational and occupational values held by college students may be manifested in at least two ways. The first is the status of the educational or occupational level sought, presumably the higher the better. The evidence in this area is reviewed in Chapter Ten. A second approach involves an examination of the reasons people have for going to college or for preferring one occupation over another. In this section, the focus is on changes in students' educational and occupational values that can be inferred from the research dealing with the relative importance of intrinsic and extrinsic reasons students have for attending college and the nature of the rewards they seek from the occupations they expect to pursue.[4]

Astin, Green, and Korn (1987) report numerically and substantively significant shifts during the period from 1967 to 1985 in the proportion of entering freshmen subscribing to intrinsic and extrinsic values. For example, while about 45 percent of the new freshmen in 1965 reported that being very well off financially was very important or essential, that proportion had climbed to over 70 percent by 1985. In contrast, the percentage for whom developing a meaningful philosophy of life was very important or essential declined from over 80 percent to 44 percent during the same period. While this study gives clear evidence of change in values across entering cohorts, it does not specifically identify these values as either educational or occupational goals. Moreover, the question of interest in our review is the extent to which college influences change *within* individuals or the same cohort.

Educational Values. Earlier literature reviews have found consistent evidence that seniors, as compared with freshmen, place greater emphasis on the intrinsic values of a liberal or general education and less emphasis on the instrumental value of education as vocational or career preparation (Feldman & Newcomb, 1969; Bowen, 1977). The research that has appeared over the last two decades provides no reason whatever to alter this general conclusion (Trent & Medsker, 1968; Beaton, 1975; Clark, Heist, McConnell, Trow, & Yonge, 1972; Musgrove, 1971 [in a British university]; Regan, 1969; Smart, Ethington, & McLaughlin, undated; Spaeth & Greeley, 1970; Suczek, 1972; Pace, 1974).

In a landmark longitudinal study of some 10,000 high school graduates from thirty-seven high schools in sixteen communities throughout the Midwest, California, and Pennsylvania, Trent and Medsker (1968) found that degree of exposure to higher education (time in attendance) was positively related to the importance attached to a broad general education. Compared to college graduates, people who never attended college or who withdrew from college at various points before graduation tended to place greater value on vocational preparation. Similar or consistent results are reported by Beaton (1975); Clark, Heist, McConnell, Trow, and Yonge (1972); Cobern, Salem, and Mushkin (1973); Heath (1968); Pace (1974); Spaeth and Greeley (1970); and Suczek (1972). The value attached to other educational purposes (some of which are facets of a liberal education), such as development of interpersonal skills, personal development, or understanding community and world problems, lags substantially behind vocational preparation and the cognitive dimensions of a liberal education as the most important educational goals. There appears to be relatively little change in the importance of these goals over the college years (Clark, Heist, McConnell, Trow, & Yonge, 1972; Trent & Medsker, 1968), although the evidence is somewhat dated.

The Clark, Heist, McConnell, Trow, and Yonge (1972) data indicate freshman-to-senior increases of from 20 to 30 percentage points in the proportion of seniors (compared to themselves as freshmen) who considered a liberal education to be the "most important purpose of college." With one exception, 60 percent or more of the seniors in eight schools subscribed to this goal as the most important one. By contrast, the freshman-to-senior percentages who endorsed "vocational training" as the most important goal dropped 10 to 30 points across the eight institutions, with fewer than a third of the seniors in all eight schools considering this the most important goal of education. More recent estimates of the degree of change in educational values over time were not identified.

Occupational Values. The evidence on occupational value change is mixed. Clark, Heist, McConnell, Trow, and Yonge (1972) found anywhere from 30 to 80 percent of the entering freshmen in their eight institutions placed a strong emphasis on intrinsic occupational values (freedom from supervision, autonomy, opportunities to be creative and to use one's talents, job challenge, and the like). This was in contrast to a range of 10 to 30 percent who placed the greatest emphasis on extrinsic values (salary, job security, opportunities for promotion, and so on). Over the college years, the percentage of students subscribing to intrinsic occupational values grew (with one exception) by less than 12 points. At the same time, the percentage endorsing extrinsic values declined over the four years in all cases except one by 14 to 15 percentage points. Change during college in the percentage endorsing the importance of service to people was less than 8 percentage points in either direction. Results consistent with these concerning intrinsic rewards are reported by Almquist and Angrist (1970) in a study of "career-salient" women and women planning sex-atypical careers, but these subjects also tended to increase in their valuing of extrinsic rewards.

Astin (1977a), in two samples, found freshman-to-senior declines of 10 to 15 percentage points in the proportion of students for whom it was important to be financially well-off. Weidman (1979), who used national data, reports consistent and moderate declines (8 to 20 percentage points) across majors in the importance of financial success and career eminence and (with minor variations) smaller increases in the value of helping others and of attaining administrative leadership. Chickering, McDowell, and Campagna (1969) found similar results. A number of other studies based on national samples (Solmon & Ochsner, 1978a, is an exception) provide similar evidence of declines in extrinsic values and/or increases in intrinsic values (Astin, 1977a; Bayer, Royer, & Webb, 1973; Bachman, O'Malley, & Johnston, 1978; Bradshaw, 1975; Kanouse et al., 1980; Kohn & Schooler, 1969; Lindsay & Knox, 1984; Smart, Ethington, & McLaughlin, undated; Strumpel, 1971). Single-institution studies have reported substantially the same findings (Caple, 1971; Chesin, 1969; Mortimer, 1975; Regan, 1969; Singer, 1974).[5]

One might be led to speculate (as did Gurin, 1971, and Bachman, O'Malley, and Johnston, 1978) that seniors may develop a certain occupational security. Confident of obtaining secure and monetarily rewarding positions, seniors may have the freedom (in a Maslovian-like hierarchy of occupational needs) to consider positions with greater intrinsic rewards. Mortimer and Lorence (1979b), however, tested this hypothesis and found no evidence to support it.

More recent research suggests stability rather than change in both intrinsic and extrinsic occupational values. For example, Anderson (1985b), in a study of occupational value change over four years (using NLS-72 data), observed general stability in both intrinsic and extrinsic occupational values. Angrist and Almquist (1975) found the stability in their respondents "remarkable," although they did observe some changes over time consistent with those noted above in educational values in their trend toward intrinsic values and away from extrinsic values. Smart, Ethington, and McLaughlin (undated), also using NLS-72 data, found evidence that declines in extrinsic occupational values may occur primarily in the freshman year, with values being essentially stable after that. Using CIRP data, however, McLaughlin and Smart (1987) report increases in extrinsic values during the college years. The discrepancies between earlier and later studies may very well reflect changes over the past twenty years in the occupational values of entering freshmen and young people in general (see, for example, Astin, 1977b; Astin, Green, & Korn, 1987; Yankelovich, 1972, 1974a, 1974b; Yankelovich & Clark, 1974), as well as differences in the ways that college affects these values. Some of the differences may also be due to variations in definitions and instruments.

There is no reason to believe or evidence to suggest that students consider the differences between intrinsic and extrinsic values to be cleanly dichotomous, with the endorsement of one set of values opposed to that of the other in either educational or occupational matters (Mentkowski & Doherty, 1984; Spaeth & Greeley, 1970). Indeed, out of their work with Stanford students in the late 1970s, Katchadourian and Boli (1985) developed a typology of college students based on students' levels of "careerism" (high or low) and intellectual orientation (high or low). Students' positions on these two dimensions suggested their placement in a four-fold matrix as "intellectuals," "strivers," "careerists," or "unconnecteds." In examining movement among the cells over a four-year period, Katchadourian and Boli found that three-quarters of the students were in the same group as seniors as they were as freshmen and that when change did occur, it was across adjacent cells, not polar opposites, thus indicating change along one or the other dimension but not along both dimensions.

None of the studies we reviewed with respect to changes in educational and occupational values included comparison groups of noncollege age-mates. This leaves maturation as a possible (but intuitively doubtful) alternative explanation. Moreover, we identified no study that compared the changes within multiple age cohorts of individuals over the last two decades. Thus, the effects of changes in educational and occupational values due to historical eras or periods or to cohort differences remain unknown.

Social and Political Attitudes and Values

Given the social and political turmoil of the last two decades, it should come as no surprise that change in students' social and political value orientations have received more research attention than any other category of attitudes and values. As noted earlier in this chapter, however, differentiating college effects from the influences of historical or generational shifts occurring in the population at large constitutes a major interpretive problem in studying attitude and value change among college students. This problem is particularly troublesome with respect to change in students' sociopolitical attitudes and values. The evidence on this topic is reviewed later in this chapter, but readers are encouraged to keep it in mind as they (and we) evaluate the available evidence.

Our review indicates that the research in this area has three general foci: (1) altruism, social conscience, humanitarianism, civic activities, and other similar "other-person" orientations in attitudes and values; (2) "liberal-conservative" orientations specifically applied in the political arena, as well as formal political party affiliation preferences and political activities (such as demonstrating for a cause, voting, discussing political affairs); and (3) general tolerance for the civil rights and civil liberties of others.

Altruism, Humanitarianism, and Civic Values. With a few exceptions (for example, Deppe, 1989, 1990; Solmon & Ochsner, 1978a, 1978b), the evidence is abundant and consistent in indicating that changes toward greater altruism, humanitarianism, and sense of civic responsibility and social conscience occur during the college years. Much of this evidence is based on nationally representative samples (Astin, 1972b, 1977a; Chickering, 1974a; Marks, 1990; McLaughlin & Smart, 1987; Pace, 1972, 1974; Pascarella, Ethington, & Smart, 1988; Pascarella, Smart, & Braxton, 1986; Peterson, 1968; Thistlethwaite, 1973). Similarly, with a few exceptions that showed nonsignificant gains (Frankland, Corbett, & Rudoni, 1980; Miller, 1973; Nelsen & Johnson, 1971), smaller-scale (and frequently but not always less rigorous) studies have produced the same consistent evidence (Bigelow & Kennedy, 1974; Greever, Tseng, & Friedland, 1974; Heath, 1968; Jones & Finnell, 1972; Lacy, 1978; Nelsen & Uhl, 1977; Newcomb, Brown, Kulik, Reimer, & Revelle, 1970, 1971; Stakenas, 1972; Suczek, 1972; Wilder, Hoyt, Doren, Hauck, & Zettle, 1978; Wilder, Hoyt, Surbeck, Wilder, & Carney, 1986).[6]

Several of the above studies afford a basis for estimating the magnitudes of the changes students undergo in this area. Astin (1977a) found relatively modest increases over four years in the percentage of students who reported that "helping others who are in difficulty" was "essential" or "very important": 1.5 percentage points in his 1966–1970 panel and 8.4 percentage points in his 1967–1971 panel. Wilder, Hoyt, Doren, Hauck, and Zettle (1978) found an increase of .35 of a standard deviation (14 percentile points) among Bucknell freshmen on the CSQ's social conscience scale.[7] Substantially larger four-year gains (.60 standard deviation, or 23 percentile points) are reported in a study (using that same CSQ scale) of three predominantly black institutions (Nelsen & Uhl, 1977). Pascarella, Smart, and Braxton (1986) found small gains (4 percentile points among white students and 10 percentile points among black students) over a nine-year period following first matriculation. McLaughlin and Smart (1987) found average increases over nine years (net of ability and socioeconomic status) of .09 of a standard deviation (4 percentile points) among men and women averaged across five types of institutions (the range was − .05 to .16 of a standard deviation). The variability in these estimates across studies suggests the roughness of their precision.

Political Attitudes and Values. The evidence on changes in students' political attitudes and values is much the same as that relating to their more generalized social and civic orientations. A number of national studies have produced results that almost invariably indicate changes during the college years in students' political attitudes and values toward more liberal political stances, greater interest in social and political issues, and greater interest and involvement in the political process (Astin, 1973b, 1977a; Astin & Kent, 1983; Bachman, 1972; Bachman, O'Malley, & Johnston, 1978; Bayer, Royer, & Webb, 1973; Beaton, 1975; Chickering, 1974a; Dey, 1989; Erikson, Luttbeg, & Tedin, 1973; Gallup, 1975a, 1975b; Hall, Rodeghier, & Useem, 1986; Hyman, Wright, & Reed, 1975; Knox, Lindsay, & Kolb, 1988; Lindsay, 1984; Molm & Astin, 1973; Phelan & Phelan, 1983; Spaeth & Greeley, 1970; Taylor & Wolfe, 1971). With a few exceptions (Braungart & Braungart, 1972; Green, Bush, & Hahn, 1980), smaller-scale studies reveal substantially the same sorts of change (Abravanel & Busch, 1975; Aldous & Tallman, 1972; Christenson & Capretta, 1968; Costantini & King, 1985; Finnie, 1970; Fotion, Bolden, & Fotion, 1978; Gaff, 1973; Harrison, Scriven, & Westerman, 1974; Jones, Rambo, & Russell, 1978; Kalish & Johnson, 1972; Little, 1970 [among Australian students]; McLeish, 1970; Rich, 1976; Riffer, 1972; Wilder, Hoyt, Doren, Hauck, & Zettle, 1978; Wilder, Hoyt, Surbeck, Wilder, & Carney, 1986; Wilson, Gaff, Dienst, Wood, & Bavry, 1975). It should be understood that in all these studies a shift toward a more liberal political orientation is not synonymous with a move toward political radicalism.

Information on the magnitudes of the changes in political attitudes and values is given or can be estimated from data in several studies. Perhaps the most persuasive evidence comes from studies by Hyman, Wright, and Reed (1975) and Erikson, Luttbeg, and Tedin (1973), both of which drew on national probability sample surveys. Both studies report percentage shifts toward the political left between high school and college graduation. These shifts ranged from 12 to 30 percentage points, although the estimate was even higher in some surveys—for example, Wilder, Hoyt, Doren, Hauck, and Zettle, 1978, report increases of .84 of a standard deviation, or 30 percentile points on the CSQ's liberalism scale (see note 7). In a more recent study based on CIRP data from over 3,200 students, however, Dey (1989) found that freshman-senior gains were substantially lower: .20 of a standard deviation (8 percentile points). Using data reported by Feldman and Newcomb (1969, vol. 2, table 2D) for studies done before 1968, Dey estimates that the average college effect size on student sociopolitical liberalism was .49, more than twice what he found in his study. These results suggest the possibility that the potential for college impact on students' sociopolitical attitudes and values may be somewhat less now than they were in the past. "Middle of the roaders" appear to be supplying the students who were changing (Astin, Green, & Korn, 1987). The percentage of seniors occupying the "far right" appears to remain relatively constant and in the minority: 9 to 25 percent over the college years (Erikson, Luttbeg, & Tedin, 1973). Thistlethwaite (1974) reports similar evidence from a study of twenty-five institutions that indicates relative stability in sociopolitical values over a one-year period. That period included the shootings at Kent State University and Jackson State College (now a university), the liberalizing effects of which on students' political attitudes appeared to be pervasive but temporary.

Civil Rights and Liberties. National studies dealing with changes during the college years in attitudes and values related to civil rights, civil liberties, racism, anti-Semitism, or general tolerance for nonconformity uniformly report shifts toward social, racial, ethnic, and political tolerance and greater support for the rights of individuals in a wide variety of areas (Bachman, 1972; Bachman, O'Malley, & Johnston, 1978; Beaton, 1975; Clark, Heist, McConnell, Trow, & Yonge, 1972; Hyman & Wright, 1979; Chickering, 1970, 1974a; Jackman, 1978; Jackman & Muha, 1984; Molm & Astin, 1973; Nunn, 1973; Nunn, Crockett, & Williams, 1978; Pace, 1972, 1974; Selznick & Steinberg, 1969; Smith, 1990; Williams, Nunn, & St. Peter, 1976). Studies based on one or a small number of institutions lead to the same conclusions (Crotty, 1967; Finney, 1967, 1971, 1974; Holt & Tygart, 1969; McMillan, 1989; Montero, 1975; Nosow & Robertson, 1973; Regan, 1969; Rich, 1977, 1980; Rich & Jolicoeur, 1978; Schein, 1969; Schonberg, 1974; Vaughan, 1972; Winter, McClelland, & Stewart, 1981).

Three national studies (Clark, Heist, McConnell, Trow, & Yonge, 1972; Hyman & Wright, 1979; Nunn, Crockett, & Williams, 1978) permit estimation of the magnitudes of the changes that appear to occur during the college years. In a study of eight quite varied institutions, Clark and his colleagues found freshman-to-senior increases that ranged from 2 to 27 percentage points among students initially high on a "civil libertarian" scale, with decreases of 5 to 26 percentage points among students initially low on the scale. Nunn and his colleagues found a difference of 26 percentage points between the proportion of college graduates classifiable as "more tolerant" of nonconformity when compared with a sample of high school graduates (84 percent versus 58 percent).

Hyman and Wright (1979) undertook a massive secondary analysis of thirty-eight national sample surveys (conducted from 1949 to 1975) of approximately 44,000 adults (ages twenty-five to seventy-two). They found educational level consistently and positively related to greater support for the civil liberties of nonconformists, as well as of more conventional individuals; for due process of law; for freedom from arbitrary legal constraints in personal and social relations; for the free flow of information, whether controversial or not; for social, political, and economic equality; and for humanitarian social programs and laws. Hyman and Wright also found education to be positively related to the importance attached to morals and good behavior as opposed to manners (see also our Chapter Eight on moral development). Overall, they found that the positive dimensions of the values in these several areas were 40 to 50 percent more prevalent among college graduates than among elementary school graduates. Moreover, the relations were generally monotonic and not limited to those who completed a full course of study at any given level of schooling: "Small increments of education anywhere along the way . . . were shown by several modes of analysis to have positive effects on values" (Hyman & Wright, 1979, p. 60), a finding consistent with Nunn, Crockett, and Williams (1978). In a single-institution study, Finney (1971, 1974) found that 38 percent of his respondents became more libertarian over a two-year period, while 26 percent became more conservative. The changes toward greater libertarianism remained into the senior year, while early shifts toward conservatism were often accompanied in the later college years by a reversal to the original, more liberal attitudes.

Religious Attitudes and Values

Feldman and Newcomb (1969, p. 23) found consistent evidence that seniors, as compared with freshmen, were "somewhat less orthodox or fundamentalist in religious orientations, somewhat more skeptical about the existence and influence of a Supreme Being, somewhat more likely to conceive of God in impersonal terms, and somewhat less favorable toward the church as an institution." The key word here is *somewhat*: While trends were clearly discernible, the magnitudes of the changes were generally small. Feldman and Newcomb also found that religious values, relative to other values, consistently declined in importance, as measured by Allport, Vernon, and Lindzey's Study of Values (1960).

One possible explanation for the modest changes observed in religiosity and religious practices is that the complexity of the phenomenon under study is not adequately reflected—and therefore measured—in terms of the rather global measures typically used. Glock (1962) and Glock and Stark (1965, chap. 2), for example, have suggested at least five dimensions (and several more subdimensions) underlying religious commitment: (1) ideological (internalized beliefs), (2) intellectual (knowledge of the basic tenets of one's religion), (3) ritualistic (the practices performed), (4) experiential (emotions related to a divinity), and (5) consequential or practical (the secular effects of beliefs, knowledge, and activities). Virtually all of the studies we identified (Campbell & Magill, 1968, is an exception) examined change in religious values or attitudes along one or both of two dimensions: (1) a generalized "religiosity" and (2) religious activities (for example, church attendance, prayer, Sunday school attendance). Because of this strong tendency in the literature, our review is similarly structured.

With some exceptions (for example, Hasting & Hoge, 1981; Kirchner & Hogan, 1972; McAllister, 1985; Rich & Jolicoeur, 1978; Smith, 1990), the literature published since 1967 fairly consistently reports statistically significant declines in religious attitudes, values, and behaviors during the college years (Arsenian, 1970; Astin, 1972b, 1973b, 1977a; Berry, Appel, & Hoffman, 1971; Chickering, 1974b; Clark, Heist, McConnell, Trow, & Yonge, 1972; Cox, 1988; Feather, 1973, 1975; Feldman & Weiler, 1976; Fengler & Wood, 1972; Finnie, 1970; Frantz, 1971; Funk & Willits, 1987; Huntley, 1967; Jones, 1970; Kalish & Johnson, 1972; Kuh, 1976; Little, 1970; May & Ilardi, 1970, 1973; McLeish, 1970; Solmon & Ochsner, 1978a, 1978b; Trent & Golds, 1967; Trent & Medsker, 1968). The shifts include changing (usually dropping) affiliation with a traditional church, a reduction in church going or prayer, alterations in beliefs about a supreme being, or a decline in general religiosity. Hoge (1974), however, while reporting an overall liberalization of religious attitudes and a reduction of traditional religious behavior over five decades since the 1920s, found no major shifts in freshman-to-senior values or attitudes.

Drops in the proportion of students with conventional religious preferences over the four-year period of college attendance appear to be moderate: -11 percent among Protestants, -6 percent among Catholics, and -1 percent among Jews (Astin, 1972b, 1977a; Solmon and Ochsner, 1978a, 1978b). Jones (1970) found declines in favorable attitudes toward "the church" of $-.27$ of a standard deviation (-11 percentile points) among both men and women, with a similar drop in favorable attitudes toward religion among men and even greater ones among women ($-.34$ of a standard deviation; -13 percentile points). Berry, Appel, and Hoffman (1971) found drops in self-reported religious activity among 831 University of Texas, Austin, seniors of $-.74$ of a standard deviation (-27 percentile points). We are reluctant to generalize too far from the particular students and institutions involved, however, for both studies were conducted at single institutions and during a particularly volatile period for students seeking to clarify personal values and attitudes, whether religious or otherwise.

Astin (1977a) also found declines of 31 to 35 percent in church and Sunday school attendance over the four years of college and 14 to 16 percent drops in reports of prayer and saying grace before meals. Clark and his colleagues (Clark, Heist, McConnell, Trow, & Yonge, 1972) and McAllister (1985), who reported no statistically significant freshman-senior declines in students' reported "need" for religion, found declines in attendance at religious observances.

While one single-institution study (May & Ilardi, 1973) suggests that these shifts may have been greater among juniors and seniors than among freshmen and sophomores, Astin's evidence indicates that the changes were reasonably steady and progressive from freshman year to senior year.

The evidence relating to changes in students' religiosity mirrors that relating to religious affiliation and behavior. Evidence from four independent samples of students who completed Allport, Vernon, and Lindzey's Study of Values' religious scale indicated freshman-to-junior or freshman-to-senior declines ranging from .38 to .86 of a standard deviation, or 15 to 30 percentile points (Arsenian, 1970; May and Ilardi, 1973). Shifts on the Omnibus Personality Inventory's religious orientation scale are consistent with those on the Study of Values. Estimated effect sizes, averaged across eight samples in fifteen schools (and reported in five studies), indicated freshman-to-senior increases of .49 of a standard deviation (19 percentile points). High scorers on this scale "are skeptical of conventional religious beliefs and practices and tend to reject most of them, especially those that are orthodox or fundamentalistic in nature" (Heist & Yonge, 1968, p. 4). These estimates of the magnitude of declines in traditional religious values are generally consistent with those reported by Bowen (1977, p. 134), who estimated drops in religious interest averaging $-.50$ of a standard deviation (-19 percentile points).

Sex or Gender Role Attitudes and Values

Major shifts have also been under way over the last twenty years in people's values and attitudes toward the marital and occupational roles of men and women. American college students are by no means immune from these extra-institutional influences, of course, and some observers might even assert that college students are in the vanguard of these forces for change.[8]

The topic has attracted substantial research attention. Etaugh (1986) identified more than 150 studies conducted between 1970 and 1985 on the biographical and personality correlates of attitudes toward women. Another substantial body of research involves time-series studies of shifting trends in group attitudes and values of college students. A review of the studies of personality and biographical correlates (except education) with sex role attitudes or of trends in those attitudes is beyond the purpose and scope of this review, however. Our primary concern is not with value or attitudinal trends among cohorts of college students, but rather with intra-individual changes that occur during, and potentially as a consequence of, college attendance.

With some exceptions (for example, Corbett, Frankland, & Rudoni, 1977; Corbett, Rudoni, & Frankland, 1981; DeFleur, Gillman, & Marshak, 1978; King & King, 1985; Martin, Osmond, & Hesselbart, 1980; Spitze, 1978; Weeks & Gage, 1984; Zuckerman, 1979), some of which might be questioned on methodological grounds, most studies indicate that during the college years students become increasingly more egalitarian, or "modern," in their views on the equality of the sexes with respect to educational and occupational opportunities and roles, as well as to the distribution of responsibilities in marriage and family relations. These conclusions are found in studies based on several national samples (Cross, 1968; Ferree, 1974; Jacobs, 1986; Mason & Bumpass, 1975; Mason, Czajka, & Arber, 1976; Orcutt & Bayer, 1978; Strumpel, 1971) but predominantly in smaller-scale or single-institution studies (Angrist, 1970; Benson & Vincent, 1980; Dambrot, Papp, & Whitmore, 1984; Dreyer, Woods, & James, 1981; Etaugh, 1975a, 1975b [based on our reanalysis of this study's data]; Etaugh & Bowen, 1976; Etaugh & Gerson, 1974; Etaugh & Spandikow, 1981; Freedman, 1967; Funk & Willits, 1987; Houser & Beckman, 1980; Hutt, 1983; Komarovsky, 1985; Leibowitz, 1975; Lloyd, 1967; McKinney, 1987; Orcutt, 1975; Parelius, 1975a, 1975b; Roper & LaBeff, 1977; Singer, 1974; Schreiber, 1978; Stein & Weston, 1976; Thornton, Alwin, & Camburn, 1983; Thornton & Freedman, 1979).

Parelius (1975a) reports cross-sectional findings based on some 350 Douglass College women that showed statistically significant freshman-to-senior increases ranging from 13 to 38 percent in women's "modern" orientations toward their roles, as well as in their work and career goals and expectations. The shifts were particularly large in women's views of their economic roles in the family relative to their husbands'. In a three-year longitudinal study, Lloyd (1967) found that 58 percent of the juniors in a women's college had changed their freshman-year choice of roles for themselves as adult women, generally toward acceptance of a dual role (inside and outside the home). Twice as many juniors as freshmen opposed confining a woman's role to the home or family. Orcutt (1975), also indexing the magnitude of change in percentage terms in a cross-sectional design, found a statistically significant shift among Florida State University women from the 74 percent "modern" women among the freshmen to the 88 percent "modern" senior women, a shift of 14 percentage points. A gain of 11 percentage points across the years (from 49 to 60 percentile points) was found when "modern" was defined differently. Etaugh (1975b) found somewhat larger freshman-to-senior differences (about .60 of a standard deviation, or 24 percentile points), with seniors having the more egalitarian attitudes toward women.

The clear weight of evidence suggests change during the college years toward more liberal and egalitarian conceptions of the equality of the sexes with respect to occupational and educational roles and opportunities, the distribution of responsibilities in marriage and child rearing, and social and political activities. One study (Corbett, Rudoni, & Frankland, 1981) suggests that the changes may be greatest among students who are initially the most conventional in their sex role views. This finding may reflect some regression to the mean between pre- and posttesting.

Net Effects of College

Cultural, Aesthetic, and Intellectual Attitudes and Values

The most convincing evidence of the net effects of college on student change in these areas above and beyond maturation and other background and personal characteristics comes from Hyman, Wright, and Reed (1975) and from Trent and Medsker (1968). Hyman, Wright, and Reed drew on fifty-four large, nationally representative surveys that were conducted between 1949 and 1971 and included some 80,000 individuals. After taking into account respondents' race (only whites were used), sex, age, religion, socioeconomic status, and rural origin, these investigators found educational level to be strongly and positively related to knowledge level, intellectual outlook, and receptivity to knowledge in such areas as current affairs, domestic and foreign policy, health, and popular culture. Similar results were reported for respondents' reading habits and continuing education interests and activities. Trent and Medsker (1968) undertook a five-year follow-up study of some 10,000 1959 high school graduates from sixteen communities throughout the United States. After controlling for ability and socioeconomic background, they found evidence consistent with that of Hyman, Wright, and Reed (1975). Trent and Medsker found aesthetic interests and attitudes among college men and women higher than among a group of their noncollege peers. The largest decrease in scores over the four-year period occurred among women who went directly from high school into homemaking, where one might expect the least exposure to and opportunity for cultural and aesthetic stimulation, as well as social, intellectual, and occupational involvement. Cobern, Salem, and Mushkin (1973) and Rich and Jolicoeur (1978), who controlled for gender, socioeconomic status, age, hometown size, religion, and political ideology, report on multi-institutional or national studies that produced findings consistent with those of Hyman, Wright, and Reed and Trent and Medsker. (Also, see Feather, 1975, who found similar evidence in a study of Australian students.)

Although the evidence of net college effects is quite limited in this area, it is consistent in indicating that college attendance has a unique impact on students' aesthetic, cultural, and intellectual attitudes, values, and interests. While we found no study to refute this conclusion, not even Hyman, Wright, and Reed (1975) controlled for initial level of cultural sophistication. The findings of their study are further constrained by reliance on a small number of single items (rather than more reliable scales) and by the use of evidence not derived from the same individuals over time. Virtually all other studies of change in this area fail to include educational attainment as a predictor variable or to control for such variables as socioeconomic status, academic aptitude and achievement, race or ethnic origin, and other individual differences that might be expected to influence both initial and subsequent levels of aesthetic, cultural, and intellectual attitudes and values.

Educational and Occupational Values

Educational Values. Research dealing with the unique contributions of college to educational value change above and beyond those of precollege values, maturation, and other potentially confounding influences is scarce. Knox, Lindsay, and Kolb (1988)[9] completed a particularly well-done study based on the NLS-72 data. After controlling race, gender, parental socioeconomic status, academic abilities, and precollege value level, as well as other previous activities, values, and personality characteristics, these researchers found that holders of a bachelor's degree were nearly three times as likely as individuals with less than two years of college to value having a good education. In addition, the former were more than twice as likely to value a good education as people with more than two years of college but less than the baccalaureate degree. Moreover, those with an advanced degree were more than twice as likely as those with a bachelor's degree to value a good education. Beaton (1975) used a sample of mature males (forty to fifty years old), all of whom had been U.S. Army Air Force aviation cadet training applicants in 1943. He found level of education in this sample to be significantly and positively, if modestly, related to the importance attached to general knowledge and negatively related to the value attached to education as career preparation. These effects held above and beyond the effects of aptitude, employment situation, and the interaction of education and aptitude. Cobern, Salem, and Mushkin (1973), who drew on various national data bases, found expenditures for education positively related to educational attainment, with the largest jumps occurring above the twelfth grade level even after controlling for income.

Occupational Values. Somewhat more information is available on the net effects of college on occupational values. In the main, the effects of educational attainment are discernible in several national, large data-based studies with moderate consistency after controlling for a variety of relevant personal and family background characteristics. Nevertheless, it appears that the educational contributions are quite small in both a relative and an absolute sense (Bachman, O'Malley, & Johnston, 1978; Kohn & Schooler, 1969; Lindsay & Knox, 1984; Smart, Ethington, & McLaughlin, undated; Strumpel, 1971; Trent & Medsker, 1968). In a smaller-scale study, Fields and Shallenberger (1987) found education, net of age, related to various dimensions of occupational attractiveness.

Lindsay and Knox (1984) have shed considerable light on the role educational attainment plays in changes in occupational values. Using data from more than 9,000 participants in the NLS-72 sample who were followed up in 1979 and controlling for sex, race, socioeconomic status, and 1979 job characteristics, Lindsay and Knox found that educational attainment had a small but statistically significant and positive effect on intrinsic occupational values in 1979 (path coefficient of .10) and a similar-sized but also significant negative direct effect on extrinsic work values (−.10). The more education people had, the more likely they were to value intrinsic occupational rewards and the less likely they were to value extrinsic rewards. On the other hand, Kanouse et al. (1980), using NLS-72 follow-up data for 1973, 1974, and 1976, found that pursuit of higher education was positively related to increases in extrinsic work values among women (especially during the first year after high school) but not among men.

More revealingly, Lindsay and Knox's (1984) analyses indicate that educational attainment plays an important reinforcing and allocational role. Respondents with higher initial intrinsic work values and lower initial extrinsic work values are more likely to attain higher levels of formal education. Moreover, while those initial values have a strong influence on work values seven years later, they are reinforced by educational attainment both directly (as noted above) and indirectly through educational attainment's effects on the kinds of jobs subsequently selected. The characteristics of these jobs, in turn, influence 1979 work values, reinforcing or accentuating values held at the time of graduation from high school.

Thus, limited but consistent evidence from generally strong studies suggests that the college experience has some influence on how students' educational and occupational values change over time. Institutional contributions above and beyond the characteristics students bring with them to college, however, appear to be rather modest, although college attendance seems to have an important indirect effect on change and stability in occupational values.

Social and Political Attitudes and Values

Altruism, Humanitarianism, and Civic Values. The evidence of the effects of college attendance on social conscience, humanitarianism, and civic values above and beyond students' precollege characteristics is generally but not entirely consistent. Hyman and Wright (1979), after controlling such factors as sex, race, age, religion, socioeconomic status, and residential origin, still found educational attainment positively related to valuing the reduction of pain and suffering, as well as to humanitarian conduct toward others. Evidence of positive college effects on social conscience and humanitarian values above and beyond a variety of background characteristics is provided in several other national studies (Curtin & Cowan, 1975; Lindsay, 1984; Marks, 1990; Thistlethwaite, 1973).

Studies by Pascarella, Smart, and Braxton (1986) and Pascarella, Ethington, and Smart (1988), both based on nationally representative samples of students who were freshmen in 1971 and were followed up nine years later, produced somewhat different results. In the earlier study, Pascarella and his colleagues found that differences in 1980 values apparently due to educational attainment level disappeared when controls for a variety of background, institutional, and occupational characteristics (including 1971 value status) were added. In the later study, Pascarella and his associates found that the highest academic degree attained had no significant *direct* effect on humanitarian and civic values for any of four groups (formed on the basis of sex and race). It did, however, have a positive but indirect effect (through occupation) for both white men and women but not for black men and women.

Although the findings are somewhat mixed, we believe the general weight of evidence supports a tentative conclusion that college attendance does have a modest net effect on social conscience and humanitararian values above and beyond the characteristics and values students bring with them to college. The evidence in these areas, however, is clearly less compelling than that in other attitude and value areas.

Political Attitudes and Values. The evidence with respect to the net effect of college on students' political attitudes and values is relatively clear and indicates that the collegiate experience has an influence above and beyond background characteristics and initial political orientations. Hyman, Wright, and Reed (1975), in their secondary analyses of national survey data gathered over a two-decade period, found level of education consistently and substantially related to being informed about public affairs and presidential elections and also to a general interest in politics. These findings held even when age, race, religion, socioeconomic status, and rural origins were controlled. Similarly, Knox, Lindsay, and Kolb (1988), using NLS-72 data and controlling race, gender, parents' socioeconomic status, academic ability, personality traits, and prior activities and values, found statistically significant (if small) associations with political activism and holding public office but not with voting or engaging in political discussions. Although there are some exceptions (Bachman, O'Malley, & Johnston, 1978; Rich, 1976, 1977; Vedlitz, 1983), substantially the same findings (or evidence consistent with them) are reported in other studies with varying degrees of control for precollege background and personal characteristics (Abravanel & Busch, 1975; Aldous & Tallman, 1972; Beaton, 1975; Christenson & Capretta, 1968; Costantini & King, 1985; Erikson, Luttbeg, & Tedin, 1973; Fotion, Bolden, & Fotion, 1978; Inglehart, 1977; Kalish & Johnson, 1972; Lindsay, 1984). On balance, then, the weight of evidence indicates the presence of reliable, if modest, college effects on increases in students' political orientations and activities above and beyond background characteristics and precollege political values and attitudes.

Civil Rights and Liberties. While Rich (1980) and Rich and Jolicoeur (1978) found little or no relation between college attendance and support for civil liberties, their findings are clearly the exception rather than the rule. Evidence of the positive effects of college on students' attitudes and opinions on civil rights and civil liberties above and beyond a variety of background characteristics, age, and occupation comes from a considerable variety of sources, both national in scope (Hyman & Wright, 1979; Inglehart, 1977; McClosky & Brill, 1983; Nunn, 1973; Nunn, Crockett, & Williams, 1978; Schreiber, 1978; Selznick & Steinberg, 1969; Smith, 1990; Weil, 1985; Williams, Nunn, & St. Peter, 1976) and smaller in scale (Crotty, 1967; Holt & Tygart, 1969; Montero, 1975). Hyman and Wright (1979), for example, after controlling a variety of relevant variables, found years of education positively and strongly related to support for civil liberties for socialists, atheists, and communists; for freedom of information; for due process of law for extremists and dissidents; for public expression; for freedom from legal constraints on intermarriage; for the value of privacy; for human values relating to abortion; and for equality of opportunity for minority groups (blacks, Jews, and Catholics). Support for these values increased consistently and dramatically with educational level. Similar findings are reported by Nunn, Crockett, and Williams (1978) and by Hall, Rodeghier, and Useem (1986). Moreover, the pattern identified by Hyman and Wright was not substantially different even during periods when public opinion was not conducive to changes toward increased libertarianism (for instance, the McCarthy era). Surprisingly, perhaps, number of years of education was unrelated to opposition to capital punishment or support for gun control laws, a finding to which we will return momentarily.

While there would appear to be consistent evidence of college effects on students' levels of support for civil rights and civil liberties and general sociopolitical tolerance—effects that have been apparent in the research literature since the 1950s (for example, Stouffer, 1955)—the issue is not as clear-cut as it might seem. This is primarily because educational level is often highly correlated with other variables that also influence tolerance. There are, for example, at least three schools of thought about why education has the apparent effects that it does (Weil, 1985). First, there is a "psychodynamic" view, which asserts that education is positively related to personal security and therefore to greater tolerance for divergent opinions and nonconformist groups. A second view, the "social class or status" view, essentially sees education as a proxy for social class, the correlation between education and tolerance being primarily an expression of class interests. Finally, the "socialization-cognitive" view attributes education's influence to the fact that the better educated, because of their easier access to an "enlightened" and presumably less prejudiced culture (through books, newspapers, and other attitude- and opinion-shaping sources), can more easily escape attitudinal narrowness and provincialism. The class or status view has not found much support in the empirical literature (Selznick & Steinberg, 1969; Weil, 1985). The psychodynamic model has not received widespread attention, but there is evidence (for example, Weil, 1985) that the liberalizing effects of education vary across national cultures, raising questions about the validity of this explanation of education's effects. The socialization-cognitive view receives the most support, as indicated by a majority of the studies of net college effects listed above, many of which support Stouffer's (1955) claim for the importance of exposure to social and cultural diversity in fostering tolerance and respect for civil liberties.

Another important issue in interpreting the evidence of education's effects on tolerance, as noted at the outset of this chapter, is the link (or lack thereof) between attitudes and values on the one hand and behavior on the other. In a well-designed study based on U.S. population samples in 1964, 1968, and 1972, Jackman (1978), after controlling for southern upbringing and rural residence, found that well-educated respondents were somewhat more likely than poorly educated individuals to support the relatively abstract principle of racial integration. The differences were negligible, however, between the well and poorly educated in support of government action to enforce legislation guaranteeing equal educational opportunity. Jackman also found that increasing years of education revealed no clear tendency toward more generalized support for governmental action in other areas.

The proposition that education may be related to support for the general principle of greater tolerance and equal rights but at the same time be less closely linked to support for action programs in these areas is consistent with one of the few anomalies in Hyman and Wright's (1979) otherwise remarkably consistent evidence linking education with increased liberalism. They found that education was *un*related to support for gun control or opposition to capital punishment. Similarly, Astin (1977a) found that the percentage of students who valued "helping others" increased over a four-year period in two national samples but that the more concrete, action-required value of Peace Corps or VISTA participation declined markedly. Taylor and Wolfe (1971), who also used national population data bases from 1948 through 1968, found that higher educational attainment levels were positively related to support for racial desegregation. There was no consistent pattern by educational level in attitudes toward government responsibility for desegregating the schools, however, or on whether "civil rights leaders were pushing too fast." Other studies (Catlin, 1978; Condran, 1979; Greeley & Sheatsley, 1974; Schreiber, 1978) also indicate differences between attitudes and action among the better educated. Greeley and Sheatsley interpret their findings to be consistent with the view that education is positively related to racial tolerance rather than as suggesting any differences between principles and action. Catlin reports inconsistencies between University of Michigan students' professed racial attitudes and receptivity to interracial contact, on the one hand, and both their actual interaction patterns and their support for affirmative action types of intervention, on the other. Schreiber found education among whites positively related to willingness to vote for a woman for president but inversely related to willingness to vote for a black for president. His evidence also indicated that education may be more salient in the early stages of an issue's life cycle, with its influence diminishing over time as awareness of norms legitimized by court decisions and laws "trickles down" to people with less education.

In a later study (also based on a national probability sample), Jackman and Muha (1984) found that on only three of forty-three attitude items dealing with intergroup attitudes (men toward women, whites toward blacks, and nonpoor toward poor) did educational attainment account for nontrivial amounts (7 to 9 percent) of the variation in attitudes. After holding constant region, age, socioeconomic status, class identification, income, and size of geographical residence, the effect size of education was reduced, although it remained positive and significant. The coefficients for educational attainment on the remaining forty items were all positive and monotonic, but none showed the same degree of dependence on education. These results indicate that liberated thinking is not a distinguishing characteristic of better-educated individuals. At the same time, however, Jackman and Muha's results do not support the view that education produces a superficial commitment to democratic principles. The content of the items on which the significant differences were identified all dealt with general policy issues (racial integration, blacks' residential rights, and women's job rights). The three items also dealt with the principle of individual rights. These results thus suggest that education may be related to support not so much for equal rights as for individual rights.

We conclude, as Jackman and Muha (1984) did, that the evidence is mixed. The general weight of the evidence continues to support the belief in a net positive college effect on support for civil rights and liberties, but recent compelling evidence to the contrary awaits replication and extension. Moreover, as Jackman and her associates' work has suggested, there may be important distinctions to be made between the espousal of socially acceptable general principles and support for individual or state action to enforce them. This constitutes an important but as yet not widely studied area of inquiry.

College Effects Versus Aging, Generation, and Period Effects. There can be little doubt that the past twenty years have witnessed substantial and significant shifts in the social, racial, political, sexual, and religious attitudes and values among students entering colleges and universities (see Astin, 1977b; Astin, Green, & Korn, 1987; Bayer & Dutton, 1975; Braungart, 1975; Hoge, Luna, & Miller, 1981; Levine, 1980; Williams, 1979) and among youth in general (for example, Yankelovich, 1972, 1974b; Yankelovich & Clark, 1974). Discussion of those trends is beyond the scope and purpose of this volume, but their very presence, as previously noted, poses a significant problem for interpreting the body of research being reviewed here and later in this chapter. Jacob (1957) had earlier suggested that college does not change student social and political values so much as it socializes students to a prevailing national social and political climate. The issue is still with us.

As noted earlier, a major methodological problem in the study of collegiate effects on students is controlling for noncollege sources of influence. These sources include (but are not limited to) normal maturation, generational effects, and period effects. Maturational (or age) effects come from simply growing older and have biological, social, and psychological dimensions (Glenn, 1980). Generational (or cohort) effects follow from the particular formative experiences of a group of individuals who have shared "the same significant life event within a given period of time" (Glenn, 1980, p. 598). Typically, that event is most commonly birth, and most "cohort analyses" form their groups according to date of birth, usually according to ten-year periods. The assumption is that one cohort may have grown up and been socialized under a different set of economic, social, and political conditions than another birth cohort. Period (or history) effects, more difficult to identify, refer to those influences that originate in the overall society and affect individuals approximately equally without regard to age. Historical effects, for example, might arise from wars or major economic or social changes.

The crux of the methodological and interpretational problem is one of "identification": "Since age is a perfect function of cohort and period, since cohort is a perfect function of age and period, and since period is a perfect function of cohort and age, it is impossible to hold two of these variables constant and vary the third" (Glenn, 1980, p. 601). Thus, when one uses cross-sectional data, aging effects are confounded with cohort effects, and when one analyzes longitudinal data, aging effects are confounded with period effects. Such confounding presents obvious problems in trying to identify net educational effects.

Studies that address the issue of education versus aging, cohort, or period effects constitute a relatively consistent body of research indicating that educational effects on social and political values are identifiable within cohorts over time. In a 1973 replication of Stouffer's (1955) classic study of national tolerance for political and ideological nonconformists, Nunn, Crockett, and Williams (1978) found that education was the single most powerful predictor of tolerance (as Stouffer had found), that tolerance increased at each successive educational level (except one) across cohorts, that younger people were more tolerant than older ones at each level of education, and that the relation between education and tolerance held even when occupational status was controlled. Davis (1975) also replicated portions of Stouffer's study with data from the 1972–1973 National Opinion Research Center's General Social Survey and found that increases in tolerance for the civil liberties of others increased 23 percent. Over half of these increases were attributable to a combination of cohort and educational effects, although the cohort influences were stronger than the educational ones. Hyman and Wright (1979) also found a consistent positive relation between education and tolerance across age cohorts. Moreover, evidence generally consistent with these findings is reported in other studies (Cutler & Bengston, 1974; Glenn, 1966, 1980; Inglehart, 1977; McClosky & Brill, 1983; Taylor, Sheatsley, & Greeley, 1978; Williams, Nunn, & St. Peter, 1976).

These findings, based on a number of independent national population samples, provide one form of evidence of the presence of educational effects on sociopolitical attitudes independent of social or cultural trends over time, but they were based (unavoidably) on cross-sectional designs and did not follow the same individuals over time. They are, however, quite consistent with the longitudinal panel studies reviewed earlier in this section that were undertaken over a two-decade period. Freshman-to-senior gains are reported in attitudes and values relating to humanitarian and civic responsibilities, general social attitudes, political attitudes and activities, and civil rights and liberties. These gains occurred consistently within cohorts of students over a twenty-year period. Indeed, Feldman and Newcomb's (1969) findings indicate that this consistency has been apparent in the literature for a substantially longer period. While faculty, students, and campus climate are not immune to changes in societal values and while campuses may mediate these changes (either intensifying or suppressing their effects) and while their starting and stopping points may have changed, the freshman-to-senior gains are consistently identifiable in different cohorts of students. The weight of these two bodies of evidence clearly suggests the presence of educational effects on students' social and political attitudes and values net of what they bring with them to college and above and beyond social and political value changes occurring in the larger society about them.

Religious Attitudes and Values

We identified only a handful of studies that examined in any rigorous fashion the net effects of college on changes in students' religious attitudes and beliefs. One of the strongest of these (Funk & Willits, 1987) used data from 549 individuals who were first tested in 1970 as high school sophomores in seventy-four school districts that lay outside the central cities of metropolitan areas in Pennsylvania (thus at least partially controlling age, race, and high school residence). These 549 people were retested in a 1981 follow-up. Controlling sex, moving out of county, and initial religious attitude, Funk and Willits found level of educational attainment (no college, some college, college degree) to be positively and significantly related to religious attitude change toward the secular. College graduates (in 1981) had the most secular scores, followed by those with some exposure to college, with people who had no college experience recording the most traditional ("sacred") attitudes toward God and religion. It is worth noting, however, that Funk and Willits did not control for occupational influences or other possibly confounding influences arising in the period of up to five years following college graduation that preceded the 1981 data collection. Thus, some of the changes they attribute to educational attainment may be at least partially accounted for by occupational and other noncollege influences. In a cross-sectional study of some 1,800 students in twelve California colleges and universities, however, and after controlling for gender, family income and education, religion, hometown size, age, and political ideology, Rich and Jolicoeur (1978) found no statistically significant relation between class year and scores on measures of religious values and religious orthodoxy.

Astin (1977a), using somewhat more indirect evidence (he had no noncollege respondents), concluded that shifts toward greater secularization are probably a function of both normal maturation and college influence. In his data, maturational effects were reflected in older students' showing less change than younger students, even after he controlled other personal and institutional characteristics. At the same time, students who lived at home reported smaller declines in religious orientation (independent of age) than those who lived in private quarters or in on-campus housing. Moreover, the changes toward secularism Astin observed were progressive and positively correlated with time enrolled (Astin, 1977a). These later findings point to college effects. Several smaller-scale, cross-sectional, and less well controlled studies report evidence consistent with a conclusion of college effects (Fengler & Wood, 1972; Frantz, 1971; Kalish & Johnson, 1972). Hoge (1970, 1974, 1976) reports somewhat different findings. Using a series of cross-sectional studies over several decades at Dartmouth College and the University of Michigan, Hoge found consistent trends toward greater secularism among cohorts of students, but changes appeared greater between cohorts than within them. This evidence suggests, at least tentatively, that some of the observed changes in religious attitudes may be more a function of changing societal values than college effects.

While the controls in all these studies were often limited, the weight of evidence generally suggests that colleges probably do have some influence on the changes in religious orientation students experience during the college years. We conclude that maturation alone cannot explain all the declines observed to occur in students' conventional religious preferences, religiosity, and religious behaviors. It is not yet possible, however, to partition with confidence the total amount of variation in religious values and attitudes into their maturational and collegiate components.

Sex or Gender Role Attitudes and Values

Several national and smaller-scale studies indicate that changes occurring during the college years might, in fact, be due to college and not simply to other influences. Mason and Bumpass (1975), for example, using a national probability sample of women under the age of forty-five in 1970, found education positively related to egalitarian views on the roles of women and men above and beyond the effects of age, race, husband's income, religion, religiosity, marital status, work history, age at marriage, and number of children. Indeed, education had the most pronounced net effect of all the variables considered. Other large-sample studies have yielded essentially the same results after controlling a selection of other, relevant variables (Houser & Beckman, 1980; Jacobs, 1986; Mason, Czajka, & Arber, 1976; Thornton & Freedman, 1979), although Jacobs found some evidence that the liberalization of attitudes may reflect external trends rather than college effects. All of these studies, save Jacobs's, were based on women only.

Funk and Willits (1987) followed 500 high school students of both sexes over a ten-year period and found college attendance to be positively related to increases in egalitarian views of gender roles above and beyond the effects of gender, migrant status (living in the same county during the study), and initial views on gender roles. The trend, consistent with other studies, was monotonic: Those with no college experience had the most "traditional" scores, followed by those with some college, with college graduates having the least traditional scores. With some exceptions (for example, Etaugh & Bowen, 1976; Martin, Osmond, & Hesselbart, 1980; Steiger, 1981), and with various sets of control variables, substantially the same results are reported in a number of single-institution studies (Dambrot, Papp, & Whitmore, 1984; Dreyer, Woods, & James, 1981; Etaugh, 1975a; Etaugh & Gerson, 1974; Lyons & Green, 1988; Orcutt, 1975; Parelius, 1975b).

On balance, the weight of evidence consistently indicates education-related changes toward more liberal views of the roles of women above and beyond those attributable to personal and background characteristics. Caution is nonetheless in order: Several of the studies that report changes in attitudes toward gender roles were based on cross-sectional designs that make it more difficult to attribute net change in student attitudes to the college experience. Moreover, even among those studies that followed the same group of students over time, in only one (Funk & Willits, 1987) were prematriculation attitudes or values themselves controlled.

Several studies point to indirect effects of education, although none test this role in any formal way (for example, with path analysis). The generational legacy of parental educational attainment is discussed elsewhere in this volume as it relates to the occupational advantages and benefits enjoyed by the children of college-educated parents (see Chapter Ten). College-educated parents may pass on a similar inheritance with respect to changes in the sex role attitudes of their children (especially daughters). Mother's education and sex role attitudes have been positively associated with the attitudes of sons and daughters (Thornton, Alwin, & Camburn, 1983); mother's education and employment status or experience have quite consistently and positively been linked to more egalitarian attitudes among sons and/or daughters (Etaugh & Gerson, 1974; Etaugh & Spiller, 1989; King & King, 1985). Related evidence consistent with these findings and reflecting the importance of a mother's educational level is reported by Troll, Neugarten, and Kraines (1969) and by Glenn and Weaver (1981).

College Effects Versus Aging, Generation, and Period Effects. The significant transformations that have occurred in this country over the past twenty years in attitudes toward the rights of men and women to equal educational and occupational opportunities and the roles of each partner in marriage and the family parallel those relating to social, political, civil rights, and civil libertarian issues. To what extent do the measured changes in sex role attitudes validly indicate attitudinal shifts attributable to the college experience rather than merely reflecting changes occurring in the society at large? Several studies shed some light on the issue.

Changes in sex role attitudes over time in the national population (Ferree, 1974; Mason, Czajka, & Arber, 1976) and in major metropolitan areas (Thornton, Alwin, & Camburn, 1983; Thornton & Freedman, 1979) have also been documented among entering college students (Astin, Green, & Korn, 1987) and among young people in general (Yankelovich, 1972, 1974a, 1974b; Yankelovich & Clark, 1974). While the evidence is virtually unanimous in indicating that age is negatively related to sex role egalitarianism (Benson & Vincent, 1980; Dambrot, Papp, & Whitmore, 1984; Helmreich, Spence, & Gibson, 1982; McBroom, 1984; Roper & LaBeff, 1977; Slevin & Wingrove, 1983; Spence & Helmreich, 1979), the differences—as in the sociopolitical domain—appear to be more cohort or period effects than maturational ones. For example, in a study based on four national opinion surveys taken between 1964 and 1974 and controlling for a number of relevant variables, Mason, Czajka, and Arber (1976) found educational attainment positively related to egalitarian views on sex roles. Thornton, Alwin, and Camburn (1983), using a 1961 probability sample taken in the Detroit, Michigan, area and followed up in 1977 and again in 1980, found age negatively related to sex role attitudes net of education and other variables, but they also found educational effects net of age and those same other variables. Dambrot, Papp, and Whitmore (1984) found essentially the same relation in a smaller-scale study. Thornton and Freedman (1979), who also used a sample of Detroit area women, found a positive association between education and attitudes above and beyond 1962 sex role attitudes and various other background variables, including age. They concluded that "the aggregate changes associated with age were due to time changes rather than to maturational effects" (p. 838).

We identified only one study that specifically sought to estimate the extent to which sex role attitudinal change is attributable to college rather than to shifting values in society at large. The task is a complicated one, and Jacobs (1986) approached it indirectly. He used several national data bases to study whether educational effects might be apparent in shifts in the extent to which sex segregation was apparent in students' choices of majors. Jacobs compared the occupational preferences of men and women entering college in various years with the final major field choices of two series of groups: one comprising several longitudinal panel groups of the same students four or more years later, the other including all degree recipients in various years as reported in National Center for Education Statistics data. Jacobs found clear evidence of the liberalization of students' sex role attitudes during the college years, but the extent of the changes varied considerably across years and appeared to follow the pattern of changing sex role attitudes among successive entering cohorts. Jacobs concluded that his findings suggest that the attitudinal liberalization apparent during the college years may be due as much (if not more) to changing societal attitudes as to the college experience. This conclusion, however, rests primarily on the degree of variation in estimates of the college effect size across years and studies. Such variations might also be attributable, at least in part, to variations across studies (due to differences in their sampling designs), as well as to variations within samples (due to respondent withdrawal over the four-year period of these longitudinal panel studies). Thus, Jacobs's findings cannot be taken as conclusive.

The role of the women's movement in individual attitude change is also unclear. Orcutt and Bayer (1978), using national longitudinal data to examine whether 1967 protest demonstration participation was related to sex role modernization in 1971, concluded that such modernization is more likely a cause rather than an effect of protest participation: "The origin of sex-role change among *individual* college students does not follow a course which parallels the origins of feminism as a *social movement*" (p. 278). Steiger (1981) reached a similar conclusion on the basis of his analyses of data from an evaluation of a women's studies program.

The evidence is ambiguous on this point, however, for Orcutt (1975) found a strong relation between student protest participation and sex role modernization. Orcutt and Bayer (1978) attribute the conflict in these findings to the timing of the studies because in the two-year period between Orcutt's (1975) data collection in 1973 and that of Orcutt and Bayer, significant developments in the feminist movement occurred and may explain the discrepancies. There is some evidence to suggest, moreover, that feminism did not begin to have a major effect on college campuses until after 1970 (Hole and Levine, 1971).

Thus, while it is difficult to differentiate cohort from period effects, the evidence tends to indicate that higher levels of educational attainment do produce greater sex role egalitarianism. This relation holds both within and across age cohorts. The dynamics of how these changes occur, however, are but poorly understood.

Between-College Effects

Cultural, Aesthetic, and Intellectual Attitudes and Values

Astin's (1977a) evidence indicates that private college students (given their personal characteristics and backgrounds) experience somewhat greater than expected increases in their artistic interests than do students at other kinds of institutions. Rich and Jolicoeur (1978) and Clark, Heist, McConnell, Trow, and Yonge (1972) found similar results. The latter researchers, in an eight-institution study, also report that although students in both selective and less selective institutions gained in cultural sophistication over the college years, the rates of gain appear not to be the same for all kinds of institutions. Not only do the selective institutions attract more culturally sophisticated students than less selective colleges and universities; the *rate* of increase is greater for their students than for students at less selective institutions. The magnitudes of the initial and subsequent differences across institutions were such that after four years of college, the seniors at less selective institutions resembled the elite institutions' freshmen. Pace (1974, 1984) also found consistent differences across institutional types, the more selective liberal arts colleges apparently producing greater gains in aesthetic activities than other types of institutions. Rich and Jolicoeur (1978), in a study of a dozen California colleges and universities, found neither size nor selectivity to be related to changes in students' cultural interests after controlling gender, socioeconomic status, religion, age, hometown size, and political ideology.

One study examined the differential effects of attending a coeducational versus a single-sex college. Smith (1990) studied 705 women entering coed institutions and 175 students entering all-women's colleges. These women participated in the 1982 CIRP survey of entering freshmen and were followed up four years later. After controlling for students' high school grade point average, academic aptitude (SAT scores), race/ethnicity, educational aspirations, and parental education and income, Smith found that women who were attending all-women's colleges enjoyed small (but statistically significant) advantages over their sisters who were attending coed institutions.

With respect to the religious affiliation of an institution, Trent and Golds (1967) found that Catholics who were attending a Catholic college or university were less likely to show gains in aesthetic values than Catholics or non-Catholics at sectarian institutions. Pace (1972) found both alumni and current students at Protestant-independent institutions more likely to report gains in their cultural and artistic interests than their counterparts at "mainline denominational" or evangelical-fundamentalist institutions.

Notwithstanding these findings, student self-selection and within-institution peer influences remain plausible alternative explanations. Bradshaw (1975), in a study based on students at 189 institutions, found general stability over time in across-institution differences in values and interests and greater differences within than between institutions. Chickering, McDowell, and Campagna (1969) report similar findings and concluded that highly similar changes in this area occur among highly different students at highly different institutions and independently of proclaimed institutional objectives and selectivity. These studies, however, relied on data for a rather narrow range of interests and activities and left a number of important variables uncontrolled. The introduction of controls for students' background characteristics tends to reduce (if not eliminate) apparent interinstitutional differences. Spaeth and Greeley (1970), for example, in a study of nearly 5,000 alumni of 135 colleges and universities seven years after graduation, found that with sex, parental socioeconomic status, and religion held constant, measures of institutional quality explained less than 1 percent of the total variance in respondents' interest in the arts or in an index of their serious reading habits. Institutional size and type of control were even less predictive.

It is entirely possible, of course, as suggested in this volume and elsewhere (for example, Astin, 1968b; Astin & Lee, 1972; Baird, Hartnett, & Associates, 1980), that the variability in students, their experiences, programs, and academic conditions *within* institutions may be relatively so much greater than that *between* schools that traditional categories (such as type of control, size, and curriculum) are too general as descriptors to be useful in predicting educational outcomes. Evidence for this position is reported by Chickering (1971a), who found changes in cultural sophistication related to general institutional environment, if not to institutional type or quality. Statistically significant increases were positively associated with institutional settings that were high on the College and University Environment Scales' (CUES) awareness scale (emphasis on an awareness of self, society, and aesthetic stimuli) or scholarship scale (emphasis on an interest in ideas, knowledge for its own sake, and intellectual discipline). Changes were negatively related to environments that were high on the CUES scales (propriety and practicality), reflecting an emphasis on conventional standards of decorum and the importance of knowing the right people, being in the right groups, or doing what is expected. Clark, Heist, McConnell, Trow, and Yonge (1972, p. 308) also suggest the potentially greater influence of campuses with relatively homogeneous student bodies: "The initial *concentration* of students with certain characteristics plays a telling part in the story of influence and effect. The larger and more similar the concentration, the greater the likelihood of a strong effect."[10]

Because of the consistent evidence that different kinds of institutions attract students with varying levels of initial cultural and intellectual sophistication, however, and (with the exception of Astin, 1977a) because of the absence of any serious controls for initial attitude or value levels and other individual differences, one cannot conclude that institutional characteristics have a differential effect on students'cultural, aesthetic, and intellectual attitudes and values. Indeed, the evidence that observed gains across institutions in this area are small suggests that institutional characteristics (with the possible exception of selectivity) are probably at best minor determinants of cultural, aesthetic, and intellectual value or attitude change. Even the effects of selectivity are small and not entirely consistent across studies.

Educational and Occupational Values

Educational Values. The evidence that focuses on differential effects across various kinds of institutions on educational and occupational values is more abundant. Insofar as educational values are concerned, Knox, Lindsay, and Kolb (1988), using NLS-72 data and net of race, sex, socioeconomic status, ability, and initial values, found no relation between the value attached to a good education and such institutional characteristics as cohesion, vocational emphasis, type of control, proportion of freshmen working, size, or selectivity. On the other hand, they found that institutional type (Carnegie classification) exerted a sometimes substantial influence on the value attached to a good education. For example, whereas attending a two-year college gives a student little advantage over a high school graduate in coming to value a good education, attending a Liberal Arts I (Carnegie type) institution increases that advantage by a factor of nearly 3. The advantages (over having only a high school diploma) of attending various other Carnegie types of institutions are: research universities, 2.5; doctorate-granting universities, about 2.2; and comprehensive universities, about 1.8.

Clark, Heist, McConnell, Trow, and Yonge (1972), however, found that the largest shifts away from extrinsic values and toward intrinsic values in education occurred at the less selective schools in their study. Indeed, the changes in these schools were such that by the senior year a majority of seniors held views similar to those of their peers in the elite institutions. Clark and his colleagues discount ceiling and differential attrition effects to explain these findings and instead conclude that a socialization process is at work, one in which students are taking on the values of students in the elite liberal arts colleges.

Spaeth and Greeley (1970) also found that general education goals were most likely to be endorsed by the graduates of selective institutions. Personal development was more likely to be favored by the alumni of lower-quality, larger schools, a finding consistent with that of Clark and his colleagues.

Occupational Values. With respect to between-college effects on occupational value change, Knox, Lindsay, and Kolb (1988) report findings similar to those relating to educational goals: Net of various relevant precollege variables, including initial values, no relationship was found for various institutional characteristics (size, type of control, or selectivity), and there was no significant relation between Carnegie type of institution and extrinsic work values. However, Carnegie type was related to intrinsic work values at statistically significant levels for all Carnegie types of institutions. The magnitudes of the effects varied considerably, however, from a low of about 1.18 times the advantage (over a high school diploma) of earning a degree from a Two-Year or Liberal Arts II college to a substantial 3.76 advantage enjoyed by Liberal Arts I college graduates.

Anderson (1985b) found that attendance at a religious institution tended to decrease extrinsic occupational values among men, but the direct effects of other college characteristics (including selectivity, type of control, and other Carnegie classifications) were unrelated to men's intrinsic values. None of the institutional characteristics tested were associated with either intrinsic or extrinsic occupational values among women. Her evidence did suggest, however, that *combinations* of institutional variables, specifically combinations of private control and a liberal arts curriculum and of private control and high selectivity, were more effective in changing values and attitudes. Yet even Anderson (p. 321) found the results "far from impressive." Weidman (1979) also failed to find any relation between institutional quality and the several aspects of occupational value change he investigated. Bradshaw (1975) found peer group influence a much more powerful predictor of occupational value change than the quality of the institution attended. His results held even when family social status and father's education were controlled.

Social and Political Attitudes and Values

Altruism, Humanitarianism, and Civic Values. With respect to social conscience, humanitarianism, and civic attitudes and values, the evidence of differential institutional effects is mixed and on balance inconclusive. Net of a wide variety of individual precollege traits and initial value status, attending a university (instead of a college) appears to have a negative effect on altruism or general civic orientation (Astin, 1977a; McLaughlin & Smart, 1987), and two-year college attendance is negatively related to changes in social responsibility (Marks, 1990). Catholic or Protestant college attendance, on the other hand, produces a large positive effect (Astin, 1977a).

Pascarella, Ethington, and Smart (1988), however, studied four groups of students (categorized according to their sex and race) using national data on nearly 4,600 students who entered college in 1971 and were followed up nine years later. After controlling a wide variety of precollege characteristics, they found no direct effects on humanitarian and civic values attributable to institutional selectivity or size or the predominant race of the student body. However, institutional size did have a negative indirect effect for all groups except black women. Findings consistent with these emerged in an earlier study (Pascarella, Smart, & Braxton, 1986) that used the same general design and national data base: changes in humanitarian and civic values were unrelated to the type (two-year or four-year), control (public or private), or selectivity of the institution attended. Nelsen and Johnson (1971), Nelsen and Uhl (1977), and Marks (1990) report findings generally consistent with those of Pascarella and his colleagues. After controlling students' background characteristics and levels of academic and social involvement, Deppe (1989, 1990) also found no statistically significant between-college effects on change in students' social concern values based on institutional size, type, control, selectivity, or predominant race or degree of racial diversity in the student body. Consistent with the evidence of Pascarella and his colleagues, Deppe's evidence indicates that the structural and organizational characteristics of institutions appear to be indirect, mediating the effects of students' level of engagement with the institution and their interpersonal interactions with peers and faculty members. Deppe's analyses suggest that these mediating effects may be somewhat stronger at private institutions than at other types.

Political Attitudes and Values. In the political arena, the research is virtually invariant in indicating that changes in students' political attitudes and values are influenced by the type of institution they attend, above and beyond the effects of precollege values and a variety of personal and background characteristics. Increases in political liberalism appear to be greatest in prestigious and highly selective institutions (Astin, 1977a; Clark, Heist, McConnell, Trow, and Yonge, 1972; Greeley & Spaeth, 1970; Knox, Lindsay, & Kolb, 1988; Spaeth & Greeley, 1970; Taylor & Wolfe, 1971). Highly selective private four-year colleges and women's colleges seem to have a particularly strong influence (Astin, 1977a). Similar results (under varying degrees of control) have been obtained in predominantly black colleges of differing selectivity (Fotion, Bolden, and Fotion, 1978; Nelsen & Johnson, 1971; Nelsen & Uhl,. 1977). Astin reports changes toward less political liberalism among students at two-year colleges, but this effect disappeared when residence (on campus versus at home) was controlled. All of these studies are somewhat dated, however, and more recent research raises a question about whether such between-college effects continue to operate today. Dey (1989), using data from some 3,200 participants in a 1983–1987 CIRP-based panel study, found that net of a variety of student background characteristics, shifts in student liberalism were unrelated to type of college, geographical location, or selectivity. Only at institutions whose entering freshmen were in the lowest quintile on liberalism was the kind of institution related (negatively) to liberalism scores in the senior year.

Relatively less is known about the causal agents or mechanisms that explain why some institutions have a different effect from others. The evidence is clear, however, that institutions differentially recruit students, and students differentially choose institutions according to their political orientations: Upon entry, students at private, prestigious, selective colleges are higher in political liberalism than their peers at other kinds of institutions (for example, Suczek, 1972; Clark, Heist, McConnell, Trow, & Yonge, 1972; Chickering, 1970; Pace, 1974; Astin, 1977a). Moreover, prestigious institutions have been shown to have more liberal faculties than other kinds of institutions (Ladd & Lipset, 1975). Comparatively few studies, however, have controlled for the effects of such differential selection. These student recruitment and faculty patterns may well create an interpersonal context that accentuates the already liberal values and attitudes of entering students. Thus, structural characteristics, such as selectivity or private control, may be proxies for a contextual setting created by undergraduates and faculty members with similar liberal political values. It would appear to be this proximal interpersonal context rather than the more distal structural characteristics that enhances changes in political values and attitudes. The evidence supporting this conclusion will be examined shortly in the section of this chapter on within-institution effects.

Civil Rights and Liberties. In the area of civil rights and liberties, the evidence indicates differences across kinds of institutions, but support for the contextual-effect hypothesis rather than the structural-effect hypothesis is fairly clear. A study of 109 colleges found strong relations between the awareness scale of the College and University Environment Scales (CUES) and participation in protests supporting civil rights and against U.S. militarism (betas of .44 and .55), net of other CUES-measured environmental characteristics (Sasajima, Davis, & Peterson, 1968). Consistent with those results, Chickering (1970) found net change over a two-year period toward increased liberalism, but the magnitude of the change varied across institutions. The amount of change toward liberalism was positively correlated with the proportion of liberal students and negatively correlated with the proportion of conservatives on the campus. Moreover, while the magnitude of the changes was nonsignificant, increases in liberalism consistently appeared to occur on campuses with goals stressing constructive citizenship and an affirmative view of emotions and impulses and, to a lesser degree, at schools with a scholarly climate. Pace (1974) and Clark, Heist, McConnell, Trow, and Yonge (1972) report similar findings with respect to institutional selectivity. A campus with a climate that emphasizes practicality, abiding by procedures, knowing the right people, and doing the expected or a campus that emphasizes group standards of politeness, courtesy, and decorum also appeared to dampen change toward increased libertarianism (Chickering, 1970). Other studies report evidence essentially consistent with our conclusion that differences in between-college contexts probably exert more influence on tolerance than do the structural characteristics of institutions (Rich, 1980; Rich & Jolicoeur, 1978).

Religious Attitudes and Values. Few studies shed any light on the effects of various kinds of colleges on changes in students' religious attitudes and values. In probably the strongest studies on this point, Astin (1972b, 1977a) found (net of other personal and background factors) significantly greater than expected decreases in conventional religious affiliation and in religiousness (that is, praying and reading the Bible) among students attending selective or prestigious schools. These declines were most evident in prestigious, nonsectarian, four-year colleges (Astin & Lee, 1972). Declines also appeared to be greater than expected at large universities and public two-year colleges. The likelihood of changing toward no religious preference was also highest at so-called elite institutions. Astin (1977a) replicated these findings in two separate follow-ups. Attending a Protestant, Catholic, or all-men's college, however, tended to suppress changes in religious affiliation. In addition, while Catholic school attendance also tended to retard declines in religiousness, somewhat greater slippage was associated with Protestant college attendance (Astin, 1977a; Trent & Golds, 1967).

Other studies provide similar evidence (Clark, Heist, McConnell, Trow, & Yonge, 1972; Pace, 1974). Clark and his colleagues found that institutional differences on religious liberalism remained even when subgroups of students initially average on the religious liberalism scale were compared across institutions, thereby controlling at least somewhat for initial religious attitudes and values. Similar differences with respect to declines in religious observances also persisted. Rich and Jolicoeur (1978), on the other hand, after controlling for a variety of relevant student background characteristics, found no relationship between the rate of decline in religious values and such institutional characteristics as size, type, or selectivity. They did, however, find reason to believe that attendance at a secular institution produced greater declines, while enrollment at a church-related college tended to produce increases in religious orthodoxy.

Nonetheless, and although the evidentiary base is small, it seems reasonable to conclude that institutional characteristics probably do play a role in the degree to which religious preferences, attitudes, values, and behaviors change during college. It seems equally clear that the nature and extent of those differences vary substantially across kinds of institutions, with selective institutions apparently exerting the strongest and most consistent effects in the direction of reduced formal religious affiliations and religiousness.

Sex or Gender Role Attitudes and Values

We uncovered no studies in the area of sex or gender role attitudes and values that examined the differential effects of institutional characteristics, such as size, selectivity, or type of control.

Within-College Effects

Studies of within-college effects on students' attitudes and values fall into a variety of categories. Typically, these inquiries focus on one or more of the following: academic major field, other academic experiences (for example, course work, study abroad), place of residence while in college, fraternity or sorority membership and other nonacademic activities, and student-faculty and student-peer interactions. As will be seen below, however, some of these sources of influence receive more attention than others, and they vary across outcome categories.

Cultural, Aesthetic, and Intellectual Attitudes and Values

Academic Major Field. Feldman and Newcomb (1969) provide an extensive review of the pre-1970 literature dealing with academic major–related differences in student values and attitudes. While these authors pursued the question of whether such differences were attributable to initial self-selection or to major field effects, they found that the available research did not directly address the question (p. 175).

Since that time, Thistlethwaite (1972, 1973) studied the effects of academic major on the attitudes and values of 1,800 students at twenty-five nationally representative universities. Holding constant initial group differences on a variety of precollege traits (including scores on each dependent variable), Thistlethwaite found virtually no evidence that varying amounts of exposure to different major fields affected either students' science orientations or their aesthetic orientations. The expected accentuation of initial major-related differences never emerged. On the basis of this evidence, Thistlethwaite suggests that the influence typically attributed to faculty members in socializing students into the culture of their academic departments may be unwarranted and perhaps be due instead to secondary school teachers' influences or to design flaws in previously published research. Feldman and Weiler (1976), in a similar study, found evidence to support Thistlethwaite's speculation (see also Feather, 1975; Lewis, 1967). In addition to finding little evidence of accentuation effects due to major departments, what effects Feldman and Weiler did find evaporated when they controlled for students being recruited into or withdrawing from a major during the period of the study. They concluded that the mixing in earlier studies of students who had and had not changed majors may account for the reported accentuation effects of a major.

Several more recent studies, however, have produced results contrary to those of Thistlethwaite (1972, 1973) and Feldman and Weiler (1976). For example, increases in students' cultural or aesthetic values, net of other influences, have been positively associated with majoring in the social sciences (Astin, 1977a), in English (Weidman, 1979), or in the liberal arts in general (Endo & Harpel, 1980). Students majoring in business, engineering, or professional programs in general are less likely to show gains in cultural or aesthetic sophistication over the college years (Astin, 1977a; Endo & Harpel, 1980, 1982; Yonge & Regan, 1975). Other, less controlled studies provide substantially the same findings (Huntley, 1967; Spaeth & Greeley, 1970; Jones & Finnell, 1972; Pace, 1986).

Differences between these two sets of studies may be attributable to the fact that Thistlethwaite and also Feldman and Weiler were interested in a specific kind of major field effect. Both studies focused on the accentuation of initial group differences, that is, on whether the initial differences between group means actually increase over time. Insofar as cultural, aesthetic, and intellectual attitudes and values are concerned, such accentuation effects appear not to occur.

Other Academic Experiences. In addition to major field, other academic program experiences have also been associated with varying levels of aesthetic, cultural, and intellectual attitude and value change. Studies of the effects of living-learning centers in this area, in contrast to those of conventional residence halls, indicate an advantage for students in the academically focused residential units (Fisher & Andrews, 1976; Magnarella, 1975; Newcomb, Brown, Kulik, Reimer, & Revelle, 1970; Pemberton, in Williams & Reilly, 1972). Newcomb and his colleagues found higher initial cultural and aesthetic interests among the residential college students (compared with two control groups), as did Fisher and Andrews (1976), and greater gains (an accentuation effect) over time. Most of these gains were attributed to increased contact with faculty and like-minded peers. These differences disappeared, however, when precollege cultural sophistication and intellectualism were controlled (Newcomb, Brown, Kulik, Reimer, & Revelle, 1971).

In a more detailed analysis of Newcomb and his colleagues' (1971) data base and after taking initial value status into account, Lacy (1978) found no direct effect on increased cultural sophistication associated with living in an innovative living-learning environment as opposed to a traditional residential setting. Lacy did find a direct positive effect on cultural sophistication associated with both the cultural or intellectual content and the frequency of contact first-year students had with their peers and faculty members. These findings indicate that a living-learning center's effects may be indirect rather than direct, mediated by the nature and frequency of the interactions they promote with faculty and peers. Endo and Harpel (1982) also report a positive association between cultural participation and the frequency of informal student-faculty interaction, even after controlling a dozen background characteristics, expectations of college, and initial cultural activity level. Their study, however, did not focus on differential effects associated with place of residence.

Gains in cultural, aesthetic, and intellectual attitudes and values have also been associated with participation in a program involving an entirely flexible class meeting schedule—even after controlling initial level of cultural sophistication (Stakenas, 1972)—and with being in an honors program (in contrast to being in a developmental studies program, although initial differences were uncontrolled) (Ory & Braskamp, 1988). In both of these studies, however, the authors attributed program effects more to students' interactions with program faculty members than to the programs themselves.

A small body of research has investigated the effects of a period of study abroad on a variety of student interests and values (Barnhart & Groth, 1987; Billigmeier & Forman, 1975; Carsello & Creaser, 1976; Flack, 1976; Hensley & Sell, 1979; James, 1976; Kafka, 1968; Kuh & Kauffman, 1985; Marion, 1980; McEvoy, 1986; Morgan, 1972, 1975; Nash, 1976; Pfnister, 1972; Salter & Teger, 1975; Stauffer, 1973; see McHugo & Jernstedt, 1979, for a review of this literature). These studies are often inconsistent in their findings, although one reasonably consistent thread indicates that study abroad produces only limited gains in students' "worldmindedness" (Hensley & Sell, 1979; Kafka, 1968; Nash, 1976; Salter & Teger, 1975; Sharma & Jung, 1984). There is even some reason to believe that overseas study programs may have fewer positive effects on students' tolerance for others than domestic off-campus study programs (that is, studying temporarily on a U.S. campus other than the one at which the student is normally enrolled). One study (Hull, Lemke, & Houang, 1977) reports no clear or general superiority of overseas study programs over off-campus domestic programs in a variety of change areas. Indeed, more changes appeared to be associated with domestic rather than overseas program participation in areas long considered the major areas of international programs' influence on students. Other studies report evidence of slight increases in students' appreciation of other cultures' art, music, and architecture. Virtually without exception, however, these studies leave pre-study-abroad characteristics, attitudes, and values uncontrolled. The introduction of such controls might produce very different results. The literature in this area of study is not distinguished for the rigor of its research designs and methods (Hull & Lemke, 1975).

Residence. Where a student lives while in college appears to make a difference. Students living in residence halls experience somewhat larger increases than commuter students in their aesthetic, cultural, and intellectual attitudes and values (Astin, 1977a; Chickering, McDowell, & Campagna, 1969; Welty, 1976). After controls have been applied for sex and precollege status on each outcome measure, freshman students' cultural orientations (for example, attending a public lecture, attending a public concert or ballet, visiting a museum, attending an art exhibition) have also been shown to be positively related to residential environments that are oriented toward interpersonal relationships or intellectual matters and negatively related to environments that facilitate dating, have an academic emphasis, or stress academic achievement (Moos, DeYoung, & Van Dort, 1976; Moos, Van Dort, Smail, & DeYoung, 1975; Moos, 1979).

The evidence on residential effects is not entirely consistent, however. Chickering and Kuper (1971) found greater increases in measures of cultural and intellectual interests among commuting students than among resident students (although precollege interest levels were not controlled).

Fraternity or Sorority Membership and Other Nonacademic Experiences. Wilder, Hoyt, Doren, Hauck, and Zettle (1978) found significant freshman-senior increases in cultural sophistication among members of Greek-letter societies and "independents" alike. Fraternity and sorority members were significantly lower in cultural sophistication than independent students upon entry to college, and these initial differences persisted throughout the college years. There was no evidence that fraternity or sorority membership worked counter to the prevailing campus culture. Miller (1973) reports similar results. However, in a subsequent replication study (Wilder, Hoyt, Surbeck, Wilder, & Carney, 1986) and after controlling gender and year of entry to college, Wilder and his colleagues found a statistically significant difference between Greeks and independents. Greek society members showed smaller gains in cultural sophistication. Students who had joined a Greek society but then had either withdrawn or become inactive showed the greatest gains of all, suggesting that something in addition to Greek membership was probably involved. It is not clear in any of these studies whether fraternity and sorority members lived in Greek society houses or in traditional residence facilities. Thus, Greek society membership status and place of residence appear to have been confounded, making any definitive conclusion problematic. (See Leemon, 1972, for an anthropological description of the rites of passage involved in the induction of new members into a fraternity and the role those rites play in member socialization.)

Increased cultural sophistication appears *not* to be related to participation in such extracurricular activities as campus organizations, part-time work, or extracurricular art, drama, music, journalism, broadcasting, or literary groups (Chickering, 1971a; Jones & Finnell, 1972). Chickering did find, however, that college climates, educational practices, and informal rather than formal peer relations and student-faculty contact were associated with increased cultural sophistication. Controls for individual differences are absent in these studies, however.

Educational and Occupational Values

Studies of within-college effects in the area of educational and occupational values focus almost exclusively on student-faculty interactions. With few exceptions, the bulk of this literature examines within-college effects on occupational values. While it is possible conceptually to differentiate frequency of faculty contact from the quality of or reasons for that contact, the corpus of relevant research is so small that such a distinction is not possible in this review. Similarly, one can reasonably ask whether student-faculty contact is, in fact, a temporally prior influence on observed value change or simply a case of students with changing values seeking out contact with faculty members. Again, however, neither the number nor the methodological rigor of the available studies permits an answer to the question.

Interaction with Faculty and Peers. With few exceptions, the findings indicate significant relations between student-faculty contact and changes in students' occupational values (Clark, Heist, McConnell, Trow, & Yonge, 1972; Chickering, 1974b), even when background, initial values, and other influences are controlled (Weidman, 1979; Anderson, 1985b). As noted earlier, regardless of institutional type or size, most students tend to shift their occupational values away from the extrinsic rewards and (to a lesser degree) toward intrinsic rewards. At larger institutions, this appears more likely to occur if the student is friendly with a particular faculty member. Indeed, in one study 80 percent of the students who reported having a faculty friend changed their preferences, as compared with 68 percent of those who had no such friend. The effects were even greater at private colleges (72 versus 48 percentile points) (Clark, Heist, McConnell, Trow, & Yonge, 1972).

Other studies indicate modest but statistically significant effects of faculty contact even after controlling precollege background characteristics. Anderson (1985b), for example, using NLS-72 data and controlling for a variety of precollege student and institutional characteristics (including students' initial values and occupational goals), reports a positive and statistically significant relation between frequency of student-faculty contact and increases in intrinsic (but not extrinsic) occupational values among women. Among men, however, faculty contact was unrelated to intrinsic or extrinsic value change. Weidman's (1979) results are consistent with Anderson's.

Students' peers can also be influential. Bradshaw (1975) found substantial influence exerted by students' peers in their academic major field. The larger the percentage of peers holding an attitude at the time of college entry, the greater was the probability that students not holding that attitude would change and adopt it and the greater the probability that those who held it would persist in holding it. Thistlethwaite (1969) and Vreeland (1970) both provide evidence consistent with Bradshaw's, indicating the potency of peers and faculty, especially within academic departments, in shaping student educational and occupational values. Mortimer (1972) found large variations in occupational values among various (Clark-Trow model) subcultural groups, patterns that persisted after controlling for father's occupation, his education, and family income.

With one exception, however, these studies are silent on the role faculty contact plays in changing educational values. Theophilides, Terenzini, and Lorang (1984b) did find frequency of student-faculty contact during the freshman year, net of a variety of background characteristics, positively related to the value attached to a liberal education. One might speculate that college's effects on educational values are probably not much different from its influence on occupational values. But while a significant body of research indicates a relationship between student-faculty contact and both career choice and educational attainment (Pascarella, 1980), the empirical evidence linking student-faculty contact and change in educational values is scarce. We deal with college effects on educational and occupational aspirations in Chapters Nine and Ten.

Residence. Beyond the findings relating to the role of interpersonal contacts in occupational and educational value change, a few studies examined, with mixed results, relations between value shifts and other aspects of the collegiate experience. Chickering (1974a), using a nationally representative data base and controlling initial values and a variety of personal and background characteristics, found a greater tendency among commuting students (who live at home with a parent or relative, as opposed to those living on campus or in private off-campus quarters) to shift their long-term occupational aspirations toward financial well-being. Resident students showed a diminished concern for financial security, business success, and a sense of obligation to others. Morstain (1973) and Moos (1979) offer additional evidence that indicates the influence of residence environment on educational and occupational values, particularly as it is shaped by the residents themselves. Anderson (1985b), however, found no association between intrinsic or extrinsic occupational values and living on campus after taking into account socioeconomic status, race, ability, high school achievement, and precollege values and occupational goals.

Social and Political Attitudes and Values

Humanitarian Values and Civil Rights and Liberties. Because of a relatively limited number of studies, the research on within-college effects on social conscience and humanitarian and civic values and on attitudes toward civil rights and liberties will be integrated here. The effects of college experiences on political attitude and value change will be discussed later in this section. In all three value domains, although no single set of within-college experiences has received extensive attention, three general sources of influence have received somewhat more notice than others: residence arrangement, academic major and course work, and student interactions with faculty and peers.

Net of various precollege characteristics and precollege status on the values being studied, living in a residence hall is consistently and positively associated with increases in altruism and support for civil liberties and racial integration. Catlin (1978), however, found no changes in interracial attitudes associated with the racial concentration of the residence hall floor on which a student lives. Commuting students, on the other hand, show smaller increases in liberalism and tend to retain their initially more conservative orientations. Students living in private, off-campus quarters resemble residence students on some issues and commuters (who live at home with a parent or relative) on others (Chickering, 1974a; Astin, 1972b; Katz & Associates, 1968). Wilder and his colleagues (1978, 1986), using several independent samples, found no differences between fraternity or sorority members and nonmembers in the degree of freshman-senior gains on the social conscience scale of the CSQ, a finding consistent with Marks (1990). With some exceptions (for example, Stakenas, 1972), there is evidence that net of precollege level of liberalism, living in an experimental living-learning setting is also associated with increases in liberalism and, to a smaller degree, social conscience (Newcomb, Brown, Kulik, Reimer, & Revelle, 1970, 1971; Lacy, 1978).

A modest but reasonably consistent body of research indicates that an academic major in the social sciences is positively associated with increases in a sense of social responsibility and support for civil rights and liberties, while majors in business, education, and engineering generally tend to show the smallest gains (Bachman, 1972; Christenson & Capretta, 1968; Rich, 1977; Crotty, 1967). When a variety of student and institutional characteristics were controlled, however, Pascarella, Ethington, and Smart (1988) and Marks (1990) found only an indirect effect (or no effect) of major on humanitarian and civic values. It thus remains unclear whether these differences are causally linked to the major field or to the initial characteristics of the students who choose those majors. Pascarella and his colleagues' research suggests that selection may explain more of the outcome than major field itself. These findings also suggest, however, that major field of study may indirectly influence humanitarian and civic values through its impact on the type of job an individual holds.

Pascarella, Ethington, and Smart (1988) found that student-faculty interaction, above and beyond the effects of a variety of student and institutional characteristics, had a significant direct effect on changes in the humanitarian and civic attitudes and values of white women, an indirect effect on white men, but no effect of any kind on black students. "Social leadership" experiences (such as being president of a student organization, serving on committees, being involved in a play) had the only consistently positive and significant direct effect on students' humanitarian and civic values nine years after college, a finding consistent with that of Astin and Kent (1983).

Political Attitudes and Values. The results of the research on within-college effects on political attitudes and activities are similar to those relating to more generalized social and humanitarian attitudes. Net of other factors, living in a college residence hall appears to be positively related to increases in political liberalism and decreases in political conservatism. Living in off-campus, private quarters produced substantially the same effects, but living at home was likely to result in lower than expected increases in political liberalism (Astin, 1972b, 1973b, 1977a; Chickering, 1974a). Moreover, these positive effects appear to be general ones, applying approximately equally to men and women, blacks and whites, high- and low-socioeconomic-status students, and students of varying ability levels. Students participating in an experimental living cluster may experience even greater increases in liberalism than students in conventional residential arrangements (Stakenas, 1972; Lacy, 1978; Newcomb, Brown, Kulik, Reimer, & Revelle, 1970).

The evidence relating to the influence of membership in fraternities and sororities is inconsistent. Astin (1977a), after extensive controls, found smaller than expected increases in liberalism associated with fraternity and sorority membership when contrasted with independents, as did Longino and Kart (1973). Wilder, Hoyt, Doren, Hauck, and Zettle (1978) and Miller (1973), using data from the College Student Questionnaire's liberalism scale, found no differences in the magnitudes of freshman-senior increases between Greeks and independents. In a later replication of this study, however, Wilder, Hoyt, Surbeck, Wilder, and Carney (1986) found evidence consistent with Astin's: The general shift toward liberalism was smaller among Greeks than among independents. But it was the students who first joined a Greek society and then withdrew or became inactive who increased the most, suggesting that the influence of Greek society membership on sociopolitical attitudes and values may be considerably more complex than previously thought. Evidence from Krasnow and Longino (1973) is consistent with this conclusion. They found that the Greek influence was a moderating one: conservative for students initially more liberal than the fraternity norm and liberalizing for new members who were more conservative than the norm.

The effects of academic major field are less clear. Social science and humanities majors appear more often than not to experience greater gains in liberalism than majors in business, engineering, mathematics, and the physical sciences (Abravanel & Busch, 1975; Bachman, 1972; Bachman, O'Malley, & Johnston, 1978; Franks, Falk, & Hinton, 1973; Phelan & Phelan, 1983; Spaeth & Greeley, 1970; Solmon & Ochsner, 1978a, 1978b). These findings emerge whether various precollege characteristics, including initial social orientation (Astin, 1977a), are controlled or not.

Thistlethwaite (1973), however, after adjusting for initial value status, found that similar one-year effects disappeared when changes over a two-year period were examined. He found that changes in the percentage of variance in political participation and in liberalism associated with major fields ranged in absolute magnitude from zero to only 3.2 percent. Thistlethwaite suggests that the inconsistencies between his results and those of others may arise from the research designs, particularly the failure in many studies to follow students who start *and* stay in the same major field during the period of the study.

Course work and other academic program involvement also appear to exert an influence on political attitudes and values, although the evidence is ambiguous (Rich, 1976; Fotion, Bolden, & Fotion, 1978; Eitzen & Brouillette, 1979; Vaughan, 1972; Nash, 1976; Chickering, 1970). Several studies have suggested that taking courses in the social sciences appeared to be related to increases in political liberalism, as well as to changes in other social attitudes and values (Eitzen & Brouillette, 1979; Farley & Newkirk, 1977; Franks, Falk, & Hinton, 1973; Hoover & Schutz, 1968; Rich, 1976, 1977). Other studies, however, found few or no differences between students in political science courses or other formal programs and those in control groups (Somit, Tanenhaus, Wilke, & Cooley, 1970; Garrison, 1968; Vaughan, 1972). Lamare (1975, p. 428) concluded from his literature review that the evidence on the relation of formal political science course work and value change is best characterized as "a pattern of reinforcement and accentuation, but not radical alteration."

Some evidence suggests that the content of a class may be less important than the manner in which it is taught. Chickering (1970) reports strong inverse relationships between change toward civil libertarianism and teaching practices in which lectures dominated and where extrinsic rewards, such as grades, were important. In contrast, greater positive changes occurred in classes that encouraged discussion and open argument and whose students gave intrinsic reasons for being enrolled (for example, "I was interested in the subject"). Eitzen and Brouillette (1979) report similar findings.

Consistent evidence, both in this area of research and elsewhere (Pascarella, 1980), suggests a relationship between student-faculty contact and attitude and value change (Astin & Kent, 1983; Chickering, 1970; Fotion, Bolden, & Fotion, 1978; Gaff, 1973). In each instance, faculty contact is positively associated with positive changes in altruism, political liberalism, or civil libertarianism. The magnitude of faculty influence is less clear, however. Students come to college with moderately well-formed attitudes and values in this area (Spaeth & Greeley, 1970; Erikson, Luttbeg, & Tedin, 1973; Gaff, 1973; Riffer, 1972; Clark, Heist, McConnell, Trow, & Yonge, 1972; Gaff, 1973; Chickering, 1974a), and these initial attitudes and values appear to predispose students to participate in activities consistent with those values. Moreover, growth appears to be greatest in those areas where students concentrate their attention (Gaff, 1973). Chickering, however, found that the accentuation effect varied by college and in some instances appeared not to occur at all. He also found that it varied according to student subgroups and, one might speculate, to the kinds of faculty members with whom students chose to have contact.

These findings and others (Astin, 1977a; Dey, 1989; Komarovsky, 1985; Lane, 1968; Lacy, 1978; Pascarella, 1980) suggest that the influence of peers may be as great as or greater than that of faculty. Place of residence while in college, for example, may mediate the influence of other variables, as has been shown in other circumstances (for example, Vreeland & Bidwell, 1965; Pascarella & Terenzini, 1980b, 1981). Similarly, as noted previously, the proportion of peers who hold liberal (or conservative) attitudes has been shown to be a source of influence on shifts in political liberalism (Chickering, 1974a; Fotion, Bolden, & Fotion, 1978; Ogle & Dodder, 1978). The evidence reported earlier relating to Greek society membership is consistent with this view.

While all of these findings indicate that the level of students' involvement in the institutional environment is positively related to value change, it has also been shown that too much involvement may be counterproductive. Intensive involvement in one aspect of college life may insulate a student from the effects of other college experiences by limiting the time and attention available for those experiences (Astin, 1977a, 1985a; Heath, 1976c).

Religious Attitudes and Values

Unlike other areas of attitude and value change among college students, specific within-college sources of influence on religious values have received comparatively little attention.

Academic Major Field. A handful of studies have examined the relationship between major academic field and changes in religious affiliation or religiosity, but the findings are not entirely consistent. Solmon and Ochsner (1978a, 1978b) report social science (especially history) and hard science majors most likely to change their religious affiliation preferences to "none" and business and education majors least likely to do so. Feldman and Weiler (1976) also found academic major (net of entering religious values) to be differentially related to change in religious liberalism, but only among women. Huntley (1967) and Feather (1975) report finding no differences across majors in the rate of decline in religiousness. Feather concluded that students tend to choose departments that will match or reinforce what he calls their entering "cognitive ecology."

Residence. Some evidence suggests that where one lives and the general ambience of an institution are related to change in religious values. Although only a few researchers have examined the effects of students' living arrangement on shifts in religious values, their findings are consistent. With some exceptions (for example, Welty, 1976), living in a residence hall or private room appears to increase the likelihood that a student, by the senior year, will express no religious preference. Living at home decreases the likelihood of any shift toward no religious preference. These findings held even when a wide variety of students' precollege characteristics and initial religious preferences and practices were controlled (Astin, 1972b, 1973b, 1977a). Moreover, smaller than expected declines (given students' precollege characteristics and religiousness) were found among students living with parents. These findings are consistent with studies by Chickering (Chickering & Kuper, 1971; Chickering, McDowell, & Campagna, 1969). The most reasonable explanation for the findings is that in living at home the student is not only reinforced in the religious value system of parents and siblings but is also insulated from any of the potentially challenging effects of close and continuing associations with other students whose religious values may be quite different. Moreover, living away from home affords students many more opportunities to test old attitudes and values against those of others and to experiment with new ones.

Differences in the environmental press of students' on-campus residence also influence changes in religious values. Moos (1979) and Moos and Lee (1979) found that students' religious interests and values, net of their sex and precollege interests and values, were positively related to a residence hall environment that promoted personal relationships or was traditionally socially oriented. Religious values were negatively affected by living in residence halls characterized by personal and academic independence. Much of the variance was explained, however, by students' characteristics, although there also was clear evidence of joint background and residence effects. These findings are consistent with the evidence reported elsewhere in this chapter indicating the importance of the interpersonal context of students' experiences. Students not only occupy collegiate settings of various kinds, but by virtue of the personal characteristics they bring to those settings, they also *define* them. Students are not only influenced by their experiences and living conditions; they are themselves individual and collective determinants of those conditions.

Additional evidence (Clark, Heist, McConnell, Trow, & Yonge, 1972) about the importance of the nature of the college context suggests a link between the religious preferences of faculty members and other students and the tendency among students to change their religious commitments. In Clark and colleagues' study, where the faculty and student body constituted a mix of the nonreligious and mildly religious, individual students' religious commitments during the college years were seen to move considerably toward the secular. Similarly, where faculty and students espoused greater commitments to a religion, the institutional climate appeared to support the maintenance of students' initial religious commitments over the four years of college. This study, however, did not control for students' religious orientations upon entering college or other background traits, faculty members' background traits, or other institutional characteristics. Hoge (1974, p. 123) believes that "the differences among students as entering freshmen were at least as great as differences attributable to college experiences; in some cases they were much greater. Differential recruitment is a more important determinant than college experiences."

Sex or Gender Role Attitudes and Values

Academic Major Field. Etaugh's (1986) review of more than 150 studies of the biographical and personality correlates of students' attitudes toward women identified nineteen that examined the relation between attitudes or values and college major or occupation. These studies generally showed that students in the humanities, arts, and social sciences were more likely to be egalitarian than majors in business, engineering, and education. Few studies, however, dealt with differential change in attitudes toward women associated with academic major. Our reanalysis of data from one cross-sectional study (Stein & Weston, 1976) indicates that freshman-senior differences (implying gains) were greater for majors in business and education than for liberal arts students, but the means for business and education seniors were still below those of liberal arts juniors. Stein and Weston concluded that attitudes toward women became more liberal by the senior year in all schools but even earlier among arts and science majors. Since precollege sex role attitudes were uncontrolled in this study, however, these findings could be due as much to self-selection and the traits students brought with them to college as to any departmental effects. Information from a study by Etaugh and Spiller (1989) indicates that academic major failed to enter a stepwise regression of sex role attitudes on a variety of variables, suggesting that major was unrelated to attitudes. Given such limited evidence, little can be concluded about differential effects in sex role attitude change associated with academic major field.

Course Work and Gender Role Attitudes. A number of studies indicate movement toward more egalitarian orientations as a consequence of college course work related to women's roles in society and the modern family (Brush, Gold, & White, 1978; Dabrowski, 1985; Davis, Morgan, & Barker, 1981; Jones & Jacklin, 1988; Lenihan & Rawlins, 1987; Olson & Gravatt, 1968; Ruble, Croke, Frieze, & Parsons, 1975; Scott, Richards, & Wade, 1977; Speizer, 1975; Steiger, 1981; Stevens & Gardner, 1983; Vedovato & Vaughter, 1980). Consistent with the findings of Stein and Weston (1976) reported above, some of this evidence suggests that students who are initially the most traditional in their views of sex roles change more than their initially more "modern" peers. Most of these studies, however, were based on opportunistic (nonrandom) samples of students who chose to take certain courses dealing with gender role attitudes and failed to control for regression effects (for example, students in these courses typically score higher initially in sex role liberalism) and other observed differences between the course and control groups. Steiger (1981), on the other hand, did control for initial attitudes and values and found that course effects persisted net of initial attitudes and age. In the other studies, however, student self-selection remains as a plausible alternative to course effects in explaining the changes that are observed. It is possible (perhaps even probable) that students in women's issues courses change more because they are less traditional to begin with and may already be in the process of changing. Moreover, no light is shed on the permanency of any course-related attitudinal or value changes.

We conclude that virtually nothing is known about the effects of specific within-college experiences on changes in the attitudes of men and women students toward appropriate sex roles, opportunities, and rights in education, occupation, or other social matters. The absence of such information no doubt reflects the relative newness of this area as a field of study; in any case, our review clearly indicates that much work remains to be done.

Conditional Effects of College

Cultural, Aesthetic, and Intellectual Attitudes and Values

Without exception, the studies reviewed deal only with variations by sex. No other individual characteristic (such as race, socioeconomic status, academic aptitude) appears to have been examined for its potentially differential effect on students' cultural, esthetic, or intellectual values and attitudes.

Most studies found that women enter college with significantly higher levels of cultural and aesthetic sophistication than do men (Chickering, McDowell, & Campagna, 1969; Kuh, 1976; Wilder, Hoyt, Doren, Hauck, &

Zettle, 1978; Spaeth & Greeley, 1970; Nelsen & Uhl, 1977). Although the direction of the changes is positive for both men and women (Chickering, McDowell, and Campagna, 1969; Cox, 1988; Spaeth and Greeley, 1970), women appear to change somewhat more than men over a four-year period (Kuh, 1976; Cox, 1988). In all these studies, however, the contrasts were conducted independently of each other and were based on bivariate statistical procedures. These studies did not address the statistical significance of the difference in the *amount* of change over time between the sexes. Three studies that did test for sex × time interactions (Nelsen & Uhl, 1977; Wilder, Hoyt, Doren, Hauck, & Zettle, 1978; Wilder, Hoyt, Surbeck, Wilder, & Carney, 1986) produced inconsistent results. The 1986 study by Wilder and his colleagues indicated that women gained more than men in cultural sophistication. However, while a statistically significant sex × time interaction is reported in Wilder and his associates' 1978 study, the nature of the interaction (whether women again gained more than men) is not reported (although there is reason to believe that they did). Nelsen and Uhl, on the other hand, found no statistically significant sex × time interaction in cultural sophistication. Thus, the research literature is equivocal on the question of differential college effects on aesthetic and cultural values and attitudes that are conditional on student characteristics.

Educational and Occupational Values

The research related to conditional college effects on educational and vocational attitudes and values is sparse, indeed. While a number of studies suggest that women are more likely than men to endorse the goal of obtaining a liberal or general education and that men appear more inclined to subscribe to occupational and vocational preparation as their major educational goal (Trent & Medsker, 1968; Knox, Lindsay, & Kolb, 1988; Katchadourian & Boli, 1985; Spaeth & Greeley, 1970), none of these studies specifically tested for whether the *rate* of value change during college was significantly different for men and women. Moreover, only Knox, Lindsay, and Kolb controlled for initial value differences between the sexes. Other studies examined effects on educational values and attitudes of socioeconomic status and race, as well as sex, but they, too, failed to test for the interaction of variables and thereby provide only weak evidence of conditional effects of college on educational and occupational values.[11]

The evidence dealing with conditional college effects on occupational attitudes and values is similarly sparse. McLaughlin and Smart (1987) tested a sex × college interaction in a national study of changing values and found that women graduates of liberal arts colleges and comprehensive colleges and universities demonstrated less growth in "business orientation" (being successful in one's career and financially well-off) than did women who attended other types of colleges and universities. These interaction effects operated above and beyond family socioeconomic status and high school academic achievement. We identified only one study (Smart, Ethington, & McLaughlin, undated) that tested a sex × time interaction. Using NLS-72 data from 1972 to 1979, Smart and his colleagues found a strong positive relation between educational attainment and extrinsic occupational values among women but not among men.

Social and Political Attitudes and Values

As with the other categories of attitudes and values, most of the research dealing with conditional effects on general social values has focused on those associated with sex, and the evidence is generally inconclusive. Several studies suggest that women gain more during college than do men in general social liberalism and altruism (Rich, 1976; Chickering, 1970), while other studies indicate the reverse (Astin, 1977a; Knox, Lindsay, & Kolb, 1988; Fotion, Bolden, & Fotion, 1978). Most studies found little or no evidence that education has different effects on the sexes (Hyman & Wright, 1979; Braungart & Braungart, 1972; Eitzen and Brouillette, 1979; Pascarella, Smart, & Braxton, 1986; Wilder, Hoyt, Doren, Hauck, & Zettle, 1978; Wilder, Hoyt, Surbeck, Wilder, & Carney, 1986). These studies showed gains in political knowledge, libertarian orientation, and other related political and social value indicators to be consistently and positively related to educational level but of approximately the same magnitudes across genders.

We identified only two studies that tested for a sex × education interaction with a nationally representative sample of students. After controlling students' precollege traits, the characteristics of the institutions they attended, and the occupations they subsequently held, Pascarella, Smart, and Braxton (1986) found that the small influence of education on the development of humanitarian and civic values was general, applying equally regardless of sex, race, college type, college control, or college selectivity. On the other hand, Marks (1990), using nationally representative data from the High School and Beyond study, found that while women began their college careers with lower levels of social responsibility than men did, after two years women exhibited a sharp increase, reaching a level of commitment to social justice equal to that of men. In smaller-scale studies, Wilder and his colleagues (Wilder, Hoyt, Doren, Hauck, & Zettle, 1978; Wilder, Hoyt, Surbeck, Wilder, & Carney, 1986) and Nelsen and Uhl (1977) tested for a sex × time interaction on the liberalism and social conscience scales of the CSQ, but there was no consistency in their results. On the basis of such limited and inconsistent evidence, one cannot conclude with any confidence that differential, sex-related college effects on social or political values do or do not exist.

Religious Attitudes and Values

Several studies report differences in changes in religious attitudes and values, differences that depend upon selected individual characteristics, most commonly students' sex. Consistently, they report declines in religious behavior to be greater among men than among women (Astin, 1977a; Kuh, 1976; Trent & Medsker, 1968; Funk & Willits, 1987; Frantz, 1971). Jewish and high-ability students also appear more likely to experience larger than average declines in religiousness (Astin, 1977a).

Only two studies were identified, however, that specifically tested for statistical interactions between sex and education. Funk and Willits (1987) followed a sample of 500 high school sophomores from seventeen school districts outside the central cities of Pennsylvania through their college years in order to study the effects of college attendance on attitude change toward gender roles and religious beliefs. They found men, overall, to be more secular than women in their religious attitudes, but the interaction of sex and education was nonsignificant, indicating no differential, sex-based college effects. Frantz (1971), using a control group of college-age individuals who were not students, also failed to find a statistically significant interaction of sex and education on students' moralism. Thus, we found no compelling evidence to suggest that college has a differential effect on men's and women's religious attitudes and values.

Sex or Gender Role Attitudes and Values

Somewhat more research exists on the conditional effects of college on students' sex or gender role attitudes, although much of it is indirect. For example, with a few exceptions (Corbett, Frankland, & Rudoni, 1977; Corbett, Rudoni, & Frankland, 1981), the attitudes and values of women were consistently shown to be more liberal and less sexist than those of men (for example, Bayer, Royer, & Webb, 1973; Cross, 1968; Etaugh, 1975a, 1975b, 1986; Etaugh & Bowen, 1976; Etaugh & Spiller, 1989; Funk & Willits, 1987; Helmreich, Spence, & Gibson, 1982; Meier, 1972; Orcutt, 1975; Orcutt & Bayer, 1978; Osmond & Martin, 1975; Roper & LaBeff, 1977; Spence & Helmreich, 1979). These differences were present at the time of admission, during the college years, and upon graduation, even when various background characteristics were controlled (Orcutt, 1975). It is important to note, however, that while most studies indicated sex-based differences in this area, we found very few that tested whether there were statistically significant differences in the rates of change over time based on sex. Funk and Willits (1987) report that amount of time in college did not interact with sex, initial attitude status, or migrant status (living in the same county during the ten-year period of study), a finding supported by Singer (1974) and Steiger (1981). Thus, while women were initially more egalitarian than men in their sex-role attitudes and while both groups grew increasingly liberal, the differences (controlling for initial attitudes) remained relatively constant over time.

Long-Term Effects of College

Cultural, Aesthetic, and Intellectual Attitudes and Values

The most persuasive evidence of college's long-term effects in the area of cultural, aesthetic, and intellectual attitudes and values comes from the secondary analyses of national opinion poll data reported by Hyman, Wright, and Reed (1975). They found that respondents' knowledge and their receptivity to knowledge in a variety of areas neither grew nor waned with age. The areas in which educational effects persisted included current affairs, contemporary public figures, domestic and foreign politics, popular culture, current health news, and participation in adult education programs. In all instances, the level of familiarity with information and the respondents' activities were directly related to years of formal education. Completion of high school had its own contribution to make above and beyond completion of elementary school, but the increases between completion of high school and completion of college were themselves substantial. The findings held even after sex, race, religion, socioeconomic status, and rural origins were controlled. It should be noted, however, that inasmuch as Hyman and his colleagues were analyzing cross-sectional and not longitudinal data, changes during the college years were never actually tested.

Longitudinal findings from several single-institution studies are, nonetheless, generally consistent with those of Hyman, Wright, and Reed (1975). Kuh (1976, 1981) tracked more than 150 alumni of a small midwestern college five and ten years after graduation. Cox (1988) and Arsenian (1970) retested groups twenty and twenty-five years after graduation, respectively. Hoge and Bender (1974) studied two groups of alumni, one tested thirteen years later and the other tracked fifteen and twenty-nine years later. Arsenian, Cox, and Kuh all found that changes in aesthetic and cultural values that occurred during the college years persisted relatively unchanged into the alumni years. Cox, however, found evidence that the apparent stability of the group mean masked considerable individual change. Hoge and Bender found similar stability in the alumni years for one group (the thirteen-year follow-up group) but a pattern of decline and then recovery to a point slightly below the senior-year level in the other group. Regrettably, all of these studies left a number of individual characteristics uncontrolled.

While the available evidence is limited, it is at least consistent in suggesting that no recidivism appears to occur (at least not to any significant degree) in graduates' attitudes and values related to cultural and intellectual matters. Neither, however, is there any evidence to suggest that the changes that occur in college are merely the early stages of a lifelong trajectory toward greater and greater cultural and aesthetic appreciation. In considering postcollege change in cultural, aesthetic, and intellectual attitudes and values, then, it seems reasonable to hypothesize that much will depend upon individuals' postcollege experiences, their occupational and social circumstances, and the attitudes and values of the people with whom they live and work. As will be seen later in this chapter, empirical evidence supports such a hypothesis in other attitudinal and value areas.

Educational and Occupational Values

Few studies (Beaton, 1975; Spaeth & Greeley, 1970) address the long-term effects of college on students' educational values. Beaton, after controlling aptitude, employment situation, and the interaction of education and aptitude, found educational attainment among mature males (forty-five to fifty years old) significantly and positively related to the importance attached to general knowledge and negatively related to the value attached to education as career preparation. Spaeth and Greeley, in a seven-year follow-up of a national sample of the class of 1961, found that 80 percent of the alumni rated a liberal education as the most important purpose of education. Education as career preparation was rated most important by about two-thirds of the sample, while service to others, friendships, and preparation for marriage and family were rated most important by less than 60 percent of the respondents. According to Spaeth and Greeley, if respondents had been forced to choose between general and career education, the overwhelming majority (70 percentile points) would have endorsed general education. They hastened to add, however, that occupational goals had not been forgotten; alumni simply placed them in a subordinate role to general education values.

A small but consistent body of research indicates that education influences postcollege occupational values directly, indirectly (through the kinds of jobs students select), and by mediating previously held values (Lindsay & Knox, 1984; Mortimer & Lorence, 1979b). In 1979, Lindsay and Knox followed up more than 9,000 participants in the National Longitudinal Study of the High School Class of 1972. Educational attainment was positively related to higher intrinsic and lower extrinsic work values in 1979 net of sex, race, socioeconomic status, precollege value levels, and postcollege employment characteristics. For both kinds of values, the strongest predictors were the values held at the time of graduation from high school in 1972 (path coefficients of .27 for intrinsic values and .63 for extrinsic ones) and, for intrinsic values, the nature of postcollege employment (.33). While the direct effects of education on both kinds of values were modest (.10 and −.10 for intrinsic and extrinsic values, respectively), the total effect of education on 1979 intrinsic values was more than twice what it was on extrinsic values (.18 versus − .08). Moreover, education's direct effect on selecting employment with high intrinsic rewards was considerable (.24; education's direct effect on selecting a high-paying job was five times less). Mortimer and Lorence (1979b) also found occupational values to be independent functions of work socialization and occupational selection. Selection and socialization effects were approximately equivalent for both intrinsic and extrinsic values ten years after graduation. Senior-year values had significant direct and indirect effects on both kinds of values ten years later, but the effect of senior-year extrinsic values was somewhat greater than that of intrinsic values. These results held even after controls were added for father's work complexity, family income, mother's education, and the student's college GPA. Our analyses of Mortimer and Lorence's data indicate gains ten years after graduation of from .25 to .65 of a standard deviation (11 to 24 percentile points) for extrinsic values and from .14 to .79 of a standard deviation (6 to 28 percentile points) for intrinsic values (both range sets are for three items within each category). Thus, it would appear that the college years set in motion changes in occupational values that subsequently exert an influence on values that is both direct and indirect (through postcollege employment). This influence is apparent at least three to ten years later, although educational effects are smaller than those of precollege value levels and the reward characteristics of postcollege employment.

Social and Political Attitudes and Values

The durability of college effects on students' social and political attitudes and values has received substantial research attention, and the results are generally consistent. Newcomb, Koenig, Flacks, and Warwick (1967), in their classic study of the political orientations among Bennington College graduates over a twenty-five-year period, found that the widespread shifts toward political liberalism that had occurred during the college years had, indeed, withstood the test of time. Whatever part of the political spectrum a student occupied upon graduation was the best predictor of political orientation a quarter-century later.

Are the effects observed by Newcomb and his colleagues generalizable to other institutions? The results of several studies suggest that they are (Astin & Kent, 1983; Fendrich, 1974; Spaeth and Greeley, 1970; Hyman, Wright, & Reed, 1975; Hyman & Wright, 1979; Weiner & Eckland, 1979). Spaeth and Greeley's results indicated relative stability over a seven-year period, and Fendrich found that the orientation toward political activism among those who had been politically active while in college persisted ten years after college. Hyman and his colleagues found results consistent across surveys and historical contexts from the late 1940s to the early 1970s, indicating that the effects of college on social, racial, and political attitudes and values persisted into older age (net of age, sex, religion, ethnicity, socioeconomic status, size of community, and region of birth). While education's effects on some values appeared to diminish after age sixty, only rarely were they extinguished, and they persisted even during historical periods uncongenial for liberals and civil libertarians (for example, the McCarthy years). Support for the relative stability of social and political values over time despite turbulent social and political periods can be found in other studies (Spaeth & Greeley, 1970; Greeley & Spaeth, 1970).

Evidence based on cohort analyses such as these still does not provide as convincing evidence as do studies that tracked the same groups of individuals over time (as did Newcomb and his colleagues) and that involved other institutions.[12] In a 1969–1970 follow-up of some 4,400 white males originally studied in 1943 as part of their U.S. Army Air Force cadet training, Beaton (1975) found education, net of aptitude and employment situation and several other variables, still positively related to more liberal political views and attitudes toward racial integration. Similarly, Lorence and Mortimer (1979) conducted a ten-year follow-up of 1966 and 1967 male graduates of the University of Michigan in a study of the effects of adolescent and adult behaviors on political liberalism. They found that, on average, college graduates became somewhat more liberal over the ten-year period following graduation but that college political opinions had the dominant impact, both direct and indirect (through students' employment experiences), on subsequent political attitudes. Lorence and Mortimer concluded that political orientation was highly stable over time (see also Capel, 1967) and that the college socialization process in this area was substantially stronger than employment-related socialization. Evidence consistent with this finding is also reported by Weiner and Eckland (1979) in a small but nationally representative study of high school sophomores followed up at age thirty.[13]

In sum, the evidence is generally consistent across studies, samples, historical contexts, and analytical designs in indicating that changes in college students' social and political attitudes and values remain relatively stable over time, perhaps into the late adult years. College clearly initiates a series of changes, but those value and attitudinal shifts appear to stabilize after college and continue relatively unchanged into later life. With the exception of certain changes after age sixty, there is very little evidence that social and political values and attitudes held at the time of college graduation revert to what they were before college.

Religious Attitudes and Values

Only a handful of studies examine the long-term effects of college on religious attitudes and values, but with one exception, they indicate that changes in this area occur during but apparently not after the college years. Where there are postcollege changes, they are slight and generally away from traditional religious values. The findings are generally the same whether alumni were tested five years (Kuh, 1976), ten years (Kuh, 1981), twenty years (Cox, 1988; Shand, 1969), or twenty-five years (Arsenian, 1970) after graduation, although there is, to be sure, some variation with respect to changes in specific areas of belief. The exception (Hoge & Bender, 1974) found shifts in both directions among sixty Dartmouth College students: an increase in religious values of .92 of a standard deviation (32 percentile points) between graduation in 1940 and fifteen years later, followed by a decline (−.33 of a standard deviation, or 13 percentile points) between 1955 and 1969. Hoge and Bender also found a statistically significant decline (.52 of a standard deviation; 20 percentile points) in a second sample of juniors and seniors tested first in 1956 and again thirteen years later.

The data in the Arsenian (1970), Cox (1988), and Hoge and Bender (1974) studies were derived from the religious scale of Allport, Vernon, and Lindzey's Study of Values, however, and warrant some caution in terms of drawing conclusions (see note 2). Moreover, each of these studies relied on univariate statistical procedures, leaving uncontrolled any differences among students on their entering and senior-year scores in the comparison of senior and alumni measurements. In addition, each of these studies was based on a sample of students from a single graduating class from a single institution, all of which were small and private. Nonetheless, while one might be reluctant to generalize these findings to larger populations of graduates from more widely varying kinds of institutions, the general consistency of the findings across independent samples, using different measures, and over varying lengths of time since graduation is noteworthy.

Sex or Gender Role Attitudes and Values

No doubt because of the relative newness of sex or gender role attitudes and values as a field of study, only three studies were identified that dealt with the durability of college effects over time. Thornton and Freedman (1979) followed 1,161 Detroit women over a fifteen-year period. In a series of three multiple classification analyses, they found evidence of a monotonic and positive relation between educational attainment level and sex role attitudes a decade and a half later, even when initial attitudes, occupational experience, and other background characteristics were controlled. Thornton, Alwin, and Camburn (1983), in an extension of that study, found additional evidence consistent with the earlier findings.

In the only longitudinal study we found specifically on college graduates on this topic, McBroom (1984) examined changes in attitudes toward women among three cohorts of students who had attended a Rocky Mountain university in 1954, 1964, and 1974. He found each cohort less traditional than the one before it, but the declines over a five-year period within each cohort were slight and approximately equal across cohorts (a range of $-.13$ to $-.22$ of a standard deviation, or 5 to 9 percentile points).

Summary and Conclusions

This chapter has sought to summarize and synthesize the research dealing with changes in students' attitudes and values in five general areas: (1) cultural, aesthetic, and intellectual; (2) educational and occupational; (3) social and political; (4) religious; and (5) sex and gender roles. That body of evidence is voluminous, varied in content, and methodologically uneven. At forest floor level it constitutes a bewildering, even intimidating, array of studies. There are, nonetheless, discernible consistencies in the evidence indicating not only that those who attend college change their value and attitudinal positions in a number of different areas but that they do so as a consequence of attending a college or university and not simply in response to normal, maturational impulses or to historical, social, or political trends. The conditions under which these changes occur and the dynamics that produce them, however, are much less apparent. The evidence in many areas is frequently more suggestive than conclusive. In what follows, we summarize our findings across outcome areas within each of the six questions that guided our research.

Change During College

When one steps back from this mass of research, a number of general consistencies are apparent. The evidence clearly shows that changes in students' attitudes and values in a variety of areas occur during the college years. In each of the five areas reviewed here, the evidence of change is moderately to highly consistent. Students gain in their cultural, aesthetic, and intellectual sophistication, while expanding their interests and activities in classical music, reading and creative writing, theater, discussions of philosophy and history, and general interest in the humanities and performing arts. These gains are estimated roughly to be on the order of 10 to 15 percentile points.

Shifts are also apparent in students' educational and occupational values. Increases of about 20 to 30 percentage points are reported in the proportion of seniors (compared to themselves as freshmen) who find intrinsic value in a liberal education and exposure to new ideas. The more instrumental and extrinsic values of education (career and vocational preparation) decline somewhat (10 to 20 percentage points). Similar (but somewhat smaller) shifts are evident in students' occupational values, where intrinsic values (such as opportunities for creativity, freedom from supervision, intellectual challenge) appear to increase (by perhaps 10 percentage points) and extrinsic values (salary, job security, opportunities for advancement) decline (10 to 20 percentage points).

Change is even more consistently apparent in students' sociopolitical attitudes and values, where modest to moderate shifts (8 percentile points and 15 to 25 percentage points) are found. Attitudes, values, and behaviors become increasingly open and "other-person" oriented as humanitarian and altruistic values develop, political tolerance and liberalism increase, and the rights of others are more quickly supported. The research is also highly consistent in indicating declines in students' traditional religious affiliations (up to −11 percentage points) and in their general religious orientations (declines of perhaps 20 percentile points over four years). Religious beliefs become more individual and less doctrinaire, and tolerance for the religious views of others appears to increase. With only slightly less consistency, the research indicates that the equality of men and women—socially, education-ally, occupationally, and within the family—becomes more accepted by students of both sexes during the college years (10 to 25 percentile points).

Indeed, as one looks across the areas of consistent change, it seems clear that colleges, as their founders and supporters might hope, appear to have a generally liberating influence on students' attitudes and values. Without exception, the nature and direction of the observed changes involve greater breadth, expansion, inclusiveness, complexity, and appreciation for the new and different. In *all* cases, the movement is toward greater individual freedom: artistic and cultural, intellectual, political, social, racial, educational, occupational, personal, and behavioral. These changes are eminently consistent with the values of a liberal education, and the evidence for their presence is compelling.

Net Effects of College

Change during the college years, of course, is not the same thing as change due to college attendance. Reassuringly, however, considering widespread popular beliefs and institutional claims about the benefits of college attendance, the research consistently indicates the presence of unique educational effects (albeit typically rather modest ones) above and beyond the characteristics students bring with them to college. Moreover, these educational effects, particularly those dealing with political, social, and sex role attitudes, appear not to be mere reflections of changes that have occurred in the larger society over the last twenty years. Even after age and selected other relevant variables are controlled, attitudes and values related to education are quite consistently apparent both within and across age cohorts. It is also worth recalling that most studies of net change are, of statistical necessity, conservative estimates of the magnitudes of educational effects (see the Appendix). In addition, some of the measures used have been constructed so as to produce relatively stable measurements over time (Winter,

1979; Winter, McClelland, & Stewart, 1981), thus perhaps underestimating the actual magnitude of change. With respect to shifts toward more open, liberal, and tolerant attitudes and values, however—whether they are general humanitarian or altruistic social values, political attitudes and behaviors, or matters of civil rights and liberties—some compelling and contrary evidence has been introduced suggesting that educational effects may be substantially less than earlier studies have indicated and many people believe. This evidence dictates some caution in our conclusions in these areas and awaits replication.

Between-College Effects

Consistent with the evidence on student change reported in other chapters of this volume, the research on differential influences associated with *where* one goes to school generally suggests that the structural characteristics of an institution (with one exception) are relatively independent of value change. Such institutional features as size, type of control (with the exception of denominational schools' effects on religious value change), mission, and curricular emphasis generally appear to be unrelated to value change in any consistent way. Where such influence is found, it is uniformly slight.

Moderately consistent evidence, on the other hand, suggests that selective, frequently private institutions, compared to their less selective sister schools, exert a relatively greater influence (net of student characteristics) on changes in students' aesthetic and cultural values and interests, their political and social values, and their religiousness. The effects of selectivity on changes in educational and occupational values and on sex role attitudes are either mixed or missing. The weight of evidence on the potency of institutional selectivity, however, is far from overwhelming and occasionally inconsistent.

A plausible explanation for the general absence of between-institution differences, as suggested in this volume and elsewhere (Astin & Lee, 1972), would seem to be that the variability in students' academic and nonacademic programs and other experiences is greater *within* than across institutions. Traditional descriptors presumed to differentiate meaningfully among institutions (for example, type of control, size, mission) may simply be too general to be useful predictors of student change. It is possible, however, that the *combination* of selectivity with small size and liberal arts emphasis may well be a more powerful set of predictors. Moreover, as Gurin (1971) has suggested, students are not immune to other sources of influence that lie outside their institution's walls, including parental values and changes occurring in society at large. Expecting greater between- than within-institution effects than we found in the research literature may be unreasonable.

Within-College Effects

Within institutions and across value areas, academic major field appears to be less influential than the interpersonal associations students have with faculty members and peers, often in the departmental context, more frequently in the residence halls. Although the effects of residence appear to be modest, their influence is most apparent in the changes in students' occupational, political, and religious attitudes and values. Studies using the organizational unit of the major department as a variable tend not to find significant differences in the amount of change over time. Major department may be too distal from students' experiences, however, for when the more proximal environment and character of students' interactions with faculty and peers in the major department are examined (regardless of the discipline), reliable differences are more likely to appear. The degree of value consensus and homogeneity among students and faculty members appears to exert an important contextual influence on student socialization and value change.

Similar evidence exists with respect to students' interactions with their peers, particularly in the place of residence. Students in residence halls are likely to change more in their sociopolitical and religious views than are students living at home or in off-campus quarters. Residence has mixed effects in cultural and aesthetic value change, while residential effects on sex role attitudes remain virtually unexplored. The dynamics and causal flow of the influence among students, peers, faculty members, departments, and residence units remain cloudy, however. Little can be said with conviction about whether these influences are exerted through the frequency of contact among the inhabitants of institutional or departmental settings, the nature of the contact, or the more contextual generalized presence of faculty members and other students who hold a certain set of educational, occupational, social, political, religious, and sex role attitudes and values toward which new students gravitate over time. Untangling this web of within-institution influences on student change remains a conceptually and technically formidable but potentially promising area of future research.

Conditional Effects of College

Not surprisingly, as our research questions become more complex, the evidence becomes more scarce. The last twenty years of research have shed little light on the question of the extent to which value and attitudinal change in any area might be dependent upon individual student characteristics. A *large* number of studies test whether women and men, independently, change in one way or another in each of the value areas reviewed here. But observing, say, that women change significantly in one way or another while men do not is *not* equivalent to testing whether the *differences in the amounts* of change for women and men are statistically significant. The number of studies testing this sex × time interaction (the only valid way to test for conditional effects) can be counted on two hands across all five areas. Where such effects have been tested, they have produced nonsignificant or inconsistent results. To be sure, detection of significant interactions is extremely difficult for statistical reasons. The fact remains, however: The literature has little to say about the differential effects of college on values and attitudes for different kinds of students.

Long-Term Effects of College

Do the effects of college on value and attitude change persist after graduation? Although the literature on this topic is small, it is relatively consistent across areas in indicating that changes that occur during college do indeed persist into the adult years. Most of the research focuses on students' humanitarian, political, racial, and civil libertarian values, however. The changes toward greater sociopolitical liberalism that begin in college appear to continue into the adult years but at a reduced rate. There is some evidence to suggest that this stability is probably due, at least in part, to reinforcement by graduates' spouses, friends, and occupational colleagues, who are likely to be similarly educated and to hold at least somewhat similar attitudes and values.

While the research consistently shows older people to be more politically conservative than younger ones, it appears that rather than older people changing their views toward a more conservative position, the liberal-conservative continuum shifts its position under them. Generally, liberal college graduates become *relatively* more conservative over time. This is not because their views are changing in a conservative direction (indeed, they tend to continue to shift toward more liberal and tolerant positions in many areas) but rather because they are being compared with younger, even *more* liberal generations of students. College-related changes persist across time and, in several studies, across historical periods.

In other attitude and value areas, there may not be a corresponding continuation of the changes initiated in college, but neither is there any evidence to suggest a return to attitudes and values held prior to college attendance. Cultural and aesthetic values and interests appear to level off after graduation, as do shifts in religious values. Still, there are some indications of slight declines in religious values over time. There is also some evidence that college both directly and indirectly sets in motion changes in occupational values that are apparent up to a decade later. Research on change in sex role attitudes is too young a field of study for there to be any convincing evidence on the durability of college effects in this area. Given the moderately strong correlations between sociopolitical and sex role attitudes, it does seem reasonable to expect that the long-term effects of college on changes in sex role attitudes would parallel those of sociopolitical shifts. This remains purely speculative, however.

Some Closing Thoughts

Our knowledge of the magnitudes of college effects across the five areas considered in this chapter, and of the processes by which change is initiated, remains disappointingly foggy. Some significant gains have been made since Feldman and Newcomb's (1969) review, but as many (perhaps more) questions remain as have been answered. At the same time, researchers are now conceptually and analytically better equipped to ask far more detailed and specific questions than were possible two decades age. Some of the six questions posed for each area of review in this book could not even have been asked twenty years ago, primarily because of the scarcity of theories and the general unavailability of the computer and statistical tools with which to test them.

Finally, glaring weaknesses—conceptual and methodological—are apparent in the existing research in the areas reviewed here. Many (but by no means all) of these weaknesses are most apparent in the early developmental stages of a field of study that has changed dramatically over the last twenty years. Many studies are atheoretical, apparently proceeding as much from mild curiosity as any systematic set of hypotheses based on some theory of how students learn or develop. Given their objectives, many studies are based on woefully weak research designs, and many employ bivariate statistical procedures that are simply incapable of adequately answering the questions put to them. Despite cautions to be wary of the tendency for group change scores to mask potentially extensive and substantial individual change (for example, Chickering, 1968; Feldman & Newcomb, 1969), *very* few studies explore changes at that level. Only a handful of studies examine the question of *when* change occurs during the college years, whether change is a more or less steady linear process or whether it develops in more episodic fashion during the college years. And most disappointing of all, only a few studies use a noncollege comparison group. Thus, most studies are unable to differentiate in any rigorous fashion between changes that occur as a consequence of college attendance and those that are due to normal maturation or to social and cultural ferment outside the academy.

The evidence is clear that changes occur during the college years and that the collegiate experience is responsible for at least *some* of those changes. But much remains to be done. It is now time for higher education researchers to look more closely and rigorously at the magnitudes, origins, timing, and durability of those changes. The questions cannot be answered in one-year studies. But they are absolutely necessary if we are to advance an understanding of the effects of college on students and if there is to be any empirical verification of popular and institutional beliefs about the benefits of college attendance.

Notes

1. Our review of studies of attitude and value change during college is not exhaustive. A number of studies have explored changes in college students' attitudes and values (or behaviors that might be taken to reflect attitudes or values) in a variety of other areas, including (but by no means limited to) aging and the elderly, drug and alcohol use and abuse, abortion, death, marriage, and sexual behavior. A review of all such areas, however, is beyond the scope and means of this study.

2. A significant portion of the evidence related to changes in students' cultural and aesthetic attitudes and values (as well as other values) is derived from three instruments, the Study of Values (Allport, Vernon, & Lindzey, 1960), the Omnibus Personality Inventory (OPI) (Heist & Yonge, 1968), and the Educational Testing Service's College Student Questionnaires (CSQ) (Peterson, 1968). The Study of Values (SOV) is a forty-four item, forced-choice instrument that measures the relative importance of an individual's values in each of six areas: theoretical, economic, aesthetic, social, political, and religious. A high score on the aesthetic scale indicates an individual who finds "highest values in harmony and form. Truth is considered equivalent to beauty, and each experience is evaluated in terms of symmetry, grace, and fitness" (May & Ilardi, 1973, p. 58). The scoring of the SOV creates certain methodological problems for any given study (points scored on one scale must necessarily be lost to one or more of the remaining scales, making it difficult to determine whether a low score on one scale reflects a "true" condition or is an artifact of a higher score on another scale; see Heist, 1968, pp. 214–218, for a succinct critique). The problem is reduced for current purposes, however, since we are concerned with the cumulative evidence over a number of studies, much of which will be based on other measures.

    Scores on the SOV aesthetic scale correlate .61 with scores on the Omnibus Personality Inventory's estheticism scale (Heist & Yonge, 1968). High scorers on the OPI's estheticism scale are interested in artistic matters and activities and have a high sensitivity to aesthetic experiences. "The content of . . . this scale extends beyond painting, sculpture, and music, and includes interests in literature and dramatics" (Heist & Yonge, 1968, p. 4).

    Research on aesthetic or cultural values that relies on the College Student Questionnaires employs their cultural sophistication scale. "Students with high scores report interest in or pleasure from such things as wide reading, modern art, poetry, classical music, discussions of philosophies of history, and so forth. Low scores indicate a lack of cultivated sensibility in the general area of the humanities" (Peterson, 1968, p. 20).

3.   "Intellectual attitudes and values" here refers to specific interest or activity areas (such as reading and writing). Chapter Four examines the research on changes in students' higher-order thinking abilities, and Chapter Six reviews the research dealing with changes in students' more generalized "intellectual" orientations toward their world. "Intellectual orientation or disposition" in that chapter refers to such characteristics as intellectual curiosity, the inclination to be skeptical or critical of information, an analytical orientation, and general intellectual flexibility and complexity.

4.   While we use the common "intrinsic versus extrinsic" dichotomy for our review, a number of studies of the structure of occupational values indicate the presence of two to five underlying dimensions (see Anderson, 1985b; Gates, 1977; Kalleberg, 1977; Kohn & Schooler, 1969; Lorence & Mortimer, 1981; Mortimer & Lorence, 1979b).

5.   Several studies have used Allport, Vernon, and Lindzey's Study of Values, which includes an economic values scale. Here high scores reflect a valuing of the useful and the practical, particularly as they relate to the business world. One study found a significant drop (-.36 of a standard deviation, or 14 percentile points) in economic values from freshman to senior year (Arsenian, 1970); others found no significant change during college (Cox, 1988; Huntley, 1967; May & Ilardi, 1970). See note 2 concerning interpretation of Study of Values scores.

6.   Several studies report data from the social values scale of the Study of Values (Allport, Vernon, & Lindzey, 1960). This scale is presumed to reflect an individual's valuing of other human beings, love in an altruistic sense. Only one of these studies (Arsenian, 1970), however, found significant gains on this scale during the college years, while the others found no changes (Baumgartel & Goldstein, 1967; Cox, 1988; Huntley, 1967; May & Ilardi, 1973). These findings are consistent with those summarized by Feldman and Newcomb (1969), who found that four of fourteen analyses reported significant social scale gains over varying amounts of time, while the remaining ten analyses found no statistically significant changes. It is possible, however, that the reasonably consistent findings of no differences were a function of the scaling constraints on the Study of Values scales (see note 2).

7.   The College Student Questionnaires' (Peterson, 1968) social conscience scale reflects "moral concern about perceived social injustice and what might be called 'institutional wrongdoing' (as in government, business, unions)" (p. 20). The CSQ's liberalism scale measures a "political-eco-

nomic-social value dimension, the nucleus of which is sympathy either for an ideology of change or for an ideology of preservation" (p. 20).

8. Differences across cohorts led Yankelovich (1974a, 1974b) to suggest that small groups of students may function as "forerunners" of the social and political attitudinal change that will eventually reshape national views on a variety of matters. According to this view, such small student groups adopt extreme positions on new values and challenge the more moderate (even conservative) views of more typical students. The larger student groups may modify their attitudes and values to some extent and carry these into the occupational and social worlds upon graduation. These views then appear among older, middle-class people, but eventually, through a series of modifications as more liberal views encounter more conventional views, they will be diffused into the population as a whole. Evidence consistent with this view has led a number of researchers to similar interpretations (Abravanel & Busch, 1975; Bayer & Dutton, 1975; Greeley & Spaeth, 1970; Kasschau, Ransford, & Bengston, 1974; Laufer & Bengston, 1974; Little, 1970; Nunn, Crockett, & Williams, 1978; Suczek, 1972). However, Davis (1980) and Taylor and Wolfe (1971) concluded that better-educated young people do not serve in this role.

9. While this study was competently conducted, Knox, Lindsay, and Kolb consider their findings preliminary and expect to report additional analyses in a forthcoming book entitled *The Way Up: The Long-Term Effects of Higher Education on Students* (W. E. Knox, telephone communication, June 1990).

10. Nelsen and Uhl (1977) studied fewer (three) and more homogeneous schools (predominantly black and in the same state) than did Chickering (1971a) and Clark, Heist, McConnell, Trow, and Yonge (1972), and their statistical controls were also more powerful. They report a significant college × time interaction on the CSQ's cultural sophistication scale, indicating that scores on this scale increased differentially by college over time. Closer inspection of their data, however, revealed that the differences were probably due to the large magnitude of freshman-year changes in one institution and thus may be institutionally specific.

11. Students from lower socioeconomic homes have been shown to be somewhat less likely to value a good education, but race appears to be unrelated to the degree of attachment to this value (Knox, Lindsay, & Kolb, 1988). Students who scored high as freshmen on a scale reflecting interest in ideas and philosophical thought were more likely than low scorers to change their educational orientation away from vocational or other goals toward a general or liberal education. It also appears that students who enrolled with a relatively strong interest in

reflective and abstract thought and with high values attached to a liberal education were less likely to change from those values and more likely to move from vocational to general education values and intrinsic occupational values during college (Clark, Heist, McConnell, Trow, & Yonge, 1972).

12. Of three such studies based on the social scale of the Study of Values, two found statistically significant drops in social values over a fifteen-year and a twenty-five-year period (Hoge & Bender, 1974; Arsenian, 1970). Two other analyses found no changes in social values after fourteen years (Arsenian, 1970, following a second cohort) and after twenty years (Cox, 1988). Study of Values scales must be interpreted cautiously, however (see note 2).

13. Experimentally induced changes in values relating to equality and freedom have been shown to be remarkably stable when retested three, five, and fifteen to seventeen months later (Rokeach, 1971).

8

Moral Development

At its very inception American higher education had a clearly defined role in developing individuals who would both think and act morally (Rudolph, 1956; Sloan, 1979, 1980). Indeed, as suggested by Morrill (1980) and Rudolph (1962), nineteenth-century American higher education had a strongly entrenched tradition of moral philosophy that was manifest in a major portion of the collegiate curriculum. In addition to what Rudolph (1962, p. 140) describes as an "impressive arsenal of weapons for making men out of boys" (such as religious revivals, dedicated and underpaid professors, unheated dormitory rooms), the religiously based liberal arts college of the early 1800s often included courses on ethics and values as part of the core curriculum (McBee, 1980). The culmination was a capstone course in moral philosophy, usually taught by the college president and required of all seniors. This course, transplanted largely from the residential universities of eighteenth-century England and Scotland, was designed to integrate the students' entire collegiate experience and send them into the larger world not only wiser but also sensitive to their moral and ethical responsibilities (Sloan, 1979). Thus, the academic curriculum and the entire campus environment clearly viewed the formation of student character as a central mission. Consistent with the classical tradition, the liberal arts college believed, as did Plato, "that education makes good men and that good men act nobly" (Adler, 1952).

In the second half of the nineteenth century, the establishment of state-supported, public institutions under the Morrill Act, the rise of research universities, and the fragmentation of knowledge that accompanied the evolution of academic disciplines contributed to major structural and curricular changes in American higher education. Direct curricular approaches to the development of student character and moral sensitivity became less evident, and faculty became more concerned with the logic, lan-

Note: An earlier and less detailed version of this chapter appeared in Nucci, L., & Pascarella, E. (1987). The influence of college on moral development. In J. Smart (Ed.), *Higher education: Handbook of theory and research,* Vol. 3. New York: Agathon.

guage, and literature of their own disciplines than with broader questions of human values and morality (Morrill, 1980).

Despite these fundamental changes, however, the tradition of liberal education and its attendant concerns with developing the whole individual still hold a prominent place in the ethos of American higher education (for example, Chickering, 1969; Heath, 1968; Sanford, 1967; Trow, 1976b; Winter, McClelland, & Stewart, 1981). There continues to be a presumption that the college experience and liberal education in particular should contribute not only to cognitive development but also to an expansion of the student's worldview and the capacity to apply reason and intellect to interpersonal, political, social, and ethical questions as well as to purely academic ones (Averill, 1983; Gamson and Associates, 1984).

A large body of research has addressed the issue of the influence of college on moral development. By far the dominant theoretical framework that guides this inquiry has been that of Lawrence Kohlberg (1958, 1964, 1969, 1971, 1976, 1981a, 1981b, 1984). The work of William Perry (1970) has also influenced some of the recent work on moral development, but Perry's is perhaps less a pure model of stages of moral development than a model that combines intellectual and ethical growth (Nucci & Pascarella, 1987). Consequently, our review of the literature on the influence of college upon moral development necessarily reflects the preeminence of Kohlbergian theory.

Because the focus of Kohlberg's theory is on the development of moral judgment, it has a substantial cognitive element. As we have seen in Chapter Two, development is described as proceeding through six stages embedded within three levels. The first two stages (Level I) are considered preconventional. At this level moral reasoning is highly egocentric in that it is based on the person's concerns for his or her own interests and for those of specific others the individual might care about. At Level II (Stages 3 and 4) conventional moral reasoning takes over. This reasoning is based on a concern with maintaining the social order. Moral judgments are guided by obedience to rules and meeting the expectations of others, particularly those in positions of authority. This orientation toward maintaining the system is replaced at Level III (Stages 5 and 6) by a postconventional or "principled" perspective. The basis of this kind of reasoning is a view of morality as a set of universal principles for making choices among alternative courses of action that would be held by any rational moral individual. These are considered "first principles" in that they exist independently of and prior to societal codification. Hence, a central emphasis in the postconventional stage is on principles for choosing the most just arrangement for individuals within society.

Although there is no necessarily direct correspondence between age and developmental stage, the body of existing evidence would place most traditional college-age freshmen (those seventeen to nineteen years old) at the conventional level of moral reasoning (for example, Keniston, 1969; Kohlberg, 1969, 1981a, 1981b; Kramer, 1968; Rest, 1979a, 1986c). If college contributes significantly to moral development beyond general age-typical experience (that is, beyond simply growing older), it should be evidenced by a greater upward shift in moral stage or by a greater proportion of postconventional (principled) reasoners among college upperclassmen than among either entering freshmen or same-age peers in the general population.

Measuring Growth in Moral Reasoning

The concept of developmental stages of moral growth as explicated by Kohlberg is a complex one and has been the subject of considerable debate (Gilligan, 1982a; Nucci & Pascarella, 1987; Shweder, Mahaptra, & Miller, 1987; Sullivan, 1977; Walker, 1984). No less complex are the problems inherent in assessing moral development. Since two instruments dominate the assessment of moral development, we will briefly describe each before turning to a review of the evidence on the influence of college. The two basic instruments used are the Moral Judgment Interview (MJI) (Colby et al., 1982; Colby, Kohlberg, Gibbs, & Lieberman, 1983) and the Defining Issues Test (DIT) (Rest, 1975, 1979c, 1983a, 1983b).

The Moral Judgment Interview that is now in use has undergone progressive revision and development over the past twenty-five years. The interview has three parallel forms. Each form consists of three hypothetical moral dilemmas followed by a series of standardized questions designed to elicit justifications for the subject's moral judgments. Scoring of the interview follows a standardized classification system designed to permit an analysis of the structure of the subject's reasoning independent of any dilemma-specific content. This scoring system yields either a global interview score in terms of estimated stage of development or a continuous scale "moral maturity" score, which is a weighted average of the total scored responses to the interview. The interrater reliability—that is, the extent to which two independent raters of the same interview arrive at the same score—is in the .84 to .98 range, while the test-retest correlations range from .96 to .99 (Colby, Kohlberg, Gibbs, & Lieberman, 1983).

In contrast to the interview format of the MJI, the Defining Issues Test is a paper and pencil test that can be group administered and quickly and objectively scored. The DIT, like the MJI, asks subjects to respond to moral dilemmas. Accompanying each dilemma are twelve issue statements that represent ways in which subjects at Levels I through III might respond. The subject is asked to indicate on a five-point scale how important each issue statement is in making a decision regarding the dilemma. On the basis of these responses, several scores are produced. The most widely used is the P-index, which is a measure of the relative importance subjects give to postconventional or principled justifications. The higher the P-index (which is expressed as a percentage), presumably the more developed the individual. As reported in Rest (1979c), average DIT reliabilities range from .78 to .81.

As perhaps indicated by the brief descriptions above, both the MJI and the DIT assess moral development in terms of one's level of moral reasoning. They are not, in and of themselves, measures of one's actual moral behavior. Nevertheless, while inconsistencies between reasoning and behavior have been found in some investigations, comprehensive reviews or discussions by Blasi (1980, 1983), Kohlberg (1981a, 1981b), Rest (1983a, 1983b), Turiel and Smetana (1984), and Turiel (1983) suggest a significant link between moral reasoning score and such behaviors as resistance to cheating, helping behavior, and civil disobedience. Evidence regarding this relationship as it applies to college students is presented in more detail later in the chapter.

Change During College

It is unlikely that increased sensitivity to moral issues develops in isolation from other cognitive and affective changes in students coinciding with college attendance. Rather, moral reasoning is perhaps most appropriately seen as an integral part of an interconnected and often mutually reinforcing network of developmental trends that characterize changes that tend to occur in college students. For example, as we have seen in earlier chapters, there is abundant evidence to suggest that students make statistically significant gains in their abilities to reason critically, flexibly, and abstractly during college. There is also a clear though modest correlation between various measures of cognitive development and level of moral reasoning (for example, de Vries & Walker, 1986; Doherty & Corsini, 1976; King, Kitchener, Wood, & Davison, 1985; Lutwak, 1984; P. Meyer, 1977; Rowe & Marcia, 1980; Smith, 1978). Some of this research has even suggested that the development of Piagetian formal (abstract) reasoning is a necessary condition for the development of principled moral judgment (Cauble, 1976; Rowe & Marcia, 1980).

Similarly, as we have seen in preceding chapters, there is substantial evidence to suggest a clear association between college attendance and a general liberalization of personality and value structures. In the vast majority of studies conducted, upperclassmen, as compared to freshmen, tend to be less authoritarian or dogmatic and more open and flexible in their perceptual processes, more autonomous and independent of authority imposed through social institutions, more tolerant and understanding of others, and more interpersonally sensitive and skilled (for example, Chickering, 1974b; Chickering & McCormick, 1973; Clark, Heist, McConnell, Trow, & Yonge, 1972; Feldman & Newcomb, 1969; Lehmann & Dressel, 1962, 1963;

Pace, 1974; Spaeth & Greeley, 1970; Trent & Medsker, 1968; Withey, 1971).
As with increases in cognitive capabilities, there is also evidence to suggest
that level of moral reasoning in college samples tends to have modest positive correlations with these and similar dimensions of personality and value
development (for example, Clouse, 1985; Czapski & Gates, 1981; de Vries
& Walker, 1986; Fishkin, Keniston, & MacKinnon, 1973; Hogan & Dickstein, 1972; Hult, 1979; Liberman, Gaa, & Frankiewicz, 1983; Lupfer, Cohn,
& Brown, 1982; Parish, Rosenblatt, & Kappes, 1979; Polovy, 1980; Sullivan, McCullough, & Stager, 1970).

Given such supportive developmental trends in the cognitive or intellectual and the personal or value orientations of college students, it seems
reasonable to hypothesize that increases in principled moral reasoning might
also accompany the experience of college. The evidence to support this
hypothesis is impressive, not only in terms of the sheer number of studies
conducted but also in terms of the extensive diversity of samples employed.
Since the Defining Issues Test has the advantage of being a paper and
pencil, group-administered measure, it is not surprising that it is the most
frequently employed instrument in cross-sectional as well as longitudinal
studies of moral development.

Studies That Use the Defining Issues Test

With few exceptions (for example, P. Meyer, 1977; White, 1973), the
cross-sectional studies that employ the DIT P-index (which, again, measures the relative importance one gives to principled moral considerations
in making a moral decision) show statistically significant age-education trends
in moral judgment. Rest (1976, 1979a, 1979c) and Rest, Davison, and Robbins (1978) have synthesized data from more than fifty published and unpublished cross-sectional studies in the United States that used the DIT.
Represented in these studies were 5,714 subjects and 136 different samples.
When the P-scores were aggregated across samples, Rest found that average P-scores tended to increase about ten points at each level of education
as a student progressed from junior high (average P-score of 21.9 percent)
to senior high (average P-score of 31.8 percent) to college (average P-score
of 42.3 percent) to graduate or professional school (average P-score of 53.8
percent). Grouping the samples by these age-education categories accounted for about 38 percent of the variations or differences in P-scores.
Remarkably similar results have been reported in other cross-sectional studies with the DIT (Cohen, 1982; Guldhammer, 1983; Martin, Shafto, & Van
Deinse, 1977; Mentowski & Strait, 1983; Ponsford, Alloway, & Mhoon, 1986;
Yussen, 1976). In all of these studies, upperclassmen or seniors tended to
give greater preference to principled moral considerations in making moral
decisions than did underclassmen or freshmen.

The strong age-education trends in DIT P-scores are not confined to

American samples. Moon (1985) reviewed and synthesized a number of studies of moral judgment development using samples from Hong Kong (Hau, 1983), Korea (Park & Johnson, 1983), Iceland (Thornlidsson, 1978), the Philippines (Villanueva, 1982), and Australia (Watson, 1983). Nearly all of these studies also showed clear developmental trends in principled thinking. Subjects who were older and who had completed higher levels of formal education (through college) tended to attribute more importance to principled moral considerations on the DIT than subjects who were younger and not as well educated. Thus, the pronounced developmental trends in principled thinking as measured by the P-index of the DIT appear to be reasonably independent of national and cultural settings.

While longitudinal studies following the same sample of subjects over time are less numerous than cross-sectional investigations, there is nevertheless considerable evidence to suggest that students tend to have significantly higher DIT P-scores as end-of-year freshmen or upperclassmen than they did as entering freshmen. Moreover, exposure to postsecondary education appears to be linked with marked increases in principled thinking even when subjects are followed beyond the typical four-year period of college.

Shaver (1985) found statistically significant freshman-to-senior P-score gains of 10.85 points for students in a conservative, religious liberal arts college. The magnitude of this freshman-to-senior increase in principled moral judgment is markedly similar to that found with other college samples. Whiteley (1982) reports modest but statistically significant increases in P-scores from the beginning to the end of the freshman year for three cohorts of students at a state university. The average P-score increase during the freshman year for all three classes was 4.08 points. When these same three samples were followed from freshman to senior year the significant P-score gain was approximately 11.14 points (Loxley & Whiteley, 1986). Thus, while the magnitude of the overall freshman-to-senior gain was quite consistent with that of Shaver (1985), about 36 to 37 percent of the gain in principled moral judgment that occurred during the four years of college did so during the freshman year. A similar pattern of change is reported by Mentkowski and Strait (1983) for two cohorts of entering freshmen who were followed up during their sophomore, junior, and senior years. Statistically significant freshman-to-sophomore and sophomore-to-senior P-score increases were found for the combined samples. The total freshman-to-senior P-score increase was 9.7 points. Of this, the freshman-to-sophomore increase was 7.37 points, while the sophomore-to-senior gain was considerably smaller (2.33 points).

Other longitudinal studies have tended to support the overall statistically significant increase in principled moral reasoning from freshman to upperclassman year or from freshman to senior year (Broadhurst, 1980; Gorman, Duffy, & Heffernan, undated; Hood, 1984; Janos, Robinson, &

Lunneborg, 1987; Kaseman, 1980; Towers, 1984). The magnitude of this increase, however, is often difficult to determine from the data presented.

Perhaps the most ambitious longitudinal investigation of changes in principled moral reasoning associated with college attendance is that conducted by Rest and his colleagues (Rest, 1986c; Rest & Thoma, 1985; Deemer, 1985). They report the findings of research that followed three cohorts of high school graduates over six and ten years, respectively. For students who had completed at least three years of college, the six-year increase in P-score was 14 points (Rest, 1986c; Rest & Thoma, 1985). Similarly, when followed up after ten years, students with at least some college had an average P-score increase of approximately 11 points (Deemer, 1985).

The only longitudinal evidence inconsistent with the general trend of increases in principled moral judgment during college is reported by McGeorge (1976) and Shaver (1987). McGeorge found positive but statistically nonsignificant gains in P-scores over a two-year period for a sample of New Zealand Teachers College students. Shaver considered changes in P-scores at a Bible college and found that from the freshman to senior year they changed little. However, this absence of an overall statistically significant freshman-to-senior gain masked the fact that P-scores actually increased significantly through the end of the sophomore year but decreased thereafter.

Studies That Use the Moral Judgment Interview

Research that has relied on Kohlberg's Moral Judgment Interview (MJI) has also shown a positive association between level of formal education and moral development with both cross-sectional data (Lei, 1981; Lei & Cheng, 1984; Mentkowski and Strait, 1983; Whitla, 1978) and longitudinal data (Colby, Kohlberg, Gibbs, & Lieberman, 1983; Loxley & Whiteley, 1986; Mentkowski & Strait, 1983). Lei and Cheng found that Taiwanese college students had higher average scores on the MJI than did secondary school students, and graduate students had higher scores than college students. The difference between college and high school students was three and one-half times as large as the difference between graduate students and college students. Further, while 70 percent of the graduate students and 34.8 percent of the college students were functioning at the higher or more principled stages of moral maturity (Kohlberg's Stages 4 and 4/5), only 17.1 percent of the secondary school students were reasoning at these stages. Mentkowski and Strait (1983) found that graduating seniors at an American institution had significantly higher moral maturity scores on the MJI than did entering freshmen. Compared to freshmen, a noticeably lower proportion of seniors were in the preconventional stages of Kohlberg's scheme, and proportionally more were in the postconventional stages.

Similar results have been reported by Whitla (1978) with a multi-institutional sample. Using a paper and pencil adaptation of the MJI, Whitla found that seniors at a private college and a state college showed significantly higher levels of moral maturity than did freshmen. At a public junior college sophomores scored significantly higher than freshmen. In all cases the freshman and upperclassman cohorts were matched on entering academic ability (SAT scores) and high school rank, though not on entering MJI scores.

In a longitudinal investigation of changes in moral development with three cohorts of entering freshmen, Loxley and Whiteley (1986) looked at changes on the Moral Judgment Interview as well as on the Defining Issues Test. Freshman-to-senior changes on the MJI were statistically significant for both men and women, but there was also a statistically significant interaction effect between amount of change and gender. This interaction indicated that the freshman-to-senior gain in principled moral reasoning for men was slightly more than twice as large as the gain for women. Since both men and women had similar freshman scores, it is unlikely that these marked differences in gains can be explained away as the result of differential regression artifacts (that is, the initially lower group gaining more than the initially higher group).

In what is probably the most ambitious longitudinal study of moral development to date, Colby, Kohlberg, Gibbs, and Lieberman (1983) followed a sample of men from two suburban Chicago schools (one predominantly upper-middle class and the other predominantly lower-middle and working class) for twenty years. The correlations between stage of moral judgment and level of formal education at four different follow-ups of the sample (ages twenty-four to thirty-six) ranged from .54 to .77, all statistically significant. While such an approach only permits an indirect assessment of gains on the MJI during college, one can reasonably infer from the strong positive correlations that such changes are taking place.

Less convincing evidence of gains in moral maturity during college is presented by Mentkowski and Strait (1983). Following two cohorts of entering freshmen through their senior year, they found an overall small and statistically nonsignificant gain on the MJI. Moreover, from the freshman to sophomore year, the change in moral maturity score was negative, while from the sophomore to the senior year, the change was positive. Such a trend is difficult to explain and may, in fact, be artifactual.

Two additional studies have used a paper and pencil version of the Kohlberg interview known as the Moral Judgment Test (MJT). This instrument attempts to assess both affective and cognitive aspects of moral judgment behavior. A cross-sectional study by Eiferman (1982) found that college seniors age thirty or older in an urban institution had significantly higher MJT scores than did freshmen age thirty or older. This finding tends to be supported by Lind's (1985, 1986) series of longitudinal investigations of German university students from various fields of study. The students were tested with the MJT in their first and third years of college. Over the two-year period there was a modest but statistically significant average gain in the group's capacity to judge social dilemmas by means of moral principles.

Summary of Evidence on Change During College

Clearly, the overwhelming weight of evidence that comes from the Defining Issues Test and the Moral Judgment Interview (and its paper and pencil adaptations) suggests that extent of principled moral reasoning is positively associated with level of formal postsecondary education and that students generally make statistically significant gains in principled moral reasoning during college. The average magnitude of these gains is extremely difficult to determine from the existing studies in that many do not provide the information necessary to make such estimates (for example, standard deviations, percentage of students advancing from one Kohlbergian stage to another). Similarly, since the studies often report different information, it is difficult to compare the size of a statistically significant increase in one sample with that in another. Given these qualifiers, however, we infer from the body of evidence that *a* major (if not *the* major) change that takes place during college is a movement from conventional moral reasoning toward postconventional moral reasoning. It would also appear that the greatest gains in principled moral reasoning occur during the first or the first and second years of college. The latter conclusion is tentative, however, because it is based on a small number of investigations.

Design Issues That Affect Interpretation of Results

As pointed out in previous chapters, simply showing that trends and changes are coincident with college attendance is quite different from demonstrating that they occur as a consequence of college attendance. As with our discussion of gains in learning and cognitive development, a number of factors potentially confound the association between increases in principled moral reasoning and college attendance reported in a large portion of the investigations reviewed.

In cross-sectional designs that simultaneously compare different cohorts of freshmen and seniors, a major confounding factor is age. This is particularly relevant when one considers that the Kohlberg model is based on the concept of life-span developmental stages. Since amount of formal education obviously varies with age, one might question whether the development of principled moral reasoning is due to exposure to college or is simply a function of maturing as one grows older. Interpreting change in moral reasoning during college has the same problem as interpreting change in many of the dimensions of cognitive growth (such as reflective judgment) that are also developmentally based.

Similarly, there may be additional confounding factors such as subject intelligence and social status. Clearly, both of these factors are positively related to college attendance (for example, Wolfle, 1980b, 1983), and there is evidence that both have a modest positive association with level of principled moral judgment (for example, Colby, Kohlberg, Gibbs, & Lieberman, 1983; Coder, 1975). Consequently, the finding that students who complete college tend to have higher levels of principled moral judgment than those whose formal education ends with high school may not represent an effect of college as such. Rather, it may be largely due to the fact that college students represent a more selective population in terms of intelligence and social status than do high school students. In the same way, changes in institutional recruitment standards over time and the natural attrition of less intellectually capable students from freshman to senior year may produce a somewhat more selective population of seniors than the population of freshmen with whom they are compared. Thus, as we have previously seen in the areas of learning and cognitive development, cross-sectional differences in moral judgment between freshmen and seniors could be a consequence of comparing samples from differentially selective populations instead of a result attributable to the collegiate experience.

Although longitudinal designs control for many of these threats to the internal validity of the findings by comparing a cohort with itself over time, the attrition of subjects from the study may yield a less variable sample that is unrepresentative of the population from which the original sample was drawn. Moreover, longitudinal studies without a control group of similar individuals who do not attend college are still potentially confounded by regression and maturation effects. Without such a control group, it is extremely difficult to disaggregate the gains in moral judgment due to the experience of college from those due to regression artifacts or normal cognitive-moral maturation in young adults.

Net Effects of College

Determining whether differential gains in moral judgment are attributable to differences in exposure to postsecondary education is a complex matter. Cross-sectional studies (such as those that compare high school seniors and college seniors) typically attempt to control for the influence of potentially confounding variables such as age and intelligence. Similarly, longitudinal studies generally include a control group of subjects who do not attend college or who have less than four years of exposure to postsecondary education. Because it is nearly impossible to control individual differences by randomly assigning subjects to different levels of exposure to college, these longitudinal studies typically rely on various forms of statistical control (partial correlation, multiple regression, analysis of covariance, and the like) to estimate the net influence of college.

Studies That Use the Defining Issues Test

Cross-sectional studies that employ the Defining Issues Test (DIT) have attempted to determine the extent to which higher levels of principled moral reasoning are attributable to level of formal education by comparing the strength of the association between DIT P-score and education with the corresponding association between P-score and age. In nearly all these studies, level of formal education had a substantially stronger association with P-score than did age. Coder (1975), for example, studied eighty-seven adults (ages twenty-four through fifty) in a religious education program and found a slightly negative ($r = -.10$) correlation between P-score and age. The correlation between P-score and level of formal education achieved by each subject, however, was substantial ($r = .25$) and statistically significant. Crowder (1976), in a study of seventy adults (ages eighteen through fifty-nine), reports findings almost exactly replicating those of Coder. Age correlated $-.05$ with P-score, whereas level of formal education and P-score were correlated .25. Consistently similar results have been reported with American samples (Dortzbach, 1975; Eiferman, 1982; Mentkowski & Strait, 1983), a Chinese sample (Hau, 1983), and an Australian sample (Watson, 1983).

In terms of determining the net effects of college on moral reasoning as measured by the DIT, the most significant longitudinal study is probably that reported by Rest & Thoma (1985). Thirty-nine subjects were tested with the DIT in high school and at two-year intervals over a six-year period following graduation from high school. When subjects were divided into "low-education" (two years or less of college) and "high-education" groups (three or more years of college), the groups showed increasingly divergent developmental pathways in terms of principled moral judgment. The high-education group showed increasing gains after high school, while the low-education group showed a leveling off. At graduation from high school, the low-education group had a P-score of 33, and the high-education group had a slightly higher P-score of 37 (a difference of only 4 points). Six years later, however, the P-score for the low-education group was 34.5, while the high-education group had a much higher P-score of 51 (a difference between groups of 16.5 points). Using analysis of covariance to control for group differences in P-score at high school graduation, Rest and Thoma found that the high-education group still had a significantly higher adjusted P-score after six years than the low-education group. Years of college education accounted for a statistically significant increase in the explained variance in P-scores of 14 percent above and beyond that due to P-score at high school graduation. Such evidence is consistent with Rest's (1979a) contention that principled moral judgment tends to increase with exposure to additional levels of formal education beyond high school. For individuals not exposed to educational environments beyond high school, however, moral judgment development tends to plateau or level off.

Generally confirmatory results are reported in a more limited longitudinal study by Kitchener, King, Davison, Parker, and Wood (1984). Samples of high school juniors, college juniors, and doctoral-level graduate students were matched on gender, hometown size, and Scholastic Aptitude Test scores. They completed the DIT in the fall of 1977 and were followed up two years later. The college undergraduates and graduate students both showed a statistically significant increase in P-score, with the gain for the latter group being somewhat more pronounced. In contrast, the high school students did not show statistically significant P-score increases over the two-year period. Analysis of covariance, controlling for verbal ability (as measured by the Concept Mastery Test), indicated that the group and time effects on P-scores persisted.

Studies That Use the Moral Judgment Interview

Evidence pertaining to the effects of college on moral reasoning as measured by the Moral Judgment Interview is mixed. In a cross-sectional study that used the MJI, Mentkowski & Strait (1983) employed analysis of covariance to statistically remove the confounding influence of student age and found that moral maturity scores between college freshmen and seniors at a single institution were statistically nonsignificant. More positive evidence, however, is reported in Colby, Kohlberg, Gibbs, and Lieberman's (1983) twenty-year longitudinal study of fifty-eight males. The study included an initial testing with the MJI during high school and five follow-ups (using three parallel forms of the MJI) over a twenty-year period. With initial intelligence (based on school records) and socioeconomic status (based on parents' occupation and education) controlled statistically, the partial correlation between level of formal education and the MJI moral maturity score was .26 (statistically significant at $p < .05$). No partial correlations, however, were computed with high school MJI score controlled.

Summary of Evidence on the Net Effects of College

In sum, the confidence with which one can attribute higher levels of moral reasoning to the college experience varies to some extent with the specific instrument used to assess moral reasoning. Studies that used the Defining Issues Test have been quite consistent in indicating that college has a discernible positive effect on the development of principled moral reasoning. Investigations that used the Moral Judgment Interview have been less consistent in their findings. Despite the differences associated with the measurement instrument employed, the weight of evidence in the total body of research is sufficient to suggest that gains in principled moral reasoning are an outcome of the collegiate experience.

This conclusion is consistent with the findings of Hyman and Wright (1979) reviewed in Chapter Five. Recall that in their analysis of thirty-eight national surveys of adults from 1949 to 1975, Hyman and Wright found that attaching importance to civil liberties and due process of law; freedom from the constraints of arbitrary laws in personal, social, economic, and political spheres; and humanitarian conduct toward others represented a profile of values most pronounced among individuals who had gone to college. This profile distinguished college from noncollege respondents even when a number of demographic characteristics (including, age, race, and social class) were taken into account. Thus, it appears that evidence indicating a net effect of college on principled moral judgment is consistent with findings from national surveys suggesting that a general humanization of values and attitudes concerning the rights and welfare of others is associated with college attendance.[1]

Between-College Effects

Evidence pertaining to differential institutional effects on the development of student moral judgment is sparse. Few studies directly address the issue. Consequently, what evidence does exist is only preliminary and suggestive. Rest (1979a) compiled what is probably the most comprehensive data set focusing on the level of college student moral judgment. His data consist of a composite sample of nearly 2,500 students from various colleges and universities across the country. Across all samples, Rest reports an average DIT P-score of 41.6. The lowest P-scores were from colleges in the southeastern United States. The two college samples from Georgia and Virginia had average DIT P-scores of 24.5 and 34.0, respectively. These were the two lowest averages in the combined college sample. Rest speculates that the particularly low scores from these two southern samples could reflect a conservative intellectual milieu that functions to inhibit the development of moral judgment. Such a conclusion is consistent with findings reported by Cady (1982) and Ernsberger (1976) in studies of level of moral judgment among clergy. Alternatively, however, such a finding could simply reflect variations in institutional selection and recruitment procedures rather than the unique effect of different institutional environments.

It is possible, of course, that there is some contextual influence associated with being in an institutional environment dominated by peers with predominantly conventional levels of moral reasoning. This is suggested by evidence reported in Shaver's (1987) comparison of freshman-to-senior DIT P-score changes in a religiously affiliated liberal arts college and a conservative Bible college. Over the four-year period there was a 10.85-point P-score increase for the liberal arts college students (freshman P-score = 41.51, senior P-score = 52.36). This compared with a slight freshman-to-senior decrease of .24 point in the P-score at the conservative Bible college, where the freshman P-score was 33.45 and the senior P-score was 33.21. Thus, not only did the Bible college students enter an institutional environment where freshmen were at less advanced stages of moral reasoning development than in the liberal arts college, but they also had a substantially lower rate of change toward principled or postconventional reasoning than their liberal arts college counterparts.

Although there are problems in comparing change scores (see the Appendix), this trend is just the reverse of what one might expect if the findings were simply the result of regression artifacts (that is, initially lower scores showing greater change toward the mean on a subsequent testing). What the Shaver study suggests instead is that different types of colleges attract or recruit students at different entering levels of moral reasoning. In turn, one impact of distinctive college environments or social contexts appears to be the accentuation of these initial differences. This is quite consistent with the idea of accentuation effects as originally defined by Feldman and Newcomb (1969). The specific mechanism that underlies this impact is difficult to identify from Shaver's study. Nevertheless, one possibility that is consistent both with Shaver's data and with theoretical expectations (Kohlberg, 1969) is the likelihood of interaction with student peers who are themselves reasoning at the postconventional or principled stages.

To further investigate differences among postsecondary institutions in level of student moral reasoning, we conducted a secondary analysis of Rest's (1979a) data on the DIT P-scores of college students. From information on sample characteristics supplied by Rest, we grouped institutions into six basic categories: (1) public research oriented universities (those in the top 100 institutions in federally funded research for fiscal year 1983 as ranked by the National Science Foundation), (2) public comprehensive universities (not in the top 100 research universities), (3) private universities, (4) private liberal arts colleges, (5) church-affiliated liberal arts colleges, and (6) two-year colleges. We then conducted a six-group analysis of covariance with DIT P-scores as the dependent measure and the year of enrollment of each institutional sample (freshman, sophomore, junior, or senior) as the statistically controlled covariate. Each separate institutional sample was considered a single data point.

The results of our analysis indicated that year of student enrollment accounted for a statistically significant portion of the variance in DIT P-scores (22.0 percent, $p < .001$), year in college being positively associated with P-scores. Statistically controlling for differences in year of enrollment across the various samples, institutional type was also associated with a statistically significant increase in the explanation of variance in P-scores (R^2 increase = 31.26 percent, $p < .001$). The adjusted P-scores for institutional type appeared to cluster in three general groups. The lowest-scoring three categories were, in ascending order, public comprehensive universities (P-score = 38.97), private universities (P-score = 40.16), and private liberal arts colleges (P-score = 40.48). Somewhat higher were two-year colleges (P-score = 43.16) and public research universities (P-score = 43.46). Highest of all were church-affiliated liberal arts colleges (P-score = 50.49). Using a subsample of institutions that could be identified, an additional analysis found a significant partial correlation (r = .37) between institutional selectivity (average SAT or ACT composite of the freshman class) and P-score, with sample year in college controlled statistically.

Whether such findings represent national trends is problematic, of course. It is difficult to determine the degree of national representativeness in Rest's data in terms of both individuals and institutions. Moreover, even assuming sample representativeness, our analyses may simply be reflecting differential college recruiting and enrollment trends rather than the net effect of institutional type or institutional selectivity on student moral reasoning. Consequently, firm conclusions about between-institution effects on student moral reasoning from our reconsideration of the Rest data are premature. What is suggested from our analyses, however, is the clear possibility that different institutional environments may have differential impacts on the development of moral reasoning in college students. Whether such impacts are adequately captured by broad institutional classifications or level of student body academic selectivity is questionable. It is likely that there are substantial variations in the press of the intellectual, social, and cultural environments of institutions within the same category or level of selectivity. Thus, identifying the true causal influences of institutional characteristics on the development of moral reasoning may entail analyses that describe how the specific experiences of college differ among institutions.

Within-College Effects

Part of this section draws on an excellent review by Barnett and Volker (1985). Their review, however, focuses on a broader view of life experiences than those that occur during college.

Individual Experiences

A small but growing body of research has investigated the specific types of college experiences systematically associated with moral reasoning or judgment. These investigations have taken several forms. One has been the large longitudinal survey approach as exemplified by the work of Barnett (1982); Biggs, Schomberg, and Brown (1977); Biggs and Barnett (1981); and Schomberg (1978). Since these scholars appear to have been analyzing the same large-sample longitudinal data set, their studies will be reviewed in chronological order.

Biggs, Schomberg, and Brown (1977) examined the relationship between precollege experiences and the level of moral judgment of 767 freshmen at the University of Minnesota. Moral judgment was assessed with the P-score of the DIT, which was administered during December of the freshman year. Using a detailed checklist of precollege experiences, the authors found that students with the highest freshman-year P-scores (compared to those with the lowest P-scores) reported that they had read greater numbers of prominent authors and books, were better acquainted with topics in the physical and social sciences and mathematics, were better informed about nationally prominent individuals and issues, and were more knowledgeable about artists, sculptors, and composers. In short, level of freshman-year moral judgment was positively associated with an academic, literary, and culturally enriched precollege environment.

Using the same sample as Biggs, Schomberg, and Brown (1977), Schomberg (1978) assessed students' involvement and success in freshman-year experiences with an expanded checklist of ten scales. The findings suggested that freshmen with initially higher principled moral judgment tended to have higher average scores for the following types of freshman-year experiences: academic and conceptual, study, artistic and literary, intercultural, social issues, and cultural affairs. Thus, freshman students who were initially high in moral judgment (compared to those with relatively lower freshman P-scores) were better read, more knowledgeable and involved in academic experiences, and more socially and culturally active throughout their freshman year.

The picture that emerges from these two studies is one that suggests self-selection into collegiate experiences that in turn function to enhance or accentuate initial levels of development. Compared to their classmates, students who enter college with relatively high levels of principled moral judgment tend to come from precollege environments that are likewise richer in terms of academic, intellectual, literary, and cultural experiences. In turn, these same students tend to engage in freshman-year experiences that are more likely to reflect a similar set of intellectual, cultural, artistic, and social interests. Whether these experiences are causally related to moral judgment development or whether they are merely linked with the true causal influence, however, cannot be clearly discerned from the designs of the studies.

Those in the Minnesota sample were followed up in their junior year by Biggs and Barnett (1981) in an effort to determine the differential impact of various college experiences on student moral judgment. Students with initially lowest quartile and initially highest quartile freshman-year DIT scores were the comparison groups. Using multiple regression to control statistically for other predictors (freshman DIT scores, social status, and so on), junior-year DIT scores for the initially low scoring group were significantly associated only with their causal attribution beliefs concerning personal responsibility. For the initially high DIT score group, junior-year DIT scores were best predicted by freshman-year scores and participation in extracurricular activities (such as residence hall groups, sports clubs, political action groups, and music groups). The latter had a statistically significant negative partial regression coefficient with junior-year moral reasoning. Thus, junior-year level of moral reasoning was negatively associated with "traditional" or "collegiate" extracurricular involvement. There were statistically significant zero-order correlations between level of acquaintance with contemporary social and political issues (for example, the environment, civil rights, drug abuse, international affairs) and junior-year moral reasoning for both the low ($r = .20$) and the high ($r = .29$) groups. These correlations became statistically nonsignificant, however, when other influences (including freshman-year moral reasoning scores) were taken into account.

Barnett (1982) reanalyzed the Minnesota data for 128 seniors and found that seniors who were in the highest quarter in freshman moral judgment (as measured by the DIT) also tended to be significantly more involved socially, politically, academically, and culturally throughout their college years than did seniors initially in the bottom quarter in freshman moral judgment. These findings are similar to those for freshmen reported by Schomberg (1978). Conversely, seniors from the lowest freshman group tended to show greater involvement in traditional campus and religious experiences during the four years of college than did seniors in the initially high moral reasoning group as freshmen. However, when Barnett classified individuals by their dominant pattern of freshman-to-senior change in moral judgment (upward, downward, or no change), no significant differences on the experience measures were indicated among groups. Thus, amount of change in moral reasoning had little systematic association with any particular type or cluster of experiences.

It seems reasonably clear from this sequential program of research on the Minnesota data that level of principled moral reasoning or judgment (at least as assessed by the Defining Issues Test) is positively associated with extent of involvement in social, political, cultural, and intellectual or academic experiences during college. Moreover, moral reasoning appears to be negatively associated with involvement in traditional campus extracurricular experiences and religious activities. With the possible exception of the negative association with traditional extracurricular activities, however, there is little in the evidence from the Minnesota data to suggest that involvement in such experiences has a causal influence on the development of moral reasoning during college. As an alternative hypothesis, such involvement during college may simply reflect the coincidental intellectual, social, and cultural interests of students who enter postsecondary education with a relatively mature level of moral judgment.

Evidence presented by Kraack (1985), as reviewed by Barnett and

Volker (1985), would tend to support the latter hypothesis, although the investigation was somewhat different in focus from the research conducted on the Minnesota sample. Kraack conducted a longitudinal study of change in moral reasoning from the beginning of the freshman year to the end of the sophomore year at Marquette University. Students completed the DIT at both times, as well as an instrument assessing their degree of campus involvement. They were also rated on involvement and leadership by university professional staff members. Controlling for initial student differences, Kraack found no statistically significant relationships between moral judgment development and work participation, involvement in noncampus activities, extent of involvement and participation in campus activities and groups (political, religious, athletic, cocurricular, publications, and so forth), or level of leadership. Similar findings are reported by Hood (1984).

A somewhat different approach to the study of the specific college or life experiences that influence the development of principled moral reasoning has involved several researchers (Rest, 1975, 1985; Rest & Deemer, 1986; Spickelmier, 1983; Volker, 1979; Whiteley, 1980; Bertin, Ferrant, Whiteley, & Yokota, 1985). These investigators have relied, to a large extent, on subjects' retrospective perceptions of experiences and individuals that have significantly influenced their moral development. Rest (1975, 1985) conducted a longitudinal study of a group of young adults that began when they were in high school and followed them every two years for four years. At the first follow-up testing (two years after high school), the subjects were asked to reflect on their experience of the previous two years and to speculate about what had influenced their moral reasoning. Responses were grouped into six categories: (1) formal instruction, reading, or study that led to expanded knowledge of world events and affairs; (2) new "real world" responsibilities (such as job, marriage, managing money); (3) maturation or sense of "just growing up"; (4) new social contacts, new friends, and an expanded world view; (5) religious experience and/or instruction; and (6) direct involvement in community or world affairs, political involvement, or assumption of leadership roles. Rest found that those subjects who cited formal instruction or new real-world responsibilities as influencing their moral development showed greater gains in DIT P-scores than did subjects not citing those experiences.

A similar study of New Zealand college students by McGeorge (1976) failed to replicate Rest's (1975) findings, and a second follow-up of the same sample four years after high school yielded somewhat inconsistent results (Rest, 1985). In the last of these investigations, subjects' responses about particularly influential experiences during the preceding four years were grouped into eighteen categories, including the six from the first follow-up. There was little consistency, however, with the findings of the first follow-up, and no specific experience was cited as influential by a majority of subjects. Rest points out that developmental theory in no way guarantees that one particular type of life experience is the preeminent cause of development in moral judgment. Rather, it may be the case that different events or experiences have different influences for different people. The absence of a predominant theme across his findings would appear to be consistent with this notion of conditional rather than general effects of "life experiences" on moral judgment.

In what appears to be a further follow-up that used Barnett's (1982) data, Spickelmier (1983) conducted retrospective interviews with twenty-four students two years after their graduation from college. The interviews were then distilled into eight experimental categories. Spickelmier found that students who had the highest DIT P-scores as freshmen, as seniors, and two years after college were also judged from the retrospective interviews to have experienced a strong educational orientation during college. (A strong educational orientation indicated a strong commitment to accomplishing educational or academic objectives rather than just having a good time in college.) Two years after college, P-scores were significantly and positively associated with college academic success, informed tolerance toward diversity, and an academically oriented postcollege environment.

Of course, such associations are potentially confounded by differential subject selection. Thus, associations between P-score gain patterns and college experiences may be more informative. Here Spickelmier reports that compared to other students interviewed, students who showed the greatest upward gain pattern in P-scores more often reported that they became more interested in academics during college and that they broke with their secondary school friends when they went to college. Unfortunately, the statistical significance of these associations was not established, nor do there appear to be any statistical controls for the possibly confounding effects of freshman-year differences in P-scores.

In what is perhaps the most methodologically sound investigation of this topic, Rest and Deemer (1986) report interview findings generally supportive of Spickelmier (1983). Their study, which appears to be a further analysis of Rest's (1975, 1985) data (but a different sample from that analyzed by Spickelmier), followed a group of young adults over the ten-year period after high school graduation. A series of extensive interviews were conducted with those sample members who had attended college. Former college students who reported high involvement in the academic and intellectual life of college had significantly greater P-score gains over the ten-year period than did those reporting lower levels of such involvement during college. This difference remained statistically significant even after high school DIT P-scores were controlled. Indeed, net of high school P-score, "academic orientation" (Rest and Deemer's term for the various dimensions of college academic and intellectual involvement) accounted for an additional 12 percent of the variance in P-scores ten years later. Examples of interview statements characteristic of a high academic orientation were "liked the professors, classes, and academic atmosphere"; "talked to interesting people"; "studied hard"; "was in an honors program"; "lived on campus"; and "had intellectual discussions with roommates." Conversely, interview statements that exemplified a low academic orientation were "took easy courses"; "lived at home"; "never had a major"; "no academic experience was of major importance"; and "didn't study hard."

Volker (1979), Whiteley (1980), and Bertin, Ferrant, Whiteley, and Yokota (1985) conducted a series of studies that generally drew on students enrolled in a residential-academic intervention designed to influence student character (Whiteley, 1982). The intervention, known as the Sierra Project, was carried out at a large public university (University of California, Irvine). Volker (1979) sampled undergraduates from the Sierra Project and from a small midwestern liberal arts college. A seventy-two-item checklist (Moral Reasoning Experience Checklist) was employed to collect student self-reports of college or other experiences they judged to be salient to their development. For both samples, only a few experiences were rated as highly salient to the individual and also significantly and positively associated with DIT P-scores. They were (1) attending a course that presented material from different perspectives, (2) learning to adjust to the life-styles of roommates, (3) work experience that exposed them to people of more mature thinking, and (4) campaigning in state, local, or national politics.

Whiteley (1980) and Bertin, Ferrant, Whiteley, and Yokota (1985) asked senior students who had participated in the Sierra Project to retrospectively identify the college experiences that most significantly influenced their moral development during the freshman year and for all four years of college. In terms of the freshman year, the majority of students mentioned experiences involving their immediate peer group that dealt with exposure to different perspectives, exposure to more mature thinking (for example, sophomore staff in the residence unit), a relationship with a person of the opposite sex, or personal spiritual experiences. In terms of the influence of their total undergraduate experience, four general themes were identified from student responses: importance of a sense of community, exposure to diversity, significance of interpersonal relationships, and development of autonomy. The specific activities or experiences indicated as having had the most important influence on moral development were living away from home, assuming additional responsibility for oneself, discussing values and morals, and getting to know different people on campus.

Senior students from the Sierra Project were also asked to identify those groups who had most significantly influenced their moral growth during college. Those most often mentioned were close friends or peers, the staff of the Sierra Project, and parents or an intimate partner. The importance of interactions with faculty appeared to have a variable influence, being important for some students but not for others. Both the Whiteley (1980) and the Bertin, Ferrant, Whiteley, and Yokota (1985) studies appear to have relied solely on the validity of students' retrospective perceptions of the experiences and individuals that had the most salient influence on moral reasoning. They did not attempt to estimate the association between those experiences and individuals recalled as most salient and actual measures of moral development.

Although there clearly are design and measurement problems with the Volker (1979), Whiteley (1980), and Bertin, Ferrant, Whiteley, and Yokota (1985) studies, they nevertheless provide at least modest support for several of Kohlberg's (1969) notions concerning salient influences on moral development. In particular, all three studies report evidence to suggest the importance of exposure to divergent perspectives (living away from home, roommates, peers, and the like) and cognitive moral conflict (such as courses presenting material from different perspectives and discussion of morals and values) as influences on moral reasoning. In this sense, the findings of these studies are consistent with Rest's (1975). Similarly, all three studies indicate the importance of exposure to more advanced stages of moral reasoning (interactions with residential staff upperclassmen in freshman dormitories, work-related experiences, and so on). Finally, there is some evidence to support the notion of social role taking (for example, assuming new personal responsibilities, adjusting to the life-style of a roommate) as an important influence on growth in moral reasoning. Rest (1975) also reports evidence to suggest the salience of new real-world responsibilities in the development of moral reasoning.

Academic Major and Residence Arrangement

There is a small body of inquiry on the association between academic major or concentration and measures of moral reasoning. The evidence from this research, however, is inconsistent. Schomberg (1975), for example, found that engineers tended to have higher levels of moral reasoning (as measured by the DIT) than did either liberal arts or agriculture majors. Gallia (1976), on the other hand, found that humanities undergraduates had higher P-scores than science majors even when other individual student differences were taken into account. The study of New Zealand college students by McGeorge (1976) reported statistically significant differences by academic major with English, language, math, and science students tending to have higher P-scores than either social science or physical education majors. It is difficult to discern a pattern in these results, and the waters become even more muddied by the fact that Bransford (1973), Dispoto (1974, 1977), and Whitla (1978) found no clear pattern in DIT P-scores among various academic majors.

Three other investigations address differences in moral reasoning according to residential or social arrangement. Marlowe and Auvenshine (1982) traced changes in DIT P-scores over a nine-month period for freshmen in a liberal arts college. They were specifically interested in whether or not fraternity-affiliated freshmen differed from nonfraternity freshmen in terms of changes in P-score over the freshman year. Their findings indicated no statistically significant differences in moral reasoning changes between the two groups. Similar results are also reported by Sanders (1990). In the research reported by Rest and Deemer (1986), living on campus (versus commuting to college) was part of an academic orientation or involvement dimension positively associated with P-score gains over a ten-year period. This association remained statistically significant even after high school P-score was controlled. At face value, such evidence suggests that residential living may facilitate the development of principled moral judgment during college. It is likely, however, that this influence is indirect. That is, living on campus increases chances for the types of academic, intellectual, and social involvement that in turn directly enhance the development of principled moral judgment.

Moral Education Interventions

A promising line of research with respect to the influence of specific college experiences on student moral judgment comes from the moral education literature. Rather than simply assessing the specific college experiences associated with moral judgment, this research generally attempts to fashion curricular or course interventions with the major goal of fostering increases in the use of principled reasoning in judging moral issues. Most of the studies reporting the results of these interventions employed the Defining Issues Test as the measure of moral development. Schlaefli, Rest, and Thoma (1985) conducted a meta-analytical review of fifty-five such studies, all of which used the DIT. The review was not limited to college students but also included junior and senior high school students and adults. Various types of interventions were included in the review (for example, group discussion of moral dilemmas, psychological development programs, social studies and humanities courses), and length of the intervention was also considered. Because of the comprehensive nature of this review, a detailed discussion of its methodology and results is warranted.

As described by Schlaefli, Rest, and Thoma (1985, pp. 342–343), the types of interventions were as follows:

1. *Dilemma Discussion:* Programs that emphasize peer discussion of controversial moral dilemmas according to the suggestions of Kohlberg (e.g. Blatt and

Kohlberg, 1975). Frequently the reports of the programs cite Galbraith and Jones (1976) as the specific guide for their "Kohlbergian" programs. These guides give specific suggestions for setting up the group discussion, selecting dilemmas for the stimulus material and the role of the teacher as discussion leader. . . . Presumably the effective condition for facilitating development in this type of treatment is providing concentrated practice in moral problem solving, stimulated by peer give and take (challenging one another's thinking, reexamining assumptions, being exposed to different points of view, building lines of argument, and responding to counter argument).

2. *Personality Development*: Programs that emphasize personal psychological development and involve some experimental activity and intense self-reflection. Initiated by Mosher and Sprinthall (1970), these programs are intended to promote personality and social development in general, of which moral development is a major strand. The programs involve subjects in diverse kinds of activities (e.g., cross-age teaching, empathy training, communication skill training, cooperation simulation games, volunteer service work, keeping logs about one's personal thoughts and feelings), but the activities all have the objective of promoting reflection about the self and self in relation to others. What one learns about oneself in these concrete activities is blended with learning the general theories of developmental psychology through assigned readings and class discussions. Frequently, one of the theories that subjects encounter is Kohlberg's theory of moral judgment development.

3. *Academic Courses*: Programs that emphasize the academic content of humanities, social studies, literature, or contemporary issues. These programs do not focus as much as the previous two groupings of programs on extended practice in moral problem solving or personal development activities. While value issues are discussed and related to real life events, emphasis is placed on learning bodies of information and the basic tenets of academic discipline. The contents of these programs are varied (criminal justice and U.S. law, great books, various topics in social studies).

4. *Short Term*: In this last group are programs where duration was short term—only three weeks or less. These programs are characterized not by type of activity in the intervention, but by the shortness of the intervention. [Schlaefli, A., Rest, J., & Thoma, S. (1985). Does moral education improve moral judgment? A meta-analysis of intervention studies using the Defining Issues Test. *Review of Educational Research, 55*, 319–352. Copyright (1985) by the American Educational Research Association. Reprinted by permission of the publishers.]

Using the procedure developed by Glass (1977), Schlaefli, Rest, and Thoma (1985) computed an effect size for each treatment and control group. This was defined as the difference between the mean of the pretest and posttest P-score divided by the average standard deviation within the groups of the study. Thus, the effect size was analogous to a standardized score or z score. Each effect size was subsequently weighted to reflect relative sample size within the total sample of experimental and control group subjects representing all studies. Consequently, an intervention with forty subjects was weighted twice as heavily in the aggregate results as one with twenty subjects. The principal findings from the synthesis indicated that dilemma discussion and personality development programs produced the strongest effects, that treatments longer than three weeks were more effective than shorter-term treatments, and that programs with adults (twenty-four years or older) produced larger effect sizes than programs with younger subjects.

Statistically significant effect sizes, however, were obtained for aggregate moral education interventions with all groups, including college students. The overall effect size for college students across all types of moral education interventions was .28. This can be considered a posttest improvement of 11 percentile points over the pretest and was statistically significant at $p < .05$. Conversely, the effect size for all control groups was .19, which failed to reach statistical significance at $p < .05$.

Although the results suggest small but statistically significant positive effects of moral education interventions on the moral judgment of college students, Schlaefli, Rest, and Thoma (1985) did not disaggregate the effects of different types of interventions for different subsamples (college students, junior high school students, and so on). To address this issue we reanalyzed the data specifically for the college student sample. Data from an additional study by Straub and Rodgers (1978) were included in our reanalysis since they were apparently not included in the original Schlaefli, Rest, and Thoma review. The inclusion of this additional study had a negligible influence on the results. Using information on each study and an identical weighting procedure, we conducted a 4 (type of intervention) × 2 (randomized versus nonrandomized design) analysis of variance with effect size as the dependent measure. Only the experimental conditions were considered, and because of unequal cell sizes, a least-squares solution was employed.

Controlling for type of intervention, we found no statistically significant difference between effect size of studies with random assignment of subjects to treatments (effect size of .34) and those without random assignment (effect size of .26). Thus, the strength of the study design was generally unrelated to the magnitude of the results for college students. This finding was consistent with the overall findings of Schlaefli, Rest, and Thoma's (1985) synthesis.

Controlling for randomized versus nonrandomized design, we found a statistically significant ($p < .05$) difference in effect size across the four types of interventions. The most effective in stimulating growth in college students' principled moral judgment were dilemma discussion (effect size of .51) and personality development (effect size of .41). These represent gains in moral reasoning during the interventions of 19.5 and 16 percentile points, respectively. Academic courses were somewhat less effective (effect size of .17).[2] By far the least effective were short-term interventions (effect size of .03). These translate into a gain of 7 and 1 percentile points, respectively. Again, these results for college students in particular closely parallel the results obtained by Schlaefli, Rest, and Thoma (1985) when adults and students from all levels of formal education were pooled.

Clearly, the small sample sizes and the attendant instability of effect sizes based on so few cases must be considered when interpreting the results of our reanalysis of Schlaefli, Rest, and Thoma's (1985) data for college students. Nevertheless, the findings do suggest that purposefully designed curricular or course interventions can have positive, if modest, effects on the development of principled moral judgment during college. In terms of research studies that use the Defining Issues Test, moral education interventions that employ dilemma discussion and those that emphasize personality development appear to be the most influential. These results need to be tempered, however, by the tendency for the two most effective interventions to include activities (for example, moral problem solving, introduction of Kohlberg's theory) that are quite similar to the criterion measure, the Defining Issues Test. Thus, a certain tautological possibility may have contributed to the findings.[3]

While the body of research focusing on the influence of educational interventions on moral judgment as measured by the Defining Issues Test is by far the most extensive, a few studies looked at the relationship between educational interventions and other measures of moral judgment. Boyd (1980) evaluated the effects of a course intervention for college sophomores designed to stimulate development in moral judgment by integrating material from an introductory philosophy course in ethics with perspectives on late-adolescent moral development taken from Kohlberg's theory. Students could choose whether or not to take the course, thus introducing the possibilities of selection bias and the interaction of selection and change as potential threats to the internal validity of the study. To counter this, Boyd used an elaborate matching procedure to achieve a reasonably equivalent control group of students who did not receive the intervention. The control group was chosen, as far as possible, from the same recruitment pool as those students in the course and was matched on grade level, age, sex, and degree of prior exposure to Kohlberg's theory. The experimental and control groups did not differ significantly on preintervention moral maturity scores from the Moral Judgment Interview. An immediate postintervention assessment showed significantly greater change toward postconventional stages of moral reasoning by the experimentals than by the controls. A follow-up posttest administered nine months later showed similar differences, but they failed to reach statistical significance.

Similar results are reported by Page and Bode (1982). They had freshman and sophomore students in three sections of an ethics course (experimental group) and one section of an introductory psychology course (control group) complete the Ethical Reasoning Inventory (ERI) at the beginning and end of a ten-week academic quarter. The ERI is another paper and pencil measure of Kohlberg's stages of moral reasoning that employs the six Kohlbergian dilemmas and prototypic statements representing Stages 1–5. (It correlates .54 with the Moral Judgment Interview and .57 with the Defining Issues Test.) The experimental ethics course focused on the rational evaluation and justification of traditional normative ethical theories. Important historical ethical theories, such as utilitarianism and Kantianism, were examined as examples of various types of ethical theories, and reasons were given for accepting or rejecting them. In order to avoid contamination of the results through increased familiarity with dilemmas or Kohlberg's theory, no discussion of Kohlberg's stages of moral development or any of the ERI dilemmas was undertaken in the course. Here Page and Bode differed in design from the earlier study by Boyd (1980), which did introduce the experimental group to Kohlberg's theory.

Since students were not randomly assigned to experimental and control conditions, Page and Bode (1982) had the internal validity problems inherent in a nonequivalent control group design (selection bias, interaction of selection and change, and so on). Fortunately, however, the experimental and control groups were almost identical in terms of pretest scores on the ERI. At the end of the ten-week quarter, the students in the experimental ethics course showed significantly greater average gain in ERI scores from pretest to posttest than did students in the control group.

In contrast to Boyd (1980) and Page and Bode (1982), who focused on a specific course, Berson (1979) investigated the effects of an experimental, value-oriented liberal arts curriculum on moral development during the freshman year. Compared to a standard course of study, the value-oriented curriculum had no significantly greater effect on moral maturity scores of the freshmen.

Faust and Arbuthnot (1978) took a somewhat different tack in their research. They were interested in the effects of a moral education intervention on college students but, in addition, anticipated that the effectiveness of such a program would depend to some extent on the student's stage of Piagetian cognitive development. To test this hypothesis, they conducted an experiment in which students were enrolled in a five-week moral education program or a control group not in the program. The moral education program was based on Blatt and Kohlberg (1975) and stressed exposure to intensive moral argument and discussion. The dependent measure was Form A of a standardized Kohlberg questionnaire. The results indicated an overall statistically significant effect on moral reasoning development that favored the moral education program. The magnitude of the effect, however, varied for students at different Piagetian reasoning stages. For those functioning primarily at the concrete stage, the advantage of the moral education program was only one-third as large as the advantage of the program for those students who were at a more advanced Piagetian stage. Such results suggest the possibility that not all college students may benefit equally from Kohlbergian moral education programs based on moral argument and discussion. Rather, Piagetian stage of cognitive development may function to set a ceiling on development in moral reasoning and, consequently, on the benefits derived from Kohlbergian moral education interventions.

Conditional Effects of College

Little research has been concerned with the question of whether the effects of college or of specific college experiences on the development of principled moral reasoning differ for different kinds of students. Two studies have conducted analyses that directly address the issue. First Loxley and Whiteley (1986) report evidence (based on the use of the DIT) to suggest that males show significantly greater increases in principled moral reasoning from the freshman to senior year than do a comparable group of women. At first glance this finding seems to suggest, as some have argued (Gilligan, 1977, 1982a), that the Kohlbergian conception of development in moral reasoning has a male bias. The Loxley and Whiteley study, however, focused on whether college had a differential impact on *changes* in moral reasoning for men and women, not on whether men scored higher than women. Furthermore, little evidence is presented in other investigations to corroborate their results. Consequently, the evidence reported by Loxley and Whiteley may hold only for the particular sample they analyzed. Overall, we are as yet unconvinced that college has a consistently stronger impact on the development of principled moral reasoning in men than in women.

The second conditional effect, reported by Faust and Arbuthnot (1978) and reviewed above, suggests that the impact on principled moral reasoning of a Kohlbergian moral education intervention depends on the student's level of Piagetian cognitive development prior to the intervention. Those initially high in cognitive development (formal reasoners) benefited substantially more from the intervention in terms of growth in moral maturity than did those initially lower in cognitive development (concrete reasoners). This finding in general is consistent both with developmental theory and with evidence suggesting that the dimensions of student development during college do not change in isolation from each other. Specifically, it supports the evidence by Cauble (1976) and Rowe and Marcia (1980), cited earlier in this chapter, that formal reasoning tends to be a necessary condition for the development of principled moral judgment.

Long-Term Effects of College

Few investigations have attempted to assess the long-term impact of college on the development of principled moral reasoning. Those that do, however, tend to be unequivocal in their findings. The longitudinal study of Colby, Kohlberg, Gibbs, & Lieberman (1983) reviewed earlier found that the MJI moral maturity score of a sample of men twenty years after high school graduation had a partial correlation of .26 with years of formal education even when high school intelligence and socioeconomic status were controlled statistically.

The evidence reported by Rest and Deemer (1986), also reviewed earlier in the chapter, is perhaps more direct. Rest and Deemer traced the DIT P-score changes of a sample of high school graduates who went to college versus a sample whose formal education ended with high school. The DIT was administered four times between graduation from high school in 1972 and 1983, approximately ten years later. Although the group that went to college started out with somewhat higher P-scores than the group that did not, the initial difference approximately doubled during the ten-year period. Thus, the two groups showed increasing divergence in developmental patterns over time. The P-scores of subjects who only completed high school tended to plateau between two and four years after high school graduation; for the next six years they actually regressed to a point only slightly above what they were at high school graduation. Conversely, the college group continued to increase in P-score over the ten-year period. The greatest increases came during the four years after high school graduation (approximately the time of one's undergraduate education). During the next six years the P-score increase for the college group was less pronounced, but in dramatic contrast to the regression for the high school group, it did not regress. These differences remained even after statistical controls were made for secondary school DIT scores.

Given the problems of bias in self-selection between college and noncollege subjects, there is some risk in attributing these differences in developmental patterns to postsecondary education. Nevertheless, the differences reported by Rest and Deemer (1986) appear to be independent of secondary school DIT scores, and the pattern of gains they report is just the opposite of what would be expected from regression artifacts. The latter finding, in particular, fits the notion of college impact as an accentuation of initial differences (Feldman & Newcomb, 1969). Moreover, Rest and Deemer's results are also consistent with the hypothesis that one of the long-term impacts of college is its capacity for allocating individuals to occupations and life-styles that further enhance or at least maintain developmental trends initiated in the undergraduate years. Thus, as compared with the group that only completed high school, those in the college sample may have maintained their P-score level between the fourth and tenth years of the study because college itself increased the likelihood of their entering postcollege environments characterized by Kohlberg's (1969) salient influences on moral development (continued intellectual challenge, exposure to divergent views and cognitive moral conflict, contact with others at the postconventional level of moral judgment, and the like).

Although individuals who attend college may be more likely to enter such occupational or life-style environments than high school graduates,

Rest and Deemer (1986) further point out that differences in posteducation environments have a statistically significant association with moral reasoning development independent of level of formal education attained. In their follow-up interview data, they identified a dimension that assessed the degree to which a person's posteducational life was characterized by a high degree of continued intellectual stimulation. For example, entering a professional job with many intellectual challenges was coded high, while entering a job with few intellectual challenges or not working at all was coded low. A regression analysis found that level of continuing intellectual stimulation accounted for a statistically significant 12 percent of the variance in tenth-year P-scores over and above that due to high school P-scores and highest level of formal education. This would suggest that while college attendance may increase the likelihood of one's entering an occupation or having a life-style characterized by high continuing intellectual stimulation, it does not necessarily guarantee it.

College and Moral Behavior

As we have stressed in this chapter, nearly all the research on the influence of college on moral development has defined moral development in terms of principled moral reasoning or judgment. There is reasonably strong evidence to indicate that college positively influences the use of principled reasoning in judging moral issues. More ambiguous is the link between college and actual moral *behavior*. Fortunately, however, there is an impressive body of evidence to suggest positive, systematic links between principled moral reasoning and what might be considered moral behavior among college students. With few exceptions (for example, Fontana & Noel, 1973; Forsyth & Berger, 1982), level of principled moral reasoning has been found to have statistically significant positive associations with resistance to cheating behavior (Dunivant, 1975; Houston, 1983; Krebs & Kohlberg, 1975; Leming, 1978, 1979; Malinowski, 1978; Malinowski & Smith, 1985; Schwartz, Feldman, Brown, & Heingartner, 1969), resistance to peer pressure (Froming & Cooper, 1976), resistance to unlawful or oppressive authority in the Milgram "shock experiment" paradigm (Kohlberg & Candee, 1984), and civil disobedience (Haan, 1975; Haan, Smith, & Block, 1968; Keniston, 1969; Candee & Kohlberg, 1987). It has also been found to be significantly and positively linked with "whistle blowing" on corruption (Brabeck, 1984a), keeping contractual promises (Jacobs, 1975; Givner & Hynes, 1983), political and social activism (Nassi, Abramowitz, & Youmans, 1983; Steibe, 1980), nonaggression (Bredemeier & Shields, 1984), and helping behavior (Andreason, 1975; McNamee, 1972, 1978; Schwartz, Feldman, Brown, & Heingartner, 1969; Staub, 1974).

From this evidence, we can offer at least the tentative hypothesis that the influence of college on moral behavior is basically indirect. College appears to foster increases in one's use of principled reasoning to judge moral issues that in turn and under certain conditions may enhance the likelihood of morally motivated behavior. Thus, the major influence of college on moral behavior may be transmitted largely through its impact on the development of principled moral reasoning. Of course, this hypothesized indirect effect is essentially an extrapolation from two independent bodies of evidence, both of which are highly correlational. While the hypothesis has a certain logical and intuitive appeal, it remains speculative and obviously requires fuller and more comprehensive verification.

Summary

Change During College

The weight of evidence from a large number of studies that used different instruments and were conducted in different cultures clearly indicates that college is linked with statistically significant increases in the use of principled reasoning to judge moral issues. Not only do upperclassmen tend to show higher levels of principled reasoning than freshmen or sophomores, but students also make nonchance increases in the use of moral reasoning during college. The relative magnitude of these gains is difficult to determine from the evidence presented. However, the exact magnitude of the gain may not be as important as the fact that the major movement from conventional to postconventional or principled judgment during college is itself an important event in moral development.

Net Effects of College

The weight of evidence also indicates that the college experience itself has a unique positive influence on increases in principled moral reasoning. This influence appears to be substantially greater in magnitude than that due merely to maturation and cannot be attributed solely to initial differences in moral reasoning, intelligence, or social status between those who attend and those who do not attend college. Of course, even with these important variables controlled statistically, one cannot be certain that all confounding influences have been taken into account. Individual differences among students related to their likelihood of attending or not attending college may be the true causal influences underlying differential change in moral reasoning rather than the college experience itself. This particular confounding influence is a potential threat to the internal validity of even the most carefully conducted longitudinal studies of the effect of college on moral reasoning.

It is also important to note that the evidence suggesting a net positive influence of college on the development of principled moral reasoning is consistent with more broadly based findings on the effects of college on values. These findings, from an extensive series of national samples, suggest that college attendance is associated with a humanizing of values and attitudes concerning the rights and welfare of others.

Between-College Effects

Evidence concerning between-college effects on moral reasoning is nearly nonexistent. Our own reanalysis of available data suggests that such differences may indeed exist. However, differences in student recruitment and selection standards among institutions make any causal conclusion drawn from such analysis highly tentative. Findings from one study are consistent with the notion that the student peer context may function to accentuate initial differences among colleges in terms of gains in principled moral reasoning. However, this finding awaits replication.

Within-College Effects

The evidence pertaining to the influence of different college experiences on principled moral judgment is somewhat equivocal in terms of offering consistent, replicable findings. This may not be too surprising in that, as Rest (1986a, 1986b) points out, developmental theory in no way guarantees that one particular type of life experience is the preeminent cause of development in principled moral reasoning. A certain specific experience, then, might foster development if it happens to a receptive and reflective individual and if it is accompanied by other experiences in a cumulative and mutually reinforcing pattern. The key role of college in fostering principled moral reasoning may therefore lie in providing a range of intellectual, cultural, and social experiences from which a range of different students might potentially benefit.

From this perspective there is modest support for what, according to Kohlberg's (1969) theories, are salient experiences in the fostering of growth in moral development. College experiences in which an individual is exposed to divergent perspectives (for example, living away from home, intellectual interactions with roommates) or is confronted with cognitive moral conflict (such as courses presenting issues from different perspectives) were reported by students as having a salient influence on their moral development. Also consistent with Kohlberg's expectations are students' specification of the importance of interactions with upperclassmen in residential facilities (that is, exposure to more advanced stages of moral reasoning) and assuming new personal responsibilities, such as social role taking. These experiences form a major part of the intellectual and interpersonal opportunities that characterize residential colleges and universities. However, it would appear to be the extent to which an individual takes advantage of these opportunities, particularly those having an intellectual or academic content, that is the key determinant of growth in moral reasoning during college.

Little consistent evidence exists to suggest that academic major or broad curricular categorizations are systematically associated with differences in the development of moral judgment. Certain specific curricular or course interventions with college students, however, do appear to foster the increased use of principled reasoning in judging moral issues. The most consistently effective interventions are those that emphasize moral dilemma discussion or personality development. This conclusion seems to hold regardless of the methodological rigor of the study. While these academic interventions would appear to enhance moral development, it is clear from the evidence reviewed that their effect, as well as the effect of any specific college experience, is smaller than the effect that can be reasonably attributed to four years of college. This conclusion is consistent with that of Rest (1986a). One possible explanation for this is that, similar to its impact on cognitive development, the influence of college on principled moral reasoning is the result not so much of any single experience but rather of the cumulative impact of a set of mutually reinforcing experiences. Another possibility is that the influence of different course interventions or specific college experiences on moral reasoning is conditional rather than general (that is, the magnitude of the influence varies for different kinds of students).

Conditional Effects of College

Almost no research has systematically looked for conditional effects. The little evidence that does exist suggests that an instructional intervention that stresses exposure to intensive moral arguments and discussion has more positive effects on principled moral judgment for subjects at high levels of cognitive development (formal reasoners) than for subjects at lower levels (concrete reasoners). This underscores the notion that moral development does not occur in isolation from other areas of student development during college but rather is a part of a network of mutually supporting changes.

Long-Term Effects of College

Evidence from ten- and twenty-year longitudinal studies is clear in identifying the positive, long-term influence of college on principled moral reasoning. The estimated advantages that accrue to those who attend college (versus those who do not) do not diminish over time but tend to increase. In large measure this may be due to the tendency for college to channel individuals into posteducation occupations and life-styles characterized by a level of continuing intellectual stimulation and challenge that either maintains or further enhances principled moral judgment. Conversely, having only a high school diploma may tend to channel one into occupational or life-style environments characterized by a relatively low level of intellectual stimulation. Thus, level of principled moral judgment may actually regress over time.

College and Moral Behavior

Finally, on the basis of two separate bodies of evidence, we have hypothesized an indirect effect of college on moral behavior or action. We have suggested that the major impact of college is to foster the increased use of principled reasoning in judging moral issues. This in turn appears to be linked systematically and perhaps causally to a range of principled behaviors, including resisting cheating, social activism, keeping contractual promises, and helping those in need. Thus, college may enhance principled behavior by first fostering an increase in one's principled moral reasoning.

Notes

1. Not all research is totally consistent with this general trend. For example, while Astin (1977a) found general freshman-to-senior increases in the value students placed on "helping others who are in difficulty," he found a corresponding decrease in the importance one attached to "participation in an organization like the Peace Corps or VISTA." Similarly, Levine (1980), employing attitudinal data, impressions of administrators, and various behavioral measures, concluded that the reasons why individuals are attending college have changed significantly from the altruistic toward the materialistic. As suggested by Rest (personal communication, 1988), it is difficult to integrate these findings with those of statistically significant gains in principled moral reasoning during college. One possibility, however, is that the findings of Levine (1980), in particular, are capturing somewhat temporary, broad-based societal fluctuations that are distinct from the more consistent trends in individual growth captured by the various instruments that assess moral reasoning. Clearly, social and economic trends may have a significant influence on the direction and extent of college effects; this may be particularly true in the areas of career choice and career values. It does not necessarily follow, however, that college is prevented from having at least some consistent influence on individual students that is independent of trends in society. With respect to impacts on moral reasoning, we suggest that the weight of reliable evidence indicates the presence of such an independent influence. We think this is particularly the case given the extensive national evidence on college attendance and values presented by Hyman and Wright (1979).

2. An unpublished study by Penn (1988), which we uncovered too late to include in this analysis, suggests that not all academic courses in this category are equally effective in enhancing moral reasoning. Specifically, Penn found that an ethics course facilitated greater DIT gains than courses in political science, religious studies (Theology of Peace and Justice), and social work. The ethics course provided a foundation in formal logic and Kohlbergian theory and then introduced students to philosophical methods of technical analysis and their application to social issues.

3. There is some evidence that an integrated curriculum that stresses decision making and the formulation of values and moral choice may be more effective than a traditional liberal arts program in enhancing moral development as measured by the DIT (Seybert & Mustapha, 1988). However, this finding has yet to be replicated.

9

Educational Attainment

Social mobility, as defined by changes in occupational status and income, is inextricably linked to postsecondary education in modern American society. Colleges and universities have been traditionally entrusted not only with the education of individuals but also with their certification. Indeed, a bachelor's degree has often been referred to as a passport to the American middle class (for example, Bowles & Gintis, 1976; Jencks & Riesman, 1968).

Much of the recent evidence concerning the centrality of educational attainment in the process of intergenerational social mobility is based on the seminal model of occupational attainment developed by Blau and Duncan (1967) and the Wisconsin social-psychological model of status attainment developed by Sewell, Hauser, and their associates (for example, Sewell, Haller, & Portes, 1969; Sewell & Hauser, 1975). These models are theoretically important because they suggest a new approach to the understanding of social mobility; they view social mobility as a process of status attainment that develops over the life cycle. This approach differs from earlier social mobility analysis in that it focuses on the extent to which the occupational status of the son or daughter is a function not only of family social status (education, occupation, and income of parents and so on) and individual ability but also of critical intervening experiences (such as influence of significant others and educational attainment). While the initial specifications of these models were concerned primarily with the explanation of occupational status, this view has been expanded by others to include both occupational status and income (for example, Duncan, 1968; Featherman & Carter, 1976; Jencks et al., 1979).

Formal schooling, typically defined either as years of schooling completed or degrees attained, plays an important dual role in these dynamic models of the status attainment process. First, it plays an indirect role by mediating the influence of the individual's background resources (for instance, family socioeconomic status) on subsequent occupational status and income. Since family socioeconomic status has an impact on college attendance beyond ability or achievement (for example, Brim, Glass, Neulinger, & Firestone, 1969; Christensen, Melder, & Weisbrod, 1975; Eckland & Henderson, 1981; Schoenfeldt, 1968; Wegner & Sewell, 1970; Wolfle, 1985b), schooling will function to convert social-origin advantages into subsequent occupational and economic advantages for an individual. Second, formal schooling is posited as having a direct effect on status attainment, an effect that is independent of an individual's social origins. This is suggested by the finding that different levels of educational attainment produce different levels of status attainment among individuals with equivalent social backgrounds (for example, Duncan, Featherman, & Duncan, 1972; Haller, 1982; Hauser & Featherman, 1977; McClendon, 1976.) Figure 9.1 presents a general model of the role of educational attainment in the status attainment process.

Thus, the major models of status attainment posit a salient role for formal schooling. A particularly crucial level of formal schooling in differentiating subsequent status attainment levels is attainment of the bachelor's degree. Indeed, as we shall see in greater detail in subsequent chapters, there is abundant evidence that the completion of a bachelor's degree is central to the determination of both occupational status and income (for example, Bowen, 1977; Jencks et al., 1979; Knox, Lindsay, & Kolb, 1988; Leslie & Brinkman, 1986; Sewell & Hauser, 1972). If educational attainment has such a pivotal influence on one's ultimate occupational and economic status, one might legitimately ask how variations in the collegiate experience affect educational attainment. This chapter synthesizes the accumulated evidence addressing this question. In doing so it departs slightly from the organization of previous chapters. In focusing on educational attainment, it makes little sense to talk about development during college or the net effects of college. This chapter is therefore concerned with between-college effects, within-college effects, conditional effects, and long-term effects of college. In the last category we concentrate largely on intergenerational effects, such as the transfer of benefits from parents to their sons and daughters.

Status attainment models and much of the status attainment research focus on formal completion of the undergraduate or graduate degree, and one cannot easily separate the process of degree attainment from that of student persistence. Persistence, whether at a particular educational institution or in the postsecondary system generally, is obviously an important determinant of a student's eventual attainment levels (for example, Kocher & Pascarella, 1988; Tinto, 1987). Indeed, individual persistence can legitimately be considered a necessary, if not sufficient, condition for degree attainment. Consequently, in reviewing the evidence on the influence of college on educational attainment, we will touch selectively on the vast body of evidence that deals with student persistence and withdrawal behavior.

Similarly, there is evidence to suggest that level of educational aspiration has an independent and significant influence on ultimate educational attainment (for example, Astin, 1975b; Pascarella, Smart, Ethington, & Nettles, 1987; Stoecker, Pascarella, & Wolfle, 1988), thus indirectly affecting occupational and economic attainments. Consequently, we will also se-

Figure 9.1. A General Model of Status Attainment.

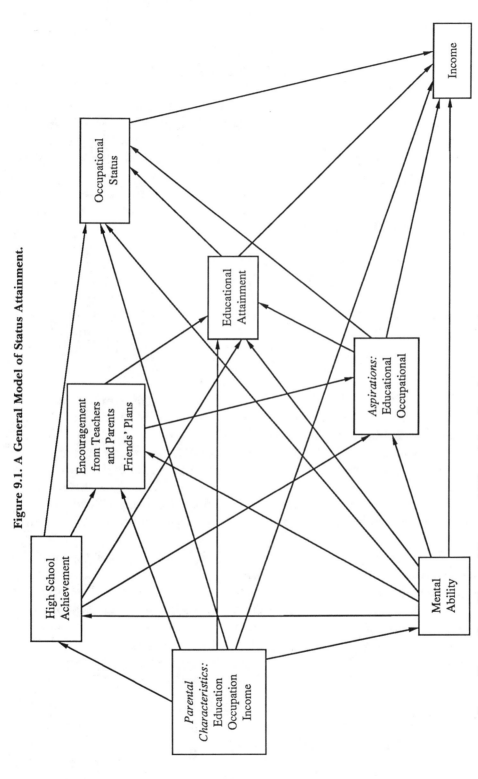

Source: Drawn from Blau and Duncan, 1967, and Sewell and Hauser, 1975.

lectively consider the evidence that college experiences influence educational aspirations.

Between-College Effects

There is a substantial amount of evidence that where one begins his or her postsecondary education has a statistically significant influence on educational aspirations, persistence, and eventual level of educational attainment. In some cases the influence of institutional characteristics is direct and clear-cut. In other cases, however, the influence is more complex, having both direct and indirect components.

Two-Year Versus Four-Year Institutions

In an early major sociological critique, Clark (1960) discussed at length the role of the two-year college in the selection and allocation of students for further education and occupational placement. His principal thesis was that the public two-year college systems could be considered a form of "tracking" in which the predominantly working- and lower-middle-class students who attend two-year institutions are "cooled out" and led away from the path to a bachelor's degree. Specifically, the cooling-out process is one in which the curriculum, the socializing agents of the college (faculty and student peers), and administrative procedures combine to lower students' educational and occupational goals (Hunt, Klieforth, & Atwell, 1977; Karabel, 1972; Shea, 1974). Consistent with this view is the notion that public two-year community colleges are, comparatively speaking, institutions of lower-social-status groups in American society (Astin, 1972a; Monk-Turner, 1982) and that rather than fostering social mobility for these groups, such colleges tend to contribute to the reproduction of existing class differences (for example, Grubb, 1984; Karabel, 1974, 1986; Pincus, 1980; Zwerling, 1976).

Such a critique may underestimate the contributions of community colleges to social mobility (for example, Cohen & Brawer, 1982), particularly when the socioeconomic attainments of community college students are compared to those whose formal education ends with high school (Nunley & Breneman, 1988). Nevertheless, there is consistent evidence that initial attendance at a two-year rather than a four-year college lowers the likelihood of one's attaining a bachelor's degree. For example, in a typical study Velez (1985) used the National Longitudinal Study of the High School Class of 1972 (NLS-72) to determine the influence of starting college at a two-year versus a four-year institution on completion of the bachelor's degree (or above) by 1979. The sample was limited to only those enrolled in academic programs; family socioeconomic status, gender, race, initial degree aspirations, academic ability, secondary school achievement, college grades, and place of residence were controlled statistically. Net of these factors, four-year college entrants had a statistically significant 18.7 percent advantage over two-year college entrants in completing a bachelor's degree within seven years after secondary school graduation.

Other analyses of the NLS-72 data with slightly different controls or subsamples have yielded consistent results with respect to the negative influence of initially enrolling in a two-year college on persistence in higher education, bachelor's degree attainment, or attendance in graduate or professional school (for example, Anderson, 1981, 1984; Breneman & Nelson, 1981; Hilton & Schrader, 1986; Levin & Clowes, 1980; National Center for Education Statistics, 1977; Robertshaw & Wolfle, 1983; Thomas & Gordon, 1983). Moreover, the same inhibiting influence on persistence and degree attainment has been found with analyses that control for salient background characteristics (academic ability, family socioeconomic status, initial degree aspirations, age, employment, and so on) conducted on samples other than the NLS-72 (for example, Alba & Lavin, 1981; Astin, 1972a, 1975b, 1977a, 1982; Folger, Astin, & Bayer, 1969; Crook & Lavin, 1989; Kohen, Nestel, & Karmas, 1978; Temple & Polk, 1986; Trent & Medsker, 1968).

Although there is some evidence that students aspiring to subbaccalaureate vocational training obtain more education if they initially enter a two-year (versus a four-year) college (Dougherty, 1987), the weight of evidence is reasonably clear that when assessed over the same period of time, baccalaureate aspirants who enter two-year colleges tend to have lower levels of educational and degree attainment than do comparable individuals who enter four-year institutions. Dougherty (1987) has suggested three mechanisms by which initial entrance into a community college hinders educational attainment: (1) high levels of attrition within the community college, (2) difficulty in transferring to four-year colleges, and (3) attrition after transfer. These three mechanisms act like a funnel in terms of their impact, and at each stage different forces may be at work. For example, attrition in the community college may be a function of those institutions' relatively low levels of prestige in the postsecondary system and the absence of residence facilities. The former may lead to a lack of student commitment to the institution (Tinto, 1975), while the latter may have an inhibiting influence on student social integration or involvement (Astin, 1973b). Similarly, problems in securing acceptance, obtaining financial aid, and transferring credits pose nontrivial administrative obstacles in transferring from two-year to four-year institutions. Finally, attrition after transfer may be precipitated by a substantial drop in grades (Kintzer & Wattenbarger, 1985) and difficulty in becoming successfully integrated into a new social setting.

Institutional "Quality"

Although the effects on educational attainment of initial entry into a two-year versus a four-year institution tend to be direct and unequivocal, this is not always the case with other institutional characteristics, such as the various indexes of so-called college "quality." Measures of college "quality" typically include one or more of the following indexes: the academic selectivity of the student body (average SAT and ACT scores, for instance; Astin & Henson, 1977), institutional resources (such as endowment or educational expenditures per student), and prestige and reputational ratings. The weight of evidence suggests that the influence of these characteristics and, in particular, selectivity on educational attainment is complex and in some ways contradictory.

In attempting to understand the influence of college "quality" on educational attainment, it is important to note that "high quality" colleges start with a distinct advantage in terms of the academic ability, educational aspirations, level and clarity of career ambition, and family financial resources of the students they recruit and enroll (for example, Astin, 1965c, 1982; Clark, Heist, McConnell, Trow, & Yonge, 1972; Hearn, 1984; Karabel & Astin, 1975). As a group, these particular students are characterized by precollege traits that make them especially likely to obtain the bachelor's degree and in many cases move on to graduate or professional school. An additional advantage of highly selective institutions is that a student's gaining admission represents a considerable achievement in itself. The harder it is to get into a college, the more committed the entering student may be to staying there and completing the degree. Kocher and Pascarella (1988), for example, found that net of secondary school achievement, family socioeconomic status, and precollege degree and occupational aspirations, the expectation of transferring during college was negatively associated with the selectivity of the four-year institution in which the student first enrolled.

These initial advantages in the precollege characteristics of the students enrolled account for much of the subsequent advantage shown by selective institutions in student persistence, bachelor's degree completion, and the percentage of graduates moving on to graduate and professional school (Astin, 1961, 1962; Clewell & Ficklen, 1986; Cope & Hannah, 1975; Tinto, 1987). At the same time, however, institutional selectivity tends to enhance various forms of persistence and educational attainment even after variations in the background characteristics of the students enrolled at different institutions are taken into account. For example, in a recent analysis of a national sample, Stoecker, Pascarella, and Wolfle (1988) sought to determine both the institutional and the individual factors accounting for bachelor's degree (or advanced degree) attainment within a nine-year period after initial college enrollment. Net of secondary school achievement, family socioeconomic status, precollege degree aspirations, commitment to the institution attended, and certain collegiate experiences (for example, grades, social involvement), a measure of student body selectivity and institutional financial resources was found to significantly and positively influence bachelor's degree attainment. Similarly, Perrucci (1980), using a sample of college graduates followed up seven years after graduation, found that undergraduate college selectivity significantly increased both graduate school enrollment and obtaining a graduate degree even when college grades, gender, and freshman and senior job expectations were controlled statistically.

Other studies that controlled for important differences in precollege traits and collegiate experiences of students in different institutions report generally, though not totally, consistent findings. Astin (1969c, 1975b), Anderson (1984), Fetters (1977), and McClelland (1990)—with independent samples—all report a substantial positive influence of college selectivity and/ or prestige on persistence or bachelor's degree attainment. Additional analyses by Kamens (1979), Anderson (1986), and Thomas (1981c), the latter two on the same NLS-72 sample, suggest a less pronounced influence. On the basis of analyses of four independent, national samples, Alexander and Eckland (1977); Ethington and Smart (1986); Henson (1980); Pascarella, Smart, Ethington, and Nettles (1987); Smart (1986); and Tinto (1980) all report that measures of institutional selectivity or prestige had small but statistically significant positive effects on general educational attainment or enrollment in graduate or professional school. The only exception to this was Sharp (1970). The findings of Spaeth (1968b), Henson (1980), and Lang (1987) further indicate that attending a selective undergraduate institution significantly increases one's chances of also attending a graduate or professional school of high "quality" or "prestige" even when student background traits and undergraduate academic performance are taken into account.

The weight of evidence, then, suggests that traditional indexes of institutional "quality" (in particular, student body selectivity) significantly enhance institutional persistence and educational attainment. It is difficult, however, to isolate the causal mechanisms that underlie this influence. In terms of institutional persistence and obtaining the bachelor's degree, Lenning, Beal, and Sauer (1980) and Tinto (1987) have suggested that an important contextual effect of selective colleges is to increase student commitment to the institution. Since the privilege of enrolling comes at such a high cost (both financially and in terms of academic effort and achievement), so too the perceived costs of leaving or failing to graduate are correspondingly high. If the student perceives that a particular college confers high adult social status on its graduates, the greater the value he or she will place on membership in it and graduation from it (Kamens, 1971).

Part of the positive net influence of college selectivity or prestige on attending graduate or professional school may also be the result of an accentuation of initial educational or career aspirations. Although selective, prestigious colleges are likely to attract students with initially high educational aspirations, there is substantial evidence that attendance at such an institution has an additional positive influence on educational aspirations and plans for graduate and professional school above and beyond initial aspirations (for example, Astin, 1977a; Astin & Panos 1969; Drew & Astin, 1972; Gurin & Epps, 1975; McClelland, 1986; Pascarella, 1985c). The accentuation of initial aspirations may be the result of a contextual influence that is manifest through high faculty expectations (Kamens, 1974) and interactions with peers who themselves have high educational aspirations (Clark, Heist, McConnell, Trow, & Yonge, 1972; Pascarella, 1984a). It is at this point, however, that the picture becomes more complicated. This is due in large measure to the fact that institutional selectivity typically has a negative influence on college grades when student ability and/or secondary school achievement are taken into account (for example, Astin, 1971b, 1977a; Alexander & Eckland, 1977; Drew & Astin, 1972; Ethington & Smart, 1986; Pascarella, Smart, Ethington, & Nettles, 1987). Since college grades are such an important determinant of degree attainment and graduate and professional school enrollment (Ethington & Smart, 1986; Pascarella, Brier, Smart, & Herzog, 1987; Spaeth, 1968b, 1970), the indirect effect of college selectivity on educational attainment (through grades) is generally negative.

This negative indirect influence of college selectivity has sometimes been referred to as the "frog-pond" or "relative deprivation" effect (Bachman & O'Malley, 1986; Davis, 1966; Werts & Watley, 1969). According to this view, a student may lower aspirations in a more competitive environment because of relatively lower academic standing. While the negative indirect impact tends to diminish the positive influence of attending a selective institution on educational attainment, it does not totally counter it. Studies that have considered this issue report that the direct positive environmental influence of institutional selectivity is substantially greater than the negative indirect frog-pond or relative deprivation effect (for example, Drew & Astin, 1972; Ethington & Smart, 1986; Stoecker, Pascarella, & Wolfle, 1988). Consequently, the net total influence of institutional selectivity and prestige on such outcomes as educational aspirations, persistence, bachelor's degree attainment, and entering graduate or professional school tends to be positive.

The supportive information supplied by each of the studies reviewed above makes it difficult to estimate the magnitude of the positive effect of college quality on various indexes of educational aspirations and attainment. What is clear, however, is that the effect is modest. We estimate that net of other factors, measures of college selectivity and prestige account on the average for no more than one or two percent of the total variance in educational aspirations, persistence, bachelor's degree attainment, and educational attainment generally.

Institutional Control: Private Versus Public

Although the currently available evidence is not totally consistent, it does suggest that attending a private rather than a public college or university has a net positive influence on bachelor's degree attainment, plans for attending graduate school, and overall level of educational attainment. Moreover, this positive influence appears to be independent of the selectivity of the college attended. In a typical study, Smart (1986) examined the educational attainment (high school through an advanced degree) of a national sample of college students over the nine-year period following their enrollment in college. Statistically controlling for family social origins, secondary school academic achievement, gender, race, precollege occupational aspirations, the selectivity and size of the undergraduate college, college major, and grade point average, Smart found that attending a private college had a modest but statistically significant positive effect on educational attainment. Other studies, based on independent national samples and employing similar statistical controls, report similar findings with respect to the influence of attending a private college or bachelor's degree attainment and plans for attending graduate or professional school (Astin & Panos, 1969; Astin, 1975b, 1977a; Porter, 1989; Thomas, 1981b). Sharp (1970) reports somewhat less pronounced results for attending graduate school, and Gurin and Epps (1975) found no statistically significant relationship between attending a private rather than a public college and changes in freshman-year educational aspirations. The Gurin and Epps sample, however, was limited to only ten primarily black institutions, so it probably does not provide an adequate representation of private and public institutions.

It is difficult to isolate the causal mechanism underlying the relationship between attendance at a private institution and persistence or degree completion. It does not appear to be simply the result of private institutions being more academically selective or prestigious than public institutions; the positive relationship between attending a private college and degree completion remains even after measures of institutional selectivity and prestige are held constant statistically. As with institutional "quality," however, student commitment may be important in accounting for the higher rates of degree attainment at private colleges. Tuition fees at private colleges can be substantially higher than at their public counterparts. If the financial investment is greater, so too may be one's commitment to realizing the benefits of that investment by completing one's degree (for example, Manski & Wise, 1983).

Certain older private institutions (such as Antioch, Haverford, Swarthmore, and Reed) may have also developed a strong sense of organizational saga based on a distinctive mission and collective perceptions of unique institutional accomplishment and purpose (Clark, 1972). This distinctiveness can often engender remarkably high levels of personal loyalty and attachment to the institution and particular pride in being identified as a graduate of it. Similarly, a substantial number of private colleges are church related. For students who follow that religious faith, there is likely to be a strong personal commitment to persisting at that institution and earning one's degree (Astin, 1975b; Clewell & Ficklen, 1986; Stobaugh, 1972; Thomas, 1988).

A final contributing factor may be that most private colleges are residential, with students living on or near campus as opposed to living at home and commuting. Public institutions, on the other hand, tend to have a higher percentage of commuting students. As will be shown later in this chapter, there is clear evidence that living on campus exerts a net positive impact on persistence and degree attainment. Thus, the residential nature of private colleges may provide those colleges with an additional advantage in terms of retaining and graduating students.

Again, it is difficult from the studies reviewed to determine the magnitude of the net positive effect of attending a private college on persistence and degree completion. Our best estimate, however, is that the effect is small, about 1 percent of the total variance in these outcomes.

Institutional Size

Evidence pertaining to the influence of institutional size, that is, student enrollment, on educational attainment is inconsistent and at times contradictory. This conclusion holds even if one gives greater inferential weight to those studies that control for student precollege characteristics and/or other institutional characteristics. For example, Astin and Panos (1969) and Anderson (1984), controlling for student precollege characteristics and other institutional traits, found that attending a large institution had a negative influence on persistence or degree attainment. Kamens (1971), however, controlled for student social class and academic ability and found that large institutions (those with a student body of more than 5,000) had lower dropout rates than smaller institutions. Other investigations that employed similar statistical controls report no relationship between measures of institutional size and bachelor's degree attainment (Anderson, 1986; Stoecker, Pascarella, & Wolfle, 1988).

A similar pattern appears when one considers the influence of institutional size on general educational attainment, plans for attending graduate school, or actual enrollment in graduate school. Controlling for student precollege characteristics, institutional selectivity, and measures of the student's collegiate experience, Smart (1986) and Ethington and Smart (1986) report that institutional size increases educational attainment and enrollment in graduate school. Conversely, Astin (1963a) controlled for a battery of twenty-one student precollege traits and found that student body size had a negative influence on seniors' motivation to seek the doctoral degree. Sharp (1970) controlled for institutional characteristics such as selectivity, resources, and control and student traits such as age and college GPA, and she found that college size had a slight negative influence on graduate school attendance for men and a slight positive influence for women. In a similarly designed set of analyses, however, Stoecker and Pascarella (1988) found almost no relationship between institutional size and the educational attainment of women when student precollege characteristics, the selectivity and gender of the institution attended, and measures of collegiate academic and social success were taken into account. Similar results are reported by Pascarella (1985c) in a study of changes in male and female educational aspirations during the first two years of college.

The inconsistent and conflicting results from this body of research suggest that the magnitude of the net direct influence of college size on educational attainment is either trivial or conditional upon the specific characteristics of the students being considered. Unfortunately, the literature is unclear as to what those conditioning characteristics might be.

An alternative hypothesis, which has some supportive documentation, is that the major consistent influence of institutional size on educational attainment is negative but indirect in its impact. For example, in estimating a causal model of the status attainment of women, Stoecker and Pascarella (1988) took into account the following variables: family social status, secondary school academic and social achievement, precollege educational and career aspirations, institutional selectivity, percentage women, college major, college grades, college social involvement, and marital status. With the influence of these variables held constant statistically, institutional size had a trivial and statistically nonsignificant direct effect on educational attainment some nine years after initial enrollment in college. Institutional size, however, did have a statistically significant negative effect on student social involvement during college, which in turn had a positive net influence on educational attainment when other variables in the model were taken into account. (As we shall see in subsequent sections of this chapter, social involvement or social integration during college is a major determinant of persistence and degree attainment.) Consequently, although institutional size did not directly influence educational attainment, it did have a statistically significant negative indirect effect through its inhibiting influence on collegiate social involvement. A similar negative indirect influence on bachelor's degree attainment was found for both black and white men and women when a measure of institutional size that included enrollment, student-faculty ratio, and public versus private control was used (Stoecker, Pascarella, & Wolfle, 1988). Though statistically significant, these indirect effects are quite small, probably accounting for no more than one-half of one percent of the total variance in attainment.

That attending a large institution (or a large public institution) has an inhibiting influence on different dimensions of social involvement or integration during college is consistent with a substantial body of evidence. This evidence indicates that the inhibiting influence persists even when controls are made for salient student precollege traits, place of residence during college, and other institutional characteristics such as selectivity, percentage of white students as compared to percentage of black students, and percentage of men as compared to percentage of women (for example, Astin, 1977a; Astin & Panos, 1969; Baird, 1987; Pascarella, 1984a, 1985d; Stoecker & Pascarella, 1988; Stoecker, Pascarella, & Wolfle, 1988). Furthermore, such evidence is also consistent with the theoretical notion of redundancy in social settings. Barker (1968), Barker and Gump (1964), and Chickering (1969) have used the term *redundancy* to refer to a condition that exists in institutions when the number of people for a given setting exceeds the opportunities for active interpersonal participation. Thus, student isolation and anonymity would be most likely in more populous institutional settings. Conversely, as institutional size decreases, it presents the student with a more psychologically manageable setting in which the opportunities for social involvement and integration are enhanced. As we have seen in earlier chapters, the influence of institutional size on social involvement has indirect but important implications for outcomes other than just persistence or educational attainment.

Institutional Racial Composition

Although a significant minority of black men and women still attend historically black institutions, the majority of black students in the United States now attend institutions in which the student body is predominantly white (Peterson et al., 1979; Thomas & Hill, 1987; Trent, 1984). This increased racial integration of American postsecondary education has not been accomplished without certain negative side effects for black students. Much evidence, for example, suggests that black students who attend predominantly white colleges and universities experience significantly greater levels of social isolation, alienation, personal dissatisfaction, and overt racism than their counterparts at historically black institutions (for example, Allen, 1987; Allen, Bobo, & Fleuranges, 1984; Bean & Hull, 1984; Bennett, 1983; Bennett & Okinaka, 1984; Blackwell, 1981; Braddock, 1981a; Burrell, 1979; Davis, 1986; Edmonds, 1984; Guloyan, 1986; Livingston & Stewart, 1987; Loo & Rolison, 1986; Suen, 1983). Given this evidence, one might hypothesize that attendance at historically black colleges enhances the persistence and educational attainment of black students, and indeed most evidence supports this hypothesis.

In a study of the factors influencing student persistence in a national sample of college students, Astin (1975b) statistically controlled for an extensive battery of salient student background and precollege traits, such as family social status, academic ability, and educational aspirations. With the influence of these factors held constant, he found that black students were significantly less likely to drop out of college if they were enrolled in a predominantly black institution. Similar results have been reported by Cross and Astin (1981). Pascarella, Smart, Ethington, and Nettles (1987), using a national sample different from Astin's (1975b) or Cross and Astin's (1981), controlled for such factors as student socioeconomic background, secondary school achievement, precollege educational aspirations, college grades, and the size, control, and academic selectivity of the undergraduate institution attended. With these influences held constant statistically, attending a predominantly black college had a statistically significant positive direct effect on educational attainment over the nine-year period after college enrollment for black men. The corresponding effect for black women was positive but not statistically significant. Similarly, Brazziel (1983) found that for the five-year period from 1975 to 1980 predominantly black undergraduate institutions were significantly overrepresented as the baccalaureate college of origin of black doctoral recipients. Indeed, nine of the top ten undergraduate producers of black doctoral recipients during this period were predominantly black colleges and universities.

Other investigations based on a national data set (NLS-72) that controlled for student precollege characteristics and other institutional characteristics report somewhat smaller direct positive effects of attending a black institution on black student persistence and educational attainment (for example, Thomas, 1981b; Thomas & Gordon, 1983). Those studies that investigated educational attainment as a longitudinal causal process, however, suggest that an additional part of the influence of attending a predominantly black institution may be indirect. For example, in an analysis of bachelor's degree attainment that used the same sample as Thomas (1981b) and Thomas and Gordon (1983), Anderson (1985a) found that attending a predominantly black college was advantageous for black students in terms of a higher level of academic achievement. This factor in turn had a positive influence on bachelor's degree attainment.

Similar results have been reported by Pascarella, Smart, and Stoecker (1989) and Stoecker, Pascarella, and Wolfle (1988), who controlled for salient student precollege characteristics and the size and selectivity of the institution attended. In the first analysis, attending a black institution had a significant positive indirect effect on educational attainment for black women, which was transmitted largely through increased academic achievement. The corresponding indirect effect for black men was similar in magnitude but nonsignificant. (The positive total effect—the direct plus the indirect effect—of attending a black institution was slightly larger for black men than for black women). In the second analysis, attending a black institution was found to have a statistically significant positive indirect effect on bachelor's degree completion for black women but not for black men. Again, the indirect effect was largely the result of the positive influence of attending a predominantly black institution on collegiate academic achievement.

Combining the direct effect and the indirect effect mediated through academic achievement, the total positive impact of black colleges on black students' educational attainment is still small. It probably averages less than 1 percent of the total variance in various indexes of attainment.

Why attending a predominantly black college modestly enhances academic achievement (particularly for black women) is difficult to determine from the evidence presented. One hypothesis is that black students may earn higher grades at predominantly black, as opposed to predominantly white, institutions because the former are not as rich in educational resources or as academically competitive as the latter (for example, Bowles & DeCosta, 1971; Sowell, 1972). Indeed, in the Pascarella, Smart, and Stoecker (1989) study the correlation between college race (predominantly black = 1; predominantly white = 0) and a measure of student body academic selectivity and resources per student was −.53. On the other hand, a strong case has been made by Fleming (1984); Nettles, Thoeny, and Gosman (1986); and Willie and Cunnigen (1981) that black students who attend predominantly black institutions benefit from a supportive social, cultural, and racial environment that enhances their successful adaptation to the academic demands of undergraduate life. Thus, black students perform better academically at black institutions not because getting good grades is easier but because the social environment enhances their successful academic adjustment. Consistent with this perspective, Pascarella, Smart, and Stoecker (1987) found that black students performed better academically at predominantly black institutions even when statistical controls were made for the academic selectivity, financial resources, size, and control of the institution attended.

Institutional Gender Composition

In many ways the issue of the influence of institutional gender composition on educational attainment (or other measures of status attainment, for that matter) is rapidly becoming a moot point. For a number of reasons—social, economic, political, and cultural—the single-sex institution has become the academic equivalent of an endangered species. Tidball (1985), for example, estimates that about 98 percent of all women now enroll in coeducational colleges. Despite this fact, there is evidence to suggest that attending a single-sex institution is associated with higher levels of persistence and educational attainment, particularly for women (for example, Astin, 1977a; El-Khawas, 1980; Nelson, 1966; Tidball & Kistiakowsky, 1976). Studies that have attempted to estimate the effect of attending a single-sex institution on educational attainment have yielded somewhat mixed results, but the weight of evidence suggests a positive net influence. Astin (1977a), for example, controlled for an extensive battery of student precollege characteristics, such as educational aspirations, family social status, and secondary school achievement, and found that colleges for women still had a net positive direct effect on both educational degree aspiration and enrolling in graduate or professional school. Similar results have been reported by Brown (1982) and Smith (1988) in studies of changes in educational plans during college and by Brown (1982) in predicting actual enrollment in graduate or professional school subsequent to college.

Less supportive evidence for the positive direct influence on educational attainment of attending a single-sex or gender-dominated college is reported by Stoecker and Pascarella (1988) and by Gruca (1988) in slightly different analyses of the same sample. Stoecker and Pascarella controlled for student precollege characteristics; the selectivity, prestige, and size of the college attended; measures of collegiate academic and social achievement; and marital status. With these influences held constant, attending a predominantly women's college had positive but statistically nonsignificant direct and indirect influences on bachelor's degree completion by women nine years after they initially enrolled in college. However, the *total* positive effect of attending a predominantly women's college (that is, the sum of the direct and indirect effects) was modest (.055) but statistically significant.

Gruca (1988) controlled for almost the same individual and institutional characteristics as Stoecker and Pascarella (1988) but was concerned with explaining educational attainment through the doctoral degree. Her analyses indicate that with all other influences controlled, the percentage of women in the institution had no statistically significant direct influence on educational attainment for either black or white women. For both groups, however, the percentage of women in the institution did have a statistically significant positive indirect effect on educational attainment. This occurred largely because attending an institution with a high percentage of women enrolled had a statistically significant positive net influence on academic achievement. The latter in turn had a direct positive influence on educational attainment, hence producing the significant indirect effect.

Whether the dominant effect is direct or mediated through intervening variables, the weight of evidence suggests that women's colleges, in particular, have tended to enhance the educational attainment of undergraduate women. The total positive effect is, on average, small, probably less than 1 percent of the variance in attainment. Nevertheless, the evidence tends to support those who claim that a women's college provides a uniquely supportive climate for women to experience themselves and other members of their gender (both students and faculty) in a wide range of intellectual and social leadership roles (for example, Monteiro, 1980; Smith, 1988; Tidball, 1980, 1986). These role models and role opportunities may not be as readily visible in coeducational institutions, where men rather than women dominate the faculty and administration (Tidball, 1980) and the environmental press is more conducive to conventional student social behaviors (participation in intercollegiate athletics, conformist social activities, and so on) (Pascarella, 1984a). Thus, other factors held constant, women's colleges may be more likely to provide the types of female role models and the opportunity for interpersonal interactions with those role models that enhance rather than inhibit female aspirations and ambition. This may, in part at least, be the causal mechanism that underlies the apparent influence of attending a women's college on educational attainment.

Other Institutional Characteristics

The previous sections have synthesized the research on the institutional characteristics for which the evidence is relatively extensive and the weight of evidence is reasonably clear. In this section we briefly review those findings that suggest the influence of other institutional characteristics (or combinations of characteristics) on educational attainment. Generally, these findings lack the extent of replication on independent samples found for the previously reviewed institutional characteristics. Nevertheless, it is worth touching briefly on these findings, if only to present a more complete portrayal of the available research in the area.

Much of this research has been conducted by Astin and his colleagues (for example, Astin & Panos, 1969; Astin, 1975b, 1977a, 1982; Panos & Astin, 1968) on successive iterations of the Cooperative Institutional Research Program data. The analytical designs of the investigations typically provided for statistical control of important student precollege characteristics, such as family social status, secondary school achievement, and educational aspirations. With these factors controlled, various institutional characteristics or environmental traits were then correlated with measures of educational attainment. Astin and his colleagues, for example, report that obtaining the bachelor's degree was positively influenced by attending a college with a high level of cohesion in the peer environment (the number of peers whom the student regarded as close friends) or where students frequently participated in college-sponsored activities and there was a high level of personal involvement with and concern for the individual student. These may be additional factors underlying the high persistence rates at small, private liberal arts colleges, where the vast majority of students reside on campus. Similarly, institutions with a highly independent and verbally aggressive student body also tended to enhance degree attainment. Conversely, bachelor's degree attainment tended to be inhibited at colleges where a high percentage of students were employed full time, changed their major, or majored in "realistic" areas such as mechanical engineering, forestry, and industrial arts.

An additional line of research has suggested that degree completion may be a function of the extent to which an institution provides supportive student personnel services. Hedlund and Jones (1970), for example, studied the relationship between the availability of student personnel and counseling services and graduation rate at twenty-one two-year colleges in New York State. With institutional size taken into account, they found that all of the colleges with a student personnel staff to day student ratio of 1:150 or less reported graduating 50 percent or more of their students in two years. In contrast, only 20 percent of the colleges with a ratio of more than 1:150 graduated 50 percent of their students in two years. A similar difference was found when only those student personnel staff members involved full-time in counseling were considered. Though the findings are provocative from a policy standpoint, the extent to which they may be confounded by differences in student body ability and other factors is not clear.

In a related study of forty institutions varying in size, control, and research orientation of the faculty, Forrest (1985) sought to determine whether graduation rate was associated with such institutional factors as emphasis on orientation and advising services and the instructional emphasis of general education courses. With entering student academic ability taken into account, Forrest found that a group of nine institutions with the most comprehensive set of orientation and advising programs had a graduation rate 9 percent higher than that of a group of nine institutions with the least comprehensive programs. (Comprehensiveness of programs was determined by the number of formal contact hours required of all freshmen in orientation activities and the degree to which freshman academic advising was administered as a distinct function.) Forrest also found that a group of nine institutions with the strongest focus on general education and individualized instruction in their general education courses had a graduation rate 8 percent higher than a group of eight institutions with the weakest emphasis on individualized instruction in general education courses. This difference held even though the two groups of colleges were quite homogeneous in terms of the academic aptitude of their entering students. (A strong emphasis on individualized instruction in general education included placing students in general education courses on the basis of their ability to handle the material and a course instructional style emphasizing problem solving and the application of skills and knowledge rather than recall.) An implication of the latter finding is that a strong institutional emphasis on teaching reasoning and problem-solving skills through general education courses enhances persistence by facilitating the students' successful adaptation to the intellectual demands of the academic program.

Transfer Between Institutions

In an analysis of the socioeconomic achievement process, Duncan, Featherman, and Duncan (1972) hypothesized that the timing of events in the life cycle can be as critical for the socioeconomic achievement of the individual as the events themselves. Tests of this hypothesis by Featherman and Carter (1976), Gaither and Dukes (1982), and Robertshaw and Wolfle (1983) indicated that with important background characteristics such as academic ability, family social status, and initial aspirations controlled statistically, delays in entering college or interruptions in one's college attendance had statistically significant negative effects on the number of years of college completed. This is not to say that withdrawing from college for a period of time cannot be a positive developmental step for an individual (for example, Johansson & Rossmann, 1973; Ochberg, 1986; Timmons, 1978). Nevertheless, the evidence is reasonably clear that educational attainment is typically enhanced when one's attendance occurs in a continuous and uninterrupted sequence from beginning to completion.

Temporal interruptions may not be the only discontinuities in the educational process with negative implications for educational attainment. Another interruption in a student's education is the transfer from one college to another (Tinto, 1987). Here we are not particularly interested in the transfer from the two-year to the four-year college, which despite the difficulties in making such a "vertical transfer," typically reflects a positive progression in the educational attainment process (for example, Dougherty, 1987; Peng, 1978). Rather, we are more concerned with transferring among four-year institutions. Such behavior is relatively frequent. Tinto (1987), for example, estimates that about 15 percent of all four-year college students will transfer at least once during the first two years after initial matriculation. Although the motivation that underlies such behavior may often reflect the student's desire to find a better fit with the institutional environment, the weight of evidence suggests that it tends to have a negative influence on educational attainment.

In an early study of the influence of college on a national sample of secondary school graduates, Trent and Medsker (1968) observed that over the four-year period 1959–1963, students who transferred from one college to another were less likely to complete their bachelor's degree than students whose entire undergraduate education was limited to the initial college of enrollment. Their analysis, however, did not control for background differences between transfer and nontransfer, so it is difficult to determine how much their observations may be confounded.

Interestingly, more recent investigations that traced educational attainment over a nine-year period and did control for student background characteristics tend to confirm Trent and Medsker's (1968) observations. Using a national sample of students who initially enrolled in four-year institutions, Pascarella (1985b) sought to determine the factors that influence bachelor's degree completion for black and white men and women. Statistically controlling for student precollege characteristics (such as degree aspirations, family social status, financial need, secondary school achievement), the characteristics of the initial college of enrollment (such as selectivity and prestige, size and control, predominant race), and measures of social and academic accomplishment during college (such as grades, social involvement), he found that the number of colleges attended had a small but statistically significant negative influence on bachelor's degree attainment over a nine-year period for all four subgroups. The negative effect was particularly pronounced for black men.

Similar results are reported by Kocher and Pascarella (1988), who used the same sample but attempted to explain overall educational attainment through the doctoral degree rather than just completion of the bachelor's degree. Controlling for many of the same variables as Pascarella (1985b) plus initial expectations of transfer and academic major, Kocher and Pascarella found that number of institutions attended had a statistically significant negative direct effect on educational attainment for male and female black and white students. In addition, these investigators found that for black men and women the number of institutions attended also had a statistically significant negative indirect effect on educational attainment, mediated through its inhibiting influence on interaction with faculty and social or leadership involvement during college.

There are data limitations in the Pascarella (1985b) and Kocher and Pascarella (1988) analyses. For example, it was impossible to determine the qualitative differences in transfer behavior (for example, from a less to a more selective college, from a public to a private college). Such differences may have a nontrivial impact on attainment. Despite this problem, the findings (along with those of Trent and Medsker, 1968) suggest that institutional continuity during one's undergraduate education has positive implications for one's educational attainment. In turn, this further suggests the potential importance of one's fit with the initial institution of enrollment.

Within-College Effects

As indicated in the preceding section, a number of the structural characteristics of the college attended (selectivity, enrollment, and so on) have statistically significant indirect effects on educational attainment through their shaping of the student's social and academic experience of college. In this section we focus on those specific college experiences or accomplishments that enhance educational attainment independently of where one attends college (even though they may be more likely to occur at some colleges than at others). The volume of literature directly or indirectly addressing this area of inquiry during the last twenty years is extensive to the point of being unmanageable. Consequently, we have been forced to be selective in our synthesis and have turned for focus to a number of relatively recent theoretical statements pertaining to student persistence and degree attainment (for example, Bean, 1980, 1985; Cope & Hannah, 1975; Pascarella, 1980; Spady, 1970, 1971; Tinto, 1975, 1982, 1987). Although these models differ in specific structural elements and nomenclature, they appear to have as a common thread the notion that persistence and thereby educational attainment are largely a function of the student's fit or match with the college environment.

Various terms have been used to represent degree of person-environment fit, including integration, involvement, congruence, and satisfaction. Operationally, however, most definitions of fit are manifest in terms of the student's interactions with the academic and social systems of the college or, indirectly, those factors that shape the nature of such interactions. Our reading of the literature suggests that these may be reasonably grouped in the following categories: academic achievement (grades), peer relationships and extracurricular involvement, interactions with faculty, academic major, residence, orientation and advising, and financial aid and work.[1]

Academic Achievement

A student's grades are probably the single most revealing indicator of his or her successful adjustment to the intellectual demands of a particular college's course of study. Without satisfactory grades, a student will not graduate from college, nor will he or she be admitted to graduate or professional school. Although heavily influenced by academic ability and intelligence, grades in college are not merely a function of those factors. Even with academic ability or intelligence taken into account, grades at the individual level are significantly influenced by such factors as personal motivation, organization, study habits, and quality of effort (for example, Astin, 1971b, 1975b; Cappella, Wagner, & Kusmierz, 1982; Corlett, 1974; Culler & Holahan, 1980; Demitroff, 1974; Hinrichsen, 1972; Lenning, Munday, Johnson, Vander Well, & Brue, 1974a, 1974b; Thompson, 1976). Thus, as a measure of successful adaptation to an academic environment, grades tend to reflect not only requisite intellectual skills but also desirable personal work habits and attitudes.

Given this, it is not particularly surprising that undergraduate grades are perhaps the single best predictor of obtaining a bachelor's degree and also of attending graduate or professional school and obtaining an advanced degree. This effect has been replicated across a number of national samples and holds even when important student precollege characteristics (such as academic ability, aspirations, secondary school achievement), the characteristics of the institution attended (such as selectivity, control), and other collegiate experiences (such as major, social involvement) are taken into account (Anderson, 1986; Ethington & Smart, 1986; Sharp, 1970; Spaeth & Greeley, 1970; Stoecker, Pascarella, & Wolfle, 1988; Tinto, 1981). Moreover, even with such factors as gender, social class, race, and undergraduate major taken into account, grades remain an important determinant of the "prestige" or ranking of the graduate school attended (Lang, 1984).

Factors Influencing Academic Achievement. Although as a measure of academic adjustment, grades are largely an amalgam of individual academic ability and other personal traits (motivation, perseverance, study skills, and the like), they are not beyond the influence of institutional interventions. Kulik, Kulik, and Shwalb (1983), for example, conducted a meta-analysis of sixty published and unpublished studies evaluating the experimental effectiveness of special college programs designed to facilitate the academic adjustment of poorly prepared students. The effects of four types of programs were reviewed: instruction in academic skills, advising and counseling programs, comprehensive support services, and remedial or developmental studies. Kulik, Kulik, and Schwalb report a statistically significant overall effect size in grades favoring the college interventions. On the average, those exposed to the interventions had a grade point average .27 of a standard deviation higher than similar students not so exposed (an advantage of 10.6 percentile points). The overall effect was greatest during the freshman year with remedial or developmental programs being significantly less effective than the other interventions. Kulik, Kulik, and Shwalb also estimated the effect of these programs on college persistence rates and found that on average those exposed to the various interventions had a statistically significant 8 percent advantage in persistence rate over similar students not exposed to the interventions. As with grades, the effect was stronger during the freshman year than thereafter. More recent research not included in the Kulik, Kulik, and Schwalb synthesis is nevertheless consistent with their conclusions concerning effects of academic adjustment interventions on both grades and persistence (for example, Abrams & Jernigan, 1984; Behrman, Dark, & Paul, 1984; Blanc, DeBuhr, & Martin, 1983; Bron & Gordon, 1986; Dubois, Kiewra, & Fraley, 1988; Kenney, 1989; Kirschenbaum & Perri, 1982; Lipsky & Ender, 1990; Martin, Blanc, & DeBuhr, 1983; Nist, Simpson, & Hogrebe, 1985; Walsh, 1985; Wilkie & Kuckuck, 1989).[2]

With a few exceptions (May, 1974; Moos & Lee, 1979), there is little evidence to suggest that when academic ability or prior achievement is held constant, different naturally occurring residence groups (those in dormitories, fraternities or sororities, or off-campus apartments) have a consistently differential influence on academic achievement (for example, Baird, 1969b; Ballou, 1985; Beal & Williams, 1968; Grosz & Brandt, 1969; Longino & Kart, 1973; Phillips, 1976; Pugh & Chamberlain, 1976). Nevertheless, residence groupings provide a readily available laboratory for enhancing the academic and interpersonal quality of student life. It is not surprising, therefore, that a second area where colleges have made a concerted effort to intervene in ways that promote student academic adjustment is the purposeful structuring of residence facilities. Here the body of evidence is extensive, but the interventions are sufficiently diverse in their approach to resist straightforward categorization and therefore simple conclusions. What can be reasonably concluded from this evidence is that when the formal and informal group norms of a residence unit function to reinforce a serious and focused study environment, academic achievement is positively influenced. This influence, however, is not particularly pervasive or dramatic in magnitude. Examples of experimental interventions that have yielded at least modest success in creating such environmental norms include special study floors with enforced quiet hours (Blimling & Hample, 1979), the use of skilled academic tutors on designated residence floors (Taylor, Roth, & Hanson, 1971), and living-learning centers designed to integrate the student's residential and intellectual life and enhance student-faculty informal interaction (Blimling & Paulsen, 1979; Pascarella & Terenzini, 1981).

There is also evidence that experimentally grouping students in residential units by academic aptitude or academic major may positively influence achievement. In the instance of ability grouping, however, it is unclear whether the achievement benefits accrue to the higher-ability students (DeCoster, 1968; Duncan & Stoner, 1977) or lower-ability students (Blai, 1971). Similarly, it is not totally clear whether all students benefit the same from homogeneous grouping by major (Schroeder & Belmonte, 1979; Schroeder & Freesh, 1977), whether men benefit more than women (Snead & Caple, 1971), whether average-ability students benefit more than high-ability students (Taylor & Hanson, 1971), or whether the effect is largely trivial when ability and personality traits are taken into account (Elton & Bate, 1966). An independent review of this literature by Buffington (1984) concludes that there is no consensus as to the benefits of homogeneous grouping in residence halls.[3]

Peer Relationships and Extracurricular Involvement

Extensive theoretical justification exists for the role of social participation in the educational attainment process. On one level this comes from the notion in theoretical models of student persistence that social participation enhances one's social integration and interpersonal bonds with the institution. Other things being equal, this increases one's commitment to and likelihood of persisting at the institution and completing one's degree (for example, Bean, 1980; Spady, 1970; Tinto, 1975, 1987). Similarly, the social-psychological life-cycle models of status attainment briefly introduced earlier in the chapter (for example, Sewell & Hauser, 1975) posit the importance of interactions with significant others as an influence on the attainment process. From this perspective participation in such things as college extracurricular activities might serve two important functions suggested by Hanks and Eckland (1976). First, it may expose students to a social network of other achievement-oriented peers, thereby generating and reinforcing higher aspirations and goals. Second, it may facilitate the realization of such aspirations and goals by allowing students to acquire the personal resources (interpersonal skills, self-confidence, specialized knowledge, and the like) that better permit such aspirations and goals to be realized.

Given this strong theoretical justification, it is not surprising that substantial research has addressed the relationship between social involvement and both persistence and educational attainment. The weight of evidence is quite clear that both the frequency and quality of students' interactions with peers and their participation in extracurricular activities are positively associated with persistence (for example, Carroll, 1988; Dukes & Gaither, 1984; Faughn, 1982; Husband, 1976; Johnson & Chapman, 1980; Kramer et al., 1985; Mallinckrodt, 1988; Mallinckrodt & Sedlacek, 1987; Nelson, Scott, & Bryan, 1984; Neuman, 1985; Seabrook, 1985; Simpson, Baker, & Mellinger, 1980; Vaughan, 1968; Waldo, 1986). It is less clear, however, that peer relationships and extracurricular involvement have a net influence on persistence when student precollege characteristics or other measures of the college experience are taken into account. For example, Endo and Bittner (1985), Munro (1981), and Pascarella and Chapman (1983a, 1983b) provide evidence to suggest a net positive effect of peer relationships and extracurricular involvement on persistence. Yet the results reported by Bean (1985); Pascarella and Terenzini (1980a); Stinson, Scherer, and Walker (1987); Terenzini and Pascarella (1977, 1978); and Thomas and Andes (1987) are less supportive.

Evidence concerning the net effect of peer relationships or extracurricular involvement on educational attainment, bachelor's degree completion, or entrance into graduate or professional school is reasonably clear. Hanks and Eckland (1976), for example, attempted to estimate the influences on educational attainment (some college to advanced degree) with a national sample of college students who were followed up fifteen years after their sophomore year in high school. Controlling for family socioeconomic status, academic aptitude, high school athletic and social participation, high school grades, and college grades, Hanks and Eckland found that a measure of collegiate social participation had a statistically significant positive effect on educational attainment for both men and women. (The measure of social participation in both high school and college included publications or creative writing, dramatics or music, debate or political groups, student government, social science or religious groups, and science or academic groups.)

More recent studies that controlled for many of the same variables but also for precollege educational aspirations report generally similar findings for bachelor's degree completion (Stoecker, Pascarella, & Wolfle, 1988), entrance into graduate or professional school (Ethington & Smart, 1986), and educational attainment through the doctoral degree (Pascarella, Ethington, & Smart, 1988). The measure of social involvement in these studies typically included items such as serving on a university or departmental committee, being president of a student organization, having a part in a play, and being editor of a student publication. As such, it has somewhat stronger loadings for leadership than does the social participation measure used by Hanks and Eckland (1976). Moreover, the scale used by Ethington and Smart (1986) also included a measure of interaction with faculty. Consequently, their findings may be somewhat ambiguous with respect to the unique influence of social involvement with peers.

It is likely, of course, that the extent to which social involvement with peers influences educational attainment depends to some extent on the characteristics of the peers with whom one interacts. Studies that provide sufficient statistical detail (for example, correlation matrices or full regression equations) to determine this, however, are rare. Nevertheless, using the statistics provided in an analysis of two separate national samples (Pascarella, 1985c; Kocher & Pascarella, 1988), we found positive correlations in the .12 to .20 range between student precollege educational aspirations and subsequent social involvement with peers during college. This suggests that those students engaging in such activities tend to have higher educational aspirations to begin with than their less involved counterparts. As such, they may constitute a viable college subculture whose group norms have a salutary influence on the aspirations of participating individuals.

Indeed, there is modest, though mixed, evidence that extracurricular involvement with peers positively influences educational aspirations. Using a national sample of white students from seventy-four four-year colleges, Pascarella (1985c) sought to determine the influences on educational aspirations at the end of the sophomore year. Controlling for such factors as academic aptitude, precollege educational aspirations, parental education, institutional selectivity and size, college grades, and social interaction with faculty, he found that an eleven-item measure of social involvement with peers had a small but statistically significant and positive direct effect on sophomore educational aspirations. Moreover, when the data were aggregated across the seventy-four institutions and all other variables were controlled, colleges with high levels of student social interaction also had high levels of sophomore student educational aspirations.

Less supportive documentation is provided by Gurin & Epps (1975), who used a sample of black students from nine black institutions. They found no significant association between the percentage of students on each campus who participated in extracurricular activities and educational aspirations at the end of the freshman year when institutional selectivity and initial aspirations were held constant. They did find, however, that net of college selectivity and initial aspirations, the diversity of extracurricular activities offered by an institution was positively and significantly linked to men's aspirations at the end of the freshman year.

While there may be several reasons for the lack of clear correspondence between these findings and those of Pascarella (1985c) (different sample, less diverse institutions, and the like), one possibility is that Gurin and Epps used a measure of extracurricular involvement aggregated at the campus level. They did not really attempt to link individual social participation with individual aspirations.

Another type of student extracurricular involvement is athletic participation. However, evidence that compares the educational attainment of athletes with other students who have similar precollege characteristics is nearly nonexistent. Analyzing a national sample of college students followed over a nine-year period, Pascarella and Smart (1990) sought to determine whether participation in intercollegiate athletics in general influenced bachelor's degree attainment. Net of such factors as family socioeconomic status, secondary school achievement, educational aspirations, college selectivity, and college grades, male intercollegiate athletes had a small but significantly greater likelihood of finishing a bachelor's degree within nine years than their nonathlete counterparts. Unfortunately, the Pascarella and Smart study could not disaggregate the impact on educational attainment of different kinds of athletic participation (for example, participation in revenue-producing sports such as football and basketball versus other sports). Furthermore, we uncovered no additional study that controlled for important precollege differences between athletes and nonathletes and replicated their findings. Consequently, we hesitate to offer a conclusion on the net effects of athletic participation on educational attainment.

Interactions with Faculty

A considerable body of evidence suggests that with the general exception of small and often selective liberal arts colleges, student-faculty contact in most institutions is largely restricted to formalized, somewhat structured situations such as the lecture, laboratory, or discussion section (Boyer, 1987; Chickering, 1969; Wood & Wilson, 1972). There may be several reasons for this. A substantial number of students may simply desire, within the limitations of academic requirements, to exclude faculty influence from their nonclassroom lives (Feldman & Newcomb, 1969). Others may have little nonclassroom contact with faculty because of the constraints of work and/or commuting to college (Chickering, 1974a). Moreover, generational and organizational status differences separate students and faculty. Such differences, when combined with the sanctions of professional norms, may lead faculty to designate substantial portions of their nonclassroom time as off-limits to undergraduates (Boyer, 1987; Malkemes, 1972; Wallace, 1967a).

Despite these impediments, there is considerable evidence that the impact on students of faculty norms, values, and attitudes, as well as faculty members' impact as role models, is enhanced when student-faculty interactions extend beyond the formal classroom setting (Pascarella, 1980). This evidence is consistent with the notion that effective social learning of normative values and attitudes often occurs in informal as well as formal settings. (Indeed, we have already seen evidence of this impact in previous chapters.) Thus, if faculty can be generally assumed to place a high value on educational attainment, one might posit that the more students interact with faculty in informal as well as formal settings, the more likely they are to be influenced by this value. Moreover, as with social interaction with peers, increased interaction between faculty and students may also serve to strengthen the personal bonds between the student and the institution, thereby increasing the likelihood of social integration and persistence.

A substantial body of research addresses these assertions. Evidence concerning the link between student-faculty interaction and institutional persistence is not totally consistent. Pascarella and Terenzini conducted a series of studies on three independent samples of freshmen as they entered the same university in three consecutive years to determine the factors that influence voluntary freshman-year persistence or withdrawal decisions (Pascarella & Terenzini, 1976, 1977, 1979a, 1979b; Terenzini & Pascarella, 1978, 1980b). Controlling for salient student precollege characteristics, such as academic aptitude, educational aspirations, initial commitment to the institution, and personality traits, as well as for freshman-year grades and extracurricular involvement, the investigators found that freshman-to-sophomore persistence was positively and significantly related to total amount of student-faculty nonclassroom contact with faculty and particularly to frequency of interactions with faculty to discuss intellectual matters. The latter finding, they concluded, suggests that the nonclassroom interactions with faculty that are most important to persistence are those that integrate the student's classroom and nonclassroom experiences. Such a conclusion is perhaps further supported by Astin's (1977a) finding that net of student precollege aptitudes and aspirations, involvement with faculty in independent research is positively associated with undergraduate persistence.

Although the potential positive influence of student-faculty informal interaction on persistence has been supported in subsequent research on independent samples (for example, Endo & Bittner, 1985; Endo & Harpel, 1979), there is also a considerable amount of evidence to suggest that the net effect of student-faculty contact on persistence is at best trivial (for example, Bean, 1980, 1985; Bean & Plascak, 1987; Kowalski, 1977; Rossmann, 1968; Voorhees, 1987). Since most of the studies were based on single-institution samples, a possible explanation for the inconsistency of the findings may be variations in measurement error or sampling characteristics across different institutional samples. Conversely, the lack of consistent findings may simply reflect the fact that interaction with faculty has differential impacts on persistence at different kinds of institutions (Pascarella, 1986a).

The weight of evidence from studies that focused on the influence of student-faculty interaction on educational aspirations and educational attainment is less equivocal. Hearn (1987), Gurin and Epps (1975), Gurin and Gaylord (1976), Pascarella (1985c), and Thistlethwaite and Wheeler (1966) report evidence to indicate that even with relevant student background characteristics and other collegiate experiences held constant, the extent of social interaction between students and faculty is significantly and positively related to educational aspirations at either the end of the freshman year, end of the sophomore year, or end of the senior year. Similarly, evidence from analyses of two independent national samples reported by Astin and Panos (1969); Kocher and Pascarella (1988); Pascarella, Smart, and Ethington (1986); and Stoecker, Pascarella, and Wolfle (1988) suggests that degree of student-faculty social contact has a significant positive association with bachelor's degree completion and educational attainment through the doctoral degree. Further, this association remains statistically significant even when controls are made for secondary school achievement, the selectivity and size of the college attended, and other measures of the college experience, such as major, grades, and extracurricular involvement.

Despite the consistency of the evidence, there is some ambiguity in interpreting the causal direction of the link between student-faculty social interaction and educational aspirations and attainment. In the studies reviewed, measures of student-faculty interaction and either educational aspirations or attainment were collected at the same time. Consequently, it is not necessarily clear that student-faculty interaction leads to higher educational aspirations and, subsequently, higher educational attainment. Rather, students with aspirations for graduate or professional school may simply be more likely to share faculty values and enjoy social interaction with them. Indeed, a study of freshman-year educational aspirations by Iverson, Pascarella, and Terenzini (1984) would tend to support the second hypothesis. They used a statistical procedure that permits one to estimate reciprocal causality, and their results suggested that educational aspirations are more likely to influence contact with faculty than contact with faculty is to influence educational aspirations.

Other evidence, however, strongly suggests that faculty have an influential causal role in students' educational aspirations, particularly their decision to attend graduate school. In what is perhaps the most comprehensive study on this topic, Baird and colleagues (Baird, 1976b; Baird, Clark, & Hartnett, 1973) surveyed a national sample of graduate students on the importance of a range of factors concerning their senior-year decisions to attend graduate or professional school. Sixty-five percent of the graduate students in arts and humanities, 62 percent in the biological or physical sciences, and 56 percent in the social sciences said that the personal encouragement of faculty was an "important" or "very important" factor. The positive influence of faculty encouragement on plans for graduate work in these disciplines held net of academic major, initial vocational choice, grades, and academic self-ratings. Faculty influence was less pronounced in decisions to attend law or medical school, yet nearly a third of these students also indicated that faculty encouragement had been "important" or "very important." Similar results have been reported for the postbaccalaureate plans of senior women at a single institution by de Wolf (1976). When matched by major and age with seniors not aspiring to graduate study, those intending to enter graduate school the next year more often indicated having been influenced by a faculty member.

It is also possible, of course, that the link between student-faculty social interaction and educational aspirations and attainment is a proxy for the extent to which specific faculty members serve as influential role models for students. (The assumption here is that students may be more likely to interact socially with such role models.) This is most clearly the case in graduate education, where personal relationships with faculty members and being treated as a junior colleague by a faculty member who acts as a mentor are significant predictors of completing the doctorate (for example, Berg & Ferber, 1983). It may also hold for the educational aspirations of undergraduates, particularly if the role model one seeks to emulate is the same gender as the student. Stake and Noonan (1985), for example, found that when they controlled for initial educational aspirations, the greatest gains in educational aspirations during the freshman year occurred for those students who chose a same-gender faculty role model they wished to emulate.

Related research has suggested that female faculty role models may be a particularly important influence on the educational aspirations of undergraduate women (Esposito, Hackett, & O'Halloran, 1987; Ridgeway, 1978; Stake, 1981). Indeed, Tidball (Tidball & Kistiakowsky, 1976; Tidball, 1986) posits the presence of female faculty role models as a potential causal mechanism that underlies the link found between the number of women faculty members in an institution and the percentage of women graduates of an institution who obtain graduate degrees. In this regard it is worth noting that women in single-sex institutions, in which female faculty are typically in the majority, report more informal interaction and higher levels of supportive interaction with faculty than do women in coeducational institutions (Monteiro, 1980).

A final interpretative point needs to be made concerning the influence of student-faculty relationships on student educational aspiration and attainment. If student-faculty interaction influences students' aspirations and thereby their educational attainment, it is likely that the nature of this influence is to accentuate or affirm rather than to fundamentally change existing aspirations. Consider the evidence reported by Pascarella (1985c) with a sample of students from seventy-four four-year institutions. He found that net of student precollege characteristics and the characteristics of the institution attended, students who developed close personal relationships with faculty during the first two years of college tended to have significantly higher precollege educational aspirations than those who did not. In turn, social interaction with faculty had a statistically significant positive influence on sophomore-year educational aspirations over and above precollege and institutional characteristics, initial educational aspirations, college grades, and social involvement with peers. This set of findings suggests that students with initially high educational aspirations are most likely to interact socially with faculty and that such interaction serves to enhance even further initial aspirations.

Academic Major

In considering the vast majority of colleges and universities, it probably makes little sense to talk about educational aspirations and attainment of students as being influenced by their experience of a single academic or social environment. Rather, as suggested by Feldman and Newcomb (1969); Hackman and Taber (1979); Simpson, Baker, and Mellinger (1980); and Weidman (1979, 1984), the individual student is more likely to identify with and interact with a number of salient subenvironments, each of which may have a unique influence on aspirations and attainment. One of these salient subenvironments is the student's academic major.

Interestingly, evidence on the net influence of academic major on educational attainment is mixed. Using a sample from the NLS-72, Thomas and Gordon (1983), for example, found that for students in four-year institutions, majoring in the hard or technical sciences (versus education and the social sciences) had a statistically significant positive effect on educational attainment even when controls were made for such factors as academic aptitude, high school achievement, precollege educational aspirations, and college grades. (The measure of educational attainment ranged from "less than two years of college" to "graduate or professional degree.") The same effect did not hold for students at two-year colleges. Similar findings for four-year college students have been reported by Sharp (1970) in a national sample of students followed up five years after they attained the bachelor's degree. In the Sharp study humanities and science majors were more likely to attend graduate or professional school than their counterparts who majored in such fields as business, education, and health.

Evidence from two other national samples has failed to support the findings of either Thomas and Gordon (1983) or Sharp (1970). Alexander and Eckland (1977) conducted their analyses on a national sample of high school sophomores who were followed up fifteen years later. Pascarella, Smart, Ethington, and Nettles (1987) analyzed a national sample of students in four-year colleges who were followed up nine years after initial enrollment. Controlling for such factors as family social status, academic ability, precollege educational aspirations, the selectivity of the institution attended, and college grades, neither study found that academic major was significantly associated with overall educational attainment (scaled from no college degree to the doctoral degree). Academic major was treated as a dichotomy in both studies. In the Alexander and Eckland study it represented the academic competency of students typically attracted to a field ("high performance" = arts, humanities, natural sciences, engineering, social sciences; "low performance" = agriculture, business, education, physical education). In the Pascarella, Smart, Ethington, and Nettles investigation it was scientific or technical major (natural sciences, engineering, and the like) versus others (for example, humanities, social sciences).

An additional analysis of essentially the same sample used by Pascarella, Smart, Ethington, and Nettles (1987) found that when a similar set of confounding influences were controlled statistically, students majoring in the social sciences were more likely to have higher levels of overall educational attainment than others (Pascarella, Ethington, & Smart, 1988). This finding is inconsistent with the findings of Sharp (1970) and Thomas and Gordon (1983).

The overall inconsistency of this body of evidence may reflect sampling and methodological differences in the studies. Yet, as we have seen in a number of other areas of research, consistent findings are yielded despite differences in sampling and methodological rigor. A better explanation for the inconsistent findings may simply be that the influence of academic major on educational aspirations and attainment is complex and multidimensional. This has been suggested by Hearn (1987), who argues that major department contextual factors—such as faculty supportiveness of students, departmental grading practices, and departmental size—need to be considered in an attempt to understand the full impact of academic major on educational attainment.

Although Hearn (1987) did not consider specific majors and used a sample limited to two institutions, his own research suggests the possibility of substantive direct and indirect influences of these contextual factors on educational aspirations and postbaccalaureate educational plans that are independent of initial educational aspirations. Evidence consistent with Hearn's findings and even further supporting his contention of the importance of the contextual effects of academic major is suggested by Stoecker, Pascarella, and Wolfle (1988) in analyses of bachelor's degree completion on a national sample of four-year college students. Controlling for student precollege characteristics (such as family socioeconomic status, secondary school academic achievement and social involvement, educational aspirations) and the characteristics of the institution attended (such as selectivity, size, race), they found that much of the consistent, statistically significant influence of a student's academic major on bachelor's degree completion was indirect, being mediated primarily through collegiate grades and to a somewhat lesser extent by interaction with faculty. Independent of these precollege characteristics and the type of institution attended, students majoring in the social sciences or the arts and humanities tended to receive higher grades and have higher levels of social interaction with faculty than students majoring in the natural sciences or technical or professional fields. Since grades and interaction with faculty, in turn, had net positive effects on degree completion, the indirect influence of majoring in the social sciences and the arts or humanities was positive.

Such evidence suggests that faculty in social science and arts or humanities departments may have grading practices and orientations toward interaction with students that independently enhance degree completion. Interestingly, the indirect effects of academic major uncovered by Stoecker, Pascarella, and Wolfle (1988) were generally consistent regardless of the student's race or gender. Conversely, the direct or unmediated effects of major were inconsistent and even contradictory across race and gender subgroups.

Another important department contextual effect on educational aspirations and attainment suggested by Hearn (1987) and others (for example, Wilson, 1978) is that of the occupational linkages of the bachelor's degree in the major discipline to the larger society and economy. As we shall see in a subsequent chapter, one's academic major is a central factor in early career economic rewards. In majors such as engineering, business, and other technical fields, the bachelor's degree alone may guarantee the graduate a reasonably high level of immediate occupational prestige and economic return. As a consequence, these majors may actually discourage further education beyond the bachelor's degree.

Hearn (1987) found evidence to support this expectation in his longitudinal analysis of educational aspirations and plans at two universities. He created a dichotomous variable indicating whether or not one's major had high status rewards in the larger occupational system (Wilson, 1978) and close links to specific occupations (Hearn & Olzak, 1981). (An example of a major high on both scales is chemical engineering.) Controlling for freshman-year educational aspirations, parental support for career plans, college grades, and other measures of departmental characteristics, majoring in a department with high status rewards and close links to a specific occupation had statistically significant negative effects on both senior-year educational aspirations and plans for graduate school for men. The effects on graduate school plans for women were also negative but not significant. This latter finding may be due, at least in part, to the pronounced tendency for women not to major in those academic areas with high status rewards (for example, Hearn & Olzak, 1981).[4]

Residence

Living on or near campus while attending college is consistently one of the most important determinants of a student's level of integration or involvement in the social system of an institution. Compared to their counterparts who live at home and must commute to college, resident students have significantly more social interaction with peers and faculty and are significantly more likely to be involved in extracurricular activities and to use campus facilities (for example, Chickering, 1974a; Chickering & Kuper, 1971; Everett, 1979; Flanagan, 1976; Nelson, 1982; Pascarella, 1984b, 1985d; Welty, 1976).[5] Moreover, as indicated by Pascarella (1985d) in his analysis of a national sample, this influence on social integration exists independently of student precollege characteristics, such as aptitude, socioeconomic status, and secondary school extracurricular involvement, as well as the size, control, and selectivity of the institution attended.

Given the links between social integration during college and both persistence and educational attainment, it is not surprising that a considerable body of inquiry has focused on the influence of residence status on these same outcomes. The weight of evidence from this research is quite clear. Even when controls were made for important precollege characteristics, such as academic aptitude, socioeconomic status, educational aspirations, and secondary school achievement, across several independent samples, living on campus still exerted a statistically significant positive influence on persistence and completion of the bachelor's degree (Anderson, 1981; Astin, 1973b, 1975b, 1977a, 1982; Chickering, 1974a; Herndon, 1984a; Pascarella & Chapman, 1983a; Velez, 1985).

As alluded to previously and as suggested by Astin (1973b), Chickering (1974a), and Pascarella (1984b), it is likely that the major causal mechanism underlying the positive influence of living on campus on persistence and degree completion is the facilitation of campus involvement. As with a number of plausible effects discussed in this and other chapters, the nature of this causal sequence probably involves the accentuation of initial differences. Regardless of the type of college attended, students who live on campus (versus those who commute) have precollege characteristics that make them more likely to obtain the bachelor's degree and to become involved in the campus social and extracurricular network (for example, Astin, 1985a; Chickering, 1974a; Pascarella, 1984b; Ryan, 1970). These precollege characteristics include higher levels of academic aptitude, family socioeconomic status, secondary school extracurricular involvement, educational aspirations, and precollege commitment to the institution attended. Consequently, living on campus may provide an additional advantage for those who enter college with individual attributes that make them more likely to exploit and benefit from this advantage.

Of course, the positive impact of living on campus on persistence and educational attainment may not be uniform. As with departmental contexts, it is likely that there are different residential contexts that differentially influence persistence and degree completion. Terenzini and Pascarella (1984), for example, found that when they controlled for individual student characteristics such as academic aptitude, socioeconomic status, and precollege educational aspirations and commitment to the institution, the average level of institutional commitment in one's residential facility had an additional positive effect on voluntary freshman-year persistence. Such a "contextual effect" may also explain Astin's (1975b) finding that net of precollege characteristics, living in a sorority or fraternity house during the freshman or sophomore year had a statistically significant positive influence on degree completion or continued persistence in college. Here, however, the contextual effect may have been manifest more in the members' commitment to the specific fraternity or sorority than to the larger institution. (See the Appendix for a fuller discussion of the methodology of estimating contextual effects.)

There is also modest evidence that it may be possible to structure the residential environment in such a way as to enhance student persistence. In Chapter Four we described a quasi-experimental study conducted by Pascarella and Terenzini (1980b) that estimated the net educational effects of a living-learning residence designed to integrate the student's academic and residential life and increase the frequency of nonclassroom interaction with faculty and the quality of interaction with both faculty and peers. Controlling for such factors as academic aptitude, secondary school academic and social achievement, educational aspirations, and socioeconomic status, Pascarella and Terenzini found that membership in the living-learning residence rather than in conventional residence facilities had a statistically significant positive influence on freshman-to-sophomore persistence. This finding was replicated on an independent sample with a similar design and statistical controls (Pascarella & Terenzini, 1981). Similar effects on persistence have been reported for experimental living-learning centers that stress the grouping of students by academic major and the use of resident upperclassmen as tutors (Schroeder & Belmonte, 1979; Schroeder & Freesh, 1977; Taylor, Roth, & Hanson, 1971).

The evidence reviewed so far clearly suggests that living on or near campus (versus commuting to college) facilitates integration into the campus social network of peers, faculty, and extracurricular activities. This integration in turn has positive implications for persistence and degree completion. At the same time, however, it should be noted that a growing proportion of the students who participate in American postsecondary education commute to college (Slade & Jarmul, 1975; Stewart, Merrill, & Saluri, 1985). Indeed, on the basis of the extrapolated national sample statistics presented by Stewart, Merrill, and Saluri, it can be argued that the commuter student has become the statistical norm in American higher education. These investigators estimate that about 60 percent of all college students live at home or with parents and commute (41 percent at private four-year colleges, 68 percent at public universities, and 76 percent at public two-year colleges). Perhaps even more significantly, trends toward the nonresidential campus hold at the institutional level as well. According to the American Council on Education's 1980 study of student housing, more than one-third of the nation's 3,000 postsecondary institutions had no student housing at all (Andersen & Atelsek, 1982).

Perhaps it goes without saying that commuter institutions present students with a substantially different social-psychological environment than do residential institutions. The fact that students live off campus and frequently work part- or full-time (for example, Chickering, 1974a; Fenske & Scott, 1972) limits the opportunity for extracurricular involvement and social interaction with faculty and peers. The student body technically exists, but it lacks the network of coherent and influential student cultures often found on residential campuses (Gusfield, Kronus, & Mark, 1970). A major implication of this is that the commuter institution's social system may simply not be potent enough to play more than a relatively trivial role in the persistence or educational attainment process. Conversely, one would expect academic factors, such as academic achievement, to be relatively important.

A substantial amount of research supports this contention, at least in explaining institutional persistence. Studies by Costa (1984); Fox (1986); Garcia (1988); Pascarella, Duby, and Iverson, 1983; Pascarella, Duby, Miller, and Rasher (1981); Rice (1983); Staman (1980); Tata (1981); and Zaccaria and Creaser (1971) have all suggested the independent importance of academic achievement in positively influencing persistence at two- and four-year commuter institutions. Conversely, with a few exceptions (for example, Neuman, 1985; Smith, 1980; Weigel, 1969), the weight of evidence is clear that various measures of social integration (including interaction with faculty, interaction with peers, and extracurricular involvement) show little if any positive relationship with persistence at commuter institutions (for example, Baumgart & Johnstone, 1977; Braxton & Brier, 1989; Carter, 1982; Fetters, 1977; Fox, 1986; Garcia, 1988; Louis, Colten, & Demeke, 1984; Pascarella & Chapman, 1983a; Pascarella, Duby, & Iverson, 1983; Roesler, 1971; Staman, 1980; White, 1972; Williamson & Creamer, 1988). This lack of a positive relationship holds regardless of the specific measure of social integration used and irrespective of whether or not student background characteristics were taken into account in the study design.[6]

Orientation and Advising

Earlier in this chapter we reviewed evidence by Forrest (1985) suggesting that institutions with a strong programmatic emphasis on orientation and advising services had higher graduation rates than institutions without such emphasis. A considerable amount of research has also addressed the influence of orientation and advising services on individual student persistence and educational attainment.

Orientation programs are fairly common at many colleges and universities in this country. Common objectives of such programs are to acquaint students with the administrative regulations and expected behaviors of the institution, to introduce them to student services, to provide opportunities for students to meet informally with faculty, to guide students in designing an academic program and/or choosing a major, to assist them in career planning, and to help them develop academic skills essential to their survival as college students (study skills, note taking, effective writing, and so on) (Titley, 1985). Clearly, there are numerous institutional variations in which factors may be emphasized, as well as in program duration and format. A common theme underlying nearly all orientation programs, however, is the facilitation of the student's successful integration into a new and unfamiliar academic and social setting.

In many ways orientation programs can be thought of as an institutionalized attempt at early student socialization that is analogous to the concept of anticipatory socialization. Anticipatory socialization, as developed by Merton (Merton, 1957; Merton & Lazarsfeld, 1972), is a process or set of experiences through which individuals come to anticipate correctly the norms, values, and behavioral expectations they will encounter in a new social setting.[7] If effective, anticipatory socialization should facilitate one's successful integration into the new setting. Thus, we might expect students exposed to orientation experiences to be more successful in becoming initially integrated into an institution's academic and social systems than their counterparts not benefiting from these experiences. Higher levels of integration, in turn, should enhance persistence.

With a few exceptions (for example, Banzinger, 1986; Rothman & Leonard, 1967; Wilkie & Kuckuck, 1989), the weight of evidence does suggest a statistically significant positive link between exposure to various orientation experiences and persistence, both from freshman to sophomore year and from freshman year through attainment of the bachelor's degree (Bron & Gordon, 1986; Cartledge & Walls, 1986; Dunphy, Miller, Woodruff, & Nelson, 1987; Farr, Jones, & Samprone, 1986; Fidler, 1985; Fidler and Hunter 1989; Gerber, 1970; Jones, 1984; Rice, 1984; Stupka, 1986). The most consistently effective program format appears to be a first-semester freshman seminar that meets as a regular class with an assigned instructor. The purpose of the seminar is to orient the student to the institution and its programs and to teach important academic survival skills. Most research in this area either uses subject-matching procedures to obtain comparison group equivalence or presents evidence to show that those attending orientation are no more advantaged than those not attending orientation on such variables as academic aptitude and secondary school achievement. Unfortunately, in nearly all the studies cited above, the student could choose whether or not to participate in orientation. The reasons why students chose to attend orientation (for example, a higher level of initial commitment to the institution) could have confounded the link between orientation and persistence. Indeed, Pascarella, Terenzini, and Wolfle (1986) found that when they controlled for such factors as precollege educational aspirations and commitment to the institution attended, in addition to academic aptitude, secondary school achievement, and socioeconomic status, exposure to orientation had only a trivial, statistically nonsignificant direct effect on persistence. However, net of precollege characteristics, orientation did have a statistically significant positive influence on freshman-year social integration and subsequent commitment to the institution. These variables in turn had statistically significant positive effects on persistence, yielding a statistically significant positive indirect effect for orientation.

It is worth noting that the orientation intervention in the Pascarella, Terenzini, and Wolfle (1986) investigation occurred during the summer before matriculation and was only a three-day program. Orientation interventions linked with stronger direct effects on persistence tend to be longer in duration and more comprehensive in scope (freshman seminars or orientation courses). Nevertheless, even short, prefreshman orientations may exert a positive indirect effect on student persistence.

Evidence concerning the influence of the frequency or quality of academic advising on persistence and educational attainment has been synthesized by Bean and Metzner (1985) and Metzner (1989). They conclude that the research results are mixed. Some studies report a statistically significant positive link between advising and measures of persistence (for example, Brigman, Kuh, & Stager, 1982; Endo & Harpel, 1979; Louis, Colten, & Demeke, 1984; Meyers, 1981; Smith, 1980; Taylor, 1982). Other studies report only a trivial and statistically nonsignificant association (Aitken, 1982; Baumgart & Johnstone, 1977; Disque, 1983; Enos, 1981; Johansson & Rossmann, 1973; Kowalski, 1977; Rossmann, 1967, 1968; Staman, 1980; Steele, 1978). Our own review of this evidence suggests little in the way of methodological rigor or measurement concerns to differentiate substantively those studies that yield a positive association from those where the link is trivial and statistically nonsignificant. Moreover, the findings did not appear to depend on whether the study was conducted at a residential or a nonresidential institution.

One possible explanation for these equivocal findings, as found with orientation, is that a considerable part of the influence exerted by advising may be indirect. This is indicated in a longitudinal study of the effects of academic advising on freshman-to-sophomore persistence by Metzner (1989). Controlling for such factors as secondary school achievement, gender, age, employment, family responsibilities, college grades, college satisfaction, and intent to leave the institution, Metzner found that the quality of advising received had only a small and statistically nonsignificant direct effect on persistence. High-quality advising, however, did have a statistically significant positive indirect effect on persistence transmitted through its positive impact on such variables as grades and satisfaction and its negative effect on intent to leave the institution. Similar results are reported by Braxton, Duster, and Pascarella (1988), although they did not test the indirect effect of advising quality on persistence for statistical significance.

Financial Aid and Work

As indicated by Tinto (1987) and others (for example, Iwai & Churchill, 1982; Manski & Wise, 1983), economic circumstances and forces may play a significant role in the educational attainment process. Students must often weigh the present "opportunity costs" of a college education, including tuition and deferred income, against the future economic benefits that accrue to those with a bachelor's degree. The required investment of frequently scarce personal economic resources suggests that factors such as financial aid and work experiences may be influential in educational attainment.

Results of research on the impact of receiving (versus not receiving) financial aid during college on persistence and bachelor's degree attainment is mixed. A number of studies suggest that receipt of general financial aid (loans, grants, scholarships, work, or some combination thereof) during college is positively associated with persistence, bachelor's degree completion, and graduate or professional school attendance (for example, Carroll, 1987; Herndon, 1984b; Heverly, 1987; Nora, 1987; Riccobono & Dunteman, 1979; Sanford, 1980; St. John, Kirshstein, & Noell, 1988; Terkla, 1984; Voorhees, 1985a, 1985b). This influence appears to hold even when controls are made for such variables as academic ability, student financial resources, secondary school achievement, educational aspirations, and college grades. Other studies, however, many of which controlled for similar variables, report that the receipt of general financial aid had only a trivial or at best a small and marginally significant influence on persistence and degree completion (for example, Bergen, Upham, & Bergen, 1970; Bergen & Zielke, 1979; Corrallo & Davis, 1977; Fields & LeMay, 1973; Jensen, 1980, 1981, 1983, 1984; McCreight & LeMay, 1982; Peng & Fetters, 1978; Selby, 1973; Stampen & Cabrera, 1986).

Murdock (1987) conducted a meta-analysis of forty-six studies that estimated the effect of general financial aid (provided by the institution, state government, or federal government) on persistence and degree attainment. Across all studies the effect size for receiving financial aid was small (.13) but statistically significant. Receipt of financial aid was also found to be significant and associated with receipt of the bachelor's degree in four years (effect size of .10) and graduation from a junior or community college in two years (effect size of .19). However, when only those studies that controlled for differences in academic ability between those receiving and those not receiving financial aid were considered, the effect size was reduced to statistical nonsignificance ($-.006$).

Thus, a synthesis of the most methodologically rigorous subset of studies suggests that receipt of general financial aid has no statistically significant net effects on persistence and degree attainment. Here the meta-analysis conclusion would seem quite consistent with the mixed findings of the studies just cited. If one assumes, however, that students with the fewest financial resources are the most likely to receive general financial aid, then one could conclude that the awarding of financial aid is reasonably successful in accomplishing its purpose. That is, by allowing recipients to persist and graduate at a rate equal to (if not better than) nonrecipients, general financial aid may be at least partially compensating for the negative effects of low socioeconomic origins on educational attainment (for example, Alexander, Riordan, Fennessey, & Pallas, 1982; Bowles, 1973; Eckland & Henderson, 1981; Peng & Fetters, 1978; Wegner & Sewell, 1970).

Another line of research has sought to determine whether different types or combinations of financial aid have differential net influences on persistence or bachelor's degree completion. Again the findings are somewhat mixed. Brooks (1981), Kreiger (1980), and Moline (1987) all found no statistically significant differences in persistence or graduation rates among students who received different types or combinations of aid. Similar results are reported by St. John, Kirshstein, and Noell (1988), who found that loans, grants, and combinations of loans, grants, and work-study programs all had a significantly positive influence at one time or another on year-to-year persistence during college. Other research, however, has suggested that some types of aid may be more beneficial than others. For example, independent analyses by Astin (1975b, 1982), Blanchfield (1971, 1972), and Hochstein and Butler (1983) have suggested that scholarships and grants have a significantly more positive effect on persistence than do loans, even when such variables as student academic aptitude, secondary school achievement, and socioeconomic origin are taken into account. Herndon (1982), on the other hand, found that net of such factors as academic aptitude, secondary school grades, and residing on or off campus, participation in college work-study programs was more effective than other forms of financial aid in discriminating persisters from dropouts. Similar results for the particularly positive effects of work-study aid, though not in any direct comparison with other forms of aid, have been reported by Astin (1975a).

Some resolution of these conflicting results is offered by Murdock (1988) in a further quantitative synthesis of the influence of financial aid on persistence. In this synthesis, Murdock compared each individual form of financial aid (grants, loans, scholarships, and work-study programs) against the combined effect of all others. The only consistently significant effect size was for scholarships (.14 of a standard deviation), indicating that scholarships were significantly (if only modestly) more effective than a composite of other forms of aid in promoting persistence. This conclusion would seem to agree with the general weight of evidence in that most studies that find significant differences among forms of aid in effects on persistence report scholarships or grants to be the most beneficial. It does not appear, however, that Murdock was able to make statistical adjustments in her synthesis for ability differences between those receiving scholarships and those receiving other forms of aid. Consequently, the effect size reported may be overestimating the true net influence of scholarship aid on persistence.

Financial aid is, of course, only one part of the economic reality confronting many students as they attempt to finance a bachelor's or other degree. Many of the same students must work while attending college (Bean & Metzner, 1985). Evidence concerning the effects on persistence and educational attainment of employment during college is shaped to some extent by where the employment occurs. The evidence is quite consistent that off-campus employment (typically measured in number of hours) has a negative influence on both year-to-year persistence in college and bachelor's degree completion (Anderson, 1981; Astin, 1975b, 1982; Ehrenberg & Sherman, 1987; Kohen, Nestel, & Karmas, 1978; Peng & Fetters, 1978; Staman, 1980; University of California, 1980). This negative effect remains even when controls are made for such factors as academic ability, secondary school achievement, socioeconomic origin, educational aspirations, gender, race, and type of college initially attended. Astin (1975b) has suggested that full-time (thirty-five to forty hours per week) off-campus employment may have more deleterious consequences for persistence and degree completion than part-time (twenty-five hours per week or less) employment. It is clear from other analyses, however, that amount of part-time off-campus employment also has a net negative influence on year-to-year persistence and an inhibiting effect on completing one's degree on time (for example, Ehrenberg & Sherman, 1987; Kohen, Nestel, & Karmas, 1978).

If persistence and educational attainment are inhibited by full- or part-time off-campus employment, the reverse appears to be true for the effects of part-time employment on campus. Studies that were based on national samples and controlled for such factors as academic aptitude, secondary school achievement, socioeconomic origins, and educational aspirations indicate that a part-time job on campus (usually in the form of a work-study arrangement) has a net positive impact on year-to-year persistence, bachelor's degree completion, timely graduation, and the probability of enrolling in graduate or professional school (Anderson, 1981; Astin, 1975a, 1982; Ehrenberg & Sherman, 1987; Velez, 1985).

Wenc (1983) and Ehrenberg and Sherman (1987) have argued that the differential effects of on-campus and off-campus work on persistence and degree attainment are due in large measure to the former experience enhancing involvement and integration in the institution while the latter experience tends to inhibit it. Anderson (1981) provides evidence to at least partially support this contention. In her analysis of the NLS-72 sample, she found that net of such factors as academic ability, educational aspirations, race, gender, and place of residence during college, regular labor-force employment tended to significantly lower one's sense of campus integration (for example, satisfaction with teachers, social life, intellectual growth). Campus integration in turn had a statistically significant positive influence on first-year persistence in college.

Conditional Effects of College

A substantial amount of research has suggested the possibility that different between- and within-college experiences may have a differential influence on educational attainment for different kinds of students. This body of research, however, has at least two problems that make it difficult to synthesize and even harder to draw firm conclusions from. First, most of the research erroneously infers conditional effects from differences found between various subgroups (men versus women, blacks versus whites, and so on) in the factors significantly associated with educational attainment. For example, a study that found grades a statistically significant influence on persistence for blacks but not for whites might conclude that grades are more important in the educational attainment process for blacks than for whites. Unfortunately, differences in sample size and simple chance sampling errors across independent samples can produce an artificial situation in which a variable has a statistically significant association with the outcomes in one subsample but not in another. More often than not such differences are due to chance; and while there are statistical procedures that help one distinguish between chance and nonchance conditional effects, they were employed in only a very few of the studies.

A second problem, likely caused in part by the first, is the paucity of replicable conditional effects across different studies. The interpretation of chance differences as though they are real differences will often increase the probability of this phenomenon in a body of evidence. This further complicates the task of synthesizing the findings and formulating reasonable conclusions. Given these problems and in order to make sense of the many inconsistent findings, we used relatively stringent criteria for making conclusions about the robustness of conditional effects. First, we only considered conditional effects in individual studies to be nonchance if they were tested for statistical significance or, lacking this, if the difference in the magnitude of variable associations between samples was so large (a ratio of 1:2) that it was unlikely to be a chance difference. Second, the weight of evidence criterion we have employed throughout this book implies that greatest credence is given to those conditional effects that were more rigorously tested and were replicated across independent samples. We considered conditional effects that lacked replication to be only suggestive in nature. In this way we hoped to give some semblance of order to the extensive but highly inconsistent and disparate body of evidence.

Institutional Characteristics by Student Characteristics

A number of investigations have sought to determine whether institutional characteristics have differential effects on educational attainment for different kinds of students. The findings of this research, however, are inconsistent and even contradictory. Alexander and Eckland (1977), Anderson (1986), Ethington and Smart (1986), Kamens (1968), and Wegner and Sewell (1970) all conducted analyses that considered gender differences in the effects of college "quality" measures on various forms of educational attainment. Alexander and Eckland (1977) and Ethington and Smart (1986) report evidence to suggest that institutional selectivity may have a stronger positive influence on educational attainment or graduate school enrollment for men than for women. Conversely, Anderson's analysis of the NLS-72 sample suggests that a measure of institutional quality that combines selectivity and financial resources may have a stronger positive influence on attainment for women than for men. Kamens (1968) and Wegner and Sewell (1970) also present evidence to suggest that measures of institutional prestige may have a differential effect on persistence and degree completion for students from different socioeconomic origins or combinations of socioeconomic origin and academic ability. The operational definitions of variables between the two studies are so different, however, that it is hazardous to compare results.

Earlier in this chapter we reviewed evidence indicating that attending a predominantly black institution enhances the educational attainment of black students. Additional analyses by Pascarella, Smart, and Stoecker (1987) and Stoecker, Pascarella, and Wolfle (1988) have attempted to determine whether there are gender differences in this effect. The occurrence of statistically nonsignificant results suggests that the effects of attending a black institution on educational attainment are generally the same for both black men and women. In a related study, Pascarella (1985b) found that initial enrollment in a large, public institution had a negative effect on bachelor's degree completion that was significantly stronger for black men than for white men. The negative effect was also significantly stronger for a pooled sample of black men and women then it was for their white counterparts. This conditional effect held irrespective of institutional selectivity and race; however, we uncovered no independent study that replicated it.

We also reviewed earlier a small body of evidence indicating that disruptions of the educational sequence, either in the form of delays, stopping out, or transferring between four-year institutions, have an inhibiting influence on degree completion. There is some additional evidence to suggest that this negative impact is not the same for all students. Again, however, the findings resist any clear conclusions and await replication. In a study of temporal discontinuities, for example, Robertshaw and Wolfle (1983) found that delaying the start of college had a stronger negative effect on the educational attainment of blacks than of whites, but interrupting one's college education (stopping out) had a more negative effect on white attainment. When gender was considered, Robertshaw and Wolfle found that both types of temporal discontinuities had a greater deleterious influence on white female attainment than on white male attainment. Pascarella's (1985b) analysis of bachelor's degree attainment indicated that institutional discontinuities (transferring from one four-year institution to another) had a significantly stronger negative influence on attainment for black men than for white men. The negative effect was similar for men and women, irrespective of race.

Finally, there is some evidence that college environmental factors may have a differential influence on educational aspirations for men and women. In Pascarella's (1984a) analyses, he found that net of precollege aptitude and educational aspirations, attending an institution with a strong environmental press for academic or intellectual competition had a significantly larger positive effect on sophomore-year aspirations for men in selective institutions (average SAT of 1075 or above) than for women generally or for men in less selective institutions. This finding, he argues, implies that academically selective institutions often provide an interpersonally competitive environment that is particularly potent in terms of its contextual effect on male aspirations. The same environmental press, however, appears to have little net consequence for female aspirations, even at those selective institutions where it is maximized.

Conversely, environmental factors that significantly influence female educational aspirations may have little impact on male aspirations. Further analyses by Pascarella (1984a) suggested that although a strong environmental press for conventional or conformist behavior had a statistically significant inhibiting influence on women's educational aspirations, the influence on male aspirations was trivial and significantly smaller in magnitude. (A conventional or conformist environment placed a strong emphasis on student conformity, traditional social activities and dating, and competitive sports.) Net of institutional selectivity, a conventional or conformist environment was least likely at small, financially well-endowed women's institutions. Thus, this conditional effect tends to reinforce the notion that women's institutions enhance women's aspirations by offering an environmental context that provides nonstereotypic role models and promotes nonconventional social roles for students (Tidball, 1986).

While a number of the conditional effects that involve institutional characteristics are conceptually intriguing, it should be emphasized that there is little evidence with respect to their replicability. Consequently, we regard any firm conclusions about the differential effects of institutional character-istics on the educational attainment of different kinds of students as pre-mature.

College Experiences by Student Characteristics

Compared to institutional characteristics, there is somewhat greater consistency in the research evidence concerning the differential effects of college experiences on the educational attainment of different kinds of stu-dents. Many of these conditional effects have been yielded in studies that attempted to validate Tinto's (1975) explanatory model of student persis-tence or withdrawal behavior. As previously indicated, Tinto's model is es-sentially a variation on the theme of person-environment fit and has as its core explanatory variables the concepts of social and academic integration in the institution attended. There is a small but growing body of evidence indicating that measures of social and academic integration tend to have a differential influence on persistence for different kinds of students.

Although this evidence is somewhat difficult to synthesize because of differences in the operational definitions of social and academic integration employed in different studies, two general conclusions appear warranted. First, at primarily residential institutions, social integration tends to have a compensatory interaction with academic integration and vice versa. Evi-dence of this conditional effect has been reported in three separate samples by Pascarella and Chapman (1983b), Pascarella and Terenzini (1983), and Pascarella and Wolfle (1985). In all three studies academic integration (as measured by such variables as grades, intellectual development, and con-tacts with faculty) had its strongest positive influence on persistence or de-gree attainment for students at the lowest levels of social integration (as measured by such variables as extracurricular involvement and informal interaction with peers). As a student's level of social integration increased, the importance of that student's academic integration for persistence or degree attainment diminished. The reverse was true for the influence of social integration on persistence or degree attainment at different levels of academic integration. Social integration had its strongest positive impact on persistence or degree attainment for students at the lowest levels of aca-demic integration, and as level of academic integration increased the im-portance of social integration diminished. There may be structural limits to this side of the conditional effect, however, in that a student must maintain a certain level of academic integration (grades) simply to be eligible to per-sist. A similar though statistically nonsignificant interaction between aca-demic and social integration has also been reported by Terenzini, Pascar-ella, Theophilides, and Lorang (1985).

A second generalization is that levels of either social or academic integration tend to have a compensatory influence on freshman-to-sophomore persistence for students who either enter a residential institution with characteristics predictive of withdrawal (for example, low family educational status, low educational aspirations) or who subsequently have low commitment to the institution or the goal of graduation from college. Pascarella and Terenzini (1979a), for example, found that the frequency of informal contact with faculty to discuss intellectual issues and the perceived quality of interaction with faculty and peers had their most positive influence on persistence for students with low initial and subsequent commitment to the goal of graduation or who came from families where parents had relatively low levels of formal education. As level of family education and graduation commitment increased, interaction with faculty and peers became less important for persistence.

A consistent set of compensatory impacts involving extracurricular participation and social interaction with peers on the one hand and commitment to the institution attended and the goal of college graduation on the other have also been reported by Pascarella and Chapman (1983b) with an independent sample of residential university students. As with the Pascarella and Terenzini (1979a) analyses, social involvement was most important in enhancing persistence for students with low levels of institutional and goal commitment. As these commitments increased, social involvement played a decreasing role in persistence or withdrawal behavior.[8]

Available research also suggests that measures of social and academic integration or institutional fit have a differential influence on persistence or educational attainment for gender and race subgroups. The evidence, however, is not always consistent. Evidence from independent samples presented by Pascarella and Terenzini (1983) and Ethington and Smart (1986) suggests that social integration or involvement had a significantly more positive impact on freshman-year persistence and attending graduate school for women than for men. Conversely, academic integration was more important for men. Somewhat at odds with these results, however, Pascarella, Ethington, and Smart (1988) and Stoecker, Pascarella, and Wolfle (1988) found little to suggest that bachelor's degree attainment for either gender is differentially influenced by level of social or academic integration.

Similarly, research concerning differences in the relative influence of social and academic integration on persistence and attainment within different racial subgroups (typically black or white students) is also inconclusive. Evidence from a number of studies has suggested that academic integration, particularly as it pertains to meeting the formal demands of the academic system, may be a more important influence on persistence for black students than is social integration (for example, Donovan, 1984; Eddins, 1982; Shaffer, 1973). Although this may be true of black students who come to college with poor academic preparation, more recent evidence has suggested that social integration and social support may be as important to the persistence and educational attainment of black students in general as is academic integration (for example, Mallinckrodt, 1988; Mallinckrodt & Sedlacek, 1987; Pascarella, 1985b; Stoecker, Pascarella, & Wolfle, 1988). Moreover, evidence reported by Pascarella and Terenzini (1979a) and Pascarella (1985b) on two separate samples has suggested that there may be no statistically significant differences between white and black students in the relative importance of social and academic integration for either persistence or bachelor's degree completion.

If one takes a more fine-grained perspective and considers the specific dimensions of social integration, there is some indication that these may vary in the magnitude of their impact on persistence and attainment by race (Mallinckrodt & Sedlacek, 1987; Pascarella, 1985b). In the Pascarella analyses, for example, formalized types of social involvement (such as serving on a university or departmental committee) may be the most influential for blacks. Conversely, more informal types of social integration (such as contact with faculty and staff) may be the most important for whites. These findings, however, await replication.

A more fine-grained analysis of subgroups based on race and gender (for example, black and white men and women) also suggests the presence of conditional effects that may be masked in analyses that simply compare blacks with whites or men with women. For example, when Stoecker, Pascarella, and Wolfle (1988) disaggregated their sample into four subgroups based on race and gender, they found that social or leadership involvement during college had a significantly more positive influence on bachelor's degree attainment for black men than for white men. For black and white women, however, the impact of this variable was about equal. Similarly, they found that majoring in the social sciences had a significantly more positive influence on degree attainment for black women than it did for black men. The same differential effect did not hold for whites. Once again, however, these findings have yet to be replicated.

Although it is hazardous to form specific conclusions from such findings until they have a more solid empirical base, they clearly suggest the potential complexity of the educational attainment process. Different types of students in the same institution may benefit differentially from different types of social and academic experiences. Furthermore, as suggested by Bean (1985), a student's integration into the social and academic system of an institution may have a differential impact on persistence at different periods during college. Bean's finding at a large residential university suggested that degree of fit with these systems was most critical during the freshman year and tended to decrease in importance thereafter. This particular finding however, may also reflect the fact that Bean's sample became less variable from the freshman year to the upperclassman years, thus attenuating associations among variables.

Another aspect of this complex picture is that nearly all of the research cited above was conducted on traditional-age college students (those eighteen to twenty-two years old) attending four-year institutions, most of them residential. Despite the fact that older, nontraditional students now constitute well over 30 percent of all college students (*Digest of Educational Statistics*, 1986), there is insufficient evidence to conclude that the factors that influence educational attainment are the same for this group as they are for their traditional-age counterparts (Bean & Metzner, 1985). A similar statement could be made for students who work, who attend college part-time rather than full-time, or who are enrolled in two-year rather than four-year institutions.

Institutional Characteristics by College Experiences

Finally, there is also a set of conditional effects suggesting that the magnitude of the influence of certain college experiences on persistence may depend on the institutional context in which they occur. Earlier in this chapter, for example, we cited a substantial body of evidence indicating that level of social involvement or integration during college has a stronger positive influence on persistence in residential schools than in commuter institutions. This is likely due in large part to the fact that at commuter institutions there is typically less of a social system in which one can become involved. On the other hand, the facilitation of social involvement during college is one of the most powerful ways in which the residential institution enhances student persistence and degree completion.

For individual students, however, the influence of residing on campus (versus commuting to college) on bachelor's degree completion may vary, depending on the type of institution attended. In an analysis of the impact of residential status on bachelor's degree completion, Astin (1973b) found that living on campus during the freshman year had its most positive impact in four-year colleges, a slightly less positive impact in four-year universities, and a trivial impact at two-year colleges. Thus, if beginning college at a four-year institution rather than at a two-year institution provides the student with a net advantage in educational attainment, that advantage may be even further accentuated if he or she lives on campus during the freshman year. It should be pointed out, however, that this finding could be the result of a methodological artifact. Very few two-year colleges have residential facilities. Consequently, the absence of variance in residing on or off campus may substantially reduce the impact of this variable on degree completion in two-year colleges.

Evidence also suggests that the positive link between receiving general financial aid and persistence or graduation is stronger at two-year and private institutions than it is at four-year or public institutions. This conclusion is based on the results of Murdock's (1988) meta-analysis of financial aid and persistence. Since Murdock's synthesis could not control for pre-college differences among students attending different types of institutions, however, these conditional effects need to be viewed with some caution. They might well reflect differential criteria for awarding financial aid at different institutions.

Long-Term Effects of College

The major long-term effect of college on educational attainment is manifest largely in the intergenerational transfer of benefits from parents to children. As suggested by Swift and Weisbrod (1965), the more fully an individual develops his or her intellectual faculties and career opportunities through investment in education, the more likely that individual is to believe in the importance of developing similar intellectual faculties and career opportunities for his or her children. Thus, other factors being equal, highly educated parents are more likely than their less-educated counterparts to raise children who themselves recognize the value of education.

Thus does education beget education; and there is abundant evidence to suggest that net of such factors as family size, parental income and occupation, and the individual's academic ability and achievement, level of parental formal education has a positive influence on the educational attainment of both sons and daughters (for example, Blau & Duncan, 1967; Brazer & David, 1962; DiMaggio & Mohr, 1985; Duncan, 1968; Hauser, 1973; Leibowitz, 1974b; Schwartz, 1985; Sewell, Hauser, & Wolf, 1980; Tinto, 1981). Part of this positive effect is direct and unmediated, and part is indirect and mediated through intervening variables in the educational attainment process such as aspirations and career plans.

Somewhat less research has addressed the issue of the impact of parents having attended or graduated from college on the educational attainment of their children. Sewell and Shah (1968a) found that net of the child's intelligence, mother's and father's attendance at college each had an independent and statistically significant positive influence on their son or daughter attending and graduating from college. Similarly, Brazer and David (1962) report that in families where the head of the spending unit was a college graduate, a child was most likely to attend college and complete the most years of college. This association remained even after statistical controls were made for such factors as occupation, earnings, race, and number of children in the family. More recent research has reported similar findings with respect to the independent positive influence of parents' college graduation on the college attendance of their sons and daughters (Christensen, Melder, & Weisbrod, 1975; Thomas, Alexander, & Eckland, 1979).

Gruca (1988) conducted what is perhaps the most comprehensive and focused study of the effects of having a bachelor's degree on the educational attainment of one's children. Gruca's sample was limited to college students and traced their attainment over the nine-year period after initial college enrollment. The variables in her model included family income, secondary school academic and social achievement, precollege educational and occupational aspirations, the selectivity and size of the institution attended, academic major, college grades, and college social involvement. With these variables held constant, one's father having a bachelor's degree or above had no statistically significant direct effects on educational attainment for black or white men or women. One's mother being a college graduate, however, had a statistically significant, positive direct effect on the attainment of black men. (The corresponding effect for black women was positive but not significant.)

When Gruca considered indirect effects, she found that having a father or mother who was a college graduate significantly, though indirectly, enhanced the educational attainment of both white men and women. These positive indirect effects were manifest largely through the net positive impact of parental college education on such salient intervening influences in the educational attainment process as parental income, precollege educational aspirations, and the selectivity of the undergraduate institution attended. The corresponding indirect effects for black men and women were similar in magnitude, particularly for college graduate fathers of black men and college graduate mothers of black women. The small black sample sizes, however, probably prevented statistical significance.

Gruca's (1988) study is not the only one to suggest that parental education has an independent influence on important intervening variables in the educational attainment process of children. Ethington and Smart (1986), Hafner (1985), Hearn (1984), and Pascarella (1984a), after analyzing separate samples, suggested that parental formal education had a statistically significant positive influence on their children's precollege educational aspirations and on the selectivity of the undergraduate institution attended, an influence that was independent of such factors as family income and the academic aptitude of the individual student.

Summary

Although educational attainment is not typically thought of as an outcome of college, it nevertheless plays a critical role in the process of individual social mobility or status attainment (for example, occupational status and income). Consequently, it is worth considering the ways in which this important mediating variable in individual social mobility is influenced by the college experience.

Between-College Effects

It is clear that where one begins one's collegiate experience has an influence on educational attainment independent of one's precollege abilities, socioeconomic status, or aspirations. The most consistent findings come from studies that consider the net effect of attending two-year rather than four-year institutions or that estimate the net effect of institutional "quality." Educational attainment tends to be enhanced by enrolling initially in a four-year rather than a two-year institution. Net of precollege differences, attending a four-year (versus a two-year) college appears to increase one's probability of obtaining a bachelor's degree within a specified time period by 15 percent, perhaps even more. Within four-year institutions, measures of institutional "quality" (for example, student body selectivity, resources per student) tend to enhance both the attainment of a bachelor's degree and enrollment in graduate or professional school. Moreover, this effect persists even when student precollege characteristics and institutional characteristics such as size, type of control, and predominant race of students are taken into account.

Though less consistent, the weight of evidence also indicates that net of student precollege characteristics, attending a private or a small college tends to have positive effects on educational attainment. These positive effects of private control and small size remain even when additional statistical controls are made for institutional selectivity and for each other (that is, a control for size when estimating the effects of private control and vice-versa). The nature of the effect of institutional size on educational attainment, however, tends to be indirect. Specifically, attendance at a small college rather than a large one tends to facilitate social involvement with faculty and peers that in turn positively influences persistence, college graduation, and graduate school enrollment.

For black students and women, attendance at a predominantly black and a predominantly women's college, respectively, appears to provide some net advantage in terms of educational attainment. This advantage may not be totally direct, however. Some evidence suggests that part of the positive effect of attendance at a black or at a women's college is indirect, specifically through the positive influence of each institution on academic achievement.

A number of different investigations have indicated that college environmental factors may also have an influence on educational attainment, one that is independent of the precollege characteristics of the students enrolled. The environmental factors that maximize attainment include a cohesive peer environment (that is, students develop close on-campus friendships), frequent participation in college-sponsored activities, and a perception that the institution has a high level of personal involvement with and concern for the individual student. Consistent with these findings is evidence suggesting that a strong institutional emphasis on supportive student personnel services (advising, orientation, the development of academic survival skills in individualized general education courses, and the like) is also linked positively with institutional persistence rates.

Educational attainment is not influenced only by the characteristics of the institution in which a student enrolls. It is also influenced by the continuity of the student's experience within that institution. An interruption in this continuity, in the form of transfer from one four-year institution to another, tends to inhibit degree attainment. This effect persists even when controls are made for important student precollege characteristics (such as aspirations, socioeconomic status, achievement) and the characteristics of the initial college attended (such as selectivity or prestige, size, control, predominant race). While the negative effect holds for both black and white students, it may be more pronounced for the former, particularly for black men.

It is important to point out that with the possible exception of attending a two-year institution as compared to a four-year institution, net between-college effects on various indexes of educational attainment are small. They probably account for no more than 1 or perhaps 2 percent of the variance in these outcomes.

Within-College Effects

Clearly, the structural and environmental characteristics of the institution attended have a substantive influence on the student's social and academic experience of college. Nevertheless, there are specific collegiate experiences or accomplishments that enhance educational attainment regardless of where one attends college. Beyond the obvious importance of academic achievement, the weight of evidence also suggests that one's level of involvement or integration in an institution's social system has significant implications for attainment. Specifically, involvement in extracurricular activities and the extent and quality of one's social interaction with student peers and faculty both have a small, positive influence on persistence, educational aspirations, bachelor's degree attainment, and graduate school attendance. This influence is largely independent of student precollege characteristics, the characteristics of the institution attended, and one's level of academic achievement during college. Thus, consistent with theoretical expectations, social interaction with significant others during college, and the encouragement received therefrom, exert an independent influence in the educational attainment process. Since the most socially integrated students also tend to have the highest precollege educational aspirations, however, the effect of social interaction or integration is perhaps best characterized as accentuating or affirming initial aspirations rather than changing them.

Limited evidence also exists to suggest that integration into the social and academic systems of an institution is more important for persistence during the freshman year than thereafter. This finding, however, may be artifactual and awaits replication.

Results of research on the direct influence of academic major on educational attainment are inconsistent. Nevertheless, major departments may provide students with salient social, intellectual, and occupationally linked contexts that have important indirect implications for educational attainment. For instance, limited evidence suggests that irrespective of student precollege characteristics and the characteristics of the institution attended, majoring in the social sciences or humanities indirectly enhances bachelor's degree completion by positively influencing grades and informal interaction with faculty. Such a finding may partially reflect the fact that faculty in the social sciences and humanities tend to have grading practices and orientations toward accessibility to students that differ from those of their colleagues in other fields of study. It also appears that those majors that can guarantee the bachelor's degree recipient a reasonably high level of immediate occupational and economic payoffs (for example, engineering, business) may actually discourage education beyond the bachelor's degree.

The evidence is quite clear that living on campus rather than commuting to college has a strong positive net effect on persistence and completion of the bachelor's degree. The causal mechanism that underlies this effect is probably the extent to which residential living facilitates involvement or integration in the social system of the institution. The self-selection process that distinguishes resident from commuter students suggests that the positive net effect of residential living on educational attainment is best characterized as the accentuation of initial differences.

Limited evidence exists to indicate that the effect on bachelor's degree completion of living on campus during the freshman year is of greater consequence in four-year colleges and universities than in two-year institutions. This finding could be the result of a methodological artifact, however. Nevertheless, the evidence quite consistently shows that the types of social integration facilitated by on-campus living play a significantly more important role in student persistence at residential institutions than at commuter institutions. In the latter, persistence is much less a function of social involvement or integration than it is of academic performance and external considerations that involve work, finances, and family responsibilities. Within residential institutions generally, it is likely that certain specific residential contexts are particularly potent in enhancing persistence. Some evidence suggests that fraternities and sororities can assume this role, particularly during the freshman or sophomore year. The most consistent findings, however, point to living-learning residences that attempt programmatically to integrate the student's academic and social life.

We have regarded orientation programs as an attempt by an institution to enhance the early socialization of entering students. If effective, such programs should facilitate academic adjustment and initial social integration, thereby increasing the likelihood of persistence and degree completion. The weight of evidence suggests that a first-semester freshman seminar designed to orient the student to the institution and to teach important academic survival skills is positively linked with both freshman-year persistence and degree completion. This positive link persists even when academic aptitude and secondary school achievement are taken into account. Moreover, even a short precollege orientation may exert a positive indirect effect on persistence by enhancing the student's initial social integration.

Evidence on the impact of academic advising on persistence is inconsistent, perhaps because of the fact that the primary influence of advising is indirect. Limited evidence suggests, for example, that high-quality advising has a positive but indirect impact on persistence through its positive effect on grades and satisfaction with college and its negative influence on intent to withdraw.

Although the findings are somewhat mixed, the weight of evidence indicates that net of differences in academic aptitude, students who receive financial aid are as likely to persist in college as those who do not receive such aid. If one assumes that financial aid is aimed at equating the financial resources of students from different family socioeconomic origins, then this conclusion tentatively implies that financial aid in general may be successfully compensating for the negative impact of low individual financial resources on persistence in college. Some evidence also exists to suggest that the influence of financial aid on persistence is stronger at two-year and private colleges than at four-year and public colleges. Although the findings with respect to the relative impact of different forms of financial aid are also mixed, the weight of evidence does suggest that scholarships have the strongest positive influence on persistence.

The influence of employment during college on persistence and educational attainment depends to a great extent upon where the employment occurs. Net of student precollege characteristics, full-time or part-time off-campus employment has a negative impact, while part-time employment on campus (usually in the form of a work-study arrangement) has a positive impact.

Conditional Effects of College

Considerable research suggests that various college characteristics or college experiences have a differential influence on persistence or educational attainment for different kinds of students. The results of this research, however, tend to be inconsistent. Replicated conditional effects of nontrivial magnitude are rare. Nevertheless, two generalizations appear warranted with respect to the influence on persistence of social and academic integration or involvement during college. First, a high level of social integration may compensate for a low level of academic integration just as a high level of academic integration may compensate for a low level of social integration. Second, levels of social and academic integration during college are most important for the persistence of students who either enter college with individual traits predictive of withdrawal or who have low commitment to the institution or the goal of graduation from college. Studies replicating these compensatory effects have been limited largely to residential institutions. It would be of interest to know whether future studies also find these effects to be present in nonresidential colleges.

Long-Term Effects of College

In terms of impact on educational attainment, the evidence is quite clear that the benefits of obtaining a college degree are passed on from one generation to the next. Having a bachelor's degree or above appears to have a positive influence on the educational attainment of sons and daughters even when controls are made for such factors as income, family size, and offspring's intelligence. The most comprehensive analysis suggests that much of this long-term impact is indirect, mediated through the influence of parental education on family financial resources, sons' and daughters' educational aspirations, and the selectivity of the undergraduate institution they attend.

Notes

1. To be sure, there is evidence to suggest that degree of overall person-college fit is positively linked with persistence (for example, Braddock, 1981a; Pervin & Rubin, 1967; Rootman, 1972). Similarly, student use of college facilities is positively associated with persistence (for example, Churchill & Iwai, 1981; Kramer & Kramer, 1968). In both cases, however, this evidence pertains almost exclusively to institutional persistence rather than educational attainment, and it is not nearly as extensive as the evidence produced by studies that focus on specific interactions and/or experiences within the academic and social systems of the institution.

2. A somewhat different type of remedial intervention, known as "attributional retraining," has also shown promise for improving student achievement. The purpose of attributional retraining is to restore a student's perceived control and self-efficacy in an academic situation, that is, to show that academic success or failure is linked to individual effort and not circumstances beyond the individual's control (Forsterling, 1985; Perry & Penner, 1989). Attributional retraining has been shown to enhance academic achievement (for example, Wilson & Linville, 1982, 1985, as reviewed by Perry & Penner, 1989), but the greatest impact may be for those who initially attribute success or failure to external rather than internal causes (Perry & Penner, 1989).

3. Clearly, there are other factors that appear to be significantly related to grades in college. These include the nature of the dominant peer culture with which the student interacts (for example, Gerst & Moos,

1972; Misner & Wellner, 1970; Moos, 1979; Schrager, 1986; Winston, Hutson, & McCaffery, 1980), the student's academic major (Astin, 1982; Stoecker, Pascarella, & Wolfle, 1988), congruence between personality characteristics and choice of major (Aderinto, 1975; Bruch & Krieshok, 1981; Reuterfors, Schneidner, & Overton, 1979; Spokane, 1985; Walsh, Spokane, & Mitchell, 1976), and the congruence between the college environment and student personality characteristics (Hayes, 1974). Grades are also related to congruence in student-faculty interests (Posthuma & Navran (1970), participation in honors programs (for example, Astin, 1977a; Pflaum, Pascarella, & Duby, 1985), the consistency between part-time work and the student's academic program (Hay, Evans, & Lindsay, 1970), and, possibly, student informal contact with faculty that focuses on intellectual matters (Pascarella, Terenzini, & Hibel, 1978; Terenzini & Pascarella, 1980a; Volkwein, King, & Terenzini, 1985). Compared to interventions designed to facilitate academic adjustment or enhance the study climate in residences, however, these associations have received little experimental verification.

4. In addition to studies that focus on the influence of academic major on educational aspirations and attainment, there is also a small body of evidence that considers the effects of varying levels of congruence or fit between a student's personality characteristics and his or her academic major. Nearly all of this research is based on Holland's (1973, 1984) theory of person-environment fit. According to this theory, congruence (typified, for example, by a person whose predominant personality type is artistic and whose major is music) should lead to higher levels of persistence and degree attainment than incongruence. The evidence addressing this proposition is somewhat mixed. Some studies find that congruence is significantly and positively related to persistence (Bruch & Krieshok, 1981; Southworth & Morningstar, 1970), while others report no significant relationship (Elton & Rose, 1981; Holcomb & Anderson, 1978).

5. Despite some findings to the contrary (for example, Hountras & Brandt, 1970; Nowack & Hanson, 1985; Trivett, 1974), the most convincing evidence suggests that living on campus or near campus (versus commuting to college) has little net positive influence on academic achievement (Blimling, 1989; Chickering, 1974a; Grosz & Brandt, 1969; Maurais, 1968; Pascarella, 1985d; Ryan, 1970; Simono, Wachowiak, & Furr, 1984; Weislogel, 1977). The latter conclusion seems to hold even when the characteristics of the institution attended are taken into account (Pascarella, 1985d). There is also single-institution evidence, as yet unreplicated, that living on campus can have a negative impact on various dimensions of general cognitive development (Pike, 1989).

6. See Bean and Metzner (1985) for a cogent and comprehensive review of the factors that influence the persistence or withdrawal behavior of

nontraditional, commuting students. Part of this section draws from that review.

7. Strictly speaking, anticipatory socialization takes place in groups not connected to the college that one will be attending (for example, high school friends). Since orientation programs are obviously tied to the college to be attended, we consider them to be institutionally sponsored attempts at early socialization that are functionally analogous to anticipatory socialization.

8. Evidence from three independent samples (Pascarella & Chapman, 1983b; Pascarella & Terenzini, 1983; Terenzini, Pascarella, Theophilides, & Lorang, 1985) has suggested a mutually compensatory interaction between commitment to the institution attended and commitment to the goal of graduation. In terms of positive influence on persistence, commitment to graduation from college is most important for individuals low in institutional commitment. Conversely, institutional commitment is most important for individuals low in commitment to graduation.

10

Career Choice
and Development

In this chapter we summarize the accumulated evidence on the influence of college on the noneconomic aspects of career. (Chapter Eleven addresses the economic returns to a college education.) Not surprisingly, this evidence indicates that college has an important impact on the type of occupation one enters. Indeed, the lack of a bachelor's degree may effectively exclude an individual from entry into a large number of jobs; and this effect is likely to increase as American society becomes more technologically complex (Boudon, 1973; Perella, 1973; Rosen, 1975). In addition to college's undeniably important implications for occupational attainment, college also shapes other dimensions of one's career. These include career choice, career progression and success, and the transfer of occupational status advantages from one generation to the next.

By definition, of course, a large portion of the evidence on the impact of college on career concerns long-term effects. Consequently, we decided not to include a separate section on long-term effects in this chapter but rather to synthesize the evidence on such effects within our other five sections. In the final section of the chapter we synthesize evidence pertaining to the intergenerational transfer of college effects from parents to children.

Change During College

Astin (1977a) has suggested that for a substantial number of students, career development during college is more a process of implementing a career than of choosing one. There is substantial evidence to support this claim in that initial career choice at the beginning of college tends to be the single best predictor of career choice at the end of college and the career or occupation actually entered (Astin, 1977a; Astin & Myint, 1971; Braxton, Brier, Herzog, & Pascarella, 1988; Ethington, Smart, & Pascarella, 1987; Pascarella, Brier, Smart, & Herzog, 1987; Tusin & Pascarella, 1985). Despite this tendency, it is clear that students frequently change their occupational plans during college (Astin & Panos, 1969; Davis, 1965; Fenske

& Scott, 1973; Hind & Wirth, 1969; Theophilides, Terenzini, & Lorang, 1984a). Feldman and Newcomb (1969) estimated that between one-third and two-thirds of all students change their career choice during college, and this is consistent with more recent national evidence presented by Astin (1977a). A large portion of such changes may be attributable to mobility across related fields or to shifts out of extremely competitive fields such as medicine and engineering (Astin, 1977a; Freiden & Staaf, 1973). Similarly, another portion of these changes may be due to the fact that students become cognizant of national or regional shifts in the employment opportunities and economic returns to different occupations (Cebula & Lopes, 1982; Florito & Dauffenbach, 1982; Freeman, 1971; Koch, 1972). In any case, a considerable amount of useful refocusing or refinement of career thinking is still occurring during college. A number of scholars have in fact addressed the issue of whether college students become more mature in their thinking about and planning for a career with increased exposure to postsecondary education.

Although assessed by several different methods and instruments, *career maturity* as it is operationally defined typically involves reference to the extent to which the individual has accomplished career developmental tasks, the ability to formulate career plans, the accuracy of knowledge about one's preferred occupation (opportunities, financial returns, training requirements, and the like), and the degree of certainty about and planning for one's career choice. A small but reasonably consistent body of evidence indicates that sophomores or upperclassmen tend to exhibit significantly higher levels of mature thinking about or planning for a career than do freshmen (Blann, 1985; Graves, 1975; Healy, Mitchell, & Mourton, 1987; Kennedy & Dimick, 1987; McCaffrey, Miller, & Winston, 1984; Ware & Apprich, 1980). The exceptions to this are studies by Loesch, Shub, and Rucker (1979) and Tilden (1976), who report that differences in level of career maturity noted between freshmen and upperclassmen were statistically nonsignificant. Somewhat mixed results are reported by Nevill and Super (1988), who found that although juniors and seniors did not differ from freshmen or sophomores on all dimensions of career maturity, they did engage in significantly more career planning.

Unfortunately, nearly all the research on the relationship between year in college and maturity of career thinking and planning is cross-sectional. Consequently, it is hazardous to attribute the more mature career thinking of upperclassmen to some internal socialization process that happens during college. Some evidence suggests that maturity in career thinking increases with age (Healy, Mitchell, & Mourton, 1987). This in itself might account for the freshman-upperclassman differences observed. Another alternative hypothesis is based on differential attrition from college. Students less advanced in their career planning may be more likely to withdraw from college than those with more advanced levels of career development. Indirect evidence for this hypothesis is perhaps suggested by the fact that degree of uncertainty about one's academic major tends to be positively linked to withdrawal from college (for example, Bucklin & Bucklin, 1970; Demitroff, 1974; Newton & Gaither, 1980).[1]

Net Effects of College

Occupational Status

As indicated in Chapter Nine, the most influential models of the socioeconomic attainment process in modern American society view formal education as playing a central role in the determination of occupational status. Not only is education seen as mediating the indirect influence of socioeconomic background; it is also considered to have an important direct effect on occupational status, irrespective of social origins.

Occupational status itself can be generally regarded as a hierarchy of occupations that reflects their perceived prestige or desirability (Duncan, 1961; Hauser & Featherman, 1977; Pineo & Porter, 1967; Siegel, 1971). The evidence is quite clear, however, that perceived occupational prestige or desirability has an overwhelming socioeconomic basis consisting largely of education and income. Duncan (1961), for example, found that about 83 percent of the variance in the perceived "prestige" of ninety U.S. occupational titles was accounted for by the typical education and income of individuals in those occupations. Almost exactly the same results have been reported in an independent analysis by Siegel (1971).

The different arrays of occupational prestige or status are themselves highly intercorrelated. Duncan, Featherman, and Duncan (1972), for example, report correlations among different ways of assessing occupational prestige in the .86 to .91 range. This suggests that the different approaches are essentially measuring the same trait and that there is a consistency or invariance in the occupational status hierarchy in the United States (Hauser & Featherman, 1977). Evidence also suggests that there is probably a single occupational prestige hierarchy for men and women (Bose, 1973; Parnes, Shea, Spitz, & Zeller, 1970).

Perhaps the most widely used measure of occupational status or prestige is the Socio-Economic Index (SEI) developed by Duncan (1961). An occupation's SEI score depends on the percentage of individuals working in that occupation who have completed a certain level of formal education or higher and the percentage with incomes at a certain level or higher. An update of the SEI, adjusted to the 1970 Census occupational codes, was completed by Hauser and Featherman (1977). It is obvious that since an occupation's SEI score is a function of its educational requirements, level of education will strongly influence an individual's score. Thus, on first consideration it would seem that any association between formal education and occupational prestige is largely tautological. This overstates the case, however, since as Jencks et al. (1979, p. 8) point out, the link between formal education and occupational status reflects a real social phenomenon. "The average education of men in a given line of work is closely related to the cognitive complexity and desirability of the work. It affects not only the social position of those who engage in the work (Duncan, 1961), but their children's life chances (Klatsky & Hodge, 1971), independent of both the individual's own education and his earnings from his work (Sewell & Hauser, 1975; Bielby, Hauser & Featherman, 1977)."

An extensive body of unequivocal evidence indicates that even when individual background characteristics (such as family social status) and abilities (for example, intelligence) are held constant, level of formal education has a strong positive impact on occupational status throughout the life span. Moreover, the clear weight of this evidence also suggests that among all measurable influences (family status, ability, aspirations, significant others, and so on), education is far and away the strongest (for example, Alexander & Eckland, 1975a; Alexander, Eckland, & Griffin, 1975; Duncan, 1968; Featherman & Carter, 1976; Fligstein & Wolf, 1978; Griffin & Kalleberg, 1981; Jencks, Crouse, & Mueser, 1983; McClendon, 1976; Porter, 1974, 1976; Sewell, Haller, & Ohlendorf, 1970; Sewell, Haller, & Portes, 1969; Sewell & Hauser, 1975, 1980; Treiman & Terrell, 1975).

The influence of educational attainment on occupational status, however, is not simply linear. Individuals appear to receive greater relative occupational status returns from some levels of formal education than from others. Evidence suggests that completing a bachelor's degree provides the single largest incremental return in terms of occupational status. Jencks et al. (1979) provide the most comprehensive evidence to support this assertion. They analyzed data from five national and six special-purpose samples to identify the determinants of occupational and economic success among men twenty-five to sixty-four years old in America. A number of the samples, though by no means all, permitted statistical control of important background variables and individual abilities such as family social status and intelligence. When these controls were made, Jencks et al. found that twelve rather than eight years of secondary school were worth a net average increase of about one-half of a standard deviation in occupational status as measured by the Duncan (1961) SEI. This converts to a 19 percent advantage in occupational status attributable to a high school over an elementary school education. In comparison, four years of college were worth a net average increase of slightly more than one standard deviation in occupational status. This converts to a 34 percentile point advantage in occupational status for completing college versus completing high school. In short, completing college appears to confer an occupational status advantage that is nearly twice as large as that obtained from completing high school.

More recent evidence, though less comprehensive than that of Jencks et al. (1979), also suggests that completing college provides relatively greater occupational status returns than earning an advanced degree. Knox, Lindsay, and Kolb (1988) analyzed the 1986 follow-up data of the National Longitudinal Study of the High School Class of 1972 to determine, among other things, the influence of educational attainment on occupational status as measured by the SEI. Controlling for race, gender, family socioeconomic status, and academic ability, they found that obtaining a bachelor's degree provided a 17.61-point increase in occupational status over and above a high school diploma. In comparison, obtaining an advanced degree was responsible for a 12.05-point increase in occupational status beyond the bachelor's degree. Thus, on average, obtaining an advanced degree returned occupational status advantages beyond the bachelor's degree that were about two-thirds of what a bachelor's degree returned in comparison with a high school diploma.

Obviously, the Knox, Lindsay, and Kolb (1988) study may have masked some differential effects by pooling all advanced degrees into a single category. Certain types of advanced degrees, M.D.s and J.D.s, for instance, may return greater occupational status advantages than others. Despite this limitation, the evidence presented by Knox, Lindsay, and Kolb, when combined with that of Jencks et al. (1979), underscores the central role of completing college in the status attainment process. The contention that a bachelor's degree is a passport to the American middle class has a strong foundation in the power of that degree to provide entry into relatively high paying professional, technical, and managerial occupations.

Moreover, although the net occupational prestige advantage of completing a college degree was stronger for younger men in the samples analyzed by Jencks et al. (1979), occupational differences among mature men with different educational levels was not just a function of college graduates obtaining higher-status jobs when they first entered the labor force. Even after controls were made for initial occupational status, family background, and intelligence, the net difference between the current occupational status of college and high school graduates was about two-thirds of the observed difference.

That college has significant short- and long-term implications for occupational and career placement is not lost on the American public and indeed may even be perceived as increasing in importance. For example, in 1978 the National Gallup Polls found that 36 percent of Americans felt college was extremely important for success; in 1982 the number increased to 58 percent (Elam, 1983).

Causal Mechanisms. The causal mechanism that underlies the power of the bachelor's degree to confer high occupational status has been the subject of considerable debate. On one side are those who believe that college, by means of a series of curricular and extracurricular experiences, imparts cognitive skills, values, personality characteristics, attitudes, and behavior patterns that are valued by employers in high-status occupations. Economists have referred to this as a "human capital" explanation for the effects of college, particularly as it influences requisite cognitive skills (for example, G. Becker, 1964; Hansen, 1970; Schultz, 1961, 1963). Sociologists, understandably, have used the term *socialization* to refer to essentially the same mechanism (Kerckhoff, 1976). The fundamental assumption underlying this explanation is that the college experience itself actually develops the cognitive and noncognitive skills, attitudes, and values necessary to succeed in complex technical, professional, and managerial occupations. There is a certain logical appeal to this argument. Clearly, college does teach some specific skills that may enable one to enter and remain in a high-status occupation. For example, a person entering the engineering profession is expected to have engineering skills that, at least in part, are probably learned in an engineering curriculum. Moreover, as we saw in Chapter Four, college also enhances the development of a number of more general cognitive skills and capabilities. Whether the particular general cognitive skills enhanced by college make the individual more likely to be successful or productive in high-status occupations, however, is less clear (Berg, 1970; Jencks et al., 1979).

Of course, college does more than impart cognitive skills; and it may well be that the important, occupationally relevant socialization that occurs in college is the development of favorable personality styles, attitudes and values, interpersonal and organizational skills, and levels of ambition, motivation, and self-confidence. These may have even greater appeal to employers than cognitive or technical skills in signifying the long-term success and productivity of the individual (H. Becker, 1964; Collins, 1974; Gordon & Howell, 1959; Hoyt & Muchinsky, 1973; Hicks, Koller, & Tellett-Royce, 1984; Useem & Miller, 1975, 1977; Rawlins & Ulman, 1974; Walberg & Sigler, 1975).[2]

Another side of this debate views college less as functioning to develop cognitive and noncognitive skills than as a screening, credentialing, or certifying institution that allocates occupational status to those with the requisite intellectual and personal traits to complete the prescribed course of study. Economists tend to refer to this explanation as "screening" (Taubman & Wales, 1974), while sociologists tend to refer to it as "certification" or "allocation" (Kerckhoff, 1976; Meyer, 1972). The essence of this explanation is that college has been granted a "charter" or "commission" by the larger society to select, sort, and confer adult status on the individual graduate quite apart from whatever he or she may have learned during college (Collins, 1979; J. Meyer, 1972, 1977). From this perspective, the high occupational status of college graduates derives not so much from the actual effects of college on the development of occupationally relevant cognitive and noncognitive skills as from what members of society (including employers) presume those effects to be. Such effects may not occur; yet the perception of society is such that a bachelor's degree generally certifies the holder as acceptable material for a middle-class occupation or position (Jencks & Riesman, 1968).

A variant of certification or screening theory posits that postsecondary education tends to recruit the most ambitious, resourceful, creative, and intellectually competent individuals in society to begin with. Graduation from college further certifies these individuals in terms of such factors as perseverance, drive, and ability to meet organizational demands. As a result, employers can use a bachelor's degree as a convenient screening device to select those employees whose intellectual capacities, ambition, and work patterns make them likely to be productive in complex high-status occupations. In this sense a college degree may simply serve to screen individuals on the basis of preexisting traits such as ability, ambition, and perseverance that are valuable employee traits in many managerial, professional, and technical jobs (Withey, 1971).

Considerable evidence exists to support the notion of the screening or certification effects of college on occupational status. Jencks et al. (1979) found that obtaining a bachelor's degree conferred a "bonus" of about five SEI points over and above the composite SEI increase one would get for four years of college without completing one's degree. Similarly, in their analysis of the NLS-72 data Knox, Lindsay, & Kolb (1988) found that with gender, race, family socioeconomic status, and academic ability held constant, obtaining a bachelor's degree was worth an SEI score more than two and a quarter times that attributable to having two or more years of college. Taken together, these findings suggest that one gains an additional occupational status advantage from college if one is certified as having completed the prescribed course of study. Put another way, the occupational status return for each year invested in college is reduced if the bachelor's degree is not earned.

Whereas evidence for some screening or certification effect of college on occupational status is reasonably clear, it is also the case that each additional year of college has an incremental, positive impact on occupational status irrespective of whether or not the bachelor's degree is completed (Jencks et al., 1979; Knox, Lindsay, & Kolb, 1988). One could obviously argue that each year of college completed is itself a certification that employers use to screen prospective employees. At the same time, however, the fact that extent of exposure to college increases occupational status regardless of degree completion suggests the possibility that college may in fact enhance cognitive and noncognitive skills that increase the likelihood of success in complex jobs. Thus, although there is ample evidence of a certification mechanism in accounting for the impact of college on occupational status, it is not clear that this impact is totally attributable to certification. Some elements of human capital or socialization are probably also at work.

Work Force Participation

In Bowen's (1977) extensive synthesis of the benefits associated with postsecondary education, he concludes that a major effect of a college education on one's career is that it enhances work force participation and stability of employment. Our review of Bowen's evidence and a synthesis of the evidence reported since Bowen's review lead us to agree with his conclusions. The weight of evidence is unequivocal in that of those seeking employment, both men and women who attend or graduate from college are more likely to participate in the work force and less likely to be unemployed than their counterparts whose formal education ends with secondary school. Moreover, those with a bachelor's degree are less likely to experience unemployment than those who attend college but do not complete their degree (for example, Calvert, 1969; Cobern, Salem, & Mushkin, 1973; Dearman & Plisko, 1981; McEaddy, 1975; Melchiori & Nash, 1983; Trent & Medsker, 1968; Wishart & Rossmann, 1977; Young, 1975, 1985; Young & Hayghe, 1984).

The differences in unemployment rates between high school and college graduates do not appear to have decreased substantially from 1960 onward despite the fact that an increasing percentage of those in the work force are college graduates. For example, in 1966 Morgan, Sirageldin, and Baerwaldt (1966), in a national study of "productive Americans," reported that bachelor's degree recipients were slightly less than half as likely to be unemployed as those having only a high school diploma. Nearly twenty years later Young (1985), using the 1984 Current Population Survey, reported that college graduates were only 33 percent as likely as high school graduates to be unemployed.

The nature of this literature makes it difficult to isolate the net effects of college on occupational stability. With few exceptions (for example, Trent & Medsker, 1968), little or no attempt has been made to control for important confounding variables such as ability, ambition, or socioeconomic origins. Nevertheless, one could make a reasonably strong argument that college indirectly contributes to occupational stability in at least two ways. First, as the evidence on occupational status clearly indicates, a college degree significantly increases one's likelihood of entering relatively high status managerial, technical, and professional occupations. This in itself has important implications for occupational stability. As suggested by Bowen (1977), managerial, technical, and professional occupations may be less sensitive than lower-status jobs to employment fluctuations that occur with changing economic conditions.[3] Moreover, since fewer of these occupations are unionized or involve physical labor, there may be less likelihood of experiencing periods of unemployment due to strikes or injury (Lando, 1975).

A second consideration is the notion that college increases the individual's "allocative ability." As defined by Schultz (1975), this is the capacity of the individual to adjust to changing economic or occupational conditions. Given an occupational disequilibrium, how effectively does the individual reallocate resources to deal with it? Schultz hypothesizes that formal education increases one's ability to deal with occupational disequilibriums largely because those with more education can bring greater intellectual and other resources to bear in the process of finding a job. Indeed, there is considerable evidence to suggest that accuracy in occupational information and efficiency in job search, as well as regional mobility to take advantage of employment opportunities, are associated with college attendance (for example, Da Vanzo, 1983; Freeman, 1973; Greenwood, 1975; Haveman & Wolfe, 1984; Lansing & Mueller, 1967; Metcalf, 1973; Mincer, 1978; Parnes & Kohen, 1975; Schwartz, 1971, 1976).

Furthermore, the college-educated individual may have an additional advantage in dealing with occupational disequilibriums in the form of acquaintanceship networks with college classmates. Evidence suggesting the importance of such networks or contacts is presented in Granovetter's (1974) study of managerial individuals who changed jobs in a major metropolitan area. Not only did the managers locate their new positions more often through personal contacts than through any other method, but a substantial number of the contacts dated back to college friendships. In this way college contacts were of continuing significance for the circulation of information and opportunities about high-status occupational positions. Consequently, such contacts may be an efficient resource not only for addressing occupational disequilibriums but also for taking advantage of opportunities to enhance one's occupational position (Useem & Miller, 1975).

Related to the notion that college enhances one's allocative ability is the idea that it provides the basic intellectual, analytical, and interpersonal competencies that permit one to effectively learn new occupationally relevant skills on the job. This intellectual and interpersonal framework for learning new skills and adapting to new responsibilities has been frequently mentioned by graduates as an important work-related benefit of college (for example, Bisconti, 1987; Bisconti & Kessler, 1980; Bisconti & Solmon, 1976; Mentkowski, 1988). Although specific skills learned in a major field, such as engineering, may be useful in a person's initial work experience, the more general intellectual and interpersonal skills learned in college may be a greater hedge against unemployment in that they permit flexibility and adaptability in a time when knowledge and jobs can rapidly become obsolescent.

Occupational Productivity and Success

In this section we review the evidence pertaining to the impact of college on occupational productivity and success, exclusive of salary or earnings. (The latter is addressed at length in Chapter Eleven.) Apart from financial returns, the two primary indicators of productivity and success employed in the literature are, typically, supervisors' ratings of productivity or effectiveness and level of advancement or rate of promotion.

Productivity. A considerable amount of research has addressed the link between formal education and occupational productivity. The findings of this research, however, tend to be inconsistent and in some cases even contradictory. For example, both Berg (1970) and Fuller (1970) found that within fairly narrowly defined blue-collar occupational categories, level of formal education had little systematic association with worker productivity. Similar results have been reported by Little (1980) for clerical workers, even with amount of occupational experience held constant. Conversely, Booth, McNally, and Berry (1978) and Hoiberg and Pugh (1978) report that formal education had a statistically significant, positive association with productivity or performance in various military occupational specialties (for example, medical corpsman, dental technician, noncommissioned officer), even when background characteristics such as age and intelligence were held constant.

Even if this evidence were less equivocal, it would still be difficult to determine the association between a college education and job productivity. Educational attainment in these studies is typically defined as years of formal education completed with no categorical breakdown into college and noncollege groups. Additionally, the occupational levels considered are those that characteristically employ only a limited number of college graduates.

The majority of studies that consider productivity differences between college and noncollege individuals in managerial, technical, or related professions yield statistically nonsignificant findings. Berliner (1971), Medoff (1977), and Medoff and Abraham (1980, 1981) report that when college and noncollege individuals hold the same jobs in a managerial field, there is little substantive difference in their productivity or effectiveness as rated by supervisors. Similar results have been reported by Greenberg and Greenberg (1976) for sales effectiveness in twelve industries.

Those investigations that do find statistically significant job productivity differences among those who attended college and those who did not tend to be contradictory. In an extensive longitudinal study of male managerial performance in a single large corporation, Howard (1986) found that college graduates, as compared to those who did not attend college, were judged by supervisors to have significantly greater general managerial effectiveness on a composite scale that included such factors as organizing and planning, leadership, decision making, energy, mental ability, personal impact, and oral communication skills. The college group was not only judged to have significantly greater potential for managerial effectiveness when first employed, but they also showed greater improvement in managerial effectiveness over time. Generally consistent results are reported by DeBack and Mentkowski (1986) in a cross-sectional study of the competencies of baccalaureate and nonbaccalaureate nurses. Conversely, in a longitudinal study of managerial effectiveness in another large corporation, Woo (1986) controlled for job grade level, tenure and experience in the firm, and geographical location and found that having a bachelor's degree actually had a statistically significant negative association with ratings of overall managerial effectiveness.

Our judgment is that the weight of evidence suggests little or no advantage in overall job productivity that can be attributed to college. Even if we give greatest weight to the longitudinal study that showed that bachelor's degree recipients were significantly more effective managers than those with less formal education (Howard, 1986), it is difficult to attribute this outcome to the influence of college rather than to differential recruitment. As compared to their counterparts with less formal education, those who attend and graduate from college may simply possess more of the personal characteristics that contribute to managerial effectiveness to begin with. A similar problem exists in interpreting the findings of DeBack and Mentkowski (1986).

Success. Evidence pertaining to the influence of college on occupational success is decidedly more consistent but by no means totally so. Howard (1986), Rosenbaum (1984), and Medoff and Abraham (1981) all present evidence indicating that bachelor's degree recipients within a large corporation have higher levels of career mobility than those with less formal education. Howard's twenty-year longitudinal analysis of a single firm (AT&T) traced the professional success of two groups of male employees: college graduates who were initially hired into first-level managerial positions and men without college degrees who were initially hired into nonmanagement positions but advanced into management positions by the age of thirty-two. The median age at the time of hiring was twenty-four for the college sample and thirty for the noncollege sample. At the end of the twenty-year period there were marked differences in the management levels attained favoring the college group. Of six management levels, the highest being vice president, the average level of the college group (3.18) was a full level above that of the noncollege group (2.14). Only 3 percent of the noncollege sample had advanced beyond the third level of management compared to 31 percent of the college men, the latter including three vice presidents. A few members of the noncollege group earned college degrees during the twenty-year period. These men attained a typical managerial level (2.56) that was higher than the noncollege sample but lower than the college group. This suggests that promotion advantages that accrue to college graduates are most pronounced when the individual enters the company with a degree.

Although it is clear from Howard's (1986) data that a bachelor's degree allocates substantial advantages in terms of corporate advancement (at least in the particular firm where her study was conducted), it is not necessarily obvious why this is so. In Howard's analyses the college group demonstrated greater managerial skill than the noncollege group, which might account for part of their advantage in promotion rate. Such a conclusion, however, may be confounded by at least two factors. First, some form of credentialing or certification may be at work in the promotion process. As a result college graduates may be regarded more favorably by their supervisors simply because of the normative expectation that those with college degrees *should* advance farther. Some evidence to support this notion is presented in Bills's (1988) analysis of the factors that influenced managers' hiring and promotion decisions in six companies. Although educational credentials were clearly more important in hiring than in advancement in the organization, 54.5 percent of the managers surveyed indicated that amount of formal education still played a "very" or "somewhat" important role in their promotion decisions.

A second and perhaps even more important confounding influence in Howard's (1986) findings is the fact that the college group had the additional advantage of being initially hired into the lower levels of a *managerial* career ladder. This in itself may have placed them on a career path characterized by opportunity for greater occupational mobility than the career path of the noncollege group. A substantial part of the greater occupational advancement enjoyed by college graduates may be attributable to initial job positioning effects rather than to their being decidedly more productive employees (Thurow, 1972). Consistent with this notion is evidence that suggests that net of tenure and race or gender composition, the percentage of bachelor's degree recipients in a job has a strong positive impact on the promotion chances associated with the job (Rosenbaum, 1984).

Rosenbaum (1984) conducted a thirteen-year longitudinal study of career mobility in another large corporation similar to the one studied by Howard (1986). Like Howard (1986), he found that having a bachelor's degree significantly enhanced career mobility and success, particularly if it was earned prior to entering the corporation. Controlling for initial job level (nonmanagement through upper-middle management), age, and tenure, Rosenbaum found that having a bachelor's degree had a statistically significant positive direct effect on subsequent job level for the first seven years of tenure in the firm, though not subsequently. An analysis was also made of a measure of job status within job level. While job level broadly defined job authority, job status defined such dimensions as salary range, benefit package, office size, and degree of autonomy in work tasks. Net of initial job status, age, race, gender, and company tenure, having a bachelor's degree had a statistically significant positive direct effect on job status thirteen years later.

Medoff and Abraham (1981) considered actual promotions of male managerial and professional personnel in a single large manufacturing firm. Controlling for years of company and noncompany experience, supervisors' performance ratings, region of the country, and job level, they found that having a bachelor's degree (versus a high school diploma only) had a statistically significant positive influence on the likelihood of promotion during a three-year period. Given this evidence, it is difficult, at first glance at least, to explain Woo's (1986) conflicting findings on a subsample of what appear to be the same data. Using essentially the same controls, Woo reports a statistically significant negative effect of a bachelor's degree on year-to-year promotion probabilities. One possible explanation for these conflicting results is that those who are hired without a bachelor's degree start at a lower job level than college graduates, and in order to work their way up to the same job level, they may receive more frequent promotions. Conversely, because college graduates are hired at initially higher job levels, promotions for them may be less frequent but more meaningful in terms of long-range consequences for eventual managerial level in the company. It may also be the case that rate of promotion in the company studied is not uniform across job grades but instead is less frequent at higher managerial levels than at lower ones. This might explain the difference noted by Woo (1986) in yearly promotion probabilities between bachelor's degree recipients and those with less formal education. As suggested by Rosenbaum's (1984) analyses, however, when those with and those without a college degree start at the same job level, the overall advancement rates of the former are clearly higher than those of the latter, at least until age thirty-five.

It is also important to note that *frequency* of yearly promotion (even if biased toward those who start at lower-level jobs in a particular company, typically those without a bachelor's degree) is by no means an unequivocal determinant of the managerial level to which one rises in a company. We found no evidence in any of the studies reviewed to suggest that those without a bachelor's degree typically rise to as high a level in a corporate management hierarchy as do college graduates.

In summary, the evidence on job productivity and career mobility reveals few substantive differences between college and noncollege employees in productivity or effectiveness within the same job level. It is undeniably the case, however, that college graduates enjoy significantly higher levels of career mobility. Initial job positioning effects, which place college graduates and those with less education on different career paths, probably account for part of these differences. Similarly, while college graduates may not demonstrate greater productivity at lower-level jobs than their noncollege counterparts, graduates may enjoy greater upward mobility in a particular company because it is expected that their cognitive and noncognitive skills will better equip them for successful adaptation to the demands of more complex, high-level managerial positions (Griliches, 1969).

This suggests one of the significant latent influences of college on career mobility. Bachelor's degree recipients end up advancing farther because college is believed to provide the general cognitive skills and personal dispositions that make such individuals more efficient learners of new occupational competencies (Bisconti, 1987; Bisconti & Kessler, 1980; Bisconti & Solmon, 1976; Mentkowski & Doherty, 1983; Pace, 1974; Wilensky & Lawrence, 1979). In short, college graduates are more promotable to higher-level positions because college has equipped them to be better on-the-job learners.[4] Of course, the effect might be basically the same if college merely "certified" the most efficient learners rather than providing a series of socializing experiences that actually enhance their learning efficiency and interpersonal skills.

Job Satisfaction

As we have seen so far in this chapter, a bachelor's degree typically confers a number of distinct occupational advantages on its owner. These include higher levels of occupational prestige (and a concomitant higher income), job stability, and career mobility. Moreover, as suggested by Lindsay and Knox (1984) and Rosenbaum (1984) college graduates seem better able to compete for jobs within occupational levels that are characterized by autonomy, individual discretion, and relatively challenging levels of complexity and ideational content. In short, within the American occupational structure, the jobs college graduates typically obtain should provide relatively high extrinsic and intrinsic rewards. Thus, we might expect a positive link between college and job satisfaction.

There is reasonably consistent evidence to support this contention, although the link is not particularly strong. In a series of studies, Quinn and associates analyzed data from eleven national surveys of male and female members of the American work force conducted between 1962 and 1977 (Quinn & Baldi de Mandilovitch, 1975, 1980; Quinn & Staines, 1979; Quinn, Staines, & McCullough, 1974). Their analyses indicated a statistically significant positive relationship between level of formal education and overall job satisfaction. The relationship, however, was modest (never accounting for more than 13 percent of the variance in job satisfaction) and not the same across all levels of education. Of the five levels of education completed (grade school or less, some high school, completed high school, some college, and completed college), there was little variance in job satisfaction among the lowest four levels. Only college graduates were consistently and substantially more satisfied with their jobs than individuals at other educational levels. Moreover, in analyses that held age constant, completion of college was probably the only increment of education that contributed appreciably to job satisfaction. Getting a college degree had a statistically significant positive association with two of six specific aspects of job satisfaction: "financial rewards" and "challenge" (the extent to which the individual was stimulated and challenged by the job and had the opportunity to exercise acquired skills at work). There was no statistically significant association between college graduation and satisfaction with resource adequacy, comfort, relationships with co-workers, or promotion, although the last was clearly in the expected direction.

Such evidence is consistent with trends in the occupational status research that suggest a credentialing bonus in job prestige attributable to obtaining the bachelor's degree. That college graduates appear to receive a similar bonus in job satisfaction may reflect the fact that obtaining the degree is a key educational credential for allocating individuals to jobs characterized by intellectual stimulation and challenge and by relatively high financial rewards.

Results generally consistent with those of Quinn and associates have also been reported by Klein and Maher (1968), Mueller (1969), and Glenn and Weaver (1982). The Klein and Maher study was based on a single-company sample of first-level managers, while the Mueller and the Glenn and Weaver studies were based on less extensive national samples of the work force than those analyzed by Quinn and associates. In all three studies the positive association between postsecondary education and overall job satisfaction was small but statistically significant.

The Glenn and Weaver (1982) analyses are interesting in that they also support the notion that education enhances job satisfaction largely by means of the characteristics of the jobs in which the more highly educated are placed. Statistically controlling for age and religious preference, Glenn and Weaver found that much of the total positive influence of education on job satisfaction was indirect, being mediated by education's direct positive effects on intrinsic and extrinsic work characteristics such as autonomy, authority, occupational prestige, and earnings.[5]

It is clear from the studies reviewed above that the overall positive influence of college on job satisfaction is modest. There are two possible explanations for this. The first is that college tends to produce conflicting influences on satisfaction with one's work. On the one hand, college tends to contribute to job satisfaction by increasing the intrinsic (autonomy, challenge, interest) and extrinsic (income) rewards of work. On the other hand, as we have seen in earlier chapters, college tends to develop the capacity for more sophisticated, complex, and critical judgments in students. Consequently, as compared to those with less formal education, college graduates may be more aware of the possible range of work options and more sensitive to unattained possibilities in their jobs and careers (Campbell, 1981).[6]

Some evidence in support of this explanation is presented by Campbell (1981) and Gordon and Arvey (1975). Campbell's analysis of overall job satisfaction among men in a series of national samples yielded a nonlinear association between education and level of job satisfaction. The group who did not go to high school had the highest level of job satisfaction, and the group with some college had the lowest level. College graduates were more satisfied than those who did not finish college but were more critical of their jobs than those with the least education. Gordon and Arvey conducted their analyses on a single-company sample and found no significant association between level of education and satisfaction with the work one actually did. They did, however, find that the more highly educated were significantly more critical of the way the company was being managed than were the less educated.

A second explanation for the modest relationship between college and job satisfaction is that the payoffs in job satisfaction that accompany increasing education can be offset when job demands do not match educational attainment. From this perspective, amount of education relative to job demands may be a more important indicator of job satisfaction than just amount of education. This has become the basis for an "overeducation" hypothesis that argues that because postsecondary education raises occupational expectations, college graduates who find themselves in jobs that do not require a college education will have a particularly high level of occupational dissatisfaction (for example, Berg, 1970; Blumberg & Murtha, 1977; Bowles & Gintis, 1976). Although there are some exceptions (for example, Sheppard & Herrick, 1972; Wright & Hamilton, 1979), the weight of evidence tends to support the presence of a statistically significant link between overeducation and job dissatisfaction (Burris, 1983; Kalleberg & Sorensen, 1973; Quinn & Baldi de Mandilovitch, 1980; Richards, 1984a; Rumberger, 1981). Not all the evidence suggests that the magnitude of the overeducation effect on job satisfaction of college graduates is particularly large or that it has extensive societal consequences (Burris, 1983; Smith, 1986). Moreover, it may not become manifest until the mismatch between educational level and job demands is substantial (for example, college graduates in jobs that typically require a secondary school diploma or less). Nevertheless, overeducation may be a factor in explaining why increased levels of postsecondary education do not always lead to increased job satisfaction.

Between-College Effects

In Chapter Nine on educational attainment we saw that a substantial body of evidence indicates that where a student attends college has a significant net impact on educational attainment. In this section we review the evidence bearing on an analogous question. Do the characteristics of the college or university attended have a nontrivial influence on the various dimensions of an individual's career independent of his or her background and precollege traits? It seems almost self-evident that the answer to this question is yes. In addition to the public folklore about different colleges and universities, there is abundant evidence to suggest that the graduates of certain kinds of institutions or even a small number of specific colleges are simply more successful or eminent than graduates of other institutions (for example, Collins, 1971; Domhoff, 1967; Hardy, 1974; Mortimer, Lorence, & Kumka, 1986; Pierson, 1969; Scientific American, 1965; Useem & Karabel, 1986; Useem & Miller, 1975, 1977). The problem, of course, is that such evidence may simply reflect the kinds of students recruited by certain types of institutions rather than being the actual result of attendance at those institutions. As has been our practice throughout this book, our concern in this section is with the net influence of different college characteristics on career.

Two-Year Versus Four-Year Institutions

In Chapter Nine we saw reasonably clear evidence that net of socioeconomic background, academic ability, and precollege aspirations, students who initially attend a two-year institution are significantly less likely to complete a bachelor's degree and have significantly lower levels of educational attainment generally than their counterparts who initially attend four-year institutions. Since educational attainment plays such a critical role in the achievement of occupational status, one might anticipate that initially attending a two-year college would have deleterious consequences for occupational status.

What little evidence there is on this matter is consistent in supporting this expectation. Breneman and Nelson (1981), analyzing the 1976 followup of the NLS-72 data, statistically controlled for a large battery of student characteristics, including race, language spoken at home, high school grades, precollege educational aspirations, and marital status. With these factors held constant, individuals who began postsecondary education in a two-year college held jobs four years later that were significantly lower in prestige (on the Duncan SEI) than those of their counterparts who began in four-year institutions.

Anderson (1984) also analyzed the NLS-72 data but examined occupational status three years later (1979 follow-up) than did the Breneman and Nelson (1981) analyses (1976 follow-up). Controlling for many of the same variables and also for gender, family socioeconomic status, precollege occupational status aspirations, college program, and academic ability, she too found that students who initially attended two-year colleges had jobs significantly lower on the Duncan SEI than did those individuals who started in four-year colleges.

It is likely that much, if not most, of the negative influence of attending a two-year college on occupational status is attributable to the fact that students who initially attend such institutions have lower levels of educational attainment than their counterparts who initially enroll in four-year colleges. It is less clear that attendance at a two-year (versus a four-year) college seriously inhibits occupational status attainment when individuals of equal educational attainment are compared. Monk-Turner (1982, 1983) used the National Longitudinal Survey of Labor Market Experience to compare the occupational attainment of community college and four-year college entrants ten years after they graduated from high school. With controls made for such variables as gender, race, family socioeconomic status, precollege educational aspirations, academic ability, and actual educational attainment, initially attending a two-year institution had a statistically significant but small negative effect on the Duncan SEI score of the job held.

Somewhat different findings, however, have been reported by Thomas and Gordon (1983) and Smart and Ethington (1985), each of whom analyzed the 1979 follow-up of the NLS-72 data. Thomas and Gordon statistically controlled for family socioeconomic status, academic ability, precollege educational and occupational aspirations, college grades, college major, and actual educational attainment. With these factors held constant, they found that attending a two-year versus a four-year college had no statistically significant effect on occupational status for any gender or racial (white, black, Hispanic) subgroups. (Attending a two-year college had a small negative effect when the samples were combined, a result that may have been due to having a much larger sample.)

Similarly, Smart and Ethington (1985) took a subsample of 1976 baccalaureate recipients from the NLS-72 data to determine differences in the job status (and other job characteristics) of those who began in four-year versus two-year institutions. With controls made for academic ability, family socioeconomic status, precollege occupational aspirations, and number of years employed, no statistically significant differences were found in the occupational status (Duncan SEI) of the job held in 1979. This finding held regardless of gender.

Taken as a body of evidence, the studies reviewed above suggest that the "cooling out" function of two-year colleges may have negative implications for occupational status *largely* because initial attendance at these institutions tends to inhibit educational attainment. Such a disadvantage is not immutable, however. Those two-year college students motivated to complete and capable of completing the bachelor's degree in the same period of time as their peers from four-year institutions do not appear to be seriously disadvantaged in competing for jobs of equal occupational status. In short, when educational attainment is held constant, any residual occupational status disadvantages attributable to initial attendance at a two-year college become quite small and perhaps trivial.

Similarly, there is little evidence to suggest that initial attendance at two- or four-year colleges has any important effects on other noneconomic measures of occupational success or satisfaction, either when educational attainment is held constant or when it is not. Smart and Ethington (1985) have provided the most extensive documentation for this claim. In their analyses of bachelor's degree recipients, they found that initially attending a two-year rather than a four-year institution had no statistically significant effect on various measures of job stability, intrinsic job satisfaction, or extrinsic job satisfaction for either sex when academic ability, family socioeconomic status, precollege occupational aspirations, and years employed were held constant. Consistent findings are reported by Breneman and Nelson (1981) for unemployment rate, even though no controls were made for educational attainment between those starting at community college versus those starting at four-year institutions.

Evidence concerning the occupational implications of attending a two-year college for those not aspiring to a bachelor's degree is practically nonexistent. We uncovered only one study that addressed this issue. Somers, Sharpe, and Myint (1971) compared the occupational status and unemployment rate of jobs secured by 1966 vocational program graduates of community colleges and graduates of postsecondary vocational or technical schools three years after program completion. Although the community college vocational students held more prestigious jobs and had a lower rate of unemployment than did their vocational or technical school counterparts, these differences became statistically nonsignificant when controls were made for student background characteristics and educational attainment.

Institutional Quality

The influence of college "quality" on career is an area of substantial research interest. This attention perhaps reflects the extent of a common cultural belief that attendance at certain colleges and universities confers distinctive advantages to an individual in the many dimensions of a career. A broad range of American society seems to believe that men and women enjoy a certain measure of career success precisely because they attend and graduate from these institutions and not others (for example, Mortimer, Lorence, & Kumka, 1986; Rynes & Boudreau, 1986).

According to human capital or socialization theory, graduates of "better" colleges attain greater occupational success because those colleges provide a more rigorous or better education. This view contends that the career success of the graduates of elite institutions is attributable to what they learn or how they are socialized in college. Conversely, those who hold to a screening or certification explanation for the effects of college argue that "high-quality" institutions produce more successful graduates because they confer greater status on their graduates and these status properties enhance the chances for occupational success (Rosenbaum, 1984). Implicit in this view is the notion that the occupational advantages conferred by a quality institution are largely a function of how that institution and its graduates are viewed by important segments of the external society (graduate and professional schools, corporate employers, and so forth). Thus, simply being admitted to a prestigious college affords the individual a considerable status attainment advantage quite apart from the quality of the educational experience provided or the actual change in the individual.

Kamens (1971, 1977) and J. Meyer (1972, 1977) have elaborated on the idea of screening or certification to propose that specific, influential segments of the external society have actually granted implicit "social charters" to colleges. These social charters often afford highly specific social statuses and career niches to graduates (Collins, 1979; Rosenbaum, 1984). Just as West Point has been granted a social charter to produce military leaders, so too many elite colleges and universities have been granted a social charter to produce highly successful graduates in a range of other careers. Thus, graduates of elite schools may benefit from a "signaling" or "labeling" effect (Spence, 1973; Karabel & McClelland, 1983; Klitgaard, 1985). A degree from such a college may identify the person as talented and capable of high-level performance. Consequently, he or she may be most likely to be hired and assigned the most challenging and rewarding jobs (Colarelli, Dean, & Konstans, 1988).

Of course, it is also likely that a major part of the impact of institutional quality on career is attributable not to influences such as socialization or chartering but instead to the types of individuals that elite colleges and universities tend to recruit and enroll. Prestigious colleges may simply enroll high-level talent and provide little in the way of socialization or chartering influences that uniquely enhance one's career. One should not dismiss this possibility too quickly. As will be seen, our synthesis of the evidence suggests that when differences in career-salient student precollege characteristics are taken into account, the effects of institutional quality on career are often small and inconsistent.

Occupational Choice. A substantial amount of evidence suggests that the dimensions of institutional quality (including selectivity, financial and academic resources, and perceived prestige) or reputation have statistically significant positive associations with a number of student background characteristics that are themselves predictive of career success. These include intelligence, academic achievement, and family financial resources (for example, Alwin, 1974, 1976; Smart, 1986; Smart & Pascarella, 1986b; Tusin & Pascarella, 1985). Furthermore, high-quality institutions also appear to attract students who enter college with significantly higher occupational aspirations than their counterparts at less selective or prestigious institutions and who are more certain of their career choice (for example, Clark, Heist, McConnell, Trow, & Yonge, 1972; Smart, 1986; Spaeth, 1970).

If selective or prestigious institutions tend to recruit ambition (along with ability and wealth), do they, as suggested by Trow (1976a), tend to encourage ambition even further? The weight of evidence from studies that address this question suggests that any net positive impact of institutional quality on the overall occupational status of one's career choice (according to the Duncan SEI or a similar index) is quite small and perhaps trivial. Spaeth (1968a, 1977) and Meyer (1970c) both report evidence to suggest that measures of college quality had no important influence on the occupational prestige level of a student's senior-year career choice when factors such as precollege career choice, family social status, and grades during college were taken into account. In contrast, Brown (1979) and Weidman (1984), controlling for essentially the same variables, found that institutional selectivity had a generally positive influence on the occupational status of senior women's career choice but (in the Weidman study) a mixed influence for the career choice of senior men. The influence was positive and statistically significant for male mathematics and history majors, statistically nonsignificant for male English majors, and significantly negative for male political science majors. Most recently, McClelland (1990) found that both men and women with initially high occupational expectations were somewhat more likely to maintain those expectations over a seven-year period after high school if they attended a selective rather than a nonselective college. Part of this finding, of course, might be due to the positive impact of college selectivity on bachelor's degree completion during the time period covered by the study.

There are at least two possible explanations for the equivocal nature of these findings. One is the presence of some form of "frog-pond" or relative deprivation mechanism. In this case, the positive environmental impact of attending an institution with many other academically gifted and ambitious students would be partially offset by the need to reassess one's academic ability and perhaps realistically lower career aspirations in light of relative performance in a competitive academic arena (Davis, 1966; Drew & Astin, 1972; Reitz, 1975).

A second explanation is that the chartering effects of elite institutions may be linked more strongly to specific occupations and careers than to some general hierarchy of occupational status (such as that measured by the Duncan SEI or similar indexes of job prestige). Kamens (1974, 1979) has provided evidence to support this explanation in studies of the influence of different measures of college quality on direction of career choice. He hypothesized that the special charter given elite or high-quality institutions provides faculty in those institutions with a stronger cultural authority to influence student career choice in a direction sanctioned by the values of the academic culture. Thus, he anticipated that irrespective of freshman career choice, students in elite institutions would be more likely than their counterparts in nonelite institutions to choose academic careers.

Controlling for such variables as initial career choice, college grades, academic ability, and family socioeconomic status, Kamens's (1974, 1979) analyses of two national samples tend to support this expectation. Net of these factors, a reputational measure of college prestige and a measure of college financial and academic resources had small but statistically significant and positive effects on student choice of a high-status academic career (for example, mathematics, natural sciences, social sciences). The effect of institutional selectivity was trivial and statistically nonsignificant. Similar results with respect to the net influence of financial resources on choice of an academic career have been reported by Astin and Panos (1969).

There is also modest evidence from Kamens's (1974) analysis to suggest that the movement toward choice of an academic career in elite institutions may come at the expense of choosing a career in the traditional free professions (law, medicine, dentistry, engineering). Astin and Panos (1969) report a similar finding with respect to the negative influence of college selectivity on choosing engineering as a career. This perhaps suggests that the very modest influence of college quality on career choice my be manifest more in the direction of choice than in the general status level of choice.

Although Kamens (1974) argues that the cultural authority granted faculty in prestigious colleges and universities may account for much of the institutional influence on student career choice, it is likely that the distribution of academic majors in such institutions may also play a role. It is reasonably clear that attendance at selective or prestigious institutions is positively linked with majoring in the liberal arts, natural sciences, and mathematics as opposed to technical, vocational, or preprofessional fields (for example, Pace, 1974; Pascarella, Brier, Smart, & Herzog, 1987; Smart, & Pascarella, 1986b). While part of this may be due to recruitment (Clark, Heist, McConnell, Trow, & Yonge, 1972) and/or environmental influences (Astin, 1977a; Astin & Panos, 1969), another part may be attributable to the simple fact that elite institutions tend to offer certain academic majors and not others. For example, they typically offer undergraduate majors such as mathematics, science, and the liberal arts that are closely linked to academic and professional careers (Jacobs, 1986). They are less likely to offer majors closely linked to such careers as elementary or secondary teaching, home economics, social work, or allied health professions.

This may at least partially explain Bielby's (1978) finding that net of family background, age, marital status, college grades, and college type (liberal arts or other), a measure of college quality based largely on selectivity had a statistically significant positive influence on women choosing sex-atypical majors and careers. Such majors and careers are those with a low percentage of women (for example, majors such as mathematics and physical science and careers such as law, medicine, and engineering). Such majors and careers tend to allocate higher occupational status and economic returns than majors and careers traditionally dominated by women (Gottlieb

& Bell, 1975; Hearn & Olzak, 1982; Polachek, 1978). Unfortunately, Bielby's analysis failed to control for such factors as academic ability and precollege career aspirations so it is difficult to separate the effects of recruitment or selection from those of actual attendance at a selective institution.

The body of evidence reviewed above suggests little to indicate that traditional measures of institutional quality have more than very small net effects on either the status level or direction of student career choice when precollege career choice is taken into account. The overall impact of an elite institution may be to maintain or perhaps slightly accentuate the status level or academic career orientation of initial choice; but as suggested by Goldstein (1974), this impact is quite small compared to that attributable to student career choice at the beginning of college. Thus, students who attend prestigious institutions may use the college experience primarily to implement rather than choose a career.

Occupational Status. To what extent does graduation from a selective or prestigious institution increase the likelihood of obtaining a high-status job? If one considers jobs in a single hierarchy of occupational prestige (such as that measured by the Duncan SEI and similar indexes), the net impact of measures of college quality is quite small and perhaps trivial. Considering only the most rigorously conducted studies (that is, those that controlled for important student background traits such as intelligence, family socioeconomic status, and precollege occupational aspirations), the evidence is mixed. Spaeth and Greeley (1970) and Perrucci (1980), employing the National Opinion Research Center 1968 follow-up of 1961 college graduates, and Sharp & Weidman (1987), using the 1979 follow-up of the NLS-72 sample, all report a statistically significant positive effect of college selectivity on subsequent job prestige. Similar results are reported by Knox, Lindsay, and Kolb (1988), who used the 1986 follow-up of the NLS-72 data, and Karabel and McClelland (1987), who used a national sample of men who were twenty to sixty-four years old in 1973. In all three samples, however, the standardized regression coefficient estimating the net influence of college selectivity on occupational prestige was quite small (less than .11 in magnitude for all analyses); and the study with the largest effect (Karabel & McClelland, 1987) failed to control for individual ability or occupational aspirations. Furthermore, similar analyses conducted on other national samples (for example, the Productive Americans Survey, the Panel Study of Income Dynamics, and the Cooperative Institutional Research Program 1971–80) found that the effects of institutional selectivity or perceived prestige on subsequent occupational status were trivial and statistically nonsignificant when individual background traits were held constant (Griffin & Alexander, 1978; Gruca & Pascarella, 1988; Jencks et al., 1979; Pascarella, Smart, & Stoecker, 1987; Trusheim & Crouse, 1981).

Such evidence suggests that traditional measures of college quality have, at best, only a very small or, quite possibly, no direct influence on overall occupational status.[7] It is notable, however, that some scholars have argued that it is misleading to assume that the process of occupational status attainment exists within an undifferentiated labor market (for example, Kalleberg & Sorensen, 1979; Tinto, 1980, 1981). There may, in fact, be a segmented labor market in which the salient factors that influence occupational status vary for different occupations or careers (for example, Crane, 1969; Hargens, 1969; Perrucci & Perrucci, 1970; Tinto, 1981; Zuckerman, 1977).

Tinto (1980, 1981) suggests that there may be reasons to suspect nontrivial differences in the degree to which college quality influences the process of status attainment in various occupations. Professional occupations, he notes, are characterized by the centrality of intellectual skills and knowledge requirements that are typically acquired in formal educational settings such as college or graduate school. Nonprofessional (for example, business-managerial) careers, on the other hand, are more likely to require the development of interests and skills that are learned in work settings. Since institutional quality is an important factor in the general undergraduate and graduate degree attainment process (a conclusion well documented by the evidence reviewed in Chapter Nine), Tinto proposed that the quality of the undergraduate institution attended would have a more important influence on occupational status attainment in professional than in nonprofessional careers. The findings from a national sample of white male college graduates broadly dichotomized into professional and business-managerial careers tends to support this premise. Net of family background, a measure of institutional selectivity had a small, positive, and statistically significant direct influence on occupational status in professional careers but not in managerial careers.

Generally similar results have been reported by Karabel and McClelland (1987). However, in their findings college selectivity had a somewhat stronger effect on the job status of men in professional and upper-level management positions than on the job status of men in lower-level white-collar or blue-collar jobs.

Unfortunately, Tinto's (1980, 1981) analyses, as well as those of Karabel and McClelland (1987), did not control for the confounding effects of precollege occupational aspirations, ability, or academic achievement. A somewhat more exacting test of Tinto's hypothesis was conducted by Smart (1986). Controlling for precollege occupational aspirations, race, and secondary school achievement, as well as family socioeconomic status, Smart found that undergraduate college selectivity had no statistically significant direct influence on occupational status in either professional or managerial careers nine years after college enrollment. For professional careers, however, college selectivity did exert a statistically significant positive indirect effect on occupational prestige through its strong impact on educational attainment. (This indirect effect was also apparent in Tinto's [1980, 1981] analyses, although it was not tested for statistical significance.) The same indirect influence was not nearly as strong for managerial careers.

The combined evidence from the Smart (1986) and Tinto (1980, 1981) studies suggests that college quality may in fact play a greater role in occupational attainment in professional careers than in nonprofessional careers. The underlying reason is likely the fact that college quality indexes tend to enhance undergraduate and graduate degree attainment, an attainment crucial to success in most professional occupations. It should be underscored that the net impact of institutional selectivity on occupational status in professional careers in both the Smart and Tinto investigations was small, probably accounting for less than 1 percent of the total variance in that outcome. Nevertheless, their findings are at least indirectly reinforced by evidence that indicates that attending a selective or prestigious undergraduate institution modestly enhances academic success in professional schools such as law and medicine (for example, Clapp & Reid, 1976; Pugh, 1969; Evans, Jones, Wortman, & Jackson, 1975), attendance at a prestigious graduate school (Henson, 1980), and the successful implementation of careers in academia (Long, Allison, & McGinnis, 1979), engineering and scientific research (Astin, 1977a), and medicine (Pascarella, Brier, Smart, & Herzog, 1987). The evidence on whether it enhances the actual implementation of a career in law is mixed. Astin's (1977a) analysis indicated that college selectivity had a negative influence on entering law school, but Braxton, Brier, Herzog, & Pascarella (1988) found that college selectivity enhanced the likelihood of becoming a lawyer within nine years after college enrollment.

There is also evidence to suggest that college quality may differentiate jobs of similar status on the basis of the perceived prestige of the company that makes the job offer. In an analysis of accountants who graduated from ninety-three colleges, Colarelli, Dean, and Konstans (1988) found statistically significant positive associations between college quality measures and receiving a job offer from a high-prestige firm. Since no controls were made for student background traits, however, it is difficult to determine whether these associations indicate institutional effects or merely marked talent and aptitude differences among students enrolled in colleges of different quality. The latter could be used by firms as an inexpensive device for screening job applicants.

Sex-Atypical Careers Among Women. Just as there is evidence to suggest that women who attend selective colleges are more likely to choose sex-atypical (that is, male-dominated) academic majors and careers than their counterparts at less selective colleges, so too is there documentation for the expectation that college selectivity will enhance women's entry into sex-atypical careers. Ethington and her colleagues (Ethington, Smart, & Pascarella, 1988; Gruca, Ethington, & Pascarella, 1988) have addressed this issue directly in analyses of a national sample of women who entered college in 1971 and were followed up nine years later. Controlling for student precollege characteristics (academic achievement, self-concept, socioeconomic status, marital plans, sex-atypical occupational aspirations, and so on), other institutional characteristics (such as percentage of women, enrollment, and private or public control), and various college experiences (including grades, major, educational attainment, and the like), these investigators found institutional selectivity to have a statistically significant positive effect on women's entrance into sex-atypical careers (for example, law, medicine, engineering, business). This finding held for black as well as white women, but it was somewhat more pronounced for women entering nonscience occupations than for women entering science occupations.

Such results are seemingly consistent with Astin's (1977a) finding that institutional selectivity negatively affects one's likelihood of becoming a homemaker. At the same time, however, they are inconsistent with Astin's additional finding that college selectivity enhances one's likelihood of becoming a nurse. Unfortunately, Astin pooled men and women in his analyses so it is difficult to determine whether the findings pertain only to women.

Occupational Productivity. A small number of studies have addressed the issue of whether attendance at a selective or prestigious college enhances one's actual job performance. The evidence from these studies is both inconsistent and unconvincing. Howard's (1986) longitudinal analysis of managerial performance and progress at AT&T found statistically significant positive correlations between measures of college quality (for example, rate of graduate student production by a college, ratings on the Gourman report [1983]) and various dimensions of managerial ability. These included factors such as nonconformity, intellectual abilities, and motivation for advancement. Since no controls appear to have been made for student background characteristics, however, it is quite possible that these associations simply reflected the fact that quality institutions tend to recruit and enroll individuals high on these and similar traits to begin with. When Howard did attempt to control for academic major and extracurricular involvement in college, college quality had a statistically significant positive association only with nonconformity.

A similar analysis by Ferris (1982) examined the relationship between a measure of college quality (based on a composite index of prestige and academic strength) and a measure of job performance (from company records) of professional accountants. Controlling for educational attainment and college grades (though not for measures of motivation or ability), Ferris found that the college quality index had no statistically significant association with job performance. These findings are quite similar to the earlier findings of Laumann and Rapoport (1968) for college graduates in technological careers. In the Laumann and Rapoport study, however, the measure of job performance was a self-reported index of achievement.

The most recent evidence we uncovered comes from a study mentioned earlier that considered the job performance of accountants from ninety-three different colleges (Colarelli, Dean, & Konstans, 1988). Measures of institutional quality (such as wealth and Gourman ratings) had no statistically significant positive associations with supervisor's ratings of performance, and institutional selectivity actually had a statistically significant negative association with job performance.

Occupational Success. If there is little compelling evidence to suggest that attendance at a selective or prestigious college makes one a more productive employee, at least in terms of nonmonetary criteria, the weight of evidence would nonetheless suggest that institutional quality may confer a slight net advantage in various other dimensions of occupational success. A series of studies by Perrucci and colleagues (Kinloch & Perrucci, 1969; Perrucci, 1969; Perrucci & Perrucci, 1970) sought to determine the institutional characteristics and college experiences contributing to the career mobility of engineers and managers. After controls were made for such factors as socioeconomic origins, grades in college, and the recruitment emphasis of the employing firm on grades and the college attended, college selectivity had a small, positive influence on the level of technical responsibility attained. (Technical responsibility was an eight-level scale ranging from minor data compilation and routine tasks through the establishment of technical policies for all operations in the organization.) The effect of college selectivity on technical responsibility was somewhat more pronounced for individuals from high socioeconomic origins than for those from lower socioeconomic origins. Although there was a slight positive relationship between college selectivity and level of supervisory responsibility achieved (Perrucci & Perrucci, 1970), it was not as clearly pronounced as the effects of selectivity on technical responsibility.

More recent evidence from three longitudinal studies of corporate managerial careers (Howard, 1986; Rosenbaum, 1984; Useem & Karabel, 1986) is consistent in suggesting that measures of college quality are in fact positively linked with the level of managerial or supervisory responsibility achieved. There seems to be some question, however, as to the time in one's career when a degree from an elite institution exerts its influence.

Useem and Karabel (1986) hypothesized that since college attendance has become essentially universal among senior managers in large American corporations, *where* one attends college will become a more salient factor in who rises to the very top positions. Evidence from senior managers in 208 major corporations tends to support this contention. With social origins and postbaccalaureate training controlled, having a bachelor's degree from one of eleven "top-ranked colleges" gave the individual a greater probability of becoming a chief executive or member of a board of directors than did having a bachelor's degree from an unranked college. (The eleven "top" colleges were taken from a ranking of undergraduate colleges conducted in 1940, about the time the members of the sample graduated from college.)

Similar results are provided in Howard's (1986) longitudinal analysis of managerial careers in a single corporation. A small but statistically significant positive correlation of .18 was found between college quality (indicated by ratings on the 1983 Gourman report) and the managerial level to which an individual rose after twenty-five years with AT&T. (All college graduates began their careers at the first managerial level.) Interestingly, the same correlation, though positive, was statistically nonsignificant for the managerial level achieved after four or eight years with the company. Howard argues that such evidence suggests that the impact of where one attends college comes later in the individual's career, when he or she is close to the highest levels of management. Implicit notions of college prestige or "top rank" may confer an advantage in terms of social, or perhaps even class, acceptability at the very highest levels of management, particularly if actual performance at this level is difficult to measure or predict.

Rosenbaum (1984) has also considered the extent to which college quality enhances the managerial level and job status (for example, autonomy, perquisites) attained in a single corporation. In contrast to Howard (1986), however, Rosenbaum found that net of age, race, sex, and company tenure, college selectivity typically exerted a statistically significant positive influence on level and status *early* in the individual's career. When initial job level and status were considered, the direct effects of college selectivity on subsequent level and status were typically reduced to statistical nonsignificance. However, because initial level and status were strong predictors of final level and status, college selectivity probably exerted a positive indirect influence on an individual's final level of managerial attainment. Thus, in Rosenbaum's analysis college selectivity enhanced career attainment largely by conferring an advantage early in one's career, most likely in terms of the initial level at which one was hired. There is little in Rosenbaum's analyses, however, to suggest that this early advantage did not persist throughout one's career in the firm.

We uncovered three longitudinal investigations that directly addressed the influence of college quality on rate of promotion within a company. In Rosenbaum's (1984) study he controlled for such factors as tenure with the company, age at entry, and managerial level and found that institutional selectivity had a small positive but statistically nonsignificant influence on promotion rates. A similar investigation in another company by Wise (1979), on the other hand, suggested that college selectivity significantly enhanced an individual's promotion probabilities even when possibly confounding influences such as college grades, college major, socioeconomic status, and initial estimates of leadership, initiative, and supervisor's ratings were taken into account. Finally, Colarelli, Dean, and Konstan's (1988) analysis of accountants' job performance found a statistically significant positive association between college quality (as measured by the Gourman ratings) and supervisor's ratings of an individual's promotability. However, institutional selectivity and promotability had an even stronger *negative* association.

Job Satisfaction. Although only a small number of studies address the question, the weight of evidence suggests that college quality may play little direct role in an individual's job satisfaction. The most comprehensive analyses pertaining to this issue have been conducted by Solmon and his colleagues (Bisconti & Solmon, 1977; Ochsner & Solmon, 1979; Solmon, Bisconti, & Ochsner, 1977). They followed up a sample of 1961 freshmen ten years after projected college graduation. All were bachelor's degree recipients. When such factors as marital status, type of job held, number of years of work experience, college grades, and college major were controlled, college selectivity had a statistically nonsignificant direct impact on job satisfaction. (Similar results have been reported by Colarelli, Dean, and Konstans, 1988.) As Bisconti and Solmon (1977) point out, however, graduates from highly selective colleges who were underemployed (for example, who worked at jobs not requiring a bachelor's degree) were less satisfied with their jobs than were graduates from less selective institutions in the same underemployment situation. This, they suggest, may have been due to the tendency for the latter students to have lower career ambitions. Thus, the discrepancy between ambition and level of employment may not be as great for underemployed individuals graduating from nonselective colleges as it is for their counterparts from selective institutions.

This may, in part at least, explain the findings of Sharp and Weidman (1987) with respect to the early job satisfaction of undergraduate humanities majors. Net of factors similar to those controlled for by Solmon and colleagues, institutional selectivity had no statistically significant direct influence on job satisfaction for women. For men, however, college selectivity had a small negative but statistically significant effect on job satisfaction when the occupational prestige and supervisory responsibility of the job held were taken into account. It may be, as suggested by McClelland (1986), that selective institutions tend to sustain relatively high levels of occupational expectations in their students. In situations where these expectations are not matched by the realities of one's occupational situation, the result may be a negative impact on job or work satisfaction. Why the same effect did not show up for women is difficult to ascertain from the analyses provided by Sharp and Weidman. One possible explanation is that women who attend selective colleges may have lower occupational prestige expectations to begin with than do their male counterparts.

It is worth pointing out that the studies reviewed above address only the direct impact of college quality on job satisfaction. While that impact appears to be minimal or perhaps slightly negative in situations of under-employment, no attempt was made to describe possible indirect effects. For example, income has a consistently positive influence on job satisfaction (Riley, 1982; Solmon, Bisconti, & Ochsner, 1977), and as we shall see in the next chapter, college quality tends to have a positive (though modest) effect on income. Consequently, a degree from a high-ranking or elite institution may exert a positive indirect effect on job satisfaction by enhancing income. The existing research literature, however, is largely silent on this and similar indirect effects.

Institutional Gender Composition

After institutional quality, which clearly dominates the research literature, institutional gender is probably the college structural characteristic most studied in terms of impact on career. While there is clear evidence that men's colleges have independently enhanced male career choices and attainment in areas such as business, law, and the professions (Astin, 1977a; Astin & Panos, 1969), most of the recent research has focused on the extent to which institutional gender influences women's career choices and career attainment in ways that ultimately affect gender equality in the workplace.

Two general questions have typically been asked in this research. First, does attending a predominantly women's institution enhance women's career interests, particularly in high-status professions or occupations that have traditionally been the preserve of men? Second, does attending a women's institution facilitate the likelihood of actually entering such careers? The findings of investigations addressing these questions are not totally consistent.

In Chapter Nine on educational attainment, we suggested that the presence of a large number of female faculty role models in women's colleges may be an important causal mechanism underlying the link found between attendance at those institutions and women's educational attainment. A similar argument has been made for an analogous link found between attendance at women's colleges and high levels of career aspirations and achievement. Evidence presented in a number of studies consistently points to the tendency for women with female teachers or female faculty role models, particularly in women's institutions, to develop greater intellectual and personal assertiveness and greater occupational self-confidence than other women (for example, Erkut & Mokros, 1984; El-Khawas, 1980; Esposito, Hackett, & O'Halloran, 1987; Fox, 1974; Sternglanz & Lyberger-Ficek, 1977; Walker, 1981). As suggested by Wright and Wright (1987), same-sex role models or mentors can be especially helpful to women in counteracting sex-stereotypic perceptions in their career aspirations and development.

Despite the fact that women's institutions may provide an environment more supportive of non-sex-stereotypic career roles for women (Smith, 1988), the small body of evidence on whether this has a net effect on career orientation or career choice appears inconsistent. Bressler and Wendell (1980) analyzed changes in occupational choices between 1967 and 1971 for a national sample of students at selective colleges and universities (average SAT score of 1100 or above). Comparing women's schools with coeducational institutions, they did find substantially more pronounced changes for women at the former than at the latter. Moreover, the changes at women's colleges were largely toward traditionally male-dominated occupations to which are ascribed relatively high levels of status and income.

Somewhat different results, however, are reported in a sixteen-institution study of women's colleges and women's career salience by Lentz (1980, 1982, 1983). Career salience measures the extent to which a person is career motivated, the degree to which an occupation is important as a source of satisfaction, and the degree of priority ascribed to the occupation among other sources of satisfaction (Masih, 1967). Lentz found that when level of college selectivity was considered, the advantages of women's colleges over coeducational colleges in the career salience of senior women could be largely explained by a similar advantage among incoming freshmen. Moreover, coeducational colleges actually achieved greater freshman-to-senior increases in the percentage of career salient women than did women's colleges.

Because Bressler and Wendell (1980) addressed somewhat different facets of career aspirations, their findings and those of Lentz (1980, 1982, 1983) may not be as inconsistent as they first appear. It may be, as suggested by Lentz, that the environment of a women's institution provides no net advantage in women's career salience over coeducational institutions. Indeed, as suggested by Blaska (1978) and Hutt (1983), increases in the importance women attach to a career may be a common freshman-to-senior change in most institutions. This however, would not necessarily preclude women's institutions from distinctively influencing the direction of career choice, as Bressler and Wendell's analyses would seem to indicate.[8]

More important, perhaps, than effects on career orientation or career choice is the impact of institutional gender on actual career attainment. The most comprehensive series of studies to address this issue was conducted by Tidball (1973, 1974, 1976, 1980, 1985, 1986) and Tidball and Kistiakowsky (1976). This research suggests that graduates of women's colleges or colleges with a high percentage of women faculty (primarily women's colleges) have demonstrated a substantially higher level of career achievement than women graduates of coeducational institutions. The evidence is impressive. For example, in a study of women achievers cited in *Who's Who in American Women* (an index of career prominence), the number of cited achievers per 1,000 women graduates per decade was compared for 59 women's and 289 coeducational institutions. For a five-decade period, the women's colleges were found to graduate twice the number of high achievers that coeducational colleges graduated (Tidball, 1973, 1974). These differences remained even after controls were made at the institutional level for selectivity, size, and faculty salaries (Tidball, 1980).

Similar results have been reported by Newcomer (1959), Oates and Williamson (1978), and Rice and Hemmings (1988), although the last study suggested that the ratio of women achievers from women's colleges was only 1.5 times that of coeducational schools in the 1970–1979 period. None of these studies implemented the same institutional controls that Tidball (1980) did.

Tidball's research also suggests that compared to coeducational institutions, women's colleges are overrepresented in the production of graduates entering male-dominated occupations. This includes research scientists and scholars (Tidball & Kistiakowsky, 1976), entrants into American medical schools (Tidball, 1985), and doctoral recipients in engineering and the physical or life sciences (Tidball, 1986). As was the case with women achievers, this overrepresentation of women's college graduates in male-dominated occupations was substantial, a ratio of 2:1 (in comparison with coeducational colleges) for medical school entrants and a ratio of 4:1 for research scientists and scholars. Furthermore, in the fifty most productive institutions of female natural science doctorates, there was a correlation of .75 between number of female bachelor's degree graduates who became doctoral scientists and the number of female faculty members. In these studies no controls appear to have been made for different institutional or individual characteristics.

Although such evidence is impressively consistent, it is hazardous to assume that it is the result of an environmental effect rather than a recruitment effect. Controls made for aggregate institutional factors such as selectivity, size, and faculty compensation simply do not provide for control of individual student precollege characteristics, which are critical influences on individual career attainment. Moreover, as both Oates and Williamson (1978) and Rice and Hemmings (1988) point out, a certain group of elite and prestigious women's colleges (the Seven Sisters) are highly overrepresented among women's colleges in their graduation of women achievers. This could be largely a function of the background characteristics of the individual students they admit.

Two recent studies that employed a national sample of college students attempted to estimate the influence of attending a women's institution on early career outcomes after controls were made for other institutional characteristics and individual traits. Gruca, Ethington, and Pascarella (1988) controlled for such influences as family socioeconomic status, secondary school achievement, educational and occupational aspirations, marital plans, institutional selectivity, college grades, and educational attainment. With these influences held constant, the percentage of women in the college attended (ranging from less than 10 percent to more than 90 percent) had no statistically significant direct or indirect effect on women entering sex-atypical careers. Such results are not inconsistent with Astin's (1977a) finding that a women's college inhibited the likelihood of one's becoming a nurse but enhanced the likelihood of one's becoming a school teacher.

The second analysis, conducted by Stoecker and Pascarella (1988), controlled for institutional size and college major in addition to the same variables for which Gruca, Ethington, and Pascarella (1988) controlled. When these influences were held constant statistically, attending a predominantly women's college had no statistically significant direct or indirect effect on the occupational status (Duncan SEI) of the job in which a woman worked. A predominantly women's institution was operationally defined as 75 percent or more women.

While these relatively recent findings suggest that most of the influence of attending a women's college on career is due to differential recruitment rather than differential socialization, they do not necessarily refute all of Tidball's findings. For example, the environment of a women's college may not have a net influence on the occupational status of the job obtained, but it may, as suggested by Tidball (1973, 1974, 1980), socialize women in ways that enhance the drive for success and prominence within occupational levels. Similarly, women's institutions, particularly selective ones, may be more closely linked to women's entrance into specific professional careers, such as medicine and scientific research, instead of others of similar occupational status or level of male domination. Allowing for these possibilities, it is still important to note that the absence of controls for *individual* student characteristics in Tidball's series of studies makes it difficult to attribute the impact to socialization rather than recruitment.

It is worth noting that certain prestigious men's colleges have also graduated a large share of high achievers. Zuckerman (1977), for example, reports that five Ivy League colleges and three other selective men's colleges were about five times as likely as colleges and universities generally to produce Nobel laureates. It is difficult, however, to attribute this productivity to socialization rather than to differential recruitment.

Institutional Racial Composition

Analyses of two national longitudinal data bases have addressed the question of the net influence of college racial composition on occupational status. Both analyses employed the Duncan SEI as the measure of occupational status or prestige. Thomas and Gordon (1983) analyzed the 1979 follow-up of the NLS-72 data. Controlling for family social status, intelligence, occupational aspirations, college type (four-year or two-year), college grades, college major, and educational attainment, Thomas and Gordon found that the predominant race of the institution attended had no statistically significant effect on the occupational status of the jobs obtained by black, Hispanic, or white students. (See also Baratz & Ficklen, 1983, for consistent findings concerning employment rates.)

Pascarella, Smart, and Stoecker (1989) conducted a similar, although somewhat more focused, study of the impact of college race on the occupational status of black men and women. Drawing their sample from the 1971–1980 Cooperative Institutional Research Program data, they controlled for family social status, secondary school achievement, precollege occupational aspirations, a measure of college selectivity and prestige, college enrollment, college major, grades, and social involvement, and educational attainment. Net of these factors, attending a predominantly black institution had extremely small and statistically nonsignificant direct and indirect effects on the occupational status of black men. For black women, however, attending a black college had a statistically significant positive direct effect and a positive but statistically nonsignificant indirect effect on occupational status. The positive direct effect for black women was significantly different from and about four times larger than the same effect for black men.

A partial explanation for the Pascarella, Smart, and Stoecker (1989) findings may be the greater tendency for black colleges (versus white colleges) to encourage black women in particular to enroll in majors typically linked to high-status careers. Thomas (1985), for example, found that net of social origins, mathematics and science preparation, occupational aspirations, and college grades, attending a black college significantly improved the likelihood that black women would major in the natural, biological, or technical sciences (versus education, social work, nursing, or other social sciences). The same effect for black men was positive but only marginally significant.

While not directly addressing the more general outcome of job status, Astin (1977a) has presented evidence that attending a black institution may also enhance the likelihood of entering at least one relatively high-status occupation. Net of student background characteristics, attending a black institution had a statistically significant positive effect on a black student's becoming a physician. Since Astin pooled men and women in his analysis, however, it is difficult to compare his findings with those of Pascarella, Smart, and Stoecker (1989).

Institutional Size

Meyer (1970b) and Kamens (1971) have both argued that larger institutions, by means of the greater number of majors and preprofessional programs they offer, typically have a wider range of links with occupational and economic groups in society. Other factors being equal, this may afford larger institutions superior status-allocating capacity than smaller institutions. As a result, one might expect larger institutions to influence student career choice and occupational attainments in the direction of relatively high-status professions, such as law, engineering, and medicine. Empirical support for this hypothesis is unconvincing, however.

Kamens (1971) analyzed data on students from ninety-nine institutions who were followed from their freshman to their junior year. Controlling for freshman occupational choice, gender, academic ability, and a measure of the "prestige" of the institution attended, Kamens found that students in large colleges were significantly more likely than their counterparts in small colleges to choose professional occupations (law, medicine, engineering, the ministry) in their junior year. This finding, however, has not been supported in analyses of two other national samples by Astin (1977a) and Astin and Panos (1969). Controlling for essentially the same variables as Kamens did plus a large battery of other student precollege characteristics, they found no statistically significant net link between institutional size and students' choice of a professional career (law, medicine, or engineering) as seniors. In this regard it is interesting to note that in a subsequent analysis by Kamens (1979), institutional "complexity" (that is, the presence of graduate academic or professional programs), a characteristic positively linked to size, had a negative influence on choice of an academic career by men and choice of a professional career by women.

Evidence concerning the net influence of institutional size on occupational status in general (Duncan SEI) is somewhat more consistent. Knox, Lindsay, and Kolb (1988), analyzing the 1986 follow-up data of the NLS-72, controlled for important student precollege traits (such as socioeconomic status, occupational aspirations, academic ability) and institutional characteristics (such as selectivity, private/public control). With these factors held constant statistically, institutional size had a statistically significant but small positive direct effect on occupational status. Smart's (1986) analysis of a national sample of students who began college in 1971 and were followed up nine years later yielded generally similar results. Net of essentially the same variables as those controlled by Knox, Lindsay, and Kolb, institutional size had a small but statistically significant positive influence on the occupational status of those in business or managerial fields but not in professional fields.

Ethington, Smart, and Pascarella's (1988) study was the only one we uncovered that considered the unique effect of institutional size on women's entrance into male-dominated occupations. Analyzing the same data as Smart (1986), Ethington, Smart, and Pascarella controlled for student precollege traits (such as socioeconomic status, high school grades, occupational aspirations), institutional characteristics (college selectivity, public/private control), and collegiate accomplishments (such as grades, leadership activities). With these influences controlled, the size of the institution attended had no statistically significant influence on the likelihood that women would enter traditionally male-dominated occupations.

Institutional Control: Public Versus Private

Much of the research on the impact of institutional control on career choice has been conducted by Astin and Panos (1969). Their extensive research indicates that public or private control has little impact on career choice apart from student precollege characteristics and other institutional influences, such as selectivity and liberal arts emphasis.

Other multi-institutional research by Gurin and Epps (1975) investigated the characteristics of ten black colleges and universities that influenced the occupational aspirations of black students. Controlling for initial occupational aspirations and the selectivity of the institution attended, these researchers found that private control positively influenced the prestige and ability demands of occupational choice at the end of the freshman year for men but not for women.

Considerably more research has attempted to estimate the unique influence of institutional control on the various dimensions of career attainment. Astin (1977a) provides the most extensive evidence on the attainment of career aspirations. His analyses suggest that net of other factors, public four-year institutions have a mixed influence. On the one hand, they significantly enhance the likelihood of implementing career plans for becoming a college teacher or engineer, but, on the other hand, they reduce the likelihood of successfully implementing plans for business, law, medicine, or nursing. More recent evidence seems to confirm Astin's finding for law, although the nature of the impact was indirect (Braxton, Brier, Herzog, & Pascarella, 1988).

Evidence concerning the influence of college control on occupational status is inconsistent and even contradictory. Net of salient student precollege characteristics and other college characteristics, such as size and selectivity, Knox, Lindsay, and Kolb (1988) found that attending a private institution significantly enhanced the occupational status (Duncan SEI) of the job obtained fourteen years after the subjects started college. Smart (1986), controlling for essentially the same individual and institutional characteristics, presents somewhat more mixed results. Attending a private college or university uniquely enhanced the occupational status of individuals entering business or managerial careers but had no statistically significant influence on the job prestige of those entering professional careers.

Sharp and Weidman (1987) analyzed the same general data as Knox, Lindsay, and Kolb (1988) did, with two exceptions. First, their sample was confined only to B.A. recipients who graduated with a humanities, social science, business, or education major. Second, they followed up the sample only seven years after the subjects entered college rather than the fourteen years of Knox, Lindsay, and Kolb. Controlling for essentially the same precollege and institutional characteristics, however, Sharp and Weidman found that attending a private institution actually had a statistically significant negative influence on the occupational status of men. The corresponding effect for women was statistically nonsignificant.

We uncovered only one study (Ethington, Smart, & Pascarella, 1988) that attempted to assess the influence of institutional control on women's entry into male-dominated occupations. In this study public or private control had no statistically significant impact on the sex atypicality of women's occupations when student precollege characteristics and other institutional characteristics were taken into account.

Liberal Arts Colleges

There is a small body of evidence to suggest that attending a liberal arts college may influence career aspirations and career choice. In Bielby's (1978) analysis of the factors influencing women's choice of sex-atypical (male-dominated) majors and careers, attending a liberal arts college was found to enhance significantly the choice of a sex-atypical major even when controls were made for the selectivity of the institution attended. Since sex-atypical majors strongly increased the likelihood of entering a sex-atypical or male-dominated occupation, a liberal arts emphasis may have indirectly enhanced the latter attainment, although the statistical significance of this indirect impact was not determined.

Such findings are consistent with those of Astin and Panos (1969), who found that net of student precollege characteristics, attending a liberal arts college enhanced the likelihood of one's majoring in the biological sciences and choosing a career in typically male-dominated fields such as academia and the physical sciences. Unfortunately, these analyses pooled men and women so it is difficult to determine whether the effect was the same for both sexes.

Gurin and Epps (1975), in their analysis of the influence of ten predominantly black colleges on career aspirations, took a somewhat different tack. Rather than categorizing institutions as liberal arts colleges or other institutional types, they estimated the level of liberal arts emphasis in each college's curriculum. With college selectivity and level of precollege career choice held constant, Gurin and Epps found that a liberal arts curricular emphasis significantly enhanced the prestige, ability demands, and nontraditionality (percentage white) of black male career choice at the end of the freshman year. Liberal arts emphasis had no statistically significant impact on the career aspirations of black women.

While there is some evidence to suggest that liberal arts colleges or a liberal arts emphasis may influence career choice and aspirations, there is little to suggest that attending a liberal arts college has much impact on occupational status. With controls made for race, gender, social status, and academic ability, Knox, Lindsay, and Kolb (1988) found that the Carnegie Classification of Institutions (Research Universities I and II, Doctoral Universities I and II, and Liberal Arts Colleges I and II) yielded no clear pattern of effects on job status. Though liberal arts colleges tended to fall below research and doctorate-granting universities and above some comprehensive universities, the overall between-category differences were slight. Similar results have been reported by Sharp and Weidman (1987).

Environmental Influences

If there is a common thread running through the evidence on the impact of college environments on career choice, it is the notion of "progressive conformity." This concept posits that net of an individual's initial career choice, the dominant peer group operates to create a greater degree of conformity among its members while at the same time opposing trends toward heterogeneity (Astin, 1965b; Holland, 1985). As Astin and Holland suggest, progressive conformity operates in two ways: It discourages students planning to pursue a relatively popular career from abandoning that choice, and it encourages students planning to pursue relatively unpopular careers to switch to more popular ones.

Evidence in support of progressive conformity is reasonably consistent. In a typical study, Astin (1965b) sought to determine the net influence of various college environmental characteristics on the senior career choices of men attending seventy-three institutions. Career choice was one of the six Holland (1985) types: realistic (for example, engineer), investigative (physician, scientific researcher), social (nurse, elementary teacher), conventional (businessperson), enterprising (lawyer, business manager), and artistic (performing artist). Environmental measures were the percentage of students on each campus with academic majors corresponding to the six Holland types. Controlling for such factors as initial career and major field choice, educational aspirations, academic aptitude, and college grades, Astin found a small but statistically significant tendency for the seniors to be planning careers consistent with the modal (or most typical) academic major in their institution. Thus, for example, net of other influences, the percentage of students in a college majoring in realistic fields and the percentage majoring in enterprising fields had significant positive associations with the likelihood of choosing realistic careers and of choosing enterprising careers, respectively. Similar results, based on essentially the same analytical approach applied to independent samples, have been reported for major field choice (Tusin, 1987) and career choice (Astin & Panos, 1969; Holland, 1968; Holland & Whitney, 1968).[9]

Smart (1988b) has extended the concept of progressive conformity beyond occupational choice during college to the actual career that an individual enters after college. In an analysis of a national sample of students followed up nine years after their initial enrollment in college, Smart controlled for such factors as gender, social status, parental occupation, precollege career choice (in Holland type), college selectivity, college grades, and educational attainment. With these factors held constant, the Holland type of the individual's occupation at the time of the follow-up was regressed on the percentage of degrees awarded by an institution in various majors. Consistent with expectations based on the progressive conformity hypothesis, the percentage of degrees awarded by an institution in the various majors had a statistically significant net positive effect on the likelihood of one's actually working in an occupation that corresponded in terms of Holland type. Thus, percentage of majors in science increased the likelihood of an individual working in an investigative occupation, percentage of majors in the social sciences increased the likelihood of a social occupation, and percentage of business majors enhanced the probability of a business occupation. Small sample sizes prevented similar analyses of other Holland types.

Geographical and Social Proximity

In his analysis of career attainment in a single corporation, Rosenbaum (1984) sought to determine whether an effect was exerted by the geographical and social proximity of the college attended. Geographical proximity simply means how close the college is to the work site. Such physical proximity alone has been found to enhance an individual's likelihood of promotion, irrespective of college selectivity (Romo & Rosenbaum, 1984). Social proximity concerns the extent of salient college activity in the community in which the firm is located, the level of information exchange and consulting activities offered by the college to the firm, and the extent to which the college's graduates are represented in company management. Rosenbaum's analyses suggest that net of age, tenure in the firm, and college selectivity, attending a college with high geographical and social proximity to the corporation significantly enhanced both job level at the time of hiring and probability of subsequent promotion. Thus, other things being equal, an individual acquired an advantage in terms of career mobility by graduating from a college that was familiar to the company.

Transfer Between Four-Year Institutions

In Chapter Nine we noted evidence that transfer between four-year institutions has a net inhibiting influence on educational attainment (Kocher & Pascarella, 1988). Consistent with expectations based on various models of status attainment, Kocher and Pascarella also anticipated that transfer between institutions would have a negative impact on job status in large measure because it impeded educational attainment. Their findings were consistent with this expectation. Controlling for such factors as socioeconomic status, academic achievement, occupational aspirations, institutional selectivity, and educational attainment, they found that extent of transfer had no statistically significant direct effect on job status (Duncan SEI) nine years after initial college enrollment. For all four subgroups (black and white men and women) considered, however, transfer had a statistically significant negative indirect impact on job status that was transmitted largely by its negative effect on educational attainment.

Within-College Effects

A large body of research has addressed the question of whether or not different internal college experiences influence an individual's career. We found no unifying thread or common theoretical perspective running through this literature. Nevertheless, the evidence appears to cluster into the following categories: academic major, academic achievement, extracurricular involvement, interaction with faculty, and work experience.

Academic Major

Job Fit. As we have suggested in previous chapters, a student's major field of study has a substantial influence on how that student experiences college. Moreover, it is clear that there are strong links between major and subsequent occupational experiences (for example, Bielby, 1978; Bills, 1988; Hearn & Olzak, 1981; Jacobs, 1986; Phelan & Phelan, 1983; Thomas, 1980). These links are by no means deterministic. As Jacobs (1986) argues, the connection between academic major and a subsequent job is often indirect for a number of occupational specialties, and the first job after college does not determine an entire career. Indeed, most evidence consistently indicates that only about 50 percent of college graduates report a close or direct relationship between their undergraduate major and their job(s) (*Digest of Educational Statistics*, 1986; Riley, 1982; Ochsner & Solmon, 1979; Solmon, 1976; Solmon, Bisconti, & Ochsner, 1977). "Nonetheless, a notable relationship between field of study and subsequent career options is indisputable, especially in certain fields" (Jacobs, 1986, p. 135; see also Florito, 1981).

The evidence concerning which majors lead to closely related jobs is reasonably consistent. Typical of the research in this area is the study by Solmon (1981) that followed up two national samples of white students seven and thirteen years after they enrolled in college. The dependent measures were the extent of perceived fit between major and job and the extent to which the individual felt that college had provided knowledge and skills he or she used in the job. Controlling for sex, marital status, college grades, educational attainment, college selectivity and control, employment sector, and length of employment, Solmon concluded that majoring in the arts, humanities, and social sciences tended to have statistically significant negative effects on both outcomes, irrespective of sex. Conversely, for both men and women, majoring in business, engineering, or other professional areas tended to have statistically significant net positive influences on both degree of major to job fit and the extent to which the major provided skills used on the job. The net influence of majoring in the biological and physical sciences was somewhat mixed, being slightly positive for women and either negative or statistically nonsignificant for men. The latter finding may reflect the fact that male physical or life science majors frequently go to medical or dental school (for example, Pascarella, Brier, Smart, & Herzog, 1987) and that the nature of daily work in these professions may have little consistent relationship with an undergraduate science major.

Solmon's (1981) findings on differences among academic majors in degree of job fit are generally consistent with other research addressing this issue (for example, Berliner, 1971; Richards, 1984b; Solmon, Bisconti, & Ochsner, 1977). Students majoring in professional preparation programs (such as engineering, teaching, business, and architecture) appear, at least early in their careers, to hold jobs that utilize major field skills more often than those who major in such areas as arts, humanities, and the social sciences.[10] Whether such a general finding has much importance, however, must be evaluated in the light of two other pieces of evidence.

First, it is unclear that net of other factors, close links between one's major field and the skills required on the job are a consistently important determinant of job satisfaction. Richards (1984a) and Smart, Elton, and McLaughlin (1986) found a statistically significant positive association between major and job fit and satisfaction, but the measures of major to job fit they used did not clearly tap the link between skills learned in the major and those required on the job. The Richards study employed a composite index that included income and education as well as major field relatedness, while Smart, Elton, and McLaughlin defined major and job fit in terms of Holland-type congruence.

Taken together, studies that look more directly at the extent to which skills learned in the major are used on the job suggest only a small and perhaps trivial relationship between major to job fit and job satisfaction (Ochsner & Solmon, 1979; Riley, 1982; Solmon, Bisconti, & Ochsner, 1977). More important to job satisfaction was the perception that individual skills (not merely those acquired in college) were fully used on the job. Where major to job fit has more than a trivial association with job satisfaction, it appears to occur quite early in one's career, before one may have been lured from a major-related job by better opportunities (Ochsner & Solmon, 1979).

A second and related piece of evidence is that the specific skills learned in one's major appear most important in preparing a person for his or her first job after graduation rather than for subsequent jobs (Bisconti, 1987;

Ochsner & Solmon, 1979). With some exceptions, as an individual's career progresses, specific skills related to his or her major field of study decline in importance in terms of effective job performance. Conversely, factors such as general intellectual skills and the ability to learn on the job increase in terms of importance for job productivity. Perhaps this is most clearly evident in the findings presented by Bisconti (1987). Bisconti asked seventy companies to select ten employees in different work areas on the basis of their "very good" or "excellent" performance. All were employed in the kinds of business and technical occupations associated with large industry. Those in the sample who had graduated about ten years prior to the study were asked to indicate those aspects of college most useful to their career. While 29 percent mentioned the specifics of a major as being important for effective performance on their first job, only 8 percent mentioned them as being important in their overall career. In contrast, 21 percent mentioned general learning in college as important for success in their first job, while 31 percent said general learning was important for overall career success. Similarly, when those who had graduated from college ten years before the study were compared to those who had graduated two years earlier, the former were between two and three times *less* likely to report that college courses had provided them with the knowledge and technical skills important to job performance.

Occupational Status. Evidence concerning the influence of academic major on occupational status is inconsistent. In a typical study, Thomas and Gordon (1983) analyzed the 1979 follow-up of the NLS-72 data. After controls were made for gender, race, socioeconomic status, academic ability, educational and occupational aspirations, college grades, and educational attainment, majoring in natural science and technical fields (compared with such majors as education and the social sciences) had a statistically significant positive direct effect on occupational status (Duncan SEI) for women but not for men. Similar results are reported for women by Stoecker and Pascarella (1988), though Anisef (1982) suggests that the occupational status benefits of a science or technical major may accrue more to men than to women.

Smart's (1986) study of early occupational status, on the other hand, suggests a somewhat different conclusion. Controlling for essentially the same characteristics as Thomas and Gordon (1983) did plus institutional selectivity and educational attainment, Smart found that majoring in the sciences had no statistically significant effect on initial occupational status (Duncan SEI) in either professional or nonprofessional careers. Moreover, when initial job status was also controlled, majoring in the natural sciences actually had a statistically significant negative influence on current job status for both career groups. A similar study conducted by Pascarella, Smart, and Stoecker (1987) used the same data base and essentially the same controls to examine the early job status of black men and women. They found little to indicate that majoring in a scientific or technical field had more than a trivial and statistically nonsignificant impact on the job status of either group. Results consistent with those of Pascarella, Smart, and Stoecker have also been reported by Griffin and Alexander (1978) in an analysis of 1955 high school male sophomores followed up in 1970.

The waters are muddied even further by the findings of Angle, Steiber, and Wissman (1980). Like the other studies reviewed, their study investigated the early status attainment of a national sample of men and women who worked full-time. Controlling for age, sex, race, a measure of family socioeconomic status, and educational attainment, these investigators found that college academic major (in six different categories) increased the explained variance in occupational status less than 1 percent. Business majors had jobs with the highest Duncan SEI score, followed in order by majors in education, social sciences, and the humanities. Jobs with the lowest prestige were held by natural science majors and those majoring in fields not included in the other categories.

Finally, Sharp and Weidman (1987) estimated the influence of academic major on the early careers of students who majored in nonscience and nontechnical fields. Their data were also from the 1979 follow-up of the NLS-72 study. For women, majoring in business, education, or the humanities (versus the social sciences) had positive effects on job status, while men's job status was positively affected by majoring in business, education, or the social sciences (versus the humanities). Unfortunately the analytical procedure that Sharp and Weidman used in their analysis (stepwise regression) meant that different confounding influences were controlled in the male versus the female sample. Moreover, no controls appear to have been made for important precollege variables such as occupational aspirations and academic achievement and ability. Consequently, the apparent impact of major on job status may have been at least partially confounded in this study.

One possible explanation for such inconsistent results is that the typical categorizations of academic major used in the studies reviewed above may have only a marginal theoretical and functional fit with the structure of occupational prestige. Furthermore, broad groupings such as natural sciences, technical, social sciences, and humanities may disguise important differences in occupational linkages among majors *within* the same grouping. These issues have been addressed in a study by Wilson and Smith-Lovin (1983) that developed a multidimensional scaling of majors according to the extent they were "targeted" toward prestige, authority (extent of supervision over others), or income. The actual scaling of majors was performed in two steps. First, expected levels of prestige, authority, and income were obtained for each occupation in the country from objective information about the national occupational structure (for example, U.S. Census public use samples). Second, ninety-seven college majors were matched with potential occupational targets by means of an occupational information system compiled by a state employment security commission. The resulting scales placed each college major on three continuums in terms of the extent to which they led to, or targeted, occupations of high prestige, authority, and income rewards. This provided for occupationally linked distinctions among majors within broad categories. For example, rather than clumping all natural science majors together, geology received a targeted prestige score of 80.0 (on the Duncan SEI) while meteorology was assigned a score of only 62.0. Conversely, the targeted income of a geology major was only 10.6 compared to a targeted income of 14.3 for a meteorology major.

Net of such factors as gender, family socioeconomic status, educational attainment, and marital status, the three measures of occupationally targeted majors constructed by Wilson and Smith-Lovin (1983) increased the explained variance in actual job prestige a statistically significant 8 percent. This stands in marked contrast to the tiny net variance increment in job prestige (less than 1 percent) associated with major when it is defined in terms of traditional categorizations (Angle, Steiber, & Wissman, 1980). Moreover, each of the three dimensions of academic major had statistically significant net direct effects on occupational prestige. The targeted prestige of a major had the strongest positive effect, followed by the targeted income of the major. The targeted authority of the major, however, had a small negative influence on job status.

Sex-Atypical Careers Among Women. The weight of evidence is clear that net of ability and socioeconomic status, women tend to be overrepresented in fields of study such as education, social work, and the social sciences and underrepresented in mathematics, natural science, engineering, and technical and professional fields (for example, Braddock, 1981b; Grevious, 1985; Jacobs, 1986; Hearn & Olzak, 1981, 1982; Polachek, 1978; Thomas, 1980). Similarly, Wilson and Smith-Lovin's (1983) and Wilson and Shin's (1983) analyses also indicate that net of family social status, family size, and sex role attitudes, women are significantly more likely to select majors that are targeted toward occupations of lower prestige, income, and authority. Since academic major is closely linked with the kind of vocation a person pursues, such choices might be expected to be an important determinant of gender equality in the work force.

Research that adequately addresses the potential causal link between undergraduate major and women's entry into sex-atypical or traditionally male-dominated occupations is sparse. Wolfson (1976) followed up a small sample of women graduates of a single institution nearly thirty years after their graduation. Patterns of careers were conceptually divided into five groups on the basis of such factors as span of occupational participation, degree of participation, and, to some extent, degree of career sex atypicality. Having a technical or vocational major rather than a liberal arts major and the percentage of men in that major significantly discriminated among the five groups. It is unclear, however, that the career grouping variable was independently measuring the sex atypicality of occupation. Moreover, no controls were made for potential confounding variables such as family social status, so it is difficult to determine how much the findings may have reflected specious rather than causal associations.

Perhaps the most rigorously conducted study to address this question is that of Bielby (1978). Employing data on a national sample of female college graduates who were followed up eight years after graduation, Bielby converted academic major to a continuum based on the percentage of men studying in those majors at the time the women finished college. Controlling for such factors as age, family social status, college selectivity, college grades, and the sex atypicality of one's first job (percentage of men in the occupation) after graduation, Bielby found that sex atypicality of major had a statistically significant positive direct influence on working in a sex-atypical job eight years after college. Moreover, sex-atypical majors also had a positive *indirect* effect on the sex atypicality of a woman's occupation. This was transmitted largely through the increased likelihood of women in sex-atypical academic majors entering sex-atypical jobs immediately after college.

Although Bielby (1978) did not control for academic ability or pre-college sex atypicality of occupational choice, his is perhaps the most direct and convincing evidence of the extent to which college major is a potential determinant of gender equality (or inequality) in the work force. More recent research has demonstrated how major choice can become part of a cumulative disadvantage accruing to women who aspire to specific sex-atypical professions. Looking only at those who aspired to becoming physicians or later became physicians, Pascarella, Brier, Smart, and Herzog (1987) found that gender had only a trivial and statistically nonsignificant direct effect on becoming a medical doctor when salient background characteristics, the selectivity of the college attended, and college grades and major were held constant. However, women were indirectly penalized because net of other factors, they were significantly less likely than men to major in the physical or life sciences as undergraduates. Since a science major strongly enhanced the likelihood of one's becoming a physician, it became part of a statistically significant inhibiting influence on women entering that profession. Thus, being female had a statistically significant negative indirect effect on occupational attainment that was at least partially explainable by major field choice.

Job Performance and Promotion. If there is any generalization that can be made from the rather small body of research on academic major and job performance and promotion, it is that over the long run liberal arts majors appear to do as well as, though no better than, those with a business or engineering degree. Some of the earliest inquiry into the link between college major and job performance and success is found in the work of Pallett and Hoyt (1968) and Calhoon and Reddy (1968). Pallett and Hoyt followed up male graduates employed in nontechnical business positions to determine whether liberal arts and business majors of similar academic aptitude differed in job performance between five and ten years after college. These investigators found only trivial and statistically nonsignificant differences between the two groups on immediate supervisor's overall ratings of job performance. Calhoon and Reddy report similar results for career mobility. In their review of three studies conducted between 1954 and 1963, two showed no statistically significant association between college major and mobility, while one suggested that liberal arts majors (versus business and engineering majors) may have had a small advantage.

Some of the most comprehensive recent evidence is based on four-year and twenty-year longitudinal studies of career development in a technical organization (AT&T) conducted by Beck (1981) and Howard (1986). Beginning in 1956 and 1977, company psychologists used a battery of tests, games, questionnaires, and interviews to develop ratings of managerial and advancement potential of college graduates recently hired into the company. Analyses of both samples indicated that humanities and social science graduates were consistently rated significantly higher than engineering, business, or science or math majors on nearly all individual and overall dimensions of managerial potential. One of the most pronounced areas of advantage was interpersonal skills. In the four-year longitudinal study no statistically significant differences were found in actual job-level advancement among those in different majors, although humanities and social science majors showed the greatest advancement and engineers the least. In the twenty-year longitudinal follow-up, however, there was a statistically significant difference among the four groups in rate of promotion over the twenty-year period. Humanities and social science majors showed the highest rate of advancement, followed in order by business, science or math, and engineering majors. The differences in career mobility were found to be statistically significant for engineering majors when compared with humanities, social science, and business majors, respectively.

Results generally consistent with those of Beck (1981) and Howard (1986) are reported in a study of managers of the Illinois Bell Telephone Company (Wade, 1984, as reviewed in Useem, 1989). While 6 and 14 percent of the managers in the lowest two managerial ranks had a liberal arts (versus an engineering or business) major, 60 percent of those in the top two managerial ranks and 32 percent of those in the third-highest category had a liberal arts major.

As suggested by Useem (1989), however, the findings of the AT&T and Illinois Bell studies may be the exception rather than the rule. His own analysis of managers in more than 500 diverse companies suggests that liberal arts and science majors (that is, humanities, social science, science, and mathematics majors) had a somewhat lower rate of advancement during the first ten years of employment than did those with a business or engineering degree. However, the former were just as likely as, though no more likely than, engineers or business majors eventually to reach the highest levels of management.

This general trend, however, masked some important differences from company to company even within the same industry. In some companies liberal arts graduates experienced accelerated advancement, while in other companies their advancement rates were somewhat lower than the rates of business or engineering graduates. Useem (1989, p. 115) attributes a substantial part of these differences to "unique educational cultures within companies that have evolved over decades of experience and recruitment." Variations in rates of advancement may also be a partial function of those areas in a company where individuals with different academic majors tended to be placed. For example, Useem found that the largest percentage of liberal arts graduates tended to be placed in sales and marketing, followed by human resources and general management. The lowest percentage were in manufacturing, planning, and research and development. If different corporate cultures place a different value on these areas, this could well influence rate of advancement.

Academic Achievement

A small body of evidence suggests that grades play a nontrivial role in career choice during college largely by signaling to a student whether he or she can successfully comply with the academic demands of fields of study linked to a career choice (Becker, Greer, & Hughes, 1968; Davis, 1966; Gallini, 1982; Spaeth, 1970; Weidman, 1984). Modification of career choice may often be in response to academic performance (Werts & Watley, 1968b). Similarly and unsurprisingly, satisfactory grades are often a prerequisite to successful implementation of a career in many fields (Astin, 1977a; Ethington, Smart, & Pascarella, 1987) and particularly in professions that require advanced training (Braxton, Brier, Herzog, & Pascarella, 1988; Pascarella, Brier, Smart, & Herzog, 1987).

Occupational Status. By far the largest body of evidence pertaining to academic achievement has addressed its influence on subsequent career outcomes; and one of the most studied of these career outcomes is occupational status or prestige. With some exceptions (for example, Thomas & Gordon, 1983), the weight of evidence is reasonably consistent in suggesting that college grades have a positive net impact on early occupational status. In a typical study, Perrucci (1980) analyzed the 1968 follow-up of a national sample of individuals who graduated from college in 1961. Controlling for gender, precollege occupational status expectations, the selectivity of the undergraduate college attended, extent of graduate education, and senior-year occupational status expectations, Perrucci found that college grades had a small but statistically significant positive direct effect on the status or prestige of the job held in 1968. The measure of job status or prestige was developed by Siegel (1971) and is similar to the Duncan SEI. Although Anisef (1982), Griffin and Alexander (1978), Harvey and Kalwa (1983), Johnson (1987), and Sharp and Weidman (1987) used somewhat different controls, all report findings similar to those of Perrucci in analyses of five independent samples. In each case the direct effect of grades on occupational status was statistically significant and positive but small in magnitude, probably accounting for no more than 1 percent of the variance in that outcome.

Other studies have also reported a statistically significant positive effect of grades on occupational status, but the pattern of effects is not always consistent across studies. Tinto (1980, 1981), who analyzed the same multi-institutional national sample as Perrucci (1980) and controlled for generally the same variables, found that college grades had a statistically significant positive direct influence on the job status of men in professional careers but not in business or managerial careers. He also found that grades had a much more pronounced positive indirect effect on job status (transmitted through senior-year prestige expectations and educational attainment) for men in professional careers than for men in business or managerial careers. Smart's (1986) analysis of a different multi-institutional national sample of students followed up nine years after initial enrollment in college reports results that are not consistent with Tinto's (1980, 1981). Part of the reason for this may be the fact that Smart pooled men and women rather than only considering men. Controlling for gender; race; family social status; precollege occupational aspirations; the size, selectivity, and control of the institution; college major; and educational attainment, Smart found that grades had a statistically significant positive direct effect on the status of the first job obtained for those in business or managerial careers but not for those in professional careers. This is just the reverse of Tinto's findings. Like Tinto, Smart found grades in college to have a statistically significant positive indirect influence on current job status, transmitted largely through the direct impact of grades on educational attainment. Unlike Tinto, however, Smart found that the indirect effect was about equal in magnitude for those in professional and business or managerial careers.

Despite differences in the findings reported by Tinto (1980, 1981) and Smart (1986), both studies underscore the importance of taking indirect influences into account when considering the impact of academic achievement on job prestige. A similar conclusion is also warranted by the earlier findings of Spaeth (1970) and the more recent findings of Pascarella, Smart, and Stoecker (1987). Because academic achievement in college is such an important determinant of educational attainment, a substantial part of its total impact on job status or prestige is likely to be transmitted through educational attainment. Failure to consider its indirect influence may lead one to underestimate the total impact of academic achievement on job status. At the same time, however, it should be stressed that even this total net influence is unlikely to explain more than 1 percent of the variance in early occupational status. Whether it would sustain even this small impact on occupational status later in one's career is debatable.

Sex-Atypical Careers Among Women. A small body of research addresses the issue of whether or not high academic achievement enhances the likelihood that women will enter sex-atypical careers. Bielby's (1978) analysis of 1961 college graduates followed up eight years later suggests that net of factors such as family social status, age, the type of institution attended, and various measures of other college accomplishments, grades had a small but statistically significant negative indirect effect on women's work force participation. For women actually in the work force, however, grades had a small, positive, and statistically significant direct effect on being employed in a sex-atypical occupation (defined according to percentage of men in the field).

Unfortunately, Bielby (1978) did not control for precollege sex atypicality of occupational choice or for a measure of prior achievement or academic ability. Consequently, the possibility exists that the direct link found between grades and sex-atypical careers is somewhat confounded. Some hint of this is suggested in the more recent findings of Ethington, Smart, and Pascarella (1988) and Gruca, Ethington, and Pascarella (1988). Analyzing data on a national sample of women who began college in 1971 and were followed up in 1980, they found that college grades had only a trivial and statistically nonsignificant direct effect on entering a sex-atypical occupation when such factors as high school grades, family social status, sex atypicality of career aspirations, institutional selectivity, and educational attainment were held constant. However, for some subgroups of women (black women and women in scientific careers), college academic achievement had a statistically significant positive indirect impact on sex atypicality of occupation, transmitted essentially through its positive influence on educational attainment. Such findings are not necessarily at odds with those of Bielby. A close inspection of her regression equations suggests that the indirect effect of grades on career sex atypicality may be nearly as large as its direct effect. Bielby, however, does not identify the variables mediating that indirect effect.

Occupational Performance and Success. In a synthesis and critique of the literature on the relationships between adult accomplishment and measures of academic ability and success, Baird (1985, p. 4) offers a cogent explanation of why society expects a positive link between academic and occupational achievement. "The student who does well in the classroom is expected to be able to do well in real-life situations. The classes and curriculums are designed to prepare students to function as citizens and workers in the general society and in specific occupations and professions. Thus, the students who do well in class should also generally do well in the social roles and occupational duties for which these classes have prepared them. From this it follows that the students who will be most likely to succeed in society and in particular occupations and professions are those . . . who have had the greatest success in academic work."

A large body of research has sought to verify the link between college grades and noneconomic measures of occupational performance and success. The vast preponderance of these studies have focused on the simple correlations between academic and occupational achievement without considering possible factors such as socioeconomic status, maturation, and ability that might confound the influence.[11] In attempting to synthesize this body of evidence, we benefited from a number of comprehensive quantitative and nonquantitative research reviews (for example, Adkins, 1975; Baird, 1985; Calhoon & Reddy, 1968; Cohen, 1984; Hoyt, 1966; O'Leary, 1980; Samson, Graue, Weinstein, & Walberg, 1984; Wingard & Williamson, 1973). Despite some minor interpretative differences, these reviews are markedly consistent in concluding that the typical correlations between college grades and noneconomic measures of both job performance (for example, supervisors' ratings) and career mobility (rate of promotion, job level obtained, and the like) are positive but quite modest in magnitude. From data presented in several of the quantitative syntheses, as well as the results of more recent research (for example, Howard, 1986), we estimate the *average* correlations of grades with performance and career mobility indexes to be as follows: .18 with job performance, .17 with rate of promotion, and .14 with the job level or level of responsibility attained in one's career. What this means is that only about 2 to 3 percent (the square of the correlations) of the differences in job performance and career mobility are explainable by differences in college grades; this is a liberal estimate because the above correlations are not adjusted for potential confounding influences.

Only a few studies have investigated the relationship between college academic achievement and measures of occupational performance and mobility while controlling for potential confounding influences. Ferris (1982) studied the first-year job performance of staff-level auditors in a large professional accounting firm. In an equation that controlled for educational attainment and a measure of the "quality" of the undergraduate institution attended, college grades had only a trivial and statistically nonsignificant influence on a job performance index taken from the firm's personnel records.

Perrucci and colleagues (Kinloch & Perrucci, 1969; Perrucci & Perrucci, 1970) and Wise (1979) have examined the influence of college grades on measures of career mobility. Perrucci and colleagues investigated the extent to which college grades influenced technical responsibility, supervisory authority, and professional involvement of engineers and managers in two samples. Controlling in various analyses for such factors as work experience, social origins, and the selectivity of the undergraduate college attended, the investigators found that grades tended to have positive relationships with all three criteria but particularly with technical responsibility and professional involvement. As suggested by Baird (1985), however, the Perrucci analyses did not control for potential confounding variables such as advanced training or individual ability and motivational influence. It is likely that even the modest associations found between grades and occupational success would be substantially reduced had these influences been taken into account.

In what is perhaps the most methodologically rigorous study of the topic, Wise (1979) analyzed data on the occupational performance of college graduates hired by a single large company over a nineteen-year period. Controlling for individual background characteristics (for example, work experience, socioeconomic status, a measure of organizational or leadership ability), the selectivity of the undergraduate college attended, advanced degrees, and academic performance in graduate school (if attended), Wise determined that undergraduate grades had a small but statistically significant positive direct effect on rate of job promotion. Such a finding suggests that at least part of the modest relationship between college achievement and career mobility may be causal in nature. It is likely, however, that any direct causal effect is quite small, probably accounting for no more than 1 or 2 percent of the total variance in promotion rate.

Baird (1985) has offered a number of reasons why the link between college grades and later occupational productivity and mobility may be small. These include the unreliability of both college grades and measures of job productivity and success; the often lengthy time interval between college and the measurement of occupational experiences, which may introduce extraneous factors into career progression; and the fact that most studies limit their sample to college graduates and thus substantially attenuate the range of academic achievement considered. It is also possible, of course, that academic success in college is simply tapping traits that have only a marginal overlap with those required for success in the exceptionally broad range of occupational activities in which graduates are employed.

Occupational Satisfaction. The existing evidence is reasonably consistent in suggesting a small positive association between college grades and occupational satisfaction. Samson, Graue, Weinstein, and Walberg (1984) conducted a quantitative synthesis of fourteen studies addressing this issue and report a statistically significant average correlation between grades and job satisfaction of .18. Cohen (1984) also conducted a meta-analytical synthesis but used a somewhat different criterion, satisfaction with career success, in selecting studies. His synthesis yielded a positive but statistically nonsignificant average correlation of .09 between grades and satisfaction with career success.

Average correlations presented in both quantitative syntheses were not adjusted for potential confounding variables. The evidence from studies that attempt to estimate the link between grades and occupational satisfaction with salient confounding influences held constant is much less consistent. Johnson (1987) found a statistically significant positive effect of major field grades on subsequent job satisfaction of black college graduates when socioeconomic status, college racial composition, and educational attainment were taken into account. Johnson's sample, however, was limited to graduates of only four institutions in a single state. Evidence from national samples suggests that any influence of college academic achievement on job satisfaction is probably trivial and statistically nonsignificant. Sharp and Weidman (1987), using the 1979 follow-up of the NLS-72 data, controlled for such factors as socioeconomic status, college major, college selectivity, and type of work. With these factors held constant, college grades had no statistically significant direct effect on job satisfaction for male college graduates and a small negative effect for female college graduates. Ochsner and Solmon (1979) and Solmon, Bisconti, and Ochsner (1977) analyzed two national cohorts of baccalaureate recipients in the 1960s and 1970s who were followed up after about four and nine years in the work force. Controlling for a set of variables quite similar to those of Sharp and Weidman, they found that grades in college had no statistically significant effect on job satisfaction for either men or women.

Our reading of this body of evidence is that the small positive correlations found between college grades and occupational satisfaction are probably specious or noncausal in nature. When potential confounding influences are controlled, the already small association between grades and job satisfaction is typically reduced to near zero.

Extracurricular Involvement

Occupational Status. A small body of research has addressed the impact of extracurricular involvement on the status of both occupational choice and occupational attainment. Weidman (1984) analyzed data from a national sample of college students who entered college in 1966 and were followed up in 1969. Controlling for such factors as freshman career choice (Duncan SEI), family socioeconomic status, race, college selectivity, and college grades, he found that extent of involvement in extracurricular activities (for example, student government, college organizations) generally had trivial and statistically nonsignificant direct effects on the status of 1969 career choice for both men and women. There were exceptions to this, but they exhibited no clear pattern. Extracurricular involvement had small negative effects for male mathematics and female history majors and a small positive effect for female English majors.

Smart's (1986) study of the factors influencing the status of one's job nine years after initial college enrollment sought to determine, among other variables, the impact of student social integration. Social integration was a scale that included measures of student extracurricular involvement and a single item assessing interaction with faculty. Net of family socioeconomic status, sex, race, secondary school grades, precollege occupational aspirations, college selectivity, academic major, grades, and educational attainment, extent of social integration had no statistically significant direct effects on occupational status nine years after college enrollment. It did, however, have a statistically significant, positive indirect effect on occupational status, mediated primarily through educational attainment. Unfortunately, the measure of social integration tapped both interaction with faculty and extracurricular involvement, making it difficult to determine which component accounted for this effect.

Women's Entry into Sex-Atypical Careers. While there is little to indicate that extracurricular involvement significantly influences women's choice of sex-atypical careers during college (Almquist & Angrist, 1970), relatively recent evidence does suggest that it may, in fact, modestly enhance entry into such careers. Using the percentage of men in the occupation as an operational definition of sex-atypical (male-dominated) occupations, Ethington, Smart, and Pascarella (1988) sought to determine whether the same measure of college social integration used by Smart (1986) had any influence on women's entry into such occupations. Net of such factors as socioeconomic status, secondary school grades, precollege occupational aspirations, college selectivity, college grades, and educational attainment, social integration had a statistically significant positive direct influence on women entering science-related, sex-atypical careers. The corresponding direct effect for sex-atypical careers in nonscience areas was also positive, but it was statistically nonsignificant. Again, however, because the measure of social integration included interaction with faculty as well as extracurricular involvement, it is difficult to ascertain which may have accounted for the impact.

A further analysis of the same data base by Braxton, Brier, Herzog, and Pascarella (1988) clarifies the situation to some extent. Their study attempted to explain entrance into one male-dominated occupation, the legal profession. Controlling for many of the same confounding influences as Ethington, Smart, and Pascarella (1988), they found that a measure of extracurricular or leadership involvement (for example, president of a student organization, member of a university committee) had a small positive direct effect on women becoming lawyers. Interestingly, the corresponding influence for men was also positive but statistically nonsignificant.

Job Performance and Promotion. With the possible exception of individuals in specific technical fields such as engineering (Hoyt & Muchinsky, 1973), the evidence is reasonably consistent in suggesting that college graduates retrospectively perceive extracurricular involvement, particularly in leadership roles, as having a substantial impact on the development of interpersonal and leadership skills important to general occupational success (for example, Bisconti & Kessler, 1980; Princeton University, 1967; Schuh & Laverty, 1983; University of North Carolina, 1967). Moreover, actual extent of participation or leadership in college extracurricular activities has statistically significant positive associations both with attainment of the first job (Nash, Rosson, & Schoemer, 1973) and with independent assessments of managerial potential (Howard, 1986). In terms of the latter criterion, it is interesting to note first that breadth of participation, or number of activities, was as good a predictor as leadership positions and, second, that of all activities, participation in student government, the school paper, and debating teams had the strongest positive correlations with the different dimensions of managerial potential. All correlations were small, however, and seldom exceeded .20 (Howard, 1986).

Given the above evidence, one might expect a modest positive relationship between college extracurricular involvement and actual occupational success. We uncovered only one study conducted in the last twenty years that addressed this question in a comprehensive manner. This was Howard's (1986) longitudinal analysis of the career development of two samples of male college graduates employed by AT&T. Her analysis uncovered little to indicate that extracurricular achievement during college was any more than a trivial predictor of occupational success. For both samples, neither extent of participation nor leadership positions in collegiate extracurricular activities had statistically significant correlations with job level attained after two, four, eight, or twenty years with the company.

Athletic Participation and Career. Some research has addressed the influence of intercollegiate athletic participation on the different dimensions of career. While the evidence from this research by no means provides a comprehensive picture, we can draw the following general conclusions. First, it appears that athletes, particularly those in revenue-producing sports such as basketball and football, tend to have lower levels of career maturity than nonathletes (Blann, 1985; Kennedy & Dimick, 1987; Sowa & Gressard, 1983). (Recall that career maturity takes into account such factors as the extent to which a person has accomplished career developmental tasks, the ability to formulate career plans, and the accuracy of knowledge and degree of certainty about one's intended career.) It would be somewhat premature, however, to attribute low levels of career maturity to athletic participation. Since none of the studies reviewed controlled for possible confounding influences, such as, level of precollege career maturity, the differences noted between athletes and nonathletes may have reflected self-selection or recruitment rather than any deleterious impact of athletic participation.

A second conclusion is that although athletic participation in college may often function to enhance the social mobility of individuals from lower socioeconomic backgrounds (Sack & Theil, 1979), the evidence on whether it influences occupational status is mixed (DuBois, 1978; Pascarella & Smart, 1990). In Pascarella and Smart's analysis of the early career experiences of intercollegiate athletes and nonathletes, athletic participation had small but statistically significant positive indirect and total effects on occupational status (Duncan SEI) when race, socioeconomic background, occupational aspirations, college grades, and educational attainment were controlled. Conversely, when DuBois controlled for many of the same variables plus age and work experience, the relationship between athletic participation and occupational status on the Duncan SEI was trivial and not statistically significant.

Finally, Howard's (1986) analysis found little relationship between college athletic participation and the various dimensions of managerial potential in her two AT&T samples. Nevertheless, retrospective perceptions of college graduates attribute athletic participation with playing a major role in their career development, particularly in the areas of competitiveness and teamwork (Bisconti & Kessler, 1980; Princeton University, 1967). Consistent with this finding, Ryan (1989) presents evidence from a national sample of college students to suggest that athletic participation has a positive net impact on the development of interpersonal and leadership skills during college.

Interaction with Faculty

Career Choice. The evidence is reasonably consistent in suggesting that faculty members can play a nontrivial role in the areas of student career interest and career choice during college. Not surprisingly, the magnitude of this role appears to be a function of the amount of informal interaction between the student and individual faculty members. In a longitudinal study at a single institution, for example, Komarovsky (1985) found that women who as seniors had the highest levels of career salience (that is, interest in and commitment to a career) had engaged in significantly more informal interaction with faculty during college than seniors with low career salience. Similarly, in an eight-institution study of the impact of faculty on student development, Wood and Wilson (1972) found that students who interacted frequently with faculty outside of class were more likely to indicate that faculty members had had a statistically significant influence on their choice of major (and thus, indirectly, on their choice of a career) than were students who had little nonclassroom interaction with faculty.

Of course, part of these associations may be attributable to student self-selection. Komarovsky (1985), for example, also found that women who as freshmen had had high levels of career salience had significantly higher levels of informal contact with faculty during college than their classmates who as freshmen had had low levels of career salience. A number of studies have employed research or analytical designs that attempt to separate the influence of differential contact with faculty on career salience or career choice from the influence of student self-selection. The weight of evidence from these investigations suggests that informal contact with faculty has a statistically significant direct effect on various dimensions of career interest and career choice above and beyond the influence of selection factors.

Komarovsky (1985) dealt with the issue of self-selection by comparing groups of women who were equally low on career salience as freshmen. She found that women who as freshmen were not interested in a career but who as seniors were, reported significantly more interaction with faculty than those women who stayed uninterested in a career throughout college. Such evidence suggests that informal interaction with faculty may at times function to change, not merely to accentuate, initial career interests. Similarly, in a multi-institutional study of the career choice of junior and senior women, Karman (1973) found that net of such factors as theoretical orientation, college grades, affinity for mathematics and science, and attitudes toward women's role in society, interaction with faculty to discuss academic issues and problems had a statistically significant positive direct effect on choice of a sex-atypical career.

Consistent with the findings of Karman (1973), Phelan's (1979) analysis of career choice during the first two years of college suggests that interaction with faculty may enhance orientation toward scientific and scholarly careers for both men and women. Analyzing data on a cohort of freshmen from forty universities, Phelan controlled for such factors as student social origins, freshman-year orientation toward a scientific or scholarly career, and a measure of academic involvement. Net of these influences and regardless of gender, amount of social interaction with faculty in one's major field had a statistically significant and positive direct effect on increases in orientation toward a scientific or scholarly career between the beginning of the freshman year and the middle of the sophomore year. Astin (1969a) has reported similar results with respect to the impact of independent research with a faculty member on interest in a professional career.

A related series of studies has addressed the influence of interaction with faculty on the prestige or ability demands of occupational choice. Gurin and colleagues (Gurin & Katz, 1966; Gurin & Epps, 1975) in a study of changes in career choice among black students during the freshman year found that net of precollege career choice, frequency of informal nonclassroom contact with faculty had a statistically significant positive influence on the prestige of career choice assessed at the end of the freshman year. Results from Weidman's (1984) analysis of a national sample are at least partially consistent with those of Gurin and colleagues. Controlling for freshman-year career choice as well as other salient factors (including social origins, race, college selectivity, and college grades), Weidman found that amount of social interaction with faculty in one's major had a statistically significant positive effect on the prestige (Duncan SEI) of senior-year career choice for three of seven subsamples analyzed (male and female history majors and male mathematics majors). The effect for English and political science majors and female mathematics majors was statistically nonsignificant.

Gender of Faculty Role Models and Women's Career Development. A small body of recent research has addressed the issue of whether women's career salience or sex-atypical career choice is enhanced more by the influence of female faculty than by male faculty. With some exceptions (for example, Kutner & Brogan, 1980), the weight of evidence suggests the possibility that female faculty members are more influential career role models and mentors for female students than are male faculty members (Basow & Howe, 1980; Esposito, Hackett, & O'Halloran, 1987; Fox, 1974; Komarovsky, 1985; Stake and Noonan, 1985; Walker, 1981; Wright & Wright, 1987). The designs in several of these studies, however, were not particularly strong. Thus, a definitive resolution of this issue probably awaits further evidence.

Work Experience During College and Career

A modest amount of research has addressed the impact of work during college on career choice and early career attainment. The weight of evidence from this research suggests that working during college, particularly in a job related to one's major or initial career aspirations, has a positive net impact on career choice, career attainment, and level of professional responsibility attained early in one's career.

Arnold (1987) sought to determine the factors that differentiated academically able women who were high vocational achievers from those who were low vocational achievers five years after they began college. Level of vocational achievement was based on aspired to and/or obtained career, plans for labor force participation, and relative importance of work versus family roles. Three independent raters used these criteria to place women into groups of high and low vocational achievers. Discriminant analysis was then employed to determine which factors best differentiated the two groups. Net of such influences as marriage and family plans, value placed on a career, family socioeconomic status, academic ability, and college selectivity, holding a job during college that was related to one's career aspirations was a strong discriminator of women who were high vocational achievers from those with low vocational achievement. Similar results have also been reported by Almquist and Angrist (1970, 1971) with respect to a positive link between holding a job during college and both women's career salience (that is, interest in and commitment to a career) and their sex atypicality of career choice. This study, however, did not effect as powerful a set of controls as did Arnold's.

A related study by Pascarella and Staver (1985) focused on the factors related to choice of one traditionally male-dominated career, scientific research, during the first two years of college. Analyzing data from a national sample of white men and women, Pascarella and Staver controlled for such factors as academic aptitude, secondary school grades, social origins, level of mathematics and science preparation in secondary school, precollege science career aspirations, majoring in the sciences, and college grades. Net of these influences, recompensed on-campus work in science (laboratory or technical assistant, for example) had a positive direct effect on science career choice two years later for both women and men. It is clear from Pascarella and Staver's results that men and women who initially aspire to be research scientists are significantly more likely than others to secure on-campus science-related work. It is also clear, however, that such work significantly enhances the likelihood of intending a science career two years later. Thus, the nature of any causal influence of work on career choice, at least from Pascarella and Staver's results, appears to be one of accentuating or strengthening of initial aspirations.

The influence of professionally related work during college on subsequent career attainment levels has been addressed in a longitudinal study of engineers by Jagacinski, LeBold, and Shell (1986). Their data were drawn from the 1981 National Engineering Career Development Survey of engineers who were employed full-time and had graduated with a degree in engineering between 1961 and 1980. The engineers were divided into those who had had engineering-related work experience during college and those who had had no such work experience. After controls were made for such factors as year of graduation, gender, and engineering field, those having had engineering-related work experience during college had higher levels of technical responsibility and satisfaction in their first job than those not having had it. The same differences, however, did not persist to the current job.

Conditional Effects of College

As in Chapter Nine on educational attainment, the search for robust conditional effects is complicated by the fact that the vast majority of studies we reviewed did not test such effects for statistical significance. Added to this is the dearth of statistically significant conditional effects that are replicable across independent samples. Consequently, we again take a relatively conservative approach, focusing on those conditional effects that are not merely the result of chance differences among samples and particularly on those that are demonstrably replicable.

College and Occupational Attainments

In terms of conditional effects, perhaps the most investigated question is whether or not different groups (such as gender or race) receive different occupational status returns from postsecondary education. This body of research has produced what seems to be the most replicable conditional effect of any in the area of the impact of college on career, namely, that nonwhite men, at least, derive greater job status benefits from postsecondary education and from graduating from college than do white men. Although there are some exceptions (for example, Gruca, 1988), this finding has been replicated on several independent samples (Featherman & Hauser, 1978; Jencks et al., 1979; Porter, 1974). This, of course, does not mean that nonwhite college graduates work in higher-status jobs than their white counterparts. It does suggest, however, that postsecondary education and college graduation are more important in the attainment of job status for nonwhites. Conversely, it also suggests that the job status penalties for not attending college may also be correspondingly greater for this group.[12]

Consistent with the evidence for white-nonwhite differences in male job status returns to postsecondary education are results reported by Gruca, Ethington, and Pascarella (1988) with respect to women entering traditionally male-dominated occupations. They found that net of other causes, the direct impact of postsecondary education on black women entering a male-dominated occupation was four times as strong as the corresponding effect for white women.

A considerable amount of research has also been concerned with gender differences in the job status returns to education. The weight of evidence suggests that educational attainment is an equally important determinant of job status for men and women (Acker, 1980; Featherman & Hauser, 1976; McClendon, 1976; Treiman & Terrell, 1975). Similarly, it would appear that the specific effects of postsecondary education on occupational status are largely independent of gender (Pascarella, Smart, & Stoecker, 1987; Sewell, Hauser, & Wolf, 1980; Thomas & Gordon, 1983). The latter conclusion needs to be modified somewhat in light of the disaggregated findings of Sewell, Hauser, and Wolf in analyses of an eighteen-year follow-up of Wisconsin high school seniors. When the outcome was the status of the first job, postsecondary education was twice as important for men as for women. Conversely, when first job status was controlled, the effect of postsecondary education on current job status was twice as great for women as for men. Consequently, the net *total* effect of college on occupational status at midlife was about the same for both sexes.[13,14]

Institutional Characteristics and Occupational Attainments

Although a number of studies have reported significant conditional effects involving race, gender, and college characteristics, this research is generally characterized by a lack of independent replication. For example, Spaeth (1977), analyzing data on 1961 college graduates followed up in 1968, found that college selectivity had a somewhat more positive impact on male than on female occupational status. This finding, however, was not generally replicated by Gruca (1988) in an analysis of a national sample of students who entered college in 1971 and were followed up in 1980.

Gruca's (1988) analysis, along with that of Pascarella, Smart, and Stoecker (1987) on the same data, did suggest that the early occupational status returns to attendance at a selective or prestigious institution differed by race and by gender within race. Specifically, whites tended to receive somewhat greater occupational status returns from attending an elite college than did blacks, while black women benefited significantly more than black men. There is also evidence from the Pascarella, Smart, and Stoecker (1987) analyses to suggest that attending a primarily black college had a significantly stronger positive influence on the early occupational status of black women than of black men. Each of the conditional effects found in these two studies, however, was based on the same sample and awaits independent replication.

A small body of research has also addressed the issue of whether the occupational returns to college selectivity differ for individuals from different socioeconomic origins. An advantage of this research is that analyses have been conducted on independent multi-institutional, national samples. Unfortunately, the results of these analyses are inconsistent. Tinto (1984) has suggested that net of other influences, greater job status returns for attendance at a selective college accrue to individuals from low rather than high social origins. Conversely, Karabel and McClelland (1987) and Perrucci and Perrucci (1970) suggest that attendance at a selective institution is most important for the job status and job technical responsibility of individuals from relatively high social origins. The findings of Alwin (1974) and McClelland (1986) suggest that impact of college selectivity on job status aspirations and attainment is largely independent of social background.

The most consistent evidence we uncovered with respect to the conditional effects of college characteristics on career concerns the differential influence of college selectivity on job status for individuals in professional as compared with business or managerial occupations. Analyzing independent samples, both Tinto (1980, 1981) and Smart (1986) report that net of other causes, college selectivity had a significantly stronger total effect on job status in professional occupations than in business or managerial ones.

Within-College Experiences and Occupational Attainments

A substantial body of research has focused on the question of whether or not college academic achievement has a differential influence on career mobility for different kinds of students. Unfortunately, this evidence provides few consistent results across independent samples, each of which was multi-institutional and national in scope. For example, Spaeth's (1977) findings suggest that college grades are worth nearly twice as much in terms of occupational status to men as to women. More recent evidence by Thomas and Gordon (1983), however, suggests that the reverse is true, and other investigations report no substantial gender differences in the net effect of college grades on job status (Kocher & Pascarella, 1988; Pascarella, Smart, & Stoecker, 1987; Sharp & Weidman, 1987). Similarly, Tinto (1984) reports that grades may have their strongest positive influence on occupational status for men from relatively high (versus low) social origins who work in professional (versus business or managerial) jobs. Harvey and Kalwa (1983), however, report essentially the opposite conditional effect with respect to social origin, and Smart's (1986) findings fail to clearly replicate Tinto's results concerning the conditional influence of working in professional occupations versus business or managerial occupations.[15]

Somewhat more consistent evidence indicates that the impact of grades on occupational attainment varies with the selectivity of the college attended. In an analysis of two generally independent subsamples of the 1971–1980 Cooperative Institutional Research Project data, Braxton, Brier, Herzog, and Pascarella (1988) and Pascarella, Brier, Smart, and Herzog (1987) found that a relatively high level of undergraduate academic achievement had a stronger positive influence on entry into high-status professions such as medicine and law if an individual had attended a selective rather than a nonselective college. Another way of saying this is that good grades may count more in terms of entrée into medicine or law if they are earned in a relatively competitive arena. Of course, this may also partially reflect the increased likelihood of high-achieving students from selective colleges gaining admission to professional schools (Henson, 1980). Consistent with this conclusion is evidence reported by McClure, Wells, and Bowerman (1986) that high academic achievement in a selective undergraduate institution is a significantly better predictor of success in a master of business administration program than similarly high achievement in a nonselective institution.

A small amount of research has also sought to determine whether major field of study has a differential influence on occupational status across gender. In an analysis of the 1979 follow-up of the NLS-72 data, Thomas and Gordon (1983) found that majoring in the natural or technical sciences was significantly more important in enhancing the early occupational status of women than of men. This finding was generally replicated on another sample by Harvey and Kalwa (1983). Less consistent results have been reported by Gruca (1988), but this may be due in large part to the fact that her analyses grouped natural science majors with technical and preprofessional majors.

A different approach to estimating gender differences in the impact of major on occupational status has been taken by Wilson and Smith-Lovin (1983). Recall from earlier in the chapter that they redefined undergraduate field of study into a multidimensional framework that indicates whether it is targeted toward jobs stressing prestige, authority, or income. According to Wilson and Smith-Lovin, majors targeted toward prestige had significantly greater occupational status payoffs for women, whereas majors targeted toward income provided significantly greater job status returns for men.

It is not readily apparent how the findings of Wilson and Smith-Lovin (1983) mesh with those of Thomas and Gordon (1983) or Harvey and Kalwa (1983). What the evidence from these studies clearly implies, however, is that there are substantial gender differences in the net impact of major field of study on subsequent occupational status.

Intergenerational Effects of College

Do individuals derive occupational status benefits from having parents who are well educated? A considerable part of the status attainment research has addressed this question, with mixed results. Net of other causes (such as father's occupation, occupational aspirations, college grades, and educational attainment), some investigations have indicated that level of parental education directly enhances sons' and daughters' occupational status (Griffin & Alexander, 1978; Sewell & Hauser, 1980; Tinto, 1984). Others have suggested that net effect may be negative (Featherman & Carter, 1976; Harvey & Kalwa, 1983). Still other investigations have reported little or no consistent intergenerational influence (Kerckhoff & Jackson, 1982; Karabel & McClelland, 1987; McClendon, 1976).

We found little in terms of differences in methodological rigor across studies that might account for these inconsistent findings. One possible conceptual explanation, however, is that the major influence of parental education on children's occupational attainment is indirect. Gruca (1988) hypothesized such an indirect impact in an analysis of the early occupational status achievements of a national sample of college students whose parents had different levels of formal education. In order to study the impact of parents having a college education, mother's and father's education was dichotomized into bachelor's degree or above and less than a bachelor's degree. After controls were made for such confounding causes as family income, secondary school achievement, precollege educational and occupational aspirations, the selectivity and size of the institution attended, college grades, and educational attainment, neither mother nor father being a college graduate had any statistically significant direct effect on the status (Duncan SEI) of an offspring's job nine years after he or she initially enrolled in college. Having college-educated parents did, however, have a number of small but statistically significant positive *indirect* effects on one's job status irrespective of race or sex. These effects occurred largely because level of parental education positively influenced a number of key intervening steps or events in the status attainment process (for example, family income, occupational and educational aspirations, educational attainment) all of which in turn had important subsequent impacts on occupational status.

There is some additional evidence from Gruca's (1988) analyses to suggest that the positive indirect job status returns to having college-educated parents may vary by race. For white men and women, the indirect positive effects on job status of having a father who was a college graduate were larger than those of having a mother who was a college graduate. For black men and women, however, the reverse was true. Having a college-educated mother had a more pronounced indirect influence on early occupational status than having a father who was a college graduate.

In addition to estimating the impact of parental education on children's occupational status achievements, a small body of inquiry has attempted to estimate the impact of parental education on a woman's work force participation and likelihood of pursuing a sex-atypical career. A particularly salient emphasis in this literature has been on the role-modeling influence of a mother on her daughter's occupational aspirations and attainments. The evidence is reasonably consistent in suggesting that mother's level of education is positively linked with a woman's work force participation (for example, Arnold, 1987; Bielby, 1978) and her likelihood of pursuing a sex-atypical career (Almquist & Angrist, 1970; H. Astin, 1969; Burlew, 1982; Levine, 1975; Lyson, 1980; O'Donnell & Andersen, 1978; Tangri, 1972). Evidence with respect to the importance of father's education is less consistent. Nagely (1971) and Werts (1967b) found a positive association between father's education and women's pursuit of a sex-atypical occupation, while O'Donnell and Andersen (1978) and Tangri (1972) did not.

A problem with many of the studies just cited is that they estimate the relationship between parental education and daughter's career choice and attainments without controlling for important confounding influences such as family income, academic ability, academic achievement, occupational aspirations, various college experiences, and educational attainment. Studies of national samples that statistically controlled for these or similar variables report little or no consistent direct impact of mother's or father's education on either women's choice of sex-atypical fields of study during college (Bielby, 1978; Peng & Jaffe, 1979) or their entry into sex-atypical occupations subsequent to college (Bielby, 1978; Gruca, Ethington, & Pascarella, 1988).

Once again, however, there is evidence to suggest that parental education has a statistically significant positive indirect influence on women's entry into sex-atypical careers. In an analysis of the factors influencing women's entry into sex-atypical careers, Gruca, Ethington, & Pascarella (1988) estimated a causal model that included such influences as family income, mother's work status, secondary school achievement, precollege educational and occupational aspirations, the selectivity and predominant gender of the undergraduate college attended, college major, college grades, and educational attainment. With these influences taken into account, having a college-educated mother (bachelor's degree or above) had a statistically significant positive indirect effect on the likelihood that either black or white women would enter a sex-atypical career. The corresponding indirect effect of having a college-educated father was statistically significant and positive for white women but not for black women. As with the indirect effect of parental education on children's occupational status (Gruca, 1988), the indirect effect of parental education on a daughter's likelihood of entering a sex-atypical career occurred largely because having college-educated parents conferred certain advantages at important intervening steps in the career choice and attainment process. These included parental income, precollege aspirations, the selectivity of the college attended, and educational attainment.

The Gruca, Ethington, and Pascarella (1988) study also suggests that differences in the indirect impact of mother's versus father's college graduation on a daughter's sex-atypical career attainment vary with race. For white women, mother's education and father's education are about equal in importance, whereas for black women it is significantly more important that the mother be a college graduate.[16]

Summary

Change During College

Although large numbers of undergraduate students use college to pursue rather than choose a career, the evidence is clear that students frequently change their career plans during college. These changes may reflect many factors, including mobility across related fields, movement from competitive to less competitive fields (or in some cases the reverse), and cognizance of national or regional shifts in the employment possibilities and/ or economic payoffs of different occupations. A consistent body of evidence exists to suggest that these shifts may also reflect the fact that students become significantly more mature, knowledgeable, and focused during college in thinking about planning for a career. Whether this is an effect of college or simply a development that occurs coincidentally with college attendance is difficult to determine. The simple fact of having to confront one's life work may have a substantial impact on the increased maturity found in seniors' thinking and planning for a career.

Net Effects of College

One of the most pronounced and unequivocal effects of college on career is its impact on the type of job one obtains. Our best estimate is that independent of an individual's background, a bachelor's degree confers about a 34 percentile point advantage in occupational status or prestige over and above graduating from high school. Although most of the research we reviewed was conducted on male samples, there is little replicable evidence to suggest that the life-span occupational status returns to a college education differ significantly by gender. The evidence also suggests that the job status advantage that accrues to college graduates is not simply a function of the first job obtained. Rather, the significant occupational status differences between high school and college graduates are sustained over the occupational life span, even when the status of one's first job is taken into account. Further, while each year of college enhances occupational status, one apparently receives a bonus for completing the baccalaureate.

The fact that a bachelor's degree significantly enhances the likelihood of entering relatively high status managerial, technical, and professional jobs has implications not only for income (to be taken up in Chapter Eleven) but also for occupational stability. The very nature of these jobs makes them less sensitive to employment fluctuations that occur with changing economic conditions. This may at least partially explain the fact that college graduates are substantially less likely than high school graduates to be unemployed. Related evidence also suggests that college-educated individuals may have additional hedges against prolonged periods of unemployment in the form of increased accuracy of occupational information and efficiency in job search, increased regional mobility to take advantage of employment opportunities, and an enhanced network of personal contacts, some of which date back to college days.

Despite the fact that college graduates derive substantial job status advantages irrespective of their background characteristics, the causal mechanism that underlies the ability of the bachelor's degree to confer these advantages is not readily apparent. One hypothesis is that the college experience imparts cognitive skills, values, personality characteristics, attitudes, and behavior patterns that employers value because these traits are required to succeed in complex technical, professional, and managerial occupations. Even if this socialization explanation is totally unfounded, however, college might still confer important job status advantages that are independent of background. Allocation of job status may depend in large measure on what employers believe a college degree certifies in terms of cognitive and noncognitive skills and values necessary for job success. If college-educated individuals are seen by employers as more likely than high school graduates to possess these requisite skills and values, they will continue to secure higher-status jobs irrespective of whether the skills and values were acquired during college. There is evidence to support either of these explanations, and it is likely that both "socialization" and "certification" contribute to the total impact of college on career.

Although college-educated individuals are more likely to obtain high-status managerial, technical, and professional jobs than those without a college education, the weight of evidence suggests little in the way of job productivity differences when the two groups hold jobs at the same level. Yet it is clear that college graduates enjoy significantly higher levels of career mobility and advancement. Part of this may be due to initial job positioning effects, which place college graduates and those with less education on different career paths. Another part may be due to the fact that those with a college education are more likely to possess (or at least are more likely to be perceived as possessing) the requisite competencies and values that equip one for successful adaptation to complex, high-level managerial positions.

College tends to produce conflicting influences on satisfaction with one's work. On the one hand, college tends to have a modest positive influence on job satisfaction by placing individuals in jobs with relatively high intrinsic (autonomy, challenge, interest) and extrinsic (income) rewards. On the other hand, college tends to develop a capacity for critical judgment and evaluation that may make college-educated individuals more sensitive to the shortcomings of their jobs. Similarly, the college educated are also quite likely to have higher expectations about the intrinsic rewards of their jobs than those with less education. The latter factors can lead to dissatisfaction in situations of "overeducation," where job demands do not require a college-level education.

Between-College Effects

Comparison of two-year and four-year institutions has produced the most pronounced and consistent between-college effect on occupational status. Net of other factors, students who begin their postsecondary education experience in two-year colleges have significantly lower job status than those who start at four-year institutions. Most of this difference, however, appears to be attributable to the adverse effect of two-year institutions on educational attainment. For individuals of equal educational attainment, whether they started at two-year or four-year institutions makes little difference in early occupational status. Similarly, for individuals of equal educational attainment, starting at a two-year or four-year institution appears to make little difference in other noneconomic dimensions of career such as employment stability or job satisfaction.

Considering only four-year institutions, the weight of evidence clearly indicates few statistically significant between-college effects on the dimensions of career choice and attainment. What effects do exist tend to be extremely small, particularly when compared to the general effect of attending rather than not attending college.[17]

The most investigated of all institutional characteristics is that of "quality," typically assessed in terms of student body selectivity or reputational and prestige indexes. Compared with other institutions, elite institutions tend to enroll students with high occupational status aspirations to begin with, and their impact appears to be one of maintaining or perhaps slightly accentuating the status level or academic career orientation of initial choice. This impact on career choice is quite small compared to that attributable to career choice at the beginning of college. It may be particularly true of students attending selective or prestigious institutions that the undergraduate experience is used more to implement than to choose a career.

Attendance at a selective college modestly increases the likelihood that women will choose sex-atypical (male-dominated) majors and careers and that they will enter sex-atypical occupations. It also appears that a degree from an elite institution confers a slight advantage in various dimensions of career mobility and success (for example, technical or supervisory responsibility, level of managerial attainment). However, with the possible exception that college selectivity may have more positive implications for attainment in the professions than in managerial or business occupations, the weight of evidence indicates that attending a selective or prestigious institution has little net impact on overall job status, job productivity, or job satisfaction.

There is evidence that men's colleges have independently enhanced male career choice and attainment in such areas as business, law, and the professions in general. The most recent research, however, has focused on the impact of women's institutions on career choice and career attainment of women. Findings from this second line of research are not totally consistent, but neither are they totally ambiguous. The weight of evidence suggests that attending a predominantly women's institution rather than a coeducational one has little or no independent impact on a woman's career salience (interest in or commitment to a career), the status or prestige level of the job she obtains, or the likelihood of her actually entering a sex-atypical career (globally defined according to a percentage of men in the field). On the other hand, women's institutions appear to enhance orientation toward a sex-atypical occupation during college, entrance into certain *spe-*

cific sex-atypical occupations (such as medicine and scientific research), and prominence or achievement within a specific occupational status level.

Net of other factors, attending a predominantly black institution rather than a predominantly white institution appears to have only a trivial and statistically nonsignificant impact on the occupational status of black men or black students generally. However, some evidence suggests that attendance at a black college may enhance the early job status of black women. A possible causal mechanism underlying this effect is suggested by evidence that black women are more likely to major in fields linked to high-status careers (for example, natural, biological, and technical sciences) in predominantly black colleges.

A small body of research has also addressed the net impact of institutional size (enrollment), control (public versus private), and liberal arts emphasis on career. The findings of this research are at best mixed. There is little consistent evidence to indicate that institutional size has any independent impact on career choice or women's entry into sex-atypical careers, but attending a large institution appears to have a small positive influence on occupational status. Similarly, institutional control appears to have little consistent impact on career choice, occupational status, or women's entry into sex-atypical careers. However, public control appears to enhance the likelihood of successfully implementing career plans for becoming an engineer or college teacher while reducing the likelihood of successfully implementing plans for law, business, medicine, or nursing. The major influence of liberal arts colleges may be in their enhancing of women's choice of sex-atypical majors and careers, although the evidence supporting this conclusion is not particularly strong. Net of other factors, attending a liberal arts college would appear to have little or no impact on occupational status.

The most consistent college environmental impact on career choice appears to be that of "progressive conformity." Progressive conformity hypothesizes that student career choice will be influenced in the direction of the dominant peer groups in an institution. A small amount of evidence indicates that irrespective of initial career choice, seniors tend to be planning careers consistent with the most typical academic majors in their institution. There is also evidence, though less of it, to suggest that independent of initial career choice, a student's likelihood of actually working in a particular occupation increases with the percentage of majors at his or her college corresponding to that occupation.

We uncovered two additional between-college effects worth noting, although they await replication. First, there is evidence to suggest that graduating from a college that has close geographical and social proximity to a firm (for example, located in the same city with frequent professional interaction) enhances one's occupational mobility in that company. This effect appears to operate independently of one's age, length of service with the company, and the selectivity of one's college. Second, transfer among four-year institutions appears to have a negative indirect effect on early occupational status irrespective of gender or race. This occurs largely because transferring from one institution to another tends to inhibit educational attainment, a key determinant of job status.

Within-College Effects

We synthesized within-college effects on career within five categories: academic major, academic achievement, extracurricular accomplishments, interaction with faculty, and work experience. The evidence is clear that certain major fields of study (for example, business, engineering, technical or professional) tend to have a closer fit with the skills required in one's first job than do others (arts, humanities, and social sciences). It is not clear, however, that the job fit of one's major is a key determinant of job satisfaction. Moreover, as an individual's career progresses, specific skills learned in a major field of study tend to decline in importance and to be replaced by more general intellectual skills and ability to learn on the job.

We found little evidence across studies that academic major as typically categorized (humanities, social sciences, natural sciences, and so on) has more than a small and inconsistent pattern of effects on job status. This may be due to the fact that traditional categorizations of major have only a marginal theoretical and functional fit with the structure of occupational status. There is some modest evidence to suggest that when academic majors are placed on a continuum in terms of how they are "targeted" toward occupations that stress prestige, supervisory authority, or income, they demonstrate a stronger impact on job status.

Although sparse, the evidence that college major independently influences the likelihood that women will enter sex-atypical careers is convincing. Net of other factors, a sex-atypical major (one that attracts a high percentage of men, such as business or mathematics) enhances the likelihood of a woman entering a sex-atypical career. Thus, academic major in college may be an important determinant of gender equality in the work force. A student's major field of study, however, may have little to do with his or her job performance or long-term career mobility, although in the private sector this may depend upon the employing company. Not a great deal of evidence pertains to these issues, but the evidence that does exist suggests that over the long run, in business at least, liberal arts majors do as well as (though not better than) those with a business or engineering degree.

The evidence is consistent in suggesting that academic achievement during college has a small but statistically significant positive impact on early occupational status. Part of this effect may be indirect, occurring because grades enhance educational attainment, a key determinant of job status. Though less extensive, there is similar evidence to suggest that college grades also enhance the likelihood of women entering sex-atypical careers. A substantial part of this influence may also be indirect, mediated through educational attainment.

On the basis of our synthesis of the existing evidence (much of it already in review form), we estimate that without other factors being controlled, college grades account for no more than 2 or 3 percent of the variance in various noneconomic indexes of job performance and career mobility. Evidence from the most rigorously conducted study suggests that at least part of the link with career mobility may be causal. This does not appear to be the case for the link between college grades and job satisfaction, however, which we interpret as spurious.

We found no evidence across studies to suggest that extracurricular involvement during college has a consistent nontrivial influence on the status of one's occupational choice or actual occupational attainment. There is some limited support, however, for the contention that social leadership involvement during college enhances the likelihood of women entering sex-atypical careers. With the exception of individuals in technical fields such as engineering, college graduates are consistent in indicating that extracurricular involvement, particularly in leadership roles, has a substantial impact on the development of interpersonal and leadership skills important to job success. It also appears to be positively linked with managerial potential. Objective assessments, however, indicate only a trivial link between career mobility and both extent of extracurricular involvement and involvement in leadership positions. There is also little consistent evidence to suggest that athletic participation has a nontrivial impact on occupational status, though it may enhance the social mobility of individuals from low socioeconomic backgrounds.

The magnitude of faculty impact on student career choice appears to vary with amount of informal contact or interaction. Net of other factors, including initial career choice, frequency of informal contact with faculty appears to enhance women's interest in a career as well as their choice of a sex-atypical career. Similarly, it also has a net positive influence on orientation toward a scientific or scholarly career and, for some students, the status of one's career choice. Although there are some problems in the designs of the extant studies, the weight of evidence also suggests that female faculty may be somewhat more influential career role models for women students than are male faculty.

The impact of work during college on career choice and career attainment has been the focus of a small body of inquiry. The existing evidence suggests that net of other factors, working during college, particularly in a job related to one's major or initial career aspirations, enhances the level of professional responsibility attained early in one's career, the likelihood of women choosing a sex-atypical career during college, and women's plans for entering the work force subsequent to college.

Conditional Effects of College

Our synthesis uncovered only four conditional effects in the impact of college on career that are generally replicable across samples. Clearly, the most consistent conditional effect is that of nonwhite men receiving significantly greater job status returns from college graduation than white men. Since most analyses in this area have employed male samples, it is not clear that the same conditional effect holds for women. However, we found little evidence to suggest that the impact of college on occupational status differs by gender.

The most consistent evidence with respect to the conditional effects of college characteristics on career concerns the differential influence of college selectivity on job status for individuals in professional occupations rather than business or managerial ones. The selectivity of the college attended appears to count for more if one enters a profession than if one pursues a business or managerial career.

We found two replicted conditional effects that involve within-college experiences. First, the impact of academic achievement on occupational attainment varies with the selectivity of the institution in which grades were earned. Good undergraduate grades appear to count more in terms of entrée into relatively high status professions such as medicine and law, and they are more predictive of success in graduate business schools if they were earned in a relatively competitive arena. Though quite modest in magnitude, this may be one hidden benefit for certain students of attending a selective institution, a benefit not captured in the literature on status attainment.

Second, it also appears that there are statistically significant gender differences in the impact of major field of study on early occupational status. One line of evidence indicates that women derive greater job status benefits from majoring in the natural or technical sciences than do men. Other evidence suggests that majors targeted toward prestige have greater job status payoffs for women, whereas majors targeted toward income have a greater payoff for men. These two sets of conditional effects are not easily reconcilable, yet they clearly indicate statistically significant gender differences in the role of academic field of study on occupational status.

Intergenerational Effects of College

The weight of evidence from the most rigorously conducted studies indicates little consistent direct intergenerational impact of parental postsecondary education on the career attainment of sons and daughters. We have suggested, however, that this may be attributable to the fact that intergenerational effects are largely indirect. There is some evidence, as yet unreplicated, to suggest that this is the case in the areas of occupational

status and women's entry into sex-atypical careers. For both these outcomes, mother's or father's graduation from college had a statistically significant positive indirect impact by influencing important intervening events
in the career attainment process such as family income, the student's aspirations, and the type of college attended. There is also some tendency for
maternal college graduation to count more for black students and for pa-
ternal graduation to be more important for whites, but this finding also
awaits replication.

A final point needs to be made. Perhaps nowhere is the long-term
impact of college more wide ranging than in its influence on an individual's
career. Attending and graduating from college is perhaps the single most
important determinant of the kind of work an individual does; and the
nature of one's work has implications for an array of outcomes that shape
one's life. These include economic resources, continuing intellectual and
personal development, values and attitudes, and perceptions of what constitutes the "good life." Thus, the influence of college on career probably
dovetails into a broad matrix of indirect but enduring impacts on the quality of life.

Notes

1. A body of evidence exists to suggest that maturity of career thinking
   and planning can be modestly improved through various career devel-
   opment courses (for example, Anderson & Binnie, 1971; Babcock &
   Kaufman, 1976; Barker, 1981; Bartsch & Hackett, 1979; Carver &
   Smart, 1985; Cooper, 1986; DiNuzzo & Tolbert, 1981; Evans & Rector,
   1978; Johnson, Smither, & Holland, 1981; Jones, 1985; Korschgen,
   Whitehurst, & O'Gorman, 1978; Lent, Larkin, & Hasegawa, 1986;
   O'Neill, Remer, & Gohs, 1984; Rayman et al., 1983; Remer, O'Neill, &
   Gohs, 1984; Slaney, 1983; Smith & Evans, 1973). These courses, however, often combine a wide variety of experiences (individual and/or
   group counseling, use of standardized career information or career-
   search inventories, writing exercises, values and goals clarification, development of career decision-making and planning skills, use of occupational or career handbooks, development of personal career profiles
   or options, individual research on specific occupations, and so forth).
   Consequently, it is difficult to categorize them efficiently to ascertain
   which elements may have the greatest impact or to determine whether
   specific experiences may have a differential influence for different kinds
   of students (Holland, Magoon, & Spokane, 1981; Johnson, Smither, &
   Holland, 1981).
2. It is also possible, of course, that one important socialization effect of
   college is to increase occupational aspirations. Jencks and his associates'
   (Jencks et al., 1979) analysis of two samples suggests that those who

attend college tend to end up in occupations of slightly higher occupational status than the occupations they aspired to in high school. Conversely, those who do not attend college tend to be working in occupations of lower status than those to which they aspired in high school. Jencks and his colleagues argue that these findings suggest that higher education may increase students' aversion to low-status occupations and, thereby, their willingness to do whatever an employer requires to obtain and keep a job in a high-status occupation. An alternative hypothesis, of course, is that amount of postsecondary education is a function of rising occupational aspirations and not the reverse.

3. Harvey and Kalwa (1983), for example, found that even when controls were made for socioeconomic origins and educational attainment, occupational status had a statistically significant and strong negative association with unemployment over a four-year period.

4. Heath (1976a, 1977b) has suggested that the critical skills for vocational success are not simply intellectual ability but rather a core group of interrelated traits that describe a psychologically mature person. These include "symbolization" (reflective intelligence), "allocentrism" (empathy and altruism), "integration" (ability to combine a variety of views), "stability," and "autonomy." Heath's longitudinal analysis of college graduates indicates that these factors rather than academic ability differentiate successful from unsuccessful vocational adaptation. This implies that college may enhance occupational success by facilitating development and growth on a wide front rather than a narrow one.

5. Some additional indirect evidence for the positive link between education and job satisfaction is suggested by the research on worker retirement patterns. While early evidence reported by Barfield and Morgan (1969) found no systematic relationship between education and retirement plans, Best (1976) found that the preference for early retirement among those currently working was negatively associated with level of education. More recently, Hardy (1984) studied actual retirement behavior by using data from a national longitudinal survey of older white males. Controlling for level of health, occupational prestige (Duncan SEI), years worked at the current job, company retirement policy (mandatory or not mandatory), income, and age, Hardy found that acquiring a college degree significantly reduced the likelihood of retirement among professional, technical, and kindred workers. Although this finding may well reflect differences in career orientations and ambition between college graduates and those with less formal education, it may also be partially attributable to the former finding their jobs more challenging, stimulating, and personally satisfying.

6. This may be augmented by the fact that college-educated employees tend to base job evaluations more on intrinsic returns (such as sense of accomplishment) than on extrinsic returns (such as wages), while the

reverse is typically true for employees with less formal education (Lindsay & Knox, 1984; Quinn & Baldi de Mandilovitch, 1980). Indeed, increases in the extent to which the intrinsic rewards of a job are valued may be one of the consistent changes in occupational attitudes to occur in college (Clark, Heist, McConnell, Trow, & Yonge, 1972; Feldman & Newcomb, 1969; Singer, 1974). See Chapter Seven.

7. Consistent with this conclusion is evidence reported by Alwin (1974, 1976) pertaining to the factors that accounted for early occupational status (Duncan SEI) among male Wisconsin high school graduates who attended college. Qualitative differences among colleges attended accounted for only about 7 percent of the explained variance in occupational status. In contrast, over 90 percent of the explained variance in occupational status was attributable to differential student selection and recruitment factors (for example, academic ability, socioeconomic background, and educational, and occupational aspirations).

8. Gurin and Epps's (1975) analysis of ten black colleges and universities found that the percentage of women in an institution was unrelated to the prestige, ability demands, and nontraditionality (percentage of whites) of one's career choice at the end of the freshman year when the level of precollege career choice was controlled. The sample of institutions, however, was small and homogeneous, with no institution having more than 68 percent or less than 32 percent women. Thus, it is difficult to conclude that the Gurin and Epps sample was not in fact one of coeducational institutions.

9. Similar to progressive conformity is the "birds of a feather" hypothesis (Davis, 1965). This hypothesis suggests that students who are unlike the majority of the other students with the same initial career choice tend to change their career plans to another field where they will be more like the other students. Werts (1967a) has provided evidence to support this hypothesis in terms of the academic ability and social class background of students with different career choices. It is also likely, however, that students tend to modify career field choice in relation to actual academic performance, not simply increased congruence with others having the same choice (Werts & Watley, 1968b). See also Gallini (1982) for similar findings with respect to major field choice.

10. It is likely, of course, that this relationship can be modified by other factors. There is at least modest evidence, for example, that students who plan careers in their major field tend to have learning styles more closely matched to the inquiry demands of the field than do students in the same major not planning careers in the major field (Kolb & Goldman, 1973).

11. For a representative list of studies, see Adams (1982); Bisconti (1978); Crooks and Campbell (1974); Howard (1986); Jacobsen, Price, de Mik,

and Taylor (1965); Lewis (1970); Mackey, Blackmon, and Andrews (1977); McClelland (1973); Muchinsky and Hoyt (1973); Munday and Davis (1974); Nash, Rosson, and Schoemer (1973); Pallett and Hoyt (1968); Taylor and Ellison (1967); Taylor, Smith, and Ghiselin (1963); and Williams and Harrell (1964).

12. Consistent with the importance of college for minorities is evidence from a 1982 study by the U.S. Commission on Civil Rights that examined the relationship between unemployment levels and education ("Education Has Little Impact on Minority Unemployment," 1982). The unemployment levels of whites as a group declined steadily as higher levels of education were attained. Among blacks and Hispanics, however, the relationship was not evident until the bachelor's degree level was reached. Thus, in terms of reducing unemployment, postsecondary education was more important for minorities than for whites.

13. Evidence concerning gender differences in the influence of postgraduate education on occupational status is mixed. Harvey and Kalwa (1983) and Spaeth (1977) have suggested that men experience a higher return than women, whereas evidence presented by Wilson and Smith-Lovin (1983) suggests that the returns for graduate education are about the same for men and women.

14. Despite some findings to the contrary (for example, Alexander & Eckland, 1975a), we found no compelling, replicable evidence to suggest that the effect of college on occupational status differs for different levels of intelligence or socioeconomic status (for example, Jencks et al., 1979).

15. There is some evidence to suggest that college grades are more important in enhancing women's entry into male-dominated careers in the sciences than in the nonsciences (Ethington, Smart, & Pascarella, 1988), but this finding awaits replication.

16. There is also evidence to suggest that having a mother in the work force, particularly in a sex-atypical occupation, acts as a salient role model influence on a daughter's orientation toward sex-atypical careers (for example, Burlew, 1982; Crawford, 1978; Lemkau, 1983; Lyson, 1984; Rosenfeld, 1978; Tangri, 1972; Pascarella & Staver, 1985). The likelihood of a mother's work force participation in a sex-atypical career probably increases with education. Thus, a college-educated mother may exert an additional positive indirect influence on her daughter's orientation toward a sex-atypical career choice by acting as an occupational role model.

17. A rough indication of this difference can be obtained by comparing relative increases in occupational status from the data analyzed by Knox, Lindsay, and Kolb (1988). The net increase in Duncan SEI score from a high school diploma to a bachelor's degree was four times as large

as the difference among four-year institutions based on Carnegie type. Using data from Olneck and Crouse (1979) with respect to job status increases attributable to a bachelor's degree, the corresponding ratio may be as high as 5 to 1. Part of this difference between the general effect of college and the effect of where one attends college may be due to differences in sample variability. It is difficult, however, to ignore the more substantive interpretation of this evidence, namely, that earning a bachelor's degree counts far more in terms of job status than where one earns it.

11

Economic Benefits of College

In this chapter we synthesize the evidence on the economic returns to a college education. Such returns are substantial,[1] and this fact probably underlies the motivation of many students who choose to attend college rather than enter the work force immediately after high school graduation (for example, "Nation Top-Heavy with Wealth," 1986; Elam, 1983; Hossler, undated). The chapter addresses the net effects of college, between-college effects, within-college effects, conditional effects of college, and the intergenerational transmission of the economic advantages of investment in postsecondary education.

Net Effects of College

Earnings

One of the safest generalizations one can make about the structure of nearly all highly developed (as well as less developed) societies is that formal education has a strong positive association with earnings, even when such factors as age, gender, and occupational category are held constant (for example, Blaug, 1970, 1972; Psacharopoulos, 1972a, 1972b, 1973, 1985). This generalization clearly holds in American society, although as suggested by status attainment research, much of the impact of formal education on earnings is transmitted indirectly through education's enhancement of occupational status (for example, Bowles, 1972; Campbell & Laughlin, 1987; Duncan, 1968; Jencks, Crouse, & Mueser, 1983; Sewell & Hauser, 1972, 1975). Whether direct or indirect, the association between education and earnings is not merely a function of the different levels of academic ability and social origin that commonly distinguish people with different levels of formal education. It persists even after such influences are taken into account (for example, Becker, 1975; Duncan, 1968; Griliches & Mason, 1973; Jencks et al., 1979; Sewell & Hauser, 1975; Renshaw, 1972; Suter & Miller, 1973). Consistent with the findings on occupational status, however, the influence of different levels of formal education on earnings is not uni-

500

formly linear. Rather, undergraduate education appears to be generally more important than secondary education and perhaps even graduate education. Furthermore, one appears to receive an additional earnings "bonus" for completing the bachelor's degree over and above the incremental advantage associated with years of college completed.

The most extensive evidence with respect to the influence of different levels of formal education on earnings is provided by Jencks et al. (1979) in an analysis of eight independent samples of men in the work force. Controlling for work experience, measures of intelligence, and socioeconomic background, these investigators estimate that a high school diploma provided a 15 to 25 percent earnings advantage over an eighth grade education. With the same factors held constant, a college graduate enjoyed an estimated earnings advantage of between 18.3 and 46.5 percent over those whose formal education ended with high school. Thus, the lower and upper estimates of the net earnings advantage of a college graduate tend to be consistently higher than the lower and upper estimates of the earnings advantage of a high school graduate over someone with an eighth grade education. Similar results are also reported by Goodman using data from the 1970 U.S. Census, one of the samples analyzed by Jencks et al. With controls for age, region of the country, and occupational status of the job held (though not for intelligence or social origins), a bachelor's degree was about twice as important as a high school diploma in increasing earnings.

Present evidence also suggests that the earnings advantage of a bachelor's degree over a high school diploma may be somewhat greater than the corresponding advantage of graduate degrees in general over the bachelor's degree. This evidence comes from two studies. First, Goodman (1979), controlling for age, job status, and region of the country, found that a bachelor's degree was substantially more important than a graduate degree in increasing earnings. (Relative importance was difficult to estimate because a graduate degree had a slight depressing effect on earnings when other factors were considered.) The second study, by Knox, Lindsay, and Kolb (1988), followed up the NLS-72 sample in 1986, some fourteen years after high school graduation. Controlling for such factors as race, gender, family socioeconomic status, and academic ability, Knox, Lindsay, and Kolb found that the net incremental earnings advantage of a graduate degree over a bachelor's degree was only about two-thirds of the corresponding earnings advantage of a bachelor's degree over a high school diploma.

There are, of course, some problems in grouping all graduate degrees together as these studies do. Certainly the marked earnings potential associated with some advanced degrees (for example, law, medicine) is masked. Nevertheless, though less pronounced, the evidence on earnings is consistent with that on occupational status in suggesting that attainment of the bachelor's degree may be the single most important educational step in the occupational and economic attainment process.

Consistent with this conclusion is the evidence suggesting that one receives an earnings "bonus" for completing the bachelor's degree, a bonus above and beyond the increment received for each year of college completed. Goodman's (1979) analysis of census data indicates that a bachelor's degree provided an earnings advantage that was nearly seven times as large as that for the first three years of college. A somewhat more rigorous analysis by Knox, Lindsay, and Kolb (1988) suggests that the advantage may be smaller but nonetheless pronounced. Net of race, gender, social status, and academic ability, they found that the earnings returns to a bachelor's degree were about 2.3 times as large as the returns to completing two or more years of college. Similarly, Hauser and Daymont (1977), in their follow-up of Wisconsin men eight to fourteen years after high school graduation, have suggested that each year of college provided a greater earnings advantage when one attained the bachelor's degree. Controlling for parental income, mental ability, and work experience, they found that the economic returns to college were approximately 6 percent per year when one did not obtain the bachelor's degree and rose to approximately 10 percent per year when one did obtain the degree (see also Martin & Morgan, 1963).

The fact that completing the bachelor's degree enhances the economic returns of college is not particularly surprising. Entry into many relatively high paying technical and managerial positions often requires the bachelor's degree. Furthermore, completing one's undergraduate degree is nearly a universal prerequisite for acceptance at professional schools typically linked to high earnings (such as business, law, and medical schools).

Private Rate of Return

The evidence establishing that college has a significant and substantial effect on earnings net of intelligence, social origins, and other factors does not necessarily provide a complete picture of the economic returns to a college education. It addresses only the economic *benefits* of postsecondary education without considering the attendant *costs*. Unlike secondary school, college often requires a financial investment on the part of the student in the form of tuition, books, and other educational fees. Moreover, for many students, the time they invest in college is a time during which they forego income that they would have earned had they entered the labor force immediately after high school (such foregone earnings are sometimes referred to as the opportunity costs of attending college). These considerations have spawned a parallel line of inquiry that we shall refer to as private rate of return research.

A simple way to estimate the private rate of return to a college education is to divide the difference between average posttax earnings of college graduates and high school graduates by the sum of the private, unsubsidized costs of education plus foregone earnings (Witmer, 1970; Walberg,

1987). Taking an example from Psacharopoulos (1973), suppose that the average annual posttax earnings of a male college graduate in 1959 were $9,255 and the corresponding earnings of a high school graduate were $6,132. Therefore, a college graduate could expect to earn on the average during his working life $3,123 more per year ($9,255 – $6,135) than he would be earning with only a high school diploma. Let's also suppose that the total private costs of a college education in 1959 plus foregone earnings were $14,768. If college were considered an investment, such an arrangement would be the equivalent of purchasing a promise to receive an average of $3,123 annually during one's working life at a present cost of $14,768. If we divide $3,123 by $14,768, we see that the average annual yield of investing in college is about 21 percent. This 21 percent is considered the private rate of return to a college education.[2,3]

A large body of research has addressed the question of the private rate of return to college graduation (for example, Becker, 1960; Bowen, 1977; Carnoy & Marenbach, 1975; Cohen & Geske, 1985; Freeman, 1975, 1977; Hines, Tweeten, & Redfern, 1970; Leslie & Brinkman, 1986, 1988; McMahon & Wagner, 1982; Mincer, 1974; Raymond & Sesnowitz, 1975; Witmer, 1980).[4] In attempting to synthesize the evidence from this research, we have the advantage of access to two existing reviews of the literature (Cohen & Geske, 1985; Leslie & Brinkman, 1986). The Cohen and Geske (1985) review synthesized evidence from nine studies that covered the time period from 1940 to 1976. Using the data supplied for each study, Cohen and Geske found that the private rate of return to a bachelor's degree ranged from about 10 to 21 percent and averaged about 13.8 percent. The Leslie and Brinkman (1986) synthesis reviewed twenty-two studies covering the time period from 1940 to 1982. The private rate of return to a bachelor's degree ranged from 7 to 18 percent and averaged 11.8 percent.

Although such rates of return compare quite favorably with "conventional benchmark rates for alternative investments" (Leslie & Brinkman, 1986, p. 214; see also McMahon & Wagner, 1982), they may overestimate the returns attributable to a bachelor's degree unless differences in background and ability are taken into account. Intellectual ability appears to be among the more important confounding influences (for example, Hansen, Weisbrod, & Scanlon, 1970). When Leslie and Brinkman synthesized thirteen studies that controlled for this variable, they estimated that about 79 percent of the private return to a bachelor's degree was independent of ability. Applying this correction, which Leslie and Brinkman (1988) caution was conservative, we obtain an estimated ability-adjusted private rate of return of 10.9 percent for the Cohen and Geske (1985) synthesis and 9.3 percent for the Leslie and Brinkman (1986) synthesis.

These are admittedly rough estimates of the economic rates of return to a bachelor's degree.[5] However, they still compare favorably to benchmark rates for alternative investments. This is particularly true if individual costs are adjusted for public and private subsidies to education (Leslie, 1984), foregone earnings are adjusted for the fact that many students work and earn wages while they attend college (Crary & Leslie, 1978; Freiden & Leimer, 1981; Parsons, 1974), and job fringe benefits are included as part of earnings (Kiker & Rhine, 1987).[6]

The syntheses by Cohen and Geske (1985) and Leslie and Brinkman (1986) also suggest that the private economic rates of return to graduate education over and above a bachelor's degree tend to be somewhat smaller than the corresponding returns to a bachelor's degree over and above a high school diploma (see also Bailey & Schotta, 1972; Hanoch, 1967; Tomaske, 1974; McMahon & Wagner, 1982). This suggestion is consistent with the status attainment research reviewed in Chapter Ten, which suggests that the net increase in earnings associated with a bachelor's degree is larger than the general increase due to graduate degrees (Goodman, 1979; Knox, Lindsay, & Kolb, 1988).[7]

Causal Mechanisms

It is one thing to determine that a bachelor's degree provides a sound economic return on one's investment. It is a somewhat different matter to determine why. Simply put, there are two major explanations for this, and they are reminiscent of our discussion of career in Chapter Ten. The first is a human capital or socialization hypothesis that suggests that college graduates earn more than high school graduates because college provides the former with the cognitive skills and/or personal traits that make them more productive employees. The second explanation is a certification or screening one. This explanation argues that college does not so much influence the cognitive and personal traits related to productivity as simply certify (by means of the bachelor's degree) those who are most likely to have such traits to begin with. Employers can then use a college education as an inexpensive screening device to select individuals who they believe possess favorable intellectual and personal traits for the highest-paying positions or career paths. Thus, part of the earnings differential noted between college graduates and those with less education might arise because the lack of education credentials is a barrier to entry into high-paying occupations.

An offshoot of the second explanation is the possibility that employers may not select or reward individuals solely on the rational basis of potential productivity. Rather, factors such as simple snobbery, image, and social class may also enter into the decision. This would mean that college graduates might end up being overly rewarded by employers for reasons unrelated to individual productivity (Jencks et al., 1979).

Consistent with our discussion in Chapter Ten, there is evidence to support both general explanations. A number of studies present evidence in support of the certification or screening explanation. Jencks et al. (1979), for example, reasoned that if the college experience actually enhances productivity potential more than high school (as posited by a human capital or socialization explanation), then the effect on earnings of an average year of college will be larger than the effect of an average year of high school. However, when these researchers controlled educational attainment, they found that the percentage effect of an extra year of college was consistently *smaller* than the percentage effect of an extra year of high school.

The evidence presented by Jencks et al. (1979) supports the certification or screening explanation essentially by failing to support the human capital or socialization explanation. More direct evidence in support of certification or screening is presented by Goodman (1979) and Knox, Lindsay, and Kolb (1988). Their work suggests that obtaining the bachelor's degree provides a substantial earnings bonus beyond the expected incremental increase for each additional year of college completed. It is highly doubtful that the final year of college actually enhances individual productivity at a higher rate than the preceding three years. Thus, the bachelor's degree may function as a certification or screening device through which employers assign those who have it to higher-paying jobs or career paths than those who do not, even though the two groups may be equally competent. Indeed, individuals who are not college graduates are disproportionately underrepresented in high-status, high-paying occupations, even when they are similar to college graduates in intellectual ability and other traits (Arrow, 1972; Taubman & Wales, 1974, 1975a). Furthermore, within the same corporation a bachelor's degree appears to provide an earnings advantage even when such factors as experience, tenure in the firm, grade level of job, and job performance ratings are held constant (Woo, 1986). Rosenbaum (1984) and Wise (1979) also document the earnings advantage of bachelor's degree recipients in a single firm but without the controls for job performance employed by Woo (1986).

Despite this evidence, it seems counterintuitive that college merely screens talent or perpetuates social class distinctions in the work force without providing some skills that make individuals more productive. In fields such as engineering, accounting, and architecture, for example, a bachelor's degree may be required not simply because it signals intellectual competence or desirable personal traits but also because it indicates the completion of a course of study that actually provides skills essential to effective job performance.

Empirical support for the human capital or socialization explanation comes mainly from observations of the magnitude of the education-earnings link over time. If college does not simply function as a screen for assigning individuals to the highest-paying jobs but rather enhances skills related to actual job productivity, then the correlation between education and earnings should not decline with work experience. (The key assumption here is that earnings reflect job productivity.) Analyses of a number of national samples have generally found that level of education does not become less important to earnings over time (Chiswick, 1973; Haller & Spenner, 1977; Haspel, 1978; Layard & Psacharopoulos, 1974; Ornstein, 1971) and may actually increase in importance with greater work experience (Lillard, 1977; Lillard & Willis, 1978; Mincer, 1974; Rosen & Taubman, 1982). Consistent with this is evidence suggesting that level of education has a positive effect on earnings, even for individuals in the same job status level (for example, Goodman, 1979; Griliches & Mason, 1972; Sewell & Hauser, 1972, 1975; Wilson & Smith-Lovin, 1983).

Such findings rest largely on the related assumptions that earnings reflect job productivity and that those with more education earn more because they are more productive. It is possible, however, that education may be related to earnings over the occupational life span for reasons unrelated to productivity (for example, differential treatment by employers based on level of education). Moreover, as we saw in Chapter Ten, there is little evidence to indicate that when they hold the same jobs, college graduates are more productive or efficient employees than those with less education. It is difficult to square this latter body of evidence with a human capital or socialization explanation for the link between education and income.

In the final analysis there is less debate about the substantial positive effect of college on earnings than about why college has this effect. A modicum of evidence exists to support both a screening or certification explanation and a human capital or socialization explanation. It is possible, of course, that both processes contribute to the causal link between higher education and earnings. In our judgment, however, neither hypothesis alone provides a completely satisfactory or unequivocal explanation.

Between-College Effects

As we have stressed throughout this book, studies that fail to control for salient differences among students who enter different types of postsecondary institutions will speciously overestimate between-college effects. The same caution clearly holds for estimation of the differential effect of institutional characteristics on earnings or income. Consequently in this section we will concentrate on those studies that provided controls for student background traits or other differences among students attending different kinds of institutions.

Two-Year Versus Four-Year Institutions

In Chapter Ten we saw that much of the negative influence on job status of beginning one's postsecondary experience at a two-year college as compared to a four-year college is attributable to the fact that two-year college entrants are significantly less likely to complete a bachelor's degree than their four-year college counterparts. For those students who successfully negotiate the not inconsequential hurdles of transfer to a four-year institution and completion of a bachelor's degree, any residual negative impact of starting at a community college is small and perhaps trivial.

Since earnings, like job status, are strongly linked to educational attainment, it seems likely that a similar trend would hold for the impact of two-year versus four-year colleges on economic returns. In fact, the evidence, based on analysis of two independent national samples, is mixed, with no clear advantage in methodological rigor to any study. Monk-Turner (1988) analyzed data from the Longitudinal Survey of Labor Market Experience on men and women followed up ten years after high school graduation (in 1976 and 1977). Net of such factors as intelligence, educational aspirations, socioeconomic background, sex, race, and educational attainment, students starting at four-year institutions had a statistically significant 6 percent wage advantage over those starting at two-year institutions. This finding, however, is not supported by two analyses of the NLS-72 data. Breneman and Nelson (1981) and Anderson (1984), controlling for many of the same factors as Monk-Turner, found no significant income penalties associated with two-year compared with four-year college attendance when the sample was followed up either four years (Breneman and Nelson) or seven years (Anderson) after high school graduation. Indeed, in the Anderson analyses community college entrants actually had slightly (though not significantly) higher net earnings than four-year college entrants.

Perhaps the soundest conclusion to be drawn from this rather sparse evidence is that when individuals of equal background traits and educational attainment are compared, any direct earnings penalties for initially attending a two-year college are quite small, at least in the early stages of one's career. Breneman and Nelson (1981) have argued that such penalties may tend to become more pronounced over the occupational life span. This may partially explain the earnings differences of two-year and four-year college entrants found by Monk-Turner (1988) in a ten-year follow-up compared with the general earnings parity between the two groups found by Breneman and Nelson (1981) and Anderson (1984) in follow-ups of four and seven years. Even if Breneman and Nelson's argument were not true, however, it is possible that there are discernible indirect economic penalties associated with initially attending a community college. These indirect penalties arise largely because initial attendance at a two-year college has substantial deleterious consequences for bachelor's degree completion, which in turn is a major determinant of entry into high-status, high-paying jobs. Such indirect effects, however, are not typically considered in the existing research.[8]

Institutional Quality

A large body of research has addressed the issue of whether or not institutional "quality" has a net impact on earnings. The findings are not totally unequivocal, but we believe the weight of evidence suggests that at least one aspect of institutional "quality," the academic selectivity of the undergraduate student body, has a statistically significant, though generally very small, net impact on earnings. The most methodologically rigorous investigations estimate the impact of institutional quality while controlling for important background factors (for example, socioeconomic origin, intelligence) and other other college and postcollege variables that might confound the link between college quality and earnings (for example, educational attainment, occupational status).

An exemplary study by Trusheim and Crouse (1981) analyzed a sample of men from the longitudinal Panel Study of Income Dynamics who were twenty-five to sixty years old in 1972. Controlling for family socioeconomic status, intelligence, a measure of achievement motivation, educational attainment, occupational status (Duncan SEI), and weeks worked per year, Trusheim and Crouse found that the academic selectivity of the college attended (average composite SAT or ACT score of freshmen) had a small but statistically significant positive direct effect on current income. A more subjective measure of college social prestige did not. Although they typically did not control for the range of confounding variables held constant by Trusheim and Crouse, analyses of fourteen independent samples have produced quite similar results (Akin & Garfinkel, 1974; Bisconti, 1978; Daniere & Mechling, 1970; Ehrenberg & Sherman, 1987; Foster & Rodgers, 1980; Jencks et al, 1979; Karabel & McClelland, 1987; McClelland, 1977; Morgan & Sirageldin, 1968; Mueller, 1988; Perrucci, 1980; Phelan & Phelan, 1983; Reed & Miller, 1970; Smart, 1988a; Solmon, 1975a, 1981; Solmon, Bisconti, & Ochsner, 1977; Wachtel, 1975a, 1976; Wales, 1973; Weisbrod & Karpoff, 1968; Wise, 1979). This body of evidence indicates that other aspects of college quality in addition to selectivity (for example, faculty salary, financial expenditures per student, reputational ranking) may also have statistically significant positive net effects on income. However, it is the academic selectivity of the college attended that demonstrates the most consistent positive impact, perhaps because this relatively objective measure is the most frequently employed index of institutional quality in the studies reviewed.

There is also a trend in this evidence suggesting that the positive effects of college selectivity or academic reputation on earnings are not linear. Analyzing data on a national sample of World War II veterans followed up in 1969 (the NBER-Thorndike data), Wales (1973) found that a college's academic reputation, based on the Gourman (1967) ratings, had a statistically significant positive impact on 1969 earnings only when it was in the top fifth of the reputational distribution. The findings of Solmon (1975a), who used the same data, are similar with respect to the statistically significant positive impact of colleges in the top quartile of the Gourman ratings but also indicate a statistically significant negative impact for colleges in the bottom quartile. Results consistent with those of Solmon are reported by Wise (1979) in an analysis of men in a single company. Net of other factors, rate of salary increase was only positively influenced when one attended a college at the very top of the selectivity distribution. Conversely, salary increase was only negatively affected when one attended a college near the bottom of the selectivity distribution.

To be sure, not all of the studies we reviewed found that college selectivity or other dimensions of quality had a positive net impact on earnings. Analyses of seven independent samples indicated a statistically nonsignificant, negative, or mixed impact of college selectivity, prestige, or resource expenditures on earnings (Angle, Steiber, & Wissman, 1980; Astin, 1977a; Griffin & Alexander, 1978; Heckman, Lazenby, & Moore, 1968; Hunt, 1963; Knox, Lindsay, & Kolb, 1988; Rogers, 1969; Sharp & Weidman, 1987). We found little in the way of methodological rigor to distinguish these studies from those that report a statistically significant positive effect of college quality indexes on earnings. Nevertheless, we believe that the weight of evidence from all studies taken together indicates a small but positive net impact of college quality (and, in particular, selectivity) on earnings. When we combine all those analyses that provide adequate statistical information, our best (and admittedly somewhat rough) estimate is that college quality explains on the average somewhere between one and one and a half percent of the differences in individual earnings above and beyond that attributable to other causes.[9]

This estimate is based essentially on the net *direct* effects of college quality on earnings. If one were to add to this the indirect effect of college quality through intervening variables such as educational attainment, the magnitude of the impact might increase. Recall from Chapter Nine on educational attainment that measures of institutional quality such as selectivity or reputation significantly enhance persistence, bachelor's degree completion, and attendance in graduate or professional school. Since educational attainment is such an important determinant of entry into high-paying jobs, it is likely that at least part of the positive impact of college quality on earnings is manifest through this indirect route (that is, college quality enhancing educational attainment, which in turn enhances earnings). Such indirect effects have not typically been estimated in the existing body of research on college quality and earnings. Recently, however, Smart's (1988a) analysis of college graduates followed up nine years after initial enrollment in college suggests that when indirect effects are considered, the overall positive impact of college quality (a composite measure of selectivity, resources, and cost) on earnings is increased between 15 and 30 percent. Much of this indirect effect is transmitted through receiving a graduate or professional degree.[10]

Causal Mechanisms. It is interesting to consider the possible causal mechanisms that underlie the small positive net influence of college quality on earnings. A human capital or socialization explanation would account for the effect by arguing that colleges with the most educational resources (academically capable and motivated students, large libraries, well-equipped laboratories, and the like) are able to foster more of the cognitive and non-cognitive skills essential to productivity than educationally less-advantaged colleges. This has an extended payoff in greater job productivity and therefore greater earnings. Conversely, a certification or screening explanation argues that elite institutions function more to enroll and certify high-level talent than to foster it. A degree from an elite institution therefore acts as an inexpensive selection or screening device. Employers can use this device to dip into a pool of talented and ambitious individuals for the highest-paying jobs or career ladders. Being a graduate of certain elite institutions may also lead to preferential treatment by employers for reasons unrelated to demonstrated job productivity.

The strongest evidence mustered in support of the human capital or socialization explanation comes from studies that demonstrate that the effect of college selectivity on earnings increases over time. (The assumption here is that employers will only increase the financial rewards to graduates of elite colleges if they consistently demonstrate greater job productivity.) Solmon (1975a), using a national sample of World War II veterans, found that net of factors such as intelligence, educational attainment, occupation, and labor force experience, the impact on earnings of aspects of college quality such as selectivity, Gourman rankings, and faculty salary becomes more pronounced later in the individual's career (see also Symonette, 1981). Similar results have also been reported by Rosenbaum (1984) and Wise (1979) in longitudinal studies of careers within two large corporations. In the Wise analysis college selectivity actually had no significant link with starting salary. It did, however, have a significant positive effect on *rate* of salary increase, even when controls were made for the job responsibilities of the position to which a person was initially assigned.

Other studies are somewhat less supportive of the notion that graduates of elite colleges are paid more because they are more productive employees. In a single-corporation study of accountants, Ferris (1982) found that a reputational measure of college quality was a statistically significant predictor of starting salary, but that this link became nonsignificant with experience and advancement in the firm. Similarly, in analyses of men from the Panel Study of Income Dynamics, Trusheim and Crouse (1981) found that neither college selectivity nor college social prestige had a statistically significant effect on income growth over a three-year period.

The findings of Ferris (1982) and Trusheim and Crouse (1981) are more consistent with the expectation that the earnings advantage enjoyed by graduates of selective or prestigious colleges is due to factors other than simple job productivity (for example, preferential treatment in the initial job assignment or assignment to career ladders with greater earnings potential). Furthermore, their results are also quite consistent with the evidence on college quality and job effectiveness. Evidence summarized in Chapter Ten on career indicates that college selectivity or prestige has little or no impact on an individual's actual job productivity or performance. When that evidence is combined with the results of Ferris (1982) and Trusheim and Crouse (1981), we find a rather compelling reason to believe that graduates of elite colleges may earn more for reasons not always linked to their job performance. Even if one were to dismiss this evidence totally, however, and assume that graduates of elite colleges earn more over the long term simply because they are more productive employees, it would still be risky to conclude that this is an institutional effect. A degree from an elite college or university might function more to screen and certify the talent and ambition necessary for effective long-term job performance than to foster this talent or ambition in any distinctive way. Thus, although the finding in some studies that the link between college quality and earnings strengthens over time is frequently cited in support of a human capital or socialization explanation, the finding is not necessarily incompatible with a screening or certification explanation.

Institutional Type

A small body of research has sought to determine whether institutional type has a net effect on earnings. All of the studies in this area have defined institutional type in terms of the eight Carnegie categories or some variation on that typology. The weight of evidence from this research points to a statistically significant net earnings differential among individuals attending the different types of institutions, but the pattern is only partially consistent across investigations.

The two major studies on this topic have been conducted by Solmon and Wachtel (1975), with a national sample of World War II veterans followed up in 1969 (the NBER-Thorndike data), and Knox, Lindsay, and Kolb (1988), with the 1986 follow-up of the NLS-72. Solmon and Wachtel controlled for educational attainment, experience in the labor force, intelligence, and type of career. With these variables held constant, attendance at colleges in the different Carnegie types explained an additional 1 percent of the variance in 1969 earnings. The highest net earnings were received by men who had attended major research universities and large doctorate-granting institutions, while the lowest earnings were received by those who had attended small doctorate-granting institutions, comprehensive colleges with a limited selection of programs, and nonselective liberal arts colleges. Knox, Lindsay, and Kolb, in an analysis that combined men and women, controlled for gender, race, family socioeconomic status, and academic abilities. With these factors held constant, the highest net earnings were received by those who had attended major research universities and small doctorate-granting institutions, while the lowest net earnings accrued to those who had attended nonselective liberal arts colleges and large doctorate-granting universities.

Readily apparent from these two analyses of major national data bases are clear points of agreement and contradiction. In both studies individuals from major research universities tended to earn relatively high incomes, while those from nonselective liberal arts colleges tended to earn relatively low incomes. Yet the net earnings received by those who had attended large doctorate-granting institutions ranked quite high in the Solmon and Wachtel (1975) study but quite low in the Knox, Lindsay, and Kolb (1988) investigation. Conversely, individuals who had attended small doctorate-granting institutions had relatively high earnings in the Knox, Lindsay, and Kolb study but relatively low earnings in the Solmon and Wachtel analysis.

Perhaps the major conclusion yielded by this research is that a significant net earnings advantage accrues to individuals who attended major research universities (Carnegie type Research I) and that a correspondingly small disadvantage accrues to those who attended nonselective liberal arts colleges. Although other investigations cluster the Carnegie types in different ways, they tend to support this conclusion, particularly with respect to the small earnings advantage of those who attended major research universities (for example, McMahon & Wagner, 1982; Sharp & Weidman, 1987). Of course, any earnings advantage accruing to graduates of major research universities or disadvantage accruing to graduates of nonselective liberal arts colleges may partially reflect differences in the salient measures of institutional quality linked to earnings (selectivity, academic reputation, financial resources, and so on). Solmon and Wachtel's (1975) analysis, for example, found substantial differences among the eight Carnegie institutional categories on such factors as student body selectivity, academic reputational rankings, and faculty compensation. Major research universities generally ranked highest of all institutional types on these indexes, whereas nonselective liberal arts colleges typically ranked at or near the bottom. We suspect that any net earnings differences among the Carnegie institutional types would be dramatically reduced if measures of institutional quality were taken into account.

Institutional Size

In Chapter Ten we reported evidence supporting the hypothesis that large institutions, because of their wider range of programatic links with occupational groups in the society, enhance the occupational status attainment of their students. A small body of research has addressed the issue of whether institutional size is also linked with earnings. The studies we reviewed that controlled for salient confounding influences were fairly consistent in suggesting that institutional size has a small positive and significant net effect on earnings early in one's career. Gruca (1988) analyzed data from a national sample of individuals who began college in 1971 and were followed up in 1980. With controls for student background characteristics, the selectivity of the institution attended, college major and grades, and educational attainment and occupational status, the enrollment of the institution attended had a statistically significant positive direct effect on 1980 earnings for both white men and women. The corresponding effects for black men and women were similar in magnitude but statistically nonsignificant, probably because of smaller sample sizes. Similar results with a somewhat different sample from the same data base are reported by Smart (1988a).

Knox, Lindsay, and Kolb (1988), using the 1986 follow-up of the NLS-72 sample, regressed 1986 annual earnings on a model that controlled for (among other factors) gender, race, socioeconomic status, academic ability, educational attainment, and the institution's selectivity, control (private versus public), and vocational emphasis. With these influences held constant, student enrollment had a small but positive and statistically significant direct effect on earnings.[11]

It is important to point out that as with college quality, the net impact of institutional size is small, probably accounting for little more than 1 percent of the variance in earnings in either study. At the same time, however, both Gruca (1988) and Knox, Lindsay, and Kolb (1988) controlled for institutional selectivity in their analyses. Thus, it is unlikely that the modest effect of institutional size was a proxy for the effects of college quality on earnings.

Institutional Control (Public Versus Private)

A small body of research has estimated the effect of institutional control on earnings while specifically controlling for salient confounding influences. The results of this research are mixed, and there is little in the way of differences in methodological rigor between studies to assist us in giving more weight to some findings than to others. Solmon (1981) analyzed data from two national samples of college students, one of which entered college in 1961 and was followed up in 1974 and the other of which entered in 1970 and was followed up in 1977. Controlling for such factors as college major and grades, marital status, length of employment, college selectivity, and educational attainment, Solmon found that attending a private institution had a small but statistically significant negative effect on earnings for both men and women.

Just the opposite, however, is reported by Knox, Lindsay, and Kolb (1988) in their analysis of the 1986 follow-up of the NLS-72 data. Net of race, gender, academic ability, socioeconomic status, educational attainment, and the selectivity, size, and vocational emphasis of the college attended, private control had a small but statistically significant positive effect on 1986 earnings.

The waters are muddied even further by the findings of Sharp and Weidman (1987) in their analysis of the 1979 follow-up of humanities graduates in the NLS-72 data and Solmon (1975a) in his analysis of a national sample of World War II veterans followed up in 1955 and 1969. Both studies found that institutional control had no significant impact on earnings net of individual traits and other institutional characteristics.

Institutional Gender and Race Composition

We found little evidence to suggest that attending a women's college rather than a coeducational institution has more than a trivial net impact on a woman's early career earnings when background characteristics, college achievement, educational attainment, and institutional selectivity are taken into account (Stoecker & Pascarella, 1988). Some evidence does suggest that graduates of predominantly black colleges have lower earnings than their counterparts from predominantly white institutions (for example, Baratz & Ficklen, 1983). It is questionable, however, whether such differences would remain if salient confounding influences were controlled. Pascarella, Smart, and Stoecker (1987) found that predominant college race had no statistically significant impact on the early career earnings of black men and women when individual factors such as socioeconomic status, high school achievement and aspirations, and institutional factors such as selectivity, prestige, and size were held constant.

Transfer Between Four-Year Institutions

In Chapter Ten we described how the inhibiting influence on educational attainment of transfer between four-year institutions has negative consequences for early occupational status. It seems reasonable, therefore, to expect that institutional transfer might also have deleterious consequences for income in the early career. Modest support for this expectation can be found in Kocher and Pascarella's (1988) analysis of a national sample of students who began college in 1971 and were followed up in 1980. Net of such influences as socioeconomic status, occupational aspirations, the selectivity of the first college attended, undergraduate major and grades, educational attainment, and occupational status, transferring between four-year institutions had a statistically significant negative direct effect on the 1980 earnings of white men and a statistically significant negative indirect effect on the 1980 earnings of black women. The corresponding effects for white women and black men were also negative but not statistically significant.

Within College Effects

A fairly large body of research addresses the question of whether or not different college experiences influence an individual's earnings. As with Chapter Ten on career, however, we found no common theoretical perspective or unifying thread running through this literature. The evidence, nevertheless, primarily clusters into the following categories: academic major, academic achievement, extracurricular involvement, and work experience.

Academic Major

Academic major in college clearly has an impact on early career earnings that cannot be totally accounted for by differences in the background characteristics of students selecting different fields of study. Two typical studies were conducted by Griffin and Alexander (1978) and Phelan and Phelan (1983). Griffin and Alexander analyzed a national sample of men first surveyed in 1955 as high school sophomores and followed up in 1970. Statistical controls were made for such factors as academic ability, family socioeconomic status, occupational aspirations, college selectivity, college grades, educational attainment, and occupational status. With these factors held constant, men who had majored in engineering or business had significantly higher 1970 earnings than those who had majored in other fields of study.

Phelan and Phelan (1983) analyzed the 1977 follow-up of a national sample of students who began college in 1970. With controls for family socioeconomic status, high school academic achievement, race, gender, college grades, and a college typology that was largely a measure of selectivity, the effects of college major on earnings were quite consistent with those of Griffin and Alexander (1978). Individuals who had majored in business, engineering, and professional fields had the highest net 1970 earnings, while those who had majored in the humanities and social sciences had the lowest. Physical science and other majors had net earnings in the middle.

Although the vast preponderance of investigations on other samples controlled for somewhat different sets of confounding influences, these studies report results remarkably consistent with those of Griffin and Alexander (1978) and Phelan and Phelan (1983) (Angle & Wissmann, 1981; Daymont & Andrisani, 1984; Gardner & Hwang, 1987; Groat, Chilson, &

Neal, 1982; Koch, 1972; Kocher & Pascarella, 1988; McMahon & Wagner, 1982; Raymond & Sesnowitz, 1983; Reed & Miller, 1970; Seeborg, 1975; Smart, 1988a; Solmon, 1981; Weinstein & Srinivasan, 1974; Wise, 1979).[12] This consistency of results holds regardless of whether the analyses were based on independent national samples (of which there were eight), single-institution samples (of which there were six), or single-company samples (of which there was one). Moreover, the findings are also consistent regardless of whether the outcome was actual earnings or the estimated private rate of return to different academic fields of study.

The generalization that appears warranted from this evidence is that certain undergraduate fields of study tend to provide consistently an advantage in earnings or return on educational investment, at least during the early stages of one's career. These particular fields of study are characterized by a relatively well defined body of knowledge and skills, an emphasis on scientific or quantitative methods of inquiry, and, quite often, an applied orientation (for example, Smart, 1988a). To some extent the findings on field of study and earnings may reflect the fact that employers use undergraduate major as a sorting device, either for purposes of hiring or for assigning individuals with equal amounts of education to different-paying positions. From this perspective those in such majors as engineering, business, or the natural sciences may have several advantages. Employers may believe that students selecting those fields are typically brighter than those in other majors, that they have more useful interests and abilities, or that their academic training is more rigorous and more immediately relevant to a range of jobs (Solmon, 1981).

A related explanation is that the earnings differential across undergraduate majors is largely a function of prevailing market conditions, and marketability may be in the minds of those who hire employees. Thus, companies may be more likely to hire engineers and business majors at higher salaries than other college graduates because they believe their company needs engineers and business majors.

From another perspective the findings on field of study and earnings may also reflect the simple fact that individuals choose their major with specific occupational and economic goals in mind (Wilson, 1978). The quite reasonable assumption here is that certain fields of study are expected or known to be linked to jobs with relatively high earnings (Cebula & Lopes, 1982; Florito & Dauffenbach, 1982; Koch, 1972; McMahon & Wagner, 1981; Wilson & Smith-Lovin, 1983). Thus, academic major is a vehicle by which students "target" their college training toward jobs with different economic payoffs (Wilson & Smith-Lovin, 1983).

Wilson and Smith-Lovin (1983) provide documentation for this "targeted education" explanation in an analysis of the 1968 follow-up of a national sample of 1961 college graduates. College majors (fields of study) were placed on a continuum in terms of the extent to which they typically lead to specific occupations with different average wages. (The specific procedures for doing this are described in Chapter Ten.) Majors typically linked to occupations with relatively high average earnings are business, engineering, several of the physical sciences, and preprofessional majors in medicine and dentistry. Majors in the humanities, social sciences, and education are typically linked to jobs with relatively low earnings. When controls were made for such factors as socioeconomic status, sex role attitudes, educational attainment, marital status, number of children, occupational status, and work experience, the continuum of majors had a statistically significant positive effect on the 1968 earnings of both men and women.

The idea that the content of one's undergraduate training is a determinant of earnings has been used to explain gender and race differences in earnings. There is clear evidence that women are substantially less likely than men and that minorities are somewhat less likely than whites to select majors linked to high economic rewards (for example, Angle & Wissmann, 1981; Daymont & Andrisani, 1984; Ferber & McMahon, 1979; Solmon, 1981; Trent, 1984; Wilson & Shin, 1983; Wilson & Smith-Lovin, 1983). In the case of gender, however, controlling for college major typically reduces sex differences in earnings, but it does not eliminate them (Angle & Wissmann, 1981; Daymont & Andrisani, 1984; Wilson & Smith-Lovin, 1983). There is evidence for a similar conclusion with respect to the effect of racial differences in earnings (for example, Reed & Miller, 1970), but the research does not appear to be as extensive as that focusing on gender differences.

A final point should be made about the net impact of field of study on earnings. Nearly all the studies reviewed in this section deal with the impact of major on earnings during the early stages of one's career, typically in the first ten years. As in Chapter Ten, the specific skills learned in one's major seem most important in preparing for one's first job after graduation rather than for subsequent jobs (Bisconti, 1987; Ochsner & Solmon, 1979). Moreover, there is clear evidence that in terms of long-term career mobility within the same technically oriented company, humanities and social science majors do as well as if not better than those with science, business, or engineering degrees (Beck, 1981; Howard, 1986). Consequently, it seems reasonable to expect that the impact of major field may be substantially reduced or perhaps changed when later career earnings is the criterion. The evidence here is sparse. However, a longitudinal study by Harrell and Harrell (1984) provides at least some support for this expectation. They found that after twenty years, engineers had lower salaries than economics, business, and English majors.

Academic Achievement

In Chapter Ten we saw that grades in college have small but significant and positive associations with measures of job productivity and career mobility. It seems reasonable to assume, therefore, that there will also be a significant positive link between college grades and earnings. A large body of evidence, consisting basically of two types of studies, has addressed this issue. One type of study estimates the simple correlation between academic achievement in college and subsequent earnings.[13] Typically, such studies do not address the factors that might confound the link between college grades and earnings (ability, socioeconomic status, aspirations, college selectivity, and so on). As with the evidence on grades and the noneconomic dimensions of career, we are aided in synthesizing this research by the presence of a number of quantitative and nonquantitative reviews of the literature (for example, Adkins, 1975; Baird, 1985; Calhoon & Reddy, 1968; Cohen, 1984; Nelson, 1975; Samson, Graue, Weinstein, & Walberg, 1984). These reviews are quite consistent in concluding that the average correlation between college grades and earnings is statistically significant and positive but quite modest in magnitude. There is some (though perhaps not serious) disagreement across the reviews as to the exact magnitude of the average correlation. From the designs and data presented in the quantitative syntheses, as well as our review of a number of the original investigations, we estimate the average correlation between college grades and earnings to be about .15. (Interestingly, this is somewhere between the estimates provided by the two most comprehensive quantitative syntheses: Cohen, 1984; Samson, Graue, Weinstein, & Walberg, 1984.) This means that only about 2.3 percent (that is, the square of the average correlation) of the differences in income are explainable by differences in college grades, and this itself may represent an inflated estimate because the correlation is not adjusted for potential confounding influences.

The second type of study puts greater emphasis on determining whether or not the positive link between academic achievement and earnings is causal. This is typically accomplished through statistical control of potential confounding influences such as academic ability, socioeconomic status, aspirations, college major, educational attainment, and occupational status. With some exceptions (for example, Griffin & Alexander, 1978), the weight of evidence from analyses of national samples is reasonably consistent in indicating that college grades have a small but statistically significant positive direct effect on early career earnings. In a typical study, Phelan and Phelan (1983) analyzed data on a national sample of men and women who began college in 1970 and were followed up in 1977. Net of such factors as secondary school grades, family socioeconomic status, race, gender, college type and selectivity, and college major, grades during college had a small but statistically significant positive impact on 1977 earnings. Studies on seven other national samples that controlled for similar variables, as well as for such factors as intelligence, educational attainment, occupational status, and region of employment, report findings generally consistent with those of Phelan and Phelan (for example, Astin, 1977a; Ehrenberg & Sherman, 1987; Hunt, 1963; Kinloch & Perrucci, 1969; Kocher

& Pascarella, 1988; Penley, Gould, & de la Vina, 1984; Perrucci, 1980; Sharp & Weidman, 1987; Smart, 1988a; Solmon, 1981; Solmon, Bisconti, & Ochsner, 1977).

Some research has also been conducted on more focused samples. Typically, these studies are based on alumni from a single college or from a few colleges similar in geographical location or institutional type. Again, the weight of evidence suggests that when such factors as family socioeconomic status, gender, race, college major, educational attainment, and work experience are held constant, college grades continue to have a positive effect on earnings (for example, Gardner & Hwang, 1987; Johnson, 1987; Lauman & Rapoport, 1968; Perrucci, 1969; Perrucci & Perrucci, 1970; Seeborg, 1975). This effect, however, is very small. Taking into account nonsupportive findings with business graduate students (for example, Dreher, Dougherty, & Whiteley, 1985; Pfeffer, 1977), the evidence is less consistent than that found with national samples.

There is also some evidence on the impact of college grades on earnings of employees within the same company. The findings, however, are inconsistent. Ferris (1982) studied the careers of staff accountants in a large accounting firm. Controlling for educational attainment and a measure of the prestige and academic strength of the undergraduate college attended, he found that college grades had no statistically significant impact on initial or subsequent salary. In contrast, Wise (1979) found that although college academic achievement had no impact on the starting salary of college graduates working in a large corporation, it did have a statistically significant positive effect on rate of salary increase over a three- to twenty-two-year period. This effect held regardless of high school grades, family socioeconomic status, college selectivity, college major, educational attainment, length of experience with the company, a measure of the individual's leadership and organizational ability, and the job responsibilities of the position to which the individual was initially assigned.

Since the Wise (1979) study focused on employees who worked for the same corporation for three to twenty-two years, it is one of the few investigations to indicate that college grades may have an independent impact on earnings beyond one's early career (for example, after the first ten years). Other evidence, however, is less consistent. For example, Taubman and Wales (1974) examined the factors influencing after-tax income of the top five executives of fifty of the seventy largest manufacturing firms in the country. Controlling for factors similar to those held constant by Wise, they found that outstanding academic performance in college actually had a negative effect on long-term earnings.

Given the entire body of evidence, we are led to conclude that grades in college probably do have a net positive direct effect on early career earnings. Evidence concerning a longer-term net effect is less extensive and also inconsistent. It is likely, however, that any such causal influence is small, probably accounting on the average for no more than 1 percent of the variance in individual income above and beyond other factors. At the same time, it is also possible that the studies reviewed underestimate the total impact of grades on earnings because they tend to ignore possible indirect influences. Studies by Kocher and Pascarella (1988); Pascarella, Smart, and Stoecker (1987); and Smart (1988a) on a national sample of 1971 college entrants followed up in 1980 report that college achievement often had a statistically significant positive indirect effect on early career earnings through its enhancement of educational attainment. When added to the direct effect, this indirect effect may increase the overall positive net impact of grades on earnings by as much as one-third.[14]

Extracurricular Involvement

A small body of research has investigated the link between collegiate extracurricular involvement and earnings. With some exceptions (for example, Havemann & West, 1952), the weight of evidence suggests that there may be a small positive and statistically significant correlation between involvement in extracurricular activities, particularly in a leadership role, and subsequent earnings (Calhoon & Reddy 1968; Jepsen, 1951; Walters & Bray, 1963). The evidence is less consistent, however, when statistical controls are made for potential confounding influences. In an early study, Hunt (1963) analyzed data on national samples of college students collected in 1947 by *Time* magazine. Controlling for such factors as years since graduation, parental education, academic ability, type of work, college grades, and various dimensions of institutional quality, he found that involvement in college extracurricular activities had a statistically significant positive effect on earnings in one sample but not in another.

More recent research on a national sample of individuals who began college in 1971 and were followed up in 1980 (Kocher & Pascarella, 1988) suggests that any direct influence of leadership positions or other indicators of extracurricular success is trivial when salient confounding influences are taken into account. After controls were made for such factors as family socioeconomic status, high school academic and social achievement, occupational aspirations, institutional selectivity, college grades and major, educational attainment, and occupational status, a measure of extracurricular leadership or success had no statistically significant direct impact on 1980 income for black or white men and women. (The measure of extracurricular leadership or success consisted of items such as being president of a student organization, being editor of a school publication, having a major part in a play, or winning a varsity letter.) There was some indication that for white women and black men extracurricular achievement had a statistically significant positive indirect effect on 1980 earnings through its enhancement of educational attainment. This, however, was not replicated for black men in a study that used a slightly different sample and operational definitions of variables (Pascarella, Smart, & Stoecker, 1987).

We uncovered only two studies that estimated the impact of intercollegiate athletic participation on earnings and that also employed reasonably adequate statistical control of confounding influences. In one study—of the early career earnings of men who had attended three public institutions—DuBois (1978) controlled for age, father's occupational prestige, race, college grades, work experience, and educational attainment. Net of these factors, intercollegiate athletic participation had no significant influence on earnings. Similar findings are reported by Pascarella and Smart (1990), who employed similar controls and analyzed data from a national sample of black and white men.

Work Experience During College

Evidence on the influence of work during college on postcollege earnings is inconsistent and prevents the forming of firm conclusions. Stephenson (1982) used the National Longitudinal Study of Young Men to estimate the postcollege wage determinants during the 1966–1971 period for a sample of white male college graduates. Earnings for 1971 were regressed on such factors as academic aptitude, health limits on work, military service, region of the country in which the person resided, and time since graduation. With these factors held constant, full- or part-time employment during college had a small but statistically significant positive effect on postcollege earnings. Forgey (1973) reports similar results for graduates of five junior colleges, though without the controls adopted by Stephenson.

A refinement of Stephenson's (1982) results is suggested by San (1986), who used a subsample of the same data. Controlling for many of the same variables as Stephenson did, San found that the relationship between work during college and earnings during the first five years after college was nonlinear. Work of twenty-seven hours per week or less during college had a positive influence on postcollege earnings, but work in excess of this amount adversely affected earnings. There was little to suggest that this effect was significantly altered by whether one worked on or off campus.

Other studies have shown less support for the link between work during college and postcollege earnings. Hunt's (1963) analysis of the 1947 *Time* magazine surveys found that supporting oneself during college had no statistically significant effect on subsequent earnings net of ability, social origins, college quality, and college grades. Similar results are reported by Ehrenberg and Sherman (1987) in an analysis of men in the NLS-72 sample. With such factors as academic ability, family socioeconomic status, race, college selectivity, college grades, and average regional earnings in the state of employment held constant, weekly hours of work during college had no statistically significant impact on early career earnings.

A possible explanation for these inconsistent results is that the studies reviewed above did not differentiate the extent to which work during college was related to the individual's postcollege employment. In Chapter Ten we saw modest evidence that work during college closely related to postcollege occupation increased the technical responsibility held early in one's career. It seems a reasonable expectation that a similar relationship might exist between college work and early career earnings. We found no study, however, that addressed this question with adequate methodological rigor.

Conditional Effects of College

Racial Differences in the Effects of College

A small body of research has focused on the question of whether white and nonwhite students receive equal economic returns on their investment in postsecondary education.[15] Often blacks have been the comparison group, and typically the category "nonwhite" includes a majority of black students. The general trend in this research suggests that in the 1940s, 1950s, and 1960s the private rate of return to a bachelor's degree for black or other nonwhite men was consistently lower than that for white men (Carnoy & Marenbach, 1975; Hanoch, 1967; Hines, Tweeten, & Redfern, 1970; Niemi, 1974). More recently, however, there is evidence to suggest that in relative terms this gap is closing, at least in the case of younger black men (Adams & Nestel, 1976; Garcia & Garcia, 1978). For women, the trend appears to be less variable over time. Black and other nonwhite women appear to have consistently higher private rates of return from a bachelor's degree than their white counterparts (Carnoy & Marenbach, 1975; Christian & Stroup, 1981; Hines, Tweeten, & Redfern, 1970; Hoffer, 1973; Niemie, 1974).

A related line of research has focused only on the relative earnings benefits of college that accrue to whites and nonwhites without considering the costs and other factors involved in the private rate of return estimates. Virtually all of this research has been conducted with male samples. Here the most rigorously conducted studies suggest a possible change over time in the relative importance of a bachelor's degree for white and nonwhite or black men. Analyses of the 1961 Occupational Changes in a Generation sample and data from the 1960 and 1970 census suggest that in the early and mid 1960s white and nonwhite men derived roughly the same relative earnings benefits from completion of a bachelor's degree (Jencks et al., 1979; Smith & Welch, 1977). Analyses of more recent data, the 1971 Panel Study of Income Dynamics by Jencks et al. (1979) and the 1973 Occupational Changes in a Generation sample by Featherman and Hauser (1978), suggest that by the early 1970s nonwhite or black men began to enjoy somewhat greater relative earnings benefits from completing college than did their white counterparts. The most recent analysis, by Hoffman (1984), used an update of the Panel Study of Income Dynamics to estimate the 1971 and 1977 earnings of two cohorts of black and white men age twenty-one to thirty-five. Net of such factors as years of work experience and place of residence (South versus North, urban versus nonurban, and the like), the relative income returns to a bachelor's degree for black men were 13 percent higher than those for white men in 1971 but were 89 percent higher in 1977.

Taken in total, the results of these studies suggest that since about 1970, black and other nonwhite men may be receiving a greater relative earnings return from a bachelor's degree than are white men. Such findings, of course, do not mean that black or other nonwhite college graduates will actually earn more than white college graduates. They only suggest that obtaining a college degree is a more important determinant of the earnings of black and other nonwhite men than of their white counterparts.[16]

As indicated by Cohen and Geske (1985), there have been a number of attempts to attribute the relative increase in the economic returns of college to blacks or other nonwhites to various public policies. These include affirmative action, federally funded equal opportunity and educational assistance programs, and vigorous university recruitment of minority students (for example, Jud & Walker, 1982; Link, Ratledge, & Lewis, 1976; Welch, 1973). Others, however, have argued that education generally has done little to improve the social mobility of minorities (for example, Levin, 1977a, 1977b; Thurow, 1975). This latter group may have a point because there is a downside to the increased economic returns accruing to nonwhites when they earn a college degree. Specifically, education less than a bachelor's degree appears to have substantially *less* relative economic benefit to black men than to white men (Featherman & Hauser, 1978; Hoffman, 1984). Thus, compared to whites, black and other nonwhite men may actually derive lower economic returns from formal education unless they are able to earn the bachelor's degree (Jencks et al., 1979).

Gender Differences in the Effects of College

The clear majority of studies on the economic returns of college have analyzed male samples. As women have become an increasingly larger part of the work force, particularly over the past three decades, some attention has focused on whether they receive the same relative economic returns from their investment in higher education as do men. Our conclusion from this research is that the nature of any gender differences in the private rate of return to a bachelor's degree depends upon race. In short, over four census years (1940, 1950, 1960 and 1970), the private rate of return for white men has been somewhat higher than that for white women. Conversely, the rate of return for black and other nonwhite men has been consistently lower than that for black and other non-white women (Carnoy & Marenbach, 1975; see also Hines, Tweeten, & Redfern, 1970; Niemi, 1974). Indeed, over the four census years, black and other nonwhite women have had the highest private rate of return of any group.

Such findings are only partially consistent with those of studies that estimate gender differences in earnings while controlling for potential confounding influences. (As suggested in the previous section, studies of earnings focus on benefits, while estimates of private rate of return embrace costs as well as benefits.) The evidence from these investigations suggests that irrespective of race, women derive relatively greater earnings benefits from postsecondary education than do men. For example, Campbell and Laughlin (1987), analyzing the 1987 National Longitudinal Survey of Labor Market Experience of young adults, controlled for such factors as academic ability, race, family socioeconomic status, U.S. region of residence, and years of work in the current job. With these influences held constant, the effect of a bachelor's degree on the early career earnings of white women was nearly 84 percent greater than the corresponding effect for white men. Similar though less pronounced results are reported for the relative impact on earnings of years of postsecondary education completed or degree attainment (for example, Angle & Wissmann, 1981; Glenn & Taylor, 1984; Gruca, 1988; Malkiel & Malkiel, 1973).

The differences in the results of these two types of studies may well be a function of the different economic criteria used. One criterion includes both costs and benefits, while the other is restricted essentially to benefits. Another possibility is that the different findings reflect methodological differences in the nonschooling variables held constant. These were extensive in estimates of simple earnings, but they were minimal in estimates of private rate of return. Despite these issues, it is important to note a consistent finding across both the private rate of return studies and the simple earnings estimates developed by Campbell and Laughlin (1987). Specifically, of all groups, nonwhite women appear to derive the greatest economic benefits from a bachelor's degree.

Ability and Socioeconomic Status Differences in the Effects of College

A small body of research has sought to determine whether the impact of college on earnings differs for various levels of intellectual or academic ability. Nearly all this research has been based on male samples with inconsistent results. For example, Hause (1972), employing the NBER-Thorndike data on World War II veterans, found that men at relatively high levels of intellectual ability received greater income returns for similar amounts of postsecondary education than did men with relatively lower levels of intellectual ability. Taubman and Wales (1975b), however, did not find this conditional effect when they reanalyzed the same data, possibly because of a somewhat different operational definition of ability. Research on other samples has found little to indicate that the effect of amount of postsecondary education on earnings varies either consistently or substantially with intellectual ability (for example, Jencks et al., 1979; Hauser & Daymont, 1977).

A similar conclusion can probably be made with respect to variations in the effects of college on earnings for individuals from different socioeconomic origins. Wachtel's (1975b) analysis of the NBER-Thorndike data suggests that the rate of return to a college education is greater for men from higher social origins than for those from lower ones. However, Jencks and his colleagues' (Jencks et al., 1979) extensive multisample analyses indicate no consistent differences in the effects of education on earnings by level of socioeconomic origin.

Institutional Characteristics

Since college quality is probably the single institutional characteristic most studied in relation to the economic returns of college, it is also the major institutional characteristic considered with respect to conditional effects. We found one conditional effect involving college quality that was clearly replicated across independent samples. The impact of college selectivity on earnings appears to be more pronounced for men from relatively high socioeconomic backgrounds (for example, managerial, professional) than for men from lower social origins (blue-collar, for instance). This has been reported by Perrucci and Perrucci (1970), with a national sample of engineering graduates, and by Karabel and McClelland (1987), with a national sample of men from the 1973 Occupational Changes in a Generation Survey.[17] Such a finding is consistent with the hypothesis that attending a selective or prestigious college is part of a process of cumulative advantage. Not only are students from advantaged socioeconomic backgrounds more likely than individuals from less advantaged social origins to attend elite undergraduate institutions (for example, Hearn, 1984; Karabel & Astin, 1975), but the former may be more likely to convert the status conferred by such an institution into greater economic success (Karabel & McClelland, 1987).

A second conditional effect involving college quality has shown less consistent replication across independent samples. Solmon (1973, 1975a), using the NBER-Thorndike data on World War II veterans, found that measures of college quality such as selectivity, resources, and academic reputation had a slightly more pronounced positive impact on earnings for men with high tested academic ability than for men with relatively lower academic ability. Similar results have also been reported by Weisbrod and Karpoff (1968) with a sample of men from a single company (AT&T). The

Weisbrod and Karpoff study, however, used rank in college class as a proxy measure for academic ability, so it is not clear that they were assessing the same individual trait as Solmon.

Other investigations have failed to support the findings of Solmon (1973, 1975a) and Weisbrod and Karpoff (1968). Daniere and Mechling (1970), analyzing a national sample of male college graduates, found that instructional cost per student (a variable highly correlated with college selectivity and prestige) had a less pronounced impact on the earnings of students with high academic ability than it did on the earnings of those with middle-level academic ability. Similarly, both Wise (1979), analyzing another corporation-specific sample, and Pascarella and Smart (1989), analyzing a national sample of college students, found that the effects of college selectivity on earnings were independent of a student's collegiate grade point average. Grades, of course, are typically the basic component of class rank (as used by Weisbrod and Karpoff). Such differences in variable definitions plus the inconsistent findings when essentially the same variable is used make it difficult to form a conclusion about this body of evidence.

It is worth noting that we uncovered no consistent evidence to suggest that the effects of college quality on earnings differ for different gender or race subgroups. There is some evidence that college selectivity or prestige enhances earnings more in the private employment sector than in the public one (Smart, 1988a) and more in managerial and professional occupations than in blue-collar jobs (Karabel & McClelland, 1987). However, these particular conditional effects await replication. Thus, at present, they are best considered as tentative findings. The literature is largely silent on conditional effects involving institutional characteristics other than quality indexes.

College Experiences

A small body of research has addressed the issue of conditional effects on earnings that involve such factors as gender, academic major, and grades. This evidence is best characterized as lacking a coherent theoretical or conceptual theme. Indeed, an inspection of the references at the end of each published article or paper would suggest that these studies are largely unaware of each other. Accordingly, it is not particularly surprising that we found no consistently replicable findings on which to develop a generalization.

For example, a number of studies have sought to determine whether the effects of academic major on earnings differ by gender (for example, Angle & Wissmann, 1981; Gardner & Hwang, 1987; Gruca, 1988; Wilson & Smith-Lovin, 1983). Wilson and Smith-Lovin found that majors targeted toward high earnings (such as engineering, business, scientific/premedical) had a significantly stronger positive effect on the subsequent earnings of men than of women. Using many of the same majors, however, Gruca's (1988) analyses uncovered no evidence of statistically significant gender differences in effects on income. Angle and Wissmann (1981) report that majoring in the humanities or education provides greater relative income returns to women than to men. Conversely, Gardner and Hwang (1987) found that men derive relatively greater income returns from majoring in the humanities, as well as from majoring in the social and natural sciences. Gender differences among other majors were small and statistically nonsignificant. About the best that can be said from such evidence is that there may be gender differences in the impact of college major on earnings. The pattern of such differences, however, is as yet unclear.

Similar ambiguity is evident in the findings of studies considering other conditional effects. Gardner and Hwang (1987), for example, found that the effect of grades on salary depended on major (and vice versa). The pattern, however, was so complex that it resisted interpretation. Seeborg (1975) and Pascarella and Smart (1989) found that the effect of college grades on earnings was largely independent of a student's major.

These examples typify what is currently a disjointed and atheoretical body of evidence. We hesitate to offer any firm conclusions about conditional effects of college experiences on earnings.

Intergenerational Effects on Earnings

In Chapter Nine on educational attainment and Chapter Ten on career, we reviewed evidence suggesting that having a college education provides a net advantage to one's sons or daughters in terms of increased educational attainment and, to a somewhat lesser extent, of occupational status. Our interpretation of this evidence is that much of the statistically significant intergenerational effect on an offspring's educational attainment is indirect and that perhaps all of the statistically significant intergenerational effect on the offspring's occupational status is indirect.

A substantial body of research has also focused on the intergenerational effects of parental education on the economic attainments of sons and daughters. As with the corresponding inquiry on occupational status, evidence pertaining to the direct effect of parental education on sons' and daughters' earnings is inconsistent. A number of studies on various national and more focused samples have suggested that net of influences such as family income, intellectual ability, race, the quality of the college attended, academic major, or educational attainment, parental education has a statistically significant positive direct effect on sons' and daughters' earnings (for example, Bowles, 1972; Phelan & Phelan, 1983; Seeborg, 1975; Taubman, 1975; Taubman & Wales, 1975a; Wales, 1973). Other investigations that controlled for similar confounding influences, however, suggest that the direct impact of parental education on sons' or daughters' earnings or wealth is essentially trivial and statistically nonsignificant (for example, Campbell & Henretta, 1980; Griffin & Alexander, 1978; Hunt, 1963; Karabel & McClelland, 1987; Penley, Gould, & de la Vina, 1984; Reed & Miller, 1970; Rumberger, 1983; Sewell & Hauser, 1972).

Only a minority of the studies cited above have considered the net direct effect of having college-educated parents on the economic success of sons or daughters. Here, too, the evidence is inconsistent and perhaps even contradictory. Using the NBER-Thorndike data on World War II veterans, Taubman and Wales (1975a) found that net of other factors, having a father who attended college had a marginally significant effect on 1955 earnings and a small but statistically significant direct effect on 1969 earnings. On the basis of alumni data from a single institution, Seeborg (1975) reports similar findings for the net effect of having a college-educated mother on the earnings of both men and women.

Less supportive evidence is reported by Reed and Miller (1970), who analyzed supplementary census data on college graduates from 1967, and by Gruca (1988), with data on a national sample of college students who began college in 1971 and were followed up in 1980. Reed and Miller found that net of factors such as age, academic major, race, father's occupation, college selectivity, and region of residence, having a father who completed four years of college had only a trivial and nonsignificant influence on a man's current earnings. Similarly, when controlling for many of the same variables plus high school achievement, college grades, and occupational status, Gruca found that having a father who was a college graduate had no statistically significant direct influence on the 1980 earnings of either white or black men or women. Having a mother who was a college graduate had the same trivial direct effect for black men and whites of either sex and actually had a statistically significant negative direct effect on the earnings of black women.

In terms of methodological rigor there seems little to choose between studies with statistically significant and nonsignificant findings. Consequently, the inconsistent findings lead us to conclude that parental postsecondary education may have little or no direct impact on the economic success of children when salient confounding factors are taken into account. At the same time, there is at least a modicum of evidence to suggest that the schooling of parents positively influences the earnings and economic well-being of their children through indirect routes such as available family financial resources and educational attainment (for example, Gruca, 1988; Leibowitz, 1974b, 1977a; Michael, 1982; Parsons, 1975; Rumberger, 1983).

As far as we know, Gruca's (1988) analysis is the only study to estimate the indirect effects of parental postsecondary education on the early career earnings of children. Though her findings await replication, they support the hypothesis that a statistically significant, if not major, part of the intergenerational transfer of economic benefits associated with college attendance is through indirect routes. As indicated above, Gruca's analyses found only one statistically significant direct effect of parental postsecondary education on children's earnings, and that was negative. However, having a mother who was a college graduate had a statistically significant positive indirect effect on the early career earnings of all four groups considered, black and white men and women. Having a father who was a college graduate had a similar indirect effect on the earnings of white, though not black, men and women. The indirect route by which parental postsecondary education exerted this influence was largely through increased family financial resources, the selectivity of the college one attended, and, in some instances, educational attainment.

Summary

Net Effects of College

Attaining the bachelor's degree has important implications for an individual's lifetime earnings. Our best estimate is that net of factors such as intelligence, socioeconomic background, and work experience, a bachelor's degree provides somewhere between a 20 and 40 percent advantage in earnings over a high school diploma. This earnings advantage appears somewhat larger than the advantage associated either with a high school diploma versus an eighth grade education or with graduate degrees in general versus a bachelor's degree. Thus, the evidence on earnings is consistent with that on occupational status in suggesting that completing the bachelor's degree may be the single most important educational step in the occupational and economic attainment process. Consistent with this conclusion is evidence indicating that one receives an earnings "bonus" for completing the bachelor's degree above and beyond the increment received for each year of college completed. This most likely reflects the fact that the bachelor's degree is a prerequisite not only for entrance into many high-status technical and managerial positions but also for acceptance at professional schools (business, law, medical, and so on) linked to high earnings.

A second approach to the study of the economic impact of college has included estimates of costs (for example, tuition, books, foregone earnings). This research has produced a private rate of return index that is basically the difference between the average posttax earnings of college and high school graduates divided by the sum of the unsubsidized costs of a college education plus foregone earnings. Expressed as a percentage, it can be thought of as an estimate of financial return on investment. Our synthesis of the evidence suggests that when adjusted for ability differences, the private rate of return to a bachelor's degree (versus a high school diploma) averages somewhere between 9.3 and 10.9 percent. This estimate compares favorably to benchmark rates for alternative investments. Moreover, it would probably increase if individual costs were adjusted for public and private subsidies to education, foregone earnings were adjusted for work during college, and fringe benefits were included as part of earnings.[18]

As with our discussion of occupational status, the causal mechanism(s) underlying the substantial impact of bachelor's degree attainment on earnings is (are) not readily apparent. We found some evidence to support a human capital or socialization explanation. This posits that the link between education and earnings is attributable to the fact that college imparts cognitive skills, values, and attitudes that make the individual a more productive (and therefore a more highly paid) employee. At the same time, however, we also found support for the argument that college serves a screening or certification function such that those without a bachelor's degree are effectively barred from entry into high-status/high-income careers. Consistent with this, additional evidence suggests that bachelor's degree recipients receive preferential treatment in the form of higher earnings for reasons unrelated to greater productivity. Our reading of this total body of evidence is that both human capital or socialization and screening or certification may be part of any causal link between postsecondary education and earnings. Neither hypothesis alone provides a completely satisfactory explanation.

Between-College Effects

Only a small body of studies has addressed the net impact of initially attending a two-year rather than a four-year institution on earnings. The weight of evidence from this research suggests that when individuals of equal background traits and educational attainment are compared, any direct earnings penalties for attending a two-year college are quite small early in the career, though they may increase slightly with longer work experience. It is likely, however, that initial attendance at a two-year college may have a discernible negative indirect effect on earnings due in large measure to its inhibiting effect on educational attainment.

A large body of research has estimated the net effect of different dimensions of college quality on earnings. Our synthesis suggests that, net of other factors, college quality (and particularly selectivity) has a small positive direct effect on earnings. The best estimate of the magnitude of this effect is that quality indexes account for between one and one and a half percent of the variance in individual earnings above and beyond other factors. There is some evidence that this effect is nonlinear; only those colleges at the very top of the distribution of selectivity or academic reputation may significantly enhance earnings.

Estimates of direct effects may underestimate the total positive impact of institutional quality measures on earnings. Additional evidence indicates that institutional quality may also have a positive indirect effect on earnings by enhancing educational attainment and attendance at prestigious professional schools. We conclude that the evidence is more supportive of a screening (as opposed to a human capital or socialization) explanation for the apparent impact of college quality on earnings.

There is a much smaller volume of research on the impact of institutional characteristics other than quality on earnings. The most consistent finding from this research is that larger institutions tend to have a modest positive effect on earnings that is independent of student background characteristics and the selectivity of the student body. There is parallel evidence to suggest that major research universities, most of which are large, also have a positive influence on earnings; but it is difficult to separate this effect from that of institutional quality. We found little consistent evidence to suggest that institutional control (private versus public) or the predominant racial or gender composition of an institution has a statistically significant impact on earnings when other factors are controlled.

There is modest support for the expectation that transfer between four-year institutions will have negative consequences for early career earnings. The negative effects are both direct and indirect (through educational attainment), but they are not as consistent as the corresponding negative effects of institutional transfer on occupational status.

Within-College Effects

According to clear and consistent evidence, major field of study has a significant impact on early career earnings that cannot be accounted for by differences in the characteristics of students selecting different majors. The majors that enhance earnings tend to be characterized by a relatively well defined body of knowledge and skills, an emphasis on scientific or quantitative methods of inquiry, and often an applied orientation. Examples are such majors as engineering, business, several of the physical sciences, and preprofessional majors oriented toward medicine and dentistry. These majors tend to have close links to occupations with relatively high average earnings. Differences in the academic field of study chosen during college tend to explain part but not all of the lower earnings of women and racial minorities.

Nearly all of the studies on the influence of academic major on earnings focus on earnings during the early career. The evidence is less convincing that the same majors are linked with higher earnings in the later stages of one's career.

The weight of evidence from a large body of research indicates that academic achievement during college has a positive direct impact on early career earnings that is independent of student background characteristics, the selectivity of the institution attended, and major field of study. Evidence with respect to a longer-term effect is less extensive and inconsistent. Any direct causal impact of grades on early career earnings appears small, probably explaining no more than 1 percent of the differences in individual earnings. This might be increased by as much as one-third if the indirect effect of grades on earnings, through educational attainment, were also taken into account.

We uncovered little consistent evidence to suggest that extracurricular accomplishment or athletic participation had a significant impact on earnings when important confounding influences were controlled. Similarly, evidence with respect to the influence of work during college on postcollege earnings is inconsistent. We suspect that the inconsistent findings in the latter body of evidence may be at least partially due to the fact that the studies reviewed do not typically consider the degree to which work during college is related to the individual's postcollege employment.

Conditional Effects of College

The bulk of research on conditional effects is concerned with whether college graduation has a differential influence on the private rate of return or on the earnings of different gender or racial groups. While earlier rate of return studies have suggested that white men derive a higher economic return from a bachelor's degree than nonwhite men, more recent evidence suggests that this gap has narrowed substantially. When the criterion is simple earnings, the trend in the evidence suggests that since about 1970, a bachelor's degree has had a stronger positive influence on the earnings of black and other nonwhite men than it has had on the earnings of white men. This is consistent with findings on the effects of a bachelor's degree on occupational status. It is important here to restress that this does not mean that nonwhite male college graduates have higher average occupational status or earnings than their white counterparts. Rather, it indicates that earning a bachelor's degree plays a more important role in the occupational and economic attainments of nonwhite men than of white men.

The nature of any gender differences in the private rate of return to a bachelor's degree appears to depend upon race. White men have typically had higher rates of return than white women, whereas the rate of return for black or other nonwhite men has typically been lower than that for their female counterparts. With earnings as the criterion, the evidence is reasonably consistent in suggesting that irrespective of race, women derive greater economic benefits from postsecondary education than do men. Across both rate of return and simple earnings estimations, however, black and other nonwhite women consistently derive the greatest relative benefits of all subgroups from postsecondary education.

A small amount of research has also sought to determine whether the impact of college on earnings differs for individuals with different levels of academic ability or for individuals who come from different socioeconomic backgrounds. The findings of this research are inconsistent, leading us to conclude that the economic returns to college are probably the same irrespective of one's academic aptitude or social origins.

The effects of institutional selectivity on earnings appear to be most pronounced for men from relatively high socioeconomic backgrounds and are less so for men from lower social origins. We found no compelling evidence, however, to indicate that the effect of college "quality" on earnings varies consistently for individuals from different race or gender groups or for individuals with different levels of academic aptitude or collegiate academic achievement. The latter finding is interesting in that it suggests that the effect of grades on earnings does not depend on the selectivity of the institution in which they were earned. Conversely, it suggests that students do not need a particularly distinguished record of academic achievement to realize the modest earnings benefits of attendance at a selective undergraduate college.

There is evidence to suggest that the economic impact of college selectivity or prestige is more pronounced in the private employment sector and in managerial and professional occupations than in the public sector or in blue-collar jobs. These conditional effects, however, await replication. A series of findings also indicate gender differences in the impact of college major on earnings. However, the exact pattern of such differences is inconsistent.

Intergenerational Effects

Evidence pertaining to the direct effect of parental postsecondary education on the earnings of sons and daughters is inconsistent. One study, however, suggests that this may be due to the fact that parental postsecondary education enhances the economic circumstances of children through indirect routes. Specifically, having parents who are college graduates increases family financial resources, the selectivity of the college attended, and in some instances educational attainment. These, in turn, have positive implications for early career earnings of both sons and daughters.

Notes

1. The evidence in support of this, based on the simple lifetime earnings differential between college graduates and high school graduates, is dramatic and unequivocal (for example, Adams & Jaffe, 1971; "Smoking, Education Level Linked," 1989; Haller, 1982; Henderson & Ottinger, 1985; "Education Has Little Impact on Minority Employment," 1982; Katona, Dunkelberg, Hendricks, & Schmiedeskamp, 1970; Miller & Glick, 1956; Morgan & David, 1963; Ottinger, 1984; Pace, 1979;

Ramirez & Soriano, 1981; Romano, 1986; Shaycoft, 1973; U.S. Bureau of the Census, 1970).

2. Another kind of rate of return is the "social" rate of return to higher education. This is typically calculated by means of pretax earnings (since from a societal point of view, taxes are counted in the national income) and the full costs, including public subsidies, of an individual's education (Walberg, 1987). Although the social rate of return has been addressed by a number of scholars (for example, Cohen & Geske, 1985; Leslie & Brinkman, 1986; McMahon & Wagner, 1982), the major purpose of this book (to synthesize the impact of college on students) leads us to focus on the individual or private rate of return to college.

3. Obviously the private rate of return is only an estimate and often a very rough estimate of the economic returns on investment in education. For a thorough discussion of some of the issues involved in calculating rates of return and what they mean, see Leslie and Brinkman (1986).

4. For other representative estimates of the private rate of return to a college education, see Baktari and Grasso (1985), Belanger and Lavallee (1980), Freeman (1976, 1980), Freeman and Hollomon (1975), Grasso (1977), Hanoch (1967), Hansen (1963), Hoffer (1973), Kolstad (1982), Liberman (1979), Mattila (1982), National Center for Education Statistics (1982), Nolen (1975), Psacharopoulos (1973), Raymond and Sesnowitz (1983), Rogers (1969), Rumberger (1980, 1984), Schwartz and Thornton (1980), Tomaske (1974), and Witmer (1976, 1983).

5. Although Leslie and Brinkman (1988) suggest that such ability adjustments may produce overly conservative estimates of returns to college, it could also be argued that they are overly liberal because such factors as an individual's socioeconomic status and ambition are not also taken into account (Griffin, 1976). Unfortunately, the literature yielded no clear analog to Leslie and Brinkman's correction for ability that might also allow us to adjust the private rate of return for socioeconomic status or ambition.

6. A sharp decline in the private rate of return to college was noted by Freeman (1976, 1977, 1979, 1980) in the late seventies. He attributed this essentially to an increasing percentage of college graduates in the work force (cohort size) and a downturn in the business cycle. Evidence from a number of studies, however, has suggested that such a decline may have been a temporary market adjustment to changes in supply and demand for college graduates and that the relative economic position of college graduates did not decline, even though their job skills may not have been fully utilized (for example, Baktari & Grasso, 1985; Cline, 1982; Clogg & Shockey, 1984; McMahon & Wagner, 1982; Rumberger, 1980, 1984; Schwartz & Thornton, 1980; Witmer, 1980). Longer-term rates of return (such as those computed a decade or so

after graduation) tend to show no decline in the relative market value of a college education (McMahon & Wagner, 1982). Moreover, recent evidence presented by Murphy and Welch (1989) suggests that by 1985 the rate of return had risen to a historical high. This, they posit, is due to an increasing demand for college-trained workers.

7. The private rates of return to elementary and secondary education are generally larger than those due to college (Leslie & Brinkman, 1986). This is to be expected, however, as both the private costs of elementary and secondary education and foregone earnings are minimal.

8. Another line of research compares the net earnings of community college students intending vocational or technical degrees with those of similar students in postsecondary vocational or technical schools. The findings of this research are contradictory. Wilms (1980) found that net of such factors as sex, socioeconomic background, educational attainment, and job experience, vocational or technical school attenders had significantly higher earnings than community college attenders. Somers, Sharpe, and Myint (1971), however, found that net of many of the same factors, individuals who had attended community colleges had significantly higher earnings than those who had attended vocational or technical schools. As Dougherty (1987) suggests, it is difficult to chose between conflicting findings because neither study has the edge in methodological rigor.

9. Although the preponderance of research in this area is based on white men, we found little to suggest statistically significant differences in the magnitude of the impact of college quality on earnings for white men, white women, black men, and black women (for example, Gruca, 1988).

10. Another potential (though unestimated) indirect effect of college quality on earnings comes through the prestige of the graduate school attended. Henson's (1980) analyses, for example, indicate that graduation from an elite undergraduate college significantly enhances the likelihood of entrance into a prestigious graduate or professional school. In turn, Kingston (1981) reports findings indicating that graduates of prestigious business or law schools have higher starting salaries than graduates of other business or law schools.

11. Consistent with these results, Astin (1977a) found that salary in school teaching was also positively influenced by attending a large institution and negatively influenced by attending a small institution. See also a pilot study by Hunt (1963).

12. A small number of studies have found no statistically significant relationship between academic major and earnings (for example, Penley, Gould, & de la Vina, 1984; Simonds, 1962, as reviewed in Calhoon & Reddy, 1968).

13. For a representative list of studies see American Telephone and Telegraph Company (1962); Jepsen (1951); Harrell (1969, 1970, 1972); Havemann and West (1952); LeBold, Thoma, Gillis, and Hawkins (1960); Lewis and Nelson (1983a,b); Muchinsky and Hoyt (1973); Walters and Bray (1963); Weinstein and Srinivasan (1974); Wise (1979).

14. It is interesting to speculate on the causal mechanisms that a human capital or socialization view or a screening or certification view might posit as underlying this net link between college grades and earnings. From a human capital or socialization perspective grades in college might indicate the extent to which an individual has mastered the cognitive and subject matter skills that make him or her a more productive and therefore more highly paid employee. A screening or certification explanation, on the other hand, might posit that grades merely help an employer sort job candidates according to individual traits linked to job productivity such as native intelligence, motivation, and work effort. Thus, grades provide another convenient screening device by which employers might select the most intelligent and motivated people for the most important and highest-paying positions.

15. This section draws heavily, though not exclusively, on a comprehensive review by Cohen and Geske (1985).

16. Some research has also addressed the question of differences in the economic returns to college for whites and American citizens of Mexican origin. This evidence is mixed. Some studies suggest that the returns are about the same (Penley, Gould, & de la Vina, 1984; Raymond & Sesnowitz, 1975), while others suggest that Anglos tend to derive greater returns than Mexican-Americans (Raymond and Sesnowitz, 1983). Evidence from the Raymond & Sesnowitz (1983) study also suggests that academic major may be a determinant of group differences in returns, with Mexican-Americans deriving greater returns from an education major while Anglos derive greater returns from other majors. The total body of evidence, however, is too sparse and inconsistent to form the basis of a firm conclusion.

17. Less supportive evidence on this point is reported by Laumann and Rapoport (1968). Their sample, however, was based on graduates of three technical institutions. Consequently, we are inclined to give it less weight relative to findings based on separate national samples.

18. Even if such adjustments were made, the private rate of return might still tend to underestimate the actual economic payoffs of college compared to other investment options. Several potentially important factors remain unconsidered. First is the relative security of the investments. An individual can get "wiped out" in the stock market or real estate speculations, and many businesses fail; but an individual has a college degree and its attendant advantages for a lifetime. A second consideration is that the idea of taking money and investing it in areas

other than college may be founded on hypothetical and unrealistic conditions. It assumes that individuals do, in fact, have the money to invest and are willing to do so. It may be unrealistic to expect that many people would endure the personal sacrifices they make for college to place their money in a deferred annuity or a money market account. Finally, as a personal investment, funds are available for the pursuit of a college education through grants, scholarships, and loans that are not as readily available for other types of investments. (We are indebted to an anonymous reviewer of the manuscript for these additional points.)

12

Quality of Life
After College

In Chapter Eleven we synthesized evidence pertaining to the economic benefits associated with college attendance. In this chapter we review the accumulated evidence pertaining to the impact of college on a range of nonmonetary benefits. Much of this research has been conducted by economists who employ such terms as *nonmarket* (Haveman & Wolfe, 1984) and *consumption* (Schultz, 1961, 1963; Lazear, 1977; Lucas, 1977) to characterize these benefits. A basic assumption is that increased formal education may raise "productivity in non-labor-market activities" such as consumer behavior, child care, family planning, health, and leisure that provide noneconomic but, nevertheless, real benefits (Michael, 1982, p. 141). A related, though distinctive, line of inquiry has a more sociological orientation and focuses on what might be called national social indicators. Among other things, this body of inquiry has sought to estimate the impact of formal education on such broad-based outcomes as "life satisfaction" or "subjective well-being" (Andrews & Withey, 1976; Campbell, 1981; Witter, Okun, Stock, & Haring, 1984).

    In this chapter we do not make a major distinction between these two lines of research. Rather, we believe that they cluster together as indicators of an individual's quality of life. Within this basic rubric, we synthesize evidence pertaining to the impact of college on subjective well-being, health, marriage, attainment of desired family size, nurturance of children, consumer behavior, savings and investment behavior, and leisure. Since the vast preponderance of this research deals only with the impact of different levels of formal education on the quality of life, the chapter will focus primarily on the net effects of college.[1] Any between-college, within-college, or conditional effects of college are discussed in the context of the net effects of college.

Net Effects of College

Subjective Well-Being

    A substantial body of research on national samples has investigated the link between amount of formal education and various indexes of subjective well-being or life satisfaction (for example, Andrews & Withey, 1976; Bryant & Marquez, 1986; Campbell, 1981; Campbell, Converse, & Rodgers, 1976; Clemente & Sauer, 1976; Diener, 1984; Flanagan, 1975; Freudiger, 1980; Glenn & Weaver, 1981; Gurin, Veroff, & Feld, 1960; Mitchell, 1976; Palmore, 1979; Palmore & Luikart, 1972; Spreitzer & Snyder, 1974; Toseland & Rasch, 1979–1980; Witter, Okun, Stock, & Haring, 1984). This research has tended to employ general indicators that ask individuals to report their overall perceptions of well-being in terms of such factors as happiness, life satisfaction, morale, or quality of life. The findings of this research are consistent in suggesting that educational attainment has a small but statistically significant positive association with subjective well-being. This association is substantially reduced, however, when a person's socioeconomic circumstances (for example, occupational status, income) are taken into account.

This conclusion is perhaps best documented by the findings of a quantitative synthesis of the research on the link between education and subjective well-being conducted by Witter, Okun, Stock, and Haring (1984). They analyzed 176 effect sizes, in the form of correlations, from ninety studies covering five different operationalizations of subjective well-being (life satisfaction, morale, well-being, quality of life, and happiness). For all studies, the average correlation between educational attainment and subjective well-being was .14, which was statistically significant. There is additional evidence to suggest that the association between educational attainment and subjective well-being is significantly stronger for older (sixty-five years or over, $r = .18$) than for younger (under sixty-five years, $r = .11$) individuals and for women ($r = .16$) than for men ($r = .11$). While statistically significant, however, these age and gender differences are not very large. No statistically significant differences in the link between educational attainment and subjective well-being were noted between black ($r = .12$) and white ($r = .14$) samples.

If one were to square the overall correlation of .14 reported by Witter, Okun, Stock, and Haring (1984), the result would indicate that educational attainment explains, on the average, only about 2 percent of the variance in subjective well-being. Even this figure probably overestimates the magnitude of the direct causal effect of education on well-being, as it does not take into account potential confounding influences. Some additional analyses by Witter and colleagues, for example, found that the association between education and well-being was reduced to .11 when income was controlled, to .06 when occupational status was controlled, and to .06 when a composite index of socioeconomic status was taken into account. Effecting controls for the latter two factors (occupational status and composite socioeconomic status) actually reduced the link between educational attainment and subjective well-being to the point where it was no longer statistically significant. This result strongly suggests that any direct causal effect of educational attainment on subjective well-being is very small and possibly trivial, although it does not preclude education from having a statistically significant, though quite likely small, indirect effect on perceived well-being. As noted in Chapters Ten and Eleven, educational attainment, particularly the completion of a bachelor's degree, is a major determinant of both occupational status and income. In turn, an individual's socioeconomic circumstances appear to be a significant, if modest, determinant of perceived well-being and satisfaction with life (for example, Andrews & Withey, 1976; Campbell, 1981). Thus, we might expect education to enhance certain elements of subjective well-being indirectly by improving the socioeconomic conditions and therefore the resources, opportunities, and material gratification available in one's life. That this effect is in all likelihood small is probably attributable to the fact that the socioeconomic circumstances in which people live account for a small part of their sense of well-being or satisfaction with life (Campbell, 1981).

Although substantially less evidence focuses specifically on the effects of postsecondary education on subjective well-being, the findings of the research that does exist suggest little that is different from the effects of education generally. The two most comprehensive investigations were conducted by Campbell (1981) and Glenn and Weaver (1981), with data from the same series of national surveys. Campbell used responses of individuals over the age of eighteen from the 1957 to 1978 surveys, whereas Glenn and Weaver used responses from individuals age twenty-five to fifty-four from the 1973 to 1978 surveys. With no controls for confounding influences, having a bachelor's degree (versus less formal education) had a slight positive association with a global measure of happiness (that is, "taking all things together, how would you say things are these days—would you say that you are very happy, pretty happy, or not too happy?"). The effect of having a bachelor's degree (versus a high school diploma) on global happiness was not statistically significant for any racial or gender subgroup, however, when controls were made for such factors as socioeconomic origin, age, income, occupational prestige, and marital status.

We interpret this finding as suggesting that graduating from college has only a trivial direct causal influence on overall subjective well-being. As with educational attainment generally, however, it is quite possible that being a college graduate indirectly enhances feelings of general well-being by improving one's socioeconomic circumstances. Still, the literature is largely silent with respect to the estimation of such an indirect influence.

The national surveys analyzed by Campbell (1981) and Glenn and Weaver (1981) are noteworthy in that they also asked individuals to report on different dimensions of life satisfaction or well-being: excitement in life, subjective health, and satisfaction with community, nonwork activities, family life, friendships, and health. Controlling for such factors as socioeconomic origin, age, income, occupational prestige, and marital status, Glenn and Campbell found that being a college graduate (versus a high school graduate) had few nontrivial effects on any of these different dimensions of perceived well-being. Out of twenty-eight possible regression coefficients, only three were statistically significant. Net of the factors listed above, being a college graduate had a significant positive direct effect on the subjective health of white men, the excitement in life of white women, and the satisfaction with friendships of black women. College graduation had only a trivial net impact on the various dimensions of well-being or satisfaction reported by black men.

Such findings are quite clear in suggesting that being a college graduate has only a very small and inconsistent impact on overall subjective well-being and the various dimensions that comprise it. As we have suggested above, part of this may be due to the fact that although a college degree may substantially enhance one's socioeconomic circumstances, this in itself may have only a partial and limited relationship with what constitutes life satisfaction or sense of well-being. In areas such as the fulfillment of occupational or economic aspirations, college graduates may have an advantage, but in domains such as the quality of friendships and perhaps family life, they probably do not (Campbell, 1981).

Another possible explanation for the findings is that one of the impacts of college is to foster a more critical perspective in individuals. Thus, as compared to those whose formal education ends with high school, college-educated individuals may simply be more sophisticated and critical in their judgments of life satisfaction. In this sense a college education probably works both for and against judgments of personal well-being. It clearly places individuals in advantaged positions with respect to income and job status, but it may also lead them to make more complex and critical judgments about the quality of their lives (Campell, 1981). Recall that we have offered a similar explanation for the absence of a strong link between postsecondary education and job satisfaction.

A final explanation is more methodological in nature. The measures of happiness or life satisfaction employed in the body of studies just reviewed tend to be based on rather general and perhaps superficial questionnaire or survey items. Consequently, they may not be particularly sensitive to the different ways in which happiness or life satisfaction can be defined by different groups of people. The important impact of college may not be that it makes the college educated distinguishable from those with less education on the same general continuum of happiness or life satisfaction. Instead, college may influence those who experience it to define happiness or life satisfaction and its attainment in fundamentally different ways than their noncollege counterparts.

Health

A substantial amount of research has addressed the link between educational attainment and health status (for example, Auster, Leveson, & Sarachek, 1969; Cobern, Salem, & Mushkin, 1973; Edwards & Grossman,

1979; Feldstein, 1979; Fuchs, 1974; Grossman, 1976; Grossman & Jacobowitz, 1981; Hinkle et al., 1968; Kitagawa & Hauser, 1973; Lee, 1982; Leigh,
1981; Orcutt, Franklin, Mendelsohn, & Smith, 1977; Rosensweig & Schultz,
1982). The general conclusion from this research is that amount of formal
education attained is positively and significantly linked to both individual
and family health and that at the aggregate level it is negatively related to
mortality (Haveman & Wolfe, 1984). Moreover, this link is apparently
nonspecious and persists even after controls are made for potential confounding influences.

Grossman (1976) presents what is perhaps the most compelling evidence for the net impact of postsecondary education on individual health
status in an analysis of forty-six-year-old men who were World War II veterans (the NBER-Thorndike data). Health status at age forty-six was based
on a rather complex scaling of the relationship between qualitative or perceived health and observed work weeks lost due to ill health (see Michael,
1982). With such factors as age, health status as a teenager, socioeconomic
origins, income, job satisfaction, intellectual ability, and a measure of obe-
sity held constant, each year of postsecondary education increased health
status at age forty-six by about 1 percent and decreased the probability of
death between ages thirty-two and forty-six by about 0.4 percent.[2, 3] Generally similar results with respect to postsecondary education and mortality
rate are reported by Kitagawa and Hauser (1973). Furthermore, net of many
of the same confounding influences (including income), findings consistent
with those of Grossman are reported in estimates of the net effect of educational attainment in general on various health indexes. These include the
positive impact of mother's educational attainment on children's health
(Edwards & Grossman, 1979; Grossman, 1982), the negative impact of
mother's education on infant mortality (Grossman & Jacobowitz, 1981), and
the negative influence of the educational level of one's state or county of
residence on mortality rate (Auster, Leveson, & Sarachek, 1969; Orcutt,
Franklin, Mendelsohn, & Smith, 1977).

Haveman and Wolfe (1984) have attributed the link between educational attainment and health to a number of factors. These include schooling's contributions to occupational and residential choices and health information acquisition. In terms of the acquisition of health information, the
findings of Hyman, Wright, and Reed (1975) indicate a clear positive association between education and the extent to which an individual stays informed about health matters. This could be expected to influence not only
health habits but also the use of health services. There is substantial evidence, for example, that college-educated individuals, as compared to those
with less formal education, are significantly less likely to smoke ("For Class
of '92, Less U.S. Aid," 1989; Hinkle et al., 1968; U.S. Bureau of Labor
Statistics, 1966) or to be obese (Hinkle et al., 1968).

More recent national evidence on education and smoking is dramatic. As of 1985 high school graduates were about 1.23 times as likely to smoke as those with some college and about 1.87 times as likely to smoke as college graduates (Pierce, Fiore, Novotny, Hatziandreu, & Davis, 1989). There is some question about the causal nature of this link in that differences in smoking prevalence are discernible before people complete their education. Adolescents who later go on to college smoke less than those who do not (Farrell & Fuchs, 1982; Johnson, O'Malley, & Bachman, 1987). At the same time, however, there is clear documentation between 1974 and 1985 that of those who actually smoked, college graduates were about twice as likely as high school graduates to have quit (Pierce, Fiore, Novothy, Hatziandreu, & Davis, 1989). Similarly, there is also clear and consistent evidence that college-educated individuals make more extensive use of health services than the less educated (Cobern, Salem, & Mushkin, 1973; Kukla, Veroff, & Douvan, 1979; Powers, 1976). Clearly, the link between educational attainment and use of health services could be a function of economic circumstances; yet at least some evidence suggests that the association persists even when income is held constant (U.S. Bureau of Labor Statistics, 1966, as reviewed in Bowen, 1977). It also appears that the negative link between education and smoking persists after income is controlled (U.S. Bureau of Labor Statistics, 1966).

Marriage

Although there is evidence that college-educated individuals marry at a somewhat later age than those with less education (for example, Berelson & Steiner, 1964) and that they are likely to choose mates with similar educational levels (for example, Fetters, 1975), it is not clear that educational attainment directly enhances marital stability or happiness. Analyses of national samples by Blood and Wolfe (1960) and Udry (1974) all report evidence to suggest a positive link between educational attainment and marital satisfaction or happiness. A more recent national study by Campbell, Converse, and Rodgers (1976), however, found that reported marital satisfaction actually varied inversely with amount of education among both husbands and wives. Glenn and Weaver (1978) found only a trivial relationship between education and marital happiness in three national surveys when statistical controls were introduced for such factors as age, age at first marriage, employment outside the home, and job prestige.

One possible explanation for these somewhat equivocal findings is that the relationship between educational attainment and marital happiness may be complex, with both positive and negative forces at work. By leading individuals to marry later in life and perhaps be more discriminating with respect to the overall compatibility of a spouse, schooling may, as suggested by Michael (1982, p. 137), facilitate "a more nearly optimal sorting of men and women in the marriage market." This should lead to increased marital happiness and stability. On the other hand, since one function of higher education is to increase sophistication of perspective and judgment, those with a college education may be more constrained than others in their expressions of marital happiness. Indeed, as indicated by Campbell (1981) in his analysis of successive national surveys, college-educated men and women are less likely than others to express either complete dissatisfaction or complete satisfaction with their marriages. Such responses would tend to suppress the magnitude of the association between educational attainment and marital happiness or satisfaction.

The question of whether or not educational attainment enhances actual marital stability has been addressed by Becker, Landes, and Michael (1977), who used a national sample of households interviewed in 1967. Controlling for such factors as current age, age at marriage, number of children, and earnings, these authors found that educational attainment had only a trivial and statistically nonsignificant direct influence on the stability of first or subsequent marriages. For men, however, educational attainment had a statistically significant direct effect on earnings that in turn had a statistically significant negative effect on the probability of divorce. Such evidence suggests that postsecondary education, while not affecting marital stability directly, nevertheless has a modest positive impact on it through indirect routes.

Attainment of Desired Family Size

Family size can have an important impact on the quality of family life in that, other things being equal, it has implications for the distribution of economic resources and parental care among children. From an economic perspective smaller families can permit a greater human capital investment in each offspring. As reported in the extensive reviews of Bowen (1977) and Haveman and Wolfe (1984), there is considerable evidence to indicate that educational attainment is negatively related to both desired and actual family size (for example, Becker, 1964; Easterlin, 1968, 1975; Michael, 1973; Mincer, 1974; Ryder & Westhoff, 1971; Willis, 1973). Moreover, this association persists even when controls are made for income and other family demographic characteristics (Michael, 1975b).

Bowen (1977) has suggested that one underlying reason for such findings is that more highly educated parents may have a greater interest than those with less education in placing a larger percentage of their financial resources and care into the rearing of each child. He also presents evidence from Gallup (1975a) to suggest that desire for smaller families may actually be an effect of college attendance. In cross-sectional comparisons of national samples of freshmen and seniors, Gallup found that seniors desired somewhat smaller families (2.3 children on the average) than freshmen (2.7 children on the average). As we have seen in previous chapters, however, there are some reasonable explanations for such differences other than college attendance. These include maturation and the natural attrition of students from freshman to senior year.

Quite apart from differences in desired and actual family size based on educational attainment, there is also a small body of evidence to suggest that educational attainment is positively linked to the effectiveness with which parents obtain their desired family size through fertility control (Haveman & Wolfe, 1984). Evidence from a number of studies, for example, has suggested that college-educated women are more likely than those with less education to use some form of contraception, to employ the most efficient contraceptive techniques, and to do so at an earlier age (for example, Freedman, Whelpton, & Campbell, 1959; Rosensweig & Seiver, 1980; Ryder & Westhoff, 1971; Whelpton, Campbell, & Patterson, 1966). Michael's (1973) analysis of the 1965 National Fertility Survey, moreover, provides some of the most compelling evidence that college-educated women tend to employ more effective forms of contraception than do women with lower educational attainment. Contraceptives marketed in the United States in the mid 1960s varied considerably in their efficiency in reducing the risk of unwanted conception. In Michael's study each contraceptive technique was scaled according to its average demonstrated effectiveness. Data analysis involved regressing the monthly probability of conception (based on the contraceptive technique used) on such factors as a woman's age, race, religion, educational attainment, and intended level of fertility. Net of other variables in the equation, educational attainment had a statistically significant negative effect on probability of conception (or, inversely, a positive effect on the efficiency of the contraceptive technique employed) for white non-Catholic women. Women who were high school graduates had a 1.5 year longer expected time to conception than women with a grade school education. In turn, college educated women had a 0.8 year longer expected time to conception than high school graduates (Michael, 1982).

Such findings, of course, might at least partially reflect the fact that women with different levels of education might also differ in the economic resources they can apply to the acquisition of differentially effective contraceptive devices.[4] Despite this possible limitation, however, Michael's (1973) analysis lends support to the hypothesis that higher education enhances one's proficiency in becoming informed about and evaluating new technologies. As a result, he or she is more likely than individuals with less education to adopt those technologies that are most effective and to use them correctly. In terms of the latter point, it should be stressed that the *absolute* effectiveness of many contraceptive techniques depends upon the care and regularity with which they are used (Michael, 1975b).

Nurturance of Children

If a basic reason underlying the smaller families of college-educated parents is their desire to place a greater human capital investment in each child, then we should expect college-educated parents to devote more time to their children than do parents with less education. With some possible exceptions (for example, Lindert, 1977), the weight of evidence from most time-use or time-budgeting studies would tend to confirm this expectation. Leibowitz (1974a, 1975), Morgan (1974), and Hill and Stafford (1974, 1977, 1980) present evidence from a number of national surveys to suggest that college-educated parents actually devote significantly more time to child care than do those with less education. For example, although Leibowitz (1975) found little difference between women with a high school education and college-educated women in the aggregate amount of time devoted to "home production" (cleaning, cooking, home maintenance, child care, and so on), she found sharp differences in the proportion of that time devoted to child care. College-educated women spent about 25 percent more time in child care than did women with less education, and the husbands of college-educated women spent between 30 and 40 percent more time in child care than did other husbands.

There is also evidence presented by Hill and Stafford (1980) that college-educated women spend more time than other women spend in preschool child-care activities that focus on learning and other experiences that enhance development. These include teaching, reading, talking, and transportation.[5] This finding holds even when a mother is working twenty hours or more per week. The implication here is that college-educated women may be more proficient in reallocating available time to child care. They may also, of course, have greater discretionary economic resources at their disposal that could be used to purchase services such as house cleaning that allow them more personal time for their children.

Qualitative differences in the child-care activities given priority by mothers with different educational attainment levels may at least partially explain the link between parental education and the cognitive development of young children. For example, Leibowitz (1977b), analyzing data pursuant to the evaluation of *Sesame Street,* sought to determine whether parental inputs accounted for children's cognitive development. Net of such factors as family size, socioeconomic status, race, language, work force participation of the mother, the presence of work-saving devices (dryer, dishwasher, and the like), and place of residence (inner city, suburban, rural), mother's level of education had a statistically significant positive effect on a measure of verbal development among children three to five years old. When child-care activities were introduced into the equation, however, one specific activity, namely, reading with the child, had a significant positive impact on verbal development. The introduction of child-care activities to the equation also reduced the effect of mother's education to statistical nonsignificance. The latter finding suggests that at least part of the impact of mother's education on the cognitive development of the child is through the indirect route of engaging the child in developmentally enriching activities.[6, 7]

In addition to qualitative and quantitative differences in the time spent with children, there is also evidence reviewed by Bowen (1977) to indicate that differences in educational attainment are associated with differences in the proportion of available income spent on developmentally oriented experiences or resources. As compared to those with less education, college-educated parents tend to spend relatively more of their income on such things as education (though not all of it for children), books, magazines, and other reading materials (Cobern, Salem, & Mushkin, 1973; Fetters, 1975). Furthermore, parents' own personal behavior would tend to reinforce their children's involvement in these experiences or use of these resources. Evidence based on a series of national surveys, for example, indicates that compared to those with less formal education, college-educated individuals are more likely to take an adult education course, read news magazines, read books, and have a library card. They are somewhat less likely to watch television daily (Hyman, Wright, & Reed, 1975; Powers, 1976). Such trends may have the aggregate effect of producing a more developmentally enriched home environment for children.

Consumer Behavior

There appear to be statistically significant differences in the allocation of consumer expenditures across different levels of education. Evidence reviewed by Bowen (1977) indicates that college-educated people are guided by somewhat different values in their consumption than individuals of equal income but less formal education. With income held constant, those with a college education spent a greater percentage of their income on housing, reading, and education but a lower percentage on food, clothing, alcohol, tobacco, and transportation (U.S. Bureau of Labor Statistics, 1966; Linden, 1967).

Beyond educational differences in consumer values, there may also be educational differences in efficiency in consumption. Perhaps the most informative and innovative study to address this issue has been conducted by Michael (1972, 1975a), who used the Bureau of Labor Statistics Consumer Expenditure Surveys of 1950 and 1960-1961. Michael hypothesized that formal education produces facts and ideas, the capacity to acquire new information and process it efficiently, and the ability to evaluate new ideas and technologies. As a result, people with more education should be able to make consumption choices more efficiently (that is, to require less time and resource costs). As succinctly described by Bowen (1977, p. 204), this hypothesis would be confirmed if "the consumption patterns of more-educated persons differed from those of less-educated persons (when incomes were equal) in the same way that consumption patterns of high-income persons differed from those with lower incomes (when level of education was equal). Additional education would then operate in the same way as additional income to achieve a higher standard of consumption."

To test this hypothesis, Michael (1972, 1975a) estimated the association between education and income elasticities for a range of consumption items (food, clothing, services, and so forth). An elasticity is essentially an unstandardized regression weight. Therefore, the education elasticity was the effect of increases in education on the amount of a particular item consumed (holding income constant), while the income elasticity was the effect of changes in income on the amount of a particular item consumed (holding education constant). The positive association found between the two sets of elasticities suggests that increased education shifts consumer budget allocations in much the same way as does income. Thus, increased education leads people to increase their consumer efficiency in the same way as if they had more income at their disposal.

The Michael (1972, 1975a) analyses are based on rather old data and as far as we know have not been replicated. Moreover, they do not speak directly to consumption differences between college-educated individuals and those with less formal education. Despite these limitations, the analyses nevertheless suggest that education may indeed function to enhance the efficiency and effectiveness with which individuals make consumer decisions.[8]

Savings and Investment Behavior

In Chapter Eleven we reviewed a substantial body of evidence indicating that having a college education is a strong determinant of one's income or earnings. There is also evidence to suggest that college-educated individuals are more likely than those with less education but similar income levels to save and invest in ways that enhance their future economic condition. Although this soil has been well tilled by Bowen (1977), Haveman and Wolfe (1984), and Michael (1982), a brief review of the evidence seems warranted.

An early investigation by Kosobud and Morgan (1964) indicated that net of an individual's income, education had a positive link with the percentage of income saved. Perhaps the most comprehensive and compelling evidence of the impact of higher education on saving and investment behavior has come from Solmon's (1975b) analyses of a national survey of families taken between 1957 and 1959. In Solmon's first set of analyses, he sought to determine whether educational level influences the percentage of income saved. Savings measures were regressed on such factors as family size, income after taxes, value of consumer durables purchased, age of family head, and wife's income and education. With controls in place for the other variables in the equation, the findings offer strong support for the expectation that those with more formal education tend to save more out of a given income than do those with less formal education. Net of other factors, those with a high school education or less had the lowest propensity to save out of income, those with at least one graduate degree had the highest, and groups with some college or four years of college fell in between. Although these trends held with both definitions of savings used, they were stronger with full savings than with marginal savings.[9]

A second set of analyses conducted by Solmon (1975b) sought to examine the relationship between educational attainment and a series of attitudes about savings objectives, efficiency in investment practices, and risk. Controlling for such factors as income, age, family size, and occupation, Solmon found that families with a high level of formal education as opposed to those with a relatively lower level were likely to place significantly more weight on long-term saving oriented toward child welfare (educating children, providing an inheritance, and the like) and significantly less on building up a business or providing for emergencies. Net of similar factors, educational attainment was also associated with an individual's perspectives on investment. When asked about their judgment as to the best investment hedges against inflation, college-educated individuals were less likely than those with less education to choose fixed income securities (such as savings accounts) and to avoid debt. However, they were more likely than the less educated to select the purchase of real or financial assets (stocks, real estate, mutual funds, and so forth). Solmon argues that these differences are not totally attributable to the greater willingness of college-educated individuals to incur higher risks for a higher yield. Rather, because the acquisition of real or financial assets is a better long-term hedge against inflation, the decision also reflects a more informed investment decision.[10]

On the basis of his aggregate findings, Solmon (1975b) concludes that the more highly educated were more willing to accept risk, more informed and rational in their approach to investments, and more likely (as evidenced in their savings behavior) to plan ahead with a long-term perspective. Of course, it might be a bit risky to attribute all of these traits to the college experience. The fact that those attending college are prepared to invest in tuition and forego earnings may mean that postsecondary education tends to attract individuals with a long-term horizon to begin with. College may function largely to enhance or accentuate this outlook by imparting cognitive and information-processing skills (Solmon, 1975b).

Leisure

It is quite clear that college graduates have different patterns of leisure activity than those with less formal education. These patterns have been reviewed succinctly by Bowen (1977, p. 208): "In their use of discretionary nonworking time, they [college graduates] tend to be less addicted to television than others and more selective in the programs they watch; they are more inclined to read, engage in adult education, attend cultural events, and participate in the arts; they are more interested in the pursuit of hobbies and other interests; they are more likely to take part in community and civic affairs; and they are more likely to take vacations (Powers, 1976; Baumol and Bowen, 1966; Cobern, Salem, and Mushkin, 1973; Morgan, Sirageldin, and Baerwaldt, 1966; Strumpel, 1976; Withey, 1971)."[11]

One potential confounding factor in these findings is income. College-educated individuals may be more likely than others to participate in many of these "meritorious" or cultured leisure activities (Lazear, 1977) because they are better able to acquire them. As suggested by Bowen (1977), however, as well as by our own reading of the studies he cites, the link between higher education and leisure activities remains even after controls are introduced for income. Even if this link cannot be accounted for by income, it is still risky to conclude that it is solely an effect of college attendance. The designs of the studies reviewed were typically not able to control for the very real possibility that college may tend to attract individuals with an orientation toward certain leisure activities (reading, cultural events, art, civic involvement) to begin with. College may function to accentuate these initial orientations and, by enhancing one's economic circumstances, even further increase the likelihood that they will be translated into behavior.

Summary

Subjective Well-Being

A substantial body of evidence from national samples indicates a small positive association between educational attainment and perceptions of global happiness, life satisfaction, or (as we have chosen to call it) subjective well-being. The direct causal effects of education on subjective well-being, however, are probably trivial; when controls are introduced for income and occupational status, the link between education and well-being becomes statistically nonsignificant. A similar conclusion is warranted for the specific impact of college on subjective well-being. When other factors are taken into account, college has little consistent direct effect on overall subjective well-being and the various dimensions that comprise it. One possible explanation for this finding is that there are socioeconomic and intellectual impacts associated with postsecondary education that work both for and against perceptions of subjective well-being or life satisfaction. On the one hand, a college education clearly provides socioeconomic advantages that positively influence some, though not all, of the elements of well-being. This influence may be manifest largely through indirect routes. On the other hand, one of the cognitive impacts of college is that it may lead individuals to make more complex and critical judgments about the quality of their lives. Another possible explanation is that college and noncollege groups may not differ on some general continuum of overall subjective well-being but rather may define subjective well-being and its attainment in different ways.

Health

Net of factors such as income, age, and prior health status, a college education appears to have a consistent positive impact on subsequent health status and a negative impact on probability of death during a given period of time. Such benefits are not just limited to individual health alone but appear to extend to other family members, including children. In addition to place of residence and occupational factors, one possible causal explanation for these findings is that college-educated people remain better informed about health care services. Evidence suggests that the latter trend holds irrespective of income.

Marriage

Evidence on the impact of postsecondary education on reported marital happiness is inconsistent. As with subjective well-being, inconsistencies may be attributable to the conflicting influence of education on expressed satisfaction with one's marital life. College-educated individuals marry later in life and may be more discriminating with respect to the overall compatibility of a spouse. Conversely, college may foster a more sophisticated and critical sense of judgment that makes individuals more circumscribed in their expressions of marital satisfaction.

We found little to suggest that educational attainment has other than a trivial direct impact on actual marital stability when background and demographic factors are taken into account. However, there is evidence, for men at least, that education may have a discernible positive indirect effect on marital stability through its substantial impact on earnings.

Family Size

There is consistent evidence that educational attainment is negatively linked to both desired and actual family size; and this association persists even when controls are made for income and other family demographic characteristics. College-educated couples appear to achieve smaller families, at least in part, through more effective fertility control. Net of other factors, they are not only more likely to use some form of contraception, but they are also more likely than those with less education to use more effective forms of contraception. Such evidence, although it may be partially confounded by variations in available economic resources, is consistent with the hypothesis that college-educated individuals are more proficient than others in evaluating new technologies and selecting the most effective ones.

Nurturance of Children

Several scholars have hypothesized that a basic reason underlying the smaller families of college-educated parents is their desire to place a greater human capital investment in each child. While it is difficult to attribute motivation, the weight of evidence we reviewed would tend to support this hypothesis. College-educated parents not only spend more nonwork time in child-care activities than do those with less education, but the time they spend is qualitatively different. Compared to those with less education, college-educated mothers spend more time with their preschool children in activities such as teaching, reading, talking, and transportation. There is additional evidence that qualitative differences in child-care activities associated with different levels of educational attainment may at least partially account for the positive link often found between parental, particularly mother's, education and the cognitive development of young children.

The designs of the studies we reviewed make it difficult to attribute quantitative and qualitative differences in child-care activities solely to the effect of college attendance. Part of the effect may be explained by economic resource differences that permit college-educated parents to purchase services that free up time for more developmentally oriented child-care activities. Irrespective of causal attribution, however, the developmental climate for a child in a home with college-educated parents is likely to be enriched even further by the fact that the child's parents spend a greater *percentage* of available income on developmentally oriented experiences or resources (education, books, magazines, and the like). These parents may also provide effective role models by being active users of these resources themselves.

Consumer Behavior

More highly educated people not only appear to be guided by different consumption values but also appear to be more efficient consumers than those with less formal education but equal income. Although the latter finding does not speak directly to the impact of college, it is of some importance in that it suggests that formal education may provide the information acquisition and processing skills that enable individuals to make more effective consumer decisions.

Savings and Investment Behavior

A small body of evidence suggests that college-educated individuals may be more efficient in their savings and investment behavior than those who are similar in income, family size, and other demographic characteristics but who have less formal education. Compared to the latter group, those with a college education save more out of a given income, place greater emphasis on long-term saving aimed at the future welfare of their children, and are more likely to choose investment options that are generally a better hedge against inflation even though they involve higher risk.

Leisure

The weight of evidence suggests that college-educated individuals are somewhat more cultured in their tastes for leisure activity. They are more likely than those with less formal education, for example, to read, engage in adult education, attend cultural or artistic events, and participate in civic or community affairs. They are somewhat less likely to watch television. In many of these areas such differences persist even when controls are made for income.

Causal Inference

It is important to point out that all of the "quality of life" outcomes synthesized in this chapter can be considered indicators of the long-term or enduring effects of college. Because of the intervening time period between college attendance and the measurement of specific outcomes, it is often difficult to make attributional statements about the direct impact of the college experience. We believe there are two possible reasons for this. First, it is likely that a substantial part of the impact of college on quality of life indexes is indirect. Specifically, college has a strong impact on the socioeconomic conditions of an individual's life. As such the college-educated person may have a greater pool of discretionary resources with which to acquire the products, services, and time linked to various quality of life indexes (better health, more effective fertility control, nurturant child care, cultured leisure).

It is also important to emphasize that although some studies find a significant link between college attendance (or educational attainment) and various quality of life indexes when income and other demographic characteristics are held constant, it is still risky to conclude that this reflects the impact of the college experience. With a few exceptions, such as health status, the studies synthesized in this chapter did not (or could not) control for various precollege attitudes, orientations, values, or cognitive functioning levels that might influence subsequent quality of life indexes. Consequently, what are interpreted as outcomes of the socialization occurring during college may in fact be at least partially due to differences in the background characteristics of those who attend and those who do not attend college.

A Final Thought

On the basis of much of the research reviewed in this chapter, one could argue that investigators have largely defined quality of life from a middle- or, perhaps, upper-middle-class perspective. Although health and subjective well-being probably cut across social class in terms of desirability, outcomes such as smaller families, a long-term perspective in investment and savings behavior, cultured leisure, and nurturant child-care activities such as reading, teaching, and transportation may be particularly important values of the American middle and upper-middle class. This is not to say that these values or outcomes are any less worthy than others. However, they are certainly not the only indexes by which one might define and assess the quality of life.

Notes

1. Several parts of this chapter draw substantially from existing literature reviews by Bowen (1977), Haveman and Wolfe (1984), and Michael (1982).
2. Grossman (1976) also provides evidence that wife's educational attainment enhances the current health status of her husband, net of his schooling, age, prior health, and earnings. One possible reason for this is that women have traditionally provided their families with medical care (Haveman & Wolfe, 1984; Sindelar, 1979). Thus, if schooling increases women's ability to acquire relevant health information and their inclination to use health care services, this benefit is likely to be passed on to family members.
3. Aside from the enjoyment of better health and a longer life expectancy as ends in themselves, higher education's impact on health may also have positive economic consequences in that those with a college education may be less likely to miss work because of ill health (Lando, 1975).
4. If increased economic resources permit women to acquire more effective contraceptive methods, then one could in fact argue that education has a potential indirect effect on adoption of effective contraception methods through its impact on income.
5. The notion of differences in time spent transporting children from place to place is interesting. As suggested by Hill and Stafford (1980) and also by Michael (1982), this could reflect differences in the provision of developmentally enriching experiences or a suburban residence. One cannot easily distinguish between these two causes from Hill and Stafford's data.
6. For additional evidence concerning the impact on early childhood cognitive development of parental interaction with children in the areas of

reading, writing, story telling, and specific instruction, see Leibowitz (1974b).

7. For other evidence pertaining to the net positive impact of parental education on the cognitive development of children, see Cobern, Salem, and Mushkin (1972); Leibowitz (1974b); Murnane (1981); Wolfle (1983); and Stariha (1989).

8. Consistent with the notion that the more highly educated are more proficient in their consumer behavior is the finding by Mandell (1972) that those with a college education are significantly more likely than those with less education to use credit cards. This association persists with a partial, though not complete, control for income. However, as Mandell points out, credit card companies actively solicit college graduates to make use of their cards. This confounds an interpretation of a more informed choice by college-educated people (Michael, 1982).

9. Full savings constituted net additions to business assets, postschool investments in human capital, and the value of durable consumer goods purchased. Marginal or conventional savings represented the change in financial assets and property other than housing minus change in debt not related to housing.

10. Consistent with the conclusion that better-educated people are more informed investors is evidence presented by Barlow, Brazer, and Morgan (1966), as reviewed in Bowen (1977), that such individuals also are more likely than those with less formal education to seek professional investment advice and to delegate management of their investments to asset managers. Of course, to the extent that they have higher earnings than others, college-educated people may be better able to pay for such services.

11. See also Guthrie, Seifert, and Kirsch (1986).

13

How College
Makes a Difference:
A Summary

How *does* college affect students? In responding to this question, we are reminded of a wonderful story told about Bernard Berelson (Menges, 1988). Berelson had published (with Gary Steiner) *Human Behavior: An Inventory of Scientific Findings* (1964) in which they synthesized over a thousand "verified generalizations" about human behavior. In reflecting on his work, Berelson is said to have offered three general conclusions (Menges suggests these were Berelson's "meta-findings"). Our conclusions about how college students change are the same as Berelson's about human change: "(1) some do, some don't; (2) the differences aren't very great; and (3) it's more complicated than that" (Menges, 1988, p. 259).

In the preceding ten chapters we have reviewed the evidence on a wide range of specific college outcomes. This chapter is our summary or, if you will, our own "meta-findings." It attempts a comprehensive synthesis of what we know about the impact of college on students; in short, it seeks to provide a general answer to this question: In what areas and through what kinds of conditions, activities, and experiences does college affect students?

In shaping this global synthesis we employ a somewhat different organizational framework than that used in Chapters Three through Twelve. In each of those chapters the evidence pertaining to a specific category of outcome (for example, learning, moral development, psychosocial development) was, where appropriate, summarized across six fundamental questions: (1) Do students change during the college years, and if so, how much and in what directions? (this is the "change" question); (2) To what extent are these changes attributable to college attendance as distinct from other sources, such as normal maturation or noncollege experiences? (the "net effects" question); (3) Are these changes differentially related to the kind of institution attended? (the "between-college effects" question); (4) Are these changes related to differences in students' experiences on any given campus? (the "within-college effects" question); (5) Are these changes differentially related to students' characteristics? (the "conditional effects" question); and (6) Is college's influence durable? (the "long-term effects" question).

In the present chapter, this organizational framework is inverted. Here we synthesize the evidence that addresses each of the six fundamental questions posed by the book across the various outcome categories. This will provide a somewhat different perspective than preceding chapters have given in that the focal emphasis will be on the various impacts of college on a broad spectrum of outcomes rather than on how a specific category of outcome may be influenced by various elements of the college experience.

In addition to the main objective of providing a comprehensive summary of major conclusions, this chapter also does some other things. First, it attempts, where possible, to draw comparisons between our conclusions and the major conclusions of previous comprehensive syntheses of the impact of college on students, primarily the work of Feldman and Newcomb (1969) and Bowen (1977). Second, where possible, it tries to articulate the extent to which the evidence is supportive of the major theses or models of student development and the impact of college. Finally, the chapter suggests important areas for future research and comments on methods of inquiry that may be most useful in increasing our understanding of the impact of college.

Change During College

Consistent with the composite findings of Feldman and Newcomb (1969) and Bowen (1977), our synthesis of the evidence indicates that the college years are a time of student change on a broad front. A number of the shifts we observed appear to be fairly substantial in magnitude. Indeed, the changes that occur during college from freshman to senior year are generally the largest "effects" we noted in our synthesis. It is the breadth of change and development, however, that is perhaps the most striking characteristic of the evidence. Students not only make statistically significant gains in factual knowledge and in a range of general cognitive and intellectual skills; they also change on a broad array of value, attitudinal, psychosocial, and moral dimensions. There is some modest tendency for changes in intellectual skills to be larger in magnitude than changes in other areas, but the evidence is quite consistent in indicating that the changes coincident with the college years extend substantially beyond cognitive growth. Thus, the change that occurs during the college years does not appear to be concentrated in a few isolated areas. Rather, the research portrays the college student as changing in an integrated way, with change in any one area appearing to be part of a mutually reinforcing network or pattern of change in other areas. Such a tendency in the evidence is generally consistent with the theoretical models of Chickering (1969) and Heath (1968), both of whom envision maturation during college as holistic in nature and embracing many facets of individual change.

There are some very clear directions to this overall pattern of change in college. The nature of the changes that occur and our best estimates of their average magnitude are shown in Tables 13.1 through 13.4. We turn now to a brief summary of those changes.

Learning and Cognitive Change

As shown in Table 13.1, students make gains from freshman to senior year on a variety of different dimensions of learning and cognition. Modest advances are evidenced in general verbal and quantitative skills, and fairly substantial advances are demonstrated in knowledge of the specific subject matter related to one's major field of study. These conclusions, particularly the latter, are not very surprising. Indeed, more surprising would be the discovery that such changes did *not* occur during college. Less intuitively obvious, perhaps, are the gains that students make on a range of general intellectual competencies and skills that may be less directly or explicitly tied to a college's formal academic program. Compared to freshmen, seniors are not only more effective speakers and writers, they are also more intellectually advanced. This intellectual change includes an improved ability to reason abstractly or symbolically and to solve problems or puzzles within a scientific paradigm, an enhanced skill in using reason and evidence

Table 13.1. Summary of Estimated Freshman-to-Senior *Changes: Learning and Cognitive Development.*

	Estimated Magnitude of Change	
Outcome	Effect Size [a]	Percentile Point Difference [b]
General verbal skills	.56	21
General quantitative skills	.24	10
Specific subject matter knowledge	.84	31
Oral communication skills	.60	22
Written communication skills	.50	19
Piagetian (formal) reasoning	.33	13
Critical thinking	1.00	34
Use of reason and evidence to address ill-structured problems (reflective judgment, informal reasoning)	1.00	34
Ability to deal with conceptual complexity	1.20	38

[a] Effect size = (senior mean minus freshman mean) divided by freshman standard deviation.

[b] Effect size converted to the equivalent percentile point under the normal curve. This is the percentile point difference between the freshman- and senior-year means when the freshman mean is set at the 50th percentile.

to address issues and problems for which there are no verifiably correct answers, an increased intellectual flexibility that permits one to see both the strengths and weaknesses in different sides of a complex issue, and an increased capacity for cognitively organizing and manipulating conceptual complexity.

It is likely that gains in college on such dimensions as abstract reasoning, critical thinking, reflective judgment, and intellectual and conceptual complexity also make the student more functionally adaptive. That is, other things being equal, this enhanced repertoire of intellectual resources permits the individual to adapt more rapidly and efficiently to changing cognitive and noncognitive environments. Put another way, the individual becomes a better learner. It is in this area, we believe, that the intellectual development coincident with college has its most important and enduring implications for the student's postcollege life.

Attitudes and Values

Table 13.2 shows our estimates of the typical freshman-to-senior changes during college in the general area of values and attitudes. A number of these changes are quite consistent with the changes noted in the area of learning and cognitive development. Students not only become more cognitively advanced and resourceful, but they also make gains in their aesthetic, cultural, and intellectual sophistication, gains that are complemented by increased interests and activities in such areas as art, classical music, reading, and creative writing; discussion of philosophical and historical issues; and the humanities and performing arts. Similarly, there are clear gains in the importance students attach to liberal education and exposure to new ideas. In short, the enhancement of cognitive skills during college appears to be concurrent with an increased valuing of and interest in art, culture, and ideas.

If one theme underlying changes in values and attitudes during college is that they tend to be supportive of or at least consistent with observed changes in cognitive growth, a second theme is that the changes also coalesce around a general trend toward liberalization. Considering consistent changes in the areas of sociopolitical, religious, and gender role attitudes and values, it would appear that there are unmistakable and sometimes substantial freshman-to-senior shifts toward openness and a tolerance for diversity, a stronger "other-person orientation," and concern for individual rights and human welfare. These shifts are combined with an increase in liberal political and social values and a decline in both doctrinaire religious beliefs and traditional attitudes about gender roles. The clear movement in this liberalization of attitudes and values is away from a personal perspective characterized by constraint, narrowness, exclusiveness, simplicity, and

Table 13.2. Summary of Estimated Freshman-to-Senior *Changes: Attitudes and Values.*

| | Estimated Magnitude of Change | | |
Outcome	Effect Size[a]	Percentile Point Difference[b]	Percentage Point Difference Between Freshmen & Seniors[c]
Aesthetic, cultural, and intellectual values	.25–.40	10–15	
Value placed on liberal education			+20 to +30%
Value placed on education as vocational preparation			−10 to −30%
Value placed on intrinsic occupational rewards			+12%
Value placed on extrinsic occupational rewards			−10 to −15%
Altruism, social and civic conscience, humanitarianism	.10–.50	4–19	+ 2 to + 8%
Political and social liberalism	.20	8	+15 to +25%
Civil rights and liberties			+ 5 to +25%
Religiosity, religious affiliation	−.49	19 (in religiosity)	Up to −11% in conventional religious preferences
Traditional views of gender roles			−10 to −25%

[a]Effect size = (senior mean minus freshman mean) divided by freshman standard deviation.

[b]Effect size converted to the equivalent percentile point under the normal curve. This is the percentile point difference between the freshman- and senior-year means when the freshman mean is set at the 50th percentile.

[c]Percentage point increase or decrease of seniors (versus freshmen) holding a particular view or position.

intolerance and toward a perspective with an emphasis on greater individual freedom, breadth, inclusiveness, complexity, and tolerance.

A third unifying thread that characterizes attitude and values change during college is a shift away from the instrumental or extrinsic values of education and occupation toward a higher valuing of intrinsic rewards. Compared to freshmen, seniors attach greater importance to the value of a liberal education and less importance to the value of a college education as vocational preparation. Consistently, seniors (as compared to freshmen) also place greater value on the intrinsic characteristics of a job (intellectual challenge, autonomy, and so forth) and less value on extrinsic rewards (salary, job security, and the like).

At first glance such changes may seem inconsistent with what was clearly an increasing trend between 1970 and 1985 toward vocationalism or materialism in the reasons underlying an individual's decision to attend college (Astin, Green, & Korn, 1987). The motivation for attending college and the changes that occur during college, however, may be largely independent of each other. Thus, even if succeeding cohorts of recent freshmen have increasingly chosen to attend college for its instrumental or extrinsic returns, it would still appear that the freshman-to-senior changes that occur during college lead to an increased value being placed on the nonvocational aspects of one's educational experience and the intrinsic rewards of one's prospective work.

Psychosocial Changes

The motif noted earlier of the interrelatedness of student change during the college years is apparent in the several areas of student psychosocial change summarized in Table 13.3. While the changes in these areas are, on the whole, more modest than those relating to learning and cognitive development, they are approximately the same size as the shifts in attitudes and values. Moreover, their general character and direction are clearly

Table 13.3. Summary of Estimated Freshman-to-Senior *Changes: Self and Relational Systems in Psychosocial Development.*

	Estimated Magnitude of Change		
Outcome	Effect Size[a]	Percentile Point Difference[b]	Percentage Point Difference Between Freshmen & Seniors[c]
Self Systems			
Identity status			+15 to +25% (in reaching identity achievement status)
Ego development	.50	19	
Self-concept			
Academic			+4 to +14% (rating self "above avg.")
Social			+7% (rating self "above avg.")
Self-esteem	.60	23	
Relational Systems			
Autonomy, independence, and locus of control	.36	14	
Authoritarianism	−.81	29	
Ethnocentrism	−.45	17	
Intellectual orientation	.30	12	
Interpersonal relations	.16	6	
Personal adjustment and psychological well-being	.40	16	
Maturity and general personal development	Not available		

[a] Effect size = (senior mean minus freshman mean) divided by freshman standard deviation.

[b] Effect size converted to the equivalent percentile point under the normal curve. This is the percentile point difference between the freshman- and senior-year means when the freshman mean is set at the 50th percentile.

[c] Percentage point increase or decrease of seniors (versus freshmen) holding a particular view or position.

consistent with those of the other two areas. Gains in various kinds of substantive knowledge and in cognitive competence may provide both a basis and the intellectual tools for students to examine their own identities, self-concepts, and the nature of their interactions with their external world.

Thus, perhaps as a partial consequence of their cognitive gains, students appear to move toward greater self-understanding, self-definition, and personal commitment, as well as toward more refined ego functioning. Similarly, students' academic and social self-images, as well as their self-esteem, while perhaps somewhat bruised initially, not only recover but become more positive over the college years.

The psychosocial changes experienced during the college years extend beyond the inner world of the self to include the relational aspects of students' lives: the manner in which they engage and respond to other people and to other aspects of their external world. As students become better learners, they also appear to become increasingly independent of parents (but not necessarily of peers), gain in their sense that they are in control of their world and what happens to them, and become somewhat more mature in their interpersonal relations, both in general and in their intimate relations with others, whether of the same or opposite sex. They also show modest gains in their general personal adjustment, sense of psychological well-being, and general personal development and maturity. Moreover, consistent with the observed shifts toward greater openness in attitudes and values, the evidence quite consistently indicates that students gain in their general intellectual disposition or orientation toward their world, their willingness to challenge authority, their tolerance of other people and their views, their openness to new ideas, and their ability to think in nonstereotypic ways about others who are socially, culturally, racially, or ethnically different from them.

Moral Development

As suggested in Table 13.4, there is clear and consistent evidence that students make statistically significant gains during college in the use of principled reasoning to judge moral issues. This finding holds across different measurement instruments and even different cultures. The absence of descriptive statistics in much of the evidence, however, makes it difficult if not impossible to estimate with confidence the magnitude of the freshman-to-senior change in the same way that we have done for other outcomes. As we have stressed in Chapter Eight on moral development, the magnitude of the freshman-to-senior gain may not be as important as the fact that the major shift during college is from conventional to postconventional or principled judgment. (The former is based strongly on morality as obedience to rules and meeting the expectations of those in authority, while the latter is based strongly on a view of morality as a set of universal

Table 13.4. Summary of Estimated Freshman-to-Senior *Changes: Moral Development.*

	Estimated Magnitude of Change		
Outcome	Effect Size[a]	Percentile Point Difference[b]	Percentage Point Difference Between Freshmen & Seniors[c]
Use of principled reasoning in judging moral issues	Difficult to estimate magnitude of effect, but major change during college is from the use of "conventional" to "postconventional" or "principled" reasoning		

[a]Effect size = (senior mean minus freshman mean) divided by freshman standard deviation.

[b]Effect size converted to the equivalent percentile point under the normal curve. This is the percentile point difference between the freshman- and senior-year means when the freshman mean is set at the 50th percentile.

[c]Percentage point increase or decrease of seniors (versus freshmen) holding a particular view or position.

principles of social justice existing independently of societal codification.) This shift in and of itself represents a major event in moral development.

The freshman-to-senior changes in moral judgment noted in our synthesis are perhaps another example of how change during college on one dimension is typically consistent with change in other areas. Measures of moral reasoning are themselves positively correlated not only with areas of general cognitive development that increase during college (such as abstract reasoning, critical thinking, and reflective judgment) but also with the general liberalization of personality and value structures coinciding with college attendance (for example, decreases in authoritarianism or dogmatism; increases in autonomy, tolerance, and interpersonal sensitivity; increased concern for the rights and welfare of others). Thus, the enhancement of principled moral judgment during college is embedded within an interconnected and perhaps mutually reinforcing network of cognitive, value, and psychosocial changes that occur at approximately the same time.

Some Final Thoughts on Change During College

Our conclusions about the changes that occur during college differ in only minor ways from those of Feldman and Newcomb (1969) and Bowen (1977). Indeed, taken as a total body of evidence, all three syntheses suggest that a reasonably consistent set of cognitive, attitudinal, value, and psychosocial changes have occurred among college students over the last four or five decades. Students learn to think in more abstract, critical, complex, and reflective ways; there is a general liberalization of values and attitudes combined with an increase in cultural and artistic interests and activities; progress is made toward the development of personal identities and more positive self-concepts; and there is an expansion and extension of interpersonal horizons, intellectual interests, individual autonomy, and general psychological maturity and well-being. Thus, it can be said that the nature and direction of freshman-to-senior changes appear to be reasonably stable and to some extent predictable.

In some instances our estimate of the *magnitude* of freshman-to-senior changes differs from estimates of previous syntheses, particularly Bowen's (1977). Since the differences are quite modest, however, we are inclined to attribute them to chance variations in the bodies of literature reviewed and perhaps even different typologies or operational definitions of outcomes. At any rate, it would seem that the consistency in the nature and direction of changes across syntheses is a much more salient and noteworthy characteristic of the evidence than are small differences in estimates of the magnitude of the changes across the same syntheses.

It may also be the case that the absolute magnitude of freshman-to-senior changes is not as educationally important as either the qualitative nature or the breadth and scope of the changes. One danger in focusing on quantitative estimates of change such as effect size is that one tends to consider change as happening on a continuum where all change is smoothly continuous and equally important. Many developmental theorists would argue that development does not always happen in such even and equivalent fashion (for example, Kitchener & King, 1990; Kohlberg, 1969; Perry, 1970; Rest, 1986b). Moreover, not all changes are equivalent in size or importance: Some shifts are particularly critical to development irrespective of whether or not they are reflected in a large quantitative change on some continuous scale. For example, the qualitative shift during college from a style of reasoning based on beliefs to one relying on evidence in making judgments represents a key prerequisite to rational problem solving. Similarly, the shift from conventional to principled reasoning during college represents a major qualitative advance in moral development. On both of these dimensions of development, the qualitative nature of the change is likely to be of greater consequence than the magnitude of the change.

We would also suggest that the magnitude of change on any particular dimension or set of dimensions during college may not be as significant as the pronounced breadth of interconnected changes we noted in our synthesis. As posited by major models of student development (for example, Chickering, 1969; Heath, 1968), the evidence indicates not only that individuals change on a broad developmental front during college but also that the changes are of a mutually consistent and supporting nature. Although there may be insufficient empirical grounds to speak of changes in one area causing or permitting changes in other areas, it is clear from the body of evidence we reviewed that the changes coincident with college attendance involve the whole person and proceed in a largely integrated manner. Certainly the notion of broad-based integrative change during college is not a new finding, but the evidence we reviewed was sufficiently compelling to warrant its reaffirmation.

There are, of course, at least three nontrivial problems endemic to the study of freshman-to-senior change. The first stems from the fact that the evidence is based largely on studies measuring typical or average change in some sample (longitudinal studies) or typical or average differences between samples (cross-sectional studies). By focusing on average group shifts or differences, the findings of such studies tend to mask individual differences in patterns of change. Some students may change substantially during college, some may change little or not at all, and some may actually shift in a direction counter to the typical movement of the group. Moreover, some students may change in one way on certain variables and in opposite ways on other variables. Thus, although the average change may be our best estimate of the dominant shift or development occurring in a group, it is not without limitations.

A second problem, one that we have emphasized throughout the book, is that freshman-to-senior change during college does not necessarily reflect the impact of college. Many of the dimensions on which change occurs during college may have a developmental base. If so, this means that individuals tend to exhibit more sophisticated levels of development through the process of maturation or simply growing older. Consequently, similar individuals not attending college might well change in essentially the same ways as college students over the same time period. In the absence of a control group of noncollege attenders (a typical weakness in most studies of change during college), it is essentially impossible to separate the changes due to college attendance from those attributable to natural maturation.

The focus on change during college as an indication of college impact can also be misleading in another way. Just as the presence of change does not necessarily indicate the impact of college, so too the absence of change does not necessarily indicate the absence of college impact. One important consequence of college attendance may be to fix development at a certain level and prevent reversion or regression (Feldman & Newcomb, 1969). If such were the case on a specific trait, little or no freshman-to-senior change would be noted. Those not attending college, however, might well regress or change in a negative direction. We will see an example of this as we turn to a summary of the net effects of college.

Finally, it is important to differentiate change from development. Whereas *change* simply means that some fact or condition at $Time_2$ is different from what it was at $Time_1$, *development* implies ordered, predictable, even hierarchical shifts or evolution have taken place in fundamental, intra-individual structures or processes. In many areas of observed change during college, it is tempting simply to conclude that observed change reflects some form of internal growth or development in the individual, that an inner restructuring has taken place, and that the senior is functioning with an advanced set of inner rules or perspectives not present in the typical freshman. This is a particular temptation when the changes that occur are consistent with those posited by developmental models or theories. The danger inherent in this assumption is that what we commonly refer to as development may in large measure be the result of an individual's response to the anticipated norms of new social settings or social roles. Different categories of people may be socialized to think and behave differently in society, and a substantial part of this categorization may have its basis in educational level. Thus, for example, college-educated men and women may have certain psychosocial traits and values and may think about controversial issues in certain ways not necessarily because of some inner developmental restructuring but because they have been socialized to behave and think in ways consistent with dominant cultural norms for educated adults.

This is not to say that the changes that occur during college merely represent the learning of social or cultural norms instead of important developmental steps. Rather, it is to suggest that we need to be wary of the tendency to equate the learning of social or cultural norms with development. It behooves us to bear in mind that change during the college years is produced by multiple influences, some internal (and perhaps ontogenetic) and others external to the individual. Theories can overly restrict as well as focus vision.

Net Effects of College

Because self-selection, as opposed to random assignment, determines who attends and who does not attend college, studies that seek to estimate the unique or net impact of college (as distinct from normal maturation, mere aging, or other noncollege sources of change) employ some rather creative research designs or, more typically, statistical controls. Although the causal inferences one can make from such studies are not of the same order of certitude as those made from randomized experiments, we can nevertheless arrive at a reasonably valid set of tentative conclusions about the changes or outcomes observed that are attributable to college attendance and not to rival explanations. It is worth recalling, however, that change during the college years involves a complex, weblike network. Change in one area may cause or be accompanied by change in other areas as well. Given this interrelatedness, estimates of change and of college's net effect in each discrete area no doubt understate college's overall, cumulative impact.

Tables 13.5 through 13.8 array those dimensions on which the weight of evidence offers support for claims about college's unique or net impact. (When we use the term *unclear* in the column reporting the magnitude of net effects in this and all subsequent tables in the chapter, we are acknowledging that the studies do not allow such estimates or that the evidence, though generally consistent, is still sufficiently complex to make an estimate of effect size hazardous.) As Tables 13.5 through 13.8 show, we judge the evidence on net impact to be more compelling for some outcomes than for others. Specifically, there is more extensive and consistent evidence to support the net impact of college on learning and cognition, moral reasoning, and career and economic returns than in the areas of attitudes, values, and psychosocial characteristics. This does not necessarily mean that college has a stronger impact on the former outcomes than on the latter ones. Indeed, we had a difficult time estimating the magnitude of the net impact of college in nearly all areas of our synthesis. Some of these differences could be more a reflection of variations in the extent and quality of the available evidence across different areas of inquiry than of major differences in the actual impact of college. More likely, they are real. It would probably be unreasonable to expect uniform changes across substantive areas. Students vary considerably in the characteristics they bring with them to college, not only in a wide variety of personal, educational, and family background traits but also in their readiness and capacity for change. Moreover, higher educational institutions do not invest their energies and resources equally across areas of change.

Learning and Cognitive Changes

Table 13.5 shows those learning and cognitive development outcomes that the weight of evidence suggests are significantly influenced by college attendance. Perhaps the clearest generalization to be made from this evidence is that on nearly all of the dimensions on which we find freshman-to-senior change, a statistically significant part of that change is attributable to college attendance, not to rival explanations. College not only appears to enhance general verbal and quantitative skills as well as oral and written communication, but it also has a statistically significant positive net effect on general intellectual and analytical skills, critical thinking, the use of reason and evidence in addressing ill-structured problems, and intellectual flexibility. These effects cannot be explained away by maturation or differences between those who attend and those who do not attend college in intelligence, academic ability, or other precollege characteristics.

These conclusions about the net effects of college on learning and cognitive development are limited by those dimensions that individual scholars have chosen to investigate. It is perhaps useful to think of these dimensions of net college effects as analogous to geological probes designed to define the nature and extent of mineral or oil deposits. They sample and begin to define the boundaries, but they may not capture the fullness of the phenomenon being measured. From this perspective, it is reasonable to conclude that college attendance positively influences a wide range of cognitive skills and intellectual functioning. The existing research, however,

Table 13.5. Summary of Estimated *Net* Effects of College: *Learning and Cognitive Development*.

Outcome	Strength of Evidence	Direction of Effect	Major Rival Explanations Controlled	Magnitude of Net Effect
General verbal skills	Strong	Positive	Precollege verbal skills, race, socioeconomic status	.26 to .32 SD (10 to 13 percentile point advantage)
General quantitative skills	Strong	Positive	Precollege quantitative skills, race, socioeconomic status	.29 to .32 SD (11 to 13 percentile point advantage)
Oral communication skills	Moderate	Positive	Age, academic ability	Unclear[a]
Written communication skills	Moderate	Positive	Age, academic ability	Unclear
General intellectual and analytical skill development	Moderate	Positive	Age, verbal ability, quantitative ability	Community college graduates higher than incoming freshmen; magnitude of effect unclear
Critical thinking	Strong	Positive	Precollege critical thinking, academic aptitude, socioeconomic status, educational aspirations	Freshman-year net effect, .44 SD (17 percentile point advantage); magnitude of net four-year effect unclear
Use of reason and evidence to address ill-structured problems (reflective judgment, informal reasoning)	Moderate to strong	Positive	Age, academic ability	Unclear
Intellectual flexibility	Moderate to strong	Positive	Age, intelligence, academic aptitude	Unclear

[a]"Unclear," as used in this table, means we are acknowledging that the studies do not allow such estimates or that the evidence, though generally consistent, is still sufficiently complex to make an estimate of effect size hazardous.

probably provides only a rough outline of the types of learning and cognitive development enhanced by college without necessarily tapping the full range or richness of effects.

As briefly alluded to in the previous section on change during college, research on college's net effects illustrates the potentially misleading nature of change. The net positive effect of college on general quantitative skills, for example, occurred not because students who attended college made greater gains than those who did not attend. Instead, the effect was largely attributable to the fact that college attendance tended to anchor quantitative skills at precollege levels while those not attending college actually regressed. Thus, an important net effect of college may be to stabilize an individual's development on certain dimensions and to prevent the regressions that might occur in the absence of college attendance.

Attitudes and Values

Evidence concerning the net impact of college on attitudes and values is summarized in Table 13.6. Although the weight of this evidence is not totally consistent and certainly not without rival explanations, it nevertheless suggests that a statistically significant, if modest, part of the broad-based attitudinal and value changes that occur during college can be attributed to the college experience. Perhaps of equal importance, the net effects of college, particularly in the areas of social, political, and sex role values, appear not to be simple reflections of trends in the larger society across the last two decades. Rather, college attendance seems to have an impact on attitudes and values in these areas, an impact that is generally consistent both within and across age cohorts.

This is not to say that what occurs during college happens in total isolation from cultural and social forces. Clearly, student values are significantly affected by those dominant in society, and general societal changes make unambiguous attributions of change to college more difficult. Nevertheless, college attendance would appear to influence political, social, and gender role attitudes and values in consistent ways regardless of cultural and societal trends.

A note of caution needs to be made with respect to this conclusion, because there is some evidence to suggest that recent college effects on social and political values may be less pronounced than earlier studies have indicated. Whether this is a chance fluctuation or the precursor of an important generational effect, however, awaits replication of the findings on future samples.

Psychosocial Changes

Table 13.7 summarizes the evidence relating to college's psychosocial net effects. As can be seen there, virtually nothing can be said with confi-

Table 13.6. Summary of Estimated _Net_ Effects of College: _Attitudes and Values._

Outcome	Strength of Evidence	Direction of Effect	Major Rival Explanations Controlled	Magnitude of Net Effect[a]
Aesthetic, cultural, and intellectual values	Moderate	Positive	Age, gender, religion, socioeconomic status, residential origin	Unclear[a]
Value placed on liberal education	Strong	Positive	Aptitude, race, gender, family socioeconomic status, precollege values	Graduates two to three times more likely to value education than are people with less education
Value placed on education as vocational preparation	Moderate	Negative	Aptitude, occupation, interaction thereof	Unclear
Value placed on intrinsic occupational rewards	Strong	Positive	Gender, race, socioeconomic status, job characteristics	Unclear, probably small
Value placed on extrinsic occupational rewards	Strong	Negative	Gender, race, socioeconomic status, job characteristics	Small
Social liberalism	Weak	Positive	Gender, race, age, religion, socioeconomic status, residential origin, cohort, aging and period effects	Unclear
Political liberalism	Strong	Positive	Gender, race, age, religion, socioeconomic status, residential origin, cohort, aging and period effects	Unclear
Civil rights and liberties	Mixed	Positive	Age, income, socioeconomic status, religion	Unclear, probably small
Secularism	Weak	Positive	Gender, race, initial religious attitudes	Unclear
Gender roles (toward the "modern")	Strong	Positive	Initial gender role values, gender, age, race, income, religion, marital status, work history, number of children, period and cohort effects	Unclear

[a]"Unclear," as used in this table, means we are acknowledging that the studies do not allow such estimates or that the evidence, though generally consistent, is still sufficiently complex to make an estimate of effect size hazardous.

Table 13.7. Summary of Estimated *Net* Effects of College: *Psychosocial Development*.

Outcome	Strength of Evidence	Direction of Effect	Major Rival Explanations Controlled	Magnitude of Net Effect
Identity and ego development	Very weak	Positive	Few	Unknown
Self-concept: Academic	Strong	Positive	Gender, race, prior achievement, socioeconomic status, degree aspirations	Small, indirect
Self-concept: Social	Strong	Positive	Gender, race, prior achievement, socioeconomic status, degree aspirations	Small, indirect
Self-concept: Self-esteem	Strong	Positive	Ability, achievement, socioeconomic status, race, precollege self-esteem	Small
Autonomy, independence, and internal locus of control	Weak to moderate (strong for locus of control)	Positive	Ability, socioeconomic status, precollege locus of control	Unclear[a] (small for locus of control)
Authoritarianism, dogmatism, and ethnocentrism	Moderate	Negative	Gender, ability, socioeconomic status	Unclear
Intellectual orientation	Moderate	Positive	Gender, ability, socioeconomic status	Unclear
Interpersonal relations	Weak	Mixed	None	Unclear
Personal adjustment and psychological well-being	Strong	Positive	Socioeconomic status, family situation, religiosity	Small
Maturity and general personal development	No evidence	Unknown	None	Unclear

[a] "Unclear," as used in this table, means we are acknowledging that the studies do not allow such estimates or that the evidence, though generally consistent, is still sufficiently complex to make an estimate of effect size hazardous.

dence about the net effects of college on changes in students' identity statuses or their stages of ego development. The research literature simply does not deal with the effects of college in these areas in any methodologically rigorous or generalizable way. The vast majority of studies are concerned with structural rather than process questions, with whether hypothesized statuses or stages exist and the characteristics of the individuals at any given stage rather than with the variables (including education) that influence status or stage change. Where change is examined, educational and age or maturational effects remain confounded.

Persuasive evidence exists to indicate that college attendance is reliably and positively related to increases in students' academic and social self-concepts, as well as their self-esteem. After holding constant a variety of relevant precollege characteristics, educational attainment is consistently and positively related to increases in students' perceptions of themselves relative to their peers in both academic areas (for example, writing and mathematical abilities, general academic abilities, intellectual self-confidence) and social areas (leadership abilities, popularity in general and with the opposite sex, general social self-confidence, and the like). Net college effects are also apparent in the increases students experience in their self-esteem: the general regard in which they hold themselves and their abilities, the extent to which they consider themselves to be capable, significant, worthy, or of value. After precollege self-concepts or self-esteem and other background characteristics have been controlled, however, college's effects in each of these areas appear to be small. Moreover, college's influence on students' self-concepts appears to be *indirect* rather than direct, being mediated through certain characteristics students bring with them to college and through the kinds of academic and interpersonal experiences they have once on campus.

The net effects of college on changes in the ways students relate to people, institutions, and conditions in their external world are somewhat less limited. Consistent with the net gains made in cognitive areas, we can attribute to college (with moderate to considerable confidence) declines in authoritarianism and dogmatism and increases in students' internal sense (locus) of control, intellectual orientation, personal adjustment, and general psychological well-being. College's contributions to the declines in authoritarianism and dogmatism appear to be strong, but its effects in the other areas are much more modest, even small. Because of methodological limitations, however, few claims (if any) can be made with confidence about college's net effects on changes in students' levels of autonomy or independence, the maturity of their interpersonal relations, or their overall maturity and personal development.

Moral Development

Table 13.8 reveals that college has a net positive effect on the use of principled reasoning in judging moral issues. This effect holds even when controls are made for maturation and for differences between those who attend and those who do not attend college in level of precollege moral reasoning, intelligence, and socioeconomic status. The net impact of college on actual moral behavior is less clear. On the basis of a synthesis of two separate bodies of research, however, we hypothesize a positive indirect effect. College enhances the use of principled moral reasoning, which in turn is positively linked to a variety of principled actions. These include resistance to cheating, social activism, keeping contractual promises, and helping behavior. The acceptance of this hypothesis is tentative, however, and awaits fuller empirical support.

Long-Term Effects of College

Nearly all of the considerable body of research on the long-term effects of college is concerned with estimating the enduring impact of attending versus not attending college. Consequently, it has much in common, both conceptually and methodologically, with research that attempts to estimate the net effects of college. Indeed, one could reasonably regard evidence on the enduring impact of college attendance essentially as an estimate of the net effects of college extended over time. For this reason we depart from the typical pattern of most chapters and summarize the evidence on the long-term effects of college here rather than near the end of this chapter.

Our synthesis of the evidence suggests that college has a rather broad range of enduring or long-term impacts. These include not only the more obvious impacts on occupation and earnings but also influences on cognitive, moral, and psychosocial characteristics, as well as on values and attitudes and various quality of life indexes (for example, family, marriage, consumer behavior). Moreover, it would also appear that the impacts extend beyond the individuals who attend college to the kinds of lives their sons and daughters can expect.

It is clear that part of the long-term impact of college (for example, on job status and income) can be traced directly back to college attendance or degree attainment. Another part of this impact, however, may be an indirect result of the socioeconomic positioning and kinds of life interests, experiences, and opportunities made more likely by being a college graduate. As suggested by Withey (1971) and Bowen (1977), part of the impact of college arises out of the distinctive kinds of lives led by the people who attend and graduate from college. Such indirect routes of influence are a major consideration in understanding the long-term and full impact of college. In short, our conclusion about the nature of the long-term effects of college is generally consistent with that of Feldman and Newcomb (1969). The distinctive effects of college tend to persist in large measure as a result of living in postcollege environments that support those effects.

Table 13.8. Summary of Estimated *Net* Effects of College: *Moral Development*.

Outcome	Strength of Evidence	Direction of Effect	Major Rival Explanations Controlled	Magnitude of Net Effect[a]
Use of principled reasoning in judging moral issues	Strong	Positive	Age, precollege differences in moral reasoning, intelligence, socioeconomic status	Unclear[a]
Principled behavior or action	Weak	Positive		Hypothesized effect is indirect and probably small

[a]"Unclear," as used in this table, means we are acknowledging that the studies do not allow such estimates or that the evidence, though generally consistent, is still sufficiently complex to make an estimate of effect size hazardous.

Socioeconomic Outcomes

The impact of college on socioeconomic outcomes (occupation and earnings) is a function not only of what happens during college but also of how college graduates are themselves regarded by employers. It is difficult to separate these two influences, but it is quite clear that obtaining a bachelor's degree has a strong net influence on one's socioeconomic attainments. We should perhaps avoid the temptation to make too much of these influences. Most prediction models of status attainment explain somewhat less than 50 percent of the individual differences in occupational status or earnings. Nevertheless, as summarized in Table 13.9, the evidence we reviewed is consistent in indicating that a bachelor's degree remains a major, if not *the* major, prerequisite for entrée into relatively high status and high paying technical, managerial, and professional jobs.

The socioeconomic impact of being a college graduate is not realized exclusively at the early stages in one's career, however. A college degree continues to provide advantages throughout one's working life. These are manifest as enhanced earnings, an increased likelihood of stable employment, and generally higher levels of career mobility and attainment. Moreover, despite periodic fluctuations, the private economic rate of return on investment in a bachelor's degree compares favorably to benchmark rates for alternative ways of investing one's money. In short, our reading of the body of evidence is quite consistent with that of Bowen (1977): A bachelor's degree continues to be a primary vehicle by means of which one gains an advantaged socioeconomic position in American society.

With respect to the importance of college graduation on other major indexes of socioeconomic attainment, such as occupational status and income, two additional observations are relevant. First, there is replicated evidence to suggest that in terms of the relative incremental advantage it confers, a bachelor's degree is typically the single most important educational rung on the socioeconomic attainment ladder. Second, although there are discernible between- and within-college effects, the occupational and economic impacts of completing one's bachelor's degree are typically more pronounced than the impacts due either to where one completes it or to the nature of one's educational experiences while doing so (for example, major field of study, academic achievement, extracurricular involvement).

The way in which a bachelor's degree positions one occupationally and economically represents an important long-term impact of college in and of itself. But this socioeconomic positioning effect has additional implications for other long-term impacts. One stems from the simple fact that the jobs that college graduates typically hold are characterized by a rela-

Table 13.9. Summary of Estimated *Long-Term* Effects of College: *Socioeconomic Outcomes*.

Outcome	*Strength of Evidence*	*Direction of Effect*	*Major Rival Explanations Controlled*	*Magnitude of Net Effect*
Occupational status	Strong	Positive	Socioeconomic status, aspirations, intelligence	Bachelor's degree confers 1 SD (34 percentile point) advantage over high school diploma
Stability of employment	Moderate	Positive	Socioeconomic status	Unclear,[a] probably large
Career mobility and attainment	Strong	Positive	Initial job level	Unclear
Earnings	Strong	Positive	Socioeconomic status, aspirations, occupational status, intelligence, work experience	Bachelor's degree confers 20 to 40 percentage point advantage over high school diploma
Private rate of return	Strong	Positive	Intelligence, costs of education, foregone earnings	Bachelor's degree confers 9.3 to 11% return on investment

[a]"Unclear," as used in this table, means we are acknowledging that the studies do not allow such estimates or that the evidence, though generally consistent, is still sufficiently complex to make an estimate of effect size hazardous.

tively high level of earnings. This permits the acquisition of a variety of material and nonmaterial resources and opportunities (including books, travel, cultural experiences, household maintenance, medical care, and additional education) that have potential impact on other long-term outcomes. A second implication stems from the fact that college graduates tend to be employed in jobs characterized by relatively high levels of social interaction and self-direction. Such job traits may provide an important continuing influence on trends in cognitive and psychosocial changes partially shaped during the college experience.

Learning and Cognitive Development

As indicated in Table 13.10, the body of evidence on the long-term impact of college on indexes of learning and cognitive characteristics is not without methodological problems. Nevertheless, there is clear evidence from extensive national samples to indicate that college graduates have a substantially larger general knowledge base across a wide range of topics than do individuals whose education ends with high school. Similarly, in an impressive set of national surveys, alumni were consistent in reporting that college had a major positive influence both on their specific and their general knowledge base and on their ability to think critically, analytically, and clearly.

As suggested by the retrospective perceptions of graduates, part of this enduring impact can probably be traced directly to what transpires in college. A substantial amount of factual learning and general intellectual development obviously occurs during that time. Yet it is likely that what happens during college represents only part of the story. Another part is probably the result of differences in the kinds of posteducation lives that college and high school graduates lead. The former are more likely to engage in intellectually challenging activities (serious reading, attending cultural events, participating in continuing education, and the like, and to be employed in the kinds of intellectually challenging jobs that further enlarge their knowledge base and continue to enhance their intellectual development. Moreover, even if college crystallizes one's interest in lifelong learning, the economic advantages linked to a college degree contribute in part by increasing one's ability to purchase the goods and services required. It is probably this complex interplay of mutually supporting direct and indirect influences (that is, what happens during college, postcollege experiences, and the ability to acquire material and nonmaterial opportunities) that most fully accounts for the long-term impact of college on knowledge acquisition and more general cognitive advances.

Table 13.10. Summary of Estimated *Long-Term* Effects of College: *Learning and Cognitive Development.*

Outcome	Strength of Evidence	Direction of Effect	Major Rival Explanations Controlled	Magnitude of Net Effect[a]
General knowledge	Moderate	Positive	Race, gender, age, initial socioeconomic status, current socioeconomic status, religion, geographical origin	Unclear[a]
General cognitive competencies and skills (e.g., critical thinking and analytical skills, ability to think clearly, oral communication skills)	Moderate	Positive	Age	Unclear

[a]"Unclear," as used in this table, means we are acknowledging that the studies do not allow such estimates or that the evidence, though generally consistent, is still sufficiently complex to make an estimate of effect size hazardous.

Attitudes and Values

The most notable conclusion from the body of research on the long-term effects of college on attitudes and values, summarized in Table 13.11, is that nearly all of the trends that occur during college tend either to persist or to stabilize in the years following college. Certainly there are exceptions to this conclusion. Intervening experiences in such areas as work, marriage and family, military service, and graduate education are potentially profound influences on one's attitudes and values. Nevertheless, for college students as a group, the intellectual, aesthetic, social, political, religious, educational, and occupational attitudes and values one holds as a graduating senior appear to be an important determinant of the attitudes and values one holds throughout the adult years.

Part of this long-term impact may be directly traceable to the college experience. College may, in fact, function to influence a broad range of attitudes and values in directions that may be relatively impervious to subsequent influence and thus tend to persist throughout adult life. It is unlikely, however, that the total enduring impact of college on attitudes or values is confined to the college years. Perhaps more important is the fact that college tends to channel graduates into postcollege lives that often reinforce trends shaped by the college experience. This indirect impact on attitudes and values may manifest itself in a variety of ways. For example, one's attitudes and values may be influenced by the type of job one holds; by the attitudes and values of a spouse, professional acquaintances, and friends with a similar level of education; or by the nature of one's leisure time interests and activities (cultural opportunities, travel, civic involvement, reading, and so on), which is often shaped by interests and available financial resources. In short, the kinds of postcollege lives college graduates lead may transmit an important indirect long-term impact of college on attitudes and values.

The long-term effect of college on attitudes and values may also involve an intergenerational legacy; the attitudes and values that students develop at least partially as a consequence of their college experiences are passed on to their children. For example, a small body of evidence has found a positive link between a mother's education and nontraditional gender role attitudes in children, particularly daughters. This may be a less obvious part of the indirect impact of a mother's education on her daughter's conceptions of herself and on the likelihood of her entering a traditionally male-dominated occupation.

Psychosocial Changes

The nature and extent of college's long-term effects on students' psychosocial characteristics are summarized in Table 13.12. As can be seen

Table 13.11. Summary of Estimated _Long-Term_ Effects of College: _Attitudes and Values_.

Outcome	Strength of Evidence	Direction of Effect	Major Rival Explanations Controlled	Magnitude of Net Effect[a]
Aesthetic, cultural, and intellectual values	Moderate	Stable over time	Gender, race, religion, socioeconomic status	Unclear[a]
Value placed on liberal education	Moderate	Positive	Aptitude, employment situation	Unclear
Value placed on education as vocational preparation	Moderate	Negative	Aptitude, employment situation	Unclear
Value placed on intrinsic occupational rewards	Strong	Positive	Gender, race, socioeconomic status, precollege values, college GPA	Unclear
Value placed on extrinsic occupational rewards	Strong	Negative	Gender, race, socioeconomic status, precollege values, college GPA	Unclear
Political and social attitudes	Moderate	Stable over time	Aptitude, age, race, gender, religion, socioeconomic status, region, historical period	Unclear; part of effect probably indirect through employment situation
Secularism	Weak	Stable over time	None	Unclear
Gender roles (toward the "modern")	Weak	Positive	Initial attitudes, various background characteristics, occupational experience	Unclear

[a] "Unclear," as used in this table, means we are acknowledging that the studies do not allow such estimates or that the evidence, though generally consistent, is still sufficiently complex to make an estimate of effect size hazardous.

Table 13.12. Summary of Estimated *Long-Term* Effects of College: *Psychosocial Changes*.

Outcome	Strength of Evidence	Direction of Effect	Major Rival Explanations Controlled	Magnitude of Net Effect
Identity and ego development	Virtually no evidence			
Self-concept: Academic	Strong	Positive	Gender, race, precollege self-concept, achievement, socioeconomic status, degree aspirations, occupational status	Small; stronger among whites than among blacks
Self-concept: Social	Strong	Positive	Gender, race, precollege self-concept, achievement, socioeconomic status, degree aspirations, occupational status	Small; stronger among whites than among blacks
Self-concept: Self-esteem	Strong	Positive	Race, gender, socioeconomic status, ability, precollege self-esteem	Small
Autonomy, independence, and internal locus of control	Moderate	Positive	Gender, race, socioeconomic status, aptitude, precollege locus of control	Unclear,[a] but probably small and perhaps indirect
Authoritarianism, dogmatism, and ethnocentrism	Weak	Stable over time	None	Unclear
Intellectual orientation	Weak	Stable over time; some declines possible	None	Unclear
Interpersonal relations	Weak	Positive	None	Unclear
Personal adjustment and psychosocial well-being	Moderate	Positive	Income, occupational status	Unclear
Maturity and general personal development	Weak	Positive	Unclear	Unclear

[a]"Unclear," as used in this table, means we are acknowledging that the studies do not allow such estimates or that the evidence, though generally consistent, is still sufficiently complex to make an estimate of effect size hazardous.

there, the research literature is silent on the extent to which college has any identifiable long-term effect on identity status or ego stage development. While there is ample evidence that identity and ego development do not end with the college years, education's role in those changes remains virtually unexamined and thus unknown. Even though the research base is small, however, it is methodologically strong and consistent in indicating that college does have a positive and unique effect on students' academic and social concepts, as well as on their self-esteem. These effects are discernible up to a decade after matriculation, although they appear to be small and largely indirect, mediated through the higher-status jobs college graduates tend to obtain compared to those held by people with less education. Moreover, college's long-term effects on self-concepts appear to be greater among white students than among black students. Nine years after entry, college attendance appears to have no measurable effects—positive or negative, direct or indirect—on the self-concepts of black males.

With a few exceptions, the research base exploring long-term changes in the several facets of students' relational systems is severely constrained either by idiosyncratic samples or by designs that do not control plausible rival hypotheses (sometimes by both). Limited but sound nationally based evidence indicates that educational attainment is positively related to increases in individuals' internal locus of control seven and nine years after high school graduation, but occupational effects were left uncontrolled, leaving claims of college's long-term effects open to challenge. The evidence in the other areas of relational change is explored by single-institution studies with only marginal generalizability. What evidence exists suggests little postcollege change in level of authoritarianism or in intellectual orientation, slight declines in anxiety and the willingness to express impulses, and gains in personal integration, psychological well-being, and general maturity. Thus, although the evidence is limited, there is some basis for believing that education at least has no deleterious effects on overall psychosocial status and probably has some decidedly beneficial ones, even though they may be slight and indirect.

Moral Development

As indicated in Table 13.13, there is strong evidence for an enduring impact of college on the use of principled moral reasoning, at least through the first six years after graduation. Students attending college not only make greater gains in the use of principled reasoning during college than individuals whose formal education ends with high school, but the gap between the two groups continues to widen in the years subsequent to college. These different patterns of change cannot be accounted for by initial differences in moral development or differential regression effects. Again, we see evidence that part of this long-term impact is directly attributable to trends

Table 13.13. Summary of Estimated *Long-Term* Effects of College: *Moral Development*.

Outcome	Strength of Evidence	Direction of Effect	Major Rival Explanations Controlled	Magnitude of Net Effect[a]
Use of principled reasoning in judging moral issues	Strong	Positive	Precollege level of principled reasoning, regression artifacts	Unclear[a]

[a] "Unclear," as used in this table, means we are acknowledging that the studies do not allow such estimates or that the evidence, though generally consistent, is still sufficiently complex to make an estimate of effect size hazardous.

shaped by the college experience. Another part, however, is indirectly attributable to college through differences between high school and college graduates in posteducational environments, particularly in the area of continuing intellectual stimulation (reading, cultural events, travel, job demands, and so on). There is clear evidence that the level of continuing intellectual stimulation in one's posteducational life has a strong positive impact on further advances in principled moral reasoning.

Quality of Life Indexes

Problems in research design and the inability to control important confounding influences make causal attributions about the long-term impact of college on various quality of life indexes somewhat tenuous. As shown in Table 13.14, the overall quality of evidence is not particularly strong. Consequently, we consider the findings as more suggestive than conclusive.

Having said this, it nevertheless remains true that college-educated individuals consistently rank higher than those with less education on a clear majority of the quality of life indexes considered. Compared to those with less education, the college educated tend to have better overall health and a lower mortality rate, have smaller families and be more successful in achieving desired family size through informed and effective use of contraceptive devices, and spend a greater portion of time in child care, particularly in activities of a developmentally enriching nature (such as teaching, reading, and talking). They also tend to be more efficient in making consumer choices, save a greater percentage of their income, make more effective long-term investment of discretionary resources, and spend a greater proportion of discretionary resources and leisure time on developmentally enriching activities (reading, participation in arts and cultural events, involvement in civic affairs, and so forth).

It is likely that at least part of the impact of college on these indexes of life quality is indirect, being mediated through the socioeconomic advantages that tend to accrue to the college educated. Having the economic resources to pay for desired goods and services is not without important consequences for the quality of one's life. At the same time, the positive link between educational level and many quality of life indexes remains even after economic resources are held constant. This suggests the possibility at least that college may also have a direct impact on quality of life by enhancing such characteristics as the ability to acquire new information and process it effectively, the ability to evaluate new ideas and technologies, the capacity to plan rationally and with a long-term perspective, the willingness to accept reasonable risk, and the developmental and cultural level of one's leisure interests and tastes. It should be pointed out, however, that with some exceptions, such as health status, the absence of controls for initial

Table 13.14. Summary of Estimated *Long-Term* Effects of College: *Quality of Life Indexes*.

Outcome	Strength of Evidence	Direction of Effect	Major Rival Explanations Controlled	Magnitude of Net Effect
Health status	Moderate	Positive	Income, age, prior health status, socioeconomic status	College graduates have 4% advantage in health status and 1.6% advantage in mortality rate over high school graduates[a]
Marital stability	Weak	Positive	Age, age at marriage, job prestige, number of children, income	Probably indirect and small
Family size	Moderate	Positive	Income, family demographic traits	Unclear[b]
Nurturance of children	Weak	Positive	Mother employed	Unclear
Consumer behavior or efficiency	Moderate	Positive	Income	Unclear
Savings and investment efficiency	Moderate	Positive	Age, income, family size, occupation	Unclear
Cultured leisure	Weak	Positive	Income	Unclear
Job satisfaction	Weak	Positive	Age, religious preference	Unclear, but probably small
Marital satisfaction	Moderate	Mixed	Age, age at first marriage, employment outside home, job status	Very small
Subjective well-being (life satisfaction)	Moderate	Mixed	Age, income, job status, socioeconomic status origins	Very small

[a]These estimates were obtained by multiplying by four the advantage attributable to each year of college completed.
[b]"Unclear," as used in this table, means we are acknowledging that the studies do not allow such estimates or that the evidence, though generally consistent, is still sufficiently complex to make an estimate of effect size hazardous.

traits makes it difficult to separate the direct impact of college from the confounding influence of preexisting differences between those who attend and those who do not attend college.

It is interesting that even though college-educated individuals clearly rank higher on a broad array of quality of life indicators, they do not, on the average, express appreciably greater satisfaction with their lives than do those with less education. We would suggest that this does not signify the absence of impact but rather reflects the fact that the impact of college has dimensions that function both to increase and to diminish expressions of satisfaction with one's life. On the one hand, the clear job status and economic returns to college are likely to have a positive impact on some dimensions of life satisfaction, particularly the intrinsic (for example, autonomy, challenge) and extrinsic (for example, earnings) aspects of one's work. This probably explains a major part of the modest direct impact of college on job satisfaction. On the other hand, one probable impact of college is that it tends to foster a more critical perspective in individuals. Consequently, as compared to those with less education, college-educated men and women may be more sophisticated, skeptical, analytical, and critical in their judgments of some facets of job satisfaction, marital satisfaction, and overall sense of well-being.

Intergenerational Effects

An often overlooked element of the long-term impact of college is the intergenerational transmission of benefits. Indeed, there is evidence to support the expectation that the net benefits of a college education are not restricted to the individual who receives them but are passed along to his or her sons and daughters. Most of the evidence on intergenerational effects concerns the socioeconomic achievements of offspring. These are summarized in Table 13.15. Having college-educated parents modestly enhances one's educational attainment, job status, early career earnings, and, if one is a woman, the likelihood of entering a male-dominated occupation. The last of these has consequences for gender equality in the work force in that male-dominated occupations are traditionally linked with relatively high status and earnings.

What is perhaps most notable about these intergenerational impacts, however, is that with the possible exception of offsprings' educational attainment, they manifest themselves essentially through indirect routes. Having college-educated parents positively affects the socioeconomic achievement of sons and daughters largely by influencing important intervening variables in the status attainment process. Such variables include family income, career aspirations, the type of college attended, and in some instances educational attainment. Through this complex matrix of indirect influences,

Table 13.15. Summary of Estimated *Long-Term* Effects of College: *Intergenerational Effects.*

Outcome	Strength of Evidence	Direction of Effect	Major Rival Explanations Controlled	Magnitude of Net Effect
Educational attainment of children	Strong	Positive	Family income, intelligence, aspirations, race, gender	Unclear;[a] effect may be both direct and indirect and is probably small
Occupational status	Moderate	Positive	Family income, intelligence, aspirations, race, gender	Unclear; effect is probably indirect and small
Daughters entering male-dominated occupations	Moderate	Positive	Family income, academic achievement, aspirations, race	Unclear; effect is probably indirect and small
Earnings of children	Moderate	Positive	Family income, academic achievement, aspirations, race, gender	Unclear; direct effects mixed; effect is probably indirect and small

[a]"Unclear," as used in this table, means we are acknowledging that the studies do not allow such estimates or that the evidence, though generally consistent, is still sufficiently complex to make an estimate of effect size hazardous.

a college education is likely to make nontrivial contributions to the socio-economic positioning of one's children.

Although the causal linkage is less clearly established, it is also likely that having college-educated parents may enhance the cognitive development of young children through the indirect route of the home environment. Compared to those with less education, college-educated parents, particularly mothers, spend more time with their children in developmentally enriching activities such as reading and teaching. Differences in such home activities may at least partially account for the positive link found between parental and, in particular, mother's education and the cognitive development of preschool children.

There is also reason to believe that the long-term effects of college via the intergenerational legacy also extend to the attitudes and values parents pass along to their children. Ample evidence indicates that successive generations and cohorts of students are increasingly more liberal in their social, political, religious, and sexual attitudes and values. These generational shifts are, of course, highly correlated with increases in average educational attainment levels over the past half-century. Thus, it would appear that as children are raised by successively better educated generations of parents who have themselves increased to varying degrees in social and political tolerance, humanitarianism, and sense of civic responsibility, the children's attendance at college leads to even greater differences relative to grandparents and great-grandparents. The long-term trend of these intergenerational legacies appears to be not only toward greater socioeconomic security and well-being but also toward greater cognitive growth and openness, tolerance, and concern for human rights and liberties.

Between-College Effects

Our interpretation of the body of evidence across all outcomes is that the net impact of attending (versus not attending) college tends to be substantially more pronounced than any differential impact attributable to attending different kinds of colleges. This conclusion is generally consistent with that of Bowen (1977), and several factors may contribute to such a conclusion.

First, estimates of between-college effects are based on much more selective and homogeneous samples than estimates of the net effect of attending college. The former are based only on college students, while the latter typically also include those who do not attend college. Restriction in the variability of a sample can attenuate the magnitude of associations among variables. This might naturally lead to smaller effects in between-college studies than in studies that assess the net effect of college.

A second possibility, similar to the first, is that the statistical procedures commonly used to analyze net college effects are essentially conserva-

tive ones. When institutional differences are under study, researchers typically control students' background characteristics by means of regression,
covariance analysis, or partial regression techniques before estimating the
amount of residual variance that can be explained by differences in institutional characteristics. With such procedures, however, any variance *jointly*
due to the effects of students' backgrounds and institutional characteristics
is attributed entirely to student differences. Consequently, institutional effects may be underestimated to some unknown degree. Thus, the failure to
find differential institutional effects may to some extent be an artifact of
the analytical procedures used.

Third, it is entirely possible (perhaps probable) that more variability
exists *within* institutional classifications than across them. Categories that
appear to be homogeneous (for instance, private four-year colleges) may
very well be far more heterogeneous than they seem (see, for example,
Astin & Lee, 1972). Under such conditions, detection of statistically significant differences becomes more unlikely.

Fourth, and perhaps most likely, the weight of evidence may well
reflect the fact that the dimensions along which American colleges are typically categorized, ranked, and studied (such as size, type of control, curricular emphasis, and selectivity) are simply not linked with major differences
in *net* impacts on students. To be sure, there are clear and unmistakable
differences among postsecondary institutions in a wide variety of areas, including size and complexity, control, mission, financial and educational resources, the scholarly productivity of faculty, reputation and prestige, and
the characteristics of the students enrolled. At the same time, however,
American colleges and universities also resemble one another in a number
of important respects. It may be that despite their structural and organizational differences, their similarities in curricular content, structures, and
sequencing; instructional practices; overall educational goals; faculty values;
out-of-class experiences; and other areas do in fact produce essentially similar effects on students, although the "start" and "end" points may be very
different across institutions.

Finally, some of the conventional institutional characteristics may
combine to produce measurable differences in institutional environments.
There is evidence in several areas that institutional context—a college or
university's educational and interpersonal climate (and subclimates)— may
more powerfully differentiate among institutions in the extent of their influence on student change than do the typical descriptors. Different con-
ceptualizations of institutional "environments" and analyses of subenvironments may reveal greater between-institution differences than are now
apparent in the research literature (see Baird, 1988).

Yet overall, the body of evidence reviewed casts considerable doubt
on the premise that the conventional, if substantial, structural, resource,
and qualitative differences among schools are translated into correspond-

ingly large differences in average educational effects. In short, similarities in between-college effects would appear to vastly outweigh the differences.

Of course, this is a general conclusion based on the total body of evidence. Although no specific institutional characteristic or set of characteristics appears to have a consistent impact across outcomes, there are, in fact, some modest between-college effects in certain areas. We turn now to a brief summary of these effects, which are shown in Tables 13.16 through 13.23.

Two-Year Versus Four-Year Colleges

It is clear that the two-year community college has played a major positive role in the social mobility of many individuals. This is particularly apparent when the socioeconomic attainments of community college students are compared to those of people whose education ends with high school. Nevertheless, there is reasonably strong evidence in support of Clark's (1960) argument that community colleges can also function to "cool out" students' educational aspirations. As indicated in Table 13.16, compared to similar students who begin in four-year institutions, community college students are significantly less likely to complete a bachelor's degree. This may be traceable in part to the social-psychological climate of community colleges, but it is probably also partially attributable to the structural obstacles and educational discontinuities involved in transferring to four-year institutions.

Because initial attendance at a two-year college is linked with a lower likelihood of completing a bachelor's degree, such attendance may have an indirect negative impact on occupational status and perhaps earnings. Such occupational and economic disadvantages are not inevitable, however. For those who can complete their bachelor's degree in the same period of time as similar students in four-year colleges, any negative impact of two-year college attendance on occupational status or earnings is quite small and perhaps trivial. Similarly, when individuals of equal educational attainment are compared, there is little to indicate that those starting out at two-year colleges are penalized in terms of job stability, unemployment rate, or job satisfaction.

College Quality

The educational impact of various measures of college quality has clearly dominated the research on between-college effects. Perhaps this is due to the expectation that those highly interrelated resource dimensions along which college quality has traditionally been defined (student body selectivity, prestige, or reputation; financial expenditures per student; library size; and the like) should be significant determinants of impact. Thus,

Table 13.16. Summary of Estimated Between-College Effects: Two-Year Versus Four-Year Colleges.

Outcome	Strength of Evidence	Direction of Effect	Major Rival Explanations Controlled	Magnitude of Effect
Bachelor's degree completion	Strong	Negative for two-year institutions	Academic ability, high school achievement, family socioeconomic status, degree aspirations, college grades, work, age, place of residence	About a 15% or greater disadvantage in likelihood of bachelor's degree completion during a specified time period
Occupational status	Moderate	Negative for two-year institutions	Academic ability, high school achievement, family socioeconomic status, degree aspirations, college grades, educational attainment	Direct effect small and perhaps trivial; most of effect indirect, transmitted by degree completion, and probably small
Earnings	Weak	Inconclusive	Intelligence, educational aspirations, family socioeconomic status, sex, race, educational attainment	Direct effect probably trivial, although disadvantage to two-year institutions may become more pronounced over time; small indirect effect through educational attainment likely but untested

those institutions with the most selective student bodies, the highest prestige, the most money, and the best facilities might reasonably be expected to provide the best education.

In considering the net impact of college quality, it is perhaps useful to divide outcomes into two broad categories that we might term developmentally oriented outcomes (learning, cognitive development, values, psychosocial change, and so on) and socioeconomic-oriented outcomes (career aspirations, educational attainment, occupational status, career mobility, and earnings, for example). What is clear from Table 13.17 is that college quality dimensions (most typically defined in terms of selectivity and prestige) have less extensive impacts on developmentally oriented outcomes than on socioeconomic-oriented ones.

In the category of developmentally oriented outcomes there is some weak to moderately consistent evidence that college selectivity has a small positive impact on aesthetic, cultural, and intellectual values; political and social liberalism; and secularism. In addition, selectivity may be inversely related to academic self-concept, but the effect is small and indirect, being mediated by grade performance. Beyond these small effects, however, there is little consistent evidence to indicate that college selectivity, prestige, or educational resources have any important net impact on students in such areas as learning, cognitive and intellectual development, other psychosocial changes, the development of principled moral reasoning, or shifts in other attitudes and values. Nearly all of the variance in learning and cognitive outcomes is attributable to individual aptitude differences among students attending different colleges. Only a small and perhaps trivial part is uniquely due to the quality of the college attended.

In various preceding chapters and earlier in this chapter, we described several possible methodological explanations for this rather counterintuitive conclusion. There are also explanations of a more substantive nature. For example, some evidence indicates wide variability in the cognitive effects of different departments within colleges at any particular level of student body selectivity. This suggests the possibility of considerably greater variability in cognitive impacts *within* colleges of similar selectivity than *between* colleges of different selectivity. Thus, differences in students' individual experiences within a particular college may be a more salient influence on learning and cognitive gains than any global or average measure of college quality.

Related to the preceding point, it may simply be that traditional definitions of college quality focus more on resource wealth than on those aspects of student life and experience that have important effects on learning and cognitive outcomes. There is at least some indication that certain aspects of college environments (for example, curricular flexibility, informal interaction with faculty and peers, a general education emphasis in the curriculum) have consistent though small net positive effects on learning

Table 13.17. Summary of Estimated Between-College Effects: College Quality (Primarily Selectivity and Prestige).

Outcome	Strength of Evidence	Direction of Effect	Major Rival Explanations Controlled	Magnitude of Effect
Aesthetic, cultural, and intellectual values	Weak	More positive at selective schools	Gender, socioeconomic status, religion	Unclear,[a] but probably quite small; effect may be somewhat more pronounced when selectivity is combined with private control
Political and social liberalism	Moderate	More positive at selective schools	Gender, socioeconomic status, ability, initial values, various other background variables	Unclear, but probably small; effect may be somewhat more pronounced when selectivity is combined with private control
Secularism	Moderate	More positive at selective schools	Gender, race, socioeconomic status, ability, initial level of religiosity, various other background characteristics	Unclear
Academic self-concept	Moderate	More negative at selective schools	Gender, race, socioeconomic status, ability, initial self-concept, various other precollege characteristics	Unclear, but probably indirect, mediated by GPA

Table 13.17. Summary of Estimated Between-College Effects: College Quality (*Primarily Selectivity and Prestige*). Cont'd.

Outcome	Strength of Evidence	Direction of Effect	Major Rival Explanations Controlled	Magnitude of Effect
Educational aspirations and educational attainment	Strong	Positive in direction of selectivity, prestige, and financial resources	Initial aspirations, secondary school achievement, family socioeconomic status, college grades, job expectations, college size	Moderate and positive direct effect; small negative indirect effect transmitted through college grades; overall, small positive total effect, accounting for about 1 to 2% of variance
Choice of academic career	Moderate	Positive in direction of college reputation and financial resources	Initial career choice, academic ability, college grades, family socioeconomic status	Unclear, but probably quite small
Choice of sex-atypical majors and careers for women	Moderate	Positive in direction of selectivity	Family socioeconomic status, age, marital status, college grades, college type (liberal arts or other)	Small
Entrance into sex-atypical careers for women	Moderate	Positive in direction of selectivity	Race, initial career aspirations, self-concept, secondary school achievement, family socioeconomic status, college gender, college control, college grades, major	Small; perhaps somewhat stronger in non-science careers than in science careers

Outcome				
Career mobility and success	Moderate	Positive in direction of selectivity and prestige	Family socioeconomic status, educational attainment, age, race, gender, college grades, recruitment emphasis of employer	Small
Occupational status in professional career	Moderate	Positive in direction of selectivity	Family socioeconomic status, initial career aspirations, secondary school achievement	Small; unclear whether effect is direct or indirect through educational attainment; evidence for all careers indicates no consistent effect on occupational status
Earnings	Moderate to strong	Positive in direction of selectivity in particular but also prestige and financial resources	Intelligence, family socioeconomic status, achievement motivation, college grades, educational attainment, occupational status	Small direct effect slightly larger than 1% of earnings variance; indirect effect through educational attainment may increase this by one-third; only most selective or prestigious colleges may account for this effect

[a] "Unclear," as used in this table, means we are acknowledging that the studies do not allow such estimates or that the evidence, though generally consistent, is still sufficiently complex to make an estimate of effect size hazardous.

and cognition, as well as on psychosocial and attitudinal change. This suggests that to understand between-college impacts on cognitive growth, we need to focus less on a college's resources and more on such factors as curricular experiences and course work patterns, the quality of teaching, the frequency and focus of student-faculty nonclassroom interaction, the nature of peer group and extracurricular activities, and the extent to which institutional structures and policies facilitate student academic and social involvement. It is likely that colleges of equal selectivity, prestige, and financial resources may differ substantially in these more proximal influences on student development.

Finally, factors such as student body selectivity may have a latent impact on cognitive and psychosocial change that is activated only when embedded in a supportive social-psychological context. Feldman and Newcomb (1969), Chickering (1969), and Heath (1968) have suggested that a social-psychological context maximizing impact would be characterized by factors such as small size, a cohesive peer environment, and frequent informal contact with faculty (presumed to be found most often at small, selective liberal arts colleges). To these factors we would add a common or shared intellectual experience in the college's curriculum and a common valuing of the life of the mind.

If college quality does not play a major role in influencing developmentally oriented outcomes, particularly those in cognitive areas, it would nevertheless appear to have a more extensive set of impacts on an individual's career. Part of this impact begins during college. Students who enroll in elite institutions tend to begin college with relatively high educational and occupational status aspirations. The overall net effect of attendance at such institutions is to maintain or modestly accentuate initial aspirations. For example, attending a selective or prestigious college has small positive net impacts on educational aspirations, plans for graduate or professional school, and choice of an academic career, particularly in high-status disciplines, and choice of sex-atypical majors and careers among women. Thus, elite colleges not only recruit ambition, but they tend to nurture it, at least to a modest extent.

In addition to influencing aspirations and plans, attendance at an elite institution modestly enhances a range of actual socioeconomic attainments. These include bachelor's degree completion, attending graduate or professional school (particularly a school with high prestige), entering sex-atypical careers if one is a woman, level of managerial attainment, occupational status (at least in professional careers such as law and medicine), and earnings. It is tempting from such evidence to conclude, as did Wolfle (1971), that if one's goal is "success" then it matters much where one goes to college. This needs to tempered, however, by two facts. First, a substantial portion of the evidence is inconsistent. Second, the magnitude of the effect that can actually be attributed to college quality and not other influences is quite small, a good deal smaller than is commonly believed.

For example, in the area of earnings, where the evidence is perhaps the most extensive and the impact the largest, even our most liberal estimate is that less than 2 percent of the differences in earnings is attributable to college quality. This means that in excess of 98 percent of the differences in individual earnings is due to influences other than where one goes to college.

Thus, while a selective or prestigious college can modestly enhance one's chances of success, the preponderance of any socioeconomic advantage popularly attributed to attending the "best" colleges is more likely due to the kinds of students those colleges enroll. From the standpoint of *incremental improvements* in one's chances for success, it probably matters much more on the average that one *completes* a bachelor's degree than where one attends college.

College Type

Estimating the net impact of different college types is complicated by the fact that type itself is often confounded with other institutional characteristics. Indeed, the evidence that major research universities and selective liberal arts colleges have a positive impact on earnings is quite likely confounded by the fact that these institutions also tend to have academically selective student bodies. As shown in Table 13.18, there is modest evidence to suggest that even when student body selectivity is held constant, private colleges tend to have small positive effects on educational aspirations and educational attainment, and liberal arts colleges tend to enhance the likelihood that women will choose sex-atypical majors and careers. Similarly and not surprisingly, church-related colleges tend to have a negative influence on the development of secular values and attitudes and smaller-than-average effects on certain kinds of psychosocial changes (for example, authoritarianism) during college.

Beyond these few small impacts, however, institutional categorizations such as the Carnegie classification appear to tell us little about differences in between-college impacts. Perhaps even more than indexes of college quality, classifications such as research university, comprehensive private university, and liberal arts college may, as suggested, simply conceal so much between-college variability within each classification that consistent impacts on students cannot be found.

College Size

The impact of institutional size (that is, enrollment) varies with the outcome considered, as shown in Table 13.19. On the one hand, attending

Table 13.18. Summary of Estimated _Between-College_ Effects: _College Type._

College Characteristic or Outcome	Strength of Evidence	Direction of Effect	Major Rival Explanations Controlled	Magnitude of Net Effect
Private Versus Public Colleges				
Aesthetic, cultural, and intellectual values	Moderate	Positive in the direction of private control	Gender, race, ability, socioeconomic status, degree aspirations, other background traits	Unclear[a]
Educational aspirations and educational attainment	Moderate	Positive in the direction of private control	Family socioeconomic status, secondary school achievement, gender, race, initial occupational aspirations, college selectivity and size, college grades	Small, probably accounting for no more than 1% of variance
Implementation of career choice	Moderate	Mixed	Initial career choice, family socioeconomic status, gender, college selectivity	Small tendency for public institutions to significantly enhance implementation of career plans for college teaching and engineering but to negatively affect plans for business, law, medicine, nursing

Liberal Arts Colleges

Women's choice of sex-atypical majors and careers	Moderate	More positive for liberal arts colleges	College selectivity, initial career choice	Small
Value attached to a liberal education	Moderate	More positive for liberal arts colleges	Gender, race, socioeconomic status, ability, initial values	Unclear
Value attached to intrinsic occupational awards	Moderate	More positive for liberal arts colleges	Gender, race, socioeconomic status, ability, initial values	Unclear

Church-Related Colleges

Secularism	Moderate	Negative in direction of church-related colleges	Initial religious orientation	Small
Humanitarian and altruistic social values	Moderate	More positive at church-related colleges	Sex, race, socioeconomic status, ability, initial values	Unclear, but stronger at church-related schools
Authoritarianism, dogmatism, and ethnocentrism	Weak	Smaller declines at Catholic colleges	Ability	Unclear

a"Unclear," as used in this table, means we are acknowledging that the studies do not allow such estimates or that the evidence, though generally consistent, is still sufficiently complex to make an estimate of effect size hazardous.

Table 13.19. Summary of Estimated _Between-College_ Effects: _College Size._

Outcome	Strength of Evidence	Direction of Effect	Major Rival Explanations Controlled	Magnitude of Effect
Educational attainment	Weak	Negative	Family socioeconomic status, educational aspirations, college selectivity, major, grades, social involvement	Direct effect trivial; small negative indirect effect transmitted through social involvement probably accounting for less than 1% of variance
Occupational status	Strong	Positive	Family socioeconomic status, academic ability, occupational aspirations, college selectivity	Small
Earnings	Strong	Positive	Family socioeconomic status, occupational aspirations, aptitude, college selectivity, college major, grades	Small
Social self-concept	Moderate	Negative	Gender, race, socioeconomic status, ability, degree aspirations, college experiences, other institutional characteristics	Small, indirect

a large institution tends to have small positive direct impacts on both occupational status and income, impacts that remain even when college selectivity is held constant. Conversely, institutional size appears to have small negative impacts on bachelor's degree completion, educational attainment, and the development of social self-image during college. These impacts also hold irrespective of student body selectivity but tend to be manifest through indirect routes. Other factors being equal, attending a large institution tends to inhibit a student's level of social involvement (extracurricular activities, interaction with faculty, and the like) during college, and social involvement is a nontrivial determinant of such outcomes as educational attainment and self-concept.

College Racial and Gender Composition

Although the total body of evidence on standardized test performance (for example, Graduate Record Examination, National Teacher Examinations) is as yet inconclusive, attending a predominantly black (versus a predominantly white) college appears to have a modest positive impact on cognitive development and educational attainment for black students and a small positive effect on occupational status and on both academic and social self-image among black women (see Table 13.20). It is somewhat difficult to identify the causal mechanism underlying these findings. It has been hypothesized, however, that black colleges provide a social-psychological environment more conducive to black students' social integration and personal development than do predominantly white colleges.

Similarly, as further indicated in Table 13.20, there is also evidence to suggest that single-sex colleges tend to enhance students' socioeconomic aspirations and career attainments. This is particularly true for women. Net of college selectivity and individual factors, attending a women's college appears to enhance educational aspirations and attainment, choice of sex-atypical (male-dominated) careers, and the achievement of prominence in a field. Although there is little support for impacts on occupational status and earnings generally, graduates of women's colleges are strongly overrepresented in the high-status, male-dominated occupations of medicine, scientific research, and engineering.

As with college racial composition, it is difficult to identify the causal mechanism that underlies such results. However, there is at least some support for the hypothesis that the critical factor is the presence in women's colleges of large numbers of female teachers as role models. The presence in large numbers of successful same-sex role models may be especially important to college women in overcoming sex-stereotypic attitudes in career aspirations and attainment.

Table 13.20. Summary of Estimated Between-College Effects: College Racial and Gender Composition.

College Characteristic or Outcome	Strength of Evidence	Direction of Effect	Major Rival Explanations Controlled	Magnitude of Effect
Racial Composition				
Cognitive development (critical thinking, concept attainment) of black students	Weak	Positive in direction of black colleges	Socioeconomic status, academic aptitude	Unclear[a]
Bachelor's degree completion and educational attainment of black students	Moderate	Positive in direction of black colleges	Family socioeconomic status, educational aspirations, academic ability, college selectivity and size, college grades	Small direct effect; possibly small indirect effect
Occupational status of black women	Weak	Positive in direction of black colleges	Family socioeconomic status, occupational aspirations, college selectivity and size, college grades, educational attainment	Small
Academic and social self-concepts of black students	Moderate	Positive in direction of black colleges	Gender, socioeconomic status, ability, initial self-concept, aspirations	Unclear; probably small indirect effect but only for black women

Gender Composition

Educational aspirations and educational attainment of women	Moderate	Positive in direction of women's colleges	Family socioeconomic status, educational aspirations, secondary school achievement, college selectivity, college grades	Small; effect may be both direct and indirect; effect on aspirations probably stronger than effect on attainment
Implementation of career choice for men	Moderate	Positive in direction of men's colleges	Family socioeconomic status, initial career choice	Small positive effect on entering business, law, and the professions in general
Women's choice of sex-atypical careers	Weak	Positive in direction of women's colleges	College selectivity	Unclear
Women's entry into specific sex-atypical occupations (such as medicine, scientific research, engineering)	Moderate	Positive in direction of women's colleges	Unclear	Strong overrepresentation of women's college graduates in these fields
Women's achievement of prominence in a field	Moderate	Positive in direction of women's colleges	College selectivity, size, and faculty salary	Moderate to strong overrepresentation of women's college graduates who achieve prominence

[a]"Unclear," as used in this table, means we are acknowledging that the studies do not allow such estimates or that the evidence, though generally consistent, is still sufficiently complex to make an estimate of effect size hazardous.

College Environments

In our discussion of the apparent absence of impact of college quality on learning and cognitive development, we reviewed evidence suggesting that more proximal aspects of the college environment (for example, student-faculty interaction, curricular emphasis) may account for a large part of any between-college effects. As shown in Table 13.21, there is also reasonably consistent evidence to indicate that college environmental factors may influence both educational attainment and career choice and possibly aesthetic and cultural values and levels of authoritarianism, internal locus of control, and general psychosocial adjustment. The environmental factors that maximize persistence and educational attainment include a peer culture in which students develop close on-campus friendships, participate frequently in college-sponsored activities, and perceive their college to be highly concerned about the individual student, as well as a college emphasis on supportive services (including advising, orientation, and individualized general education courses that develop academic survival skills). It is possible, of course, that these environmental characteristics may be at least partially determined by other institutional traits, such as enrollment or the academic preparation of the student body. Nevertheless, it is worth noting that some of these environmental influences on educational attainment persist even after college size and student body selectivity are taken into account.

The most consistent college environmental impact on career choice is that of "progressive conformity." Progressive conformity holds that career choice will be influenced in the direction of the dominant peer groups in a college. The weight of evidence we reviewed tends to support this hypothesis. Irrespective of initial career choice, there is a small but persistent tendency for seniors to plan and subsequently enter careers consistent with the most typical academic majors at their institution.

Environmental effects are also evident in certain areas of psychosocial change. For example, decreases in authoritarianism and increases in general psychosocial adjustment and maturity appear to be greater on campuses where there is an emphasis on intrinsic motivations, student involvement in classroom discussions and course decision making, and general involvement with faculty in an academic community.

Geographical and Social Proximity

Between-college effects on socioeconomic outcomes may depend as much, if not more, on how individual institutions are regarded by employers as on any distinctive cognitive and noncognitive skills they impart to students. This may in part explain the modest occupational and economic advantages enjoyed by graduates of elite schools. In addition to the status-allocating power of public reputation, another way in which a college may

Table 13.21. Summary of Estimated *Between-College* Effects: *College Environments.*

Outcome	Strength of Evidence	Direction of Effect	Major Rival Explanations Controlled	Magnitude of Net Effect
Learning (typically on standardized measures such as the Graduate Record Examination)	Moderate	Positive in direction of (1) frequent student-faculty interaction, (2) degree of curricular flexibility, (3) faculty formal education level	Academic aptitude, major field of study	Very small
Cognitive development (such as critical thinking, adult reasoning skills)	Moderate	Positive in direction of general education emphasis in curriculum	College selectivity	Small to moderate
Educational attainment	Moderate	Positive in direction of (1) cohesive peer environment, (2) participation in college activities, (3) perception of personal concern for student, (4) emphasis on supportive student personnel services	Family socioeconomic status, secondary school achievement, educational aspirations, college size and selectivity	Unclear,[a] but probably small
Aesthetic, cultural, and intellectual attitudes and values	Weak	Positive in direction of campuses high in awareness and scholarship; negative on campuses high in propriety and practicality	None	Unclear
Internal locus of control	Moderate	Positive in direction of cohesive peer environment	Gender, race, socioeconomic status, ability, initial level of internality	Unclear

Table 13.21. Summary of Estimated *Between-College* Effects: *College Environments*. Cont'd

Outcome	Strength of Evidence	Direction of Effect	Major Rival Explanations Controlled	Magnitude of Net Effect
Authoritarianism and dogmatism	Weak	Negative in direction of schools with liberal campus climate, large proportion of nonconformists, student involvement in class activities, emphasis on intrinsic motivations	Gender, ability, socioeconomic status	Unclear
Personal adjustment and psychological well-being	Weak	Positive in direction of campus with high proportion of "expressive" students, classroom participation, emphasis on complex mental activities, intrinsic awards	Gender, socioeconomic status, ability	Unclear
Career choice and career entered	Strong	Positive in direction of "progressive conformity" hypothesis	Initial career choice, major field choice, educational aspirations, academic aptitude, college grades	Small

[a]"Unclear," as used in this table, means we are acknowledging that the studies do not allow such estimates or that the evidence, though generally consistent, is still sufficiently complex to make an estimate of effect size hazardous.

confer an occupational advantage on a graduate is through its geographical and social proximity to a prospective employer. (See Table 13.22.) A college that is geographically close to a company, that has frequent professional and consultative interactions with the company, and whose graduates are represented in the company's management tends to confer on its graduates employed by that company an advantage in initial job level and promotion rate. This advantage, moreover, appears to function independently of the selectivity of the college.

Thus, the occupational impact of where one attends college may not be independent of one's employment context. Indeed, the career mobility of graduates of certain colleges may be at least partially influenced by the dominant managerial culture of an employing organization.

Transfer Between Four-Year Institutions

Educational attainment is not only influenced by the type of institution in which one enrolls; it is also affected by the continuity of one's experience in that institution. An interruption in this continuity in the form of transfer from one four-year institution to another tends to inhibit degree attainment (see Table 13.23). This holds irrespective of race and gender but is particularly pronounced for black men. Not surprisingly, the inhibiting influence of transfer on degree attainment leads to a consistent set of negative indirect effects on occupational status and a less consistent set of negative impacts on earnings. Thus, institutional continuity in one's postsecondary educational experience not only enhances degree attainment but also has additional positive implications for early occupational and economic attainments. This suggests the potential importance of one's fit with the initial college of enrollment.

Within-College Effects

As evidenced in Chapters Three through Twelve, an extensive variety of within-college effects on students have been examined. Although a substantial number of individual studies have proceeded from a theoretical base, the evidence as a whole is not founded on a common set of conceptual or theoretical themes. Consequently, we organize the synthesis of this large body of research around our own understanding of the common threads running through the evidence. First, we offer several conclusions about the evidence as a whole. Second, we offer our conclusions about the major determinants of within-college effects, as organized under the categories of residence, major field of study, the academic experience, interpersonal involvement, extracurricular involvement, and academic achievement.

Table 13.22. Summary of Estimated *Between-College* Effects: *Geographical and Social Proximity*.

Outcome	Strength of Evidence	Direction of Effect	Major Rival Explanations Controlled	Magnitude of Net Effect
Initial job level and promotion rate	Weak	Positive in direction of proximity	College selectivity, age, tenure in firm	Unclear,[a] but probably small

[a] "Unclear," as used here, means we are acknowledging that the studies do not allow such estimates or that the evidence, though generally consistent, is still sufficiently complex to make an estimate of effect size hazardous.

Table 13.23. Summary of Estimated Between-College Effects: *Transfer Between Four-Year Institutions.*

Outcome	Strength of Evidence	Direction of Effect	Major Rival Explanations Controlled	Magnitude of Net Effect
Educational attainment, occupational status, and earnings	Weak	Negative in direction of transfer	Family socioeconomic status, aspirations, expectations of transfer, selectivity of first college attended, college grades	Moderate negative direct effect on educational attainment; small negative indirect effect on occupational status transmitted through educational attainment; small negative direct and indirect effects on earnings

General Conclusions

The types of within-college experiences that maximize impact are not independent of the kind of college attended. Certain experiences that maximize change are more likely at some institutions than at others. For example, a social context that enhances frequent student-faculty informal interaction is more likely at small, primarily residential colleges than at large universities with a mix of residential and commuter students. Nevertheless, nearly all of the important within-college impacts persist irrespective of the institutional context in which they occur.

Similarly, many of the experiences that maximize impact are not independent of the kinds of students who engage in them. For example, students who are most likely to develop close informal relationships with faculty members are also likely to aspire to graduate or professional school when they enter college. The net impact of their informal interaction with faculty would be to even further strengthen their plans. Thus, consistent with Feldman and Newcomb's (1969) conclusion, we found many within-college effects to be essentially the accentuation of initial student characteristics. Certain experiences tend to attract students with certain traits or dispositions and, in turn, tend to accentuate the traits or dispositions that drew those students to the experiences in the first place.

A third generalization is that within-college effects, like between-college effects, tend to be substantially smaller in magnitude than the overall net effect of college attendance. As with the research on between-college effects, there are several possible methodological reasons for this. Substantive explanations, however, are perhaps more valid. Most theoretical models of development in no way guarantee that any single experience will be an important determinant of change for all students. A majority of important changes that occur during college are probably the cumulative result of a set of interrelated experiences sustained over an extended period of time. Consequently, research that focuses on the impact of a single or isolated experience, a characteristic of most investigations of within-college influences, is unlikely to yield strong effects.

A final generalization concerns empirical support for theoretical models of college impact. In Chapter Two we briefly summarized the major elements of several such theories. On the basis of the extensive body of evidence reviewed, much of which would confirm expectations based on those theories, one of the most inescapable and unequivocal conclusions we can make is that the impact of college is largely determined by the individual's quality of effort and level of involvement in both academic and nonacademic activities. This is not particularly surprising; indeed, the positive effects of both the quality and extent of involvement have been repeatedly stressed by Astin (1984) and Pace (1984, 1987).

Such a conclusion suggests that the impact of college is not simply the result of what a college does for or to a student. Rather, the impact is a result of the extent to which an individual student exploits the people, programs, facilities, opportunities, and experiences that the college makes available. Students are not simply the recipients of institutional effects. They themselves bear a major responsibility for the impact of their own college experience. From this perspective it is the individual student who perhaps most determines the extent to which college makes a difference.

Although this conclusion stresses the salience of individual student involvement, it in no way means that individual campus policies and programs are unimportant. Indeed, we would strongly argue the contrary. If individual effort or involvement is the critical determinant of college impact, then a key question focuses on the ways in which a campus can shape its intellectual and interpersonal environments to invite increased student involvement. In the next sections we summarize salient within-college influences, some of which may provide colleges with programmatic or policy levers by which student involvement can be maximized.

Residence

Living on campus (versus commuting to college) is perhaps the single most consistent within-college determinant of impact (see Table 13.24). This is not particularly surprising because residential living creates a social-psychological context for students that is markedly different from that experienced by those who live at home or elsewhere off campus and commute to college. Simply put, living on campus maximizes opportunities for social, cultural, and extracurricular involvement; and it is this involvement that largely accounts for residential living's impact on student change. To be sure, those who live on campus may, as a group, be psychologically more open to many of the impacts of college to begin with than are their commuting counterparts. Even with this initial difference held constant, however, residential living is positively, if modestly, linked to increases in aesthetic, cultural, and intellectual values; a liberalizing of social, political, and religious values and attitudes; increases in self-concept, intellectual orientation, autonomy, and independence; gains in tolerance, empathy, and ability to relate to others; persistence in college; and bachelor's degree attainment.

Since the facilitation of campus social involvement or participation is the probable causal mechanism underlying the impact of living on campus, it is not surprising that the majority of the demonstrated effects of living on campus are in the areas of student values, attitudes, and psychosocial development. There is little compelling evidence to suggest that the knowledge acquisition or general cognitive effects of college are significantly related to living on campus compared with commuting to college. Indeed, there is at least a modicum of evidence to suggest that a high level of in-

Table 13.24. Summary of Estimated _Within-College_ Effects: _Residence._

Outcome	Strength of Evidence	Direction of Effect	Major Rival Explanations Controlled	Magnitude of Net Effect[a]
Aesthetic, cultural, and intelletual values	Moderate	Positive in direction of on-campus residence	Gender, race, socioeconomic status, ability, initial values	Unclear
Sociopolitical attitudes and values	Moderate	Positive in direction of on-campus residence	Gender, race, socioeconomic status, ability	Unclear
Secularism	Moderate	Positive in direction of on-campus residence	Gender, race, socioeconomic status, ability, initial values	Unclear
Self-concepts	Weak to moderate	Positive in direction of on-campus residence	Gender, race, socioeconomic status, ability, initial concepts	Unclear, but probably small and indirect via interpersonal relations
Autonomy, independence, internal locus of control	Weak	Positive in direction of on-campus residence	Gender, ability	Unclear
Intellectual orientation	Moderate	Positive in direction of on-campus residence	Gender, ability, initial levels	Unclear, but probably small and indirect, mediated by interpersonal relations and residence environment
Persistence and degree attainment	Strong	Positive in direction of on-campus residence, especially in living-learning center	Gender, ability, socioeconomic status, educational aspirations, high school achievement	Unclear
Moral development	Weak	Positive in direction of on-campus residence	Initial level of moral development	Unclear

[a] "Unclear," as used in this table, means we are acknowledging that the studies do not allow such estimates or that the evidence, though generally consistent, is still sufficiently complex to make an estimate of effect size hazardous.

volvement in dormitory life and activities can actually function to isolate an individual from the intellectual life of a college and inhibit some aspects of cognitive growth.

It is likely that the impact of living on campus is not monolithic. Considerable evidence suggests discernible differences in the social and intellectual climate of different residences on the same campus. With a few exceptions (such as college grades), unfortunately, there is little consistent evidence linking differences in the climate of residences to various college outcomes. Not surprisingly, what evidence we do have suggests that those residence climates with the strongest impacts on cognitive development and persistence are typically the result of purposeful programmatic efforts to integrate the student's intellectual and social life during college. Moreover, as will be discussed in greater detail below, residential effects may well be indirect ones, mediated through the interpersonal experiences students have with peers and faculty members that are shaped by the residential setting.

It is important to be aware of two limitations if one is to place the impact of living on campus in its proper perspective. First, it is quite clear that over half of all students in American postsecondary education commute to college and if current trends continue that proportion is likely to increase. Similarly, fully a third of the nation's colleges and universities have no residential facilities, and given financial and student demographic exigencies, they are unlikely to ever have them. For this major group of students and institutions the potential educational benefits of living on campus are largely moot. Developing programs and policies that approximate the student involvement facilitated by residential living is a major challenge for those who educate commuter students or who administer commuter campuses.

A second limitation involves the somewhat narrow view many scholars have taken in assessing the impact of place of residence during college. The focus has been largely on outcomes traditionally valued by the academic community (intellectual values, tolerance, liberalization of social attitudes, and the like). Less sensitivity has been shown to the types of learning and maturing that may occur when the individual must successfully attend to work and family as well as to educational responsibilities. A far larger percentage of commuter students than of resident students are confronted with these additional responsibilities. As a result, the challenges that they face but that their resident counterparts are less likely to confront may lead to comparatively greater growth in areas not now explored by studies of traditional residential students.

Major Field of Study

One's major field of study creates a potentially important subenvironment during college. It not only focuses one's intellectual efforts in a particular direction, but it also has an influence on the kinds of students and faculty with whom one interacts. Consequently, it might be expected that in addition to what one learns, academic major would also have a significant impact on such outcomes as values, attitudes, and psychosocial change. The total body of evidence, however, suggests that the impacts of academic major are markedly stronger and more consistent in cognitive areas than in noncognitive ones.

As might be expected, and as indicated in Table 13.25, the cognitive impact of major field of study is selective. Students tend to demonstrate the highest levels of learning on subject matter tests most congruent with their academic major. Similarly, they tend to demonstrate the greatest proficiency on measures of general cognitive development when the content of problems is most consistent with their academic major or the disciplinary emphasis of their course work. Thus, for example, social science majors outperform others on tests of social science content and on measures of abstract reasoning and critical thinking applied to social science tasks and problems. The same tendencies hold for science and humanities majors. Beyond these selective impacts, however, we found little consistent evidence that one's major has more than a trivial net impact on one's general level of intellectual or cognitive outcomes.

In contrast, the impact of major field of study on noncognitive outcomes is substantially less apparent or consistent. The effects of major field on changes in students' identity status or ego development stage remain unexamined. Students majoring in the natural or physical sciences, mathematics, or technical fields appear to enjoy slightly greater gains in developing a positive academic self-concept, but major field is unrelated to changes in social self-concept. Similarly, the weight of evidence consistently indicates that few if any differential changes in any of the facets of students' relational systems or in attitudinal and value areas are attributable to academic major. As with the research on the effects of residence in these areas, however, there is some evidence to suggest that departmental environment, whatever the department, may be more important than the characteristics of the discipline in shaping psychosocial and attitudinal changes among students. The interpersonal climate and value homogeneity and consensus within a department appear to be particularly important. The salience of interpersonal relations is discussed at greater length below.

Major field of study does have a number of statistically significant links to the occupational structure in American society. Consequently, what one majors in during college has potentially important implications for the occupation one enters and the economic rewards one receives from his or her work. For example, majors in such areas as business, engineering, some preprofessional programs, and some natural sciences increase the likelihood that one will enter a job with skill requirements consistent with one's academic training, that women will enter relatively high status, male-domi-

Table 13.25. Summary of Estimated Within-College Effects: Major Field of Study.

Outcome	Strength of Evidence	Direction of Effect	Major Rival Explanations Controlled	Magnitude of Net Effect
Content learning and cognitive development	Strong	Students perform highest on subject matter tests and on measures of general cognitive development most consistent with their academic major	Unclear	Unclear,[a] but probably moderate to large
Academic self-concept	Strong	Positive in favor of sciences, math, technical majors	Gender, race, ability, socioeconomic status, high school achievement, initial self-concept, other precollege traits	Unclear, but departmental environment may be more important than the discipline
Women's entry into sex-atypical occupations	Strong	Positive in direction of high percentage of men in the major (e.g., business, engineering, natural sciences)	Age, socioeconomic status, college selectivity, college grades	Unclear, but probably moderate
Earnings	Strong	Positive in direction of business, engineering, and preprofessional majors	Socioeconomic status, race, gender, academic aptitude, college grades, occupational aspirations, educational attainment, college selectivity	Unclear, but probably moderate; also unclear whether earnings advantage extends over one's total career

[a] "Unclear," as used in this table, means we are acknowledging that the studies do not allow such estimates or that the evidence, though generally consistent, is still sufficiently complex to make an estimate of effect size hazardous.

nated occupations, and that one will enjoy advantages in early career earnings. These major field impacts tend to persist above and beyond differences in student background traits linked to different majors, as well as level of academic achievement during college.

The occupational impacts of one's academic major, however, appear to be strongest in the earliest stages of one's career. As an individual's career matures, the impact of undergraduate field of study decreases in importance. For example, the specific skills learned in one's major are most important for productivity in the first job after graduation. Thereafter, they diminish in importance and are replaced in importance by general intellectual skills and the ability to learn on the job. Similarly, over the long term, career mobility and occupational attainment levels of liberal arts majors in the private business sector appear to equal (though not excel) those of business or engineering majors. While the existing evidence on earnings is less extensive, it suggests the same trend.

The Academic Experience

Although the body of research on the impacts of the college academic experience is extensive, it clearly does not match the large volume of research conducted with elementary and secondary school students. Nevertheless, we believe that the former permits four general conclusions (see Table 13.26).

Perhaps the strongest conclusion that can be made is the least surprising. Simply put, the greater the student's involvement or engagement in academic work or in the academic experience of college, the greater his or her level of knowledge acquisition and general cognitive development. Though less extensive, evidence also suggests that academic involvement enhances declines in authoritarianism and dogmatism and increases in autonomy and independence, intellectual orientation, and the use of principled moral reasoning.

If level of involvement were totally determined by individual student motivation, interest, and ability, the above conclusion would be uninteresting as well as unsurprising. However, a substantial amount of evidence indicates that there are instructional and programmatic interventions that not only increase a student's active engagement in learning and academic work but also enhance knowledge acquisition and some dimensions of both cognitive and psychosocial change. Instructional strategies such as note taking, peer teaching, and various individualized learning approaches (for example, personalized system of instruction, audio-tutorial instruction, computer-based instruction) are based to a large extent on increasing students' active engagement in learning. Each has been shown to enhance knowledge acquisition under experimental conditions. The evidence on interventions

Table 13.26. Summary of Estimated Within-College Effects: *The Academic Experience*.

Outcome	Strength of Evidence	Direction of Effect	Major Rival Explanations Controlled	Magnitude of Net Effect
Knowledge acquisition	Strong	Positive in direction of greater student involvement, individualized instructional strategies, instructor skill, and course structure	Aptitude, motivation; many of the studies of individualized instruction are based on randomized experiments	Individualized instruction produces positive effects of .15 to .49 SD (6 to 19 percentile points) over traditional methods; correlations of course achievement with instructor skill and course structure are about .50 and .47, respectively
Cognitive development	Strong	Positive in direction of greater student involvement, emphasis on inductive learning, academic experiences providing for challenge and/or integration	Academic aptitude, secondary school achievement, socioeconomic status	Small to moderate
Sociopolitical and gender role attitudes and values	Weak to moderate	Positive in direction of course work and special programs	Few	Unclear[a]
Academic self-concept	Moderate	Positive in direction of participation in honors program, academic integration with peers and faculty	Gender, race, socioeconomic status, ability, aspirations, initial self-concept	Unclear

Table 13.26. Summary of Estimated *Within-College Effects: The Academic Experience.* Cont'd

Outcome	Strength of Evidence	Direction of Effect	Major Rival Explanations Controlled	Magnitude of Net Effect
Relational psychosocial areas (primarily autonomy and independence, nonauthoritarianism, intellectual disposition, general personal development and maturity)	Weak to moderate	Positive in direction of living-learning program participation	Gender, ability, initial levels	Unclear, but may be more indirect than direct, via interpersonal relations and program environment
Moral development	Strong	Positive in direction of instructional interventions stressing dilemma discussion and personality development	Unclear, but studies include several randomized experiments	Dilemma discussion effect size of .51 SD (19.5 percentile point gain); personality development effect size of .41 SD (16 percentile point gain)

[a]"Unclear," as used in this table, means we are acknowledging that the studies do not allow such estimates or that the evidence, though generally consistent, is still sufficiently complex to make an estimate of effect size hazardous.

that influence cognitive development is less extensive. Nevertheless, the learning-cycle or inquiry approach, which stresses inductive learning based on concrete activities, shows evidence of enhancing the development of abstract reasoning and perhaps cognitive complexity. Similarly, there is at least modest evidence to suggest that critical thinking and the use of principled moral reasoning may be enhanced by instruction that stresses active student discussion at a relatively high cognitive level and instruction that engages students in problem solving.

A second general conclusion is that change in a wide variety of areas is stimulated by academic experiences that purposefully provide for challenge and/or integration. For example, cognitive-developmental instruction, which presents the student with cognitive conflict and forces the altering of previously held values and constructs for reasoning, shows evidence of uniquely stimulating growth in postformal reasoning abilities. Similarly, a curricular experience in which students are required to integrate learning from separate courses around a central theme appears to elicit greater growth in critical thinking than does the same curricular experience without the integrative requirement.

A third conclusion is that student learning is unambiguously linked to effective teaching, and we know much about what effective teachers do and how they behave in the classroom. Although a number of teacher behaviors are positively associated with student learning (rapport with students, interpersonal accessibility to students, feedback to students, and the like), two stand out as being particularly salient. These are instructor skill (particularly clarity of presentation) and structuring of the course (for example, class time is structured and organized efficiently). What is perhaps most important is that many of the elements of both dimensions of effective teaching can themselves be learned.

Finally, there is evidence in support of differential course work impacts. This conclusion is perhaps the most tentative in that the research is in its initial stages and the mapping of consistent and replicable patterns of results is still somewhat unclear. Nevertheless, it is quite possible that, irrespective of academic ability, the pattern and sequence of courses taken as an undergraduate may influence not only the subject matter content of what is learned but also more general cognitive abilities. To the extent that replicable findings are derived from this inquiry, it may be possible to plan one's academic program in ways that are most likely to maximize cognitive impact. While the effects of different course work patterns and sequences on psychosocial changes have not been examined, a number of studies indicate that course work in certain areas (the social sciences, for instance) may have a positive influence on increases in political liberalism and in other social attitudes and values (such as sex roles). And a substantial body of research points to course-related or special-program-related effects on a number of psychosocial characteristics. Studies in this research area are highly heterogeneous in focus and methodological rigor, however, making summary conclusions difficult.

Interpersonal Involvement

A large part of the impact of college is determined by the extent and content of one's interactions with major agents of socialization on campus, namely, faculty members and student peers. The influence of interpersonal interaction with these groups is manifest in intellectual outcomes as well as in changes in attitudes, values, aspirations, and a number of psychosocial characteristics (see Table 13.27).

The educational impact of a college's faculty is enhanced when their contacts with students extend beyond the formal classroom to informal nonclassroom settings. Net of student background characteristics, extent of informal contact with faculty is positively linked with a wide range of outcomes. These include perceptions of intellectual growth during college, increases in intellectual orientation, liberalization of social and political values, growth in autonomy and independence, increases in interpersonal skills, gains in general maturity and personal development, educational aspirations and attainment, orientation toward scholarly careers, and women's interest in and choice of sex-atypical (male-dominated) careers.

With some exceptions, much of the research on which these conclusions are based uses rather distal and often surface measures of student-faculty interaction. Nevertheless, we do know that the impact of student-faculty informal contact is determined by its content as well as by its frequency. The most influential interactions appear to be those that focus on ideas or intellectual matters, thereby extending and reinforcing the intellectual goals of the academic program.

Just as the impact of student-faculty informal contact is not independent of its content or focus, so too it is not independent of the characteristics of the individuals involved. The students most likely to engage in nonclassroom interaction with faculty appear to be those most open to the influence of faculty to begin with. Thus, their ensuing interactions with faculty would tend to accentuate existing interests, aspirations, and values. Similarly, certain types of faculty may be more accessible or influential than others. There is clear evidence, for example, that faculty members who frequently meet with students outside of class give cues about their accessibility through their classroom behaviors. Somewhat less consistent evidence suggests that female faculty may be more influential than male faculty as role models for female students.

Consistent with evidence on the impact of student-faculty interaction, students' interactions with their peers also have a strong influence on many aspects of change during college. Included are such areas as intellectual development and orientation; political, social, and religious values; academic and social self-concept; intellectual orientation; interpersonal skills; moral development; general maturity and personal development; and educational aspirations and educational attainment. As one might expect, the degree of peer influence varies across outcomes, with some evidence suggesting that fellow students exert greater influence on change in attitudinal and psychosocial areas than in learning or cognitive ones, where the weight of faculty influence appears greater.

The direction of this impact appears to depend largely on the characteristics of the peers with whom students interact. For example, shifts in students' identities appear to follow from exposure to a wide diversity of other students who presumably challenge currently held beliefs and self-conceptions and who force introspection and reflection, leading perhaps to alterations in identity status or ego development stage. In contrast, principled moral reasoning and more general cognitive complexity are enhanced through interactions with peers who are themselves functioning at more sophisticated levels of moral reasoning and intellectual complexity. Similarly, declines in authoritarianism and dogmatism are greatest among students on campuses with large numbers of nonconforming students. Findings consistent with these are reported in other psychosocial areas. The homogeneity of the peer group may not invariably be an asset, however. Like-mindedness is a distinguishing characteristic of peer groups, and a small body of evidence (dealing primarily with residence groups) suggests that the peer group can insulate against change in certain areas even as it stimulates change in others.

Details about the causal mechanisms behind the influence of these interpersonal interactions remain unclear, however. For example, little can be said with confidence about whether interpersonal effects are more closely related to the frequency of students' contact with peers and faculty members or to the nature of the contact. The influence may also originate in the more generalized context and climate created by the presence of individuals who possess knowledge, skills, psychosocial characteristics, and attitudes and values that differ to varying degrees from those of the student and toward or away from which the student may shift. Moreover, the causal direction of the influence remains uncertain. We do not yet know, for example, whether the manifest associations between student-faculty contact and various kinds of change are a function of faculty influence on students or of certain student characteristics (for example, eagerness to learn) that predispose them to seek out certain kinds of faculty members who rather than initiating change accentuate or reinforce changes already under way. In all likelihood, the causal flow is reciprocal, but at present that proposition remains more a belief than an empirically substantiated fact.

Table 13.27. Summary of Estimated *Within-College* Effects: *Interpersonal Involvement*.

Outcome	Strength of Evidence	Direction of Effect	Major Rival Explanations Controlled	Magnitude of Net Effect
Learning and cognitive growth (self-reported)	Moderate	Positive in relation to faculty and (to lesser degree) student interaction	Gender, race, ability, socioeconomic status, degree aspirations, secondary school achievement, major field	Unclear,[a] probably small
Aesthetic, cultural, and intellectual interests	Weak to moderate	Positive	Openness to change, initial values	Unclear
Occupational values	Moderate	Positive toward intrinsic and away from extrinsic values associated with faculty contact	Gender, race, ability, prior achievement, educational goals, initial values	Unclear
Sociopolitical attitudes and values	Moderate	Positive in relation to peer and faculty contact	Gender, race, ability, socioeconomic status, initial values, degree aspirations, other traits	Unclear
Secularism	Weak	Positive in relation to concentration of faculty and peers with same values	Ability, socioeconomic status	Unclear
Identity and ego development	Weak	Positive in relation to contact with and diversity of peers	None	Unclear
Academic and social self-concepts	Strong	Positive in relation to integration in academic and social systems, peers, faculty contact	Gender, race, ability, socioeconomic status, institutional characteristics	Unclear

Intellectual orientation	Moderate	Positive in relation to peer and faculty interaction	Gender, ability, initial level	Unclear
Moral development	Moderate	Positive in relation to peer interactions, contact with divergent perspectives and with peers at higher stages of moral development	Unclear	Unclear
General maturity and personal development	Moderate	Positive in relation to faculty and peer interactions	Gender, race, ability, high school achievement, major, parents' education, degree aspirations	Unclear
Educational aspirations, persistence, and attainment	Strong	Positive in relation to peer interactions and out-of-class student-faculty interaction	Gender, secondary school achievement, socioeconomic status, aptitude, educational aspirations, initial institutional and degree commitments, other college experiences	Unclear

[a]"Unclear," as used in this table, means we are acknowledging that the studies do not allow such estimates or that the evidence, though generally consistent, is still sufficiently complex to make an estimate of effect size hazardous.

Extracurricular Involvement

From one perspective extracurricular involvement may be seen as a more formalized manifestation of one's interpersonal involvement during college. Thus, part of its impact may stem from an individual's participation in an influential peer culture. This may explain why extracurricular involvement has a positive impact on educational attainment (see Table 13.28). As a group, students who frequently participate in extracurricular activities tend to enter college with relatively high educational aspirations. Consequently, they may constitute a peer culture within the institution, a culture whose group norms tend to accentuate the educational aspirations of participating members.

Interestingly, we found little additional consistent evidence to suggest that extracurricular involvement per se has a broad-based impact on student development or change. To a great extent, however, this probably reflects the fact that the vast majority of studies make no clear distinction between peer involvement and extracurricular involvement. Indeed, the terms are often conceptually interchangeable in the body of evidence. Even though it may not be captured in the designs of the studies reviewed, it is quite likely that a major portion of the influential interactions that students have with peers takes place in the multifaceted extracurriculum.

From another perspective, extracurricular involvement, particularly in leadership positions, has at least modest implications for one's career. This may stem from the fact that such involvements enhance self-confidence along with interpersonal and leadership skills. Thus, net of background characteristics, holding extracurricular leadership positions during college increases the likelihood that women will enter male-dominated occupations. Similarly, alumni are reasonably consistent in reporting that involvement in extracurricular activities, particularly in leadership roles, significantly enhanced interpersonal and leadership skills important to job success. We found no consistent evidence, however, that extracurricular accomplishment has an independent influence on job status, career mobility, or earnings.

Academic Achievement

Although grades are limited as a reliable and valid measure of what is learned during college, they nevertheless reflect a number of personal traits that have implications for job productivity and success. These include requisite intellectual skills, personal motivation and effort, and the willingness and ability to meet organizational norms. The independent impact of undergraduate grades on various indexes of occupational success is small, but it is persistent. Net of individual background characteristics, as well as college selectivity and major field of study, undergraduate grades have a

Table 13.28. Summary of Estimated *Within-College* Effects: *Extracurricular Involvement.*

Outcome	Strength of Evidence	Direction of Effect	Major Rival Explanations Controlled	Magnitude of Net Effect
Educational persistence and attainment	Moderate	Positive	Gender, ability, high school achievement, socioeconomic status, educational aspirations	Small
Women's choice of sex-atypical careers	Moderate	Positive	Socioeconomic status, secondary school grades, initial occupational aspirations, college grades, college selectivity, educational attainment	Unclear[a]
Social self-concept	Strong	Positive, related to involvement in leadership activities	Gender, race, ability, high school achievement, socioeconomic status, degree aspirations, major, initial self-concept, various other precollege characteristics, selected institutional characteristics	Unclear

[a]"Unclear," as used in this table, means we are acknowledging that the studies do not allow such estimates or that the evidence, though generally consistent, is still sufficiently complex to make an estimate of effect size hazardous.

positive influence on the status or prestige of the job entered, career mobility, and earnings (see Table 13.29). Part of this effect is direct, but part
is also indirect, being transmitted through the strong impact of grades on
educational attainment. Thus, good undergraduate grades do give an individual a modest career advantage, at least in the early stages.

In some areas, such as entrance into the relatively high status professions of medicine and law, good grades appear to count more if they are
earned at a selective undergraduate college. In terms of income, however,
grades appear to count the same irrespective of college selectivity or even
major field of study.

Selective or General Involvement?

It seems clear that involvement tends to be selective in its influence
on change during college. By this we mean that there is some tendency for
college impact to be commensurate with involvement in activities that are
consistent with and support specific outcomes. Thus, intellectual development is most clearly influenced by classroom involvement or the quality of
effort put forth in one's academic work. Conversely, changes in attitudes,
values, and psychosocial dimensions may, on the whole, be more a function
of one's interpersonal involvement.

Despite this clear tendency, there is also evidence to suggest a certain
wholeness to the college experience, particularly in its impacts on intellectual development. Intellectual growth may be primarily a function of one's
academic involvement and effort, but the content and focus of one's interpersonal and extracurricular involvements can have a moderating influence
on that growth. Indeed, in some areas of intellectual development, such as
critical thinking, there is evidence to suggest that it is the student's breadth
of involvement in the intellectual and social experience of college, not any
particular type of involvement, that counts most. Thus, although the weight
of evidence indicates that the links between involvement and change tend
to be specific, the greatest impact may stem from the student's total level of
campus engagement, particularly when academic, interpersonal, and extracurricular involvements are mutually supporting and relevant to a particular educational outcome.

Conditional Effects of College

Despite many undoubtedly sincere statements in the postsecondary
education literature about the need to respect individual student differences, relatively little attention has been paid to the assessment of conditional effects—changes that are differentially related to the interaction of
students' characteristics and either the duration or nature of the collegiate
experience. To be sure, there are isolated exceptions to this conclusion, for

Table 13.29. Summary of Estimated *Within-College* Effects: *Academic Achievement*.

Outcome	Strength of Evidence	Direction of Effect	Major Rival Explanations Controlled	Magnitude of Net Effect
Occupational status	Strong	Positive	Gender, occupational aspirations, socioeconomic status, college selectivity, educational attainment	Small; grades probably account for about 1% of variance; part of effect is indirect via effect on educational attainment
Job performance and career mobility	Moderate	Positive	Socioeconomic status, work experience, college selectivity, educational attainment	Small; grades probably account for no more than 1% of variance
Earnings	Strong	Positive	Socioeconomic status, race, gender, secondary school grades, college selectivity, academic ability, educational attainment, occupational status, region of country where employed	Small; grades probably account for about 1% of variance; part of effect is indirect via effect on educational attainment

example, in research on instructional methods. By and large, however, the research has been more interested in assessing the average impact of various college experiences on all students than in determining whether different college environments or experiences have different effects on different kinds of students.

The presence of conditional effects is most pronounced in two areas of research on college impact: learning and cognitive development and the socioeconomic outcomes of college. (See Table 13.30.) In the area of learning and cognitive development there is reasonably strong evidence that certain kinds of students benefit more from one instructional approach than another. For example, instructional approach may interact with student personality traits. Students high in need for independent achievement or internal locus of control appear to learn more when instruction stresses independence, self-direction, and participation. Conversely, students high in the need for conforming or dependent achievement or external locus of control appear to benefit more from more highly structured, teacher-directed instructional formats.

It seems reasonable that other types of instruction may also interact with individual student personality traits. Here the emerging work of Perry and colleagues with remedial instructional interventions, such as attributional retraining, shows considerable promise (Perry & Dickens, 1984; Perry & Magnusson, 1987; Perry & Penner, 1984; Perry & Tunna, 1988).

There is additional evidence to suggest that instruction interacts not only with personality but also with the student's level of cognitive development. For example, instruction stressing inductive learning based on concrete activities (learning-cycle or inquiry approach) appears to have its most pronounced benefits on the development of abstract reasoning for students functioning at initially lower (concrete) levels of reasoning.

What may be most important is not the findings we have to date but rather what they suggest. We should fully expect that individual student differences will moderate the effects of college instruction. Not all students will benefit equally from the same classroom settings and instructional approaches. A more comprehensive mapping of these interactions between student traits and the instructional process may allow for a more precise and effective application of different instructional approaches.

In terms of socioeconomic outcomes, perhaps the clearest set of conditional effects concerns race. Unfortunately, the analyses are largely limited to male samples, but it would appear that in terms of occupational status, nonwhite or black men derive somewhat greater relative benefits from a bachelor's degree than do white men. The evidence on earnings is less consistent but suggests that since about 1970 nonwhite or black men may also be receiving somewhat greater relative benefits from a bachelor's degree than are their white counterparts.

Gender effects are less clear and for private economic rate of return may depend on race. Of all groups, nonwhite women appear to receive the greatest economic return on investment from a bachelor's degree. In terms of incremental effects on earnings, a bachelor's degree is probably more valuable to a woman than to a man. What men and women major in during college can also have a differential impact on early occupational status. For example, women are less likely than men to major in the natural sciences or technical fields (for example, engineering), but they receive incrementally greater occupational status benefits from doing so than do their male counterparts.

What is perhaps most seductive about the conditional effects of college based on race and gender is that college appears to function in a compensatory manner. That is, it confers incrementally different socioeconomic benefits in a manner that should produce greater racial and gender equality. What should be kept in mind, however, is that the groups who would benefit most from obtaining a bachelor's degree (racial and ethnic minorities) or from majoring in scientific or technical fields (women) are at a distinct disadvantage when it comes to doing either. Thus, while the benefits may be greater, the chances of obtaining them are smaller.

A note of caution is in order here. As indicated by the above conclusions, our reading of the evidence suggests that replicable conditional effects involving gender and race are largely limited to socioeconomic outcomes. This in no way precludes the possibility, even the likelihood, that there may be significant gender or racial differences in the processes of intellectual and personal maturation. Our synthesis, however, was concerned with a different question: specifically, whether or not the magnitude of the impact of college on intellectual and personal maturation varies for gender or racial groups. We found little in the way of replicable evidence to indicate that this is the case.

A final set of conditional effects concerns the influence of college selectivity on various indexes of career attainment. Although the general effect of college selectivity on occupational status is quite small and perhaps trivial, there is reasonably consistent evidence that selectivity matters for occupational status in professional careers but may be of questionable value for business or managerial careers. Consistent with this evidence is the finding that good undergraduate grades have a more positive impact on entry into professional careers (for example, medicine and law) if they were earned at selective rather than at less selective institutions. Thus, part of the explanation for why college selectivity has trivial or at best small effects on overall occupational prestige and career mobility is that its impact is of greater consequence in some career paths than in others.

A similar conditional effect is that the positive net impact of college selectivity on earnings is stronger for men from relatively high family socioeconomic backgrounds (managerial, professional) than for men from lower socioeconomic origins (blue-collar). Such a finding suggests that attendance

Table 13.30. Summary of Estimated *Conditional* College Effects.

Outcome	Strength of Evidence	Direction of Effect	Major Rival Explanations Controlled	Magnitude of Net Effect
Effects Conditional on Student Characteristics				
Learning	Moderate	Students high in need for independent achievement or internal locus of control do better in courses stressing self-direction and independent learning; students with high need for conforming or dependent achievement or external locus of control do better in structured, teacher-directed courses	Results based on randomized experiments	Moderate
Cognitive development (formal reasoning)	Weak	Less-advanced reasoners benefit more from learning-cycle or inquiry approach to instruction; students advance most via instuctional methods matched to their reasoning level	Initial level of formal reasoning	Unclear[a]
Occupational status	Strong	Nonwhite males derive greater benefits than whites from a bachelor's degree; women derive greater benefits than men from majoring in natural science and technical fields	Socioeconomic status, intelligence, educational aspirations, grades, occupational aspirations	Unclear

Earnings	Strong	Since about 1970 black and other nonwhite men have derived greater relative earnings benefits from a bachelor's degree than have white men; women derive greater relative earnings benefits than men from each year of college completed and from a bachelor's degree	Socioeconomic status, academic ability, place of residence, years of work experience	Moderate to substantial
Private rate of return	Moderate	White men enjoy somewhat higher private economic rate of return on a bachelor's degree than do nonwhite (primarily black) men, but this gap may be closing; black and other nonwhite women have a higher rate of return on a bachelor's degree than do white women	Unclear	Moderate
Effects Conditional on Institutional Characteristics				
Occupational status	Moderate	College selectivity may have stronger positive impact on occupational status in professional careers than in nonprofessional careers	Socioeconomic status, secondary school achievement, occupational aspirations, race	Small; effect may be both direct and indirect through educational attainment
Earnings	Moderate	College selectivity may have stronger positive impact on earnings for men from relatively high family socioeconomic backgrounds than for men from relatively low family socioeconomic backgrounds	Socioeconomic status, educational attainment, occupational status, race	Small

[a]"Unclear," as used in this table, means we are acknowledging that the studies do not allow such estimates or that the evidence, though generally consistent, is still sufficiently complex to make an estimate of effect size hazardous.

at a selective college may be part of the process of cumulative advantage in American society. Students from advantaged social backgrounds are not only more likely to attend elite undergraduate colleges than their counterparts from less advantaged social origins; they may also be more likely to convert the status conferred by such an institution into greater economic success.

Some Final Thoughts

When asked why he robbed banks, Willie Sutton, the notorious bank robber, is reputed to have replied: "Because that's where the money is." In developing this synthesis we have gone "where the evidence is," and that evidence is not without some bias. It is based almost exclusively on samples of traditional college students who are age eighteen to twenty-two, who attend four-year institutions full-time, and who live on campus. It has also tended to focus on nonminority students, although there have been some recent major exceptions to this. The research methodologies have almost exclusively been quantitative and positivistic in their orientation.

If there is a major future direction for research on the impact of college, it will be to focus on that growing proportion of students whom we have typically classified as nontraditional, although they are rapidly becoming the majority participants in the American postsecondary system. These include minority and older students, those who commute to college and quite likely work part- or full-time, and those who attend college part-time. Some of our most cherished notions about the determinants of impact may have little relevance to these students. Indeed, we may need to revise our traditional ideas about what the impact of college really means for nontraditional students. Specifying the effects of college for the vast numbers of nontraditional students who now populate American postsecondary education may be the single most important area of research on college impacts in the next decade. In mounting such a research effort, it may be necessary to be particularly sensitive to the impressive diversity of students classified as nontraditional. For example, in a national study of older students, Lenning and Hanson (1977) found that the category "older student" masks great variability in many individual traits and motivations that might well determine in what ways and to what extent postsecondary education will exert an influence on these students. Failure to take such diversity into account when studying the impact of college on nontraditional students could easily produce trivial or inconsistent general effects that mask important conditional effects.

The positivistic, quantitative paradigm has served us well. The vast preponderance of what we know about the impact of college has been learned from this approach to inquiry. Yet although the broad framework is in place, there is still much important fine-grained work to be done. We suspect that the most informative future research on the impact of college must take a number of directions.

First, greater attention needs to be given to the *rigorous* examination of net college effects. The drop in the volume of relevant research when one moves from studies of change *during* college to studies of change *due to* college is striking and a source of some concern. Current claims about the benefits of college attendance frequently extend well beyond the empirical evidence to support them. Controlling the numerous alternative, noncollege sources of influence can be a daunting undertaking. It will require greater use of noncollege control groups, more specific theories, and more extensive use of relevant theories in the design of studies. Such careful theoretical preparation and grounding is not one of the distinctive characteristics of most of the research done over the past two decades, but higher education as a field of inquiry has clearly started down that road, and we wish to encourage its continuation. Theory-based research will not only be more sharply focused and parsimonious but is also likely to reflect more fully the complexity of college impacts.

Second and relatedly, researchers need to make greater efforts to estimate the *magnitudes* of college's net effects. While it may be meaningful to report simply whether an independent variable is related to a dependent variable at some level of statistical significance, it is much more meaningful, as well as theoretically and practically more informative, also to estimate the strength of that relation. Many of the studies we reviewed failed to report even the most basic information (for example, means *and* standard deviations) that might be used to estimate effect sizes. Reporting estimated effect size can reasonably be expected to lead to theories that are more parsimonious and better reflect the reality of college impact, and to substantially improve the effective allocation of scarce resources to programs intended to enhance desired institutional impacts on student outcomes.

Third, greater attention in the preparation of research studies needs to be given to bodies of theory and evidence in fields not always reflected in past and present studies. This need is particularly acute in studies of students' noncognitive, psychosocial changes. Psychological paradigms have dominated this area of study over the past twenty years, although important inroads and contributions have been made by scholars trained as sociologists and anthropologists. An alarming number of studies reflect little familiarity with the knowledge base outside the author's main disciplinary paradigm. Whether many of the observed changes are due to developmental, psychosocial restructuring within students or to the learning, through the socialization process, of competencies, attitudes, values, and behaviors valued by important others remains very much an open and vital question.

Fourth, future theory-based research should consider indirect as well as direct effects. As much of the evidence we have reviewed suggests, it is entirely possible that we may be underestimating or even misrepresenting the impact of many college influences by failing to consider their indirect effects. Because some source of influence in the causal chain is one step removed from having a direct effect on a given outcome makes it no less theoretically or practically important. Indeed, its consideration may add substantially to our knowledge of educational effects. Of course, any consideration of indirect effects means that one must typically conceptualize research questions in terms of theoretical models; but such a process is likely to reflect the complexity of college impacts more fully.

A fifth direction for future research is to focus on conditional effects. We found few replicable conditional effects in the body of evidence. This is probably because such effects have not been assessed either routinely or consistently rather than because they do not exist. We still strongly suspect that students' individual characteristics frequently mediate the impact of college; not all students benefit equally from the same experience. If certain experiences are indeed shown to be especially beneficial for particular kinds of students, it may be possible to craft more developmentally specific and effective programs and policies.

Sixth, more attention needs to be given to the analysis of the *timing* of change during the college experience. Most studies of change focus on the freshman year or on freshman-senior differences. Only a handful of studies have monitored change on an annual, sequential basis. Thus, we know little about whether change is mostly linear and monotonic or primarily episodic and discontinuous over the college years. Moreover, it seems reasonable to suggest (and there is some basis for believing) that the pacing of change varies across outcomes areas. Designing maximally effective educational interventions requires knowing *when* an intervention will make a difference and when it will not.

A seventh important direction of future research on college impact should be a greater dependence on naturalistic and qualitative methodologies. When employed judiciously, such approaches are capable of providing greater sensitivity to many of the subtle and fine-grained complexities of college impact than more traditional quantitative approaches. Naturalistic inquiries may be particularly sensitive to the detection of the kinds of indirect and conditional effects just discussed. We anticipate that in the next decade important contributions to our understanding of college impact will be yielded by naturalistic investigations.

While there are a number of topics on which important research remains to be done, one in particular stands out as a significant focus for future inquiry. This is the impact of the academic program and the teaching-learning process. How do different teaching and instructional approaches influence not only how much content is learned but also what higher-order thinking skills are developed? How and in what ways does the academic program influence values and personal change? Are there particular teaching or instructional approaches that are differentially effective for different kinds of students? What is the connection between the intellectual competencies acquired through the academic experience and those required in one's career? Answers to these and similar questions would constitute a major contribution to our understanding of the impact of college.

14

Implications
of the Research
for Policy and Practice

What do the nearly 3,000 studies conducted over the past twenty years on the effects of college on students have to say that can inform policy and enhance educational programs and practices? While a number of responses to this question, some rather narrowly focused, are possible, in this final chapter we discuss the more global and comprehensive ones, those that cut across many of the topical areas covered in this review. We first examine a number of the policy issues raised and then suggest some of the administrative and programmatic implications of the conclusions summarized in Chapter Thirteen.

Implications for Institutional and Public Policy

The evidence raises policy issues in three general areas: equalities and inequalities in postsecondary educational outcomes, institutional tolerance for individual student differences, and the tensions between educational effectiveness and economic efficiency. By "educational equalities and inequalities," we do not refer to issues of equal access to enrollment in a higher educational institution of *some* kind, as in states that guarantee all of their high school graduates a place somewhere in the state's postsecondary educational system. Rather, we use the phrase, much as Astin does, in reference to the equality of access to the *benefits* of higher education, without regard to race, sex, or socioeconomic status. As Astin (1985a, p. 82) puts it: "The real issue . . . is whether certain types of students are being denied access to educational opportunities that would confer greater benefits than the opportunities that are available to them." In a variation on that theme, one can also ask about the extent to which presumably different kinds of institutions, after holding constant the characteristics of their entering students, offer educational programs and experiences that produce correspondingly different educational outcomes.

Equalities in Educational Outcomes

Four-Year Colleges and Universities. The evidence we have reviewed on between-college effects (those attributable to differences in institutional characteristics) raises serious questions about what we mean by college "quality," the current pecking order presumably based on it, how much parents pay for it, and what they get for their money. Are institutions really all that different in "quality," if by that we mean their ability to promote educationally desirable change in students? Among four-year institutions, our review consistently suggests that they are not. After holding constant students' entering characteristics, where students attend college appears to matter much less than what happens to them after they enroll. Across a considerable range of cognitive, psychosocial, and economic outcomes, few statistically significant differences in college impact are associated with such organizational and structural characteristics as institutional size, type of control, curricular emphasis, or selectivity. Where differences do exist, they tend to be small. The apparently general character of college effects on student change clearly implies that a substantial number of non-"elite" four-year institutions may be able to compete quite successfully with substantially more prominent and resource-rich institutions in diverse, educationally significant areas.

These findings and conclusions support Astin's (1985a) argument that many current notions of institutional quality may be misleading, particularly those based on resources (library holdings, endowment, faculty degrees, and so on), simpleminded outcomes (such as the quality of an institution's graduates unadjusted for their precollege characteristics), or reputation. Such conceptions imply institutional advantages and greater personal benefits that may be more mythical than real. When such notions of quality, singly or in the aggregate, receive public and presumably authoritative expression in the form of institutional rankings reported in the news media, they may be not only misleading but pernicious. Such contrasts do a disservice to non-"elite" institutions, to the students and faculty members of those schools, and to high school students and parents who rely on such rankings when choosing a college. The evidence also clearly points out the need for more useful taxonomies, for better measures of college effectiveness and quality, for more circumspection in our beliefs and claims about the benefits of attendance at different kinds of institutions, and for moderation and candor in our recruiting literature. The quality of undergraduate education may be much more a function of what colleges do programmatically than it is of the human, financial, and educational resources at their disposal.

To be sure, there is evidence to suggest that, on average, students attending elite colleges may derive some small net advantages in career mobility and earnings. The key words, however, are *may* and *small*. It is unlikely that the net socioeconomic advantages of attending one of the "best" colleges are anywhere near as certain or pronounced as the predominant public mythology would lead one to believe. Certainly a degree from an elite school might open certain career doors, but the probability is low that educational pedigree alone can "make" or "break" a career.

Astin's (1985a) argument that "talent development" should be the proper work of undergraduate education has considerable appeal, focusing as it does on students and what institutions do to advance student learning beyond what it is when the student enters a college or university rather than on resources or structural characteristics that do not meaningfully differentiate among institutions insofar as educational outcomes are concerned. Such a philosophy of higher education, however, implies substantial shifts in current educational values (see Astin, 1987; Palmer, 1987) and policies and in the ways most institutions (large or small) and public postsecondary educational systems currently do business. Such a philosophy also implies greater recognition of the roles different categories of institutions play and the status and support we accord those institutions. Some of these shifts are discussed in this chapter.

Predominantly Black and Single-Sex Institutions. As America has moved over the past twenty years toward being a more racially tolerant, integrated society, a debate has grown over whether historically and predominantly black institutions should continue to receive state or federal financial support. Proponents of that support argue that it is needed to maintain the financial and therefore educational viability of a group of institutions with important historical, social, educational, and symbolic significance in the lives of black Americans. Opponents of continued support assert that such public expenditures serve to preserve racial separation in education and to retard progress toward a truly integrated and race-blind society. Although the evidence is not without its flaws, it is reasonably consistent in suggesting that attendance at a predominantly black institution is not associated with any educational disadvantage and also that such attendance may provide black students with benefits they would not receive from predominantly white colleges and universities. Holding constant a variety of student precollege characteristics, the positive benefits for black students of attending a predominantly black versus a predominantly white institution include modestly larger increases in certain areas of cognitive development, brighter prospects for completing a baccalaureate degree program, and, indirectly, the higher postcollege earnings associated with degree completion. Among black women, attendance at predominantly black (versus white) institutions is also associated with slightly higher occupational status and more positive academic and social self-concepts.

Similarly, attendance at single-sex institutions appears to provide certain educational benefits less likely on coeducational campuses. Even with student background characteristics and institutional selectivity held constant, a woman attending an all-women's college, compared with her coed-college counterpart, is more likely to emerge with higher educational aspirations, to attain a higher degree, to enter a sex-atypical career, and to achieve prominence in her field. Men attending all-male institutions are more likely than men at coeducational institutions to enter certain occupations (for example, business, law, and the professions in general).

Thus, with respect to predominantly black and single-sex (especially all-women) institutions, the research evidence of the last twenty years provides a modestly strong educational argument for their preservation and public support (see also Alterman, 1989; Nettles & Baratz, 1985). There may yet come a time when racial and sex equity issues no longer constitute significant items on America's public policy agenda, but until that time, these special-population institutions appear to function in ways likely to bring the races and sexes socially, educationally, occupationally, and economically closer together.

Inequalities in Educational Outcomes

While one of the prominent findings of our review is the relative generality of college effects across kinds of four-year institutions, for certain outcomes and for certain students, the kind of college attended may matter a great deal. This important caveat applies particularly to minority and lower-socioeconomic-status students and involves residential and commuter colleges, two- and four-year schools, and predominantly white institutions.

Residential Versus Commuter Schools. If one subscribes to the view that a college education should involve changes not just in substantive learning and cognitive and intellectual competence but in a variety of interpersonal and psychosocial areas as well, then the available evidence quite consistently indicates that commuter institutions are not as well equipped as residential campuses to facilitate those changes. Residential institutions, compared with commuter schools, are more likely to provide their students with the kinds of interpersonal academic and social experiences associated with change in a wide variety of attitudinal and psychosocial areas, including increases in cultural and esthetic attitudes and values; in social, political, and religious tolerance; in self-understanding and personal independence; and in persistence and degree attainment. To say that commuter institutions have less impact than residential institutions in these areas is not to diminish the substantial contributions they make to the enhancement of the lives of significant numbers of students who might otherwise miss the benefits of higher education altogether. The issue is the character of the education delivered: The opportunities for cognitive and psychosocial changes widely accepted as desirable educational outcomes are constrained on commuter campuses in comparison with those on residential campuses. Residence units afford a natural and continuous meeting place for people involved in common activities and educational pursuits. Residence halls and the greater involvement in campus life that the entire residential campus experience affords are powerful socializing and educative agents. On residential campuses, students encounter, confront, question, examine, analyze, challenge, criticize, reflect, differentiate, and evaluate to an extent unequalled on commuter campuses. As a consequence, they also tend to change in a variety of ways and to an extent unapproached by students on commuter campuses.

The significance of this inequality becomes all the more striking and urgent when one considers that more than half of America's college students commute, and even more are likely to do so in the future. Similarly, approximately a third of America's colleges and universities are commuter campuses. Given economic pressures and, for many, limited or nonexistent space for new buildings, current commuter institutions are unlikely to open residential facilities in the foreseeable future.

Ways must be found and resources provided to bring the educational experience of commuter college students closer to that of their residential campus peers. The absence of residence facilities is a significant obstacle, but there is reason to believe that if the gaps cannot be closed entirely, they can at least be narrowed. Recommendations to accomplish this end have included significant redesign of admissions, orientation, and academic advising programs and processes to emphasize personal and program planning; orientation programs for the parents or spouses of commuter college students to acquaint them with the pressures and expectations students will be facing; curricular design and course structures more suited to individual student differences and needs; an emphasis on good teaching; career-related clubs and other activities that bring students and faculty into more frequent contact outside of class; short residential experiences (for example, on weekends or during vacation periods); and even the reconceptualization of institutional excellence as talent development (see Astin, 1985a, pp. 189–191; Baird, 1976c; Chickering, 1974a, chap. 9).

Two-Year Versus Four-Year Schools. Because few public two-year colleges have residence facilities, the educational inequalities facing commuter students also confront most two-year college students. These inequalities are compounded, however, by additional constraints on the capacity of two-year colleges to provide educational benefits in certain cognitive, psychosocial, and economic areas.

There can be little doubt that the growth of the community college sector has significantly expanded traditionally disadvantaged groups' access to postsecondary education. The research is clear about the socioeconomic and other advantages enjoyed by two-year college graduates over people with only a high school diploma. But the evidence also consistently indicates that the advantages are even greater for baccalaureate degree holders when compared with two-year college graduates. So great are the differences that three decades ago Clark (1960) argued that community colleges, despite their many positive and facilitative functions, can also serve to "cool out" high-aspiration but low-achieving and/or low-socioeconomic-status students, discouraging continued enrollment and reducing the likelihood that two-year students would enjoy educational benefits equal to those of four-year college graduates. More recently, Karabel (1972, 1986; Brint & Karabel, 1989) and Astin (1977a) have commented on the paradox of the proliferation of public community colleges and the evidence that because of demonstrably lower persistence and baccalaureate degree attainment rates, community colleges may not really serve well the interests of students aspiring to a bachelor's degree and to the careers that require it. Providing equal access to participation in the postsecondary educational system is only half of the solution to educational inequities. The other half requires equal access to opportunities to enjoy the full benefits of postsecondary participation.

The research published in the last two decades has consistently found— even after holding constant a variety of relevant personal, academic, and family background characteristics and when studying only students in "college transfer" programs—that students entering a four-year institution are substantially more likely than two-year college entrants to persist in their education, to complete a baccalaureate degree, and to attend graduate or professional school. Lower degree attainment rates are compounded in reduced expectations in other areas, including occupational status and income. Although where one enters college makes little difference *once the baccalaureate degree is earned*, the fact remains that students at two-year colleges are substantially less likely than their peers at four-year colleges to complete a bachelor's degree program and to reap the associated benefits. The magnitude of the problem expands, moreover, when we recall the evidence in our review of the intergenerational effects of college attendance. Parents with higher educational attainment levels pass on to their children certain educational, economic, and occupational advantages in terms of precollege backgrounds, schooling, and educationally and occupationally relevant attitudes, values, and expectations. Thus, the children of better-educated parents indirectly derive certain benefits from their parents' education, beginning their own intellectual, economic, and occupational development with advantages that have not been available to children whose parents are not as well educated. It follows, of course, that if there are intergenerational benefits, there are also intergenerational liabilities, which are being compounded in each succeeding generation.

Despite such evidence (about which they are doubtless unaware), significant numbers of high school graduates, their parents, and policymakers continue to believe that attendance at a two-year college followed by transfer to a four-year college for completion of the baccalaureate degree is the low-cost equivalent of the full tour of duty at a four-year institution. This misperception, of course, is particularly damaging among minority and economically disadvantaged groups, for whom the two-year college is the most likely point of entry into the postsecondary educational system. These are the same groups for whom the need for educational and occupational benefits may be greatest and among whom the promise of those benefits may be the most alluring. It is a cruel irony, then, that while the incremental socioeconomic benefits of a bachelor's degree are greatest for these groups (compared to white or higher socioeconomic groups), the likelihood of their obtaining those benefits is lowest. Astin (1977a, p. 247) puts it bluntly: "For the eighteen-year-old going directly to college from high school, the public community college does not represent an 'equal educational opportunity' compared with other types of institutions."

Thus, with respect to both two-year and commuter colleges (but primarily the former), the issue is one of educational and social equity, of deciding whether as a matter of public policy such discrepancies in educational impacts should continue or whether ways can be found to narrow the gaps. As Astin (1977a) has suggested, the presumed economic advantages of two-year (versus four-year) and commuter (versus residential) institutions to state and local governments in terms of cost per student might well be more apparent than real if costs *per degree granted* were used as the yardstick.

The matter goes well beyond capital and operational costs to the public, however. The calculus of the public "economy" of two-year and commuter campuses must also somehow take into account the indirect costs to students and their families in the form of reduced prospects for degree attainment, lower postcollege occupational status and earnings, and fewer opportunities for gains in a variety of widely accepted cognitive and psychosocial outcomes. These personal and family costs, when aggregated, can lead to substantial additional economic, social, and political costs, particularly in light of current projections for substantial growth in minority group populations over the next decade.

Failure on the part of educators and public policymakers to acknowledge that two-year and four-year colleges do *not* lead to the same set of educational and economic outcomes and failure to act on that recognition will mean that unequal educational opportunity will continue, not in the opportunities to participate in higher education but in the opportunities to reap the full benefits of participation. It will mean the perpetuation of the very inequities in educational and social mobility the community college movement was intended to eliminate. It will mean the continued loss of talented individuals and at the least a reduction in their contributions to our educational, cultural, economic, social, and political systems. The burdens of those losses may be compounded by greater demands for welfare and unemployment supports and other social services, the loss of tax revenues, and larger numbers of underemployed individuals living unnecessarily limited lives. Over a long period of time, it could mean the diminishment or loss of a historic national faith in the efficacy of education as a vehicle for improving one's own and one's children's station in life.

As has been suggested elsewhere (for example, Bernstein, 1986; Brint & Karabel, 1989; Donovan, Schaier-Peleg, & Forer, 1987; Palmer, 1986), it appears that the time has come to reconsider the role of two-year colleges' transfer programs. Kinnick & Kempner (1988) suggest at least two alternative courses of action are open. One is to acknowledge the current inequalities and remove the transfer function from the mission of public two-year colleges. Resources and energies could then be redirected and concentrated on the other multiple dimensions of the public two-year college's mission (vocational and technical training, adult literacy, continuing education, community economic development, and the like). Or resources could be redirected to four-year institutions, which would be charged with full responsibility for meeting the demand for education at the baccalaureate degree level. Such a course, however, would in all likelihood even further disadvantage those individuals who, for whatever reasons, would be unable to enroll in a four-year institution or who might initially seek only a two-year degree (or less) but subsequently switch into a transfer program.

A second, more realistic and responsible course of action would be to initiate serious and coordinated efforts at local, state, and federal levels to revitalize the apparently moribund transfer function of two-year colleges. Such regeneration would necessitate revised public-funding formulas and structures. Under most state funding formulas, community colleges are budgeted at lower levels than four-year institutions. Additionally, their missions preclude their access to the additional revenue-generating capacity available to upper-division and graduate-level instruction and research, which also benefit lower-division programs and students. Revitalization would in addition require elimination of some of the obstacles to transferring that contribute to the current inequalities in outcomes. The removal of barriers would require more energetic, systematic, and coordinated efforts at articulation at two points: between the high schools and community colleges and between the community colleges and four-year institutions. Community colleges would have to set and make clear to high schools the nature of the courses and academic skills students entering a college transfer program should have, as well as the curricular and performance standards they would be expected to meet. Four-year institutions would have to do likewise for community colleges (see Commission for Educational Quality, 1985).

At two-year colleges, efforts would also probably involve more intensive remedial programs in reading, writing, mathematical, and general learning skills; more effective academic and personal support programs for transfer candidates; curricula and course offerings that would unequivocally satisfy four-year institutions' admissions and academic major requirements; and increased rigor in instruction and grading. At four-year colleges, easing the transition from two-year to four-year institutions and increasing the likelihood of degree completion would require simpler and more flexible admissions procedures, admissions criteria not limited to standardized test scores and prior academic performance records, greater flexibility in transfer credit policies and criteria (not standards), easier access to larger amounts and more varied forms of financial aid, more equitable opportunities for on-campus housing, and more sustained and aggressive academic and personal support programs, including remedial programs in basic academic skills. More detailed discussions and recommendations for revitalizing the transfer function of two-year colleges are given by Bernstein (1986); Cohen and Brawer (1987, 1989); Donovan, Schaier-Peleg, and Forer (1987); Kintzer and Wattenbarger (1985); Palmer (1986); Pincus and Archer (1989); Richardson and Bender (1985); and Wechsler (1989). Levine and Associates (1989) discuss changes in current practices that will be needed to accommodate higher education's increasingly diverse clientele. (See Palmer, 1986, for a review of related literature.)

White Campuses and Nonwhite Students. The notion of educational inequality has another set of policy implications, primarily at the institutional level, relating to the sociopsychological climate of many predominantly white institutions as it is experienced by nonwhite students. It is clear that many of the most important effects of college occur through students' interpersonal experiences with faculty members and other students. It is equally clear that the academic, social, and psychological worlds inhabited by most nonwhite students on predominantly white campuses are substantially different in almost every respect from those of their white peers. On some (perhaps many) campuses, minority students feel a powerful need to band together for psychological and social support of one another, sometimes in defense against the tacit and not-so-tacit condescension and hostility some feel from white faculty, students, and staff alike. While confirming evidence may be scarce, it does not seem unreasonable to suggest that under such conditions the educational experiences and outcomes of college for nonwhite students are probably also very different from those for white students, perhaps significantly so. Certainly, more research is needed to clarify the nature of the college experience and its effects on cognitive and psychosocial change among nonwhite students.

If this speculation is anywhere near accurate, it is not too soon to begin reviewing and changing institutional policies and programs that create or tolerate activities or conditions that are academically and socially uncongenial, if not downright hostile, to nonwhite students. These would in-clude (but not be limited to) policies and programs relating to increased minority faculty and staff recruitment and retention, institution-wide fac-ulty and staff recruitment and rewards, student housing and financial aid, social organizations, instructors' classroom attitudes and behaviors, and any other conditions that sustain or permit educational inequalities for minority students on predominantly white campuses. But it is not enough, of course, simply to identify and eliminate aversive policies, programs, and conditions. Good educational practice, as well as fundamental fairness, also calls for the development of new policies, programs, and conditions that will create campuswide and specific learning environments and an institutional "tone" that is congenial to *all* students (this includes remedial or developmental studies students as well) (see Allen, 1987).

Organizational Tolerance for Individual Differences

Students manifestly differ in their educational and career goals, mo-tivational levels, readiness to learn, prior preparation, and developmental status in both cognitive and noncognitive areas and in a range of other ways. This heterogeneity exists across institutions (even among those in presumably homogeneous categories) and, indeed, within any given insti-tution. How, then, does one reconcile such student heterogeneity with the homogeneity of most institutions in their academic and administrative or-ganizational structures, curricular content and structures, course content and sequences, instructional methods, housing designs and programming, nonclassroom activities, and campus life generally?

While much has been made of the importance of recognizing and adapting educational programs and experiences so that they are more re-sponsive to individual differences among students, there is little evidence to suggest that the challenge has been taken seriously on more than a hand-ful of campuses. Part of the fault for this may lie with researchers, who with a few exceptions have given little attention to the ways in which col-lege's effects might vary for different kinds of students. With respect to learning and cognitive development, however, the evidence is convincing that certain kinds of students benefit more from certain kinds of instruc-tional approaches than they do from others. These differential effects ap-pear to be related to students' personality or psychosocial orientations. For example, compared to their peers, students with a higher need for inde-pendent achievement and students with a stronger internal locus of control appear to learn more in instructional settings that give them the freedom to guide their own course of study and learning and that involve them more directly in the design and implementation of their learning experi-ences. On the other hand, students high in dependence and in the need for structure and guidance from external authorities appear to learn better in more structured, instructor-centered learning settings. In short, there is good reason to believe that not all students respond in the same fashion to the same instructional format.

Similarly, our review indicates that individualized instructional approaches that accommodate variations in students' learning styles and rates consistently appear to produce greater subject matter learning than do more conventional approaches, such as lecturing. These advantages are especially apparent with instructional approaches that rely on small, modularized content units, require a student to master one instructional unit before proceeding to the next, and elicit active student involvement in the learning process. Perhaps even more promising is the evidence suggesting that these learning advantages are the same for students of different aptitudes and different levels of subject area competence. Probably in no other realm is the evidence so clear and consistent.

Nonetheless, whether out of ignorance of the evidence or for other (most likely financial) reasons, the largest proportion of instruction on most campuses, particularly at the lower-division level, continues to be delivered in conventional lecture and recitation formats. Course content continues to be presented in ways that make students passive participants in their learning, in content units tailored across disciplines to the same number of class periods of the same duration, meeting the same prespecified number of times during a semester or a quarter, betraying a reliance on academic content packaging bereft of variety and flexibility. Considerations other than course objectives, content, and student learning dictate the character of most college instructional settings. One can and must acknowledge that other factors impinge on course and curriculum design: Individualized instruction is more expensive in terms of credit-hour costs, as well as more demanding of faculty time and energy. While these considerations cannot be ignored, it seems clear that current course and curriculum planning are not heavily influenced by individual variations in students' learning styles or readiness to learn. Quite the contrary: Modern colleges and especially universities seem far better structured to process large numbers of students efficiently than to maximize student learning.

Change in these circumstances can be induced in several ways: for example, through state-level program initiation and review processes, through increased funding for individualized instruction programs, and through incremental budgetary support for other programmatic initiatives that reflect institutional efforts to respect individual differences in the learning process more fully. Some of these possibilities are discussed below. Others are given in the several reports on improving undergraduate education that have been published in recent years (see, for example, Association of American Colleges, 1985; Astin, 1985a; Bennett, 1984; Boyer, 1987; Study Group on the Conditions of Excellence in American Higher Education, 1984).

Economy, Efficiency, and Effectiveness

More than a decade ago, Astin (1977a, chap. 9) identified seven policy trends that ran counter to what his extensive analyses suggested would
be sound educational policy: (1) expansion of the public sector, (2) the trend
toward larger institutions, (3) the disappearance of single-sex colleges, (4)
the proliferation of public community colleges, (5) the deemphasis of the
residential experience, (6) open admissions, and (7) the denigration of the
grade point average. The preceding discussion makes clear that some of
these conflicts remain between current policies and what is now known about
sound educational practice, particularly those relating to two-year and residential colleges.

The underlying determinant in these policy-research paradoxes is, of
course, economic. Larger schools generate economies of scale. Two-year
and commuter campuses are less expensive to construct and maintain than
residential campuses of comparable size. Single-sex institutions can no longer
compete for enrollments with coeducational institutions. As we have seen,
these public policies have resulted in fundamental educational inequalities
in both the experiences and outcomes of college for significant numbers of
students.

We are not confident that state and federal policymakers can or will
soon abandon costs as a basis for policy-making. It is entirely possible, however, to shift the emphasis of public policy at least somewhat more toward
educational effectiveness. Indeed, that shift is already under way in increased state interest in colleges' and universities' "assessment" activities.
Many states now have some agency or legislative requirement (or milder
prod) for the examination of institutional influences on student cognitive
and noncognitive outcomes. States' efforts span a considerable range, from
Tennessee's budgetary performance incentives to the more common, gentle,
and flexible requirement that annual reports or other reporting mechanisms discuss what an institution knows about its impact on its students. We
believe that the potential of such institutional assessment efforts for increasing the impact of college on students is substantial and should be encouraged.

We also believe, however, that state-level policies and incentives are
limited in what they can accomplish. To be effective, specific institutional
changes must be determined internally if the hoped for alterations are to
receive the support they will need to be successful. Thus, we believe a more
immediately promising course of action lies in the concerted efforts of individual institutions, with state encouragement and support, to restructure
themselves philosophically and programmatically in order to ameliorate some
of the inequalities identified above and to increase their present educationally positive impact on students. We now turn to some of the ways that
might be accomplished.

Implications for Institutional Practice

Our review indicates two persistent themes in the research literature on college effects. The first is the central role of other people in a student's life, whether students or faculty, and the character of the learning environments they create and the nature and strength of the stimulation their interactions provide for learning and change of all kinds. The second theme is the potency of students' effort and involvement in the academic and nonacademic systems of the institutions they attend. The greater the effort and personal investment a student makes, the greater the likelihood of educational and personal returns on that investment across the spectrum of college outcomes.

Thus, the major implication of our review for individual campuses and their faculty and administrators is to shape the educational and interpersonal experiences and settings of their campus in ways that will promote learning and achievement of the institution's educational goals and to induce students to become involved in those activities, to exploit those settings and opportunities to their fullest.

Kuh and colleagues (Kuh et al., in press), on the basis of their case studies of fourteen institutions reputed to be particularly effective in promoting student involvement in the life of the campus and in their own learning and personal development, identify five characteristics common to those "involving" institutions: "clear institutional missions and educational purposes; campus environments that are compatible with the institution's mission and philosophy; opportunities for meaningful student involvement in learning and personal development activities; an institutional culture (history, tradition, rituals, language) that reinforces the importance of student involvement; and policies and practices consistent with institutional aspirations, mission, and culture." The authors provide detailed descriptions of these characteristics and give examples drawn from the institutions they studied. Chickering (1969, chaps. 8–13) identifies similar "conditions for impact" on students, including clear and consistent educational and institutional objectives; an institutional size that affords students opportunities to participate in a variety of activities; curriculum, teaching, and evaluation practices that strive for variety and active student involvement; residence hall arrangements that promote intellectual diversity and meaningful interchange among students; student and faculty interactions; and a student culture that reinforces rather than counterbalances institutional efforts to educate undergraduates. Discussion of the role of these conditions in any detail is beyond the scope of this volume, but readers are encouraged to refer to the original sources, as well as to Baird (1976c), who provides useful guidance for purposefully shaping environments in order to improve educational outcomes. The following sections offer suggestions based on our review that might be helpful in increasing students' involvement in their own learning.

Admissions and Faculty Recruitment and Rewards

Student admissions and faculty hiring decisions can be powerful tools in shaping an institution's intellectual and interpersonal climate and the nature of the influence it exerts on students. Taking full advantage of that power, however, may mean a thorough review and redefinition of the processes, criteria, and standards for both student and faculty recruitment and decision making. If admissions decisions are based solely on applicants' academic credentials and their promise for successful grade performance, important opportunities to enroll students with special talents or gifts that would enrich the academic or interpersonal climate of the school may be lost. Moreover, there is mounting evidence that traditional admissions criteria (test scores and grades) are not the best predictors of college performance and retention for all students. For example, certain student personal, attitudinal, and behavioral characteristics are better predictors of minority student performance than are standardized test scores (see, for example, Nettles, Thoeny, & Gosman, 1986). The ease with which admissions criteria can be redefined and with which nonmachine-processable information can be incorporated into the admissions decision-making process will, of course, be inversely related to the number of applications. The nature of the community of students, faculty, and staff and the homogeneity of the interests, abilities, attitudes, and values they share are, however, powerful instruments of education and socialization. The influences on the character of that community that are exerted by each new class of students should not be left to chance.

Institutional climate is also heavily influenced, of course, by faculty members and by their activities that are rewarded, such as the relative weight given to teaching and research in the faculty reward system. Significant involvement in students' out-of-class lives cannot be expected from faculty members who are recruited because of their research potential and whose research is more quickly, visibly, and amply rewarded than their involvement with undergraduate students. Faculty recruitment and reward processes may have to be redesigned to reflect an institution's serious interest in student learning in all areas. For example, when new faculty members are recruited, they might be asked to submit evidence of their teaching abilities and other student-oriented activities, as well as their research bibliographies. Candidates might be required to meet with and to make presentations to students as well as faculty members. Such attention to teaching ability and interest in students in the selection process would send new faculty members a clear message about the importance the institution attaches to instruction. The presumption, of course, is that such values would also be reflected subsequently in promotion, tenure, and compensation decisions. Clearly, in many colleges and universities good teaching is its own reward, but even here there may be more tangible ways for institutions to acknowledge professorial excellence and effort in the classroom. Whatever steps are taken, ways must be found to give faculty members more incentives to become involved in student learning, both in and out of the classroom.

Orientation

One of the major transitions from high school to college involves the unlearning of past attitudes, values, and behaviors and the learning of new ones (Feldman & Newcomb, 1969). For students going away to college, it also means cutting loose from past social networks and established identities. In their place, new identities and interpersonal networks must be constructed, and new academic and social structures, attitudes, values, and behaviors must be learned. This represents a major social and psychological transition and a time when students may be more ready to change than at any other point in their college career.

Orientation programs serve an important early socialization function. These programs involve a series of experiences by means of which individuals come to anticipate and understand the value and behavioral norms that characterize their new social setting and that will be expected of them as members of that community. If successful, the orientation process can lead to earlier and more enduring involvement in the academic and social systems of an institution. It is also reasonable to expect that student involvement will be greatest if new students can be immediately linked with people who are already invested in the institution, whether faculty members or other students. New students' initial encounters with the institution may have profound effects on subsequent levels of involvement, and these encounters should be carefully designed to socialize students to the institution's highest educational values and goals. Introducing students to available support services, key administrators, student social life, and major and degree requirements, as well as their early course registration, is important for students and institutions. If these introductions define an orientation program, however, then once-in-a-lifetime opportunities to orient students to the institution's intellectual and cultural life and values may be lost. Intentionally or not, institutional values are on display during orientation, and the program's activities send subtle but powerful messages to new students about what and who is valued (and not valued) on a campus.

Scholars and administrators are increasingly coming to realize that the most effective orientation programs are not limited to the first few days or weeks of the first semester. Rather, orientation activities are being extended throughout the initial semester and, indeed, throughout the entire freshman year. Upcraft, Gardner, and their associates (1989) provide a more detailed examination of this extended orientation process, as well as discussions of specific ways to increase institutional impact during students' first year of college.

Instruction

The evidence unequivocally indicates that greater content learning and cognitive development occur in classrooms where students are engaged in and by the instructional and learning processes. Greater gains in non-authoritarianism, tolerance, independence, intellectual disposition, reflective judgment, and other dimensions of psychosocial change also appear to accompany academic involvement. Promoting such involvement, however, requires awareness of a student's cognitive and affective developmental status and then serious, systematic efforts to devise learning experiences that take into account the student's level of understanding, ways of structuring information, and learning style (see, for example, Chickering, 1976, pp. 88–107; Rodgers, 1980, 1983).

Student engagement can be influenced by a variety of mechanisms but probably most directly by the instructional methods adopted. Substantial advantages over traditional teaching formats have been shown to be associated with a variety of individualized approaches, particularly the personalized system of instruction, or Keller Plan, which involves (among other things) having more-advanced students assume helping roles when other students have difficulties with course material. Other types of individualized instruction have also been shown to be effective. These include audio-tutorial, computer-assisted, and programmed instruction approaches.

Similarly, instruction stressing inductive learning based on concrete activities appears with some consistency to promote gains in abstract reasoning and cognitive complexity. Classroom activities that require student participation—question-and-answer exchanges, topical discussions, assignments that call upon higher-order thinking, problem-solving activities, in-class presentations, and student involvement in decisions about course content and activities—appear to promote course involvement. Student engagement can also be enhanced through the use of qualified undergraduates in peer tutoring programs.

Other recommendations include the creation of learning communities around specific themes and increased use of instructional technologies and other mechanisms for bringing students and faculty into more frequent contact (Study Group, 1984) and interdisciplinary seminars focused on contemporary problems (Astin, 1985a). The Association of American Colleges (AAC) (1985) has recommended greater integration of students' courses of study with the extracurriculum, including community service, political participation, and other civic activities, as well as similar interactions with business, corporate, professional, governmental, and arts organizations. The AAC has also recommended greater use of artist- and writer-in-residence programs, temporary faculty appointments for people outside the traditional faculty ranks, and more creative use of college work-study programs. The common theme in all these recommendations is that where stronger and clearer links can be forged between students' lives and course content skills, student engagement and change are likely to follow (see also Boyer, 1987, pt. 3, especially chap. 9).

It is also reasonable to expect that good teaching will generate academic involvement, and we know a good deal about what effective teachers do in the classroom. They have good rapport with their students. They signal their accessibility in and out of the classroom. They give students formal and informal feedback on their performance. But even more important is instructor skill. Effective teachers have a thorough command of their subject matter, the ability to present sophisticated and complex material in ways that students can follow, the ability to organize course content and structure classroom activities in an efficient manner, and the ability to send clear learning stimuli through such devices as examples and analogies that clarify key points, relate one topic to another, and signal the transition from one topic to another. These instructor and instructional-style characteristics have consistently been linked with increased student achievement.

Most important, these characteristics are teachable to and learnable by faculty members. Institutions that wish to increase their instructional effectiveness can do so if the will is there and if institutional and faculty value systems are conducive to that goal. Significant improvements in the quality of instruction, however, may require alteration in faculty recruiting, hiring, and reward policies, particularly at larger schools, where the economies of scale dominate educational decision making. Instructional support programs may also be needed to teach faculty these key pedagogical skills.

Departmental Climate

Students' content learning is highest in those areas that are most closely related to their academic major. Similarly, the cognitive or intellectual skills that they develop most fully are those closest to the nature and methods of their major field. Beyond these unsurprising conclusions, major field per se appears to have little effect on other kinds of change. However, a growing body of evidence suggests that while the specific department or nature of the discipline may have little impact in noncognitive areas, the organizational and interpersonal climate of the department may very well have a significant impact. Departmental influence on personal and educational changes is observable in those departments where faculty and students share common attitudes and values; where interpersonal exchanges are frequent, friendly, and not rigidly hierarchical; and where there is a departmental esprit de corps.

Thus, it appears that student involvement may also be enhanced through the conscious and systematic efforts of academic departments to create environments that attract and engage students in both intellectual and interpersonal learning. This is not a simplistic recommendation for hand-holding or for new or specially designed programs to bring students and faculty into greater contact. Rather, it is a suggestion for shaping departmental, as well as institutional, climates in ways that will promote desirable educational outcomes (see Baird, 1976c). It suggests the elevation of the mentor's role. Much will depend, of course, on the presence of faculty members who are genuinely interested in students and willing to make the necessary personal efforts to engage them intellectually and personally in and out of class. The need here is for faculty members who neither intimidate nor are intimidated by students and their questions but who enjoy engaging with students in the learning process. Departmental climates can be scrutinized during the normal program review process. Where climates not conducive to student learning are identified, they can be altered through a variety of mechanisms, including resource allocation processes, faculty recruitment and hiring criteria and standards, and faculty recognition, promotion, tenure, and compensation policies.

Residence Units

As noted earlier, living on campus (as opposed to commuting) is associated with higher levels of integration in the academic and social systems of an institution and, in turn, with changes in a variety of value, attitudinal, and psychosocial areas. Moreover, our estimates of the average effect sizes may to some extent underestimate the influences of residence, based as they are on research using rather global characterizations of residence settings. The evidence also indicates that the effects of the programmatic, structural, and organizational characteristics of residence halls appear to be indirect, exerting their influence through the interpersonal relations and experiences they spawn.

Given this body of evidence, one might reasonably conclude that the particular nature of residence hall programming may be less important than the fact that it occurs at all and that it initiates and sustains students' intellectual and interpersonal involvement. The truly important traits of educationally effective residence units may well be the characteristics, interests, values, attitudes, and orientations of the students who live there; the frequency and nature of their contacts with one another and with faculty within the unit; and the general intellectual and social-psychological context they collectively create. The most consistent evidence linking residence with specific kinds of change points to the greater impact of those halls in which there are systematic and purposeful efforts to integrate students' academic and social lives (for example, in living-learning centers) in ways that extend and reinforce learning in other areas. Many campuses have such facilities, but on most they are by no means the modal residential setting. To the extent that living-learning center philosophies, activities, and climates can be developed in other residence units, their educational and psychosocial benefits can be extended to more students. Baird (1976c, pp. 12–16) provides advice on how residential influence might be increased. As Vreeland and Bidwell (1965) and Vreeland (1970) make clear, however, groups have complex value systems, and the dynamics that operate within them are not easily shaped. Students' peers, particularly their close friends, appear to exert the greatest shaping influence.

Psychological Size

To a certain extent, all of the preceding discussion boils down to the issue of psychological size. With a few exceptions, institutional size by itself does not appear to be a salient determinant of student change. There is evidence, however, that size is indirectly influential through the kinds of interpersonal relations and experiences it promotes or discourages. A number of steps have already been proven effective in increasing student engagement and reducing the psychological size of larger institutions by affording opportunities for students to become involved with smaller groups of individuals, some of whom may be like-minded while others are not. Such downsizing can include cluster colleges and other purposeful housing arrangements, architectural alterations, academic organizations (for example, honors programs, discipline-based clubs, peer tutoring programs), cocurricular activities, work-study and other on-campus employment programs, intramural athletics, and so on. Astin (1985a, chap. 7) and the Study Group on the Conditions of Excellence in American Higher Education (1984) provide more detailed recommendations for increasing student involvement.

Whatever form engagement might take, however, students should be helped *early* in their academic careers to find academic and social niches where they can feel that they are a part of the institution's life, where friendships can be developed, and where role models (whether student or faculty) can be observed and emulated. Because of the interconnectedness of areas of change noted earlier, the simple fact of involvement, as long as it is educationally productive, may be as important to educational changes as the specific area of the involvement.

Finally, as noted previously, student attrition rates are highest during the first two years of college, particularly during the first year. Thus, efforts such as those suggested above to increase students' involvement in the educational process and life of the institution should be concentrated in the first two years. Upcraft, Gardner, and their associates (1989) examine a wide variety of ways in which students' first year in college can be educationally enhanced.

Cumulative Versus Specific Effects

We have already noted that the effects of specific within-college programs, conditions, or experiences consistently appear to be smaller than the overall net effect of college. This is no surprise since it is probably unreasonable to expect any single experience to be a significant determinant of change for all students. Nonetheless, this conclusion implies that the enhancement of the educational impact of a college is most likely if policy and programmatic efforts are broadly conceived and diverse. It also implies, however, that they should be consistent and integrated. There appear to be only a few specific programmatic or policy levers that administrators can hope to pull and produce a significant effect across the campus. Indeed, it may be potentially more productive for faculty, administrators, and researchers to conceive of the environment of any given campus not as unitary and global but rather as an amalgam of many diverse subenvironments, each of which has influence (Baird, 1988). Furthermore, while the impact of any single subenvironment may be small or modest, the cumulative effect of all subenvironments—if they are mutually supportive—can be substantial.

Thus, instead of singular, large, specially designed, and campuswide programs to achieve a particular institutional goal, efforts might more profitably focus on ways to embed the pursuit of that goal in *all* appropriate institutional activities. For example, while special speakers and campuswide meetings may be one way to increase racial tolerance, it may be even more effective if awareness of and sensitivity to the issue permeate the selection of course content; the cultural activities of the campus (such as speakers, plays, concerts, art shows); student admissions and faculty and administrator hiring and reward systems; committee appointments; selection of trustees; swift and unambiguous responses to activities or incidents that are racially tainted; and so on. In short, rather than seeking single large levers to pull in order to promote change on a large scale, it may well be more effective to pull more small levers more often.

Finally, the research makes clear the important influences faculty members have on student change in virtually all areas. There can be little doubt about the need for faculty members' acceptance of their roles and responsibilities for student learning and for their active involvement in students' lives. At the same time, while the literature on administrator involvement in student change is only indirect, we believe that administrators exercise significant control over campus affairs and climates. Presidents, vice-presidents, deans, and department heads, consciously or unconsciously and explicitly or implicitly, set a tone and standards for students, faculty, and staff at large. Enhancement of institutional learning environments and efforts to increase student involvement will require the active and visible support of administrators at all levels but particularly of presidents and vice-presidents. For significant changes to occur, a collective act of institutional will is needed. Changes in an institution's philosophy of education, its organizational arrangement, or its programmatic efforts may originate among students, faculty, or staff as collectivities, but they are much more likely to occur and to have effect if they are initiated and guided by senior administrators, who are responsible for institutional acts.

We have already noted the determining influence of financial considerations in decisions affecting educational policies and practices. By and large, faculty members do not make those decisions; campus and system administrators, trustees, and legislators do. In the last analysis, a shift in the decision-making orientation of middle- and executive-level administrators is needed. We believe that shift should be toward what might be called learning-centered management, an orientation to decision making that consistently and systematically takes into account the potential consequences of alternative courses of administrative action for student learning. (The origin of this idea appears in Astin, 1979.) Financial considerations cannot, of course, be ignored, but neither should they be absolutely and invariably determinant. Colleges and universities are distinctive in their preeminent focus on the facilitation of undergraduate student learning. If they are to be faithful to that portion of their common mission, the impact of administrative decisions on student learning, broadly defined, must be a constant consideration.

APPENDIX:

Methodological
and Analytical Issues
in Assessing
the Influence of College

This appendix is designed to provide an introduction to some of the more important methodological and analytical issues in estimating the influence of college. It covers the following basic topics: the problem of estimating unique or net effects, attributing student change to college attendance, attributing student change to the type of college attended or to different experiences within the same institution, analytical approaches useful in assessing the impact of college (that is, residual scores and partial correlation), different multiple correlation and regression procedures (including commonality analysis, hierarchical and stepwise analysis, and causal modeling), issues in the appropriate unit of analysis, the use of change scores, and conditional versus general effects.

The Problem of Estimating Unique or Net Effects

One of the most basic and persistent questions in educational research has been how one determines the extent to which student change or development can be attributed to the educational experience itself and not to other factors or competing influences. We will refer to this as the unique or net effects question, although more recently it has been referred to by other names, such as the value-added question (Astin, 1985a, 1985b; Ewell, 1985a, 1985b; Pascarella, 1986b). At the very heart of this question is an attempt to separate that part of student change that is caused by the particular educational experience under investigation from the part that is due to other influences, such as student background abilities or normal maturation over time. It has been axiomatic in the educational research community that the most valid approach for estimating the causal link between two variables and thus the net effect of one on the other is through the random assignment of individual subjects (or an alternatively appropriate

657

unit of analysis) to experimental and control groups (for example, Astin, 1970c, 1970d; Borg & Gall, 1983; Campbell, 1967; Campbell & Stanley, 1963; Cochran & Cox, 1957; Cook & Campbell, 1979; Cronbach, 1982; Kerlinger & Pedhazur, 1973; Linn, 1986; Linn & Werts, 1977; Rubin, 1974; Stanley, 1967).

Unfortunately, the necessary conditions for a true or randomized experiment are extremely difficult to obtain in actual field settings where self-selection rather than random assignment is the rule. This is no less a problem in research on the influence of college than it is in educational research generally. Indeed, a basic and perhaps *the* basic problem in assessing the unique influence of college on students is the issue of student self-selection or recruitment. An overwhelming body of evidence suggests that characteristics are not randomly distributed to college and noncollege groups (for example, Anderson, Bowman, & Tinto, 1972; Astin, 1975c; Bachman & O'Malley, 1986; Blau & Duncan, 1967; Bowles & Gintis, 1976; Braddock, 1980; Brim, Glass, Neulinger, & Firestone, 1969; Peng, Bailey, & Eckland, 1977; Sewell, 1971; Sewell & Shah, 1967, 1968b; Taubman & Wales, 1973; Thomas, Alexander, & Eckland, 1979; Trent & Medsker, 1968; Wolfle, 1985b), to different types of colleges (for example, Alexander & Eckland, 1977; Astin, 1961, 1962, 1965c, 1982; Feldman & Newcomb, 1969; Hearn, 1984; Karabel & Astin, 1975; Medsker & Trent, 1972; Bohrnstedt, 1967; Burns, 1974; Smart & Pascarella, 1986b), or to different academic and social experiences within the same institution (for example, Astin, 1971b, 1977a, 1984; Bohrnstedt, 1967; Burns, 1974; Pascarella, 1980, 1985b; Pascarella, Smart, Ethington, & Nettles, 1987). This means that in estimating the influence of college on student development, one is confronted with the particularly knotty problem of separating the influence due to collegiate experiences alone from that due to the particular characteristics of the individuals participating in those experiences.

It is typically the case that student background characteristics (academic aptitude, prior achievement, family socioeconomic status, aspirations, personality orientations, and the like) are not merely the best predictors of many of the outcomes associated with college; they are also a major determinant of whether or not one attends college and, if so, the type of college attended and the extent and quality of involvement in different academic and social experiences during college. Because individual student background characteristics influence both categories of variables (the collegiate experience and outcome measures), they satisfy the requirements for the classical definition of a confounding variable—that is, a variable so associated with both the independent (collegiate experience) and dependent (outcome) variables that it may be confused with the effect of the independent variable (for example, Cohen & Cohen, 1975; Cronbach, 1982; Kerlinger, 1979; Kerlinger & Pedhazur, 1973; Pedhazur, 1982). In short, student background characteristics may masquerade as college effects. Another way of saying this is that the associations between college experience and outcomes may be spurious or noncausal because both are dependent upon mutually antecedent causes such as individual student background characteristics (Linn & Werts, 1969).

This problem is demonstrated graphically in Figure A.1. As Figure A.1 shows, a substantial part of the relationship between college experience and college outcomes (that is, the area defined by $A + B$) is confounded by the joint relationship between student background and both college experience and college outcomes (area B). Determining or estimating the unique or net influence of college experience on college outcomes (that is, $[A + B] - B$) is a nontrivial analytical problem, and we now turn to some ways in which the issue has been addressed.

Attributing Student Change to College Attendance

One fairly common methodological approach in estimating the influence of college attendance (versus nonattendance) on students has been to treat those attending or graduating from college as the experimental or "treated" group while designating those whose formal education stops with secondary school as the natural control group (for example, Colby, Kohlberg, Gibbs, & Lieberman, 1983; Hyman & Wright, 1979; Hyman, Wright, & Reed, 1975; Plant, 1962; Rest & Thoma, 1985; Telford & Plant, 1963; Trent & Medsker, 1968; Wolfle & Robertshaw, 1982). The problem, of course, is that the control group (those not attending college) may be so fundamentally different in important individual characteristics from the treated group (those exposed to college) that simple comparison of outcome differences is often meaningless. Thus, for example, if given a mea-

Figure A.1. Schematic View of Variable Relationships in Estimating College Effects.

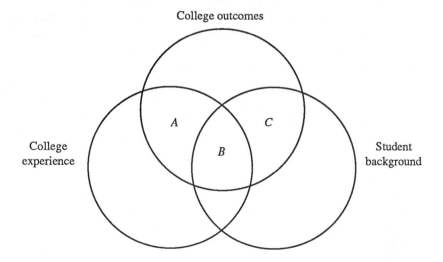

sure of vocabulary or verbal learning, college graduates would likely score higher than high school graduates. A substantial part of this difference, however, would probably be due to the fact that when they graduated from high school both groups also differed in the same direction in verbal ability. Indeed, to some extent it is higher levels of verbal ability that led the college group to be admitted to college in the first place.

One way of dealing with this problem is to attempt to match or equate college and noncollege groups on important background characteristics, that is, to select for the control group those high school–only subjects who are similar in verbal ability to their counterparts who attended college (King, Kitchener, & Wood, 1985; Kitchener & King, 1981; Pascarella, 1989). Though this approach is workable when subjects are being matched on a small number of variables (for example, one to three), it can quickly become impractical if one attempts to match subjects on an extensive number of variables. Another, more common approach has been to use analytical procedures such as partial correlations, regression analysis, or analysis of covariance to "statistically equate" the comparison groups (for example, Robertshaw & Wolfle, 1982; Wolfle, 1983). What these approaches typically accomplish is to statistically remove (or "partial out" or "covary out") the confounded part of the relationship between the independent and dependent variables. The unconfounded "part" of the correlation that remains is often interpreted as the unique or net association between the independent and dependent variables (Cohen & Cohen, 1975).

Such statistical procedures are discussed and expanded upon later in this appendix. It is important to point out at this juncture, however, that these statistical procedures are not a totally adequate substitute for random assignment of subjects to treatments (Elashoff, 1969; Linn & Slinde, 1977; Lord, 1967, 1969). Indeed, as suggested by Lord (1967, p. 305), "There simply is no logical or statistical procedure that can be counted on to make proper allowances for uncontrolled preexisting differences among groups." Moreover, statistical control (like control by matching) is further limited to those variables for which data are available. Other important but unmeasured variables may remain uncontrolled and therefore lead to problems in interpretation and attribution. Despite these significant limitations, the vast preponderance of research on the influence of college on students has had to rely on less than ideal statistical controls in estimating the net effects of college experiences (Astin, 1970a, 1970b; Feldman, 1969, 1971b; Pascarella, 1982; Wolfle, 1985a).

Even if one is able to match groups or statistically equate them on important background characteristics, the college versus noncollege comparison may still be confounded by differences in motivational factors that lead some individuals to invest in college while others go from high school directly to the labor force. This is a subtle and therefore pernicious threat to the validity of the findings that has been referred to as the "interaction of selection and change" or "the interaction of selection and the dependent variable" (Campbell & Stanley, 1963). What it suggests is that the complex set of motivations underlying a person's choice of a particular experience (such as attending college) may itself be an important determinant of many of the outcomes typically associated with the experience.

For example, consider two high school graduates of equal ability and family socioeconomic position, with one choosing college and the other not. The college graduate may eventually have a higher level of income not just because a college degree provides entry into higher-salaried professions but also because of the higher level of ambition, drive, or need to achieve that led him or her to choose to attend college in the first place. Underlying ambitions, drives, and achievement needs may be particularly difficult to assess; and if they cannot be assessed, then confounding effects cannot be statistically removed. Often this leads one to attribute to the collegiate experience an effect that is more appropriately attributed to the individual characteristics of those who attend college.

With few exceptions (for example, Stanley, 1967), there may be no naturally occurring and easily accessible control group of noncollege individuals. This has apparently been recognized by researchers who have attempted to assess the effects of college on students without employing control groups of individuals not exposed to college. One typical design is the simple pretest-posttest longitudinal design in which the same panel or sample of students is followed over a specified period of time, such as freshman to senior year, and measured on the same instrument. The students are essentially their own control group, and the difference between mean freshman and senior scores on some measure of interest (moral reasoning, reflective judgment, or critical thinking, for instance) is used as an estimate of the effect of college. Unfortunately, even if one assumes the reasonable reliability of change scores (an unsafe assumption; see Cronbach & Furby, 1970), such mean changes may reflect not only the influence of college but also the effects of confounding noncollege influences such as external events (history), the practice effect (taking the same instrument or test twice), and possibly even regression (to-the-mean) artifacts if the group is extremely low or high on the first testing. In many instances, however, the most troublesome confounding variable associated with simple longitudinal panel designs having no control group is that of age or maturation. From the perspective of many developmental theorists, a considerable portion of the maturing that occurs coincidentally with college attendance may be explainable by the fact that students grow older as they attend college (for example, Erikson, 1968; Kohlberg, 1969; Loevinger, 1976; Perry, 1970). This, of course, implies that average freshman-to-senior changes may well overestimate the net influence of college attendance (McMillan, 1986).

Another problem with this design is mortality or attrition in student responses from freshman to senior year. Students willing to be in a study or to respond to a questionnaire instrument as freshmen may not always be as willing to do so as seniors. Since it is necessary to have pre- and post-measures for each student, those for whom freshman-to-senior comparisons are possible may not be representative of the institutional population to whom the results are to be inferred. This, of course, may speak more to the generalizability of the findings (external validity) than to the extent to which the differences can be attributed to the college experience and not alternative or competing hypotheses (internal validity).

In an effort to gain some control over the confounding effects of student maturation, a number of cross-sectional (cohort) designs have been suggested as an alternative to the longitudinal pretest-posttest panel design without control group. Consider the cross-sectional design where freshmen are compared with seniors on a measure of critical thinking. The freshmen, who have not been exposed to college, act as a control group for the seniors, who have theoretically benefited from four years of exposure to it. (To better reflect the entire college experience, the measure of critical thinking might be given to freshmen upon enrollment in college and seniors in the final semester or quarter of their senior year.)

Since this design is comparing different cohorts on the same measure, the potential confounding influences of regression artifacts or of being assessed twice on the same measure are largely controlled. There is still the problem of age differences between freshmen and seniors. In a cross-sectional design, however, it is at least possible to adjust statistically for the effects of age. Other weaknesses in this design remain, of course. First, because of attrition, seniors may represent a more selective population in terms of academic ability and related traits than freshmen, although this may vary with the patterns and determinants of attrition at different colleges. Second, there is the possibility that differential recruitment or admission criteria may be used for the seniors versus the current freshmen. (For example, if the college used a more stringent set of standards for admitting the senior cohort than it did in admitting the current freshmen, the former might represent a more academically select and motivated group than the latter.) Thus, to increase the validity of the findings yielded by such cross-sectional designs, one may need to adjust statistically for aptitude or prior achievement as well as for age (Mentkowski & Strait, 1983; Whitla, 1978).

Another cross-sectional design that attempts to disaggregate the effects of college from the effects of maturation without having to depend on statistical adjustments for age is suggested by Goulet (1975) and exemplified in the work of Strange (1978). This design requires that nonoverlapping cohorts of different ages be assessed on the dependent measure of interest at different points in their college career. For example, traditional-age freshmen (age eighteen), nontraditional-age freshmen (for example, age twenty-two), traditional-age seniors (age twenty-two), and nontraditional-age seniors (for example, age twenty-six) might all be administered the measure of critical thinking. The effects of maturation independent of college could be obtained by comparing average scores of samples of different ages but with the same amount of exposure to college (for example, freshmen age eighteen with freshmen age twenty-two and seniors age twenty-two with seniors age twenty-six). Conversely, the influence of college independent of age could be estimated by comparing average scores of samples of the same age but with different levels of exposure to college (for example, freshmen age twenty-two and seniors age twenty-two). While this design is quite powerful in detecting and holding constant the effects of age, it does not guarantee that the estimated differences associated with differential exposure to college can, in fact, be attributed to the net influence of college. Other factors, such as differential selectivity or recruitment effects between freshmen and senior samples, may still introduce uncontrolled bias in the results.

Attributing Student Change to Type of College Attended or Different Experiences Within the Same Institution

The design and analysis issues that confront researchers in their attempt to separate the influence of type of college attended or specific collegiate experiences from the confounding effects of individual subject differences are essentially the same as those in attempts to separate the effects of college attendance (versus nonattendance) from individual differences. Specifically, different types of colleges tend to recruit and enroll different kinds of students. Consequently, in comparing student outcomes associated with attendance at different kinds of institutions, it is difficult to separate recruitment effects from socialization effects; the former are the result of differential selection, while the latter refer to the actual effects of attending different colleges (Chickering, 1971b; Hauser, 1971; Kamens, 1971; Withey, 1971). Similarly, because different types of students tend to have different levels of involvement in college (for example, Astin, 1984; Pace, 1984) and to become involved in different types of academic and social experiences during college (for example, Apostal, 1970; Astin, 1977a; Astin & Panos, 1969), separating the influence of a specific set of college experiences from the influence of individual student differences is a nontrivial matter. Thus, for example, obtaining a valid estimate of the net influence of academic major on formal (Piagetian) reasoning is extremely difficult if one ignores the likelihood that students choosing different academic majors may differ substantially in level of formal reasoning to begin with.

Analytical Approaches to Assessing the Influence of College

A number of different analytical models have been used in estimating the influence of college on student development. While these methods differ somewhat in emphasis, they have in common a concern with separating the influence of college or different collegiate experiences (socialization) from the effects of individual student differences and self-selection (recruitment). We will discuss each of these approaches separately. Since our major purpose is didactic, we will emphasize intuitive and visual or geometric explanations rather than mathematical ones. We will also illustrate our discussion with an example based on plausible, though fictitious, data. We hope that this approach will aid the general reader of studies on the influence of college in better understanding and evaluating the meaning of results from different analyses.

Example Data

For our illustrative example, let's assume that we are interested in studying the influence of student-faculty informal contact on the development of intellectual orientation during the freshman year. To do so, we plan and conduct a longitudinal panel investigation in which we collect data at three points from the same sample of 1,000 students attending ten institutions that are comparable in student selectivity but differ substantially in enrollment size. At the beginning of the freshman year or prior to enrollment, all members of the sample are tested on a measure of intellectual orientation (IO_1). During January and February of the freshman year, a questionnaire is sent to members of the sample to obtain a measure of the frequency of their informal, nonclassroom contact with faculty to discuss intellectual or course-related matters (IWF). Finally, in May of the freshman year, we again test members of the sample on the measure of intellectual orientation (IO_2). Since we are also interested in the effects of institutional size or enrollment $(SIZE)$, we collect data on this from institutional records and assign the appropriate institutional value to each student's data file.

Thus, our final set of data would consist of four measures for each student:

1. Precollege intellectual orientation (IO_1)
2. The size of the institution attended $(SIZE)$
3. Frequency of informal contact with faculty (IWF)
4. End-of-freshman-year intellectual orientation (IO_2)

Clearly, if this were an actual study, we might also be interested in other student preenrollment traits or other measures of institutional characteristics and freshman-year experiences. For didactic simplicity, however, we will limit our example data to the four variables noted.

The correlations among the four variables in our fictitious study are shown in Table A.1. As can be seen, the size of the institution attended, informal contact with faculty, and postfreshman intellectual orientation are

Table A.1. Matrix of Correlations.

Variable	M	SD	SIZE	IWF	IO_2
1. Precollege intellectual orientation (IO_1)	40.50	6.85	−.08	.13	.60
2. Institutional size (SIZE)	9,500	2.45		−.24	−.15
3. Informal interaction with faculty (IWF)	6.83	2.42			.33
4. Postfreshman intellectual orientation (IO_2)	51.53	7.16			

all associated to varying degrees with precollege intellectual orientation. Thus, the relationships between both institutional size and informal contact with faculty, on the one hand, and postfreshman intellectual orientation, on the other, are confounded by precollege intellectual orientation. (The reader is referred back to Figure A.1 for a visual representation of a confounded relationship.) The analytical issue, then, becomes one of estimating that part of the relationship between measures of college experience (for example, IWF) and college output (for example, IO_2) that is unconfounded by student background (for example, IO_1). This is represented by area A in Figure A.1.

Use of Residual Scores

One early approach to estimating the unconfounded relationship between college experience and college output has been advocated and refined by Astin, largely in connection with his influential input-environment-output model for assessing college impacts (Astin, 1963a, 1963b, 1965a, 1968b, 1968c, 1990; Astin & Panos, 1966, 1969). In this model, *input* refers to the traits or characteristics that students bring to college (precollege intellectual orientation in our example data), *environment* refers to the college environment or students' college experiences (institutional size and informal interaction with faculty in our example data), and *output* refers to the college outcome being explained or predicted (postfreshman intellectual orientation in the example data). The analytical procedure involves two steps. In the first step, student outputs are regressed on student inputs, and the regression equation produced is used to compute a predicted or expected output. This predicted output is then subtracted from actual or observed output to yield a residual output. Since predicted and residual scores are uncorrelated or statistically independent of each other, the residual score represents variation in output statistically purged or independent of the influence of input. Measures of the college experience are then correlated (step 2) with the residual output (RIO_2) to yield a "part" correlation representing the net or unique association of college experience and output. The square of this part correlation (r^2) represents the portion or percentage (when multiplied by 100) of the residual variance in output that is systematically shared with college experience but not with student input. This relationship is portrayed by area *A* in Figure A.2, where *IWF* represents the college experience variable and RIO_2 (enclosed by the solid line) represents the residual variance in IO_2, with variance shared with IO_1 removed statistically.

In our example, both the independent *(IWF)* and dependent *(IO_2)* variables are continuous in nature. It is also possible, however, to compute a part correlation between a categorical independent variable (for example, college exposure versus noncollege exposure) and the residual variance in a continuous dependent measure. This residual score/part correlation procedure with a categorical independent variable is typically referred to as the analysis of covariance (Cohen & Cohen, 1975).

Figure A.2. Use of Residualized Outcome Score (Part Correlation).

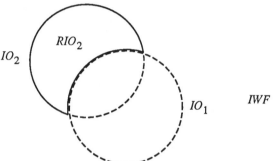
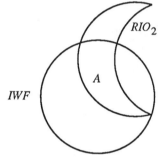

Step 1: IO_2 is regressed on IO_1 to obtain residual variance in IO_2 (RIO_2 enclosed by the solid line), which is statistically independent of IO_1

Step 2: RIO_2 is correlated with *IWF* to yield *part* correlation

A related procedure using residual scores is the partial correlation. In the partial correlation both college experience *(IWF)* *and* output *(IO_2)* are residualized on input *(IO_1)*. The two sets of residual scores represented geometrically by areas RIO_2 *and* $RIWF$ would then be correlated. The square of the partial correlation would represent the percentage of residual variance in IO_2 (RIO_2) systematically associated with residual variance in *IWF* ($RIWF$). In our example the squared partial correlation between $RIWF$ and RIO_2, statistically controlling for IO_1, equals .10, or 10 percent, of the residual variance. A visual portrayal of the partial correlation is shown in Figure A.3. As the figure illustrates, the square of the partial correlation is area *A,* which corresponds to area *A* in the part correlation (see Figure A.2). Figures A.2 and A.3 differ only in that the total variance in *IWF* is correlated with the residual variance in IO_2 (RIO_2) in Figure A.2, and the residual variances in *IWF* ($RIWF$) and IO_2 (RIO_2) are correlated in Figure A.3. Comparing Figures A.2 and A.3, it is questionable that the partial correlation

Figure A.3. Partial Correlation.

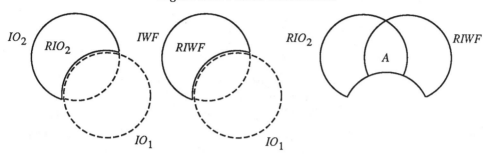

Step 1: Both IO_2 and IWF are regressed on IO_1 to obtain residual variance in IO_2 (RIO_2) and IWF ($RIWF$), both of which are statistically independent of IO_1

Step 2: RIO_2 and RIWF are correlated to obtain *partial* correlation

provides any more stringent statistical control over confounding variables than does the part correlation (Cohen & Cohen, 1975). Indeed, both part and partial correlations will, in fact, have the same level of statistical significance.

As pointed out by Feldman (1971b) and Werts (1968), the residual score procedure, in both its part and partial correlation forms, statistically removes any joint association between input and the college experience. Consequently, the variance in output that could be *jointly* attributable to the influence of input and the college experience is automatically attributed to the variable partialed out (typically and in the present case, input). This means that the residual score procedure may overestimate the influence of input and provide a very conservative estimate of the influence of college experience. This may not always be undesirable, however. As suggested by Feldman (1971b), there may be situations in which the analyst has a sound theoretical rationale for attributing the shared portion of variance in student outcome to student input and intentionally does so. When this happens, value connotations attached to the words *overestimation* and *underestimation* are inappropriate (Feldman, 1971b, p. 135). Fuller discussions of the use of residual scores in computing and interpreting part and partial correlations are found in Astin (1970a), Creager (1969), Feldman (1971b), and Werts and Watley (1968a).

Clearly, the use of residual scores as a mechanism to gain some measure of control over confounding input variables has been a major methodological advance in the study of college impact. There are, however, some problems with this approach. One is the reliability of residual scores, which may be a particular problem when one uses the two-step part correlation procedure (Kerlinger & Pedhazur, 1973). Perhaps more important, however, is the fact that the use of residual scores allows one to explain only the percentage of the residual variance in the criterion measure. This means that squared part or partial correlations based on residual scores do not represent the portion of total variance in college output uniquely associated with college experience. Rather, they represent association with that portion of the variance in college output that remains after covariation with input has been removed. Thus, the squared part and partial correlations based on residual scores will be larger in magnitude than they would be if the baseline were the total variance in the output criterion. How much larger sometimes depends on the correlation between input and output.

Multiple Correlation and Regression Procedures

Frequently, the analyst is interested in explaining or partitioning the total variance in some college outcome measures. The most useful set of approaches for accomplishing this is multiple correlation and regression analysis (for example, Cohen, 1968; Darlington, 1968; Draper & Smith, 1966; Kerlinger & Pedhazur, 1973; Pedhazur, 1975, 1982). This procedure allows one to estimate the percentage of total variance in a criterion measure systematically associated with a set of independent variables. It also allows for partitioning of the explained variance into different unique and common (or joint) components, depending upon the analyst's understanding of the conceptual model being estimated. Thus, in our present example the explained variance (R^2) in IO_2 is a function of IO_1, *SIZE*, and *IWF*. The actual R^2 achieved for our fictitious data is .4266, or 42.66 percent. This means that approximately 43 percent of the variance in IO_2 is systematically associated with our three independent variables and that approximately 57 percent $(1 - R^2)$ is due to errors of measurement and other influences not specified in our regression model.

It is worth noting that the R^2 for our data (43 percent) is less than it would be if we had simply summed the squared simple correlations between each independent variable and IO_2 as shown in Table A.1; that is, $.60^2 + (-.15^2) + .33^2 = .49$. This difference is due to the intercorrelations, or multicolinearity, among the independent variables (also shown in Table A.1). Because of this multicolinearity, the independent variables are, at least in part, laying claim to some of the same variance in IO_2. The computation of R^2 is designed to take this redundant association into account. An excellent and readable discussion of the computations involved in obtaining R^2 is provided by Cohen and Cohen (1975).

Commonality Analysis

In addition to estimating the variance explained by our total set of three predictors, we are also interested in the proportion of the variance that can be attributed to each of the independent variables. One procedure that has received a reasonable amount of use is commonality analysis. The purpose of commonality analysis is to "identify proportions of variance in the dependent variable that may be attributed uniquely to each of the independent variables, and proportions of variance to be attributed to various combinations of independent variables" (Pedhazur, 1975, p. 252).

To obtain the unique variance estimate for each independent variable, a residualizing procedure analogous to that discussed above is carried out. In this procedure, however, each independent variable in the equation is residualized on all other independent predictors variables to produce a measure that is purged of any association with other independent variables. These residualized independent variables are then correlated with the total variance in the criterion measure. This is portrayed in Figure A.4 for the relationship between *IWF* (residualized on IO_1 and *SIZE*) and IO_2. Figure A.4 shows the squared semipartial correlation (area *A*) between *IWF* (residualized on IO_1 and *SIZE*) and total variance in IO_2. Thus, it can be thought of as the unique or net relationship between *IWF* and IO_2, with IO_1 and *SIZE* controlled statistically. The net variance in IO_2 associated with IO_1 and with *SIZE* is computed in the same manner.

Figure A.4. Multiple Correlation/Regression and the Semipartial Correlation.

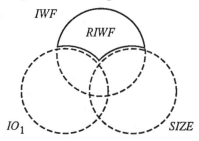
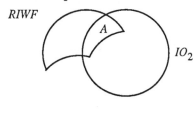

Step 1: Each independent variable, in this case *IWF*, is regressed on all other independent variables to obtain residual variance in *IWF* (*RIWF* enclosed by the solid line); *RIWF* is statistically independent of both IO_1 and *SIZE*

Step 2: Each residualized independent variable, in this case *RIWF*, is correlated with the *total* variance in the dependent variable (IO_2) to yield a semipartial correlation

Another way to conceptualize the unique or net criterion variance associated with a specific independent variable is to think of it as the proportion of the total variance that is explained above and beyond that associated with all other independent predictors. Consequently, if we are interested in the net or unique variance in IO_2 associated with *IWF*, we might compute two R^2s. The first would be the R^2 associated with the regression of IO_2 on IO_1 and *SIZE*, while the second would be the R^2 associated with the regression of IO_2 on IO_1, *SIZE*, and *IWF*. The difference between the R^2s of the two equations would represent the variance in IO_2 associated with *IWF*, *net* of IO_1 and *SIZE*. An analogous set of regression equations would be computed to estimate the unique variance in IO_2 associated with IO_1 and *SIZE*, respectively.

The joint or common variance among sets of predictor variables is essentially that which cannot be uniquely attributed to the individual independent variables. In our fictitious example the common variance is the difference between the R^2 in IO_2 associated with IO_1, *SIZE*, and *IWF* and the sum of the unique variance increments with each individual independent variable. Table A.2 shows the unique and common variance increments based on regression analysis of the correlation matrix in Table A.1. As Table A.2 shows, of the 42.66 percent of the total variance in IO_2 explained by IO_1*1*, *SIZE*, and *IWF*, 5.35 percent is the common variance or that which could not be attributed uniquely to any of the three independent variables.

Table A.2. Unique and Common Variance Increments.

Source	Increment
IO_1	31.47%
SIZE	0.19%
IWF	5.65%
Common variance increment	5.35%
Total variance explained (R^2)	42.66%

It is also possible to calculate the common or joint variance estimates in a dependent measure that can be attributed to any particular subset of independent variables that may be of interest. Reasonably straightforward rules for writing commonality formulas that use various combinations of simple regression equations are provided by Kerlinger and Pedhazur (1973), Mood (1969, 1971), and Wisler (1969).

Commonality analysis has a great deal of intuitive appeal and at first glance seems a perfectly logical and straightforward method for determining the relative importance of a variable in explaining criterion variance. Needless to say, however, there are problems with such a conclusion. A major limitation of commonality analysis is that the unique variance estimates are highly influenced by the degree of intercorrelation or multicolinearity among the independent variables (Creager, 1969). Although not particularly acute in our fictitious example, it is often the case that student input characteristics are substantially correlated with measures of both college characteristics and the college experience. (This is particularly true when institutions are the unit of analysis.) In the situation where the independent variables are themselves highly intercorrelated with each other, it is not uncommon to get large increments of joint variance and relatively trivial increments of unique variance. This makes it quite difficult to talk about the relative importance of a specific variable. Because of the way in which the unique contribution of a variable is affected by its intercorrelations with other independent variables, there is some question as to its appropriateness for assessing the substantive importance of individual variables in regression analyses (Astin, 1990; Pedhazur, 1975; Tukey, 1954).

As suggested by Pedhazur (1975), the critics of variance partitioning have questioned both its validity and its usefulness in terms of policy decisions. As an alternative, they have advocated a regression coefficient approach, which has as its purpose the estimation of the "effects" of each of the independent variables on the criterion measure (for example, Blalock, 1968; Linn, Werts, & Tucker, 1971; Werts, 1970; Werts & Watley, 1968a). In our fictitious example, the regression equation would be as follows:

$$IO_2 = a + b_1 (IO_1) + b_2(SIZE) + b_3(IWF) + \text{error},$$

where a = the intercept or constant; b_1, b_2, and b_3 = the regression coefficients associated with the independent variables or predictors; and error = causes of IO_2 not specified in the equation plus errors of measurement.

In the multiple regression case, the regression coefficients or weights come in two forms. In the equation shown above, the b weights are metric (or unstandardized) partial regression coefficients. Thus a b weight indicates the expected change in IO_2 for a unit increase in the independent variable with which it is associated, while the influence of all other independent variables in the equation is statistically held constant. In their standardized form, the beta regression weights indicate the expected standard deviation change in the dependent measure (IO_2) associated with one standard deviation increase in an independent variable, while all other variables are held constant (Pedhazur, 1975). As such, b weights are in raw-score terms and to some extent reflect the relative scale or metric of the independent and dependent variables. Beta weights, on the other hand, put all variables on the same scale and thus provide a scale-free estimate of a variable's effect on the dependent measure. In our fictitious data, the respective metric (b) and standardized (B) coefficients are as follows:

	Metric (b)	Standardized (B)
IO_1	.590	.564
SIZE	$-.0001$	$-.046$
IWF	.727	.246

Which of the two regression coefficients $(b$ or B$)$ should bear the interpretative burden in regression analysis has been the topic of considerable debate (for example, Blalock, 1964, 1968; Bowles & Levin, 1968; Cain & Watts, 1970; Hanushek & Kain, 1972; Schoenberg, 1972; Werts & Watley, 1968a). A principal problem of beta (B) weights is that they are not particularly stable across different samples, whereas *b* weights are. Thus, in comparing the relative effect of a variable *between* two different samples, the metric *b* weight is preferable (Pedhazur, 1982). Similarly, because the beta weight is essentially scale-free, there is some doubt about its usefulness in terms of policy. For example, within the same sample, relative beta weights may indicate that years of formal education are more important in explaining annual salary (say, in dollars) than is intelligence. One cannot, however, use the beta weight to estimate the average income benefits of one additional year of education, net of other factors. To do this, one needs to rely on the *b* weight. Because the *b* weight represents the partial influence of an independent variable on a dependent variable in terms of the actual units in which they are measured, it provides a direct estimate of the average dollar increase in income associated with each additional year of formal education (for example, Linn, Werts, & Tucker, 1971; Pedhazur, 1975; Smith, 1972).

A counterargument can be made, however, concerning the relative usefulness of *b* and beta weights in assessing the relative contribution or effects of independent variables *within* a sample. In this case, the metric regression weight is limited because of the very fact that its magnitude is a function of the scale units employed in measuring independent and dependent variables. Consequently, the relative magnitudes of *b* weights for several independent variables may have little correspondence to the relative importance of those variables in terms of effects on the dependent measure. In the schooling-intelligence-income illustration, for example, schooling may be measured on a 1–17 scale (where 16 = a bachelor's degree and 17 = some graduate study; or 0–1, where 1 = college graduate and 0 = nongraduate), while intelligence may be measured on a much more variable scale, say, 90–150.

When one is primarily interested in the relative effects of different independent variables *within the same sample,* it may be more appropriate to allow the beta or standardized regression weights to bear the interpretative burden. On the other hand, if one is interested in comparing the relative effects of the same variable *between or among different samples* (for example, between men and women), the metric regression weight is a more useful index (Blalock, 1967; Kerlinger & Pedhazur, 1973; Pedhazur, 1975, 1982; Smith, 1972; Wright, 1960).

Regression Coefficients and Causality

There is a tendency in much literature on the influence of college to speak of regression coefficients as estimates of the net effect of the independent variable on a dependent measure. Given the above definitions of metric and standardized regression coefficients, this seems a natural interpretative conclusion. In an important discussion of the meaning of regression coefficients, however, Pedhazur (1975, 1982) makes an important distinction between the causal meaning of regression coefficients derived from experimental data and those yielded by correlational data.

The easiest way to illustrate this distinction is through an admittedly contrived example. Suppose we randomly provide half the entering freshmen in a particular college with a dictionary-thesaurus combination and withhold it from the remaining half. At the end of the freshman year we give the entire class a test of vocabulary and find that those who received the dictionary thesaurus scored significantly and substantially higher than the nonrecipients. The unstandardized regression equation would tell us the average advantage in vocabulary test achievement accruing to those freshmen provided with the dictionary thesaurus (group coded 1) versus those not provided with it (group coded 0). Given this randomized, true experiment, we could estimate (by means of the b weight) the typical improvement in vocabulary achievement we might get by routinely providing all incoming freshmen with a dictionary thesaurus.

Conversely, suppose in a correlational, panel study we find that net of precollege level of vocabulary achievement, having a dictionary thesaurus has a net positive association with vocabulary achievement at the end of the freshman year. In this situation we have not been able to manipulate and control the conditions under which the relationship between having a dictionary thesaurus and outcome vocabulary achievement is observed. Consequently, the regression coefficient allows us *only* to estimate the average difference in vocabulary achievement between freshmen who own a dictionary thesaurus and those who do not, net of precollege vocabulary achievement. We cannot tell from the regression coefficient whether purposefully providing freshmen with a dictionary thesaurus would produce the same effect (Pedhazur, 1975).

In short, we cannot interpret regression coefficients from naturally occurring correlational data as though the variables they are associated with had been purposefully manipulated under experimental conditions. It would be misleading, therefore, to interpret them as the change in the dependent variable that we can *expect* from a purposeful unit increase in the independent variable, net of other independent variables. Regression coefficients from correlational data can be quite useful in identifying *possibly* causal associations among variables. In the vast majority of investigations on the influence of college, however, the regression coefficients are, in and of themselves, insufficient evidence for causality.

Hierarchical and Stepwise Regression Analysis

In the approach to regression or commonality analysis discussed above, all independent variables in the model are entered into the equation at the same time. It is worth briefly mentioning two other approaches to regression analysis that are concerned with the order in which independent variables enter a regression equation. The first is termed hierarchical regression, and it is often used when the researcher can posit an explicit causal or temporal ordering or hierarchy to the independent variables (for example, Chapman & Pascarella, 1983; Pascarella & Terenzini, 1980a; Terenzini & Pascarella, 1978).

For example, suppose in our fictitious data we are interested only in whether measures of the college environment and experience (for example, institutional size and informal contact with faculty) account for a substantive increase in the explained variance in freshman-year intellectual orientation over and above the individual's level of precollege intellectual orientation. Consistent with our question, we would solve the regression analyses in two steps. In the first step, IO_2 would be regressed on IO_1, and in the second step, $SIZE$ and IWF would be added to the equation. The increase in R^2 from step 1 to step 2 would represent the unique contribution of college environment and experience variables ($SIZE$ and IWF) over and above that due to input (IO_1). (In the actual data, the R^2 in IO_2 increases from .360 with only IO_1 in the equation to .426 with $SIZE$ and IWF added, or an R^2 increase due to $SIZE$ and IWF of .066 or 6.6 percent.) Hierarchical analysis makes no attempt to find the joint or common variance due to input (IO_1) and college environment and experience ($SIZE$ and IWF). Rather, it attributes any joint influence to input alone. As such, hierarchical approaches provide a conservative or lower-bounds estimate of the output variance associated with college environment or experience. This, however, may accurately reflect the analyst's conceptualization of the process.

Although hierarchical analysis enters variables or sets of variables in steps, it does so in accordance with a conceptual or causal hierarchy specified by the researcher. Thus, it must be distinguished from another type of analysis, termed stepwise regression, with which it is sometimes confused. In stepwise analyses, variables are entered (or removed) in steps, but the criteria and order of entry (or removal) are empirically rather than conceptually determined. In one type of stepwise analysis, for example, the computer searches first for the independent variable with the largest simple or zero-order correlation with the dependent measure and enters it into the regression equation in step 1. In step 2, the computer searches the *remaining* independent variables and selects the one with the largest partial correlation with the dependent variable (net of the variable already in the equation) and adds it to the equation. This step-by-step, empirically driven procedure continues until a specified criterion for entry is no longer met (for example, the R^2 increase is no longer statistically significant or is less than 1 percent, and so on).

The basic purpose of stepwise analysis is to develop a parsimonious accounting of variance in the dependent variable (that is, an optimal accounting with the fewest and most important predictors). This has a lot of intuitive appeal, but stepwise analysis has some serious limitations. The most important of these is that it capitalizes on chance covariation in a sample. The easiest way to show this is through an example. Suppose in sample 1 we have ten independent variables, but the two variables with the highest simple correlations with the dependent measure are A ($r = .31$) and B ($r = .30$). In sample 2, with the same set of independent variables, the two respective highest correlations are $A = .30$ and $B = .31$ (just the reverse). In a stepwise analysis conducted with sample 1, variable A would enter the equation first and, if A and B are highly correlated, B might never enter the equation. In sample 2, variable B would enter first, and if B and A are correlated sufficiently, A might never be selected for inclusion. Moreover, in sample 1 the variables entering the equation would be strongly determined not only by their correlation with the dependent variable but also by how much they covary with A. In sample 2, however, an important factor determining the final equation would be correlations between the remaining independent variables and variable B. If these respective correlation patterns differ, the result could be quite different equations in sample 1 and sample 2 even when the same independent variables are being considered.

What this comes down to is that regression equations determined by stepwise analysis can be unstable across independent samples. Indeed, as a rule of thumb, it is probably wise to trust stepwise-determined equations only when the results have been validated on another independent sample (Kerlinger & Pedhazur, 1973).

Causal Modeling

Regression analysis provides the same level of statistical control as the use of residual scores and partial correlations. In addition, it permits partitioning of the total variance in the dependent measure and provides (through regression coefficients) ways of estimating the net magnitude of the influence of each independent variable on the dependent measure. Due in large part to these and related advantages, regression analysis has generally replaced the use of residual scores and partial correlations in studies concerned with the influence of college.

Despite its utility as a general data analytical system, however, regression analysis in the forms discussed above is largely predictive rather than explanatory in nature. For example, when we regress IO_2 on IO_1, $SIZE$, and IWF in our fictitious data set, the resultant regression equation allows us to determine the unique and joint variance increments in IO_2 associated with the three predictors. It also allows us to estimate the net change in IO_2 associated with unit changes in each of the three predictors. It does not, however, provide much information in terms of explaining the interactive process through which student precollege traits (for example, IO_1), institutional characteristics (for example, *SIZE*), and individual collegiate experiences (for example, *IWF*) influence one another as well as freshman-year outcomes (for example, IO_2). Moreover, simple regression analysis does not really help us understand the various mechanisms through which the joint or common influences among independent variables may have an effect on the dependent measure.

Causal modeling is a use of regression analysis that focuses on explanation rather than prediction and provides an efficient method for determining the indirect as well as the direct influences of each independent variable in a theoretically guided causal system (Anderson & Evans, 1974; Duncan, 1966, 1975; Feldman, 1971a; Heise, 1969; Werts & Linn, 1970; Wolfle, 1977, 1980a; Wright, 1934, 1954). As argued by Wright (1934) and discussed by Wolfle (1985a), the purpose of causal modeling is not to accomplish the impossible (that is, to attribute experimental causality from correlational data). Rather, its purpose is to determine the extent to which an *a priori* system of hypothesized causal effects is supported by actual data. Thus, causal relationships exist in models not because they are "proven" by regression coefficients but because theories posit them. From this perspective, if regression coefficients tend to support the presence of a hypothesized causal relationship, this suggests only the *possibility* that the observed relationship may be causal. One does not confirm a causal relationship with regression coefficients in causal modeling; one only "fails to disconfirm it" (for example, Cliff, 1983; Kenny, 1979; Wolfle, 1985a).

As suggested in a comprehensive and readable discussion of causal modeling by Wolfle (1985a), the use of causal models in research on the influence of college may have two important advantages. First, causal modeling requires that the researcher give considerable thought to the theoretical structure of the problem. This means that he or she must not only specify the relevant independent and dependent variables but must also be explicit about the presumed causal ordering and patterns of cause and effect in the model. Often this is accomplished by drawing a path diagram of the causal model in which causal arrows reflect relationships among variables suggested by theory or relevant literature. The explicitness of causal modeling can be important in preventing the misinterpretation of results. As Wolfle (1985a, p. 383) puts it, the "researcher may, of course, be wrong but he won't be misunderstood."

The second advantage of causal modeling is that it moves beyond typical regression analysis and allows the researcher to investigate not only the direct unmediated causal effects of each independent variable but also their indirect effects through intervening variables in the model (Finney, 1972; Wolfle, 1985a). It is in the investigation of indirect effects that causal modeling provides substantively more information than do typical regression analyses. The estimation of direct effects in a causal model can be achieved through the simple regression of the dependent variable on all independent variables in the model. Thus, direct effects in causal models are the same as standardized regression weights in regression analysis, and both are analogous to the unique variance estimates in commonality analysis. The indirect effects in causal modeling, however, can be thought of as a way to further understand and disaggregate the joint or common variance among independent variables (Alwin & Hauser, 1975; Feldman, 1971a).

Decomposition of Effects in Causal Modeling. There are three types of effects in causal modeling. (Note that the terms *path analysis* and *structural equations modeling* are often used interchangeably with *causal modeling.*) These types are direct effects, indirect effects, and total effects. The direct effects have been defined above, the indirect effects are the sum of the products of direct effects through intervening variables, and the total effects are the sum of the direct and indirect effects. The difference between the simple or zero-order correlation between an independent and a dependent variable and the total effect of that independent variable can be considered the spurious or noncausal part of the relationship.

A simple way to understand indirect effects is to visualize three billiard balls: *A*, *B*, and *C*. If ball *A* strikes ball *B*, which in turn strikes ball *C*, then ball *A* can be thought of as having an indirect effect on ball *C* through ball *B*. Thus ball *A* has an effect on ball *C* even though it may never strike it directly. Similarly, college grades may not directly influence income. Nevertheless, they clearly have a strong positive influence on degree attainment, which in turn is a key determinant of income. Consequently, grades in college may have an important indirect effect on income through educational attainment.

The easiest way to demonstrate the decomposition of effects in a causal model is through the use of an example. Again, we will use the fictitious correlation matrix found in Table A.1. The difference, however, is that this time we will posit a hypothetical causal structure to the variables. Let's suppose that on the basis of some theory, we hypothesize that the enrollment of the institution attended *(SIZE)* is a function of precollege level of intellectual orientation, with students initially high in intellectual orientation tending to select and attend smaller schools. In turn, informal contact with faculty *(IWF)* is hypothesized as being a function of both precollege intellectual orientation and institutional size. The former is hypothesized as positively influencing informal contact with faculty, while institutional size is hypothesized to inhibit faculty contact. Finally, end-of-freshman-year intellectual orientation *(IO$_2$)* is posited as being positively influenced by IO_1 and *IWF* and negatively influenced by *SIZE*. A visual portrayal of the model is shown in Figure A.5. In the model, IO_1 is considered an exogenous variable because it is determined by effects outside the model. *SIZE*, *IWF*, and IO_2 are considered endogenous variables and are determined by exogenous variables and all other causally antecedent endogenous variables in the model.

Figure A.5. Proposed Causal Model.

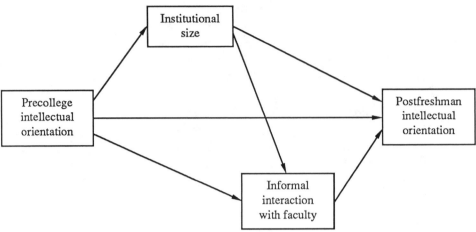

In order to estimate the direct and indirect effects specified by the model, it is necessary to solve a series of regression equations that define the structure of effects in the model. These "structural equations" for the model shown in Figure A.5 are as follows:

$$SIZE = a + B_1(IO_1) + \text{error}$$
$$IWF = a + B_1(IO_1) + B_2(SIZE) + \text{error}$$
$$IO_2 = a + B_1(IO_1) + B_2(SIZE) + B_3(IWF) + \text{error},$$

where B equals the standardized regression or path coefficient and a is a constant. Thus, the structural equations provide all the direct effects, which in turn can be used to compute indirect effects. Figure A.6 shows the ap-

Figure A.6. Path Coefficients.

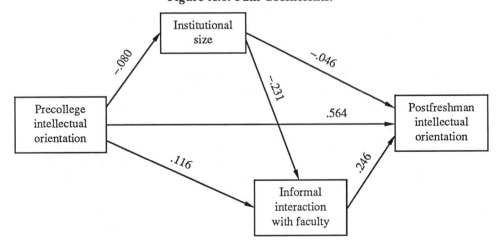

propriate direct effects (beta weights) for each causal path computed for our fictitious correlation matrix. The decomposition of causal effects on IO_2 is summarized in Table A.3. As this table shows, the direct or unmediated effects of IO_1 (.564) and IWF (.246) on IO_2 were positive and substantial; both were also statistically significant. The direct effect of $SIZE$ (-.046), however, was small and nonsignificant.

Had we ended our analysis here, essentially the results of a simple multiple regression, we would have concluded that both precollege intellectual orientation and informal contact with faculty may causally influence freshman-year intellectual orientation but that the size of the institution attended is essentially unimportant. This would have been misleading, however, since as we can see from Figure A.6, $SIZE$ has a substantial (-.231) negative effect on IWF, which in turn positively influences IO_2 (.246). Based on our computational definition of indirect effects (the sum of the products of direct effects through intervening variables), the indirect effect of $SIZE$ on IO_2 through $IWF = (-.231) \times (.246) = -.057$. Though modest, this indirect effect is larger than the direct effect and is statistically significant, while the latter is not. (The statistical significance of indirect effects can now be computed quite simply via a computer program developed by Wolfle and Ethington, 1985, based on the work of Sobel, 1982.)

This example demonstrates an important analytical advantage of causal modeling over simple regression analysis. By permitting one to estimate indirect (mediated) as well as the direct (unmediated) effects, it provides a more complete estimate of a variable's total influence on the criterion. In this sense it addresses and helps illuminate the nature of a variable's influence through its joint covariation with other independent variables (that is, the joint or common variance from a commonality analysis). In doing so, it may alter one's conclusions about the importance of a variable's impact versus the estimate one would get from an examination of direct effects only. In the present case, the total effect of $SIZE$ on IO_2 —that is, the sum of the direct (-.046) and indirect (-.057) effects—is -.103, which is also statistically significant. This suggests that in our hypothetical example, the enrollment of the institution attended has a modest negative influence on the development of intellectual orientation, primarily by inhibiting student informal contact with faculty. Our conclusion based on direct effects only

Table A.3. Direct, Indirect, and Total Effects.

Variable	Direct Effect	Indirect Effect	Total Effect
IO_1	.564[a]	.036	.600[a]
$SIZE$	−.046	−.057[a]	−.103[a]
IWF	.246[a]		.246[a]

[a] $p < .01$.

would have essentially dismissed any influence of *SIZE* on IO_2 as trivial and statistically nonsignificant.

It is worth noting that there are different ways of computing indirect and total effects in a causal model. Indirect effects can be computed as shown above. In complex models, however, the summing of the products of direct effects through the various paths leading to the dependent measure can be tedious and fraught with computational errors. A simpler way is to compute direct effects and total effects and then subtract the former from the latter to get indirect effects. Direct effects, of course, can be obtained from the simple regression of the dependent measure on all relevant independent measures. Total effects and their statistical significance can be obtained by using "reduced form" regression equations (Alwin & Hauser, 1975). These are simply the regression of the dependent measure on the variable of interest and all causally concurrent or antecedent variables in the model. Intervening variables between the variable of interest and the dependent measure are not in the equation—thus the term *reduced form*. For example, the total effect of IO_1 on IO_2 is simply the regression of IO_2 on IO_1. The independent variable here is exogenous, so it has no causal antecedents defined by the model. The total effect of *SIZE* is obtained from the regression of IO_2 on IO_1 and *SIZE*. Finally, since *IWF* has no indirect effect on IO_2 through intervening variables in the model, its direct effect is also its total effect.

Problems in the Use of Causal Modeling. While causal models have great potential for increasing the information gained about the process of collegiate influence on student development, a number of problems are inherent in their use. The first of these focuses on the issue of adequate model specification. This means that in constructing causal models the researcher must give considerable thought both to including all important relevant variables in the model and to specifying their appropriate causal ordering. If important causal influences are excluded, the result is often seriously biased or inflated path coefficients. For example, with IO_1 and *SIZE* also in the equation, the direct effect of *IWF* on IO_2 is .246. However, if IO_1 is left out, the direct effect of *IWF* on IO_2 jumps spuriously to .312. On the other hand, if the model specifies an inappropriate or implausible causal ordering in the variables, the indirect effects can be misleading and perhaps even meaningless.

What determines an adequately specified model, of course, is the soundness of its theoretical structure. Indeed, as noted by Duncan (1975, p. 149), quoted in Wolfle (1985a), "The study of structural equation [causal] models can be divided into two parts: the easy part and the hard part." The easy part is the solution of structural equations and the computation of direct, indirect, and total effects. The hard part is the construction of causal models that reflect sound social theory.

In addition to adequate model specification, a second assumption of causal modeling, and indeed of ordinary least-squares multiple regression generally, is recursiveness. *Recursiveness* refers to the assumption of unidirectional causal influence (for example, A influences B but not vice versa) in the model and the absence of causal feedback loops. Thus, in the example data, informal contact with faculty is presumed to influence freshman-year intellectual orientation, but the reverse is not hypothesized. The only way to ensure that causal feedback loops (or correlated errors) are not present is to collect longitudinal data in a manner that reflects the causal ordering of variables in the model. For example, in our fictitious study, measures of IO_1 were collected prior to measures of IWF, which in turn preceded the collection of data relevant to IO_2. This means that while IWF may causally influence IO_2, the reverse is not possible (for example, Kenny, 1979). If, however, independent measures such as IWF and dependent measures such as IO_2 had been collected simultaneously on the same instrument (a practice quite common in educational research), the direction of causal effects could be ambiguous. Does informal interaction with faculty influence intellectual orientation, or do increases in intellectual orientation lead students to seek out more frequent nonclassroom interaction with faculty?

Consistent with what we know about the developmental nature of student growth and maturation during college (for example, Chickering, 1969; Feldman, 1972; Heath, 1968), causal models assume longitudinality in the data being analyzed. In the absence of carefully collected *longitudinal* data, it is extremely hazardous to assume the presence of unidirectional causal effects. Moreover, when there is simultaneous assessment of the dependent variable and independent causal variables on the same instrument (that is, cross-sectional data), the frequent result is a correlation between those independent causes and errors of measurement on the dependent variable. This violates one of the assumptions of any ordinary least-squares regression analysis and can lead to biased regression coefficients (Pedhazur, 1982).

This problem has led to the development of nonrecursive causal models in which the researcher actually hypothesizes the presence of causal loops or two-way causality (Anderson, 1978). Estimating nonrecursive causal models requires the use of a procedure termed two-stage least-squares regression analysis. One of the assumptions of two-stage least squares is the presence of "instrumental" exogenous variables. By definition, an instrumental exogenous variable is one that causally influences one of the dependent (endogenous) variables in the causal loop but has zero effect on the other (Anderson, 1978; Wolfle, 1985a). Once these instrumental exogenous variables are identified and the causal model is specified, existing two-stage least-squares regression programs, such as those available in the Statistical Analysis System (SAS), can be used to estimate the direction and strength of causal influences. Unfortunately, given the considerable correlations among student precollege traits, institutional characteristics, and measures of the collegiate experience in research on college influence, it is extremely difficult to find exogenous variables that meet the assumption of also being instrumental variables. Wolfle (1985a, p. 395) has suggested that this problem may make "most nonrecursive models implausible for social science applications." Nevertheless, there are a few uses of nonrecursive models and two-stage least-squares regression in research on the college student (for example, Bean & Bradley, 1986; Bean & Kuh, 1984; Iverson, Pascarella, & Terenzini, 1984).

A third important issue in the use of causal models is measurement error. One of the assumptions of any regression analysis is that both the independent and dependent variables are measured without error; however, this is almost never the case. In the presence of measurement error, regression or path coefficients will be biased, and it is extremely difficult to determine both the magnitude and the direction of the biases (Maruyama & Walberg, 1982; Stage, 1989, 1990). Recently, however, there have been a number of advances with maximum likelihood estimation procedures such as linear structural relations (LISREL) (Joreskog, 1973; Joreskog & Sorbom, 1979, 1983). These procedures permit correction for differential measurement errors and thus yield less biased regression coefficients than do ordinary least-squares regression approaches. As such, they represent an important refinement in the application of causal modeling to questions of the influence of college on student development.

The Unit of Analysis

An important question in investigations of the influence of college on student development is the appropriate unit of analysis. This is most apparent when one is analyzing multi-institutional samples where data are collected at the individual level but where it is also possible to obtain average scores at the institutional or other level of aggregation (for example, the Cooperative Institutional Research Program data, the National Longitudinal Study of the High School Class of 1972, High School and Beyond). It is also possible, however, that one needs to consider the appropriate unit of analysis even when the data come from single-institution samples. What, for example, are the effects of classroom climate or residential unit composition on student learning (for example, Pascarella & Terenzini, 1982; D. Smith, 1977; Terenzini & Pascarella, 1984)?

The unit of analysis issue has been a complex and somewhat controversial one in research on the influence of college. It is often the case that scholars interested in essentially the same question have in various studies used institutions, departments, or individuals as the unit of analysis. Consider, for example, studies of the influence of different college characteristics on student learning (for example, Astin, 1968c; Ayres, 1983; Ayres & Bennett, 1983; Centra & Rock, 1971; Hartnett & Centra, 1977). Variation in the unit of analysis has perhaps contributed to the lack of consistent findings in several areas of inquiry (for example, Pascarella, 1985a). As suggested in a sophisticated and cogent discussion by Burstein (1980a), the issue is not so much that one unit of aggregation is more appropriate than another. Rather, the issue needs to be understood in light of the fact that different units of aggregation or analysis are asking different questions of the data. When the institution is the unit of analysis, for example, one is essentially asking what the average influence of certain college characteristics (student body selectivity, average faculty salary, and so on) is on average student development. Thus, one is primarily concerned with average effects among or between institutions. When individuals are the unit of analysis, however, the question is typically whether differences in individual students' collegiate experiences (for instance, academic major, extracurricular involvement, interaction with faculty) lead to differences in specified outcomes. Here the focus is on the effects of different experiences or exposures among or between individual students, even if the data are multi-institutional in form.

By focusing on one question, both institutional and individual levels of aggregation tend to ignore other questions. Aggregating at the level of the institution tends to mask possibly substantial variations between individual students' experiences within the same institution (Cronbach, 1976). Assuming, for example, that an aggregate or global measure of the college environment accurately portrays a homogeneous stimulus experienced by all students in the institution ignores substantial evidence of influential subenvironments in an institution, subenvironments that are more proximal to the student's daily experience (for example, Baird, 1974; Berdie, 1967; Lacy, 1978; Newcomb & Wilson, 1966; Pascarella, 1976; Phelan, 1979; Weidman, 1979). Conversely, using individuals as the unit of analysis tends to ignore the dependencies (or correlations) of individual subject experiences within institutions; that is, the shared educational experience among individual students within the same college leads to the nonindependence of individual behaviors within the college (Burstein, 1980a). Thus, for example, institutional enrollment (size) may facilitate certain types of student-faculty relationships in a small liberal arts college that are quite different from the nature of the student-faculty relationships typically found in large research universities. These types of relationships may differentiate small and large institutions even when individual differences in student characteristics are taken into account. Moreover, as suggested by Burstein (1980a), standard statistical estimation techniques such as ordinary least-squares regression analysis can yield flawed or biased estimates in the presence of within-group dependencies.

Because of the dilemmas inherent in choosing one level of aggregation or unit of analysis over another, a number of scholars have suggested the appropriateness of using multilevels of analysis guided by appropriate theory (for example, Astin, 1970b; Burstein, 1980a, 1980b; Cooley, Bond, & Mao, 1981; Cronbach, 1976; Cronbach & Webb, 1975; Terenzini & Pascarella, 1984; Rogosa, 1978). In such analyses, both between-student and between-aggregation effects could be estimated when one has multi-institutional (or even multimajor, multiclassroom, or multiresidential arrangement) data. (The appropriate level of aggregation, of course, depends on the substantive question being asked.) Routine use of a multilevel approach such as this might be one way to permit a more valid and informative comparison of results across studies. It would also permit one to compare differences in the aggregate effects of college (or some other unit of aggregation) with the effects of individual student characteristics and experiences. As suggested by Burstein (1980a), variables can have different meanings at different levels of analysis. Studies that choose colleges as the unit of analysis are asking different questions than studies that use the individual as the unit of analysis; consequently, we should expect different results.

Contextual Analysis

One way of combining aggregate and individual levels of analysis simultaneously is through a procedure known as contextual analysis. Contextual analysis is essentially the study of the influence of group- or aggregate-level variables on individual-level outcomes (Erbring & Young, 1980; Firebaugh, 1978, 1980; Lazarsfeld & Menzel, 1961). In this procedure the individual is the true unit of analysis, but instead of focusing only on the developmental effects of individual college experiences, one also attempts to estimate the effect of being a member of a particular group or aggregation (for example, college academic major, residential unit, classroom).

In its simplest form, contextual analysis can be defined by the following regression equation:

$$Y_{ij} = a + b_1 X_{ij} + b_2 \overline{X}_j + \text{error},$$

where Y_{ij} might represent the academic achievement (for instance, Graduate Record Examination Scores) of the ith student in college j, X_{ij} might be a measure of academic aptitude for the same student, and $\overline{X}_j$ would be the average (mean) value of student academic aptitude in college j. In short, X_{ij} might be thought of as a measure of student input or background, while $\overline{X}_j$ could be considered an estimate of college context or environment. The error or random disturbance term represents errors of measurement plus all causes of Y_{ij} (achievement) unspecified by the equation, such as student motivation and efficiency of study habits (Hanushek, Jackson, & Kain, 1974). The coefficients a (constant) and b_1 and b_2 (regression coefficients) can be estimated by ordinary least-squares regression procedures. A contextual or environmental effect is said to occur in this equation if the aggregate measure of student body aptitude has a significant regression coefficient with individual GRE achievement net of individual aptitude. If the coefficient for the contextual effect is positive, it would suggest that attending a college with a student body composed of "bright" students tends positively to influence a student's standardized academic achievement above and beyond his or her own academic aptitude.

One might posit the causal mechanism underlying the above example as due to the tendency for college faculty to gear the cognitive and conceptual level of instruction to the academic capacities of the students being taught or to the generally "higher" intellectual level of student discourse inside or outside the classroom. Hypothetically, then, students in more selective colleges might benefit from instruction (or an overall environment) geared to higher-level cognitive processes such as analysis, synthesis, and evaluation (Bloom, 1956), the results of which are manifest in higher GRE scores. In positing such a causal mechanism, however, we are again confronted by the disconcerting likelihood that selection (input) and aggregation (environmental) effects are substantially correlated. As such, it is extremely difficult, if not impossible, to accurately estimate and separate the effects of the latter from those of the former (Cronbach, Rogosa, Floden, & Price, 1977; Werts & Linn, 1971). In the above specification of the model, the unique effects of context or environment (as indicated by b_2) are likely to be quite conservative. Thus, a significant regression coefficient for average student body aptitude is reasonably convincing evidence of a unique contextual or environmental influence (Burstein, 1980a).

Frog-Pond Effects

Another approach to the combining of individual and aggregate level data is the "frog-pond" or relative deprivation effect as suggested by the work of Davis (1966), Alexander and Eckland (1975b), and Bassis (1977). This approach suggests that in order to understand individual behavior, one needs to be cognizant not only of individual attributes but also of how individual attributes position one in relationship to an important reference or peer group. In the above example of aptitude and achievement, the regression equation might be specified as follows:

$$Y_{ij} = a + b_1 X_{ij} + b_2(\overline{X}_j - X_{ij}) + \text{error}$$

In this specification, hypothetical GRE achievement for an individual student (Y_{ij}) is posited as a function of individual academic aptitude (X_{ij}) and the difference between individual aptitude and the average college aptitude ($\overline{X}_j - X_{ij}$). A significant regression coefficient would indicate that a student's academic ability relative to the student average at the college attended has an influence on GRE achievement above and beyond individual aptitude alone. The sign of the regression coefficient would indicate whether the effect is generally beneficial to students below ($+$) or above ($-$) the college average.

As demonstrated by Burstein (1980a, 1980b), a regression equation including individual, contextual, and frog-pond effects is not estimable by standard means because the variables representing the three effects have a linear dependency. (The coefficients in an equation with any combination of two of the three effects represented, however, can be estimated.) Burstein (1980a) has suggested a way to deal with this problem. Specifically, he suggests that the investigator obtain more direct measures of the contextual or frog-pond effects. This means giving considerable thought to the specific and underlying causal mechanisms at work. For example, research conducted by Terenzini and Pascarella (1984) found that net of individual levels of institutional commitment, freshman-year persistence was independently and positively influenced by the average level of institutional commitment in the student's residence unit (contextual).

It is also possible that the student's level of institutional commitment relative to that of his or her residential unit peers (frog pond) would add significantly to an understanding of individual persistence or withdrawal behavior (an influence not estimated by Terenzini & Pascarella, 1982). That this effect operates through the influence of social involvement or integration is suggested by the theoretical work of Tinto (1975, 1982, 1987). Thus, instead of entering an unestimable frog-pond term operationalizing the student's standing relative to the average institutional commitment of the residence unit, one could substitute relative standing on level of social involvement. The equation then might be specified as follows:

$$P_{ij} = a + b_1 (IC_{ij}) + b_2 (\overline{IC}_j) + b_3 (\overline{SI}_j - SI_{ij}),$$

where

P_{ij} = an individual student's persistence or withdrawal behavior,
IC_{ij} = an individual student's level of institutional commitment,
$\overline{IC}_j$ = average level of institutional commitment in a particular student's residence unit,
$(\overline{SI}_j - SI_{ij})$ = an individual student's level of social integration relative to the average in his or her residence unit.

Burstein's (1980a) argument for focusing on direct measures of aggregate and/or frog-pond effects underscores a major conceptual problem in multilevel analysis. This problem, which has been forcefully articulated by analysts such as Hauser (1970, 1974) and Firebaugh (1978), is that contextual or frog-pond effects estimated atheoretically are often mechanistic and distally related to the underlying social-psychological processes they were designed to represent (Burstein, 1980a). For example, contextual or frog-pond effects estimated at the institutional level may have little relevance to and therefore little impact on individual cognitive development during college. Greater understanding may come from estimating contextual and relative standing effects at levels of aggregation that are not only theoretically justifiable but also more proximal and directly related to student learning (for example, classrooms, peer groups, roommates). In short, the most informative multilevel analyses are likely to be those "based on theories in which the source and form of group effects are measured directly" (Burstein, 1980a, p. 207).

It may be, of course, that aggregate effects at almost any level are simply too psychologically remote (or too globally measured) to have important direct effects on student development. Instead, the major aggregate-level influences on student development in college may be indirect, transmitted through their shaping of the individual student's interaction with important agents of socialization on campus, such as peers and faculty.

Change Scores

A substantial amount of the more recent research on the influence of college has a developmental focus and attempts to estimate how exposure to different collegiate experiences or environments leads to differential change on some trait over time. For example, do students who reside on campus tend to change more in critical thinking than students who commute to campus? One way in which this type of question has traditionally been approached is to compare pre- to postdifferences (such as freshman-to-senior scores) on an appropriate measure between groups of interest. If, for example, students residing on campus tend to change more in critical thinking than do those commuting to campus, one might conclude that the residential experience increases the impact of college, at least on critical thinking.

This is an intuitively appealing approach. There are, however, two problems with the use of change scores: reliability and the fact that the magnitude of the change or gain is typically correlated with the initial score (Linn, 1986). Reliability is an issue because change scores incorporate the unreliability of both the pre- and posttest measures (Thorndike & Hagen, 1977). This can be a major problem when difference scores are used to make decisions about individuals, but it may not be a major issue when group comparisons are being made (Cronbach, 1970; Linn, 1986). The second problem with change scores, their correlation with the initial score, however, can confound attempts to attribute differential change to exposure to a particular group or educational experience. If one simply compared changes in critical thinking between residents and commuters, it would be extremely difficult, if not impossible, to determine whether the differential changes were due to differences in actual residence status or simply to differences in initial critical thinking status between the two groups.

Comparing simple change or gain scores cannot correct for the lack of random assignment to different groups or collegiate experiences. A better (though not totally adequate) approach would be to employ change or gain in critical thinking as a dependent measure in a regression model that includes both a measure of group membership (for example, 1 = residents, 0 = commuters) and initial level of critical thinking. This would indicate whether or not residence arrangement is significantly associated with critical thinking gains when the influence of initial critical thinking status is partialed out. It is of interest to note, however, that one need not use change scores to obtain essentially the same information. Exactly the same results in terms of the statistical significance of residence status would be obtained if senior-year critical thinking were regressed on a model containing both residence status and initial freshman-year critical thinking (Linn, 1986; Linn & Slinde, 1977). Similarly, in the fictitious example we have been using throughout this appendix, essentially the same *net associations* for *SIZE* and *IWF* would be obtained in either of the following regression equations:

$$IO_2 - IO_1 = IO_1 + SIZE + IWF + \text{error}$$
$$IO_2 = IO_1 + SIZE + IWF + \text{error}$$

In what has come to be regarded as a classic paper, Cronbach and Furby (1970, p. 80) have suggested that "investigators who ask questions regarding gain scores would ordinarily be better advised to frame their questions in other ways." In fact, as suggested above, questions about gain or change can typically be reformulated without sacrificing information. Regression analyses that treat the pretest (precollege) scores no differently from other independent variables in the model and use the posttest (senior-year) scores as the dependent variable provide essentially the same information while avoiding many of the problems associated with change scores (Linn & Slinde, 1977).

This is not to suggest that change should not be studied. Recent work by Bryk and Raudenbush (1987) and Willett (1988), as reviewed by Light, Singer, and Willett (1990), has suggested that the study of change becomes more valid and less ambiguous when it is measured over more than two time points. Light, Singer, and Willett (1990, p. 147) argue that assessing change over three, four, or even more time points permits one to trace the "shape of each student's growth trajectory" rather than just the difference between the beginning and end points. The use of multiple estimates of student status over time is a promising new methodological approach to the assessment of change or growth.

Conditional Versus General Effects

The analytical procedures we have discussed in the preceding sections have all assumed that the net effects of each independent variable on the dependent variable are general. That is, the effect is the same for all students irrespective of their status on other independent variables (Kerlinger & Pedhazur, 1973). Thus, in our fictitious example we are assuming that the net direct effect of *IWF* on IO_2 is the same regardless of the student's level on IO_1 or the size of the institution attended. This assumption certainly has the appeal of parsimony (that is, other things being equal, the simplest explanation is often the optimal one). On the other hand, it can be argued that assuming only general effects in one's analytical approach ignores individual differences among students attending the same institution or exposed to the same educational or instructional experience. These individual differences among students may interact with different institutional, instructional, curricular, or other educational experiences to produce "conditional" rather than general effects. In a conditional effect, the magnitude of the influence of certain educational experiences on the dependent measure may vary for students with different individual characteristics. Thus, for example, the magnitude of the direct effect of *IWF* on IO_2 may vary, depending upon the student's precollege level of intellectual orientation (IO_1) or on other individual traits such as gender or race.

It is also possible that there may be patterns of conditional relationships or interactions that involve different levels of aggregation (Bryk & Thum, 1989; Raudenbush & Bryk, 1988). In a contextual analysis, for example, individual aptitude may influence achievement differently depending upon the aggregate level of institutional, departmental, or residence unit aptitude. Similarly, there may be interactions among college experience variables that do not directly involve individual differences among student precollege characteristics. The influence of informal contact with faculty on intellectual orientation, for example, may vary in magnitude in institutions of different size enrollment. Conditional effects of the various types described above may be masked by analyses that consider general effects only. Under certain circumstances this may lead the researcher to conclude that the effects of specific educational experiences are trivial or nonsignificant when, in fact, they may have statistically significant and nontrivial influences for certain subgroups in the sample. Thus, a narrow focus on aggregate means or tendencies as an index of college impact may mask important changes in individuals or student subgroups. (See Clark, Heist, McConnell, Trow, & Yonge [1972] or Feldman & Newcomb [1969, pp. 53–58] for a more extensive discussion of this point.)

The concept of conditional effects determined by the interaction of individual differences among students with different methods of teaching or the presentation of course content has a respected tradition in instructional research. Here it is typically referred to as aptitude (or trait) × treatment interaction (Berliner & Cahen, 1973; Cronbach & Snow, 1977). Underlying its application in instructional research is the more general perspective, stemming from the psychology of individual differences, that not all individuals will benefit equally from the same educational experience. Applications of the investigation of conditional effects with postsecondary samples are provided by Romine, Davis, and Gehman (1970) for college environments and achievement; by Holland (1963) for career choice and academic achievement; by Pfeifer (1976) for race and grades; by Andrews (1981), Born, Gledhill, and Davis (1972), Buenz and Merrill (1968), Domino (1968), Daniels and Stevens (1976), Gay (1986), Horak and Horak (1982), Parent, Forward, Canter, and Mohling (1975), Pascarella (1978), Peterson (1979), Ross and Rakow (1981), and Stinard and Dolphin (1981) for different instructional approaches; by Cosgrove (1986) for the effects of programmatic interventions; by Bean (1985), Pascarella and Terenzini (1979a), and Terenzini, Pascarella, Theophilides, and Lorang (1985) in research on student persistence and withdrawal behavior in college; and by Chapman and Pascarella (1983) on students' levels of social and academic integration in college.

The computational procedure for estimating conditional effects involves the addition of a cross-product term to a general effects equation. Thus, if one is interested in the interaction of IO_1 and IWF, the required regression would be the following:

$$IO_2 = IO_1 + SIZE + IWF + (IO_1 \times IWF) + \text{error}$$

Because the cross-product of $IO_1 \times IWF$ is composed of variables already in the equation, its introduction produces a high level of multicolinearity or intercorrelation among the independent variables. Since this can lead to biased and unstable regression coefficients, the estimation of conditional effects is usually conducted via a hierarchical regression approach (Overall & Spiegel, 1969). In this approach, the general effects IO_1, $SIZE$, and IWF (sometimes called main effects) would be entered in the first step. This would be followed by the addition of the cross-product or interaction term in the second step. If the cross-product of $IO_1 \times IWF$ is not associated with a significant increase in R^2, one can then eliminate the cross-product term from the equation and interpret the equation in terms of its general effects results. If, however, the cross-product is associated with a significant increase in R^2, it suggests the presence of a significant conditional effect (that is, the magnitude of the influence of IWF on IO_2 varies with the student's precollege status on IO_1).

This being the case, the results yielded by the general effects equation would be misleading. Rather, one would interpret the nature of the $IO_1 \times IWF$ interaction to determine variations in the effects (unstandardized regression coefficient) of *IWF* on IO_2 at different levels of IO_1. Cohen and Cohen (1975) provide a simple computational formula for interpreting the nature of a conditional effect when the two interacting variables are continuous in nature. This formula can also be applied when one variable is categorical (for example, treatment versus control) and one is a continuous covariate (for example, aptitude). In the latter case an additional analysis can be conducted to determine the range of the continuous variable (aptitude) for which significant differences in the dependent variable exist between treatment and control groups (Johnson & Fay, 1950; Serlin & Levin, 1980).

A final point needs to be made about the estimation of conditional effects. The presence of replicable aptitude × treatment interaction effects has not been particularly common in experimental instructional research. Thus, in correlational data where one needs to rely on less effective statistical controls, the presence of conditional effects can often be artifacts idiosyncratic to the particular sample being analyzed. Considerable caution is therefore recommended in substantively interpreting conditional effects in correlational data. The most trustworthy are those suggested by theory and replicable across independent samples.

Final Note

At about the time this volume went into production, two potentially important books on the methodology of research and assessment in higher education were published. The first, by Light, Singer, and Willett (1990), uses case studies of actual investigations in postsecondary settings to introduce and explicate in greater detail many of the issues in research methodology touched upon in this appendix. The second, by Astin (1990), is a detailed treatment of many of the important conceptual, methodological, and analytical issues involved in assessing the impact of college and the impact of different experiences in college. Of particular relevance to the present discussion is Astin's own technical appendix on the statistical analysis of longitudinal data. Therein, he deals with many of the statistical and analytical issues we have just discussed, though from a somewhat different perspective. He also demonstrates how elements of regression analysis and causal modeling are combined to assess college effects within his input-environment-output model. Both books provide important conceptual, methodological, and analytical tools for scholars interested in the impact of college on students.

References

Abrams, H., & Jernigan, L. (1984). Academic support services and the success of high-risk students. *American Educational Research Journal, 21,* 261–274.

Abravanel, M., & Busch, R. (1975). Students' beliefs about how to influence the government. *Journal of Higher Education, 46,* 567–584.

Acker, J. (1980). Women and stratification: A review of recent literature. *Contemporary Sociology, 9,* 25–35.

Adams, A., & Nestel, G. (1976). Interregional migration, education, and poverty in the urban ghetto: Another look at black-white earnings differentials. *Review of Economics and Statistics, 58,* 156–166.

Adams, E. (1982). *General management hire validation studies.* Morristown, NJ: American Telephone and Telegraph Company.

Adams, G., & Fitch, S. (1982). Ego stage and identity status development: A cross-sequential analysis. *Journal of Personality and Social Psychology, 43,* 547–583.

Adams, G., & Fitch, S. (1983). Psychological environments of university departments: Effects on college students' identity status and ego stage development. *Journal of Personality and Social Psychology, 44,* 1266–1275.

Adams, G., & Shea, J. (1979). The relationship between identity status, locus of control, and ego development. *Journal of Youth and Adolescence, 8,* 81–89.

Adams, G., Shea, J., & Fitch, S. (1979). Toward the development of an objective assessment of ego-identity status. *Journal of Youth and Adolescence, 8,* 223–237.

Adams, W., & Jaffe, A. (1971). Economic returns on the college investment. *Change, 3,* 8 ff.

Adelman, C. (1984). *The standardized test scores of college graduates, 1964–1982.* Washington, DC: National Institute of Education.

Aderinto, K. (1975). Academic achievement of college freshmen using Holland's constructs. In *Summaries, abstracts, and research reports.* Washington, DC: American Personnel and Guidance Association.

Adkins, D. (1975). *The great American degree machine.* New York: McGraw-Hill.

Adler, M. (1952). *The great ideas: A syntopicon of great books of the western world* (Vol. 1). Chicago: Encyclopaedia Britannica.

Adorno, T., Frenkel-Brunswick, E., Levinson, D., & Sanford, N. (1950). *The authoritarian personality.* New York: Harper & Row.

Aiello, N., & Wolfle, L. (1980). *A meta-analysis of individualized instruction in science.* Paper presented at the meeting of the American Educational Research Association, Boston.

Ainsworth, C., & Maynard, D. (1976). The impact of roommate personality on achievement: An exploratory study and model of analysis. *Research in Higher Education, 4,* 291–301.

Aitken, N. (1982). College student performance, satisfaction, and retention. *Journal of Higher Education, 53,* 32–50.

Akin, J., & Garfinkel, I. (1974). *Economic returns to education quality.* Madison: University of Wisconsin, Institute for Research on Poverty.

Alba, R., & Lavin, D. (1981). Community colleges and tracking in higher education. *Sociology of Education, 54,* 223–237.

Alberti, R. (1972). Influence of the faculty on college student development. *Journal of College Student Personnel, 13,* 18–23.

Aldous, J., & Tallman, I. (1972). Immediacy of situation and conventionality as influences on attitudes toward war. *Sociology and Social Research, 56,* 356–367.

Aleamoni, L., & Yimer, M. (1973). An investigation of the relationship between colleague rating, student rating, research productivity, and academic rank in rating instructional effectiveness. *Journal of Educational Psychology, 64,* 274–277.

Alexander, K., & Eckland, B. (1975a). Basic attainment process: A replication and extension. *Sociology of Education, 48,* 457–495.

Alexander, K., & Eckland, B. (1975b). Contextual effects in the high school attainment process. *American Sociological Review, 40,* 402–416.

Alexander, K., & Eckland, B. (1977). High school context and college selectivity: Institutional constraints in educational stratification. *Social Forces, 56,* 166–188.

Alexander, K., Eckland, B., & Griffin, L. (1975). The Wisconsin model of socioeconomic achievement: A replication. *American Journal of Sociology, 81,* 324–342.

Alexander, K., Riordan, C., Fennessey, J., & Pallas, A. (1982). Social background, academic resources, and college graduation: Recent evidence from the national longitudinal survey. *American Journal of Education, 90,* 315–333.

Alfert, E., & Suczek, R. (1971). Personality development and cultural change. *Journal of Higher Education, 42,* 21–26.

Alishio, K., & Schilling, K. (1984). Sex differences in intellectual and ego development in late adolescence. *Journal of Youth and Adolescence, 13,* 213–224.

Allen, W. (1986). *Gender and campus race differences in black student academic performance, racial attitudes and college satisfaction.* Atlanta: Southern Education Foundation.

Allen, W. (1987). Black colleges vs. white colleges: The fork in the road for black students. *Change, 19,* 28–34.

Allen, W., Bobo, L., & Fleuranges, P. (1984). *Preliminary report: 1982 undergraduate survey of black undergraduate students attending predominantly white, state-supported activities.* Ann Arbor, MI: National Study of Black College Students, Center for Afro-American and African Studies.

Allport, G., Vernon, P., & Lindzey, G. (1960). *Study of Values: Manual* (3rd ed.). Boston: Houghton Mifflin.

Allred, G., & Graff, T. (1980). Improving students' interpersonal communication. *Journal of College Student Personnel, 21,* 155–162.

Almquist, E., & Angrist, S. (1970). Career salience and atypicality of occupational choice among college women. *Journal of Marriage and the Family, 32,* 242–249.

Almquist, E., & Angrist, S. (1971). Role model influences on college women's career aspirations. *Merrill-Palmer Quarterly, 17,* 263–279.

Alterman, E. (1989, November 5). Black universities: In demand and in trouble. *New York Times Magazine,* pp. 61–63, 80–86.

Alwin, D. (1972). *College effects on educational and socioeconomic achievements.* Unpublished doctoral dissertation, University of Wisconsin, Madison.

Alwin, D. (1974). College effects on educational and occupational attainments. *American Sociological Review, 39,* 210–221.

Alwin, D. (1976). Socioeconomic background, colleges and postcollegiate achievements. In W. Sewell, R. Hauser, & D. Featherman (Eds.), *Schooling and achievement in American society.* Orlando, FL: Academic Press.

Alwin, D., & Hauser, R. (1975). The decomposition of effects in path analysis. *American Sociological Review, 40,* 37–47.

American Telephone and Telegraph Company. (1962). *College achievement and progress in management.* New York: Author, Personnel Research Section.

Anaya, G. (1989). *Students' perceived cognitive change.* Paper presented at the meeting of the American Educational Research Association, San Francisco.

Andersen, C., & Atelsek, F. (1982). *Assessment of college student housing and physical plant* (Higher Education Panel Report No. 55). Washington, DC: American Council on Education.

Anderson, C., Bowman, M., & Tinto, V. (1972). *Where colleges are and who attends: Effects of accessibility on college attendance.* New York: McGraw-Hill.

Anderson, D., & Binnie, A. (1971). Effects of a group vocational guidance class with community college students. *Vocational Guidance Quarterly, 20,* 123–128.

Anderson, J. (1978). Causal models in educational research: Nonrecursive models. *American Educational Research Journal, 15,* 81–97.

Anderson, J., & Evans, F. (1974). Causal models in educational research: Recursive models. *American Educational Research Journal, 11,* 29–39.

Anderson, K. (1981). Post–high school experiences and college attrition. *Sociology of Education, 54,* 1–15.

Anderson, K. (1984). *Institutional differences in college effects.* Unpublished paper, Florida Atlantic University, Boca Raton.

Anderson, K. (1985a). *Black and white college entrants: College selection/recruitment and educational attainment.* Unpublished report, Florida Atlantic University, Boca Raton.

Anderson, K. (1985b). College characteristics and change in students' occupational values: Socialization in American colleges. *Work and Occupations, 12,* 307–328.

Anderson, K. (1986). *College contexts, student involvement, and educational attainment.* Paper presented at the meeting of the American Educational Research Association, San Francisco.

Anderson, R., & Darkenwald, G. (1979). *Participation and persistence in American adult education.* New York: College Entrance Examination Board.

Andreason, A. (1975). *The effects of social responsibility, moral judgment, and conformity on helping behavior.* Unpublished doctoral dissertation, Brigham Young University, Provo, UT.

Andrews, F., & Withey, S. (1976). *Social indicators of well-being: Americans' perceptions of life quality.* New York: Plenum Press.

Andrews, J. (1981). Teaching format and student style: Their interactive effects on learning. *Research in Higher Education, 14,* 161–178.

Angle, J., Steiber, S., & Wissmann, D. (1980). Educational indicators and occupational achievement. *Social Science Research, 9,* 60–75.

Angle, J., & Wissmann, D. (1981). Gender, college major, and earnings. *Sociology of Education, 54,* 25–33.

Angrist, S. (1970). Variations in women's adult aspirations during college. *Journal of Marriage and the Family, 34,* 465–468.

Angrist, S., & Almquist, E. (1975). *Careers and contingencies: How college women juggle with gender.* New York: Dunellen.

Anisef, P. (1982). University graduates revisited: Occupational mobility attainments and accessibility. *Interchange, 13,* 1–19.

Annis, L. (1983). The processes and effects of peer tutoring. *Human Learning, 2,* 39–47.

Apostal, R. (1970). Personality types and preferred college subculture. *Journal of College Student Personnel, 11,* 206–209.

Archer, S. (1982). The lower age boundaries of identity. *Child Development, 53,* 1551–1556.

Arlin, P. (1975). Cognitive development in adulthood: A fifth stage? *Developmental Psychology, 11,* 602–606.

Arnold, K. (1987). *Values and vocations: The career aspirations of academically gifted females in the first five years after high school.* Paper presented at the meeting of the American Educational Research Association, Washington, DC.

Aronson, S. (1971). A comparison of cognitive vs. focused-activities techniques in sensitivity group training. *Dissertation Abstracts International, 32,* 548-B. (University Microfilms No. 71–18, 394)

Arrow, K. (1972). *Higher education as a filter* (Tech. Rep. No. 71). Stanford, CA: Stanford University, Institute for Mathematical Studies in the Social Sciences.

Arsenian, S. (1970). Change in evaluative attitudes during twenty-five years. *Journal of Applied Psychology, 54,* 302–304.

Association of American Colleges. (1985). *Integrity in the college curriculum: A report to the academic community.* Washington, DC: Association for American Colleges.

Astin, A. (1961). A re-examination of college productivity. *Journal of Educational Psychology, 52,* 173–178.

Astin, A. (1962). Influences on the student's motivation to seek advanced training: Another look. *Journal of Educational Psychology, 53,* 303–309.

Astin, A. (1963a). Differential college effects on the motivation of talented students to obtain the Ph.D. degree. *Journal of Educational Psychology, 54,* 63–71.

Astin, A. (1963b). Further validation of the environmental assessment technique. *Journal of Educational Psychology, 54,* 217–226.

Astin, A. (1963c). Undergraduate institutions and the production of scientists. *Science, 141,* 334–338.

Astin, A. (1965a). Classroom environment in different fields of study. *Journal of Educational Psychology, 56,* 275–282.

Astin, A. (1965b). Effects of different college environments on the vocational choices of high aptitude students. *Journal of Counseling Psychology, 21,* 28–34.

Astin, A. (1965c). Who goes where to college? In A. Astin (Ed.), *Who goes where to college?* Chicago: Science Research Associates.

Astin, A. (1968a). Personal and environmental determinants of student activism. *Measurement and Evaluation in Guidance, 1,* 149–162.

Astin, A. (1986b). *The college environment.* Washington, DC: American Council on Education.

Astin, A. (1968c). Undergraduate achievement and institutional "excellence." *Science, 161,* 661–668.

Astin, A. (1969a). A preliminary evaluation of the undergraduate research participation program of the National Science Foundation. *Journal of Educational Research, 62,* 217–221.

Astin, A. (1969b). What goes into academic planning? New research has implications for academic planning and the quest for "excellence." *College & University Business, 47,* 31–33.

Astin, A. (1969c). Recent findings from the ACE Research Program: Implications for college choice and admissions. *College and University, 44,* 341–356.

Astin, A. (1969d). Comment on "A student's dilemma: Big fish–little pond or little fish–big pond." *Journal of Counseling Psychology, 16,* 20–22.

Astin, A. (1970a). Are the "best" colleges really better? *Think, 36,* 26–28.

Astin, A. (1970b). How colleges are rated. *Change, 2,* 85 ff.

Astin, A. (1970c). The methodology of research on college impact (I). *Sociology of Education, 43,* 223–254.

Astin, A. (1970d). The methodology of research on college impact (II). *Sociology of Education, 43,* 437–450.

Astin, A. (1971a). Open admission and programs for the disadvantaged. *Journal of Higher Education, 42,* 629–647.

Astin, A. (1971b). *Predicting academic performance in college.* New York: Free Press.

Astin, A. (1972a). *College dropouts: A national study.* Washington, DC: American Council on Education.

Astin, A. (1972b). The measured effects of higher education. *Annals of the American Academy of Political and Social Science, 404,* 1–20.

Astin, A. (1973a). Measurement and determinants of the outputs of higher education. In L. Solmon & P. Taubman (Eds.), *Does college matter? Some evidence on the impacts of higher education.* New York: Academic Press.

Astin, A. (1973b). The impact of dormitory living on students. *Educational Record, 54,* 204–210.

Astin, A. (1975a). Financial aid and student persistence (HERI Research Rep. No. 75-2). Los Angeles: Higher Education Research Institute.

Astin, A. (1975b). *Preventing students from dropping out.* San Francisco: Jossey-Bass.

Astin, A. (1975c). The myth of equal access. *Chronicle of Higher Education, 11,* 24.

Astin, A. (1977a). *Four critical years: Effects of college on beliefs, attitudes, and knowledge.* San Francisco: Jossey-Bass.

Astin, A. (1977b). The new realists. *Psychology Today, 11,* 50 ff.

Astin, A. (1979). Student-oriented management: A proposal for change. In *Evaluating educational quality.* Washington, DC: Council on Postsecondary Accreditation.

Astin, A. (1982). *Minorities in American higher education: Recent trends, current prospects, and recommendations.* San Francisco: Jossey-Bass.

Astin, A. (1984). Student involvement: A developmental theory for higher education. *Journal of College Student Personnel, 25,* 297–308.

Astin, A. (1985a). *Achieving educational excellence: A critical assessment of priorities and practices in higher education.* San Francisco: Jossey-Bass.

Astin, A. (1985b). The value added debate . . . continued. *American Association for Higher Education Bulletin, 38,* 11–12.

Astin, A. (1987, September/October). Competition or cooperation? *Change,* pp. 12–19.

Astin, A. (1990). *Assessment for excellence: The philosophy and practice of assessment and evaluation in higher education.* New York: Macmillan.

Astin, A., Green, K., & Korn, W. (1987). *The American freshman: Twenty-year trends, 1966–1985.* Los Angeles: University of California, Graduate School of Education, Higher Education Research Institute.

Astin, A., & Henson, J. (1977). New measures of college selectivity. *Research in Higher Education, 6,* 1–9.

Astin, A., & Holland, J. (1961). The Environmental Assessment Technique: A way to measure college environments. *Journal of Educational Psychology, 52,* 308–316.

Astin, A., & Lee, C. (1972). *The invisible colleges: A profile of small, private colleges with limited resources.* New York: McGraw-Hill.

Astin, A., & Panos, R. (1966). A national research data bank for higher education. *Educational Record, 47,* 5–17.

Astin, A., & Panos, R. (1969). *The educational and vocational development of college students.* Washington, DC: American Council on Education.

Astin, H. (1969). *The woman doctorate in America: Origins, career and family.* New York: Russell Sage Foundation.

Astin, H., & Kent, L. (1983). Gender roles in transition: Research and policy implications for higher education. *Journal of Higher Education, 54,* 309–324.

Astin, H., & Myint, T. (1971). Career development of young women during the post-high school years. *Journal of Counseling Psychology, 18,* 369–393.

Atkinson, D., Morten, G., & Sue, D. (1983). *Counseling American minorities: A cross-cultural perspective* (2nd ed.). Dubuque, IA: Wm. C. Brown.

Attiyeh, T., & Lumsden, K. (1972). Some modern myths in teaching economics: The U.K. experience. *American Economic Review, 62,* 429–433.

Aulston, M. (1974). Black transfer students in white colleges. *NASPA Journal, 12,* 116–123.

Auster, R., Leveson, I., & Sarachek, D. (1969). The production of health: An exploratory study. *Journal of Human Resources, 4,* 411–436.

Averill, L. (1983). *Learning to be human: A vision for the liberal arts.* Port Washington, NY: Associated Faculty Press.

Ayers, J., & Turck, M. (1976). Longitudinal study of change in teacher dogmatism. *College Student Journal, 10,* 84–87.

Ayres, Q. (1982). Racial desegregation, higher education, and student achievement. *Journal of Politics, 44,* 337–364.

Ayres, Q. (1983). Student achievement at predominantly white and predominantly black universities. *American Educational Research Journal, 20,* 291–304.

Ayres, Q., & Bennett, R. (1983). University characteristics and student achievement. *Journal of Higher Education, 54,* 516–532.

Babcock, R., & Kaufman, M. (1976). Effectiveness of a career course. *Vocational Guidance Quarterly, 24,* 261–266.

Bachman, J. (1972). *Young men in high school and beyond: A summary of findings from the youth in transition project.* (Contract No. OE-5-85-054). Washington, DC: Office of Education, Bureau of Research. (ERIC Document Reproduction Service No. ED 063 568)

Bachman, J., & O'Malley, P. (1977). Self-esteem in young men: A longitudinal analysis of the impact of educational and occupational attainment. *Journal of Personality and Social Psychology, 35,* 365–380.

Bachman, J., & O'Malley, P. (1986). Self-concepts, self-esteem, and educational experiences: The frog pond revisited (again). *Journal of Personality and Social Psychology, 50,* 35–46.

Bachman, J., O'Malley, P., & Johnston, J. (1978). *Youth in transition: Vol. 4. Adolescence to adulthood—Change and stability in the lives of young men.* Ann Arbor: University of Michigan, Institute for Social Research.

Bailey, D., & Schotta, C. (1972). Private and social rates of return to education of academicians. *American Economic Review, 62,* 19–31.

Bailey, J. (1979). The effects of instructional paradigm on the development of critical thinking of college students in an introductory botany course. *Dissertation Abstracts International, 40,* 3138A.

Bailey, K., & Minor, S. (1976). Self-image and congruence in freshmen, seniors, and graduate students. *Journal of Genetic Psychology, 129,* 301–309.

Baird, L. (1969a). Big school, small school: A critical examination of the hypothesis. *Journal of Educational Psychology, 60,* 253–260.

Baird, L. (1969b). The effects of college residence groups on students' self-concepts, goals, and achievements. *Personnel and Guidance Journal, 47,* 1015–1021.

Baird, L. (1974). The practical utility of measures of college environments. *Review of Educational Research, 44,* 307–329.

Baird, L. (1976a). *Using self-reports to predict student performance.* New York: College Entrance Examination Board.

Baird, L. (1976b). Who goes to graduate school and how they get there. In J. Katz & R. Hartnett (Eds.), *Scholars in the making: The development of graduate and professional students.* Cambridge, MA: Ballinger.

Baird, L. (1976c). Structuring the environment to improve outcomes. In O. Lenning (Ed.), *Improving educational outcomes* (New Directions for Higher Education No. 16). San Francisco: Jossey-Bass.

Baird, L. (1985). Do grades and tests predict adult accomplishment? *Research in Higher Education, 23,* 3–85.

Baird, L. (1987). *The undergraduate experience: Commonalities and differences among colleges.* Paper presented at the meeting of the Association for the Study of Higher Education, San Diego.

Baird, L. (1988). The college environment revisited: A review of research and theory. In J. Smart (Ed.), *Higher education: Handbook of theory and research* (Vol. 4). New York: Agathon.

Baird, L., Clark, M., & Hartnett, R. (1973). *The graduates: A report on the characteristics and plans of college seniors.* Princeton, NJ: Educational Testing Service.

Baird, L., Hartnett, R., & Associates (1980). *Understanding student and faculty life: Using campus surveys to improve academic decision making.* San Francisco: Jossey-Bass.

Baker, M. (1978). Desk-top kits in the teaching of introductory chemistry in the community college: An approach based on the Piagetian model. *Dissertation Abstracts International, 38,* 4709A.

Baker, T. (1976a). The dimensions of nonauthoritarianism. *Journal of Personality Assessment, 40,* 626–634.

Baker, T. (1976b). The weakening of authoritarianism in black and white college students. *Sociology and Social Research, 60,* 440–460.

Baktari, P., & Grasso, J. (1985). An empirical study of new high school and college graduates' wages using alternative labor market models. *Review of Higher Education, 8,* 193–210.

Baldwin, J. (1980). An Africentric model of black personality. In *Proceedings of the Fourteenth Annual Convention of the Association of Black Psychologists.* Washington, DC: Association of Black Psychologists.

Baldwin, J. (1981). Notes on an Africentric theory of black personality. *Western Journal of Black Studies, 5,* 172–179.

Baldwin, J. (1984). African self-consciousness and the mental health of African-Americans. *Journal of Black Studies, 15,* 177–194.

Baldwin, J., Duncan, J., & Bell, Y. (1987). Assessment of African self-consciousness among black students from two college environments. *Journal of Black Psychology, 13,* 27–41.

Ballou, R. (1985). Freshmen in college residence halls: A study of freshman academic performance at five liberal arts colleges. *Journal of College and University Student Housing, 15,* 27–30.

Banks, J. (1981). The stages of ethnicity: Implications for curriculum reform. In J. Banks (Ed.), *Multi-ethnic education: Theory and practice.* Boston: Allyn & Bacon.

Banta, T., Lambert, E., Pike, G., Schmidhammer, J., & Schneider, J. (1987). Estimated student score gain on the ACT COMP Exam: Valid tool for institutional assessment? *Research in Higher Education, 27,* 195–217.

Banzinger, G. (1986). *Evaluating the freshman seminar course and developing a model of intervention with freshmen.* Unpublished manuscript, Marietta College, Marietta, OH.

Baratz, J., & Ficklen, M. (1983). *Participation of recent black college graduates in the labor market and in graduate education* (Research Rep., Education Policy Research Institute). Princeton, NJ: Educational Testing Service.

Barfield, R., & Morgan, J. (1969). *Early retirement.* Ann Arbor: University of Michigan Press.

Bargh, J., & Schul, Y. (1980). On the cognitive benefits of teaching. *Journal of Educational Psychology, 72,* 593–604.

Barker, R. (1968). *Ecological psychology: Concepts for studying the environment of human behavior.* Stanford, CA: Stanford University Press.

Barker, R., & Associates (1978). *Habitats, environments, and human behavior: Studies in ecological psychology and eco-behavioral science.* San Francisco: Jossey Bass.

Barker, R., & Gump, P. (1964). *Big school small school.* Stanford, CA: Stanford University Press.

Barker, S. (1981). An evaluation of the effectiveness of a college career guidance course. *Journal of College Student Personnel, 22,* 354–358.

Barlow, R., Brazer, H., & Morgan, J. (1966). *Economic behavior of the affluent.* Washington, DC: Brookings Institution.

Barnes, C. (1980). *Questioning: The untapped resource.* Paper presented at the meeting of the American Educational Research Association, Boston.

Barnes, C. (1983). Questioning in college classrooms. In C. Ellner & C. Barnes (Eds.), *Studies of college teaching: Experimental results, theoretical interpretations, and new perspectives.* Lexington, MA: D. C. Heath.

Barnes, M. (1943). Gains on the ACE during freshman-sophomore years. *School and Society, 57,* 250–252.

Barnett, R. (1982). *Change in moral judgment and college experience.* Unpublished master's thesis, University of Minnesota, Minneapolis and St. Paul.

Barnett, R., and Volker, J. (1985). *Moral judgment and life experiences.* Unpublished manuscript, University of Minnesota, Minneapolis and St Paul.

Barnhart, R., & Groth, L. (1987). The assessment of college student growth resulting from an international course and study experience. *College Student Journal, 21,* 78–85.

Barrall, M., & Hill, D. (1977). A survey of college students' exposure to and preference for eight instructional options. *Research in Higher Education, 7,* 315–327.

Barrows, T., Ager, S., Bennett, M., Braun, H., Clark, J., Harris, L., & Klein, S. (1981). *College students' knowledge and beliefs: A survey of global understanding.* Princeton, NJ: Educational Testing Service.

Barrows, T., Clark, J., & Klein, S. (1980). What students know about their world. *Change, 12,* 10 ff.

Barrows, T., Klein, S., Clark, J., & Hartshorne, N. (1981). *What college students know and believe about their world.* New Rochelle, NY: Change Magazine Press.

Barton, K., Cattell, R., & Vaughan, G. (1973). Changes in personality as a function of college attendance or work experience. *Journal of Counseling Psychology, 20,* 162–165.

Bartsch, K., & Hackett, G. (1979). Effect of a decision-making course on locus of control, conceptualization, and career planning. *Journal of College Student Personnel, 20,* 230–235.

Basmajian, R. (1978). The relationship between Piagetian cognitive maturity and scholastic success of students enrolled in an audio-tutorial biology program. *Dissertation Abstracts International, 39,* 210A.

Basow, S., & Howe, K. (1980). Role-model influence: Effects of sex and sex-role attitude in college students. *Psychology of Women Quarterly, 4,* 558–572.

Basseches, M. (1980). Dialectical schemata: A framework for the empirical study of the development of dialectical thinking. *Human Development, 23,* 400–421.

Basseches, M. (1984). *Dialectic thinking and adult development.* Norwood, NJ: Ablex.

Bassis, M. (1977). The campus as a frog pond: A theoretical and empirical reassessment. *American Journal of Sociology, 82,* 1318–1326.

Bauer, G. (1976). Performance and satisfaction as a function of person/environment fit. *Dissertation Abstracts International, 36,* 5223B–5224B.

Baumgart, N., & Johnstone, J. (1977). Attrition at an Australian university. *Journal of Higher Education, 48,* 553–570.

Baumgartel, H., & Goldstein, J. (1967). Need and value shifts in college training groups. *Journal of Applied Behavioral Science, 3,* 87–101.

Baumol, W., & Bowen, W. (1966). *Performing arts: The economic dilemma.* New York: Twentieth Century Fund.

Baumrind, D. (1986). Sex differences in moral reasoning: Response to Walker's (1984) conclusion that there are none. *Child Development, 5,* 511–521.

Baxter Magolda, M. (1987a). Comparing open-ended interviews and standardized measures of intellectual development. *Journal of College Student Personnel, 28,* 443–448.

Baxter Magolda, M. (1987b). The affective dimension of learning: Faculty-student relationships that enhance intellectual development. *College Student Journal, 21,* 46–58.

Baxter Magolda, M. (1988). *The impact of the freshman year on epistemological development: Gender differences.* Paper presented at the meeting of the American Educational Research Association, New Orleans.

Baxter Magolda, M., & Porterfield, W. (1985). A new approach to assess intellectual development on the Perry scheme. *Journal of College Student Personnel, 26,* 343–351.

Bayer, A., Drew, D., Astin, A., Boruch, R., & Creager, J. (1970, February). *The first year of college: A follow-up normative report* (ACE Research Rep. No. 5). Washington, DC: American Council on Education.

Bayer, A., & Dutton, J. (1975). Trends and attitudes on political, social, and collegiate issues among college students: Mid-1960s to mid-1970s. *Journal of Higher Education, 47,* 159–171.

Bayer, A., Royer, J., & Webb, R. (1973). *Four years after college entry* (ACE Research Rep. No. 8). Washington, DC: American Council on Education.

Beach, L. (1968). *Student interaction and learning in small self-directed groups* (Final report). Washington, DC: Department of Health, Education, and Welfare.

Beal, P., & Williams, D. (1968). *An experiment with mixed-class housing assignments at the University of Oregon.* Eugene, OR: Student Housing Research, ACUHO Research and Information Committee.

Bean, J. (1980). Dropouts and turnover: The synthesis and test of a causal model of student attrition. *Research in Higher Education, 12,* 155–187.

Bean, J. (1985). Interaction effects based on class level in an explanatory model of college student dropout syndrome. *American Educational Research Journal, 22,* 35–64.

Bean, J., & Bradley; R. (1986). Untangling the satisfaction-performance relationship for college students. *Journal of Higher Education, 57,* 293–412.

Bean, J., & Hull, D. (1984). *The determinants of black and white student attrition at a major southern state university.* Paper presented at the meeting of the American Educational Research Association, New Orleans.

Bean, J., & Kuh, G. (1984). *The reciprocity between student-faculty informal contact and the undergraduate grade-point average of university students.* Paper presented at the meeting of the Association for the Study of Higher Education, Chicago.

Bean, J., & Metzner, B. (1985). A conceptual model of nontraditional undergraduate student attrition. *Review of Educational Research, 55,* 485–540.

Bean, J., & Plascak, F. (1987). *Traditional and nontraditional undergraduate student attrition at an urban liberal arts college.* Paper presented at the meeting of the American Educational Research Association, Washington, DC.

Beaton, A. (1975). The influence of education and ability on salary and attitudes. In F. Juster (Ed.), *Education, income, and human behavior.* New York: McGraw-Hill.

Beck, R. (1981). *Career patterns: The liberal arts major in Bell System management.* Washington, DC: Association of American Colleges.

Becker, G. (1960). Underinvestment in college education. *American Economic Review, 50,* 346–354.

Becker, G. (1964). *Human capital: A theoretical and empirical analysis with special reference to education.* New York: Columbia University Press.

Becker, G. (1975). *Human capital: A theoretical and empirical analysis with special reference to education* (2nd ed.). New York: National Bureau of Economic Research.

Becker, G., Landes, E., & Michael, R. (1977). An economic analysis of marital instability. *Journal of Political Economy, 85,* 1141–1188.

Becker, H. (1964). What do they really learn at college? *Transaction, 1,* 14–17.

Becker, H., Greer, B., & Hughes, E. (1968). *Making the grade: The academic side of college life.* New York: John Wiley & Sons.

Beckham, B. (1987). Strangers in a strange land: The experience of blacks on white campuses. *Educational Record, 68,* 74–78.

Beckman, V. (1956). An investigation of the contributions to critical thinking made by courses in argumentation and discussion in selected colleges. *Dissertation Abstracts International, 16,* 2551A.

Beeken, L. (1982). *The general education component of the curriculum through transcript analysis at three Virginia community colleges.* Unpublished doctoral dissertation, Virginia Polytechnic Institute and State University, Blacksburg.

Behrman, J., Dark, V., & Paul, S. (1984). The effects of a structured learning skills intervention on long-term academic performance. *Journal of College Student Personnel, 25,* 326–331.

Behuniak, P., & Gable, P. (1981). A longitudinal study of self-concept and locus of control for persisters in six college majors. *Educational Research Quarterly, 6,* 3–12.

Belanger, C., & Lavallee, L. (1980). Economic returns to schooling decisions. *Research in Higher Education, 12,* 23–35.

Belenky, M., Clinchy, B., Goldberger, N., & Tarule, J. (1986). *Women's ways of knowing.* New York: Basic Books.

Benezet, L. (1976). *College organization and student impact.* Washington, DC: Association of American Colleges.

Bennett, C. (1983). *A study of interracial contact experience and attrition among black undergraduates at a predominantly white university.* Paper presented at the meeting of the American Educational Research Association, Montreal.

Bennett, C., & Okinaka, A. (1984). *Explanation of black student attrition in predominantly black universities.* Paper presented at the meeting of the American Educational Research Association, New Orleans.

Bennett, M. (1975–1976). A study of the relationship between curricula taken and the critical thinking abilities of high school seniors and University of Illinois freshmen, sophomores, and seniors majoring in elementary education. *Dissertation Abstracts International, 36,* 5799A.

Bennett, S., & Hunter, J. (1985). A measure of success: The WILL program four years later. *Journal of the National Association of Women Deans, Administrators, and Counselors, 48,* 3–11.

Bennett, W. (1984). *To reclaim a legacy.* Washington, DC: National Endowment for the Humanities.

Benson, P., & Vincent, S. (1980). Development and validation of the Sexist Attitudes Toward Women Scale (SATWS). *Psychology of Women Quarterly, 5,* 276–291.

Benton, S. (1982). *Rating college teaching: Criterion validity studies of student evaluation-of-instruction instruments* (AAHE-ERIC Higher Education Research Rep. No. 1). Washington, DC: American Association for Higher Education.

Benware, C., & Deci, E. (1984). Quality of learning with an active versus passive motivational set. *American Educational Research Journal, 21,* 755–765.

Berdie, R. (1967). A university is a many faceted thing. *Personnel and Guidance Journal, 45,* 768–775.

Berdie, R. (1971). Self-claimed and tested knowledge. *Educational and Psychological Measurement, 31,* 629–636.

Berdie, R. (1974). College courses and changes in dogmatism. *Research in Higher Education, 2,* 133–143.

Berelson, B., & Steiner, G. (1964). *Human behavior: An inventory of scientific findings.* New York: Harcourt Brace Jovanovich.

Berg, H., & Ferber, M. (1983). Men and women graduate students: Who succeeds and why? *Journal of Higher Education, 54,* 629–648.

Berg, I. (1970). *Education and jobs: The great training robbery.* New York: Praeger.

Bergen, G., Upham, J., & Bergen, M. (1970). Do scholarships affect academic achievement? *Journal of College Student Personnel, 11,* 383–384.

Bergen, M., & Zielke, D. (1979). Educational progress of basic education opportunity grant recipients compared to non-recipients. *Journal of Student Financial Aid, 9,* 19–22.

Bergquist, W., Gould, R., & Greenberg, E. (1981). *Designing undergraduate education: A systematic guide.* San Francisco: Jossey-Bass.

Berliner, D., & Cahen, L. (1973). Trait-treatment interaction and learning. In F. Kerlinger (Ed.), *Review of research in education* (Vol. 1). Itasca, IL: F. E. Peacock.

Berliner, H. (1971). Real economic benefits of higher education. *Personnel Journal, 50,* 124–131.

Bernstein, A. (1986). The devaluation of transfer: Current explanations and possible causes. In L. Zwerling (Ed.), *The community college and its critics* (New Directions for Community Colleges No. 54). San Francisco: Jossey-Bass.

Berry, M., Appel, V., & Hoffman, R. (1971). *Significant collegiate sources of influence* (Research Monograph No. 2). Austin: University of Texas, Division of Student Affairs, Research and Development Programs.

Berson, R. (1979). *Ethics and education in the freshman year: Impact and implications of an experimental, value-oriented curriculum.* Unpublished doctoral dissertation, Columbia University, New York.

Bertin, B., Ferrant, E., Whiteley, J., & Yokata, N. (1985). Influences on character development during the college years: The retrospective view of recent graduates. In J. Dalton (Ed.), *Promoting values education in student development.* Washington, DC: National Association of Student Personnel Administrators.

Best, F. (1976). *The effect of work and free-time scheduling upon worker time-income trade-off preferences.* Washington, DC: Quality of Life Research Associates.

Bielby, D. (1978). Career sex-atypicality and career involvement of college women: Baseline evidence from the 1960s. *Sociology of Education, 51,* 7–28.

Bielby, W., Hauser, R., & Featherman, D. (1977). Response errors of black and nonblack males in models of the intergenerational transmission of economic status. *American Journal of Sociology, 82,* 1242–1288.

Bietter, J. (1970–1971). A study to determine the effect of selected variables on the critical thinking ability of social studies methodology students at the University of Idaho. *Dissertation Abstracts International, 31,* 3383A.

Bigelow, G., & Kennedy, W. (1974). Attitudes of Kent State students before and after the events of May 4, 1970. *Journal of College Student Personnel, 15,* 17–21.

Biggs, D., & Barnett, R. (1981). Moral judgment development of college students. *Research in Higher Education, 14,* 91–102.

Biggs, D., Schomberg, S., & Brown, J. (1977). Moral judgment development of freshmen and their precollege experiences. *Research in Higher Education, 7,* 329–339.

Billigmeier, R., & Forman, D. (1975). Göttingen in retrospect: A longitudinal assessment of the University of California's education abroad program in Göttingen by 1956–66 participants. *International Review of Education, 21,* 217–230.

Bills, D. (1988). Educational credentials and promotions: Does schooling do more than get you in the door? *Sociology of Education, 61,* 52–60.

Bird, C. (1975). *The case against college.* New York: David McKay.

Birnbaum, R. (1983). *Maintaining diversity in higher education.* San Francisco: Jossey-Bass.

Bisconti, A. (1978). *Who will succeed? College graduates as business executives* (Special Topic Series No. 3). Bethlehem, PA: CPC Foundation.

Bisconti, A. (1987). *Effective job performance: How does college education contribute?* Paper presented at the meeting of the American Educational Research Association, Washington, DC.

Bisconti, A., & Kessler, J. (1980). *College and other stepping stones: A study of learning experiences that contribute to effective performance in early and long-run jobs.* Bethlehem, PA: CPC Foundation.

Bisconti, A., & Solmon, L. (1976). *College education on the job—The graduates' viewpoint.* Bethlehem, PA: CPC Foundation.

Bisconti, A., & Solmon, L. (1977). *Job satisfaction after college . . . The graduates' viewpoint.* Bethlehem, PA: CPC Foundation.

Blackburn, R., Armstrong, E., Conrad, C., Didham, J., & McKune, T. (1976). *Changing practices in undergraduate education.* Berkeley, CA: Carnegie Council for Policy Studies in Higher Education.

Blackwell, J. (1981). *Mainstreaming outsiders: The production of black professionals.* Bayside, NY: General Hall.

Blai, B. (1971). *Roommate-impact upon academic performance.* Bryn Mawr, PA: Harcum Junior College.

Blake, A., & Nordland, F. (1978). Science instruction and cognitive growth in college students. *Journal of Research in Science Teaching, 15,* 413–419.

Blake, L. (1976). *A measure of developmental change: A cross-sectional study.* Paper presented at the annual meeting of the American Psychological Association, Washington, DC.

Blalock, H. (1964). *Causal inferences in nonexperimental research.* Chapel Hill: University of North Carolina Press.

Blalock, H. (1967). Path coefficients versus regression coefficients. *American Journal of Sociology, 72,* 675–676.

Blalock, H. (1968). Theory building versus regression coefficients. In H. Blalock & A. Blalock (Eds.), *Methodology in social research.* New York: McGraw-Hill.

Blanc, R., DeBuhr, L., & Martin, D. (1983). Breaking the attrition cycle: The effects of supplemental instruction on undergraduate performance and attrition. *Journal of Higher Education, 54,* 80–90.

Blanchfield, W. (1971). College dropout identification: A case study. *Journal of Experimental Education, 40,* 1–4.

Blanchfield, W. (1972). College dropout identification: An economic analysis. *Journal of Human Resources, 7,* 540–544.

Blann, F. (1985). Intercollegiate athletic competition and students' educational and career plans. *Journal of College Student Personnel, 26,* 115–118.

Blasi, A. (1980). Bridging moral cognition and moral action: A critical review of the literature. *Psychological Bulletin, 88,* 1–45.

Blasi, A. (1983). Moral cognition and moral action: A theoretical perspective. *Developmental Review, 3,* 178–210.

Blaska, B. (1978). College women's career and marriage aspirations: A review of the literature. *Journal of College Student Personnel, 19,* 302–305.

Blatt, M., & Kohlberg, L. (1975). The effects of a classroom moral discussion upon children's level of moral judgment. *Journal of Moral Education, 4,* 129–161.

Blau, P., & Duncan, O. (1967). *The American occupational structure.* New York: Free Press.

Blaug, M. (1970). *An introduction to the economics of education.* London: Allen Lane, Penguin Press.

Blaug, M. (1972). The correlation between education and earnings: What does it signify? *Higher Education, 1,* 53–76.

Blimling, G. (1989). A meta-analysis of the influence of college residence halls on academic performance. *Journal of College Student Development, 30,* 298–308.

Blimling, G., & Hample, D. (1979). Structuring the peer environment in residence halls to increase academic performance in average-ability students. *Journal of College Student Personnel, 20,* 310–316.

Blimling, G., & Paulsen, F. (1979). The Educational Development Group Enrichment (EDGE) program: A comprehensive model for student development in residence halls. *Journal of the National Association of Women Deans, Administrators, and Counselors, 42,* 24–33.

Blocher, D. (1978). Campus learning environments and the ecology of student development. In J. Banning (Ed.), *Campus ecology.* Cincinnati, OH: National Association of Student Personnel Administrators.

Block, J., & Burns, R. (1976). Mastery learning. In L. Shulman (Ed.), *Review of research in education* (Vol. 4). Itasca, IL: F. E. Peacock.

Blood, R., & Wolfe, D. (1960). *Husbands and wives: The dynamics of married living.* New York: Free Press.

Bloom, A. (1987). *The closing of the American mind.* New York: Simon & Schuster.

Bloom, B. (1956). *Taxonomy of educational objectives: The classification of educational goals: Handbook I. Cognitive domain.* London: Longmans, Green.

Bloom, B. (1964). *Stability and change in human characteristics.* New York: John Wiley & Sons.

Bloom, B. (1968). Mastery learning. In *Evaluation comment* (Vol. 1, No. 2). Los Angeles: University of California, Center for the Study of Evaluation of Instructional Programs.

Bloom, B., Englehart, M., Furst, E., Hill, W., & Krathwohl, D. (1956). *Taxonomy of educational objectives: Handbook I. Cognitive domain.* New York: David McKay.

Blumberg, P., & Murtha, J. (1977). College graduates and the American dream. *Dissent, 24,* 45–53.

Blume, F. (1981). The role of personal growth groups at Johnson College. *Journal of Humanistic Psychology, 21,* 47–61.

Blunt, M., & Blizard, P. (1975). Recall and retrieval of anatomical knowledge. *British Journal of Medical Education, 9,* 255–263.

Boaz, R. (1978). *Participation in adult education, final report 1975.* Washington, DC: National Center for Education Statistics.

Bohrnstedt, G. (1967). *Social mobility aspirations and fraternity membership.* Paper presented at the meeting of the American Sociological Association, San Francisco.

Bok, D. (1978). The president's report. *Official Register of Harvard University, 75.*

Booth, R., McNally, M., & Berry, N. (1978). Predicting performance effectiveness in paramedical occupations. *Personnel Psychology, 31,* 581–593.

Borg, W., & Gall, M. (1983). *Educational research: An introduction* (4th ed.). New York: Longman.

Borgers, S. (1979). Effect of counselor involvement on dogmatism scores of teacher education students. *Humanist Educator, 17,* 160–166.

Born, D., Gledhill, S., & Davis, M. (1972). Examination performance in lecture-discussion and personalized instruction courses. *Journal of Applied Behavior Analysis, 5,* 33–43.

Bose, C. (1973). *Jobs and gender: Sex and occupational prestige.* Baltimore: Johns Hopkins University, Center for Metropolitan Planning and Research.

Boudon, R. (1973). *Education, opportunity and social inequality: Changing prospects in western societies.* New York: John Wiley & Sons.

Bourne, E. (1978a). The state of research on ego identity: A review and appraisal. Part 1. *Journal of Youth and Adolescence, 7,* 223–251.

Bourne, E. (1978b). The state of research on ego identity: A review and appraisal. Part 2. *Journal of Youth and Adolescence, 7,* 371–392.

Bowen, H. (1977). *Investment in learning: The individual and social value of American higher education.* San Francisco: Jossey-Bass.

Bowen, H. (1980). *The costs of higher education: How much do colleges and universities spend per student and how much should they spend?* San Francisco: Jossey-Bass.

Bowen, H. (1981). Cost differences: The amazing disparity among institutions of higher education in educational costs per student. *Change, 13,* 21–27.

Bowles, F., & DeCosta, F. (1971). *Between two worlds: A profile of Negro higher education.* New York: McGraw-Hill.

Bowles, S. (1972). Schooling and inequality from generation to generation. *Journal of Political Economy, 80,* S219–S251.

Bowles, S. (1973). Understanding unequal economic opportunity. *American Economic Review, 63,* 346–356.

Bowles, S., & Gintis, H. (1976). *Schooling in capitalist America.* New York: Basic Books.

Bowles, S., & Levin, H. (1968). The determinants of scholastic achievement—An appraisal of some recent evidence. *Journal of Human Resources, 3,* 3–24.

Boyd, D. (1980). The condition of sophomoritis and its educational cure. *Journal of Moral Education, 10,* 24–39.

Boyer, E. (1987). *College: The undergraduate experience in America.* New York: Harper & Row.

Brabeck, M. (1983a). Critical thinking skills and reflective judgment development: Redefining the aims of higher education. *Journal of Applied Developmental Psychology, 4,* 23–34.

Brabeck, M. (1983b). Moral judgment: Theory and research on differences between males and females. *Developmental Review, 3,* 274–291.

Brabeck, M. (1984a). Ethical characteristics of whistle blowers. *Journal of Research in Personality, 18,* 41–53.

Brabeck, M. (1984b). Longitudinal studies of intellectual development during adulthood: Theoretical and research models. *Journal of Research and Development in Education, 17,* 12–27.

Brabeck, M., & Wood, P. (1983). *A longitudinal study of reflective judgment development, critical thinking skills and related life experiences.* Unpublished manuscript.

Brabeck, M., & Wood, P. (1990). Cross-sectional and longitudinal evidence for differences between well-structured and ill-structured problem-solving abilities. In M. Commons, D. Sinnott, F. Richards, & C. Armon (Eds.), *Beyond formal operations: Vol. 2. Comparisons and applications of adolescent and adult developmental models.* New York: Praeger.

Braddock, J. (1980). The perpetuation of segregation across levels of education: A behavioral assessment of the contact-hypothesis. *Sociology of Education, 53,* 178–186.

Braddock, J. (1981a). Desegregation and black student attrition. *Urban Education, 15,* 403–418.

Braddock, J. (1981b). The major field choices and occupational career orientations of black and white students. In G. Thomas (Ed.), *Black students in higher education.* Westport, CT: Greenwood Press.

Bradshaw, T. (1975). The impact of peers on student orientations to college: A contextual analysis. In M. Trow (Ed.), *Teachers and students: Aspects of American higher education.* New York: McGraw-Hill.

Bragg, A. (1976). *The socialization process in higher education* (AAHE-ERIC Higher Education Research Rep. No. 7). Washington, DC: American Association for Higher Education.

Branch-Simpson, G. (1985). A study of the patterns in the development of black students at the Ohio State University. *Dissertation Abstracts International, 45,* 2422A.

Bransford, C. (1973). *Moral development in college students.* Unpublished manuscript, St. Olaf College, Northfield, MN.

Braungart, R. (1975). Youth and social movements. In S. Dragastin & G. Elder, Jr. (Eds.), *Adolescence in the life cycle: Psychological change and social context.* Washington, DC: Hemisphere.

Braungart, R., & Braungart, M. (1972). *Social and political correlates of protest attitudes and behavior among college youth: A case study.* Paper presented at the meeting of the Southern Sociological Society, New Orleans.

Brawer, F. (1973). *New perspectives on personality development in college students.* San Francisco: Jossey-Bass.

Braxton, J., and Brier, E. (1989). Melding organizational and interactional theories of student attrition: A path analytic study. *Review of Higher Education, 13,* 47–61.

Braxton, J., Brier, E., Herzog, L., & Pascarella, E. (1988). *Occupational attainment in the professions: The effects of college origins and college experiences on becoming a lawyer.* Paper presented at the meeting of the Association for the Study of Higher Education, St. Louis.

Braxton, J., Duster, M., & Pascarella, E. (1988). Causal modeling and path analysis: An introduction and illustration in student attrition research. *Journal of College Student Development, 29,* 263–272.

Braxton, J., & Nordvall, R. (1985). Selective liberal arts colleges: Higher quality as well as higher prestige? *Journal of Higher Education, 56,* 538–554.

Brazer, H., & David, M. (1962). Social and economic determinants of the demand for education. In S. Mushkin (Ed.), *Economics of higher education.* Washington, DC: U.S. Office of Education.

Brazziel, W. (1983). Baccalaureate college of origin of black doctorate recipients. *Journal of Negro Education, 32,* 102–109.

Bredemeier, B., & Shields, D. (1984). The utility of moral stage analysis in the investigation of athletic aggression. *Sociology of Sport Journal, 1,* 138–149.

Bredemeier, M., Bernstein, G., & Oxman, W. (1982). Ba fa ba fa dogmatism/ethnocentrism: A study of attitude change through simulation-gaming. *Simulation and Games, 13,* 413–436.

Breneman, D., & Nelson, S. (1981). *Financing community colleges.* Washington, DC: Brookings Institution.

Bressler, M., & Wendell, P. (1980). The sex composition of selective colleges and gender differences in career aspirations. *Journal of Higher Education, 51,* 650–663.

Brethower, D. (1977). Research in learning behavior: Some implications for college teaching. In S. Scholl & S. Inglis (Eds.), *Teaching in higher education.* Columbus: Ohio Board of Regents.

Brigman, S., Kuh, G., & Stager, S. (1982). Those who choose to leave: Why students voluntarily withdraw from college. *Journal of the National Association of Women Deans, Administrators, and Counselors, 45,* 3–8.

Brim, O., Glass, D., Neulinger, J., & Firestone, I. (1969). *American beliefs and attitudes about intelligence.* New York: Russell Sage Foundation.

Brim, O., & Wheeler, S. (1966). *Socialization after childhood: Two essays.* New York: John Wiley & Sons.

Brint, S., & Karabel, J. (1989). *The diverted dream: Community colleges and the promise of educational opportunity in America, 1900–1985.* New York: Oxford University Press.

Broadhurst, B. (1980). *Report: The Defining Issues Test.* Unpublished manuscript, Colorado State University, Fort Collins.

Bron, G., & Gordon, M. (1986). Impact of an orientation center on grade point average and attrition. *College Student Journal, 20,* 242–246.

Brooks, J. (1981). Academic performance and retention rates of participants in the college work study program and recipients of national direct student loans. *Dissertation Abstracts International, 41,* 3440A.

Brown, M. (1979). *Independent and interactive effects of significant institutional variables on the career aspirations of college women.* Paper presented at the meeting of the American Educational Research Association, San Francisco.

Brown, M. (1982). Career plans of college women: Patterns and influences.

In P. Perun (Ed.), *The undergraduate woman: Issues in educational equity.* Lexington, MA: Lexington Books.

Brown, R. (1968). Manipulation of the environmental press in a college residence hall. *Personnel and Guidance Journal, 46,* 555–560.

Brown, R., & Barr, M. (1990). Student development: Yesterday, today and tomorrow. In L. Moore (Ed.), *Evolving theoretical perspectives about students* (New Directions for Student Services No. 51). San Francisco: Jossey-Bass.

Brown, R., & DeCoster, D. (1982). *Mentoring-transcript systems for promoting student growth.* San Francisco: Jossey-Bass.

Brown, R., Winkworth, J., & Braskamp, L. (1973). Student development in a coed residence hall: Promiscuity, prophylactic, or panacea? *Journal of College Student Personnel, 14,* 98–104.

Bruch, M., & Krieshok, T. (1981). Investigative vs. realistic Holland types and adjustment in theoretical engineering majors. *Journal of Vocational Behavior, 18,* 162–173.

Brush, L., Gold, A., & White, M. (1978). The paradox of intention and effect: A women's studies course. *Signs: Journal of Women in Culture and Society, 3,* 870–883.

Bryant, F., & Marquez, J. (1986). Educational status and the structure of subjective well-being in men and women. *Social Psychology Quarterly, 49,* 142–153.

Bryk, A., & Raudenbush, S. (1987). Applications of hierarchical linear models to assessing change. *Psychological Bulletin, 101,* 147–158.

Bryk, A., & Thum, A. (1989). The effects of high school organization on dropping out: An exploratory investigation. *American Educational Research Journal, 26,* 353–383.

Bucklin, R., & Bucklin, W. (1970). *The psychological characteristics of the college persister and leaver: A review.* Washington, DC: U.S. Department of Health, Education, and Welfare. (ERIC Document Reproduction Service No. ED 049 709)

Buenz, R., & Merrill, I. (1968). Effects of effort on retention and enjoyment. *Journal of Educational Psychology, 59,* 154–158.

Buffington, S. (1984). Homogeneous grouping and roommate matching: A review of the literature. *Journal of the Indiana University Personnel Association,* 25–32.

Burbach, H., & Thompson, M. (1971). Alienation among college freshmen: A comparison of Puerto Rican, black, and white students. *Journal of College Student Personnel, 12,* 248–252.

Burlew, A. (1982). The experiences of black females in traditional and non-traditional professions. *Psychology of Women Quarterly, 6,* 312–326.

Burns, R. (1974). The testing of a model of critical thinking ontogeny among Central State College undergraduates. *Dissertation Abstracts International, 54,* 5467A.

Burrell, L. (1979). *Perception of administrators and minority students of minority student experience on predominantly white campuses*. Barre, VT: Northgut Studio Press.

Burris, V. (1983). The social and political consequences of overeducation. *American Sociological Review, 48,* 454–467.

Burstein, L. (1980a). The analysis of multilevel data in educational research and evaluation. In D. Berliner (Ed.), *Review of research in education* (Vol. 8). Washington, DC: American Educational Research Association.

Burstein, L. (1980b). The role of levels of analysis in the specification of educational effects. In R. Dreeben & J. Thomas (Eds.), *The analysis of educational productivity: Vol. I. Issues in microanalysis.* Cambridge, MA: Ballinger.

Burton, R., & Polmantier, P. (1973). Intellectual attitude development of students in a teacher education program. *Journal of College Student Personnel, 14,* 352–354.

Byrne, B. (1984). The general/academic self-concept nomological network: A review of construct validation research. *Review of Educational Research, 54,* 427–456.

Cade, S. (1979). A comparison of the developmental impact of homogeneous and heterogeneous housing conditions on freshmen. *Journal of College and University Student Housing, 9,* 18–21.

Cady, M. (1982). *Assessment of moral development among clergy.* Unpublished honors thesis, Augsburg College, Minneapolis.

Cain, G., & Watts, H. (1970). Problems in making policy inferences from the Coleman Report. *American Sociological Review, 35,* 228–242.

Calhoon, R., & Reddy, A. (1968). The frantic search for predictors of success: 50 years of confusion and contradiction. *Journal of College Placement, 28,* 54–66.

Calvert, R. (1969). *Career patterns of liberal arts graduates.* Cranston, RI: Carroll Press.

Campbell, A. (1981). *The sense of well-being in America.* New York: McGraw-Hill.

Campbell, A., Converse, P., Miller, W., & Stokes, D. (1960). *The American voter.* New York: John Wiley & Sons.

Campbell, A., Converse, P., & Rodgers, W. (1976). *The quality of American life.* New York: Russell Sage Foundation.

Campbell, D. (1965). *A study of college freshmen—Twenty-five years later.* Minneapolis: University of Minnesota, Cooperative Research Program.

Campbell, D. (1967). *The effects of college on students: Proposing a quasi-experimental approach.* Evanston, IL: Northwestern University.

Campbell, D., & Magill, D. (1968). Religious involvement and intellectuality among university students. *Sociological Analysis, 29,* 79–93.

Campbell, D., & Stanley, J. (1963). Experimental and quasi-experimental designs for research on teaching. In N. Gage (Ed.), *Handbook of research on teaching.* Chicago: Rand McNally.

Campbell, L., & Williamson, J. (1973). Dogmatism in student teachers. *Educational Forum, 37*, 489.

Campbell, P., & Laughlin, S. (1987). *Climbing toward equity: The postsecondary advantage*. Paper presented at the meeting of the American Educational Research Association, Washington, DC.

Campbell, R., & Henretta, J. (1980). Status claims and status attainment: The determinants of financial well-being. *American Journal of Sociology, 86*, 618–629.

Campbell, T. (1978). An evaluation of a learning cycle intervention strategy for enhancing the use of formal operational thought by beginning college physics students. *Dissertation Abstracts International, 38*, 3903A.

Candee, D., & Kohlberg, L. (1987). Moral judgment and moral action: A reanalysis of Haan, Smith, and Block's (1968) free speech movement data. *Journal of Personality and Social Psychology, 52*, 554–564.

Canelos, J., & Ozbeki, M. (1983). Application of the Keller instructional strategy of personalized instruction for the improvement of problem-solving learning in technical education. *Journal of Instructional Psychology, 10*, 61–69.

Capel, W. (1967). Continuities and discontinuities in attitudes of the same persons measured through time. *Journal of Social Psychology, 73*, 125–136.

Caple, R. (1971). Freshman students' expectancy of the campus climate at a community college. *Journal of College Student Personnel, 12*, 20–25.

Caple, R. (1987a). The change process in developmental theory: A self-organization paradigm. Part 1. *Journal of College Student Personnel, 28*, 4–11.

Caple, R. (1987b). The change process in developmental theory: A self-organization paradigm. Part 2. *Journal of College Student Personnel, 28*, 100–104.

Capoor, M., & Gelfman, A. (1988). *Assessment of college outcomes with the value-added approach*. Paper presented at the meeting of the Association for Institutional Research, Phoenix, AZ.

Cappella, B., Wagner, M., & Kusmierz, J. (1982). Relation of study habits and attitudes to academic performance. *Psychological Reports, 50*, 593–594.

Carnoy, M., & Marenbach, D. (1975). The returns to schooling in the U.S., 1939–69. *Journal of Human Resources, 10*, 83–88.

Carp, A., Peterson, R., & Roelfs, P. (1974). Adult learning interests and experiences. In K. Cross, J. Valley, & Associates, *Planning nontraditional programs: An analysis of issues for postsecondary education*. San Francisco: Jossey-Bass.

Carroll, C. (1987). *The effects of grants on college persistence*. Washington, DC: U.S. Department of Education, Office of Educational Research and Improvement.

Carroll, J. (1963). A model of school learning. *Teachers College Record, 64*, 723–733.

Carroll, J. (1988). Freshman retention and attrition factors at a predominantly black urban community college. *Journal of College Student Development, 29,* 52–59.

Carsello, C., & Creaser, J. (1976). How college students change during study abroad. *College Student Journal, 10,* 276–278.

Carter, B. (1982). *Exit interview summary, fall 1981.* Indianapolis: Indiana University–Purdue University, Office of Student Services.

Carter, R., & Helms, J. (1987). The relationship of black value-orientations to racial identity attitudes. *Measurement and Evaluation in Counseling and Development, 19,* 185–195.

Cartledge, C., & Walls, D. (1986). *COL 105: The freshman experience in staying alive.* Unpublished manuscript, Columbus College, Columbus, GA.

Carver, D., & Smart, D. (1985). The effects of a career and self-exploration course for undecided freshmen. *Journal of College Student Personnel, 26,* 37–43.

Catlin, J. (1978). The impact of interracial living on the racial attitudes and interaction patterns of white students. *Dissertation Abstracts International, 38,* 6559A.

Cauble, M. (1976). Formal operations, ego identity, and principled morality: Are they related? *Developmental Psychology, 12,* 363–364.

Cebula, R., & Lopes, J. (1982). Determinants of student choice of undergraduate major field. *American Educational Research Journal, 19,* 303–312.

Centra, J. (1968). Student perceptions of residence hall environments: Living learning vs. conventional units. *Journal of College Student Personnel, 9,* 266–272.

Centra, J. (1970). Black students at predominantly white colleges: A research description. *Sociology of Education, 43,* 325–339.

Centra, J. (1977). Student ratings of instruction and their relationship to student learning. *American Educational Research Journal, 14,* 17–24.

Centra, J. (1979). *Determining faculty effectiveness: Assessing teaching, research, and service for personnel decisions and improvements.* San Francisco: Jossey-Bass.

Centra, J. (1981). *Research productivity and teaching effectiveness.* Princeton, NJ: Educational Testing Service.

Centra, J., Linn, R., & Parry, M. (1970). Academic growth in predominantly Negro and predominantly white colleges. *American Educational Research Journal, 7,* 83–98.

Centra, J., & Rock, D. (1971). College environments and student academic achievement. *American Educational Research Journal, 8,* 623–634.

Chapman, D., & Pascarella, E. (1983). Predictors of academic and social integration of college students. *Research in Higher Education, 19,* 295–322.

Charkins, R., O'Toole, D., & Wetzel, J. (1985). Linking teacher and student learning styles with student achievement and attitudes. *Journal of Economic Education, 16,* 111–120.

Cheatham, H., Slaney, R., & Coleman, N. (1990). Institutional effects on the psychosocial development of African-American college students. *Journal of Counseling Psychology, 37*, 453–458.

Cheatham, H., Tomlinson, S., & Ward, T. (1990). The African self-consciousness construct and African American students. *Journal of College Student Development, 31*, 492–499.

Chesin, S. (1969). Effects of differential housing on attitudes and values. *College Student Survey, 3*, 62–66.

Chew, C., & Ogi, A. (1987). Asian American college student perspectives. In D. Wright (Ed.), *Responding to the needs of today's minority students* (New Directions for Student Services No. 38). San Francisco: Jossey-Bass.

Cheydleur, F. (1945, August). Criteria of effective teaching in basic French courses. *Bulletin of the University of Wisconsin.*

Chiappetta, E. (1976). A review of Piagetian studies relevant to science instruction at the secondary and college level. *Science Education, 60*, 253–262.

Chickering, A. (1967). Institutional objectives and student development in college. *Journal of Behavioral Science, 3*, 287–304.

Chickering, A. (1968). FD's and SD's: Neglected data in institutional research. In C. Fincher (Ed.), *Institutional research and academic outcomes.* Tallahassee, FL: Association for Institutional Research.

Chickering, A. (1969). *Education and identity.* San Francisco: Jossey-Bass.

Chickering, A. (1970). Civil liberties and the experience of college. *Journal of Higher Education, 41*, 599–606.

Chickering, A. (1971a). Cultural sophistication and college experience. *Educational Record, 52*, 125–128.

Chickering, A. (1971b, January 16). The best colleges have the least effect. *Saturday Review*, pp. 48–50, 54.

Chickering, A. (1972). Undergraduate academic experience. *Journal of Educational Psychology, 63*, 134–143.

Chickering, A. (1974a). *Commuting versus resident students: Overcoming educational inequities of living off campus.* San Francisco: Jossey-Bass.

Chickering, A. (1974b). The impact of various college environments on personality development. *Journal of the American College Health Association, 23*, 82–93.

Chickering, A. (1976). Developmental change as a major outcome. In M. Keeton & Associates, *Experiential learning: Rationale, characteristics, and assessment.* San Francisco: Jossey-Bass.

Chickering, A., & Havighurst, R. (1981). The life cycle. In A. Chickering & Associates, *The modern American college: Responding to the new realities of diverse students and a changing society.* San Francisco: Jossey-Bass.

Chickering, A., & Kuper, E. (1971). Educational outcomes for commuters and residents. *Educational Record, 52*, 255–261.

Chickering, A., & McCormick, J. (1973). Personality development and the college experience. *Research in Higher Education, 1*, 43–70.

Chickering, A., McDowell, J., & Campagna, D. (1969). Institutional differences and student development. *Journal of Educational Psychology, 60*, 315–326.

Chiswick, B. (1973). Schooling, screening, and income. In L. Solmon & P. Taubman (Eds.), *Does college matter? Some evidence on the impacts of higher education*. Orlando, FL: Academic Press.

Christensen, S., Melder, J., & Weisbrod, B. (1975). Factors affecting college attendance. *Journal of Human Resources, 10*, 174–188.

Christenson, R., & Capretta, R. (1968). The impact of college on political attitudes: A research note. *Social Science Quarterly, 49*, 315–320.

Christian, V., & Stroup, R. (1981). The effect of education on relative earnings of black and white women. *Economics of Education Review, 1*, 113–122.

Churchill, W., & Iwai, S. (1981). College attrition, student use of facilities, and consideration of self-reported personal problems. *Research in Higher Education, 14*, 353–365.

Churchman, C. (1971). *The design of inquiring systems: Basic concepts of systems and organizations*. New York: Basic Books.

Clapp, T., & Reid, J. (1976). Institutional selectivity as a predictor of applicant selection and success in medical school. *Journal of Medical Education, 51*, 850–852.

Clark, B. (1960). The "cooling-out" function in higher education. *American Journal of Sociology, 65*, 569–576.

Clark, B. (1972). The organizational saga in higher education. *Administrative Science Quarterly, 17*, 178–184.

Clark, B., Heist, P., McConnell, M., Trow, M., and Yonge, G. (1972). *Students and colleges: Interaction and change*. Berkeley: University of California, Center for Research and Development in Higher Education.

Clark, B., & Trow, M. (1966). The organizational context. In T. Newcomb & E. Wilson (Eds.), *College peer groups: Problems and prospects for research*. Chicago: Aldine.

Claxton, C., & Murrell, P. (1987). *Learning styles: Implications for improving educational practices* (ASHE-ERIC Higher Education Report No. 4). Washington, DC: Association for the Study of Higher Education.

Clemente, F., & Sauer, W. (1976). Life satisfaction in the United States. *Social Forces, 54*, 621–631.

Clewell, B., & Ficklen M. (1986). *Improving minority retention in higher education: A search for effective institutional practices*. Princeton, NJ: Educational Testing Service.

Cliff, N. (1983). Some cautions concerning the application of causal modeling methods. *Multivariate Behavioral Research, 18*, 115–126.

Clinchy, B., & Zimmerman, C. (1982). Epistemology and agency in the development of undergraduate women. In P. Perun (Ed.), *The undergraduate woman: Issues in educational equity*. Lexington, MA: D. C. Heath.

Cline, H. (1982). The measurement of change in the rate of return to education: 1967–1975. *Economics of Education Review, 2,* 275–293.

Cline, M., & Michael, E. (1978). An evaluation of a personalized system of instruction in psychology at the community college level. *Community/Junior College Research Quarterly, 3,* 1–12.

Clogg, C., & Shockey, J. (1984). Mismatch between occupation and schooling: A prevalence measure, recent trends and demographic analysis. *Demography, 21,* 235–257.

Clouse, B. (1985). Moral reasoning and Christian faith. *Journal of Psychology and Theology, 13,* 190–198.

Cobern, M., Salem, C., & Mushkin, S. (1973). *Indicators of educational outcomes, Fall 1972* (DHEW Publication No. OE 73-11110). Washington, DC: U.S. Government Printing Office.

Cochran, W., & Cox, G. (1957). *Experimental designs* (2nd ed.). New York: John Wiley & Sons.

Coder, R. (1975). *Moral judgment in adults.* Unpublished doctoral dissertation, University of Minnesota, Minneapolis and St. Paul.

Cogan, J., Torney-Purta, J., & Anderson, D. (1988). Knowledge and attitudes toward global issues: Students in Japan and the United States. *Comparative Education Review, 32,* 282–297.

Cohen, A. (1986). What do our students know? *Community College Review, 13,* 6–11.

Cohen, A., & Brawer, F. (1982). *The American community college.* San Francisco: Jossey-Bass.

Cohen, A., & Brawer, F. (1987). *The collegiate function of community colleges: Fostering higher learning through curriculum and student transfer.* San Francisco: Jossey-Bass.

Cohen, A., & Brawer, F. (1989). *The American community college* (2nd ed.). San Francisco: Jossey-Bass.

Cohen, E. (1982). Using the Defining Issues Test to assess stage of moral development among sorority and fraternity members. *Journal of College Student Personnel, 23,* 324–328.

Cohen, H., Hillman, D., & Agne, R. (1978). Cognitive level and college physics achievement. *American Journal of Physics, 46,* 1–14.

Cohen, J. (1968). Multiple regression as a general data analytic system. *Psychological Bulletin, 70,* 426–443.

Cohen, J., & Cohen, P. (1975). *Applied multiple regression/correlation analysis in the behavioral sciences.* Hillsdale, NJ: Lawrence Erlbaum.

Cohen, P. (1972). Validity of student ratings of psychology courses: A research synthesis. *Teaching of Psychology, 9,* 78–82.

Cohen, P. (1981). Student ratings of instruction and student achievement: A meta-analysis of multisection validity studies. *Review of Educational Research, 51,* 281–309.

Cohen, P. (1984). College grades and adult achievement: A research synthesis. *Research in Higher Education, 20,* 281–293.

Cohen, P., Ebeling, B., & Kulik, J. (1981). A meta-analysis of outcome studies of visual-based instruction. *Educational Communication and Technology Journal, 29,* 26–36.

Cohn, E., & Geske, T. (1985). *Benefit-cost analysis of investment in higher education* (Working Papers in Economics). Columbia: University of South Carolina, College of Business Administration, Division of Research.

Colarelli, S., Dean, R., & Konstans, C. (1988). *The influence of college characteristics on early career outcomes of accountants.* Unpublished manuscript, Central Michigan University, Mount Pleasant.

Colby, A., Kohlberg, L., Gibbs, J., Candee, D., Speicher-Dubin, B., Kauffman, K., Hewer, A., & Power, C. (1982). *The measurement of moral judgment: A manual and its results.* New York: Cambridge University Press.

Colby, A., Kohlberg, L., Gibbs, J., Candee, D., Speicher-Dubin, B., & Power, C. (1978). *Assessing moral judgment stages: A manual.* Cambridge, MA: Moral Education Research Foundation.

Colby, A., Kohlberg, L., Gibbs, J., & Lieberman, M. (1983). A longitudinal study of moral judgment. *Society for Research on Child Development Monograph, 48*(1–2, Serial No. 200).

Coleman, J. (1960). The adolescent subculture and academic achievement. *American Journal of Sociology, 65,* 337–347.

Coles, H. (1983). *College student perceptions: Four-year follow-up of 1976 freshmen: Part 1. Academic and career plans and experiences.* Buffalo: State University of New York, Division of Student Affairs, Student Testing.

College degree increases lifetime earnings by 40 percent. (1983, March 15). *Higher Education Daily,* p. 5.

College Entrance Examination Board. (1968). *Score distributions: General examinations, college-level examination program, candidates tested through the United States Armed Forces Institute, July 1965–December 1966.* New York: Author.

Collins, R. (1971). Functional and conflict theories of stratification. *American Sociological Review, 36,* 1002–1119.

Collins, R. (1974). Where are educational requirements for employment highest? *Sociology of Education, 47,* 419–442.

Collins, R. (1979). *The credential society: An historical sociology of education and stratification.* Orlando, FL: Academic Press.

Commission for Educational Quality. (1985). *Access to quality undergraduate education.* Atlanta: Southern Regional Education Board.

Condran, J. (1979). Changes in white attitudes toward blacks: 1963–1977. *Public Opinion Quarterly, 43,* 463–476.

Constantinople, A. (1967). Perceived instrumentality of the college as a measure of attitudes toward college. *Journal of Personality and Social Psychology, 5,* 196–201.

Constantinople, A. (1969). An Eriksonian measure of personality development in college students. *Developmental Psychology, 1,* 357–372.

Constantinople, A. (1970). Some correlates of average level of happiness among college students. *Developmental Psychology, 2,* 447.

Cook, T., & Campbell, D. (1979). *Quasi-experimentation: Design and analysis issues for field settings.* Chicago: Rand McNally.

Cook, T., & Leviton, L. (1980). Reviewing the literature: A comparison of traditional methods with meta-analysis. *Journal of Personality, 48,* 449–472.

Cooker, P., & Caffey, C. (1984). Addressing the cognitive and affective needs of college athletes: Effects of group counseling on self-esteem, reading skills, and coaches' perceptions of attitude. *Journal of Sport Psychology, 6,* 377–384.

Cooley, W., Bond, L., & Mao, B. (1981). Analyzing multilevel data. In R. Berk (Ed.), *Educational evaluation methodology: The state of the art.* Baltimore: Johns Hopkins University Press.

Cooper, H. (1982). Scientific guidelines for conducting integrative research reviews. *Review of Educational Research, 52,* 291–302.

Cooper, S. (1986). The effects of group and individual vocational counseling on career indecision and personal indecisiveness. *Journal of College Student Personnel, 27,* 39–42.

Coopersmith, S. (1967). *The antecedents of self-esteem.* New York: W. H. Freeman.

Cope, R., & Hannah, W. (1975). *Revolving college doors: The causes and consequences of dropping out, stopping out, and transferring.* New York: John Wiley & Sons.

Corbett, M., Frankland, E., & Rudoni, D. (1977). Sexism among college students: Do males and females differ? *Youth & Society, 9,* 171–190.

Corbett, M., Rudoni, D., & Frankland, E. (1981). Change and stability in sexism among college students: A three-year panel study. *Sex Roles, 7,* 233–246.

Corey, S. (1936). Attitude differences between college classes: A summary and criticism. *Journal of Educational Psychology, 27,* 321–330.

Corlett, D. (1974). Library skills, study habits and attitudes, and sex as related to academic achievement. *Educational and Psychological Measurement, 34,* 967–969.

Corno, L., & Snow, R. (1986). Adapting teaching to individual differences among learners. In M. Wittrock (Ed.), *Handbook of research on teaching* (3rd ed.). New York: Macmillan.

Corrallo, S., & Davis, J. (1977). *Impact of financial aid on postsecondary entrance and persistence.* Paper presented at the meeting of the American Educational Research Association, New York.

Coscarelli, W., & Schwen, T. (1979). Effects of three algorithmic representations on critical thinking, laboratory efficiency, and final grade. *Educational Communication and Technology Journal, 27,* 58–64.

Cosgrove, T. (1986). The effects of participation in a mentoring-transcript program on freshmen. *Journal of College Student Personnel, 27,* 119–124.

Costa, A. (1984). Selected correlates of achievement and persistence of adult community college students. *Dissertation Abstracts International, 44,* 2989A.

Costantini, E., & King, J. (1985). Affirmative action: The configuration, concomitants, and antecedents of student opinion. *Youth and Society, 16,* 499–525.

Costin, F., Greenough, W., & Menges, R. (1971). Student ratings of college teaching: Reliability, validity, and usefulness. *Review of Educational Research, 41,* 511–535.

Cottle, T. (1974). The felt sense of studentry. *Interchange, 5,* 31–41.

Cox, S. (1988). *A longitudinal study of values preferences change as an index of adult development in Berea College students and alumni.* Paper presented at the meeting of the American Educational Research Association, Washington, DC.

Crane, D. (1969). Social class origins and academic success. *Sociology of Education, 41,* 1–17.

Crary, L., & Leslie, L. (1978). The private costs of postsecondary education. *Journal of Educational Finance, 4,* 14–28.

Crawford, J. (1978). Career development and career choice in pioneer and traditional women. *Journal of Vocational Behavior, 12,* 129–139.

Creager, J. (1969). *On methods for analysis of differential input and treatment effects on educational outcomes.* Paper presented at the meeting of the American Educational Research Association, Los Angeles.

Crimmel, H. (1984). The myth of the teacher-scholar. *Liberal Education, 70,* 184–198.

Cronbach, L. (1970). *Essentials of psychological testing* (3rd ed.). New York: Harper & Row.

Cronbach, L. (1976). *Research on classrooms and schools: Formulation of questions, design, and analysis.* Stanford, CA: Stanford University, Stanford Evaluation Consortium.

Cronbach, L. (1982). *Designing evaluations of education and social programs.* San Francisco: Jossey-Bass.

Cronbach, L., & Furby, L. (1970). How we should measure "change"—Or should we? *Psychological Bulletin, 74,* 68–80.

Cronbach, L., Rogosa, D., Floden, R., & Price, G. (1977). *Analysis of covariance in non-randomized experiments: Parameters affecting bias.* Stanford, CA: Stanford University, Stanford Evaluation Consortium.

Cronbach, L., & Snow, R. (1977). *Aptitudes and instructional methods: A handbook for research on interactions.* New York: Irvington.

Cronbach, L., & Webb, N. (1975). Between-class and within-class effects in a reported aptitude × treatment interaction: Reanalysis of a study by G. L. Anderson. *Journal of Educational Psychology, 67,* 717–727.

Crook, D., & Lavin, D. (1989). *The community-college effect revisited: The long-term impact of community-college entry on B.A. attainment.* Paper presented at the meeting of the American Educational Research Association, San Francisco.

Crooks, L., & Campbell, J. (1974). *Career progress of MBAs: An exploratory study six years after graduation.* Princeton, NJ: Educational Testing Service.

Cross, K. (1968). College women: A research description. *Journal of the National Association of Women Deans, Administrators, and Counselors, 32,* 12–21.

Cross, K. (1971). *Beyond the open door: New students to higher education.* San Francisco: Jossey-Bass.

Cross, K. (1976). Beyond education for all, toward education for each. *College Board Review, 99,* 5–10.

Cross, K. (1981). *Adults as learners: Increasing participation and facilitating learning.* San Francisco: Jossey-Bass.

Cross, K., & Astin, H. (1981). Factors influencing black students' persistence in college. In G. Thomas (Ed.), *Black students in higher education.* Westport, CT: Greenwood Press.

Cross, W., Jr. (1971a). Discovering the black referent: The psychology of black liberation. In J. Dixon & B. Foster (Eds.), *Beyond black or white.* Boston: Little, Brown.

Cross, W., Jr. (1971b). The Negro-to-black conversion experience: Toward a psychology of black liberation. *Black World, 20,* 13–27.

Cross, W., Jr. (1978). Models of psychological nigrescence: A review. *Journal of Black Psychology, 5,* 13–31.

Cross, W., Jr. (1979). The Negro-to-black conversion experience: An empirical analysis. In A. Boykin, A. Franklin, & J. Yates (Eds.), *Research directions of black psychologists.* New York: Russell Sage Foundation.

Cross, W., Jr. (1980). Models of psychological nigrescence: A literature review. In R. Jones (Ed.), *Black psychology* (2nd ed.). New York: Harper & Row.

Cross, W., Jr. (1985). Black identity: Rediscovering the distinction between personal identity and reference group orientation. In M. Spencer, G. Brookins, & W. Allen (Eds.), *Beginnings: The social and affective development of black children.* Hillsdale, NJ: Lawrence Erlbaum.

Crotty, W. (1967). Democratic consensual norms and the college student. *Sociology of Education, 40,* 200–218.

Crowder, J. (1976). *The Defining Issues Test and correlates of moral judgment.* Unpublished master's thesis, University of Maryland, College Park.

Culbert, S., Clark, J., & Bobele, H. (1968). Measures of changes toward self-actualization in two sensitivity training groups. *Journal of Counseling Psychology, 15,* 53–57.

Culler, R., & Holahan, C. (1980). Test anxiety and academic performance: The effects of study-related behaviors. *Journal of Educational Psychology, 72,* 16–20.

Cunningham, J., & Lawson, D. (1979). *The myth of the all-university GPA: An analysis of sources of apparent grade inflation.* Paper presented at the meeting of the Association for Institutional Research, San Diego.

Curtin, R., & Cowan, C. (1975). Public attitudes toward fiscal programs. In B. Strumpel, C. Cowan, F. Juster, & J. Schmiedeskamp (Eds.), *Survey of Consumers 1972–73.* Ann Arbor: University of Michigan, Institute for Social Research.

Cutler, N., & Bengston, V. (1974). Age and political alienation: Maturation, generation and period effects. *Annals of the American Academy of Political and Social Sciences, 415,* 160–175.

Czapski, D., & Gates, L. (1981). Love and justice: An examination of affective and cognitive aspects of moral judgment development. *Educational and Psychological Research, 1,* 215–221.

Dabrowski, I. (1985). Liberating the "deviant" feminist image through education. *Social Behavior and Personality, 13,* 73–81.

Dalgaard, K. (1982). Some effects of training on teaching effectiveness of untrained university teaching assistants. *Research in Higher Education, 17,* 39–50.

Dambrot, F., Papp, M., & Whitmore, C. (1984). The sex-role attitudes of three generations of women. *Personality and Social Psychology Bulletin, 10,* 469–473.

Daniels, R., & Stevens, J. (1976). The interaction between internal-external locus of control and two methods of college instruction. *American Educational Research Journal, 13,* 103–113.

Daniere, A., & Mechling, J. (1970). Direct marginal productivity of college education in relation to college aptitude of students and production costs of institutions. *Journal of Human Resources, 5,* 51–70.

Dannefer, D. (1984a). Adult development and social theory: A paradigmatic reappraisal. *American Sociological Review, 49,* 100–116.

Dannefer, D. (1984b). The role of the social in life-span developmental psychology, past and future: Rejoinder to Baltes and Nesselroade. *American Sociological Review, 49,* 847–850.

Darlington, R. (1968). Multiple regression in psychological research and practice. *Psychological Bulletin, 69,* 161–182.

Da Vanzo, J. (1983). Repeat migration in the U.S.: Who moves back and who moves on? *Review of Economics and Statistics, 65,* 552–559.

Davidson, J. (1974). Empirical development of a measure of black identity. *Dissertation Abstracts International, 35,* 7076A.

Davis, B., Morgan, C., & Barker, D. (1981). The relationship of special programs to social change. *Journal of the National Association of Women Deans, Administrators, and Counselors, 44,* 3–9.

Davis, D., Belcher, M., & McKitterick, T. (1986). Comparing the achievement of students taught by part-time versus full-time faculty. *Community/ Junior College Quarterly of Research and Practice, 10,* 65–72.

Davis, H. (1977). A comparison of academic achievement of black PE majors at predominantly black and predominantly white institutions. *Journal of Physical Education and Recreation, 48,* 24–25.

Davis, J. (1965). *Undergraduate career decisions: Correlates of occupational choice.* Chicago: Aldine.

Davis, J. (1966). The campus as frog pond: An application of the theory of relative deprivation to career decisions of college men. *American Journal of Sociology, 72,* 17–31.

Davis, J. (1975). Communism, conformity, cohorts, and categories: American tolerance in 1954 and 1972–73. *American Journal of Sociology, 81,* 491–513.

Davis, J. (1980). Conservative weather in a liberalizing climate: Change in selected NORC General Social Survey items. *Social Forces, 58,* 1129–1156.

Davis, J., & Borders-Patterson, A. (1973). *Black students in predominantly white North Carolina colleges and universities.* (Research Rep. No. 2). New York: College Entrance Examination Board.

Davis, R. (1986). *Social support networks and undergraduate student academic-success related outcomes: A comparison of black students on black and white campuses.* Paper presented at the meeting of the American Educational Research Association, San Francisco.

Daymont, T., & Andrisani, P. (1984). Job preferences, college major, and the gender gap in earnings. *Journal of Human Resources, 19,* 408–428.

Dearman, N., & Plisko, V. (1981). *The condition of education, 1981 edition.* Washington, DC: National Center for Education Statistics.

DeBack, V., & Mentkowski, M. (1986). Does the baccalaureate make a difference? Differentiating nurse performance by education and experience. *Journal of Nursing Education, 25,* 275–285.

DeCoster, D. (1968). Effects of homogeneous housing assignments for high ability students. *Journal of College Student Personnel, 8,* 75–78.

DeCoster, D. (1979). The effects of residence hall room visitation upon academic achievement for college students. *Journal of College Student Personnel, 20,* 520–525.

Deemer, D. (1985). *Research in moral development.* Paper presented at the meeting of the American Educational Research Association, Chicago.

DeFleur, L., Gillman, D., & Marshak, W. (1978). Sex integration of the U.S. Air Force Academy. *Armed Forces and Society, 4,* 607–622.

DeLisi, R., & Staudt, J. (1980). Individual differences in college students' performance on formal operations tasks. *Journal of Applied Developmental Psychology, 16,* 121–131.

Demitroff, J. (1974). Student persistence. *College and University, 49,* 553–565.

Denham, M., & Land, M. (1981). Research brief-effect of teacher verbal fluency and clarity on student achievement. *Technical Teachers Journal of Education, 8,* 227–229.

Dent, P., & Lewis, D. (1976). The relationship between teaching effectiveness and measures of research quality. *Educational Research Quarterly, 1,* 3–16.

Deppe, M. (1989). *The impact of racial diversity and involvement on college students' social concern values.* Paper presented at the meeting of the Association for the Study of Higher Education, Atlanta.

Deppe, M. (1990). The impact of racial diversity and involvement on college students' social concern values (Doctoral dissertation, Claremont Graduate School, 1989). *Dissertation Abstracts International, 50,* 2397A.

Dettloff, J. (1982). *Predicting achievement in community college science students.* Unpublished doctoral dissertation, University of Michigan, Ann Arbor.

de Vries, B., & Walker, L. (1986). Moral reasoning and attitudes toward capital punishment. *Developmental Psychology, 22,* 509–513.

de Wolf, V. (1976). *Factors related to postgraduate educational aspirations of women college graduates.* Paper presented at the meeting of the American Psychological Association, Washington, DC.

Dey, E. (1989). *College impact and student liberalism revisited: The effect of student peers.* Unpublished manuscript, University of California, Graduate School of Education, Higher Education Research Institute, Los Angeles.

Diamond, M., & Shapiro, J. (1973). Changes in locus of control as a function of encounter group experiences. *Journal of Abnormal Psychology, 82,* 514–518.

Dickstein, E. (1977). Self and self-esteem: Theoretical foundations and their implications for research. *Human Development, 20,* 129–140.

Diener, E. (1984). Subjective well-being. *Psychological Bulletin, 95,* 542–575.

Digest of educational statistics 1985–1986. (1986). Washington, DC: U.S. Department of Education.

Dignan, M., & Adams, D. (1979). Locus of control and human sexuality education. *Perceptual and Motor Skills, 49,* 778.

DiMaggio, P., & Mohr, J. (1985). Cultural capital, educational attainment, and marital selection. *American Journal of Sociology, 90,* 1231–1261.

DiNuzzo, T., & Tolbert, E. (1981). Promoting the personal growth and vocational maturity of the re-entry woman: A group approach. *Journal of the National Association of Women Deans, Administrators, and Counselors, 45,* 26–31.

Dispoto, R. (1974). *Socio-moral reasoning and environmental activity, emotionality and knowledge.* Unpublished doctoral dissertation, Rutgers University, New Brunswick, NJ.

Dispoto, R. (1977). Moral valuing and environmental variables. *Journal of Research in Science Teaching, 14,* 273–280.

Disque, C. (1983). The relationship of student characteristics and academic integration to college freshman attrition. *Dissertation Abstracts International, 43,* 3820A–3821A.

Doherty, W., & Corsini, D. (1976). Creativity, intelligence, and moral development in college women. *Journal of Creative Behavior, 10,* 276–284.

Domhoff, G. (1967). *Who rules America?* Englewood Cliffs, NJ: Prentice-Hall.

Domino, G. (1968). Differential prediction of academic achievement in conforming and independent settings. *Journal of Educational Psychology, 59,* 256–260.

Domino, G. (1971). Interactive effects of achievement orientation and teaching style on academic achievement. *Journal of Educational Psychology, 62,* 427–431.

Donald, J., & Bateman, D. (1989). *Developing students' ability to think critically.* Paper presented at the meeting of the American Educational Research Association, San Francisco.

Donovan, J. (1970). A study of ego identity formation. *Dissertation Abstracts International, 31,* 4986B.

Donovan, R. (1984). Path analysis of a theoretical model of persistence in higher education among low-income black youth. *Research in Higher Education, 21,* 243–252.

Donovan, R., Schaier-Peleg, B., & Forer, B. (1987). *Transfer: Making it work.* Washington, DC: American Association of Community and Junior Colleges.

Dortzbach, J. (1975). *Moral judgment and perceived locus of control: A cross-sectional developmental study of adults, aged 25–74.* Unpublished doctoral dissertation, University of Oregon, Eugene.

Dougherty, K. (1987). The effects of community colleges: Aid or hinderance to socioeconomic attainment? *Sociology of Education, 60,* 86–103.

Douvan, E., & Adelson, J. (1966). *The adolescent experience.* New York: John Wiley & Sons.

Doyle, K. (1975). *Student evaluation of instruction.* Lexington, MA: D. C. Heath.

Draper, N., & Smith, H. (1966). *Applied regression analysis.* New York: John Wiley & Sons.

Dreher, G., Dougherty, T., & Whiteley, B. (1985). Generalizability of MBA degree and socioeconomic effects on business school graduates' salaries. *Journal of Applied Psychology, 70,* 769–773.

Dressel, P., & DeLisle, F. (1969). *Undergraduate curriculum trends.* Washington, DC: American Council on Education.

Dressel, P., & Mayhew, L. (1954). *General education: Explorations in evaluation.* Westport, CT: Greenwood Press.

Drew, D., & Astin, A. (1972). Undergraduate aspirations: A test of several theories. *American Journal of Sociology, 77,* 1151–1164.

Dreyer, N., Woods, N., & James, S. (1981). ISRO: A scale to measure sex-role orientation. *Sex Roles, 7,* 173–182.

Drum, D. (1980). Understanding student development. In W. Morrill & J. Hurst (Eds.), *Dimensions of intervention for student development.* New York: John Wiley & Sons.

Dubin, R., & Taveggia, T. (1968). *The teaching-learning paradox.* Eugene: University of Oregon, Center for the Advanced Study of Educational Administration.

Dubois, N., Kiewra, K., & Fraley, J. (1988). *Differential effects of a learning strategy course with a cognitive orientation.* Paper presented at the meeting of the American Educational Research Association, New Orleans.

DuBois, P. (1978). Participation in sports and occupational attainment: A comparative study. *Research Quarterly, 49,* 28–37.

Duby, P. (1981). *Attributions and attributional change: Effects of a mastery learning instructional approach.* Paper presented at the meeting of the American Educational Research Association, Los Angeles.

Dukes, F., & Gaither, G. (1984). A campus cluster program: Effects on persistence and academic performance. *College and University, 59,* 150–166.

Dumont, R., & Troelstrup, R. (1980). Exploring relationships between objective and subjective measures of instructional outcomes. *Research in Higher Education, 12,* 37–51.

Dumont, R., & Troelstrup, R. (1981). Measures and predictors of educational growth with four years of college. *Research in Higher Education, 14,* 31–47.

Duncan, B. (1976). Minority students. In J. Katz & R. Hartnett (Eds.), *Scholars in the making: The development of graduate and professional students.* Cambridge, MA: Ballinger.

Duncan, C., & Stoner, K. (1977). The academic achievement of residents living in a scholar residence hall. *Journal of College and University Student Housing, 6,* 7–9.

Duncan, O. (1961). A socioeconomic index for all occupations. In A. Reiss (Ed.), *Occupations and social status.* New York: Free Press.

Duncan, O. (1966). Path analysis: Sociological examples. *American Journal of Sociology, 72,* 1–16.

Duncan, O. (1968). Ability and achievement. *Eugenics Quarterly, 15,* 1–11.

Duncan, O. (1975). *Introduction to structural equation models.* Orlando, FL: Academic Press.

Duncan, O., Featherman, D., & Duncan, B. (1972). *Socioeconomic background and achievement.* New York: Seminar Press.

Dunivant, N. (1975). *Moral judgment, psychological development, situational characteristics and moral behavior: A mediational interactionist model.* Unpublished doctoral dissertation, University of Texas, Austin.

Dunkin, M., & Barnes, J. (1985). Research on teaching in higher education. In M. Wittrock (Ed.), *Handbook of research on teaching* (3rd ed.). New York: Macmillan.

Dunlop, D., & Fazio, F. (1976). Piagetian theory and abstract preferences of college science students. *Journal of College Science Teaching, 5,* 297–300.

Dunphy, L., Miller, T., Woodruff, T., & Nelson, J. (1987). Exemplary retention strategies for the freshman year. In M. Stodt & W. Klepper (Eds.), *Increasing retention: Academic and student affairs administrators in partnership.* (New Directions in Higher Education No. 60). San Francisco: Jossey-Bass.

Easterlin, R. (1968). *Population, labor force and long swings in economic growth: The American experience.* New York: National Bureau of Economic Research.

Easterlin, R. (1975). Relative economic status and the American fertility swing. In E. Sheldon (Ed.), *Family economic behavior.* Philadelphia: Lippincott.

Eckland, B., & Henderson, L. (1981). *College attainment four years after high school.* National Longitudinal Study Sponsored Reports Series. Washington, DC: National Center for Education Statistics.

Eddins, D. (1982). *A causal model of the attrition of specially admitted black students in higher education.* Paper presented at the meeting of the American Educational Research Association, New York.

Eddy, E. (1959). *The college influence on student character.* Washington, DC: American Council on Education.

Edmonds, G. (1984). Needs assessment strategy for black students: An examination of stressors and program implications. *Journal of Non-White Concerns, 12,* 48–56.

Edmonson, J., & Mulder, F. (1924). Size of class as a factor in university instruction. *Journal of Educational Research, 9,* 1–12.

Education has little impact on minority unemployment, study finds. (1982, November 29). *Higher Education Daily,* p. 2.

Educational Testing Service. (1954). *Institutional testing program: Summary statistics 1953–1954* (ETS Archives Microfiche No. 40). Princeton, NJ: Author.

Educational Testing Service. (1976). *Undergraduate assessment program guide.* Princeton, NJ: Author.

Educational Testing Service. (1978). *Undergraduate assessment program guide.* Princeton, NJ: Author.

Edwards, H. (1970). *Black students.* New York: Free Press.

Edwards, K., & Tuckman, B. (1972). Effect of differential college experiences in developing the students' self- and occupational concepts. *Journal of Educational Psychology, 63,* 563–571.

Edwards, L., & Grossman, L. (1979). The relationship between children's health and intellectual development. In S. Mushkin (Ed.), *Health: What is it worth?* Elmsford, NY: Pergamon Press.

Ehrenberg, R., & Sherman, D. (1987). Employment while in college, academic achievement, and postcollege outcomes: A summary of results. *Journal of Human Resources, 22,* 1–23.

Eiferman, D. (1982). *Moral judgment in adult urban college students.* Paper presented at the East Coast Forum on Urban Higher Education Research, New York.

Eisert, D., & Tomlinson-Keasey, C. (1978). Cognitive and interpersonal growth during the college freshman year: A structural analysis. *Perceptual and Motor Skills, 46,* 995–1005.

Eitzen, D., & Brouillette, J. (1979). The politicization of college students. *Adolescence, 14,* 123–134.

Elam, S. (1983). The Gallup education surveys: Impressions of a poll watcher. *Phi Delta Kappan, 64,* 14–22.

Elashoff, J. (1969). Analysis of covariance: A delicate instrument. *American Educational Research Journal, 6,* 383–401.

Elfner, E., McLaughlin, R., Williamsen, J., & Hardy, R. (1985). *Assessing goal related student outcomes.* Paper presented at the annual meeting of the Association for Institutional Research, Portland, OR.

El-Khawas, E. (1980). Differences in academic development during college. In *Men and women learning together: A study of college students in the late 70s.* Report of the Brown Project. Providence, RI: Brown University.

Ellis, V. (1968). Students who seek psychiatric help. In J. Katz & Associates, *No time for youth: Growth and constraint in college students.* San Francisco: Jossey-Bass.

Ellison, A., & Simon, B. (1973). Does college make a person healthy and wise? In L. Solmon & P. Taubman (Eds.), *Does college matter?* New York: Academic Press.

Elton, C. (1969). Patterns of change in personality test scores. *Journal of Counseling Psychology, 16,* 95–99.

Elton, C. (1971). Interaction of environment and personality: A test of Holland's theory. *Journal of Applied Psychology, 55,* 114–118.

Elton, C., & Bate, W. (1966). The effect of housing policy on grade-point average. *Journal of College Student Personnel, 7,* 73–77.

Elton, C., & Rose, H. (1969). Differential change in male personality test scores. *Journal of College Student Personnel, 10,* 373–377.

Elton, C., & Rose, H. (1981). *Retention revisited: With congruence, differentiation, and consistency.* Unpublished manuscript, University of Kentucky, Lexington.

Endo, J., & Bittner, T. (1985). *Using an integrated marketing and attrition model from a student information system to examine attrition after one year.* Unpublished manuscript, Office of Academic Planning and Budget, University of Colorado, Boulder.

Endo, J., & Harpel, R. (1979). *A longitudinal study of attrition.* Boulder: University of Colorado. (ERIC Document Reproduction Service No. ED 174 095)

Endo, J., & Harpel, R. (1980). *A longitudinal study of student outcomes at a state university.* Paper presented at the meeting of the Association for Institutional Research, Atlanta.

Endo, J., & Harpel, R. (1982). The effect of student-faculty interaction on students' educational outcomes. *Research in Higher Education, 16,* 115–138.

Endo, J., & Harpel, R. (1983). *Student-faculty interaction and its effect on freshman year outcomes at a major state university.* Paper presented at the meeting of the Association for Institutional Research, Toronto.

Eniaiyeju, P. (1983). The comparative effects of teacher-demonstration and self-paced instruction on concept acquisition and problem-solving skills of college level chemistry students. *Journal of Research in Science Teaching, 20,* 795–801.

Enos, P. (1981). Student satisfaction with faculty academic advising and persistence beyond the freshman year in college. *Dissertation Abstracts International, 42,* 1985A.

Enwieme, X. (1976). The incidence of formal operations of students in eight subject areas of the Nustep program at the University of Nebraska, Lincoln Campus. *Dissertation Abstracts International, 37,* 2761A.

Enyeart, M. (1981). Relationships among propositional logic, analogical reasoning and Piagetian level. *Dissertation Abstracts International, 41,* 3974A.

Epps, E. (1972). *Black students in white schools.* Worthington, OH: Jones.

Erbring, L., & Young, A. (1980). Individuals and social structure: Contextual effects as endogenous feedback. In E. Borgatta & D. Jackson (Eds.), *Aggregate data analysis and interpretation.* Beverly Hills, CA: Sage.

Erikson, E. (1956). The problem of ego identity. *Journal of the American Psychoanalytic Association, 4,* 56–121.

Erikson, E. (1959). Identity and the life cycle. *Psychological Issues Monograph, 1*(1), 1–171. New York: International Universities Press.

Erikson, E. (1963). *Childhood and society* (2nd ed.). New York: W. W. Norton.

Erikson, E. (1968). *Identity: Youth and crisis.* New York: W. W. Norton.

Erikson, R., Luttbeg, N., & Tedin, K. (1973). *American public opinion: Its origins, content, and impact* (2nd ed.). New York: W. W. Norton.

Erkut, S., & Mokros, J. (1984). Professors as models and mentors for college students. *American Educational Research Journal, 21,* 399–417.

Ernsberger, D. (1976). *Intrinsic-extrinsic religious identification and level of moral development.* Unpublished doctoral dissertation, University of Texas, Austin.

Erwin, T. (1982). Academic status as related to the development of identity. *Journal of Psychology, 110,* 163–169.

Erwin, T. (1983). The influences of roommate assignments upon students' maturity. *Research in Higher Education, 19,* 451–459.

Erwin, T., & Delworth, U. (1980). An instrument to measure Chickering's vector of identity. *NASPA Journal, 17,* 19–24.

Erwin, T., & Delworth, U. (1982). Formulating environmental constructs that affect students' identity. *NASPA Journal, 20,* 47–55.

Erwin, T., & Kelly, K. (1985). Changes in students' self-confidence in college. *Journal of College Student Personnel, 26,* 395–400.

Esposito, D., Hackett, G., & O'Halloran, S. (1987). *The relationship of role model influences to the career salience and educational and career plans of college women.* Paper presented at the meeting of the American Educational Research Association, Washington, DC.

Etaugh, C. (1975a). Biographical predictors of college students' attitudes toward women. *Journal of College Student Personnel, 16,* 273–276.

Etaugh, C. (1975b). Stability of college students' attitudes toward women during one school year. *Psychological Reports, 36,* 125–126.

Etaugh, C. (1986, August). *Biographical and personality correlates of attitudes toward women: A review.* Paper presented to the meeting of the American Psychological Association, Washington, DC.

Etaugh, C., & Bowen, L. (1976). Attitudes toward women: Comparison of enrolled and nonenrolled college students. *Psychological Reports, 38,* 229–230.

Etaugh, C., & Gerson, A. (1974). Attitudes toward women: Some biographical correlates. *Psychological Reports, 35,* 701–702.

Etaugh, C., & Spandikow, D. (1981). Changing attitudes toward women: A longitudinal study of college students. *Psychology of Women Quarterly, 5,* 591–594.

Etaugh, C., & Spiller, B. (1989). Attitudes toward women: Comparison of traditional-aged and older college students. *Journal of College Student Development, 30,* 41–46.

Ethington, C., & Smart, J. (1986). Persistence to graduate education. *Research in Higher Education, 24,* 287–303.

Ethington, C., Smart, J., & Pasacrella, E. (1987). Entry into the teaching profession: Test of a causal model. *Journal of Educational Research, 80,* 156–163.

Ethington, C., Smart, J., & Pascarella, E. (1988). Influences on women's entry into male-dominated occupations. *Higher Education, 17,* 545–562.

Ethington, C., & Wolfle, L. (1986). Sex differences in quantitative and analytical GRE performance: An exploratory study. *Research in Higher Education, 25,* 55–67.

Evans, D., Jones, P., Wortman, R., & Jackson, E. (1975). Traditional criteria as predictors of minority student success in medical school. *Journal of Medical Education, 50,* 934–939.

Evans, J., & Rector, A. (1978). Evaluation of a college course in career decision making. *Journal of College Student Personnel, 19,* 163–168.

Everett, C. (1979). *An analysis of student attrition at Penn State.* University Park: Pennsylvania State University, Office of Planning and Budget.

Ewell, P. (1984). *The self-regarding institution: Information for excellence.* Boulder, CO: National Center for Higher Education Management Systems.

Ewell, P. (Ed.). (1985a). *Assessing educational outcomes* (New Directions for Institutional Research No. 47). San Francisco: Jossey-Bass.

Ewell, P. (1985b). The value-added debate . . . continued. *American Association for Higher Education Bulletin, 38,* 12–13.

Ewell, P. (1988). Outcomes, assessment, and academic improvement: In search of usable knowledge. In J. Smart (Ed.), *Higher education: Handbook of theory and research* (Vol. 4). New York: Agathon.

Ewell, P. (1989). Institutional characteristics and faculty/administrator perceptions of outcomes: An exploratory analysis. *Research in Higher Education, 30,* 113–136.

Eysenck, H. (1978). An exercise in mega-silliness. *American Psychologist, 33,* 517.

Fannin, P. (1977). Ego identity status and sex role attitude, work role salience, atypicality of college major, and self-esteem in college women. *Dissertation Abstracts International, 38,* 7203A–7204A.

Farley, L., & Newkirk, M. (1977). Measuring attitudinal change in political science courses. *Teaching Political Science, 4,* 185–198.

Farr, W., Jones, J., & Samprone, J. (1986). *The consequences of a college preparatory and individual self-evaluation program on student achievement and retention.* Unpublished manuscript, Georgia College, Milledgeville.

Farrell, P., & Fuchs, V. (1982). Schooling and health: The cigarette connection. *Journal of Health Economics, 1,* 217–230.

Faughn, S. (1982). *Significant others: A new look at attrition.* Paper presented at the meeting of the American College Personnel Association, Detroit.

Faust, D., & Arbuthnot, J. (1978). Relationship between moral and Piagetian reasoning and the effectiveness of moral education. *Developmental Psychology, 14,* 435–436.

Feather, N. (1973). Value change among university students. *Australian Journal of Psychology, 25,* 57–70.

Feather, N. (1975). *Values in education and society.* New York: Free Press.

Feather, N. (1980). Values in adolescence. In J. Adelson (Ed.), *Handbook of Adolescent Psychology.* New York: John Wiley & Sons.

Featherman, D., & Carter, T. (1976). Discontinuities in schooling and the socioeconomic life cycle. In W. Sewell, R. Hauser, & D. Featherman (Eds.), *Schooling and achievement in American society.* Orlando, FL: Academic Press.

Featherman, D., & Hauser, R. (1976). Sexual inequalities and socioeconomic achievement in the U.S., 1962–1973. *American Sociological Review, 41,* 462–483.

Featherman, D., & Hauser, R. (1978). *Opportunity and change.* Orlando, FL: Academic Press.

Feldman, K. (1969). Studying the impacts of college on students. *Sociology of Education, 42,* 207–237.

Feldman, K. (1971a). Measuring college environments: Some uses of path analysis. *American Educational Research Journal, 8,* 51–70.

Feldman, K. (1971b). Some methods for assessing college impacts. *Sociology of Education, 44,* 133–150.

Feldman, K. (1972). Some theoretical approaches to the study of change and stability of college students. *Review of Educational Research, 42,* 1–26.

Feldman, K. (1976). The superior college teacher from the students' view. *Research in Higher Education, 5,* 243–288.

Feldman, K. (1984). Class size and college students' evaluations of teachers and courses: A closer look. *Research in Higher Education, 21,* 45–116.

Feldman, K. (1987). Research productivity and scholarly accomplishment of college teachers as related to their instructional effectiveness: A review and exploration. *Research in Higher Education, 26,* 227–298.

Feldman, K. (1989). The association between student ratings of specific instructional dimensions and student achievement: Refining and extending the synthesis of data from multisection validity studies. *Research in Higher Education, 30,* 583–645.

Feldman, K. (in press). An afterword for "The association between student ratings of specific instructional dimensions and student achievement: Refining and extending the synthesis of data from multisection validity studies." *Research in Higher Education.*

Feldman, K., & Newcomb, T. (1969). *The impact of college on students.* San Francisco: Jossey-Bass.

Feldman, K., & Weiler, J. (1976). Changes in initial differences among major-field groups: An exploration of the "accentuation effect." In W. Sewell, R. Hauser, & D. Featherman (Eds.), *Schooling and achievement in American society.* Orlando, FL: Academic Press.

Feldstein, P. (1979). *Health care economics.* New York: John Wiley & Sons.

Felmlee, D. (1988). Return to school and women's occupational attainment. *Sociology of Education, 61,* 29–41.

Fendrich, J. (1974). Activists ten years later: A test of generational unit continuity. *Journal of Social Issues, 30,* 95–118.

Fengler, A., & Wood, V. (1972). The generation gap: An analysis of attitudes on contemporary issues. *Gerontologist, 12,* 124–128.

Fennema, E., & Sherman, J. (1977). Sex-related differences in mathematics achievement, spatial visualization and affective factors. *American Educational Research Journal, 14,* 51–71.

Fennimore, F. (1968). Reading and the self-concept. *Journal of Reading, 11,* 447 ff.

Fenske, R., & Scott, C. (1972). *A comparison of freshmen who attend college in their home community and freshmen who migrate to college.* Iowa City, IA: American College Testing Program.

Fenske, R., & Scott, C. (1973). College students' goals, plans, and background characteristics: A synthesis of three empirical studies. *Research in Higher Education, 1,* 101–118.

Ferber, M., & McMahon, W. (1979). Women's expected earnings and their investment in higher education. *Journal of Human Resources, 14,* 405–420.

Ferree, M. (1974). A woman for president? Changing responses 1958–1972. *Public Opinion Quarterly, 38,* 390–399.

Ferris, K. (1982). Educational predictors of professional pay and performance. *Accounting, Organizations and Society, 7,* 225–230.

Fetters, W. (1975). *National longitudinal study of the high school class of 1972: Student questionnaire and test results by sex, high school program, ethnic category and father's education* (DHEW, National Center for Education Statistics, NCES75-208). Washington, DC: U.S. Government Printing Office.

Fetters, W. (1977). *Withdrawal from institutions of higher education: An appraisal with longitudinal data involving diverse institutions.* Washington, DC: U.S. Government Printing Office.

Fidler, P. (1985). *Research summary—University 101.* Columbia: University of South Carolina.

Fidler, P., and Hunter, M. (1989). How seminars enhance student success. In M. Upcraft, J. Gardner, & Associates, *The freshman year experience: Helping students survive and succeed in college.* San Francisco: Jossey-Bass.

Fields, C., & LeMay, M. (1973). Student financial aid: Effects on educational decisions and academic achievement. *Journal of College Student Personnel, 14,* 425–429.

Fields, M., & Shallenberger, W. (1987). The influence of age and education on perceptions of occupational attractiveness. *Journal of Occupational Psychology, 60,* 339–342.

Finkelstein, M. (1984). *The American academic profession: A synthesis of social inquiry since World War II.* Columbus: Ohio State University Press.

Finney, H. (1967). Development and change of political libertarianism among Berkeley undergraduates. *Dissertation Abstracts International, 27,* 4628A.

Finney, H. (1971). Political libertarianism at Berkeley: An application of perspectives from the new student left. *Journal of Social Issues, 27,* 35–61.

Finney, H. (1974). Political dimensions of college impact on civil-libertarianism and the integration of political perspective: A longitudinal analysis. *Sociology of Education, 47,* 214–250.

Finney, J. (1972). Indirect effects in path analysis. *Sociological Methods and Research, 1,* 175–186.

Finnie, B. (1970). The statistical assessment of personality change. In J. Whiteley & H. Sprandel (Eds.), *The growth and development of college students.* Washington, DC: American Personnel and Guidance Association.

Firebaugh, G. (1978). A rule for inferring individual-level relationships from aggregate data. *American Sociological Review, 43,* 555–572.

Firebaugh, G. (1980). Assessing group effects: A comparison of two methods. In E. Borgatta & D. Jackson (Eds.), *Aggregate data analysis and interpretation.* Beverly Hills, CA: Sage.

Fischer, C., & Grant, G. (1983). Intellectual levels in college classrooms. In C. Ellner & C. Barnes (Eds.), *Studies of college teaching: Experimental results, theoretical interpretations and new perspectives.* Lexington, MA: D. C. Heath.

Fisher, J. (1981). Transitions in relationships style from adolescence to young adulthood. *Journal of Youth and Adolescence, 10,* 11–23.

Fisher, R., & Andrews, J. (1976). The impact of self-selection and reference group identification in a university living-learning center. *Social Behavior and Personality, 4,* 209–218.

Fishkin, J., Keniston, K., & MacKinnon, C. (1973). Moral reasoning and political ideology. *Journal of Personality and Social Psychology, 27,* 109–119.

Fitch, S., & Adams, G. (1983). Ego identity and intimacy status: Replication and extension. *Developmental Psychology, 19,* 839–845.

Flack, M. (1976). Results and effects of study abroad. *Annals of the American Academy of Political and Social Sciences, 424,* 107–117.

Flanagan, D. (1976). The commuter student in higher education. *NASPA Journal, 13,* 35–41.

Flanagan, J. (1975). Education's contribution to the quality of life of a national sample of 30 year olds. *Educational Researcher, 4,* 13–16.

Flanders, N. (1970). *Analyzing teaching behavior.* Reading, MA: Addison-Wesley.

Flavell, J. (1963). *The developmental psychology of Jean Piaget.* New York: Van Nostrand.

Fleming, J. (1981). Special needs of blacks and other minorities. In A. Chickering & Associates, *The modern American college.* San Francisco: Jossey-Bass.

Fleming, J. (1982). Sex differences in the impact of college environments on black students. In P. Perun (Ed.), *The undergraduate woman: Issues in educational equity.* Lexington, MA: D. C. Heath.

Fleming, J. (1984). *Blacks in college: A comparative study of students' success in black and in white institutions.* San Francisco: Jossey-Bass.

Fleming, J. (1986). *Academic influences on self-esteem in college students.* Paper presented at the meeting of the American Educational Research Association, San Francisco.

Fligstein, N., & Wolf, W. (1978). Sex similarities in occupational status attainment: Are the results due to the restriction of the sample to employed women? *Social Science Research, 7,* 197–212.

Florito, J. (1981). The school-to-work transition of college graduates. *Industrial and Labor Relations Review, 35,* 103–114.

Florito, J., & Dauffenbach, R. (1982). Market and nonmarket influences on curriculum choice by college students. *Industrial and Labor Relations Review, 36,* 88–101.

Flory, C. (1940). The intellectual growth of college students. *Journal of Educational Research, 33,* 443–451.

Folger, J., Astin, H., & Bayer, A. (1969). *Human resources and higher education.* Staff Report of the Commission on Human Resources and Advanced Education. New York: Russell Sage Foundation.

Follman, J. (1974). Student ratings and student achievement. *JSAS Catalogue of Selected Documents in Psychology, 4,* 136. (Ms. No. 791)

Fontana, A., & Noel, B. (1973). Moral reasoning in the university. *Journal of Personality and Social Psychology, 27,* 419–429.

For class of '92, less U.S. aid: Survey indicates increased stress on college freshmen. (1989, January 9). *Chicago Tribune.*

Forgey, G. (1973). Work really does pay off. *Community and Junior College Journal, 43,* 52.

Forrest, A. (1982). *Increasing student competence and persistence: The best case for general education.* Iowa City, IA: American College Testing Program.

Forrest, A. (1985). Creating conditions for student and institutional success. In L. Noel, D. Levitz, & D. Saluri (Eds.), *Increasing student retention: Effective programs and practices for reducing the dropout rate.* San Francisco: Jossey-Bass.

Forrest, A., & Steele, J. (1978). *College outcome measures project.* Iowa City, IA: American College Testing Program.

Forrest, A., & Steele, J. (1982). *Defining and measuring general education knowledge and skills.* Iowa City, IA: American College Testing Program.

Försterling, F. (1985). Attributional retraining: A review. *Psychological Bulletin, 98,* 495–512.

Forsyth, D., & Berger, R. (1982). The effects of ethical ideology on moral behavior. *Journal of Social Psychology, 117,* 53–56.

Foster, E., & Rodgers, J. (1980). Quality of education and student earnings. *Higher Education, 8,* 21–37.

Foster, P. (1981). Clinical discussion groups: Verbal participation and outcomes. *Journal of Medical Education, 56,* 831–838.

Foster, P. (1983). Verbal participation and outcomes in medical education: A study of third-year clinical-discussion groups. In C. Ellner & C. Barnes (Eds.), *Studies in college teaching: Experimental results, theoretical interpretations and new perspectives.* Lexington, MA: D. C. Heath.

Fotion, J., Bolden, W., & Fotion, N. (1978). Political attitudes of students in three predominantly black colleges. *Journal of Negro Education, 47,* 395–401.

Foulds, M. (1971). Changes in locus of internal-external control: A growth group experience. *Comparative Group Studies, 2,* 293–300.

Foulds, M., Guinan, J., & Hannigan, P. (1974). Marathon group: Changes in scores on the California Psychological Inventory. *Journal of College Student Personnel, 15,* 474–479.

Foulds, M., Guinan, J., & Warehime, R. (1974). Marathon group: Changes in perceived locus of control. *Journal of College Student Personnel, 15,* 8–11.

Fox, G. (1974). Some observations and data on the availability of same-sex role models as a factor in undergraduate career choice. *Sociological Focus, 7,* 15–30.

Fox, R. (1986). Application of a conceptual model of college withdrawal to disadvantaged students. *American Educational Research Journal, 23,* 415–424.

Frankland, E., Corbett, M., & Rudoni, D. (1980). Value priorities of college students. *Youth and Society, 11,* 267–293.

Franks, D., Falk, R., & Hinton, J. (1973). Differential exposure to courses in two majors and differences in value responses. *Sociology of Education, 46,* 361–369.

Frantz, T. (1971). Student and non-student change. *Journal of College Student Personnel, 12,* 49–53.

Freedman, M. (1965). Personality growth in the college years. *College Board Review, 56,* 25–32.

Freedman, M. (1967). *The college experience.* San Francisco: Jossey-Bass.

Freedman, R., Whelpton, P., & Campbell, A. (1959). *Family planning, sterility, and population growth.* New York: McGraw-Hill.

Freeman, R. (1971). *The market for college trained manpower.* Cambridge, MA: Harvard University Press.

Freeman, R. (1973). Decline of labor market discrimination and economic analysis. *American Economic Review, 63,* 280–286.

Freeman, R. (1975). Overinvestment in college training? *Journal of Human Resources, 10,* 287–311.

Freeman, R. (1976). *The over-educated American.* Orlando, FL: Academic Press.

Freeman, R. (1977). Decline in economic rewards to college education. *Review of Economics and Statistics, 59,* 18–29.

Freeman, R. (1979). The effect of demographic factors on age-earning profiles. *Journal of Human Resources, 14,* 289–318.

Freeman, R. (1980). The facts about the declining economic value of college. *Journal of Human Resources, 15,* 124–142.

Freeman, R., & Hollomon, J. (1975). The declining value of college going. *Change, 7,* 24 ff.

Freeman, W. (1984). Relative long-term benefits of a PSI and a traditional-style remedial chemistry course. *Journal of Chemical Education, 61,* 617–619.

Freiden, A., & Leimer, D. (1981). The earnings of college students. *Journal of Human Resources, 16,* 152–156.

Freiden, A., & Staaf, R. (1973). Scholastic choice: An economic model of student behavior. *Journal of Human Resources, 8,* 396–404.

Freudiger, P. (1980). Life satisfaction among American women. *Dissertation Abstracts International, 40,* 6438A.

Frey, P., Leonard, D., & Beatty, W. (1975). Student ratings of instruction: Validation research. *American Educational Research Journal, 12,* 435–447.

Friedlander, J. (1980). *The importance of quality of effort in predicting college student attainment.* Unpublished doctoral dissertation, University of California, Los Angeles.

Friedlander, J. (1982). *Measuring the benefits of liberal arts education in Washington's community colleges.* Research report, Center for the Study of Community Colleges, ERIC Clearinghouse for Community Colleges.

Friedlander, J., & Pace, C. (1981). *Influences of amount of time spent versus quality of time spent on college student development.* Paper presented at the meeting of the American Educational Research Association, Los Angeles.

Friedrich, R., & Michalak, S. (1983). Why doesn't research improve teaching? Some answers from a small liberal arts college. *Journal of Higher Education, 54,* 145–163.

Froming, W., & Cooper, R. (1976). *Predicting compliance behavior from moral judgment scales.* Unpublished manuscript, University of Texas, Austin.

Fry, P. (1974). Developmental changes in identity status of university students from rural and urban backgrounds. *Journal of College Student Personnel, 15,* 183–190.

Fry, P. (1976). Changes in youth's attitudes toward authority: The transition from university to employment. *Journal of Counseling Psychology, 23,* 66–74.

Fry, P. (1977). A reply to David R. Matteson's "Two transitions and two crises in youth." *Journal of Counseling Psychology, 24,* 81–82.

Fuchs, V. (1974). *Who shall live?* New York: Basic Books.

Fuller, W. (1970). *Education, training, and worker productivity: Study of skilled workers in two firms in south India.* Unpublished doctoral dissertation, Stanford University, Stanford, CA.

Funk, R., & Willits, F. (1987). College attendance and attitude change: A panel study, 1970–81. *Sociology of Education, 60,* 224–231.

Fuqua, A. (1983). *Moral reasoning and formal operational thought: A comparison of science majors and religion majors in three church-related colleges.* Unpublished doctoral dissertation, Vanderbilt University, Nashville, TN.

Furedy, C., & Furedy, J. (1985). Critical thinking: Toward research and dialogue. In J. Donald & A. Sullivan (Eds.), *Using research to improve teaching* (New Directions for Teaching and Learning No. 23). San Francisco: Jossey-Bass.

Gadzella, G., & Fournet, G. (1975). Differences and changes among college classes (freshman through graduate levels) in self-rating of a quality student. *Journal of Educational Psychology, 67,* 243–252.

Gaff, J. (1973). Making a difference: The impacts of faculty. *Journal of Higher Education, 44,* 605–622.

Gaff, J. (1983). *General education today: A critical analysis of controversies, practices, and reforms.* San Francisco: Jossey-Bass.

Gage, N. (1974). Students' ratings of college teaching: Their justification and proper use. In N. Glasman & B. Killiat (Eds.), *Second UCSB conference on effective teaching.* Santa Barbara: University of California, Graduate School of Education and Office of Instructional Development.

Gaither, G., & Dukes, F. (1982). *A study of selected factors associated with the prediction and prevention of minority attrition.* Paper presented at the meeting of the Association for Institutional Research, Denver.

Galbraith, R., & Jones, T. (1976). *Moral reasoning: A teaching handbook for adapting Kohlberg to the classroom.* Minneapolis: Greenhaven Press.

Gallia, T. (1976). *Moral reasoning in college science and humanities students: Summary of a pilot study.* Unpublished manuscript, Glassboro State College, Glassboro, NJ.

Gallini, J. (1982). Evidence of an adaptive level grading practice through a causal approach. *Journal of Experimental Education, 50,* 188–194.

Gallo, P. (1978). Meta-analysis—A mixed meta-phor? *American Psychologist, 33,* 515–517.

Gallup, G. (1975a). *Attitudes of college students on political, social, and economic issues.* Princeton, NJ: Gallup Poll.

Gallup, G. (1975b). Students discontented with business; remain social, political liberals. In *Gallup Opinion Index, Report No. 123.* Princeton, NJ: Princeton Opinion Press.

Gamson, Z. (1966). Utilitarian and normative orientations toward education. *Sociology of Education, 39,* 46–73.

Gamson, Z. & Associates. (1984). *Liberating education.* San Francisco: Jossey-Bass.

Garcia, G., & Garcia, R. (1978). Higher education: What is the payoff? *National Association of College Admission Counselors Journal, 22,* 24–26.

Garcia, M. (1988). *Community college student persistence: A field application of the Tinto model.* Unpublished manuscript, Montclair State College, Upper Montclair, NJ.

Gardner, P., & Hwang, H. (1987). *An investigation of the components of starting salary for recent college graduates.* Paper presented at the meeting of the American Educational Research Association, Washington, DC.

Garrison, C. (1968). Political involvement and political science: A note on the basic course as an agent of political socialization. *Social Science Quarterly, 49,* 305–314.

Gates, D. (1977). Job satisfaction, job characteristics, and occupational level. *Dissertation Abstracts International, 38,* 3762-A. (University Microfilms No. 77–27, 252)

Gay, G. (1984). Implications of selected models of ethnic identity development for educators. *Journal of Negro Education, 54,* 43–52.

Gay, G. (1986). Interaction of learner control and prior understanding in computer-assisted video instruction. *Journal of Educational Psychology, 78,* 225–227.

Gelman, R., & Baillargeon, R. (1983). A review of some Piagetian concepts. In J. Flavell & E. Markman (Eds.), *Handbook of child psychology: Cognitive development* (Vol. 3). New York: John Wiley & Sons.

George, R., & Marshall, J. (1972). Personality differences among community college students. *College Student Journal, 6,* 30–36.

Gerber, S. (1970). Four approaches to freshman orientation. *Improving College and University Teaching, 18,* 57–60.

Gergen, K. (1971). *The concept of self.* New York: Holt, Rinehart & Winston.

Gerst, M., & Moos, R. (1972). Social ecology of university student residences. *Journal of Educational Psychology, 63,* 513–525.

Getzels, J., & Jackson, P. (1962). *Creativity and intelligence.* New York: John Wiley & Sons.

Gibbs, J. (1973). Black students/white university: Different expectations. *Personnel and Guidance Journal, 51,* 463–469.

Gibbs, J. (1974). Patterns of adaptation among black students at a predominantly white university. *American Journal of Orthopsychiatry, 44,* 728–740.

Gibbs, J. (1975). Use of mental health services by black students at a predominantly white university: A three-year study. *American Journal of Orthopsychiatry, 45,* 430–445.

Gifford, B. (1974). Effects of various residence hall administrative structures on students. *Journal of College Student Personnel, 15,* 133–137.

Gilligan, C. (1977). In a different voice: Women's conceptions of self and of morality. *Harvard Educational Review, 47,* 481–517.

Gilligan, C. (1982a). *In a different voice: Psychological theory and women's development.* Cambridge, MA: Harvard University Press.

Gilligan, C. (1982b). New maps of development: New visions of maturity. *American Journal of Orthopsychiatry, 52,* 199–212.

Gilligan, C. (1986a). Remapping development: The power of divergent data. In L. Cirillo & S. Wapner (Eds.), *Value presuppositions in theories of human development.* Hillsdale, NJ: Lawrence Erlbaum.

Gilligan, C. (1986b). Reply by Carol Gilligan. In L. Kerber, C. Greeno, E Maccoby, Z. Luria, C. Stack, & C. Gilligan, "On 'In a different voice': An interdisciplinary forum." *Signs: Journal of Women in Culture and Society, 11,* 324–333.

Givner, N., & Hynes, K. (1983). An investigation of change in medical students' ethical thinking. *Medical Education, 17,* 3–7.

Glass, G. (1977). Integrating findings: The meta-analysis of research. In L. Shulman (Ed.), *Review of research in education.* Itasca, IL: F. E. Peacock.

Glass, G., Cahen, L., Smith, M., & Filby, N. (1982). *School class size.* Beverly Hills, CA: Sage.

Glass, G., McGaw, B., & Smith, M. (1981). *Meta-analysis in social research.* Beverly Hills, CA: Sage.

Glatfelter, M. (1982). Identity development, intellectual development, and their relationship in reentry women students. *Dissertation Abstracts International, 43,* 3543A.

Glenn, N. (1966). The trend in differences in attitudes and behavior by educational level. *Sociology of Education, 39,* 255–275.

Glenn, N. (1980). Values, attitudes, and beliefs. In O. Brim & J. Kagan (Eds.), *Constancy and change in human development.* Cambridge, MA: Harvard University Press.

Glenn, N., & Taylor, P. (1984). Education and family income: A comparison of white married men and women in the U.S. *Social Forces, 63,* 169–183.

Glenn, N., & Weaver, C. (1978). A multivariate, multisurvey study of marital happiness. *Journal of Marriage and the Family, 40,* 269–282.

Glenn, N., & Weaver, C. (1981). Education's effects on psychological well-being. *Public Opinion Quarterly, 45,* 22–39.

Glenn, N., & Weaver, C. (1982). Further evidence on education and job satisfaction. *Social Forces, 61,* 46–55.

Glock, C. (1962). On the study of religious commitment. *Religious Education, 42,* 98–110.

Glock, C., & Stark, R. (1965). *Religion and society in tension.* Chicago: Rand McNally.

Goethals, G., & Klos, D. (1970). *Experiencing youth: First person accounts.* Boston: Little, Brown.

Goldberg, L. (1972). Student personality characteristics and optimal college learning conditions: An extensive search for trait-by-treatment interaction effects. *Instructional Science, 1,* 153–210.

Goldberger, N. (1980). *Meeting the developmental needs of the early college students: The Simon's Rock experience.* Great Barrington, MA: Simon's Rock of Bard College.

Golden, R., & Smith, D. (1983). Potential benefits of academic units in the college residence hall: An issue revisited. *Journal of College and University Student Housing, 13,* 8–13.

Goldman, J., & Olczak, P. (1976). Effects of an innovative academic program upon self-actualization and psychosocial maturity. *Journal of Educational Research, 69,* 333–334.

Goldman, J., & Olczak, P. (1980). Effect of an innovative educational program upon self-actualization and psychosocial maturity: A replication and follow-up. *Social Behavior and Personality, 8,* 41–47.

Goldman, R., & Hewitt, B. (1975). Adaptation-level as an explanation for differential standards in college grading. *Journal of Educational Measurement, 12,* 149–161.

Goldman, R., & Hudson, D. (1973). A multivariate analysis of academic abilities and strategies for successful and unsuccessful college students in different major fields. *Journal of Educational Psychology, 65,* 364–370.

Goldman, R., & Warren, R. (1973). Discriminant analysis of study strategies connected with college grade success in different major fields. *Journal of Educational Measurement, 10,* 39–47.

Goldman, R., & Widawski, M. (1976). A within-subjects technique for comparing college grading standards: Implications in the validity of the evaluation of college achievement. *Educational and Psychological Measurement, 36,* 381–390.

Goldscheider, F., & Da Vanzo, J. (1986). Semiautonomy and leaving home in early adulthood. *Social Forces, 65,* 187–201.

Goldschmid, B., & Goldschmid, M. (1974). Individualizing instruction in higher education: A review. *Higher Education, 3,* 1–24.

Goldschmid, B., & Goldschmid, M. (1976). Peer teaching in higher education: A review. *Higher Education, 5,* 9–33.

Goldstein, M. (1974). Academic careers and vocational choices of elite and non-elite students at an elite college. *Sociology of Education, 47,* 441–450.

Gondola, J., & Tuckman, B. (1985). Effects of a systematic program of exercise on selected measures of creativity. *Perceptual and Motor Skills, 60,* 53–54.

Goodman, J. (1979). The economic returns of education: An assessment of alternative models. *Social Science Quarterly, 60,* 269–283.

Gordon, M., & Arvey, R. (1975). The relationship between education and satisfaction with job content. *Academy of Management Journal, 18,* 888–892.

Gordon, R., & Howell, J. (1959). *Higher education for business.* New York: Columbia University Press.

Gorman, M., Duffy, J., & Heffernan, M. (undated). *The effect of service experience on the moral development of college students.* Unpublished report, Boston College, Chestnut Hill, MA.

Gottlieb, D., & Bell, M. (1975). Work expectations and work realities: A study of graduating college seniors. *Youth and Society, 7,* 69–83.

Gould, R. (1972). The phases of adult life. *American Journal of Psychiatry, 5,* 521–531.

Goulet, L. (1975). Longitudinal and time-lag designs in educational research: An alternate sampling model. *Review of Educational Research, 45,* 505–523.

Gourman, J. (1967). *The Gourman report.* Phoenix, AZ: Continuing Education Institute, Inc.

Gourman, J. (1983). *The Gourman report: A rating of undergraduate programs in American and international universities.* Los Angeles: National Education Standards.

Graffam, D. (1967). Dickinson College changes personality. *The Dickinson Alumnus, 44,* 2–7.

Grandy, J. (1988). Assessing changes in student values. In C. Adelman (Ed.), *Performance and judgment: Essays on principles and practice in the assessment of college student learning* (DOE Publication No. OR 88-514). Washington, DC: U.S. Government Printing Office.

Granovetter, M. (1974). *Getting a job: A study of contacts and careers.* Cambridge, MA: Harvard University Press.

Grant, W., & Eigenbrod, F. (1970). Behavioral changes influenced by structured peer group activities. *Journal of College Student Personnel, 11,* 291–295.

Grasso, J. (1977). *On the declining labor market value of schooling.* Paper presented at the meeting of the American Educational Research Association, New York.

Graves, T. (1975). A study of vocational maturity and college students' certainty and commitment to career choice. *Dissertation Abstracts International, 35,* 7056A.

Greeley, A., & Sheatsley, P. (1974). Attitudes toward racial integration. In L. Rainwater (Ed.), *Social problems and public policy: Inequality and justice.* Chicago: Aldine.

Greeley, A., & Spaeth, J. (1970). Political change among college alumni. *Sociology of Education, 43,* 106–113.

Greeley, A., & Tinsley, H. (1988). Autonomy and intimacy development in college students: Sex differences and predictors. *Journal of College Student Development, 29,* 512–520.

Green, J., Bush, D., & Hahn, J. (1980). The effects of college on students' partisanship: A research note. *Journal of Youth and Adolescence, 9,* 547–552.

Greenberg, J., & Greenberg, H. (1976). Predicting sales success—Myths and reality. *Personnel Journal, 55,* 621–627.

Greenwood, M. (1975). Research on internal migration in the U.S.: A survey. *Journal of Economic Literature, 13,* 397–433.

Greever, K., Tseng, M., & Friedland, B. (1974). Measuring change in social interest in community college freshmen. *Individual Psychologist, 11,* 4–6.

Gressler, L. (1976). The effect of research courses upon the attitudes and critical thinking abilities of graduate students. *Dissertation Abstracts International, 37,* 3994A.

Grevious, C. (1985). A comparison of occupational aspirations of urban black college students. *Journal of Negro Education, 54,* 35–42.

Griffin, L. (1976). Specification biases in estimates of socioeconomic returns to schooling. *Sociology of Education, 49,* 121–139.

Griffin, L., & Alexander, K. (1978). Schooling and socioeconomic attainments: High school and college influences. *American Journal of Sociology, 84,* 319–347.

Griffin, L., & Kalleberg, A. (1981). Stratification and meritocracy in the United States: Class and occupational recruitment patterns. *British Journal of Sociology, 32,* 1–37.

Griffith, J. (1984). *Reflective judgment scores, Davidson College students.* Unpublished manuscript, Davidson College, Davidson, NC.

Griliches, Z. (1969). Capital-skill complementarity. *Review of Economics and Statistics, 51,* 465–468.

Griliches, Z. (1976). Wages of very young men. *Journal of Political Economy, 84* (Pt. 2), S69–S86.

Griliches, Z., & Mason, W. (1972). Education, income, and ability. *Journal of Political Economy, 80* (Pt. 2), S74–S103.

Griliches, Z., & Mason, W. (1973). Education, ability, and income. In A. Goldberger & O. Duncan (Eds.), *Structural equation models in the social sciences.* New York: Seminar Press.

Groat, H., Chilson, D., & Neal, A. (1982). Sex stratification among three cohorts of recent university graduates. *Sociology and Social Research, 66,* 269–288.

Gross, E., & Grambasch, P. (1968). *University goals and academic power.* Washington, DC: American Council on Education.

Grossman, M. (1976). The correlation between health and schooling. In N.

Terleckyj (Ed.), *Household production and consumption*. New York: Columbia University Press.

Grossman, M. (1982). *Determinants of children's health* (Report PHS 81-3309). Washington, DC: National Center for Health Services.

Grossman, M., & Jacobowitz, S. (1981). Variations in infant mortality rates among counties in the United States: The roles of public policies and programs. *Demography, 18,* 695–713.

Grosz, R., & Brandt, K. (1969). Student residence and academic performance. *College and University, 44,* 240–243.

Grubb, N. (1984). The bandwagon once more: Vocational preparation for high-tech occupations. *Harvard Educational Review, 54,* 429–451.

Gruca, J. (1988). *Intergenerational benefits of college for sex-atypical career attainment in women.* Unpublished manuscript, University of Illinois, Chicago.

Gruca, J., Ethington, C., & Pascarella, E. (1988). Intergenerational effects of college graduation on career sex-atypicality in women. *Research in Higher Education, 29,* 99–124.

Gruca, J., & Pascarella, E. (1988). *The impact of college graduation on the next generation: A path analytic model.* Unpublished manuscript, University of Illinois, Chicago.

Guinan, J., & Foulds, M. (1970). Marathon group: Facilitator of personal growth? *Journal of Counseling Psychology, 17,* 145–149.

Guldhammer, A. (1983). Factors in the college experience relating to moral judgment development. *Dissertation Abstracts International, 43,* 2250A.

Guller, I. (1969). Increased stability of self-concept in students served by a college counseling center. *Personnel and Guidance Journal, 47,* 546–551.

Guloyan, E. (1986). An examination of white and non-white attitudes of university freshmen as they relate to attrition. *College Student Journal, 20,* 396–402.

Gurin, G. (1971). The impact of the college experience. In S. Withey (Ed.), *A degree and what else? Correlates and consequences of a college education.* New York: McGraw-Hill.

Gurin, G., Veroff, J., & Feld, S. (1960). *Americans view their mental health.* New York: Basic Books.

Gurin, P., & Epps, E. (1975). *Black consciousness, identity and achievement: A study of students in historically black colleges.* New York: John Wiley & Sons.

Gurin, P., & Gaylord, C. (1976). Sex-role constraints: The college-educated black woman. In D. McGuigan (Ed.), *New research on women and sex roles at the University of Michigan.* Ann Arbor: University of Michigan, Center for Continuing Education of Women.

Gurin, P., & Katz, D. (1966). *Motivation and aspiration in the Negro college* (DHEW, Office of Education, Project No. 5-0787). Ann Arbor: University of Michigan, Institute for Social Research, Survey Research Center.

Gusfield, J., Kronus, S., & Mark, H. (1970). The urban context and higher education: A delineation of issues. *Journal of Higher Education, 41,* 29–43.

Guskey, T. (1987). *Improving student learning in college classrooms.* Springfield, IL: Charles Thomas.

Guskey, T., Benninga, J., & Clark, C. (1984). Mastery learning and students' attributions at the college level. *Research in Higher Education, 20,* 491–498.

Guskey, T., & Easton, J. (1983). The characteristics of very effective teachers in urban community colleges. *Community/Junior College Quarterly of Research and Practice, 7,* 265–274.

Guskey, T., & Monsaas, J. (1979). Mastery learning: A model for academic success in urban junior colleges. *Research in Higher Education, 11,* 263–274.

Gustav, A. (1969). Retention of course material over varying intervals of time. *Psychological Reports, 25,* 727–730.

Guthrie, J., Seifert, M., & Kirsch, I. (1986). Effects of education, occupation, and setting on reading practices. *American Educational Research Journal, 23,* 151–160.

Haan, N. (1975). Hypothetical and actual moral reasoning in a situation of civil disobedience. *Journal of Personality and Social Psychology, 32,* 255–270.

Haan, N., Smith, M., & Block, J. (1968). The moral reasoning of young adults: Political-social behavior, family background, and personality correlates. *Journal of Personality and Social Psychology, 10,* 183–201.

Hackman, J., & Taber, T. (1979). Patterns of undergraduate performance related to success in college. *American Educational Research Journal, 16,* 117–138.

Haemmerlie, F. (1985). Role of immediate feedback in a personalized system of instruction: Evidence of a negative impact. *Psychological Reports, 56,* 947–954.

Hafner, A. (1985). *Gender differences in college students' educational and occupational aspirations, 1971–1983.* Paper presented at the meeting of the American Educational Research Association, Chicago.

Hall, R., Rodeghier, M., & Useem, B. (1986). Effects of education on attitude to protest. *American Sociological Review, 51,* 564–573.

Hall, W., Cross, W., & Freedle, R. (1972). Stages in the development of black awareness: An empirical investigation. In R. Jones (Ed.), *Black psychology.* New York: Harper & Row.

Hall, W., Freedle, R., & Cross, W. (1972). *Stages in the development of black identity* (ACT Research Rep. No. 50). Iowa City, IA: American College Testing Program.

Haller, A. (1982). Reflections on the social psychology of status attainment. In R. Hauser, D. Mechanic, A. Haller, & T. Hauser (Eds.), *Social structure and behavior.* New York: Academic Press.

Haller, A., & Spenner, K. (1977). Occupational income differentials in status attainment. *Rural Sociology, 42,* 517–535.

Hancock, B. (1981). The effect of guided design on the critical thinking ability of college level administrative science students. *Dissertation Abstracts International, 42,* 4275A.

Hancock, B., Coscarelli, W., & White, G. (1983). Critical thinking and content acquisition using a modified guided design process for large course sections. *Educational and Psychological Research, 3,* 139–149.

Hanks, M., and Eckland, B. (1976). Athletics and social participation in the educational attainment process. *Sociology of Education, 49,* 271–294.

Hanoch, G. (1967). An economic analysis of earnings and schooling. *Journal of Human Resources, 2,* 310–329.

Hansen, W. (1963). Total and private rates of return to investment in schooling. *Journal of Political Economy, 61,* 128–140.

Hansen, W. (1970). *Education, income and human capital.* New York: Columbia University Press.

Hansen, W., Weisbrod, B., & Scanlon, W. (1970). Schooling and earnings of low achievers. *American Economic Review, 50,* 409–418.

Hansford, B., & Hattie, J. (1982). The relationship between self and achievement/performance measures. *Review of Educational Research, 52,* 123–142.

Hanson, G. (Ed.). (1982). *Measuring student development* (New Directions for Student Services, No. 20). San Francisco: Jossey-Bass.

Hanson, G. (1988). *Educational goal attainment: A longitudinal study.* Paper presented at the meeting of the Association for Institutional Research, Phoenix, AZ.

Hanushek, E., Jackson, J., & Kain, J. (1974). Model specification, use of aggregate data and the ecological correlation fallacy. *Political Methodology, 1,* 89–107.

Hanushek, E., & Kain, J. (1972). On the value of *Equality of educational opportunity* as a guide to public policy. In F. Mosteller & D. Moynihan (Eds.), *On equality of educational opportunity.* New York: Vintage Books.

Hardin, L. (1977). A study of the influence of a physics personalized system of instruction versus lecture on cognitive reasoning, attitudes, and critical thinking. *Dissertation Abstracts International, 38,* 4711A–4712A.

Hardy, K. (1974). Social origins of American scientists and scholars. *Science, 185,* 497–506.

Hardy, M. (1984). Effects of education on retirement among white male wage-and-salary workers. *Sociology of Education, 57,* 84–98.

Hargens, L. (1969). *Occupations and the social structure.* Englewood Cliffs, NJ: Prentice-Hall.

Harper, F. (1975). *Black students: White campus.* Washington, DC: American Personnel and Guidance Association Press.

Harrell, T. (1969). The personality of high earning MBAs in big business. *Personnel Psychology, 22,* 457–463.

Harrell, T. (1970). The personality of high earning MBAs in small business. *Personnel Psychology, 23,* 369–375.

Harrell, T. (1972). High earning MBAs. *Personnel Psychology, 25*, 523–530.

Harrell, T., & Harrell, M. (1984). *Stanford MBA careers: A 20 year longitudinal study* (Research paper No. 723). Stanford, CA: Stanford University, Graduate School of Business.

Harris, J. (1970). *Gain scores on the CLEP General Examination and an overview of research.* Paper presented at the meeting of the American Educational Research Association, Minneapolis.

Harris, J., & Hurst, P. (1972). Does college assure academic growth? *Change, 4,* 8–9, 60.

Harris, R. (1983). Changing women's self-perceptions: Impact of a psychology of women course. *Psychological Reports, 52,* 314.

Harrison, A., Scriven, E., & Westerman, J. (1974). Traditional vs. emergent—A study of value change. *Intellect, 102,* 398–400.

Hartnett, R. (1976). Departments within colleges differ in impact. *Findings, 3,* 5–8.

Hartnett, R., & Centra, J. (1977). The effects of academic departments on student learning. *Journal of Higher Education, 48,* 491–507.

Hartson, L. (1936). Does college training influence test intelligence? *Journal of Educational Psychology, 27,* 481–491.

Harvey, E., & Kalwa, R. (1983). Occupational status attainments of university graduates. *Canadian Review of Sociology and Anthropology, 20,* 435–453.

Harvey, O., Hunt, D., & Schroder, H. (1961). *Conceptual systems and personality organization.* New York: John Wiley & Sons.

Harvey, P., & Lannholm, G. (1960). *Achievement in three major fields during the last two years of college* (Graduate Record Examination Special Report 60-Z). Princeton, NJ: Educational Testing Service.

Haspel, A. (1978). The questionable role of higher education as an occupational screening device. *Higher Education, 7,* 279–294.

Hasting, P., & Hoge, D. (1981). Religious trends among college students, 1948–79. *Social Forces, 60,* 517–531.

Hatch, D. (1970). Differential impact of college on males and females. In *Women on campus: 1970 a symposium.* Ann Arbor: University of Michigan, Center for Continuing Education for Women.

Hau, K. (1983). *A cross-cultural study of a moral judgment test (the D.I.T.).* Unpublished master's thesis, Chinese University, Hong Kong.

Haukoos, G., & Penick, J. (1983). The influence of classroom climate on science process and content achievement of community college students. *Journal of Research in Science Teaching, 20,* 629–637.

Hause, J. (1972). Earnings profile: Ability and schooling. *Journal of Political Economy, 80,* S108–S138.

Hauser, R. (1970). Context and consex: A cautionary tale. *American Journal of Sociology, 75,* 645–664.

Hauser, R. (1971). *Socioeconomic background and educational performance.* Rose Monograph Series. Washington, DC: American Sociological Association.

Hauser, R. (1973). Disaggregating a social-psychological model of educational attainment. In A. Goldberger & O. Duncan (Eds.), *Structural equation models in the social sciences*. New York: Seminar Press.

Hauser, R. (1974). Contextual analysis revisited. *Sociological Methods and Research, 2*, 365–375.

Hauser, R., & Daymont, T. (1977). Schooling, ability, and earnings: Cross-sectional findings 8 to 14 years after high school graduation. *Sociology of Education, 50*, 182–206.

Hauser, R., & Featherman, D. (1977). *The process of stratification: Trends and analyses*. New York: Academic Press.

Hauser, S. (1976). Loevinger's model and measure of ego development: A critical review. *Psychological Bulletin, 83*, 928–955.

Hauser, S., & Kassendorf, E. (Eds.). (1983). *Black and white identity formation* (2nd ed.). Malabar, FL: R. E. Krieger.

Haveman, R., & Wolfe, B. (1984). Schooling and well-being: The role of nonmarket effects. *Journal of Human Resources, 19*, 377–407.

Havemann, E., & West, P. (1952). *They went to college*. San Diego: Harcourt Brace Jovanovich.

Haven, E. (1964). *The sophomore norming sample for the general examinations of the college-level examination program* (Statistical Report SR-64-63). Princeton, NJ: Educational Testing Service.

Hay, J., Evans, K., & Lindsay, C. (1970). Student part-time jobs: Relevant or nonrelevant. *Vocational Guidance Quarterly, 19*, 113–118.

Hayden, V. (1978). A study of the effects of traditional biology and selected biological science curriculum study (BSCS) minicourses on the attitudes, achievement levels, and critical thinking abilities of students at Alcorn State University. *Dissertation Abstracts International, 39*, 2167A.

Hayes, A. (1981). An investigation of the effects of dilemma content on level of reasoning in the reflective judgment interview. *Dissertation Abstracts International, 42*, 2564B.

Hayes, E. (1974). Environmental press and psychological need as related to academic success of minority group students. *Journal of Counseling Psychology, 21*, 299–304.

Healy, C., Mitchell, J., & Mourton, D. (1987). Age and grade differences in career development among community college students. *Review of Higher Education, 10*, 247–258.

Heaps, R., & Thorstenson, C. (1972). Self-concept changes immediately and one year after survival training. *Therapeutic Recreation Journal, 8*, 60–63.

Hearn, J. (1980). Major choice and the well-being of college men and women: An examination from developmental, structural, and organizational perspectives. *Sociology of Education, 53*, 164–178.

Hearn, J. (1984). The relative roles of academic, ascribed, and socioeconomic characteristics in college destinations. *Sociology of Education, 57*, 22–30.

Hearn J. (1987). Impacts of undergraduate experiences on aspirations and plans for graduate and professional education. *Research in Higher Education, 27,* 119–141.

Hearn, J., & Olzak, S. (1981). The role of college major departments in the reproduction of sexual inequality. *Sociology of Education, 54,* 195–205.

Hearn, J., & Olzak, S. (1982). Sex differences in the implications of the links between major departments and the occupational structure. In P. Perun (Ed.), *The undergraduate woman: Issues in educational equity.* Lexington, MA: Lexington Books.

Heath, D. (1965). *Explorations of maturity: Studies of mature and immature college men.* New York: Appleton-Century-Crofts.

Heath, D. (1968). *Growing up in college.* San Francisco: Jossey-Bass.

Heath, D. (1976a). Adolescent and adult predictors of vocational adaptation. *Journal of Vocational Behavior, 9,* 1–19.

Heath, D. (1976b). Competent fathers: Their personalities and marriages. *Human Development, 19,* 26–39.

Heath, D. (1976c). What the enduring effects of higher education tell us about a liberal education. *Journal of Higher Education, 47,* 173–190.

Heath, D. (1977a). Academic predictors of adult maturity and competence. *Journal of Higher Education, 48,* 613–632.

Heath, D. (1977b). *Maturity and competence: A transcultural view.* New York: Gardner.

Heath, D. (1977c). Prescription for collegiate survival: Return to liberally educate today's youth. *Liberal Education, 63,* 338–350.

Heath, D. (1978). A model of becoming a liberally educated and mature student. In C. Parker (Ed.), *Encouraging development in college students.* Minneapolis: University of Minnesota Press.

Heath, R. (1964). *The reasonable adventurer.* Pittsburgh, PA: University of Pittsburgh Press.

Heath, R. (1973). Form, flow and full-being response. *The Counseling Psychologist, 4,* 56–63.

Heckman, R., Lazenby, R., & Moore, L. (1968). *College graduate progress study.* Dearborn, MI: Ford Motor Company.

Hedegard, J., & Brown, D. (1969). Encounters of some Negro and white freshmen with a public multiversity. *Journal of Social Issues, 25,* 131–144.

Hedlund, D., & Jones, J. (1970). Effect of student personnel services on completion rates in two-year colleges. *Journal of College Student Personnel, 11,* 196–199.

Hegarty, E. (1978). Levels of scientific enquiry in university science laboratory classes: Implications for curriculum deliberations. *Research in Science Education, 8,* 45–47.

Heidbreder, E. (1946). The attainment of concepts: I. Terminology and methodology. *Journal of General Psychology, 35,* 173–189.

Heilweil, M. (1973). The influences of dormitory architecture on resident behavior. *Environment and Behavior, 5,* 377–412.

Heise, D. (1969). Problems in path analysis and causal inference. In E. Borgatta & G. Bohrnstedt (Eds.), *Sociological methodology 1969.* San Francisco: Jossey-Bass.

Heist, P. (1968). Considerations in the assessment of creativity. In P. Heist (Ed.), *The creative college student: An unmet challenge.* San Francisco: Jossey-Bass.

Heist,. P., McConnell, T., Matsler, F., & Williams, P. (1961). Personality and scholarship. *Science, 133,* 362–367.

Heist, P., & Yonge, G. (1968). *Omnibus Personality Inventory manual (Form F).* New York: Psychological Corporation.

Helmreich, R., Spence, J., & Gibson, R. (1982). Sex-role attitudes: 1972–1980. *Personality and Social Psychology Bulletin, 8,* 656–663.

Helms, J. (Ed.). (1990a). *Black and white racial identity: Theory, research, and practice.* New York: Greenwood.

Helms, J. (1990b). Introduction: Review of racial identity terminology. In J. Helms (Ed.), *Black and white racial identity: Theory, research, and practice.* New York: Greenwood.

Helms, J. (1990c). An overview of black racial identity theory. In J. Helms (Ed.), *Black and white racial identity: Theory, research, and practice.* New York: Greenwood.

Henderson, C., & Ottinger, C. (1985). College degrees—still a ladder to success? *Journal of College Placement, 45,* 35 ff.

Henry, M., & Renaud, H. (1972). Examined and unexamined lives. *The Research Reporter, 7,* 5–8.

Hensley, T., & Sell, D. (1979). A study abroad program: An examination of impacts on student attitudes. *Teaching Political Science, 6,* 387–412.

Henson, J. (1980). Institutional excellence and student achievement: A study of college quality and its impact on educational and career achievement. *Dissertation Abstracts International, 41,* 958A.

Heppner, P., & Krause, J. (1979). A career seminar course. *Journal of College Student Personnel, 20,* 300–305.

Herndon, S. (1982). A longitudinal study of financial aid persisters, dropouts, and stopouts: A discriminant analysis. *Dissertation Abstracts International, 42,* 4736A–4737A.

Herndon, S. (1984a). Recent findings concerning the relative importance of housing to student retention. *Journal of College and University Student Housing, 14,* 27–31.

Herndon, S. (1984b). The impact of financial aid on student persistence. *Journal of Student Financial Aid, 14,* 3–9.

Hess, A., & Bradshaw, H. (1970). Positiveness of self-concept and ideal self as a function of age. *Journal of Genetic Psychology, 117,* 57–67.

Hesse-Biber, S. (1985). Male and female students' perceptions of their academic environment and future career plans: Implications for higher education. *Human Relations, 38,* 91–105.

Heston, J. (1950). Educational growth as shown by retests on the graduate record examination. *Educational and Psychological Measurement, 10,* 367–370.

Heverly, M. (1987). *Community college student persistence: Longitudinal tracking of multiple cohorts.* Paper presented at the annual meeting of the Association for Institutional Research, Kansas City, MO.

Hicks, M., Koller, S., & Tellett-Royce, N. (1984). Liberal arts students and their skills. *Journal of College Placement, 44,* 31–35.

Hicks, R. (1974). The relationship between publishing and teaching effectiveness. *California Journal of Educational Research, 25,* 140–146.

Hill, R., & Stafford, F. (1974). Allocation of time to pre-school children and educational opportunity. *Journal of Human Resources, 9,* 323–343.

Hill, R., & Stafford, F. (1977). Family background and lifetime earnings. In F. Juster (Ed.), *The distribution of economic well-being.* Cambridge, MA: Ballinger.

Hill, R., & Stafford, F. (1980). Parental care of children: Time diary estimates of quantity, predictability, and variety. *Journal of Human Resources, 15,* 219–239.

Hiller, J., Fisher, G., & Kaess, W. (1969). A computer investigation of verbal characteristics of effective classroom lecturing. *American Educational Research Journal, 6,* 661–675.

Hilton, T., & Schrader, W. (1986). *Pathways to graduate school: An empirical study based on national longitudinal data.* Paper presented at the annual meeting of the American Educational Research Association, San Francisco.

Hind, R., & Wirth, T. (1969). The effect of university experience on occupational choice among undergraduates. *Sociology of Education, 42,* 50–70.

Hines, C., Cruickshank, D., & Kennedy, J. (1982). *Measures of teacher clarity and their relationships to student achievement and satisfaction.* Paper presented at the annual meeting of the American Educational Research Association, New York.

Hines, C., Cruickshank, D., & Kennedy, J. (1985). Teacher clarity and its relationship to student achievement and satisfaction. *American Educational Research Journal, 22,* 87–99.

Hines, F., Tweeten, L., & Redfern, M. (1970). Social and private rates of return to investment in schooling, by race-sex groups and regions. *Journal of Human Resources, 5,* 318–340.

Hinkle, L., Whitney, L., Lehman, E., Dunn, J., Benjamin, B., King, R., Plakun, A., & Flehinger, B. (1968). Occupation, education, and coronary heart disease. *Science, 161,* 238–246.

Hinrichsen, J. (1972). Prediction of grade point average from estimated study behaviors. *Psychological Reports, 31,* 974.

Hipple, J. (1973). Personal growth outcomes due to human relations training experiences. *Journal of College Student Personnel, 14,* 156–164.

Hirsch, E. (1987). *Cultural literacy: What every American needs to know.* Boston: Houghton Mifflin.

Ho, M. (1987). *Family therapy with ethnic minorities.* Newbury Park, CA: Sage.

Hochstein, S., & Butler, R. (1983). The effects of the composition of a financial aid package on student retention. *Journal of Student Financial Aid, 13,* 21–26.

Hodge, R., Siegel, P., & Rossi, P. (1964). Occupational prestige in the United States, 1925–63. *American Journal of Sociology, 70,* 286–302.

Hodgson, J., & Fischer, J. (1979). Sex differences in identity and intimacy development in college youth. *Journal of Youth and Adolescence, 8,* 437–450.

Hoffer, S. (1973). Private rates of return to higher education for women. *Review of Economics and Statistics, 55,* 482–486.

Hoffman, S. (1984). Black-white differences in returns to higher education: Evidence from the 1970s. *Economics of Education Review, 3,* 13–21.

Hogan, R., & Dickstein, E. (1972). A measure of moral values. *Journal of Consulting and Clinical Psychology, 39,* 210–214.

Hoge, D. (1970). College students' value patterns in the 1950's and 1960's. *Sociology of Education, 44,* 170–197.

Hoge, D. (1974). *Commitment on campus: Changes in religion and values over five decades.* Philadelphia: Westminster.

Hoge, D. (1976). Changes in college students' value patterns in the 1950's, 1960's, and 1970's. *Sociology of Education, 49,* 155–163.

Hoge, D., & Bender, I. (1974). Factors influencing value change among college graduates in adult life. *Journal of Personality and Social Psychology, 54, 29,* 572–585.

Hoge, D., Luna, C., & Miller, D. (1981). Trends in college students' values between 1952 and 1979: A return of the fifties? *Sociology of Education,* 263–274.

Hoiberg, A., & Pugh, W. (1978). Predicting navy effectiveness: Expectations, motivation, personality, aptitude, and background variables. *Personnel Psychology, 31,* 841–852.

Holcomb, W., & Anderson, W. (1978). Expressed and inventoried vocational interests as predictors of college graduation and vocational choice. *Journal of Vocational Behavior, 12,* 290–296.

Hole, J., & Levine, E. (1971). *The rebirth of feminism.* New York: Quadrangle.

Holland, J. (1959). A theory of vocational choice. *Journal of Counseling Psychology, 14,* 319–324.

Holland, J. (1963). Explorations of a theory of vocational choice and achievement II: A four year predictive study. *Psychological Reports, 12,* 547–594.

Holland, J. (1966). *The psychology of vocational choice: A theory of personality types and model environments.* Waltham, MA: Blaisdell.

Holland, J. (1968). Explorations of a theory of vocational choice: VI. A longitudinal study using a sample of typical college students. *Journal of Applied Psychology, Monograph Supplement, 52.* 37 pp.

Holland, J. (1973). *Making vocational choices: A theory of careers.* Englewood Cliffs, NJ: Prentice-Hall.

Holland, J. (1984). *Making vocational choices: A theory of careers* (2nd ed.). Englewood Cliffs, NJ: Prentice-Hall.

Holland, J. (1985). *Making vocational choices: A theory of vocational personalities and work environments.* Englewood Cliffs, NJ: Prentice-Hall.

Holland, J., Magoon, T., & Spokane, A. (1981). Counseling psychology: Career interventions and related research and theory. *Annual Review of Psychology, 32,* 279–305.

Holland, J., & Whitney, D. (1968). *Changes in the vocational plans of college students: Orderly or random?* (ACT Research Rep. No. 25). Iowa City, IA: American College Testing Program.

Holloway, D. (1976). A study of the effects of the Thirteen Colleges Curriculum Program open-ended laboratory experiences on the critical thinking abilities and attitudes toward science of college freshmen. *Dissertation Abstracts International, 36,* 4222A.

Holt, N., & Tygart, C. (1969). Political tolerance and higher education. *Pacific Sociological Review, 12,* 27–33.

Holt, R. (1980). Loevinger's measure of ego development: Reliability and national norms for male and female short forms. *Journal of Personality and Social Psychology, 39,* 909–920.

Hood, A. (1984). Student development: Does participation affect growth? *Bulletin of the Association of College Unions-International, 54,* 16–19.

Hood, A. (1986a). The Erwin Identity Scale. In A. Hood (Ed.), *The Iowa Student Development Inventories.* Iowa City, IA: Hitech Press.

Hood, A. (Ed.). (1986b). *The Iowa student development inventories.* Iowa City, IA: Hitech Press.

Hood, A., & Jackson, L. (1986a). Assessing the development of competence. In A. Hood (Ed.), *The Iowa Student Development Inventories.* Iowa City, IA: Hitech Press.

Hood, A., & Jackson, L. (1986b). The Iowa Managing Emotions Inventory. In A. Hood (Ed.), *The Iowa Student Development Inventories.* Iowa City, IA: Hitech Press.

Hood, A., & Jackson, L. (1986c). The Iowa Developing Autonomy Inventory. In A. Hood (Ed.), *The Iowa Student Development Inventories.* Iowa City, IA: Hitech Press.

Hood, A., & Mines, R. (1986). Freeing of interpersonal relationships. In A. Hood (Ed.), *The Iowa Student Development Inventories*. Iowa City, IA: Hitech Press.

Hood, A., Riahinejad, A., & White, D. (1986). Changes in ego identity during the college years. *Journal of College Student Personnel, 27,* 107–113.

Hoover, K., Baumann, V., & Schafer, S. (1970). The influence of class-size variation on cognitive and affective learning of college freshmen. *Journal of Experimental Education, 38,* 39–43.

Hoover, K., & Schutz, R. (1968). Student attitude change in an introductory education course. *Journal of Educational Research, 61,* 300–303.

Horak, V., & Horak, W. (1982). The influence of student locus of control and teaching method on mathematics achievement. *Journal of Experimental Education, 51,* 18–21.

Horn, J. (1970). Organization of data on life-span development of human abilities. In L. Goulet & P. Baltes (Eds.), *Life-span developmental psychology: Research and theory*. New York: Academic Press.

Horn, J., & Donaldson, G. (1976). On the myth of intellectual decline in adulthood. *American Psychologist, 31,* 701–719.

Hossler, D. (undated). *College enrollment: The impact of perceived economic benefits*. Chicago: Loyola University.

Hountras, P., & Brandt, K. (1970). Relation of student residence to academic performance in college. *Journal of Educational Research, 63,* 351–354.

House, J. S. (1977). The three faces of social psychology. *Sociometry, 40,* 161–177.

Houser, B., & Beckman, L. (1980). Background characteristics and women's dual-role attitudes. *Sex Roles, 6,* 355–366.

Houston, J. (1983). Kohlberg-type moral instruction and cheating behavior. *College Student Journal, 17,* 196–204.

Howard, A. (1986). College experiences and managerial performance. *Journal of Applied Psychology Monographs, 71,* 530–552.

Hoyt, D. (1966). The relationship between college grades and adult achievement: A review of the literature. *Educational Record, 47,* 70–75.

Hoyt, D., & Muchinsky, P. (1973). Occupational success and college experiences of engineering graduates. *Engineering Education, 63,* 622–623.

Hoyt, D., & Spangler, R. (1976). Faculty research involvement and instructional outcomes. *Research in Higher Education, 4,* 113–122.

Hudelson, E. (1928). *Class size at the college level*. Minneapolis: University of Minnesota Press.

Huebner, L. (Ed.). (1979). *Redesigning campus environments* (New Directions for Student Services No. 8). San Francisco: Jossey-Bass.

Huebner, L. (1980). Interaction of student and campus. In U. Delworth, G. Hanson, & Associates (Eds.), *Student services: A handbook for the profession*. San Francisco: Jossey-Bass.

Huebner, L. (1989). Interaction of student and campus. In U. Delworth, G. Hanson, & Associates (Eds.), *Student services: A handbook for the profession* (2nd ed.). San Francisco: Jossey-Bass.

Hughes, M., & Winston, R., Jr. (1987). Effects of fraternity membership on interpersonal values. *Journal of College Student Personnel, 28,* 405–411.

Hull, W., & Lemke, W. (1975). The assessment of off-campus higher education. *International Review of Education, 21,* 195–206.

Hull, W., Lemke, W., & Houang, R. (1977). *The American undergraduate, off-campus and overseas: A study of the educational validity of such programs* (CIEE Occasional Paper No. 20). New York: Council on International Educational Exchange.

Hult, R. (1979). The relationship between ego identity status and moral reasoning in university women. *Journal of Psychology, 103,* 203–207.

Hult, R., Cohn, S., & Potter, D. (1984). An analysis of student note-taking effectiveness and learning outcomes in the college lecture setting. *Journal of Instructional Psychology, 11,* 175–181.

Hummel-Rossi, B. (1976). The determinants of intellectual commitment in university students. *Character Potential, 11,* 164–173.

Hunt, D. (1966). A conceptual systems change model and its application to education. In O. Harvey (Ed.), *Experience, structure and adaptability.* New York: Springer.

Hunt, D. (1970). A conceptual level matching model for coordinating learner characteristics with educational approach. *Interchange, 1,* 68–72.

Hunt, D. (1971). *Matching models in education: The coordination of teaching method with student characteristics.* Toronto: Ontario Institute for Studies in Education.

Hunt, D. (1976). Teacher's adaptation: Reading and flexing to students. *Journal of Teacher Education, 27,* 268–275.

Hunt, D., Butler, L., Noy, J., & Rosse, M. (1978). *Assessing conceptual level by the paragraph completion method.* Toronto: Ontario Institute for Studies in Education.

Hunt, S. (1963). Income determinants for college graduates and the return to educational investment. *Yale Economic Essays, 3,* 305–357.

Hunt, T., Klieforth, A., & Atwell, C. (1977). Community colleges: A democratizing influence? *Community College Review, 4,* 15–24.

Hunter, E. (1942). Changes in scores of college students on the American Council Psychological Examination at yearly intervals during the college course. *Journal of Educational Research, 36,* 284–291.

Huntley, C. (1967). Changes in values during the four years of college. *College Student Survey, 1,* 43–48.

Hursh, B., & Borzak, L. (1979). Towards cognitive development through field studies. *Journal of Higher Education, 50,* 63–78.

Husband, R. (1976). *Significant others: A new look at attrition.* Paper presented at the meeting on Future Solutions to Today's Problems, Association for Innovation in Higher Education, Philadelphia.

Huston-Stein, A., & Baltes, P. (1976). Theory and method in life-span developmental psychology: Implications for child development. In H. Reese (Ed.), *Advances in child development and behavior* (Vol. 3). New York: Academic Press.

Hutt, C. (1983). College students' perceptions of male and female career patterns. *Journal of College Student Personnel, 24,* 240–246.

Hyman, H., & Wright, C. (1979). *Education's lasting influence on values.* Chicago: University of Chicago Press.

Hyman, H., Wright, C., & Reed, J. (1975). *The enduring effects of education.* Chicago: University of Chicago Press.

Inglehart, R. (1977). *The silent revolution: Changing values and political styles among western politics.* Princeton, NJ: Princeton University Press.

Inhelder, B., & Piaget, J. (1958). *The growth of logical thinking from childhood to adolescence.* New York: Basic Books.

Inkeles, A. (1966). Social structure and the socialization of competence. *Harvard Educational Review, 36,* 265–283.

Insel, P., & Moos, R. (1974). Psychological environments: Expanding the scope of human ecology. *American Psychologist, 29,* 179–186.

Itzkowitz, S., & Petrie, R. (1986). The student Developmental Task Inventory: Scores of northern versus southern students. *Journal of College Student Personnel, 27,* 406–412.

Itzkowitz, S., & Petrie, R. (1988). Northern black urban college students and the revised Student Developmental Task Inventory. *Journal of Multicultural Counseling and Development, 16,* 63–72.

Iverson, B., Pascarella, E., & Terenzini, P. (1984). Informal faculty-student contact and commuter college freshmen. *Research in Higher Education, 21,* 123–136.

Iwai, S., & Churchill, W. (1982). College attrition and the financial support systems of students. *Research in Higher Education, 17,* 105–113.

Jackman, M. (1978). General and applied tolerance: Does education increase commitment to racial integration? *American Journal of Political Science, 22,* 302–324.

Jackman, M., & Muha, M. (1984). Education and intergroup attitudes: Moral enlightenment, superficial democratic commitment, or ideological refinement? *American Sociological Review, 49,* 751–769.

Jackson, B. (1975). Black identity development. In L. Golubschick & B. Persky (Eds.), *Urban social and educational issues.* Dubuque, IA: Kendall-Hunt.

Jackson, G. (1980). Methods for integrative reviews. *Review of Educational Research, 50,* 438–460.

Jackson, T. (1961). The effects of intercollegiate debating on critical thinking ability. *Dissertation Abstracts International, 21,* 3556A.

Jacob, P. (1957). *Changing values in college: An exploratory study of the impact of college teaching.* New York: Harper & Row.

Jacobi, M., Astin, A., & Ayala, F. (1987). *College student outcomes assessment:*

A talent development perspective (ASHE-ERIC Higher Education Report No. 7). Washington, DC: Association for the Study of Higher Education.

Jacobs, J. (1986). The sex-aggregation of fields of study: Trends during the college years. *Journal of Higher Education, 57,* 134–154.

Jacobs, M. (1975). *Women's moral reasoning and behavior in a contractual form of prisoner's dilemma.* Unpublished doctoral dissertation, University of Toledo, Toledo, OH.

Jacobsen, T., Price, P., de Mik, G., & Taylor, C. (1965). *An exploratory study of predictors of physician performance* (DHEW Research Project No. OE-3-10-136). Washington, DC: U.S. Office of Education.

Jagacinski, C., LeBold, K., & Shell, K. (1986). The relationship between undergraduate work experience and job placement of engineers. *Engineering Education, 76,* 232–236.

Jakobsen, L. (1986). Greek affiliation and attitude change: Developmental implications. *Journal of College Student Personnel, 27,* 523–527.

James, L., & Jones, A. (1974). Organizational climate: A review of theory and research. *Psychological Bulletin, 81,* 1096–1112.

James, N. (1976). Students abroad: Expectations versus reality. *Liberal Education, 62,* 599–607.

Janos, P., Robinson, N., & Lunneborg, C. (1987). *The academic performance and adjustment status of early college entrants, non-accelerated peers, and college classmates.* Unpublished manuscript, University of Washington, Seattle.

Jencks, C., Bartlett, S., Corcoran, M., Crouse, J., Eaglesfield, D., Jackson, G., McClelland, K., Mueser, P., Olneck, M., Schwartz, J., Ward, S., & Williams, J. (1979). *Who gets ahead? The determinants of economic success in America.* New York: Basic Books.

Jencks, C., Crouse, J., & Mueser, P. (1983). The Wisconsin model of status attainment: A national replication with improved measures of ability and aspiration. *Sociology of Education, 56,* 3–19.

Jencks, C., & Riesman, D. (1968). *The academic revolution.* New York: Doubleday.

Jensen, E. (1980). *Persistence in college: The impact of financial assistance to students.* Paper presented at the annual meeting of the American Educational Research Association, Boston.

Jensen, E. (1981). Student financial aid and persistence in college. *Journal of Higher Education, 52,* 280–293.

Jensen, E. (1983). Financial aid and educational outcomes: A review. *College and University, 58,* 287–302.

Jensen, E. (1984). Student financial aid and degree attainment. *Research in Higher Education, 20,* 117–127.

Jepsen, V. (1951). Scholastic proficiency and vocational success. *Educational and Psychological Measurement, 11,* 616–628.

Johansson, C., & Rossmann, J. (1973). Persistence at a liberal arts college: A replicated five-year longitudinal study. *Journal of Counseling Psychology, 20,* 1–9.

Johnson, J. (1969). Change in student teacher dogmatism. *Journal of Educational Research, 62,* 224–226.

Johnson, J., Smither, R., & Holland, J. (1981). Evaluating vocational interventions: A tale of two career development seminars. *Journal of Counseling Psychology, 28,* 180–183.

Johnson, K., & Ruskin, R. (1977). *Behavioral instruction: An evaluative review.* Washington, DC: American Psychological Association.

Johnson, K., Sulzer-Azaroff, B., & Mass, C. (1977). The effects of internal proctoring upon examination performance in a personalized instruction course. *Journal of Personalized Instruction, 1,* 113–117.

Johnson, L., O'Malley, P., & Bachman, J. (1987). *National trends in drug use and related factors among American high school students and young adults, 1975–1986.* Rockville, MD: National Institute on Drug Abuse.

Johnson, M., & Lashley, K. (1988). Influence of Native Americans' cultural commitment on preferences for counselor ethnicity. *Journal of Multicultural Counseling and Development, 17,* 115–122.

Johnson, P., & Fay, L. (1950). The Johnson-Neyman technique, its theory and application. *Psychometrika, 15,* 349–367.

Johnson, R. (1987). Factors related to the postbaccalaureate careers of black graduates of selected four-year institutions in Alabama. In A. Pruitt (Ed.), *In pursuit of equality in higher education.* Dix Hills, NY: General Hall.

Johnson, R., & Chapman, D. (1980). *Involvement in academic and social activities and its relationship to student persistence—A study across institutional types.* Paper presented at the meeting of the Association for Institutional Research, Atlanta.

Johnson, T. (1981). The relationships among college science students' achievement, engaged time, and personal characteristics. *Dissertation Abstracts International, 42,* 3534A.

Johnson, T., & Butts, D. (1983). The relationships among college science student achievement, engaged time, and personal characteristics. *Journal of Research in Science Teaching, 20,* 357–366.

Jones, G., & Jacklin, C. (1988). Changes in sexist attitudes toward women during introductory women's and men's studies courses. *Sex Roles, 18,* 611–622.

Jones, J. (1974). An experimental study of four interdisciplinary approaches to promoting critical thinking skills and personal development in the college classroom. *Dissertation Abstracts International, 35,* 5216A.

Jones, J., & Finnell, W. (1972). Relationships between college experiences and attitudes of students from economically deprived backgrounds. *Journal of College Student Personnel, 13,* 314–318.

Jones, L. (1987). Adapting to the first semester of college: A test of Heath's model of maturing. *Journal of College Student Personnel, 28,* 205–211.

Jones, S. (1984). *Evaluating the impact of freshman orientation on student persistence and academic performance.* Fort Lauderdale, FL: Nova University. (ERIC Document Reproduction Service No. ED 241 085)

Jones, S. (1985). The impact of career counseling on freshman student retention, grade point average and career maturity. *College Student Affairs Journal, 6,* 38–54.

Jones, V. (1970). Attitudes of college students and their changes: A 37-year study. *Genetic Psychology Monographs, 81,* 3–80.

Jones, V. (1982). *Report on the use of the COMP Objective Test and Activity Inventory to assess Nazareth College general evaluation outcomes.* Kalamazoo, MI: Nazareth College. (ERIC Document Reproduction Service No. ED 219 025)

Jones, W., Rambo, W., & Russell, D. (1978). The effect of prior information on attitude change. *Journal of Social Psychology, 106,* 203–205.

Jordan-Cox, C. (1987). Psychosocial development of students in traditionally black institutions. *Journal of College Student Personnel, 28,* 504–512.

Joreskog, K. (1973). A general method for estimating a linear structural equation system. In A. Goldberger & O. Duncan (Eds.), *Structural equation models in the social sciences.* New York: Seminar Press.

Joreskog, K., & Sorbom, D. (1979). *Advances in factor analysis and structural equation models.* Cambridge, MA: ABT Books.

Joreskog, K., & Sorbom, D. (1983). *LISREL VI: Analysis of linear structural relationships by maximum likelihood and least-squares methods.* Chicago: National Educational Resources.

Josselson, R. (1973). Psychodynamic aspects of identity formation in college women. *Journal of Youth and Adolescence, 2,* 3–52.

Josselson, R. (1980). Ego development in adolescence. In J. Adelson (Ed.), *Handbook of Adolescent Psychology.* New York: John Wiley & Sons.

Josselson, R. (1987). *Finding herself: Pathways to identity development in women.* San Francisco: Jossey-Bass.

Jud, D., & Walker, J. (1982). Racial differences in returns to schooling and experience among prime-age males: 1967–1975. *Journal of Human Resources, 17,* 623–632.

Juhasz, A., & Walker, A. (1988). The impact of study abroad on university students' self-esteem and self-efficacy. *College Student Journal, 22,* 329–341.

Kafka, E. (1968). The effects of overseas study on worldmindedness and other selected variables of liberal arts students. *Dissertation Abstracts International, 29,* 481A–482A.

Kagerer, R. (1974). Toward an affective outcome of higher education. *Journal of Educational Measurement, 11,* 203–208.

Kalish, R., & Johnson, A. (1972). Value similarities and differences in three generations of women. *Journal of Marriage and the Family, 34,* 49–54.

Kalleberg, A. (1977). Work values and job rewards: A theory of job satisfaction. *American Sociological Review, 42,* 124–143.

Kalleberg, A., & Sorensen, A. (1973). The measurement of the effects of overtraining on job attitudes. *Sociological Methods and Research, 2,* 215–238.

Kalleberg, A., & Sorensen, A. (1979). Sociology of labor markets. *Annual Review of Sociology, 5,* 351–379.

Kamens, D. (1968). *Social class, college contexts, and educational attainment: Social class and college dropout.* Paper presented at the meeting of the American Sociological Association, Boston.

Kamens, D. (1971). The college "charter" and college size: Effects on occupational choice and college attrition. *Sociology of Education, 44,* 270–296.

Kamens, D. (1974). Colleges and elite formation: The case of prestigious American colleges. *Sociology of Education, 47,* 354–378.

Kamens, D. (1977). Legitimating myths and educational organization: The relationship between organizational ideology and formal structure. *American Sociological Review, 42,* 208–219.

Kamens, D. (1979). Student status aspirations: A research note on the effects of colleges. *Youth & Society, 11,* 83–91.

Kammer, P. (1984). Changes in beginning counseling students' self-perceptions. *Counseling and Values, 28,* 122–127.

Kanouse, D., Haggstrom, G., Blaschke, T., Kahan, J., Lisowski, W., & Morrison, P. (1980). *Effects of postsecondary experiences on aspirations, attitudes, and self-conceptions.* Santa Monica, CA: Rand Corporation. (ERIC Document Reproduction Service No. ED 214 430)

Karabel, J. (1972). Community colleges and social stratification. *Harvard Educational Review, 42,* 521–562.

Karabel, J. (1974). Protecting the portals: Class and the community college. *Social Policy, 5,* 12–18.

Karabel, J. (1986). Community colleges and social stratification in the 1980s. In L. S. Zwerling (Ed.), *The community college and its critics* (New Directions for Community Colleges No. 54). San Francisco: Jossey-Bass.

Karabel, J., & Astin, A. (1975). Social class, academic ability, and college quality. *Social Forces, 53,* 381–398.

Karabel, J., & McClelland, K. (1983). *The effects of college rank on labor market outcomes.* Paper presented at the meeting of the American Sociological Association, Detroit.

Karabel, J., & McClelland, K. (1987). Occupational advantage and the impact of college rank on labor market outcomes. *Sociological Inquiry, 57,* 323–347.

Karman, F. (1973). *Women: Personal and environmental factors in career choice.* Paper presented at the meeting of the American Educational Research Association, New Orleans.

Karp, D., & Yoels, W. (1976). The college classroom: Some observations on the meanings of student participation. *Sociology and Social Research, 60,* 421–439.

Karplus, R. (1974). *Science curriculum improvement study: Teacher's handbook.* Berkeley, CA: Lawrence Hall of Science.

Kaseman, T. (1980). *A longitudinal study of moral development of the West Point class of 1981*. West Point, NY: United States Military Academy, Department of Behavioral Sciences and Leadership.

Kasschau, P., Ransford, H., & Bengston, V. (1974). Generational consciousness and youth movement participation: Contrasts in blue collar and white collar youth. *Journal of Social Issues, 30,* 69–94.

Katchadourian, H., & Boli, J. (1985). *Careerism and intellectualism among college students: Patterns of academic and career choice in the undergraduate years*. San Francisco: Jossey-Bass.

Katona, G., Dunkelberg, W., Hendricks, G., & Schmiedeskamp, J. (1970). *1969 Survey of consumer finances*. Ann Arbor: University of Michigan, Institute for Social Research.

Katz, A. (1974). Schooling, age, and length of unemployment. *Industrial and Labor Relations Review, 28,* 597–605.

Katz, J. (1974). Coeducational living: Effects upon male-female relationships. In D. DeCoster & P. Mable (Eds.), *Student development and education in college residence halls*. Washington, DC: American College Personnel Association.

Katz, J., & Associates. (1968). *No time for youth: Growth and constraint in college students*. San Francisco: Jossey-Bass.

Keeley, S., Browne, M., & Kreutzer, J. (1982). A comparison of freshmen and seniors on general and specific essay tests of critical thinking. *Research in Higher Education, 17,* 139–154.

Kegan, R. (1979). The evolving self: A process conception for ego psychology. *Counseling Psychologist, 8,* 5–34.

Kegan, R. (1980). Making meaning: The constructive-developmental approach to persons and practice. *Personnel and Guidance Journal, 58,* 373–380.

Kegan, R. (1982). *The evolving self*. Cambridge, MA: Harvard University Press.

Keller, F. (1968). Good-bye teacher. *Journal of Applied Behavior Analysis, 1,* 79–89.

Keniston, K. (1969). Moral development, youthful activism, and modern society. *Youth and Society, 1,* 110–127.

Keniston, K. (1970). Youth: A "new" stage of life. *American Scholar, 39,* 631–654.

Keniston, K. (1971a). *Youth and dissent: The rise of a new opposition*. New York: Harcourt Brace Jovanovich.

Keniston, K. (1971b). Youth as a stage of life. In S. Feinstein, P. Giovacchini, & A. Miller (Eds.), *Adolescent psychiatry: Vol. 3. Developmental and clinical studies*. New York: Basic Books.

Kennedy, S., & Dimick, K. (1987). Career maturity and professional sports expectations of college football and basketball players. *Journal of College Student Personnel, 28,* 293–297.

Kenney, P. (1989). *Effects of supplemental instruction on student performance in a college-level mathematics course.* Paper presented at the meeting of the American Educational Research Association, San Francisco.

Kenny, D. (1979). *Correlation and causality.* New York: John Wiley & Sons.

Kerber, L., Greeno, C., Maccoby, E., Luria, Z., Stack, C., & Gilligan, C. (1986). On "In a different voice": An interdisciplinary forum. *Signs: Journal of Women in Culture and Society, 11,* 304–333.

Kerckhoff, A. (1976). The status attainment process: Socialization or allocation? *Social Forces, 55,* 368–381.

Kerckhoff, A., & Jackson, R. (1982). Types of education and the occupational attainments of young men. *Social Forces, 61,* 24–45.

Kerlinger, F. (1979). *Behavioral research: A conceptual approach.* New York: Holt, Rinehart & Winston.

Kerlinger, F. (1986). *Foundations of behavioral research* (3rd ed.). New York: Holt, Rinehart & Winston.

Kerlinger, F., & Pedhazur, E. (1973). *Multiple regression in behavioral research.* New York: Holt, Rinehart & Winston.

Key, V. (1961). *Public opinion and American democracy.* New York: Alfred Knopf.

Khalili, H., & Hood, A. (1983). A longitudinal study of change in conceptual level in college. *Journal of College Student Personnel, 24,* 389–394.

Kiernan, I., & Daniels, R. (1967). Signs of social change through an exploratory study of 23 Negro students in a community college. *Journal of Negro Education, 36,* 129–135.

Kiewra, K. (1983). The relationship between notetaking over an extended period and actual course-related achievement. *College Student Journal, 17,* 381–385.

Kiker, B., & Rhine, S. (1987). Fringe benefits and the earnings equation: A test of the consistency hypothesis. *Journal of Human Resources, 22,* 126–137.

Killian, C., & Warrick, C. (1980). Steps to abstract reasoning: An interdisciplinary program for cognitive development. *Alternative Higher Education, 4,* 189–200.

Kilson, M. (1973a, September 2). The black experience at Harvard. *New York Times Magazine,* pp. 13, 31–32, 34, 37.

Kilson, M. (1973b, April). Blacks at Harvard: Crisis and change. *Harvard Bulletin.*

Kimball, R., & Gelso, C. (1974). Self-actualization in a marathon growth group: Do the strong get stronger? *Journal of Counseling Psychology, 21,* 38–42.

King, J., Biggs, S., & Lipsky, S. (1984). Students' self-questioning and summarizing as reading study strategies. *Journal of Reading Behavior, 16,* 205–218.

King, L., & King, D. (1985). Sex-role egalitarianism: Biographical and personality correlates. *Psychological Reports, 57,* 787–792.

King, M., Walder, L., & Pavey, S. (1970). Personality change as a function of volunteer experience in a psychiatric hospital. *Journal of Consulting and Clinical Psychology, 35,* 423–425.

King, P. (1977). *The development of reflective judgment and formal operational thinking in adolescents and young adults.* Unpublished doctoral dissertation, University of Minnesota, Minneapolis and St. Paul.

King, P. (1978). William Perry's theory of intellectual and ethical development. In L. Knefelkamp, C. Widick, & C. Parker (Eds.), *Applying new developmental findings* (New Directions for Student Services No. 4). San Francisco: Jossey-Bass.

King, P. (1986). Formal reasoning in adults: A review and critique. In R. Mines & K. Kitchener (Eds.), *Adult cognitive development.* New York: Praeger.

King, P., Kitchener, K., Davison, M., Parker, C., & Wood, P. (1983). The justification of beliefs in young adults: A longitudinal study. *Human Development, 26,* 106–116.

King, P., Kitchener, K., & Wood, P. (1985). The development of intellect and character: A longitudinal-sequential study of intellectual and moral development in young adults. *Moral Education Forum, 10,* 1–13.

King, P., Kitchener, K., Wood, P., & Davison, M. (1985). *Relationships across developmental domains: A longitudinal study of intellectual, moral, and ego development.* Paper presented at the conference Beyond Formal Operations 2: The Development of Adolescent and Adult Thought and Perception, Harvard University, Cambridge, MA.

King, P., & Parker, C. (1978). *Assessing intellectual development in the college years: A report of the Instructional Improvement Project, 1976–1977.* Unpublished manuscript, University of Minnesota, Minneapolis and St. Paul.

King, P., Taylor, J., & Ottinger, D. (1989). *Intellectual development of black college students on a predominantly white campus.* Paper presented at the meeting of the Association for the Study of Higher Education, Atlanta.

King, P., Wood, P., & Mines, R. (1990). Critical thinking among college and graduate students. *Review of Higher Education, 13,* 167–186.

King, S. (1970). The clinical assessment of change. In J. Whiteley & H. Sprandel (Eds.), *The growth and development of college students.* Washington, DC: American Personnel and Guidance Association.

King, S. (1973). *Five lives at Harvard: Personality change during college.* Cambridge, MA: Harvard University Press.

Kingston, P. (1981). The credential elite and the credential route to success. *Teachers College Record, 82,* 589–600.

Kinloch, G., & Perrucci, R. (1969). Social origins, academic achievement, and mobility channels: Sponsored and contest mobility among college graduates. *Social Forces, 48,* 36–45.

Kinnick, M., & Kempner, K. (1988). Beyond "front door" access: Attaining the bachelor's degree. *Research in Higher Education, 29,* 299–318.

Kintzer, F., & Wattenbarger, J. (1985). *The articulation/transfer phenomenon:*

Patterns and directions. Washington, DC: American Association of Community and Junior Colleges, National Center for Higher Education.

Kirchner, J., & Hogan, R. (1972). Student values: A longitudinal study. *Psychology, 9,* 36–39.

Kirschenbaum, D., & Perri, M. (1982). Improving academic competence in adults: A review of recent research. *Journal of Counseling Psychology, 29,* 76–94.

Kitabchi, G. (1985). *Multivariate analyses of urban community college student performance on the ACT College Outcomes Measures Program test.* Paper presented at the meeting of the American Educational Research Association, Chicago.

Kitagawa, E., & Hauser, P. (1973). *Differential mortality in the United States: A study of socioeconomic epidemiology.* Cambridge, MA: Harvard University Press.

Kitchener, K. (1977). *Intellectual development in late adolescents and young adults: Reflective judgment and verbal reasoning.* Unpublished doctoral dissertation, University of Minnesota, Minneapolis and St. Paul.

Kitchener, K. (1978). Intellectual development in late adolescents and young adults: Reflective judgment and verbal reasoning. *Dissertation Abstracts International, 39,* 936B.

Kitchener, K. (1982). Human development and the college campus: Sequences and tasks. In G. Hanson (Ed.), *Measuring student development* (New Directions for Student Services No. 20). San Francisco: Jossey-Bass.

Kitchener, K. (1983). Educational goals and reflective thinking. *Educational Forum, 47,* 75–95.

Kitchener, K. (1986). The reflective judgment model: Characteristics, evidence, and measurement. In R. Mines & K. Kitchener (Eds.), *Adult cognitive development.* New York: Praeger.

Kitchener, K., & King, P. (1981). Reflective judgment: Concepts of justification and their relationship to age and education. *Journal of Applied Developmental Psychology, 2,* 89–116.

Kitchener, K., & King, P. (1985). *The reflective judgment model: Ten years of research.* Paper presented at the symposium Beyond Formal Operations 2: The Development of Adolescent and Adult Thought and Perception, Harvard University, Cambridge, MA.

Kitchener, K., & King, P. (1990). The reflective judgment model: Ten years of research. In M. Commons, C. Armon, L. Kohlberg, F. Richards, T. Grotzer, & J. Sinnott (Eds.), *Adult development: Models and methods in the study of adolescent and adult thought.* New York: Praeger.

Kitchener, K., King, P., Davison, M., Parker, C., & Wood, P. (1984). A longitudinal study of moral and ego development in young adults. *Journal of Youth and Adolescence, 13,* 197–211.

Kitchener, K., King, P., Wood, P., & Davison, M. (1985). *A longitudinal-sequential study of epistemic cognition in young adults.* Unpublished manuscript.

Kitchener, K., King, P., Wood, P., & Davison, M. (1989). Sequentiality and consistency in the development of reflective judgment: A six year longitudinal study. *Journal of Applied Developmental Psychology, 10,* 73–95.

Kitchener, K., & Kitchener, R. (1981). The development of natural rationality: Can formal operations account for it? In J. Meacham & N. Santilli (Eds.), *Social development in youth: Structure and content.* Basel: S. Karger.

Kitchener, K., & Wood, P. (1987). Development of concepts of justification in German university students. *International Journal of Behavioral Development, 10,* 171–185.

Klassen, P. (1983–1984). Changes in personal orientation and critical thinking among adults returning to school through weekend college: An alternative evaluation. *Innovative Higher Education, 8,* 55–67.

Klatsky, S., & Hodge, R. (1971). A canonical correlation analysis of occupational mobility. *Journal of the American Statistical Association, 66,* 16–22.

Kleeman, J. (1974). The Kendall College human potential seminar model: Research. *Journal of College Student Personnel, 15,* 89–95.

Klein, S., & Maher, J. (1968). Education level, attitudes, and future expectations among first-level management. *Personnel Psychology, 21,* 43–53.

Klitgaard, R. (1985). *Choosing elites.* New York: Basic Books.

Knapp, C. (1977). Education and differences in postschool human investment. *Economic Inquiry, 15,* 283–289.

Knefelkamp, L. (1974). *Developmental instruction: Fostering intellectual and personal growth in college students.* Unpublished doctoral dissertation, University of Minnesota, Minneapolis and St. Paul.

Knefelkamp, L., Parker, C., & Widick, C. (1978). Jane Loevinger's milestones of development. In L. Knefelkamp, C. Widick, & C. Parker (Eds.), *Applying new developmental findings* (New Directions for Student Services No. 4). San Francisco: Jossey-Bass.

Knefelkamp, L., Widick, C., & Parker, C. (Eds.). (1978). *Applying new developmental findings* (New Directions for Student Services No. 4). San Francisco: Jossey-Bass.

Knoop, R. (1981). Age and correlates of locus of control. *Journal of Psychology, 108,* 103–106.

Knox, W. (1971). A comparative study of fraternity and non-fraternity members on selected personality variables. *Dissertation Abstracts International, 32,* 2421A.

Knox, W., Lindsay, P., & Kolb, M. (1988). *Higher education institutions and young adult development.* Unpublished manuscript, University of North Carolina at Greensboro.

Koch, J. (1972). Student choice of undergraduate major field of study and private internal rates of return. *Industrial and Labor Relations Review, 26,* 680–685.

Kocher, E., & Pascarella, E. (1988). *The effects of institutional transfer on status attainment.* Paper presented at the meeting of the American Educational Research Association, New Orleans.

Kohen, A., Nestel, G., & Karmas, C. (1978). Factors affecting individual persistence rates in undergraduate college programs. *American Educational Research Journal, 5,* 233–252.

Kohlberg, L. (1958). *The development of modes of moral thinking and choice in the years ten to sixteen.* Unpublished doctoral dissertation, University of Chicago.

Kohlberg, L. (1964). Development of moral character and moral ideology. In M. Hoffman (Ed.), *Review of child development research* (Vol. 1). New York: Russell Sage Foundation.

Kohlberg, L. (1969). Stage and sequence: The cognitive-developmental approach to socialization. In D. Goslin (Ed.), *Handbook of socialization theory and research.* Chicago: Rand McNally.

Kohlberg, L. (1971). Stages of moral development. In C. Beck, B. Crittenden, & E. Sullivan (Eds.), *Moral education.* Toronto: University of Toronto Press.

Kohlberg, L. (1972).The cognitive-developmental approach to moral education. *Humanist, 32,* 13–16.

Kohlberg, L. (1975). A cognitive-developmental approach to moral education. *Phi Delta Kappan, 56,* 670–677.

Kohlberg, L. (1976). Moral stages and moralization: The cognitive-developmental approach. In T. Lickona (Ed.), *Moral development and behavior: Theory, research and social issues.* New York: Holt, Rinehart & Winston.

Kohlberg, L. (1981a). *Essays on moral development: Vol. 1. The philosophy of moral development: Moral stages and the idea of justice.* New York: Harper & Row.

Kohlberg, L. (1981b). *The meaning and measurement of moral development.* Worcester, MA: Clark University Press.

Kohlberg, L. (1984). *Essays on moral development: Vol. 2. The psychology of moral development: The nature and validity of moral stages.* New York: Harper & Row.

Kohlberg, L., & Candee, D. (1984). The relationship of moral judgment to moral action. In W. Kurtines & J. Gewirtz (Eds.), *Morality, moral behavior, and moral development.* New York: Wiley-Interscience.

Kohlberg, L., Levine, C., & Hewer, A. (1983). *Moral stages: A current formulation and a response to critics* (Contributions to Human Development Series, Vol. 10). New York: Karger.

Kohn, M., & Schooler, C. (1969). Class, occupations and orientation. *American Sociological Review, 34,* 659–678.

Kohn, M., & Schooler, C. (1978). The reciprocal effects of the substantive complexity of work and intellectual flexibility: A longitudinal assessment. *American Journal of Sociology, 84,* 24–52.

Kohn, M., & Schooler, C. (Eds.). (1983). *Work and personality: An inquiry into the impact of social stratification.* Norwood, NJ: Ablex.

Kolb, D. (1976). *Learning styles inventory technical manual.* Boston: McBer.

Kolb, D. (1981). Learning styles and disciplinary differences. In A. Chickering & Associates, *The modern American college: Responding to the new realities of diverse students and a changing society.* San Francisco: Jossey-Bass.

Kolb, D. (1984). *Experiential learning: Experience as the source of learning development.* Englewood Cliffs, NJ: Prentice-Hall.

Kolb, D., & Goldman, M. (1973). *Toward a typology of learning styles and learning environments: An investigation of the impact of learning styles and discipline demands on the academic performance, social adaptation and career choices of MIT seniors* (Working Paper 688-773). Boston: MIT Sloan School of Management.

Kolodiy, G. (1975). The cognitive development of high school and college science students. *Journal of College Science Teaching, 5,* 20–22.

Kolstad, A. (1982, November 5). Does college pay? Wage rates before and after leaving school. *National Center for Education Statistics Bulletin.*

Komarovsky, M. (1985). *Women in college: Shaping new feminine identities.* New York: Basic Books.

Korn, H. (1986). *Psychological models explaining the impact of college on students.* Ann Arbor: University of Michigan, School of Education, National Center for Research to Improve Postsecondary Teaching and Learning.

Korn, J. (1968). Personality scale changes from the freshman year to the senior year. In J. Katz & Associates, *No time for youth: Growth and constraint in college students.* San Francisco: Jossey-Bass.

Korschgen, A., Whitehurst, C., & O'Gorman, D. (1978). The effect of values clarification on self-understanding. *Journal of College Student Personnel, 19,* 407–409.

Kosobud, R., & Morgan, J. (1964). *Consumer behavior of individual families over two and three years.* Ann Arbor: University of Michigan, Survey Research Center.

Kowalski, C. (1977). *The impact of college on persisting and nonpersisting students.* New York: Philosophical Library.

Kraack, T. (1985). *The relation of moral development to involvement and leadership experiences.* Unpublished doctoral dissertation, University of Minnesota, Minneapolis and St. Paul.

Kramer, D. (1983). Post-formal operations? A need for further conceptualization. *Human Development, 26,* 91–105.

Kramer, G., et al. (1985). Why students persist in college: A categorical analysis. *NACADA Journal, 5,* 1–17.

Kramer, L., & Kramer, M. (1968). The college library and the drop-out. *College and Research Libraries, 29,* 310–312.

Kramer, R. (1968). *Moral development in young adulthood.* Unpublished doctoral dissertation, University of Chicago.

Krasnow, R., & Longino, C. (1973). Reference and membership group influence of fraternities on student political orientation change. *Journal of Social Psychology, 91,* 163–164.

Krate, R., Leventhal, G., & Silverstein, B. (1974). Self-perceived transformation of Negro-to-black identity. *Psychological Reports, 35,* 1071–1075.

Krebs, R., & Kohlberg, L. (1975). Moral judgment and ego controls as determinants of resistance to cheating. In L. Kohlberg & E. Turiel (Eds.), *Recent research in moral development.* New York: Holt, Rinehart & Winston.

Kreiger, T. (1980). A longitudinal study of the relationship between federal financial aid packaging and retention for the members of the freshman class of 1974–1975 at Troy State University. *Dissertation Abstracts International, 41,* 960A.

Kroger, J., & Haslett, S. (1988). Separation-individuation and ego identity status in late adolescence: A two-year longitudinal study. *Journal of Youth and Adolescence, 17,* 59–79.

Kuh, G. (1976). Persistence of the impact of college on attitudes and values. *Journal of College Student Personnel, 17,* 116–122.

Kuh, G. (1977). Factors associated with postcollege changes in personality characteristics. *Journal of College Student Personnel, 18,* 362–370.

Kuh, G. (1981). *Persistence of college related changes in personality functioning ten years after graduation.* Paper presented at the meeting of the American Educational Research Association, Los Angeles.

Kuh, G. (1985). The case for attendance: The outcomes of higher education. *Journal of College Admissions, 7,* 3–9.

Kuh, G. (1987). *A brief for incorporating organizational theory in student affairs preparation and research.* Paper presented at the meeting of the Association for the Study of Higher Education, Baltimore.

Kuh, G., & Kauffman, N. (1985). The impact of study abroad on personal development. *Journal of International Student Personnel, 2,* 6–10.

Kuh, G., Krehbiel, L., & MacKay, K. (1988). *Personal development and the college student experience: A review of the literature.* Trenton, NJ: New Jersey Department of Higher Education, College Outcomes Evaluation Program.

Kuh, G., Schuh, J., Whitt, E., Andreas, R., Lyons, J., Strange, C., Krehbiel, L., & MacKay, K. (in press). *Involving colleges: Encouraging student learning and personal development through out-of-class experiences.* San Francisco: Jossey-Bass.

Kuh, G., Whitt, E., & Shedd, J. (1988). *Student affairs work, 2001: A paradigmatic odyssey* (ACPA Media Publication No. 42). Alexandria, VA: American College Personnel Association.

Kuhn, D., & Brannock, J. (1977). Development of the isolation of variables scheme in experimental and "natural experiment" contexts. *Developmental Psychology, 13,* 9–14.

Kukla, R., Veroff, J., & Douvan, E. (1979). Social class and the use of professional help for personal problems: 1957 and 1976. *Journal of Health and Social Behavior, 20,* 2–16.

Kulik, C., Kulik, J., & Bangert-Drowns, R. (1990). Effectiveness of mastery learning programs: A meta-analysis. *Review of Educational Research, 60,* 265–299.

Kulik, C., Kulik, J., & Shwalb, B. (1983). College programs for high-risk and disadvantaged students: A meta-analysis of findings. *Review of Educational Research, 53,* 397–414.

Kulik, J. (1982). Individualized systems of instruction. In H. Mitzel (Ed.), *Encyclopedia of educational research* (5th ed.) (Vol. 2). New York: Free Press.

Kulik, J. (1983). What can science educators teach chemists about teaching chemistry? A symposium: How can chemists use educational technology effectively? *Journal of Chemical Education, 60,* 957–959.

Kulik, J., Cohen, P., & Ebeling, B. (1980). Effectiveness of programmed instruction in higher education. *Educational Evaluation and Policy Analysis, 2,* 51–64.

Kulik, J., Jaksa, P., & Kulik, C. (1978). Research on component features of Keller's personalized system of instruction. *Journal of Personalized Instruction, 3,* 2–14.

Kulik, J., & Kulik, C. (1979). College teaching. In P. Peterson & H. Walberg (Eds.), *Research on teaching: Concepts, findings and implications.* Berkeley, CA: McCutcheon.

Kulik, J., Kulik, C., & Carmichael, K. (1974). The Keller plan in science teaching. *Science, 83,* 379–383.

Kulik, J., Kulik, C., & Cohen, P. (1979a). A meta-analysis of outcome studies of Keller's personalized system of instruction. *American Psychologist, 34,* 307–318.

Kulik, J., Kulik, C., & Cohen, P. (1979b). Research on audio-tutorial instruction: A meta-analysis of comparative studies. *Research in Higher Education, 11,* 321–341.

Kulik, J., Kulik, C., & Cohen, P. (1980). Effectiveness of computer-based college teaching. A meta-analysis of findings. *Review of Educational Research, 50,* 525–544.

Kulik, J., & McKeachie, W. (1975). The evaluation of teachers in higher education. In F. Kerlinger (Ed.), *Review of research in education* (Vol. 3). Itasca, IL: F. E. Peacock.

Kurfiss, J. (1977). Sequentiality and structure in a cognitive model of college student development. *Developmental Psychology, 13,* 565–571.

Kurfiss, J. (1988). *Critical thinking: Theory, research, practice, and possibilities* (ASHE-ERIC Higher Education Report No. 2). Washington, DC: Association for the Study of Higher Education.

Kutner, N., & Brogan, D. (1980). The decision to enter medicine: Motivations, social support, and discouragements for women. *Psychology of Women Quarterly, 5,* 341–357.

LaBouvie-Vief, G. (1980). Beyond formal operations: Uses and limits of pure logic in life-span development. *Human Development, 23,* 141–161.

LaCounte, D. (1987). American Indian students in college. In D. Wright (Ed.), *Responding to the needs of today's minority students* (New Directions for Student Services No. 38). San Francisco: Jossey-Bass.

Lacy, W. (1978). Interpersonal relationships as mediators of structural effects: College student socialization in a traditional and an experimental university environment. *Sociology of Education, 51,* 201–211.

Ladd, E., & Lipset, S. (1975). *The dividend academy: Professors and politics.* New York: McGraw-Hill.

Lamare, J. (1975). Using political science courses to inculcate political orientations. *Teaching Political Science, 2,* 409–432.

Lambert, M., Segger, J., Staley, J., Spencer, B., & Nelson, D. (1978). Reported self-concept and self-actualizing value changes as a function of academic classes with wilderness experiences. *Perceptual and Motor Skills, 46,* 1035–1040.

Lamont, L. (1979). *Campus shock: A firsthand report on college life today.* New York: E. P. Dutton.

Land, M. (1979). Low-inference variables of teacher clarity: Effects on student concept learning. *Journal of Educational Psychology, 71,* 795–799.

Land, M. (1980). Teacher clarity and cognitive level of questions: Effects on learning. *Journal of Experimental Education, 49,* 48–51.

Land, M. (1981a). Actual and perceived teacher clarity: Relations to student achievement in science. *Journal of Research in Science Teaching, 18,* 139–143.

Land, M. (1981b). Combined effect of two teacher clarity variables on student achievement. *Journal of Experimental Education, 50,* 14–17.

Land, M., & Smith, L. (1979a). Effects of a teacher clarity variable on student achievement. *Journal of Educational Research, 72,* 196–197.

Land, M., & Smith, L. (1979b). The effect of low inference teacher clarity inhibitors on student achievement. *Journal of Teacher Education, 30,* 55–57.

Land, M., & Smith, L. (1981). College student ratings and student behavior: An experimental study. *Journal of Social Studies Research, 5,* 19–22.

Lando, M. (1975). The interaction between health and education. *Social Security Bulletin, 38,* 16–22.

Lane, R. (1968). Political education in the midst of life's struggles. *Harvard Educational Review, 38,* 468–494.

Lang, D. (1984). Education, stratification, and the academic hierarchy. *Research in Higher Education, 21,* 329–352.

Lang, D. (1987). Stratification and prestige hierarchies in graduate and professional education. *Sociological Inquiry, 57,* 12–31.

Lannholm, G. (1952). Educational growth during the second two years of college. *Educational and Psychological Measurement, 12,* 645–653.

Lannholm, G., & Pitcher, B. (1959). *Mean score changes on the Graduate Re-*

cord Examination Area Tests for college students tested three times in a four-year period. Unpublished manuscript, Educational Testing Service, Princeton, NJ.

Lansing, J., & Mueller, E. (1967). *The geographic mobility of labor.* Ann Arbor: University of Michigan, Institute for Social Research.

Lara, J. (1981). *Differences in quality of academic effort between successful and unsuccessful community college transfer students.* Los Angeles: University of California.

Laufer, R., & Bengston, V. (1974). Generations, aging, and social stratification: On the development of generational units. *Journal of Social Issues, 30,* 181–205.

Laughlin, J. (1976). A sacred cow—class size. *College and University, 51,* 339–347.

Laumann, F., & Rapoport, R. (1968). The institutional effect on career achievement of technologists: A multiple classification analysis. *Human Relations, 28,* 227–239.

LaVoie, J. (1976). Ego identity formation in middle adolescence. *Journal of Youth and Adolescence, 5,* 371–385.

Lawrence, G. (1982). *People types and tiger stripes* (2nd ed.). Gainesville, FL: Center for Applications of Psychological Type.

Lawrence, G. (1984). A synthesis of learning style research involving the MBTI. *Journal of Psychological Type, 8,* 2–15.

Lawrenz, F. (1985). Aptitude-treatment effects of laboratory grouping methods for students of differing reasoning ability. *Journal of Research in Science Teaching, 22,* 279–287.

Lawson, A. (1985). A review of research on formal reasoning and science teaching. *Journal of Research in Science Teaching, 22,* 569–617.

Lawson, A., Nordland, F., & DeVito, A. (1974). Piagetian formal operational tasks: A crossover study of learning effect and reliability. *Science Education, 58,* 267–276.

Lawson, A., & Snitgen, D. (1982). Teaching formal reasoning in a college biology course for preservice teachers. *Journal of Research in Science Teaching, 19,* 233–248.

Lawson, J. (1980). *The relationship between graduate education and the development of reflective judgment: A function of age or educational experience?* Unpublished doctoral dissertation, University of Minnesota, Minneapolis and St. Paul.

Layard, R., & Psacharopoulos, G. (1974). The screening hypothesis and the returns to education. *Journal of Political Economy, 82,* 983–998.

Lazarsfeld, P., & Menzel, H. (1961). On the relation between individual and collective properties. In A. Etzioni (Ed.), *Complex organizations: A sociological reader.* New York: Holt, Rinehart & Winston.

Lazear, E. (1977). Education: Consumption or production? *Journal of Political Economy, 85,* 569–598.

Learned, W., & Wood, B. (1938). *The student and his knowledge: A report to the Carnegie Foundation on the results of the high school and college examinations of 1928, 1930, and 1932* (Bulletin No. 29). New York: The Carnegie Foundation for the Advancement of Teaching.

Learner, R. (1986). *Concepts and theories of human development* (2nd ed.). New York: Random House.

LeBold, W., Thoma, E., Gillis, J., & Hawkins, G. (1960). *A study of the Purdue University engineering graduate* (Engineering Extension Series Bulletin No. 99). West Lafayette, IN: Purdue University.

Lee, L. (1982). Health and wage: A simultaneous equation model with multiple discrete indicators. *International Economic Review, 23,* 199–122.

Leemon, T. (1972). *The rites of passage in a student culture: A study of the dynamics of transition.* New York: Teachers College Press.

Lefcourt, H. (1982). *Locus of control: Current trends in theory and research* (2nd ed.). Hillsdale, NJ: Lawrence Erlbaum.

Lehmann, I. (1963). Changes in critical thinking, attitudes, and values from freshman to senior years. *Journal of Educational Psychology, 54,* 305–315.

Lehmann, I. (1968). Changes from freshman to senior years. In K. Yamamoto (Ed.), *The college student and his culture.* Boston: Houghton Mifflin.

Lehmann, I., & Dressel, P. (1962). *Critical thinking, attitudes, and values in higher education.* East Lansing: Michigan State University.

Lehmann, I., & Dressel, P. (1963). *Changes in critical thinking, ability, attitudes, and values associated with college attendance.* East Lansing: Michigan State University.

Lei, T. (1981). *The development of moral, political, and legal reasoning in Chinese societies.* Unpublished master's thesis, University of Minnesota, Minneapolis and St. Paul.

Lei, T., & Cheng, S. (1984). *An empirical study of Kohlberg's theory and scoring system of moral judgment in Chinese society.* Unpublished manuscript, Harvard University, Center for Moral Education, Cambridge, MA.

Leib, J., & Snyder, W. (1967). Effects of group discussions on underachievement and self-actualization. *Journal of Counseling Psychology, 14,* 282–285.

Leibowitz, A. (1974a). Education and home production. *American Economic Review, 64,* 243–250.

Leibowitz, A. (1974b). Home investments in children. *Journal of Political Economy, 82,* S111–S131.

Leibowitz, A. (1975). Education and the allocation of women's time. In F. Juster (Ed.), *Education, income, and human behavior.* New York: McGraw-Hill.

Leibowitz, A. (1977a). Family background and economic success: A review of the evidence. In P. Taubman (Ed.), *Kinometrics: Determinants of socioeconomic success within and between families.* Amsterdam: North Holland.

Leibowitz, A. (1977b). Parental inputs and children's achievement. *Journal of Human Resources, 12*, 242–251.

Leigh, J. (1981). Hazardous occupations, illness, and schooling. *Economics of Education Review, 1*, 381–388.

Leming, J. (1978). Cheating behavior, situational influence and moral development. *Journal of Educational Research, 71*, 214–217.

Leming, J. (1979). *The relationship between principled moral reasoning and cheating behavior under threat and non-threat situations.* Paper presented at the meeting of the American Educational Research Association, San Francisco.

Lemkau, J. (1983). Women in male-dominated professions: Distinguishing personality and background characteristics. *Psychology of Women Quarterly, 8*, 144–165.

Lenihan, G., & Rawlins, M. (1987). The impact of a women's studies program: Challenging and nourishing the true believers. *Journal of the National Association of Women, Deans, Administrators, and Counselors, 50*, 3–10.

Lenning, O., Beal, P., & Sauer, K. (1980). *Retention and attrition: Evidence for action and research.* Boulder, CO: National Center for Higher Education Management Systems.

Lenning, O., & Hanson, G. (1977). Adult students at two-year colleges: A longitudinal study. *Community/Junior College Research Quarterly, 1*, 271–287.

Lenning, O., Lee, Y., Micek, S., & Service, A. (1977). *A structure for the outcomes of postsecondary education.* Boulder, CO: National Center for Higher Education Management Systems.

Lenning, O., Munday, L., Johnson, O., Vander Well, A., & Brue, E. (1974a). *Nonintellective correlates of grades, persistence and academic learning in college: The published literature through the decade of the sixties* (Monograph No. 14). Iowa City, IA: American College Testing Program.

Lenning, O., Munday, L., Johnson, O., Vander Well, A., & Brue, E. (1974b). *The many faces of college success and their nonintellectual correlates* (Monograph No. 15). Iowa City, IA: American College Testing Program.

Lenning, O., Munday, L., & Maxey, J. (1969). Student educational growth during the first two years of college. *College and University, 44*, 145–153.

Lent, R., Larkin, K., & Hasegawa, C. (1986). Effects of a "focused interest" career course approach for college students. *Vocational Guidance Quarterly, 34*, 151–159.

Lentz, L. (1980). The college choice of career salient women: Coeducational or women's. *Journal of Educational Equity and Leadership, 1*, 28–35.

Lentz, L. (1982). *College selectivity, not college type, is related to graduate women's career aspirations.* Paper presented at the meeting of the American Educational Research Association, New York.

Lentz, L. (1983). Differences in women's freshman versus senior career salience ratings at women's and coeducational colleges. *Review of Higher Education, 6*, 181–193.

Leon, G. (1974). Personality change in the specially admitted disadvantaged student after one year in college. *Journal of Clinical Psychology, 30,* 522–528.

Leslie, L. (1984). Changing patterns in student financing of higher education. *Journal of Higher Education, 55,* 313–346.

Leslie, L., & Brinkman, P. (1986). Rates of return to higher education. In J. Smart (Ed.), *Higher education: Handbook of theory and research* (Vol. 2). New York: Agathon.

Leslie, L., & Brinkman, P. (1988). *The economic value of higher education.* New York: American Council on Education and Macmillan.

Levin, B., & Clowes, D. (1980). Realization of educational aspirations among blacks and whites in two- and four-year colleges. *Community/Junior College Research Quarterly, 4,* 185–193.

Levin, H. (1977a). A decade of policy developments in improving education and training for low income populations. In R. Haveman (Ed.), *A decade of federal antipoverty programs.* Orlando, FL: Academic Press.

Levin, H. (1977b). A radical critique of educational policy. *Journal of Education Finance, 3,* 9–31.

Levin, M. (1967). Congruence and development changes in authoritarianism in college students. In J. Katz (Ed.), *Growth and constraint in college students.* Stanford, CA: Stanford University, Institute for the Study of Human Problems.

Levine, A. (1975). Forging a feminine identity: Women in four professional schools. *American Journal of Psychoanalysis, 35,* 63–67.

Levine, A. (1978). *Handbook on undergraduate curriculum.* San Francisco: Jossey-Bass.

Levine, A. (1980). *When dreams and heroes died: A portrait of today's college student.* San Francisco: Jossey-Bass.

Levine, A., & Associates (1989). *Shaping higher education's future: Demographic realities and opportunities, 1901–2000.* San Francisco: Jossey-Bass.

Levinson, D. (with Darrow, C. N., Klein, E. B., Levinson, M. H., & McGee, B.). (1978). *The seasons of a man's life.* New York: Knopf.

Levinson, D., Darrow, C., Klein, E., Levinson, M., & McGee, B. (1974). The psychosocial development of men in early adulthood and mid-life transition. In D. Ricks, A. Thomas, & M. Roff (Eds.), *Psychopathology* (Vol. 3). Minneapolis: University of Minnesota Press.

Lewin, K. (1936). *Principles of topological psychology.* New York: McGraw-Hill.

Lewin, K. (1951). *Field theory in social science.* New York: Harper & Row.

Lewis, J. (1970). *A study of the achievements and activities of selected liberal arts graduates.* Unpublished doctoral dissertation, University of Iowa, Iowa City.

Lewis, J., & Nelson, K. (1983a). The achievements of university alumni from five academic areas. *Journal of Instructional Psychology, 10,* 163–167.

Lewis, J., & Nelson, K. (1983b). The relationship between college grades and three factors of adult achievement. *Educational and Psychological Measurement, 43,* 577–580.

Lewis, L. (1967). Two cultures: Some empirical findings. *Educational Record, 48,* 260–267.

Liberman, D., Gaa, J., & Frankiewicz, R. (1983). Ego and moral development in an adult population. *Journal of Genetic Psychology, 142,* 61–65.

Liberman, J. (1979). *The rate of return to schooling: 1958–1976.* Faculty Working Paper. Chicago: University of Illinois, Department of Finance.

Lieberman, M., Yalom, I., & Miles, M. (1973). *Encounter groups: First facts.* New York: Basic Books.

Light, R., & Pillemer, D. (1982). Numbers and narrative: Combining their strengths in research reviews. *Harvard Educational Review, 52,* 1–26.

Light, R., Singer, J., & Willett, J. (1990). *By design: Planning research on higher education.* Cambridge, MA: Harvard University Press.

Lillard, L. (1977). Inequality: Earnings vs. human wealth. *American Economic Review, 67,* 42–53.

Lillard, L., & Willis, R. (1978). Dynamic aspects of earning mobility. *Econometrica, 46,* 985–1012.

Lind, G. (1985). Moral competence and education in democratic society. In G. Zecha & P. Weingartner (Eds.), *Conscience: An interdisciplinary view.* Dordrecht, the Netherlands: Reidel.

Lind, G. (1986). Growth and regression in cognitive-moral development. In C. Harding (Ed.), *Moral dilemmas: Philosophical and psychological issues in the development of moral reasoning.* Chicago: Precedent.

Linden, F. (Ed.) (1967). *Market profiles of consumer products.* New York: National Industrial Conference Board.

Linder, F. (1986). *Locus of control and value orientations of adult learners in postsecondary education.* Paper presented at the meeting of the American Educational Research Association, San Francisco. (ERIC Document Reproduction Service No. ED 272 093)

Lindert, P. (1977). Sibling position and achievement. *Journal of Human Resources, 12,* 198–219.

Lindsay, P. (1984). High school size, participation in activities, and young adult social participation. Some enduring effects of schooling. *Educational Evaluation and Policy Analysis, 6,* 73–83.

Lindsay, P., & Knox, W. (1984). Continuity and change in work values among young adults: A longitudinal study. *American Journal of Sociology, 89,* 918–931.

Link, C., Ratledge, E., & Lewis, K. (1976). Black-white differences in returns to schooling: Some new evidence. *American Economic Review, 66,* 221–223.

Linn, R. (1986). Quantitative methods in research on teaching. In M. Wittrock (Ed.), *Handbook of research on teaching* (2nd ed.). New York: Macmillan.

Linn, R., & Slinde, J. (1977). The determination of the significance of change between pre- and post-testing periods. *Review of Educational Research, 47,* 121–150.

Linn, R., & Werts, C. (1969). Assumptions in making causal inferences from part correlations, partial correlations, and partial regression coefficients. *Psychological Bulletin, 72,* 307–310.

Linn, R., & Werts, C. (1977). Analysis implications of the choice of a structural model in the nonequivalent control group design. *Psychological Bulletin, 84,* 299–324.

Linn, R., Werts, C., & Tucker, L. (1971). The interpretation of regression coefficients in a school effects model. *Educational and Psychological Measurement, 31,* 85–93.

Linsky, A., & Straus, M. (1975). Student evaluations, research productivity, and eminence of college faculty. *Journal of Higher Education, 46,* 89–102.

Lipsky, S., & Ender, S. (1990). Impact of a study skills course on probationary students' academic performance. *Journal of the Freshman Year Experience, 2,* 7–15.

Little, A. (1980). *Is education related to productivity?* (Bulletin 11). Sussex, England: Institute of Developmental Studies.

Little, G. (1970). *The university experience: An Australian study.* Carlton, Victoria: Melbourne University Press.

Livingston, M., & Stewart, M. (1987). Minority students on a white campus: Perception is truth. *NASPA Journal, 24,* 39–49.

Lloyd, B. (1967). Retouched picture: Follow-up of a questionnaire portrait of the freshman coed. *Journal of the National Association of Women Deans and Counselors, 30,* 174–177.

Locke, D., & Zimmerman, N. (1987). Effects of peer-counseling training on psychological maturity of black students. *Journal of College Student Personnel, 28,* 525–532.

Locke, E. (1977). An empirical study of lecture note taking among college students. *Journal of Educational Research, 71,* 93–99.

Loeffler, D., & Feidler, L. (1979). Woman—A sense of identity: A counseling intervention to facilitate personal growth in women. *Journal of Counseling Psychology, 26,* 51–57.

Loesch, L., Shub, P., & Rucker, B. (1979). Vocational maturity among community college students. *Journal of College Student Personnel, 20,* 140–144.

Loevinger, J. (1966). The meaning and measure of ego development. *American Psychologist, 21,* 195–206.

Loevinger, J. (1976). *Ego development: Conceptions and theories.* San Francisco: Jossey-Bass.

Loevinger, J. (1979). Construct validity of the Sentence Completion Test of Ego Development. *Applied Psychological Measures, 3,* 281–311.

Loevinger, J., Cohn, L., Redmore, C., Bonneville, L., Streich, D., & Sargent, M. (1985). Ego development in college. *Journal of Personality and Social Psychology, 48,* 947–962.

Loevinger, J., Wessler, R., & Redmore, (1970a). *Measuring ego development: Vol. 1. Construction and use of a sentence completion test* San Francisco: Jossey-Bass.

Loevinger, J., Wessler, R., & Redmore, C. (1970b). *Measuring ego development: Vol. 2. Scoring manual for women and girls* (Vol. 2). San Francisco: Jossey-Bass.

Logan, G. (1976). Do sociologists teach students to think more critically? *Teaching Sociology, 4,* 29–48.

Lokitz, B., & Sprandel, H. (1976). The first year: A look at the freshman experience. *Journal of College Student Personnel, 17,* 274–279.

Long, J., Allison, P., & McGinnis, R. (1979). Entrance into the academic career. *American Sociological Review, 44,* 816–830.

Longino, C., & Kart, C. (1973). The college fraternity: An assessment of theory and research. *Journal of College Student Personnel, 14,* 118–125.

Look, C., & Rolison, G. (1986). Alienation of ethnic minority students at a predominantly white university. *Journal of Higher Education, 57,* 58–77.

Lord, F. (1967). A paradox in the interpretation of group comparisons. *Psychological Bulletin, 68,* 304–305.

Lord, F. (1969). Statistical adjustments when comparing pre-existing groups. *Psychological Bulletin, 72,* 336–337.

Lorence, J., & Mortimer, J. (1979). Work experience and political orientation: A panel study. *Social Forces, 58,* 651–676.

Lorence, J., & Mortimer, J. (1981). Work experience and work involvement. *Sociology of Work and Occupations, 8,* 297–326.

Louis, K., Colten, M., & Demeke, G. (1984). *Freshman experiences at the University of Massachusetts at Boston.* Boston: University of Massachusetts. (ERIC Document Reproduction Service No. ED 242 251)

Loxley, J., & Whiteley, J. (1986). *Character development in college students* (Vol. 2). Schenectady, NY: Character Research Press.

Lucas, R. (1977). Hedonic wage equations and psychic wages in the returns to schooling. *American Economic Review, 67,* 549–558.

Lupfer, M., Cohn, B., & Brown, L. (1982). *Jury decisions as a function of level of moral reasoning.* Unpublished manuscript, Memphis State University, Memphis, TN.

Lutwak, N. (1984). The interrelationship of ego, moral, and conceptual development in a college group. *Adolescence, 19,* 675–688.

Lyle, E. (1958). An exploration in the teaching of critical thinking in general psychology. *Journal of Educational Research, 52,* 129–133.

Lynch, A. (1987). Type development and student development. In J. Provost & S. Anchors (Eds.), *Applications of the Myer-Briggs Type Indicator in higher education.* Palo Alto, CA: Consulting Psychologists Press.

Lynch, M., Ogg, W., & Christensen, M. (1975). Impact of a life planning workshop on perceived locus of control. *Psychological Reports, 37,* 1219–1222.

Lyons, D., & Green, S. (1988). Sex role development as a function of college experiences. *Sex Roles, 18,* 31–40.

Lyson, T. (1980). Factors associated with the choice of a typical or atypical curriculum among college women. *Sociology and Social Research, 64,* 559–571.

Lyson, T. (1984). Sex differences in the choice of a male or female career line. *Women and Occupations, 11,* 131–146.

Maccoby, E., & Jacklin, C. (1974). *The psychology of sex differences.* Stanford, CA: Stanford University Press.

Mackey, J., Blackmon, C., & Andrews, J. (1977). Does academic achievement make a difference in student teaching? *Phi Delta Kappan, 59,* 272–273.

Macomber, F., & Siegel, L. (1957). A study of large-group teaching procedures. *Educational Record, 38,* 220–229.

Madison, P. (1969). *Personality development in college.* Reading, MA: Addison-Wesley.

Magnarella, P. (1975). The University of Vermont's Living Learning Center: A first year appraisal. *Journal of College Student Personnel, 16,* 300–305.

Maier, N., & Casselman, G. (1971). Problem solving ability as a factor in selection of major in college study: Comparison of the processes of "idea getting" and "making essential distinctions" in males and females. *Psychological Reports, 28,* 503–514.

Malinowski, C. (1978). *Moral judgment and resistance to the temptation to cheat.* Paper presented at the meeting of the American Psychological Association, Toronto.

Malinowski, C., & Smith, C. (1985). Moral reasoning and moral conduct: An investigation prompted by Kohlberg's theory. *Journal of Personality and Social Psychology, 49,* 1016–1027.

Malkemes, L. (1972). *An application of Parson's LIGA scheme: The faculty-student system of interaction.* Unpublished doctoral dissertation, University of Colorado, Boulder.

Malkiel, G., & Malkiel, J. (1973). Male-female pay differentials in professional employment. *American Economic Review, 63,* 693–705.

Mallinckrodt, B. (1988). Student retention, social support, and dropout intention: Comparison of black and white students. *Journal of College Student Development, 29,* 60–64.

Mallinckrodt, B., & Sedlacek, W. (1987). Student retention and use of campus facilities by race. *NASPA Journal, 24,* 28–32.

Mandell, L. (1972). *Credit card use in the United States.* Ann Arbor: University of Michigan, Institute for Social Research.

Manis, J. (1985). *Some correlates of self-esteem, personal control, and occupational settlement: An overview of findings from CEW surveys of educated women* (CEW Research Rep. No. 18). Ann Arbor: University of Michigan, Center for the Study of Higher Education and the Program in Adult and Continuing Education.

Manski, C., & Wise, D. (1983). *College choice in America.* Cambridge, MA: Harvard University Press.

Marcia, J. (1965). Determination and construct validity of ego identity status. *Dissertation Abstracts International, 25,* 6763A.

Marcia, J. (1966). Development and validation of ego-identity status. *Journal of Personality and Social Psychology, 3,* 551–558.

Marcia, J. (1967). Ego identity status: Relationship to change in self-esteem, "general maladjustment," and authoritarianism. *Journal of Personality, 35,* 118–133.

Marcia, J. (1976). Identity six years after: A follow-up study. *Journal of Youth and Adolescence, 5,* 145–160.

Marcia, J. (1980). Identity in adolescence. In J. Adelson (Ed.), *Handbook of adolescent psychology.* New York: John Wiley & Sons.

Marcia, J., & Friedman, M. (1970). Ego identity status in college women. *Journal of Personality, 38,* 249–263.

Marion, P. (1980). Relationships of student characteristics and experiences with attitude changes in a program of study abroad. *Journal of College Student Personnel, 21,* 58–64.

Marion, P., & Cheek, N. (1985). Relationships between student characteristics and perceived outcomes of a university education. *NACADA Journal, 5,* 53–60.

Marks, H. (1990). *The college experience: Differential gender effects on the development of social responsibility.* Paper presented at the meeting of the American Educational Research Association, Boston.

Markus, H. (1977). Self-schemata and processing information about the self. *Journal of Personality and Social Psychology, 35,* 151–175.

Marlowe, A., & Auvenshine, C. (1982). Greek membership: Its impact on the moral development of college freshmen. *Journal of College Student Personnel, 23,* 53–57.

Marron J., & Kayson, W. (1984). Effects of living status, gender, and year in college on college students. *Psychological Reports, 55,* 811–814.

Marsh, H. (1984). Students' evaluations of teaching: Dimensionality, reliability, validity, potential biases, and utility. *Journal of Educational Psychology, 76,* 707–754.

Marsh, H. (1986a). Applicability paradigm: Students' evaluation of teaching effectiveness in different countries. *Journal of Educational Psychology, 78,* 465–473.

Marsh, H. (1986b). Verbal and math self-concept: An internal/external frame of reference model. *American Educational Research Journal, 23,* 129–149.

Marsh, H., Fleiner, H., & Thomas, C. (1975). Validity and usefulness of student evaluations of instructional quality. *Journal of Educational Psychology, 67,* 833–839.

Marsh, H., & Parker, J. (1984). Determinants of student self-concept: Is it better to be a relatively large fish in a small pond even if you don't learn to swim as well? *Journal of Personality and Social Psychology, 46,* 213–231.

Martin, D., Blanc, R., & DeBuhr, L. (1983). *Supplemental instruction: A model for student academic support.* Kansas City: University of Missouri.

Martin, D., & Morgan, J. (1963). Education and income. *Quarterly Journal of Economics, 77,* 423–437.

Martin, J., & Redmore, C. (1978). A longitudinal study of ego development. *Developmental Psychology, 14,* 189–190.

Martin, P., Osmond, M., & Hesselbart, S. (1980). The significance of gender as a social and demographic correlate of sex role attitudes. *Sociological Focus, 13,* 383–396.

Martin, R., & Light, H. (1984). Education: Its positive impact on women. *College Student Journal, 18,* 401–405.

Martin, R., Shafto, M., & Van Deinse, W. (1977). The reliability, validity and design of the Defining Issues Test. *Developmental Psychology, 13,* 460–468.

Martinez, C., Jr. (1988). Mexican Americans. In L. Comas-Diaz & E. Griffith (Eds.), *Clinical guidelines in cross-cultural mental health.* New York: John Wiley & Sons.

Martinson, W., & Zerface, J. (1970). Comparison of individual counseling and a social program with non-daters. *Journal of Counseling Psychology, 17,* 36–40.

Maruyama, G., & Walberg, H. (1982). Causal modeling. In M. Mitzel (Ed.), *Encyclopedia of educational research* (5th ed.). New York: Free Press.

Masih, L. (1967). Career saliency and its relation to certain needs, interests and job values. *Personnel and Guidance Journal, 45,* 653–658.

Mason, K., & Bumpass, L. (1975). U.S. women's sex-role ideology, 1970. *American Journal of Sociology, 80,* 1212–1219.

Mason, K., Czajka, J., & Arber, S. (1976). Change in U.S. women's sex-role attitudes, 1964–1974. *American Sociological Review, 41,* 573–596.

Matteson, D. (1974). Changes in attitudes toward authority figures with the move to college: Three experiments. *Developmental Psychology, 10,* 340–347.

Matteson, D. (1975). Statuses and sex differences. In D. Matteson (Ed.), *Adolescence today: Sex roles and the search for identity.* Homewood, IL: Dorsey.

Matteson, D. (1977). Exploration and commitment: Sex differences and methodological problems in the use of identity status categories. *Journal of Youth and Adolescence, 6,* 353–374.

Mattila, J. (1982). Determinants of male school enrollments: A time series analysis. *Review of Economics and Statistics, 64,* 242–251.

Maurais, R. (1968). *A statistical analysis of the effects of housing environment on grade point average.* (ERIC Document Reproduction Service No. ED 027 874)

May, E. (1974). Type of housing and achievement of disadvantaged university students. *College Student Journal, 8,* 48–51.

May, W., & Ilardi, R. (1970). Change and stability of values in collegiate nursing students. *Nursing Research, 19,* 359–362.

May, W., & Ilardi, R. (1973). Value changes in college students. *College Student Journal, 7,* 57–61.

McAllister, E. (1985). Religious attitudes of women college students: A follow-up study. *Adolescence, 20,* 797–804.

McArthur, C. (1970). Rorschachs and Harvard men. In J. Whiteley & H. Sprandel (Eds.), *The growth and development of college students.* Washington, DC: American Personnel and Guidance Association.

McBee, M. (1980). The values development dilemma. In M. McBee (Ed.), *Rethinking college responsibilities for values* (New Directions for Higher Education No. 31). San Francisco: Jossey-Bass.

McBroom, W. (1984). Changes in sex-role orientations: A five-year longitudinal comparison. *Sex Roles, 11,* 583–592.

McCaffrey, S., Miller, T., & Winston, R. (1984). Comparison of career maturity among graduate students and undergraduates. *Journal of College Student Personnel, 25,* 127–132.

McClaran, D., & Sarris, R. (1985). Attitudes, knowledge, and behavior before and after an undergraduate health and lifestyle course. *Journal of the American College Health Association, 33,* 220–222.

McClelland, D. (1973). Testing for competence rather than for intelligence. *American Psychologist, 28,* 1–14.

McClelland, K. (1977). The "productive Americans" survey. In C. Jencks & L. Rainwater (Eds.), *The effects of family background, test scores, personality traits and schooling on economic success* (Final report to the National Institute of Education, Appendix C, Grant #NIE-G-74-0077). Springfield, VA: National Technical Information Service.

McClelland, K. (1986). *The effects of college rank among highly ambitious students: Do gender and social origins make a difference?* Paper presented at the meeting of the American Educational Research Association, San Francisco.

McClelland, K. (1990). Cumulative disadvantage among the highly ambitious. *Sociology of Education, 63,* 102–121.

McClendon, M. (1976). The occupational status attainment process of males and females. *American Sociological Review, 41,* 52–64.

McClosky, H., & Brill, A. (1983). *Dimensions of tolerance: What Americans believe about civil liberties.* New York: Russell Sage Foundation.

McClure, R., Wells, C., & Bowerman, B. (1986). A model of MBA student performance. *Research in Higher Education, 25,* 182–193.

McConnell, T. (1934). Changes in scores on the psychological examination of the American Council on Education from freshman to senior year. *Journal of Educational Psychology, 25,* 66–69.

McConnell, T. (1972). Do colleges affect student values? *Change, 4,* 9 ff.

McCreight, K., & LeMay, M. (1982). A longitudinal study of the achievement and persistence of students who receive basic educational opportunity grants. *Journal of Student Financial Aid, 12,* 11–15.

McCullers, J., & Plant, W. (1964). Personality and social development: Cultural influences. *Review of Educational Research, 34,* 599–610.

McEaddy, B. (1975). Educational attainment of workers, March 1974. *Monthly Labor Review, 98,* 64–69.

McEvoy, T. (1986). Cosmopolitanism. *Journal of Higher Education, 57,* 84–91.

McGeorge, C. (1976). Some correlates of principled moral thinking in young adults. *Journal of Moral Education, 5,* 265–273.

McGinn, P., Viernstein, M., & Hogan, R. (1980). Fostering the intellectual development of verbally gifted adolescents. *Journal of Educational Psychology, 72,* 494–498.

McHugo, G., & Jernstedt, G. (1979). The affective impact of field experience education on college students. *Alternative Higher Education, 3,* 188–206.

McIntire, D. (1973). *College roommate system affects grades.* Unpublished report, West Virginia Wesleyan College, Buckhannon.

McKeachie, W. (1962). Procedures and techniques of teaching: A survey of experimental studies. In N. Sanford (Ed.), *The American college: A psychological and social interpretation of higher learning.* New York: John Wiley & Sons.

McKeachie, W. (1978). *Teaching tips: A guidebook for the beginning college teacher* (7th ed.). Lexington, MA: D. C. Heath.

McKeachie, W. (1980). Class size, large classes, and multiple sections. *Academe, 66,* 24–27.

McKeachie, W., & Lin, Y. (1978). A note on validity of student ratings of teaching. *Educational Research Quarterly, 4,* 45–47.

McKeachie, W., Pintrich, P., Lin, Y., & Smith, D. (1986). *Teaching and learning in the college classroom: A review of the research literature.* Ann Arbor: University of Michigan, National Center for Research to Improve Postsecondary Teaching and Learning.

McKinney, K. (1987). Age and gender differences in college students' attitudes toward women: A replication and extension. *Sex Roles, 17,* 353–358.

McKinnon, J., & Renner, J. (1971). Are colleges concerned with intellectual development? *American Journal of Physics, 39,* 1047–1052.

McLaughlin, G., & Smart, J. (1987). Baccalaureate recipients: Developmental patterns in personal values. *Journal of College Student Personnel, 28,* 162–168.

McLeish, J. (1968). *The lecture method* (Cambridge Monograph on Teaching Methods No. 1). Cambridge, England: Cambridge Institute of Education.

McLeish, J. (1970). *Students' attitudes and college environments.* Cambridge, England: Cambridge Institute of Education.

McLeish, J. (1973). Changes in students in relation to college environments. *Research in Higher Education, 1,* 245–262.

McMahon, W., & Wagner, A. (1981). Expected returns to investment in higher education. *Journal of Human Resources, 16,* 274–285.

McMahon, W., & Wagner, A. (1982). The monetary returns to education as partial social efficiency. In W. McMahon & T. Geske (Eds.), *Financing education: Overcoming inefficiency and inequity.* Urbana: University of Illinois Press.

McMeen, J. (1983). *The role of the chemistry inquiry-oriented laboratory approach in facilitating cognitive growth and development.* Unpublished doctoral dissertation, Vanderbilt University, Nashville, TN.

McMillan, J. (1986). Beyond value added: Improvement alone is not enough. Unpublished manuscript, Virginia Commonwealth University, Richmond.

McMillan, J. (1987). Enhancing college students' critical thinking: A review of studies. *Research in Higher Education, 26,* 3–29.

McMillan, J. (1989). *Conceptualizing and assessing college student values.* Paper presented to the meeting of the American Educational Research Association, San Francisco.

McMorris, R., & Ambrosino, R. (1973). Self-report predictors: A reminder. *Journal of Educational Measurement, 10,* 13–17.

McNamee, S. (1972). *Moral behavior, moral development, and needs in students and political activists.* Unpublished doctoral dissertation, Case Western Reserve University, Cleveland, OH.

McNamee, S. (1978). Moral behavior, moral development, and motivation. *Journal of Moral Education, 7,* 27–32.

McSwine, B. (1971). Black visions, white realities. *Change, 3,* 28–34.

McWilliams, S. (1979). Effects of reciprocal peer counseling on college students' personality development. *Journal of the American College Health Association, 27,* 210–213.

Meador, B. (1971). Individual process in a basic encounter group. *Journal of Counseling Psychology, 18,* 70–76.

Medoff, J. (1977). *The earnings function: A glimpse inside the black box* (National Bureau of Economic Research Working Paper No. 224). New York: National Bureau of Economic Research.

Medoff, J., & Abraham, K. (1980). Experience, performance, and earnings. *Quarterly Journal of Economics, 95,* 703–736.

Medoff, J., & Abraham, K. (1981). Are those paid more really more productive? The case of experience. *Journal of Human Resources, 16,* 186–216.

Medsker, L., & Trent, J. (1972). Factors related to type of college attended. In K. Feldman (Ed.), *College and student.* New York: Pergamon Press.

Meier, H. (1972). Mother-centeredness and college youths' attitudes toward social equality for women: Some empirical findings. *Journal of Marriage and the Family, 34,* 115–121.

Meilman, P. (1979). Cross-sectional age changes in ego identity status during adolescence. *Developmental Psychology, 15,* 230–231.

Melchiori, G., & Nash, N. (1983). *The impact of higher education: An analysis of the research.* Paper presented at the meeting of the Association for Institutional Research, Toronto.

Mele, F. (1978). A biology problem-solving program's effect on college students' transition from concrete to formal thought. *Dissertation Abstracts International, 38,* 7290A.

Menges, R. (1988). Research on teaching and learning: The relevant and redundant. *Review of Higher Education, 11,* 259–268.

Mentkowski, M. (1988). Paths to integrity: Educating for personal growth and professional performance. In S. Srivastva & Associates, *Executive integrity: The search for high human values in organizational life.* San Francisco: Jossey-Bass.

Mentkowski, M., & Doherty, A. (1983). *Careering after college: Establishing the validity of abilities learned in college for later careering and professional performance* (Final report to the National Institute of Education: Overview and Summary). Milwaukee, WI: Alverno College, Office of Research and Evaluation.

Mentkowski, M., & Doherty, A. (1984). Abilities that last a lifetime: Outcomes of the Alverno experience. *American Association for Higher Education Bulletin, 36,* 5–6, 11–14.

Mentkowski, M., & Strait, M. (1983). *A longitudinal study of student change in cognitive development, learning styles, and generic abilities in an outcome-centered liberal arts curriculum* (Final report to the National Institute of Education, Research Report No. 6). Milwaukee, WI: Alverno College, Office of Research and Evaluation.

Merlino, A. (1977). A comparison of the effectiveness of three levels of teacher questioning on the outcomes of instruction in a college biology course. *Dissertation Abstracts International, 37,* 5551A.

Merton, R. (1957). *Social theory and social structure.* New York: Free Press.

Merton, R., & Lazarsfeld, P. (1972). A professional school for training in social research. In P. Lazarsfeld (Ed.), *Qualitative analysis.* Newton, MA: Allyn and Bacon.

Metcalf, D. (1973). Pay dispersion, information, and returns to search in a professional labor market. *Review of Economic Studies, 40,* 491–505.

Metzner, B. (1989). Perceived quality of academic advising: The effect on freshman attrition. *American Educational Research Journal, 26*, 422–442.

Meyer, J. (1970a). High school effects on college intentions. *American Journal of Sociology, 76*, 59–70.

Meyer, J. (1970b). The charter: Conditions of diffuse socialization in schools. In W. Scott (Ed.), *Social processes and social structure: An introduction to sociology*. New York: Holt, Rinehart & Winston.

Meyer, J. (1970c). *The effects of college quality and size on student occupational choice*. Final Report. Washington, DC: U.S. Office of Education, Bureau of Research.

Meyer, J. (1972). The effects of the institutionalization of colleges in society. In K. Feldman (Ed.), *College and student*. New York: Pergamon Press.

Meyer, J. (1977). The effects of education as an institution. *American Journal of Sociology, 83*, 55–77.

Meyer, P. (1977). Intellectual development: Analysis of religious content. *Counseling Psychologist, 6*, 47–50.

Meyers, E. (1981). A comparative analysis of persisters, permanent dropouts, dropouts who transfer and stopouts at St. Cloud State University. *Dissertation Abstracts International, 42*, 105A.

Michael, R. (1972). *The effect of education on efficiency in consumption*. New York: Columbia University Press for the National Bureau of Economic Research.

Michael, R. (1973). Education and the derived demand for children. *Journal of Political Economy, 81* (Pt. 2), S128–S164.

Michael, R. (1975a). Education and consumption. In F. Juster (Ed.), *Education, income, and human behavior*. New York: McGraw-Hill.

Michael, R. (1975b). Education and fertility. In F. Juster (Ed.), *Education, income, and human behavior*. New York: McGraw-Hill.

Michael, R. (1982). Measuring non-monetary benefits of education: A survey. In W. McMahon & T. Geske (Eds.), *Financing education*. Urbana: University of Illinois Press.

Michelson, W. (1970). *Man and his urban environment: A sociological approach*. Reading, MA: Addison-Wesley.

Mickler, M., & Zippert, C. (1987). Teaching strategies based on learning styles of adult students. *Community/Junior College Quarterly of Research and Practice, 11*, 33–37.

Miller, H., & Glick, P. (1956). Educational level and potential income. *American Sociological Review, 21*, 307–312.

Miller, L. (1973). Distinctive characteristics of fraternity members. *Journal of College Student Personnel, 14*, 126–129.

Miller, T., & Winston, R. (1990). Assessing development from a psychosocial perspective. In D. Creamer & Associates, *College student development theory and practice for the 1990s* (Media Publication No. 49). Alexandria, VA: American College Personnel Association.

Milliones, J. (1974). Construction of the Developmental Inventory of Black Consciousness. *Dissertation Abstracts International, 35,* 1241A.

Milliones, J. (1980). Construction of a black consciousness measure: Psychotherapeutic implications. *Psychotherapy: Theory, Research, and Practice, 17,* 175–182.

Milton, O. (1972). *Alternatives to the traditional: How professors teach and how students learn.* San Francisco: Jossey-Bass.

Mincer, J. (1974). *Schooling, experience, and earnings.* New York: Columbia University Press.

Mincer, J. (1978). Family migration decisions. *Journal of Political Economy, 85,* 749–773.

Mines, R. (1980). *Levels of intellectual development and associated critical thinking skills in young adults.* Unpublished doctoral dissertation, University of Iowa, Iowa City.

Mintzes, J. (1975). The A-T approach 14 years later: A review of recent research. *Journal of College Science Teaching, 5,* 247–252.

Mintzes, J. (1982). Relationships between student perceptions of teaching behavior and learning outcomes in college biology. *Journal of Research in Science Teaching, 19,* 789–794.

Misner, M., & Wellner, W. (1970). Factors associated with scholastic productivity in high and low achieving sororities. *Journal of College Student Personnel, 11,* 445–448.

Mitchell, R. (1976). Paths to happiness: Residence locality and interpersonal relationships. *Dissertation Abstracts International, 37,* 3944A.

Moffatt, M. (1989). *Coming of age in New Jersey: College and American culture.* New Brunswick, NJ: Rutgers University Press.

Moline, A. (1987). Financial aid and student persistence: An application of causal modeling. *Research in Higher Education, 26,* 130–147.

Moll, M., & Allen, R. (1982). Developing critical thinking skills in biology. *Journal of College Science Teaching, 12,* 95–98.

Molm, C., & Astin, A. (1973). Personal characteristics and attitude changes of student protesters. *Journal of College Student Personnel, 14,* 239–249.

Monk-Turner, E. (1982). *Education, occupation and income: The effects of attending a community college on the labor market outcomes of young men and women.* Unpublished doctoral dissertation, Brandeis University, Waltham, MA.

Monk-Turner, E. (1983). Sex, educational differentiation and occupational status. *Sociological Quarterly, 24,* 393–404.

Monk-Turner, E. (1988). Educational differentiation and status attainments: The community college controversy. *Sociological Focus, 21,* 141–151.

Monroe, S. (1973, February). Guest in a strange house: A black at Harvard. *Saturday Review of Education,* 45–48.

Monteiro, L. (1980). The college academic environment: Student-faculty interaction. In *Men and women learning together: Study of college students in the late 70's.* Report of the Brown Project. Providence, RI: Brown University.

Montero, D. (1975). Support for civil liberties among a cohort of high school graduates and college students. *Journal of Social Issues, 31,* 123–136.

Montgomery, J., McLaughlin, G., Fawcett, L., Pedigo, E., & Ward, S. (1975). The impact of different residence hall environments upon student attitudes. *Journal of College Student Personnel, 16,* 379–384.

Mood, A. (1969). Macro-analysis of the American educational system. *Operations Research, 17,* 770–784.

Mood, A. (1971). Partitioning variance in multiple regression analyses as a tool for developing learning models. *American Educational Research Journal, 8,* 191–202.

Moon, Y. (1985). *A review of cross-cultural studies on moral judgment development using the Defining Issues Test.* Paper presented at the meeting of the American Educational Research Association, Chicago.

Moore, G. (1972). The dot and the elephant. *Change, 4,* 33–41.

Moore, L. (Ed.). (1990). *Evolving theoretical perspectives on students* (New Directions for Student Services No. 51). San Francisco: Jossey-Bass.

Moore, L., & Upcraft, M. (1990). Theory in student affairs: Terminology, evolving perspectives. In L. Moore (Ed.), *Evolving theoretical perspectives on students* (New Directions for Student Services No. 51). San Francisco: Jossey-Bass.

Moore, W. (1989). The Learning Environment Preferences: Exploring the construct validity of an objective measure of the Perry scheme of intellectual development. *Journal of College Student Development, 30,* 504–519.

Moos, R. (1976). *The human context: Environmental determinants of behavior.* New York: John Wiley & Sons.

Moos, R. (1978). Social environments of university student living groups: Architectural and organizational correlates. *Environment and Behavior, 10,* 109–126.

Moos, R. (1979). *Evaluating educational environments: Procedures, measures, findings, and policy implications.* San Francisco: Jossey-Bass.

Moos, R., DeYoung, A., & Van Dort, B. (1976). Differential impact of university student living groups. *Research in Higher Education, 5,* 67–82.

Moos, R., & Lee, E. (1979). Comparing residence hall and independent living settings. *Research in Higher Education, 11,* 207–221.

Moos, R., & Otto, J. (1975). The impact of coed living on males and females. *Journal of College Student Personnel, 16,* 459–467.

Moos, R., Van Dort, B., Smail, P., & DeYoung, A. (1975). A typology of university student living groups. *Journal of Educational Psychology, 67,* 359–367.

Morgan, E. (1972). The American college student in Switzerland: A study of cross-cultural adaptation and change. *Dissertation Abstracts International, 33,* 529A.

Morgan, E. (1975). Study abroad: A process of adaptation and change. *International Review of Education, 21,* 207–215.

Morgan, J. (1974). *Five thousand American families—patterns of economic progress.* Ann Arbor: University of Michigan, Institute for Social Research.

Morgan, J., & David, M. (1963). Education and income. *Quarterly Journal of Economics, 77,* 423–437.

Morgan, J., & Sirageldin, I. (1968). A note on the quality dimension in education. *Journal of Political Economy, 76,* 1069–1077.

Morgan, J., Sirageldin, I., & Baerwaldt, N. (1966). *Productive Americans: A study of how individuals contribute to economic progress.* Ann Arbor: University of Michigan, Institute for Social Research.

Morrill, R. (1980). *Teaching values in college: Facilitating development and ethical, moral, and value awareness in students.* San Francisco: Jossey-Bass.

Morstain, B. (1973). Change in students' educational attitudes: A study of an experimental living-learning program. *Research in Higher Education, 1,* 141–148.

Mortensen, L., & Moreland, W. (1985). Critical thinking in a freshman introductory course: A case study. In J. Jeffrey & G. Erickson (Eds.), *To improve the academy* (Vol. 5). Stillwater, OK: POD/New Forums Press.

Mortimer, J. (1972). Family background and college influences upon occupational value orientations and the career decision. *Dissertation Abstracts International, 33,* 2518A.

Mortimer, J. (1975). Occupational value socialization in business and professional families. *Sociology of Work and Occupations, 2,* 29–53.

Mortimer, J., & Lorence, J. (1979a). Occupational experience and the self-concept: A longitudinal study. *Social Psychology Quarterly, 42,* 307–323.

Mortimer, J., & Lorence, J. (1979b). Work experience and occupational value socialization: A longitudinal study. *American Journal of Sociology, 84,* 1361–1385.

Mortimer, J., & Lorence, J. (1981). Self-concept stability and change from late adolescence to early adulthood. *Research in Community and Mental Health, 2,* 5–42.

Mortimer, J., Lorence, J., & Kumka, D. (1986). *Work, family and personality.* Norwood, NJ: Ablex.

Mortimer, J., & Simmons, R. (1978). Adult socialization. In R. Turner, J. Coleman, & R. Fox (Eds.), *Annual review of sociology* (Vol 4). Palo Alto, CA: Annual Reviews.

Mosher, R., & Sprinthall, N. (1970). Psychological education in secondary schools: A program to promote individual and human development. *American Psychologist, 25,* 911–924.

Moshman, D., Johnston, S., Tomlinson-Keasey, C., Williams, V., & Eisert, D. (1984). ADAPT: The first five years. In R. Fuller (Ed.), *Piagetian programs in higher education.* Lincoln: University of Nebraska.

Moss, H., & Sussman, E. (1980). Longitudinal study of personality development. In O. Brim & J. Kagan (Eds.), *Constancy and change in human development.* Cambridge, MA: Harvard University Press.

Muchinsky, P., & Hoyt, D. (1973). Academic grades as a predictor of occupational success among engineering graduates. *Measurement and Evaluation in Guidance, 6,* 93–103.

Mueller, A. (1924). Class size as a factor in normal school instruction. *Education, 45,* 203–227.

Mueller, E. (with Hybels, J., Schmiedeskamp, J., Sonquist J., & Staelin, C.). (1969). *Technological advance in an expanding economy: Its impact on a cross-section of the labor force.* Ann Arbor: University of Michigan, Institute for Social Research.

Mueller, R. (1988). The impact of college selectivity on income for men and women. *Research in Higher Education, 29,* 175–191.

Mulford, C. (1967). Self-actualization in a small college environment. *Journal of College Student Personnel, 8,* 100–104.

Mullins, R., & Perkins, E. (1973). Increased self-actualization as a result of an intensive one semester academic program. *Journal of Educational Research, 66,* 210–214.

Munday, L., & Davis, J. (1974). *Varieties of accomplishment after college: Perspectives on the meaning of academic talent.* Iowa City, IA: American College Testing Program.

Munro, B. (1981). Dropouts from higher education: Path analysis of a national sample. *American Educational Research Journal, 18,* 133–141.

Munro, G., & Adams, G. (1977). Ego-identity formation in college students and working youth. *Developmental Psychology, 13,* 523–524.

Murdock, T. (1987). It isn't just money: The effects of financial aid on student persistence. *Review of Higher Education, 11,* 75–101.

Murdock, T. (1988). *Financial aid and persistence: An integrative review of the literature.* Paper presented at the meeting of the National Association of Student Personnel Administrators, St. Louis.

Murnane, R. (1981). New evidence on the relationship between mother's education and children's cognitive skills. *Economics of Education Review, 1,* 245–252.

Murphy, K., & Welch, F. (1989). Wage premiums for college graduates: Recent growth and possible explanations. *Educational Researcher, 18,* 17–26.

Murray, H. (1938). *Exploration in personality.* New York: Oxford University Press.

Murray, H. (1951). Toward a classification of interaction. In T. Parsons & E. Shils (Eds.), *Toward a general theory of action.* Cambridge, MA: Harvard University Press.

Murray, H. (1965). Classroom teaching behaviors related to college teaching effectiveness. In J. Donald & A. Sullivan (Eds.), *Using research to improve teaching.* San Francisco: Jossey-Bass.

Musgrove, F. (1971). A widening gap between students of science and arts. *Educational Research, 13,* 113–118.

Myers, I. (1980a). *Introduction to type.* Palo Alto, CA: Consulting Psychologists Press.

Myers, I. (1980b). *Gifts differing.* Palo Alto, CA: Consulting Psychologists Press.

Myers, I., & McCaulley M. (1985). *Manual: A guide to the development and use of the Myers-Briggs Type Indicator.* Palo Alto, CA: Consulting Psychologists Press.

Nachman, M., & Opochinsky, S. (1958). The effects of different teaching methods: A methodological study. *Journal of Educational Psychology, 49,* 245–249.

Nagely, D. (1971). Traditional and pioneer working mothers. *Journal of Vocational Behavior, 1,* 331–341.

Najmaie, M., & Dolphin, W. (1983). Academic achievement after self-paced testing: A long-term study. *Psychological Reports, 52,* 791–798.

Nash, D. (1976). The personal consequences of a year of study abroad. *Journal of Higher Education, 47,* 191–203.

Nash P., Rosson, J., & Schoemer, J. (1973). Grades and extra-curricular activities: How important are they in landing the first job? *Journal of College Placement, 33,* 73–76.

Nassi, A., & Abramowitz, S. (1979). Transition or transformation? Personal and political development of former Berkeley free-speech movement activists. *Journal of Youth and Adolescence, 8,* 21–35.

Nassi, A., Abramowitz, S., & Youmans, J. (1983). Moral development and politics a decade later: A replication and extension. *Journal of Personality and Social Psychology, 45,* 1127–1135.

Nation top-heavy with wealth. (1986, July 19). *Chicago Tribune.*

National Center for Education Statistics. (1977). *Withdrawal from institutions of higher education.* Washington, DC: U.S. Government Printing Office.

National Center for Education Statistics. (1980). *Preliminary data, participation in adult education, 1978.* Washington, DC: U.S. Office of Education.

National Center for Education Statistics. (1982). *Does college pay? Wage rates before and after leaving school* (NCES Bulletin No. 82-238b). Washington, DC: Author.

National Institute of Education Study Group (1984). *Involvement in learning: Realizing the potential of American higher education.* Washington, DC: National Institute of Education.

Neimark, E. (1975). Intellectual development during adolescence. In F. Horowitz (Ed.), *Review of child development research.* Chicago: University of Chicago Press.

Nelsen, E., & Johnson, N. (1971). *Attitude changes on the College Student Questionnaires: A study of students enrolled in predominantly black colleges and uni-*

versities. Paper presented at the meeting of the American Educational Research Association, New York.

Nelsen, E., & Uhl, N. (1977). The development of attitudes and social characteristics of students attending predominantly black colleges: A longitudinal study. *Research in Higher Education, 7*, 299–314.

Nelson, A. (1966). College characteristics associated with freshman attrition. *Personnel and Guidance Journal, 44*, 1046–1050.

Nelson, A. (1975). *Undergraduate academic achievement in college as an indication of occupational success* (PS 75-5). Washington, DC: Personnel Measure Research and Development Center, U.S. Civil Service Commission. (ERIC Document Reproduction Service No. 137 381)

Nelson, J. (1982). Institutional assessment of a private university by commuter and resident students. *Dissertation Abstracts International, 43*, 90A–91A.

Nelson, R., Scott, T., & Bryan, W. (1984). Precollege characteristics and early college experiences as predictors of freshman year persistence. *Journal of College Student Personnel, 25*, 50–54.

Nettles, M., & Baratz, J. (1985, March/April). Black colleges: Do we need them? *Change*, pp. 58–60.

Nettles, M., Thoeny, A., & Gosman, E. (1984). *Comparing and predicting the college performance of black and white students*. Paper presented at the meeting of the Association for the Study of Higher Education, Chicago.

Nettles, M., Thoeny, A., & Gosman, E. (1986). Comparative and predictive analyses of black and white students' college achievement and experience. *Journal of Higher Education, 57*, 289–318.

Neugarten, B. (1964). *Personality in middle and later life*. New York: Atherton.

Neugarten, B. (1968). *Middle age and aging*. Chicago: University of Chicago Press.

Neugarten, B. (1969). Continuities and discontinuities of psychological issues into adult life. *Human Development, 12*, 121–130.

Neugarten, B. (1975). Adult personality: Toward a psychology of life cycle. In W. Sze (Ed.), *The human life cycle*. New York: Jason Aronson.

Neugarten, B. (1977). Personality and aging. In J. Birren & K. Schaie (Eds.), *Handbook of the psychology of aging*. New York: Van Nostrand Reinhold.

Neugarten, B., & Datan, N. (1973). Sociological perspectives on the life cycle. In P. Baltes & K. Schaie (Eds.), *Life-span developmental psychology: Personality and socialization*. New York: Academic Press.

Neuman, W. (1985). *Persistence in the community college: The student perspective*. Unpublished doctoral dissertation, Syracuse University, Syracuse, NY.

Nevill, D., & Super, D. (1988). Career maturity and commitment to work in university students. *Journal of Vocational Behavior, 32*, 139–151.

Newcomb, T. (1968). Student peer group influence. In K. Yamamoto (Ed.), *The college student and his culture: An analysis*. Boston: Houghton Mifflin.

Newcomb, T., Brown, D., Kulik, J., Reimer, D., & Revelle, W. (1970). Self-selection and change. In J. Gaff (Ed.), *The cluster college*. San Francisco: Jossey-Bass.

Newcomb, T., Brown, D., Kulik, J., Reimer, D., & Revelle, W. (1971). The University of Michigan's residential college. In P. Dressel (Ed.), *The new colleges: Toward an appraisal*. Iowa City, IA: American College Testing Program and American Association for Higher Education.

Newcomb, T., Koenig, K., Flacks, R., & Warwick, D. (1967). *Persistence and change: Bennington College and its students after 25 years*. New York: John Wiley & Sons.

Newcomb, T., & Wilson, E. (1966). *College peer groups*. Chicago: Aldine.

Newcomer, M. (1959). *A century of higher education for American women*. New York: Harper & Row.

Newman, F. (1971). *Report on higher education*. Washington, DC: U.S. Department of Health, Education, and Welfare.

Newman, P., & Newman, B. (1978). Identity formation and the college experience. *Adolescence, 13*, 311–326.

Newton, L., & Gaither G. (1980). Factors contributing to attrition: An analysis of program impact on persistence patterns. *College and University, 55*, 237–251.

Nichols, R. (1964). Effects of various college characteristics on student aptitude test scores. *Journal of Educational Psychology, 55*, 45–54.

Nichols, R. (1967). Personality change and the college. *American Educational Research Journal, 4*, 173–190.

Nie, N. (1983). *Statistical package for the social sciences (Version X)*. New York: McGraw-Hill.

Niemi, A. (1974). Racial and ethnic differences in returns to educational investment in California and Texas. *Economic Inquiry, 12*, 398–402.

Nist, S., Simpson, M., & Hogrebe, M. (1985). The relationship between the use of study strategies and test performance. *Journal of Reading Behavior, 17*, 15–28.

Nolen, S. (1975). The economics of education: Research-results and needs. *Teachers College Record, 77*, 51–79.

Nora, A. (1987). *Campus-based aid programs as determinants of retention among Hispanic community college students*. Houston: University of Houston, Institute for Higher Education Law and Governance.

Northrop, L. (1975). Relationships among career maturity, achievement motivation, anxiety, independence and decisiveness in college students. *Dissertation Abstracts International, 37*, 958B.

Nosow, S., & Robertson, S. (1973). Changing socio-political attitudes of college students, 1967–71. *College Student Journal, 7*, 7–14.

Nowack, K., & Hanson, A. (1985). Academic achievement of freshmen as a function of residence hall housing. *NASPA Journal, 22*, 22–28.

Nucci, L., & Pascarella, E. (1987). The influence of college on moral development. In J. Smart (Ed.), *Higher education: Handbook of theory and research* (Vol. 3). New York: Agathon.

Nunley, C., & Breneman, D. (1988). Defining and measuring quality in community college education. In J. Eaton (Ed.), *Colleges of choice: The enabling impact of the community college.* New York: American Council on Education.

Nunn, C. (1973). Support of civil liberties among college students. *Social Problems, 20,* 300–310.

Nunn, C., Crockett, H., & Williams, J. (1978). *Tolerance for nonconformity.* San Francisco: Jossey-Bass.

Oates, M., & Williamson, S. (1978). Women's colleges and women achievers. *Signs: Journal of Women in Culture and Society, 3,* 795–806.

Ochberg, R. (1986). College dropouts: The developmental logic of psychosocial moratoria. *Journal of Youth and Adolescence, 15,* 287–302.

Ochsner, N., & Solmon, L. (1979). *College education and employment: The recent graduates.* Bethlehem, PA: CPC Foundation.

O'Donnell, J., & Andersen, D. (1978). Factors influencing choice of major and career of capable women. *Vocational Guidance Quarterly, 26,* 214–221.

Offer, D., & Offer, J. (1975). *From teen-age to young manhood.* New York: Basic Books.

Ogle, N., & Dodder, R. (1978). Increased tolerance and reference group shifts: A test in the college environment. *Educational Research Quarterly, 4,* 48–57.

Ohlde, C., & Vinitsky, M. (1976). Effects of values-clarification workshop on value awareness. *Journal of Counseling Psychology, 23,* 489–491.

Okes, I. (1976). *Participation in adult education: Final report, 1972.* Washington, DC: National Center for Education Statistics.

Olczak, P., & Goldman, J. (1975). The relationship between self-actualization and psychosocial maturity. *Journal of Clinical Psychology, 31,* 415–419.

O'Leary, B. (1980). *College grade point average as an indicator of occupational success: An update* (PRR 80-23). Washington, DC: Personnel Research and Developmental Center, U.S. Office of Personnel Management.

Olivas, M. (Ed.). (1986). *Latino college students.* New York: Teachers College Press.

Olneck, M., & Crouse, J. (1979). The IQ meritocracy reconsidered: Cognitive skill and adult success in the United States. *American Journal of Education, 88,* 1–31.

Olsen, H. (1972). Effects of changes in academic roles on self-concept of academic ability of black and white compensatory education students. *Journal of Negro Education, 41,* 365–369.

Olson, D., & Gravatt, A. (1968). Attitude change in a functional marriage course. *Family Coordinator, 17,* 99–104.

O'Malley, P., & Bachman, J. (1979). Self-esteem and education: Sex and cohort comparisons among high school seniors. *Journal of Personality and Social Psychology, 37,* 1153–1159.

O'Neill, C., Remer, P., & Gohs, D. (1984). Multiple outcome evaluation of a life-career development course. *Journal of Counseling Psychology, 31,* 532–540.

Orcutt, G., Franklin, S., Mendelsohn, R., & Smith, J. (1977). Does your probability of death depend on your environment? *American Economic Review, 67,* 260–264.

Orcutt, J. (1975). The impact of student activism on attitudes toward the female sex role. *Social Forces, 54,* 382–392.

Orcutt, J., & Bayer, A. (1978). Student protest and sex-role attitude change, 1967–1971: A log-linear analysis of longitudinal data. *Sex Roles, 4,* 267–280.

Orlofsky, J. (1977). Sex-role orientation, identity formation, and self-esteem in college men and women. *Sex Roles, 3,* 561–575.

Orlofsky, J., Marcia, J., & Lesser, I. (1973). Ego identity status and the intimacy versus isolation crisis of young adulthood. *Journal of Personality and Social Psychology, 27,* 211–219.

Ornstein, M. (1971). *Entry into the American labor force* (Report No. 113). Baltimore: Johns Hopkins University.

Ory, J., & Braskamp, L. (1988). Involvement and growth of students in three academic programs. *Research in Higher Education, 28,* 116–129.

Osmond, M., & Martin, P. (1975). Sex and sexism: A comparison of male and female sex-role attitudes. *Journal of Marriage and the Family, 37,* 744–758.

Ottinger, C. (Ed.). (1984). *Fact book on higher education, 1984–1985.* Washington, DC: American Council on Education.

Overall, J., & Spiegel, D. (1969). Concerning least-squares analysis of experimental data. *Psychological Bulletin, 72,* 311–322.

Owings, M., & Fetters, W. (1983). *An examination of the influence of different environmental factors on the postsecondary cognitive development of young adults.* Paper presented at the meeting of the American Educational Research Association, Montreal.

Pace, C. (1969). *College and University Environment Scales (CUES) technical manual* (2nd ed.). Princeton, NJ: Educational Testing Service.

Pace, C. (1972). *Education and evangelism: A profile of Protestant colleges.* New York: McGraw-Hill.

Pace, C. (1974). *The demise of diversity? A comparative profile of eight types of institutions.* Berkeley, CA: The Carnegie Commission on Higher Education.

Pace, C. (1976). *Evaluating higher education* (Topical Paper No. 1). Tucson: University of Arizona, College of Education, Higher Education Program.

Pace, C. (1979). *Measuring outcomes of college: Fifty years of findings and recommendations for the future.* San Francisco: Jossey-Bass.

Pace, C. (1980). Measuring the quality of student effort. *Current Issues in Higher Education, 2,* 10–16.

Pace, C. (1983). *College student experiences: A questionnaire* (2nd ed.). Los Angeles: University of California, Higher Education Research Institute.

Pace, C. (1984). *Measuring the quality of college student experiences.* Los Angeles: University of California, Higher Education Research Institute.

Pace, C. (1986). *Separate paths to separate places* (Report No. 3). Los Angeles: University of California, Graduate School of Education, Higher Education Research Institute, Project on the Study of Quality in Undergraduate Education.

Pace, C. (1987). *Good things go together.* Los Angeles: University of California, Center for the Study of Evaluation.

Pace, C. (1990). *The undergraduates: A report of their activities and progress in college in the 1980s.* Los Angeles: University of California, Center for the Study of Evaluation.

Pace, C., & Stern, G. (1958). An approach to the measurement of psychological characteristics of college environments. *Journal of Educational Psychology, 49,* 269–277.

Page, R., and Bode, J. (1982). Inducing changes in moral reasoning. *Journal of Psychology, 112,* 113–119.

Pallas, A., & Alexander, K. (1983). Sex differences in quantitative SAT performance: New evidence on the differential coursework hypothesis. *American Educational Research Journal, 20,* 165–182.

Pallett, J., & Hoyt, D. (1968). College curriculum and success in general business. *Journal of College Student Personnel, 9,* 238–245.

Palmer, J. (1984). Do college courses improve basic reading and writing skills? *Community College Review, 12,* 20–28.

Palmer, J. (1986). Bolstering the community college transfer function: An ERIC review. *Community College Review, 14,* 53–63.

Palmer, P. (1987, September/October). Community, conflict, and ways of knowing. *Change,* pp. 20–25.

Palmore, E. (1979). Predictors of successful aging. *The Gerentologist, 19,* 427–431.

Palmore, E., & Luikart, C. (1972). Health and social factors related to life satisfaction. *Journal of Health and Social Behavior, 13,* 68–80.

Panos, R., & Astin, A. (1968). Attrition among college students. *American Educational Research Journal, 5,* 57–72.

Parelius, A. (1975a). Change and stability in college women's orientation toward education, family, and work. *Social Problems, 22,* 420–432.

Parelius, A. (1975b). Emerging sex-role attitudes, expectations, and strains among college women. *Journal of Marriage and the Family, 37,* 146–153.

Parent, J., Forward, J., Canter, R., & Mohling, J. (1975). Interactive effects of teaching strategy and personal locus of control on student performance and satisfaction. *Journal of Educational Psychology, 67,* 764–769.

Parham, T., & Helms, J. (1981). The influence of black students' racial identity attitudes on preference for counselor's race. *Journal of Counseling Psychology, 28,* 250–257.

Parham, T., & Helms, J. (1985a). Attitudes of racial identity and self-esteem of black students: An exploratory investigation. *Journal of College Student Personnel, 26,* 143–147.

Parham, T., & Helms, J. (1985b). Relation of racial identity attitudes to self-actualization and affective states of black students. *Journal of Counseling Psychology, 32,* 431–440.

Parish, T. (1988a). Enhancing college students' social skills and self-concepts. *College Student Journal, 22,* 203–205.

Parish, T. (1988b). Helping college students take control of their lives. *College Student Journal, 22,* 64–69.

Parish, T., Rosenblatt, R., & Kappes, B. (1979). The relationship between human values and moral judgment. *Psychology, 16,* 1–5.

Park, J., & Johnson, R. (1983). *Moral development in rural and urban Korea.* Unpublished manuscript, Hankook University of Foreign Studies, Seoul, Korea.

Parker, C. (1977). On modeling reality. *Journal of College Student Personnel, 18,* 419–425.

Parker, C., & Schmidt, J. (1982). Effects of college experience. In H. Mitzel (Ed.), *Encyclopedia of educational research* (5th ed.). New York: Free Press.

Parker, J., & Thorndike, R. (1989). *Effects of age and education on cognitive development.* Paper presented at the meeting of the American Educational Research Association, San Francisco.

Parnes, H., & Kohen, A. (1975). Occupational information and labor market status: The case of young men. *Journal of Human Resources, 10,* 44–55.

Parnes, H., Shea, J., Spitz, R., & Zeller, F. (1970). *Dual careers* (Vol. 1) (Manpower Research Monograph No. 21). Washington, DC: U.S. Department of Labor.

Parnes, S., & Noeller, R. (1973). Applied creativity: The creative studies project: IV. Personality findings and conclusions. *Journal of Creative Behavior, 7,* 15–36.

Parrott, R., & Hewitt, J. (1978). Increasing self-esteem through participation in a goal-attainment program. *Journal of Clinical Psychology, 34,* 955–957.

Parsons, D. (1974). The cost of school time, foregone earnings, and human capital formation. *Journal of Political Economy, 82,* 251–266.

Parsons, D. (1975). Intergenerational wealth transfer and educational decisions of male youth. *Quarterly Journal of Economics, 89,* 603–617.

Parsons, T., & Platt, G. (1970). Age, social structure, and socialization in higher education. *Sociology of Education, 43,* 1–38.

Pascarella, E. (1976). Perceptions of the college environment by students in different academic majors in two colleges of arts and sciences. *Research in Higher Education, 4,* 165–176.

Pascarella, E. (1977a). Interaction of motivation, mathematics preparation, and instructional method in a PSI and conventionally taught calculus course. *AV Communication Review, 25,* 25–41.

Pascarella, E. (1977b). Student motivation as a differential predictor of course outcomes in personalized system of instruction and conventional instructional methods. *Journal of Educational Research, 71,* 21–26.

Pascarella, E. (1978). Interactive effects of prior mathematics preparation and level of instructional support in college calculus. *American Educational Research Journal, 15,* 275–285.

Pascarella, E. (1980). Student-faculty informal contact and college outcomes. *Review of Educational Research, 50,* 545–595.

Pascarella, E. (1982). Perspectives on quantitative analysis for research in postsecondary education. *Review of Higher Education, 5,* 197–211.

Pascarella, E. (1984a). College environmental influences on students' educational aspirations. *Journal of Higher Education, 55,* 751–771.

Pascarella, E. (1984b). Reassessing the effects of living on-campus versus commuting to college: A causal modeling approach. *Review of Higher Education, 7,* 247–260.

Pascarella, E. (1985a). College environmental influences on learning and cognitive development: A critical review and synthesis. In J. Smart (Ed.), *Higher education: Handbook of theory and research* (Vol. 1). New York: Agathon.

Pascarella, E. (1985b). Racial differences in factors associated with bachelor's degree completion: A nine-year follow-up. *Research in Higher Education, 23,* 351–373.

Pascarella, E. (1985c). Students' affective development within the college environment. *Journal of Higher Education, 56,* 640–663.

Pascarella, E. (1985d). The influence of on-campus living versus commuting to college on intellectual and interpersonal self-concept. *Journal of College Student Personnel, 26,* 292–299.

Pascarella, E. (1986a). A program for research and policy development on student persistence at the institutional level. *Journal of College Student Personnel, 27,* 100–107.

Pascarella, E. (1986b). *Are value-added analyses valuable?* Paper presented at the Educational Testing Service Invitational Conference on Assessment in Higher Education, New York.

Pascarella, E. (1989). The development of critical thinking: Does college make a difference? *Journal of College Student Development, 30,* 19–26.

Pascarella, E. (undated). *Academic and interpersonal experience as mediators of the structural effects of college.* Unpublished manuscript, University of Illinois, Chicago.

Pascarella, E., Brier, E., Smart, J., & Herzog, L. (1987). Becoming a physician: The influence of the undergraduate experience. *Research in Higher Education, 26,* 180–201.

Pascarella, E., & Chapman, D. (1983a). A multi-institutional, path analytic validation of Tinto's model of college withdrawal. *American Educational Research Journal, 20,* 87–102.

Pascarella, E., & Chapman, D. (1983b). Validation of a theoretical model of college withdrawal: Interaction effects in a multi-institutional sample. *Research in Higher Education, 19,* 25–48.

Pascarella, E., Duby, P., & Iverson, B. (1983). A test and reconceptualization of a theoretical model of college withdrawal in a commuter institution setting. *Sociology of Education, 56,* 88–100.

Pascarella, E., Duby, P., Miller, V., & Rasher, S. (1981). Preenrollment variables and academic performance as predictors of freshman year persistence, early withdrawal, and stopout behavior in an urban, nonresidential university. *Research in Higher Education, 15,* 329–349.

Pascarella, E., Duby, P., Terenzini, P., & Iverson, B. (1983). Student-faculty relationships and freshman year intellectual and personal growth in a nonresidential setting. *Journal of College Student Personnel, 24,* 395–402.

Pascarella, E., Ethington, C., & Smart, J. (1988). The influence of college on humanitarian/civic involvement values. *Journal of Higher Education, 59,* 412–437.

Pascarella, E., & Smart, J. (1989). *Is the effect of grades on early career income general or conditional? A research note.* Unpublished manuscript, University of Illinois, Chicago.

Pascarella, E., & Smart, J. (1990). *Impacts of intercollegiate athletic participation for black-American and white-American men: Some further evidence.* Unpublished manuscript, University of Illinois, Chicago.

Pascarella, E., Smart, J., & Braxton, J. (1986). Postsecondary educational attainment and humanitarian and civic values. *Journal of College Student Personnel, 27,* 418–425.

Pascarella, E., Smart, J., & Ethington, C. (1986). Long-term persistence of two-year college students. *Research in Higher Education, 24,* 47–71.

Pascarella, E., Smart, J., Ethington, C., & Nettles, M. (1987). The influence of college on self-concept: A consideration of race and gender differences. *American Educational Research Journal, 24,* 49–77.

Pascarella, E., Smart, J., & Stoecker, J. (1987). *College racial composition and the early educational, occupational, and economic attainments of black men and women.* Paper presented at the meeting of the American Educational Research Association, Washington, DC.

Pascarella, E., Smart, J., & Stoecker, J. (1989). College race and the early status attainment of black students. *Journal of Higher Education, 60,* 82–107.

Pascarella, E., & Staver, J. (1985). The influence of on-campus work in science on science career choice during college: A causal modeling approach. *Review of Higher Education, 8,* 229–245.

Pascarella, E., & Terenzini, P. (1976). Informal interaction with faculty and freshman ratings of academic and non-academic experience of college. *Journal of Educational Research, 70,* 35–41.

Pascarella, E., & Terenzini, P. (1977). Patterns of student-faculty informal interaction beyond the classroom and voluntary freshman attrition. *Journal of Higher Education, 48,* 540–552.

Pascarella, E., & Terenzini, P. (1978). Student-faculty informal relationships and freshman year educational outcomes. *Journal of Educational Research, 71,* 183–189.

Pascarella, E., & Terenzini, P. (1979a). Interaction effects in Spady's and Tinto's conceptual models of college dropout. *Sociology of Education, 52,* 197–210.

Pascarella, E., & Terenzini, P. (1979b). Student-faculty informal contact and college persistence: A further investigation. *Journal of Educational Research, 72,* 214–218.

Pascarella, E., & Terenzini, P. (1980a). Predicting freshman persistence and voluntary dropout decisions from a theoretical model. *Journal of Higher Education, 51,* 60–75.

Pascarella, E., & Terenzini, P. (1980b). Student-faculty and student-peer relationships as mediators of the structural effects of undergraduate residence arrangement. *Journal of Educational Research, 73,* 344–353.

Pascarella, E., & Terenzini, P. (1981). Residence arrangement, student/faculty relationships, and freshman-year educational outcomes. *Journal of College Student Personnel, 22,* 147–156.

Pascarella, E., & Terenzini, P. (1982). Contextual analysis as a method for assessing residence group effects. *Journal of College Student Personnel, 23,* 108–114.

Pascarella, E., & Terenzini, P. (1983). Predicting voluntary freshman year persistence/withdrawal behavior in a residential university: A path analytic validation of Tinto's model. *Journal of Educational Psychology, 75,* 215–226.

Pascarella, E., Terenzini, P., & Hibel, J. (1978). Student-faculty interactional settings and their relationship to predicted academic performance. *Journal of Higher Education, 49,* 450–463.

Pascarella, E., Terenzini, P., & Wolfle, L. (1986). Orientation to college and freshman year persistence/withdrawal decisions. *Journal of Higher Education, 57,* 155–175.

Pascarella, E., & Wolfle, L. (1985). *Persistence in higher education: A nine-year test of a theoretical model.* Paper presented at the meeting of the American Educational Research Association, Chicago.

Pedhazur, E. (1975). Analytic methods in studies of educational effects. In F. Kerlinger (Ed.), *Review of research in education* (Vol. 3). Itasca, IL: F. E. Peacock.

Pedhazur, E. (1982). *Multiple regression in behavioral research: Explanation and prediction* (2nd ed.). New York: Holt, Rinehart & Winston.

Pelowski, J. (1979). A study of the impact of the cross-cultural education program, the winter term abroad, on the alumnae of Lake Erie College for Women from 1953–1978. *Dissertation Abstracts International, 40,* 3818A.

Peng, S. (1978). Transfer students in institutions of higher education. *Research in Higher Education, 8,* 319–342.

Peng, S., Bailey, J., & Eckland, B. (1977). Access to higher education: Results from the National Longitudinal Study of the High School Class of 1972. *Educational Researcher, 6,* 3–7.

Peng, S., & Fetters, W. (1978). Variables involved in withdrawal during the first two years of college: Preliminary findings from the National Longitudinal Study of the High School Class of 1972. *American Educational Research Journal, 15,* 361–372.

Peng, S., & Jaffe, J. (1979). Women who enter male-dominated fields of study in higher education. *American Educational Research Journal, 16,* 285–293.

Penley, L., Gould, S., & de la Vina, L. (1984). The comparative salary position of Mexican American college graduates in business. *Social Science Quarterly, 65,* 444–454.

Penn, W. (1988). *Teaching ethics: A non-Socratic approach.* Unpublished manuscript, St. Edwards University, Austin, TX.

Perella, V. (1973). Employment of recent college graduates. *Monthly Labor Review, 96,* 41–50.

Perkins, D. (1985). Postprimary education has little impact on informal reasoning. *Journal of Educational Psychology, 77,* 562–571.

Perkins, D. (1986). *Reasoning as it is and could be: An empirical perspective.* Paper presented at the meeting of the American Educational Research Association, San Francisco.

Perkins, D., Allen, R., & Hafner, J. (1983). Difficulties in everyday reasoning. In W. Maxwell (Ed.), *Thinking: The frontier expands.* Hillsdale, NJ: Lawrence Erlbaum.

Perkins, D., Bushey, B., & Farady, M. (1986). *Learning to reason* (Final Report to the National Institute of Education, Grant NIE-G-83-0028). Cambridge, MA: Harvard University.

Perrucci, C. (1969). Engineering and the class structure. In R. Perrucci & J. Gerstl (Eds.), *The engineers and the social system.* New York: John Wiley & Sons.

Perrucci, C. (1980). Gender and achievement: The early careers of college graduates. *Sociological Focus, 13*, 99–111.

Perrucci, R., & Perrucci, C. (1970). Social origins, educational contexts, and career mobility. *American Sociological Review, 35*, 451–463.

Perry, R., & Dickens, W. (1984). Perceived control in the college classroom: The effect of response outcome contingency training and instructor expressiveness on students' attributions and achievement. *Journal of Educational Psychology, 76*, 966–981.

Perry, R., & Magnusson, J. (1987). Effective instruction and students' perceptions of control in the college classroom: Multiple lectures effects. *Journal of Educational Psychology, 79*, 453–460.

Perry, R., & Penner, K. (1989). *Enhancing academic achievement in college students through attributional retraining.* Paper presented at the meeting of the American Educational Research Association, San Francisco.

Perry, R., & Tunna, K. (1988). Perceived control, type A/B behavior, and instructional quality. *Journal of Educational Psychology, 80*, 102–110.

Perry, W. (1970). *Forms of intellectual and ethical development in the college years: A scheme.* New York: Holt, Rinehart & Winston.

Perry, W. (1981). Cognitive and ethical growth. In A. Chickering & Associates, *The modern American college: Responding to the new realities of diverse students and a changing society.* San Francisco: Jossey Bass.

Pervin, L. (1967). A twenty-college study of student × college interaction using TAPE (transactional analysis of personality and environment): Rationale, reliability, and validity. *Journal of Educational Psychology, 58*, 290–302.

Pervin, L. (1968a). The college as a social system: Student perceptions of students, faculty, and administration. *Journal of Educational Research, 61*, 281–284.

Pervin, L. (1968b). Performance and satisfaction as a function of individual-environment fit. *Psychological Bulletin, 69*, 56–68.

Pervin, L., & Rubin, D. (1967). Student dissatisfaction with college and the college dropout: A transactional approach. *Journal of Social Psychology, 72*, 285–295.

Peterson, C. (1973). The development and achievement of equal opportunity program students. *Journal of College Student Personnel, 14*, 34–37.

Peterson, M., et al. (1979). *Black students on white campuses: The impacts of increased black enrollments.* Ann Arbor: University of Michigan, Institute for Social Research.

Peterson, P. (1979). Aptitude × treatment interaction effects of teacher structuring and student participation in college instruction. *Journal of Educational Psychology, 71*, 521–533.

Peterson, R. (1968). *College Student Questionnaires: Technical manual* (rev. ed.). Princeton, NJ: Educational Testing Service.

Pfeffer, J. (1977). Effects of an MBA and socioeconomic origins on business school graduates' salaries. *Journal of Applied Psychology, 62,* 698–705.

Pfeifer, C. (1976). Relationship between scholastic aptitude, perception of university climate and college success for black and white students. *Journal of Applied Psychology, 61,* 341–347.

Pflaum, S., Pascarella, E., & Duby, P. (1985). The effects of honors college participation on academic performance during the freshman year. *Journal of College Student Personnel, 26,* 414–419.

Pfnister, A. (1972). *Impact of study abroad on the American college undergraduate.* Paper presented at the meeting of the National Association for Foreign Student Affairs. (ERIC Document No. ED 063 882)

Phares, E. (1973). *Locus of control: A personality determinant of behavior.* Morristown, NJ: General Learning Press.

Phares, E. (1976). *Locus of control in personality.* Morristown, NJ: General Learning Press.

Phelan, T., & Phelan, J. (1983). Higher education and early life outcomes. *Higher Education, 12,* 665–680.

Phelan, W. (1979). Undergraduate orientations toward scientific and scholarly careers. *American Educational Research Journal, 16,* 411–422.

Phillips, M. (1976). The influence of residential setting on the academic achievement of college students: A review. *Journal of College and University Student Housing, 6,* 33–37.

Piaget, J. (1964). *Judgment and reasoning in the child.* Totowa, NJ: Littlefield, Adams.

Piaget, J. (1972). Intellectual evolution from adolescence to adulthood. *Human Development, 15,* 1–12.

Pierce, J., Fiore, M., Novotny, T., Hatziandreu, E., & Davis, R. (1989). Trends in cigarette smoking in the United States: Educational differences are increasing. *Journal of the American Medical Association, 261,* 56–60.

Pierson, G. (1969). *The education of American leaders: Comparative contributions of U.S. colleges and universities.* New York: Praeger.

Pike, G. (1989). Background, college experiences, and the ACT-COMP exam: Using construct validity to evaluate assessment instruments. *Review of Higher Education, 13,* 91–117.

Pike, G., & Banta, T. (1989). *Using construct validity to evaluate assessment instruments: A comparison of the ACT-COMP exam and the ETS Academic Profile.* Paper presented at the meeting of the American Educational Research Association, San Francisco.

Pike, G., & Phillippi, R. (1988). *Relationships between self-reported coursework and performance on the ACT-COMP exam: An analysis of the generalizability of the differential coursework methodology.* Paper presented at the meeting of the Association for the Study of Higher Education, St. Louis.

Pillemer, D., & Light, R. (1980). Synthesizing outcomes: How to use research evidence from many studies. *Harvard Educational Review, 50,* 176–195.

Pincus, F. (1980). The false promises of community colleges: Class conflict and vocational education. *Harvard Educational Review, 50,* 332–361.

Pincus, F., & Archer, E. (1989). *Bridges to opportunity: Are community colleges meeting the transfer needs of minority students?* New York: Academy for Educational Development and College Entrance Examination Board.

Pineo, P., & Porter, J. (1967). Occupational prestige in Canada. *Canadian Review of Sociology and Anthropology, 4,* 24–40.

Plant, W. (1958a). Changes in ethnocentrism associated with a two-year college experience. *Journal of Genetic Psychology, 92,* 189–197.

Plant, W. (1958b). Changes in ethnocentrism associated with a four-year college education. *Journal of Educational Research, 49,* 162–165.

Plant, W. (1962). *Personality changes associated with a college education* (DHEW, Cooperative Research Branch Project 348 [SAE 7666]). San Jose, CA: San Jose State College.

Plant, W. (1965). Longitudinal changes in intolerance and authoritarianism for subjects differing in amount of college education over four years. *Genetic Psychology Monographs, 72,* 242–287.

Plant, W., & Minium, E. (1967). Differential personality development in young adults of markedly different aptitude levels. *Journal of Educational Psychology, 58,* 141–152.

Plant, W., & Telford, C. (1966). Changes in personality for groups completing different amounts of college over two years. *Genetic Psychology Monographs, 74,* 3–36.

Plummer, O., & Koh, Y. (1987). Effects of "aerobics" on self-concepts of college women. *Perceptual and Motor Skills, 65,* 271–275.

Podd, M. (1972). Ego identity status and morality: The relationship between two developmental constructs. *Developmental Psychology, 6,* 497–507.

Pohlmann, J., & Beggs, D. (1974). A study of validity of self-report measures of academic growth. *Journal of Educational Measurement, 11,* 115–119.

Polachek, S. (1978). Sex differences in college major. *Industrial and Labor Relations Review, 31,* 498–508.

Polite, C., Cochrane, R., & Silverman, B. (1974). Ethnic group identification and differentiation. *Journal of Social Psychology, 92,* 149–150.

Polkosnik, M., & Winston, R. (1989). Relationships between students' intellectual and psychosocial development: An exploratory investigation. *Journal of College Student Development, 30,* 10–19.

Pollio, H. (1984). *What students think about and do in college lecture classes* (Teaching-Learning Issues No. 53). Knoxville, TN: University of Tennessee Learning Research Center.

Polovy, P. (1980). A study of moral development and personality relationships in adolescents and young adult Catholic students. *Journal of Clinical Psychology, 36,* 752–757.

Ponsford, R., Alloway, L., & Mhoon, J. (1986). *Self-esteem and moral judgments in a Christian liberal arts college: Class comparisons.* Paper presented at the meeting of the Western Psychological Association, Seattle.

Porter, J. (1974). Race, socialization, and mobility in educational and early occupational attainment. *American Sociological Review, 39,* 303–316.

Porter, J. (1976). Socialization and mobility in educational and early occupational attainment. *Sociology of Education, 49,* 23–33.

Porter, O. (1989). *The influence of institutional control on the persistence of minority students: A descriptive analysis.* Paper presented at the meeting of the American Educational Research Association, San Francisco.

Posthuma, A., & Navran, L. (1970). Relation of congruence in student-faculty interests to achievement in college. *Journal of Counseling Psychology, 17,* 352–356.

Postlethwaite, S., Novak, J., & Murray, H. (1972). *The audio-tutorial approach to learning.* Minneapolis: Burgess.

Pounds, A. (1987). Black students' needs on predominantly white campuses. In D. Wright (Ed.), *Responding to the needs of today's minority students* (New Directions for Student Services No. 38). San Francisco: Jossey Bass.

Powell, J. (1985). The residues of learning: Autobiographical accounts by graduates of the impact of higher education. *Higher Education, 14,* 127–147.

Powers, J. (1976). *An inquiry into the effects of a college education on the attitudes, competencies and behavior of individuals.* Claremont, CA: Claremont Graduate School.

Prager, K. (1982). Identity development and self-esteem in young women. *Journal of Genetic Psychology, 141,* 177–182.

Prager, K. (1986). Identity development, age, and college experience in women. *Journal of Genetic Psychology, 147,* 31–36.

Prather, J., & Smith, G. (1976). *Faculty grading patterns* (Report No. 76-12). Atlanta: Georgia State University, Office of Institutional Planning.

Prather, J., Smith, G., & Kodras, J. (1979). A longitudinal study of grades in 144 undergraduate courses. *Research in Higher Education, 10,* 11–24.

Prather, J., Williams, J., & Wadley, J. (1976). *The relationship of major field of study with undergraduate course grades: A multivariate analysis controlling for academic and personal characteristics and longitudinal trends* (Report OIP-77-3). Atlanta: Georgia State University, Office of Institutional Research.

Presby, S. (1978). Overly broad categories obscure important differences between therapies. *American Psychologist, 33,* 514–515.

Priest, R., Prince, H., & Vitters, A. (1978). The first coed class at West Point in performance and attitudes. *Youth and Society, 10,* 205–224.

Princeton University (1967). *Twenty-five years out.* Princeton, NJ: Princeton University Alumni Office.

Provost, J., & Anchors, S. (1987). *Applications of the Myers-Briggs Type Indicator in higher education.* Palo Alto, CA: Consulting Psycholgists Press.

Psacharopoulos, G. (1972a). Rates of return around the world. *Comparative Education Review, 16,* 54–67.

Psacharopoulos, G. (1972b). The economic returns to higher education in twenty-five countries. *Higher Education, 1,* 141–158.

Psacharopoulos, G. (1973). *Returns to education.* San Francisco: Jossey-Bass.

Psacharopoulos, G. (1985). Returns to education: A further international update and implications. *Journal of Human Resources, 20,* 583–604.

Pugh, R. (1969). Undergraduate environment as an aid in predicting law school achievement. *Journal of Educational Research, 62,* 271–274.

Pugh, R., and Chamberlain, P. (1976). Undergraduate residence: An assessment of academic achievement in a predominantly university community. *Journal of College Student Personnel, 17,* 138–141.

Pyle, K. (1981). Institution cross-cultural service/learning: Impact on student development. *Journal of College Student Personnel, 22,* 509–514.

Quevedo-Garcia, E. (1987). Facilitating the development of Hispanic college students. In D. Wright (Ed.), *Responding to the needs of today's minority students* (New Directions for Student Services No. 38). San Francisco: Jossey-Bass.

Quinn, R., & Baldi de Mandilovitch, M. (1975). *Education and job satisfaction: A questionable payoff.* Ann Arbor: University of Michigan, Survey Research Center.

Quinn, R., & Baldi de Mandilovitch, M. (1980). Education and job satisfaction, 1962–1977. *Vocational Guidance Quarterly, 29,* 100–111.

Quinn, R., & Staines, G. (1979). *The 1977 quality of employment survey.* Ann Arbor: University of Michigan, Survey Research Center.

Quinn, R., Staines, G., & McCullough, M. (1974). *Job satisfaction: Is there a trend?* Washington, DC: U.S. Department of Labor.

Rabinowitz, M., & Glaser, R. (1985). Cognitive structure and process in highly competent performance. In F. Horowitz & M. O'Brien (Eds.), *The gifted and talented: Developmental perspectives.* Washington, DC: American Psychological Association.

Rago, J. (1973). The influence of undergraduate residence upon student personal development. *College Student Journal Monograph, 7.* 11 pp.

Ramirez, A., & Soriano, F. (1981). Causal attributions of success and failure among Chicano university students. *Hispanic Journal of Behavioral Sciences, 3,* 397–407.

Ramseur, H. (1975). *Continuity and change in black identity: A study of black students at an interracial college.* Unpublished doctoral dissertation, Harvard University, Cambridge, MA.

Ratcliff, J. (1988). *Assessment and curriculum reform: Research issues, models, and methods.* Invited symposium presented at the meeting of the Association for the Study of Higher Education, St. Louis.

Ratcliff, J., & Associates (1988). *Development and testing of a cluster-analytic model for identifying coursework patterns associated with general learned abilities of students* (Progress Report No. 6). Ames: Iowa State University, College of Education.

Raudenbush, S., & Bryk, A. (1988). Methodological advances in analyzing the effects of schools and classrooms on student learning. In E. Rothkopf (Ed.), *Review of research in education* (Vol. 15). Washington, DC: American Educational Research Association.

Rawlins, V., & Ulman, L. (1974). The utilization of college-trained manpower in the United States. In M. Gordon (Ed.), *Higher education and the labor market*. New York: McGraw-Hill.

Rayman, J., Bernard, C., Holland, J., & Barnett, D. (1983). The effects of a career course on undecided college students. *Journal of Vocational Behavior, 23,* 346–355.

Raymond, R., & Sesnowitz, M. (1975). The returns to investments in higher education: Some new evidence. *Journal of Human Resources, 10,* 139–514.

Raymond, R., & Sesnowitz, M. (1983). The rate of return to Mexican Americans and Anglos on an investment in a college education. *Economic Inquiry, 21,* 400–411.

Redmore, C. (1983). Ego development in the college years: Two longitudinal studies. *Journal of Youth and Adolescence, 12,* 301–306.

Redmore, C., & Loevinger, J. (1979). Ego development in adolescence: Longitudinal studies. *Journal of Youth and Adolescence, 8,* 1–20.

Redmore, C., & Waldman, K. (1975). Reliability of a sentence completion measure of ego development. *Journal of Personality Assessment, 39,* 236–243.

Reed, R., & Miller, H. (1970). Some determinants of the variation in earnings for college men. *Journal of Human Resources, 5,* 177–190.

Regan, M. (1969). Student change: The new student and society. *NASPA Journal, 6,* 127–135.

Reid, E. (1974). Effects of co-residential living on the attitudes, self-image, and role expectations of college women. *American Journal of Psychiatry, 131,* 551–554.

Reif, R. (1984). The development of formal reasoning patterns among university science and mathematics students. *Dissertation Abstracts International, 45,* 766A.

Reitz, J. (1975). Undergraduate aspiration and career choice: Effects of college selectivity. *Sociology of Education, 48,* 303–323.

Remer, P., O'Neill, C., & Gohs, D. (1984). Multiple outcome evaluation of a life-career development course. *Journal of Counseling Psychology, 31,* 532–540.

Renner, J., & Lawson, A. (1975). Intellectual development in preservice elementary school teachers: An evaluation. *Journal of College Science Teaching, 5,* 89–92.

Renner, J., Paske, W. (1977). Comparing two forms of instruction in college physics. *American Journal of Physics, 45,* 851–859.

Renshaw, E. (1972). Are we overestimating the return from a college education? *School Review, 80,* 459–475.

Rest, J. (1975). Longitudinal study of the Defining Issues Test: A strategy for analyzing developmental change. *Developmental Psychology, 11,* 738–748.

Rest, J. (1976). *Moral judgment related to sample characteristics* (Tech. Rep. No. 2). Minneapolis: University of Minnesota.

Rest, J. (1979a). *Development in judging moral issues.* Minneapolis: University of Minnesota Press.

Rest, J. (1979b). *Revised manual for the Defining Issues Test.* Minneapolis: Moral Research Projects.

Rest, J. (1979c). *The impact of higher education on moral judgment development* (Tech. Rep. No. 5). Minneapolis: Moral Research Projects.

Rest, J. (1981). *The impact of higher education on moral judgment development.* Paper presented at the meeting of the American Educational Research Association, Los Angeles.

Rest, J. (1983a). Morality. In J. Flavell & E. Markman (Eds.), *Handbook of child psychology: Vol. 3. Cognitive development.* New York: John Wiley & Sons.

Rest, J. (1983b). Morality. In P. Mussen (Ed.), *Carmichael's manual of child psychology.* New York: John Wiley & Sons.

Rest, J. (1985). *Moral development in young adults.* Unpublished manuscript, University of Minnesota, Minneapolis and St. Paul.

Rest, J. (1986a). *Discussion of the Sierra Project.* Presentation at the meeting of the Society for Moral Education, Chicago.

Rest, J. (Ed.). (1986b). *Moral development: Advances in research and theory.* New York: Praeger.

Rest, J. (1986c). Moral development in young adults. In R. Mines & K. Kitchener (Eds.), *Adult cognitive development.* New York: Praeger.

Rest, J., Davison, M., & Robbins, S. (1978). Age trends in judging moral issues: A review of cross-sectional, longitudinal, and sequential studies of the Defining Issues Test. *Child Development, 49,* 263–279.

Rest, J., & Deemer, D. (1986). Life experiences and developmental pathways. In J. Rest, (Ed.). *Moral development: Advances in research and theory.* New York: Praeger.

Rest, J., & Thoma, S. (1985). Relation of moral judgment development to formal education. *Developmental Psychology, 21,* 709–714.

Reutefors, D., Schneider, L., & Overton, T. (1979). Academic achievement: An examination of Holland's congruence, consistency, and differentiation predictions. *Journal of Vocational Behavior, 14,* 181–189.

Riahinejad, A., & Hood, A. (1984). The development of interpersonal relationships in college. *Journal of College Student Personnel, 25,* 498–502.

Riccobono, J., & Dunteman, G. (1979). *National longitudinal study of the high school class of 1972: Preliminary analyses of student financial aid.* Arlington, VA: National Center for Education Statistics. (ERIC Document Reproduction Service No. ED 170 303)

Rice, J., & Hemmings, A. (1988). Women's colleges and women achievers: An update. *Signs: Journal of Women in Culture and Society, 13,* 546–559.

Rice, R. (1983). *USC-Lancaster: A retention study for a two-year commuter campus.* Lancaster: University of South Carolina. (ERIC Document Reproduction Service No. ED 231 440)

Rice, R. (1984). *Does University 101 work? You bet: Research documenting the effectiveness of University 101 upon retention and student study habits and attitudes.* Unpublished manuscript, University of South Carolina, Lancaster.

Rich, H. (1976). The effect of college on political awareness and knowledge. *Youth and Society, 8,* 67–80.

Rich, H. (1977). The liberalizing influence of college: Some new evidence. *Adolescence, 12,* 199–211.

Rich, H. (1980). Tolerance for civil liberties among college students. *Youth and Society, 12,* 17–32.

Rich, H., & Jolicoeur, P. (1978). *Student attitudes and academic environments: A study of California higher education.* New York: Praeger.

Richards, E. (1984a). Early employment situations and work role satisfaction among recent college graduates. *Journal of Vocational Behavior, 24,* 305–318.

Richards, E. (1984b). Undergraduate preparation and early career outcomes: A study of recent college graduates. *Journal of Vocational Behavior, 24,* 279–304.

Richardson, J. (1981). Problem solving instruction for physics. *Dissertation Abstracts International, 42,* 3536A.

Richardson, R., & Bender, L. (1985). *Students in urban settings: Achieving the baccalaureate degree* (ASHE-ERIC Higher Education Report No. 6). Washington, DC: Association for the Study of Higher Education.

Ridgeway, C. (1978). Predicting college women's aspirations from evaluations of the housewife and work role. *Sociological Quarterly, 19,* 281–291.

Riffer, S. (1972). Determinants of university students' political attitudes or demythologizing campus political activism. *Review of Educational Research, 42,* 561–571.

Riley, S. (1982). The applicability of undergraduate education in jobs. *Higher Education, 11,* 155–175.

Robbins, R. (1981). Improving student reasoning skills in science classes. *Engineering Education, 72,* 208–212.

Robbins, S. (1976). Outdoor wilderness survival and sociological effects upon students in changing human behavior. *Dissertation Abstracts International, 37,* 1473–A. (University Microfilms No. 76-18,350)

Robertshaw, D., & Wolfle, L. (1982). The cognitive value of two-year colleges for whites and blacks. *Integrated Education, 19,* 68–71.

Robertshaw, D., & Wolfle, L. (1983). Discontinuities in schooling and educational attainment. *Higher Education, 12,* 1–18.

Robin, A. (1976). Behavioral instruction in the college classroom. *Review of Educational Research, 46,* 313–354.

Rock, D. (1972). *The use of taxonomic procedures to identify both overall college effects and those effects which interact with student ability.* Paper presented at the meeting of the American Educational Research Association, Chicago.

Rock, D., Baird, L., & Linn, R. (1972). Interaction between college effects and students' aptitudes. *American Educational Research Journal, 9,* 149–161.

Rock, D., Centra, J., & Linn, R. (1970). Relationships between college characteristics and student achievement. *American Educational Research Journal, 7,* 109–121.

Rodgers, R. (1980). Theories underlying student development. In D. Creamer (Ed.), *Student development in higher education: Theories, practices, and future directions* (ACPA Media Publication No. 27). Alexandria, VA: American College Personnel Association.

Rodgers, R. (1983). Using theory in practice. In T. Miller, R. Winston, & W. Mendenhall (Eds.), *Administration and leadership in student affairs.* Muncie, IN: Accelerated Development.

Rodgers, R. (1989). Student development. In U. Delworth, G. Hanson, & Associates (Eds.), *Student services: A handbook for the profession* (2nd ed.). San Francisco: Jossey-Bass.

Rodgers, R. (1990a). Using theory in practice in student affairs. In T. Miller, R. Winston, & W. Mendenhall (Eds.), *Administration and leadership in student affairs: Actualizing student development in higher education* (2nd ed.). Muncie, IN: Accelerated Development.

Rodgers, R. (1990b). Recent theories and research underlying student development. In D. Creamer & Associates, *College student development theory and practice for the 1990s* (Media Publication No. 49). Alexandria, VA: American College Personnel Association.

Rodgers, R. (1990c). An integration of campus ecology and student development: The Olentangy project. In D. Creamer & Associates, *College student development theory and practice for the 1990s* (Media Publication No. 49). Alexandria, VA: American College Personnel Association.

Roesler, E. (1971). *Community college and technical institute follow-up study of students enrolled during one or more quarters: Fall 1970 to fall 1971.* Washington, DC: U.S. Department of Health, Education, and Welfare. (ERIC Document Reproduction Service No. ED 072 770)

Rogers, R. (1969). Private rates of return to education in the U.S.: A case study. *Yale Economic Essays, 9,* 89–134.

Rogosa, D. (1978). Politics, process, and pyramids. *Journal of Educational Statistics, 3*, 79–86.

Rokeach, M. (1960). *The open and closed mind: Investigations into the nature of belief systems and personality systems.* New York: Basic Books.

Rokeach, M. (1971). Long-range experimental modification of values, attitudes, and behavior. *American Psychologist, 26*, 453–459.

Romano, R. (1986). What is the payoff to a community college degree? *Community/Junior College Quarterly of Research and Practice, 10*, 153–164.

Romig, J. (1972). An evaluation of instruction by student-led discussion in the college classroom. *Dissertation Abstracts International, 32*, 6816A.

Romine, B., Davis, J., & Gehman, W. (1970). The interaction of learning, personality traits, ability, and environment: A preliminary study. *Educational and Psychological Measurement, 30*, 337–347.

Romo, F., & Rosenbaum, J. (1984). *College old-boy connections and promotions.* Unpublished paper, Yale University, New Haven, CT.

Rootman, I. (1972). Voluntary withdrawal from a total adult socializing organization: A model. *Sociology of Education, 45*, 258–270.

Roper, B., & LaBeff, E. (1977). Sex roles and feminism revisited: An intergenerational attitude comparison. *Journal of Marriage and the Family, 39*, 113–119.

Roper Organization. (1974) *The Virginia Slims American woman's opinion poll* (Vol. 3). New York: Author.

Rosen, S. (1975). Measuring the obsolescence of knowledge. In F. Juster (Ed.), *Education, income, and human behavior.* New York: McGraw-Hill.

Rosen, S., & Taubman, P. (1982). Changes in life cycle earnings: What do social security data show? *Journal of Human Resources, 17*, 321–338.

Rosenbaum, J. (1984). *Career mobility in a corporate hierarchy.* New York: Academic Press.

Rosenberg, F., & Simmons, R. (1975). Sex differences in the self-concept in adolescence. *Sex Roles, 1*, 147–159.

Rosenberg, M. (1979). *Conceiving the self.* New York: Basic Books.

Rosenfeld, R. (1978). Women's intergenerational occupational mobility. *American Sociological Review, 43*, 36–46.

Rosenshine, B. (1982). *Teaching functions in instructional programs.* Washington, DC: National Institute of Education.

Rosensweig, M., & Schultz, T. (1982). The behavior of mothers as inputs to child health. In V. Fuchs (Ed.), *Economic aspects of health.* Chicago: University of Chicago Press.

Rosensweig, M., & Seiver, D. (1980). *Education and contraceptive choice: A conditional demand framework.* Unpublished manuscript, University of Minnesota, Minneapolis and St. Paul.

Ross, S., & Rakow, E. (1981). Learner control versus program control as adaptive strategies for selection of instructional support on math rules. *Journal of Educational Psychology, 73*, 745–753.

Rossmann, J. (1967). An experimental study of faculty advising. *Personnel and Guidance Journal, 46,* 160–164.

Rossmann, J. (1968). Released time for faculty advising: The impact upon freshmen. *Personnel and Guidance Journal, 47,* 356–363.

Rossmann, J. (1976). Teaching, publication, and rewards at a liberal arts college. *Improving College and University Teaching, 24,* 238–240.

Rothman, A., & Preshaw, R. (1975). Is scientific achievement a correlate of effective teaching performance? *Research in Higher Education, 3,* 29–34.

Rothman, L., & Leonard, D. (1967). Effectiveness of freshman orientation. *Journal of College Student Personnel, 8,* 300–304.

Rotter, J. (1966). Generalized expectancies for internal versus external controls of reinforcement. *Psychological Monographs, 80* (Whole No. 609).

Rotter, J. (1975). Some problems and misconceptions related to the construct of internal versus external control of reinforcement. *Journal of Consulting and Clinical Psychology, 43,* 56–67.

Rowe, I., & Marcia, J. (1980). Ego identity status, formal operations, and moral development. *Journal of Youth and Adolescence, 9,* 87–99.

Rowe, M., & Deture, L. (1975). A summary of research in science education—1973. *Science Education, 59,* 1–85.

Rubin, D. (1974). Estimating causal effects of treatments in randomized and nonrandomized studies. *Journal of Educational Psychology, 66,* 688–701.

Ruble, D., Croke, J., Frieze, I., & Parsons, J. (1975). A field study of sex-role attitude change in college women. *Journal of Applied Social Psychology, 5,* 110–117.

Rudolph, F. (1956). *Mark Hopkins and the log: Williams College, 1836–1872.* New Haven, CT: Yale University Press.

Rudolph, F. (1962). *The American college and university.* New York: Vintage Books.

Rumberger, R. (1980). The economic decline of college graduates: Fact or fallacy? *Journal of Human Resources, 15,* 99–112.

Rumberger, R. (1981). *Overeducation in the U.S. labor market.* New York: Praeger.

Rumberger, R. (1983). The influence of family background on education, earnings, and wealth. *Social Forces, 61,* 755–773.

Rumberger, R. (1984). The changing economic benefits of college graduates. *Economics of Education Review, 3,* 3–11.

Ryan, F. (1989). Participation in intercollegiate athletics: Affective outcomes. *Journal of College Student Development, 30,* 122–128.

Ryan, J. (1970). College freshmen and living arrangements. *NASPA Journal, 8,* 127–130.

Ryan, T. (1969). Research: Guide for teaching improvement. *Improving College and University Teaching, 17,* 270–276.

Ryder, N., & Westhoff, C. (1971). *Reproduction in the United States, 1965.* Princeton, NJ: Princeton University Press.

Rynes, S., & Boudreau, J. (1986). College recruiting in large organizations: Practice, evaluation, and research implications. *Personnel Psychology, 39,* 729–757.

Rysberg, J. (1986). Effects of modifying instruction in a college classroom. *Psychological Reports, 58,* 965–966.

Sack, A., & Thiel, R. (1979). College football and social mobility: A case study of Notre Dame football players. *Sociology of Education, 52,* 60–66.

St. John, E., Kirshstein, R., & Noell, J. (1988). *The effects of student financial aid on persistence.* Paper presented at the meeting of the American Educational Research Association, New Orleans.

Sakalys, J. (1982). Effects of a research methods course on nursing students' research attitudes and cognitive development. *Dissertation Abstracts International, 43,* 2254A.

Salter, C., & Teger, A. (1975). Change in attitudes toward other nations as a function of the type of international contact. *Sociometry, 38,* 213–222.

Samson, G., Graue, M., Weinstein, T., & Walberg, H. (1984). Academic and occupational performance: A quantitative synthesis. *American Educational Research Journal, 21,* 311–321.

San, G. (1986). The early labor force experience of college students and their post-college success. *Economics of Education Review, 5,* 65–76.

Sanders, C. (1990). Moral reasoning of male freshmen. *Journal of College Student Development, 31,* 5–8.

Sanford, N. (1956). Personality development during the college years. *Personnel and Guidance Journal, 35,* 74–80.

Sanford, N. (1962). Developmental status of the entering freshman. In N. Sanford (Ed.), *The American college: A pyschological and social interpretation of the higher learning.* New York: John Wiley & Sons.

Sanford, N. (1967). *Where colleges fail: A study of the student as a person.* San Francisco: Jossey Bass.

Sanford, T. (1979). Residual effects of self-help aid on the lives of college graduates. *Journal of Student Financial Aid, 9,* 3–10.

Sanford, T. (1980). The effects of student aid on recent college graduates. *Research in Higher Education, 12,* 227–243.

Sasajima, M., Davis, J., & Peterson, R. (1968). Organized student protest and institutional climate. *American Educational Research Journal, 5,* 291–304.

SAS Institute (1985). *SAS user's guide: Basics* (Version 5). Cary, NC: Author.

Saunders, P. (1980). The lasting effects of introductory economics courses. *Journal of Economic Education, 12,* 1–14.

Schaie, K., & Parham, I. (1976). Stability of adult personality traits: Fact or fable? *Journal of Personality and Social Psychology, 34,* 146–158.

Schein, L. (1969). Institutional characteristics and student attitudes. *College Student Survey, 3*, 67–70.

Schenkel, S., & Marcia, J. (1972). Attitudes towards premarital intercourse in determining ego identity status in college women. *Journal of Personality, 3*, 472–482.

Schlaefli, A., Rest, J., & Thoma, S. (1985). Does moral education improve moral judgment? A meta-analysis of intervention studies using the Defining Issues Test. *Review of Educational Research, 55*, 319–352.

Schmidt, J. (1983). The intellectual development of traditionally and non-traditionally aged college students: A cross sectional study with longitudinal follow-up. *Dissertation Abstracts International, 44*, 2681A.

Schmidt, J. (1985). Older and wiser? A longitudinal study of the impact of college on intellectual development. *Journal of College Student Personnel, 26*, 388–394.

Schmidt, J., & Davison, M. (1981). Does college matter? Reflective judgment: How students tackle the tough questions. *Moral Education Forum, 6*, 2–14.

Schmidt, J., & Davison, M. (1983). Helping students think. *Personnel and Guidance Journal, 61*, 563–569.

Schmidt, M. (1970). Personality change in college women. *Journal of College Student Personnel, 11*, 414–418.

Schmidt, M. (1971). Relationships between sorority membership and changes in selected personality variables and attitudes. *Journal of College Student Personnel, 12*, 208–213.

Schneider, J. (1971). College students' belief in personal control, 1966–1970. *Journal of Individual Psychology, 27*, 188.

Schoenberg, R. (1972). Strategies for meaningful comparison. In H. Costner (Ed.), *Sociological methodology 1972*. San Francisco: Jossey-Bass.

Schoenfeldt, L. (1968). Education after high school. *Sociology of Education, 41*, 350–369.

Schomberg, S. (1975). *Some personality correlates of moral maturity among community college students*. Unpublished manuscript, University of Minnesota, Minneapolis and St. Paul.

Schomberg, S. (1978). *Moral judgment development and its association with freshman year experiences*. Unpublished doctoral dissertation, University of Minnesota, Minneapolis and St. Paul.

Schonberg, W. (1974). Modification of attitudes of college students over time: 1923–1970. *Journal of Genetic Psychology, 125*, 107–117.

Schrager, R. (1986). The impact of living group social climate on student academic performance. *Research in Higher Education, 25*, 265–276.

Schreiber, E. (1978). Education and change in American opinions on a woman for president. *Public Opinion Quarterly, 42*, 171–182.

Schroeder, C. (1973). Sex differences and growth toward self-actualization during the freshman year. *Psychological Reports, 32*, 416–418.

Schroeder, C. (1980a). Redesigning college environments for students. In F. Newton & K. Ender (Eds.), *Student development practices*. Springfield, IL: Charles Thomas.

Schroeder, C. (1980b). The impact of homogeneous housing on environmental perceptions and student development. *Journal of College and University Student Housing, 10,* 10–15.

Schroeder, C., & Belmonte, A. (1979). The influence of residential environment on prepharmacy student achievement and satisfaction. *American Journal of Pharmaceutical Education, 43,* 16–19.

Schroeder, C., & Freesh, N. (1977). Applying environmental management strategies in residence halls. *NASPA Journal, 15,* 51–57.

Schroeder, C., & LeMay, M. (1973). The impact of coed residence halls on self-actualization. *Journal of College Student Personnel, 14,* 105–110.

Schubert, D. (1975a). A subcultural change of MMPI norms in the 1960s due to adolescent role confusion and glamorization of alienation. *Journal of Abnormal Psychology, 84,* 406–411.

Schubert, D. (1975b). Increase of apparent adjustment in adolescence by further ego identity formation and age. *College Student Journal, 7,* 3–6.

Schuh, J., & Laverty, M. (1983). The perceived long-term influence of holding a significant student leadership position. *Journal of College Student Personnel, 24,* 28–32.

Schultz, T. (1961). Investment in human capital. *American Economic Review, 51,* 1–17.

Schultz, T. (1963). *The economic value of education.* New York: Columbia University Press.

Schultz, T. (1975). The value of the ability to deal with disequilibria. *Journal of Economic Literature, 13,* 827–846.

Schustereit, R. (1980). Team teaching and academic achievement. *Improving College and University Teaching, 28,* 85–89.

Schwartz, A. (1971). On efficiency of migration. *Journal of Human Resources, 6,* 193–205.

Schwartz, A. (1976). Migration, age, and education. *Journal of Political Economy, 84,* 701–720.

Schwartz, E., & Thornton, R. (1980). Overinvestment in college training? *Journal of Human Resources, 15,* 121–123.

Schwartz, J. (1985). Student financial aid and the college enrollment decision: The effects of public and private grants and interest subsidies. *Economics of Education Review, 4,* 129–144.

Schwartz, S., Feldman, K., Brown, M., & Heingartner, A. (1969). Some personality correlates of conduct in two situations of moral conflict. *Journal of Personality, 37,* 41–57.

Scientific American. (1965). *The big business executive, 1964: A study of his social and educational background.* New York: Author.

Scott, R., Richards, A., & Wade, M. (1977). Women's studies as change agent. *Psychology of Women Quarterly, 1*, 377–379.

Scott, S. (1975). Impact of residence hall living on college student development. *Journal of College Student Personnel, 16*, 214–219.

Seabrook, T. (1985). *Attrition and retention of first year students at a college of advanced education.* Unpublished master's thesis, University of New South Wales, Australia.

Sedlacek, W. (1987). Black students on white campuses: 20 years of research. *Journal of College Student Personnel, 28*, 484–495.

Seeborg, M. (1975). The effect of curricular choice on alumni income. *Journal of Behavioral Economics, 7*, 151–172.

Selby, J. (1973). Relationships existing among race, student financial aid, and persistence in college. *Journal of College Student Personnel, 14*, 38–40.

Selznick, G., & Steinberg, J. (1969). *The tenacity of prejudice: Anti-Semitism in contemporary America.* New York: Harper & Row.

Semmes, C. (1985). Minority status and the problem of legitimacy. *Journal of Black Studies, 15*, 259–275.

Serlin, R., & Levin, J. (1980). Identifying regions of significance in aptitude-by-treatment interaction research. *American Educational Research Journal, 17*, 389–399.

Sewell, W. (1971). Inequality of opportunity for higher education. *American Sociological Review, 36*, 793–809.

Sewell, W., Haller, A., & Ohlendorf, G. (1970). The educational and early occupational attainment process: Replications and revisions. *American Sociological Review, 35*, 1014–1027.

Sewell, W., Haller, A., & Portes, A. (1969). The educational and early occupational attainment process. *American Sociological Review, 34*, 82–92.

Sewell, W., & Hauser, R. (1972). Causes and consequences of higher education: Models of the status attainment process. *American Journal of Agricultural Economics, 54*, 851–861.

Sewell, W., & Hauser, R. (1975). *Education, occupation, and earnings: Achievement in the early career.* New York: Academic Press.

Sewell, W., & Hauser, R. (1980). The Wisconsin longitudinal study of social and psychological factors in aspirations and achievements. In A. Kerckhoff (Ed.), *Research in the sociology of education and socialization* (Vol. 1). Greenwich, CT: JAI Press.

Sewell, W., Hauser, R., & Wolf, W. (1980). Sex, schooling and occupational status. *American Journal of Sociology, 86*, 551–583.

Sewell, W., & Shah, V. (1967). Socioeconomic status, intelligence, and the attainment of higher education. *Sociology of Education, 40*, 1–23.

Sewell, W., & Shah, V. (1968a). Parents' education and children's educational aspirations and achievements. *American Sociological Review, 33*, 191–209.

Sewell, W., & Shah, V. (1968b). Social class, parental encouragement, and educational aspirations. *American Journal of Sociology, 73,* 559–572.

Seybert, J., & Mustapha, S. (1988). *Moral reasoning in college students: An evaluation of two curricular approaches.* Paper presented at the meeting of the American Educational Research Association, New Orleans.

Sgan, M. (1970). Letter grade achievement in pass-fail courses. *Journal of Higher Education, 41,* 638–644.

Shaffer, P. (1973). Academic progress of disadvantaged minority students: A two-year study. *Journal of College Student Personnel, 14,* 41–46.

Shand, J. (1969). Report on a twenty-year follow-up study of the religious beliefs of 114 Amherst College students. *Journal for the Scientific Study of Religion, 8,* 167–168.

Sharma, M., & Jung, L. (1984). The influence of institutional involvement in international education on United States students. *International Review of Education, 30,* 457–467.

Sharon, A. (1971). Adult academic achievement in relation to formal education and age. *Adult Education Journal, 21,* 231–237.

Sharp, L. (1970). *Education and employment: The early careers of college graduates.* Baltimore: Johns Hopkins University Press.

Sharp, L., & Weidman, J. (1987). *Early careers of undergraduate humanities majors.* Paper presented at the meeting of the American Educational Research Association, Washington, DC.

Shavelson, R., & Bolus, R. (1982). Self-concept: The interplay of theory and methods. *Journal of Educational Psychology, 74,* 3–17.

Shavelson, R., Burstein, L., & Keesling, J. (1977). Methodological considerations in interpreting research on self-concept. *Journal of Youth and Adolescence, 6,* 295–307.

Shavelson, R., Hubner, J., & Stanton, G. (1976). Self-concept: Validation of construct interpretations. *Review of Educational Research, 46,* 407–441.

Shaver, D. (1985). A longitudinal study of moral development at a conservative, religious liberal arts college. *Journal of College Student Personnel, 26,* 400–404.

Shaver, D. (1987). Moral development of students attending a Christian, liberal arts college and a Bible college. *Journal of College Student Personnel, 28,* 211–218.

Shaycoft, M. (1973). Factors affecting a factor affecting career. *Vocational Guidance Quarterly, 22,* 96–104.

Shea, B. (1974). *Inequality of outcomes: Two-year educations.* Paper presented at the meeting of the Society for the Study of Social Problems, Montreal.

Sheehy, G. (1974). *Passages: Predictable crises of adult life.* New York: E. P. Dutton.

Sheppard, H., & Herrick, N. (1972). *Where have all of the robots gone?* New York: Free Press.

Sherif, M., & Sherif, C. (1970). Black unrest as a social movement toward an emerging self-identity. *Journal of Social and Behavioral Sciences, 15*, 41–52.

Shields, L. (1972). Student maturity in a college of education. *Educational Research, 14,* 101–109.

Shoff, S. (1979). The significance of age, sex, and type of education on the development of reasoning in adults. *Dissertation Abstracts International, 40,* 3910A.

Shostrom, E. (1966). *The Personal Orientation Inventory.* San Diego: Educational and Industrial Testing Service.

Shuch, M. (1975). The use of calculators versus hand computations in teaching business arithmetic and the effects on the critical thinking ability of community college students. *Dissertation Abstracts International, 36,* 4299A.

Shweder, R., Mahaptra, M., & Miller, J. (1987). Culture and moral development. In J. Kagan and S. Lamb (Eds.), *The emergence of morality in young children.* Chicago: University of Chicago Press.

Siegel, L., Adams, J., & Macomber, F. (1960). Retention of subject matter as a function of large-group instructional procedures. *Journal of Educational Psychology, 51,* 9–13.

Siegel, P. (1971). *Prestige in the American occupational structure.* Unpublished doctoral dissertation, University of Chicago.

Silvey, H. (1951). Changes in test scores after two years in college. *Educational and Psychological Measurement, 11,* 494–502.

Simmons, H. (1959). Achievement in intermediate algebra associated with class size at the University of Wichita. *College and University, 34,* 309–315.

Simon, A., & Ward, L. (1974). The performance on the Watson-Glaser Critical Thinking Appraisal of university students classified according to sex, type of course pursued, and personality score category. *Educational and Psychological Measurement, 34,* 957–960.

Simonds, R. (1962). College majors vs. business success. *Business Topics.*

Simono, R., Wachowiak, D., & Furr, S. (1984). Student living environments and their perceived impact on academic performance: A brief follow-up. *Journal of College and University Student Housing, 14,* 22–24.

Simpson, C., Baker, K., & Mellinger, G. (1980). Conventional failures and unconventional dropouts: Comparing different types of university withdrawals. *Sociology of Education, 53,* 203–214.

Sindelar, J. (1979). *Why women use more medical care than men.* Unpublished doctoral dissertation, Stanford University, Stanford, CA.

Singer, J. (1974). Sex and college class differences in attitudes toward autonomy in work. *Human Relations, 27,* 493–499.

inger, S. (1968). Review and discussion of the literature on personality development during college. In J. Katz (Ed.), *Growth and constraint in college students.* Stanford, CA: Stanford University, Institute for the Study of Human Problems.

Skager, R., Holland, J., & Braskamp, L. (1966). *Changes in self-ratings and life goals among students at colleges with different characteristics.* Iowa City, IA: American College Testing Program, Research and Development Division.

Slade, I., & Jarmul, L. (1975). Commuting college students: The neglected majority. *College Board Review, 95,* 16–21.

Slaney, R. (1983). Influence of career indecision on treatments exploring the vocational interests of college women. *Journal of Counseling Psychology, 30,* 55–63.

Slavin, R. (1984). Meta-analysis in education: How has it been used? *Educational Researcher, 13,* 6–15.

Slevin, K., & Wingrove, C. (1983). Similarities and differences among three generations of women in attitudes toward the female role in contemporary society. *Sex Roles, 9,* 609–624.

Sloan, D. (1979). The teaching of ethics in the American undergraduate curriculum, 1876–1976. *Hastings Center Report, 9,* 21–41.

Sloan, D. (1980). The teaching of ethics in the American undergraduate curriculum, 1876–1976. In D. Callahan & S. Bok, (Eds.), *The teaching of ethics.* New York: Plenum Press.

Smart, J. (1985). Holland environments as reinforcement systems. *Research in Higher Education, 23,* 279–292.

Smart, J. (1986). College effects on occupational status attainment. *Research in Higher Education, 24,* 73–95.

Smart, J. (1988a). College influences on graduates' income levels. *Research in Higher Education, 29,* 41–59.

Smart, J. (1988b). *Life history influences on Holland vocational type development.* Unpublished manuscript, University of Illinois, Chicago.

Smart, J., Elton, C., & McLaughlin, G. (1986). Person-environment congruence and job satisfaction. *Journal of Vocational Behavior, 29,* 216–225.

Smart, J., & Ethington, C. (1985). Early career outcomes of baccalaureate recipients: A study of native four-year and transfer two-year college students. *Research in Higher Education, 22,* 185–193.

Smart, J., Ethington, C., & McLaughlin, G. (undated). *Postsecondary educational attainment and the development of self-concept and career orientation.* Unpublished manuscript, Virginia Polytechnic Institute and State University.

Smart, J., & McLaughlin, G. (1986). *Outcomes assessment and the quality of student involvement.* Paper presented at the meeting of the Association for Institutional Research, Orlando, FL.

Smart, J., & Pascarella, E. (1986a). Self-concept development and educational degree attainment. *Higher Education, 15,* 3–15.

Smart, J., & Pascarella, E. (1986b). Socioeconomic achievements of former college students. *Journal of Higher Education, 57,* 529–549.

Smith, A. (1978). Lawrence Kohlberg's cognitive stage theory of the development of moral judgment. In L. Kneffelkamp, C. Widick, & C. Parker (Eds.), *Applying new developmental findings* (New Directions for Student Services No. 4). San Francisco: Jossey-Bass.

Smith, A. (1980). A study of selected variables among student persisters and nonpersisters enrolled in the general and the community and technical colleges. *Dissertation Abstracts International, 41,* 963A.

Smith, C. (1970). *A comparative study of two methods of teaching physical science to college freshmen with disadvantaged backgrounds.* Unpublished doctoral dissertation, University of Mississippi, University.

Smith, D. (1977). College classroom interactions and critical thinking. *Journal of Educational Psychology, 69,* 180–190.

Smith, D. (1981). *Instruction and outcomes in an undergraduate setting.* Paper presented at the meeting of the American Educational Research Association, Los Angeles.

Smith, D. (1988). *Women's colleges and coed colleges: Is there a difference for women?* Unpublished manuscript, Claremont Graduate School, Claremont, CA.

Smith, D. (1990). Women's colleges and coed colleges: Is there a difference for women? *Journal of Higher Education, 61,* 181–197.

Smith, H. (1986). Overeducation and underemployment: An agnostic review. *Sociology of Education, 59,* 85–99.

Smith, H. (1987). Comparative evaluation of three teaching methods of quantitative techniques: Traditional lecture, Socratic dialogue, and PSI format. *Journal of Experimental Education, 55,* 149–154.

Smith, J., & Welch, F. (1977). Black-white male wage ratios: 1960–1970. *American Economic Review, 67,* 323–338.

Smith, L. (1971). A 5-year follow-up study of high ability achieving and nonachieving college freshmen. *Journal of Educational Research, 64,* 220–222.

Smith, L. (1977). Aspects of teacher discourse and student achievement in mathematics. *Journal for Research in Mathematics Education, 8,* 195–204.

Smith, L. (1982). A review of two low-inference teacher behaviors related to performance of college students. *Review of Higher Education, 5,* 159–167.

Smith, L., & Edmonds, E. (1978). Teacher vagueness and pupil participation in mathematics learning. *Journal for Research in Mathematics Education, 9,* 228–232.

Smith, L., & Land, M. (1980). Student perception of teacher clarity in mathematics. *Journal for Research in Mathematics Education, 11,* 137–146.

Smith, M. (1972). *Equality of educational opportunity: The basic findings reconsidered.* In F. Mosteller & D. Moynihan (Eds.), *On equality of educational opportunity.* New York: Random House.

Smith, R., & Evans, J. (1973). Comparison of experimental group guidance and individual counseling as facilitators of vocational development. *Journal of Counseling Psychology, 20,* 202–208.

Smoking, education level linked. (1989, January 6). *Chicago Tribune.*

Snead, R., & Caple, R. (1971). Some effects of the environmental press in university housing. *Journal of College Student Personnel, 12,* 189–192.

Snyder, B. (1968). The education of creative science students. In P. Heist (Ed.), *The creative college student: An unmet challenge.* San Francisco: Jossey-Bass.

Sobel, M. (1982). Asymptotic confidence intervals for indirect effects in structural equation models. In S. Leinhardt (Ed.), *Sociological Methodology 1982.* San Francisco: Jossey-Bass.

Solmon, L. (1973). The definition and impact of college quality. In L. Solmon & P. Taubman (Eds.), *Does college matter? Some evidence on the impacts of higher education.* Orlando, FL: Academic Press.

Solmon, L. (1975a). The definition of college quality and its impact on earnings. *Explorations in Economic Research, 2,* 537–587.

Solmon, L. (1975b). The relation between schooling and savings behavior: An example of the indirect effects of education. In F. Juster (Ed.), *Education, income, and human behavior.* New York: McGraw-Hill.

Solmon, L. (1976). *The utilization of undergraduate education in careers* (Comments, pp. 1–4). Los Angeles: Higher Education Research Institute.

Solmon, L. (1981). New findings on the links between college education and work. *Higher Education, 10,* 615–648.

Solmon, L., Bisconti, A., & Ochsner, N. (1977). *College as a training ground for jobs.* New York: Praeger.

Solmon, L., & Ochsner, N. (1978a). New findings on the effects of college. In *Current issues in higher education: 1978 National Conference Series.* Washington, DC: American Association for Higher Education.

Solmon, L., & Ochsner, N. (1978b). Attitude changes of college graduates. In D. Drew (Ed.), *Increasing student development options in college* (New Directions for Education, Work, and Careers No. 4). San Francisco: Jossey-Bass.

Solmon, L., & Taubman, P. (1973). *Does college matter? Some evidence on the impacts of higher education.* Orlando, FL: Academic Press.

Solmon, L., & Wachtel, P. (1975). The effects on income of type of college attended. *Sociology of Education, 48,* 75–90.

Somers, G., Sharpe, L., & Myint, T. (1971). *The effectiveness of vocational and technical programs.* Madison: University of Wisconsin, Center for Studies in Vocational and Technical Education. (ERIC Document Reproduction Service No. ED 055 190)

Somit, A., Tanenhaus, J., Wilke, W., & Cooley, R. (1970). The effect of the introductory political science course on student attitudes toward personal political participation. In R. Sigel (Ed.), *Learning about politics: A reader in political socialization.* New York: Random House.

Sommer, R. (1969). *Personal space: The behavioral basis of design.* Englewood Cliffs, NJ: Prentice-Hall.

Southworth, J., & Morningstar, M. (1970). Persistence of occupational choice and personality congruence. *Journal of Vocational Behavior, 13,* 45–53.

Sowa, C., & Gressard, C. (1983). Athletic participation: Its relationship to student development. *Journal of College Student Personnel, 24,* 236–239.

Sowell, T. (1972). *Black education: Myths and tragedies.* New York: David McKay.

Spady, W. (1970). Dropouts from higher education: An interdisciplinary review and synthesis. *Interchange, 1,* 64–85.

Spady, W. (1971). Dropouts from higher education: Toward an empirical model. *Interchange, 2,* 38–62.

Spaeth, J. (1968a). Occupational prestige expectations among male college graduates. *American Journal of Sociology, 73,* 548–558.

Spaeth, J. (1968b). The allocation of college graduates to graduate and professional schools. *Sociology of Education, 41,* 342–349.

Spaeth, J. (1970). Occupational attainment among male college graduates. *American Journal of Sociology, 75,* 632–644.

Spaeth, J. (1977). Differences in the occupational achievement process between male and female college graduates. *Sociology of Education, 50,* 206–217.

Spaeth, J., & Greeley, A. (1970). *Recent alumni and higher education: A survey of college graduates.* New York: McGraw-Hill.

Speizer, J. (1975). An evaluation of the changes in attitudes toward women which occur as a result of participation in a women's studies course. *Dissertation Abstracts International, 36,* 1404A. (University Microfilm No. 75–20,968)

Spence, J., & Helmreich, R. (1979). Comparison of masculine and feminine personality attributes and sex-role attitudes across age groups. *Developmental Psychology, 15,* 583–584.

Spence, M. (1973). Job market signaling. *Quarterly Journal of Economics, 87,* 355–374.

Spickelmier, J. (1983). *College experience and moral judgment development.* Unpublished doctoral dissertation, University of Minnesota, Minneapolis and St. Paul.

Spitze, G. (1978). Role experiences of young women: A longitudinal test of the role hiatus hypothesis. *Journal of Marriage and the Family, 40,* 471–479.

Spokane, A. (1985). A review of research on person-environment congruence in Holland's theory of careers. *Journal of Vocational Behavior, 26,* 306–343.

Spreitzer, E., & Snyder, E. (1974). Correlates of life satisfaction among the aged. *Journal of Gerontology, 29,* 454–458.

Stadtman, V. (1980). *Academic adaptations.* San Francisco: Jossey-Bass.

Stage, F. (1987). *Reciprocal causation and mixed effects within the Tinto model of college student withdrawal.* Paper presented at the meeting of the Association for the Study of Higher Education, Baltimore.

Stage, F. (1989). An alternative to path analysis: A demonstration of LIS-REL using students' commitment to an institution. *Journal of College Student Development, 30,* 129–135.

Stage, F. (1990). LISREL: An introduction and application in higher education. In J. Smart (Ed.), *Higher education: Handbook of theory and research* (Vol. 6). New York: Agathon.

Stake, J. (1981). The educator's role in fostering female career aspirations. *Journal of the National Association of Women Deans, Administrators, and Counselors, 45,* 3–10.

Stake, J., & Gerner, M. (1985). *The effect of women's studies on self-esteem and career interests.* Paper presented at the meeting of the American Psychological Association, Los Angeles.

Stake, J., & Noonan, M. (1985). The influence of teacher models on the career confidence and motivation of college students. *Sex Roles, 12,* 1023–1031.

Stakenas, R. (1972). Student-faculty contact and attitude change: Results of an experimental program for college freshmen. In K. Feldman (Ed.), *College and student: Selected readings in the social psychology of higher education.* New York: Pergamon Press.

Stallings, W., & Singhal, S. (1970). Some observations on the relationships between research productivity and student evaluations of courses and teaching. *American Sociologist, 5,* 141–143.

Staman, E. (1980). Predicting student attrition at an urban college. *Dissertation Abstracts International, 40,* 4440A.

Stampen, J., & Cabrera, A. (1986). Explaining the effects of student aid on attrition. *Journal of Student Financial Aid, 16,* 28–40.

Stampen, J., & Cabrera, A. (in press). The targeting and packaging of student aid and its effect on attrition. *Economics of Education Review.*

Stanley, J. (1967). A design for comparing the impact of different colleges. *American Educational Research Journal, 4,* 217–228.

Stariha, W. (1989). *Productivity factors influencing the achievement and interest in mathematics of college-bound seniors.* Unpublished doctoral dissertation, University of Illinois, Chicago.

Stark, J., & Morstain, B. (1978). Educational orientations of faculty in liberal arts colleges: An analysis of disciplinary differences. *Journal of Higher Education, 49,* 420–437.

Stark, P., & Traxler, A. (1974). Empirical validation of Erikson's theory of identity crisis in late adolescence. *Journal of Psychology, 86,* 25–33.

Staub, E. (1974). Helping a distressed person: Social, personality and stimulus determinants. In L. Berkowitz (Ed.), *Advances in experimental social psychology* (Vol. 7). New York: Academic Press.

Stauffer, M. (1973). The impact of study abroad experience on prospective teachers. *Dissertation Abstracts International, 34,* 2448A.

Steel, L., & Wise, L. (1979). *Origins of sex differences in high school mathematics achievement and participation.* Paper presented at the meeting of the American Educational Research Association, San Francisco.

Steele, J. (1986). *Assessing reasoning and communication skills of postsecondary students.* Paper presented at the meeting of the American Educational Research Association, San Francisco.

Steele, J. (1989). Evaluating college programs using measures of student achievement and growth. *Educational Evaluation and Policy Analysis, 11,* 357–375.

Steele, M. (1978). Correlates of undergraduate retention at the University of Miami. *Journal of College Student Personnel, 19,* 349–352.

Steele, S. (1989, February). The recoloring of campus life: Student racism, academic pluralism, and the end of a dream. *Harper's* pp. 47–55.

Steibe, S. (1980). *Level of fairness reasoning and human values as predictions of social justice related behavior.* Unpublished doctoral dissertation, University of Ottawa, Ottawa, Canada.

Steiger, J. (1981). The influence of the feminist subculture in changing sex-role attitudes. *Sex Roles, 7,* 627–633.

Stein, S., & Weston, L. (1976). Attitudes toward women among female college students. *Sex Roles, 2,* 199–202.

Stephenson, B., & Hunt, C. (1977). Intellectual and ethical development: A dualistic curriculum intervention for college students. *Counseling Psychologist, 6,* 39–42.

Stephenson, S. (1982). Work in college and subsequent wage rates. *Research in Higher Education, 17,* 165–178.

Stern, G. (1970). *People in context: Measuring person-environment congruence in education and industry.* New York: John Wiley & Sons.

Sternglanz, S., & Lyberger-Ficek, S. (1977). Sex differences in student-teacher interaction in the college classroom. *Sex Roles, 3,* 345–352.

Stevens, G., & Gardner, S. (1983). Women's study courses: Do they change attitudes? *Psychological Reports, 53,* 81–82.

Stewart, A. (1977). *Analysis of argument: An empirically derived measure of intellectual flexibility.* Boston: McBer.

Stewart, S., Merrill, M., & Saluri, D. (1985). Students who commute. In L. Noel, R. Levitz, D. Saluri, & Associates, *Increasing student retention/Effective programs and practices for reducing the dropout rate.* San Francisco: Jossey-Bass.

Stewart, W. (1977). A psychosocial study of the formation of the early adult life structure in women. *Dissertation Abstracts International, 38,* 381B.

Stikes, C. (1975). A conceptual map of black student development problems. *Journal of Non-White Concerns in Personnel and Guidance, 4,* 24–30.

Stikes, C. (1984). *Black students in higher education.* Carbondale: Southern Illinois University Press.

Stinard, T., & Dolphin, W. (1981). Which students benefit from self-paced mastery instruction and why. *Journal of Educational Psychology, 73,* 754–763.

Stinson, M., Scherer, M., & Walker, G. (1987). Factors affecting persistence of deaf college students. *Research in Higher Education, 27,* 244–258.

Stobaugh, C. (1972). *The effect of college environment on student output* (Organizational Research Tech. Rep. 72-31). Seattle: University of Washington, Department of Psychology.

Stoecker, J., & Pascarella, E. (1988). *Institutional gender and the early educational, occupational, and economic attainments of women.* Paper presented at the meeting of the American Educational Research Association, New Orleans.

Stoecker, J., Pascarella, E., & Wolfle, L. (1988). Persistence in higher education: A nine-year test of a theoretical model. *Journal of College Student Development, 29,* 196–209.

Stonewater, J., & Daniels, M. (1983). Psychosocial and cognitive development in a career decision-making course. *Journal of College Student Personnel, 24,* 403–410.

Stouffer, S. (1955). *Communism, conformity, and civil liberties.* New York: Doubleday.

Strange, C. (1978). *Intellectual development, motive for education, and learning styles during the college years: A comparison of adult and traditional age college students.* Unpublished doctoral dissertation, University of Iowa, Iowa City.

Strange, C. (1986). Greek affiliation and goals of the academy: A commentary. *Journal of College Student Personnel, 27,* 519–523.

Strange, C. (1987). *Bridging the gap between theory and practice in student affairs professional preparation.* Paper presented at the meeting of the Association for the Study of Higher Education, Baltimore.

Strange, C., & King, P. (1981). Intellectual development and its relationship to maturation during the college years. *Journal of Applied Developmental Psychology, 2,* 281–295.

Strange, C., & King, P. (1990). The professional practice of student development. In D. Creamer & Associates, *College student development theory and practice for the 1990s* (Media Publication No. 49). Alexandria, VA: American College Personnel Association.

Straub, C. (1987). Women's development of autonomy and Chickering's theory. *Journal of College Student Personnel, 28,* 198–204.

Straub, C., and Rodgers, R. (1978). Fostering moral development in college women. *Journal of College Student Personnel, 19,* 430–436.

Straub, C., & Rodgers, R. (1986). An exploration of Chickering's theory and women's development. *Journal of College Student Personnel, 27,* 216–224.

Strumpel, B. (1971). Higher education and economic behavior. In S. Withey (Ed.), *A degree and what else? Correlates and consequences of a college education.* New York: McGraw-Hill.

Strumpel, B. (1976). *Economic means for human needs.* Ann Arbor: University of Michigan, Institute for Social Research.

Study Group on the Conditions of Excellence in American Higher Education. (1984). *Involvement in learning: Realizing the potential of American higher education.* Washington, DC: National Institute of Education.

Stupka, E. (1986). *Student persistence and achievement: An evaluation of the effects of an extended orientation course.* A research study sponsored by the Northern California Cooperative Institutional Research Group.

Suczek, R. (1972). *The best laid plans.* San Francisco: Jossey-Bass.

Sue, S., & Sue, D. (1971). Chinese-American personality and mental health. *Amerasia Journal, 1,* 36–49.

Suen, H. (1983). Alienation and attrition of black college students on a predominantly white campus. *Journal of College Student Personnel, 24,* 117–121.

Suksiringarm, P. (1976). An experimental study comparing the effects of BSCS and the traditional biology on achievement, understanding of science, critical thinking ability, and attitude toward science of first year students at the Sakon Nakorn Teacher's College, Thailand. *Dissertation Abstracts International, 37,* 2764A.

Sullivan, A. (1985). Two types of research on the evaluation and improvement of university teaching. In J. Donald & A. Sullivan (Eds.), *Using research to improve teaching* (New Directions for Teaching and Learning No. 23). San Francisco: Jossey-Bass.

Sullivan, A., & Skanes, G. (1974). Validity of student evaluation of teaching and the characteristics of successful instructors. *Journal of Educational Psychology, 66,* 584–590.

Sullivan, E. (1977). A study of Kohlberg's structural theory of moral development: A critique of liberal social science ideology. *Human Development, 20,* 352–376.

Sullivan, E., McCullough, G., & Stager, M. (1970). A developmental study of the relationship between conceptual, ego, and moral development. *Child Development, 41,* 399–411.

Sullivan, K., & Sullivan, A. (1980). Adolescent-parent separation. *Developmental Psychology, 16,* 93–98.

Suter, L., & Miller, H. (1973). Income differences between men and career women. *American Journal of Sociology, 78,* 962–974.

Swift, W., & Weisbrod, B. (1965). On the monetary value of education's intergenerational benefits. *Journal of Political Economy, 73,* 643–649.

Symonette, H. (1981). *Does type of college attended matter? Decomposing the college-earnings association.* Madison: University of Wisconsin, Center for Demography and Ecology.

Tamir, P., & Kempa, R. (1977). College students' cognitive preferences in science. *Journal of Educational Research, 70,* 210–218.

Tangri, S. (1972). Determinants of occupational role innovation among college women. *Journal of Social Issues, 28,* 177–199.

Tata, C. (1981). *The effect of an intrusive advisement program on first-term freshman attrition.* Paper presented at the meeting of the Association for Institutional Research, Minneapolis.

Taubman, P. (1975). *Sources of inequality in earnings.* Amsterdam: North Holland.

Taubman, P., & Wales, T. (1973). Higher education, mental ability, and screening. *Journal of Political Economy, 81,* 28–55.

Taubman, P., & Wales, T. (1974). *Higher education and earnings: College as an investment and a screening device.* New York: McGraw-Hill.

Taubman, P., & Wales, T. (1975a). Appendix B: Mental-ability tests and factors. In F. Juster (Ed.), *Education, income, and human behavior.* New York: McGraw-Hill.

Taubman, P., & Wales, T. (1975b). Education as an investment and a screening device. In F. Juster (Ed.), *Education, income, and human behavior.* New York: McGraw-Hill.

Taylor, C., & Ellison, R. (1967). Biographical predictors of scientific performance. *Science, 155,* 1075–1080.

Taylor, C., Smith, W., & Ghiselin, B. (1963). The creative and other contributions of one sample of research scientists. In C. Taylor & F. Barron (Eds.), *Scientific creativity: Its recognition and development.* New York: John Wiley & Sons.

Taylor, D., Sheatsley, P., & Greeley, A. (1978). Attitudes toward racial integration. *Scientific American, 238,* 42–49.

Taylor, E., & Wolfe, A. (1971). Political behavior. In S. Withey (Ed.), *A degree and what else? Correlates and consequences of a college education.* New York: McGraw-Hill.

Taylor, R. (1976). Black youth and psychosocial development: A conceptual framework. *Journal of Black Studies, 6,* 353–372.

Taylor, R. (1977). The orientational others and value preferences of black college youth. *Social Science Quarterly, 57,* 797–810.

Taylor, R., & Hanson, G. (1971). Environmental impact on achievement and study habits. *Journal of College Student Personnel, 12,* 445–454.

Taylor, R., Roth, J., & Hanson, G. (1971). Experimental housing and tutoring: Effects on achievement and attrition. *Journal of College Student Personnel, 12,* 271–278.

Taylor, W. (1982). A five-year attrition study of an undergraduate class at the University of Tennessee at Chattanooga. *Dissertation Abstracts International, 43,* 695A.

Telford, C., & Plant, W. (1963). *The psychological impact of the public two-year college on certain non-intellectual functions* (DHEW Cooperative Research Branch Project SAE 8646). San Jose, CA: San Jose State College.

Telford, C., & Plant, W. (1968). The psychological impact of the public junior college. In K. Yamamoto (Ed.), *The college student and his culture.* Boston: Houghton Mifflin.

Temple, M., & Polk, K. (1986). A dynamic analysis of educational attainment. *Sociology of Education, 59,* 79–84.

Terenzini, P., & Pascarella, E. (1977). Voluntary freshman attrition and patterns of social and academic integration in a university: A test of a conceptual model. *Research in Higher Education, 6,* 25–43.

Terenzini, P., & Pascarella, E. (1978). The relation of students' precollege characteristics and freshman year experience to voluntary attrition. *Research in Higher Education, 9,* 347–366.

Terenzini, P., & Pascarella, E. (1980a). Student/faculty relationships and freshman year educational outcomes: A further investigation. *Journal of College Student Personnel, 21,* 521–528.

Terenzini, P., & Pascarella, E. (1980b). Toward the validation of Tinto's model of college student attrition: A review of recent studies. *Research in Higher Education, 12,* 271–282.

Terenzini, P., & Pascarella, E. (1984). Freshman attrition and the residential context. *Review of Higher Education, 7,* 111–124.

Terenzini, P., Pascarella, E., & Lorang, W. (1982). An assessment of the academic and social influences on freshman year educational outcomes. *Review of Higher Education, 5,* 86–110.

Terenzini, P., Pascarella, E., Theophilides, C., & Lorang, W. (1985). A replication of a path analytic validation of Tinto's theory of college student attrition. *Review of Higher Education, 8,* 319–340.

Terenzini, P., Theophilides, C., & Lorang, W. (1984a). Influences on students' perceptions of their academic skill development during college. *Journal of Higher Education, 55,* 621–636.

Terenzini, P., Theophilides, C., & Lorang, W. (1984b). Influences on students' perceptions of their personal development during the first three years of college. *Research in Higher Education, 21,* 178–194.

Terenzini, P., & Wright, T. (1987a). Influences on students' academic growth during four years of college. *Research in Higher Education, 26,* 161–179.

Terenzini, P., & Wright, T. (1987b). *The influence of academic and social integration on students' personal development during four years of college.* Paper presented at the meeting of the Association for Institutional Research, Kansas City, MO.

Terenzini, P., & Wright, T. (1987c). Students' personal growth during the first two years of college. *Review of Higher Education, 10,* 259–271.

Terkla, D. (1984). *Does financial aid enhance undergraduate persistence?* Paper presented at the joint meeting of the Association for the Study of Higher Education/American Educational Research Association–Division J, San Francisco.

Terranova, C. (1976). The effectiveness of a summer freshman orientation conference. *Measurement and Evaluation in Guidance, 9,* 70–74.

Theodory, G., & Day, R. (1985). The association of professors' style, trait anxiety, and experience with students' grades. *American Educational Research Journal, 22,* 123–133.

Theophilides, C., Terenzini, P., & Lorang, W. (1984a). Freshman and sophomore experiences and changes in major. *Review of Higher Education, 7,* 261–278.

Theophilides, C., Terenzini, P., & Lorang, W. (1984b). The relation between freshman experience and perceived importance of four major educational goals. *Research in Higher Education, 20,* 235–252.

Thistlethwaite, D. (1959a). College environments and the development of talent. *Science, 130,* 71–76.

Thistlethwaite, D. (1959b). College press and student achievement. *Journal of Educational Psychology, 50,* 183–191.

Thistlethwaite, D. (1960). College press and changes in study plans of talented students. *Journal of Educational Psychology, 51,* 222–234.

Thistlethwaite, D. (1962). Fields of study and development of motivation to seek advanced training. *Journal of Educational Psychology, 53,* 53–64.

Thistlethwaite, D. (1969). Some ecological effects of entering a field of study. *Journal of Educational Psychology, 60,* 284–293.

Thistlethwaite, D. (1972). *Effects of university subcultures on student attitudes.* Nashville, TN: Vanderbilt University.

Thistlethwaite, D. (1973). Accentuation of differences in values and exposures to major field of study. *Journal of Educational Psychology, 65,* 279–293.

Thistlethwaite, D. (1974). Impact of disruptive external events on student attitudes. *Journal of Personality and Social Psychology, 30,* 228–242.

Thistlethwaite, D., & Wheeler, N. (1966). Effects of teaching and peer subcultures upon student aspirations. *Journal of Educational Psychology, 57,* 35–47.

Thomas, C. (1971). *Boys no more: A black psychoanalyist's view of community.* Encino, CA: Glencoe.

Thomas, G. (1980). Race and sex group equity in higher education: Institutional and major field enrollment statuses. *American Educational Research Journal, 17,* 171–181.

Thomas, G. (1981a). *Black students in higher education: Conditions and experiences of the 1970s.* Westport, CT: Greenwood Press.

Thomas, G. (1981b). College characteristics and black students' four-year college graduation. *Journal of Negro Education, 50,* 328–345.

Thomas, G. (1981c). Student and institutional characteristics as determinants of the prompt and subsequent four-year college graduation of race and sex groups. *Sociological Quarterly, 22,* 327–345.

Thomas, G. (1985). College major and career inequality: Implications for black students. *Journal of Negro Education, 54,* 537–547.

Thomas, G., Alexander, K., & Eckland, B. (1979). Access to higher education: The importance of race, sex, social class, and academic credentials. *School Review, 87,* 133–156.

Thomas, G., & Gordon, S. (1983). *Evaluating the payoffs of college investments for black, white, and hispanic students* (Report No. 344). Baltimore: Johns Hopkins University, Center for Social Organization of Schools.

Thomas, G., & Hill, S. (1987). *Black colleges and universities in U.S. higher education: Present roles, contributions, and future prospects.* Paper presented at the meeting of the American Educational Research Association, Washington, DC.

Thomas, J., & Andes, J. (1987). Affiliation and retention in higher education. *College and University, 62,* 322–340.

Thomas, R. (1988). *Student retention at liberal arts colleges: The development and test of a model.* Paper presented at the meeting of the National Association of Student Personnel Administrators, St. Louis.

Thomas, R., & Chickering, A. (1984). *Education and identity* revisited. *Journal of College Student Personnel, 25,* 392–399.

Thomas, W., & Grouws, D. (1984). Inducing cognitive growth in concrete-operational college students. *School Science and Mathematics, 84,* 233–243.

Thompson, M. (1976). The prediction of academic achievement by a British study habits inventory. *Research in Higher Education, 5,* 365–372.

Thorndike, R., & Hagen, E. (1977). *Measurement and evaluation in psychology and education* (4th ed). New York: John Wiley & Sons.

Thornlidsson, T. (1978). *Social organization, role-taking, elaborated language and moral judgment in an Icelandic setting.* Unpublished doctoral dissertation, University of Iowa, Iowa City.

Thornton, A., Alwin, D., & Camburn, D. (1983). Causes and consequences of sex-role attitudes and attitude change. *American Sociological Review, 48,* 211–227.

Thornton, A., & Freedman, D. (1979). Changes in the sex role attitudes of women, 1962–1977: Evidence from a panel study. *American Sociological Review, 44,* 831–842.

Thrasher, F., & Bloland, P. (1989). Student development studies: A review of published empirical research, 1973–1987. *Journal of Counseling and Development, 67,* 547–554.

Thurow, L. (1972). Education and economic equality. *Public Interest, 28,* 66–81.

Thurow, L. (1975). *Generating inequality: Mechanisms of distribution in the U.S. economy.* New York: Basic Books.

Tidball, M. (1973). Perspective on academic women and affirmative action. *Educational Record, 54,* 130–135.

Tidball, M. (1974). The search for talented women. *Change, 6,* 51–52, 64.

Tidball, M. (1976). On liberation and competence. *Educational Record, 57,* 101–110.

Tidball, M. (1980). Women's colleges and women achievers revisited. *Signs: Journal of Women in Culture and Society, 5,* 504–517.

Tidball, M. (1985). Baccalaureate origins of entrants into American medical schools. *Journal of Higher Education, 56,* 385–402.

Tidball, M. (1986). Baccalaureate origins of recent natural science doctorates. *Journal of Higher Education, 57,* 606–620.

Tidball, M., & Kistiakowsky, V. (1976). Baccalaureate origins of American scientists and scholars. *Science, 196,* 646–653.

Tilden, A. (1976). A cross validation of the Career Development Inventory and a study of vocational maturity in college students. *Dissertation Abstracts International, 37,* 2088A.

Timmons, F. (1978). Freshman withdrawal from college: A positive step toward identity formation? A follow-up study. *Journal of Youth and Adolescence, 7,* 159–173.

Tinto, V. (1975). Dropout from higher education: A theoretical synthesis of recent research. *Review of Educational Research, 45,* 89–125.

Tinto, V. (1980). College origins and patterns of status attainment: Schooling among professional and business-managerial occupations. *Sociology of Work and Occupations, 7,* 457–486.

Tinto, V. (1981). Higher education and occupational attainment in segmented labor markets: Recent evidence from the United States. *Higher Education, 10,* 499–516.

Tinto, V. (1982). Limits of theory and practice in student attrition. *Journal of Higher Education, 53,* 687–700.

Tinto, V. (1984). Patterns of educational sponsorship to work: A study of modes of early occupational attainment from college to professional work. *Work and Occupations, 11,* 309–330.

Tinto, V. (1987). *Leaving college: Rethinking the causes and cures of student attrition.* Chicago: University of Chicago Press.

Titley, B. (1985). Orientation programs. In L. Noel, R. Levitz, & D. Saluri (Eds.), *Increasing student retention: Effective programs and practices for reducing the dropout rate.* San Francisco: Jossey-Bass.

Toder, N., & Marcia, J. (1973). Ego identity status and response to conformity pressure in college women. *Journal of Personality and Social Psychology, 26,* 287–294.

Toldson, I., & Pasteur, A. (1975). Developmental stages of black self-discovery: Implications for using black art forms in group interaction. *Journal of Negro Education, 44,* 130–138.

Tomaske, J. (1974). Private and social rates of return to education of academicians: Note. *American Economic Review, 64,* 220–224.

Tomlinson-Keasey, C., & Eisert, D. (1978a). Can doing promote thinking in the college classroom? *Journal of College Student Personnel, 19,* 99–105.

Tomlinson-Keasey, C., & Eisert, D. (1978b). Second year evaluation of the

ADAPT program. In R. Fuller (Ed.), *Multidisciplinary Piagetian-based programs for college freshmen: ADAPT.* Lincoln: University of Nebraska.

Tomlinson-Keasey, C., Williams, V., & Eisert, D. (1978). Evaluation report of the first year of the ADAPT program. In R. Fuller (Ed.), *Multidisciplinary Piagetian-based programs for college freshmen: ADAPT.* Lincoln: University of Nebraska.

Toseland, R., & Rasch, J. (1979–1980). Correlates of life satisfaction: An AID analysis. *International Journal of Aging and Human Development, 10,* 203–211.

Towers, K. (1984). *A longitudinal study of moral judgment development using Kohlberg's model and Rest's DIT.* Paper presented at the meeting of the American College Personnel Association, Baltimore.

Tracey, T., & Sedlacek, W. (1987). *A comparison of white and black student academic success using noncognitive variables.* Paper presented at the meeting of the American Educational Research Association, Washington, DC.

Tracy, J. (1975). Assessing the effects of a supervised, experimental program of instruction on the self-concept and grade point average of students on academic probation. *Dissertation Abstracts International, 36,* 2037A–2038A.

Trank, D., & Steele, J. (1983). Measurable effects of a communication skills course: An initial study. *Communication Education, 32,* 227–236.

Treiman, D., & Terrell, K. (1975). Sex and the process of status attainment: A comparison of working women and men. *American Sociological Review, 40,* 174–200.

Trent, J., & Craise, J. (1967). Commitment and conformity in the American college. *Journal of Social Issues, 23,* 34–51.

Trent, J., & Golds, J. (1967). *Catholics in college: Religious commitment and the intellectual life.* Chicago: University of Chicago Press.

Trent, J., & Medsker, L. (1968). *Beyond high school: A psychological study of 10,000 high school graduates.* San Francisco: Jossey-Bass.

Trent, W. (1984). Equity considerations in higher education: Race and sex differences in degree attainment and major field from 1976 through 1981. *American Journal of Education, 92,* 280–305.

Treppa, J., & Fricke, L. (1972). Effects of a marathon group experience. *Journal of Counseling Psychology, 19,* 466–467.

Trivett, D. (1974). The commuting student. *College & University Bulletin, 26,* 3–6.

Troll, L., Neugarten, B., & Kraines, R. (1969). Similarities in values and other personality characteristics in college students and their parents. *Merrill-Palmer Quarterly, 15,* 323–336.

Trow, M. (1976a). "Elite higher education": An endangered species? *Minerva, 4,* 355–376.

Trow, M. (1976b). Higher education and moral development. *American Association of University Professors Bulletin, 62,* 20–27.

Trow, M. (1977). *Aspects of American higher education.* New York: McGraw-Hill.

Trusheim, D., & Crouse, J. (1981). Effects of college prestige on men's occupational status and income. *Research in Higher Education, 14,* 283–304.

Tukey, J. (1954). Causation, regression, and path analysis. In O. Kempthorne, T. Bancroft, T. Gowen, & J. Lush (Eds.), *Statistics and mathematics in biology.* Ames: Iowa State College Press.

Turiel, E. (1983). *The development of social knowledge: Morality and convention.* Cambridge, England: Cambridge University Press.

Turiel, E., & Smetana J. (1984). Social knowledge and action: The coordination of domains. In J. Gewirtz & W. Kurtines (Eds.), *Morality, moral development, and moral behavior.* New York: John Wiley & Sons.

Turner, R. (1975). Is there a quest for identity? *Sociological Quarterly, 16,* 148–161.

Tusin, L. (1987). *The relationship of academic and social self-concepts with women's choice of teaching as a career: A longitudinal model.* Unpublished doctoral dissertation, University of Illinois, Chicago.

Tusin, L., & Pascarella, E. (1985). The influence of college on women's choice of teaching as a career. *Research in Higher Education, 22,* 115–134.

Udry, J. (1974). *The social context of marriage* (3rd ed.). Philadelphia: Lippincott.

University of California. (1980). *Retention and transfer: University of California undergraduate enrollment study.* Berkeley: University of California, Office of the Vice President. (ERIC Document Reproduction Service No. ED 215 597)

University of Massachusetts Counseling Center. (1972). The effects of three types of sensitivity groups on changes in measures of self-actualization. *Journal of Counseling Psychology, 19,* 253–254.

University of North Carolina. (1967). *The Yackety Yack, '42.* Chapel Hill: University of North Carolina Alumni Office.

Upcraft, M., Gardner, J., & Associates (1989). *The freshman year experience: Helping students survive and succeed in college.* San Francisco: Jossey-Bass.

Urahn, S., & Nettles, M. (1987). *Student financial aid and educational outcomes: Is there a difference between grants and loans?* Paper presented at the meeting of the Association for the Study of Higher Education, San Diego.

U.S. Bureau of Labor Statistics. (1966). *Survey of consumer expenditures, 1960–61* (Suppl. 2 to Bureau of Labor Statistics Report No. 237-93). Washington, DC: U.S. Government Printing Office.

U.S. Bureau of the Census. (1970). Annual mean income, lifetime income, and educational attainment of men in the United States, for selected years, 1956–1968. *Current population reports* (Ser. P-60, No. 74). Washington, DC: Author.

Useem, M. (1989). *Liberal education and the corporation: The hiring and advancement of college graduates.* Hawthorne, NY: Aldine de Gruyter.

Useem, M., & Karabel, J. (1986). Pathways to top corporate management. *American Sociological Review, 51,* 184–200.

Useem, M., & Miller, S. (1975). Privilege and domination: The role of the upper class in American higher education. *Social Science Inquiry, 14,* 115–145.

Useem, M., & Miller, S. (1977). The upper class in higher education. *Social Policy, 7,* 28–31.

Vaillant, G. (1977). *Adaptation to life.* Boston, MA: Little, Brown.

Valine, W. (1976). A four-year follow-up study of underachieving college freshmen. *Journal of College Student Personnel, 17,* 309–312.

Van Damme, J., & Masui, C. (1980). *Locus of control and other student characteristics in interaction with the personalized system of instruction versus lectures* (Report No. 20). Katholieke Universiteit Leuven, Departement Pedagogische Wetenschappen Afdcling Didactier en Psychopedagogiek, Leuven, Belgium.

Vander Wilt, R., & Klocke, R. (1971). Self-actualization of females in an experimental orientation program. *Journal of the National Association of Women Deans, Administrators, and Counselors, 34,* 125–129.

Vaughan, C. (1972). The relationship between student alienation and participation in extracurricular activities. *Journal of College Student Personnel, 13,* 31–38.

Vaughan, R. (1968). Involvement in extracurricular activities and dropout. *Journal of College Student Personnel, 9,* 60–61.

Vedlitz, A. (1983). The impact of college education on political attitudes and behaviors: A reappraisal and test of the self-selection hypothesis. *Social Science Quarterly, 64,* 145–153.

Vedovato, S., & Vaughter, R. (1980). Psychology of women courses changing sexist and sex-typed attitudes. *Psychology of Women Quarterly, 4,* 587–590.

Velez, W. (1985). Finishing college: The effects of college type. *Sociology of Education, 58,* 191–200.

Villanueva, E. (1982). *Validation of a moral judgment instrument for Filipino students.* Unpublished doctoral dissertation, University of the Philippines, Quezon City.

Volker, J. (1979). *Moral reasoning and college experience* (Higher Education and Cognitive-Social Development Project, Report No. 4). Minneapolis: University of Minnesota.

Volkwein, J., King, M., & Terenzini, P. (1985). *A study of the academic performance and intellectual growth of transfer students: The role of the faculty.* Paper presented at the meeting of the Association for the Study of Higher Education, Chicago.

Volkwein, J., King, M., & Terenzini, P. (1986). Student-faculty relationships and intellectual growth among transfer students. *Journal of Higher Education, 57,* 413–430.

Volkwein, J., Wright, T., & Agrotes, M. (1987). *The impact of college experiences on the intellectual growth of transfer students.* Paper presented at the conference of the North East Association for Institutional Research, Rochester, NY.

Von Wittich, B. (1972). The impact of the pass-fail system upon achievement of college students. *Journal of Higher Education, 43,* 499–508.

Voorhees, R. (1985a). Financial aid and persistence: Do federal campus-based aid programs make a difference? *Journal of Student Financial Aid, 15,* 21–30.

Voorhees, R. (1985b). Student finances and campus-based financial aid: A structural model analysis of the persistence of high need freshmen. *Research in Higher Education, 22,* 65–92.

Voorhees, R. (1987). Toward building models of community college persistence: A logit analysis. *Research in Higher Education, 26,* 115–129.

Vreeland, R. (1970). The effects of houses on students' attitudes and values. In J. Whiteley & H. Sprandel (Eds.), *The growth and development of college students* (Student Personnel Series No. 12). Washington, DC: American Personnel and Guidance Association.

Vreeland, R., & Bidwell, C. (1965). Organizational effects on student attitudes: A study of the Harvard houses. *Sociology of Education, 38,* 233–250.

Vreeland, R., & Bidwell, C. (1966). Classifying university departments: An approach to the analysis of their effects upon undergraduates' values and attitudes. *Sociology of Education, 39,* 237–254.

Wachtel, P. (1975a). The effect of school quality on achievement, attainment levels, and lifetime earnings. *Explorations in Economic Research, 2,* 502–536.

Wachtel, P. (1975b). The returns to investment in higher education: Another view. In F. Juster (Ed.), *Education, income, and human behavior.* New York: McGraw-Hill.

Wachtel, P. (1976). The effect on earnings of school and college investment expenditures. *Review of Economics and Statistics, 63,* 326–331.

Wade, O. (1984). *Remarks.* Conference on the Humanities and Careers in Business, Northwestern University, Evanston, IL.

Wagner, H. (1970). Adolescent problems resulting from the lengthened educational period. *Adolescence, 5,* 339–344.

Waite, J. (1975). A study comparing college science students' performance on Piagetian type tasks, including cross-cultural comparisons. *Dissertation Abstracts International, 35,* 5954A.

Walberg, H. (1985). Synthesis of research on teaching. In M. Wittrock (Ed.), *Third handbook of research on teaching.* Washington, DC: American Educational Research Association.

Walberg, H. (1987). Learning and life-course accomplishments. In C. Schooler & W. Schaie (Eds.), *Cognitive function and social structure over the life course.* Norwood, NJ: Ablex.

Walberg, H., & Sigler, J. (1975). Business views education in Chicago. *Phi Delta Kappan, 56,* 610–612.

Waldo, M. (1986). Academic achievement and retention as related to students' personal and social adjustment in university residence halls. *Journal of College and University Student Housing, 16,* 19–23.

Wales, T. (1973). The effect of college quality on earnings: Results from the NBER-Thorndike data. *Journal of Human Resources, 8,* 306–317.

Walizer, M., & Herriott, R. (1971). *The impact of college on students' competence to function in a learning society* (ACT Research Report No. 47). Iowa City, IA: American College Testing Program.

Walker, A. (1981). *Influence of female role models on career-related attitudes.* Paper presented at the meeting of the Eastern Psychological Association, New York.

Walker, L. (1984). Sex differences in the development of moral reasoning: A critical review. *Child Development, 55,* 677–691.

Wallace, W. (1963). *Peer groups and student achievement: The college campus and its students* (Report No. 91). Chicago: University of Chicago, National Opinion Research Center.

Wallace, W. (1967a). Faculty and fraternities: Organizational influences on student achievement. *Administrative Science Quarterly, 11,* 643–670.

Wallace, W. (1967b). Student culture research: Application and implications for structure and continuity in the liberal arts college. *NASPA Journal, 5,* 149–154.

Walsh, R. (1985). Changes in college freshmen after participation in a student development program. *Journal of College Student Personnel, 26,* 310–314.

Walsh, W. (1973). *Theories of person-environment interaction: Implications for the college student* (ACT Monograph No. 20). Iowa City, IA: American College Testing Program.

Walsh, W. (1975). Some theories of person/environment interaction. *Journal of College Student Personnel, 16,* 107–113.

Walsh, W., Spokane, A., & Mitchell, E. (1976). Consistent occupational preferences and academic adjustment. *Research in Higher Education, 4,* 123–129.

Walters, R., & Bray, D. (1963). Today's search for tomorrow's leaders. *Journal of College Placement, 24,* 22–23.

Ware, M., & Apprich, R. (1980). Variations in career cognition measures among groups of college women. *Measurement and Evaluation in Guidance, 13,* 179–183.

Warren, J. (1975). Alternatives to degrees. In D. Vermilye (Ed.), *Learner-*

centered reform: Current issues in higher education 1975. San Francisco: Jossey-Bass.

Warren, J. (1984). The blind alley of value added. *American Association for Higher Education Bulletin, 37,* 10–13.

Waterman, A. (1982). Identity development from adolescence to adulthood: An extension of theory and a review of research. *Developmental Psychology, 18,* 341–358.

Waterman, A., & Archer, S. (1979). Ego identity status and expressive writing among high school and college students. *Journal of Youth and Adolescence, 8,* 327–341.

Waterman, A., Geary, P., & Waterman, C. (1974). A longitudinal study of changes in ego identity status from the freshman to the senior year at college. *Developmental Psychology, 10,* 387–392.

Waterman, A., & Goldman, J. (1976). A longitudinal study of ego identity development at a liberal arts college. *Journal of Youth and Adolescence, 5,* 361–369.

Waterman, A., Kohutis, E., & Pulone J. (1977). The role of expressive writing in ego identity formation. *Developmental Psychology, 13,* 286–287.

Waterman, A., & Waterman, C. (1971). A longitudinal study of changes in ego identity status during the freshman year at college. *Developmental Psychology, 5,* 167–173.

Waterman, A., & Waterman, C. (1972). The relationship between freshman ego identity status and subsequent academic behavior: A test of the predictive validity of Marcia's categorization system for identity status. *Developmental Psychology, 6,* 179.

Waterman, A., & Waterman, C. (1974). Ego identity status and decision styles. *Journal of Youth and Adolescence, 3,* 1–6.

Waterman, C., Buebel, M., & Waterman, A. (1970). The relationship between resolution of the identity crisis and outcomes of previous psychosocial crises. *Proceedings of the 78th Annual Convention of the American Psychological Association, 5,* 467–468.

Waterman, C., & Nevid, J. (1977). Sex differences in the resolution of the identity crisis. *Journal of Youth and Adolescence, 6,* 337–342.

Watkins, D. (1987). Academic locus of control: A relevant variable at tertiary level? *Higher Education, 16,* 221–229.

Watson, G., & Glaser, E. (1980). *Watson-Glaser Critical Thinking Appraisal.* San Antonio, TX: Psychological Corporation.

Watson, W. (1983). *A study of factors affecting the development of moral judgment.* Unpublished manuscript, Monash Chirering, Clayton, Victoria, Australia.

Watson, W. (1984). A study of the Piagetian cognitive development of science and humanities college students from the freshman to the senior year. *Dissertation Abstracts International, 44,* 2423A.

Weathersby, R. (1981). Ego development. In A. Chickering & Associates, *The modern American college: Responding to the new realities of diverse students and a changing society.* San Francisco: Jossey-Bass.

Webb, S. (1971). Estimated effects of four factors on academic performance before and after transfer. *Journal of Experimental Education, 39,* 78–84.

Webster, D. (1985). Does research productivity enhance teaching? *Educational Record, 66,* 60–62.

Webster, D. (1986). Research productivity and classroom teaching effectiveness. *Instructional Evaluation, 9,* 14–20.

Wechsler, H. (1989). *The transfer challenge: Removing barriers, maintaining commitment.* Washington, DC: Association of American Colleges.

Weeks, M., & Gage, B. (1984). A comparison of the marriage-role expectations of college women enrolled in a functional marriage course in 1961, 1972, and 1978. *Sex Roles 11,* 377–388.

Wegner, E., & Sewell, W. (1970). Selection and context as factors affecting the probability of graduation from college. *American Journal of Sociology, 75,* 665–679.

Weidman, J. (1979). Nonintellective undergraduate socialization in academic departments. *Journal of Higher Education, 50,* 48–62.

Weidman, J. (1984). Impacts of campus experiences and parental socialization on undergraduates' career choices. *Research in Higher Education, 20,* 445–476.

Weidman, J. (1989a). Undergraduate socialization: A conceptual approach. In J. Smart (Ed.), *Higher education: Handbook of theory and research* (Vol. 5). New York: Agathon.

Weidman, J. (1989b). The world of higher education: A socialization-theoretical perspective: In K. Hurrelmann & U. Engel (Eds.), *The social world of adolescents: International perspectives.* New York: Aldine.

Weidman, J., & Friedman, R. (1984). The school-to-work transition for high school dropouts. *Urban Review, 16,* 25–42.

Weidman, J., Phelan, W., & Sullivan, M. (1972). The influence of educational attainment on self-evaluation of competence. *Sociology of Education, 45,* 303–312.

Weidman, J., & White, R. (1985). Postsecondary "high-tech" training for women on welfare: Correlates of program completion. *Journal of Higher Education, 56,* 555–568.

Weigel, M. (1969). *A comparison of persisters and non-persisters in a junior college.* Coon Rapids, MN: Anoka-Ramsey State Junior College. (ERIC Document Reproduction Service No. ED 044 115)

Weil, F. (1985). The variable effects of education on liberal attitudes: A comparative-historical analysis of anti-Semitism using public opinion survey data. *American Sociological Review, 50,* 458–474.

Weiland, A., & Kingsbury, S. (1979). Immediate and delayed recall of lecture material as a function of note taking. *Journal of Educational Research, 72,* 228–230.

Weiner, T., & Eckland, B. (1979). Education and political party: The effects of college or social class? *American Journal of Sociology, 84,* 911–928.

Weinstein, A., & Srinivasan, V. (1974). Predicting managerial success of master of business administration (MBA) graduates. *Journal of Applied Psychology, 59,* 207–212.

Weisbrod, D., & Karpoff, P. (1968). Monetary returns to college education, student ability, and college quality. *Review of Economics and Statistics, 50,* 491–497.

Weislogel, L. (1977). *Academic over- and under-achievement and residence patterns: An associative study.* (ERIC Document Reproduction Service No. ED 149 696)

Welch, F. (1973). Black-white differences in returns to schooling. *American Economic Review, 63,* 893–907.

Welfel, E. (1982). How students make judgments: Do educational level and academic major make a difference? *Journal of College Student Personnel, 23,* 490–497.

Welfel, E., & Davison, M. (1983). *Four years later: A longitudinal study of the development of reflective judgment during the college years.* Chicago: Spencer Foundation .

Welfel, E., & Davison, M. (1986). The development of reflective judgment during the college years: A 4-year longitudinal study. *Journal of College Student Personnel, 27,* 209–216.

Wells, L., & Marwell, G. (1976). *Self-esteem: Its conceptualization and measurement.* Beverly Hills, CA: Sage.

Wells, S. (1976). Evaluation criteria and the effectiveness of instructional technology in higher education. *Higher Education, 5,* 253–275.

Welty, J. (1976). Resident and commuter students: Is it only the living situation? *Journal of College Student Personnel, 17,* 465–468.

Wenc, L. (1983). Using student aid in retention efforts. In R. Fensker, R. Huff, & Associates, *Handbook of student financial aid: Programs, procedures, and policies.* San Francisco: Jossey-Bass.

Werts, C. (1967a). Career changes in college. *Sociology of Education, 40,* 90–95.

Werts, C. (1967b). Career choice patterns. *Sociology of Education, 40,* 348–358.

Werts, C. (1968). The partitioning of variance in school effects studies. *American Educational Research Journal, 5,* 311–318.

Werts, C. (1970). The partitioning of variance in school effects studies: A reconsideration. *American Educational Research Journal, 7,* 127–132.

Werts, C., & Linn, R. (1970). Path analysis: Psychological examples. *Psychological Bulletin, 74,* 193–212.

Werts, C., & Linn, R. (1971). Considerations when making inferences within the analysis of covariance model. *Educational and Psychological Measurement, 31,* 407–416.

Werts, C., & Watley, D. (1968a). Analyzing college effects: Correlation vs. regression. *American Educational Research Journal, 5,* 585–598.

Werts, C., & Watley, D. (1968b). Determinants of changes in career plans during college. *Sociology of Education, 41,* 401–405.

Werts, C., & Watley, D. (1969). A student's dilemma: Big fish–little pond or little fish–big pond. *Journal of Counseling Psychology, 16,* 14–19.

West, M., & Kirkland M. (1986). Effectiveness of growth groups in education. *Journal for Specialists in Group Work, 11,* 16–24.

Whelpton, P., Campbell, A., & Patterson, J. (1966). *Fertility and family planning in the United States.* Princeton, NJ: Princeton University Press.

Whitbourne, S., Jelsma, B., & Waterman, A. (1982). An Eriksonian measure of personality development in college students: A reexamination of Constantinople's data and a partial replication. *Developmental Psychology, 18,* 369–371.

Whitbourne, S., & Tesch, S. (1985). A comparison of identity and intimacy statuses in college students and alumni. *Developmental Psychology, 21,* 1039–1044.

Whitbourne, S., & Waterman, A. (1979). Psychosocial development during the adult years: Age and cohort comparisons. *Developmental Psychology, 15,* 373–378.

White, C. (1973). *Moral judgment in college students: The development of an objective measure and its relationship to life experience dimensions.* Unpublished doctoral dissertation, University of Georgia, Athens.

White, C., & Burke, P. (1987). Ethnic role identity among black and white college students. *Sociological Perspectives, 30,* 310–331.

White, J. (1972). Individual and environmental factors associated with freshman attrition at a multi-campus community college. *Dissertation Abstracts International, 32,* 3709A.

White, K. (1980). Problems and characteristics of college students. *Adolescence, 15,* 23–41.

White, K., & Ferstenberg, A. (1978). Professional specialization and formal operations: The balance task. *Journal of Genetic Psychology, 133,* 97–104.

Whiteley, J. (1980). A developmental intervention in higher education. In V. Erickson & J. Whiteley (Eds.), *Developmental counseling and teaching.* Pacific Grove, CA: Brooks/Cole.

Whiteley, J. (1982). *Character development in college students* (Vol. 1). Schenectady, NY: Character Research Press.

Whiteley, J., & Yokota, N. (1988). *Development in the freshman year and over four years of undergraduate study* (Monograph Series No. 1). Columbia: University of South Carolina, Center for the Study of the Freshman Year Experience.

Whitla, D. (1978). *Value added: Measuring the impact of undergraduate educa-

tion. Cambridge, MA: Harvard University, Office of Instructional Research and Evaluation.

Whitla, D. (1981). *Value added and other related matters*. Washington, DC: U.S. Department of Education, National Commission on Excellence in Education. (ERIC Document Reproduction Service No. ED 228 245)

Wicker, A. (1973). Undermanning theory and research: Implications for the study of psychological and behavioral effects of excess populations. *Representative Research in Social Psychology, 4,* 190–191.

Wicker, A., & Kirmeyer, S. (1976). From church to laboratory of national park: A program of research on excess and insufficient populations. In S. Wapner, B. Kaplan, & S. Cohen (Eds.), *Experiencing the environment*. New York: Plenum Press.

Widick, C. (1975). An evaluation of developmental instruction in a university setting. *Dissertation Abstracts International, 36,* 2041A.

Widick, C., Knefelkamp, L., & Parker, C. (1975). The counselor as developmental instructor. *Counselor Education and Supervision, 14,* 286–296.

Widick, C., Knefelkamp, L., & Parker, C. (1980). Student development. In U. Delworth, G. Hanson, & Associates, *Student services: A handbook for the profession*. San Francisco: Jossey-Bass.

Widick, C., Parker, C., & Knefelkamp, L. (1978b). Douglas Heath's model of maturing. In L. Knefelkamp, C. Widick, & C. Parker (Eds.), *Applying new developmental findings* (New Directions for Student Services No. 4). San Francisco: Jossey-Bass.

Widick, C., Parker, C., & Knefelkamp, L. (1978c). Erik Erikson and psychosocial development. In L. Knefelkamp, C. Widick, & C. Parker (Eds.), *Applying new developmental findings* (New Directions for Student Services No. 4). San Francisco: Jossey-Bass.

Widick, C., Parker, C., & Knefelkamp, L. (1978c). Erik Erikson and psychosocial development. In L. Knefelkamp, C. Widick, & C. Parker (Eds.), *Applying new developmental findings* (New Directions for Student Services No. 4). San Francisco: Jossey-Bass.

Widick, C., & Simpson, D. (1978). Developmental concepts in college instruction. In C. Parker (Ed.), *Encouraging development in college students*. Minneapolis: University of Minnesota Press.

Wilder, D., & Hoyt, A. (1986). Greek affiliation and attitude change: A reply to Jakobsen and Strange. *Journal of College Student Personnel, 27,* 527–530.

Wilder, D., Hoyt, A., Doren, D., Hauck, W., & Zettle, R. (1978). The impact of fraternity or sorority membership on values and attitudes. *Journal of College Student Personnel, 19,* 445–449.

Wilder, D., Hoyt, A., Surbeck, B., Wilder, J., & Carney, P. (1986). Greek affiliation and attitude change in college students. *Journal of College Student Personnel, 27,* 510–519.

Wilensky, H., & Lawrence, A. (1979). Job assignment in modern societies:

A reexamination of the ascription-achievement hypothesis. In A. Hawley (Ed.), *Societal growth: Processes and implications*. New York: Free Press.

Wilkie, C., & Kuckuck, S. (1989). A longitudinal study of the effects of a freshman seminar. *Journal of the Freshman Year Experience, 1,* 7–16.

Willett, J. (1988). Questions and answers in the measurement of change. In E. Rothkopf (Ed.), *Review of research in education* (Vol. 15). Washington, DC: American Educational Research Association.

Williams, D., Cook, P., & Jensen, R. (1984). *Class size and achievement among college students.* Paper presented at the meeting of the American Educational Research Association, New Orleans.

Williams, D., Cook, P., Quinn, B., & Jensen, R. (1985). University class size: Is smaller better? *Research in Higher Education, 23,* 307–318.

Williams, D., & Reilly, R. (1972). The impact of residence halls on students. *Journal of College Student Personnel, 13,* 402–410.

Williams, F., & Harrell, T. (1964). Predicting success in business. *Journal of Applied Psychology, 48,* 164–167.

Williams, H., Turner, C., Debreuil, L., Fast, J., & Berestiansky, J. (1979). Formal operational reasoning by chemistry students. *Journal of Chemical Education, 56,* 599–600.

Williams, I. (1975). An investigation into the developmental stages of black consciousness. *Dissertation Abstracts International, 35,* 2488B.

Williams, J., Nunn, C., & St. Peter, L. (1976). Origins of tolerance: Findings from a replication of Stouffer's *Communism, conformity, and civil liberties. Social Forces, 55,* 394–408.

Williams, R. (1979). Change and stability in values and value systems: A sociological perspective. In M. Rokeach (Ed.), *Understanding human values.* New York: Free Press.

Williamson, D., & Creamer, D. (1988). Student attrition in 2- and 4-year colleges: Application of a theoretical model. *Journal of College Student Development, 29,* 210–217.

Willie, C., & Cunnigen, D. (1981). Black students in higher education: A review of studies, 1965–1980. In R. Turner & J. Short (Eds.). *Annual review of sociology* (Vol. 7). Palo Alto, CA: Annual Reviews.

Willie, C., & Levy, J. (1972). On white campuses, black students retreat into separatism. *Psychology Today, 5,* 50–52, 76.

Willie, C., & McCord, A. (1972). *Black students at white colleges.* New York: Praeger.

Willingham, W., Young, J., & Morris, M. (1985). *Success in college: The role of personal qualities and academic ability.* New York: College Entrance Examination Board.

Willis, R. (1973). A new approach to the economic theory of fertility behavior. *Journal of Political Economy, 81,* S14–S64.

Willis, S., Blieszner, R., & Baltes, P. (1981). Intellectual training research in aging: Modification of performance on the fluidability of figural relations. *Journal of Educational Psychology, 73,* 41–50.

Wilms, W. (1980). *Vocational education and social mobility.* Los Angeles: University of California. (ERIC Document Reproduction Service No. 183 966)

Wilson, A. (1987). Teaching formal thought for improved chemistry achievement. *International Journal of Science Education, 9,* 197–202.

Wilson, J. (1974). *Impact of cooperative education upon personal development and growth of values: Final report to the Braitmayer Foundation.* Boston: Northeastern University, Cooperative Education Research Center.

Wilson, K. (1978). Toward an improved explanation of income attainment: Recalibrating education and occupation. *American Journal of Sociology, 84,* 684–697.

Wilson, K. (1985). *The relationship of GRE general test item-type part scores to undergraduate grades* (Report No. ETS-RR-84-38, GREB-81-22P). Princeton, NJ: Educational Testing Service.

Wilson, K., & Shin, E. (1983). Reassessing the discrimination against women in higher education. *American Educational Research Journal, 20,* 529–551.

Wilson, K., & Smith-Lovin, L. (1983). Scaling the prestige, authority, and income potential of college curricula. *Social Science Research, 12,* 159–186.

Wilson, R., Anderson, S., & Fleming, W. (1987). Commuter and resident students' personal and family adjustment. *Journal of College Student Personnel, 28,* 229–233.

Wilson, R., Gaff, J., Dienst, R., Wood, L., & Bavry, J. (1975). *College professors and their impact on students.* New York: Wiley-Interscience.

Wilson, R., Wood, L., & Gaff, J. (1974). Social-psychological accessibility and faculty-student interaction beyond the classroom. *Sociology of Education, 47,* 74–92.

Wilson, T., & Linville, P. (1982). Improving the academic performance of college freshmen: Attributional therapy revisited. *Journal of Personality and Social Psychology, 42,* 367–376.

Wilson, T., & Linville, P. (1985). Improving the performance of college freshmen with attributional techniques. *Journal of Personality and Social Psychology, 49,* 287–293.

Wingard, J., & Williamson, J. (1973). Grades as predictors of physicians' career performance: An evaluative literature review. *Journal of Medical Education, 48* (Pt. 1), 311–322.

Winston, R., Jr., Hutson, G., & McCaffrey, S. (1980). Environmental influences on fraternity academic achievement. *Journal of College Student Personnel, 21,* 449–455.

Winston, R., Jr., & Miller, T. (1987). *Student Developmental Task and Lifestyle Inventory manual.* Athens, GA: Student Development Associates.

Winston, R., Jr., Miller, T., & Prince, J. (1979). *Assessing student development: A preliminary manual for the Student Development Task Inventory (revised, sec-*

ond edition) and the Student Developmental Profile and Planning Record. Athens, GA: Student Development Associates.

Winston, R., Jr., & Saunders, S. (1987). The Greek experience: Friend or foe of student development? In R. Winston, Jr., W. Nettles III, & J. Opper, Jr. (Eds.), *Fraternities and sororities on the contemporary college campus* (New Directions for Student Services No. 40). San Francisco: Jossey-Bass.

Winteler, A. (1981). The academic department as environment for teaching and learning. *Higher Education, 10,* 20–35.

Winter, D. (1979). Defining and measuring the competencies of a liberal arts education. In *Current Issues in Higher Education* (Vol. 5). Washington, DC: American Association for Higher Education.

Winter, D., McClelland, D. (1978). Thematic analysis: An empirically derived measure of the effects of liberal arts education. *Journal of Educational Psychology, 70,* 8–16.

Winter, D., McClelland, D., & Stewart, A. (1981). *A new case for the liberal arts: Assessing institutional goals and student development.* San Francisco: Jossey-Bass.

Wise, D. (1979). *Academic achievement and job performance: Earnings and promotions.* New York: Garland.

Wishart, P., & Rossmann, J. (1977). *Career patterns, employment and earnings of graduates of 11 ACM colleges.* Chicago: Associated Colleges of the Midwest.

Wisler, C. (1969). Partitioning the explained variance in regression analysis. In G. Mayeske et al., *A study of our nation's schools.* Washington, DC: U.S. Department of Health, Education, and Welfare, Office of Education.

Withey, S. (1971). *A degree and what else? Correlates and consequences of a college education.* New York: McGraw-Hill.

Witkin, H. (1962). *Psychological differentiation.* New York: John Wiley & Sons.

Witkin, H. (1976). Cognitive style in academic performance and in teacher-student relations. In S. Messick & Associates, *Individuality in learning.* San Francisco: Jossey-Bass.

Witmer, D. (1970). Economic benefits of college education. *Review of Educational Research, 40,* 511–523.

Witmer, D. (1976). Is the value of college really declining? *Change, 8,* 46–47, 60–61.

Witmer, D. (1980). Has the golden age of American higher education come to an abrupt end? *Journal of Human Resources, 15,* 113–120.

Witmer, D. (1983). Income predictions. *Review of Higher Education, 7,* 35–47.

Witmer, D., & Wallhaus, R. (1975). *What we know about educational productivity.* Paper presented at the meeting of the Association for Institutional Research, St. Louis.

Witter, R., Okun, M., Stock, W., & Haring, M. (1984). Education and subjective well-being: A meta-analysis. *Educational Evaluation and Policy Analysis, 6,* 165–173.

Wolfle, D. (1971). *The uses of talent.* Princeton, NJ: Princeton University Press.

Wolfle, L. (1977). An introduction to path analysis. *Multiple Linear Regression Viewpoints, 8,* 36–61.

Wolfle, L. (1980a). Strategies of path analysis. *American Educational Research Journal, 17,* 183–209.

Wolfle, L. (1980b). The enduring effects of education on verbal skills. *Sociology of Education, 53,* 104–114.

Wolfle, L. (1983). Effects of higher education on achievement for blacks and whites. *Research in Higher Education, 19,* 3–9.

Wolfle, L. (1985a). Applications of causal models in higher education. In J. Smart (Ed.), *Higher education: Handbook of theory and research* (Vol. 1). New York: Agathon.

Wolfle, L. (1985b). Postsecondary educational attainment among whites and blacks. *American Educational Research Journal, 22,* 501–525.

Wolfle, L. (1987). Enduring cognitive effects of public and private schools. *Educational Researcher, 16,* 5–11.

Wolfle, L. (in press). Effects of postsecondary education on self-esteem. *Research in Higher Education.*

Wolfle, L., & Ethington, C. (1985). GEMINI: Program for analysis of structural equations with standard errors of indirect effects. *Behavior Research Methods, Instruments, and Computers, 17,* 581–584.

Wolfle, L., & Robertshaw, D. (1982). Effects of college attendance on locus of control. *Journal of Personality and Social Psychology, 43,* 802–810.

Wolfson, K. (1976). Career development patterns of college women. *Journal of Counseling Psychology, 23,* 119–125.

Woo, J. (1986). Graduate degrees and job success: Managers in one U.S. corporation. *Economics of Education Review, 5,* 227–237.

Wood, L., & Wilson, R. (1972). Teachers with impact. *Research Reporter, 7,* 1–4.

Wood, P. (1983). Inquiring systems and problem structure: Implications for cognitive development. *Human Development, 26,* 249–265.

Worley, B. (1978). Personal growth and self-discovery: A product of the exchange experience. *Journal of the National Association of Women Deans, Administrators, and Counselors, 41,* 69–71.

Wortman, P. (1983). Meta-analysis: A validity perspective. *Annual Review of Psychology, 34,* 223–260.

Wright, C., & Wright, S. (1987). The role of mentors in the career development of young professionals. *Family Relations, 36,* 204–208.

Wright, D. (1987). Minority students: Developmental beginnings. In D. Wright (Ed.), *Responding to the needs of today's minority students* (New Directions for Student Services No. 38). San Francisco: Jossey-Bass.

Wright, E. (1973). A study of student leaves of absence. *Journal of Higher Education, 44,* 235–247.

Wright, J., & Hamilton, R. (1979). Education and job attitudes among blue-collar workers. *Sociology of Work and Occupations, 6,* 59–83.

Wright, S. (1934). The method of path coefficients. *Annals of Mathematical Statistics, 5,* 161–215.

Wright, S. (1954). The interpretation of multivariate systems. In O. Kempthorne, T. Bancroft, J. Gowen, & D. Lush (Eds.), *Statistics and mathematics in biology.* Ames: Iowa State College Press.

Wright, S. (1960). Path coefficients and path regressions: Alternative or complementary concepts? *Biometrics, 16,* 189–202.

Wylie, R. (1974). *The self-concept: Vol. 1. A review of methodological considerations and measuring instruments* (rev. ed.). Lincoln: University of Nebraska Press.

Wylie, R. (1979). *The self-concept: Vol. 2. Theory and research on selected topics* (rev. ed.). Lincoln: University of Nebraska Press.

Wyne, M., White, K., & Coop, R. (1974). *The black self.* Englewood Cliffs, NJ: Prentice-Hall.

Yankelovich, D. (1972). *Changing values on campus: Political and personal attitudes of today's college student.* New York: Washington Square Press.

Yankelovich, D. (1974a). *Changing youth values in the 70's: A study of American youth.* New York: John D. Rockefeller 3rd Foundation.

Yankelovich, D. (1974b). *The new morality: A profile of American youth in the 70s.* New York: McGraw-Hill.

Yankelovich, D., & Clark, R. (1974, September). College and noncollege youth values. *Change,* pp. 45–46, 64.

Yarbrough, S., Ragan, T., & Wilson, R. (1984). Developmental levels of disadvantaged college freshmen. *College Student Affairs Journal, 5,* 12–19.

Yeany, R., Waugh, M., & Blalock, A. (1979). The effects of achievement diagnosis with feedback on the science achievement and attitude of university students. *Journal of Research in Science Teaching, 16,* 465–472.

Yonge, G., & Regan, M. (1975). A longitudinal study of personality and choice of major. *Journal of Vocational Behavior, 7,* 41–65.

Young, A. (1975). Students, graduates, and dropouts in the labor market, October, 1974. *Monthly Labor Review, 98,* 33–36.

Young, A. (1985). One-fourth of the adult labor force are college graduates. *Monthly Labor Review, 108,* 43–46.

Young, A., & Hayghe, H. (1984). More U.S. workers are college graduates. *Monthly Labor Review, 107,* 46–49.

Young, E., & Jacobson, L. (1970). Effects of time extended marathon group experiences on personality characteristics. *Journal of Counseling Psychology, 17,* 247–251.

Yussen, S. (1976). Moral reasoning from the perspective of others. *Child Development, 47,* 551–555.

Zaccaria, L., & Creaser, J. (1971). Factors relating to persistence in an urban commuter university. *Journal of College Student Personnel, 12,* 256–261.

Zirkle, K., & Hudson, G. (1975). The effects of residence hall staff members on maturity development for male students. *Journal of College Student Personnel, 16,* 30–33.

Zuckerman, D. (1979). The impact of education and selected traits on sex-role related goals and attitudes. *Journal of Vocational Behavior, 14,* 248–254.

Zuckerman, H. (1977). *Scientific elite.* New York: Macmillan.

Zwerling, L. (1976). *Second best: The crisis of the community college.* New York: McGraw-Hill.

Name Index

Subject Index

A

Ability, and economic benefits, 524–525

Academic achievement: and career development, 470–475, 497–498; and economic benefits, 517–520, 536; factors influencing, 388–390; and job satisfaction, 474–475; meta-findings on, 624, 626–629; and occupational performance and success, 472–474, 497–498; and occupational status, 470–472; and sex-atypical careers among women, 472; within-college effects on, 388–390, 421–422, 470–475, 497–498, 517–520, 536, 624, 626–629

Academic experience, meta-findings on, 616–620

Academic major. *See* Major fields

Academic skills. *See* Subject matter competence

Accent on Developing Abstract Processes of Thought (ADAPT), 142, 143, 145–146

Accommodation or assimilation, in cognitive-structural theories, 28

Achievement Test, 64

Administrators, learning-centered management by, 656

Admissions, issues of, 649

Adult students. *See* Older students

Advising services, and educational attainment, 385, 402–405, 419–420, 423

Aesthetics. *See* Cultural, aesthetic, and intellectual values

Aging, generation, and period effects, net effects of college versus, 290–292, 295–297

Allocative ability, and work force participation, 432

Altruism, humanitarianism, and civic values: between-college effects on, 300–301; change during college in, 277, 332–333; net effects on, 286–287; within-college effects on, 310–311

Alverno College, ego development study at, 179

American College Testing (ACT) Program: and cognitive skills, 115–116, 120, 128, 135, 136–137, 141; and economic benefits, 508; and educational attainment, 374; and moral development, 349; and subject matter competence, 64, 65, 67, 86

American Council on Education, 63, 119, 180, 183, 402

American Educational Research Association, 8

American Telephone and Telegraph Company (AT&T): and career development, 434–435, 449, 451, 469, 477, 478; and economic benefits, 525, 536

Analysis of Argument (AOA) Test, 126, 132, 135, 138

Antioch University, as distinctive, 377

Asian Americans, psychosocial development of, 26, 210

Assessment of Performance of Colleges and Universities (APCU), 240

Association for Institutional Research, 8

Association for the Study of Higher Education, 8

Association of American Colleges (AAC), 4, 646, 651–652

Athletic participation: and career development, 477–478; and cognitive skills, 151–152; and educational attainment, 393

Attitudes and values: and aging, generation, and period effects, 290–292, 295–297; analysis of changes in, 269–334; background on, 269–270; between-college effects on, 297–304, 327; change during college in, 270–283, 325–326, 331, 559–561; concepts of, 269–270; conclusions on, 330–331; conditional effects on, 316–320, 328–329; cultural, aesthetic, and intellectual, 271–273, 283–284, 297–299,